ENGINEERING CHEMISTRY

Prasanta Rath

School of Applied Sciences
KIIT University
Bhubaneswar, Odisha

CENGAGE

Australia • Brazil • India • Mexico • Singapore • United Kingdom • United States

Cengage

Engineering Chemistry

Prasanta Rath

ISBN-13: 978-81-315-2669-9
ISBN-10: 81-315-2669-0

Cengage Learning India Pvt. Ltd.
T-303, 3rd Floor
DAV Complex, Plot 3
Mayur Vihar Phase 1
Delhi-110091

Cengage Learning is a leading provider of customized learning solutions with office locations around the globe, including Andover, Melbourne, Mexico City, Stamford (CT), Toronto, Hong Kong, New Delhi, Seoul, Singapore, and Tokyo. Locate your local office at: **www.cengage.com/global**

Cengage Learning products are represented in Canada by Nelson Education, Ltd.

For product information, visit **www.cengage.co.in**

Printed by:
Rajiv Book Binding House
D-1518, DSHDC Industrial Complex, Narela, New Delhi 110040

Dedicated to

Lord Jagannath

PREFACE

The book covers the topics taught to graduate level engineering students of different Indian Universities. The engineering chemistry syllabi enlist topics from all the branches of chemistry, viz., inorganic, organic, physical, analytical, and material sciences. Therefore, there is a need of a book which will exclusively cover all the topics prescribed by these technological universities.

This book consolidates all these topics and presents the concepts in a simple, comprehensive, and illustrative manner. It emphasizes more on fundamental aspects in chemistry to help the students to increase their logical ability and self-confidence in making the algorithm for new problems. Emphasis has also been given to provide an exposure to the students the possible varieties of problems pertaining to a particular aspect.

The text has been organized in a format to suit classroom teaching. This approach will definitely help the students a lot. A particular methodological approach has been followed while dealing with conceptual and theoretical aspects of all topics. At the end, quite a good number of questions are given for practice. Solving these questions will boost the confidence of learners as well as give them a feel of the typical questions asked in the examination.

I express my sincere gratitude to Dr A. Samanta, Founder, KIIT Group of Institutions and KISS, for his continuous inspiration and encouragement. I am grateful to my colleagues Dr B.B. Patra, Dr K.G. Mishra, Dr B.B. Kar, Dr K. Parashar, Dr T.K. Bastia, Dr D. Behera, and Dr I. Chakraborty for their valuable suggestions during the preparation of the subject matter for the book. Thanks to Dr Bastia for his hardship in editing the chapters. I also thank Dr Chakraborty for his help in developing the portions of green chemistry, spectroscopy, and photochemistry. I deeply acknowledge my parents for their never-ending encouragement. It is my pleasure to thank my wife Nibedita and my daughter Pranita for their moral support, patience, and understanding during the preparation of the book.

I must thank my friends Mr Pabak K. Nanda, Mr Girish K. Mishra, Dr Alekh K. Sutar, Dr Anil Mohapatra, Dr. Arun K. Rout, and Mr S.N. Brahma for their constant encouragement.

I am thankful to Cengage Learning India and the entire editorial team for their cooperation and interest during the entire work. I humbly request my students and teachers to send their constructive criticism and suggestions in order to enable me to incorporate them in the next edition to make this book error free and more useful.

Lastly, I am highly indebted to one and all who have been directly or indirectly consulted during the preparation of the book.

I hope this book will serve its purpose and create interest towards the subject in its readers. Any suggestion and constructive criticism for further development of the book are most welcome.

Prasanta Rath

E-Mail:prathfch@gmail.com

CONTENTS

CHAPTER 7: SOLID STATE CHEMISTRY

CHAPTER 8: SURFACE CHEMISTRY

CHAPTER 10: STEREOCHEMISTRY AND ORGANIC REACTION MECHANISM

CHAPTER 11: ANALYTICAL CHEMISTRY

CHAPTER 14: FUEL AND COMBUSTION

CHAPTER

1 Structure and Bonding

Chapter Outline

- Maxwell Theory of Radiation (Classical Theory)
- Blackbody Radiation
- Photoelectric Effect
- Atomic Spectrum
- de Broglie's Concept
- Heisenberg Principle
- Schrödinger Wave Equation
- Particle in One-Dimensional Box
- Representation of Orbitals
- Molecular Orbital Theory
- Molecular Orbital Treatment of Metallic Bond (Band Theory)

The development of science in real sense started in the year 1803 with Dalton's idea of atom that "atom is the smallest indivisible particle which aggregates to form matter." The word *atom* has been derived from Greek word *átomos*, meaning indivisible. Much of the development in the modern atomic theory was based on two broad types of research performed during the late 1800s and early 1900s. Research first dealt with the more fundamental particles which form atom and also the approximate arrangement of these particles in an atom based on classical mechanics. The second broad area of research dealt with the interaction of matter with energy in the form of light, which led to a further detailed description of the arrangement of particles in atoms. This second approach is based on quantum mechanics.

Maxwell Theory of Radiation (Classical Theory)

Clark Maxwell (1856) put forward this theory. The theory successfully explains the mode of propagation of electromagnetic radiation and optical phenomena such as refraction, diffraction, and interference. The salient features of the theory are as follows:

1. The radiant energy, i.e., energy in the form of radiation, propagates in the form of continuous waves.
2. The energy of a radiation is proportional to its intensity, i.e., the square of amplitude of the wave.
3. The color of a radiation depends on its wavelength.
4. A body can emit or absorb energy continuously.
5. A black body radiates at a particular wavelength independent of temperature.

Towards the end of the nineteenth century, some phenomena were recorded which classical theory failed to explain. The important ones being energy distribution in blackbody spectrum, photoelectric effect, and line spectrum emitted by excited atoms.

Blackbody Radiation

Conceptually, a black body is one which absorbs all the radiation falling on it. Though it is not possible to have a perfect black body, an approximation can be a hollow spherical body having a pinhole and a conical projection just opposite to it, the inner surface of which is coated with lamp black (Ferry's black body; Fig. 1.1). When certain radiation is allowed to enter into the spherical body through the pinhole, the radiation suffers a number of internal deflections and is assumed to be completely absorbed. Such bodies absorb and incandescently re-emit radiation in a characteristic, continuous spectrum. At room temperature, black bodies emit mostly in infrared wavelengths. But as the temperature increases past a few hundred degrees Celsius, black bodies start to emit visible wavelengths, appearing red, orange, yellow, and blue with increasing temperature. By the time an object is white, it emits substantial ultraviolet radiation. To study energy distribution in a blackbody spectrum, let us consider Fig. 1.2, which shows a graph plotted by taking spectral energy density, i.e., the energy emitted per unit surface area as a function of wavelength at different temperatures.

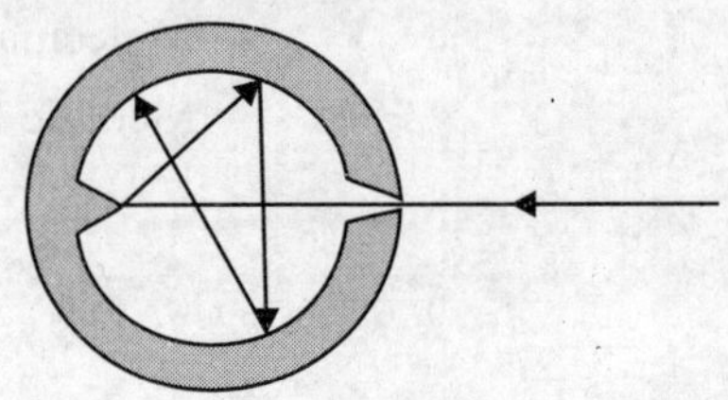

Fig. 1.1 Ferry's black body

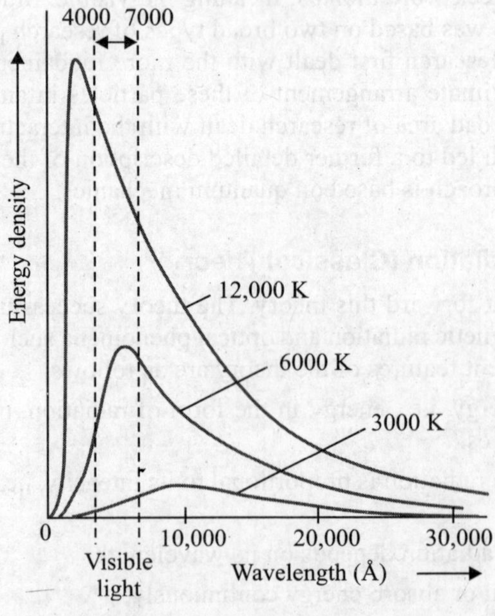

Fig. 1.2 Energy distribution curves

The significant features of the curves shown in Fig. 1.2 are as follows:

1. At a particular temperature, energy is not uniformly distributed among wavelengths.
2. The energy density increases with increase in wavelength, approaches a maximum, and subsequently decreases with further increase in wavelength.
3. For any wavelength, energy density is higher at higher temperature.
4. With increase in temperature, the wavelength corresponding to highest energy density shifts towards the lower wavelength side which is identified as *blue shift* (as per Wien's displacement law).
5. The total area below the curve corresponds to the total energy radiated. This area increases with increase in temperature (as per Stefan–Boltzmann law).

Note:

1. **Wien's displacement law**: The dominant wavelength at which a blackbody emits is inversely proportional to the temperature in absolute scale.

$$\lambda_{max} \propto \frac{1}{T}$$

$$= \frac{b}{T}$$

where "*b*" is Wien's constant having value 2.898×10^{-3} mK.

This law explains why a black body appears red, then orange, then yellow, and then even blue with the increase in temperature.

2. **Stefan–Boltzmann law**: The total energy flux emitted by a blackbody remains proportional to the fourth power of temperature in absolute scale.

$$E \propto T^4$$

$$= \sigma T^4$$

where σ is Stefan's constant which has a value 5.672×10^{-8} $Js^{-1}m^{-2}$ K^{-4}.

As per the law the area enclosed below a curve, i.e., the total energy emitted increases with the increase in temperature. Thus, it explains the growth in height of the curves with rise in temperature.

Let us try to look into the explanations suggested with respect to the classical and the quantum theory.

Classical theory

A black body radiates at a particular wavelength irrespective of temperature as energy is not related to wavelength, rather it is related to intensity. *Rayleigh* and *Jeans* developed a relation based on the classical theory between energy density and wavelength to account for the blackbody spectrum. According to them, the spectral energy density in the wavelength range λ and $(\lambda + d\lambda)$ is given by

$$dE = \frac{8\pi kT}{\lambda^4} d\lambda \qquad ...[1.1]$$

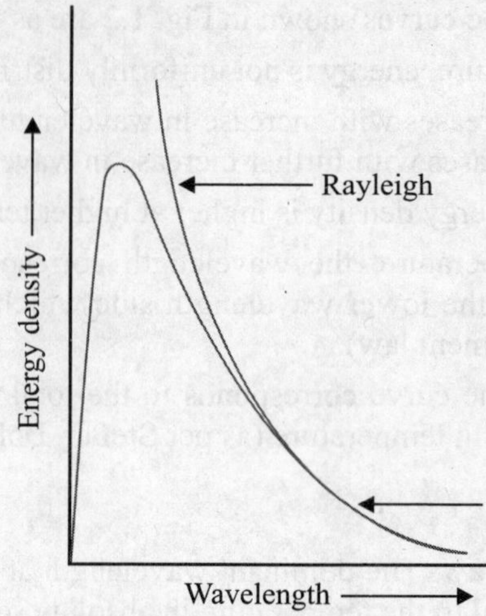

Fig. 1.3 Comparison of experimental blackbody spectrum and Rayleigh–Jeans law

It is quite evident from the relation that with decrease in wavelength, energy density increases and as it tends to zero, energy density tends to infinity without passing through the maximum (Fig. 1.3). In other words, oscillators of very short wavelengths are highly excited even at low temperature. This absurd result, which implies that a large amount of energy is radiated in the high-frequency region, is known as *ultraviolet catastrophe*. Therefore, the law is only successful in explaining the variation of energy density at higher values of wavelength but leads to an absurd result at very small wavelengths.

Quantum theory

To explain the blackbody spectrum, Max Planck in 1901 proposed a new theory, known as the *quantum theory* of radiation with the following features:

1. The energy of oscillators is limited to discrete values and cannot be varied arbitrarily, which eliminates the possibility of ultraviolet catastrophe.
2. An oscillator gains or losses energy in the form of small packets known as quanta.
3. The energy of a quantum is proportional to the frequency of oscillation, i.e. $E = h\nu$, where h is Planck's constant and has a value 6.627×10^{-34} J s.

Planck developed an expression to account for the blackbody spectrum on the basis of his quantum theory. According to him, the energy density in the wavelength range λ and $(\lambda + d\lambda)$ is given by

$$dE = \frac{8\pi hc}{\lambda^5}\left[\frac{1}{e^{hc/\lambda kT} - 1}\right] d\lambda \qquad ...[1.2]$$

Case I

At higher wavelengths, $\dfrac{hc}{\lambda kT}$ is very small; thus,

$$\frac{hc}{e^{\lambda kT}} = 1 + \frac{hc}{\lambda kT} + \cdots$$

Substituting this in relation [1.2], we get

$$dE = \frac{8\pi hc}{\lambda^5}\left(\frac{1}{\frac{hc}{\lambda}}\right) d\lambda$$

$$= \frac{8\pi hc}{\lambda^4} d\lambda$$

which is same as the Rayleigh expression, i.e., at higher wavelengths Planck's idea matches with Rayleigh and Jean's idea.

Case II

At very small wavelengths, $e^{\frac{hc}{\lambda kT}}$ tends to become infinite before λ^5 becomes zero, i.e.,

$$e^{\frac{hc}{\lambda kT}} \longrightarrow \infty$$

$$\text{Thus, } dE = \frac{8\pi hc}{\lambda^5}\left(\frac{1}{\infty}\right) d\lambda = 0$$

That is, the curve has to pass through a maximum and thereafter energy density decreases. It finally becomes zero as the wavelength approaches zero (Fig. 1.3). This is exactly what is observed in the distribution of energy among wavelengths in the blackbody spectrum.

Photoelectric Effect

The ejection of electrons from a metal surface as certain radiation of appropriate frequency interacts with it is known as photoelectric effect (Fig. 1.4). The electrons emitted are known as photo-electrons.

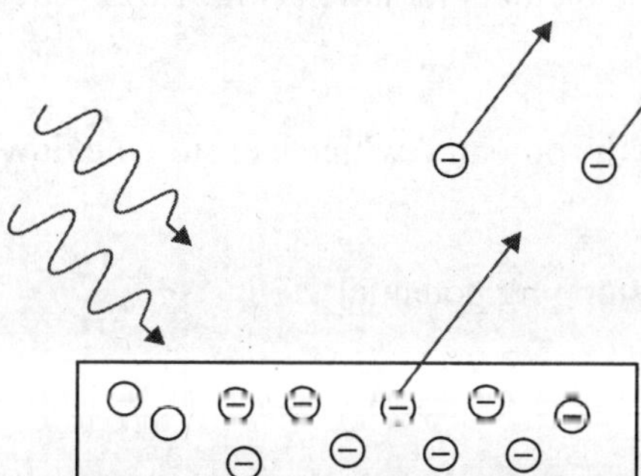

Fig. 1.4 Ejection of electrons from a metal surface

The laws of photoelectric effect are as follows:

1. Light radiation with only a very specific frequency or more than it (threshold or cut-off frequency) can cause ejection of an electron.
2. The velocity and energy of photoelectrons are proportional to the frequency.
3. The number of photoelectrons emitted is proportional to the intensity of incident radiation.

Again let us look into the suggestions made by the classical and the new theory.

Classical theory

As per this theory, it is possible to have photoelectric effect by striking a radiation with a frequency even less than the cut-off frequency on a metal surface. However, in practice, it does not happen. Again as per the classical theory, the velocity and the kinetic energy of photoelectrons should depend on intensity and not on frequency (Fig. 1.5).

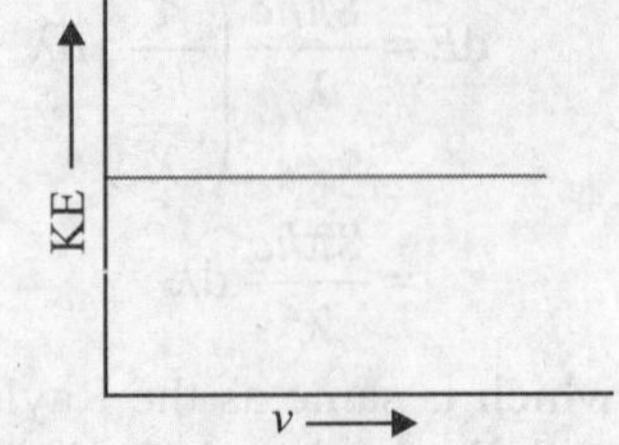

Fig. 1.5 Dependence of KE on frequency of incident radiation (classical concept)

Quantum theory

Einstein in 1905 explained the photoelectric effect on the basis of Planck's quantum theory. As per this theory, energy with only a very specific frequency (threshold frequency) can cause ejection of electrons. This is due to the fact that energy can neither be absorbed nor be emitted continuously; rather it happens so in the form of discrete packets.

Einstein suggested the following expression to account for the photoelectric effect:

$$h\nu = h\nu_0 + \frac{1}{2}mv^2 \quad ...[1.3]$$

where ν is the frequency of radiation striking on the metal surface,

ν_0 is the cut-off or threshold frequency,

$h\nu_0$ is the threshold energy [also known as work function (w_0)],

and $1/2\ mv^2$ is the kinetic energy of the ejected electron.

From relation [1.3], KE = $h\nu - h\nu_0 = h(\nu - \nu_0)$. Thus, KE depends on the frequency of the incident radiation (Fig. 1.6).

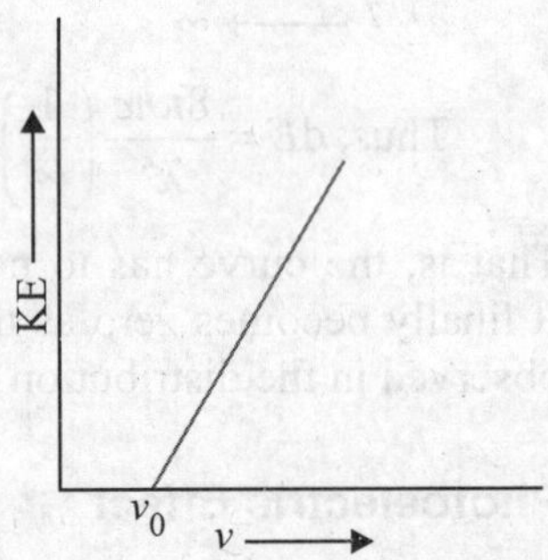

Fig. 1.6 Dependence of KE on frequency of incident radiation (quantum mechanical concept)

Note:

Stopping potential: It is the potential which can stop the flow of electrons emitted with their maximum velocity.

$\frac{1}{2}mv^2 = eV_s$; V_s is the stopping potential

Example 1.1

When light of wavelength of 400 nm strikes on the surface of sodium, electrons with a kinetic energy of 1.05 × 10⁵ J mol⁻¹ are emitted. Find the minimum energy required to remove an electron from sodium.

Solution

$$\text{KE of electron} = \frac{1.05 \times 10^5}{6.02 \times 10^{23}} = 1.74 \times 10^{-19}\ \text{J atom}^{-1}$$

From Einstein's photoelectric equation, we get

$$h\nu_0 = h\nu - \text{KE}$$

$$= h\frac{c}{\lambda} - \text{KE}$$

$$= \frac{6.62 \times 10^{-34} \times 3 \times 10^8}{400 \times 10^{-9}} 1.74 \times 10^{-19}$$

$$= 3.225 \times 10^{-19}\ \text{J}$$

Example 1.2

A light of wavelength 300 nm strikes on a certain metal with work function of 3 eV. Calculate the velocity of the ejected electron and the stopping potential.

Solution

$$h\nu = w_0 + \frac{1}{2} mv^2$$

$$\frac{1}{2} mv^2 = h\frac{c}{\lambda} = - w_0$$

$$= \frac{6.627 \times 10^{-34} \times 3 \times 10^8}{300 \times 10^{-9}} - 3 \times 1.6 \times 10^{-19}$$

$$= 1.826 \times 10^{-19}\ \text{J}$$

$$v = \sqrt{\frac{2 \times 1.826 \times 10^{-19}}{9.1 \times 10^{-31}}} = 6.33 \times 10^5\ \text{m s}^{-1}$$

Now, $\frac{1}{2} mv^2 = eV_s$

$$V_s = \frac{1}{2}\frac{mv^2}{e} = \frac{9.1 \times 10^{-31} \times (6.33 \times 10^5)^2}{2 \times 1.6 \times 10^{-19}} = 1.14\ \text{V}$$

Atomic Spectrum

Atomic spectrum appears as a line spectrum which can be explained only with respect to "quantum jumps" made by electrons during their excitation and de-excitation from one electronic level to another. As per the classical theory, an atomic spectrum should appear as a band spectrum.

de Broglie's Concept

As per *Louis de Broglie (1924)*, every material particle in motion has dual character, i.e., both particle and wave character. de Broglie developed an empirical relation to have the wavelength of the matter wave associated with the material particles in motion:

$$\text{Wavelength } (\lambda) = \frac{h}{mv} \quad \text{...[1.4]}$$

where m is the mass of the particle, v is the velocity of the particle, and h is Planck's constant.

Derivation

de Broglie's idea is an extension of Einstein's idea of the dual character of light. Let us consider a light photon. Its energy can be expressed in terms of Planck's relation as well as Einstein's mass–energy conversion relation as:

$$E = h\nu \qquad ...[1.5]$$

$$= mc^2 \qquad ...[1.6]$$

Now, from the above two relations, we get

$$h\nu = mc^2$$

$$h\frac{c}{\lambda} = mc^2$$

$$\lambda = \frac{h}{mc} \qquad ...[1.7]$$

For a material particle moving with velocity v, relation [1.7] takes the form

$$\lambda = \frac{h}{mv}$$

Physical significance

Let us find the wavelength of a macroscopic and a microscopic particle to look into the significance.

Case I

For a macroscopic particle like a bullet of mass 100 g moving with a velocity, say, 1000 m s^{-1}, the wavelength is

$$\lambda = \frac{6.627 \times 10^{-34}}{0.1 \times 10^{3}} = 6.627 \times 10^{-36} \text{ m}$$

⇒ The wavelength is too small to have any physical significance.

Case II

For a microscopic particle like an electron moving with a velocity, say, one hundredth of the velocity of light, the wavelength is

$$\lambda = \frac{6.627 \times 10^{-34}}{9.1 \times 10^{-31} \times 3 \times 10^{6}} = 2.427 \times 10^{-10} \text{ m}$$

$$= 2.427 \text{ Å}$$

Thus, the wavelength is appreciable.

Thus, the de Broglie concept has physical significance for only microscopic particles in motion.

Verification of Dual Character

Particle character

The particle character of microscopic particles such as electrons can be verified by observing the scintillations produced upon their striking on a fluorescent screen.

Wave character

The wave character of microscopic particles such as an electron can be the verified by the *Davission and Germer* experiment. The experiment was originally suggested to verify the wave character of an electron. In this experiment, a beam of electrons obtained from a heated filament is allowed to strike on a nickel crystal. The nickel crystal operates like a natural grating, and a characteristic diffraction pattern is observed on a photographic plate placed behind the crystal. This experiment confirms that the electron is capable of exhibiting diffraction, which is characteristic of a wave. This is how it establishes the wave character of electrons.

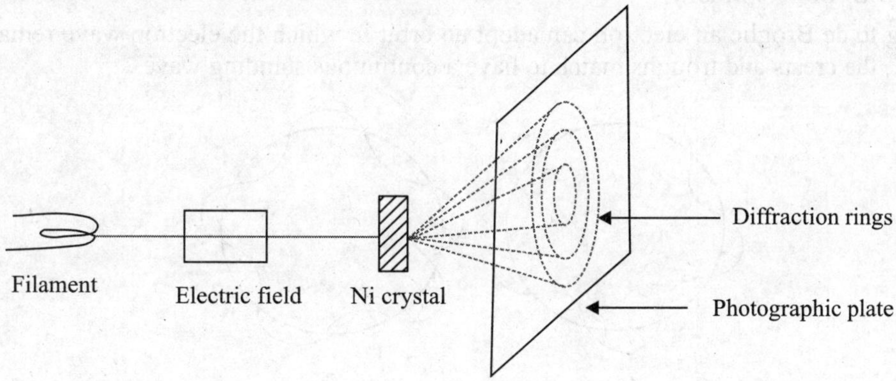

Fig. 1.7 Davission–Germer experimental setup

Mathematically,

$$eV = \frac{1}{2}mv^2$$

$$v^2 = \frac{2eV}{m}$$

$$v = \sqrt{\frac{2eV}{m}} \qquad \text{...[1.8]}$$

Again, $\lambda = \dfrac{h}{mv}$

$$= \frac{h}{m\sqrt{\dfrac{2eV}{m}}}$$

$$= \frac{h}{\sqrt{2eVm}} \qquad \text{...[1.9]}$$

In expression [1.9], all parameters are constants except the potential difference. Therefore, for an electron, the equation can be reduced by substituting the constants as

$h = 6.62 \times 10^{-34}$ J s, $e = 1.6 \times 10^{-19}$ C, and $m = 9.1 \times 10^{-31}$ kg

Now,

$$\lambda = \frac{6.62 \times 10^{-34}\ \text{J s}}{\sqrt{2 \times 1.6 \times 10^{-19}\ \text{C} \times V \times 9.1 \times 10^{-31}\ \text{kg}}}$$

$$= \frac{12.26}{\sqrt{V}}\ \text{Å} \qquad \text{...[1.10]}$$

The value of λ, obtained from relation [1.10], is in well agreement with the wavelength obtained experimentally by substituting Θ, the diffraction or glancing angle in Bragg's equation, $\lambda = 2d \sin \Theta$ (d is the lattice spacing, which for the Ni crystal is 2.87Å). This again confirms the wave nature of an electron as well as the validity of de Broglie's expression.

Analogy with Bohr's theory

According to de Broglie an electron can adopt an orbit in which the electron wave remains in phase, i.e., the crests and troughs match to have a continuous standing wave.

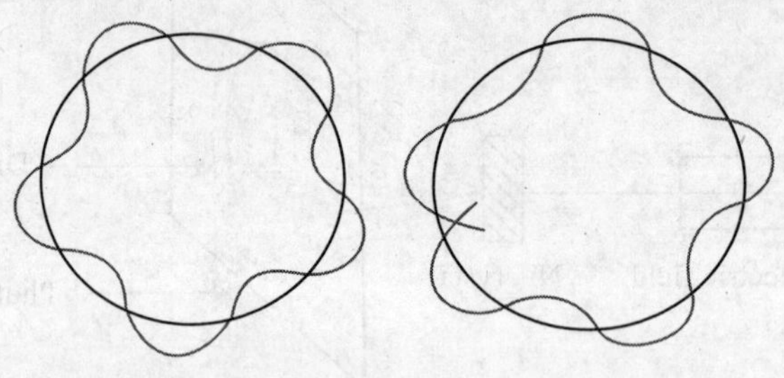

(a) (b)

Fig. 1.8 Electron waves in orbits: (a) in phase (b) out of phase

Mathematically, the condition required to have an electron wave in phase is that the circumference of the orbit must be an integral multiple of the wavelength:

$$2\pi r = n\lambda$$

$$= n\frac{h}{mv}$$

$$mvr = n\frac{h}{2\pi} \qquad \text{...[1.11]}$$

This is nothing but Bohr's assumption of quantization of angular momentum used to have the allowed orbits for electron.

Example 1.3

Calculate the wavelength of an α-particle moving with a velocity of 10^4 m s^{-1}.

Solution

$$\lambda = \frac{h}{mv}$$

$$= \frac{6.627 \times 10^{-34}}{4 \times 1.67 \times 10^{-27} \times 10^4} = 10^{-11} \text{ m}$$

Example 1.4

Calculate the wavelength of the electron that revolves in the second Bohr's orbit of a hydrogen atom.

Solution

$$v_n = 2.18 \times 10^6 \frac{Z}{n} \text{ m s}^{-1}$$

$$= \frac{2.18 \times 10^6}{2} = 1.09 \times 10^6 \text{ m s}^{-1}$$

Now, $\lambda = \frac{h}{mv}$

$$= \frac{6.627 \times 10^{-34}}{9.108 \times 10^{-31} \times 1.09 \times 10^6}$$

$$= 6.675 \times 10^{-10} \text{ m}$$

Example 1.5

An electron moves with a kinetic energy of 2.5 eV. Find the wave length of the electron.

Solution

$$\lambda = \frac{h}{\sqrt{2m \times \text{KE}}}$$

$$= \frac{6.629 \times 10^{-34}}{\sqrt{2 \times 9.108 \times 10^{-31} \times 1.602 \times 10^{-19} \times 2.5}}$$

$$= 1.23 \times 10^{-9} \text{ m}$$

Example 1.6

Calculate the wavelength of an electron that has been accelerated from rest through the potential difference of 10 kV.

Solution

$$\lambda = \frac{12.26}{\sqrt{V}} \text{ Å}$$

$$= \frac{12.26}{\sqrt{10^4}} \text{ Å}$$

$$= 0.0123 \text{ Å}$$

Example 1.7

Through what potential a beam of electrons be accelerated so that its wavelength becomes equal to 1.54 Å.

Solution

$$\lambda = \frac{h}{\sqrt{2eVm}}$$

or $V = \frac{h^2}{2em\lambda^2}$

$$= \frac{(6.627 \times 10^{-34})^2}{2 \times 1.602 \times 10^{-19} \times 9.108 \times 10^{-31} \times (1.54 \times 10^{-10})^2}$$

$$= 63.3 \text{ V}$$

Heisenberg Principle

In 1927, Werner Heisenberg from quantum mechanics showed that it is impossible to measure the position and momentum of a microscopic particle in motion simultaneously with absolute accuracy. To account for his principle, he developed the following expression:

$$\Delta x \, \Delta p \geq \frac{h}{4\pi} \qquad \text{...[1.12]}$$

where Δx and Δp are the uncertainty or error in the measurement of the position and the momentum, respectively.

Again, $p = mv$. Thus, substituting in relation [1.12], we get

$$\Delta x \, \Delta v \geq \frac{h}{4\pi m} \qquad \text{...[1.13]}$$

Physical significance

The physical significance of the principle can be explained by the consideration of interaction of light with both microscopic and macroscopic particles.

Case I

In case of macroscopic objects, the impact of light photon fails to bring any alteration in the position and velocity. Therefore, it is possible to know precisely the position and velocity of the object at a time, keeping the product of uncertainties in position and velocity negligible. Let us find the product for a cricket ball of mass 100 g.

$$\Delta x \, \Delta v \geq \frac{h}{4\pi m}$$

$$= \frac{6.627 \times 10^{-27}}{4 \times 3.14 \times 100} = 0.53 \times 10^{-29} \text{ cm}^2 \text{ s}^{-1}$$

Hence, the product in the uncertainties is too small to have any physical significance.

Case II

Let us try to find the position and velocity of a microscopic particle such as an electron. To find the position of the electron, a microscope is adjusted and a beam of light is thrown on it so that the photon strikes and the reflected photon can be seen in the microscope. To observe an object, the wavelength of the incident light should be less than its size. Thus, to visualize electron, light of very short wavelength, i.e., high energy is required. When such a high-energy photon strikes with the electron it transfers some of its energy to the electron. The result being the electron is deviated from its intended path and its velocity and momentum become uncertain. Therefore, the exact position and the velocity of a microscopic particle cannot be simultaneously determined. In other words, the magnitude of the product of uncertainties is significant. Let us find the product for the electron.

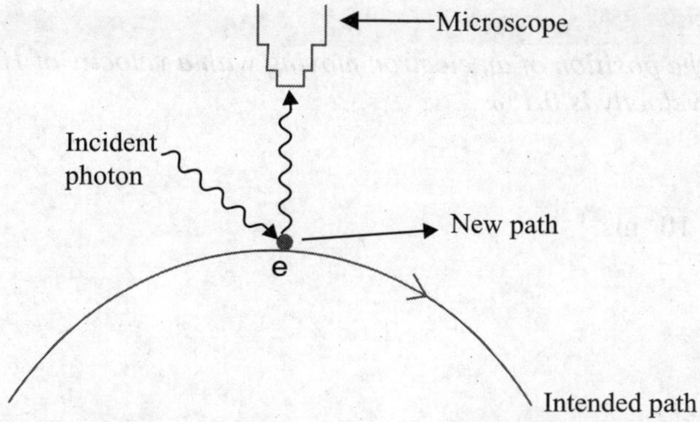

Fig. 1.9 Impact of photon on a microscopic particle such as electron

$$\Delta x\,\Delta v = \frac{h}{4\pi m}$$

$$= \frac{6.627 \times 10^{-27}}{4 \times 3.14 \times 9.108 \times 10^{-28}} = 0.579\ \text{cm}^2\ \text{s}^{-1}$$

Hence, the product in the uncertainties is appreciably large and cannot be neglected.

Conclusion

Like de Broglie concept, Heisenberg's uncertainty principle holds good for all objects but is of significance only for microscopic particles in motion. The reason for this is quite obvious. The energy of the photon is not sufficient to bring change in the position and velocity of macroscopic objects upon striking with them.

Example 1.8

"Electron cannot exist within the nucleus." Justify on the basis of Heisenberg's uncertainty principle.

Solution

By contradiction let us assume that electron can remain within nucleus. As the diameter of the atomic nucleus is of the order of 10^{-15} m, the maximum uncertainty in its position will be 10^{-15} m. Taking the mass of electron as 9.108×10^{-31} kg, the minimum uncertainty in velocity can be calculated by applying uncertainty principle as follows:

$$\Delta x\,\Delta v = \frac{h}{4\pi m}$$

or $$\Delta v = \frac{h}{4\pi m \times \Delta x}$$

$$= \frac{6.627 \times 10^{-34}}{4 \times 3.14 \times 9.108 \times 10^{-31} \times 10^{-15}}$$

$$= 6 \times 10^{10}\ \text{m s}^{-1}$$

This value is much higher than the velocity of light and hence is not possible. Thus the assumption taken in the beginning is wrong and electron can't remain within nucleus.

Example 1.9

Calculate the error in the position of an electron moving with a velocity of 10^6 m s^{-1}. The error in the measurement of velocity is 0.1%.

Solution

$$\Delta v = \frac{10^6 \times 0.1}{100} = 10^3 \text{ ms}^{-1}$$

$$\text{Now, } \Delta x \times \Delta v = \frac{h}{4\pi m}$$

$$\text{or} \quad \Delta x = \frac{h}{4\pi m \times \Delta v}$$

$$= \frac{6.627 \times 10^{-34}}{4 \times 3.14 \times 9.108 \times 10^{-31} \times 10^3}$$

$$= 5.791 \times 10^{-8} \text{ m}$$

Example 1.10

The uncertainty in position and velocity of a material particle in motion are 10^{-8} and 5.3×10^{-20} m, respectively. Find the mass of the particle.

Solution

$$\Delta x \times \Delta v = \frac{h}{4\pi m}$$

$$\text{or} \quad m = \frac{h}{4\pi \times \Delta x \times \Delta v}$$

$$= \frac{6.627 \times 10^{-34}}{4 \times 3.14 \times 10^{-8} \times 5.3 \times 10^{-20}}$$

$$= 9.952 \times 10^{-8} \text{ kg}$$

Schrödinger Wave Equation

To support uncertainty principle, E. Schrödinger utilized de Broglie's concept of matter wave and incorporated the wavelength expression into general classical wave equation. By this he developed a wave equation for a moving particle which is known as Schrödinger's wave equation. When the same is considered for "e" in an atom, it provides probability of finding "e" at different points in space around nucleus.

Considering the oscillation along one axis, say *X*-axis, the equation of standing wave is

$$\psi = A \sin \frac{2\pi x}{\lambda} \quad \text{...[1.14]}$$

where ψ is the wave function.

Now, differentiating with respect to x, we get

$$\frac{d\psi}{dx} = \frac{2\pi}{\lambda} A \cos \frac{2\pi x}{\lambda}$$

Again, taking the second derivative,

$$\frac{d^2\psi}{dx^2} = -\frac{2\pi}{\lambda} A \sin\frac{2\pi x}{\lambda} \times \frac{2\pi}{\lambda}$$

$$= -\frac{4\pi^2}{\lambda^2} A \sin\frac{2\pi x}{\lambda}$$

$$= -\frac{4\pi^2}{\lambda^2}\psi \qquad \text{...[1.15]}$$

Extending the relation to three dimension, we get

$$\frac{d^2\psi}{dx^2} + \frac{d^2\psi}{dy^2} + \frac{d^2\psi}{dz^2} = -\frac{4\pi^2}{\lambda^2}\psi$$

or $$\nabla^2\psi + \frac{4\pi^2}{\lambda^2}\psi = 0$$

or $$\nabla^2\psi + 4\pi^2\frac{m^2v^2}{h^2}\psi = 0 \qquad \left[\text{putting } \lambda = \frac{h}{mv}\right]$$

or $$\nabla^2\psi + 4\pi^2\, 2\frac{m^2v^2}{2h^2}\psi = 0$$

or $$\nabla^2\psi + 8\pi^2 m\frac{\text{KE}}{h^2}\psi = 0$$

or $$\nabla^2\psi + \frac{8\pi^2 m}{h^2}(E - V)\psi = 0 \qquad \text{...[1.16]}$$

where E is the total energy and V is the potential energy. Relation [1.16] is known as Schrödinger equation.

An alternate form

Multiplying $\left(-\frac{h^2}{8\pi^2 m}\right)$ to the relation, we get

$$-\frac{h^2}{8\pi^2 m}\nabla^2\psi - (E - V)\psi = 0$$

or $$\left(V - \frac{h^2}{8\pi^2 m}\nabla^2\right)\psi = E\psi$$

or $$\hat{H}\psi = E\psi \qquad \text{...[1.17]}$$

where $\hat{H}$ is the Hamiltonian operator.

Conversion of Schrödinger equation from Cartesian to polar co-ordinates

As an atom is considered to be spherical, spherical co-ordinates are more convenient to use than Cartesian co-ordinates. The relation between both these systems is shown in Fig. 1.10.

The value of Ψ at any point P is described in terms of polar co-ordinates r, θ, and φ. The relation between the Cartesian and polar co-ordinates can be developed by simple geometrical consideration. r is the radial distance of the point P from O and is called radius vector. θ is the angle between radius vector and Z-axis. A perpendicular is dropped on XY plane so that OP′ makes an angle of φ with X-axis which is known as longitudinal angle or azimuthal angle.

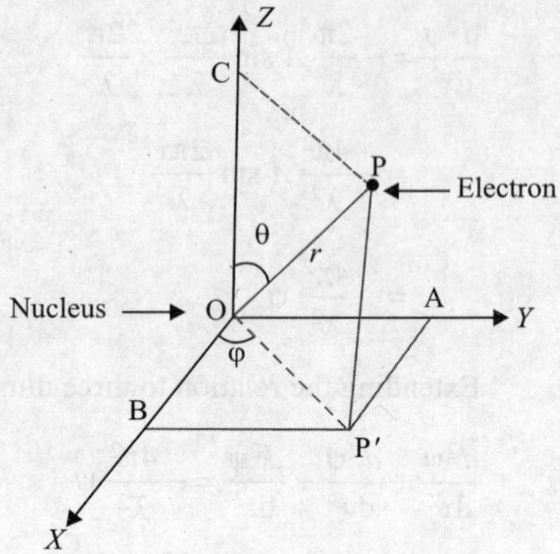

Fig. 1.10

From Δ OPC,

$$\cos\theta = \frac{OC}{OP}$$

or $OC = OP\cos\theta$

or $z = r\cos\theta$ ...[1.18]

Again, $\sin\theta = \dfrac{PC}{OP}$

or $PC = OP\sin\theta = r\sin\theta = OP'$ ...[1.19]

Now in Δ OP′B, $\sin\varphi = \dfrac{BP'}{OP'}$

or $BP' = OP'\sin\varphi = r\sin\theta\sin\varphi$

or $y = r\sin\theta\sin\varphi$ ...[1.20]

In the same triangle,

$$\cos\varphi = \frac{OB}{OP'}$$

or $OB = OP'\cos\varphi = r\sin\theta\cos\varphi$

or $x = r\sin\theta\cos\varphi$ ...[1.21]

On transforming relation [1.16] into polar co-ordinates, we get

$$\frac{1}{r^2}\left[\frac{\partial}{\partial r}\left(r^2\frac{\partial}{\partial r}\right)+\frac{1}{\sin\theta}\frac{\partial}{\partial\theta}\left(\sin\theta\frac{\partial}{\partial\theta}\right)+\frac{1}{\sin^2\theta}\frac{\partial^2}{\partial\varphi^2}\right]\psi+\frac{8\pi^2 m}{h^2}(E-V)\,\psi=0 \quad ...[1.22]$$

This relation [1.22] is Schrödinger equation in terms of polar co-ordinates.

Born Interpretation of Wave Function

The German scientist Max Born interpreted the wave functions in reference to the uncertainty principle. According to him, it is very difficult to establish absolutely that a particular electron is in a particular place at a particular time. Rather, over a long period of time, the electron has a certain probability of being in a certain region. This probability can be determined from the wave function ψ. Specifically, Born stated that the probability P of an electron being in a certain region between points a and b in space is

$$P = \int_a^b |\psi|^2 \, d\tau$$

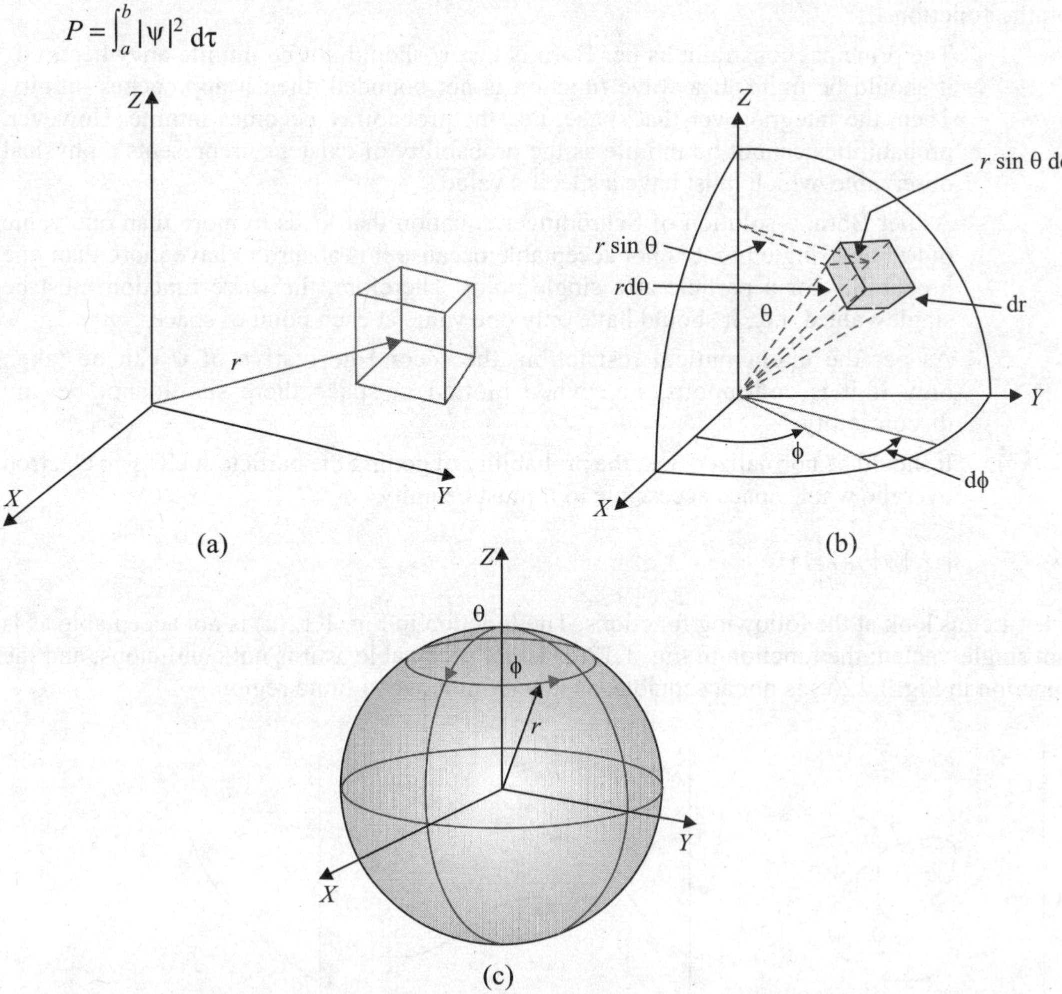

Fig. 1.11 (a) Small volume element in Cartesian coordinates, (b) polar coordinates, and (c) variation range of r, θ, and φ

If ψ is complex, then $|\psi|^2$ is replaced by $\psi\psi^*$, where ψ^* is the complex conjugate of ψ. In Cartesian coordinates, $d\tau$ is $dx\, dy\, dz$, and in spherical coordinates, it is $r^2 \sin\theta\, dr\, d\theta\, d\varphi$, and the integral is evaluated over the interval of interest (between points a and b, in this case). If one thinks of the probability over the whole space, then the limits of integration will be from $-\infty$ to $+\infty$ in Cartesian coordinates, while in spherical polar coordinates, r varies from 0 to ∞, θ varies from 0 to π, and φ varies from 0 to 2π [Fig. 1.11(c)]. The Born interpretation also requires that the probability be evaluated over a definite *region*, not at a specific point, in space. Thus, we should think of $|\psi|^2$ as an indicator of the *probability* that the electron will be in a certain region of space.

Eigen Functions and Values

Schrödinger equation has a number of solutions for ψ out of which a few are acceptable which satisfy the following conditions. The acceptable solutions are known as eigen functions, whereas the corresponding values of energies are known as eigen values. The conditions are imposed with reference to Born interpretation and mathematical restrictions on the function.

1. The principal constraint as per Born is that ψ should not be infinite anywhere, i.e., it should be finite. If a wave function is not bounded, then it approaches infinity. Then, the integral over that space, i.e., the probability becomes infinite. However, probabilities cannot be infinite as the probability of existence represents a physical observable which must have a specific value.
2. As per Born, a solution of Schrödinger equation that leads to more than one value of $|\psi|^2$ at a single point is not acceptable because it is absurd to have more than one probability for a particle at a single point. Therefore, the wave function must be single-valued, i.e., it should have only one value at each point of space.
3. As per the mathematical restriction, the second derivative of ψ can be taken only if it is continuous, i.e., when plotted in space there should not be any discontinuity.
4. It should be normalized, i.e., the probability of getting the particle such as an electron over the whole space accessible to it must be unity.

$$\int_{-\infty}^{+\infty} |\psi|^2 \, d\tau = 1$$

Let us look at the following functions. The function in Fig. 1.12(a) is not acceptable as is not single-valued; the function in Fig. 1.12(b) is not acceptable as it is not continuous; and the function in Fig. 1.12(c) is not acceptable, as it is infinite over a finite region.

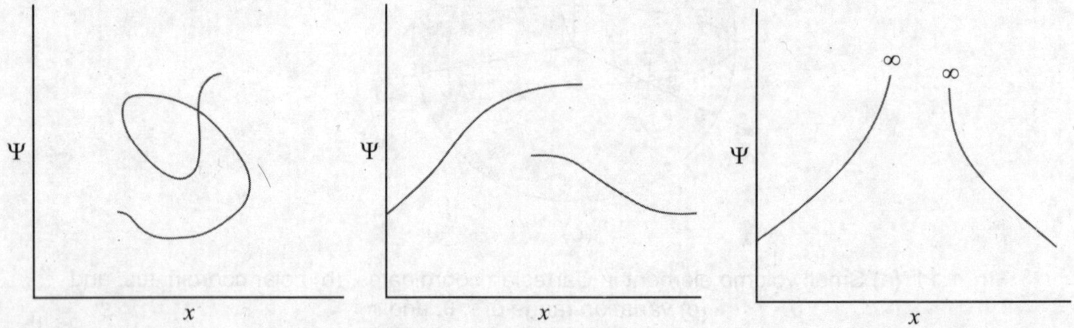

(a) (b) (c)

Fig. 1.12

Significance of ψ

1. It is a solution of Schrödinger equation.
2. It represents the amplitude of an electron wave.
3. Describes the variation of amplitude of an electron wave with distance and direction.
4. Although a number of values are there, only a few are acceptable which are known as eigen functions.
5. Each eigen function corresponds to an atomic orbital in case of an atom and a molecular orbital in case of a molecule.

Significance of ψ^2

Represents the probability of finding an electron with a specified energy from place to place in a given region of space around the nucleus.

Particle in One-Dimensional Box

Let us illustrate the properties of wave mechanics and wave functions by using the Schrödinger wave equation to describe a simple hypothetical model "particle in a box." The reason for this treatment is of three fold. The first one being to illustrate the mathematics of wave mechanics, the second one being to give characteristics of wave functions, and finally the third one being to show how energy quantization arises.

A particle with mass M is free to move along one direction arbitrarily say x-axis between the values $x = 0$ and $x = L$. The potential energy $V(x)$ of the particle is zero at all points along its path except at the end points where it is infinitely large. Thus, it is assumed that the particle is kept in a one-dimensional box with impenetrable walls, and the probability of getting the particle outside is zero.

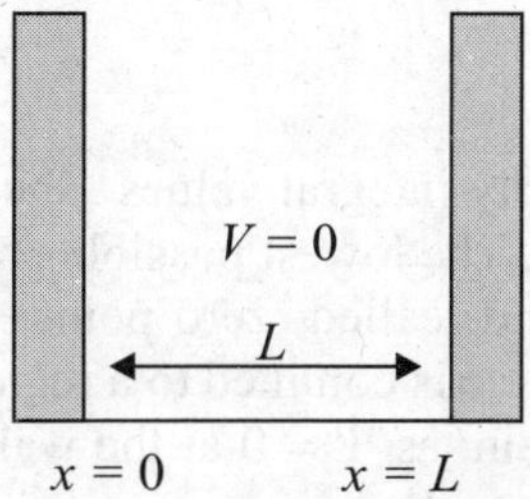

Fig. 1.13 Particle in one-dimensional box

$$V(x) = \begin{cases} \infty & x < 0 \\ 0 & 0 \le x \le L \\ \infty & x > L \end{cases}$$

The Schrödinger equation for the motion of the particle is

$$\frac{d^2\Psi}{dx^2} + \frac{8\pi^2 m}{h^2}(E - V)\,\Psi = 0$$

or $$\frac{d^2\Psi}{dx^2} + \frac{8\pi^2 m}{h^2}E\,\Psi = 0$$

or $$\frac{d^2\Psi}{dx^2} + k^2\,\Psi = 0$$

where $$k^2 = \frac{8\pi^2 m}{h^2}E \qquad \text{...[1.23]}$$

The general solution of the equation is,

$$\Psi(x) = A \sin kx + B \cos kx \qquad \text{...[1.24]}$$

Now, to be a valid wave function, Ψ must satisfy certain boundary conditions. Firstly, it must be a continuous function of x, and since $\Psi = 0$ for $x < 0$, $\Psi(0) = 0$:

$$\Psi(0) = A \sin(0) + B \cos(0) = 0$$

$\Rightarrow$ $B = 0$

At the other wall, $\Psi(L) = 0$

$$\Psi(L) = A \sin(kL) + B \cos(kL) = 0$$

$\Rightarrow$ $A \sin(kL) = 0$

$\Rightarrow$ $kL = n\pi$, where n can have only integral values, i.e., 1, 2, 3, ...

$$\Rightarrow \quad k = \frac{n\pi}{L} \qquad ...[1.25]$$

Substituting k in relation [1.23], we get

$$E = \frac{k^2 h^2}{8\pi^2 m} = \frac{\left(\frac{n\pi}{L}\right)^2 h^2}{8\pi^2 m}$$

$$= \frac{n^2 h^2}{8mL^2} \qquad ...[1.26]$$

As the constant n can have only integral values , the energy associated with the motion of the particle in a box is quantized. The lowest possible energy which the particle can possess is for $n = 1$, i.e., $E_1 = h^2/8\ mL^2$, and called zero point energy. Interestingly, the zero point energy is not zero. Thus, if the particle is confined to a region it always remains in motion, i.e., possesses some kinetic energy. Again, as $\Psi = 0$ at the walls, but smooth, continous and non-zero everywhere, then it must be curved.

From relations [1.24] and [1.25], we get

$$\Psi = A \sin \frac{n\pi}{L} x \qquad ...[1.27]$$

The value of constant A can be evaluated by finding the total probability of finding the particle from $x = 0$ to L which is unity.

$$\int_0^L \Psi\Psi^* \, dx = 1$$

or $$\int_0^L \left[A \sin \frac{n\pi}{L}\right]^2 dx = 1$$

or $$A^2 \int_0^L \sin^2\left(\frac{n\pi x}{L}\right) dx = 1$$

or $$\frac{A^2}{2} \int_0^L \left[1 - \cos\left(\frac{2n\pi x}{L}\right)\right] dx = 1 \qquad \left[\because \sin^2\theta \frac{1}{2}(1 - \cos 2\theta)\right]$$

or $$\frac{A^2}{2} \left[\int_0^L dx - \int_0^L \cos \frac{2n\pi x}{L} dx\right] = 1$$

or $$\frac{A^2}{2} \left[\int_0^L dx\right] = 1$$

or $$\frac{A^2}{2}L = 1$$

or $$A = \sqrt{\frac{2}{L}} \qquad \text{...[1.28]}$$

Now, the wave function for the particle in one-dimensional box is

$$\Psi(x) = \sqrt{\frac{2}{2}} \sin \frac{n\pi}{L} x \qquad (\text{for } n = 1, 2, 3, \ldots) \qquad \text{...[1.29]}$$

The corresponding energy levels are

$$E = \frac{n^2 h^2}{8mL^2}$$

This analysis leads to a series of solutions to the Schrödinger equation. The wave functions of the four lowest states along with their corresponding energies are as follows.

n	Wave function	Energy
1	$\Psi_1 = \sqrt{\frac{2}{L}} \sin \frac{\pi}{L} x$	$E = \frac{h^2}{8mL^2}$ (Zero-point energy)
2	$\Psi_2 = \sqrt{\frac{2}{L}} \sin \frac{2\pi}{L} x$	$E = \frac{h^2}{2mL^2}$
3	$\Psi_3 = \sqrt{\frac{2}{L}} \sin \frac{3\pi}{L} x$	$E = \frac{9h^2}{8mL^2}$
4	$\Psi_4 = \sqrt{\frac{2}{L}} \sin \frac{4\pi}{L} x$	$E = \frac{2h^2}{mL^2}$

Thus, for a bound system, the energies are quantized, because boundary conditions require that n assumes only integer values. The solutions can be conveniently represented by a plot of wave functions and probability distribution. The following facts regarding the plot must be noted:

1. Note that each wave function goes to zero at the edges of the box. In addition, it also becomes zero at various points within the box. The number of times it becomes zero is equal to $(n - 1)$. The point at which $\Psi = 0$ is known as node.
2. The number of nodes increases with increase of n.
3. The probability density is not uniform at all positions. For $n = 1$, the particle is most likely to be present near the center of the box. For $n = 2$, the probability of finding the particle is zero in the center of the box. The distribution becomes more and more uniform with increase of n. For very high value of "n," the distribution is completely uniform. Therefore, for higher values of "n," particle spends equal time at all points which is nothing but the classical behavior.
4. The separation between adjacent energy levels with quantum numbers "n" and "$n + 1$" is

$$E_{n+1} - E_n = \frac{(n+1)^2 h^2}{8mL^2} - \frac{n^2 h^2}{8mL^2}$$

$$= (2n+1)\frac{h^2}{8mL^2}$$

This separation decreases as the length of the container increases and becomes very small when the container has macroscopic dimensions. The separation of adjacent levels tends to zero when the walls are infinitely far apart. Therefore, on removal of boundary condition, the energy levels behave as continuum.

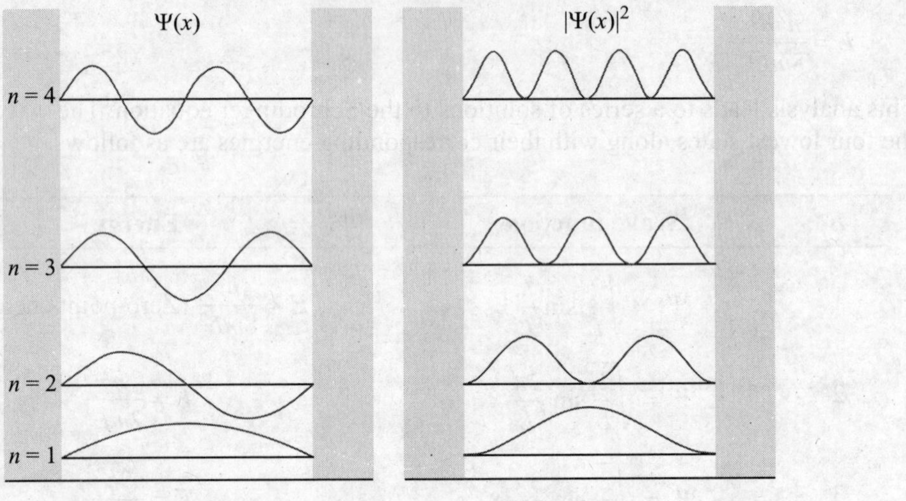

Fig. 1.14 Quantization of energy levels in a one-dimensional box

Example 1.11

Assuming an electron to be confined in a one-dimensional box 2.0 nm in length, find the lowest three energy levels for the electron. Also find the wavelength of the radiation emitted during de-excitation of electron from the first excited state to ground state.

Solution

$$E = \frac{n^2 h^2}{8mL^2}$$

For electron,

For $n = 1$, $E_1 = \dfrac{(6.627 \times 10^{-34})^2}{8 \times 9.11 \times 10^{-31} \times (2.0 \times 10^{-9})^2} = 1.506 \times 10^{-20}$ J

Similarly, For $n = 2$, $E_2 = 6.024 \times 10^{-20}$ J and for $n = 3$, $E_3 = 1.355 \times 10^{-19}$ J

$$\frac{hc}{\lambda} = E_2 - E_1$$

or $\quad \dfrac{hc}{\lambda} = 6.024 \times 10^{-20} - 1.506 \times 10^{-20} = 4.518 \times 10^{-20}$

or $$\lambda = \frac{6.627 \times 10^{-34} \times 3 \times 10^{8}}{4.518 \times 10^{-20}} = 4.4 \times 10^{-6} \text{ m}$$

Note:

1. **Validity of de-Broglie relation for particle in 1D-box**

$$E = \frac{p^2}{2m} \text{ [as } E \text{ is Kinetic Energy]}$$

Again, from de-Broglie relation, $p = \frac{h}{\lambda}$

Since the particle is in motion within boundary conditions, i.e., $x = 0$ and $x = L$, one can write,

$$n\lambda = 2L$$

or $$\lambda = \frac{2L}{n}$$

Now, substituting p and λ, $E = \frac{p^2}{2m} = \frac{n^2h^2}{8mL^2}$

This relation is same as obtained in 1D-box.

The point to be marked is that this approach cannot justify the non zero value of n.

2. **Justification of uncertainty principle from zero point energy**: Zero point energy is not zero. This suggests that even at 0 K the particle remains in motion. Thus, its position cannot be precisely determined even at 0 K. Ultimately momentum can not be determined. Hence, the fact that zero point energy is not zero supports uncertainty principle.

Representation of Orbitals

For representation of an orbital on pen and paper one has to plot the corresponding wave function Ψ as a function of polar co-ordinates r, θ, and φ. Now, it is not possible to plot all the four parameters at a time. In practice, the variables Ψ, r, and φ are separated into the product of three functions.

$$\Psi(r, \theta, \varphi) = R(r) \cdot \Theta(\theta) \cdot \varphi(\varphi)$$
$$= R_{n,l}(r) . Y_{l,m}(\theta, \varphi)$$

where n is the principal quantum number, l is the Azimuthal quantum number, and m is the magnetic quantum number.

Radial Plots

Radial wave function

$R(r)$ denotes the radial wave function, which provides the variation of the amplitude of the electron wave with respect to the distances from the nucleus. Some important facts regarding this can be summarized as follows:

1. It is characterized by only two quantum numbers, n and l, where n and l correspond to principal and azimuthal quantum numbers, respectively.
2. The general form of the radial wave function is $R_{n,l}(r) = Np(r)e^{-kr}$., where N is a positive normalizing constant, $p(r)$ is a polynomial in r, and k is a positive constant.

3. A particular distance from the nucleus where $R_{n,l}(r)$ becomes zero is called a *radial (or spherical) node.* Possible number of radial nodes = $(n - l - 1)$.
4. The sign of $R_{n,l}(r)$ depends on the behavior of $p(r)$. As the exponential factor has a negative sign in the exponent, $R_{n,l}(r)$ approaches zero as r goes to infinity.

Some exact radial wave functions solved for hydrogen and hydrogen like atoms are as follows. Here, a_0 is Bohr's radius. Remember for hydrogen, $Z = 1$.

For 1*s* orbital, $R_{1,0}(r) = 2\left(\frac{z}{a_0}\right)^{3/2} e^{-Zr/a_0}.$

For 2*s* orbital, $R_{2,0}(r) = \frac{1}{2\sqrt{2}}\left(\frac{z}{a_0}\right)^{3/2}\left(2 - \frac{zr}{a_0}\right) e^{-Zr/2a_0}.$

For 2*p* orbital, $R_{2,1}(r) = \frac{1}{2\sqrt{6}}\left(\frac{z}{a_0}\right)^{3/2}\left(\frac{zr}{a_0}\right) e^{-Zr/2a_0}.$

For 3*s* orbital, $R_{3,0}(r) = \frac{2}{81\sqrt{3}}\left(\frac{z}{a_0}\right)^{3/2}\left(27 - \frac{18Zr}{a_0} + \frac{2z^2r^2}{a_0^2}\right) e^{-Zr/3a_0}.$

For 3*p* orbital, $R_{3,1}(r) = \frac{4}{81\sqrt{6}}\left(\frac{z}{a_0}\right)^{3/2}\left(\frac{6Zr}{a_0} - \frac{z^2r^2}{a_0^2}\right) e^{-Zr/3a_0}.$

For 3*d* orbital, $R_{3,2}(r) = \frac{4}{81\sqrt{30}}\left(\frac{z}{a_0}\right)^{3/2}\left(\frac{Zr}{a_0}\right)^2 e^{-Zr/3a_0}.$

Let us look at the plots of some radial wave functions.

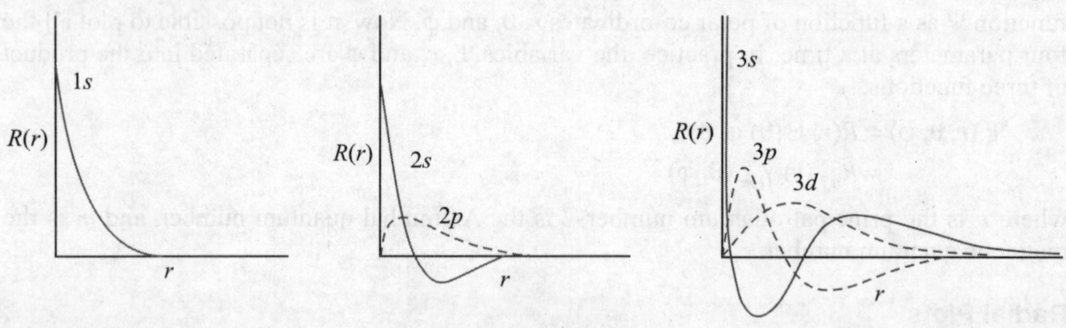

Fig. 1.15

Radial probability function

These plots never correspond to the probability of getting an electron at a distance r from the nucleus. The reason is twofold. In the plot, $R_{n,l}(r)$ becomes maximum at $r = 0$, i.e., the probability of getting an electron is maximum in the nucleus, which is not acceptable. Again, $R_{n,l}(r)$ has both positive and negative values, but probability cannot be negative. Therefore, instead of $R_{n,l}(r)$, $R^2(r)$ is taken into account. $R^2(r)$ is known as the radial probability function, which provides the probability of finding an electron at a distance r from the nucleus. Let us look at some radial probability function plots.

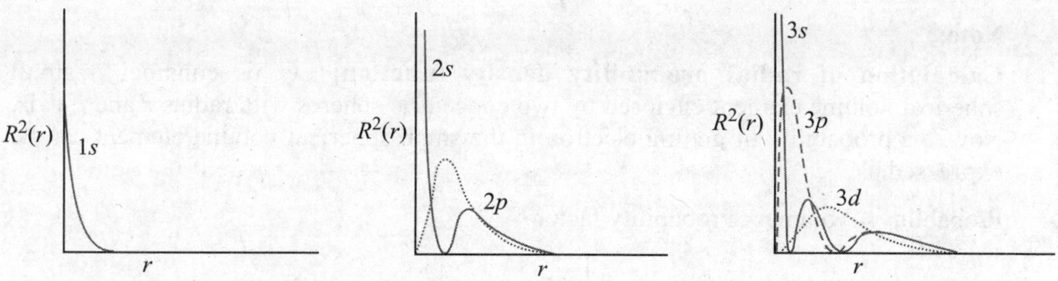

Fig. 1.16

Radial probability density function

If the probability density is related to $R^2(r)$ instead of $R_{n,l}(r)$, then also one problem persists that for *s*-orbitals, still the curves show maximum probability in the nucleus ($r \approx \theta$), which is not possible in reality, although in this case the curves never show any negative value. The problem can be sorted out by taking radial probability density function $4\pi r^2 R^2(r)$. Some important facts regarding this can be summarized as follows:

1. All the orbitals have zero radial probability at $r = 0$.
2. The curves start from the origin, and the area covered under an envelope of a particular curve increases from left to right so that the area of the last envelope is the maximum.
3. The peak of the last envelope of each curve provides the distance from the nucleus where the probability of finding the electron is the maximum.
4. The point at which $4\pi r^2 R^2(r) = 0$ is called the radial node. The number of radial nodes, as mentioned above, is equal to $n - l - 1$.
5. The more the number of radial nodes for an orbital, the larger is the size of that orbital and the more diffused it becomes.
6. Thus, the relative penetrating power of different orbitals belonging to the same value of *n* follows the order: $s > p > d > f$. This means that the *s*-orbital is more penetrating into the nucleus than the p-orbital, and so on (Fig. 1.17).

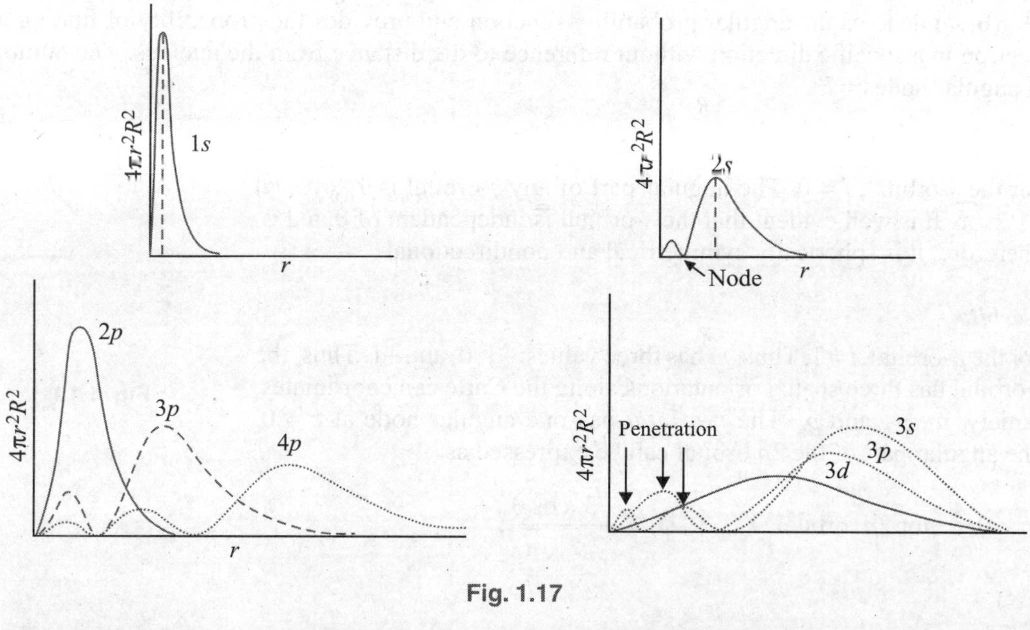

Fig. 1.17

Note:

Calculation of radial probability density function: Let us consider a small spherical volume element enclosed by two concentric spheres with radius r and $r + dr$. Now, the probability of getting electron in the small spherical volume element can be expressed as:

Probability = Volume × Probability factor

$$= \left[\frac{4}{3}\pi(r+dr)^3 - \frac{4}{3}\pi r^3\right] \times R^2$$

$$= \left[\frac{4}{3}\pi(r^3 + dr^3 + 3r^2dr + 3dr^2 r) - \frac{4}{3}\pi r^3\right] \times R^2$$

$$= \left[\frac{4}{3}\pi 3r^2dr\right] \times R^2$$

$$= 4\pi r^2 dr R^2$$

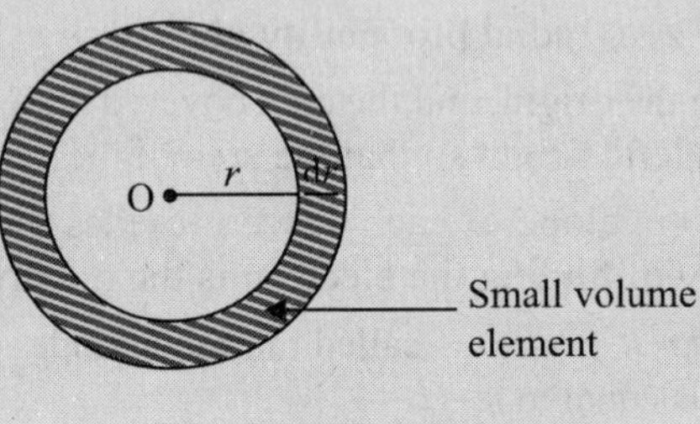

Fig. 1.18

Angular Plots

$Y_{l,m}$ (θ, φ) is the angular wave function. It is characterized by two quantum numbers, l and m, where l and m correspond to azimuthal and magnetic quantum numbers, respectively. $Y^2_{l,m}$(θ, φ) denotes the angular probability function and provides the probability of finding an electron in a specific direction without reference to the distance from the nucleus. The number of angular nodes = l.

s-orbital

For the *s*-orbital, $l = 0$. The angular part of any *s*-orbital is $Y_{0,0}$ (θ, φ) $= 1/2\sqrt{\pi}$. It is well evident that the *s*-orbital is independent of θ and φ. Therefore, it is spherically symmetrical and nondirectional.

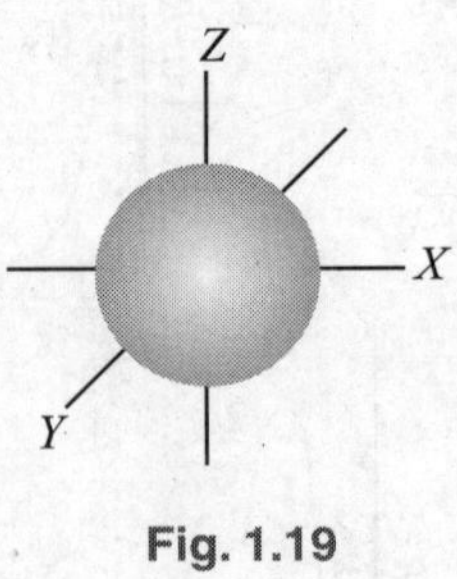

Fig. 1.19

p-orbital

For the *p*-orbital, $l = 1$. Thus, m has three values: –1, 0, and +1. Thus, the *p*-orbital has three spatial orientations along the Cartesian coordinates, namely, p_x, p_y, and p_z. The *p-orbital* has one angular node at $r = 0$. The angular part of the 2*p* orbital can be expressed as

1. for $2p_z$ orbital, $Y_{1,0}(\theta, \varphi) = \dfrac{\sqrt{3}}{2}\dfrac{\cos\theta}{\sqrt{\pi}}$;

2. for $2p_x$ orbital, $Y_{1,+1}(\theta, \varphi) = \dfrac{\sqrt{3}}{2}\dfrac{\sin\theta\cos\varphi}{\sqrt{\pi}}$; and

3. for $2p_y$ orbital, $Y_{1,-1}(\theta, \varphi) = \dfrac{\sqrt{3}}{2}\dfrac{\sin\theta\sin\varphi}{\sqrt{\pi}}$.

Analysis of the wave functions reveals the following points:

1. These orbitals have maximum values along their respective coordinate axes. $2p_z$ [$Y_{1,0}(\theta, \varphi)$] attains maximum when $\theta = 0$, i.e., when $\cos\theta = 1$. At $\theta = 0$, $Y_{1,+1}(\theta, \varphi)$ and $Y_{1,-1}(\theta, \varphi)$ become zero.
2. At $\theta = 90°$ and $\varphi = 0$, $\sin\theta\cos\varphi = 1$; the wave function $Y_{1,+1}(\theta, \varphi)$ becomes maximum along the *X*-axis.
3. At $\theta = 90°$ and $\varphi = 90°$, $\sin\theta\sin\varphi = 1$; the wave function $Y_{1,-1}(\theta, \varphi)$ becomes maximum along the *Y*-axis.
4. On either side of the nucleus along the Cartesian coordinates, the wave functions have opposite signs. This is readily understood from the limits of variation of θ (from 0 to π) and φ (from 0 to 2π).

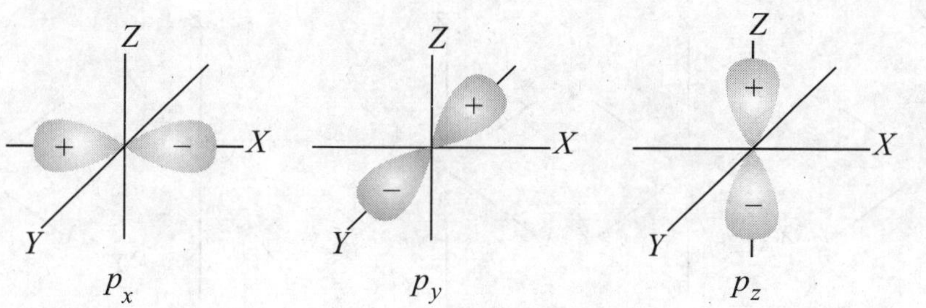

Fig. 1.20

***d*-orbital**

For the *d*-orbital, $l = 2$. Thus, *m* has five values: –2, –1, 0, +1, and +2. Thus, the *d*-orbital has five spatial orientations along the Cartesian coordinates, namely, d_{xy}, d_{yz}, d_{z^2}, d_{zx}, and $d_{x^2-y^2}$. The *d-orbital* has two angular nodes at $r = 0$. The angular part of the 3*d* orbital can be expressed as

1. for orbital, $3d_{xy} = Y_{2,2}(\theta, \varphi) = \dfrac{\sqrt{15}}{4}\dfrac{1}{\sqrt{\pi}}\sin^2\theta\sin 2\varphi$;

2. for $3d_{yz}$ orbital, $Y_{2,-1}(\theta, \varphi) = \dfrac{\sqrt{30}}{2\sqrt{2}}\dfrac{1}{\pi}\sin\theta\cos\theta\sin\varphi$;

3. for $3d_{z2}$ orbital, $Y_{2,0}(\theta, \varphi) = \dfrac{\sqrt{5}}{4\sqrt{\pi}}(3\cos^2\theta - 1)$;

4. for $3d_{zx}$ orbital, $Y_{2,1}(\theta, \varphi) = \dfrac{\sqrt{30}}{2\sqrt{2}}\dfrac{1}{\pi}\sin\theta\cos\theta\cos\varphi$; and

5. for $3d_{x2-y2}$ orbital, $Y_{2,1}(\theta, \varphi) = \dfrac{\sqrt{15}}{4}\dfrac{1}{\sqrt{\pi}}\sin^2\theta\cos 2\varphi$.

Analysis of the wave functions reveals the following points:

1. The d_{xy} orbital has $\sin^2 \theta \sin 2\varphi$. Therefore, such a wave function reduces to 0 along the Z-axis as $\theta = 0°$, along the X-axis as $\theta = 90°$ but $\varphi = 0°$, and along the Y-axis as $\theta = 90°$ and $\varphi = 90°$. The wave function becomes maximum on the XY-plane at 90° to the Z-axis, i.e., $\theta = 90°$, but at 45° from either the X- or the Y-axis, i.e., $\varphi = 45°$. Since the XY-plane has four quadrants, the orbital has four lobes—one in each of the four quadrants having alternate positive and negative signs.
2. Similar discussions can be made for d_{yz} and d_{zx} orbitals which lie in the YZ- and ZX-planes, respectively.
3. The d_{z2} orbital becomes maximum at $\theta = 0°$. At $\theta = 90°$, the orbital has a negative value. The orbital remains concentrated along the Z-axis with a positive sign and, in addition, along a ring around the nucleus in the XY-plane with a negative sign.
4. d_{x2-y2} reduces to zero when $\theta = 0°$ or 180°, i.e., along the Z-axis. It becomes maximum at $\theta = 90°$ and $\varphi = 0°$, i.e., along the X-axis, and also at θ and φ both 90°. Therefore, the orbital is concentrated along the X- and the Y-axes. The orbital has four lobes having alternate positive and negative signs.

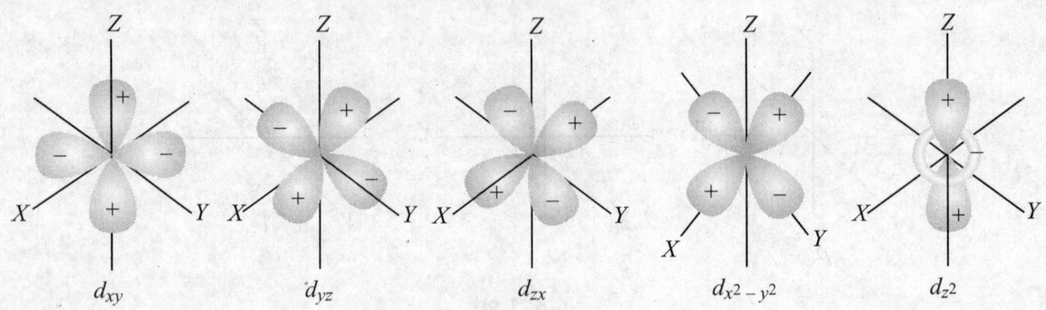

Fig. 1.21 Angular probability curves

Molecular Orbital Theory

To overcome the limitations of VBT, Hund and Mulliken put forward a new theory to explain formation of covalent bonds known as molecular orbital (MO) theory. Salient features of MO theory being:

1. As the combining atoms approach each other their atomic orbitals with same or nearly same energy and appropriate symmetry undergo linear combination to form a completely new set of orbitals known as molecular orbitals.
2. The number of molecular orbitals formed is equal to the number of atomic orbitals participating in linear combination.
3. The molecular orbital formed by addition overlap (when atomic orbitals remain in phase) of atomic orbitals is called bonding molecular orbital. Such an orbital posseses less energy than the combining atomic orbitals.
4. The molecular orbital formed by subtraction overlap (when atomic orbitals remain in different phase) of atomic orbitals is called antibonding molecular orbital. Such an orbital posseses more energy than the combining atomic orbitals.
5. Unlike atomic orbitals, molecular orbital is polycentric.

6. The shapes of molecular orbitals depend on the shapes of atomic orbitals from which they are generated.
7. Filling of molecular orbitals follows the same rules used for filling of atomic orbitals.

Linear Combination of Atomic Orbitals

Molecular orbitals of a molecule, i.e., solutions to the molecular Schrodinger equation can be obtained by a method known as linear combination of atomic orbitals (LCAO). As per this method, linear combination is brought about by taking the summation or differences of atomic orbital wave functions. For diatomic molecules, such a wave function takes the form,

$$\Psi = N(C_A \Psi_A \pm C_B \Psi_B) \qquad ...[1.30]$$

where Ψ is the wave function of MO; Ψ_A, Ψ_B are wave functions of AOs belonging to atom *A* and *B*, respectively; C_A, C_B are adjustable coefficients (for identical atoms $C_A = C_B = 1$); and *N* is the normalizing factor chosen to ensure that $\int \Psi\Psi^* \, d\tau = 1$, i.e., probability of finding an electron in the whole space in unity.

$$N = \frac{1}{\sqrt{\sum C_i^2}}$$, where C_i is the coefficient of the AOs (for identical atoms $N = 1/\sqrt{2}$)

The equation clearly shows that linear combination of Ψ^a and Ψ^b gives rise to two MOs. One is obtained by taking the sum of two AO wave functions, i.e., wave functions $\Psi^b = N(C_A \Psi_A + C_B \Psi_B)$ resulting in an increased electron density between the two nuclei. This is the bonding MO which has a lower energy than the combining AOs. The other MO namely *a* is obtained by taking the difference of two AO wave function, i.e., wave functions $\Psi^a = N(C_A \Psi_A - C_B \Psi_B)$. It has a node with zero electron density between the nuclei due to cancellation of two wave functions and has a higher energy. It is, therefore, the antibonding MO. The following energy level diagram (Fig. 1.22) is helpful in understanding the processes.

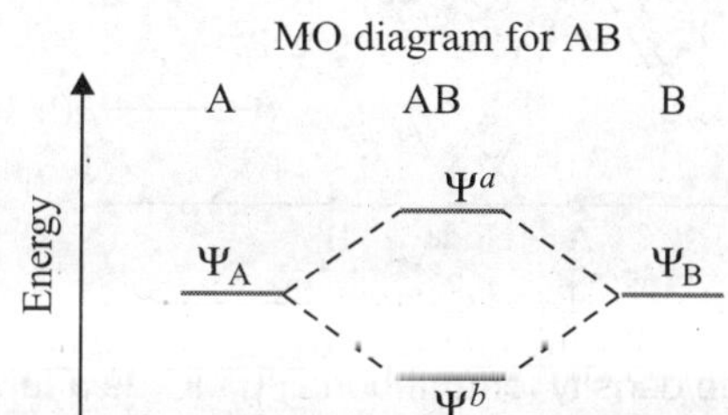

Fig. 1.22 Formation of bonding and antibonding MOs in diatomic molecules

Significance of Bonding and Anti-Bonding MOs

Taking squares of the bonding MO wave function (Ψ^b), we get

$$(\Psi^b)^2 = \Psi_A^2 + \Psi_B^2 + 2\Psi_A \Psi_B \qquad \text{(For identical atoms } C_A = C_B = 1) \qquad ...[1.31]$$

The terms Ψ_A^2 and Ψ_B^2 indicate electronic charge densities of wave functions Ψ_A and Ψ_B belonging to isolated atoms *A* and *B*, respectively. $(\Psi^b)^2$ is the electronic charge density of the wave function Ψ^b, i.e., the bonding MO. Thus, the more is the value of $(\Psi^b)^2$, the more is the charge density between the two combining nuclei. Again from the equation it is also evident that $(\Psi^b)^2 > \Psi_A{}^2 + \Psi_B{}^2$ by a term, $2\,\Psi_A\,\Psi_B$. This term $2\,\Psi_A\,\Psi_B$ results from the overlap of AO's and is called overlap integral. Larger is the overlap integral more is the charge density between the nuclei and stable is the bond formed. The plot of electron charge density as a function of inter-nuclear distance for bonding MO is shown below.

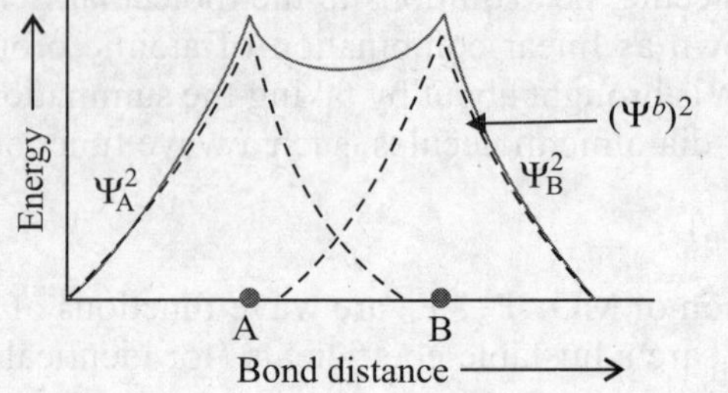

Fig. 1.23 Plot of electron charge density for bonding MO as a function of internuclear distance

Again, taking square of the antibonding MO wave function (Ψ^a), we get

$$(\Psi^a)^2 = \Psi_A{}^2 + \Psi_B{}^2 - 2\Psi_A\Psi_B \qquad ...[1.32]$$

It is evident from the above equation that $(\Psi^b)^2 < \Psi_A{}^2 + \Psi_B{}^2$ by a term $2\Psi_A\,\Psi_B$. Thus, in antibonding MO, there is less charge density between the nuclei. It is, therefore, the energy of the antibonding MO is more than the sum of the energies of the two interacting atoms *A* and *B*. The plot of electron charge density is shown below. The charge density touches the axis at midpoint between the nuclei. This midpoint is called a node and at this point the electron charge density is zero.

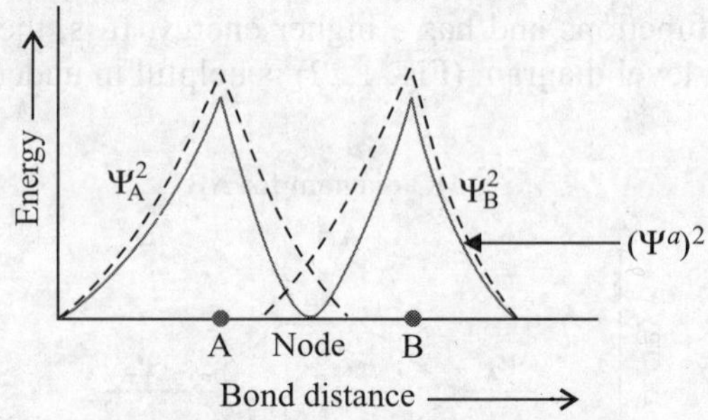

Fig. 1.24 Plot of electron charge density for anti-bonding MO as a function of internuclear distance

Formation of MOs

From* s*-atomic orbitals

Let $\Psi_{1s(A)}$, $\Psi_{1s(B)}$ describe the 1*s* atomic orbitals on the two atoms. Now as the atoms come close these two atomic orbital wave functions undergo linear combination to form two MOs (Fig. 1.25). If the wave functions have same sign, i.e., they are in one phase then they add up to give the bonding MO. On the other hand, if they are different in their signs i.e., they remain in different phases then they cancel each other to form antibonding MO. Here, +ve and –ve signs refer to signs of the wave functions, which determine their relative phases and have no relation with charge (if one of the wave functions is assigned with +ve sign, the other may be either +ve or –ve). The two MOs are as follows:

$$\Psi^b = N\,[C_A\,\Psi_{1s(A)} + C_B\,\Psi_{1s(B)}];\ \Psi^a = N\,[C_A\Psi_{1s(A)} - C_B\Psi_{1s(B)}]$$

For a homonuclear diatomic molecule, both atoms are identical. Thus, $C_A = C_B = 1$ and $N = 1/\sqrt{2}$ and therefore the MO's take the form

$$\Psi^b = \frac{1}{\sqrt{2}}\,[\Psi_{1s(A)} + \Psi_{1s(B)}];\ \Psi^a = \frac{1}{\sqrt{2}}\,[\Psi_{1s(A)} + \Psi_{1s(B)}]$$

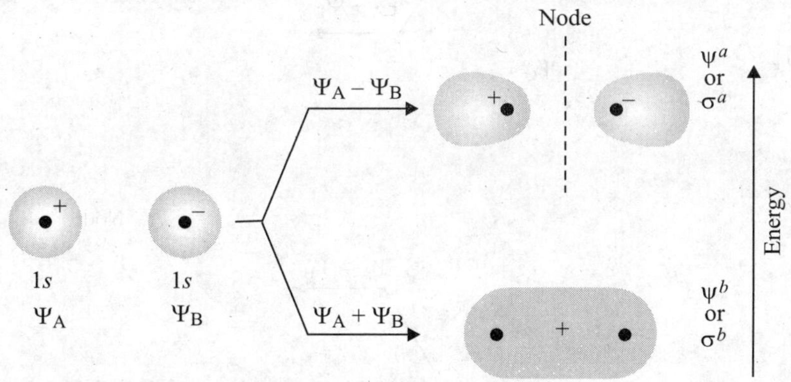

Fig. 1.25 MOs from *s*-orbitals

From p-atomic orbitals

With respect to *p*-orbitals, there arise two different cases:

Case I

Let *Z*-axis be the internuclear or molecular axis. Now the linear combination of p_z AOs leads to the the formation of MOs which remain symmetrical about the molecular axis and therefore known as σ-MOs. Again if the waves are in one phase, they form bonding MO and if in different phase, they form antibonding MO (Fig. 1.26).

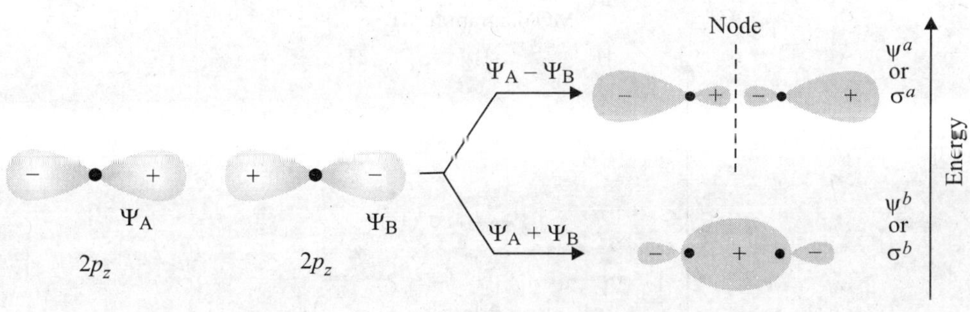

Fig. 1.26 Molecular orbitals formed from $2p_z$-orbitals

Case II

Combination of other *p*-orbitals which have their lobes oriented perpendicular to the internuclear axis leads to formation of MOs that are not symmetrical about the internuclear axis. Such MO's are known as π-MOs. Here also the possibility of bonding and antibonding MO formation is there (Fig. 1.27).

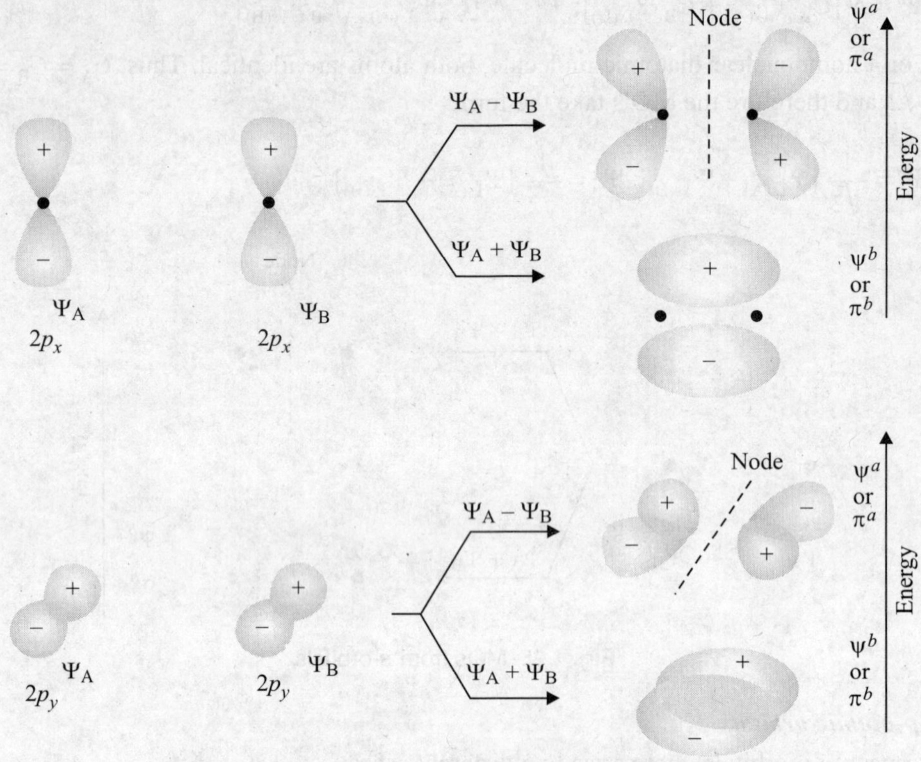

Fig. 1.27 Molecular orbitals formed from $2p_x$ and $2p_y$ orbitals

MO Treatment of Diatomic Molecules

For homonuclear diatomic molecules

H_2 molecule

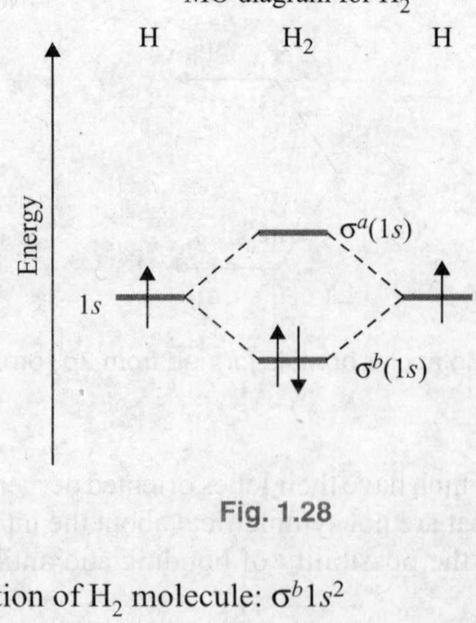

Fig. 1.28

Electronic configuration of H_2 molecule: $\sigma^b 1s^2$

$$\text{Bond order} = \frac{1}{2}\,[\text{Number of electrons in bonding MOs}(N_b) - \text{Number of electrons in antibonding MOs}(N_a)]$$

$$= \frac{1}{2}(2-0) = 1$$

Hence, there exists a single covalent bond between two hydrogen atoms.
Magnetic behavior is diamagnetic due to lack of unpaired electrons.

Example 1.12

Draw the molecular energy level diagram for H_2^+ molecular ion. Give the electronic configuration, find bond order and also comment on its magnetic behavior.

Solution

Energy level diagram is same as in Fig. 1.25.

Electronic configuration of H_2 molecule: $\sigma^b 1s^2$

$$\text{Bond order} = \frac{1}{2}(N_b - N_a)$$

$$= \frac{1}{2}(1-0) = \frac{1}{2}$$

Magnetic behavior is paramagnetic due to the presence of one unpaired electron.

N_2 molecule

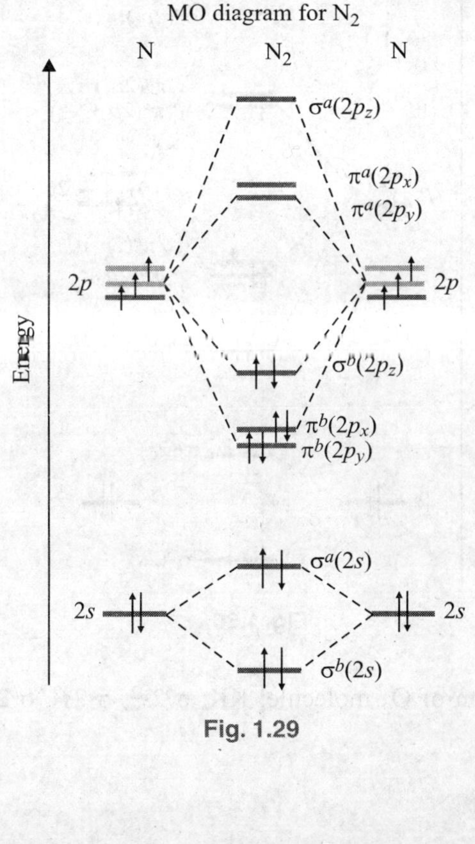

Fig. 1.29

Electronic configuration of N_2 molecule: KK, $\sigma^b 2s^2$, $\sigma^a 2s^2$, $\pi^b 2p_x^{\,2} = \pi^b 2p_y^{\,2}$, $\sigma^b 2p_z^{\,2}$

$$\text{Bond order} = \frac{1}{2}(N_b - N_b)$$

$$= \frac{1}{2}(8 - 2) = 3$$

Hence, there exists triple covalent bond between two nitrogen atoms.

Magnetic behavior is diamagnetic due to lack of unpaired electrons.

Orbital mixing

Molecular orbitals with nearly same energies interact if they have appropriate symmetries. These secondary mixing lowers the energy of the lower orbital and raises the energy of the higher one. In case of homonuclear diatomic molecules, where atomic number (Z) of the element is ≤ 7, the σ^a $2s$ and σ^b $2p_z$ are very close with respect to their energies. Due to match symmetry they participate in secondary mixing which lowers the energy of σ^a $2s$ and at the same time increases the energy of $\sigma^b 2p_z$. The result being $\sigma^b 2p_z$ goes higher in energy with respect to energies of π^b - MO's. On the other hand, if $Z > 7$, then σ^a $2s$ and $\sigma^b 2p_z$ differ much in their energies which does not allow the secondary mixing.

O_2 molecule

MO diagram for O_2

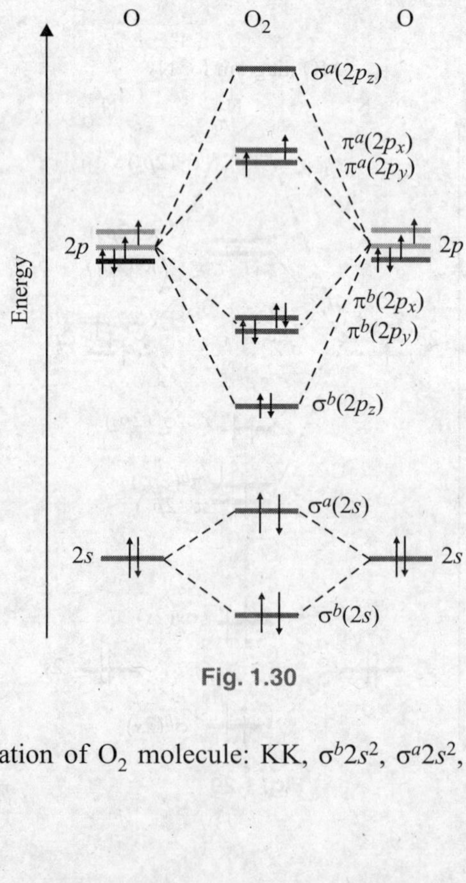

Fig. 1.30

Electronic configuration of O_2 molecule: KK, $\sigma^b 2s^2$, $\sigma^a 2s^2$, $\sigma^b 2p_z^{\,2}$, $[\pi^b\ 2p_x^{\,2} = \pi^b\ 2p_y^{\,2}]$, $[\pi^b\ 2p_x^{\,1} = \pi^b\ 2p_y^{\,1}]$

$$\text{Bond order} = \frac{1}{2}(N_b - N_a)$$
$$= \frac{1}{2}(8-4) = 2$$

Hence, there exists a double covalent bond between two oxygen atoms.

Magnetic behavior is paramagnetic due to presence of two unpaired electrons.

> **Note:**
>
> Paramagnetism of O_2 can be explained only with respect to MO treatment. This observation serves as an evidence for the failure of VBT.

Example 1.13

Draw the molecular energy level diagram for O_2^- molecular ion. Give the electronic configuration, find bond order, and also comment on its magnetic behavior.

Solution

The MO energy level diagram is same as that for O_2.

Electronic configuration of O_2^- molecule: KK, $\sigma^b 2s^2$, $\sigma^a 2s^2$, $\sigma^b 2p_z^{\ 2}$, $[\pi^b 2p_x^{\ 2} = \pi^b 2p_y^{\ 2}]$, $[\pi^a 2p_x^{\ 2} = \pi^a 2p_y^{\ 1}]$

$$\text{Bond order} = \frac{1}{2}(N_b - N_a)$$
$$= \frac{1}{2}(8-5) = 1.5$$

Magnetic behavior is paramagnetic due to the presence of one unpaired electrons.

Example 1.14

Arrange the following species in increasing order of their bond dissociation energies. Also account for the trend O_2^+, O_2, O_2^-, and O_2^{2-}.

Solution

Let us find the bond order in the different species.

In O_2^+, BO $= \frac{1}{2}(8-3) = 2.5$; in O_2, BO $= \frac{1}{2}(8-4) = 2.0$; in O_2^-, BO $= \frac{1}{2}(8-5) = 1.5$ and in O_2^{2-}, BO $= \frac{1}{2}(8-6) = 1.0$. As the bond dissociation energy is proportional to the bond order, the required order is $O_2^{2-} < O_2^- < O_2 < O_2^+$.

For heteronuclear diatomic molecules

The wave functions describing MO's in heteronuclear diatomic molecules can be obtained from the linear combination of AOs Ψ_A and Ψ_B.

$$\Psi = N(C_A \Psi_A \pm C_B \Psi_B) \qquad [\text{here } C_A \neq C_B]$$

The result being the electron distribution in the internuclear region is not symmetrical. Let us assume electronegativity of atom A is greater than that of B. In such a case energy of $\Psi_B >$

Ψ_A. Atom A with wave function Ψ_A makes a greater contribution to the bonding MO (Ψ^b) as it is having lower energy and lies close to Ψ^b. On the other hand, atom B with wave function Ψ_B makes a greater contribution to the antibonding MO (Ψ^a).

HF molecule

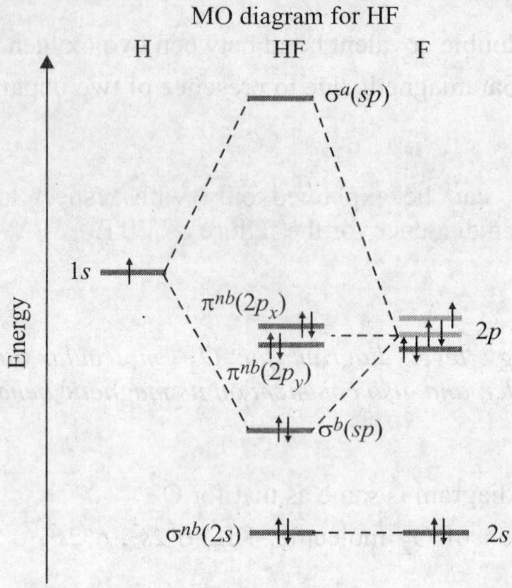

Fig. 1.31

Electornic configuration: $\sigma^{nb}1s^2$, $\sigma^{nb}2s^2$, σ^b1sp^2, $\pi^{nb}2p_x{}^2 = \pi^{nb}2p_y{}^2$

Bond order = 1/2(2 – 0) = 1

Magnetic behaviour diamagnetic.

CO molecule

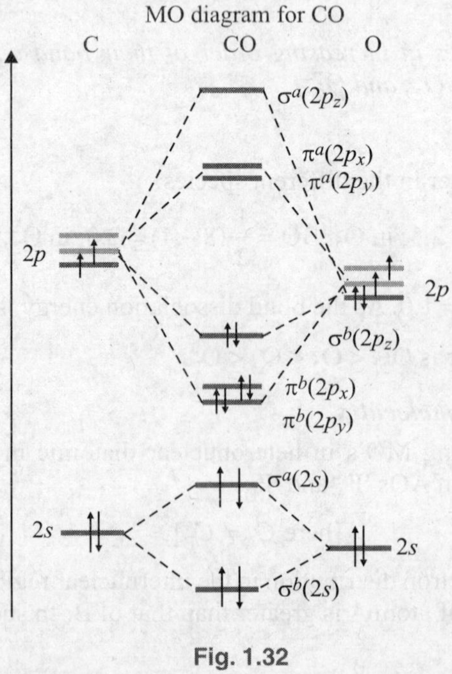

Fig. 1.32

Electronic configuration of CO molecule: $\sigma^b1s^2, \sigma^a1s^2, \sigma^b2s^2, \sigma^a2s^2, \pi^b2p_x^{\;2} = \pi^b2p_y^{\;2}, \sigma^b2p_z^{\;2}$.

Bond order $= \frac{1}{2}(N_b - N_a) = \frac{1}{2}(8 - 2) = 3$

Magnetic behavior is diamagnetic due to lack of unpaired electrons.

NO molecule

MO diagram for NO

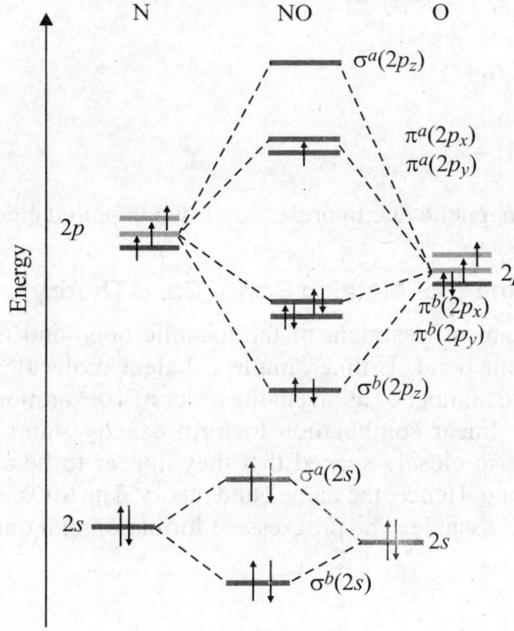

Fig. 1.33

Electronic configuration of NO molecule: $\sigma^b1s^2, \sigma^a1s^2\ \sigma^b2s^2\ \sigma^a2s^2, \sigma^b2p_z^{\;2}, \pi^b2p_x^{\;2} = \pi^b2p_y^{\;2}$, $\pi^a2p_x^{\;1} = \pi^a2p_y^{\;0}$.

Bond order $= \frac{1}{2}(N_b - N_a)$

$= \frac{1}{2}(8 - 3) = 2.5$

Magnetic behavior is paramagnetic due to presence of one unpaired electrons.

Example 1.15

Draw the molecular orbital energy level diagram for NO^+ and NO^-. Write down their electronic configuration and find bond order in both the cases. Also predict their magnetic behavior.

Solution

The molecular orbital energy level diagram for NO^+ and NO^- are same as that of NO.

Electronic configuration of NO^+ molecular ion: $\sigma^b\ 1s^2, \sigma^a1s^2, \sigma^b2s^2, \sigma^a2s^2, \sigma^b2p_z^{\;2}$, $[\pi^b2p_x^{\;2} = \pi^b2p_y^{\;2}]$.

$$\text{Bond order} = \frac{1}{2}(N_b - N_a)$$

$$= \frac{1}{2}(8-2) = 3$$

Magnetic behavior is diamagnetic due to presence of one unpaired electron.

Electronic configuration of NO^- molecular ion: $\sigma^b 1s^2$, $\sigma^a 1s^2$, $\sigma^b 2s^2$, $\sigma^a 2s^2$, $\sigma^b 2p_z^2$, $[\pi^b 2p_x^2 = \pi^b 2p_y^2]$, $[\pi^a 2p_x^1 = \pi^a 2p_y^1]$

$$\text{Bond order} = \frac{1}{2}(N_b - N_a)$$

$$= \frac{1}{2}(8-4) = 2$$

Magnetic behavior is paramagnetic due to presence of two unpaired electrons.

Molecular Orbital Treatment of Metallic Bond (Band Theory)

This is the quantum mechanical treatment of the metallic bond and is similar to molecular orbital approach of covalent bond. Unlike simple covalent molecules during formation of metallic crystal, a very large number of atoms in the order of 10^{23} or more are brought together so that their AOs undergo linear combination to form exactly same number of MOs. The energies of these MOs are so closely spaced that they appear to be a continuum known as quasi-continuous energy band. Hence, the name band theory. The MOs formed are delocalized, i.e., belong to the crystal as a whole. The progressive formation of a quasi-continuous band is shown in Fig. 1.34.

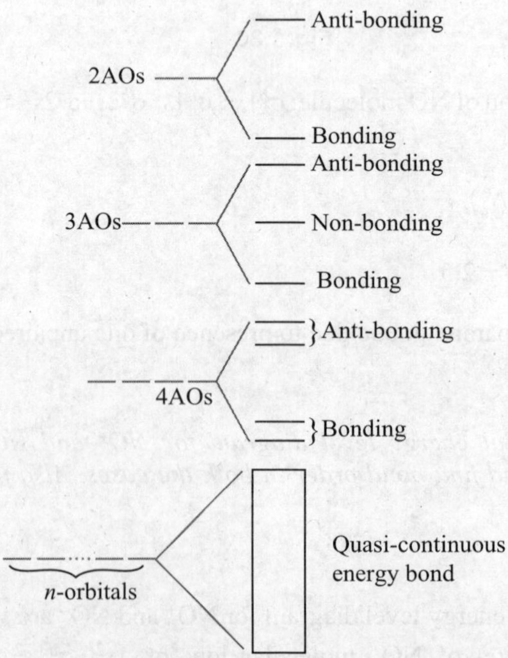

Fig. 1.34 Formation of MO band in metals

Let us look into a specific example of Li metal. The electronic configuration of Li is $1s^2$, $2s^1$, $2p^0$. When n-Li atoms come close to form Li crystal, three energy bands are formed.

1s band

This band is formed by combination of large n of "1s" AOs of Li atoms and hence contains n number of energy levels. This band is completely filled and carries $2n$ electrons. This is inner shell band and is not influenced by surrounding atoms, therefore narrow at equilibrium interatomic distance.

2s band

This band is formed by combination of 2s orbitals of n atoms. This band has n levels. This band is half filled and contains "n-electrons." The upper half is completely filled while the lower half remains vacant. This is a valency band and is significantly influenced by surrounding atoms. It is quite spared out at equilibrium distance. Due to close spacing of energy levels, electrons can move to energy levels in upper half at room temperature.

2p band

n atoms of Li give $3n$ levels in $2p$ band. $2s$ and $2p$ levels are so close in energy that the bands overlap and the electrons of $2s$ band gets additional energy levels differing slightly in energies to move about. The total capacity of this overlapped band is $8n$ electrons and is therefore 1/8th filled.

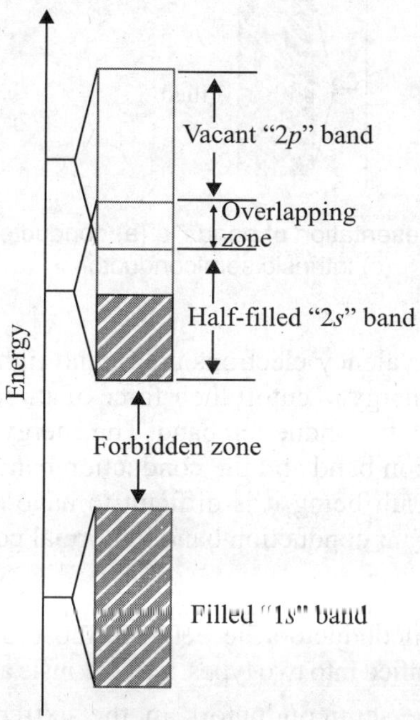

Fig. 1.35 Different bands in Li metal

Note:

1. The energy level in a quasi-continuous bond below which all the levels are filled is known as fermi level.
2. The band in which electrons can move is called permitted band or Brillouin zone.
3. The energy bands formed from the valence shell orbitals are known as valency bands. The valency bands which are completely filled are non-conduction bands and those which are partially filled are called conduction band.

Conduction Behavior

Let us apply the band theory to explain the conduction behavior of different solids.

Conductors

In a conductor, plenty of electrons are available for free movement and thereby for electric conduction. In terms of band theory, conduction band of a conductor is partly filled and contains a large number of electrons. These electrons can be easily promoted to nearby vacant levels in the same band by providing a very small amount of electric or thermal energy. This explains high electrical and thermal conductivity of metals.

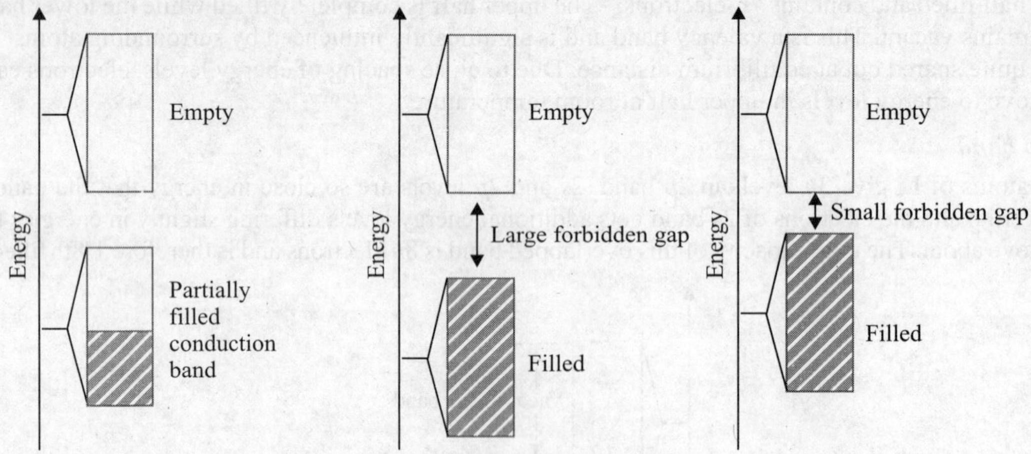

Fig. 1.36 Schematic presentation of bands in (a) conductor, (b) insulator, and (c) intrinsic semiconductor

Non-conductors or insulators

Insulator is a material in which valency electrons are bound tightly to their parent atom and hence require sufficiently large energy to cutoff their force of attraction with nuclei. In terms of energy bands an insulator has empty conduction band. The energy gap between the completely filled valency shell non-conduction band and the conduction band is very large. Such a gap is known is forbidden gap. The result being it is difficult to have promotion of electrons from filled nonconduction band to vacant conduction band in normal condition.

Semiconductors

The electrical properties of semiconductors lie between those of conductors and insulators. Semi conductors are broadly classified into two types, viz., intrinsic and extrinsic semi-conductors.

Intrinsic semiconductors: the semiconductors in the extremely pure form are called *intrinsic semiconductors*, e.g., Ge, Si etc. In terms of energy bands semiconductors have filled valency shell nonconduction band and empty conduction band. However, the forbidden gap between these bands is small enough to have promotion of electrons from filled valency band to empty nonconduction band even at room temperature. This is the reason for low conductivity. With rise of temperature the width of forbidden gap decreases which results in a hike in conductivity.

Extrinsic semiconductors: Semiconductors prepared by adding impurities to intrinsic semiconductors or insulators are called *extrinsic semiconductors*. On the basis of the nature of impurity added, these are further classsified into two types:

1. ***n*-type extrinsic semiconductors**

Such semiconductors are obtained by doping with an impurity in which atoms carry more number of external electrons than parent atoms. The extra electrons from impurity remain in a delocalized energy level which is known as donor impurity level and is placed just below the empty conduction band. These extra electrons can be easily excited to the empty conduction band (Fig. 1.37). As electrons are responsible for conduction, these semiconductors are called *n*-type semiconductors. For example, doping of group 15 element P, As, or Sb with group 14 elements, i.e., pure Ge or Si produces semiconductors of Ge or Si.

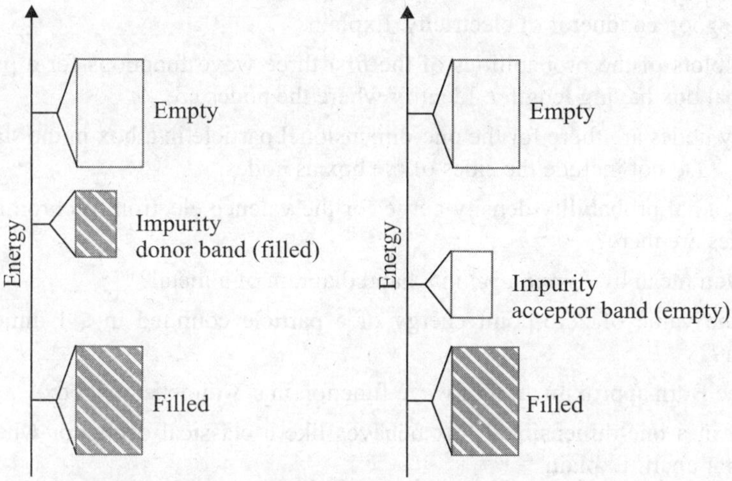

Fig. 1.37 Schematic presentation of bands in extrinsic semiconductors

2. ***p*-type extrinsic semiconductors**

Such semiconductors are obtained by doping with impurity in which atoms carry less number of external electrons than parent atoms. Thus, positive holes are created in the valency bands of the parent element. These holes remain in acceptor impurity level and are placed close to filled valency band (Fig. 1.37). The electrons from the filled valency band can be easily promoted to the empty acceptor level carrying +ve holes. Under the influence of applied field, an electron from adjacent atom migrates into the hole creating another hole. As this continuous the hole migrates in a direction opposite to that of electron. Therefore, here current flow is attributed to migration of +ve holes and hence the name *p*-type semiconductor. For example, doping of group 13 elements such as Al or Ga with group 14 elements, i.e., pure Ge or Si produces semiconductors of Ge or Si.

QUESTIONS

1. State Heisenberg's uncertainty principle.
2. NO is paramagnetic and NO^+ is diamagnetic. Justify using MO configuration.
3. Hydrogen forms diatomic molecule but helium does not. Explain.
4. What is eigen function and eigen value?
5. Show schematically the different bands present in a *p*-type extrinsic semiconductor.

6. When would the wavelength associated with an electron be equal to that of proton?
7. Write the Schrodinger's time-independent wave equation.
8. What are the rules for linear combination of atomic orbitals?
9. What is the significance of Ψ^2?
10. What is linear combination of atomic orbitals (LCAO) principle?
11. Why Mg behaves as a metal even if it has filled orbitals?
12. What is the physical significance of an electronic wave function?
13. Molecular oxygen is paramagnetic in nature. Explain.
14. Metals are good conductor of electricity. Explain.
15. Construct plots of the probabilities of the first three wave functions for a particle in a one-dimensional box having length l. Identify where the nodes are.
16. How many nodes are there for the one-dimensional particle in a box in the state described by ψ_5 and ψ_{10}? Do not include the sides of the box as nodes.
17. Draw the radial probability density curve for the valence electron of chromium. How many radial nodes are there?
18. What do you mean by *Fermi level* in a band diagram of a metal?
19. What is the value of zero-point energy of a particle confined in a 1-dimensional box of dimension l?
20. What is the Born approximation of wave function in a 3-dimensional box.
21. A particle in a one-dimensional box behaves like a classical oscillator when the walls are infinitely far apart. Explain.
22. What is correspondence principle?
23. The Ge_xAs_y semiconductor has more conductivity value than that of silicon semiconductor at room temperature. Explain on the basis of MO diagram.
24. Comment on the acceptability of the following two wave functions:

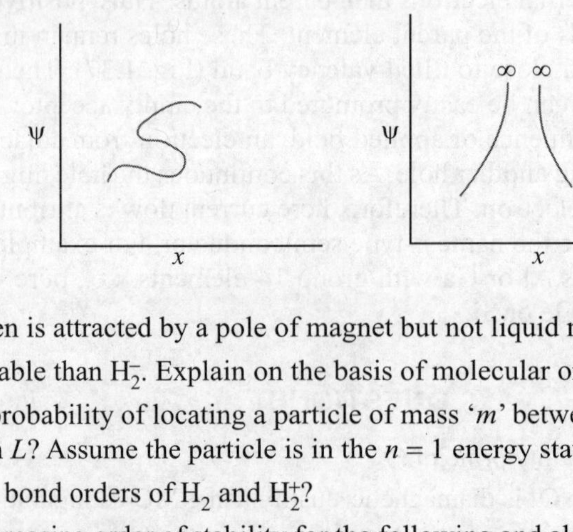

25. Liquid oxygen is attracted by a pole of magnet but not liquid nitrogen. Explain.
26. H_2^+ is more stable than H_2^-. Explain on the basis of molecular orbital theory.
27. What is the probability of locating a particle of mass 'm' between $x = L/4$ and $x = L/2$ in a 1-D box of length L? Assume the particle is in the $n = 1$ energy state.
28. What are the bond orders of H_2 and H_2^+?
29. Write the decreasing order of stability for the following and also justify the order –H_2, H_2^+, H_2^-.
30. On the basis of uncertainty principle, explain why electrons can't exist within the nuclei of atoms.
31. Write a short note on applications of Schrodinger's equation.

32. Explain energy distribution in blackbody spectrum on the basis of quantum theory.
33. Justify the wave nature of electron in reference to Davission–Germer experiment.
34. Show that, $\left(V - \frac{h^2}{8\pi^2 m}\nabla^2\right)\Psi = E\Psi$
35. Show that the energy levels for a particle in a one-dimensional box is quantized.
36. What do you mean by bonding and anti-bonding molecular orbitals? Discuss the molecular orbital diagram of CO and find out its bond order.
37. What are the salient features of molecular orbital theory? Explain the significance of bonding and anti-bonding orbitals.
38. Explain how blackbody radiation led to failure of classical mechanics.
39. Which has more dissociation energy: O_2 or O_2^+? Discuss on the basis of MO theory.
40. Explain the terms conductor, insulator, and semiconductor on the basis of molecular orbital diagrams.
41. Write down the MO configuration of O_2, N_2, F_2, and compare their bond dissociation energies and magnetic properties.
42. Justify the order of stability of O_2^{2+}, O_2^{2-}, O_2^-, O_2 by molecular orbital theory. Compare their bond orders, bond lengths, and magnetic properties using their molecular orbital electronic configuration.
43. Write down the Schrodinger wave equation for a 3-dimensional form. Mention the conditions for acceptable wave function.
44. Verify the uncertainty principle for a particle in a one-dimensional box.
45. Show that the normalization constants for the general form of the wave function $\psi = \sin (n\pi x/a)$ are the same and do not depend on the quantum number n.
46. Explain metallic bonding in terms of band theory.
47. For a particle in a one-dimensional box, show that $h\psi = E\psi$.
48. Show that the 1s wave function of hydrogen atom given by $\psi_{1s} = \frac{1}{\sqrt{\pi}} a_0^{3/2} e^{r/a_0}$ is normalized, where a_0 is Bohr's radius.
49. Prove that for a particle in a one-dimensional box at $n = 1$ level, the product of uncertainties in momentum and position is constant, i.e., equal to h.

$$\left[\textit{Hint: } \frac{p^2}{2m} = \frac{n^2h^2}{8ma^2} \text{ or } p = \pm\frac{nh}{2a};\ \Delta p = \frac{nh}{a} \text{ and } \Delta x = a\right]$$

50. What do you mean by LCAO principle? With the help of this, explain how bonding and anti-bonding molecular orbitals are formed involving p–orbitals.

NUMERICAL PROBLEMS

1. Calculate the wavelength of He atom whose speed is equal to its RMS velocity.
2. Calculate the wavelength of CO_2 molecule moving with a velocity of 250 m s^{-1}.
3. A proton is moving with a kinetic energy 5×10^{-27} J. Find the wavelength.
4. The uncertainty in momentum of a particle is 3.5×10^{-2} kg m s^{-1}. Find the uncertainty in its position.

5. Calculate the kinetic energy of an electron emitted from a surface of a metal, by the irradiation of light of frequency $5.5 \times 10^{17}\ s^{-1}$. The work function of the said metal is 3.62×10^{-12} ergs.
6. Calculate KE and the velocity of the photoelectron when a light of wavelength 190 nm falls on a metal surface. The work function is 2.05 eV. Also calculate the stopping potential.
7. A laser used to read CD emits light of wavelength 600 nm. Calculate the number of photons emitted by it in each second if its power is 0.1 W.
8. The speed of a projectile of mass 1 g is known to within 1 μm s^{-1}. Calculate the minimum uncertainty in its position.
9. If the wavelength of an electron is 1 nm, what is the velocity of the electron?
10. Light of 350 nm strikes a metal surface with a work function of 3.2 eV. Calculate (a) The kinetic energy of the most energetic electron and (b) the stopping potential.
11. Calculate the spacing of the energy levels of a dust particle of mass 0.01 g which is enclosed in a box of side 0.1 m and moving with a velocity of 1 m s^{-1}. Prove that the quantized energy levels cannot be distinguished.
12. Calculate the maximum velocity of electron emitted from the surface of sodium metal if the photon of wavelength 210 nm strikes on it. The work function of the metal is 6.5×10^{-12} ergs.
13. Compare wavelength associated with an object with mass 6×10^{27} kg and a velocity 3×10^4 m s^{-1} with that of an electron moving with a velocity of 6×10^5 m s^{-1}.
14. Calculate the uncertainty in the velocity of a bullet weighing 10 g whose position is known with ± 0.01 mm.
15. The kinetic energy of a subatomic particle is 5.65×10^{25} J. Calculate the frequency of the particle wave.
16. Calculate the voltage required to accelerate an electron to have a velocity $1.42 \times 10^9\ ms^{-1}$. What will be the de Broglie wavelength?
17. An alpha particle in a one-dimensional box of width 2×10^{-10} m undergoes a transition from the ground state to the first excited state. Find the transition energy.
18. The energy required for the ionization of a certain atom is 3.44×10^{-16} J. The absorption of a photon of unknown wavelength ionizes the atom and ejects an electron with velocity $1.03 \times 10^6\ ms^{-1}$. Find the wavelength of the incident radiation.
19. How many photons per second of IR radiation are produced by an IR lamp that consumes energy at the rate of 150 W and is 20% efficient in converting this energy to IR radiation? Assume that the wavelength of the radiation is 1500 nm.
20. Find the energy required to promote an election placed in a 1-dimensional box of length 2 Å from the ground state to the first excited state. Express the result in electron volt.
21. Calculate the voltage required to accelerate an electron to have a velocity of $1.87 \times 10^9\ ms^{-1}$. What will be the de-Broglie wave length?
22. Calculate the uncertainty in velocity for a particle with mass 7×10^{-18} kg if the uncertainty in position is 0.1 nm.
23. What is the de-Broglie wavelength of an electron travelling at 1% of the speed of light?
24. Calculate the velocity of an electron that has been accelerated by a potential difference of 1V.

CHAPTER

2 Coordination Compounds

Chapter Outline

- Addition Compounds
- Terminologies
- IUPAC Nomenclature
- Werner's Theory
- Bonding in Complexes (VBT and CFT)

Complexes or coordination compounds have lots of importance in chemistry and biochemistry. To mention a few, in electroplating, $K[Ag(CN)_2]$ is used for silver plating; in metallurgy, during the extraction of gold and silver; in photography, AgBr forms soluble complex with sodium thiosulfate; in analytical chemistry, i.e., during complexometric titration for the estimation of hardness; in physiology and biochemistry, heme, the oxygen-carrying component of red blood cells, is basically a complex of iron; the part of chlorophyll that converts sunlight into chemical energy within green plants is a magnesium complex; in treatment of metal poisoning, lead can be removed from the body in the form of soluble $Pb[Na_2\ EDTA]$ complex in urine by injecting the patient with $Ca[Na_2EDTA]$. Our primary focus in this chapter is on bonding in complexes.

Addition Compounds

The compounds obtained upon evaporation of solutions containing two or more simple salts in molecular proportions are known as addition or molecular compounds, for example—

Double salts:

$$K_2SO_4 + Al_2(SO_4)_3 + 24H_2O \longrightarrow \underset{\text{Potash alum}}{K_2SO_4 \cdot Al_2(SO_4)_3 \cdot 24H_2O}$$

$$(NH_4)_2SO_4 + FeSO_4 + 6H_2O \longrightarrow \underset{\text{Mohr's salt}}{(NH_4)_2SO_4 \cdot FeSO_4 \cdot 6H_2O}$$

Coordination compounds:

$$CuSO_4 + 4NH_3 \longrightarrow \underset{\text{Tetrammine copper sulfate}}{CuSO_4 \cdot 4NH_3}$$

$$Fe(CN)_2 + 4KCN \longrightarrow \underset{\text{Potassium ferrocyanide}}{Fe(CN)_2 \cdot 4KCN}$$

The addition compounds can be classified into two types on the basis of their behavior in solution phase.

Double Salts

The addition compounds which are stable in solid state but dissociate to provide all of their constituent ions upon dissolution in water or any other polar solvents are known as double salts. Therefore, such a salt behave similar to simple salts in solution. For example, potash alum upon dissolution in water provides K^+, Al^{3+}, SO_4^{2-} ions.

Coordination Compounds

The addition compounds which do not provide all of their constituent ions in solution are known as coordination or complex compounds. In such compounds, some of the constituent ions lose their identity. For example, potassium ferrocyanide upon dissolution in water provides only K^+ and $[Fe\,(CN)_6]^{4-}$. Here Fe^{2+} and CN^- ions lose their identities and a complex ion $[Fe\,(CN)_6]^{4-}$ is formed instead.

Terminologies

Ligand

The molecules or ions which remain directly attached to the central metal in a complex compound through coordinate linkages are known as ligands. The atom of the ligand which actually donates the electron pair for coordination is known as donor or coordinating atom. For example, in ferrocyanide ion, CN^- ions are ligands and "C" is the coordinating atom.

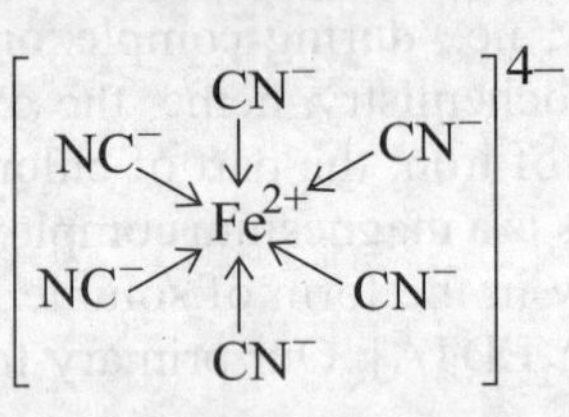

Ligands are classified usually on the basis of their number of donor sites into the following two categories:

1. Monodentate ligands: Such a ligand carries only one donor site. For example, $\ddot{N}H_3$, $(Ph)_3\,\ddot{P}$, $H_2\ddot{O}:$, $C_3H_3\ddot{N}$ or *py*, F^-, $\ddot{N}H_2^-$, etc.

2. Polydentate ligands: Such a ligand carries more than one donor sites. For example

Ligand	Name
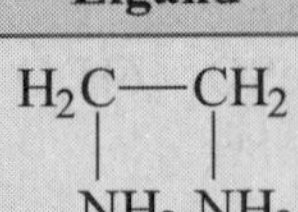	Ethylenediamine (en)
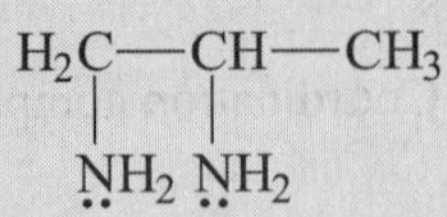	Propylenediamine (pn)

Ligand	Name
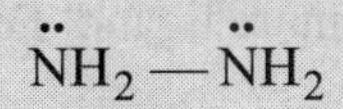	Hydrazine
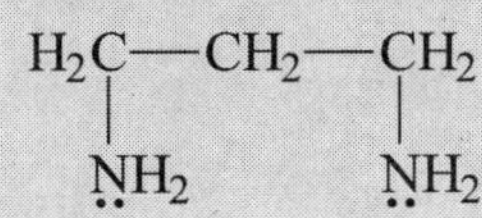	Trimethylenediamine (tn)
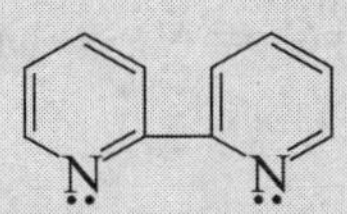	Bipyridine (bipy)
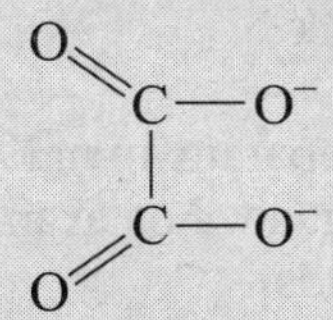	Oxalate (ox)
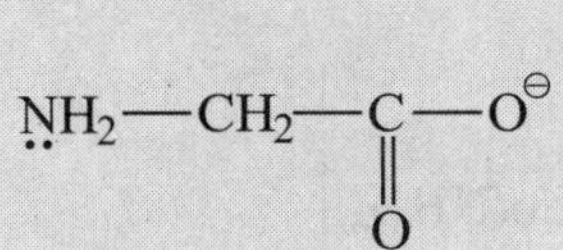	Glycinate (gly)
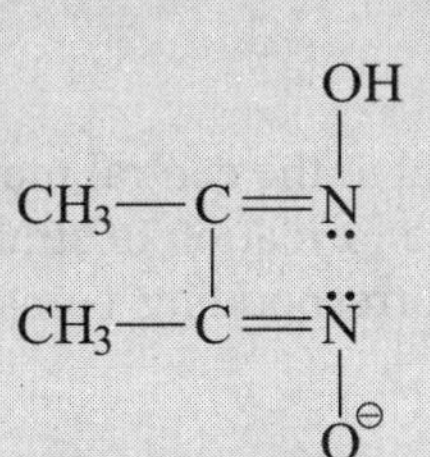	Dimethylglyoximate (dmg)
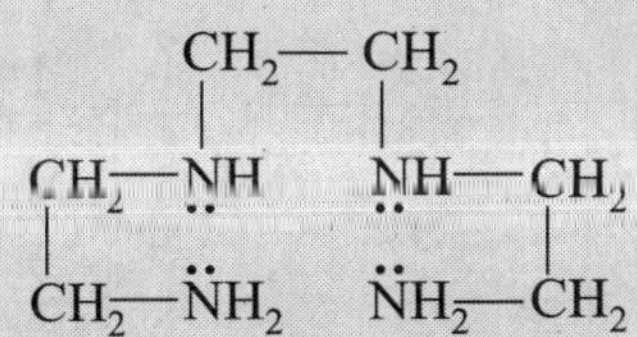	Triethylenetetramine (trien)
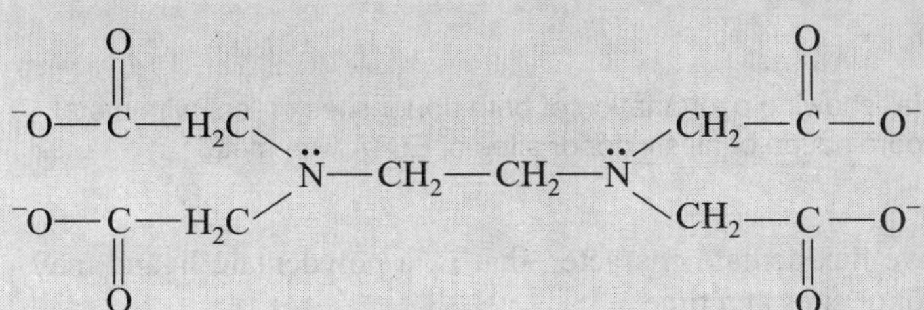	Ethylenediaminetetraacetate (EDTA)

Note:

1. A ligand which possesses two or more donor atoms but can coordinate only through one donor atom at a time is known as ambidentate ligand. For example,

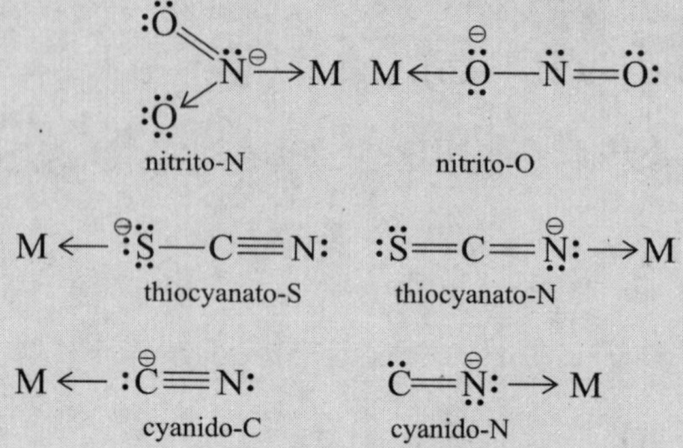

2. A ligand which remains attached to two separate metal atoms/ions making a bridge between them is known as bridging ligand. For examples, in the following examples, "NH_2" and "OH" are bridging ligands.

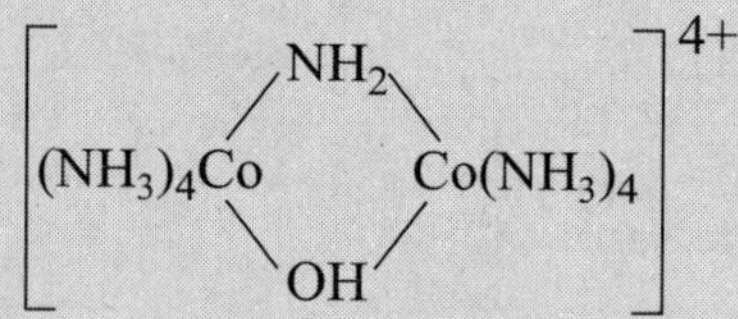

3. A polydentate ligand which remains attached to the central metal atom/ion through two or more of its donor sites resulting in the formation of strainless ring structures are known as chelating ligands, and the corresponding complexes are known as chelates. For example,

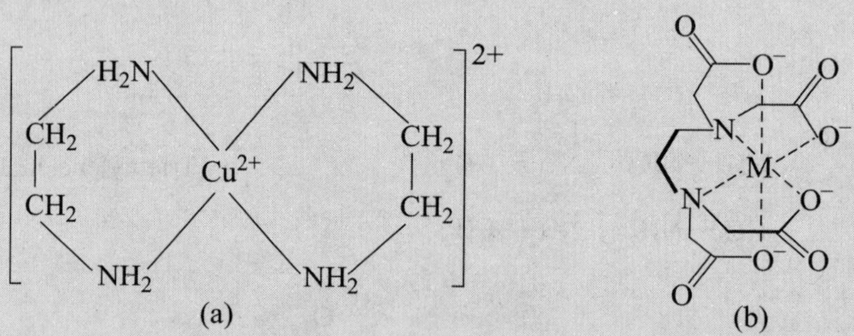

Fig. 2.1 Formation of chelates: (a) showing coordination of both donor sites of "en" with metal and (b) showing the coordination of all six donor sites of EDTA with metal

4. Polydentate ligands have flexidentate character, that is, a polydentate ligand may use some or all of its donor sites at a time.

Coordination Number

Coordination number of the central metal atom/ion is the number of donor sites of the ligands which remain attached to it through coordinate linkage. For example, $[Fe^{2+}(CN)_6]^{4-}$: coordination number is 6; $[Cu^{2+}(en)_2]^{2+}$: coordination number is 4; $[Co(NH_3)_5Cl]^4 Br_2$: coordination number is 6. Coordination number of some common transition metals are given in the following table:

Metal ion	Coordination number	Metal ion	Coordination number
Fe^{2+}	6	Au^{+}	2, 4
Co^{2+}	4, 6	Al^{3+}	4, 6
Ni^{2+}	4, 6	Cr^{3+}	6
Cu^{2+}	4, 6	Fe^{3+}	6
Zn^{2+}	4	Co^{3+}	6
Pt^{2+}	4	Au^{3+}	4
Cu^{+}	2, 4	Pt^{4+}	6
Ag^{+}	2		

Coordination Sphere

The central metal atom/ion along with the ligands attached to it are placed within square brackets and is known as coordination or inner sphere. The portion outside the square brackets is known as ionization or outer sphere. The species in the inner sphere are nonionizable, whereas those in the outer sphere are ionizable.

$$\underbrace{[Co(NH_3)_5Cl]}_{\text{Inner sphere}}\ \overbrace{Br_2}^{\text{Outer sphere}} \longrightarrow [Co(NH_3)_5Cl]^{2+} + 2Br^-$$

Sidgwick Concept of Effective Atomic Number

As per Sidgwick, effective atomic number (EAN) it is the total number of electrons present with the central atom/ion including those gained from ligands during bonding and in many cases it is equal to the atomic number of the nearest noble gas. This concept is known as effective atomic number rule.

$$EAN = Z - O.S. + 2 \times C.N.$$

where Z is the atomic number of the central metal, O.S. is the oxidation state, and C.N. is the coordination number.

Let us find EAN for central metal in some complexes:

$[Fe^{2+}(CN)_6]^{4-}$

$EAN = 26 - 2 + 2 \times 6 = 36$

$[Cu^{2+}(en)_2]^{2+}$

$EAN = 29 - 2 + 2 \times 4 = 35$

Application of EAN

EAN rule can be utilized to predict the magnetic behavior of a complex. If EAN of central metal equals the atomic number (Z) of the nearest noble gas, then the corresponding complex is diamagnetic otherwise paramagnetic. The difference between the EAN and the atomic number of the nearest noble gas corresponds to the number of unpaired electrons. The magnetic moment can be calculated by using the formula,

$$\mu_{eff} = \sqrt{n(n+2)}\ \text{BM}$$

where n is the number of unpaired electrons.

Example 2.1

Comment on the magnetic behavior of $[Fe^{3+}(CN)_6]^{3-}$ on the basis of EAN rule. Also, calculate the magnetic moment.

Solution

$$\text{EAN} = 26 - 3 + 2 \times 6 = 35$$

As EAN $\neq Z$ of the nearest noble gas, the complex ion is paramagnetic.

Number of unpaired electrons, $n = 36 - 35 = 1$

Now, $\mu_{eff} = \sqrt{1(1+2)}\ \text{BM} = 1.732\ \text{BM}$

IUPAC Nomenclature

1. The name of the cation is written first followed by the name of the anion.
2. During naming of complex ions following rules must be followed:
   (a) Names of ligands are arranged in alphabetic order.
   (b) Repetition of a ligand is indicated by using prefixes such as di, tri, and tetra. In case the ligand name itself carries a number, then its repetition is indicated by using prefixes such as bis, tris, and tetrakis.
   (c) Neutral ligands are given their usual names with a few exceptions as given below.

Ligand	Name
H_2O	aqua/aquo
CO	carbonyl
NO	nitrosyl
NH_3	amine

   (d) Names of positive ligands end with suffix "–ium."

Ligand	Name
NH_4^+	ammonium
$NH_2—NH_3^+$	hydrazinium
NO^+	nitrosylium

(e) Negative ligands which end with -ite, -ate, or -ide are usually named by replacing "e" with "o."

Ligand	Name	Name in complex
SO_4^{2-}	sulfate	sulfato
SO_3^{2-}	sulfite	sulfito
S^{2-}	sulfide	sulfido
NO_3^-	nitrate	nitrato
ONO^-	nitrite	nitrito
N^{3-}	nitride	nitrido
N_3^-	azide	azido
NH_2^-	amide	amido
NH^{2-}	imide	imido
CO_3^{2-}	carbonate	carbonato
CH_3COO^-	acetate	acetato
SCN^-	thiocyanate	thiocynato
H^-	hydride	hydrido
$C_2O_4^{2-}$	oxalate	oxalato
F^-	fluoride	fluorido
Br^-	bromide	bromido
I^-	iodide	iodido
OH^-	hydroxide	hydroxido
O^{2-}	oxide	oxido
NC^-	cyanide	cyanido
CN^-	isocyanide	isocyaido

(f) The point of attachment of an ambidentate ligand is specified by the ligating site after the name of the ligand.

(g) A bridging ligand is indicated by using a prefix μ, and its repetition is indicated by using prefixes such as di-μ and tri-μ.

(h) If bridging and nonbridging ligands are same, then bridging ligands are named first.

(i) Ligands are named first followed by the central atom along with its oxidation state in roman numerical within parenthesis.

3. Positive and neutral complexes have no special ending. Negative complex ions end with suffix "-ate."

Let us illustrate the rules with some examples:

$Ca_2[Fe(CN)_6]$: calcium hexacyanidoferrate(II)

$NH_4[Ni(H_2O)F_5]$: ammonium aquapentafluoridonicklate(IV)

$Na_3[Ag(S_2O_3)_2]$: sodium dithiocyanatoargentate(I)

$[Fe(H_2O)_6]SO_4$: hexaaquairon(II) sulfate

$[Co(NH_3)_5Cl]\ Br_2$: pentaamminechloridocobalt(III) bromide

$[Co(en)_3]_2\ (SO_4)_3$: tris(ethylenediamine)cobalt(III) sulfate

$[Ni(dmg)_2]$: bis(dimethylglyoximato)nickel(II)

$[Pt(en)Cl_4]$: tetrachloridoetylenediamineplatinum(IV)

$[Pt(py)_4]\ [PtCl_4]$: tetrapyridineplatinum(II) tetrachloridoplatinate(II)

$[Ag(NH_3)_2]\ [PtCl_4]$: diamminesilver (II) tetrachloridoplatinate(II)

$[Co(NH_3)_2][PtCl_4]$: diamminecobalt(II) tetrachloridoplatinate(II)

$[Co(NH_3)_5ONO]\ Br_2$: pentaamminenitrito-O-cobalt(III) bromide

$[Co(NH_3)_5NO_2]\ Br_2$: pentaamminenitrito-N-cobalt(III) bromide

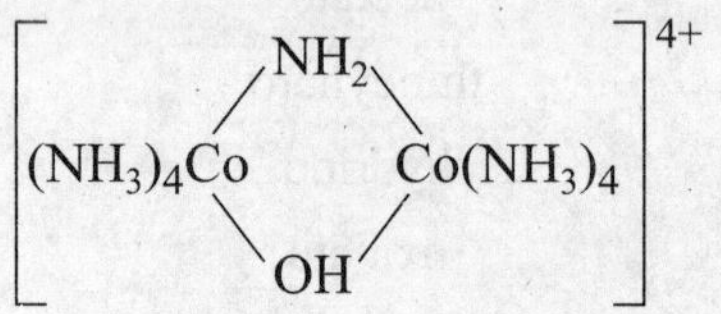

tetraamminecobalt(III)-μ-amido-μ-hydroxotetraamminecobalt(III)

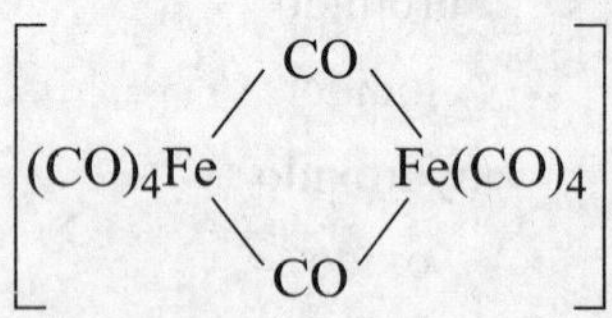

μ-dicarbonyloctacarbonyldiiron(0)

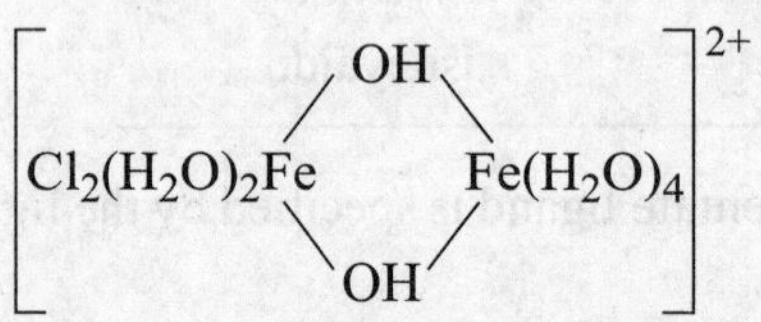

diaquadichloroiron(III)-μ-dihydroxidotetraaquairon(III)

Werner's Theory

Werner in 1893 put forward the first theory to explain the structure and properties of complexes. The salient features of this theory are as follows:

1. In complexes the central metal exhibits two types of valencies, viz., primary and secondary valencies.
2. Primary valency corresponds to the oxidation state of the central metal.
   (a) It is satisfied by only anions, and the attachment to the central metal is shown by dotted lines.

(b) These are ionizable, that is, when added to polar solvent, they dissociate to release free ions.

(c) These are nondirectional and do not decide the geometry of complex.

3. Secondary valency corresponds to the coordination number of the central metal.

(a) It is satisfied by both neutral molecules and anions, and the attachment to the central metal is shown by solid lines.

(b) These are nonionizable.

(c) These are directional in nature and remain oriented towards specific directions in space providing specific geometry to the complex compounds.

4. Every metal has a tendency to satisfy both of its valencies. In the due process the anions sometimes play dual role, that is, satisfy both primary and secondary valencies. The attachment to the central metal is shown by the combination of dotted and solid lines. These are nonionizable and directional.

Werner's concept can be illustrated by taking the example of Co(III) ammine complexes. The different possible complexes along with Werner and IUPAC representations (below) are given as follows:

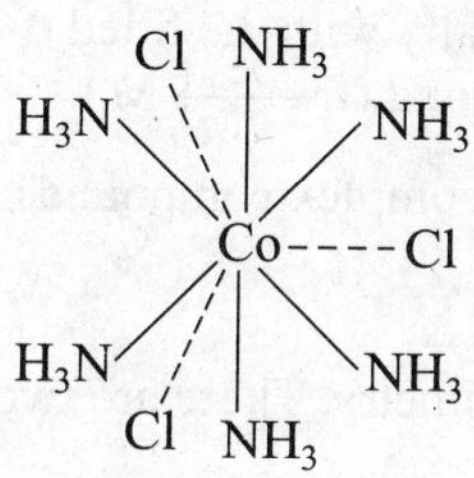

$[Co(NH_3)_6]Cl_3$

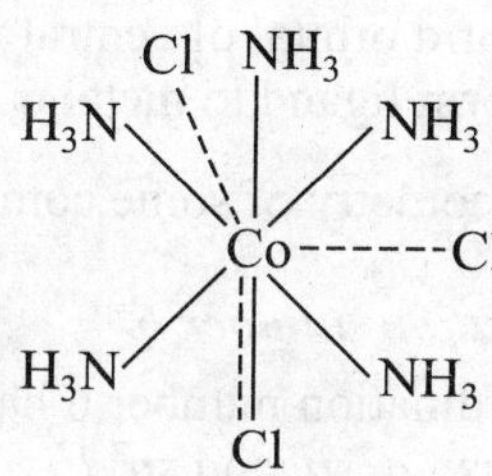

$[Co(NH_3)_5Cl]Cl_2$

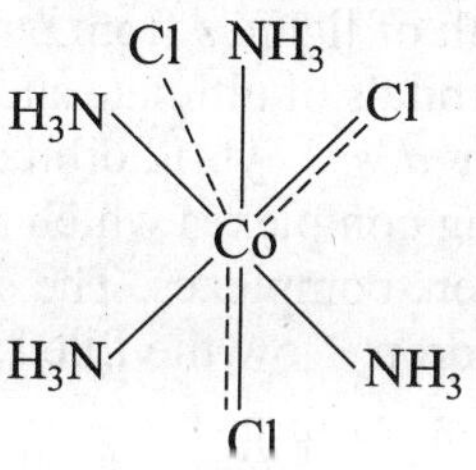

$[Co(NH_3)_4Cl_2]Cl$

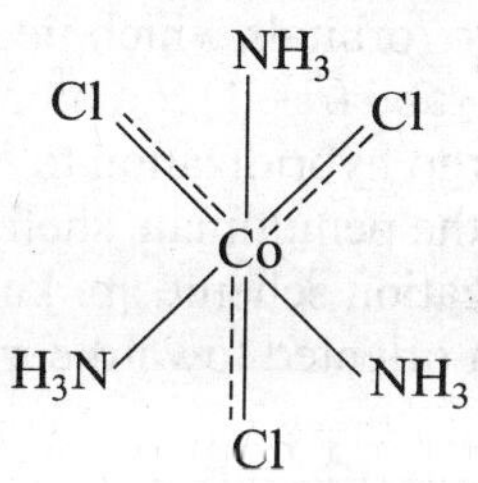

$[Co(NH_3)_4Cl_3]$

Bonding in Complexes

Valence Bond Theory

Valence bond theory (VBT) has been developed by L. Pauling and J.L. Slater in 1935. The salient features of the theory are as follows:

1. The central metal atom/ion makes available a number of empty atomic orbitals equal to its coordination number for hybridization.
2. The empty atomic orbitals hybridize to form exactly the same number of equivalent hybrid orbitals which remain oriented towards specific directions in space

providing definite geometry to a complex. The relationship between coordination number and possible hybridization scheme along with the shape of complex are given as follows:

Coordination number	Type of hybridization	Shape of complex
2	sp	Linear
3	sp^2	Trigonal planar
4	sp^3	Tetrahedral
4	dsp^2/sp^2d	Square planar
5	dsp^3	Trigonal bipyramidal
6	d^2sp^3/sp^3d^2	Octahedral

3. In the process of making available the vacant orbitals for hybridization the nonbonding electrons often get rearranged in the metal orbitals which remain out of hybridization.
4. A ligand must have at least one σ-orbital containing a lone pair of electrons.
5. The vacant hybrid orbital of central metal overlap axially with the filled σ-orbital of the ligand to form ligand to metal σ-type coordinate bond ($L \xrightarrow{\sigma} M$).

Let us discuss the geometry of some common varieties of complex compounds:

Complexes with coordination number 6

The complexes with coordination number 6 have octahedral geometry. There are two possible hybridization schemes, viz., d^2sp^3 and sp^3d^2.

d^2sp^3 (inner orbital octahedral complexes)

In d^2sp^3 hybridization, two orbitals which lie directly in the path of ligands from penultimate shell, that is, $(n-1)\, d_{x^2-y^2}$ and $(n-1)\, d_{z^2}$, along with *s*- and *p*-orbitals of ultimate shell, that is, ns, np_x, np_y, and np_z undergo hybridization to form six equivalent d^2sp^3 hybrid orbitals. As the *d*-orbitals used belong to the penultimate shell, the corresponding complexes which utilize the above-mentioned hybridization scheme are known as inner sphere complexes. The six hybrid orbitals so formed remain oriented toward corners of an octahedron. Now the filled orbital of ligands overlap axially with these vacant hybrid orbitals of metal to form $L \xrightarrow{\sigma} M$ bonds. Let us discuss some examples.

$[Fe(CN_6)]^{3-}$ [hexacyanoferrate (III) ion]: In this complex, the central metal iron remains in +3 oxidation state having five unpaired electrons. However, experimental evidence, that, is magnetic moment measurement supports the presence of only one unpaired electron. Therefore, in the processes of making the inner shell *d*-orbitals available for hybridization, two electrons of $3\, d_{x^2-y^2}$ and $3\, d_{z^2}$ rearrange themselves, that is, pair up with the other 3*d*-orbitals which are out of hybridization. Thus, the Fe^{3+} ion remains with one unpaired electron. Now $3\, d_{x^2-y^2}$, $3\, d_{z^2}$ along with 4s, $4p_x$, $4p_y$, and $4p_z$ atomic orbitals of iron undergo hybridization to form six equivalent d^2sp^3 hybrid orbitals which remain oriented toward corners of an octahedron. Finally, the filled σ-orbitals of CN^- ions overlap with the vacant hybrid orbitals to form six $NC^- \xrightarrow{\sigma} Fe^{3+}$ coordinate bonds. The bonding scheme is as follows:

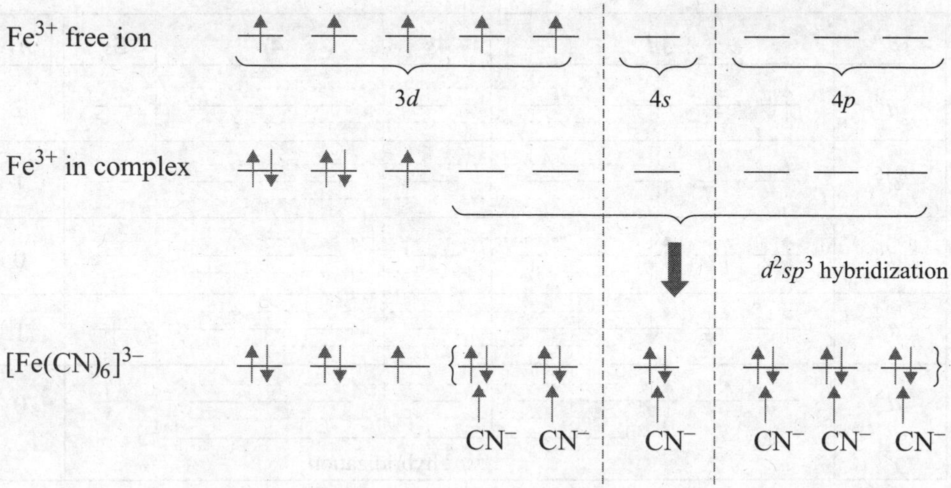

$[Co(NH_3)_6]^{3+}$ [hexaamminecobalt (III) ion]: In this complex, the central metal cobalt remains in +3 oxidation state having four unpaired electrons. However, experimentally, it has been found to be diamagnetic. In the processes of making the inner shell *d*-orbitals available for hybridization, two electrons of 3 $d_{x^2-y^2}$ and 3 d_{z^2} rearrange themselves, that is, pair up with the other 3*d*-orbitals which are out of hybridization. Thus, the Co^{3+} ion remains with no unpaired electron. Now 3 $d_{x^2-y^2}$, 3 d_{z^2} along with 4*s*, $4p_x$, $4p_y$, and $4p_z$ atomic orbitals of cobalt undergo hybridization to form six equivalent d^2sp^3 hybrid orbitals which remain oriented toward corners of an octahedron. Finally, the filled σ-orbitals of NH_3 molecules overlap with the vacant hybrid orbitals of Co to form six $H_3N \xrightarrow{\sigma} Co^{3+}$ coordinate bonds. The bonding scheme is as follows:

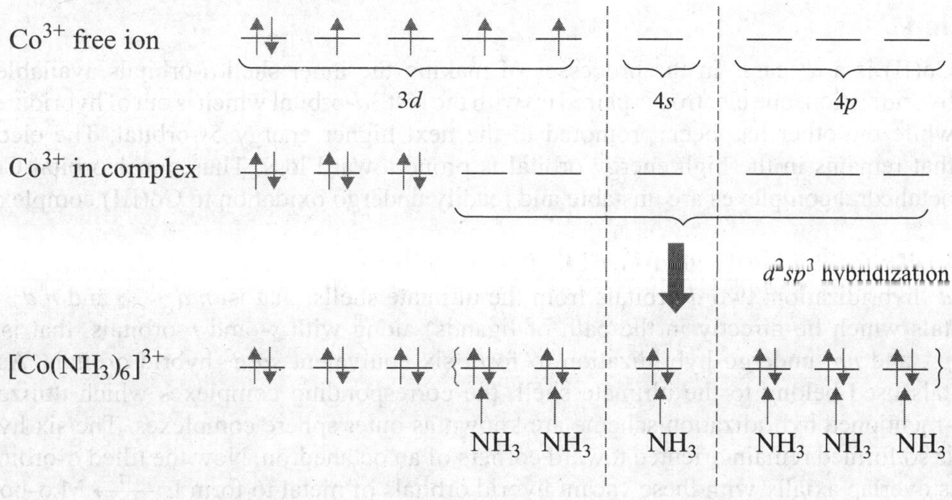

General distribution scheme

General scheme for the formation of inner orbital octahedral complexes of d^4, d^5, d^6, d^7, and d^8 ions (the distribution of *d*-electrons in only complex ions are given) of the first transition series, 3*d*-series elements, is as follows:

d^n	3d	4s	4p	5s	n
d^4	↑↓ ↑ ↑ [— —]	[—]	[— — —]	—	2
d^5	↑↓ ↑↓ ↑ [— —]	[—]	[— — —]	—	1
d^6	↑↓ ↑↓ ↑↓ [— —]	[—]	[— — —]	—	0
d^7	↑↓ ↑↓ ↑↓ [— —]	[—]	[— — —]	↑	1
d^8	↑↓ ↑↓ ↑↓ [— —]	[—]	[— — —]	↑↓	0
	d^2sp^3 hybridization				

Note:

d^6 and d^8 inner sphere octahedral complexes are always diamagnetic.

Other examples

$[Cr(NH_3)_6]^{3+}$, $[Mn(CN)_6]^{3-}$, $[Co(NO_2)_6]^{3-}$, $[Pt(NH_3)_6]^{4+}$

Example 2.2

Inner orbital octahedral Co(II) complexes such as $[Co\,(NO_2)_6]^{4-}$ and $[Co\,(CN)_6]^{4-}$ are unstable and get readily oxidized to corresponding Co(III) complexes. Explain.

Solution

Co(II) is a d^7 case. In the processes of making the inner shell *d*-orbitals available for hybridization, one electron is paired up with the rest 3*d*-orbital which is out of hybridization while the other has been promoted to the next higher energy 5*s*-orbital. The electron that remains in the high energy orbital is prone toward loss. Thus, inner orbital Co(II) octahedral complexes are unstable and readily undergo oxidation to Co(III) complexes.

sp^3d^2 hybridization (outer orbital octahedral complexes)

In sp^3d^2 hybridization, two *d*-orbitals from the ultimate shells, that is, $n\,d_{x^2-y^2}$ and $n\,d_{z^2}$ (the *d*-orbitals which lie directly in the path of ligands) along with *s*- and *p*-orbitals, that is, *ns*, np_x, np_y, and np_z undergo hybridization to form six equivalent sp^3d^2 hybrid orbitals. As the *d*-orbitals used belong to the ultimate shell, the corresponding complexes which utilize the above-mentioned hybridization scheme are known as outer sphere complexes. The six hybrid orbitals so formed remain oriented toward corners of an octahedron. Now the filled σ-orbital of ligands overlap axially with these vacant hybrid orbitals of metal to form $L \xrightarrow{\sigma} M$ σ-bonds. Let us discuss some examples.

$[FeF_6]^{3-}$ [hexafluoroferrate (III) ion]: In this complex, the central metal iron remains in +3 oxidation state. Experimental evidence, that is, magnetic moment measurement is in support of the presence of five unpaired electrons. Now $4d_{x^2-y^2}$ and $4d_{z^2}$ along with 4*s*, $4p_x$, $4p_y$, and $4p_z$ undergo hybridization to form six equivalent sp^3d^2 hybrid orbitals which remain oriented toward corners of an octahedron. Finally, the filled σ-orbitals of F^- ions overlap with the vacant hybrid orbitals to form six, $F^- \xrightarrow{\sigma} Fe^{3+}$ coordinate bonds. The bonding scheme is as follows:

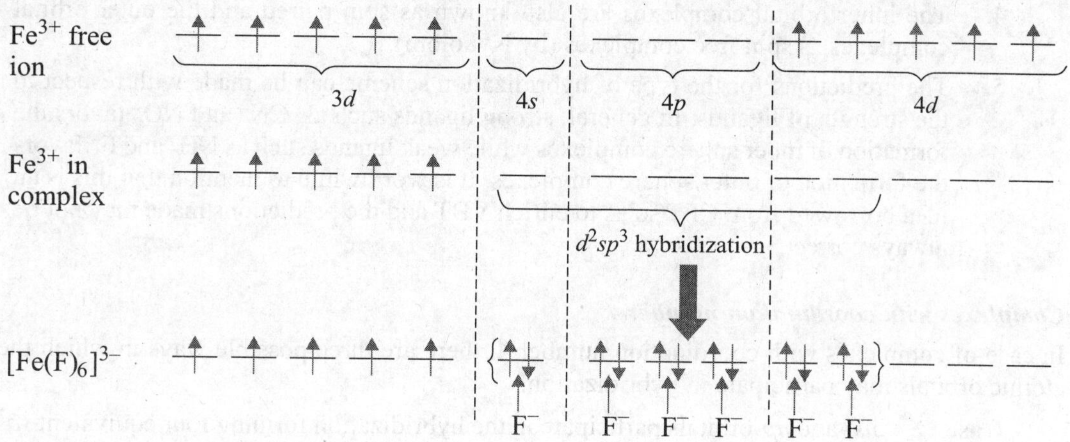

General distribution scheme

General scheme for the formation of outer orbital octahedral complexes of d^4, d^5, d^6, d^7, and d^8 ions (the distribution of *d*-electrons in only complex ions are given) of the first transition series, that is, 3*d*-series elements is as follows:

d^n	3*d*	4*s*	4*p*	4*d*	*n*
d^4	↑ ↑ ↑ ↑ __	__	__ __ __	__ __ __ __ __	4
d^5	↑ ↑ ↑ ↑ ↑	__	__ __ __	__ __ __ __ __	5
d^6	↑↓ ↑ ↑ ↑ ↑	__	__ __ __	__ __ __ __ __	4
d^7	↑↓ ↑↓ ↑ ↑ ↑	__	__ __ __	__ __ __ __ __	3
d^8	↑↓ ↑↓ ↑↓ ↑ ↑	__	__ __ __	__ __ __ __ __	2
		sp^3d^2 hybridization			

Other examples

$[Cr(H_2O)_6]^{3+}$, $[Mn(H_2O)_6]^{2+}$, $[Co(H_2O)_6]^{2+}$, $[Ni(NH_3)_6]^{2+}$, $[Cu(NH_3)_6]^{2+}$, etc.

Note:

1. In inner orbital complexes, the number of unpaired electrons is less than that in the free metal ion. Therefore, the experimental value of magnetic moment (μ_{exp}) is always less than that calculated from spin only formula, that is, μ_s.
2. In outer orbital complexes, the metal ion has same electronic configuration in both free and complex. Thus, μ_{exp} values are comparable with μ_s.

3. The classification of complexes into *inner* and *outer* orbitals is primarily based on the magnetic moment measurement.
4. The inner orbital complexes are also known as spin paired and the outer orbital complexes as spin free complexes (by Nyholom).
5. The predictions for the type of hybridization scheme can be made with respect to the strength of ligands. In general, strong ligands such as, CN^- and NO_2^- favors the formation of inner sphere complexes while weak ligands such as NH_3 and F^- favors the formation of outer sphere complexes. It is worthwhile to mention that this is an idea borrowed from CFT so as to enrich VBT and the predictions made may not be always correct.

Complexes with coordination number 4

In case of complexes with coordination number 4, there are three possible ways in which the atomic orbitals may participate in hybridization.

Case I: *ns*- and *np*-orbitals participate in the hybridization forming four equivalent sp^3 hybrid orbitals which remain oriented toward corners of a tetrahedron.

Case II: Here $(n-1)d_{x^2-y^2}$, ns, np_x, and np_y participate in hybridization forming four equivalent dsp^2 hybrid orbitals leading to square planner geometry.

Case III: ns, np_x, np_y, and $nd_{x^2-y^2}$ participate in hybridization forming four equivalent sp^2d hybrid orbitals leading to square planner geometry.

Note:

Square planner geometry can be obtained from octahedral by removing the two axial ligands, say, along the *z*-axis. Therefore, the *d*-orbital which has its lobe oriented along *x*- and *y*-axes, that is, $d_{x^2-y^2}$, is utilized for hybridization. In addition, np_x and np_y orbitals are used.

Let us discuss some examples in both square planner and tetrahedral geometries.

Square planner geometry

$[Ni(CN)_4]^{2-}$-[tetracyanonickelate (II) ion]: In this complex, experimental evidence is in favor of diamagnetism. Both sp^3 and dsp^2 hybridization schemes may be taken into account. However, sp^3 hybridization scheme is not acceptable, as it carries two unpaired electrons. Thus, dsp^2 scheme is acceptable as it accounts for the diamagnetic behavior of the complex and the geometry is square planner.

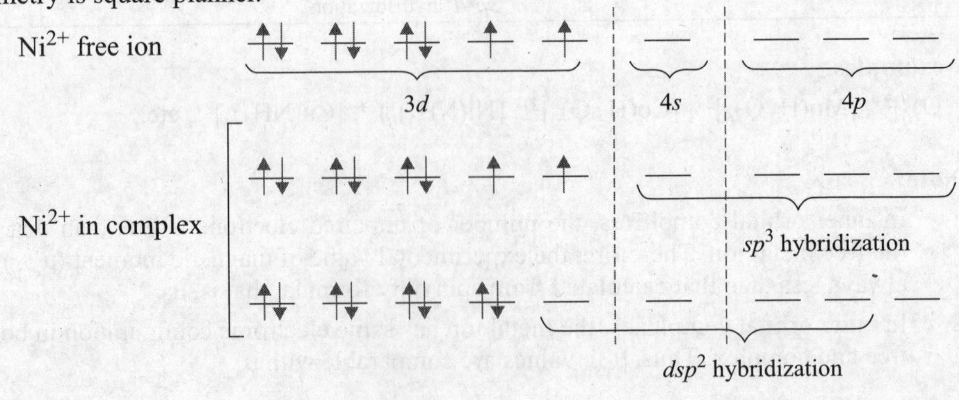

$[Cu(NH_3)_4]^{2+}$ [tetraamminecopper(II) ion]: In this complex, the magnetic moment is experimentally found to be close to 1.73 BM corresponding to the presence of one unpaired electron. In addition, experimental evidence is not in support of tetrahedral geometry. All possible hybridization schemes may be considered. It is interesting to note that all the schemes have one unpaired electron with them. sp^3 scheme is straightway rejected as tetrahedral geometry is not acceptable. In dsp^2 scheme, one electron is to be promoted to high energy 4*p* orbital so as to make the 3 $d_{x^2-y^2}$ available for hybridization. This makes the complex unstable and susceptible toward oxidation through the loss of the electron present in 4*p*-orbital. But Cu (II) is very stable and easy oxidation to Cu (III) is almost impossible. Therefore, dsp^2 scheme is cancelled. The most acceptable scheme is sp^2d, imparting square planner geometry.

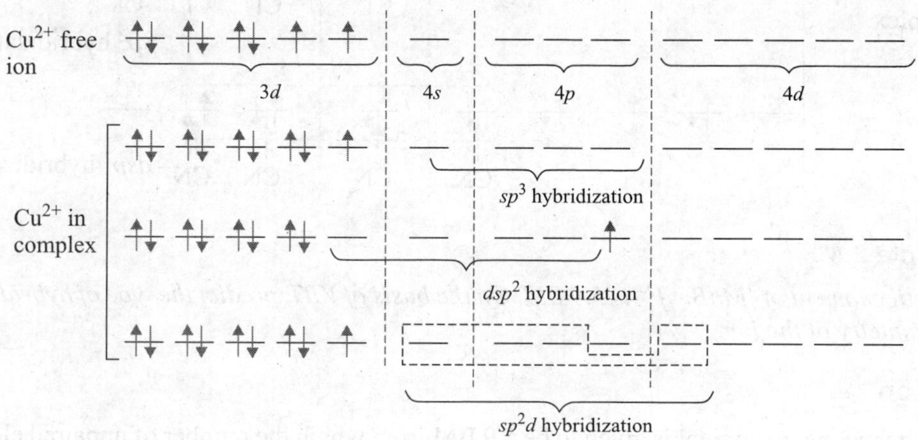

Other examples

$[Pd(Cl)_4]^{2-}$, $[Pt(NH_3)_4]^{2+}$, $[Cu(en)_2]^{2+}$, etc.

Tetrahedral geometry

$[Ni(CO)_4]$ [tetracarbonylnickel(0)]: Experimental evidence is in support of diamagnetism. In this case the two 4*s*-electrons are forced to pair up with 3*d*-orbitals. This results in sp^3 hybridization and tetrahedral structure.

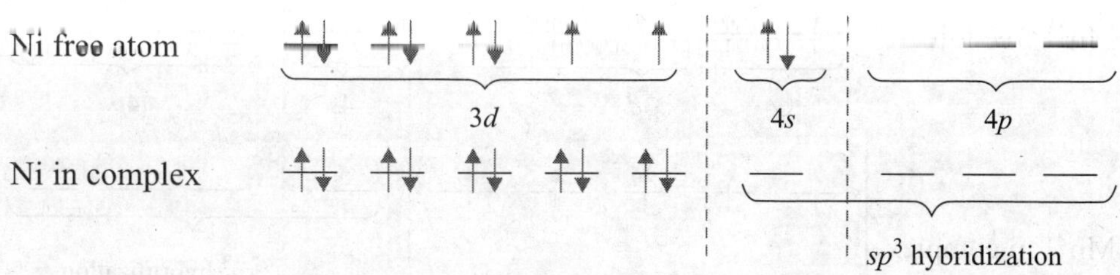

Other examples

$[FeCl_4]^{2-}$, $[Zn(NH_3)_4]^{2+}$, etc.

Example 2.3

$[NiCl_4]^{2-}$ is paramagnetic while $[Ni(CN)_4]^{2-}$ is diamagnetic. Explain.

Solution

Ni^{2+} is sp^3 hybridized in $[NiCl_4]^{2-}$ carrying 2 unpaired electrons leading to paramagnetism while the same is dsp^2 hybridized in $[Ni(CN)_4]^{2-}$ carrying no unpaired electrons leading to diamagnetism.

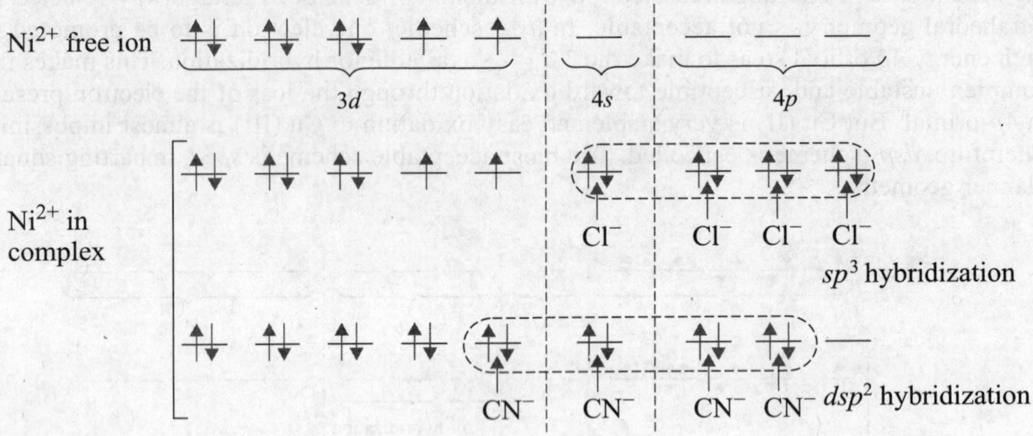

Example 2.4

Magnetic moment of $[MnBr_4]^{2-}$ is 5.9 BM. On the basis of VBT, predict the type of hybridization and geometry of the ion.

Solution

The magnetic moment is given to be 5.9 BM from which the number of unpaired electrons can be computed as follows:

$$\sqrt{n\,(n+2)} = 5.9$$

Solving the relation, $n = 5$, that is, the number of unpaired electrons are five. Again as the coordination number of Mn in the complex is 4, it will have either tetrahedral geometry with sp^3 or square planner geometry with dsp^2 hybridization. Let us look into both these possibilities.

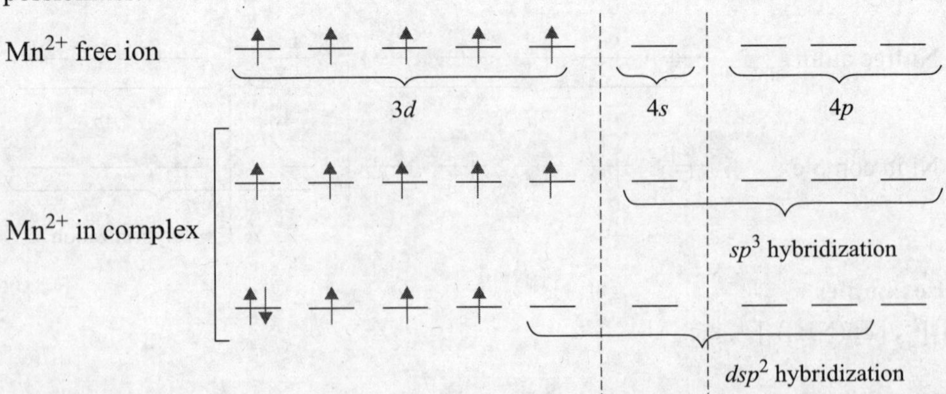

sp^3 hybridization carries 5 unpaired electrons is the accepted one.

Limitations of VBT

1. It does not account for the relative stabilities of different shapes and coordination numbers.
2. The classification of complexes on the basis of their magnetic behavior is not satisfactory and often misleading.
3. It fails to explain the finer details of magnetic properties including orbital contribution. This theory does not consider the orbital contribution.
4. It fails to interpret/account for the color of complexes.
5. It is silent regarding the rates and mechanism of reactions involving the complex compounds.
6. In this the importance of ligands is not properly stressed.

Crystal Field Theory (CFT)

This theory has been developed by Brethe and Van Vleck. The salient features of this theory are as follows:

1. The central metal cation remains surrounded by ligands which carry one or more lone pairs of electrons.
2. The ionic ligands are regarded as point charges, whereas the neutral ligands are regarded as point dipoles.
3. The bonding between metal cation and ligands is purely electrostatic in nature.
4. The theory does not consider any orbital overlap.

Grouping of d-orbitals in different crystal fields

Octahedral crystal field

In a free metal ion all the five *d*-orbitals are degenerate. In an octahedral crystal field, the central metal ion remains surrounded by six ligands at the corners of an octahedron. During the formation of an octahedral complex, the ligands approach along the three axes as shown in Figure 2.2. In the processes there develops repulsion among the electrons in *d*-orbitals of the central metal and the negative point charge or negative end of dipole of the ligands. If all the ligands remain at an equal distance from the *d*-orbitals, the energy of all the *d*-orbitals will raise to the same extent, that is, the orbitals still remain degenerated although they posses more energy than their ground state. This idea of spherically symmetrical crystal field is a hypothetical one. As the lobes of e_g set of orbitals, that is, d_{z^2} and $d_{x^2-y^2}$, lie directly in the path of ligands experience more repulsion than those of t_{2g} set of orbitals, that is, d_{xy}, d_{yz}, and d_{zx}, which have their lobes in between axes. Thus, the energy of e_g set of orbitals is increased while t_{2g} set of orbitals is decreased. To summarize, under the influence of crystal field, the degeneracy of *d*-orbitals is lifted so as to form two sets of *d*-orbitals, viz., t_{2g} set, which is triply degenerate and has lower energy, and e_g set, which is doubly degenerate and has higher energy. This phenomenon of lifting of degeneracy of *d*-orbitals is known as crystal field splitting. The energy gap between the two sets of orbitals is denoted by Δ_0 or 10 Dq and is known as crystal field splitting energy. The energy of t_{2g} set of orbital is $0.4\Delta_0$ or 4 Dq less than the hypothetical spherical crystal field whereas the energy of e_g set of orbital is $0.6\Delta_0$ or 6 Dq more than the hypothetical spherical crystal field.

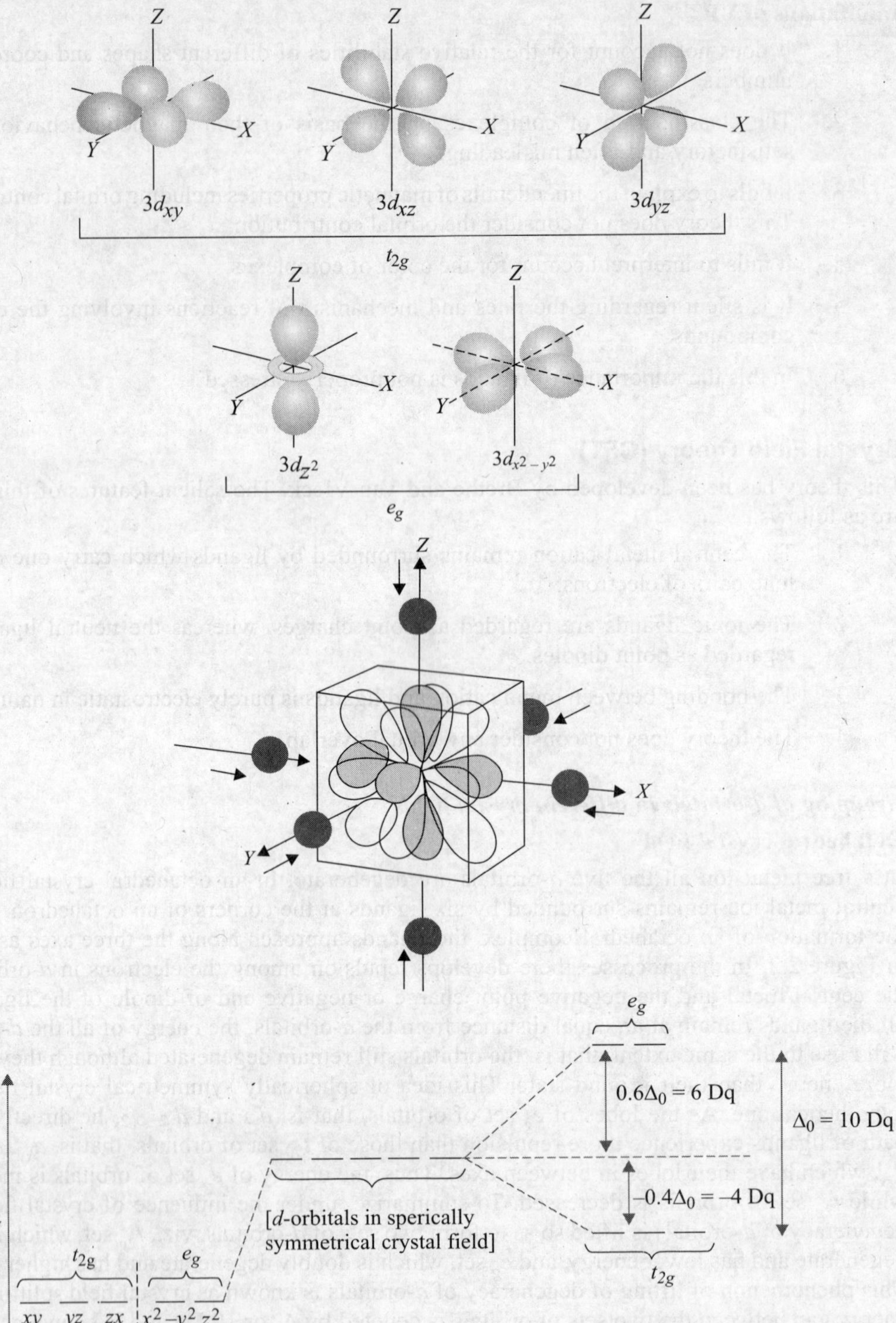

Fig. 2.2 Spatial orientation of different *d*-orbitals and lifting of degeneracy in octahedral crystal field

Tetrahedral crystal field

In order to understand the grouping of *d*-orbitals in a tetrahedral crystal field, it is convenient to imagine the tetrahedron to be placed inside a cube. The ligands are placed at the alternate corners while the metal ion is placed at the center. During the formation of the complex, the ligands approach inbetween the three axes, as shown in Figure 2.3. As the lobes of t_2 set of orbitals d_{xy}, d_{yz}, and d_{zx} lie relatively close to the path of ligands, it experiences more repulsion than those of *e* set of orbitals, that is, d_{z^2} and $d_{x^2-y^2}$, which have their lobes directed along the axes. Thus, the energy of t_2 set of orbitals is increased, while the energy of *e* set orbital is decreased. To summarize, under the influence of tetrahedral crystal field, the degeneracy of *d*-orbitals is lifted so as to form two sets of *d*-orbitals, viz., *e* set, which is doubly degenerate and has lower energy, and t_2 set, which is tripely degenerate and has higher energy. The energy gap is denoted by Δ_t (10 Dq). The relative energies of both the set of orbitals are shown in Figure 2.3.

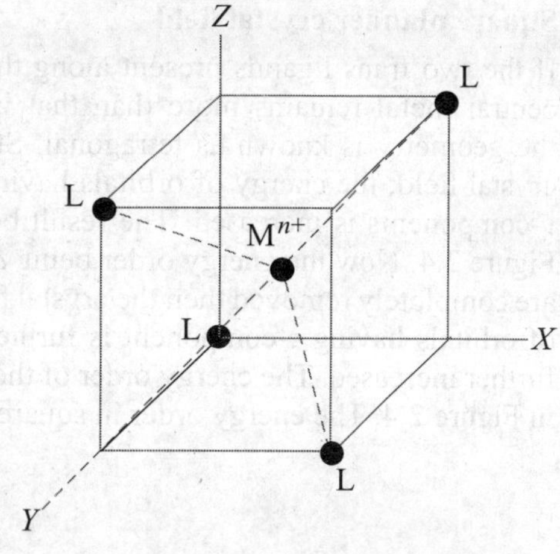

Fig. 2.3(a) Tetrahedral crystal field

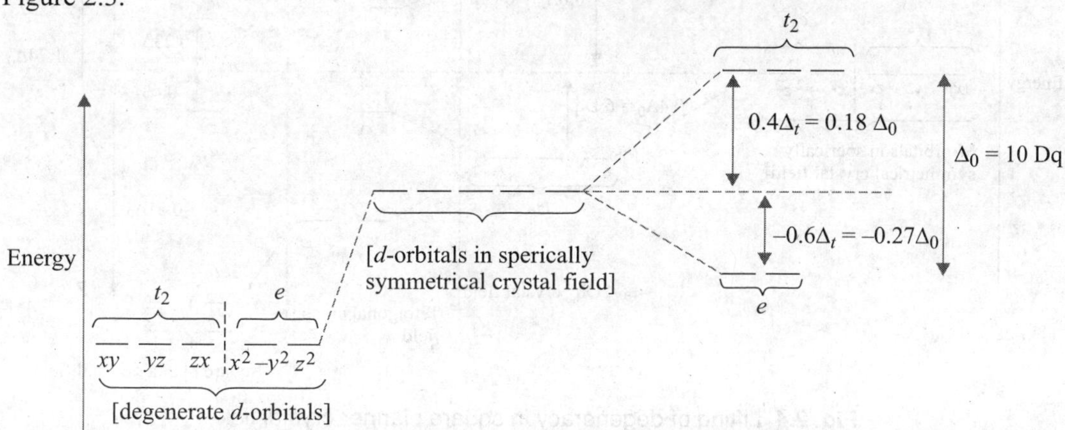

Fig. 2.3(b) Lifting of degeneracy in tetrahedral crystal field

Note:

1. Here $\Delta_t < \Delta_0$. The reason is twofold.
   (a) In tetrahedral field, the t_2 set of orbitals are close to ligands, but do not point directly toward ligands. But in octahedral field, all six ligands point directly towards the lobes of t_2 set of orbitals.
   (b) In tetrahedral field, there are only 4 ligands, whereas in octahedral field, there are 6 ligands.
2. The other factors being equal the energy gap in tetrahedral crystal field is almost half the magnitude of that in an octahedral crystal field. It has been found that $\Delta_t = 0.45\ \Delta_0$.
3. The subscript g is not used in tetrahedral crystal field, as a tetrahedron has no center of symmetry.

Square planner crystal field

If the two trans ligands present along the z-axis are moved away so that their distance from central metal remains more than that is for other four ligands lying in the xy plane, then the geometry is known as tetragonal. Starting with octahedral splitting pattern in tetragonal crystal field, the energy of orbitals having z-component is decreased and those having x- and y-components is increased. The result being four set of d-orbitals are generated as shown in Figure 2.4. Now the energy order being $d_{yz} = d_{zx} < d_{xy} < d_{z^2} < d_{x^2-y^2}$. Now if two trans ligands are completely removed then the crystal field becomes square planner. In such a filed the energy of orbitals having z-component is further decreased and those having x- and y-component is further increased. The energy order of the different group of orbitals is again changed as shown in Figure 2.4. The energy order in square planner crystal field is $d_{yz} = d_{zx} < d_{z^2} < d_{xy} < d_{x^2-y^2}$.

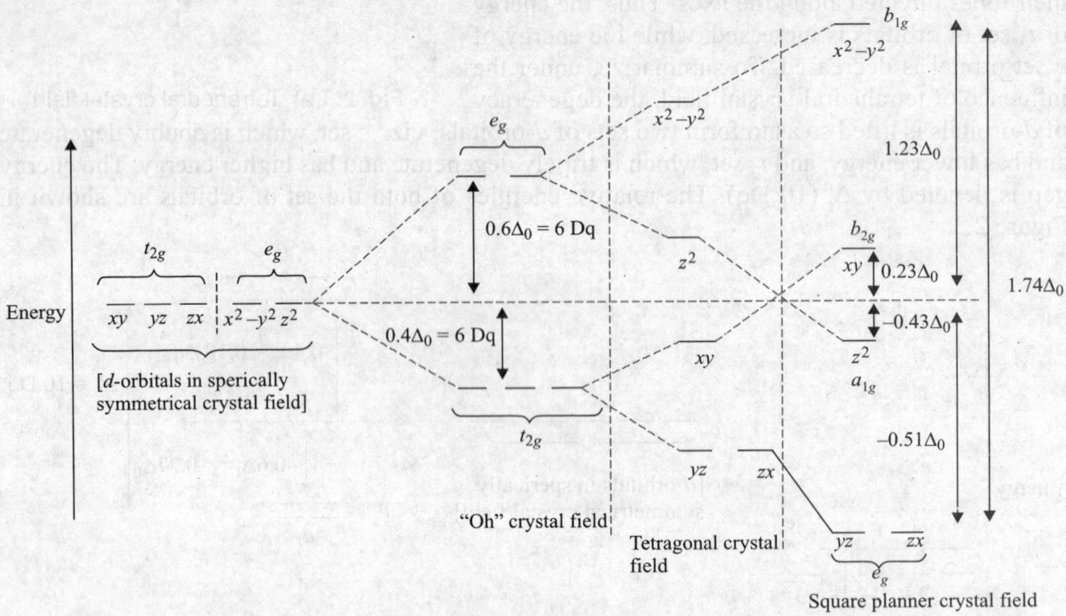

Fig. 2.4 Lifting of degeneracy in square planner crystal field

Note:

Mulliken symbols for atomic/molecular orbitals

Symbol	*Property*
a	Non-degenerate, Symmetric with respect to principal C_n-axis.
b	Non-degenerate, Unsymmetric with respect to principal C_n-axis.
e	Doubly degenerate
t	Triply degenerate
Subscript "g"	Symmetric with respect to inversion centre
Subscript "u"	Unsymmetric with respect to inversion centre
Subscript "1"	Symmetric with respect to C_2-axis perpendicular to C_n-axis.
Subscript "2"	Unsymmetric with respect to C_2-axis perpendicular to C_n-axis.
Superscript (′)	Symmetric with respect to mirror plane horizontal to the principal rotational axis.
Superscript (″)	Unsymmetric with respect to mirror plane horizontal to the principal rotational axis.

***Factors affecting magnitude of* Δ**

The factors can be discussed under two main headings:

1. **Nature of metal**

   (a) **Charge:** If the same metal carries different charges, that is, remains in different oxidation states, then the more the charge, the more is Δ_0. The reason being the metal ion with higher charge polarize the ligands more effectively and bring them more closer resulting in larger splitting. For example,

   Δ_0 for $[Fe^{2+}H_2O)_6]^{2+} = 10400\ cm^{-1}$

   Δ_0 for $[Fe^{3+}(H_2O)_6]^{3+} = 13700\ cm^{-1}$

Note:

If different metals with same number of *d*-electrons and geometry around them carry different charges, then also the one with higher charge will have larger value of Δ_0. For example,

Δ_0 for $[V^{2+}(H_2O)_6]^{2+} = 12400\ cm^{-1}$

Δ_0 for $[Cr^{3+}(H_2O)_6]^{3+} = 17400\ cm^{-1}$

   (b) **Number of *d*-electrons:** If the metal ions have same charge but carries different number of *d*-electrons, then lesser the number of *d*-electrons, more is Δ_0. For example,

   Δ_0 for $[Co^{2+}(H_2O)_6]^{2+} = 9300\ cm^{-1}$

   Δ_0 for $[Ni^{2+}(H_2O)_6\ ]^{2+} = 8500\ cm^{-1}$

   (c) **Principal quantum number of *d*-orbital:** Δ_0 increases significantly with the increase in principal quantum number of the *d*-orbital of the metal ion, for example,

   Δ_0 for $[Co^{3+}(H_2O)_6]^{3+} = 23000\ cm^{-1}$

   Δ_0 for $[Rh^{3+}(H_2O)_6]^{3+} = 34000\ cm^{-1}$

   Δ_0 for $[Ir^{3+}(H_2O)_6]^{3+} = 41000\ cm^{-1}$

2. **Nature of ligand:**

   The strength of ligands in order to lift the degeneracy of *d*-orbitals is expressed in terms of a series known as spectrochemical series. The spectrochemical series with some common ligands is as follows: $I^- < Br^- < Cl^- < F^- < OH^- < ox^{2-} < H_2O < NH_3 <$ en $< CN^- < NO_2^- <$ CO. The ligands in the left-hand side of the series are weak ligands, whereas the ligands toward the right-hand side are strong ligands. For example,

   Δ_0 for $[Ni^{2+}(H_2O)_6]^{2+} = 8500\ cm^{-1}$

   Δ_0 for $[Ni^{2+}(NH_3)_6]^{2+} = 10800\ cm^{-1}$

   Δ_0 for $[Ni^{2+}(en)_3]^{2+} = 11500\ cm^{-1}$

Note:

The position of ligands in spectrochemical series cannot be explained with respect to crystal field theory. However, subsequent developments, particularly ligand field theory provides the explanation for the same. As per this theory, the π-acceptor ligands which are capable of forming $M \xrightarrow{\pi} L$ backbonding in addition to usual $L \xrightarrow{\sigma} M$ bond increases the splitting gap, whereas the π-donor ligands which forms $L \xrightarrow{\pi} M$ bonds decreases the splitting gap. The ligands which are neither π-donor nor π-acceptor remain inbetween.

$$\underbrace{I < Br^- < Cl < F^-}_{\text{Strongly } \pi\text{-donor}} < | \underbrace{OH < ox^{2-}}_{\text{Weakly } \pi\text{-donor}} < | \underbrace{H_2O < NH_3 < en}_{\text{Having no } \pi \text{ bonding ability}} < | \underbrace{NO_2^- < CN^- < CO}_{\pi\text{-acceptor ligands}}$$

3. **Geometry of the complex:** The magnitude of Δ also depends on the geometry of the complex. $\Delta_{SP} > \Delta_o > \Delta_t$

Distribution of d-electrons

In octahedral crystal field: There arise the following two cases:

Case I: If the ligands generate a strong field so that the crystal field splitting energy becomes more than pairing energy, that is, $\Delta_0 > P$, then electrons prefer to pair up in the t_{2g} set of orbitals before entering into e_g orbitals. The result being the first six electrons go to t_{2g} set and the remaining four electrons enter into e_g orbitals. In each individual set of orbitals Hund's rule is obeyed. The complexes with strong field ligands are known as strong field or spin paired or low spin complexes.

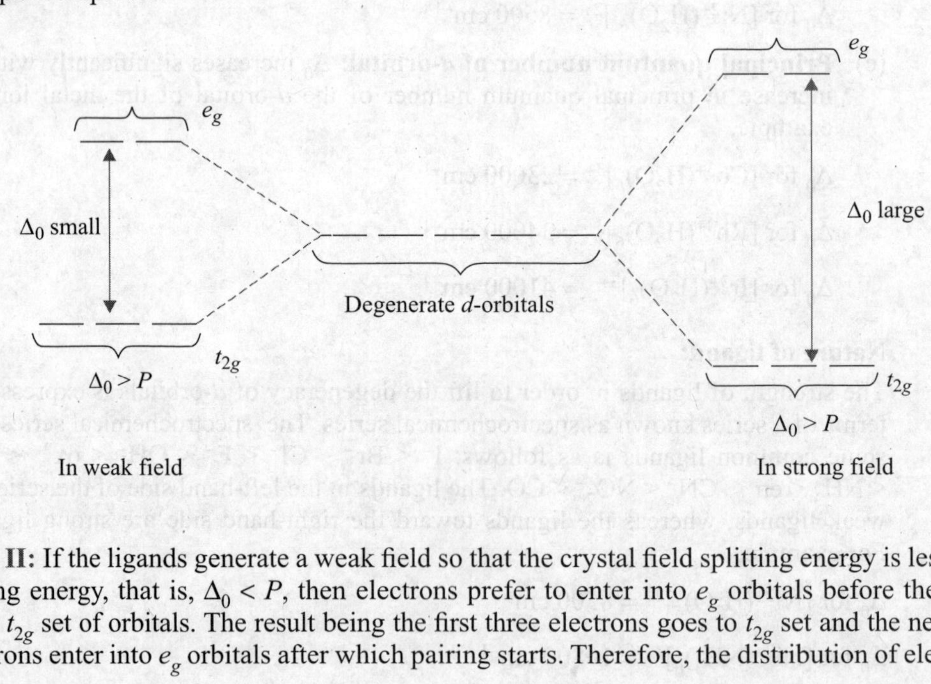

Case II: If the ligands generate a weak field so that the crystal field splitting energy is less than pairing energy, that is, $\Delta_0 < P$, then electrons prefer to enter into e_g orbitals before they pair up in t_{2g} set of orbitals. The result being the first three electrons goes to t_{2g} set and the next two electrons enter into e_g orbitals after which pairing starts. Therefore, the distribution of electrons is as per Hund's rule throughout. Such complexes are known as weak field or spin free or high spin complexes. The distribution of electrons in both strong and weak field cases along with the number of unpaired electrons are as follows:

d^n ions	Strong field complexes ($\Delta_0 > P$)	Number of unpaired electrons	Weak field complexes ($\Delta_0 < P$)	Number of unpaired electrons
d^1	$t_{2g}^1\, e_g^0$	1	$t_{2g}^1\, e_g^0$	1
d^2	$t_{2g}^2\, e_g^0$	2	$t_{2g}^2\, e_g^0$	2
d^3	$t_{2g}^3\, e_g^0$	3	$t_{2g}^3\, e_g^0$	3
d^4	$t_{2g}^4\, e_g^0$	2	$t_{2g}^3\, e_g^1$	4
d^5	$t_{2g}^5\, e_g^0$	1	$t_{2g}^3\, e_g^2$	5
d^6	$t_{2g}^6\, e_g^0$	0	$t_{2g}^4\, e_g^2$	4
d^7	$t_{2g}^6\, e_g^1$	1	$t_{2g}^5\, e_g^2$	3
d^8	$t_{2g}^6\, e_g^2$	2	$t_{2g}^6\, e_g^2$	2
d^9	$t_{2g}^6\, e_g^2$	1	$t_{2g}^6\, e_g^3$	1
d^{10}	$t_{2g}^6\, e_g^4$	0	$t_{2g}^6\, e_g^4$	0

Note:

Remember that strength of ligand is not the only factor that decides the field to be generated during the mutual interaction of central metal atom/ion and ligands. Sometimes weak ligands may generate a strong field, e.g., $[Ni^{4+}F_6]^{2-}$. Here the oxidation state of metal is very high and therefore interaction with a weak ligand like fluoride generates a strong field.

Distribution of *d*-electrons in tetrahedral crystal field: In case of tetrahedral complexes, Δ_t is generally less than pairing energy (P), that is, $\Delta_t > P$. Thus, the electrons prefer to go to t_2 set of orbitals before they pair up in lower energy e set of orbitals. The result being the first two electrons goes to e set and the next three electrons enter into t_2 orbitals after which pairing starts. Therefore, the distribution of electrons is as per Hund's rule throughout and only high spin tetrahedral complexes are known. The distribution of electrons in tetrahedral crystal field (only high spin) along with the unpaired electrons is as follows:

d^n ions	Distribution of *d*-electrons in tetrahedral field	Number of unpaired electrons
d^1	$e^1\ t_2^0$	1
d^2	$e^2\ t_2^0$	2
d^3	$e^2\ t_2^1$	3
d^4	$e^2\ t_2^2$	4
d^5	$e^2\ t_2^3$	5
d^6	$e^3\ t_2^3$	4
d^7	$e^4\ t_2^3$	3
d^8	$e^4\ t_2^4$	2
d^9	$e^4\ t_2^3$	1
d^{10}	$e^4\ t_2^6$	0

Crystal field stabilization energy

In octahedral crystal field: Let us consider a hypothetical configuration $t_{2g}^p\ e_g^q$. The change in energy for the said configuration is known as crystal field stabilization energy (CFSE) since it stabilizes *d*-orbitals by lowering their energies.

CFSE = Loss in energy due to *p*-electrons + gain in energy due to *q*-electrons + gain in energy due to pairing

$= p\,(-0.4\Delta_0) + q\,(+0.6\Delta_0) + mP$

$= p\,(-4\text{ Dq}) + q\,(+6\text{ Dq}) + mP$

where *m* is the total number of paired electrons and *P* is the mean pairing energy.

In tetrahedral crystal field: For hypothetical configuration $e^p\ t_2^q$,

CFSE = Loss in energy due to *p*-electrons + gain in energy due to *q*-electrons + gain in energy due to pairing

$= p\,(-0.6\Delta_t) + q\,(+0.6\Delta_t) + mP$

$= p\,(-0.27\Delta_0) + q\,(+0.18\Delta_0) + mP$

$= p\,(-6\text{ Dq}) + q\,(+4\text{ Dq}) + mP$

Example 2.5

Calculate CFSE for the complex $[Mn(H_2O)_6]^{3+}$ in both strong and weak fields. Given $\Delta_0 = 21000$ cm^{-1} and the pairing energy is 28800 cm^{-1}.

Solution

Mn^{3+} is a d^{4-} case. The distribution of electrons in both strong and weak fields is shown as follows:

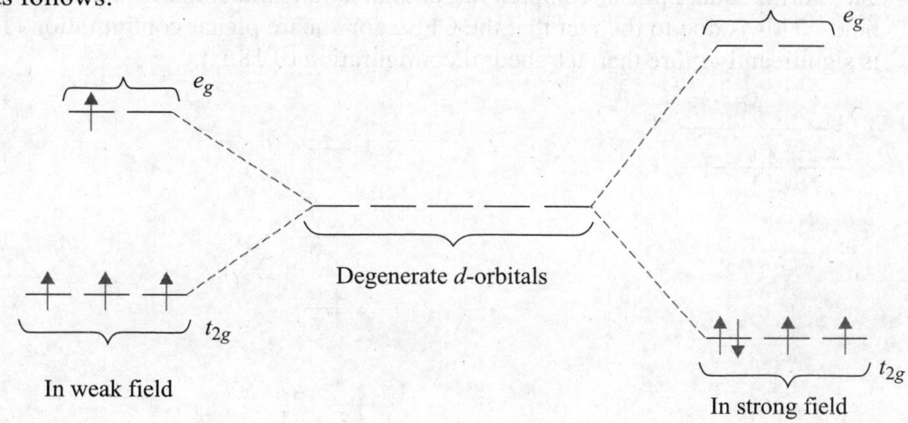

Weak field:

$CFSE = 3\,(-0.4\Delta_0) + 0.6\Delta_0 = -0.6\Delta_0 = -0.6 \times 21000\ cm^{-1} = -12600\ cm^{-1}$

Strong field:

$CFSE = 4\,(-0.4\Delta_0) + P = -1.6\Delta_0 + P = -1.6 \times 21000\ cm^{-1} + 28800\ cm^{-1} = -4800\ cm^{-1}$

Applications of CFT

1. **Stability of oxidation states:** CFSE can be utilized to predict the preferential stabilities of certain oxidation states of a metal through coordination with certain ligands. Let us look into some examples.

   Being a weak ligand water is expected to form high spin octahedral complexes with both Co^{2+} and Co^{3+}. However, experimental evidences confirm that water stabilizes Co^{2+} to more extent than Co^{3+}. This is due to the fact that Co^{2+} (d^7) with electronic distribution $t_{2g}^5\,e_g^2$ has a much higher value of CFSE ($0.80\Delta_0$) than Co^{3+} (d^6) with electronic distribution $t_{2g}^4\,e_g^2$ ($CFSE = 0.4\Delta_0$).

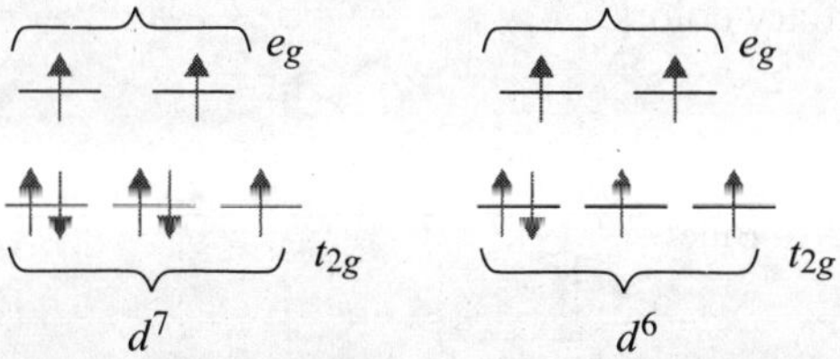

   In the above example, if water is replaced with ammonia, which is a strong ligand, it stabilizes Co^{3+} in preference to Co^{2+}. In strong field configuration, Co^{3+} has much higher value of CFSE ($2.4\Delta_0$) than Co^{2+} ($CFSE = 1.8\Delta_0$).

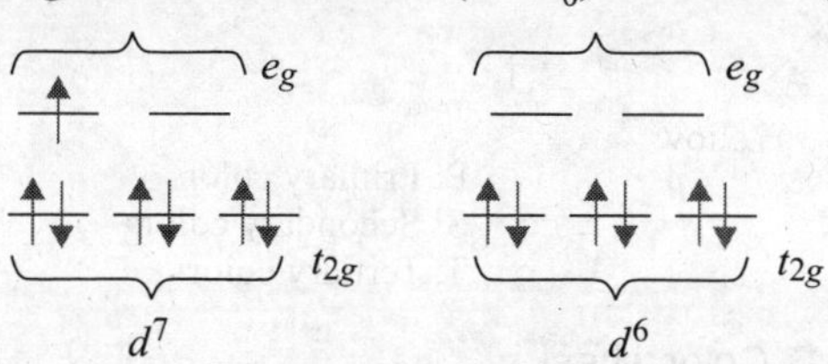

2. **Preferential geometry:** CFSE values also help to decide the preferential geometry of a complex. For example,
Cu^{2+} forms square planar complex rather than tetrahedral complex in both the crystal fields. This is due to the fact that the CFSE for square planar configuration ($1.22\Delta_0$) is significantly more than tetrahedral configuration ($0.18\Delta_0$).

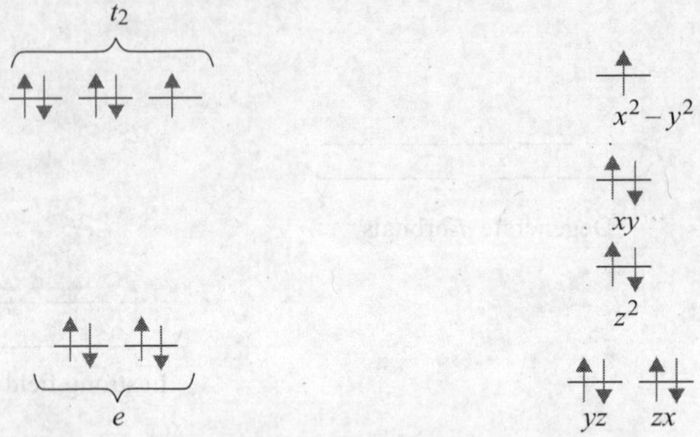

Tetrahedral crystal field
$CFSE = 4(-0.6\Delta_0) + 5(+0.4\Delta_0) = -0.18\Delta_0$

Square planar crystal field
$CFSE = 4(-0.51\Delta_0) + 2(-0.43\Delta_0) + 2(+0.23\Delta_0) + 1.23\Delta_0 = -1.22\Delta_0$

3. **Preferential coordination number:** In addition to geometry it also helps to find the relative stabilities of coordination numbers. For example, Cu^{2+} forms preferably four coordinated complexes. This is due to the fact that CFSE for C.N. four $1.22\Delta_0$ for square planar geometry is significantly higher than CFSE for C.N. six $0.6\Delta_0$.
4. **Color of complex compounds:** Most of the transition metal complexes are colored, as they have characteristic absorbance in the visible region (4000–7000 Å) of the complete electromagnetic spectrum. The color of the complex depends on the transmitted light, which is the complimentary color of the light absorbed. An approximate relation between the absorbed and transmitted light can be obtained from the following color wheel. The opposite colors are complimentary colors. For example, if a complex absorbs red color, then it appears green and vice-versa. Red, blue, and yellow are primary colors, whereas violet green and orange are secondary colors. The other six colors are tertiary colors.

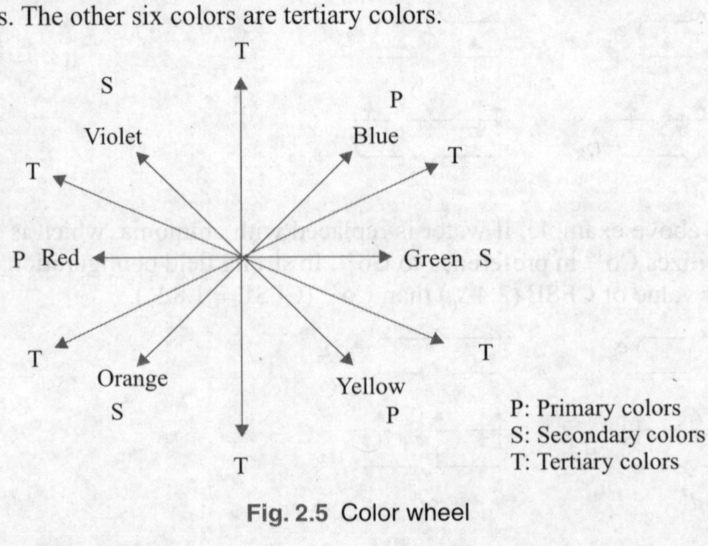

Fig. 2.5 Color wheel

Explanation for origin of color: In different crystal fields, the degeneracy of *d*-orbitals is lifted and the orbitals get grouped into different sets. As the orbitals belong parentally to one subshell, the energy gap among them is small and the energy required for the transition of electron from one set of orbitals to another is available in the visible region of complete electromagnetic spectrum. Thus, when ordinary light is allowed to fall on the complex, it absorbs certain radiation to bring transition of electron from lower energy *d*-orbitals to that of higher energy *d*-orbitals (*d–d* transition). The complimentary color is observed as the color of the complex. The relation between the absorbed color and the transmitted color can be roughly obtained from the color wheel.

Note:

1. Electronic transitions obey the following selection rules:
   (a) *Spin selection rule*: As per the rule during electronic transition, $\Delta S = 0$, that is, the allowed transitions must involve the promotion of electrons without change in their spin.
   (b) *Laporte selection rule*: It states that there must be a change in parity during transition. If the molecule has a center of symmetry, transitions within a given set of *d*-orbitals are forbidden.
2. Relaxation of the rules can occur through:
   (a) *Spin–orbit coupling*: This gives rise to weak spin forbidden bands.
   (b) *Vibronic coupling*: An octahedral complex may have allowed vibrations where the molecule is asymmetric. Absorption of light at that moment is then possible.
   (c) *Orbital mixing*: *p*-orbitals of π-acceptor and π-donor ligands can mix with the *d*-orbitals, so transitions remain no longer purely *d–d*.
3. The presence of unpaired electron(s) and possibility of transition from *d*-orbitals of lower energy to those of higher energy imparts color to a complex.
4. If both of these facilities exist but still the complex is colorless, then λ_{abs} lies outside the visible region. If crystal field is strong, λ_{abs} goes to ultraviolet region and if the crystal field is a weak one, then it goes to infrared region.
5. d^0 and d^{10} complexes are colorless due to the absence of *d–d* transitions.
6. *Charge transfer spectrum*: There are certain compounds such as $KMnO_4$ and $K_2Cr_2O_7$ in which the central metal do not carry any *d*-electron but have characteristic color. The reason is attributed to charge transfer spectrum from filled ligand orbital to vacant metal orbital.

Example 2.6

(a) *$[Ti^{3+}(H_2O)_6]^{3+}$ is purple in color. Explain.*
(b) *$[Zn^{2+}(H_2O)_6]^{2+}$ is colorless.*
(c) *$[Ni^{2+}(H_2O)_6]^{2+}$ is green but $[Ni^{4+}(CN)_6]^{2-}$ is colorless.*
(d) *Assign the colors orange and blue to the complexes $[Co(Cl)_6]^{3-}$ and $[Co(NH_3)_6]^{3+}$.*

Solution

(a) In this complex Ti^{3+} is having one solitary electron in t_{2g} set of orbitals. It absorbs at about 5000 Å units to have a transition from $t_{2g} \rightarrow$ eg. In other words, it absorbs in green region of visible spectrum and the observed color is therefore purple.

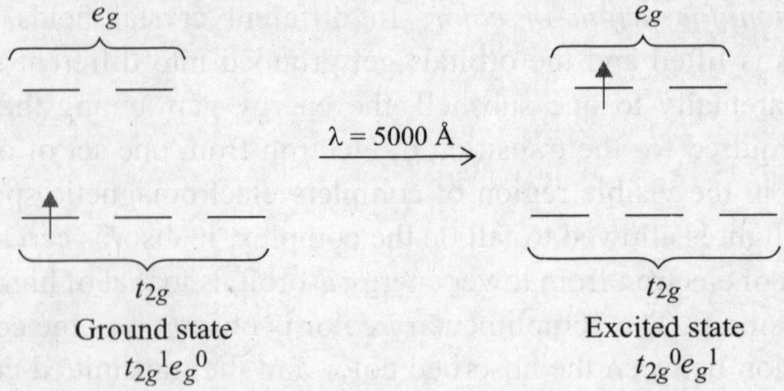

(b) In this complex, Zn^{2+} is having 10 electrons in *d*-orbitals. Therefore, $t_{2g} \rightarrow e_g$ transition is not possible and the complex is colorless.

(c) In $[Ni^{2+} (H_2O)_6]^{2+}$, the Ni^{2+} is having 8 electrons in the *d*-orbitals with an electronic configuration of $t_{2g}{}^6e_g{}^2$. The complex absorbs in red region of visible spectrum to have transition from $t_{2g} \rightarrow e_g$ and the observed color is green. However in $[Ni^{4+} (CN)_6]^{2-}$, the ligand is a strong one and in addition Ni remains with the oxidation state of +4 both of which results in a very strong field. The result being transition requires higher energy and λ_{abs} goes to the UV region. Ultimately, the complex becomes colorless.

(d) In both the complexes, Co remains in +3 oxidation state, which is a d^6 case. Thus, it gets absorb in the visible region. In $[Co(NH_3)_6]^{3+}$, NH_3 is a relatively strong ligand and the Δ_0 value is expected to be more than $[Co(Cl)_6]^{3-}$. Therefore, $[Co(NH_3)_6]^{3+}$ absorbs at a lower wavelength and the complimentary color falls at relatively higher wavelength, that is, the orange region of the visible spectrum.

6. **Magnetic property:** Paramagnetism arises due to the presence of unpaired electrons in the substance. The more is the number of unpaired electrons, the more is the paramagnetism. The resultant magnetic moment is contributed by the spin and orbital magnetic moments.

Thus,

$$\mu_{total} = \mu_{orbital} + \mu_{spin}$$
$$= [\sqrt{l\,(l+1)} + 2\sqrt{s\,(s+1)}]\frac{eh}{4\pi mc}$$
$$= [\sqrt{l\,(l+1)} + 2\sqrt{s\,(s+1)}]\ \text{BM}$$

where *e* is the charge of the electron, *c* is the velocity of light, and *m* the the mass of the electron. BM is the unit of magnetic moment and is read as Bohr Magneton. 1 BM = 9.27 × 10^{-21} erg/G.

In case of transition metal ions of 3*d*-series, the crystal field, that is, the ligands which remain surrounding the metal restrict the movement of electron around the nucleus in orbitals. The result being the orbital contribution is quenched and becomes negligible. Therefore, the effective magnetic moment can be expressed by spin only formula.

$$\mu_{spin} = \mu_{eff} = [2\sqrt{s\,(s+1)}]\frac{eh}{4\pi mc}$$
$$= [2\sqrt{s\,(s+1)}]\ \text{BM}$$

$$= \left[2\sqrt{\frac{n}{2}\left(\frac{n}{2}+1\right)}\right] \text{ BM}$$

$$= \sqrt{n\,(n+2)} \text{ BM}$$

where n is the number of unpaired electrons.

Example 2.7

Find the value of magnetic moment in the following complex ions $[Co(F)_6]^{3-}$ and $[Co(NH_3)_6]^{3+}$.

Solution

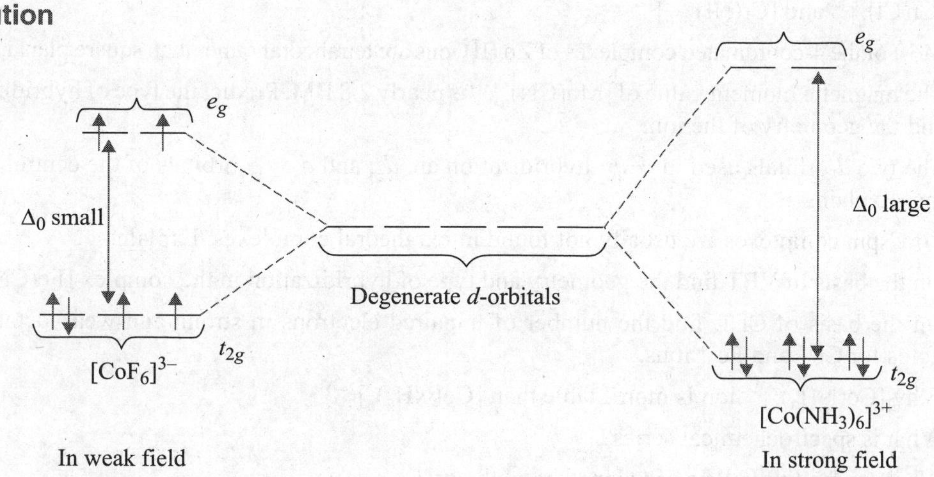

In $[Co(NH_3)_6]^{3+}$ the number of unpaired electrons is 0. The complex is diamagnetic with zero magnetic moment. On the other hand, in $[Co(F)_6]^{3-}$ the number of unpaired electrons is 4. Therefore, the complex ion is paramagnetic and magnetic moment can be calculated as follows:

$$\mu_{spin} = \sqrt{n\,(n+2)} \text{ BM}$$

$$= \sqrt{4\,(4+2)} \text{ BM}$$

$$= 4.9 \text{ BM}$$

Limitations of CFT

1. It gives emphasis only on *d*-orbitals of metal and does not consider the influence of other metal orbitals and π-orbitals of ligands.
2. It fails to justify the position of ligands in spectrochemical series.
3. It gives no account for the partly covalent nature of metal–ligand bonds.

QUESTIONS

1. $[Ni(CN)_4]^{2-}$ is square planar, while $[Zn(CN)_4]^{2-}$ is tetrahedral. Explain.
2. $[Ni(NH_3)_4]^{2+}$ can exist both in tetrahedral form and in square planar form. Explain.
3. In presence of weak field, Co (II) forms both octahedral and tetrahedral complexes, while Ni (II) rarely forms tetrahedral complexes. Explain.

4. Fe (III) forms both octahedral and tetrahedral complexes, while Cr (III) forms only octahedral complexes. Explain.
5. $[Co(NO_2)_6]^{4-}$ is easily oxidized to $[Co(NO_2)_6]^{3-}$. Explain.
6. $[Co(H_2O)_6]^{2+}$ is more stable than $[Co(H_2O)_6]^{3+}$. Explain.
7. $[Cu(NH_3)_4]^{2+}$ cannot be oxidized easily. Explain.
8. $[NiF_6]^{2-}$ is diamagnetic, whereas $[CoF_6]^{3-}$ is paramagnetic. Explain.
9. Most of the 4-coordinated complexes of Ni (II) ions are square planar rather than tetrahedral, why?
10. Arrange the following complexes in the increasing order of their Δ_0 values: $[Cr(CN)_6]^{3-}$, $[Cr(Cl)_6]^{3-}$ and $[Cr(NH_3)_6]^{3+}$.
11. Most of the 4-coordinated complexes of Zn (II) ions are tetrahedral rather than square planar, why?
12. The magnetic moment value of $[Mn(CN)_6]^{3-}$ is nearly 2.8 BM. Predict the type of hybridization and the geometry of the ion.
13. The two *d*-orbitals used in d^2sp^3 hybridization are d_{z^2} and $d_{x^2-y^2}$ orbitals of the central atom/ion. Explain.
14. Low spin complexes are usually not found in tetrahedral complexes. Explain.
15. On the basis of VBT find the geometry and type of hybridization in the complex $[Fe(CN)_6]^{4-}$.
16. On the basis of CFT, find the number of unpaired electrons in strong and weak octahedral fields for Cr^{3+} and Fe^{2+} ions.
17. Why $[Co(NH_3)_6]^{3+}$ ion is more stable than $[Co(NH_3)_6]^{2+}$?
18. What is spectrochemical series?
19. What are the limitations of valency bond theory?
20. What is the oxidation state of the metal atom in $[Co(NH_3)_4Cl_2]Cl$ and how many moles of ions are formed when 1 mole of this compound dissolves in water?
21. "Cobalt yellow" is a pigment used in oil paints and contains the coordination compound $K_3[Co(NO_2)_6]$. How many unpaired electrons are there on the cobalt atom in this compound? Note that NO_2^- is a strong-field ligand.
22. All coordination compounds which contain a Zn^{2+} transition metal ion are colorless. Explains this observation?
23. Which of the following compounds would be paramagnetic: (a) $[Sc(NH_3)_6]^{3+}$ (high spin), (b) $[Zn(OH)_4]^{2-}$ (tetrahedral), (c) $[Co(NH_3)_6]^{3+}$ (high spin), and (d) $[Fe(CN)_6]^{4-}$ (low spin).
24. What is a bridging ligand? Explain with a suitable example.
25. What is a chelating ligand? Explain with a suitable example.
26. $K_3[Fe(CN)_6]$ is colored/colorless, explain on the basis of CFT.
27. Among titanium tetra-halides, TiF_4 and $TiCl_4$ are colorless while, $TiBr_4$ is orange, and TiI_4 is dark brown. Explain the trend.
28. $[Cu(MeCN)_4]^+$ is colorless while $[Cu(Phen)_2]^+$ is dark orange though both are d^{10} systems. Explain.
29. Assign colors yellow and violet to the solutions of two complexes $[Co(H_2O)_6]^{3+}$ and $[Co(CN)_6]^{3-}$.
30. An octahedral metal complex absorbs light that is 535 nm. What is the crystal field splitting "Δ" for the complex? What color is it?

31. Cu (II) ions form square planar complexes rather than tetrahedral or octahedral complexes. Explain.
32. $[Fe(CN)_6]^{4-}$ is colorless, whereas $[Fe(H_2O)_6]^{2+}$ is colored. Explain on the basis of CFT.
33. What are the salient features of CFT? Show through a diagram, the splitting of *d*-orbitals in octahedral and tetrahedral crystal fields.
34. On the basis of VBT, find the geometry and type of hybridization involved in the complex $[Cu(CN)_4]^{2-}$. What is the oxidation state of the central metal ion and the magnetic behavior of the complex?
35. Explain bonding in coordination compounds on the basis of Werner's theory?
36. On the basis of CFT decide the geometry of the following complex ions: $[Pt(NH_3)_4]^{2+}$ and $[NiCl_4]^{2-}$.
37. Explain the origin of color in complexes with suitable examples. What are the selection rules? Also explain the relaxation of selection rules.
38. Discuss the factors which affect Δ_0 with suitable examples.
39. What are the salient features of VBT? Inner sphere Co(II) octahedral complex is unstable and readily gets oxidized to Co(III) complex. Explain.
40. List the basic postulates of Werner's theory. How will you explain the bonding in $CoCl_3 \cdot 3NH_3$ and $CoCl_3 \cdot 5NH_3$?
41. What are primary and secondary valencies? Explain on the basis of Werner's theory why cobalt amine complex $CoCl_3 \cdot 4NH_3$ upon treatment with $AgNO_3$ solution precipitates only one Cl^- ion, although it has three Cl^- ions.
42. The magnetic moment of $[MnBr_4]^{2-}$ is nearly 3.87 BM. Predict the type of hybridization and geometry of the ion.
43. The magnetic moment of $[Mn(CN)_6]^{3-}$ is nearly 2.8 BM. Predict the type of hybridization and geometry of the complex.
44. If a solution appears yellow, what wavelength of light does it absorb? Would you expect it to be low spin or high spin?

NUMERICAL PROBLEMS

1. Calculate the value of $\mu_{spin\ only}$ for the complex that gives the brown ring, $[Fe(H_2O)_5NO]^{2+}$, in nitrate test
2. Δ_0 for $[Mn(H_2O)_6]^{3+}$ is found to be 21,000 cm^{-1} from electronic spectrum. The pairing energy of Mn(III) is 28,800 cm^{-1}. Predict whether the complex is high/low spin.
3. Calculate CFSE in kJ mol^{-1} for $[Ti(H_2O)_6]^{3+}$ ion for which *d–d* transition leads to a single broad absorption peak at 20,300 cm^{-1}. Also draw the splitting diagram.
4. If the frequency of the radiation absorbed by a complex ion in the visible region is $5.3 \times 10^{14}\ s^{-1}$. What is the color of the complex ion ?
5. $[Co(NH_3)_6]^{3+}$ has a absorption maximum at 437 nm. What is the color of the ion?
6. Calculate CFSE for following complexes: $[Cu(NH_3)_6]^{2+}$ and $[Fe(CN)_6]^{4-}$.
7. On the basis of CFT, calculate magnetic moment and CFSE of the $[Cu(NH_3)_4]^{2+}$ complex.
8. Calculate the CFSE and magnetic moment of the complex $[Cu(NH_3)_4]^{2+}$.

CHAPTER 3

Chemical Thermodynamics

Chapter Outline

- Terminologies
- First Law of Thermodynamics
- Internal Energy (*U*)
- Enthalpy (*H*)
- Heat Capacity
- Types of Heat (Enthalpy) of Process
- Hess' Law by G.H. Hess (1840)
- Kirchhoff's Equation
- Joule–Thomson Effect
- Entropy
- Second Law of Thermodynamics
- Concept of Free Energy in Chemical Reactions
- Maxwell Relations
- Partial Molar Properties

The word *thermodynamics* was first coined by mechanical engineers, suggesting the evolution of a new subject dealing with conversion of thermal energy into mechanical energy in engines that drove the industrial revolutions. Nowadays thermodynamics has a broader scope and it deals with all possible forms of energies and energy transformations that occur in different systems. In addition, it also helps in understanding the equilibrium state, in deciding the feasibility of a process under a given set of conditions and providing support to a number of generalizations in physical chemistry. The largest contribution of thermodynamics is that it systematises the information obtained from various experiments and allows drawing conclusions about other aspects of the behavior of the system than that measured.

Thermodynamics is based on three fundamental generalizations known as the laws of thermodynamics, which sum up our experience with energy and natural process. From these laws, logical deductions can be made that are applicable to almost all aspects of physical science. These laws are permanent in the sense that these are not shared by our energy changing views of the nature of atoms and molecules and are developed independent of atomic and molecular theories. The understanding of thermodynamic functions on a molecular basis, although not at all necessary for the study of thermodynamics, is an important part as far as chemical science is concerned.

Terminologies

System and Surroundings

System refers to the part of the universe in which one has interest. Every system remains separated from rest of the universe, i.e., *surroundings* by a boundary which may be real or imaginary. The classification of system can be done with respect to the homogeneity and nature of the boundary that separates it from the surroundings. On the basis of *homogeneity*, system is of two types.

1. **Homogeneous**: It is a system which is uniform throughout and consists of only one phase, e.g., a system carrying mixture of two or more gases, mixture of miscible liquids, etc.
2. **Heterogeneous**: This system is not uniform throughout and consists of more than one phase, e.g., mixture of the immiscible liquids, mixture of two or more solids, etc.

   On the basis of the *nature of boundary*, system is of three types.

   (i) ***Open system***: Boundary allows the exchange of both matter and energy.

   (ii) ***Closed system***: Boundary allows only the exchange of energy.

   (iii) ***Insulated (isolated system)***: Boundary allows the exchange of neither energy nor matter.

Properties of System

The physically measurable parameters that enable us to define a system are known as properties of a system or thermodynamic properties or sometimes macroscopic properties as every system is composed of quite a large number of particles. These properties can be grouped into two broad categories on the basis of the fact that whether they depend on the amount of matter contained in the system or not.

1. **Extensive properties**

   These are dependent on the amount of matter contained in the system, e.g., volume, mass, internal energy, enthalpy, entropy, free energy, heat capacity, etc.
2. **Intensive properties**

   These are independent of the amount of matter contained in the system, e.g., density, temperature, pressure, specific heat, concentration, surface tension, etc.

State and State Variables

State refers to the condition of existence of a system and is characterised by the constancy of the microscopic properties. Any change in one or more of the macroscopic properties, bring a change in the state of the system. Therefore the macroscopic properties are also known as *state variables.*

Note: As the state variables are inter-related, it is not necessary to mention all variables to define a state. Only independent variables are required to be mentioned.

State and Path Functions

The property of a system which is uniquely determined by the present state of the system and not at all by the previous history of the system is known as a state function, e.g., internal energy, enthalpy, entropy, free energies, etc. In contrast, a path function is that which does depend on the previous history of the system, i.e., path adopted as the system is generated, e.g., heat, work, etc.

Note: Mathematically, a property is said to be state function only when dZ is an exact differential. An exact differential is an infinitesimal quantity which upon integration gives a result independent of the path between initial and the final states, i.e.,

$$\Delta Z = \int_i^f dZ$$

Condition of exactness

Let $Z = f(x, y)$

The complete differential of Z

$$dZ = \left(\frac{\partial Z}{\partial x}\right)_y dx + \left(\frac{\partial Z}{\partial y}\right)_x dy \qquad \text{...[3.1]}$$

In differential equation form,

$$dZ = P(x, y)dx + Q(x, y)dy \qquad \text{...[3.2]}$$

$$\text{where } P(x, y) = \left(\frac{\partial Z}{\partial x}\right)_y \text{ and } Q(x, y) = \left(\frac{\partial Z}{\partial y}\right)_x$$

The differential expression 'dZ' is said to be exact/perfect if,

$$\left(\frac{\partial P}{\partial y}\right)_x = \left(\frac{\partial Q}{\partial x}\right)_y \qquad \text{...[3.3]}$$

$$\text{or} \quad \left[\frac{\partial}{\partial y}\left(\frac{\partial Z}{\partial x}\right)_y\right]_x = \left[\frac{\partial}{\partial x}\left(\frac{\partial Z}{\partial y}\right)_x\right]_y \qquad \text{...[3.4]}$$

This condition of exactness is also known as *Euler's reciprocity condition.*

Mathematically, a property say (Z) is a path function only when dZ is an inexact differential. An inexact differential is an infinitesimal quantity that upon integration gives a result depending on the path adopted between the initial and the final state 3, i.e.,

$$Z = \int_{i,\ \text{Path}}^f dZ$$

ΔZ is not written, as Z is not a state function and be expressed as $Z_f - Z_i$.

Condition of inexactness

From relation [3.4],

$$\left[\frac{\partial}{\partial y}\left(\frac{\partial Z}{\partial x}\right)_y\right]_x \neq \left[\frac{\partial}{\partial x}\left(\frac{\partial Z}{\partial t}\right)_x\right]_y \qquad \text{...[3.5]}$$

Example 3.1

Show that volume of an ideal gas is a state function.

Solution

For an ideal gas, $PV = nRT$

or $V = \dfrac{nRT}{P}$

$V = f(P, T)$

If V is a state function, then dV should be an exact differential, i.e., should satisfy the following condition.

$$\left[\frac{\partial}{\partial T}\left(\frac{\partial V}{\partial P}\right)_T\right]_P = \left[\frac{\partial}{\partial P}\left(\frac{\partial V}{\partial T}\right)_P\right]_T \qquad ...[1]$$

$$\left(\frac{\partial V}{\partial P}\right)_T = \left[\frac{\partial}{\partial P}\left(\frac{nRT}{P}\right)\right]_T$$

$$= nRT\frac{\partial}{\partial P}\left(\frac{1}{P}\right)$$

$$= -\frac{nRT}{P^2}$$

$$\left[\frac{\partial}{\partial T}\left(\frac{\partial V}{\partial P}\right)_T\right]_P = \frac{\partial}{\partial T}\left(-\frac{nRT}{P^2}\right)$$

$$= -\frac{nR}{P^2} \qquad ...[2]$$

$$\left(\frac{\partial V}{\partial T}\right)_P = \left[\frac{\partial}{\partial T}\left(\frac{nRT}{P}\right)\right]_P$$

$$= \frac{nR}{P}\left(\frac{\partial T}{\partial T}\right)$$

$$= \frac{nR}{P}$$

$$\left[\frac{\partial}{\partial P}\left(\frac{\partial V}{\partial T}\right)_P\right]_T = \frac{\partial}{\partial P}\left(\frac{nR}{P}\right)$$

$$= -\frac{nR}{P^2} \qquad ...[3]$$

Thus, relation [1] is satisfied, which confirms that V is state function for an ideal gas.

Note: Relations between partial derivatives:

1. $\left(\frac{\partial x}{\partial y}\right)_z = \left(\frac{1}{\frac{dy}{dx}}\right)_z$

2. $\left(\frac{\partial x}{\partial y}\right)_z \left(\frac{\partial y}{\partial z}\right)_x \left(\frac{\partial z}{\partial x}\right)_y + 1 = 0$, this relation is known as cyclic rule

Example 3.2

Verify cyclic rule for 1 mol of an ideal gas.

Solution

For 1 mol of an ideal gas, $PV = RT$

or $\quad PdV + VdP = RdT$ ...[1]

The cyclic rule can be written as

$$\left(\frac{\partial P}{\partial T}\right)_V \left(\frac{\partial T}{\partial V}\right)_P \left(\frac{\partial V}{\partial P}\right)_T + 1 = 0 \qquad ...[2]$$

At constant volumem $dV = 0$, thus relation [1] becomes

$VdP = RdT$

or $\quad V\left(\frac{\partial P}{\partial T}\right)_V = R$

or $\quad \left(\frac{\partial P}{\partial T}\right)_V = \frac{R}{V}$ ...[3]

At constant pressure, $dP = 0$, thus relation [1] becomes

$PdV = RdT$

or $\quad P = R\left(\frac{\partial T}{\partial V}\right)_P$

or $\quad \left(\frac{\partial T}{\partial V}\right)_P = \frac{P}{R}$ [4]

At constant temperature, $dT = 0$, thus relation [1] becomes

$PdV + VdP = 0$

or $\quad P\left(\frac{\partial V}{\partial P}\right)_T = -V$

or $\quad \left(\frac{\partial V}{\partial P}\right)_T = -\frac{V}{P}$ ...[5]

$$\left(\frac{\partial P}{\partial T}\right)_V \left(\frac{\partial T}{\partial V}\right)_P \left(\frac{\partial V}{\partial P}\right)_T + 1 = \frac{R}{V} \times \frac{P}{R} \times -\frac{V}{P} + 1 = 0$$

Hence proved.

Thermodynamic Process

The operation by virtue of which a system moves from one state to another is known as thermodynamic process.

Types of processes

On the basis of the condition maintained during the process, they can be classified as follows:

1. **Isothermal**: Such a process is carried out at constant temperature. Temperature is kept constant by extracting or supplying heat to the system.
2. **Adiabatic**: No heat exchange between system and surroundings is allowed during such a process. Here temperature may change.
3. **Isobaric**: Pressure of the system remains constant during the process.
4. **Isochoric**: Volume of the system remains constant.

Figure 3.1 shows the P–V indicator diagram which explains the different process.

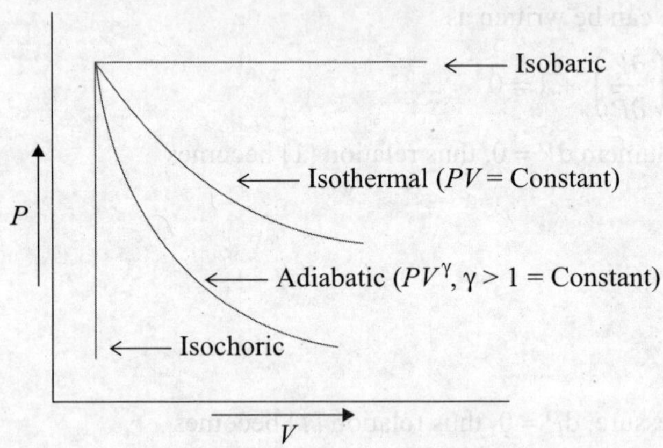

Fig. 3.1 Indicator diagram

On the basis of nature, the thermodynamic processes can be classified as follows:

Reversible processes

A process which can be made to proceed in the reverse direction so that it passes through the same states as in the direct processe and at the end both system and surrounding attain the initial condition is called a reversible process.

Characteristics

1. Driving and opposing forces differ by infinitesimally small amount.
2. Such a process occurs infinitesimally slowly, i.e., so slowly that it always appears to be in equilibrium.
3. An *absolute reversible* process cannot be realized in practice. For example, frictionless motion, resistanceless current flow, etc.
4. When carried between same initial and final conditions, the optimum efficiency is obtained in reversible process.

Irreversible processes

A process which cannot be made to retrace its path with modification of conditions is known as irreversible process or spontaneous process.

Characteristics

1. Driving and opposing forces differ by an appreciable amount.
2. Rate is not a factor here. An irreversible process may be very slow or very fast.
3. All processes occuring in nature are irreversible processes. For example, any spontaneous chemical change, diffusion of gases into one another, work done against friction, current flow against resistance, etc.
4. When carried between same initial and final conditions, the optimum efficiency is always less than that of reversible process.

Concept of Heat and Work

Energy change can take place in different forms. In thermodynamics, the two popular forms are heat and work.

Heat

1. Heat is a form of energy.
2. In terms of molecular interpretation, heat is the transfer of energy that makes use of thermal molecular motion in the surroundings. Therefore it is regarded as the random form of energy.
3. Energy change takes place in the form of heat when there is a temperature gradient between system and surroundings.
4. It is an extensive property.
5. It is a path function, i.e., dq is not an exact differential.
6. Heat absorbed by a system is +ve, while heat released by a system is –ve.

Work

1. Work is also a form of energy.
2. In terms of molecular interpretation, work is the transfer of energy that makes use of organized molecular motion in surroundings. Therefore it is regarded as the organized form of energy.
3. Energy change takes place in the form of heat when there is a temperature gradient between system and surroundings.
4. It is an extensive property.
5. It is a path function, i.e., dw is not an exact differential.
6. Work done on the system is +ve, while work done by the system is –ve.

Note:

1. Work (*isothermal reversible*) $= nRT \ln \dfrac{V_2}{V_1} = nRT \ln \dfrac{P_1}{P_2}$

2. Work (*isothermal irreversible*) $= P_2 (V_2 - V_1)$

$$= nRT\left(1 - \frac{P_2}{P_1}\right)$$

3. Work (*adiabatic reversible*) $= \dfrac{nR(T_2 - T_1)}{1 - \gamma}$

4. Work done in a reversible process is always more than that of irreversible process.

$$W_{rev} = nRT \ln \frac{P_1}{P_2}$$

$$= nRT \ln \left[1 - 1 + \frac{P_1}{P_2}\right]$$

$$= nRT \ln \left[1 - \left(1 - \frac{P_1}{P_2}\right)\right]$$

$$= -nRT\left[1 - \frac{P_1}{P_2}\right] \qquad [\because \ln(1 - n) \cong -n]$$

$$= nRT\left(\frac{P_1}{P_2} - 1\right) \qquad \text{...(1)}$$

$$W_{rev} - W_{irr} = nRT\left(\frac{P_1}{P_2} - 1\right) - nRT\left(1 - \frac{P_2}{P_1}\right)$$

$$= nRT\left(\frac{P_1^2 - 2P_1P_2 + P_2^2}{P_1P_2}\right)$$

$$= \frac{nRT}{P_1P_2}(P_1 - P_2)^2$$

As, $(P_1 - P_2)^2 > 0$

$\Rightarrow W_{rev} - W_{irr} > 0$

$\Rightarrow W_{rev} > W_{irr}$

Subscripts 1 and 2 correspond to initial and final states. Positive and negative signs in the relation are utilized depending on the fact whether work is done on the system or by the system.

First Law of Thermodynamics

It may be stated in different ways.

1. Energy can neither be created nor be destroyed in a process, however it can be converted from one form to another.
2. Whenever certain quantity of one form of energy disappears, exactly equivalent quantity of some other form must appear.
3. The sum total of all forms of energy of an isolated system remains constant.

4. The sum total of all forms of energy of the universe, i.e., system and surroundings taken together is constant.

Mathematical formulation

Let us consider a system that takes q amount of heat to do some work. Now a part of the heat is utilized in doing work w and the rest gets dissipated in the system which increases its internal energy by an amount ΔU. As per the first law,

$$q = w + \Delta U$$

Internal Energy (*U*)

The energy possessed by a system by virtue of its existence is known as its internal energy and is denoted by U. It originates from individual particles which aggregate to form the whole system. It is contributed by different molecular motions and non-bonding interactions such as translational, vibrational, rotational, nuclear and electronic energies. The following aspects are important in reference to internal energy.

1. It is an extensive property.
2. It is a state function i.e., dU is an exact differential.
3. Its absolute value cannot be measured. The difficulty lies in the correct evaluation of contributing factors.
4. In thermodynamics, ΔU is given importance instead of absolute U.
5. *Physical significance*: Let us consider a process that occurs at constant volume, then no work is done. Now from the first law,

   $$q_v = \Delta U$$

   where q_v is the heat of process at constant volume.

Change in internal energy is nothing but the heat of the process/reaction at constant volume

Enthalpy (*H*)

If a process occurs at constant pressure then the total energy content includes the energy due to work done by or on the system in addition to the internal energy of the system. In such a case, new thermodynamic function is introduced to account for the total energy content which is known as enthalpy. Thus enthalpy can be written as:

$$H = U + PV$$

The following points are important in reference to enthalpy:

1. It is an extensive property.
2. It is a state function, i.e., dH is an exact differential.
3. Like internal energy, the absolute value of enthalpy also cannot be measured.
4. In thermodynamics, ΔH is given importance instead of absolute H.
5. *Physical significance*: Let us consider a process that occurs at constant pressure.

   $$\begin{aligned}\Delta H &= H_f - H_i \\ &= (U_f + PV_f) - (U_i + PV_i) \\ &= \Delta U + P\Delta V \\ &= \Delta U + w \qquad \text{...[3.6]}\end{aligned}$$

From the first law,

$$q = w + \Delta U \quad ...[3.7]$$

Comparing the above relations [3.6] and [3.7],

$$q_p = \Delta H$$

where q_p is the heat of process at constant pressure.

Change in enthalpy is nothing but the heat of the process/reaction at constant pressure

6. Sign of ΔH can be considered as one of the criterion of spontaneity. A process accompanied by decrease of enthalpy tends to be spontaneous.

Relation between q_p and q_v

$$\Delta H = \Delta U + P\Delta V$$

or $q_p = q_v + P\Delta V$ ...[3.8]

Now let's consider a hypothetical reaction,

$$aA + bB \longrightarrow cC + dD$$

Change in number of moles = $(c + d) - (a + b) = \Delta n$

ΔV = Change in number of moles × volume occupied by one mole of gas

or $\Delta V = \Delta n \times \text{V}$

or $P\Delta V = P(\Delta n \times \text{V})$

$$= PV(\Delta n)$$

$$= \Delta nRT \quad ...[3.9]$$

Substituting in relation [3.8], we get

$$q_p = q_v + \Delta nRT \quad ...[3.10]$$

Example 3.3

The heat liberated on complete combustion of 7.8 g of benzene is 327 kJ at 27 °C measured at constant volume. Calculate the heat of combustion of benzene at constant pressure at the same temperature.

Solution

The reaction for combustion of benzene is

$$C_6H_{6(l)} + (15/2)\,O_{2\,(g)} \longrightarrow 6CO_{2\,(g)} + 3H_2O_{(l)}$$

$$\Delta n = 6 - (15/2) = -(3/2)$$

$$q_v = \frac{-327 \times 78}{7.8} = -3270\text{ kJ}$$

$$q_p = q_v + \Delta nRT$$

$$= -3270 + (-3/2) \times 8.3 \times 10^{-3} \times 300$$

$$= -3273.7\text{ kJ}$$

Heat Capacity

The *heat capacity* of a system is the amount of heat required to raise the temperature of the whole mass by 1°C. On the other hand, the *specific heat* is the amount of heat required to raise the temperature of unit mass of it by 1°C. It can be expressed as

$$\text{Heat capacity} = \frac{q}{\Delta T} \qquad ...[3.11]$$

$$\text{Specific heat, } C = \frac{q}{m \times \Delta T}, \ m \text{ is mass.} \qquad ...[3.12]$$

$$\text{Molar specific heat, } C = \frac{q}{\Delta T}, \text{ mass is 1 mol} \qquad ...[3.13]$$

$$\text{For a small change, } C = \frac{\mathrm{d}q}{\mathrm{d}T} \qquad ...[3.14]$$

Case I: At constant volume

Here no work is done and therefore all the heat given is utilized in doing work. Thus, from the first law,

$$\mathrm{d}q = \mathrm{d}U$$

$$C_V = \left[\frac{\partial U}{\partial T}\right]_V \qquad ...[3.15]$$

or $\mathrm{d}U = C_V \mathrm{d}T$ ...[3.16]

For a finite change, $\Delta U = C_V(T_2 - T_1)$

For n moles of ideal gas, $\Delta U = nC_V(T_2 - T_1)$ ...[3.17]

Case II: At constant pressure

Here heat given is utilized in two ways, i.e., both in raising temperature and in doing useful work. Thus the heat capacity at constant pressure is invariably more than the same at constant volume. From the first law,

$$\mathrm{d}H = \mathrm{d}U + P\mathrm{d}V$$

Comparing, $\mathrm{d}q = \mathrm{d}H$

Substituting in relation [3.14], we get

$$C_P = \left[\frac{\partial H}{\partial T}\right]_P \qquad ...[3.18]$$

or $\mathrm{d}H = C_P \mathrm{d}T$ ...[3.19]

For a finite change, $\Delta U = C_P(T_2 - T_1)$

For n moles of ideal gas, $\Delta U = nC_P(T_2 - T_1)$ ...[3.20]

Relation Among Heat Capacities

1. ***For an ideal gas***

$$C_P - C_V = R$$

Proof:

$$U = f(T, V)$$

or $$\mathrm{d}U = \left(\frac{\partial U}{\partial T}\right)_V \mathrm{d}T + \left(\frac{\partial U}{\partial V}\right)_V \mathrm{d}V$$

or $$\left(\frac{\partial U}{\partial T}\right)_P = \left(\frac{\partial U}{\partial T}\right)_V + \left(\frac{\partial U}{\partial T}\right)_T + \left(\frac{\partial U}{\partial T}\right)_P \quad ...[3.21]$$

Now, $$C_P - C_V = \left[\frac{\partial H}{\partial T}\right]_P - \left[\frac{\partial U}{\partial T}\right]_V$$

$$= \left[\frac{\partial U}{\partial T}\right]_P + P\left[\frac{\partial V}{\partial T}\right]_P - \left[\frac{\partial U}{\partial T}\right]_V$$

$$= \left(\frac{\partial U}{\partial T}\right)_V + \left(\frac{\partial U}{\partial V}\right)_T\left(\frac{\partial V}{\partial T}\right)_P + P\left[\frac{\partial V}{\partial T}\right]_P - \left[\frac{\partial U}{\partial T}\right]_V$$

$$= \left(\frac{\partial V}{\partial T}\right)_P\left[\left(\frac{\partial U}{\partial V}\right)_T + P\right]$$

$$= P\left(\frac{\partial V}{\partial T}\right)_P \quad ...[3.22]$$

For an ideal gas, $\left(\frac{\partial U}{\partial V}\right)_T = 0$

Again, for 1 mol of an ideal gas, $PV = RT$

or $$V = \frac{RT}{P}$$

or $$\left(\frac{\partial V}{\partial T}\right)_P = \frac{R}{P}$$

Substituting in relation [3.22], we get

$$C_P - C_V = P \times \frac{R}{P} = R$$

2. ***For a real gas***

$q = f(T, V)$

or $$dq = \left(\frac{\partial q}{\partial V}\right)_T dV + \left(\frac{\partial q}{\partial T}\right)_T dT$$

$$- T\left(\frac{\partial S}{\partial V}\right)_T dV + C_V dT$$

or $$\left(\frac{\partial q}{\partial T}\right)_P = T\left(\frac{\partial S}{\partial V}\right)_T\left(\frac{\partial V}{\partial T}\right)_P + C_V$$

or $$C_P - C_V = T\left(\frac{\partial S}{\partial V}\right)_T\left(\frac{\partial V}{\partial T}\right)_P$$

$$= T\left(\frac{\partial P}{\partial T}\right)_V\left(\frac{\partial V}{\partial T}\right)_P \quad ...[3.23]$$

$$\left[\left(\frac{\partial S}{\partial V}\right)_T = \left(\frac{\partial P}{\partial T}\right)_V \text{, from Maxwell relation (3.97)}\right]$$

For a real gas, $\left[P + \frac{a}{V^2}\right][V - b] = RT$ or $PV - Pb + \frac{a}{V} - \frac{ab}{V^2} = RT$

Differentiating with respect to T at constant V.

$$\left(\frac{\partial P}{\partial T}\right)_V V - \left(\frac{\partial P}{\partial T}\right)_V b = R$$

or $$\left(\frac{\partial P}{\partial T}\right)_V = \frac{R}{V - b} \quad \text{...[3.24]}$$

Again differentating w.r.t. T at constant P

$$p\left(\frac{\partial V}{\partial T}\right)_P - \frac{a}{V^2}\left(\frac{\partial V}{\partial T}\right)_P + \frac{2ab}{V^3}\left(\frac{\partial V}{\partial T}\right)_P = R$$

or $$\left(\frac{\partial V}{\partial T}\right)_P = \frac{R}{P - \frac{a}{V^2} + \frac{2ab}{V^3}} \quad \text{...[3.25]}$$

Substituting in relation [3.23], we get

or $$C_P - C_V = \frac{R}{V - b} \times \frac{R}{P - \frac{a}{V^2} + \frac{2ab}{V^3}}$$

$$= \frac{RT}{V - b} \times \frac{R}{\left[P + \frac{a}{V^2}\right] - \frac{2a}{V^3}(V - b)}$$

$$= \frac{RT}{V - b} \cdot \frac{R}{\frac{RT}{V - b} - \frac{2a}{V^3}(V - b)}$$

$$= \frac{RT}{V - b} \times \frac{R}{\frac{RT}{V - b}\left[1 - \frac{2a(V - b)^2}{RTV^3}\right]}$$

$$\cong R\left[1 + \frac{2a}{RTV}\right] \quad \text{[Neglecting } b \text{ in comparision to } V\text{]}$$

$$= R\left[1 + \frac{2aP}{R^2T^2}\right] \quad \text{...[3.26]}$$

From relation [3.26], it follows that the difference of C_p and C_V increases linearly with pressure. This difference also depends on the nature of the gas through the constant a. The larger the value of a, the more is the difference between C_p and C_V.

Relation [3.26] is not valid for conditions of low temperature and high pressure. In such a case, let us moidify the relation.

$$C_p - C_V = \frac{RT}{V-b} \times \frac{R}{\frac{RT}{V-b} - \frac{2a}{V^3}(V-b)}$$

$$= \frac{RT}{V-b} \times \frac{R(V-b)}{RT - \frac{2a}{V^3}(V-b)^2}$$

$$= \frac{RT}{V-b} \times \frac{V-b}{T}\left[1 - \frac{2a}{V^3RT}(V-b)^2\right]^{-1}$$

$$= \frac{RT}{V-b} \times \frac{V-b}{T}\left[1 + \frac{2a}{V^3RT}(V-b)^2\right]$$

$$\simeq R\left[1 + \frac{2a}{V^3RT}(V^2 - 2Vb)\right]$$

$$\simeq R\left[1 + \frac{2aP}{R^2T^2} - \frac{4abp^2}{R^3T^3}\right] \quad ...[3.27]$$

3. **Ratio of specific heats (γ)**

$$\gamma = \frac{C_P}{C_V}$$

In general, $C_V = \frac{3}{2}R + x$ and $C_P = \frac{5}{2}R + x$,

here x is compensating factor for vibrational and rotational degrees of freedom. The value of x varies from gas to gas.

For mono-atomic gases, $x = 0$, thus

$$\gamma = \frac{\frac{5R}{2}}{\frac{3R}{2}} = 1.667$$

For diatomic gases in most cases, $x = R$, thus

$$\gamma = \frac{\frac{7R}{2}}{\frac{5R}{2}} = 1.40$$

For polyatomic gases in most cases $x = 3R/2$, thus

$$\gamma = \frac{\frac{5R}{2} + \frac{3R}{2}}{\frac{3R}{2} + \frac{3R}{2}} = 1.33$$

Example 3.4

Calculate the values of ΔU and ΔH during heating of 32 g of oxygen from 0°C to 100°C. C_P and C_V on an average are 7.0 and 5.0 cal mol^{-1} degree^{-1}, respectively.

Solution

$n = 2$ mol

$$\Delta U = nC_V(T_2 - T_1) = 2 \times 5.0\ (373 - 273) = 2000 \text{ cal}$$
$$\Delta H = nC_P(T_2 - T_1) = 2 \times 7.0\ (373 - 273) = 2800 \text{ cal}$$

Example 3.5

Calculate the amount of heat required to raise the temperature of 90 g of water from 25°C to 100°C. Molar heat capacity of water is 18.0 cal mol^{-1}degree^{-1}.

Solution

$$C = \frac{q}{\Delta T}$$

or $q = C \times \Delta T$

$= n \times C \times \Delta T$, for n moles

$= 5 \times 18 \times (373 - 298) = 6750$ cal

Types of Heat (Enthalpy) of Process

Heats of reactions are named after the names of the reaction or processes involved. Therefore we come across several types. Some of them are as follows:

1. **Heat of formation (ΔH_F)**

   The *heat of formation* of a compound may be defined as the heat change during the formation of one mole of the same from its constituent elements. When all components of the reaction remain in their standard states, i.e., under 1 atm pressure and a specified temperature, the corresponding heat of formation is known as the *standard heat of formation* ($\Delta H°_F$). For example,

$$\frac{1}{2}H_{2(g)} + O_{2(g)} \longrightarrow H_2O_{(l)};\ \Delta H°_F = -68.84 \text{ kcal}$$

$$2C_{(s)} + 3H_{2(g)} + \frac{1}{2}O_{2(g)} \longrightarrow C_2H_5OH_{(l)};\ \Delta H°_F = -66.26 \text{ kcal}$$

$$6C_{(s)} + 3H_{2(g)} \longrightarrow C_6H_{6\,(g)};\ \Delta H°_F = +11.86 \text{ kcal}$$

Note:

1. The standard state of a substance is the purest form under 1 atm pressure and at a specified temperature (If not specified temperature is always the average room temperature, i.e., 298 K)
2. Though it is difficult to find the absolute values of standard heat (enthalpy) of a compound, the relative values can be calculated with the convention that the standard enthalpies of elements are zero.

$$\frac{1}{2}H_{2(g)} + O_{2(g)} \longrightarrow H_2O_{(l)};\ \Delta H°_F = -68.84 \text{ kcal}$$

$$\Delta H^\circ_F(H_2O) = \Sigma H^\circ(\text{Products}) - (\text{Reactants})$$
$$= H^\circ(H_2O) - \left[\frac{1}{2} H^\circ(H_{2(g)}) + H^\circ(O_{2(g)})\right]$$
$$= H^\circ(H_2O), \text{ standard enthalpies of elements are taken as zero}$$

The above analysis shows that the standard heat of a compound is equal to its heat of formation.

3. Knowing the values of ΔH°_F of reactants and products, the heat of any reaction (ΔH°) can be calculated by using the relation:
$\Delta H^\circ = \Sigma\Delta H^\circ_F\,(\text{Products}) - \Sigma\Delta H^\circ_F(\text{Reactants})$

Example 3.6

Find the standard heat change during combustion of 1 mol of ethyl alcohol. Given the standard heat of formations of $C_2H_5OH_{(l)}$, $CO_{2(g)}$ and $H_2O_{(l)}$ are –66.36, –94.05 and –68.32 kcal mol^{-1}, respectively.

Solution

The reaction is, $C_2H_5OH_{(l)} + 3O_{2(g)} \longrightarrow 2CO_{2(g)} + 3H_2O_{(l)}$

$$\Delta H^\circ = \Sigma\Delta H^\circ_F\,(\text{Products}) - \Sigma\Delta H^\circ_F(\text{Reactants})$$
$$= [2\Delta H^\circ_F(CO_{2(g)}) + 3\Delta H^\circ_F(H_2O_{(l)})] - [\Delta H^\circ_F(C_2H_5OH_{(l)}) + 3\Delta H^\circ_F(O_{2(g)})]$$
$$= [2 \times (-94.05) + 3 \times (-68.32)] - [-66.36 + 0]$$
$$= -326.7 \text{ kcal mol}^{-1}$$

2. **Heat of combustion (ΔH_C)**
The *heat of combustion* of a compound is defined as the heat change during the complete combustion of one mole of the same in excess oxygen.
$C_{(s)} + O_{2\,(g)} \longrightarrow CO_{2\,(g)};\ \Delta H_C = -94.3$ kcal
$CH_{4\,(g)} + 2O_{2(g)} \longrightarrow CO_{2\,(g)} + 2H_2O_{\,(l)};\ \Delta H_C = -212.8$ kcal
$C_{12}H_{22}O_{11\,(s)} + 12O_{2\,(g)} \longrightarrow 12CO_{2\,(g)} + 11H_2O_{\,(l)};\ \Delta H_C = -1349$ kcal

Note:

1. The heat of combustion is always negative.
2. Calorific value: The efficiency of any food or fuel is compared by calorific value which may be defined as the heat released during the complete combustion of 1 g of food/fuel in excess oxygen. Some common foods/fuels along with their calorific values are as follows.

Food	Calorific value (cal/g)
Milk	0.65
Butter	7.40
Cheese	3.10
Beans	0.20
Cabbage	0.10
Potatoes	0.80
Tamatos	0.15
Apple	0.45
Banana	0.80

Fuel	Calorific value (kcal/g)
Hydrogen	33.9
Gasoline	11.3
Diesel	10.7
Wood	3.6
Coal (lignite)	4.4
Coal (anthracite)	7.8
Natural gas	13.0
Ethanol	7.1
Butane	11.8

3. **Heat of neutralization**

The *heat of neutralization* is defined as the heat change accompanying the complete neutralization of 1 g equivalent of an acid by 1 g equivalent of a base or vice-versa in dilute solutions.

$$HCl_{(aq)} + NaOH_{(aq)} \longrightarrow NaCl_{(aq)} + H_2O_{(l)};\ \Delta H = -13.7 \text{ kcal}$$

$$HNO_{3(aq)} + NaOH_{(aq)} \longrightarrow NaNO_{2(aq)} + H_2O_{(l)};\ \Delta H = -13.7 \text{ kcal}$$

Note:

1. When acid and base both are strong, the heat of neutralization is always –13.7 kcal. This is because of the fact that no heat is utilized for the purpose of dissociation of the electrolytes and the heat released is simply due to interaction of 1 mol of H^+ and 1 mol of OH^- ions to form 1 mol of H_2O.
2. If one of them or both are weak electrolytes, then heat of neutralization is always less than –13.7 kcal. The reason being some heat is utilized in dissociation of the weak component.

$$CH_3COOH_{(aq)} + NaOH_{(aq)} \longrightarrow CH_3COONa_{(aq)} + H_2O_{(l)};\ \Delta H = -13.2 \text{ kcal}$$

Here acetic acid is a weak electrolyte and +0.5 kcal heat is utilized in its dissociation.

4. **Heat of solution (ΔH_{Sol})**

The *heat of solution* of a compound is defined as the heat change during the complete dissolution of 1 mol of the same in excess solvent.

$$KCl_{(s)} + H_2O_{(l)} \longrightarrow KCl_{(aq)};\ \Delta H_{Sol} = -4.4 \text{ kcal}$$

Note: The value of heat of a solution depends upon the amount of solvent available and approaches a limiting value at infinite dilution. Infinite dilution is such dilution after which further dilution does not bring any change in enthalpy.

5. **Heat of phase transition**

The process which involves the change in the state of matter is known as phase change or transition. The corresponding heat change is known as heat of phase transition. It can be of the following four types:

(a) *Heat of fusion* (ΔH_{Fusion})

The *heat of fusion* (ΔH_{Fusion}) of a compound is defined as the heat change during the conversion of one mole of a solid substance into liquid at its melting point.

$$H_2O_{(s)} \longrightarrow H_2O_{(l)};\ \Delta H_{Fusion} = +1.43 \text{ kcal}$$

(b) *Heat of vaporization* (ΔH_V)

The *heat of vaporization* (ΔH_V) of a compound is defined as the heat change during the conversion of one mole of a liquid substance into vapor at its boiling point.

$$H_2O_{(l)} \longrightarrow H_2O_{(v)};\ \Delta H_V = +9.71 \text{ kcal}$$

(c) *Heat of sublimation* (ΔH_S)

The *heat of sublimation* (ΔH_S) of a compound is defined as the heat change during the conversion of one mole of a solid substance directly into vapor at a temperature below its melting point.

$$I_{2(s)} \longrightarrow I_{2(g)};\ \Delta H_S = +14.92 \text{ kcal}$$

(d) *Heat of transition* (ΔH_T)

The *heat of transition* (ΔH_T) of an element is defined as the heat change during the conversion of one mole of an element from one allotropic form to another.

$C_{(Dimond)} \longrightarrow C_{(Graphite)}$; $\Delta H_T = +3.3$ kcal

Hess' Law By G.H. Hess (1840)

The heat change accompanying a process (chemical reaction) remains independent of the fact that whether it takes place in one step or in several steps.

Mathematical formulation

Let a reactant "A" changes to product "C" in a step where the heat change is ΔH. In an alternate path, the reactant "A" first goes to "B" and then from "B" to final product "C". The corresponding heat changes in the alternate path being ΔH_1 and ΔH_2, respectively.

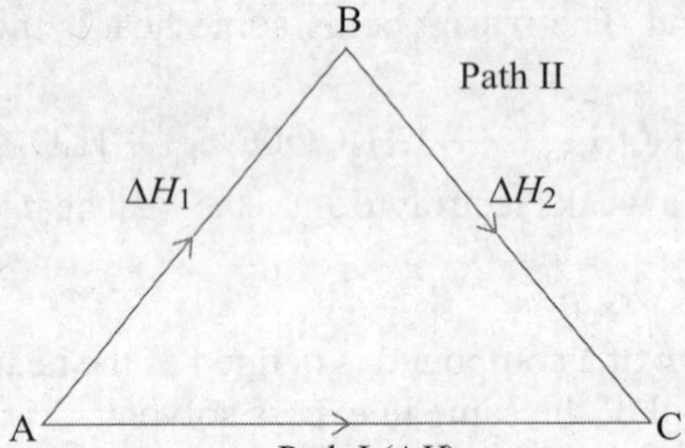

By the law, $\Delta H = \Delta H_1 + \Delta H_2$

Justification

Let's couple the two paths of the hypothetical example given above to have a cyclic process. In path I, A changes to C, say ΔH is the heat evolved. In path II, C returns back to A and the heat ($\Delta H_1 + \Delta H_2$) is absorbed.

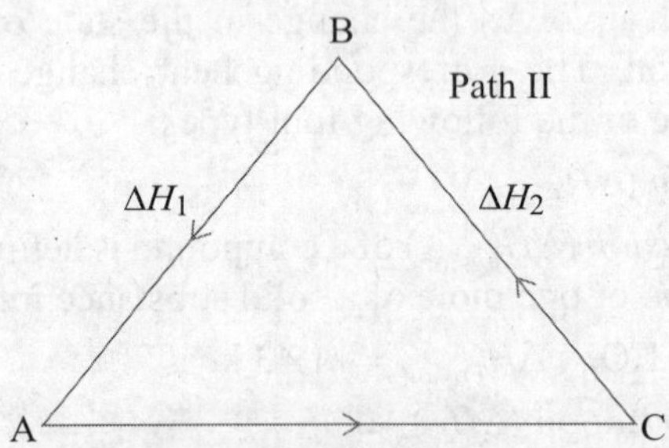

By contradiction, say $\Delta H \neq \Delta H_1 + \Delta H_2$. Then let's assume $\Delta H > \Delta H_1 + \Delta H_2$. Now in completion of one cycle $\Delta H - (\Delta H_1 + \Delta H_2)$ heat is generated. By repeating the cycle several times, the requisite amount of energy can be generated. This result is in direct conflict with the first law of thermodynamics which says construction of perpetual motion machine is impossible. Thus ΔH cannot be greater than ($\Delta H_1 + \Delta H_2$). Similarly it can be shown that ΔH can also not be lesser than ($\Delta H_1 + \Delta H_2$). Therefore the assumption $\Delta H \neq \Delta H_1 + \Delta H_2$ is not correct, rather $\Delta H = \Delta H_1 + \Delta H_2$.

Some important results of Hess' law

1. The thermo-chemical equations can be operated algebraically, i.e., can be added, one equation can be subtracted from another and an equation can be multiplied by some factor.
2. The enthalpy change of a forward and reverse reaction is same in magnitude and differs only in sign.

Applications

Hess' law finds its wide application in those cases where direct experimental measurement of heat change is not possible. The manipulation of thermo-chemical equations is the key to applying this law.

1. *To find heat of formation*

There are many compounds which cannot be prepared directly from their elements. ΔH_f in such cases can be estimated with the use of Hess' law.

Example 3.7

If the heat of formation of $CO_{2(g)}$ and $H_2O_{(l)}$ are -393.5 and -285.8 kJ mol^{-1}, respectively and heat of combustion of $C_3H_8(g)$ is -2220.2 kJ mol^{-1}, find the standard heat of formation of $C_3H_8(g)$.

Solution

Required equation is $3C_{(s)} + 4H_{2(g)} \longrightarrow C_3H_{8\,(g)}$; $\Delta H = ?$ ...[1]

Given, $C_{(s)} + O_{2(g)} \longrightarrow CO_{2(g)}$; $\Delta H = -393.5$ kJ ...[2]

$H_{2(g)} + \frac{1}{2}O_{2(g)} \longrightarrow H_2O_{(l)}$; $\Delta H = -285.8$ kJ ...[3]

$C_3H_{8(g)} + 5\,O_{2(g)} \longrightarrow 3CO_{2(g)} + 4H_2O_{(l)}$; $\Delta H = -2220.2$ kJ ...[4]

The required equation can be obtained by,

$3 \times$ Eq [2] + $4 \times$ Eq [3] − Eq [4]

$[C_{(s)} + O_{2(g)} \longrightarrow CO_{2\,(g)}] \times 3$; $\Delta H = -\,393.5 \times 3 = -1180.5$ kJ

$[H_{2\,(g)} + \frac{1}{2}O_{2(g)} \longrightarrow H_2O_{(l)}] \times 4$; $\Delta H = -285.8 \times 4 = -1143.2$ kJ

(+)

$3C_{(s)} + 4H_{2\,(g)} + 5O_{2\,(g)} \longrightarrow 3CO_{2(g)} + 4H_2O_{(l)}$; $\Delta H = -\,2323.7$ kJ

$C_3H_{8(g)} + 5O_{2(g)} \longrightarrow 3CO_{2\,(g)} + 4H_2O_{\,(l)}$; $\Delta H = -2220.2$ kJ

(−)

$3C_{(s)} + 4\,H_{2\,(g)} \longrightarrow C_3H_{8\,(g)}$; $\Delta H = -10.35$ kJ

The heat of formation of $C_3H_{8\,(g)}$ is -10.35 kJ mol^{-1}.

2. *To find lattice energy*

This approach was developed by Born and Haber in 1919 which correlates the lattice energy of a crystal to other thermo-chemical data. The underlying principle in this approach is Hess' law. The method can be explained by taking the following illustrative examples.

Illustration I

Let us find the lattice energy of NaCl. The formation reaction is one where NaCl is prepared directly from its elements (path I). Otherwise in path II, it can be prepared through several steps. The Born–Haber cycle designed for the purpose is as follows. The heat changes involved in all the steps are mentioned therein.

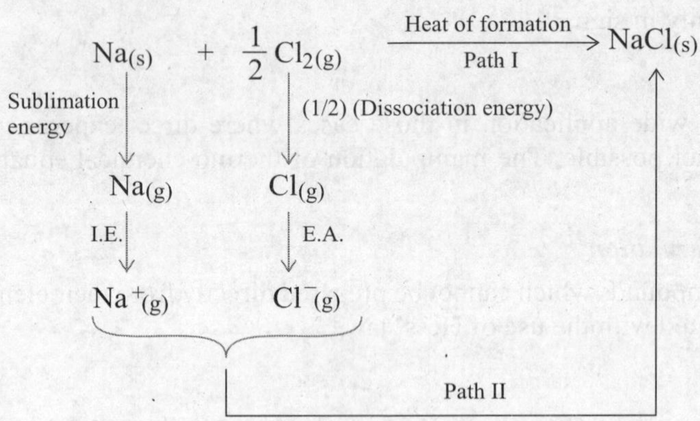

Fig. 3.2 Born–Haber cycle for NaCl

According to Hess' law the overall energy change in a process depends only on th eenergy of the initial and final states and not on the route adopted. Therefore, applying Hess' law,

$$\Delta H_F = \Delta H_S + \text{I.E.} + \frac{1}{2}\Delta H_D + \text{E.A.} + U$$

where ΔH_S is the heat of sublimation of sodium, I.E. is the ionization energy of sodium, ΔH_D is the heat of dissociation of chlorine, E.A. is the electron affinity and U is the lattice energy of NaCl. All values are to be used along with their signs.

Illustration II

Let us design Born–Haber cycle for calculation of lattice energy of $CaCl_2$.

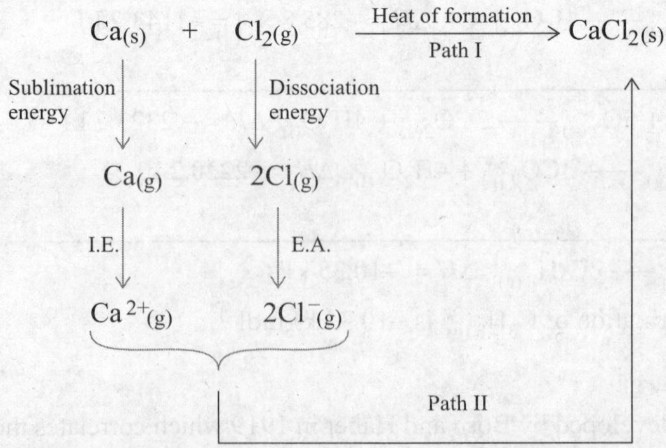

Fig. 3.3 Born–Haber cycle for $CaCl_2$

Applying Hess' law,

$$\Delta H_F = \Delta H_S + \text{I.E.}_1 + \text{I.E.}_2 + \Delta H_D + 2\text{E.A.} + U$$

where ΔH_S is the heat of sublimation of calcium, I.E.$_1$ and I.E.$_2$ are the first and second ionization energies of calcium, ΔH_D is the heat of dissociation of chlorine, E.A. is the electron affinity of fluorine and U is the lattice energy of $CaCl_2$. All values are to be used along with their signs.

Example 3.8

Heat of formation of NaCl is –410 kJ mol^{-1}. The heat of sublimation of sodium, ionization energy of Na, heat of dissociation of chlorine gas and electron affinity of chlorine are 108.8, 493.7, 242.7, and –368.2 kJ mol^{-1}, respectively. Find the lattice energy of NaCl.

Solution

Refer to Fig. 3.2.

From Born–Haber cycle,

$$\Delta H_F = \Delta H_S + \text{I.E.} + \frac{1}{2}\Delta H_D + \text{E.A.} + U$$

or $$-410 = 108.8 + 493.7 + \frac{1}{2} \times 242.7 - 368.2 + U$$

or $$U = 765.6 \text{ kJ mol}^{-1}$$

3. *To find standard heat of reaction*

Knowing the standard enthalpies of formation of reactants and products, it is possible to find the standard heat of a reaction by use of the Hess' cycle as given below.

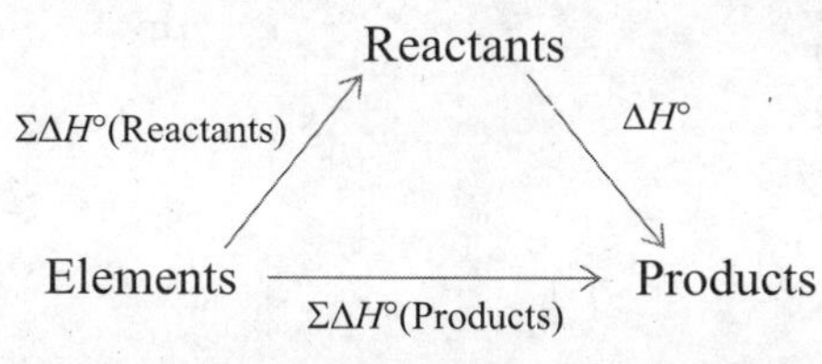

$$\Sigma\Delta H^\circ_F \text{(Products)} = \Sigma\Delta H^\circ_F - \Sigma\Delta H^\circ_F \text{(Reactants)}$$

or $$\Delta H^\circ = \Sigma\Delta H^\circ_F \text{(Products)} - \Sigma\Delta H^\circ_F \text{(Reactants)}$$

Example 3.9

The standard heats of formation of $CH_{4(g)}$, $CO_{2(g)}$ and $H_2O_{(g)}$ are –76.2, –394.8, and –241.6 kJ mol^{-1}, respectively. Calculate the amount of heat evolved during the burning of 1 m^3 of CH_4 measured under normal conditions.

Solution

Reaction is $CH_{4(g)} + 2O_{2(g)} \longrightarrow CO_{2(g)} + 2H_2O_{(g)}$

$$\Delta H^\circ = \Sigma\Delta H^\circ\text{(Products)} - \Sigma\Delta H^\circ\text{(Reactants)}$$

$$= [(-394.8) + 2 \times (-241.6)] - [-76.2 + 0]$$

$$= -801.8 \text{ kJ}$$

22.41 or 22.4×10^{-3} m^3 of CH_4 on burning gives energy = 801.8 kJ

1 m^3 of CH_4 on burning gives energy $= \dfrac{801.8}{22.4 \times 10^{-3}} = 35.79 \times 10^3$ kJ

Kirchhoff's Equation

Kirchhoff's equation provides the dependence of heat of a process on temperature. Let's consider a hypothetical reaction,

$$a\text{A} + b\text{B} \longrightarrow l\,\text{L} + m\text{M}$$

Now, $\Delta H = \Sigma H_P - \Sigma H_R$

$$= (lH_\text{L} + mH_\text{M}) - (aH_\text{A} + bH_\text{B})$$

Differentiating, with respect to T at a constant pressure,

$$\left[\frac{\partial(\Delta H)}{\partial T}\right]_P = \left[l\left(\frac{\partial H_L}{\partial T}\right)_P - m\left(\frac{\partial H_M}{\partial T}\right)_P\right] - \left[a\left(\frac{\partial H_A}{\partial T}\right)_P - b\left(\frac{\partial H_B}{\partial T}\right)_P\right]$$

$$= (lC_{P,\,L} + mC_{P,\,M}) - (aC_{P,\,A} + bC_{P,\,B})$$

$$= \Delta C_P$$

or $\quad d(\Delta H) = \Delta C_P dT$ ...[3.28]

This relation is known as Kirchhoff's equation. This is a differential equation. Let us integrate this one. Following two cases may be considered.

Case 1

When temperature range is small, C_P can be taken to be independent of temperature.

$$\int_{\Delta H_2}^{\Delta H_2} d(\Delta H) = \Delta C_P \int_{T_1}^{T_2} dT$$

or $\quad \Delta H_2 - \Delta H_1 = \Delta C_P(T_2 - T_1)$

or $\quad \Delta H_2 = \Delta H_1 + \Delta C_P(T_2 - T_1)$ ...[3.29]

Case 2

When temperature range is large, C_P cannot be taken to be independent of temperature. In such a case it can be expressed in terms of a power series of temperature, that is

$C_P = \alpha + \beta T + \gamma T^2 + \cdots$ ...[3.30]

where α, β, γ, ... are constants for a given species.

Now,

$$\Delta C_P = [(l\alpha_L + m\alpha_M) - (a\alpha_A + b\alpha_B)] + [(l\beta_L + m\beta_M) - (a\beta_A + b\beta_B)]T + [(l\gamma_L + m\gamma_M) - (a\gamma_A + b\gamma_B)]T^2 + \cdots$$

$= \Delta\alpha + \Delta\beta T + \Delta T^2 + \cdots$ ...[3.31]

Substituting ΔC_P in relation [3.28] and integrating,

$$\int_{\Delta H_2}^{\Delta H_2} d(\Delta H) = \int_{T_1}^{T_2} (\Delta\alpha + \Delta\beta T + \Delta\gamma T^2 + \cdots)dT$$

or $\Delta H_2 - \Delta H_1 = \Delta\alpha \int_{T_1}^{T_2} dT + \Delta\beta \int_{T_1}^{T_2} T dT + \Delta\gamma \int_{T_1}^{T_2} T^2 dT + \cdots$

or $\Delta H_2 = \Delta H_1 + \Delta\alpha(T_2 - T_1) + \frac{\Delta\beta}{2}(T_2^2 - T_1^2) + \frac{\Delta\gamma}{2}(T_2^3 - T_1^3) + \cdots$ ...[3.32]

This relation is known as integrated form of Kirchhoff's equation.

Example 3.10

The heat of a reaction $N_2 + 3H_2 \longrightarrow 2NH_3$ at 27°C is −91.94 kJ. What will be its value at 47°C? The molar heat capacities at constant pressure and 27°C for N_2, H_2 and NH_3 are 28.45, 28.32 and 37.07 J, respectively.

Solution

$$N_2 + 3H_2 \longrightarrow 2NH_3;\ \Delta H_1 = -91.94 \text{ kJ}$$

$$\Delta C_P = 2C_{P,NH_3} - (C_{P,N_2} - C_{P,H_2})$$

$$= 2 \times 37.07 - (28.45 + 3 \times 28.32)$$

$$= -39.27 \text{ J}$$

Now, $\Delta H_2 = \Delta H_1 + \Delta C_P(T_2 - T_1)$

$$= -91940 - 39.27\,(320 - 300)$$

$$= -92.73 \text{ kJ}$$

Example 3.11

The heat of formation of H_2O vapor is −58 kcal at 500 K. What will be the heat of formation at 1000 K? Given that C_{P,H_2}, C_{P,O_2} and C_{P,H_2O} are $6.94 - 0.2 \times 10^{-3}\,T$, $6.15 + 3.2 \times 10^{-3}\,T$ and $7.25 + 2.28 \times 10^{-3}\,T$, respectively.

Solution

$$H_{2(g)} + \frac{1}{2}O_{2(g)} \longrightarrow H_2O_{(g)};\ \Delta H_1 = -58 \text{ kcal}$$

By Kirchhoff's equation,

$$\Delta H_2 = \Delta H_1 + \int_{500}^{1000} \Delta C_P\, dT$$

$$\Delta C_P = C_{P,H_2O} - \left(C_{P,H_2} + \frac{1}{2}C_{P,O_2}\right)$$

$$= 7.25 + 2.28 \times 10^{-3}T - [6.94 - 0.2 \times 10^{-3}T + \frac{1}{2}(6.15 + 3.2 \times 10^{-3}T)]$$

$$= -3.39 + 0.880 \times 10^{-3}T$$

Now, $\Delta H_2 = -58 + \int_{500}^{1000} (-3.39 + 0.880 \times 10^{-3}\,T)dT$

$$= -58 - 3.39(1000 - 500) + \frac{0.88 \times 10^{-3}}{2}[(1000)^2 - (500)^2]$$

$$= -1378.38 \text{ kcal}$$

Example 3.12

Calculate the change in enthalpy of 1 mol of $CO_{2(g)}$ if it is heated from 300 to 1000 K. Given, $C_P = a + bT + cT^2$, where $a = 26.86\ J\ mol^{-1}\ K^{-1}$, $b = 6.966 \times 10^{-3}\ J\ mol^{-1}\ K^{-2}$ and $c = 8.243 \times 10^{-7}\ J\ mol^{-1}\ K^{-3}$.

Solution

$$\Delta H = \int_{300}^{1000} (a + bT + cT)^2 d$$

$$= 700a + \left[\frac{1000^2 - 300^2}{2}\right] b + \left[\frac{1000^3 - 300^3}{3}\right] c$$

$$= 700 \times 26.86 + \left[\frac{1000^2 - 300^2}{2}\right] 6.966 \times 10^{-3} + \left[\frac{1000^3 - 300^3}{3}\right] \times 8.243 \times 10^{-6}$$

$$= 22.239 \text{ kJ mol}^{-1}$$

Joule–Thomson Effect

The phenomenon of change in temperature upon adiabatic expansion from a region of high pressure to a region of extremely low pressure is known as the Joule–Thomson effect. All gases, except H_2 and He, show cooling effect. H_2 and He get warmed up under similar circumstances. However, at very low temperature, i.e., below −80°C for H_2 and below −240°C for He, these gases also show usual cooling behavior. Such a temperature below which a gas becomes cooler on adiabatic expansion is known as *inversion temperature*.

Joule–Thomson Coefficient (μ_{JT})

The experimental set up used for derivation of relation between the fall of pressure of a gas on adiabatic expansion and the resulting change in temperature is shown in Fig. 3.4. Let V_1 be the volume of a gas enclosed between the piston A, and the porous plug at pressure P_1 be the forced to expand to a volume V_2 at pressure P_2 by moving the piston inward.

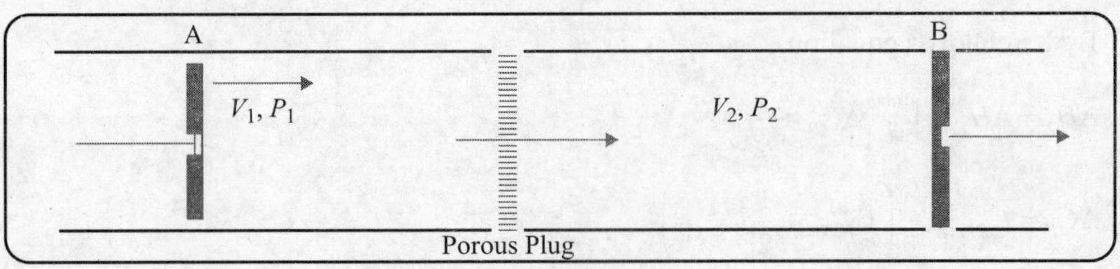

Fig. 3.4 Porous plug experiment

Work done on the system by the piston = $+P_1V_1$
Work done by the system on the piston = $-P_2V_2$
Net work done by the system = $-P_2V_2 + P_1V_1$

In an adiabatic expansion, the system is not in a position to absorb heat from the surroundings. Therefore, the system works at the expense of its internal energy. Let the change in the internal energy be from U_1 to U_2.

$$U_2 - U_1 = -P_2V_2 + P_1V_1$$

or $$U_2 + P_2V_2 = U_1 + P_1V_1$$

or $$H_2 = H_1$$

or $$\Delta H = 0$$

Here an important conclusion can be drawn that adiabatic expansion of a real gas occurs with *constant enthalpy*.

Taking $H = f(P, T)$, the exact differential dH can be expressed as

$$\mathrm{d}H = \left(\frac{\partial H}{\partial P}\right)_\mathrm{T} \mathrm{d}P + \left(\frac{\partial H}{\partial T}\right)_\mathrm{P} \mathrm{d}T$$

or $$\mathrm{d}H = \left(\frac{\partial H}{\partial P}\right)_\mathrm{T} \mathrm{d}P + C_\mathrm{P}\mathrm{d}T \qquad [3.33]$$

As $\Delta H = 0$, the relation [3.33] becomes

$$\left(\frac{\partial H}{\partial P}\right)_\mathrm{T} \mathrm{d}P + C_\mathrm{P}\mathrm{d}T = 0$$

or $$\left(\frac{\partial T}{\partial P}\right)_\mathrm{H} = -\frac{\left(\frac{\partial H}{\partial P}\right)_\mathrm{T}}{C_\mathrm{P}}$$

or $$\mu_\mathrm{JT} = -\frac{\left(\frac{\partial H}{\partial P}\right)_\mathrm{T}}{C_\mathrm{P}} \qquad [3.34]$$

where μ_JT is known as Joule–Thomson coefficient. Let us see for ideal and real gases.

1. **Joule–Thomson coefficient for ideal gas**

$$\mu_\mathrm{JT} = -\frac{1}{C_\mathrm{P}}\left(\frac{\partial H}{\partial P}\right)_\mathrm{T}$$

$$= -\frac{1}{C_\mathrm{P}}\left[\frac{\partial(U+PV)}{\partial P}\right]_\mathrm{T}, \text{ as } H = U + PV$$

$$= -\frac{1}{C_\mathrm{P}}\left[\left(\frac{\partial U}{\partial P}\right)_\mathrm{T} + \left(\frac{\partial(PV)}{\partial P}\right)_\mathrm{T}\right]$$

$$= -\frac{1}{C_\mathrm{P}}\left[\left(\frac{\partial U}{\partial V} \times \frac{\partial V}{\partial P}\right)_\mathrm{T} + \left(\frac{\partial(PV)}{\partial P}\right)_\mathrm{T}\right]$$

$$= -\frac{1}{C_\mathrm{P}}\left[\left(\frac{\partial U}{\partial V}\right)_\mathrm{T}\left(\frac{\partial V}{\partial P}\right)_\mathrm{T} + \left(\frac{\partial(PV)}{\partial P}\right)_\mathrm{T}\right] \qquad [3.35]$$

For an ideal gas, there exists no force of attraction among the molecules of the gas. Therefore, there is no expenditure of energy during the expansion and $\left(\frac{\partial U}{\partial V}\right)_T = 0$. Also, $\left(\frac{\partial (PV)}{\partial P}\right)_T = 0$

Now, relation [3.33] reduces to $\mu_{JT} = 0$

Thus, Joule–Thomson coefficient for ideal gas is zero.

2. **Joule–Thomson coefficient for real gases**

   Let a real gas expand in vacuum so that no external work is done. However, still some work is done in separating the gas molecules against the van der Walls forces that exist between the molecules of a real gas. In an adiabatic system, work is done at the cost of kinetic energy of molecules. If temperature is kept constant, then work done is stored as potential energy in the system, increasing its energy. Thus, for a real gas, $(\partial U/\partial V)_T$ is positive. However, $(\partial V/\partial P)_T$ is negative as volume invariably decreases as the pressure increases at constant temperature. Thus, the factor $(\partial U/\partial V)_T (\partial V/\partial P)_T$ is negative. Again, at ordinary temperature when the pressure is not too high, the value PV decreases as the pressure increases, i.e., $[\partial(PV)/\partial P]_T$ is negative except for H_2 and He.

   Now, the result being at ordinary temperature and low to moderate pressure, the complete term within brackets of relation [3.35] is negative. As heat capacity is always positive, μ_{JT} is positive under the above-mentioned conditions. The result shows that if ΔP is negative, i.e., with fall of pressure, then ΔT is also negative, i.e., there is a fall in temperature.

Calculation

van der Walls equation for one mole of gas is

$$\left(P + \frac{a}{V^2}\right)(V - b) = RT$$

$$PV - Pb + \frac{a}{V} - \frac{ab}{V^2} = RT \qquad [3.36]$$

When pressure is not too high, the term $\frac{ab}{V^2}$ can be neglected. Now, the van der Walls equation can be expressed as

$$PV = RT - \frac{a}{V} + bP$$

or $$PV = RT - \frac{aP}{RT} + bP$$

or $$V = \frac{RT}{P} - \frac{a}{RT} + b \qquad [3.37]$$

Differentiating relation [3.37] with respect to temperature at constant pressure, we get

$$\left(\frac{\partial V}{\partial T}\right)_P = \frac{R}{P} + \frac{a}{RT^2} \qquad [3.38]$$

Rearranging relation [3.37], we get

$$RT = \frac{aP}{RT} + P(V - b)$$

Dividing both sides by PT, we get

$$\frac{R}{P} = \frac{V-b}{T} + \frac{a}{RT^2}$$

Now, substituting $\frac{R}{P}$ in relation [3.38], we get

$$\left(\frac{\partial V}{\partial T}\right)_P = \frac{V-b}{T} + \frac{a}{RT^2} + \frac{a}{RT^2}$$

or $$T\left(\frac{\partial V}{\partial T}\right)_P - V = \frac{2a}{RT} - b \qquad [3.39]$$

Again, from a very well-known relation,

$$V = T\left(\frac{\partial V}{\partial T}\right)_P + \left(\frac{\partial H}{\partial P}\right)_T \qquad [3.40]$$

From relations [3.39] and [3.40], we get

$$-\left(\frac{\partial H}{\partial P}\right)_T = \frac{2a}{RT} - b \qquad [3.41]$$

From relations [3.34] and [3.41], we get

$$C_P \times \mu_{JT} = \frac{2a}{RT} - b$$

or $$\mu_{JT} = \frac{1}{C_P}\left[\frac{2a}{RT} - b\right] \qquad [3.42]$$

Thus, μ_{JT} is positive as long as $\frac{2a}{RT} > b$. The coefficient becomes zero when $\frac{2a}{RT} = b$, while negative when $\frac{2a}{RT} < b$. As a, b, and R are constants, the sign of μ_{JT} depends only upon the temperature at which expansion takes place. The temperature at which it changes sign is the inversion temperature, i.e., at this temperature, $\mu_{JT} = 0$.

$$\frac{1}{C_P}\left[\frac{2a}{RT} - b\right] = 0$$

or $$\frac{2a}{RT} - b = 0$$

or $$T = T_i = \frac{2a}{Rb} \qquad [3.43]$$

where T_i is the inversion temperature.

Example 3.13

The van der Walls constants a and b for O_2 are 1.360 atm l^2 mol^{-2} and 0.0318 $l mol^{-1}$. Find its inversion temperature.

Solution

$$T_i = \frac{2a}{Rb}$$

$$= \frac{2 \times 1.360}{0.0821 \times 0.0318}$$

$$= 1042 \text{ K}$$

The inversion temperature is 1042 K.

Entropy

Entropy is the measure of randomness or disorderness at the molecular level of a system and is denoted by *S*. It is an extensive property and a state function.

Derivation of Entropy from Carnot Cycle

Let us look at the indicator diagram of Carnot cycle.

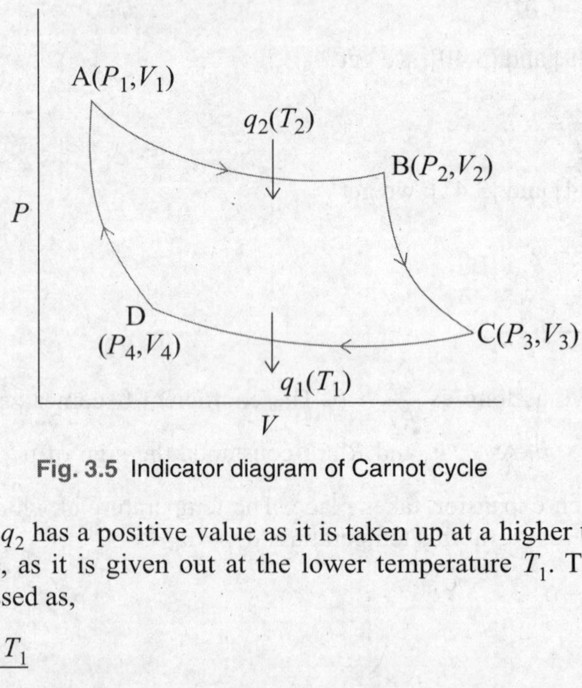

Fig. 3.5 Indicator diagram of Carnot cycle

In a Carnot cycle, q_2 has a positive value as it is taken up at a higher temperature T_2 and q_1 has a negative value, as it is given out at the lower temperature T_1. The thermodynamic efficiency can be expressed as,

$$\eta = \frac{q_2 - q_1}{q_2} = \frac{T_2 - T_1}{T_2}$$

or $$1 - \frac{q_1}{q_2} = 1 - \frac{T_1}{T_2}$$

or $$\frac{q_1}{q_2} = \frac{T_1}{T_2}$$

or $$\frac{q_1}{T_1} = \frac{q_2}{T_2}$$

or $-\dfrac{q_1}{T_1} = \dfrac{q_2}{T_2}$ [Using appropriate sign convention]

or $\sum \dfrac{q}{T} = 0$ ...[3.44]

Thus, when the isothermal and adiabatic processes in a Carnot cycle are carried out infinitesimally slowly, i.e., reversibly, the summation of q terms is equal to zero. Now, any reversible cycle can be regarded as made up of a number of Carnot cycles. This can be shown by drawing a series of isothermal and adiabatic curves drawn across the diagram. For each cycle, the sum of two q/T terms involved is zero.

Hence, for all the Carnot cycles equivalent to the general reversible cycle ABA as shown in Fig. 3.6, it follows that

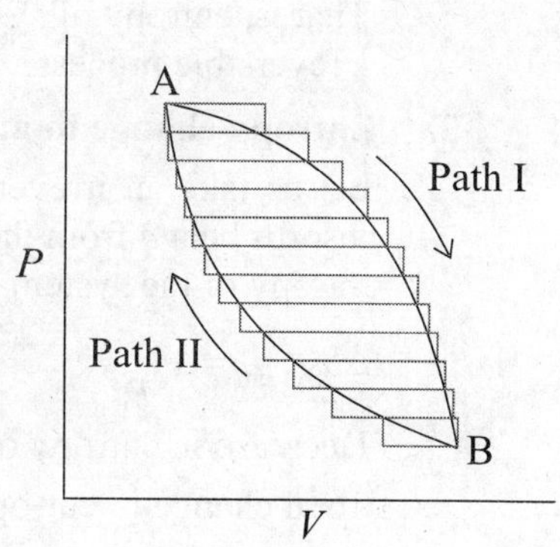

Fig. 3.6

$$\sum \frac{q}{T} = 0 \qquad \text{...[3.45]}$$

where the sum includes two terms for each of the individual Carnot cycles. Since an infinite number of small Carnot cycles are required to duplicate the process ABA, it is convenient to write equation [3.45] in the form,

$$\sum \frac{dq}{T} = 0 \qquad \text{...[3.46]}$$

The integration of relation [3.46] applicable to the complete cycle ABA may be divided into two parts, one for the path from A to B, and the other back from B to A. Thus,

$$\sum \frac{dq}{T} = \int_A^B \frac{dq}{T} + \int_B^A \frac{dq}{T} = 0$$

or $\displaystyle\int_A^B \frac{dq}{T}\text{ (Path I)} = -\int_B^A \frac{dq}{T}\text{ (Path II)}$

$$= \int_A^B \frac{dq}{T}\text{ (Path II)} \qquad \text{...[3.47]}$$

These integrals are independent of the path from A to B. The values of the integrals are determined by some function at states A and B and are independent of the manner in which the systems are brought to these states, such a function is called *entropy*.

Entropy Calculations

1. **Entropy change in a reversible process**

   Let us take a reversible isothermal process in which the system absorbs heat q from the surroundings at temperature T. Then, the increase in entropy of the system is given by

   $$\Delta S_{\text{System}} = +\frac{q}{T}$$

   At the same time, the surroundings lose the same quantity of heat, i.e., q at temperature T. Thus, decrease in entropy of the surroundings, $\Delta S_{\text{surroundings}} = -\dfrac{q}{T}$

Total change in entropy in the process

$\Delta S_{\text{system}} + \Delta S_{\text{surroundings}}$

or $\Delta S = \frac{q}{T} - \frac{q}{T} = 0$

That is, entropy of system and surroundings taken together remains constant during a reversible process.

2. **Entropy change in an irreversible process**

Let us take an irreversible process in which the system, at lower temperature T_1, absorbs heat q from the surroundings, at higher temperature T_2. Then, the increase in entropy of the system is given by

$$\Delta S_{\text{System}} = +\frac{q}{T_1}$$

Decrease in entropy of the surroundings, $\Delta S_{\text{Surroundings}} = -\frac{q}{T_2}$

Total change in entropy in the process

$\Delta S_{\text{system}} + \Delta S_{\text{surroundings}}$

$$\text{or} \quad \Delta S = \frac{q}{T_1} - \frac{q}{T_2} = q\left[\frac{T_2 - T_1}{T_1 T_2}\right]$$

As $T_2 > T_1$, $\Delta S > 0$, i.e., entropy increases in an irreversible processes.

Conclusion

The entropy of system and surroundings taken together remains constant during a reversible process while the same tends to increase during an irreversible process. This conclusion is often regarded as a statement for the *second law of thermodynamics* in terms of entropy.

3. **Entropy change accompanying different processes involving ideal gas system**

(a) **Temperature and volume as variables**

$$\mathrm{d}S = \frac{\mathrm{d}p}{T} = \frac{\mathrm{d}U + P\mathrm{d}V}{T} = \frac{\mathrm{d}U}{T} + P\frac{\mathrm{d}V}{T} = \frac{C_V\mathrm{d}T}{T} + R\frac{\mathrm{d}V}{T}$$

Integrating within appropriate limits,

$$\int_{S_1}^{S_2} \mathrm{d}S = C_V \int_{T_1}^{T_2} \frac{\mathrm{d}T}{T} + R\int_{V_1}^{V_2} \frac{\mathrm{d}V}{T}$$

$$\text{or} \quad S_2 - S_1 = [\ln T_2 - \ln T_1] + [\ln V_2 - \ln V_1]$$

$$\text{or} \quad \Delta S = C_V \ln\frac{T_2}{T_1} + R\ln\frac{V_2}{V_1} \qquad \text{...[3.48]}$$

For n moles of gas,

or $$\Delta S = 2.303\, n\, C_V \log \frac{T_2}{T_1} + 2.303\, R \log \frac{V_2}{V_1} \quad ...[3.49]$$

(b) **Temperature and pressure as variables**

$$\frac{P_1V_1}{T_1} = \frac{P_2V_2}{T_2}$$

or $$\frac{V_2}{V_1} = \frac{P_1T_2}{P_2T_1} \quad ...[3.50]$$

Substituting in relation [3.48],

$$\Delta S = 2.303\, C_V \log \frac{T_2}{T_1} + 2.303\, R \log \frac{P_1T_2}{P_2T_1}$$

$$= 2.303\, C_V \log \frac{T_2}{T_1} + 2.303\, R \log \frac{P_1}{P_2} + 2.303\, R \log \frac{T_2}{T_1}$$

$$= 2.303\, (C_V + R) \log \frac{T_2}{T_1} + 2.303\, R \log \frac{P_1}{P_2}$$

$$= 2.303\, C_P \log \frac{T_2}{T_1} + 2.303\, R \log \frac{P_1}{P_2} \quad ...[3.51]$$

For n moles of gas,

$$\Delta S = 2.303\, nC_P \log \frac{T_2}{T_1} + 2.303\, nR \log \frac{P_1}{P_2} \quad ...[3.52]$$

Case I

For isothermal process, there is no change in temperature. Hence, the equations from relations [3.49] and [3.52] reduce to

$$\Delta S = 2.303\, nR \log \frac{V_2}{V_1} \quad ...[3.53]$$

$$= 2.303\, nR \log \frac{P_1}{P_2} \quad ...[3.54]$$

Case II

For isobaric process, there is no change in pressure. Hence, the equation from relation [3.52] reduces to

$$\Delta S = 2.303\, nC_P \log \frac{T_2}{T_1} \quad ...[3.55]$$

Case III

For isochoric process, there is no change in volume. Hence, the equation from relation [3.49] reduces to

$$\Delta S = 2.303\, nC_V \log \frac{T_2}{T_1} \quad ...[3.56]$$

Example 3.14

Ten moles of an ideal gas expands from a volume of 2 l to 4 l isothermally. Find the entropy change accompanying the expansion.

Solution

$$\Delta S = 2.303nR \log \frac{V_2}{V_1}$$
$$= 2.303 \times 10 \times 8.314 \times \log \frac{4}{2}$$
$$= 57.44 \text{ J K}^{-1}$$

Example 3.15

Two moles of a mono-atomic ideal gas expands reversibly from temperature of 25°C and 1 atm pressure to a temperature of 50°C and 0.5 atm pressure. Find the entropy change.

Solution

$$\Delta S = 2\left[2.303\ C_P \log \frac{T_2}{T_1} + 2.303\ R \log \frac{P_1}{P_2}\right]$$
$$= 2\left[2.303 \times \frac{5}{2} \times 8.314 \times \log \frac{323}{298} + 2.303 \times 8.314 \times \log \frac{1}{0.5}\right]$$
$$= 34.5 \text{ J K}^{-1}$$

(c) **Entropy changes during mixing of ideal gases**

Let us consider 1 mol of an ideal gas. The entropy change can be expressed as,

$$dS = \frac{C_V dT}{T} + R\frac{dV}{V}$$
$$= \frac{(C_P - R)dT}{T} + R\frac{dV}{V}$$

On integration,

$$S = C_P \ln T - R \ln T + R \ln V + S^\circ$$
$$= C_P \ln T - R \ln T + R \ln R + R \ln T - R \ln P + S^\circ$$
$$= C_P \ln T - R \ln P + R \ln R + S^\circ$$
$$= C_P \ln T - R \ln P + S^{\circ\prime} \qquad \text{...[3.57]}$$

Let us consider a number of gases, i.e., n_1 moles of gas 1, n_2 moles of gas 2 and so on. Let their partial pressures be $p_1, p_2, ...,$ etc. respectively. Then

$$S_1 = [C_P \ln T - R \ln p_1 + S^{\circ\prime}]$$
$$S_2 = [C_P \ln T - R \ln p_2 + S^{\circ\prime}]$$

Now, total entropy

$$S_T = \Sigma n_i\,[C_P \ln T - R \ln p_i + S^{\circ\prime}] \qquad \text{...[3.58]}$$

Now if each gas is taken under pressure P, then total entropy

$$S_T = \Sigma n_i[C_P \ln T - R \ln P + S^{\circ\prime}] \qquad \text{...[3.59]}$$

Entropy of mixing is the difference between the entropy of the mixture of gases and the sum of the entropies of the separate gases, each at a pressure P. Thus

$$\Delta S_{\text{Mix}} = \Sigma n_i[C_P \ln T - R \ln P + S^{\circ\prime}] - \Sigma n_i[C_P \ln T - R \ln p_i + S^{\circ\prime}]$$
$$= \Sigma n_i[C_P \ln T - R \ln P + S^{\circ\prime}] - \Sigma n_i[C_P \ln T - R \ln \chi_i P + S^{\circ\prime}]$$
$$= -\Sigma n_i R \ln \chi_i \qquad \text{...[3.60]}$$

Now, ΔS_{Mix} per mole of mixture $= -\Sigma \chi_i R \ln \chi_i$ ...[3.61]

Example 3.16

Two grams of H_2 and 16 g of He are mixed at 298 K and 1 atm pressure. Calculate the entropy of mixing per mole of the mixture formed, assuming ideal behavior for the gases.

Solution

$$n_1 = 1 \text{ mol}$$
$$n_2 = 4 \text{ mol}$$
$$\chi_1 = 0.2, \chi_2 = 0.8$$
$$\Delta S_{\text{Mix}} = -\Sigma \chi_i R \ln \chi_i$$
$$= -[0.2 \times 8.314 \times \ln 0.2 + 0.8 \times 8.314 \times \ln 0.8]$$
$$= 4.156 \text{ J K}^{-1}$$

Example 3.17

Show that during the mixing of two ideal gases the ΔS will be maximum when $\chi_1 = \chi_2 = 0.5$.

Solution

$$\Delta S_{\text{Mix}} = -R[\chi_1 \ln \chi_1 + \chi_2 \ln \chi_2]$$
$$= -R[\chi_1 \ln \chi_1 + (1-\chi_1)\ln(1-\chi_1)] - R\,[\chi_1 \ln \chi_1 + (1-\chi_1)\ln(1-\chi_1)]$$

Differentiating with respect to χ_1, we get

$$\frac{\partial \Delta S_{\text{Mix}}}{\partial \chi_1} = -R\left[\ln \chi_1 + \frac{\chi_1}{\chi_1} + \ln(1-\chi_1) + \frac{1-\chi_1}{1-\chi_1}\right]$$

For entropy of mixing to be maximum, the derivative should be zero.

$$\frac{\partial \Delta S_{\text{Mix}}}{\partial \chi_1} = 0$$

or $\quad -R\left[\ln \chi_1 + \frac{\chi_1}{\chi_1} - \ln(1-\chi_1) - \frac{1-\chi_1}{1-\chi_1}\right] = 0$

or $\quad \ln \chi_1 - \ln(1-\chi_1) = 0$

or $\quad \chi_1 = 1 - \chi_1$

or $\quad 2\chi_1 = 1$

or $\quad \chi_1 = 0.5$ and $\chi_2 = 1 - \chi_1 = 0.5$

(d) **Entropy change during phase changes**

Entropy change during a phase change can be calculated by using the basic relation with substitution of q_{rev} by the corresponding heat change.

e.g, entropy of fusion, $\Delta S_{\text{fusion}} = \dfrac{\Delta H_{\text{fusion}}}{T}$, where T is the melting point.

Note: To conclude, let us consolidate the characteristic features regarding entropy:

1. It is the measure of randomness at molecular level of a system.
2. It is an extensive property.
3. It is a state function.

4. The entropy of system and surroundings taken together remains constant during a reversible process while the same tend to increase during an irreversible process. This is the statement for the *second law of thermodynamics*.
5. The entropy of a perfectly crystalline substance at absolute zero temperature is zero, this is the statement for the *third law of thermodynamics*.
6. Entropy of a substance is highest in the gaseous phase. The order being $S_{Gas} > S_{Liquid} > S_{Solid}$.
7. A process is spontaneous in the direction of increase of entropy. In other words, $\Delta S > 0$ is one of the *criterion of spontaneity*.

Limitations of First Law

The first law of thermodynamics has the following major limitations:

1. It fails to provide the extent of convertibility of one form of energy to another.
2. It fails to provide the direction of feasibility of a process.

Second Law of Thermodynamics

Like the first law, second law of thermodynamics can also be stated in different ways. Some of the popular forms are:

1. It is impossible to take heat from a hotter reservoir and convert it absolutely into work by a cyclic process without transferring a part of heat to a cooler reservoir—Kelvin statement.
2. It is impossible for a cyclic process to transfer heat from a body at a lower temperature to one at higher temperature without at the same time converting a portion of work to heat—Clausius statement.
3. The entropy of system and surroundings taken together remains constant during a reversible process while the same tends to increase during an irreversible process.
4. The total entropy of the universe tends to increase always.

Concept of Free Energy in Chemical Reactions

Neither energy nor randomness factor alone decides the feasibility of a process. Therefore they should be considered together for convenient measure of the driving force for a process. The thermodynamic functions which consider both energy and randomness together are known as free energy functions. They are of two types viz. Helmholtz work function (A) and Gibb's free energy function (G).

Work Function (*A*) or Helmholtz Function

The maximum amount of energy isothermally available to a system that can be converted into useful work is known as work function or Helmholtz function. It is denoted by A (Arbeit: Germanv measuring work). A is an extensive property and also a state function, i.e., 'dA' is an exact differential.

Mathematically,

$$A = U - TS \qquad ...[3.62]$$

where U is the internal energy, i.e., total energy; TS is unavailable energy or random energy; and A is the available energy for useful work

Physical significance

Let us consider an isothermal process involving change from state 1 to state 2. Then relation [3.62] can be written as

$$A_1 = U_1 - TS_1 \quad ...[3.63]$$

$$A_2 = U_2 - TS_2 \quad ...[3.64]$$

Subtracting relation [3.64] from [3.63],

$$A_2 - A_1 = (U_2 - U_1) - T(S_2 - S_1)$$

or $\Delta A = \Delta U - T\Delta S$

$$= \Delta U - T\frac{q_{rev}}{T}$$

$$= \Delta U - q_{rev} \quad ...[3.65]$$

Again from first law, $\Delta U = q_{rev} - W$ ...[3.66]

Substituting

$$\Delta A = q_{rev} - W - q_{rev}$$

or $-\Delta A = W$ ...[3.67]

As the process is a reversible one, W represents maximum work. Now decrease in work function is nothing but the maximum work that can be obtained from the system which includes both mechanical and non-mechanical work, i.e., *gross work*.

Free Energy (*G*) or Gibb's Function

It is the maximum amount of energy isothermally available to a system that can be converted to useful work. It is denoted by G (after the name of J.W. Gibb). G is an extensive property and a state function, i.e., dG is an exact differential.

Mathematically,

$$G = H - TS \quad ...[3.68]$$

Physical significance

Let us consider the reversible change of a system from state (1) to (2). Then relation [3.68] can now be written as,

$$G_1 = H_1 - TS_1 \quad ...[3.69]$$

$$G_2 = H_2 - TS_2 \quad ...[3.70]$$

Now, $G_2 - G_1 = (H_2 - H_1) - T(S_2 - S_1)$

or $\Delta G = \Delta H - T\Delta S$

$$= \Delta U + P\Delta V - T\Delta S$$

$$= -\Delta A + P\Delta V$$

or $-\Delta G = W - P\Delta V$ ...[3.71]

Therefore, decrease in free energy is nothing but the maximum work obtainable from a system other than that due to change in volume, i.e., *net work*.

Variation of free energy with temperature and pressure

$$G = H - TS$$

$$= U + PV - TS$$

On differentiation,

$$\begin{aligned} dG &= dU + PdV + VdP - SdT - TdS \\ &= dq + VdP - SdT - TdS \\ &= TdS + VdP - SdT - TdS \\ &= VdP - SdT \end{aligned} \qquad ...[3.72]$$

At constant temperature,

$$dG = VdP \qquad ...[3.73]$$

At constant pressure,

$$dG = -SdT \qquad ...[3.74]$$

Relation [3.73] represents the variation of free energy with pressure while relation [3.74] represents the variation with temperature.

Variation of Free Energy with Pressure for an Ideal Gas

From relation [3.73]

$$dG = VdP$$

On integration,

$$\int_{G_1}^{G_2} dG = \int_{P_1}^{P_2} VdP$$

or $$\int_{G_1}^{G_2} dG = \int_{P_1}^{P_2} \frac{nRT}{P}\, dP$$

or $$G_2 - G_1 = nRT \ln \frac{P_2}{P_1}$$

or $$\Delta G = nRT \ln \frac{P_2}{P_1} \qquad ...[3.75]$$

$$= nRT \ln \frac{V_1}{V_2} \qquad ...[3.76]$$

Example 3.18

Five moles of an ideal gas expand isothermally from 1 l to 10 l at 300 K. Calculate the change in free energy of the gas.

Solution

$$\begin{aligned} \Delta G &= nRT \ln \frac{V_1}{V_2} \\ &= 5 \times 8.314 \times 300 \ln \frac{1}{10} \\ &= -28.72 \text{ kJ} \end{aligned}$$

van't Hoff Isotherm

van't Hoff isotherm provides a quantitative relation for free energy change accompanying a chemical reaction.

From relation [3.73],

$$dG = VdP$$

or $$dG = \frac{RT}{P} \text{ (for 1 mol of ideal gas, } PV = RT)$$

On integration,

$$\int dG = \int \frac{RT}{P} dP$$

or $$G = G^\circ + RT \ln P \quad ...[3.77]$$

G°, integration constant, is known as standard free energy.

Now, let us consider a hypothetical reaction,

$$aA + bB \longrightarrow lL + mM$$

The free energy change of the reaction,

$$\Delta G = \Sigma G(\text{Products}) - \Sigma G(\text{Reactants})$$
$$= [lG_L + mG_M] - [aG_A + bG_B]$$
$$= [l(G^\circ_L + RT \ln P_L) + m(G^\circ_M + RT \ln P_M)] - [a(G^\circ_A + RT \ln P_A + b(G^\circ_B + RT \ln P_B)]$$
$$= [(lG^\circ_L + mG^\circ_M) - (aG^\circ_A + bG^\circ_B)] + [RT \ln (P_L)^l + RT \ln (P_M)^m] - [RT \ln (P_A)^a + RT \ln (P_B)^b]$$
$$= \Delta G^\circ + RT \ln \frac{P_L^{\,l}\, P_M^{\,m}}{P_A^{\,a}\, P_B^{\,b}}$$
$$= \Delta G^\circ + RT \ln Q_P \quad ...[3.78]$$

At equilibrium, $\Delta G = 0$

Relation [3.78] reduces to

$\Delta G^\circ = -RT \ln K_P$ (K_P is the equilibrium constant in terms of pressure) ...[3.79]

Substituting back in relation [3.78], we get

$$\Delta G = -RT \ln K_P + RT \ln Q_P \quad ...[3.80]$$

Relations [3.78] and [3.80] are van't Hoff isotherms.

van't Hoff Isochore

Temperature dependence of equilibrium constant can be obtained by combining Gibbs–Helmholtz equation with van't Hoff reaction isotherm. The relation is known as van't Hoff reaction isochore.

From Gibbs–Helmholtz equation, we get

$$\Delta G = \Delta H + T\left[\frac{\partial(\Delta G)}{\partial T}\right]_P$$

or $$-\Delta H = T\left[\frac{\partial(\Delta G)}{\partial T}\right]_P - \Delta G$$

Dividing both sides by T^2,

$$-\frac{\Delta H}{T^2} = \frac{T\left[\frac{\partial(\Delta G)}{\partial T}\right]_P - \Delta G}{T^2} \quad ...[3.81]$$

The right-side of the relation can be obtained by the differentiation of ($\Delta G/T$) with respect to T at constant pressure.

$$\left[\frac{\partial\left(\frac{\Delta G}{T}\right)}{\partial T}\right]_P = \frac{T\left[\frac{\partial(\Delta G)}{\partial T}\right]_P - \Delta G}{T^2} \quad ...[3.82]$$

Comparing relations [3.80] and [3.82], we get

$$\left[\frac{\partial\left(\frac{\Delta G)}{T}\right)}{\partial T}\right]_P = \frac{-\Delta H}{T^2} \quad \text{...[3.83]}$$

Again, from van't Hoff reaction isotherm

$\Delta G° = - RT \ln K_P$

Combining with relation [3.83] at equilibrium, we get

$$\frac{\Delta H}{RT^2} = \left[\frac{\partial(\ln K_P)}{\partial T}\right]_P \quad \text{...[3.84]}$$

Relation [3.84] is known as van't Hoff isochore. For real application, this is to be integrated after the variable separation,

$$\int_{K_{P_1}}^{K_{P_2}} \partial(\ln K_P) = \frac{\Delta H}{R}\int_{T_1}^{T_2} \frac{\partial T}{T^2}$$

or $\ln K_{P_2} - \ln K_{P_1} = \frac{\Delta H}{R}\left[\frac{1}{T_1} - \frac{1}{T_2}\right]$

or $\ln \frac{K_{P_2}}{K_{P_1}} = \frac{\Delta H}{R}\left[\frac{T_2 - T_1}{T_1 T_2}\right]$ ...[3.85]

Note:

Relation between K_P and K_C is $K_P = K_C\,(RT)^{\Delta n}$, where K_P is equilibrium constant in terms of pressure and K_C is the equilibrium in terms of concentration.

Example 3.19

$\Delta G°$ for $\frac{1}{2}N_2 + \frac{3}{2}H_2 \rightleftharpoons NH_3$ is –16.5 kJ mol^{-1} at 300K. Find out K_P for the reaction. Also find K_C.

Solution

$- \Delta G° = R_T \ln K_P$

or $\ln K_P = \frac{16.5 \times 10^3}{8.314 \times 298}$

$K_P = 779.4 \text{ atm}^{-1}$

$$K_C = \frac{K_P}{(R_T)^{\Delta n}} = \frac{779.4}{(0.0821 \times 300)^{-1}}$$

$= 19.2 \text{ mol}^{-1}$

Example 3.20

The equilibrium constant (K_P) for a reaction at 327°C and 427°C are 10^{-12} and 10^{-7}, respectively. Calculate the enthalpy of the reaction.

Solution

$$\ln \frac{K_{P_2}}{K_{P_1}} = \frac{\Delta H}{R}\left[\frac{T_2 - T_1}{T_1 T_2}\right]$$

or $$\ln \frac{10^{-7}}{10^{-12}} = \frac{\Delta H}{2.303 \times 8.314}\left[\frac{700 - 600}{700 \times 600}\right]$$

or $\Delta H = 402.09$ kJ

Example 3.21

K_P for a reaction is 1.6×10^{-4} atm^{-2} at 400°C. What will be the K_P at 500°C ? Heat of reaction in this temperature range is −25.0 kcal.

Solution

$$\ln \frac{K_{P_2}}{1.6 \times 10^{-4}} = \frac{-25.0 \times 10^3}{1.98}\left[\frac{773 - 673}{773 \times 673}\right]$$

or $K_{P_2} = 1.46 \times 10^{-5}$ atm^{-2}

Gibbs–Helmholtz Equation

This equation provides the temperature dependence of free energy.

From relation [3.72]

$dG = VdP - SdT$

At constant pressure, $dG = -SdT$ ...[3.86]

Let us consider an isobaric change in which initial state is characterised by (S_1, G_1, T_1) and final state by (S_2, G_2, T_2). Now, with change in temperature, initial and final free energy change by an amount of dG_1 and dG_2, respectively.

Using relation [3.86]

$dG_1 = -S_1 dT$

$dG_2 = -S_2 dT$

Now, $dG_2 \quad dG_1 = (S_2 \quad S_1)dT$

or $d(\Delta G) = -\Delta S dT$

or $$\left[\frac{\partial(\Delta G)}{\partial T}\right]_P = -\Delta S \qquad ...[3.87]$$

But,

$\Delta G = \Delta H - T\Delta S$

Substituting $-\Delta S$, we get

$$\Delta G = \Delta H + T\left[\frac{\partial(\Delta G)}{\partial T}\right]_P \qquad ...[3.88]$$

This equation is known as Gibbs–Helmholtz equation and is applicable to all processes occurring at constant pressure.

Note:

1. $$\Delta G - T\left[\frac{\partial(\Delta G)}{\partial T}\right]_P = \Delta H$$

   Dividing by T^2 on both sides

$$\frac{\Delta G - T\left[\frac{\partial(\Delta G)}{\partial T}\right]_P}{T^2} = \frac{\Delta H}{T^2}$$

or $$-\left[\frac{\partial\left(\frac{\Delta G)}{T}\right)}{\partial T}\right]_P = \frac{\Delta H}{T^2}$$

or $$\left[\frac{\partial\left(\frac{\Delta G)}{T}\right)}{\partial T}\right]_P = \frac{\Delta H}{T^2} \qquad \text{...[3.89]}$$

   This is another form of Gibbs–Helmholtz equation.

2. *Criterion of spontaneity*

   Gibbs–Helmholtz equation ($\Delta G = \Delta H - T\Delta S$) can be utilized for prediction of spontaneity of a process under different conditions. At constant temperature and pressure, a chemical reaction is spontaneous in the direction of decrease of free energy, i.e., $\Delta G_{T,P} < 0$. A graphical presentation of dependence of ΔG (spontaneity) on temperature for different combinations of ΔH and ΔS is shown as follows.

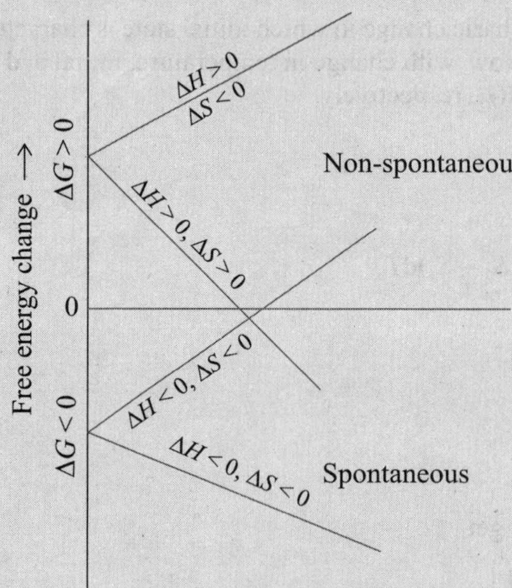

Fig. 3.7 Determination of spontaneity

Applications

1. **To predict spontaneity**

   If $\Delta G_{T,P} < 0$, then the reaction is spontaneous.

Example 3.22

For a reaction $M_2O_{(s)} \rightarrow 2M_{(s)} + \frac{1}{2}O_2(g)$; $\Delta H = 30$ kJ mol^{-1} and $\Delta S = 0.07$ kJ^{-1} mol^{-1} at 1 atm. Calculate upto which temperature, the reaction would not be spontaneous?

Solution

For a non-spontaneous process $\Delta G > 0$

or $\quad \Delta H - T\Delta S > 0$

or $\quad \Delta H > T\Delta S$

or $\quad T < \dfrac{\Delta H}{\Delta S}$

or $\quad T < \dfrac{30}{0.07}$

or $\quad T < 428.6$ K

2. **To find thermodynamic parameters during electrochemical cell operation.**

   During cell operation, decrease in free energy appears as electrical energy. Therefore,

$$-\Delta G = nFE \qquad \text{...[3.90]}$$

Again substituting ΔG in relation [3.88]

$$-nFE = \Delta H - nFT\left(\frac{\partial E}{\partial T}\right)_P$$

or $$\Delta H = nF\left[T\left(\frac{\partial E}{\partial T}\right)_P - E\right]_P \qquad \text{...[3.91]}$$

Comparing relation [3.91] with $\Delta H = \Delta G + T\Delta S$

$$\Delta S = nF\left(\frac{\partial E}{\partial T}\right)_P \qquad \text{...[3.92]}$$

Relations [3.90], [3.91], and [3.92] can be utilized to find free energy change, enthalpy change and entropy change during cell operation.

Example 3.23

Find the thermodynamic parameters accompanying the operation of standard cadmium cell. The cell potential and temperature coefficient of the cell are 1.018 at 25°C and -5×10^{-5} VK^{-1}, respectively.

Solution

$$\Delta G = -2 \times 96500 \times 1.018 \text{ J}$$
$$= -196.47 \text{ kJ}$$

$$\Delta H = 2 \times 96500\,[298\,(-5 \times 10^{-5}) - 1.018]\ \text{J}$$
$$= -199.35\ \text{kJ}$$
$$\Delta S = 2 \times 96500\,(-5 \times 10^{-5})\ \text{J K}^{-1}$$
$$= -9.65\ \text{J K}^{-1}$$

3. **To find enthalpy change at constant pressure.**
Gibbs–Helmholtz equation can be used to find ΔH accompanying a reaction, provided the values of free energy change at two different temperatures are known.

Example 3.24

The free energy change for a given reaction is –90 kJ at 25°C and –85 kJ at 35°C. Calculate the change in enthalpy for the reaction at 30°C.

Solution

$$\left[\frac{\partial(\Delta G)}{\partial T}\right]_P = \frac{-85-(-90)}{308-298} = 0.5\ \text{kJ K}^{-1}$$

$$\Delta G \text{ at } 30°\text{C} = \frac{-90+(-85)}{2} = -87.5\ \text{kJ}$$

Now from Gibbs–Helmholtz equation

$$\Delta G = \Delta H + T\left[\frac{\partial(\Delta G)}{\partial T}\right]_P$$

or $$\Delta H = \Delta G - T\left[\frac{\partial(\Delta G)}{\partial T}\right]_P$$
$$= -87.5 - 303 \times 0.5$$
$$= -239\ \text{kJ}$$

Clapeyron–Clausius Equation

It finds its application in cases where two phases of a particular substance remain in equilibrium. Let's consider a system where two phases, say 1 and 2, of a particular substance are in equilibrium. Let G_1 and G_2 be their free energies/mole at temperature T and pressure P.

$$\text{Phase 1} \rightleftharpoons \text{Phase 2}$$

As the two phases are in equilibrium, $G_1 = G_2$. Let the temperature and pressure of the system be raised to $T + \text{d}T$ and $P + \text{d}P$ so that the new free energies of phases 1 and 2 become $G_1 + \text{d}G_1$ and $G_2 + \text{d}G_2$, respectively. As the two phases are still in equilibrium,

$$G_1 + \text{d}G_1 = G_2 + \text{d}G_2$$

or $$\text{d}G_1 = \text{d}G_2$$

or $$V_1\text{d}P - S_1\text{d}T = V_2\text{d}T - S_2\text{d}T$$

or $$(V_2 - V_1)\text{d}P = (S_2 - S_1)\text{d}T$$

or $$\frac{\text{d}P}{\text{d}T} = \frac{\Delta S}{V_2 - V_1} \qquad \text{...[3.93]}$$

where V_1 and V_2 are the molar volumes of the substance in phases 1 and 2, respectively. Similarly S_1 and S_2 are the molar entropies in phases 1 and 2, respectively. Now, let the heat change in reversible manner per mole of the substance during phase change at temperature T be q. Then entropy change can be expressed as, $\Delta S = q/T$. Substituting in relation [3.93]

$$\frac{dP}{dT} = \frac{q}{T(V_1 - V_1)} \quad \text{...[3.94]}$$

Relation [3.94] is known as Clapeyron–Clausius equation.

Case 1

For liquid–vapor equilibrium

Let's consider the equilibrium between the liquid and vapor phases of a particular substance.

$$\text{Liquid} \rightleftharpoons \text{Vapor}$$

Applying Clapeyron–Clausius equation,

$$\frac{dP}{dT} = \frac{\Delta H_V}{T(V_g - V_l)} \quad \text{...[3.95]}$$

where ΔH_V is the molar heat of vaporization and V_g and V_l are the volumes of gas and liquid phases of the substance, respectively. As $V_g >> V_l$, $V_g - V_l = V_g$. Thus the above relation can also be written as

$$\frac{dP}{dT} = \frac{\Delta H_V}{TV_g}$$

$$= \frac{\Delta H_V}{T\frac{RT}{P}} \left[\text{Assuming ideal behavior of vapor, } V_g = \frac{RT}{P}\right]$$

$$= P\frac{\Delta H_V}{RT^2}$$

or $$\frac{dP}{P} = \frac{\Delta H_V}{RT^2}\, dT$$

Integrating within appropriate limits,

$$\int_{P_1}^{P_2} \frac{dP}{P} = \frac{\Delta H_V}{R} \int_{T_1}^{T_2} \frac{dT}{T^2}$$

or $$\ln \frac{P_2}{P_1} = \frac{\Delta H_V}{R}\left[\frac{T_2 - T_1}{T_1 T_2}\right] \quad \text{...[3.96]}$$

Relation [3.96] is known as integrated form of Clapeyron–Clausius equation.

Case 2

For solid–vapor equilibrium

Similarly approach can be made to derive the Clapeyron–Clausius equation. The equation can be written as,

$$\frac{dP}{dT} = \frac{\Delta H_S}{T(V_g - V_S)} \quad \text{...[3.97]}$$

$$\ln \frac{P_2}{P_1} = \frac{\Delta H_S}{P_1}\left[\frac{T_2 - T_1}{T_1 T_2}\right] \quad \text{...[3.98]}$$

Relation [3.97] is the differential form while relation [3.98] is the integrated form. DH_S is the heat of sublimation per mole of the substance.

Applications

1. **To find the latent heat of vaporization:** If the vapor pressure of a liquid is known at two different temperatures, then its latent heat of vaporization can be calculated by using the Clapeyron–Clausius equation.

Example 3.25

The vapor pressure of water at 95°C and 100°C are 634 and 760 mm of Hg, respectively. Calculate the latent heat of vaporization per mole of water.

Solution

Using the Clapeyron–Clausius relation

$$\ln \frac{P_2}{P_1} = \frac{\Delta H_V}{R}\left[\frac{T_2 - T_1}{T_1 T_2}\right]$$

or $$\ln \frac{760}{634} = \frac{\Delta H_V}{1.98}\left[\frac{373 - 368}{373 \times 368}\right]$$

or $\Delta H_V = 9.89 \text{ kcal mol}^{-1}$

2. **To find boiling point or freezing point:** Knowing the boiling or freezing point at one pressure, the same at some other pressure can be calculated by using the Clapeyron–Clausius equation.

Example 3.26

Water boils at 100°C at 1 atm pressure. At what temperature will water boil at a pressure of 2 atm. Given that latent heat of vaporization of water is 536 cal g^{-1}.

Solution

$\Delta H_V = 536 \times 18 \text{ cal mol}^{-1}$

Using the Clapeyron–Clausius relation

$$\ln \frac{2}{1} = \frac{536 \times 18}{1.98}\left[\frac{T_2 - 373}{373 T_2}\right]$$

or $T_2 = 277.66$ K

3. **To find the vapor pressure:** Knowing the the vapor pressure at a particular temperature, the same at some other temperature can be calculated.

Example 3.27

The vapor pressure of water at 95°C is 634 mm of Hg. What will be the vapor pressure at 150°C? Given $\Delta H = 41.27$ kJ mol^{-1}.

Solution

Using the Clapeyron–Clausius relation

$$\ln \frac{P_2}{634} = \frac{41270}{8.314}\left[\frac{423 - 368}{423 \times 368}\right]$$

or $\ln \frac{P_2}{634} = 1.754$

or $P_2 = 3663$ mm of Hg

Maxwell Relations

Certain variables in thermodynamics, such as entropy, are hard to measure experimentally. Maxwell relations provide a way to exchange variables and thereby equate the rate of change of such a variable with those of experimentally measurable quantities such as temperature, pressure and volume. Maxwell relations can be derived from basic equations of state.

For thermodynamic function, U

From the first law of thermodynamics,

$$dq = dU + PdV$$

or $dU = dq - PdV \quad \left[\text{as, } dS = \frac{dq}{T}\right]$

$$= TdS - PdV \qquad \text{...[3.99]}$$

At constant volume, $\left(\frac{\partial U}{\partial S}\right)_V = T$

Differentiating with respect to V keeping S constant,

$$\frac{\partial^2 U}{(\partial S)(\partial V)} = \left(\frac{\partial T}{\partial V}\right) S \qquad \text{...[3.100]}$$

Again at constant entropy, $\left(\frac{\partial P}{\partial S}\right)_S = -P$

Differentiating with respect to S keeping V constant,

$$\frac{\partial^2 U}{(\partial V)(\partial S)} = -\left(\frac{\partial P}{\partial S}\right) V \qquad \text{...[3.101]}$$

As U is a state function, left hand sides are same. Comparing relations [3.100] and [3.101],

$$\left(\frac{\partial T}{\partial V}\right)_S = -\left(\frac{\partial P}{\partial S}\right)_V \qquad \text{...[3.102]}$$

For thermodynamic function, H

$$H = U + PV$$

or $dH = dU + PdV + VdP$

or $dH = dq + VdP$

$$= TdS + VdP \qquad \text{...[3.103]}$$

Now, in a very similar manner, another Maxwell relation can be developed.

$$\left(\frac{\partial T}{\partial P}\right)_S = \left(\frac{\partial V}{\partial S}\right)_P \qquad \text{...[3.104]}$$

For thermodynamic function, G

$$G = H - TS$$

or $dG = dH - T\,dS - S\,dT$

$$= TdS + VdP - TdS - SdT$$

$$= VdP - SdT \qquad \text{...[3.105]}$$

The Maxwell relation becomes,

$$\left(\frac{\partial S}{\partial P}\right)_T = \left(\frac{\partial V}{\partial T}\right)_P \qquad ...[3.106]$$

For thermodynamic function, A

$$A = U - TS$$

or $\quad dA = dU - TdS - SdT$

$$= -PdV - SdT \qquad ...[3.107]$$

The Maxwell relation becomes,

$$\left(\frac{\partial S}{\partial V}\right)_T = \left(\frac{\partial P}{\partial T}\right)_V \qquad ...[3.108]$$

Mnemonic device for obtaining Maxwell relations

The following mnemonic diagram is quite useful in deriving Maxwell relations. The diagram consists of a square with two diagonal arrows pointing upwards. A mnemonic popularly used to write the thermodynamic square and remember the *Maxwell relations* is "**G**ood **P**hysicists **H**ave **S**tudied **U**nder **V**ery **F**ine **T**eachers". One has to move clockwise.

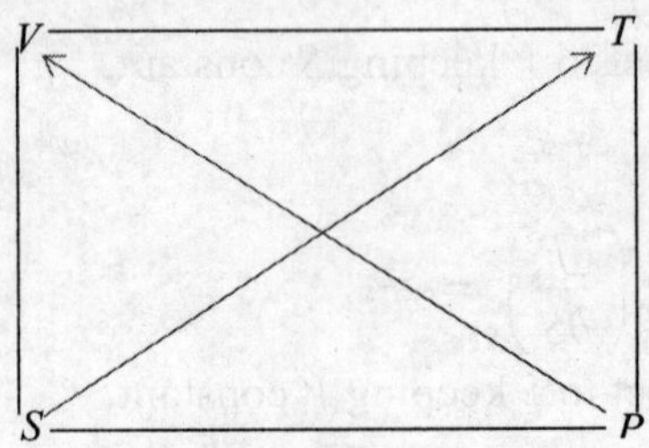

Fig. 3.8

The partial derivative of two neighboring properties (e.g., V and T) corresponds to the partial derivative of the two properties on the opposite side of the square (e.g., S and P). The arrows denote the negative sign; if both are pointed the same way, then the sign is positive.

Considering left and right sides,

$$\left(\frac{\partial S}{\partial V}\right)_T = \left(\frac{\partial P}{\partial T}\right)_V$$

$$\left(\frac{\partial V}{\partial S}\right)_P = \left(\frac{\partial T}{\partial P}\right)_S$$

Considering top and bottom sides,

$$\left(\frac{\partial T}{\partial V}\right)_S = -\left(\frac{\partial P}{\partial S}\right)_V$$

$$\left(\frac{\partial S}{\partial P}\right)_T = -\left(\frac{\partial V}{\partial T}\right)_P$$

Thermodynamic equations of state

Using appropriate Maxwell relation and combined form of the first and the second law of thermodynamics, it is possible to derive two equations of state of thermodynamics.

$$\left(\frac{\partial U}{\partial V}\right)_T = T\left(\frac{\partial P}{\partial T}\right)_V - P \qquad ...[3.109]$$

$$\left(\frac{\partial H}{\partial P}\right)_T = V - T\left(\frac{\partial V}{\partial T}\right)_P \qquad ...[3.110]$$

Relations [3.109] and [3.110] are known as first and second thermodynamic equations of state, respectively.

Derivation

From relation [3.99],

$dU = TdS - PdV$

Differentiating with respect to *V*, keeping temperature constant,

$$\left(\frac{\partial U}{\partial V}\right)_T = T\left(\frac{\partial S}{\partial V}\right)_T - P$$

From Maxwell relation [3.108],

$$\left(\frac{\partial U}{\partial V}\right)_T = T\left(\frac{\partial S}{\partial V}\right)_T - P, \text{ first thermodynamic equation of state}$$

Again from relation [3.103]

$dH = T\,dS + V\,dP$

Differenting with respect to *P*, keeping temperature constant,

$$\left(\frac{\partial H}{\partial P}\right)_T = T\left(\frac{\partial S}{\partial P}\right)_T + V$$

From Maxwell relation [3.106],

$$\left(\frac{\partial H}{\partial P}\right)_T = V - T\left(\frac{\partial V}{\partial T}\right)_P, \text{ second thermodynamic equation of state}$$

Partial Molar Quantities

In an open system, there is every possibility of change in composition. Therefore, in such a system the state must involve composition along with temperature and pressure. Now, any extensive thermodynamic property *Z* can be expressed as

$$Z = (T, P, n_1, n_2, \ldots, n_i)$$

As d*Z* is an exact differential, it can be expressed as

$$dZ = \left(\frac{\partial Z}{\partial P}\right)_{T, n_1, n_2, \ldots, n_i} dP + \left(\frac{\partial Z}{\partial T}\right)_{P, n_1, n_2, \ldots, n_i} dT + \left(\frac{\partial Z}{\partial n_1}\right)_{T, P, n_2, \ldots, n_i} dn_1$$

$$+ \left(\frac{\partial Z}{\partial n_2}\right)_{T, P, n_1, n_3, \ldots, n_i} dn_2 + \cdots + \left(\frac{\partial Z}{\partial n_i}\right)_{T, P, n_1, n_2, \ldots, n_{i-1}} \qquad [3.111]$$

$(\partial Z/\partial n_i)_{T, P, n_1, n_2, \ldots, n_{i-1}}$ is the partial molar quantity of component "*i*" and may be defined as the change of the property with the change in the amount of *i*th component when temperature, pressure, and the amount of other components of the system are constant. It is represented as $\overline{Z_i}$.

This is an intensive property. To be specific, $(\partial H/\partial n_i)_{T, P, n_1, n_2, \ldots, n_{i-1}} = \overline{H}_i$. is known as partial molar enthalpy and $(\partial S/\partial n_i)_{T, P, n_1, n_2, \ldots, n_{i-1}} = \overline{S}_i$ is known as partial molar entropy.

Chemical Potential

The partial molar free energy $(\overline{G})$ is known as chemical potential and is designated as μ. Thus, the partial molar property of component "*i*" in the mixture is the change in free energy of the system with the change in the amount of the same component when temperature, pressure, and the amount of other components of the system are constant. It is expressed as

$$\mu_i = \left(\frac{\partial G}{\partial n_i}\right)_{T, P, n_1, n_2, \ldots, n_{i-1}} \quad [3.112]$$

Note:

1. It is an intensive property.
2. At equilibrium, it must have the same value throughout the system.
3. If at all the chemical potential of a substance is not uniform throughout the system, then the matter will spontaneously flow from a region of higher potential to that at a lower potential.

Gibbs–Duhem Equation

For a multicomponent system, free energy is a function of temperature, pressure, and composition.

$$G = f(T, P, n_1, n_2, \ldots, n_i)$$

Now, d*G* can be expressed as

$$dZ = \left(\frac{\partial G}{\partial P}\right)_{T, n_1, n_2, \ldots, n_i} dP + \left(\frac{\partial G}{\partial T}\right)_{P, n_1, n_2, \ldots, n_i} dT + \left(\frac{\partial G}{\partial n_1}\right)_{T, P, n_1, n_2, \ldots, n_i} dn_1$$

$$+ \left(\frac{\partial G}{\partial n_2}\right)_{T, P, n_1, n_3, \ldots, n_i} dn_2 + \cdots + \left(\frac{\partial G}{\partial n_i}\right)_{T, P, n_1, n_3, \ldots, n_{i-1}} dn_1$$

or $$dG = \left(\frac{\partial G}{\partial P}\right)_{T, n_1, n_2, \ldots, n_i} dP + \left(\frac{\partial G}{\partial T}\right)_{P, n_1, n_2, \ldots, n_i} dT + \mu_1 dn_1 + \mu_2 dn_2 + \cdots + \mu_i dn_i \quad [3.113]$$

At constant temperature and pressure, relation [3.113] becomes

$$(dG)_{T, P} = \mu_1 dn_1 + \mu_2 dn_2 + \ldots + \mu_i dn_i \quad [3.114]$$

For system with definite composition having, $n_1, n_2, \ldots, n_i$ moles of the constituents 1, 2,…, *i*, respectively, the integration of relation [3.114] gives

$$(G)_{T, P, N} = \mu_1 n_1 + \mu_2 n_2 + \ldots + \mu_i n_i \quad [3.115]$$

On differentiation of the above equation at constant temperature and pressure but varying composition, we have

$$(dG)_{T,P} = \mu_1 dn_1 + n_1 d\mu_1 + \mu_2 dn_2 + n_2 d\mu_2 + \ldots + \mu_i dn_i + n_i d\mu_i$$

or $$(dG)_{T,P} = (\mu_1 dn_1 + \mu_2 dn_2 + \ldots + \mu_i dn_i) + (n_1 d\mu_1 + n_2 d\mu_2 + \ldots + n_i d\mu_i) \quad [3.116]$$

Comparing the results of relations [3.114] and [3.116], we get

$$n_1 d\mu_1 + n_2 d\mu_2 + \ldots + n_i d\mu_i = 0$$

or $$\Sigma n_i d\mu_i = 0 \quad [3.117]$$

Relation [3.117] is known as Gibbs–Duhem equation.

Effect of Temperature and Pressure

For a closed system, when there is no change in the number of moles of various substances present, relation [3.113] can be expressed as

$$dG = \left(\frac{\partial G}{\partial P}\right)_{T,N} dP + \left(\frac{\partial G}{\partial T}\right)_{P,N} dT \quad [3.118]$$

Again, $dG = VdP - SdT$

Comparing the coefficients, we get

$$\left(\frac{\partial G}{\partial T}\right)_{P,N} = -S \quad [3.119]$$

$$\left(\frac{\partial G}{\partial P}\right)_{T,N} = V \quad [3.120]$$

1. Now for effect of temperature on chemical potential of any constituent, let us differentiate relation [3.112] with respect to temperature. Thus,

$$\frac{\partial^2 G}{\partial n_i \partial T} = \left(\frac{\partial \mu_i}{\partial T}\right)_{P,N} \quad [3.121]$$

Again, differentiating relation [3.119] with respect to n_i, we get

$$\frac{\partial^2 G}{\partial T \partial n_i} = -\left(\frac{\partial S}{\partial n_i}\right)_{T,P,N} = -\overline{S}_i$$

or $$\frac{\partial^2 G}{\partial T \partial n_i} = -\overline{S}_i \quad [3.122]$$

As dG is an exact differential, the order of differentiation is immaterial; therefore, relations [3.121] and [3.122] are equivalent so that

$$\left(\frac{\partial \mu_i}{\partial T}\right)_{P,N} = -\overline{S}_i \quad [3.123]$$

Relation [3.123] provides the variation of chemical potential of any constituent i of the system with temperature.

2. Now for effect of pressure on chemical potential of any constituent, let us differentiate relation [3.112] with respect to pressure. Thus,

$$\frac{\partial^2 G}{\partial n_i \partial P} = \left(\frac{\partial \mu_i}{\partial P}\right)_{T,N} \quad [3.124]$$

Again, differentiating relation [3.120] with respect to n_i,

$$\frac{\partial^2 G}{\partial P\, \partial n_i} = -\left(\frac{\partial V}{\partial n_i}\right)_{T, P, N} = -\bar{V}_i$$

or $$\frac{\partial^2 G}{\partial P\, \partial n_i} = \bar{V}_i \quad [3.125]$$

As dG is an exact differential, the order of differentiation is immaterial; therefore, relations [3.124] and [3.125] are equivalent so that

$$\left(\frac{\partial \mu_i}{\partial P}\right)_{T, N} = -\bar{V}_i \quad [3.126]$$

Relation [3.126] provides the variation of chemical potential of any constituent i of the system with pressure.

Chemical Potential of an Ideal Gas

It is well known that d$G = V$d$P - S$dT

At constant temperature $(dG)_T = V dP$

Integrating in the limits of a specified change from 1 atm to pressure P,

$$\int_{G^0}^{G} (dG)_T = \int_1^P V dP$$

or $$G - G^0 = \int_1^P \frac{nRT}{P} dP$$

or $$G = G^0 + nRT \ln P$$

Dividing both sides by n,

$$\frac{G}{n} = \frac{G^0}{n} + RT \ln P$$

or $$\mu = \mu^0 + RT \ln P \quad [3.127]$$

where μ is the chemical potential, and μ^0 is the standard chemical potential. Thus, chemical potential of an ideal gas is dependent on pressure.

In a mixture of ideal gases, chemical potential of any component can be expressed as

$$\mu_i = \mu_i^0 + RT \ln p_i \quad [3.128]$$

where p_i is the partial pressure of ith component.

As partial pressure remain proportional to mole fraction as well as molar concentration of the ith component, relation [3.128] can be expressed as

$$\mu_i = \mu_i^0 + RT \ln \chi_i \quad [3.129]$$

$$= \mu_i^0 + RT \ln [i] \quad [3.130]$$

Non-ideal Mixtures or Solutions

In non-ideal system, chemical potential of ith component can be expressed as

$$\mu_i = \mu_i^0 + RT \ln \gamma_i \chi_i \quad [3.131]$$

$$= \mu_i^0 + RT \ln f_i [i] \quad [3.132]$$

where γ_i and f_i are the activity coefficients, i.e., effective mole fraction and concentration, respectively. The product of $\gamma_i \chi_i$ and $f_i [i]$ are known as activity and is denoted by a_i. As the system tends to ideal behavior, γ or $f \rightarrow 1$.

Example 3.28

Find the change in chemical potential of a substance if the partial pressure of an ideal gas changes from 0.25 atm to 1 atm.

Solution

Chemical potential at initial and final conditions can be expressed as

$$\mu_1 = \mu^0 + RT \ln P_1$$

$$\mu_2 = \mu^0 + RT \ln P_2$$

Change in potential,

$$\mu_2 - \mu_1 = (\mu^0 + RT \ln P_1) - (\mu^0 + RT \ln P_2)$$

$$= RT \ln \frac{P_2}{P_1}$$

$$= 8.314 \times 298 \times \ln \frac{0.25}{1}$$

$$= 8.314 \times 298 \times (-1.386)$$

$$= -3.434 \text{ J mol}^{-1}$$

QUESTIONS

1. What is the physical significance of free energy change (ΔG)?
2. Write down van't Hoff reaction isotherm giving the significance of all the terms involved there in.
3. Define Hess' law of heat of summation.
4. A reaction is said to be spontaneous if it satisfies a thermodynamic condition. What condition is it?
5. Explain how ΔG of a cell process occurring in an electrochemical cell is related to the emf of the cell.
6. How is standard free energy change related to the equilibrium constant?
7. For a reaction both ΔH and ΔS are positive. Under what condition will the reaction be spontaneous?
8. Define enthalpy of neutralization.
9. What is cyclic rule?
10. What are the characteristics of reversible process?
11. State and explain heat of formation with a suitable example.
12. What do you mean by heat of hydration? Give an example.
13. What do you mean by intensive properties? Justify that the emf of a cell is an intensive property.
14. What do you mean by extensive and intensive properties of the system? Explain with examples.
15. What is the composition for getting the maximum during the mixing of two ideal gases?
16. What are the limitations of the 1st law of thermodynamics?

17. Give the statement of the 2nd law of thermodynamics in terms of entropy.
18. What is calorific value of a fuel? Explain with examples.
19. What are the criteria of spontaneity of chemical reactions?
20. Why is enthalpy of neutralization of weak acid and strong base always less than −13.7 kcal.
21. Given $G = H - TS$. Show that the change in free energy of the system with temperature is the measure of decrease in the entropy of the system at constant pressure.
22. Using Gibbs–Helmholtz equation show that

$$E = \frac{-\Delta H}{nF} + T\left(\frac{\partial E}{\partial T}\right)_P,$$

where E is the emf and ΔH is the change in enthalpy of the system.

23. Show that $\left(\frac{\partial G}{\partial T}\right)_P = -S$
24. Show that $\left(\frac{\partial G}{\partial P}\right)_T = V$
25. Show that $\left[\frac{\partial\left(\frac{\Delta G)}{T}\right)}{\partial T}\right]_P = -\frac{\Delta H}{T^2}$
26. Design Born–Haber cycle to find lattice energy of CaO crystal. Explain different energy terms present in the cycle.
27. Derive relation between molar heat capacities for a real gas.
28. Define heat of a reaction. Derive integrated form of Kirchhoff's equation to provide the effect of temperature on heat of a reaction.
29. Derive Clapeyron–Clausius equation for liquid–vapor equilibrium.
30. Derive van't Hoff reaction isotherm.
31. What do you mean by lattice energy? Discuss the Born–Haber cycle for lattice energy.
32. Prove that $C_P - C_V = \left[P + \left(\frac{\partial U}{\partial V}\right)_T\right]\left(\frac{\partial V}{\partial T}\right)_P.$
33. What do you mean by bond energy? Write down the factors affecting bond energy.
34. If $\partial U = T\partial S - P\partial T$, then show that

$$\left[\frac{\partial T}{\partial V}\right]_S = -\left[\frac{\partial P}{\partial S}\right]_V.$$

35. State and explain Hess's law.
36. Derive Gibb's Helmholtz equation in terms of free energy change and enthalpy change. With the help of the above equation, explain how the emf of the cell can be calculated.
37. Show that for one mole of an ideal gas,

$$\left(\frac{\partial P}{\partial V}\right)_T\left(\frac{\partial V}{\partial T}\right)_P\left(\frac{\partial T}{\partial P}\right)_V = -1.$$

38. For one mole of an ideal gas, writing V as a function of temperature, show that ∂V is an exact differential.

39. If $T = f(P, V)$, then prove that dT is a perfect differential.
40. Write a short note on Born-Haber cycle.
41. Prove $\left[\frac{\partial S}{\partial P}\right]_T = -\left[\frac{\partial V}{\partial T}\right]_P$ and $\left[\frac{\partial V}{\partial S}\right]_P = -\left[\frac{\partial T}{\partial P}\right]_S$.
42. Show that $\left[\frac{\partial H}{\partial P}\right]_T = V - T\left[\frac{\partial V}{\partial T}\right]_P$
43. What is a state function?
44. What is the entropy of a perfectly crystalline substance at absolute zero temperature?
45. What is Joule–Thomson effect?
46. What do you mean by Joule–Thomson coefficient?
47. Why H_2 and He show heating effect during Joule–Thomson expansion under normal condition?
48. Joule–Thomson coefficient, i.e., μ_{JT}, for an ideal gas is zero. Explain.
49. Show that for a real gas, μ_{JT} depends only upon the temperature at which isoenthalpic expansion takes place.
50. What do you mean by inversion temperature?
51. Show that inversion temperature of a gas can be expressed as $\frac{2a}{Rb}$.
52. Explain partial molar property. Is it an extensive or intensive property?
53. What do you mean by chemical potential?
54. Show that the variation of chemical potential of any constituent i of the system with pressure is equal to partial molar volume.
55. Show that $\left(\frac{\partial \mu_i}{\partial T}\right)_{P,N} = -\bar{S}_i$.
56. Derive Gibbs–Duhem equation.
57. Derive integrated form of Kirchhoff's equation.
58. Show that $\Delta H_2 = \Delta H_1 + \Delta C_P(T_2 - T_1)$.
59. Derive an expression to find the lattice energy of CaF_2 on the basis of Born-Haber cycle.
60. Show that during cell operation, entropy change can be expressed as

$$\Delta S = nF\left(\frac{\partial E}{\partial T}\right)_P$$

where $(\partial E/\partial T)_P$ is the temperature coefficient of emf of the cell, n is the number of moles of electrons involved in the cell reaction, and F is the Faraday.
61. Derive an expression to give the simultaneous effect of temperature and pressure on free energy change.
62. Derive an expression to find enthalpy change accompanying a cell reaction during the operation of an electrochemical cell.
63. Show that the entropy of mixing of ideal gases $\Delta S_{mix} > 0$.
64. Show that per mole of a mixture of ideal gases is equal to $-\Sigma\chi_i \ln \chi_i$.

NUMERICAL PROBLEMS

1. Calculate the equilibrium constant K_{eq} for the following reaction at 27°C.
   $2Ag^+ + Zn \rightleftharpoons Zn^{+2} + 2Ag$, where the standard emf of the cell is 1.56 V.
2. Calculate ΔG when 1 mol of an ideal gas expands isothermally and reversibly from 3 atm to 1 atm at 300 K.
3. The equilibrium constant for a reaction is 2.5×10^6. Calculate free energy change at 27°C.
4. Calculate the change in Gibb's and Helmholtz free energy when 4 mol of an ideal gas is expanded isothermally and reversibly from 5 atm to 1 atm at 300 K.
5. Two moles of a gas is isothermally expanded from 100 atm to 10 atm at 27°C. What is the amount of work done during the expansion?
6. Calculate ΔG for isothermal reversible compression of a mole of ideal gas from 1 atm to 50 atm at 303 K.
7. What is the value of ΔG for liquid water vaporizing at 373 K and 1 atm pressure?
8. Two moles of a perfect gas expanded from a pressure of 20 Nm^{-2} to 1 Nm^{-2} at 300 K. What will be the free energy change of the gas?
9. Calculate the free energy change which occurs when one mole of an ideal gas expands reversibly and isothermally at 300 K from an initial volume of 5 l to 50 l.
10. Calculate the free energy change accompanying the compression of 1 mol of CO_2 at 57°C from 5 atm to 50 atm assuming ideal behavior for CO_2.
11. Using the following data calculate the enthalpy of formation of $CaF_{2(s)}$ and explain its stability. Estimated lattice energy of $CaF_{2(s)}$, enthalpy of atomization of $Ca_{(s)}$, ionization energy of $Ca_{(g)}$, enthalpy of atomization of $F_{2(g)}$, electron affinity of $F_{(g)}$ and enthalpy of $CaF_{2(s)}$ are −795, 201, 590, 79, −335 and −1243 kJ mol^{-1}, respectively.
12. At NTP, 2.8 l of oxygen was mixed with 19.6 l of hydrogen. Calculate the increase in entropy assuming ideal gas behavior.
13. Calculate the free energy change when 5 mol of oxygen at 300 K and 5 bar pressure expands isothermally to 1 bar pressure.
14. For a gaseous reaction at 300 *K*, $\partial H - \partial U = -4.98$ kJ. Assuming $R = 8.35\ JK^{-1}$ mol^{-1}, find ∂n_g.
15. Calculate the entropy change in melting 5 g of ice at 0°C. Given that molar heat of fusion of ice is 1440 cal.
16. When the heat for the combustion of glucose at constant pressure is −651 kcal at 17°C, calculate the heat of reaction for the same at constant volume.
17. The molar heat of combustion of $C_2H_{2(g)}$, $C_{(graphite)}$, and $H_{2(g)}$ are 310.62, 94.05, and 68.32 kcal, respectively. Calculate the heat of formation of $C_2H_{2(g)}$.
18. The heat of reaction for
    $N_{2(g)} + 3H_{2(g)} \rightleftharpoons 2NH_{3(g)}$
    at 27°C is −91.94 kJ. What will be its value at 50°C? The molar heat capacities at constant pressure and 27°C for $N_{2(g)}$, $H_{2(g)}$, and $NH_{3(g)}$ are 28.45, 28.32, and 37.07 J, respectively.
19. Calculate the temperature at which the reaction given below will be at equilibrium. Given that $\Delta H = 30.5$ kJ mol^{-1} and $\Delta S = 0.06$ kJ K^{-1} mol^{-1}.
    $Ag_2O_{(s)} \longrightarrow 2Ag_{(s)} + 1/2\ O_{2(g)}$

20. At 300 K, the standard enthalpies of formation of $C_6H_5COOH_{(s)}$, $CO_{2(g)}$, and $H_2O_{(l)}$ are $-408, -393$, and -286 kJ mol^{-1}, respectively. Calculate the heat of combustion of benzoic acid at constant pressure and at constant volume.

21. Calculate the change in free energy accompanying the vaporization of one mole liquid water at 100°C and 0.1 atm pressure. Will the process be spontaneous?

22. For the reaction, $Ag_2O_{(s)} \longrightarrow 2\ Ag_{(s)} + \frac{1}{2} O_{2(g)}$ at 1 atm pressure, $\Delta H = 30.6$ kJ mol^{-1} and $\Delta S = 0.66$ kJ K^{-1}. Calculate the temperature at which the reaction would be in equilibrium.

23. Find the change in chemical potential of ethanol at 300 K upon addition of a solute assuming ideal behavior. Given that the mole fraction of the solute is 0.02.

24. The equilibrium constant for a reaction is 10 at 473 K and 2.5 at 373 K. Find standard enthalpy of the reaction and also calculate the standard entropy change at 373 K.

25. At what temperature will water boil when the atmospheric pressure is 600 mm of Hg? Given latent heat of vaporization is 545.5 cal g^{-1}.

26. Find the entropy change during mixing of 2 mol of NH_3, 3 mol of CH_4, and 1.5 mol of N_2 at 298 K assuming ideal behavior.

27. Five moles of an ideal gas expands reversibly from a temperature of 273 to 373 K at constant pressure. Calculate the entropy change accompanying the pressure.

CHAPTER 4 Chemical Equilibrium

Chapter Outline

- Characteristic Facts of Equilibrium
- Law of Mass Action
- Law of Chemical Equilibrium
- Le Chatelier's Principle
- Thermodynamics of Chemical Equilibrium
- Concepts of Acid and Base
- Ionic Product of Water
- Concept of pH
- Buffer
- Indicators
- Acid–Base Titrations
- Common Ion Effect
- Solubility Product
- Salt Hydrolysis

Reversible reactions when carried in closed system, where exchange of matter with surroundings is not allowed, do not go up to completion, i.e., they proceed to a certain point and then virtually stop having a considerable amount of unutilized reactant/s. This state of a reversible reaction at which the reaction virtually stops, and no further change in the composition of reaction mixture takes place until and unless some external stress is imposed in the form of change of concentration, temperature, or pressure is known as chemical equilibrium. At chemical equilibrium, the rates of forward and reverse reactions become identical. The approach of equilibrium can be confirmed by the constancy of some observable properties, such as the concentration of some species, pressure of some gaseous components formed during the reaction, intensity of color of some species involved, and so on.

Characteristic Facts of Equilibrium

1. Chemical equilibrium is possible only in a closed system, i.e., a system which does not allow the exchange of matter with surroundings.
2. The approach of equilibrium can be confirmed by the constancy of some observable properties.
3. Equilibrium can be approached either starting with reactants or with products.
4. It is dynamic in nature, i.e., both forward and reverse reactions continue to occur even after the attainment of the state of equilibrium.
5. Equilibrium once established, continues to remain as such until it is not subjected to any type of external stress.

6. The thermodynamic condition for equilibrium is free energy change, i.e., $\Delta G = 0$.
7. A catalyst speeds up the rate of both forward and reverse reactions to the same extent.

Thus, the use of a catalyst does not change equilibrium point, rather it only quickens the approach of equilibrium.

Law of Mass Action

It was proposed by Cato Maximilian Guldberg and Peter Waage in 1864. As per this law "the rate of a reaction is directly proportional to the product of the active masses of the reactants with each term raised to the power equal to its stoichiometric coefficients." For an ideal system, the active mass may be taken equal to the molar concentration.

Let us consider a hypothetical reaction,

$$aA + bB \longrightarrow lL + mM$$

Applying the law of mass action, we get

$$\text{Rate} \propto [A]^a [B]^b$$

$$= k [A]^a [B]^b \quad ...[4.1]$$

where k is the rate or velocity constant and $[i]$ represents the concentration of the ith component in mole liter^{-1}.

Note:

1. *Active mass* or *activity* (a) is a measure of the "effective concentration" of a species in a mixture. By convention, activity is treated as a dimensionless quantity, although its actual value depends on customary choices of standard state for the species.
2. The activity of pure substances in condensed phases, i.e., in solid or liquid, is normally taken as unity. For gases, the effective partial pressure is referred to as fugacity.
3. Activities, in practice, are often replaced by molar concentrations. But there are circumstances, particularly in nonideal systems, where activity and the concentration are significantly different, and as such, it is not correct to approximate with molar concentrations. For example, in a solution of 0.02 M potassium hydrogen iodate, the activity is 40% lower than the calculated hydrogen ion concentration, resulting in a much higher pH than expected.
4. The difference between activity and other measures of composition arises because molecules in nonideal gases or solutions interact with each other, either to attract or to repel each other. The activity of an ion is particularly influenced by its surroundings.
5. The *standard state* of a material, which may be a pure substance, mixture, or solution, is a reference point used to calculate its properties under different conditions. In principle, the choice of standard state is arbitrary, although IUPAC recommends a conventional set of standard states for general use. It recommends the use of 1 bar as the standard pressure. Strictly speaking, temperature is not a part of the "standard state" definition—a standard state can be ascribed to any specified temperature. However, thermodynamic quantities are compiled most commonly at 298.15 K (exactly 25°C). The standard state should not be confused with the standard temperature and pressure (STP) as defined for gases.

Law of Chemical Equilibrium

Let us consider a hypothetical reversible reaction,

$$aA + bB \rightleftharpoons lL + mM$$

Applying the law of mass action to the forward reaction, we get

$$\text{Rate} \propto [A]^a [B]^b$$
$$= k_f [A]^a [B]^b$$

where k_f is the rate constant for the forward reaction.

Again applying the law to the reverse reaction, we get

$$\text{Rate} \propto [L]^l [M]^m$$
$$= k_r [L]^l [M]^m$$

where k_r is the rate constant for the reverse reaction.

At equilibrium,

Rate of forward reaction = Rate of reverse reaction

or $\quad k_f [A]^a [B]^b = k_r [L]^l [M]^m$

or $$\frac{k_f}{k_r} = K_C = \frac{[L]^l [M]^m}{[A]^a [B]^b} \qquad \text{...[4.2]}$$

The relation [4.2] is known as the law of chemical equilibrium. K_C is known as the equilibrium constant and is a measure of the extent to which the forward or reverse reaction has taken place at the approach of equilibrium.

Equilibrium Constant in Terms of Partial Pressures

When all components involved in the reaction remain in the gaseous form, then the equilibrium constant can also be expressed in terms of partial pressures of different components. Thus, for the same hypothetical reaction, as mentioned above, the equilibrium constant in terms of partial pressure can be expressed as

$$K_P = \frac{(p_L)^l (p_M)^m}{(p_A)^a (p_B)^b} \qquad \text{...[4.3]}$$

where p_i term refers to the partial pressure of ith component.

Relation between K_P and K_C

Let us consider a hypothetical reaction,

$$aA + bB \rightleftharpoons lL + mM$$

Equilibrium constant in terms of partial pressure,

$$K_P = \frac{(p_L)^l (p_M)^m}{(p_A)^a (p_B)^b} \qquad \text{...[4.4]}$$

Partial pressure of any component can be expressed as

$$p_i = \left(\frac{n_i}{V}\right) RT$$

$$= [i]\, RT$$

Substituting this value in relation [4.4], we get

$$K_P = \frac{(p_L)^l\,(p_M)^m}{(p_A)^a\,(p_B)^b}$$

$$= \frac{([L]\,RT)^l\,([M]\,RT)^m}{([A]\,RT)^a\,([B]\,RT)^b}$$

$$= \frac{[L]^l\,[M]^m}{[A]^a\,[B]^b} \times \frac{(RT)^{l+m}}{(RT)^{a+b}}$$

$$= K_C \times (RT)^{\Delta n} \qquad ...[4.5]$$

Here Δn is the change in the number of moles of gaseous components as the reactants get converted into products.

Case I: If $\Delta n = 0$, then $K_C = K_P$.

Case II: If $\Delta n > 0$, then $K_C < K_P$.

Case III: If $\Delta n < 0$, then $K_C > K_P$.

Example 4.1

At 500 K, the equilibrium constant K_C for the reaction,

$$PCl_5 \rightleftharpoons PCl_3 + Cl_2$$

is 4×10^{-2} mol l^{-1}. Find K_P of the reaction.

Solution

$$PCl_5 \rightleftharpoons PCl_3 + Cl_2$$

$$\Delta n = 2 - 1 = 1$$

$$R = 0.082 \text{ L atm mol}^{-1} \text{ K}^{-1}$$

$$T = 500 \text{ K}$$

$$K_P = K_C \times (RT)^{\Delta n}$$

$$= 4 \times 10^{-2}\,(0.082 \times 500)$$

$$= 1.64 \text{ atm}$$

Characteristics of equilibrium constant

1. The equilibrium constant is a measure of the extent to which the forward or reverse reaction has taken place at the approach of equilibrium.
2. The equilibrium constant has a definite value for a given reaction at a specified temperature.
3. The value of equilibrium constant is independent of the concentration of reactants and products.

4. The equilibrium constant is inverted if the equation for the reaction is reversed.
5. The use of catalyst does not change the value of equilibrium constant.
6. If the equation of a reversible reaction is multiplied by a factor, then the equilibrium constant is raised to the same factor.

   [e.g., if $HI \rightleftharpoons \frac{1}{2} H_2 + \frac{1}{2} I_2$ has an equilibrium constant K, then the equilibrium constant for the reaction $2HI \rightleftharpoons H_2 + I_2$ will be $K' = K^2$]
7. If a reversible reaction is obtained by the addition of two or more such reactions, then the equilibrium constant of the resultant reaction is the product of equilibrium constants of the individual reactions.

   [e.g., let us consider the following steps of a reaction $R \rightleftharpoons P$ with their respective equilibrium constants:

   Step I: $R \rightleftharpoons I, K_1$

   Step II: $I \rightleftharpoons P, K_2$

   Then for the net reaction, $R \rightleftharpoons P$, the equilibrium constant can be expressed as $K = K_1 \times K_2$]
8. Equilibrium constant has no unit when $\Delta n = 0$. However, when $\Delta n \neq 0$, it has a specific unit.

   [e.g., for the reaction, $H_2 + I_2 \rightleftharpoons 2HI$, the equilibrium constant K has no unit. But for the reaction, $N_2 + 3H_2 \rightleftharpoons 2NH_3$, K has a specific unit which can be developed as follows:

$$K = \frac{[NH_3]^2}{[N_2][H_2]}$$

$$= \frac{[mol/1]^2}{[mol/1][mol/1]^3}$$

$$= [mol^{-2}\ 1^2]$$

Example 4.2

The equilibrium constant of the reaction $SO_{3\,(g)} \rightleftharpoons SO_{2\,(g)} + \frac{1}{2} O_{2\,(g)}$ is 0.15 at 298 K. Find the equilibrium constant for $2SO_{2\,(g)} + O_{2\,(g)} \rightleftharpoons 2SO_{3\,(g)}$.

Solution

$$SO_{3\,(g)} \rightleftharpoons SO_{2\,(g)} + \frac{1}{2} O_{2\,(g)};\ K_1$$

For $2SO_{3\,(g)} \rightleftharpoons 2SO_{2\,(g)} + O_{2\,(g)};\ K_2 = K_1^2$

By reversing the reaction, $2SO_{2\,(g)} + O_{2\,(g)} \rightleftharpoons 2SO_{3\,(g)};\ K = \frac{1}{K_1^2}$

$$K = \frac{1}{K_1^2}$$

$$= \frac{1}{(0.15)^2}$$

$$= 44.44 \text{ mol}^{-1}\text{l}^{-1}$$

Note:

Concentration quotient: The ratio of the product of active masses of products to that of reactants with each term raised to the power equal to its stoichiometric coefficients is known as the concentration quotient and is denoted by Q_C. For a hypothetical reaction,

$$a\text{A} + b\text{B} \rightleftharpoons l\text{L} + m\text{M}$$

$$Q_C = \frac{[\text{L}]^l\,[\text{M}]^m}{[\text{A}]^a\,[\text{B}]^b} \qquad \text{...[4.6]}$$

When equilibrium concentrations of all the components are substituted in the relation, then Q_C becomes K_C. The numerical value of Q_C helps in predicting the direction in which the reaction should proceed.

If $Q_C = K_C$, the reaction remains in equilibrium.

If $Q_C < K_C$, the net reaction occurs in forward direction.

If $Q_C > K_C$, the net reaction occurs in backward direction.

Evaluation of Equilibrium Constants

Homogeneous equilibria

The equilibria in which all components remain in the same phase are known as homogeneous equilibria.

Case I: $\Delta n = 0$

In such a case, $K_C = K_P$. Let us see the whole process of evaluation by taking a specific example of combination of hydrogen and iodine to form hydrogen iodide. Let us first find K_C.

	$H_{2(g)}$ +	$I_{2(g)}$	$\rightleftharpoons$	$2HI_{(g)}$
Initial	a/V	b/V		0 mol l^{-1}
Equilibrium	$(a-x)/V$	$(b-x)/V$		$2x/V$ mol l^{-1}

Now, $$K_C = \frac{[\text{HI}]^2}{[\text{H}_2][\text{I}_2]}$$

$$= \frac{[2x/V]^2}{[(a-x)/V]\,[(b-x)/V]}$$

$$= \frac{4x^2}{(a-x)(b-x)} \qquad \text{...[4.7]}$$

Now, let us find K_P in the same reaction.

	$H_{2(g)}$	+ $I_{2(g)}$	$\rightleftharpoons$ $2HI_{(g)}$
Initial	a	b	0 mol
Equilibrium	$a - x$	$b - x$	$2x$ mol

Total number of moles $= a - x + b - x + 2x = a + b$

Now, $p_{HI} = \dfrac{2x}{a+b}P$

$$p_{H_2} = \frac{a-x}{a+b}P, \quad p_{I_2} = \frac{b-x}{a+b}P$$

$$K_P = \frac{(p_{HI})^2}{(p_{H_2})(P_{I_1})}$$

$$= \frac{\left(\dfrac{2x}{a+b}P\right)^2}{\left(\dfrac{a-x}{a+b}P\right)\left(\dfrac{b-x}{a+b}P\right)}$$

$$= \frac{4x^2}{(a-x)(b-x)} \qquad \text{...[4.8]}$$

Case II: $\Delta n \neq 0$

Here $K_C \neq K_P$. Let us see the whole process of evaluation by taking a specific example of combination of nitrogen and hydrogen to form ammonia. Let us go for K_C in the beginning.

	$N_{2(g)}$	+ $3H_{2(g)}$	$\rightleftharpoons$ $2NH_{3(g)}$
Initial	a/V	b/V	0 mol l^{-1}
Equilibrium	$(a - x)/V$	$(b - 3x)/V$	$2x/V$ mol l^{-1}

Now, $K_C = \dfrac{[NH_3]^2}{[N_2][H_2]}$

$$= \frac{[2x/V]^2}{[(a-x)/V][(b-3x)/V]^3}$$

$$= \frac{4x^2V^2}{(a-x)(b-3x)} \qquad \text{...[4.9]}$$

Now, let us go for K_P

	$N_{2(g)}$	+ $3H_{2(g)}$	$\rightleftharpoons$ $2NH_{3(g)}$
Initial	a	b	0 mol
Equilibrium	$a - x$	$b - 3x$	$2x$ mol

Total number of moles $= a - x + b - 3x + 2x = a + b - 2x$

$$\text{Now, } p_{NH_3} = \frac{2x}{a+b-2x} P$$

$$p_{N_2} = \frac{a-x}{a+b-2x} P, \qquad p_{H_1} = \frac{b-3x}{a+b-2x} P$$

$$K_P = \frac{(p_{NH_3})^2}{(p_{N_2})(P_{H_2})}$$

$$= \frac{\left(\frac{2x}{a+b-2x} P\right)^2}{\left(\frac{a-x}{a+b-2x} P\right)\left(\frac{b-3x}{a+b-2x} P\right)^3}$$

$$= \frac{4x^2 (a+b-2x)^2}{(a-x)(b-3x)P^2} \qquad \text{...[4.10]}$$

Heterogeneous equilibria

The equilibria in which all components do not remain in the same phase are known as heterogeneous equilibria. Here, the activity of pure solid and liquid are not included in the rate expression, e.g., decomposition of calcium carbonate to calcium oxide and carbon dioxide. Here, calcium carbonate and calcium oxide remain in solid phase while carbon dioxide remains in gaseous phase.

$$CaCO_{3(s)} \rightleftharpoons CaO_{(s)} + CO_{2(g)}$$

Here $K_C = [CO_2]$ ...[4.11]

and $K_P = p_{CO_2}$ ...[4.12]

Example 4.3

One mole of nitrogen is mixed with three moles of hydrogen in a 5 l flask. If 25% of nitrogen is converted into ammonia by the reaction $N_2 + 3H_2 \rightleftharpoons 2\,NH_3$, calculate K_C.

Solution

	$N_{2(g)}$	+	$3H_{2(g)}$	$\rightleftharpoons$	$2NH_{3(g)}$
Initial	1/5		3/5		0 mol l^{-1}
Equilibrium	0.75/5		2.25/5		0.50 mol l^{-1}
	= 0.15		= 0.45		= 0.10 mol l^{-1}

$$\text{Now, } K_C = \frac{[NH_3]^2}{[N_2][H_2]}$$

$$= \frac{(0.10)^2}{(0.15)(0.45)^3}$$

$$= 0.74\ l^2\ \text{mol}^{-2}$$

Example 4.4

In the dissociation of HI, 25% is dissociated at equilibrium. Find K_P for the reaction $HI \rightleftharpoons \frac{1}{2}H_2 + \frac{1}{2}I_2$.

Solution

	$HI_{(g)}$	$\rightleftharpoons$	$1/2\ H_{2(g)}$	+	$1/2\ I_{2(g)}$
Initial,	$1/V$		0		0 mol l^{-1}
At equilibrium	$(1-\alpha)/V$		$\alpha/2V$		$\alpha/2V$ mol l^{-1}

$$K_C = \frac{[H_2]^{1/2}\,[I_2]^{1/2}}{[HI}$$

$$= \frac{[\alpha/2V]^{1/2}\,[\alpha/2V]^{1/2}}{(1-\alpha)/V}$$

$$= \frac{\alpha}{2(1-\alpha)} = \frac{0.25}{2(1-0.25)}$$

$$= 0.167 = K_P \text{ as } \Delta n = 0$$

Example 4.5

Two moles each of hydrogen and iodine were heated in a 1 l flask at 500°C till the equilibrium was reached. Find the concentrations of each component at equilibrium. Given that equilibrium constant is 46.

Solution

	H_2	+	I_2	$\rightleftharpoons$	2HI
Initial	2.0		2.0		0 mol l^{-1}
Equilibrium	$2.0 - x$		$2.0 - x$		$2x$ mol l^{-1}

Now, $K_C = \dfrac{(2x)^2}{(2.0-x)\,(2.0-x)}$

or $\quad 46 = \dfrac{(2x)^2}{(2.0-x)\,(2.0-x)}$

or $\quad 42x^2 - 184x + 184 = 0$

or $\quad x = 1.54$ (2.84 not acceptable)

At equilibrium,

$[H_2] = 0.46$,

$[I_2] = 0.46$, and

$[HI] = 0.92$.

Example 4.6

The value of K_P for the reaction $H_2 + I_2 \rightleftharpoons HI$ at 450° C is 50. If the initial pressure of both H_2 and I_2 is 0.5 atm, find partial pressures of each component at equilibrium.

Solution

	H_2	+	I_2	$\rightleftharpoons$	2HI
Initial	0.5		0.5		0 atm
At equilibrium	$0.5 - x$		$0.5 - x$		$2x$ atm

$$K_P = \frac{(2x)^2}{(0.5-x)\,(0.5-x)}$$

$$\text{or} \quad 50 = \frac{(2x)^2}{(0.5-x)\,(0.5-x)}$$

$$\text{or} \quad \frac{2x}{(0.5-x)} = 7.07$$

$$\text{or} \quad x = 0.39$$

At equilibrium,

$$p_{H_2} = 0.5 - 0.39 = 0.11 \text{ atm} = p_{I_2}, \text{ and } p_{HI} = 2 \times 0.39 = 0.78 \text{ atm.}$$

Example 4.7

I mole of N_2 and 3 moles of PCl_5 are placed in a 100 l flask and is heated to 200°C. The equilibrium pressure is 2 atm. Find the degree of dissociation and K_P, assuming ideal behavior.

Solution

	$PCl_{5(g)}$	$\rightleftharpoons$	$PCl_{3(g)}$	+	$Cl_{2(g)}$
Initial	3		0		0 mol
Equilibrium	$3 - x$		x		x mol

Total moles present at equilibrium = $4 + x$

Total pressure at equilibrium = 2 atm

$$PV = nRT$$

$$\text{or} \quad 2 \times 100 = (4 + x) \times 0.082 \times 473$$

$$\text{or} \quad x = 1.156$$

$$\text{Now, } \alpha = \frac{1.156}{3.0} = 0.385$$

$$= 38.5\ \%$$

$$\text{Again, } K_P = \frac{p_{PCl_3}\, p_{Cl_2}}{p_{PCl_5}}$$

$$= \frac{1.844 \times 1.156}{1.156} = 1.844$$

Example 4.8

When 4 g of solid NH_4HS is introduced into a 1 l evacuated flask at 27°C, 30% of the solid decomposed into gaseous ammonia and hydrogen sulphide. Calculate K_C for the reaction at 27°C. What would happen to the equilibrium when more solid NH_4HS is introduced into the flask?

Solution

Moles of NH_4HS introduced into flask = 4/51 = 0.078

$\alpha = 30\%$, i.e., $\alpha = 0.3$.

$$NH_4HS_{(s)} \rightleftharpoons NH_{3(g)} + H_2S_{(g)}$$

$$0.078\,(1-0.3) \qquad 0.078 \times 0.3 \qquad 0.078 \times 0.3$$

Now, $K_C = [NH_3]\,[H_2S]$

$= 0.023 \times 0.023$

$= 5.29 \times 10^{-4}$

The addition of $NH_4HS_{(s)}$ does not change the position of equilibrium.

Le Chatelier's Principle

This principle was proposed by French Chemist Henery Le Chatelier. It predicts the effect of stress on a system in equilibrium. It states that if a system in equilibrium is subjected to some external stress, the system adjusts itself internally so as to undo the stress, i.e., the system shifts in a direction so as to reduce the outside stress. The external stress can be in the form of the change of concentration, change of pressure, change of temperature, use of catalyst, or addition of noble gas.

Effect of Concentration

The concentration of a species in a reaction can be changed by the addition or the removal of that component from the reaction mixture. If some species is added to the reaction mixture, then the equilibrium shifts in a direction so as to consume that species. Therefore, the addition of reactant/s shift/s the equilibrium in the forward direction, while the addition of product/s shift/s the equilibrium in the reverse direction. Similarly, the removal of some species from the reaction mixture shifts the equilibrium in a direction so as to generate the same.

For example, in the following reaction

$$N_{2(g)} + 3H_{2(g)} \rightleftharpoons 2NH_{3(g)}$$

the addition of N_2, H_2, or both shifts the equilibrium in the forward direction, favoring the formation of ammonia. The formation of ammonia is also favored by the removal of ammonia.

Effect of Temperature

The temperature gradient between system and surroundings drives the heat flow. Increase in temperature allows heat to enter into the system. As per the principle, the system tries to utilize the extra heat and this is possible with the shifting of equilibrium in the endothermic direction. Similarly, the lowering of temperature shifts the equilibrium in the exothermic direction.

For example,

$$N_{2(g)} + 3H_{2(g)} \rightleftharpoons 2NH_{3(g)} + 93\text{ kJ}$$

In the above reaction, the formation of ammonia is favored by the lowering of temperature, as in this direction, the reaction is exothermic.

Note:

Though low temperature favors the yield of ammonia, during its manufacture in Haber's process, a temperature of ~450°C is maintained. This fact is sometimes treated as the limitation of Le Chatelier's principle. In fact, this is not a limitation, as here the process is optimized for the minimum costing.

Explanation:

Being a molecular reaction, it proceeds too slowly even in the presence of a catalyst. To make the reaction proceed with an appreciable rate, a high temperature of ~450°C is used. At this temperature, the yield is ~15% as compared to ~90% at room temperature. For a comparative account, the following graph may be considered. The graph provides the simultaneous effect of the temperature and pressure on the percentage of NH_3 at equilibrium (Fig. 4.1).

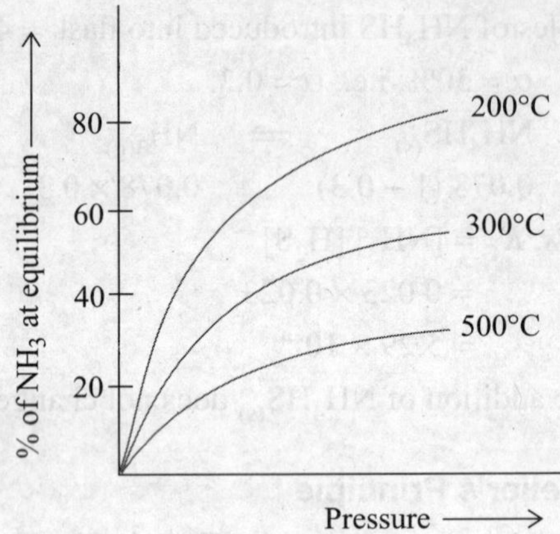

Fig. 4.1 Percentage yield of NH_3 at equilibrium at different temperatures

Effect of Pressure

An increase in pressure tends to decrease the volume. Therefore, a hike in pressure shifts the equilibrium in the direction in which there is a decrease in volume or number of moles. On the other hand, a decrease in pressure shifts the equilibrium in a direction in which there is an increase in the number of moles.

For example,

$$\underbrace{N_{2(g)} + 3H_{2(g)}}_{\text{4 moles}} \rightleftharpoons \underbrace{2NH_{3(g)}}_{\text{2 moles}}$$

An increase in pressure shifts the equilibrium in the forward direction, favoring the formation of NH_3.

Note:

If there is no change in the number of moles as one move from reactants to products, then the change in pressure does not impart any effect on the equilibrium, e.g., the equilibrium in the following reaction is not disturbed by change in pressure.

$$\underbrace{H_{2(g)} + I_{2(g)}}_{\text{2 moles}} \rightleftharpoons \underbrace{2HI_{(g)}}_{\text{2 moles}}$$

Effect of Catalyst

The use of a catalyst increases the rate of the forward as well as the reverse reaction to the same extent. Therefore, its use does not alter the equilibrium rather quickens the approach of equilibrium, e.g., the Haber's process for the manufacture of ammonia is catalyzed by finely divided iron mixed with molybdenum. One more example is the contact process for the manufacture of sulphuric acid where V_2O_5 is used as the catalyst.

$$N_{2(g)} + 2H_{2(g)} \xrightleftharpoons{\text{Fe–Mo}} 2NH_{3(g)}$$

$$2SO_{2(g)} + O_{2(g)} \xrightleftharpoons{V_2O_5} 2SO_{3(g)}$$

Effect of Addition of Noble Gas

At a constant volume, the addition of a noble gas increases the total pressure, but does not change the partial pressures of different gaseous components present in the reaction mixture. Therefore, equilibrium is not disturbed. However at a constant pressure, the addition of a noble gas makes a hike in the pressure, which ultimately shifts the equilibrium in the direction so as to utilize the pressure. This is possible only when the equilibrium shifts in the direction in which there is a decrease in volume.

For example,

$$N_{2(g)} + 3H_{2(g)} \rightleftharpoons 2NH_{3(g)}$$

Here, the addition of a noble gas at a constant pressure favors the yield of ammonia by shifting the equilibrium in the forward direction.

Example 4.9

Apply Le-Chatelier's principle so as to predict the optimum conditions for the maximum yield of (a) sulphuric acid in Contact process and (b) nitric acid in Birkeland–Eyde process.

Solution

(a) The basic reaction involved in the contact process is the oxidation of sulfur dioxide. The reaction is as follows:

$$\underbrace{2SO_{2(g)} + O_{2(g)}}_{2\text{ mol}} \xrightleftharpoons{V_2O_5} \underbrace{2SO_{3(g)}}_{2\text{ mol}} + 176\text{ kJ}$$

The optimum conditions are:

1. Low temperature favors the yield. However in practice, ~500°C is used. The reason is same as that mentioned in Haber's processes.
2. High pressure
3. Using V_2O_5 as the catalyst

(b) The basic reaction involved in the Birkeland–Eyde processes is the oxidation of nitrogen. The reaction is as follows:

$$\underbrace{N_{2(g)} + O_{2(g)}}_{2\text{ mol}} \xrightleftharpoons{Cu(NO_3)_2} \underbrace{2NO_{(g)}}_{2\text{ mol}} - 181\text{ kJ}$$

The optimum conditions are:

1. High temperature favors the yield. In practice, a temperature of ~3000°C is used.
2. Pressure has no effect.
3. Using a suitable catalyst like cupric nitrate.

Thermodynamics of Chemical Equilibrium

van't Hoff Isotherm

van't Hoff isotherm provides a quantitative relation for free energy change accompanying a chemical reaction.

$$\Delta G = \Delta G^0 + RT \ln Q \qquad \text{...[4.13]}$$

At equilibrium, $\Delta G = 0$.

Hence, relation [4.13] reduces to

$$\Delta G^0 = - RT \ln K_P \qquad \text{...[4.14]}$$

Substituting back in relation [4.13], we get

$$\Delta G = - RT \ln K_P + RT \ln Q \qquad \text{...[4.15]}$$

Relations [4.14] and [4.15] are Van't Hoff isotherms.

van't Hoff Isochore (Effect of temperature on equilibrium constant)

The temperature dependence of equilibrium constant can be obtained by combining Gibbs–Helmholtz equation with Van't Hoff reaction isotherm. The relation is known as Van't Hoff reaction isochore. The equation is as follows. For details, refer to relation [3.85] in chapter 3, Chemical Thermodynamics.

$$\ln \frac{K_{P_2}}{K_{P_1}} = \frac{\Delta H}{R}\left[\frac{T_2 - T_1}{T_1 T_2}\right] \qquad \text{...[4.16]}$$

Note:

1. For an endothermic reaction, ΔH^0 is positive. Now, increase in temperature $(T_2 > T_1)$ will make $K_{P_2} > K_{P_1}$, i.e., the reaction moves in the forward direction.
2. For an exothermic reaction, ΔH^0 is negative. Now, increase in temperature $(T_2 > T_1)$ will make $K_{P_2} < K_{P_1}$, i.e., the reaction moves in the backward direction.

Example 4.10

ΔG^0 for the reaction $N_2 + 3H_2 \rightleftharpoons 2\,NH_3$ is -33 kJ mol^{-1} at 298 K. Find K_P for the reaction.

Solution

$$\Delta G^0 = - RT \ln K_P$$

or $$\ln K_P = -\frac{\Delta G^0}{RT}$$

$$= \frac{33 \times 10^3}{8.314 \times 298}$$

or $K_P = 6.09 \times 10^5$ atm^{-2}.

Example 4.11

For the reaction $N_2 + 3H_2 \rightleftharpoons 2\,NH_3$, the equilibrium constant at 400°C is 1.6×10^{-4}. Find the same at 500°C. Given heat of reaction is -95 kJ.

Solution

$$\ln \frac{K_{P_2}}{K_{P_1}} = \frac{\Delta H}{R}\left[\frac{T_2 - T_1}{T_1 T_2}\right]$$

or $$\ln \frac{K_{P_2}}{1.6 \times 10^{-4}} = \frac{-95 \times 10^3}{8.314} = \left[\frac{773 - 673}{773 \times 673}\right]$$

$$= -2.22$$

or $$\frac{K_{P_2}}{1.6 \times 10^{-4}} = e^{-2.22}$$

$$= 0.109$$

or $K_{P_2} = 1.74 \times 10^{-5}$

Example 4.12

$I_{2(g)}$ at 1 atm pressure is 1 % dissociated into atoms at 600°C and 25% dissociated at 800°C. Find the enthalpy change for the dissociation.

Solution

	$I_{2(g)}$	$\rightleftharpoons$	$2I_{(g)}$
Initial	1		0
Equilibrium	$1 - \alpha$		2α

Total number of moles = $1 + \alpha$

$$P_I = \frac{2\alpha}{1+\alpha} P, \quad p_{I_2} = \frac{1-\alpha}{1+\alpha} P$$

Now, $$K_P = \frac{p_I^2}{P_{I_2}}$$

$$= \frac{4\alpha^2}{1-\alpha^2} P$$

At 600°C, $K_{P_1} = \frac{4(0.01)^2}{1-(0.01)^2} \times 1 = 4 \times 10^{-4}$

At 800°C, $K_{P_2} = \frac{4(0.025)^2}{1-(0.025)^2} \times 1 = 0.27$

$$\ln \frac{K_{P_2}}{K_{P_1}} = \frac{\Delta H}{R}\left[\frac{T_2 - T_1}{T_1 T_2}\right]$$

or $$\ln \frac{0.27}{4 \times 10^{-4}} = \frac{\Delta H}{1.98}\left[\frac{200}{873 \times 1073}\right]$$

or $\Delta H = 60.63$ kcal

Concepts of Acid and Base

It is not possible to have a universal definition for acids and bases. Therefore, different operational theories have been proposed by different scientists from time to time. Let us discuss some popular concepts.

Arrhenius Concept

It is the first theory that defines acids and bases which came in 1884 by S. Arrehenius. The salient features are as follows:

1. Acid is a substance that furnishes H^+ ions in aqueous solutions, e.g., HCl, HNO_3, H_2SO_4, CH_3COOH, etc.
   $$HCl_{(aq)} \rightleftharpoons H^+_{(aq)} + Cl^-_{(aq)}$$
2. Base is a substance that furnishes OH^- ions in aqueous solutions, e.g., NaOH, Ca $(OH)_2$, NH_4OH, etc.
   $$NaOH_{(aq)} \rightleftharpoons Na^+_{(aq)} + OH^-_{(aq)}$$
3. The reaction between an acid and a base simply involves the reaction between H^+ and OH^- ions to form H_2O. Such a reaction is known as neutralization reaction. Let us look into the following reaction:
   $$HCl_{(aq)} + NaOH_{(aq)} \rightleftharpoons NaCl_{(aq)} + H_2O_{(1)}$$
   $$H^+_{(aq)} + Cl^-_{(aq)} + Na^+_{(aq)} + OH^-_{(aq)} \rightleftharpoons Na^+_{(aq)} + Cl^-_{(aq)} + H_2O_{(1)}$$
   $$\underbrace{H^+_{(aq)} + OH^-_{(aq)}} \rightleftharpoons H_2O$$

Limitations of Arrhenius concept

1. The theory is limited to only aqueous solutions.
2. It fails to explain the acidic nature of substances such as CO_2, SO_3, etc., which parentally do not carry hydrogen, but in aqueous solution provides H^+ ions.
   $$CO_2 + H_2O \rightleftharpoons H_2CO_3 \rightleftharpoons H^+ + HCO_3^-$$
3. It fails to explain the basic nature of substances such as NH_3, CaO, etc., which parentally do not carry hydroxyl ions, but in aqueous solution provides OH^- ions.
   $$NH_3 + H_2O \rightleftharpoons NH_4OH \rightleftharpoons NH_4^+ + OH^-$$
4. The theory remains silent regarding the fact that H^+ ions never exist free in aqueous medium rather they exist as H_3O^+ ions.

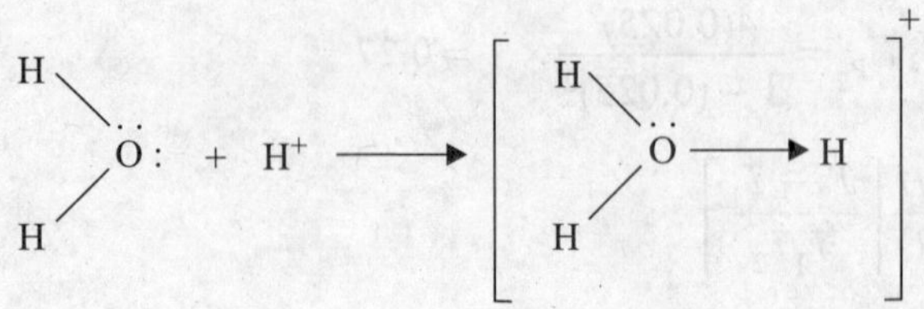

Bronsted–Lowry Concept

J.N. Bronsted and T.M. Lowry proposed this theory independently in 1923. The salient features are as follows:

1. Acid is a substance that can furnish a proton (H^+ ion) to some other substance, i.e., it is a proton donor, e.g., HCl, HNO_3, H_2S, H_3O^+, NH_4^+, HSO_4^-, etc.
2. Base is a substance that can accept a proton (H^+ ion) from some other substance, i.e., it is a proton acceptor, e.g., NH_3, H_2O, RNH_2, OH^-, Cl^-, CO_3^{2-}, etc.
3. A pair of acid and base which differ by a proton is known as conjugate acid–base pair.

$$\underbrace{HA \rightleftharpoons A^-}_{\text{Conjugate Acid–Base pair}} + H^+$$

4. An acid reacts with a base to form its conjugate base and acid respectively. This can be illustrated with the help of a specific example.

Conjuagte Acid-Base pair (NH$_3$ / NH$_4^+$)

$$\underset{\text{Acid}}{HCl} + \underset{\text{Base}}{NH_3} \rightleftharpoons \underset{\text{Acid}}{NH_4^+} + \underset{\text{Base}}{Cl^-}$$

Conjugate Acid-Base pair (HCl / Cl$^-$)

Here Cl^- is the conjugate acid of HCl, while NH_4^+ is the conjugate acid of NH_3.

Note:

1. All Arrhenius acids are Bronsted acids, but not the vice versa.
2. This theory includes both molecules and ions.
3. The strength of an acid or base depends on their ability to loose or gain proton.
4. The conjugate base of a strong acid is always weak and vice versa.
5. An additional category of substances are there, which can donate as well as accept proton. Such substances are called amphiprotic or amphoteric substances, e.g., H_2O donates proton when allowed to interact with ammonia, and on the other hand, it can also accept a proton in the presence of HCl. Other examples in the category are NH_3, HSO_4^-, HS^-, etc.

$$\underbrace{H_2O}_{\text{Acid}} + NH_3 \rightleftharpoons NH_4^+ + OH^-$$

$$\underbrace{H_2O}_{\text{Base}} + HCl \rightleftharpoons H_3O^+ + Cl^-$$

Limitations of Bronsted–Lowry concept

1. The concept fails to explain the acidic nature of non-metallic oxides such as CO_2, SO_2, P_2O_5, etc.
2. It fails to explain the basic nature of metallic oxides such as Na_2O, CaO, ZnO, etc.
3. It does not explain the acidic nature of electron deficient compounds, e.g., $AlCl_3$, BF_3, etc.

Lewis Concept

In 1923, G.N. Lewis suggested the electronic theory of acid and base. The salient features of the theory are as follows:

1. An acid is a substance that can accept an electron pair from some other substance. These include simple positive ions such as Na^+ and Fe^{2+}, etc. compounds with central atom having incomplete octet such as BF_3, $AlCl_3$, etc. compounds in which central atom remains attached to more electronegative element/s by multiple bonds such as SO_2, SO_3, CO_2, etc.
2. A base is a substance that can donate an electron pair to some other substance. These include simple negative ions such as Cl^-, OH^-, CN^-, etc. compounds with central atom carries one or more loan pair of electrons to offer such as H_2O, NH_3, RNH_2, ROH, etc.
3. An acid–base reaction simply involves the formation of a coordinate bond among them resulting in an adduct.

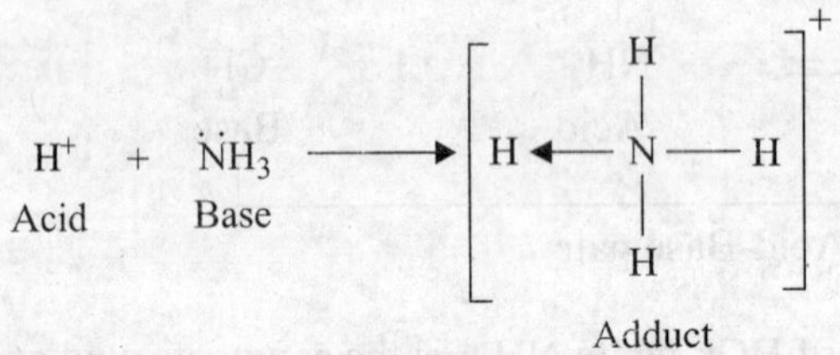

$$BF_3 + \ddot{N}H_3 \longrightarrow [F_3B \leftarrow NH_3]$$

Note:
All Bronsted bases are Lewis bases, but not vice versa.

Limitations of Lewis concept

1. The concept does not explain the behavior of protic acids such as HCl and HNO_3.
2. As per this theory, acid–base reactions should be slow, as they involve the coordinate bond formation. However in practice, these reactions are quite fast.
3. The concept remains silent regarding the relative strength of acids and bases.

Strength of Acids

The dissociation of an acid in general can be represented as

$$HA + H_2O \rightleftharpoons H_3O^+ + A^-$$

Applying the law of chemical equilibrium, we get

$$K = \frac{[H_3O^+][A^-]}{[HA][H_2O]}$$

$$\text{or} \quad K[H_2O] = \frac{[H^+][A^-]}{[HA]}; [H_3O^+] = [H^+]$$

$$\text{or} \quad K_a = \frac{[H^+][A^-]}{[HA]} \qquad ...[4.17]$$

K_a is known as the dissociation constant of acid and it has a specific value at a particular temperature. Its magnitude is a measure of acid strength. For a strong acid, the value of K_a is very high, as a strong acid dissociates to almost complete extent, while for weak acids, its value is small. The K_a values of some common acids are summarized as follows:

Acid	K_a
HCl	∞
HNO_3	∞
HCOOH	1.78×10^{-4}
CH_3COOH	1.75×10^{-5}
C_6H_5OH	1.0×10^{-5}

Relative strength

Strength of two acids can be compared by considering their dissociation constants.

	HA + H_2O	$\rightleftharpoons$	H_3O^+	+ A^-
Initial	c		0	0 M
Equilibrium	$(c - c\alpha)$		$c\alpha$	$c\alpha$ M

where α is the degree of dissociation.

$$K_a = \frac{[H^+][A^-]}{[HA]} = \frac{c\alpha \times c\alpha}{c(1-\alpha)}$$

$$= c\alpha^2 \text{ ; } 1 - \alpha \cong \alpha, (\alpha \text{ is very small})$$

$$\alpha = \sqrt{\frac{K_a}{c}} \qquad \text{... [4.18]}$$

For two weak acids with dissociation constants K_{a_1} and K_{a_2}, and corresponding degree of dissociations α_1 and α_2, the relation [4.18] can be written as

$$\alpha_1 = \sqrt{\frac{K_{a_1}}{c}}$$

$$\alpha_2 = \sqrt{\frac{K_{a_2}}{c}}$$

$$\text{Now, } \frac{\alpha_1}{\alpha_2} = \sqrt{\frac{K_{a_1}}{K_{a_2}}}$$

$$\frac{\alpha_1}{\alpha_2} = \sqrt{\frac{K_{a_1}}{K_{a_2}}} \qquad \text{...[4.19]}$$

As degree of dissociation is the measure of the tendency of an acid to furnish H^+ ions, i.e., acid strength, the above equation can be written as

$$\text{Relative strength} = \frac{\text{Strength of acid 1}}{\text{Strength of acid 2}} = \sqrt{\frac{K_{a_1}}{K_{a_2}}} \qquad \text{...[4.20]}$$

Strength of Bases

The dissociation of a base, in general, can be represented as

$$BOH \rightleftharpoons B^+ + OH^-$$

By applying the law of chemical equilibrium, we get

$$K_b = \frac{[B^+][OH^-]}{[BOH]}$$

K_b is known as the dissociation constant of base and it has a specific value at a particular temperature. Its magnitude is a measure of base strength. The K_b values of some common acids are summarized as follows:

Base	K_b
NaOH	∞
KOH	∞
NH_4OH	1.8×10^{-4}
$Ca(OH)_2$	3.7×10^{-4}
$C_6H_5NH_2$	4.4×10^{-4}

Relative strength

	BOH	$\rightleftharpoons$	B^+	+	OH^-
Initial	c		0		0 M
Equilibrium	$(c - c\alpha)$		$c\alpha$		$c\alpha$ M

where α is the degree of dissociation.

$$K_b = \frac{[B^+][OH^-]}{[BOH]} = \frac{c\alpha \times c\alpha}{c\,(1-\alpha)}$$

$$= c\alpha^2;\ 1 - \alpha \cong \alpha, \text{ as } \alpha \text{ is very small.}$$

$$\alpha = \sqrt{\frac{K_b}{c}} \qquad \text{...[4.21]}$$

For two weak bases with dissociation constants K_{b_1} and K_{b_2}, and corresponding degree of dissociations α_1 and α_2, the relation [4.21] can be written as

$$\frac{\alpha_1}{\alpha_2} = \sqrt{\frac{K_{b_1}}{K_{b_2}}} \qquad \text{...[4.22]}$$

As degree of dissociation is the measure of the tendency of an acid to furnish H^+ ions, i.e., acid strength, the above equation can be written as

$$\text{Relative strength} = \frac{\text{Strength of base 1}}{\text{Strength of base 2}} = \sqrt{\frac{K_{b_1}}{K_{b_2}}} \qquad \text{...[4.23]}$$

Ionic Product of Water

Water is a weak electrolyte and dissociates feebly to release H^+ and OH^- ions.

$$H_2O \rightleftharpoons H^+ + OH^-$$

By applying law of chemical equilibrium, we get

$$K_C = \frac{[H^+][OH^-]}{[H_2O]}$$

or $\quad K_C [H_2O] = [H^+][OH^-]$

or $\quad K_w = [H^+][OH^-]$ ...[4.24]

K_w is known as the ionic product of water, which is a constant at a given temperature. At 25°C, the value of ionic product is 1.4×10^{-14} mol^2 l^{-2}. With the increase in temperature, the equilibrium for dissociation of water shifts in the forward direction, increasing the concentrations of both H^+ and OH^- ions. Thus, K_w increases with the increase in temperature. The value of K_w at different temperatures is given as follows:

Temperature (°C)	**K_w value (mol^2 l^{-2})**
0	0.11×10^{-14}
10	0.30×10^{-14}
25	1.00×10^{-14}
40	2.92×10^{-14}
50	4.47×10^{-14}

For pure water, $[H^+] = [OH^-]$

$$K_w = [H^+][OH^-]$$
$$= [H^+]^2$$

or $\quad [H^+] = \sqrt{K_w}$

$$= \sqrt{10^{-14}}$$
$$= 10^{-7} \text{ mol l}^{-1}$$

From above relation, an important conclusion regarding the nature of aqueous solution can be made. An aqueous solution with $[H^+] > 10^{-7}$ mol l^{-1} will be acidic and that with $[H^+] < 10^{-7}$ mol l^{-1} will be basic.

Concept of pH

Hydrogen ion concentration can be used to express the nature of an aqueous solution. However, hydrogen ion concentration is often too small to realize, convey others, and use in a lengthy process of calculation. In order to avoid these difficulties, Sorensen introduced a new term pH (p stands for 'potenz' in German). It is defined as the negative logarithm of the hydrogen ion concentration in mol l^{-1} with base 10.

$$pH = -\log [H^+]$$ ...[4.25]

For pure water, $[H^+] = [OH^-] = 10^{-7}$ mol l^{-1}

We know, $pH = -\log [H^+]$

$$= -\log 10^{-7}$$
$$= 7$$

For acidic solutions, $[H^+] > 10^{-7}$ mol l^{-1}, therefore, pH < 7.

For basic solutions, $[H^+] < 10^{-7}$ mol l^{-1}, therefore, pH > 7.

pH Scale

For expressing H^+ ion concentration in terms of pH for different aqueous solutions a scale has been developed which is known as pH scale. On this scale, the pH values range from 0 to 14. The scale is shown in Fig. 4.2.

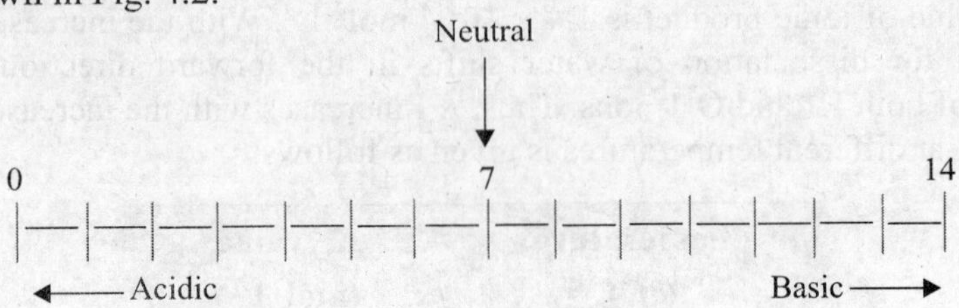

Fig. 4.2 pH scale

Effect of Temperature on pH

With the increase in temperature, the dissociation equilibrium shifts in the forward direction releasing more and more H^+ ions. This ultimately increases $[H^+]$ and thereby lowers the pH.

Note:

1. $pOH = -\log [OH^-]$
2. $pK_w = -\log K_w$
3. $pH + pOH = 14$

   At 298 K, $[H^+] [OH^-] = 10^{-14}$

   or $-\log [H^+] + \{-\log [OH^-]\} = -\log 10^{-14}$

   or $pH + pOH = 14$
4. $[H^+] = 10^{-pH}$
5. $[OH^-] = 10^{-pOH}$

pH Calculations

Type I: For strong acids

In such a case, the dissociation is almost 100 %. Therefore, H^+ ion concentration can be directly obtained.

Example 4.13

Find the pH of 0.02 M HCl.

Solution

HCl being a strong electrolyte dissociates to complete extent in aqueous solution.

HCl	$\longrightarrow$	H^+	+	Cl^-
0.02		0		0 M
0		0.02		0.02 M

$[H^+] = 0.02$ M

Now, $pH = -\log [H^+]$

$= -\log (0.02)$

$= -\log (2 \times 10^{-2})$

$= -\log 2 + 2 \log 10$

$= -0.3010 + 2$

$= 1.699$

Type II: For strong bases

In such a case, again the dissociation is almost 100 %. Therefore, OH^- ion concentration can be directly obtained. From this, pOH can be calculated and then pH can be calculated by applying the relation pH + pOH = 14.

Example 4.14

Find pH of 0.001 NaOH.

Solution

NaOH being a strong electrolyte dissociates to complete extent in aqueous solution.

NaOH	$\longrightarrow$	Na^+	+	OH^-
0.001		0		0 M
0		0.001		0.001 M

$[OH^-] = 0.001$ M

Now, $pOH = -\log [OH^-]$

$= -\log (0.001)$

$= -\log (1 \times 10^{-3})$

$= -\log 1 + 3 \log 10$

$= 3$

But pH + pOH = 14

or pH = 14 – pOH

or pH = 14 – 3 = 11

Type III: Weak acid and base

In such a case, the dissociation is not complete. Here concentration of hydrogen ion is calculated from dissociation constant or degree of dissociation.

Example 4.15

Find the pH of 0.1 M acetic acid. The dissociation constant of the acid is 1.8×10^{-5} at 298 K.

Solution

Let x be the amount of acid that has undergone dissociation. The equilibrium can be presented as follows:

$$\begin{array}{lccc} CH_3COOH & \rightleftharpoons & CH_3COO^- & + & H^+ \\ 0.1 & & 0 & & 0\text{ M} \\ (0.1 - x) & & x & & x\text{ M} \end{array}$$

$$K_a = \frac{[CH_3COO^-][H^+]}{[CH_3COOH]}$$

$$= \frac{[CH_3COO^-][H^+]}{[CH_3COOH]}$$

$$= \frac{x^2}{0.1 - x} = \frac{x^2}{0.1}$$

or $x = \sqrt{0.1\,K_a}$

$$= \sqrt{0.1(1.8 \times 10^{-5})}$$

$$= 1.34 \times 10^{-3}\text{ M}$$

Now, $pH = -\log(1.34 \times 10^{-3})$

$$= 2.87$$

Example 4.16

Find the pH of 0.002 M acetic acid assuming 2.5% dissociation at this dilution.

Solution

The dissociation equilibrium is as follows:

$$\begin{array}{lccc} CH_3COOH & \rightleftharpoons & CH_3COO^- & + & H^+ \\ 0.02 & & 0 & & 0\text{ M} \\ (0.02 - 0.02 \times 0.023) & & 0.02 \times 0.023 & & 0.02 \times 0.023\text{ M} \end{array}$$

Now, $[H^+] = 0.02 \times 0.025 = 0.0005$ M

$$pH = -\log(0.0005)$$

$$= -\log(5 \times 10^{-4})$$

$$= 4 - \log 5$$

$$= 4 - 0.699$$

$$= 3.301$$

Type IV: pH after mixing of acid and/or base

Example 4.17

Calculate the pH of a solution obtained by mixing 100 ml of 0.1 M HCl and 400 ml of 0.2 M H_2SO_4.

Solution

Meq of H^+ ions from HCl = $100 \times 0.1 = 10$

Meq of H^+ ions from $H_2SO_4 = 400 \times 0.2 \times 2 = 160$

Total Meq of H^+ ions in solution = 10 + 160 = 170

$$[H^+] = \frac{170}{500} = 0.34$$

Now, $pH = -\log 0.34$

$= 0.47$

Example 4.18

Find the pH of a solution containing 150 ml of 0.1 M HCl and 10 ml of 1 M NaOH.

Solution

	HCl	+	NaOH	⟶	NaCl	+	H_2O
Meq before reaction,	150 × 0.1 = 15		10 × 1 = 10		0		0
Meq after reaction,	5		0		10		10

$$[H^+] = \frac{5}{160} = 0.031\ M$$

$pH = -\log 0.031$

$= 1.509$

Type V: Very dilute acids ($H^+ \leq 10^{-7}$)

In such a case, the contribution of H^+ ions from both acid and H_2O is considered.

Example 4.19

Find the pH of 10^{-8} M HNO_3 solution.

Solution

HCl being a strong electrolyte dissociates completely and H^+ ions coming from H_2O are, say, x mole per liter.

$$HCl \longrightarrow \underbrace{H^+ + Cl^-}_{10^{-8}}$$

$$\underset{}{H_2O} \rightleftharpoons \underset{x}{H^+} + \underset{x}{OH^-}$$

Now at equilibrium, $[H^+] = (10^{-8} + x)$ and $[OH^-] = x$

But $K_W = [H^+]\,[OH^-] = 10^{-14}$

or $(10^{-8} + x)\,(x) = 10^{-14}$

or $x^2 + 10^{-8}\,x - 10^{-14} = 0$

or $x = \dfrac{-10^{-8} \pm \sqrt{(10^{-8})^2 - 4\,(10^{-14})}}{2}$

$= 9.5 \times 10^{-8}$ M

Thus, $[H^+] = 10^{-8} + 9.5 \times 10^{-8} = 10.5 \times 10^{-8}$ M

$$pH = -\log (10.5 \times 10^{-8})$$
$$= 6.98$$

Type VI: Finding concentration of H^+/ OH^- ions from pH

Example 4.20

The pH of a fruit juice is 1.5. Find the concentration of H^+ ions in the juice.

Solution

$$[H^+] = 10^{-pH}$$
$$= 10^{-1.5}$$
$$= 3.16 \times 10^{-2} \text{ M}$$

Example 4.21

Find the concentrations of H^+ and HCO_3^- ions in a 0.01 M solution of carbonic acid if the pH of the solution is 4.2 ($K = 4.45 \times 10^{-7}$).

Solution

$$[H^+] = 10^{-pH}$$
$$= 10^{-4.2}$$
$$= 6.31 \times 10^{-5} \text{ M.}$$

$$H_2CO_3 \rightleftharpoons H^+ + HCO_3^-$$

$$K = \frac{[H^+][HCO_3^-]}{[H_2CO_3]}$$

or $$[HCO_3^-] = \frac{K\,[H_2CO_3]}{[HCO_3^-]}$$

$$= \frac{4.45 \times 10^{-7} \times 0.01}{6.31 \times 10^{-5}}$$

$$= 7.052 \times 10^{-5}$$

Buffer

A buffer solution is the one which resists the change in its pH upon the addition of a little amount of acid or base.

Types of Buffer

Buffer solutions can be broadly classified into two categories:

1. Simple buffer: It is a solution of the salt of weak acid and weak base, e.g., solutions of CH_3COONH_4, $(NH_4)_2\,CO_3$, etc.
2. Mixed buffer: Again mixed buffer can be of two types:
   (a) Acidic mixed buffer: It is a mixture of solutions of a weak acid and its salt with a strong base, e.g., CH_3COOH and CH_3COONa, H_2CO_3 and $NaHCO_3$, etc.
   (b) Basic mixed buffer: It is a mixture of weak base and its salt with a strong acid, e.g., NH_4OH and NH_4Cl, NH_4OH and NH_4NO_3, etc.

Buffer Action

The mechanism by the virtue of which a buffer resists the change in its pH is known as buffer action. Let us try to understand the buffer action by taking examples of different buffers.

Simple buffer

The addition of acid releases H^+ ions which are taken up by CH_3COO^- ions to form acetic acid. Acetic acid being a weak electrolyte does not further dissociate appreciably. Thus, the concentration of H^+ ions remains unaltered in the solution. Further as per Le Chatelier's principle, with the consumption of acetate ions, the equilibrium shifts in the forward direction releasing more and more such ions. On the other hand, the addition of base releases OH^- ions which are consumed by NH_4^+ ions forming NH_4OH. Being a weak electrolyte, ammonium hydroxide does not further dissociate appreciably. The result being the concentration of OH^- ions remains unchanged and so also the pH.

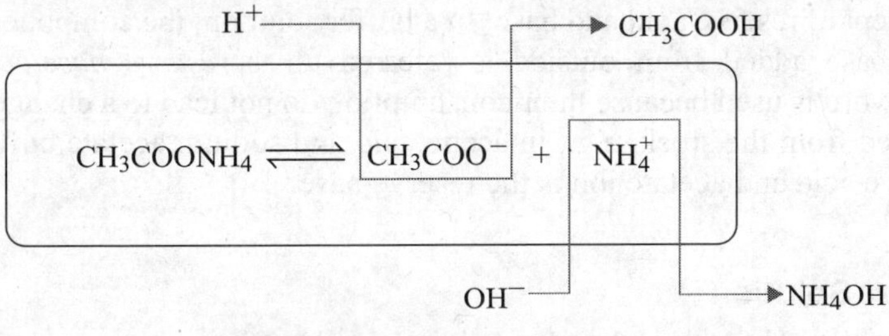

Fig. 4.3 Simple buffer

Acidic mixed buffer

The addition of acid releases H^+ ions, which are taken up by CH_3COO^- ions to form acetic acid. Acetic acid being a weak electrolyte does not further dissociate appreciably. Thus, the concentration of H^+ ions remains unaltered in the solution. On the other hand, the addition of base releases OH^- ions, which are consumed by H^+ ions forming H_2O. Being a weak electrolyte, water does not further dissociate appreciably. The result being the concentration of OH^- ions remains unchanged and so also the pH. Further as per Le Chatelier's principle, with the consumption of hydrogen ions, the equilibrium for dissociation of acetic acid shifts in the forward direction releasing more and more hydrogen ions.

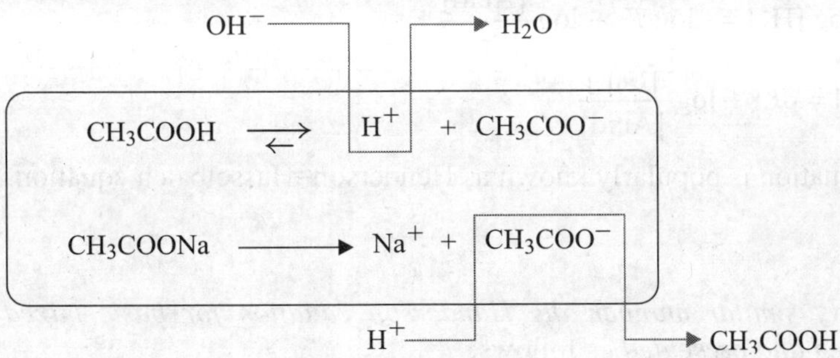

Fig. 4.4 Acidic mixed buffer

Basic mixed buffer

In a very similar manner, the buffer action of basic mixed buffer can be explained. The scheme is presented schematically in Fig. 4.5.

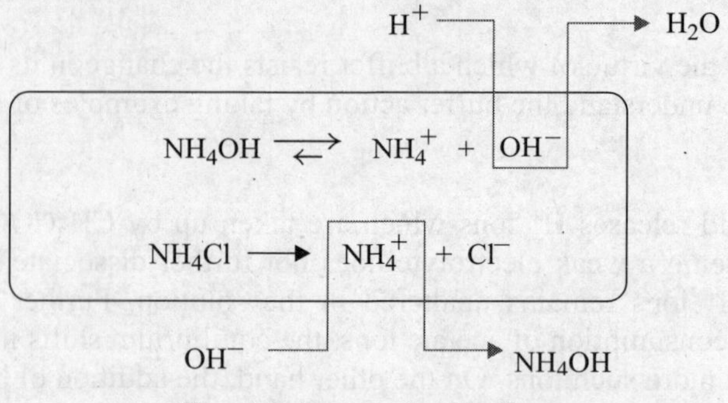

Fig. 4.5 Basic mixed buffer

> **Note:**
>
> The concept of reserve acid and base: In a buffer solution, the component that consumes the acid/base added from outside is referred to as *reserve base/acid*, respectively. Reserve word is used because their consumption do not lead to a change in pH, and they are utilized from the stock, e.g., in acetic acid and sodium acetate buffer, acetic acid is the reserve acid and acetate ion is the reserve base.

pH of a Buffer Solution

Let us first consider pH for the following acidic mixed buffer:

$$\underbrace{HA}_{\text{Acid}} \rightleftharpoons H^+ + \underbrace{A^-}_{\text{Salt}}$$

$$K_a = \frac{[H^+][A^-]}{[HA]}$$

$$\text{or} \quad [H^+] = K_a \frac{[HA]}{[A^-]}$$

$$= K_a \frac{[\text{Acid}]}{[\text{Salt}]}$$

$$\text{or} \quad -\log [H^+] = -\log K_a - \log \frac{[\text{Acid}]}{[\text{Salt}]}$$

$$\text{or} \quad \text{pH} = \text{p}K_a + \log \frac{[\text{Salt}]}{[\text{Acid}]} \qquad \ldots[4.26]$$

The above equation is popularly known as Henderson–Hasselbalch equation.

> **Note:**
>
> In a very *similar manner, the Handerson equation for basic mixed buffer can be developed and presented a*s follows:
>
> $$\text{pOH} = \text{p}K_b + \log \frac{[\text{Salt}]}{[\text{Base}]} \qquad \ldots[4.27]$$
>
> Then pH = 14 − pOH

Buffer Capacity

It is the ability of a buffer to resist the change in its pH upon the addition of an acid or a base. It may be defined as the number of moles of an acid or base added for per liter of buffer solution, so as to bring a unit change in pH.

$$\text{Buffer capacity } (\beta) = \frac{\text{Number of moles of acid or base added per liter}}{\text{Change in pH}} \quad [4.28]$$

Note:

1. pH of a buffer after the addition of an acid or a base from outside neglecting the volume change:

After the addition of an acid

Let the buffer contains a mole liter^{-1} of acid and b mole liter^{-1} of salt. Again, if x mole liter^{-1} of acid is added, it furnishes x mole liter^{-1} of H^+ ions. These excess H^+ ions combine with x mole of A^- ions, pushing the equilibrium to left, forming x mole of acid.

	HA	$\rightleftharpoons$	H^+	+	A^-
Before addition of acid	a				b
After addition of acid	$(a+x)$				$(b-x)$

Now, replacing the acid and salt concentrations in the Handerson equation

$$pH = pK_a + \log \frac{[\text{Salt}]}{[\text{Acid}]}$$

$$pH = pK_a + \log \frac{b-x}{a+x} \quad \ldots[4.29]$$

After the addition of a base

If x mole liter^{-1} of base is added, it furnishes x mole liter^{-1} of OH^- ions. These excess OH^- ions combine with x mole of H^+ ions of buffer, forming water. Thus, equilibrium shifts to the right, so as to release x mole of H^+ ions.

	HA	$\rightleftharpoons$	H^+	+	A^-
Before addition of base	a				b
After addition of base	$(a-x)$				$(b+x)$

Now, replacing the base and salt concentrations in the Handerson equation

$$pH = pK_a + \log \frac{[\text{Salt}]}{[\text{Acid}]}$$

$$= pK_a + \log \frac{b+x}{a-x} \quad \ldots[4.30]$$

2. **Maximum buffer capacity**
Buffer capacity is maximum only when the ratio of [salt]/[acid] or [salt]/[base] is unity. Buffer capacity decreases if the ratio is less than 1 or more than 1.

Type I: Finding the pH of acidic/basic buffer

Example 4.22

Find the pH of a solution obtained by mixing 2 g of acetic acid, 1.5 g of sodium acetate, and making the volume equal to 250 ml. Given that the dissociation constant of acetic acid is 1.8×10^{-5} at 298 K.

Solution

$$[CH_3COOH] = \frac{2}{60} \times \frac{1000}{250} = 0.133 \text{ M}$$

$$[CH_3COONa] = \frac{1.5}{82} \times \frac{1000}{250} = 0.073 \text{ M}$$

$$pK_a = -\log K_a$$
$$= -\log (1.8 \times 10^{-5})$$
$$= 4.745$$

Applying Henderson equation

$$pH = pK_a + \log \frac{[\text{Salt}]}{[\text{Acid}]}$$
$$= pK_a + \log \frac{[CH_3COONa]}{[CH_3COOH]}$$
$$= 4.745 + \log \frac{0.073}{0.133}$$
$$= 4.485$$

Example 4.23

A buffer solution contains 0.25 M NH_4OH and 0.5 M NH_4Cl. Calculate the pH of the buffer. The dissociation constant of the base is 1.8×10^{-5}.

Solution

$$pOH = pK_b + \log \frac{[\text{Salt}]}{[\text{Base}]}$$
$$= -\log (1.8 \times 10^{-5}) + \log \frac{0.5}{0.25}$$
$$= 4.745 + 0.301$$
$$= 5.046$$

Now, $pH = 14 - 5.046$
$$= 8.954$$

Type II: pH of buffers after addition of acid/base from outside

Example 4.24

Find the change in pH of a buffer solution containing 0.5 mole liter^{-1} each of acetic acid and sodium acetate upon the addition of (a) 0.02 mole liter^{-1} of HCl and (b) 0.02 mole liter^{-1} of NaOH. Given that the K_a of acid is 1.8×10^{-5}.

Solution

(a)

	CH_3COOH	$\rightleftharpoons$	H^+ +	CH_3COO^-
Before addition of acid	0.5			0.5
After addition of acid	(0.5 + 0.02)			(0.5 – 0.02)

$$\text{pH} = \text{p}K_a + \log\frac{[\text{Salt}]}{[\text{Acid}]}$$
$$= -\log(1.8 \times 10^{-5}) + \log\frac{0.52}{0.48}$$
$$= 4.745 + 0.035$$
$$= 4.780$$

(b)

	$CH_3\ COOH$	$\rightleftharpoons$	H^+ +	CH_3COO^-
Before addition of base	0.5			0.5
After addition of base	(0.5 – 0.02)			(0.5 + 0.02)

$$\text{pH} = \text{p}K_a + \log\frac{[\text{Salt}]}{[\text{Acid}]}$$
$$= -\log(1.8 \times 10^{-5}) + \log\frac{0.48}{0.52}$$
$$= 4.745 - 0.035$$
$$= 4.710$$

Type III: Finding buffer capacity

Example 4.25

Calculate the change in pH of a buffer solution containing 0.2 M each of NH_3 and NH_4Cl upon the addition of 0.02 M HCl assuming no change in the volume. Also, find the buffer capacity. Given that the dissociation constant of base is 1.8×10^{-5}.

Solution

	NH_4OH	$\rightleftharpoons$	NH_4^+	+ OH^-
Before addition of acid	0.2		0.2	
After addition of acid	(0.2 – 0.02)		(0.2 + 0.02)	

Now, pH before the addition of acid

$$pOH = pK_b + \log \frac{[Salt]}{[Base]}$$

$$= -\log (1.8 \times 10^{-5}) + \log \frac{0.2}{0.2}$$

$$= 4.745$$

Now, pH = 14 – 4.745 = 9.255

pH after the addition of acid

$$pOH = pK_b + \log \frac{[Salt]}{[Base]}$$

$$= -\log (1.8 \times 10^{-5}) + \log \frac{0.22}{0.18}$$

$$= 4.745 + 0.086$$

$$= 4.831$$

Now, pH = 14 – 4.831 = 9.169

Thus, change in pH = 9.255 – 9.169 = 0.086.

$$\text{Buffer Capacity } (\beta) = \frac{\text{Number of moles of acid added per litre}}{\text{Change in pH}}$$

or $$\beta = \frac{0.02}{0.086}$$

$$= 0.233$$

Type IV: To prepare a buffer of required pH

Example 4.26

A chemist needs one liter of a buffer solution of pH 5.7. How many grams of sodium formate should he add to one liter of 0.02 M formic acid to make the required buffer? Given that the dissociation constant of formic acid is 1.8×10^{-4}.

Solution

$$pH = pK_a + \log \frac{[Salt]}{[Acid]}$$

or $$5.7 = -\log (1.8 \times 10^{-4}) + \log \frac{[Salt]}{0.02}$$

or $$\log \frac{[Salt]}{0.02} = 5.7 - 3.745$$

or $$\frac{[Salt]}{0.02} = 10^{1.955} = 90.157$$

or $$[Salt] = 90.157 \times 0.02 = 1.803 \text{ M}$$

The amount of salt required per liter to have a buffer of pH 5.7 = 1.803 × 68 =122.6 g

Example 4.27

Find the composition of an acidic buffer made of HA and NaA of total molarity 0.3, having pH 4.0 and $K_a = 1.8 \times 10^{-5}$.

Solution

Let the concentration of salt be a mole liter^{-1}. Then the concentration of acid will be $(0.3 - a)$.

Now,

$$pH = pK_a + \log \frac{[\text{Salt}]}{[\text{Acid}]}$$

or $$4.0 = -\log (1.8 \times 10^{-5}) + \log \frac{a}{0.3 - a}$$

or $$4.0 = 4.745 + \log \frac{a}{0.3 - a}$$

or $$\log \frac{a}{0.3 - a} = -0.745$$

or $$\frac{a}{0.3 - a} = 10^{-0.745} = 0.18$$

or $$a = (0.3 - a) \times 0.18$$

$$= 0.046$$

Thus, [NaA] = 0.046 M

[HA] = 0.3 – 0.046 = 0.254 M

Indicators

Acid–base indicators are weak acids or bases, usually large water soluble organic compounds. The acid form of such an indicator has a characteristic color, which is different from the basic form. These two forms remain in equilibrium.

$$\underbrace{\text{H–Ind}_{(aq)}}_{\text{Color } x} + H_2O_{(1)} \rightleftharpoons H_3O^+_{(aq)} + \underbrace{\text{Ind}^-_{(aq)}}_{\text{Color } y}$$

$$K_{\text{Ind}} = \frac{[H_3O^+][\text{Ind}^-]}{[\text{H–Ind}]}$$

or $$[H_3O^+] = \frac{K_{\text{Ind}}[\text{H–Ind}]}{[\text{Ind}^-]}$$

or $$-\log [H_3O^+] = -\log K_{\text{Ind}} - \log \frac{[\text{H–Ind}]}{[\text{Ind}^-]}$$

or $$pH = pK_{\text{Ind}} + \log \frac{[\text{Ind}^-]}{[\text{H–Ind}]} \qquad \ldots[4.31]$$

Color change of indicators is not observed at a specific pH rather it occurs over a range of pH. In general, the pH range of an indicator is given as pH = $pK_{\text{Ind}} \pm 1$. Some common indicators with their pH range are given as follows:

Indicator	Color [Acid–Base medium]	pH range
Methyl orange	Red – Orange	3.1 – 4.4
Methyl red	Red – yellow	4.4 – 6.0
Phenolphthalein	Colorless – Pink	8.3–10.0
Phenol red	Yellow – Red	6.4 – 8.2
Bromothymol blue	Yellow – Blue	6.0 – 7.6

Acid–Base Titrations

The characteristics of an acid-base neutralization titration can be summarized in terms of titration curves, which are usually plotted by taking pH as a function of volume of the titrant. The curve can be plotted by theoretical calculations, and conclusions can be drawn from the same regarding the feasibility, the expected accuracy of the titration, the point of equivalence, and the choice of the proper indicator. Let us look into the nature of such a curve as shown in Fig. 4.6. The pH near the equivalence point is the characteristic of such a curve. At equivalence point, the slope [d(pH)/dV] is the highest, i.e., the second derivative [d^2(pH)/dV^2] is zero, which makes it an inflation point. The significant change in pH at equivalence point indicates that only a small drop of titrant can bring a remarkable change in pH at this point. The equivalence point is the theoretical end point, while the end point determined from color change in indicator is the experimental estimate of the equivalence point. A suitable indicator is the one which has as narrow pH range as possible that lies entirely on the steep part of the titration curve.

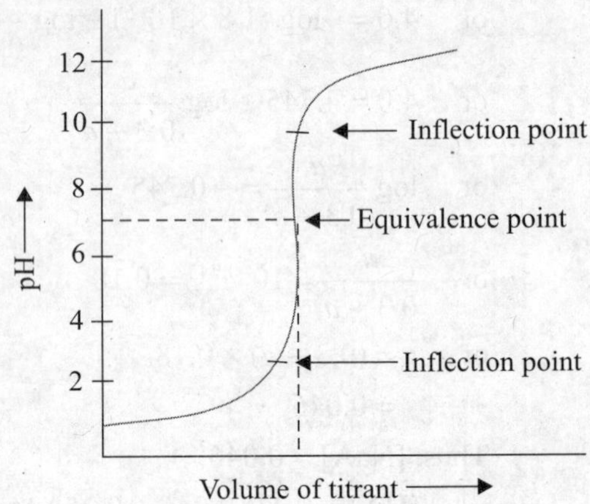

Fig. 4.6 Titration curve

Indicator Selection in Different Acid–base Titrations

1. *Strong acid–strong base titration*

Let us consider titration between 25 ml 0.1 N HCl and 0.1 N NaOH. The titration curve is shown in Fig. 4.7. In the curve, pH rises slowly in the beginning and near equivalence point pH changes abruptly from 3.0 to 9.0, and the curve appears vertical. The end point lies at pH 7.0. After this, the pH again rises slowly due to the presence of excess base. Here, indicators with pH range 3.0–9.0 such as methyl red and phenolpthalein are suitable.

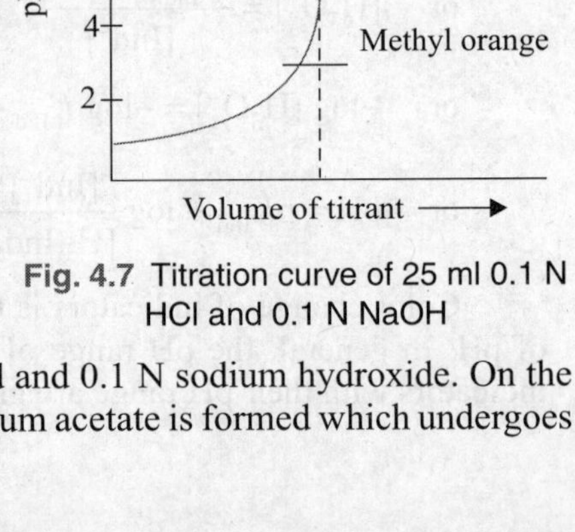

Fig. 4.7 Titration curve of 25 ml 0.1 N HCl and 0.1 N NaOH

2. *Weak acid–strong base titration*

Let us consider titration between 25 ml 0.1 N acetic acid and 0.1 N sodium hydroxide. On the addition of sodium hydroxide solution to acetic acid, sodium acetate is formed which undergoes hydrolysis to result in a basic solution. Therefore, the end point lies at a pH somewhat higher than 7.0. The titration curve is shown in Fig. 4.8. A weak acid only partially dissociates from its salt. The pH will rise normally at first, but as it reaches a zone where the solution seems to be buffered, the slope levels out. After this zone, the pH rises sharply through its equivalence point from 7.0 to 9.0 and levels out again like a strong acid/strong base reaction. Here, indicator such as Phenolphthalein is suitable.

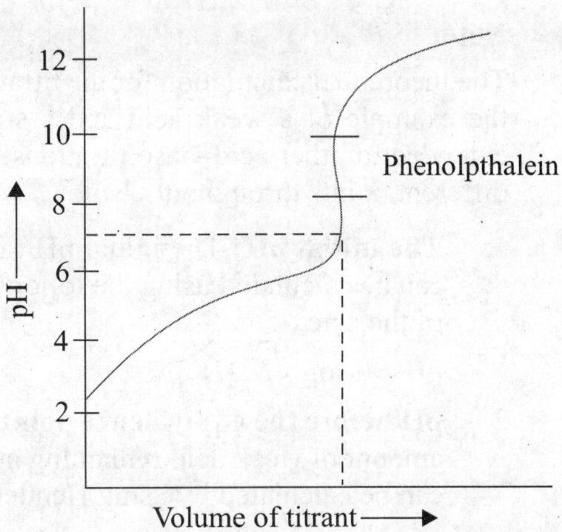

Fig. 4.8 Titration curve of 25 ml 0.1 N acetic acid and 0.1 N sodium hydroxide

2. *Strong acid – weak base titration*

Let us consider titration between 25 ml 0.1 N HCl and 0.1 N NH_4OH. On the addition of ammonium hydroxide solution to hydrochloric acid, NH_4Cl is formed which undergoes hydrolysis to result in an acidic solution. Therefore, the end point lies at a pH somewhat less than 7.0. The titration curve is shown in Fig. 4.9. In the curve, pH rises slowly in the beginning, and near equivalence point, pH changes abruptly from 3.0 to 7.0. Beyond this, pH variation is not much. Here, methyl orange with a pH range 3.1–4.4 is a suitable indicator.

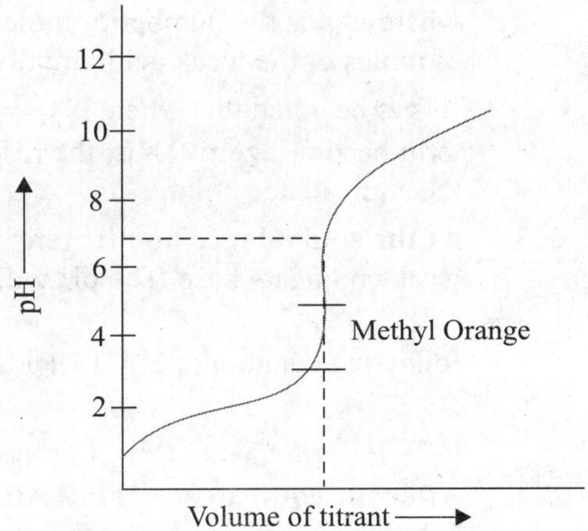

Fig. 4.9 Titration curve of 25 ml 0.1 N HCl and 0.1 N NH_4OH

3. *Weak acid–weak base titration*

Let us consider titration between 25 ml 0.1 N acetic acid and 0.1 N NH_4OH. The titration curve is shown in Fig. 4.10. Here, the vertical portion in the curve is missing and there is no sharp change of pH near equivalence point. Here, no indicator is suitable.

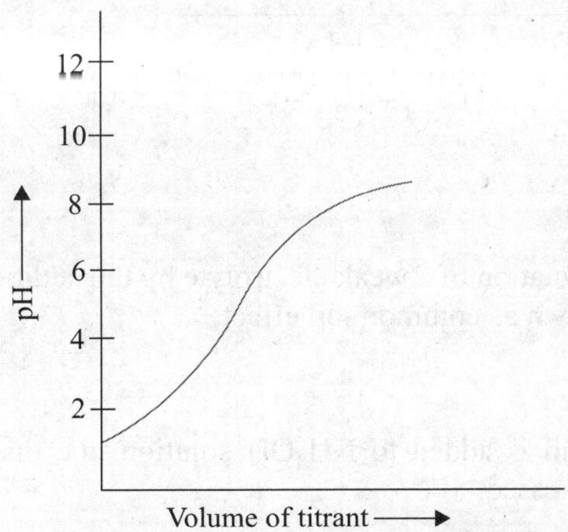

Fig. 4.10 Titration curve of 25 ml 0.1 N acetic acid and 0.1 N NH_4OH

Note:

The theoretical calculation for the titration curve can be made. Let us illustrate by taking the example of a weak acid and a strong base titration. The same approach may be extended to other acid–base titrations. The pH during the titration can be calculated at different points throughout.

1. **The initial pH:** The initial pH (approximately) for a weak acid solution in water can be calculated using the following equation. Here K_a is the dissociation constant of the acid.

   $pH = -\log\sqrt{K_a[H^+]}$

2. **pH before the equivalence point:** pH before the equivalence point depends on the amount of weak acid remaining and the amount of conjugate base formed. The pH can be calculated by using Henderson equation formatted as per the requirement.

   $$pH = pK_a + \log\left[\frac{n_{OH^-}}{n_{HA} + n_{OH^-}}\right]$$

   where n_{OH} is the number of moles of the strong base added and n_{HA} is the number of moles of the weak acid initially present.

   It is to be noted that when, $n_{OH^-} = n_{HA} + n_{OH^-}$, then the ratio becomes 1 and the log term becomes zero. Thus, the pH will be equal the pK_a, which occurs half-way to the equivalence point.

3. **At the equivalence point:** Here, the weak acid is consumed and converted into its weak conjugate base. The pH will be greater than 7 and can be calculated from the following equation: $pH = 14 + \log\sqrt{\dfrac{[HA]\,[OH^-]\,K_w}{([HA]+[OH^-])\,K_a}}$

   Here $[HA] \times V_{Acid} = [OH^-] \times V_{Base}$

4. **After the equivalence point:** After the equivalence point, the solution will contain both the conjugate base of the acid and the strong base of the titrant. However, the base of the titrant is stronger than the conjugate base of the acid, and control the pH in this region. The pH can be calculated by using the following relation:

   $$pH = 14 + \log\sqrt{\frac{[OH^-]\times V_{Base} - [HA]\times V_{Acid}}{V_{Acid} + V_{Base}}}$$

Common Ion Effect

The suppression of the dissociation of a weak electrolyte by the addition of a strong electrolyte having a common ion is known as common ion effect.

Illustrations

1. When NH_4Cl solid is added to NH_4OH solution, the dissociation of ammonium hydroxide is suppressed.

   $NH_4OH \rightleftharpoons NH_4^+ + OH^-$

$$NH_4Cl \longrightarrow \underbrace{NH_4^+}_{\text{Common ion}} + Cl^-$$

Upon the addition of NH_4Cl, the concentration of ammonium ion substantially increases. Now as per the Le Chatelier's principle, the equilibrium gets shifted in the reverse direction, so as to consume the extra ammonium ions. The result being the dissociation of NH_4OH, which is a weak electrolyte, is suppressed.

2. During qualitative analysis, dissociation of H_2S is suppressed by passing through dil. HCl solution.

$$H_2S \rightleftharpoons 2H^+ + S^{2-}$$

$$HCl \longrightarrow \underbrace{H^+}_{\text{Common ion}} + Cl^-$$

HCl is a strong electrolyte, which increases H^+ ions substantially. The equilibrium for the dissociation of H_2S shifts in the reverse direction, so as to consume the excess H^+ ions.

Solubility Product

In saturated solutions of sparingly soluble salts such as AgCl, Ag_2SO_4, and $PbSO_4$, there exists a dynamic equilibrium between the dissociated ions in solution phase, and parent insoluble salt in solid phase. For a hypothetical sparingly soluble salt A_xB_y, the equilibrium can be represented as

$$A_xB_{y\,(s)} \rightleftharpoons x\,A^{y+}{}_{(aq)} + y\,B^{x-}{}_{(aq)}$$

Applying the law of chemical equilibrium

$$K_C = \frac{[A^{y+}]^x\,[B^{x-}]^y}{[A_xB_y]}$$

$$= [A_xB_y] = [A^{y+}]^x\,[B^{x-}]^y$$

or $\quad K_{SP} = [A^{y+}]^x\,[B^{x-}]^y$

The activity of the solid is unity for which the term $[A_xB_y]$ does not appear in the final expression. K_{SP} is the solubility product constant, which is equal to the product of the molar concentration of ions present with each term raised to the power equal to the number of times it appears in the dissociation expression.

Relation between (K_{SP}) and Solubility (S)

Let us consider a saturated solution of a hypothetical electrolyte A_xB_y. Let S be the molar solubility of the electrolyte. Here, the solubility of a solute refers to the amount of the same dissolved per liter of solvent to form a saturated solution at a specified temperature.

$$A_xB_{y\,(s)} \rightleftharpoons x\,A^{y+}{}_{(aq)} + y\,B^{x-}{}_{(aq)}$$

$$\qquad\qquad xS \qquad\qquad yS$$

$[A^{y+}] = xS$ mole liter^{-1}

$[B^{x-}] = xS$ mole liter^{-1}

Now,

$$K_{SP} = [A^{y+}]^x [B^{x-}]^y$$
$$= [xS]^x [xS]^y$$
$$K_{SP} = x^x y^y S^{x+y} \quad ...[4.32]$$

For example, for AgCl, $K_{SP} = S^2$; for Ag_2SO_4, $K_{SP} = 2^2\, 1^1\, S^3 = 4S^3$; for As_2S_3, $K_{SP} = 2^2\, 3^3\, S^5 = 108\, S^3$.

Note:

1. The product of the concentration of ions as defined above is also known as ionic product (IP). When the solution is saturated, the same product is referred to as solubility product, which is a constant at a specified temperature.
2. IP can be changed by providing one or both types of ions from outside; however, K_{SP} is a constant irrespective of the source of the ions.
3. In a solution, usually IP is less than K_{SP}. For a saturated solution, IP = K_{SP}. When IP temporarily exceeds K_{SP}, the oppositely charged ions readily combine among themselves to form the electrolyte, i.e., precipitation occurs. This condition is known as the condition of precipitation.

Type I: To find K_{SP} from solubility (S) and vice versa

Example 4.28

The solubility of AgCl in water at 25°C is 1.8×10^{-3} g l^{-1}. Find K_{SP} of AgCl at the same temperature.

Solution

$$\text{Solubility of AgCl} = 1.8 \times 10^{-3}\ \text{g l}^{-1}$$
$$= \frac{1.8 \times 10^{-3}}{143.5}\ \text{mol l}^{-1}$$
$$= 1.254 \times 10^{-5}\ \text{mol l}^{-1}$$

Now, $K_{SP} = S^2$

$$= (1.254 \times 10^{-5})^2$$
$$= 1.573 \times 10^{-10}\ \text{mol}^2\ \text{l}^{-2}$$

Example 4.29

The solubility product of SrF_2 is 7.98×10^{-10} at a given temperature. Find its solubility.

Solution

$$K_{SP} = 4S^3$$

or $S = \sqrt[3]{\frac{K_{SP}}{4}}$

$$= \sqrt[3]{\frac{7.89 \times 10^{-10}}{4}}$$

$$= 5.84 \times 10^{-4} \text{ mol l}^{-1}$$

Type II: To find solubility in presence of a common ion

Example 4.30

K_{SP} of AgCl is 1.5×10^{-10} at 25°C. Find its solubility in the presence of 0.2 M $AgNO_3$.

Solution

$$AgCl \rightleftharpoons \underset{S}{Ag^+} + \underset{S}{Cl^-}$$

$$AgNO_3 \longrightarrow \underbrace{Ag^+}_{0.2} + \underbrace{NO_3^-}_{0.2}$$

$$K_{SP} = [Ag^+][Cl^-]$$

$$= (0.2 + S)(S)$$

$$= 0.2\,S \text{ [as } S << 0.2]$$

Now, $0.2\,S = 1.5 \times 10^{-10}$

or $S = 7.5 \times 10^{-10}$ mol l^{-1}

Applications

1. To test whether precipitation will occur on mixing of two solutions: After mixing of the two solutions, concentrations of both cation and anion present in the substance whose precipitation is to be tested is estimated. Subsequently, the ionic product is calculated and compared with the K_{SP}. If ionic product exceeds K_{SP}, then precipitation occurs.

Example 4.31

Equal volumes of 0.02 M calcium chloride and 0.04 M sodium sulphate are mixed. Will a precipitate form? K_{SP} of calcium sulphate is 2.4×10^{-5}.

Solution

$$[Ca^{2+}] = \frac{0.02}{2}$$

$$[SO_4^{2-}] = \frac{0.04}{2}$$

Now, IP = $[Ca^{2+}][SO_4^{2-}]$

$$= \left(\frac{0.02}{2}\right)\left(\frac{0.04}{2}\right)$$

$$= 8 \times 10^{-4}$$

Here IP > K_{SP}

Thus, precipitation of calcium sulfate will be there.

2. In qualitative analysis: The principle of solubility product along with ionic product plays an effective role in the separation of basic radicals into different groups in qualitative analysis.

(a) Gr-II (Cu^{2+}, Hg^{2+}, Pb^{2+}, Cd^{2+}, $As^{3+/5+}$, $Sn^{2+/4+}$, and Bi^{3+}): These radicals are precipitated as their sulphides by passing H_2S under pressure through the mixture solution acidified with dil. HCl.

$$H_2S \rightleftharpoons 2H^+ + \underbrace{S^{2-}}_{\text{Low conc.}}$$

$$HCl \longrightarrow \underbrace{H^+}_{\text{Common ion}} + Cl^-$$

H^+ ions obtained from HCl suppress the dissociation of weak acid, H_2S, lowering the concentration of S^{2-} ions. However, this lower concentration of sulphide ions is sufficient to make the ionic product Gr-II sulphides exceed solubility product causing their precipitation. The sulphides of other higher groups possess higher solubility product values, which cannot be achieved with this lower concentration of sulphide ions. Thus, higher group radicals remain in the solution.

(b) Gr-IIIA (Fe^{3+}, Al^{3+}, and Cr^{3+}): These radicals are precipitated as their hydroxides by adding excess NH_4OH solution in the presence of excess of NH_4Cl.

$$NH_4OH \rightleftharpoons NH_4^+ + \underbrace{OH^-}_{\text{Low conc.}}$$

$$NH_4Cl \longrightarrow \underbrace{NH_4^+}_{\text{Common ion}} + Cl^-$$

NH_4^+ ions obtained from NH_4Cl suppress the dissociation of weak base, NH_4OH, lowering the concentration of OH^- ions. However, this lower concentration of hydroxide ions is sufficient to make the ionic product of Gr-IIIA hydroxides exceed solubility product causing their precipitation. The hydroxides of other higher groups possess higher solubility product values, which cannot be achieved with this lower concentration of hydroxide ions. Thus, higher group radicals remain back in the solution.

(c) Gr-IIIB (Co^{2+}, Ni^{2+}, Zn^{2+}, and Mn^{2+}): These radicals are precipitated as their sulphides by passing H_2S gas through their ammoniacal solution saturated with NH_4Cl.

$$H_2S \rightleftharpoons 2H^+ + \underbrace{S^{2-}}_{\text{High conc.}}$$

$$NH_4OH \rightleftharpoons NH_4^+ + \underbrace{OH^-}_{\text{Low conc.}}$$

$$NH_4Cl \longrightarrow \underbrace{NH_4^+}_{\text{Common ion}} + Cl^-$$

NH_4^+ ions obtained from NH_4Cl suppress the dissociation of NH_4OH. Thus, OH^- concentration is maintained at lower level, which prevents the precipitation of Gr-IIIB radicals as their hydroxides. The OH^- ions obtained from ammonium hydroxide takes up H^+ ions obtained from H_2S to form water ($H^+ + OH^- \longrightarrow H_2O$), which does not dissociate further appreciably. As H^+ ions are removed, the dissociation equilibrium of H_2S shifts in the forward direction, increasing the concentration of sulphide ions. This high concentration of sulphide ions is enough to make the ionic product of Gr-IIIB sulphides exceed solubility product causing their precipitation. The sulphides of other higher groups possess higher solubility product values, which cannot be achieved with this lower concentration of sulphide ions. Thus, higher group radicals remain back in the solution.

(d) Gr-IV (Ca^{2+}, Sr^{2+}, and Ba^{2+}): These radicals are precipitated as their carbonates by adding saturated solution of $(NH_4)_2CO_3$ to ammoniacal mixture solution saturated with NH_4Cl.

$$(NH_4)_2CO_3 \rightleftharpoons NH_4^+ + \underbrace{CO_3^{2-}}_{\text{Low conc.}}$$

$$NH_4OH \rightleftharpoons NH_4^+ + \underbrace{OH^-}_{\text{Low conc.}}$$

$$NH_4Cl \longrightarrow \underbrace{NH_4^+}_{\text{Common ion}} + Cl^-$$

NH_4^+ ions obtained from NH_4Cl suppress the dissociation of both NH_4OH and $(NH_4)_2CO_3$. OH^- concentration is maintained at lower level, which prevents the precipitation of Gr-IV radicals as their hydroxides. However, this lower concentration of carbonate ions is sufficient to make the ionic product of Gr-IV carbonates exceed solubility product causing their precipitation. The carbonates of Gr-V radicals have higher solubility product values, which cannot be achieved with this lower concentration of carbonate ions. Thus, Gr-V radicals remain back in the solution.

Salt Hydrolysis

Upon addition to water, salts dissociate to release their constituent cations and anions. These ions then interact with water resulting in an acidic, a basic, or a neutral solution. Such a phenomenon of interaction of cations and anions of a salt with water leading to either an acidic, a basic, or a neutral solution is known as salt hydrolysis. The process can be explained by taking different types of salts.

Type I: Salts of Strong Acid and Strong Base

This category includes salts such as NaCl, KCl, and KNO_3. Such salts do not undergo hydrolysis, as the products of hydrolysis are strong electrolytes, which remain completely in their dissociated form. Therefore, the concentration of H^+ remains equal to that of OH^- ions and the solution remains neutral. Let us try to understand the process by taking the example of NaCl.

$$NaCl + H_2O \rightleftharpoons \underbrace{NaOH + HCl}_{\text{Strong electrolytes}}$$

or $$Na^+ + Cl^- + H_2O \rightleftharpoons Na^+ + OH^- + H^+ + Cl^-$$

or $$H_2O \rightleftharpoons H^+ + OH^-$$

Type II: Salts of Strong Acid and Weak Base

This category includes salts such as NH_4Cl, $CuCl_2$, and $Fe(NO_3)_3$. In case of such a salt, anion is not hydrolyzed, as the possible product is a strong electrolyte and dissociates almost completely; rather here, only cation undergo hydrolysis. The result being the solution becomes rich in H^+ ions and behaves acidic. The process can be explained by taking the example of a specific salt, say, NH_4Cl.

$$NH_4Cl + H_2O \rightleftharpoons \underbrace{NH_4OH}_{\text{Weak}} + \underbrace{HCl}_{\text{Strong}}$$

$$\text{or} \quad NH_4^+ + Cl^- + H_2O \rightleftharpoons NH_4OH + H^+ + Cl^-$$

$$\text{or} \quad NH_4^+ + H_2O \rightleftharpoons NH_4OH + \underbrace{H^+}_{\text{Free}}$$

Quantitative aspect

Hydrolysis constant

In general, the hydrolysis can be represented as

$$A^+ + H_2O \rightleftharpoons AOH + H^+$$

Now, the hydrolysis constant, $K_h = \dfrac{[AOH]\,[H^+]}{[A^+]}$ ...[4.33]

The dissociation of weak base can be written as

$$AOH \rightleftharpoons A^+ + OH^-$$

The dissociation constant of base, $K_b = \dfrac{[A^+]\,[OH^-]}{[AOH]}$ ...[4.34]

Again $K_w = [H^+]\,[OH^-]$ ...[4.35]

From relations [4.33], [4.34], and [4.35], we get

$$K_h = \frac{K_w}{K_b} \qquad \text{...[4.36]}$$

Degree of hydrolysis

	$\underbrace{A^+}$	$+ H_2O \rightleftharpoons$	AOH	$+ H^+$
Initial concentration	c		0	0
At equilibrium	$c - c\alpha$		$c\alpha$	$c\alpha$

$$K_h = \frac{[AOH]\,[H^+]}{[A^+]}$$

$$= \frac{c\alpha \cdot c\alpha}{c(1-\alpha)}$$

$$= \frac{c\alpha^2}{1-\alpha}$$

If α is very small, then $1-\alpha \cong 1$. Now, the above equation is reduced to

$$K_h = c\alpha^2$$

or $$\alpha = \sqrt{\frac{K_h}{c}}$$

$$= \sqrt{\frac{K_w}{K_b c}} \quad \ldots[4.37]$$

pH

$$[H^+] = c\alpha$$

$$= c\sqrt{\frac{K_w}{K_b c}}$$

$$= \sqrt{\frac{K_w c}{K_b}}$$

Taking negative logarithm on both sides, we get

$$-\log [H^+] = \frac{1}{2}(-\log K_w + \log K_b - \log c)$$

or $$pH = \frac{1}{2}(pK_w - pK_b - \log c) \quad \ldots[4.38]$$

Type III: Salts of Weak Acid and Strong Base

This category includes salts such as CH_3COONa, K_2CO_3, and Na_2S. In case of such a salt, cation is not hydrolyzed, as the possible product is a strong electrolyte and dissociates almost completely; rather here, only anion undergo hydrolysis. The result being the solution becomes rich in OH^- ions and behaves basic. The process can be explained by taking the example of a specific salt, say, CH_3COONa.

$$CH_3COONa + H_2O \rightleftharpoons \underbrace{CH_3COOH}_{\text{Weak}} + \underbrace{NaOH}_{\text{Strong}}$$

or $$CH_3COO^- + Na^+ + H_2O \rightleftharpoons CH_3COOH + Na^+ + OH^-$$

or $$CH_3COO^- + H_2O \rightleftharpoons CH_3COOH + \underbrace{OH^-}_{\text{Free}}$$

Quantitative aspect

Hydrolysis constant

In general, the hydrolysis can be represented as

$$B^- + H_2O \rightleftharpoons BH + OH^-$$

Now, the hydrolysis constant, $K_h = \dfrac{[BH]\,[OH^-]}{[B^-]}$ $\quad \ldots[4.39]$

The dissociation of weak base can be written as

$$BH \rightleftharpoons B^- + H^+$$

The dissociation constant of acid, $K_a = \dfrac{[B^-]\,[H^+]}{[BH]}$ ...[4.40]

Again $K_w = [H^+]\,[OH^-]$ ...[4.41]

From relations [4.39], [4.40], and [4.41],we get

$$K_h = \frac{K_w}{K_a} \qquad \text{...[4.42]}$$

Degree of hydrolysis

	$\underbrace{B^-}$	+ H_2O $\rightleftharpoons$	BH	+ OH^-
Initial concentration	c		0	0
At equilibrium	$c - c\alpha$		$c\alpha$	$c\alpha$

$$K_h = \frac{[BH]\,[OH^-]}{[B^-]}$$

$$= \frac{c\alpha \cdot c\alpha}{c(1-\alpha)} = \frac{c\alpha^2}{1-\alpha}$$

If α is very small, then $1 - \alpha \cong 1$. Now, the above equation is reduced to

$$K_h = c\alpha^2$$

or $\alpha = \sqrt{\dfrac{K_h}{c}}$

$$= \sqrt{\frac{K_w}{K_a c}} \qquad \text{...[4.43]}$$

pH

$$[OH^-] = c\alpha$$

$$= c\sqrt{\frac{K_w}{K_a c}}$$

$$= \sqrt{\frac{K_w c}{K_a}}$$

Taking negative logarithm on both sides, we get

$$-\log\,[OH^-] = \frac{1}{2}\,(-\log K_w + \log K_a - \log c)$$

or $$\text{pOH} = \frac{1}{2}(\text{p}K_w - \text{p}K_a - \log C) \qquad \ldots[4.44]$$

Here pH = 14 – pOH

Type IV: Salts of Weak Acid and Weak Base

The salts such as CH_3COONH_4, $(NH_4)_2CO_3$, and $Be_2C_2O_4$ belong to this category. In such a case, both cation and anion of salt interact with water to form weak electrolytes, i.e., both of them undergo hydrolysis. Here, the nature of solution can be predicted with respect to relative values of dissociation constants of weak acid and base generated. If $K_a > K_b$, then the solution will have some excess H^+ ions and will behave acidic. On the other hand, if $K_b > K_a$, then the solution will have some excess OH^- ions and will behave basic. Finally, if $K_a = K_b$, then the solution will be neutral.

$$CH_3COO^- + NH_4^- + H_2O \rightleftharpoons \underbrace{CH_3COOH}_{\text{Weak}} + \underbrace{NH_4OH}_{\text{Weak}}$$

Quantitative aspect

Hydrolysis constant

In general, the hydrolysis can be represented as

$$A^+ + B^- + H_2O \rightleftharpoons BH + AOH$$

$$K_h = \frac{[BH]\,[AOH]}{[A^+]\,[B^-]} \qquad \ldots[4.45]$$

Again, $K_a = \dfrac{[B^-]\,[H^+]}{[BH]}$, $K_b = \dfrac{[A^+]\,[OH^-]}{[AOH]}$, and $K_w = [H^+]\,[OH^-]$

Thus, $$K_h = \frac{K_w}{K_a K_b} \qquad \ldots[4.46]$$

Degree of Hydrolysis

	A^+	+ B^-	+ H_2O $\rightleftharpoons$	BH	+ AOH
Initial concentration	c	c		0	0
At equilibrium	$c - c\alpha$	$c - c\alpha$		$c\alpha$	$c\alpha$

$$K_h = \frac{K_w}{K_a K_b}$$

$$= \frac{c\alpha \cdot c\alpha}{c^2(1-\alpha)^2}$$

$$= \frac{\alpha^2}{(1-\alpha)^2}$$

If α is very small, then $1 - \alpha \cong 1$. Now, the above equation is reduced to

$$K_h = \alpha^2$$

or $$\alpha = \sqrt{K_h}$$

$$= \sqrt{\frac{K_w}{K_a K_b}} \quad \ldots[4.47]$$

pH

$$BH \rightleftharpoons B^- + H^+$$

$$K_a = \frac{[B^-]\,[H^+]}{[BH]}$$

or $$[H^+] = \frac{K_a\,[BH]}{[B^-]}$$

$$= \frac{K_a\,(\alpha c)}{[(1-\alpha)c]} = \frac{K_a\,(\alpha)}{1-\alpha}$$

Ignoring α as compared to unity, we get

$$[H^+] = K_a\,(\alpha)$$

$$= K_a \sqrt{\frac{K_w}{K_a K_b}}$$

$$= \sqrt{\frac{K_w K_a}{K_b}}$$

Taking negative logarithm, we get

$$-\log\,[H^+] = \frac{1}{2}(-\log K_w - \log K_a + \log K_b)$$

or $$pH = \frac{1}{2}\,pK_w + \frac{1}{2}\,pK_a - \frac{1}{2}\,pK_b \quad \ldots[4.48]$$

Case I: If $pK_a = pK_b$, then $pH = \frac{1}{2}\,pK_w = 7$

The solution remains neutral, in spite of the fact that hydrolysis has taken place, e.g., CH_3COONH_4 solution remains neutral as the dissociation constants of acetic acid and ammonium hydroxide are almost the same.

Case II: If $pK_a > pK_b$, i.e.,

If the acid is relatively weaker than base, then the solution remains basic with pH > 7, e.g., ammonium cyanide.

Case III: If $pK_a < pK_b$, i.e.,

If the base is relatively weaker than acid, then the solution remains acidic with pH < 7, e.g., ammonium oxalate.

Example 4.32

Find the pH of 0.2 M ammonium chloride. Given that the dissociation constant of ammonia is 1.8×10^{-5}.

Solution

$$\text{pH} = \frac{1}{2}(\text{p}K_\text{w} - \text{p}K_\text{b} - \log c)$$

$$= 7 - \frac{1}{2}[-\log(1.8 \times 10^{-5}) - \log 0.2]$$

$$= 7 \cdot (2.372 - 0.349)$$

$$= 7 - 2.023$$

$$= 4.977$$

Example 4.33

Find hydrolysis constant and degree of hydrolysis of ammonium chloride in 0.02 M solution. ($K_b = 1.8 \times 10^{-5}$.)

Solution

$$\alpha = \sqrt{\frac{K_\text{w}}{K_\text{b}C}} = \sqrt{\frac{10^{-14}}{1.8 \times 10^{-5} \times 0.02}}$$

$$= 1.66 \times 10^{-5}$$

$$K_\text{h} = \frac{K_\text{w}}{K_\text{b}}$$

$$= \frac{10^{-14}}{1.8 \times 10^{-5}}$$

$$= 5.55 \times 10^{-10}$$

QUESTIONS

1. Explain homogeneous and heterogeneous equilibria with suitable examples.
2. State law of mass action.
3. Why chemical equilibrium is identified as dynamic equilibrium?
4. Give the relation between K_P and K_C.
5. Give the relation between free energy change and equilibrium constant.
6. What is a Lewis acid?
7. Define Bronsted acid and base.
8. Under which condition, buffer capacity will be maximum?
9. Why phenolphthalein is not a suitable indicator for the titration of ammonium hydroxide with hydrochloric acid?
10. Write conjugate acids of CO_3^{2-}, OH^-, O^{2-}, H_2O, and HCO_3^-.
11. Write conjugate base of H_2CO_3, NH_4^+, HPO_4^{2-}, and $CH_3NH_3^+$.

12. What is a buffer solution?
13. E xplain common ion effect with a suitable example.
14. What is buffer capacity?
15. Explain effect of temperature on pH.
16. State Le Chatelier's principle.
17. Provide favorable conditions for the manufacture of ammonia in Haber's process using Le Chatelier's principle.
18. Though low temperature favors formation of ammonia in Haber's process, still a high temperature of about ~ 450°C is used in practice. Explain.
19. The constant for the equilibrium constant for a reaction is 2.5×10^6. Calculate the free energy change at 27°C.
20. What happens to the equilibrium of the following reactions, if the pressure is increased?

    $N_2 + 3H_2 \rightleftharpoons 2NH_3$

    $H_2 + I_2 \rightleftharpoons 2HI$
21. What is common ion effect? Explain it with a suitable example.
22. Predict the effect of increased pressure and temperature on the following reaction equilibria stating only if product formation will be favored, inhibited, or unchanged.

    $2SO_{2(g)} + O_{2(g)} \rightleftharpoons 2SO_{3(g)}$; $\Delta H^0 = -194.0$ kJ

    $N_{2(g)} + O_{2(g)} \rightleftharpoons 2NO_{(g)}$; $\Delta H^0 = +361.0$ kJ
23. Derive the relation between K_P and K_C by taking a hypothetical reversible reaction.
24. State and explain Le Chatelier's principle.
25. Explain Le Chatelier's principle with reference to the contact process for the manufacture of sulphuric acid.
26. Derive Van't Hoff reaction isotherm.
27. What is a buffer? Explain buffer action with a suitable example.
28. Give a comparative account of ionic product and solubility product. Also, explain the application of the concept of solubility product in explaining the precipitation of Gr-IIIA radicals.
29. What is salt hydrolysis? Explain the process by taking one example from each category of salt.
30. Gr-II radicals are precipitated as sulphides by passing H_2S through their solution in acidic medium, but for the precipitation of Gr-IIIA radicals as sulphides, they are passed through basic medium. Explain.
31. Derive the empirical relation to show the temperature dependence of the equilibrium constant of a reaction.
32. What are the characteristics of equilibrium constant? In which way is it different from rate constant?
33. What is buffer capacity? Provide some important uses of buffer.
34. Discuss different concepts of acids and bases.

NUMERICAL PROBLEMS

1. K_P is 8×10^{-9} atm at 100°C for the equilibrium $COCl_{2(g)} \rightleftharpoons CO_{(g)} + Cl_{2(g)}$; $\Delta S^\circ = 30$ cal dg^{-1}. Find the degree of dissociation of phosgene at 100°C and 2 atm pressure, ΔH° for the reaction, and at what temperature phosgene will be 0.1% dissociated at 2 atm pressure?
2. ΔH° and ΔG° for the reaction, $Br_{2(g)} \rightleftharpoons 2Br_{(g)}$ is −320 cal and −1440 cal, respectively, at 25°C. Calculate the value of K_P at 500°C assuming $\Delta C_p = 0$.
3. K_P for the reaction $N_2 + 3\ H_2 \rightleftharpoons 2\ NH_3$ at 400°C is 1.64×10^{-4}. Find K_C. Also, find ΔG° using K_P and K_C values, and interpret the difference.
4. Two moles of HI were heated in a sealed tube at 440 K till the equilibrium state was reached. HI was found to be 22 % dissociated. Calculate the equilibrium constant for the dissociation reaction, and also, calculate the standard free energy change for the reaction.
5. N_2O_4 is 25% dissociated at 37°C and one atm pressure. Calculate K_P and the percent dissociation at 0.1 atm at the same temperature.
6. K_P for $SO_{2(g)} + \frac{1}{2} O_{2(g)} \rightleftharpoons SO_{3(g)}$ is 1.7×10^{21} at 300 K. Calculate K_P and K_C for $2SO_{2(g)} + O_{2(g)} \rightleftharpoons 2\ SO_{3(g)}$.
7. The ionization constant for a certain acid HA is 4.5×10^{-4} at 298 K. What concentration of acid would be required to produce $[H_3O^+]$ of 3×10^{-3} M?
8. A mixture of SO_2 and O_2 in the molar ratio 2:1 is kept over platinum catalyst in a reaction vessel at 650°C; the total pressure at equilibrium being found to be 10 atm. 60 % of SO_2 be converted into SO_3 in this process. Calculate the equilibrium constant (K_P) for the reaction, $2SO_{2(g)} + O_{2(g)} \rightleftharpoons 2\ SO_{3(g)}$.
9. An equilibrium mixture, at 300 K, contains N_2O_4 and NO_2 at 0.28 atm and 1.1 atm, respectively. If the volume of container is doubled, calculate the new equilibrium pressure of two gases.
10. At 540 K, 0.10 moles of PCl_5 are heated in an 8 liter flask. The pressure of the equilibrium mixture is found to be 1.0 atm. Find K_P and K_C for the reaction.
11. The degree of dissociation of steam into hydrogen and oxygen at 1273 K and 1 atm pressure is 2.4×10^{-4}. Calculate K_P for the reaction at this temperature and pressure.
12. Calculate the value of log K_P for the reaction $N_{2(g)} + 3\ H_{2(g)} \rightleftharpoons 2\ NH_{3(g)}$ at 25°C. Given that the standard enthalpy of formation of ammonia is −46 kJ and standard entropies of $N_{2(g)}$, $H_{2(g)}$, and $NH_{3(g)}$ are 191, 130, and 192 JK^{-1}mol^{-1}, respectively.
13. The pH of a soft drink is 5.2. Find the concentration of H^+ and OH^- ions in the drink.
14. Calculate the pH of 1.2×10^{-3} M HCl after 100 times dilution with water.
15. Find the pH of a saturated solution of $Mg(OH)_2$. Given that K_{SP} is 8.87×10^{-12} at 298 K.
16. Find the pH and $[H_3O^+]$ of 0.5 M NH_4Br ($pK_b = 4.73$) at 298 K.
17. Calculate the change in pH of 1 liter of buffer solution containing 0.1 mol each of ammonia and ammonium chloride upon addition of (a) 0.02 mol of dissolved gaseous HCl and (b) 0.02 mol of dissolved NaOH, assuming no change in volume. (K_b for ammonia is 1.8×10^{-5}.)
18. The pK_a of a monobasic acid is 4.74 at 298 K. What will be the pH of its 0.01 M solution at this temperature?
19. The pH of HCN solution is 5.2. What is the value of K_a?

20. Calculate the composition of an acetic acid buffer of total molarity of 0.29 and having a pH of 4.4 ($K_a = 1.8 \times 10^{-5}$).
21. How much of 0.5 M ammonium hydroxide should be mixed with 100 ml of 0.2 M of ammonium chloride solution to have a buffer of pH 8.5? Given $pK_b = 4.75$.
22. Find the degree of hydrolysis, hydrolysis constant, and pH for 0.02 N solution of sodium acetate. Given $K_a = 1.9 \times 10^{-5}$.
23. K_a for ascorbic acid (HAac) is 5×10^{-5}. Find the concentration of H^+ ion and % of hydrolysis in an aqueous solution having $[Asc^-] = 0.02$ M.
24. Find the amount of ammonium nitrate required to prepare 500 ml of solution in water with pH 4.0. Given K_b for ammonium hydroxide is 1.8×10^{-5}.
25. 10 cc of 0.2 N NaOH is added to 30 cc of 0.1 N CH_3COOH. Calculate the pH of the resulting solution. K_a for acetic acid is 1.8×10^{-5}.
26. A 0.1 N aqueous solution of a monobasic organic acid is titrated with 0.1 N aqueous NaOH solution. Find the pH of the solution (a) before addition of alkali, (b) when two-third of an acid has been neutralized, and (c) at the equivalence point.
27. K_{SP} of Ag_2CrO_4 is 1.12×10^{-12}. Find its solubility in aqueous solution in the presence of 1 M $AgNO_3$ and in the presence of 1 M K_2CrO_4.
28. The solubility of $Pb(OH)_2$ in water is 6.7×10^{-5} M. Find the solubility of the same in a buffer solution of pH = 9.
29. 150 ml of 0.2 M $Pb(NO_3)_2$ and 100 ml of 0.2 M NaCl are mixed. Test if the precipitation will occur. K_{SP} of $PbCl_2$ is 1.2×10^{-5}.
30. Which compound (if any) will precipitate when 100 ml of 10^{-5} M $Ba(OH)_2$ is added to 25 ml of 10^{-5} M $Fe_2(SO_4)_3$? Given K_{SP} of $Fe(OH)_3$ and $BaSO_4$ is 2.6×10^{-10}.
31. Calculate the solubility product of lead iodide at 25°C. Its solubility at this temperature is 0.7 g l^{-1} (Molecular mass = 461 g).
32. The solubility of a sparingly soluble salt Ag_2CrO_4 is 5.2×10^{-5} mol l^{-1}. Assuming complete dissociation, calculate the solubility product of the salt.
33. A solution contains a mixture of A^+ (0.01M) and B_2^{2+} (0.1M) ions which are to be separated. Calculate the minimum concentration of iodide ion at which one of them gets precipitated completely. Also, calculate the percentage of that metal ion precipitated. (K_{SP}: AI = 8.5×10^{-17}, $B_2I_2 = 2.5 \times 10^{-26}$.)

CHAPTER

5

Chemical Kinetics

Chapter Outline

- Rate of Reaction
- Rate Law
- Order
- Molecularity
- Integrated Rate Laws
- Half-Life Time
- Study of Complex Reactions and Steady-State Approximation
- Methods of Find Order of a Reaction
- Factors Affecting the Rate of a Reaction
- Theories of Reaction Rates

Kinetics can be introduced as a complimentary topic to thermodynamics as it helps to overcome the limitations of the latter one, and together both of them are able to explain the three vital questions regarding any process, i.e., feasibility, rate, and underlying mechanism. It is the branch of chemistry which primarily addresses the question "How fast do reactions occur." It covers the mechanism of a process, the rate, and rate law along with the factors affecting rate.

Rate of a Reaction

The rate corresponds to the fact that how fast a reaction proceeds. Quantitatively, it is expressed in terms of change in concentration or any related parameter of one of the components of the reaction with respect to time. Let us look into the following two cases.

Case I

Stoichiometric coefficients are same.

$A + B \rightarrow C + D$

$$\text{Rate} = -\frac{\Delta[A]}{\Delta t} = -\frac{\Delta[B]}{\Delta t} = \frac{\Delta[C]}{\Delta t} = \frac{\Delta[D]}{\Delta t}$$

Case II

Stoichiometric coefficients are different

$aA + bB \rightarrow cC + dD$

$$\text{Rate} = -\frac{\Delta[A]}{a\Delta t} = -\frac{\Delta[B]}{b\Delta t} = \frac{\Delta[C]}{c\Delta t} = \frac{\Delta[D]}{d\Delta t}$$

Modes to express rate

Rate of a reaction can be expressed in two different ways.

Average rate

It refers to the rate over a definite span of time. As the concentration of all components change in a continuous fashion, the rate also changes continuously. Therefore, it does not provide significant information regarding the rate.

$$\text{Average rate} = \frac{\Delta x}{\Delta t}, \text{ where } x \text{ is concentration of any component}$$

Graphical evaluation

Average rate over the time span t_1 to t_2 can be calculated from the curve that has been ploted by taking concentration of any one reacting component as a function of time and can be expressed as

$$\text{Rate} = \frac{\Delta x}{\Delta t}$$

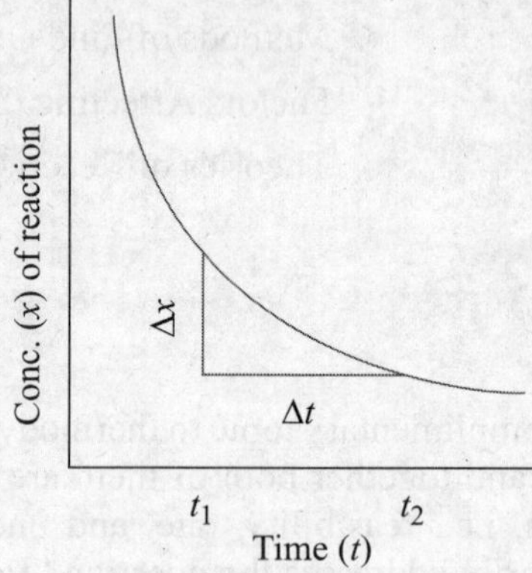

Fig. 5.1 Average rate (calculated w.r.t. a reactant)

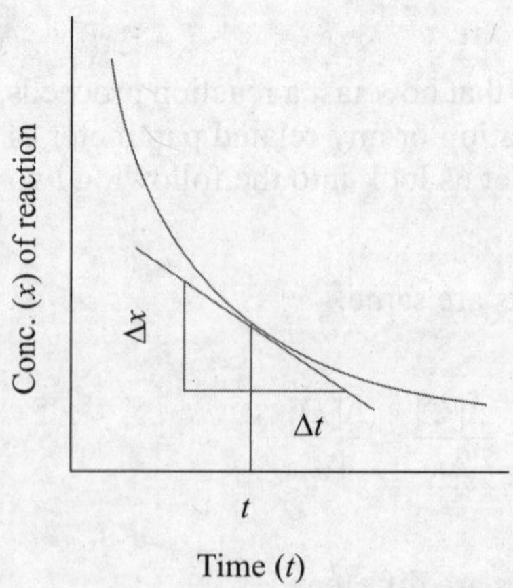

Fig. 5.2 Instantaneous rate

Instantaneous rate

The rate of a reaction at a particular instant of time. This can be expressed as

$$\text{Rate} = \lim_{\Delta t \to 0} \frac{\Delta x}{\Delta t} = \frac{dx}{dt}$$

Graphical evaluation

Instantaneous rate at time t is the slope of the tangent drawn to the curve that has been ploted by taking concentration of any one reacting component as a function of time at that temperature.

$$\text{Rate} = \frac{\Delta x}{\Delta t}$$

Rate Law

An empirical relation which provides the exact dependence of rate of a reaction on the concentration of reacting substances at a given temperature. Let us discuss the following cases.

Case I

For a simple reaction, i.e., a reaction that takes place in only one step, the rate law is nothing but same as the law of mass action. For example,

$H_2 + I_2 \longrightarrow 2HI$

Rate = $k[H_2][I_2]$

$2NO + O_2 \longrightarrow 2NO_2$

Rate = $k[NO]^2 [O_2]$

Case II

For a complex reaction, i.e., a reaction that takes place in more than one step, the rate law does not match with the law of mass action expression. In this case, rate law can be obtained by applying law of mass action to the rate controlling step, which is the slowest step. This is obvious because a reaction cannot proceed faster than the slowest step. For example,

1. $2NO_2 + F_2 \longrightarrow 2NO_2F$

Mechanism

Step I: $NO_2 + F_2 \longrightarrow NO_2F + F$ (slow)

Step II: $NO_2 + F \longrightarrow NO_2F$

As the first step is the slower one, it is the rate controlling step. Thus, the rate law becomes Rate = $k[NO_2][F_2]$

2. $2N_2O_5 \longrightarrow 4NO_2 + O_2$

Mechanism

$N_2O_5 \longrightarrow NO_2 + NO_3$ (slow)

$N_2O_5 + NO_3 \longrightarrow 3NO_2 + O_2$

Rate = $k\,[N_2O_5]$

Note:

1. **Law of mass action (by Guldberg and Waage):** The rate of a reaction is proportional to the product of active masses of the reactants with each term raised to the power equal to its stoichiometric coefficient. For ordinary systems as those of gases or dilute solutions, which do not deviate appreciably from ideal behavior,

active mass may be taken equal to molar concentration. For solids and pure liquids, the active masses or concentrations are taken as unity since the rate of reaction is independent of their amounts present.

2. In complex reactions, several reactions occur simultaneously along with the main reaction and thus the smooth progress of the main reaction is disturbed. These reactions follow a complicated kinetics. The rate expression in such a case is the resultant of several different rate expressions of the main and side reactions. The different possible cases of complex reactions and their rate expressions as per steady state principle are discussed in the latter portion of the topic.

Order

The *order of a reaction* is the sum of exponents of the concentration terms involved in the rate law. The decomposition of ammonia on the surface of molybdenum is an example of zero order reaction.

$$2NH_3 \xrightarrow{Mo} N_2 + 3\,H_2$$

Rate = $k\,[NH_3]^0$, order is zero.

Let us see a few more examples.

1. Photochemical combination of hydrogen and chlorine.

   $$H_2 + Cl_2 \xrightarrow{h\nu} 2HCl$$

   Rate = $k\,[H_2]^0\,[Cl_2]^0$, order is zero.

2. $NO_2 + CO \longrightarrow NO + CO_2$, at 200°C

   Rate = $k\,[NO_2]^2\,[CO]^0$, order is two with respect to NO_2 while it is zero with respect to CO.

3. Decomposition of hydrogen peroxide.

   $$H_2O_2 \longrightarrow H_2 + O_2$$

   Rate = $k\,[H_2O_2]^1$, order is one.

4. $2N_2O_5 \longrightarrow 4NO_2 + O_2$

   Rate = $k\,[N_2O_5]$, order is one.

5. $2NO_2 \longrightarrow 2NO + O_2$

   Rate = $k\,[NO_2]^2$, order is two.

6. $2NO + 2H_2 \longrightarrow N_2 + 2H_2O$

   Rate = $k\,[NO]^2\,[H_2]$, order is three.

7. $CH_3CHO \longrightarrow CH_4 + CO$

   Rate = $k\,[CH_3CHO]^{3/2}$, order is 3/2

Note:

1. The reaction order is "not necessarily" related to the stoichiometry of the reaction, unless the reaction is *elementary or simple*.

2. A reaction in which one of the reactant remains in large excess so that change in its concentration does not alter the rate shows an order different from the actual one. Such a reaction is called *pseudo order* reaction. For example, In acid hydrolysis of ester, water is used as solvent and taken in excess.

$$CH_3COOC_2H_5 + H_2O \xrightarrow{H^+} CH_3COOH + C_2H_5OH$$

Rate = $k\,[CH_3COOC_2H_5]$, a pseudo first order reaction.

3. For simple concerted reactions, molecularity and order are identical. Therefore, *pseudo order* reactions are sometimes also known as *pseudo molecular* reactions.

4. The order of a reaction can be zero, can be a fraction, or it can even have negative values in a few rare cases.

5. *Broken order* reactions are those in which the order is a non-integer. The chemical decomposition of ethanal to methane and carbon monoxide proceeds with an order of 1.5 with respect to ethanal. The decomposition of phosgene to carbon monoxide and chlorine has order 1 with respect to phosgene itself and order 0.5 with respect to chlorine.

6. *Mixed order* reactions are those in which the order changes in the course of a reaction as a result of changing variables such as pH. An example is the oxidation of an alcohol to a ketone by a ruthenate (RuO_4^{2-}) and a hexacyanoferrate, the latter serving as the sacrificial catalyst converting Ru (IV) back to Ru (VI). The disappearing rate of the ferrate is zero order with respect to the ferrate at the onset of the reaction (when its concentration is high and the ruthenium catalyst is quickly regenerated) but it changes to first order reaction when its concentration decreases.

   Ref: *"Ruthenium(VI)-Catalyzed Oxidation of Alcohols by Hexacyanoferrate(III): An Example of Mixed Order" Mucientes, Antonio E.; de la Peña, María A. J. Chem. Edu. 2006, 83, 1643.*

7. *Negative order reactions* are rare; for example, the conversion of ozone to oxygen. The order is 2 with respect to ozone while it is –1 with respect to oxygen.

8. Order is not a characteristic of a reaction and it may change with the modification of reaction condition. For example, acid hydrolysis of ester which is known to follow first order kinetics becomes second order when the water to ester ratio is 5:1.

Molecularity

The actual number of reacting particles (atoms, molecules or ions) participating in a simple reaction or in an elementary step of a complex reaction simultaneously to bring about the change. For example,

$NH_4NO_2 \longrightarrow N_2 + 2H_2O$, molecularity is 1.

$NO + O_2 \longrightarrow NO_2 + O_2$, molecularity is 2.

$2NO + O_2 \longrightarrow 2NO_2$, molecularity is 3.

Note:

1. Molecularity always has integral values.
2. It is a *characteristic* of a reaction.

3. The molecularity of a complex reaction as a whole has no significance rather the concept is applicable to each individual step of such a reaction. In such a case, the molecularity of the rate-controlling step may be considered as the molecularity of the reaction.
4. Molecularity does not give any idea regarding the rate and mechanism of a reaction.
5. Whatever may be the case, molecularity does not exceed three.

Integrated Rate Laws

Rate laws are differential equations which show only the dependence of the rate of a reaction on the molar concentration of reactant(s). To make it applicable to real-life problems, i.e., to get the relation between directly measured experimental quantities such as concentration and time one has to integrate it. The integrated rate laws are different for reactions of different order. Let us discuss them one by one.

Zero Order Rate Law

Let us consider a hypothetical reaction,

	A	$\longrightarrow$	Product(s)
At commencement	a		$0 \text{ mol } l^{-1}$
At certain time, t	$a - x$		$x \text{ mol } l^{-1}$

Rate $\propto (a - x)^0$

or $\dfrac{dx}{dt} = k$

or $dx = k dt$

Integrating within specified limits, we get

$$\int_0^x dx \int_0^t k dt$$

or $[x]_0^x = kt$

or $x = kt$

or $k = \dfrac{x}{t}$ ...[5.1]

The unit of rate constant is mol l^{-1} time^{-1}.

Evaluation of k

Graphical evaluation

$x = kt$

Now k can be evaluated from the slope of the obtained by plotting x as a function of t which is a straight line passing through origin. Here, slope = k.

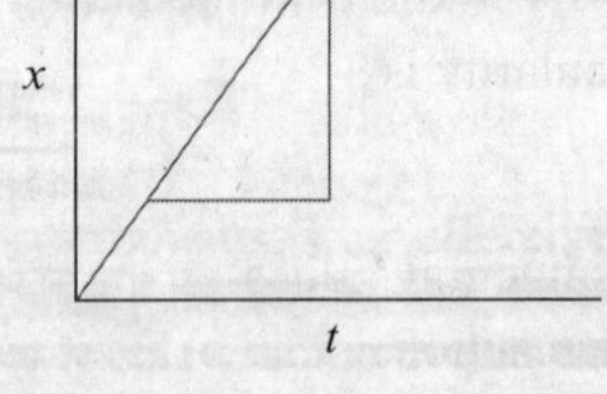

Fig. 5.3 Plot of x as a function of time

More examples

1. The decomposition of HI on the surface of gold, i.e., $2HI \longrightarrow H_2 + I_2$.
2. The decomposition of phosphine on the surface of tungsten or molybdenum at high pressure, i.e., $2PH_3 \longrightarrow 2P + 3H_2$.

First Order Rate Law

Let us consider a hypothetical reaction, i.e.,

	A	$\longrightarrow$	Product(s)
At commencement,	a		0 mol l^{-1}
At certain time t,	$a - x$		$x \text{ mol l}^{-1}$

Rate $\propto a - x$

or $\dfrac{dx}{dt} = k(a - x)$

or $\dfrac{dx}{(a - x)} = k\,dt$

Integrating within specified limits, we get

$$\int_0^x \frac{dx}{(a - x)} = \int_0^x k\,dt$$

or $\displaystyle\int_a^{(a-x)} \frac{-dz}{z} = k\int_0^t dt$; where $a - x = z$, so that $-dx = dz$

or $[-\ln z]_a^{a-x} = kt$; or $\ln a - \ln(a - x) = kt$

or $\ln \dfrac{a}{a - x} = kt$; or, $k = \dfrac{1}{t} \ln \dfrac{a}{a - x}$ ...[5.2]

The unit of rate constant is time^{-1}.

Evaluation of k

Graphical evaluation

$\ln a - \ln(a - x) = kt$

or $\ln(a - x) = \ln a - kt$

Now, k can be obtained from the slope of the line obtained by plotting $\ln(a - x)$ as a function of time.

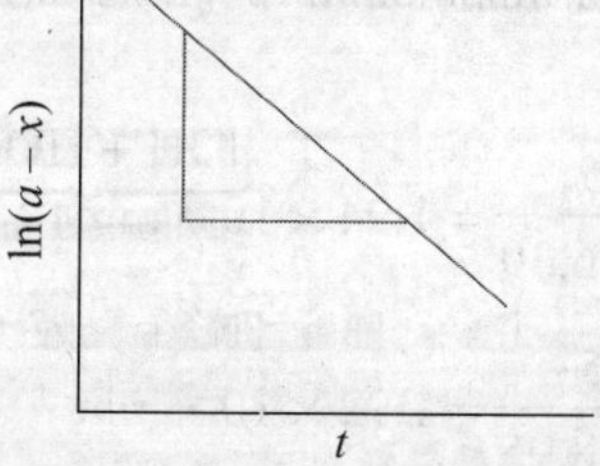

Fig. 5.4 Plot of ln $(a - x)$ as a function of time

Analytical evaluation

For the evaluation of k analytically, the relation [5.2] can be applied with a slight modification as per the experimental data available. Let us consider some typical examples.

Example 5.1

Kinetics of catalytic decomposition of hydrogen peroxide is studied by titrating H_2O_2 with $KMnO_4$ at different intervals of time. Find rate constant assuming the reaction to be first order.

Time (s)	0	600	1200
$KMnO_4$ (ml)	22.8	13.8	8.2

Solution

Let the volume of $KMnO_4$ consumed at the commencement of reaction be V_0. This is a measure of initial concentration of H_2O_2, i.e., a. Again, the volume of $KMnO_4$ consumed at any time V_t corresponds to the amount of undecomposed $KMnO_4$ at that time, i.e., $(a - x)$. Thus, the relation [5.2] now can be written as

$$k = \frac{1}{t} \ln \frac{V_0}{V_t}$$

At 600 s, $k = \dfrac{1}{600} \ln \dfrac{22.8}{13.8} = 8.37 \times 10^{-4}\ s^{-1}$

At 1200 s, $k = \dfrac{1}{1200} \ln \dfrac{22.8}{8.2} = 8.52 \times 10^{-4}\ s^{-1}$

Now the average rate constant is $8.44 \times 10^{-4}\ s^{-1}$.

Example 5.2

Kinetics of catalytic decomposition of hydrogen peroxide is studied by measuring the volume oxygen gas liberated at different intervals of time. Find the rate constant.

Time (min)	10	15	20	25	∞
Volume of O_2 (ml)	6.30	8.95	11.40	13.5	35.75

Solution

Volume of O_2 at any time V_t is x, while the volume of O_2 at the end of reaction, i.e., V_∞ is a the initial concentration of H_2O_2. Thus, the relation [5.2] becomes

$$k = \frac{1}{t} \ln \frac{V_\infty}{V_\infty - V_t}$$

At 10 min, $k = \dfrac{1}{10} \ln \dfrac{35.75}{35.75 - 6.30} = 1.94 \times 10^{-2}\ min^{-1}$

At 15 min, $k = \dfrac{1}{15} \ln \dfrac{35.75}{35.75 - 8.95} = 1.92 \times 10^{-2}\ min^{-1}$

At 20 min, $k = \frac{1}{20} \ln \frac{35.75}{35.75 - 11.40} = 1.92 \times 10^{-2}\ \text{min}^{-1}$

At 25 min, $k = \frac{1}{25} \ln \frac{35.75}{35.75 - 13.5} = 1.90 \times 10^{-2}\ \text{min}^{-1}$

Now the average rate constant is $1.92 \times 10^{-2}\ \text{min}^{-1}$

Example 5.3

Kinetics of acid hydrolysis of an ester is studied by at 25°C by withdrawing 10 ml of reaction mixture at different intervals and titrating it with a standard alkali. Find the rate constant.

Time (min)	0	75	120	260	∞
Volume of alkali (ml)	19.24	24.20	26.60	32.23	42.03

Solution

The reaction is as follows:

$$RCOOR' + H_2O \xrightarrow{H^+} RCOOH + R'OH$$

The volume of alkali consumed at commencement V_0 is ∝ moles of acid used as catalyst. Again, the volume of alkali consumed at any time V_t ∝ moles of catalyst + moles of acetic acid formed at that time. Finally at the end, V_∞ ∝ moles of catalyst + moles of acetic acid at the end. Thus, we get

$V_\infty - V_0 \propto a$, $V_t - V_0 \propto x$ and $V_\infty - V_t \propto (a - x)$, now the relation [5.2] can be written as

$$k = \frac{1}{t} \ln \frac{V_\infty - V_0}{V_\infty - V_t}$$

At 75 min, $k = \frac{1}{75} \ln \frac{42.03 - 19.24}{42.03 - 24.20} = 3.27 \times 10^{-3}\ \text{min}^{-1}$

At 120 min, $k = \frac{1}{120} \ln \frac{42.03 - 19.24}{42.03 - 26.60} = 3.25 \times 10^{-3}\ \text{min}^{-1}$

At 260 min, $k = \frac{1}{260} \ln \frac{42.03 - 19.24}{42.03 - 32.23} = 3.24 \times 10^{-3}\ \text{min}^{-1}$

Now the average rate constant is $3.25 \times 10^{-3}\ \text{min}^{-1}$.

Example 5.4

Kinetics of acid hydrolysis of cane sugar (sucrose) is studied by the following changes in optical rotation at different time intervals. Find the rate constant.

Time (min)	0	10	20	30	∞
Rotation (degrees)	+32.50	+23.80	+25.50	+22.4	−11.10

Solution

$$\underset{\substack{\text{Sucrose} \\ (+\,66.5^\circ)}}{C_{12}H_{22}O_{11}} + H_2O \xrightarrow{H^+} \underset{\substack{\text{Glucose} \\ (+52.5^\circ)}}{C_6H_{12}O_6} + \underset{\substack{\text{Fructose} \\ (-92.0^\circ)}}{C_6H_{12}O_6}$$

Dextro rotary (+66.5°) As a whole leavo rotary

In this case, the change in rotation is proportional to the amount of sucrose undergoing hydrolysis. Therefore, we have

$r_0 - r_t \propto x$, $r_0 - r_\infty \propto a$ and $(r_t - r_\infty) \propto (a - x)$

Now relation [5.2] can be written as, $k = \dfrac{1}{t}\ln\dfrac{r_0 - V_\infty}{r_t - r_\infty}$

$$\text{At 10 min, } k = \frac{1}{10}\ln\frac{32.4 - (-11.1)}{23.8 - (-11.1)} = 8.62 \times 10^{-3}\ \text{min}^{-1}$$

$$\text{At 20 min, } k = \frac{1}{20}\ln\frac{43.5}{36.6} = 8.62 \times 10^{-3}\ \text{min}^{-1}$$

$$\text{At 30 min, } k = \frac{1}{30}\ln\frac{43.5}{35.5} = 8.62 \times 10^{-3}\ \text{min}^{-1}$$

Now the average rate constant is 8.62×10^{-3} min^{-1}

Note:

Expression of rate constant for a gas phase reaction

Let us consider a hypothetical gas phase first order reaction,

	$A_{(g)}$	$\longrightarrow$	$B_{(g)}$	+	$C_{(g)}$
At initial stage	P_i		0		0
At a time, t	$P_i - x$		x		x

where P_i is the pressure in the beginning which is due to A only and at time t, the pressure due to A reduces by an amount of x. Now the partial pressure due to B and C will be x.

Thus, the total pressure at time t is the sum of partial pressures of A, B and C.

$$P_t = p_A + p_B + p_C$$
$$= (P_i - x) + x + x$$
$$= P_i + x$$

or $\quad x = P_t - P_i$

Now, $P_A = P_i - x = P_i - (P_t - P_i) = 2P_i - P_t$

For a first order reaction, $P_i \propto a$ and $P_A \propto (a - x)$

$$k = \frac{1}{t} \ln \frac{P_i}{P_A}$$

or $$k = \frac{1}{t} \ln \frac{P_i}{2P_i - P_t}$$

Example 5.5

The decomposition of N_2O_5 according to the equation $2N_2O_{5\,(g)} \longrightarrow 4NO_{2(g)} + O_{2(g)}$ is a first order reaction. After 30 min from the start of decomposition in a closed vessel, the total pressure developed is found to be 284.5 mm of Hg and on complete decomposition, the total pressure is 584.5 mm of Hg. Calculate rate constant of the reaction.

Solution

	$2N_2O_{5\,(g)}$ $\longrightarrow$	$4NO_{2\,(g)}$ +	$O_{2\,(g)}$
At commencement	a	0	0 mol
At time, t	$a - x$	$2x$	$x/2$ mol
At ∞	0	$2a$	$a/2$ mol

Number of moles is proportional to the pressure developed.

Thus,

At $t = 0$, $a = P_0$ ...[1]

At $t = 30$ min, $a + \frac{3x}{2} = P_{30} \Rightarrow a + \frac{3x}{2} = 284.5$ ...[2]

At $t = \infty$, $\frac{5a}{2} = P_\infty \Rightarrow a + \frac{5a}{2} = 584.5$ ...[3]

From relation [3], we have

$$a = \frac{2 \times 584.5}{5}$$

$$= 233.8$$

From relation [2], we get $x = \frac{2(284.5 - 233.8)}{3} \Rightarrow x = 33.8$

Now, $a - x = 200$

Substituting in the rate expression, we get

$$k = \frac{1}{t} \ln \frac{a}{a - x}$$

$$= \frac{1}{t} \ln \frac{233.8}{200}$$

$$= 5.206 \times 10^{-3}\ \text{min}^{-1}$$

Second Order Rate Law

The following are the two possibilities.

Case I

Let us consider a hypothetical reaction in which there is one reactant.

$$A \longrightarrow \text{Product(s)}$$

	A	Product(s)
At commencement,	a	0 mol l^{-1}
At certain time t	$a - x$	x mol l^{-1}

Rate $\propto (a - x)^2$

or $$\frac{dx}{dt} = k\,(a - x)^2$$

or $$\frac{dx}{(a - x)^2} = k dt$$

Integrating within specified limits, we get

$$\int_0^x \frac{dx}{(a - x)^2} = \int_0^t k dt$$

or $$\int_a^{(a-x)} \frac{-dz}{z^2} = k\int_0^t dt, \text{ where } a - x = z, \text{ so that } -dx = dz$$

or $$\left[\frac{1}{z}\right]_a^{a-x} = k, \text{ or } \frac{1}{a - x} - \frac{1}{a} = kt$$

or $$\frac{x}{a(a - x)} = kt, \text{ or } k = \frac{1}{t}\,\frac{x}{a(a - x)} \qquad \text{...[5.3]}$$

Case II:

Let us consider a hypothetical reaction, in which there are two reactants.

$$A + B \longrightarrow \text{Product(s)}$$

	A	B	Product(s)
At commencement	a	b	0 mol l^{-1}
At certain time t	$a - x$	$b - x$	x mol l^{-1}

Rate $\propto (a - x)(b - x)$

or $$\frac{dx}{dt} = k(a - x)(b - x)$$

or $$\frac{dx}{(a - x)(b - x)} = k dt$$

Integrating, we get

$$\int \frac{dx}{(a - x)(b - x)} = \int k dt$$

or $$\frac{1}{a - b}\left[\int \frac{dx}{(b - x)} - \int \frac{dx}{(a - x)}\right] = k\int dt$$

or $$\frac{1}{a - b}\left[\ln(a - x) - \ln(b - x)\right] = kt + c$$

or $$\frac{1}{a - b}\ln\frac{a - x}{b - x} = kt + c \qquad \text{...[5.4]}$$

Putting initial conditions at $t = 0, x = 0$, we get

$$c = \frac{1}{a-b} \ln \frac{a}{b}$$

Now, substituting in relation [5.4], we get

$$\frac{1}{a-b} \ln \frac{a-x}{b-x} - \frac{1}{a-b} \ln \frac{a}{b} = kt$$

or $$\frac{1}{a-b} \ln \frac{b(a-x)}{a(b-x)} = kt$$

or $$k = \frac{1}{t(a-b)} \ln \frac{b(a-x)}{a(b-x)} \qquad [5.5]$$

The unit of rate constant is $l\ mol^{-1}\ time^{-1}$.

Evaluation of k

Graphical evaluation

k can be calculated from the slope of the line by plotting

$$\frac{1}{(a-b)} \ln \frac{b(a-x)}{a(b-x)} \text{ as a function of time.}$$

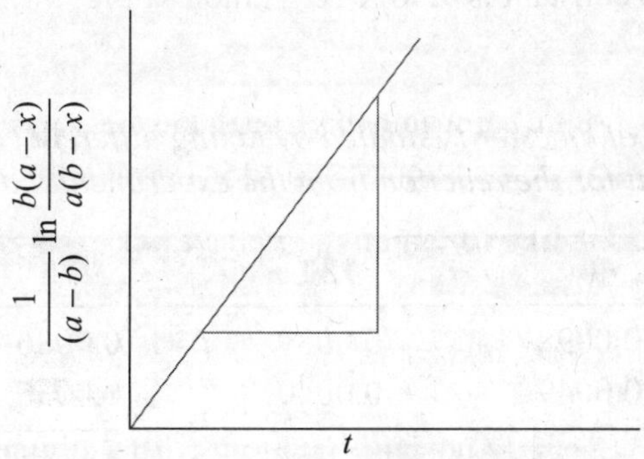

Fig. 5.5 Plot of $\frac{1}{(a+b)} \ln \frac{b(a-x)}{a(b-x)}$ as a function of time

Analytical evaluation

For the evaluation of k analytically, the relation [5.3] or [5.5] can be applied with a slight modification as per the experimental data available. Let us consider some typical examples.

Example 5.6

Kinetics of base hydrolysis of an ester is studied by taking equal concentrations of ester and base. The amount of acid used at different time intervals during the titration for a specific amount of reaction mixture is as follows. Find the rate constant.

Time (min)	0	05	10	∞
Acid used (ml)	47.65	38.90	32.60	11.85

Solution

The reaction is as follows:

$$RCOOR' + NaOH \longrightarrow RCOONa + R'OH$$

Both are in equal quantities

Thus, acid used at any point of time V_t estimates the amount of alkali that remains unused at that time which ultimately corresponds to $a - x$. The volume of acid used at the commencement V_0 corresponds to the alkali present in the beginning, i.e., a. Now the relation [5.3] becomes

$$k = \frac{1}{t}\frac{V_0 - V_t}{V_0(V_t)}$$

At 05 min, $k = \frac{1}{0.5} \times \frac{47.65 - 38.90}{47.65(38.90)} = 9.44 \times 10^{-4}\ \text{l mol}^{-1}\ \text{time}^{-1}$

At 10 min, $k = \frac{1}{10} \times \frac{47.65 - 32.60}{47.65(32.60)} = 9.69 \times 10^{-4}\ \text{l mol}^{-1}\ \text{time}^{-1}$

Now the average rate constant is $9.56 \times 10^{-4}\ \text{l mol}^{-1}\ \text{time}^{-1}$

Example 5.7

Kinetics of base hydrolysis of an ester is studied by taking different concentrations of ester and base. Find the rate constant for the reaction from the experimental data.

Time (s)	0	180	275	350
[ester] mol l^{-1}	0.0098	0.0089	0.0086	0.0072
[base] mol l^{-1}	0.0049	0.0040	0.0037	0.0030

Solution

The reaction is as follows:

$$RCOOR' + NaOH \longrightarrow RCOONa + R'OH$$

Both are in different quantities

Here V_0 for ester = a, and that for base = b, again V_t for ester corresponds to $a - x$, while that for base = $b - x$. Thus, relation [5.5] becomes

$$k = \frac{1}{t\{V_0(\text{ester}) - V_0(\text{base})\}} \ln \frac{V_0(\text{base}) \times V_t(\text{ester})}{V_0(\text{ester}) \times V_t(\text{base})}$$

At 180 s, $k = \frac{1}{180(0.0098 - 0.0049)} \ln \frac{0.0049 \times 0.0089}{0.0098 \times 0.0049} = 1.20 \times 10^{-1}\ \text{l mol}^{-1}\ \text{time}^{-1}$

At 275 s, $k = \dfrac{1}{275(0.0098 - 0.0049)} \ln \dfrac{0.0049 \times 0.0086}{0.0098 \times 0.0037} = 1.11 \times 10^{-1}\,l\,mol^{-1}\,time^{-1}$

At 350 s, $k = \dfrac{1}{350(0.0098 - 0.0049)} \ln \dfrac{0.0049 \times 0.0072}{0.0098 \times 0.0030} = 1.06 \times 10^{-1}\,l\,mol^{-1}\,time^{-1}$

Now the average rate constant is $1.12 \times 10^{-1}\,l\,mol^{-1}\,time^{-1}$

Rate Law for *n*th Order Reaction

Let us consider a hypothetical reaction,

	A	$\longrightarrow$ Product(s)
At commencement	a	0 mol l^{-1}
At certain time t	$a - x$	x mol l^{-1}

Rate $\propto (a - x)^n$

or $\dfrac{dx}{dt} = k(a - x)^n$

or $\dfrac{dx}{(a - x)^2} = k dt$

Integrating within specified limits, we get

$$\int_0^x \frac{dx}{(a - x)^n} = \int_0^t k dt$$

or $\displaystyle\int_a^{(a-x)} \frac{-dz}{z^n} = k \int_0^t dt$; where $a - x = z$, so that $- dx = dz$

or $\left[\dfrac{z^{-n+1}}{-n+1}\right]_a^{a-x} = kt$

or $\dfrac{1}{n-1}\left[\dfrac{1}{z^{n-1}}\right] = kt$

or $\dfrac{1}{n-1}\left[\dfrac{1}{(a-x)^{n-1}} - \dfrac{1}{a^{n-1}}\right] = kt$

or $k = \dfrac{1}{t(n-1)}\left[\dfrac{1}{(a-x)^{n-1}} - \dfrac{1}{a^{n-1}}\right]$ ...[5.6]

Half-Life Time

Refers to the time during which reaction is half completed.

For Zero Order Reaction

For zero order reaction, it is seen that $k = x/t$, at half-life, $x = a/2$ and $t = t_{1/2}$. Thus,

$k = \dfrac{a}{2t_{1/2}} \Rightarrow t_{1/2} = \dfrac{a}{2k}$ ...[5.7]

For First Order Reaction

$$k = \frac{1}{t}\ln\frac{a}{a-x}\text{; at half-life, } x = a/2 \text{ and } t = t_{1/2}.$$

$$= \frac{1}{t_{1/2}}\ln\frac{a}{a-a/2}$$

$$= \frac{0.693}{t_{1/2}} \text{ or } t_{1/2} = \frac{1}{k} \qquad \text{...[5.8]}$$

Note: $t_{1/2}$ is independent of the initial concentration of reactant and is characteristic of the reaction.

For Second Order Reaction

$$k = \frac{1}{t}\frac{x}{a(a-x)}\text{; at half-life, } x = a/2 \text{ and } t = t_{1/2}$$

$$= \frac{1}{at_{1/2}} \text{ or } t_{1/2} = \frac{1}{2k} \qquad \text{...[5.9]}$$

Note: $t_{1/2}$ depends inversely on the initial concentration of reactant.

For *n*th Order Reaction

$$k = \frac{1}{t(n-1)}\left[\frac{1}{(a-x)^{n-1}} - \frac{1}{a^{n-1}}\right]\text{; at half-life, } x = a/2 \text{ and } t = t_{1/2}$$

$$= \frac{1}{t_{1/2}(n-1)}\left[\frac{1}{(a-a/2)^{n-1}} - \frac{1}{a^{n-1}}\right]$$

$$= \frac{2^{n-1}-1}{t_{1/2}(n-1)a^{n-1}} \qquad \text{...[5.10]}$$

Note: $t_{1/2} \propto \frac{1}{a^{n-1}}$ ..[5.11]

Example 5.8

The decomposition of a compound, "A" follows first order kinetics. The rate constant of the reaction is 0.075 s^{-1}*. Find the half-life of "A."*

Solution

From relation [5.8], $k = \frac{0.693}{t_{1/2}}$

Thus, $t_{1/2} = \frac{0.693}{k}$

$$= \frac{0.693}{0.075}$$

$$= 9.24 \text{ s}$$

Example 5.9

The half-life of a first order reaction is 30 min. Find the rate constant of the reaction.

Solution

From relation [5.8], $k = \dfrac{0.693}{t_{1/2}}$

or $k = \dfrac{0.693}{30} = 2.31 \times 10^{-2}\ \text{min}^{-1}$

Example 5.10

For a first order reaction half-life is 15 min. How much time will be required for 75% completion of reaction?

Solution

From relation [5.8], $k = \dfrac{0.693}{t_{1/2}}$

or $k = \dfrac{0.693}{15} = 4.62 \times 10^{-2}\ \text{min}^{-1}$

Again, from relation [5.2], $k = \dfrac{1}{t} \ln \dfrac{a}{a-x}$

or $t = \dfrac{1}{k} \ln \dfrac{a}{a-x}$

$$= \frac{1}{4.62 \times 10^{-2}} \ln \frac{100}{100-75}$$

$$= \frac{1}{4.62 \times 10^{-2}} \ln 4 = 30\ \text{min}$$

Example 5.11

The half-life time for the reaction,
$NH_2NO_{2(aq)} \longrightarrow N_2O_{(g)} + H_2O_{(l)}$ which follows first order kinetics is 2.1 hour. If 6.2 g of nitramide is allowed to decompose, then calculate then time required for 99% decomposition and volume of dry N_2O produced at this point under STP.

Solution

From [5.2], $k = \dfrac{1}{t} \ln \dfrac{a}{a-x}$

Now, $t_{1/2} = \dfrac{0.693}{k}$ ...[1]

Again, $t_{99\%} = \dfrac{1}{k} \ln \dfrac{a}{a - 0.99a}$

$$= \frac{1}{k} \ln 100$$

$$= \frac{4.605}{k} \quad \text{...[2]}$$

Dividing the relations, we get

$$t_{99\%} = \frac{4.605}{0.693} t_{1/2}$$

$$= \frac{4.605}{0.693} \times 2.1 = 13.95 \text{ h}$$

Number of moles of $NH_2NO_2 = 6.2/62 = 0.1$

Now, number of moles of N_2O formed $= 0.99 \times 0.1 = 0.099$

At STP, the volume of N_2O formed $= 0.099 \times 22.4 = 2.218$ liters.

Example 5.12

In a second order reaction, the initial concentration of the reactant is 0.2 mol/l. The reaction is found to be 30% complete in 50 min. Calculate the rate constant and half-life time.

Solution

From [5.3], $k = \frac{1}{t}\frac{x}{a(a-x)}$

Here, $x = 30\%$ of initial concentration is $0.2 \times \frac{30}{100} = 0.06$

Substituting in the parent relation, $k = \frac{1}{50} \times \frac{0.06}{0.2(0.2-0.06)} = 0.043 \text{ l mol}^{-1} \text{ min}^{-1}$

Now, half-life time $= \frac{1}{ka}$

or $\quad t_{1/2} = \frac{1}{0.043 \times 0.2} = 116.28$ min

Example 5.13

Show that in case of a first order reaction, time required for 99.9% completion of a reaction is about 10 times than that required for half completion.

Solution

$$t_{1/2} = \frac{0.693}{k} \qquad \text{...[1]}$$

$$t_{99.9\%} = \frac{1}{k} \ln \frac{a}{a - 0.999a}$$

$$= \frac{1}{k} \ln \frac{a}{0.001a}$$

$$= \frac{6.930}{k} \qquad \text{...[2]}$$

Comparing relations [1] and [2], we get $\frac{t_{99.9\%}}{t_{1/2}} = 10$

Study of Complex Reactions and Steady-State Approximation

In case of complex reactions, sometimes it is difficult to choose a specific rate controlling step. In such cases, a particular approach is made which is known as steady-state approximation. The central idea is that at steady state, the change of concentration of any intermediate (a species which is formed in situ in one step and consumed in subsequent steps so that it does not appear as an end product) remains constant, i.e., the rate of its formation becomes equal to its consumption. Mathematically, $d[I]/dt = 0$, where I stands for intermediate. Different complex reactions fall into following four categories. Let us look at them.

Type I: First step is slow and rate-controlling step is followed by a rapid step.

Let us consider the reaction between NO_2 and F_2.

$$2NO_{2(g)} + F_{2(g)} \longrightarrow 2NO_2F_{(g)}$$

The proposed mechanism is as follows:

Step I $\quad NO_2 + F_2 \xrightarrow{k_1} NO_2F + F$

Step II $\quad NO_2 + F \xrightarrow{k_2} NO_2F$

Example 5.14

Show that the rate of reaction follows the equation, $-\dfrac{d[NO_2]}{dt} = 2k_1[NO_2][F_2]$

Solution

Applying steady-state approximation, we get $\dfrac{d[F]}{dt} = 0$

or $\quad k_1[NO_2][F_2] - k_2[NO_2][F] = 0$

or $\quad [F] = \dfrac{k_1}{k_2}[F_2]$ ...[5.12]

The rate of disappearance of NO_2 is given by $-\dfrac{d[NO_2]}{dt} = k_1[NO_2][F_2] + k_2[NO_2][F]$

or $\quad -\dfrac{d[NO_2]}{dt} = k_1[NO_2][F_2] + k_2[NO_2]\dfrac{k_1}{k_2}[F_2]$

$\quad = 2k_1[NO_2][F_2]$ ...[5.13]

Type II: Intermediate formed in the first step remains in equilibrium with reactants which subsequently slowly reacts in the second step.

Let us consider the reaction between nitric oxide and hydrogen, we have

$$2\,NO_{(g)} + H_{2(g)} \longrightarrow N_2O_{(g)} + H_2O_{(g)}$$

The proposed mechanism is as follows:

Step I $\quad 2NO \underset{k_{-1}}{\overset{k_1}{\rightleftharpoons}} N_2O_2$

Step II $\quad N_2O_2 + H_2 \xrightarrow{k_2} N_2O + H_2$

Apply steady-state approximation so as to find the overall rate law.

Applying steady-state approximation, $\dfrac{d[N_2O_2]}{dt} = 0$

or $k_1[NO]^2 - k_{-1}[N_2O_2] - k_2[N_2O_2][H_2] = 0$

$$\text{or} \quad [N_2O_2] = \frac{k_1[NO]^2}{k_{-1} + k_2[H_2]} \qquad [5.14]$$

Again from the rate law, we have rate = $[N_2O_2][H_2]$

Substituting,we get $[N_2O_2]$

$$\text{Rate} = k_2 \frac{k_1[NO]^2}{k_{-1} + k_2[H_2]} [H_2]$$

$$= \frac{k_1 k_2[NO]^2[H_2]}{k_{-1} + k_2[H_2]} \qquad ...[5.15]$$

This is the overall rate law based on steady-state approximation. However, this is a complicated one and needs to be simplified by choosing concentration conditions so that its validity can be confirmed. For example, if in the above case, concentration of H_2 is large enough so that $k_2[H_2] >> k_{-1}$, then the rate law becomes

$$\text{Rate} = \frac{k_1 k_2[NO]^2[H_2]}{k_2[H_2]}$$

$$= k\,[NO]^2 \qquad ...[5.16]$$

Thus, if at all the suggested mechanism is valid, then at sufficiently high concentration of H_2, the reaction should follow second order kinetics with respect to NO.

On the other hand, if $[H_2]$ is not much high so that $k_{-1} >> k_2\,[H_2]$, then the rate law becomes

$$\text{Rate} = \frac{k_1 k_2[NO]^2[H_2]}{k_{-1}}$$

$$= k[NO]^2[H_2] \qquad ...[5.17]$$

Thus, rate should be first order with respect to H_2 and second order with respect to NO to confirm the validity of the mechanism.

Type III: Reactions with more than two elementary steps with at least one slow step.

The reaction for the formation of phosgene is

$$CO + CO_2 \longrightarrow COCl_2$$

The suggested mechanism is as follows:

Step I $Cl_2 \underset{k_{-1}}{\overset{k_1}{\rightleftharpoons}} 2Cl$ (fast)

Step II $Cl + CO \underset{k_{-2}}{\overset{k_2}{\rightleftharpoons}} COCl$ (fast)

Step III $COCl + Cl_2 \xrightarrow{k_3} COCl_2 + Cl$ (slow)

Example 5.15

Show that $\frac{d[COCl_2]}{dt} = k\,[CO][Cl_2]^{3/2}$.

Solution

$$\text{Rate} = \frac{d[COCl_2]}{dt} = k_3[COCl][Cl_2] \qquad ...[5.18]$$

$$\text{From, Step I, } \frac{k_1}{k_{-1}} = \frac{[Cl]^2}{[Cl_2]} \text{ or } [Cl] = \left\{\frac{k_1}{k_{-1}}[Cl_2]\right\}^{1/2} \qquad ...[5.19]$$

$$\text{From, Step II, } \frac{k_2}{k_{-2}} = \frac{[COCl]}{[Cl][CO]} \text{ or } [COCl] = \frac{k_2}{k_{-2}}[Cl][CO] \qquad ...[5.20]$$

Substituting the value of [Cl] from relation [5.19] in relation [5.20], we get

$$[COCl] = \frac{k_2}{k_{-2}}\left\{\frac{k_1}{k_{-1}}[Cl_2]\right\}^{1/2}[CO] \qquad ...[5.21]$$

Finally, putting [COCl] in relation [5.18], we get

$$\frac{d[COCl_2]}{dt} = k_3[Cl_2]\frac{k_2}{k_{-2}}\left\{\frac{k_1}{k_{-1}}[Cl_2]\right\}^{1/2}[CO]$$

$$= k[CO][Cl_2]^{3/2}, \text{ where } k \text{ is the overall rate constant.} \qquad ...[5.22]$$

Type IV: Reaction with more than one step and more than one intermediate with comparable rate constants.

For the decomposition reaction of $N_2O_{5(g)}$ which is $2N_2O_5 \longrightarrow 4NO_2 + O_2$, the mechanistic steps are as follows:

Step I $\quad N_2O_5 \underset{k_{-1}}{\overset{k_1}{\rightleftharpoons}} NO_2 + NO_3$

Step II $\quad NO_3 + NO_2 \xrightarrow{k_2} NO + NO_2 + O_2$

Step III $\quad NO_3 + NO \xrightarrow{k_3} 2NO_2$

Example 5.16

Show that $\frac{d}{dt}[O_2] = k\,[N_2O_5]$, *where* $k = \frac{k_1k_2}{k_{-1} + 2k_2}$.

Solution

$$\text{From step II, } \frac{d}{dt}[O_2] = k_2\,[NO_3][NO_2] \qquad ...[5.23]$$

Applying steady-state approximation to NO, $k_2[NO_3][NO_2] - k_3\,[NO_3][NO] = 0$

$$\text{or} \quad [NO] = \frac{k_2}{k_3}[NO_2] \qquad ...[5.24]$$

Again, applying steady-state approximation to NO_3, we get

$$k_1[N_2O_5] - k_{-1}[NO_2][NO_3] - k_2\,[NO_3][NO_2] - k_3\,[NO_3][NO] = 0$$

$$\text{or} \quad [NO_3] = \frac{k_1[N_2O_5]}{k_{-1}[NO_2] + k_2[NO_2] + k_3[NO]} \qquad ...[5.25]$$

Substituting [NO] in relation [5.25], we get

$$[NO_3] = \frac{k_1[N_2O_5]}{k_{-1}[NO_2] + k_2[NO_2] + k_3 \times \frac{k_2}{k_3}[NO_2]}$$

$$= \frac{k_1[N_2O_5]}{k_{-1}[NO_2] + k_2[NO_2] + k_3 \times \frac{k_2}{k_3}[NO_2]}$$

$$= \frac{k_1[N_2O_5]}{[NO_2]\,[k_{-1} + 2k_2]} \qquad ...[5.26]$$

Finally, substituting $[NO_3]$ in relation [5.23], we get

$$\frac{d}{dt}[O_2] = k_2[NO_2]\frac{k_1[N_2O_5]}{[NO_2] + [k_{-1} + 2k_2]}$$

$$= k_2\frac{k_1[N_2O_5]}{[k_{-1} + 2k_2]}$$

$$= k_2[N_2O_5], \text{ where } k = \frac{k_1k_2}{k_{-1} + 2k_2} \qquad ...[5.27]$$

Note: If more than one intermediate remains present, then steady-state approximation is to be applied to individual intermediates so as to find their concentrations. Subsequently, the concentrations of intermediates are substituted in the rate law to get the overall rate.

Methods to Find Order of a Reaction

There are several methods to find order of a reaction. Let us discuss some commonly used methods.

Use of Integrated Rate Expressions

Analytical

In this method, the experimental data is substituted in integrated rate expressions of first, second, or third order. The equation that gives almost same value (within experimental error) of k, i.e., rate constant corresponds to the correct order of reaction.

Graphical

In this appropriate concentration term is plotted against time. Order can be evaluated from the nature of graph. For example, let us see the nature of graphs for zero, first, and second order reactions.

For zero order, $\underset{\downarrow\atop y}{(a - x)} = \underset{\downarrow\atop mx}{-kt} + \underset{\downarrow\atop c}{a}$

For first order, $\log(a - x) = \frac{-kt}{2.303} + \log a$

For second order, $\frac{1}{a - x} = kt + \frac{1}{a}$

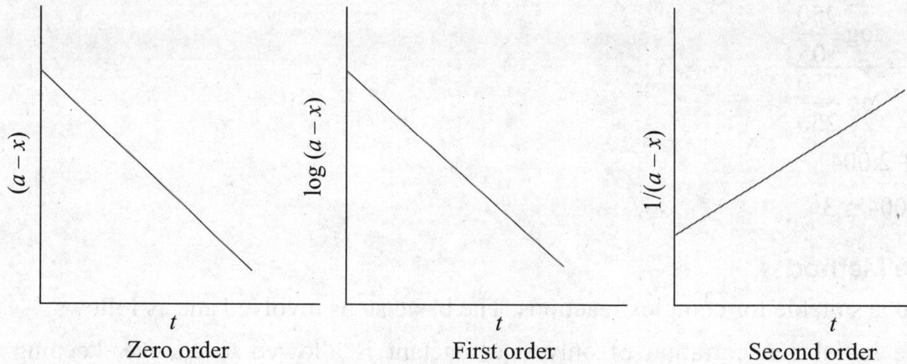

Fig. 5.6 Different plots to find order

Half-Life Method

It is a well-known fact that for nth order reaction, $t_{1/2} \propto \dfrac{1}{a^{n-1}}$.

Thus, if two experiments are carried with two different initial concentrations of reactant, then

$$\frac{(t_{1/2})_1}{(t_{1/2})_2} = \left[\frac{a_2}{a_1}\right]^{n-1}$$

Taking log of both sides, we get

$$\log \frac{(t_{1/2})_1}{(t_{1/2})_2} = (n-1)\log\left[\frac{a_2}{a_1}\right]$$

or $$n = 1 + \frac{\log \dfrac{(t_{1/2})_1}{(t_{1/2})_2}}{\log \dfrac{a_2}{a_1}} \qquad \text{...[5.28]}$$

The above expression can be utilised to find the order of a reaction.

Example 5.17

During thermal decomposition of a gaseous substance, the half-life was found to be 105 min when initial pressure was 750 mm and 950 min when the initial pressure was 250 mm. Find the order of reaction.

Solution

$$\frac{(t_{1/2})_1}{(t_{1/2})_2} = \left[\frac{a_2}{a_1}\right]^{n-1}$$

or $$\frac{105}{950} = \left[\frac{250}{750}\right]^{n-1}$$

or $$\log\frac{950}{105} = (n-1)\log\frac{750}{250}$$

or $$n = 1 + \frac{\log \frac{950}{105}}{\log \frac{750}{250}}$$

$$= 1 + 2.004$$

$$= 3.004 \cong 3$$

Initial Rate Method

This method is suitable for complex reactions. The basic steps involved ane as follows:

Step I: The initial concentration of only one reactant is allowed to change, keeping the concentration of others constant. Now the rate is determined from which order with respect to that reactant is calculated.

Step II: The procedure is repeated with respect to other reactants until the overall rate law is completely determined. The order of reaction is established from the rate law.

Example 5.18

In a reaction between A and B, the initial rate of reaction was measured for different initial concentrations of A and B as given below.

Trial	*I*	*II*	*III*
A (mol l^{-1})	*0.20*	*0.20*	*0.40*
B (mol l^{-1})	*0.30*	*0.10*	*0.05*
Rate (mol $l^{-1}s^{-1}$)	*5.07×10^{-5}*	*5.07×10^{-5}*	*7.6×10^{-5}*

Find the order of the reaction.

Solution

Let the rate expression be, rate = $k[A]^a [B]^b$.

From trials I and II, we get

$$R_I/R_{II} = \frac{5.07 \times 10^{-5}}{5.07 \times 10^{-5}} = \frac{(0.2)^a (0.3)^b}{(0.2)^a (0.1)^b}$$

or $$1 = \left[\frac{0.3}{0.1}\right]^b$$

Taking log on both sides, we get

$\log 1 = \ln(0.3)^b$, or, $b = 0$

Again, from trials I and III, we get

$$R_{III}/R_I = \frac{7.6 \times 10^{-5}}{5.07 \times 10^{-5}} = \frac{(0.4)^a (0.05)^b}{(0.2)^a (0.3)^b}$$

or $$1.5 = 2^a \left[\frac{0.05}{0.03}\right]^b$$

or $1.5 = 2^a$.

Taking log on both sides, we get

$\log 1.5 = a \log 2$

or $a = \dfrac{\log 1.5}{\log 2} = \dfrac{0.176}{0.301} = 0.58$. Or, $a \cong 0.5$

Now the rate expression becomes, rate = $k[A]^{0.5}[B]^0$

Thus, the order becomes 0.5.

Ostwald's Isolation Method

This method is similar to the initial rate method. In this method, the concentration of all of the reactants except one is taken in excess and the order is then determined with respect to the component which is not taken in excess. The procedure is then repeated with one more reactant and so on. This is known as isolation method, as the reactant which is not taken in excess is said to be kept isolated from the other reactants. The total order of the reaction is the sum of the orders of individual reactants

Factors Affecting the Rate of a Reaction

Nature of Reacting Species

Nature of reacting component is substantially important as far as rate of a reaction is concerned. It is decided by a number of contributing factors such as physical state, bond energy, solvation energy, polarity of solvent, etc. Therefore, it is difficult to generalize this effect. However individual reactions can be considered separately. For example, neutralization reactions are fast reactions.

Effect of Concentration

Concentration effect is well illustrated with respect to the rate expressions.

Effect of Temperature

Temperature has the most significant effect on the rate of a reaction. The magnitude of effect is expressed in terms of temperature coefficient, which is the ratio of rate constants that differ by 10°, i.e., temperature coefficient = (k_{T+10}/k_T).

Usually, we express temperature coefficient as (k_{308}/k_{298}) and in majority of cases it is found to lie between 2 and 3. This indicates that in majority of cases the rate of a reaction increases by twofold or even threefold with a mere 10° C rise in temperature.

Explanation

A simple explanation can be provided with respect to Maxwellian curves those describe the distribution of energies among molecules in a system. The curves show that the molecular energies remain distributed over a wide range (Fig. 5.7) at a particular temperature. Only the fraction of the reacting molecules having energy equal to or more than certain minimum value i.e., threshold energy (shown in the shaded region) are capable of causing effective collision and bring about the change. With the rise in temperature, average kinetic energy increases which bring more molecules into the higher energy range. Now, the fraction of molecules having energy becomes more as shown in the curve. The ultimate result being the number of effective collisions increases significantly and so also the rate.

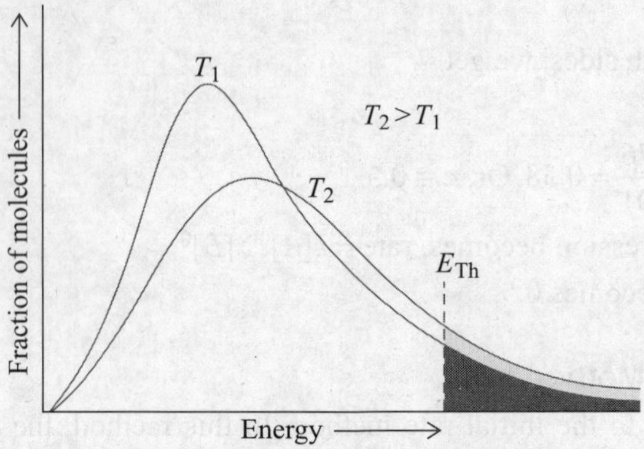

Fig. 5.7 Maxwellian distribution of energies

In order to explain the effect of temperature on reaction rate, different theories have been proposed from time to time. The significant theories are collision theory and absolute reaction rate theory which will be discussed in the latter course of the topic.

Effect of Catalyst

A catalyst alters, i.e., increases or decreases the rate of a reaction by providing an alternate path to the reaction and is recovered unchanged with respect to composition and amount at the end of the reaction. The reason is explained in detailed under section "Theories of Catalysis" (Chapter 5).

Theories of Reaction Rates

Collision Theory

According to Arrehenius and van't Hoff, the salient features are as follows:

1. Collision among the reacting particles is the essential requirement of a reaction.
2. Though collision frequency is usually very high, all collisions do not give rise to the change.
3. An effective collision is that which leads to the formation of products. This is possible when the following requirements are satisfied.
   (a) **Energy requirement:** The colliding particles must possess certain minimum energy called *threshold energy* so that bond rupture is possible.
   (b) **Orientation requirement:** The reacting particles must be properly oriented, i.e., the atoms taking part in bond breaking and making must come in contact with each other.

Mathematical treatment

As per the collision theory,

$$\text{Rate} = Z f P \qquad \text{...[5.29]}$$

where Z is the collision frequency, i.e., the number of collisions per unit volume per unit time. Thus,

$$Z = \frac{1}{\sqrt{2}} \pi \sigma^2 n^2 \bar{v}$$

where σ is the collision diameter, i.e., the closest distance between the nuclei of two colliding particles; n is the total number of molecules present per unit volume; $\overline{v}$ is the average velocity; and f is the fraction of molecules having energy equal to or more than threshold energy. Thus,

$$f = \frac{n'}{n} = e^{-E_a/RT}$$

where $e^{-E_a/RT}$ is the Boltzmann's factor; n is the number of molecules having activation energy; and P is the probability or steric factor which depends on the geometry of the molecules, i.e., proble fraction of molecules having proper orientation.

Case I: Collision among similar particles

$$\text{Average velocity} = \sqrt{\frac{8RT}{\pi M}}$$

Substituting in relation [5.29], we get

$$\text{Rate} = \frac{1}{\sqrt{2}}\pi\sigma^2 n^2 \sqrt{\frac{8RT}{\pi M}}\, e^{-E_a/RT} P$$

$$= 2\sigma^2 n^2 \sqrt{\frac{\pi RT}{M}}\, e^{-E_a/RT} P \qquad \text{...[5.30]}$$

Case II: Collision among different particles

$$\text{Total number of collisions per cc} = \frac{1}{\sqrt{2}}\pi\sigma^2 (n_a + n_b)^2 \overline{v} \qquad \text{...[5.31]}$$

Subtracting the number of collisions involving just a molecules and b molecules from this will give the number of collisions between a and b molecules. Hence,

$$Z = \frac{1}{\sqrt{2}}\pi\sigma^2 (n_a + n_b)^2 \overline{v} - \frac{1}{\sqrt{2}}\pi\sigma^2 (n_a)^2 \overline{v} - \frac{1}{\sqrt{2}}\pi\sigma^2 (n_b)^2 \overline{v}$$

$$= \sqrt{2}\,\pi\sigma^2 n_a n_b \overline{v} \qquad \text{...[5.32]}$$

$$\text{Average velocity} = \sqrt{\frac{8RT}{2\pi\mu}}$$

where μ is the reduced mass, i.e., $\mu = \dfrac{M_a M_b}{M_a + M_b}$

M_a and M_b are molecular masses.

$$\text{Collision diameter, } \sigma = \frac{\sigma_a + \sigma_b}{2}$$

Substituting in relation [5.29], we get

$$\text{Rate} = \sqrt{2}\,\pi \left(\frac{\sigma_a + \sigma_b}{2}\right)^2 n_a n_b \sqrt{\frac{8RT}{2\pi\mu}}\, e^{-E_a/RT} P$$

$$= \frac{1}{\sqrt{2}}(\sigma_a + \sigma_b)^2 n_a n_b \sqrt{\frac{\pi RT}{\mu}}\, e^{-E_a/RT} P \qquad \text{...[5.33]}$$

Explanation for the effect of temperature

There are two temperature terms in the relation [5.30], one in collision frequency and the other one in Boltzmann's factor. Let us verify the magnitude of contribution of these two terms in explaining the effect of temperature on the rate of reaction.

Collision frequency

We know that, rate $\propto Z$ and $Z \propto \sqrt{T}$. Thus, increase of collision frequency and ultimately the rate with 10°C rise in temperature is

$$\frac{r_{310}}{r_{300}} = \frac{Z_{310}}{Z_{300}} = \sqrt{\frac{310}{300}} = 1.015$$

Therefore, this factor does not have significant contribution.

Boltzmann's factor

We know that, rate $\propto$ Boltzmann factor.

Let us look at the ratio of Boltzmann's factors differing by 10°, taking a typical value of activation energy = 100 kJ/mol, we get

$$\frac{r_{310}}{r_{300}} = \frac{e^{-100 \times 10^3/310\,R}}{e^{-100 \times 10^3/300\,R}}$$

$$= e^{1.239} = 3.643$$

The result shows that this factor is very sensitive to temperature and is primarily responsible for the significant hike of rate with the increase in temperature.

Concept of activation energy

As per collision theory, there always exists an energy barrier between reactants and products. Activation energy is the excess energy than the average energy of reactants required to lift the molecules to have threshold energy so that they can cross over the energy barrier. This is shown in the energy profile for an exothermic reaction as follows.

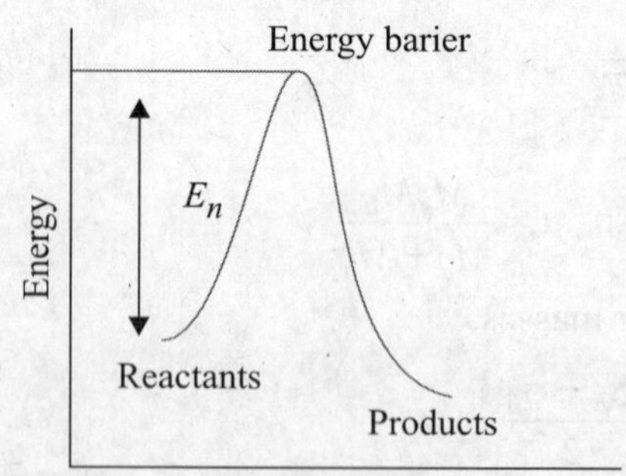

Fig. 5.8 Energy profile of a reaction showing activation energy

Arrhenius equation

Arrhenius (1889) observed that the rate constant for a large number of reactions increases exponentially with temperature and the plot of log k against $1/T$ gives a linear relation. He, therefore, suggested the empirical relation between rate constant and temperature as

$$k = A \qquad \text{...[5.34]}$$

where A is a constant known as pre-exponential factor or frequency factor, E is the activation energy, and k is the rate constant.

Evaluation of activation energy

1. **Graphical method**

$$k = Ae^{-E_a/RT}$$

Taking logarithm of both sides, we get

$$\ln k = \ln A - \frac{E_a}{RT}$$

$$\text{or} \quad \log k = -\frac{E_a}{2.303\,RT} + \log A \qquad \text{...[5.35]}$$

Now, plotting $\log k$ as a function of $1/T$ a straight line is obtained with negative slope and Y-intercept. The activation energy can be calculated from the slope, i.e., E = slope × 2.303, while intercept is $\log A$.

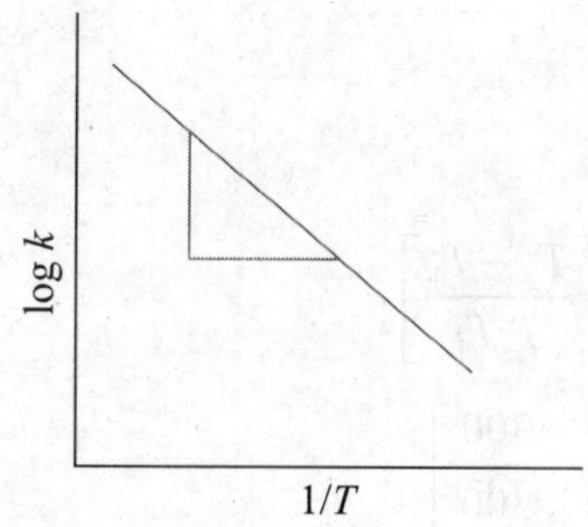

Fig. 5.9 Plot of log k as a function of $1/T$

2. **Analytical method**

Let k_1 and k_2 be the rate constants at two different temperatures T_1 and T_2, respectively. Then, from relation, we get

$$\text{At } T_1,\ \ln k_1 = \ln A - \frac{E_a}{RT_1}$$

$$\text{At } T_2,\ \ln k_2 = \ln A - \frac{E_a}{RT_2}$$

$$\ln k_2 - \ln k_1 = \frac{E_a}{R}\left[\frac{T_2 - T_1}{T_2T_1}\right]$$

$$\text{or} \quad \ln(k_2/k_1) = \frac{E_a}{R}\left[\frac{T_2 - T_1}{T_2T_1}\right]$$

$$\text{or} \quad \log(k_2/k_1) = \frac{E_a}{2.303\,R}\left[\frac{T_2 - T_1}{T_2T_1}\right] \qquad \text{...[5.36]}$$

Now knowing the rate constants at two different temperatures, one can easily calculate the activation energy by using the above relation.

Example 5.19

A reaction proceeds three times faster at 37°C as it does at 27°C. Find the activation energy.

Solution

$$\log (k_2/k_1) = \frac{E_a}{2.303\,R}\left[\frac{T_2 - T_1}{T_2 T_1}\right]$$

or $$\log 3 = \frac{E_a}{2.303 \times 1.987}\left[\frac{310 - 300}{310 \times 300}\right]$$

or $$E_a = 20.305 \text{ kcal}$$

Example 5.20

A first order reaction is 50% complete in 25 min at 27°C and in 5 min at 37°C. Calculate the activation energy.

Solution

$$k_1 = \frac{0.693}{25} = 0.0277 \text{ min}^{-1}$$

$$k_2 = \frac{0.693}{05} = 0.1386 \text{ min}^{-1}$$

Now, $$\log (k_2/k_1) = \frac{E_a}{2.303\,R}\left[\frac{T_2 - T_1}{T_2 T_1}\right]$$

or $$\log 5 = \frac{E_a}{2.303 \times 1.987}\left[\frac{310 - 300}{310 \times 300}\right]$$

or $$E_a = 29.746 \text{ kcal}$$

Example 5.21

At 300°C, the half life for a first order reaction is 350 min. The activation energy of the reaction is 100 kJ mol^{-1}. Calculate the time required for 90% completion of the reaction at 400°C.

Solution

$$k_1 = \frac{0.693}{350} = 1.98 \times 10^{-3} \text{ min}^{-1}$$

Substituting in Arrehenius equation, we get

$$\log (k_2/k_1) = \frac{E_a}{2.303\,R}\left[\frac{T_2 - T_1}{T_2 T_1}\right]$$

or $$\log (k_2/1.98 \times 10^{-3}) = \frac{100 \times 10^3}{2.303 \times 8.314}\left[\frac{673 - 573}{673 \times 573}\right]$$

or $$k_2 = 4.473 \times 10^{-2}$$

Now, $$t = \frac{2.303}{4.473 \times 10^{-2}} \log \frac{100}{10} = 51.49 \text{ min}$$

Example 5.22

A reaction is carried at 500 K. If the same reaction is carried out in the presence of a catalyst at the same rate, then the temperature required is 400 K. Calculate activation energy of the reaction if the catalyst is capable of lowering the energy barrier by 20 kJ mol^{-1}.

Solution

Let E_1 and E_2 be the activation energies in the absence and presence of catalyst, respectively. Then in the absence of catalyst, $k_1 = Ae^{-E_1/500R}$, and in the presence of the catalyst $k_2 = Ae^{-E_2/400R}$.

As the rates are same, $k_1 = k_2$

or $\quad Ae^{-E_1/500R} = Ae^{-E_2/400R}$

or $\quad \dfrac{E_1}{500\,R} = \dfrac{E_1 - 20}{400\,R}$

or $\quad E_1 = 100 \text{ kJ mol}^{-1}$

Example 5.23

At 300 K, the activation energy E_a for the decomposition of H_2O_2 has been measured to be 70.3 kJ mol^{-1}. In the presence of iodide ions, I^-, with specified concentration, the activation energy has been found to be 50.5 kJ mol^{-1}. How much faster is the decomposition when the same concentration of iodide is present in the reaction?

Solution

If k_1 and k_2 represent the reaction rate constants of decomposition in the absence of iodide and in the presence of iodide.

$$k_1 = Ae^{\frac{-70300}{8.314 \times 300}}$$

$$k_2 = Ae^{\frac{-50500}{8.314 \times 300}}$$

$$\text{Now, } k_2/k_1 = \frac{e^{\frac{-50500}{8.314 \times 300}}}{e^{\frac{-70300}{8.314 \times 300}}}$$

$$= e^{\frac{19800}{8.314 \times 300}}$$

$$= 2807$$

Thus, the rate becomes 2807 times faster in the presence of iodide.

Example 5.24

For a first order reaction, the values of frequency factor and activation energy are 4×10^{13} s^{-1} and 98.6 kJ mol^{-1}, respectively. At what temperature will its half-life be 10 min?

Solution

For a first order reaction, $k = \dfrac{0.693}{600}$ s^{-1}

$$\text{Now, } k = 4 \times 10^{13} e^{-\frac{98.6 \times 10^3}{8.314 \times T}}$$

$$\text{or} \quad \frac{0.693}{600} = 4 \times 10^{13} e^{-\frac{98.6 \times 10^3}{8.314 \times T}}$$

$$\text{or} \quad \ln \frac{0.693}{600} = \ln (4 \times 10^{13}) \times -\frac{98.6 \times 10^3}{8.314 \times T}$$

$$\text{or} \quad T = 311.35 \text{ K}$$

Example 5.25

If the activation energy of a reaction is 80.9 kJ mol^{-1}, calculate the fraction of molecules at 400°C which have enough energy to form the products.

Solution

$$f = e^{-\frac{E_a}{R \times T}}$$

$$= e^{-\frac{80.9 \times 10^3}{8.314 \times 673}}$$

$$= 5.27 \times 10^{-7}$$

Example 5.26

Calculate the number of binary collisions per cc of N_2 gas at 1 atm and 298 K. Given the diameter of N_2 molecule is 3.74 Å.

Solution

Number of molecules per cc at 298 K and 1 atm,

$$n = \frac{6.023 \times 10^{23}}{22400} \times \frac{273}{298}$$

$$= 2.46 \times 10^{19}$$

$$\text{Average velocity } (\bar{v}) = \sqrt{\frac{8RT}{\pi M}} = \sqrt{\frac{8 \times 8.314 \times 298 \times 10^7}{3.14 \times 28}} = 4.8 \times 10^4 \text{ cm s}^{-1}$$

$$\text{Now, number of binary collisions} = \frac{1}{\sqrt{2}} \pi \sigma^2 n^2 \bar{v}$$

$$= \frac{3.14}{\sqrt{2}} (3.74 \times 10^{-8})^2 \times 4.8 \times 10^4 \times (2.46 \times 10^{19})^2$$

$$= 8.98 \times 10^{28}$$

Limitations of collision theory

Some limitations of the collision theory are as follows:

1. It is restricted to gaseous phase reactions.
2. Separate treatment is required for uni- and bimolecular reactions.
3. There is no reason why rotation and vibration energies are not considered.
4. It is difficult to evaluate the steric factor *P* in case of molecules with complex geometry.

Theory for unimolecular reactions (Lindemann's time lag teory)

Collision theory apparently fails to explain the mechanism of a unimolecular reaction. The reason is twofold. *Firstly*, in unimolecular reactions, only one molecule takes part in the reaction and the reaction follows first order kinetics. However, with respect to collision theory, molecules become activated through collisions and the rate of formation of activated molecules should be proportional to the number of two-particle collisions and hence the reaction should be a bimolecular process. Thus, the theory fails to explain how a bimolecular collision can give rise to first order kinetics. *Secondly*, the theory also fails to explain how lowering of pressure can convert the first order unimolecular kinetics to second order kinetics although the rate of a first order reaction is independent of initial pressure or concentration. Both the problems were addressed by Lindemann. According to him,

1. Molecules get activation energy through collisions,
2. Activated molecules decompose only after some time has passed after collision, i.e., there is a time lag between activation and decomposition.
3. When the time lag is relatively large then there is every possibility that some of the activated molecules get deactivated through subsequent collisions to ordinary molecules.
4. The rate of decomposition is not proportional to all activated molecules rather it is proportional to fraction of activated molecules which survive the time lag.
5. The activated molecules disappear through two parallel processes, namely, through deactivation and through decomposition.

Mathematical treatment

The mechanism of a hypothetical unimolecular reaction can be written as

$$A + A \xrightarrow{k_1} A + A^*$$

$$A^* + A \xrightarrow{k_2} 2A$$

$$A^* \xrightarrow{k_3} B + C$$

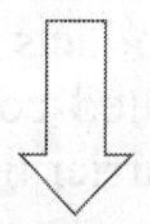

Products

where A is normal and A^* is the activated molecules.

Now, rate of reaction = $k_3\,[A^*]$

Applying steady-state principle to the activated molecules, we get

$$k_1\,[A]^2 - k_2\,[A^*][A] - k_3\,[A^*] = 0$$

or $$[A^*] = \frac{k_1[A]^2}{k_2[A] + k_3}$$

Substituting in relation, we get

$$\text{Rate} = \frac{k_1[A]^2}{k_2[A] + k_3} \qquad ...[5.37]$$

Case I

When rate of deactivation is larger than decomposition, i.e., $k_2\,[A] >> k_3$, then

$$\text{Rate} = k'[A] \qquad ...[5.38]$$

where $k' = \dfrac{k_1 k_3}{k_2}$

This is similar to that of first order and this happens if time lag is relatively large.

Case II

When the rate of decomposition is larger than deactivation, i.e., $k_3 >> k_2\,[A]$, then

$$\text{Rate} = k_1[A]^2, \qquad ...[5.39]$$

That is, at low concentration the process follows a second order kinetics.

Activated Complex Theory (by Eyring and Polani)

The salient features of the activated complex theory are as follows:

1. With the approach of reacting molecules towards each other, there occurs a continuous change in the intermolecular distance, net energy content, and configuration, i.e. rearrangement of valency bonds.
2. On reaching the equilibrium, the reactant molecules get transferred into an energy-rich intermediate having specific configuration known as transition state or activated complex.
3. The activated complex is unstable and has a transient existence.
4. The activated complex remains in dynamic equilibrium with the reactants.
5. Activated complex must possess an unstable vibrational degree of freedom to facilitate the disruption of bonds. The frequency of such a vibration is low and the average value is of the order of kT, where k is Boltzmann's constant.
6. The activated complex finally decomposes to yield the products. Thus, the rate is proportional to the frequency of decomposition of activated complex, i.e., the number of activated complex that passes over the potential barrier in unit time.
7. The activation energy is the additional energy which must be supplied to the reactant molecules to transform them to activated complex.

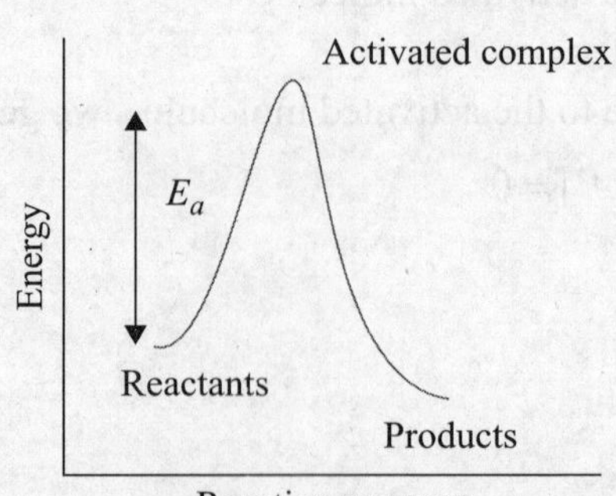

Fig. 5.10 Energy profile of a reaction showing activation energy

Mathematical treatment

Let us consider a hypothetical reaction, $A + B \longrightarrow$ Products. As per the theory, the reaction takes place as:

$$A + B \underset{}{\overset{K^{\#}}{\rightleftharpoons}} [AB]^{\#} \xrightarrow{k_2} \text{Products}$$

$$K^{\#} = \frac{[AB]^{\#}}{[A][B]}$$

or $\quad [AB^{\#}] = K^{\#}\,[A][B]$ ...[5.40]

$$\text{Rate} = [AB]^{\#} \times \text{Frequency of decomposition of activated complex}$$

$$= K^{\#}\,[A][B] \times \frac{E_{\text{Vib}}}{h}$$

$$= K^{\#}\,[A][B] \times \frac{kT}{h}$$

$$= K^{\#}\,[A][B] \times \frac{RT}{Nh} \quad \text{...[5.41]}$$

Again, rate $= k_2\,[A][B]$ ...[5.42]

Thus, $k_2\,[A][B] = K^{\#}\,[A][B] \times \dfrac{RT}{Nh}$

or $\quad k_2 = K^{\#} \times \dfrac{RT}{Nh}$ ...[5.43]

From van't Hoff reaction isotherm, we get

$$\Delta G^{\#} = -RT \ln K^{\#}$$

or $\quad \ln K^{\#} = \dfrac{-\Delta G^{\#}}{RT}$

$$= \frac{-(\Delta H^{\#} - T\Delta S^{\#})}{RT}$$

$$K^{\#} = e^{-\Delta H^{\#}/RT}\, e^{-\Delta S^{\#}/R} \quad \text{...[5.44]}$$

Substituting in relation [5.43], we get

$$k_2 = e^{-\Delta H^{\#}/RT}\, e^{-\Delta S^{\#}/R}\, \frac{RT}{Nh} \quad \text{...[5.45]}$$

Case I: For unimolecular reaction

As E_a is related to enthalpy of transition, $\Delta H^{\#}$ by the relation,

$$E_a = \Delta H^{\#} + RT - \Delta n^{\#}\, RT$$

where $\Delta n^{\#}$ is the change in number of moles as we move from reactant to its activated complex.

In unimolecular reaction, $\Delta n^{\#} = 0$

Thus, $E_a = \Delta H^{\#} + RT$

$$k_2 = e^{-(E_a - RT)/RT} e^{-\Delta S^{\#}/R} \frac{RT}{Nh}$$

or $$k_2 = e.e^{-E_a/RT} e^{-\Delta S^{\#}/R} \frac{RT}{Nh} \qquad ...[5.46]$$

Case II: For bimolecular reactions

In bimolecular reaction, $\Delta n^{\#} = -1$

$$k_2 = e^{-(E_a - 2RT)/RT} e^{-\Delta S^{\#}/R} \frac{RT}{Nh}$$

or $$k_2 = e^2\, e^{-E_a/RT} e^{\Delta S^{\#}/R} \frac{RT}{Nh} \qquad ...[5.47]$$

Now comparing relations [5.46] and [5.47] with Arrhenius equation, $k = Ae^{-E_a/RT}$, the pre-exponential factor A is related to entropy as:

$$A = e^{\Delta S^{\#}/R} \frac{RT}{Nh} f \qquad ...[5.48]$$

where $f = e$ for unimolecular reaction and $f = e^2$ for bimolecular reaction

Comparison of collision theory and transition state theory

From collision theory, rate = $Ze^{-E_a/RT} P$

From transition state theory, rate = $e^{-\Delta H^{\#}/RT} e^{\Delta S^{\#}/R} \frac{RT}{Nh}$

$$\text{Now, } Ze^{-E_a/RT} P = e^{-\Delta H^{\#}/RT} e^{\Delta S^{\#}/R} \frac{RT}{Nh}$$

or $$Ze^{-E_a/RT} P = e^{-E_a/RT} e^{\Delta S^{\#}/R} \frac{RT}{Nh}$$

or $$P = e^{\Delta S^{\#}/R} \frac{RT}{NhZ} \qquad ...[5.49]$$

Thus, the orientation factor P is related to entropy of activation.

Note:

Relation between E_a and enthalpy of transition $\Delta H^{\#}$

From van't Hoff, $$\frac{d \ln K^{\#}}{dt} = \frac{\Delta E^{\#}}{RT^2} \qquad ...[5.50]$$

$$\text{Again, } k_2 = K^{\#} \times \frac{RT}{Nh}$$

or $$\ln k_2 = \ln k^{\#} + \ln T + \ln \frac{R}{Nh}$$

Differentiating with respect to t, $$\frac{d \ln k_2}{dt} = \frac{d \ln K^{\#}}{dt} + \frac{1}{T}$$

or $$\frac{d \ln k_2}{dt} = \frac{\Delta E^{\#}}{RT^2} + \frac{1}{T} = \frac{\Delta E^{\#} + RT}{RT^2} \qquad ...[5.51]$$

From Arrhenius, $\dfrac{d \ln k_2}{dt} = \dfrac{E_a}{RT^2}$ ...[5.52]

Now comparing relations [5.51] and [5.52], $\dfrac{E_a}{RT^2} = \dfrac{\Delta E^{\#} + RT}{RT^2}$

or $E_a = \Delta H^{\#} - P\Delta V + RT$

$= \Delta H^{\#} - \Delta nRT + RT$ ...[5.53]

Advantages

1. It can be applied to all types of processes, i.e., uni-molecular, bi-molecular, etc.
2. It can be applied to reactions in solution.

Note:

Negative activation energy: A few cases are there where rates of reaction *decrease* with the increasing temperature following an approximately exponential relationship so the rate constant can still be fit to an Arrhenius expression, this results in a negative value of E_a. Elementary reactions exhibiting these negative activation energies are typically barrierless reactions, in which the reaction proceeding relies on the capture of the molecules into a potential well. Increasing the temperature leads to a reduced probability of the colliding molecules capturing one another (with more glancing collisions not leading to reaction as the higher momentum carries the colliding particles out of the potential well), expressed as a reaction cross section that decreases with increasing temperature. Negative activation energy implies it is not possible to stop the reaction from occurring. The reactants already have plenty of energy for the reaction so that the only way to prevent the reaction is to keep the reactants apart.

For example, the oxidation of nitrogen monoxide, the rate falls with an increase in temperature. This implies negative activation energy. The reason for this apparent peculiarity is that although the rate constant k does indeed increase with the increasing temperature, the mechanism is such that another constant, the equilibrium constant for one of the mechanistic steps, is also involved in the rate equation. This falls with the increasing temperature.

The reaction of nitrogen monoxide (nitrogen (II) oxide) with oxygen, i.e., $2NO(g) + O_2(g) \longrightarrow 2NO_2(g)$ is a well-known third order reaction with rate expression, rate $= k[NO]^2[O_2]$. The probability of a trimolecular reaction, where the three species collide simultaneously with the correct energy and the correct orientation in a single step, is very small. The suggested mechanism for the oxidation of NO with O_2 involves an initial dimerisation in an equilibrium reaction, followed by reaction of the dimer with the oxygen.

Step I: $2NO(g) \xrightleftharpoons{k_c} (NO)_2(g)$

Step II: $(NO)_2(g) + O_2(g) \xrightarrow{k} 2NO_2(g)$

The rate of attainment of the equilibrium in step I is very fast compared with reaction step II which is the rate limiting step. The equilibrium constant is

$K_c = [(NO)_2]/[NO]^2$

or $[(NO)_2] = K_c[NO]^2$ ...[5.54]

The rate can be expressed as:

Rate $= k\,[(NO)_2][O_2] = k\,K_c\,[NO]^2[O_2]$ ...[5.55]

Both k and K_c are temperature dependent. The constant k increases with increasing temperature, while K_c decreases with temperature (Step I involves bond formation and therefore exothermic). The hike in k is less than the fall in K_c, so that the overall value 'k K_c' also falls with an increase in temperature. The activation energy is only apparently negative; for the rate-limiting step it is, as is usual, positive.

QUESTIONS

1. Differentiate between order and molecularity.
2. For the reaction, $2A + B_2 \longrightarrow 2AB$, the rate increases by 8 times when concentrations of both are doubled and rate doubles when only concentration of B is doubled. Write down the rate law.
3. What is the order of the following reactions:
   (i) Inversion of cane sugar
   (ii) Saponification of ester
4. What is the order of reaction if half-life period and units of k depend inversely on concentration?
5. Write the equation that relates the rate constant of a reaction with its activation energy explaining all the symbols used.
6. Give one example of zero order reaction. What is the unit of a zero order rate constant?
7. What are the characteristics of first order reaction?
8. If the rate of a reaction is equal to the rate constant, what is the order of the reaction?
9. What are the characteristics of a second order reaction?
10. Explain why reactions of third and higher orders are usually not common.
11. What are the disadvantages of collision theory?
12. How does half-life period of a first order reaction vary with temperature?
13. Define temperature coefficient of a reaction.
14. Explain why collision theory fails to account for kinetics of uni-molecular reaction.
15. What is the advantage in using integrated rate laws over differential rate laws?
16. Explain the term collision frequency. On what factors does it depend?
17. Out of order and molecularity, which is the characteristic of a reaction and why?
18. What is a mixed-order reaction?
19. Explain negative-order reaction with an example.
20. State law of mass action.
21. What is order of reaction? Give two examples on fractional order reaction.
22. What do you mean by steady state approximation?
23. Give the unit of rate constant of a second order reaction with example.

24. Write down the Arrhenius equation and explain each term involved in it.
25. Explain why order of a reaction can't be predicted from overall stoichiometry.
26. What is the significance of writing + or – sign before the rate of reaction?
27. Identify the catalyst and promoter in the following reaction.

$$CO_{2(g)} + H_{2(s)} \xrightarrow[250°C]{ZnO, Cr_2O_3} CH_3OH\ (1)$$

28. Derive a relation between $\Delta H^{\#}$ and E_a.
29. Derive an expression for the rate constant of a second order reaction in which both the reactants are different.
30. Explain why increase in temperature invariably increases the rate of reaction.
31. Explain why order of a reaction cannot be predicted from overall stoichiometry?
32. How is the theory of absolute rate superior to the collision theory?
33. What are the essential requirements of a reaction to occur according to the collision theory?
34. How is the order of a reaction determined by graphical method?
35. Give the basic concept of transition state theory.
36. Derive an expression for rate constant of a bimolecular gaseous reaction on the basis of collision theory.
37. Deduce the rate expression for a second order reaction where both the concentration terms are same. What is half-life period of the reaction?
38. Derive the rate expression of a uni-molecular reaction on the basis of transition state theory.
39. Explain Lindemann's Time Lag Theory of uni-molecular reactions.
40. For the decomposition of ozone, $2O_3 \longrightarrow 3O_2$, the mechanistic steps are as follows:

Step I: $O_3 \underset{k_{-1}}{\overset{k_1}{\rightleftharpoons}} O_2 + O$

Step II: $O_3 + O \xrightarrow{k_2} 2O_2$

Show that decomposition of O_3, i.e., $-\dfrac{d[O_3]}{dt} = \dfrac{k[O_3]^2}{[O_2]}$,

where $k = \dfrac{2k_1k_2}{k_{-1}}$; assume $k_{-1}\ [O_2] >> k_2\ [O_3]$

41. For the reaction, $2NO + Cl_2 \longrightarrow 2NOCl$, the proposed mechanism is as follows:

Step I: $NO + Cl_2 \underset{k_{-1}}{\overset{k_1}{\rightleftharpoons}} NOCl_2$

Step II: $NO + NOCl_2 \xrightarrow{k_2} 2NOCl$

Show that the overall rate = $k[NO]^2\ [Cl_2]$, where $k = \dfrac{2k_1k_2}{k_{-1}}$; assume $k_2\ [NO] << k_{-1}$.

42. What is the effect of temperature on reaction rate? Give Arrhenius equation. Plot the graph showing variation in k with temperature. What can you calculate from the slope?
43. Describe a method to determine the order of a reaction.
44. How is theory of absolute rate superior to collision theory?
45. Show that for a first order reaction the time required for the successive reduction in the concentration of A by a constant factor is independent of the initial concentration of A.

NUMERICAL PROBLEMS

1. In a reaction between Cl_2 and NO, the initial rate of reaction was measured for different initial concentrations as given below,

Trial	I	II	III
Cl_2 (mol l^{-1})	0.02	0.02	0.04
NO (mol l^{-1})	0.01	0.03	0.03
Rate (mol l^{-1} s^{-1})	2.4×10^{-4}	2.16×10^{-3}	4.32×10^{-3}

Find the order of the reaction. Also calculate the rate constant.

2. In a reaction between $K_2C_2O_4$ and $HgCl_2$ i.e., $K_2C_2O_4 + 2HgCl_2 \longrightarrow 2KCl + 2CO_2 + Hg_2Cl_2$, the weights of Hg_2Cl_2 precipitated from different solutions in given time are as follows

Time	60	65	120
$K_2C_2O_4$ (mol l^{-1})	0.404	0.404	0.202
$HgCl_2$ (mol l^{-1})	0.0418	0.0836	0.0836
Hg_2Cl_2 (mol l^{-1})	0.0032	0.0068	0.0031

Write the rate expression and find the order.

3. The half-life of a reaction becomes 2.5 times if the concentration is made half. What is the order of the reaction?
4. At 300 K, a first order reaction is 50% completed in 20 min. At 350 K, the same reaction is 50% completed in 5 min. Calculate the energy of activation of the reaction.
5. In a first order reaction, the concentration of reactant after 10 and 20 min from the start was found to be 14 and 8.5 units, respectively. Calculate the initial concentration and rate constant.
6. A first order reaction has rate constant equal to 7×10^{-7} s^{-1} at 7°C and 9×10^{-1} s^{-1} at 77°C. Calculate the activation energy. Also calculate the rate constant.
7. A first order reaction has rate constant equal to 1.5×10^{-4} s^{-1} at 300 K and 7.5×10^{-4} s^{-1} at 320 K. Calculate the activation energy. Also calculate the rate constant.
8. The decomposition of a gaseous substance $AB(g) \longrightarrow A(g) + B(g)$ follows first order kinetics. Calculate:
   (i) the rate constant if pressure of *AB* falls from 0.62 atm to 0.44 atm in 50 s and
   (ii) pressure of *AB* after 75 s at the same pressure.
9. A buried piece of wood has 25.6% as much C^{14} as ordinary wood today. When did the piece get buried if the decay follows first order kinetics? (half-life is 5760 years)
10. The rate of a reaction (i) $A \rightarrow$ Pr is doubled when the temperature is raised from 300 K to 310 K. The half life period at 310 K for the reaction is 30 min. At the same temperature *B* decomposes twice as fast as *A* in another reaction, (ii) $B \rightarrow$ Pr. Calculate the rate constant of reaction (ii) at 300K if the activation energy of reaction (ii) is half that of reaction (i). Both reaction follows first order kinetics.

11. The rate constant of a reaction is found to be tripled when the temperature increases from 25°C to 60°C. Calculate the activation energy.
12. A first order reaction is 20% complete in 10 min. Calculate rate constant and time taken for 75% completion.
13. The specific rate constant of a reaction increases by a factor 4 if the temperature changed from 27°C to 47°C. Find the activation energy of the reaction.
14. A zero order reaction is 50% complete in 20 min. What percentage would be completed at the end of 30 min? Find out the time when concentration would be zero.
15. A bottle of milk stored at 30°C sours in 36 h and in 3 days when refrigerated at 5°C. Assuming the rate constant to be inversely proportional to souring time, calculate the activation energy required for souring.
16. If a first order reaction has activation energy of 105 kJ mol^{-1} and pre-exponential factor 5×10^{13}, calculate the temperature at which the half-life period will be 20 days.
17. For a reaction rate = $k\,[A]^{1/2}$. The initial concentration of A is 1 mol l^{-1}. Find out the half-life period and the rate constant if 80% of the reaction is completed in 45 min.
18. The initial concentration is 0.2 M in a second order reaction. The reaction is found to be 10% completed in 30 min Calculate the rate constant and half-life time.
19. At 25°C, the rate constant for the first order decomposition of N_2O_5 in the reaction is $N_2O_5\ (g) \longrightarrow 4NO_2\ (g) + O_2\ (g)$ is $k = 3.38 \times 10^{-5}$ s^{-1}. What is the half-life of N_2O_5? If the initial pressure is 5000 torr, then what will be the pressure 10 min after the ignition of the reaction.
20. Find the order of the reaction. $A + 2B \longrightarrow C + D$ from the following data.

Rate (mol dm^{-3} s^{-1})	[A]	[B]
0.0032	0.1	0.1
0.0096	0.3	0.1
0.0064	0.1	0.2

Which of the following mechanisms agree with the rate law?

(i) $2A \longrightarrow A_2;\ A_2 + B \longrightarrow C + D$

(ii) $A + B \longrightarrow E\,;\ E + B \longrightarrow C + D$

21. Consider a gas phase decomposition reaction, $A \longrightarrow$ Product(s) at 500°C and at an initial pressure of 350 torr. The rate of the reaction was 1.07 torr s^{-1} when 5% of the decomposition was over and 0.76 torr s^{-1}, when 20% decomposition was over. Determine the order of the reaction.
22. A second order reaction where two reactants are same is 30% completed in 500 s. How long will it take to go to 90% completion?
23. The activation energy of a certain uncatalyzed reaction at 310 K is 70 kJ mol^{-1} which is reduced to 50 kJ mol^{-1} when catalyzed by an enzyme. Find the ratio of the rate constants of the enzyme catalysed to that of uncatalyzed reactions?
24. Inversion of cane sugar follows first order kinetics. If 30% of a sample so cane sugar gets hydrolysed in 1 h, how much time will it take for 75% to be hydrolysed?

25. The plot of ln k vs. $1/T$ is a straight line and with a slope of -1.2×10^4 K. Calculate the activation energy.
26. At 380°C, the half-life period for a first-order decomposition of H_2O_2 is 360 min. The energy of activation of reaction is 200 kJ mol^{-1}. Calculate the time required for 75% decomposition at 450°C.
27. Calculate the activation energy of a chemical reaction which doubles the rate when the temperature is raised from 300 K to 310 K.
28. A second order reaction, when two reactants are same, is 30% completed in 500 seconds. How long will it take to go to 90% completion?

CHAPTER

6 Phase Rule

Chapter Outline

- Terminologies
- Phase Rule
- Water System
- Sulfur System
- Two-Component System and Reduced Phase Rule
- Eutectic System
- Pb–Ag System
- Bi–Cd System
- Fe–C System

Phase rule is considered to be an important tool to deal with the behavior of heterogeneous systems. It helps in predicting the effect of temperature, pressure, and concentration on a heterogeneous system in equilibrium. Phase rule also allows us to construct *phase diagrams* to represent and interpret phase equilibria in heterogeneous systems. This relationship was developed by an American physicist Willard Gibbs and is popularly known as *Gibb's phase rule.* The main advantages of the relation are as follows:

1. It predicts the possible equilibriums among different substances present in different phases.
2. It does not require any information regarding the molecular structure of the system and deals with the system as a whole, i.e., macroscopically.
3. It can be applied to both physical and chemical equilibria.

The rule describes a system in terms of phase, component, and degree of freedom. Therefore, before exploring the applications it is essential to understand the basic terminologies.

Terminologies

Phase

A phase is any homogeneous and physically distinct segment of a system which remains bounded by a surface and is mechanically separable from other parts of the system. Let us look into some examples.

1. A gaseous mixture, irrespective of the number of gases present, constitutes a single phase as gases are completely miscible, e.g., air which is a mixture of nitrogen, oxygen, carbon dioxide, water vapors, etc., constitutes a single phase only.
2. Two or more completely miscible liquids constitute a single phase, e.g., water and ethyl alcohol present together exists in one liquid phase only.

3. A mixture of two immiscible liquids, such as water and benzene, will exist in two distinct liquid phases. Thus, there will be two phases, each separated from the other by a well-defined bounding surface.
4. Every solid constitutes a separate phase unless a solid solution is formed, which is rare. Thus, in the system consisting of a calcium carbonate in equilibrium with its dissociation products, calcium oxide and carbon dioxide, $CaCO_{3(s)} \rightleftharpoons CaO_{(s)} + CO_{2(g)}$ there are three phases, two solid and one gaseous.

Components

The number of components of a system at equilibrium is the smallest number of independently variable constituents necessarily required to describe the composition of all phases in the system by means of a chemical equation. Let us look into some examples.

1. Water can exist in three phases, viz., solid, liquid, and vapor but the number of components is one, since the composition of every phase can be expressed in terms of the component H_2O.
2. Sulfur can exist in four phases, viz., sulfur rhombic, sulfur monoclinic, liquid, and vapor but since the composition of every phase can be expressed in terms of sulfur only, it is a one-component system.
3. In case of dissociation of calcium carbonate, i.e., $CaCO_3(s) \rightleftharpoons CaO(s) + CO_2(g)$ the number of component is two. The composition of two solid phases can be expressed as $CaCO_3$ while the gaseous phase is given by CO_2. Now the composition of different phases is as follows. $CaCO_3 = CaCO_3 + 0CO_2$, $CaO = CaCO_3 - CO_2$ and $CO_2 = 0CaCO_3 + CO_2$.
4. Decomposition of ammonium chloride in a closed vessel [$NH_4Cl_{(s)} \rightleftharpoons NH_{3(g)} + HCl_{(g)}$] consists of two phases, viz., the solid NH_4Cl and the gaseous mixture of NH_3 and HCl. However, the composition of both phases can be expressed in terms of NH_4Cl alone. This is due to the fact that the proportion of NH_3 and HCl are equivalent.

Note:

The number of components can be obtained by using the following relation:

Number of components = Number of species – Number of relation or reactions among them

Let us look into some examples:

1. In sugar solution: The number of species is two, viz., sugar and water. Here sugar does not react with water and, therefore, the number of reactions is zero. Applying the relation, the number of components is $2 - 0 = 2$.
2. Aqueous solution of NaCl: It contains three species Na^+, Cl^-, and water. However, there is one relation $NaCl(s) \rightleftharpoons Na^+_{(aq)} + Cl^-_{(aq)}$. Therefore, the number of components is $3 - 1 = 2$.

Degree of Freedom

The degree of freedom of a system is defined as the number of independent intensive variables which must be specified in order to define a system completely. Let us look into some examples.

1. A system consisting of a pure gas is evidently a one component, one phase system. The composition remains invariably 100%. Here degree of freedom is 2, i.e., the system is bivariant and requires two variables, viz., temperature and pressure to define it.
2. Consider a one-component system having two phases. The example is furnished by water in equilibrium with its vapor. The system has only one degree of freedom as at a given temperature, the equilibrium vapor pressure of water can have only one fixed value and vice versa. Therefore, one has to mention only one variable, either temperature or pressure. The system is thus monovariant.
3. If three phases of a one-component system coexist, then the system becomes non-variant, i.e., have no degree of freedom. The reason is that these three phases can coexist at one particular temperature and under one particular pressure. The mere statement that these phases coexist defines the system completely.

Phase Rule (W. Gibbs)

As per the rule if the equilibrium in a heterogeneous system is not influenced by gravity or by electrical or magnetic force, then the number of degrees of freedom (F) of the system is related to the number of components (C) and the number of phases (P) existing at equilibrium with one another by the equation

$$F = C - P + 2$$

Derivation

Let us consider a heterogeneous system in equilibrium consisting of C components distributed in P phases. The degree of freedom of the system in equilibrium can be expressed as

Total number of variables of the system – Number of variables that are defined automatically by virtue of the system being in equilibrium

Degree of freedom is the total number of variables that are defined automatically by virtue of the system being in equilibrium.

A system in equilibrium can be defined by only one temperature and one pressure, i.e., these two are fixed variables. The number of concentration or composition variables depends on the number of phases. Now, it is necessary to specify $(C - 1)$ composition variables because the composition of the remaining components can be obtained by difference. For P phases, therefore, the total number of composition variables is $P(C - 1)$. Thus,

$$\text{Total number of variables of the system} = P(C - 1) + 2 \qquad \text{...[6.1]}$$

Now, as per thermodynamics in case of a heterogeneous system in equilibrium, at a constant temperature and pressure, the chemical potential (μ) of a given component must remain same in every phase. Therefore, if there is one component in three phases, then the same fact may be written in the form of two equations $\mu_1 = \mu_2$ and $\mu_1 = \mu_3$. Thus for each component in (P) phases, $(P - 1)$ equations are known. For (C) components, the number of equations or variables that are known from the conditions of equilibrium is

$$C(P - 1) \qquad \text{...[6.2]}$$

As chemical potential is a function of temperature, pressure, and concentration, each equation represents one variable. Thus, the degrees of freedom is

$$F = P(C-1) + 2 - C(P-1)$$
$$= PC - P + 2 - CP + C$$
$$= C - P + 2 \qquad ...[6.3]$$

Limitations of Phase Rule

There are a number of limitations of phase rule.

1. The rule considers only the number of phases but not their amount.
2. It cannot be applied to the systems which are not in equilibrium and also to the systems approaching equilibrium.
3. It is applicable only to those phases of the system which remain simultaneously under identical conditions of temperature and pressure.
4. It is applicable to a single equilibrium system and does not provide any information regarding the other possible equilibriums in the system.

Example 6.1

Find the degree of freedom in partially frozen acetic acid.

Solution

Here there are two phases, i.e., solid acetic acid and acetic acid solution. The number of components is also two, i.e., acetic acid and water. Applying phase rule, we get

$$F = C - P + 2$$
$$= 2 - 2 + 2 = 2$$

Thus, the system is bivariant.

Water System

Water system is a one-component three-phase system. The three phases are water vapor, liquid, and solid.

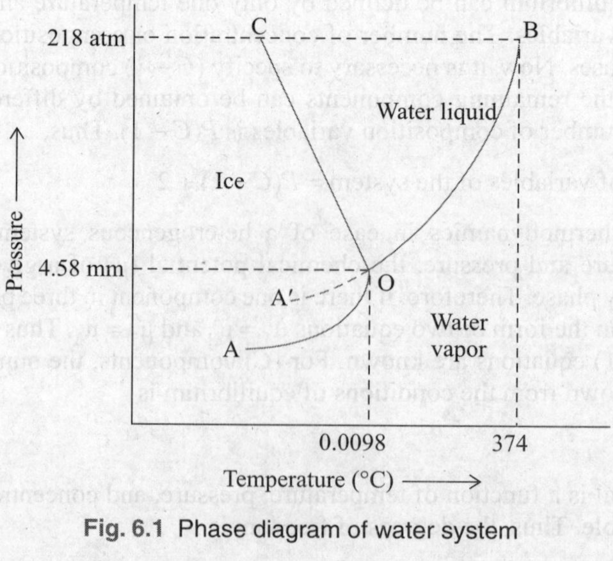

Fig. 6.1 Phase diagram of water system

Area

The areas *AOB*, *AOC*, and *BOC* represent the independent existence of vapor, solid, and liquid phases, respectively. Within any of these mentioned areas, only one phase exists and the system remains bivariant, i.e., degree of freedom is two [$F = 1 - 1 + 2 = 2$]. Therefore, to describe the system in any of these regions, only two variables temperature and pressure need to be defined both of which may change independently without causing disappearance of any phase or appearance of a new phase.

Curves/Lines

The curve *OA* represents the equilibrium between ice and vapor. It is known as sublimation curve of ice. The curve can be extended up to absolute zero temperature. The variation of vapor pressure of ice with temperature can be expressed by the Clapeyron–Clausius equation, i.e.,

$$\frac{dP}{dT} = \frac{\Delta H_S}{T(V_g - V_S)} \qquad \text{...[6.4]}$$

where ΔH_S is enthalpy of sublimation; V_g and V_S are volumes of water vapor and ice, respectively.

The curve *OB* represents the equilibrium between water liquid and vapor. It is the vapor pressure curve of water liquid. The curve extends up to a critical limit characterized by a temperature of 374°C and a pressure of 218 atm beyond which liquid and vapor phases become indistinguishable. Again the Clapeyron–Clausius equation can be utilized to provide the variation of vapor pressure with temperature, i.e.,

$$\frac{dP}{dT} = \frac{\Delta H_V}{T(V_g - V_l)} \qquad \text{...[6.5]}$$

where ΔH_V is enthalpy of vaporization; V_g and V_l are volumes of water vapor and water liquid, respectively.

The line *OC* represents the equilibrium between water liquid and ice. It is the melting point curve of ice or freezing point curve of water liquid. This line has a negative slope and remains slightly tilted toward pressure axis indicating that the melting point of ice or the freezing point of water decrease with the increase in pressure. The reason is attributed to the fact that the volume of ice is greater than that of water liquid. The variation can be expressed as

$$\frac{dP}{dT} = \frac{\Delta H_F}{T(V_l - V_S)} \qquad \text{...[6.6]}$$

where ΔH_F is enthalpy of fusion; V_l and V_s are volumes of water liquid and ice, respectively.

The line *AO'* represents the metastable equilibrium between water liquid and vapor. It is the vapor pressure curve of water liquid. When water liquid is cooled below its freezing point, it gets transferred in to a supercooled liquid state. However, this state is not stable and readily the whole thing solidifies on slight disturbance. The metastable vapor pressure of supercooled water is higher than vapor pressure of ice. All these curves/lines are univariant [$F = 1 - 2 + 2 = 2$] as all of them represent equilibrium between two phases.

Triple Point

The point at which all the three curves, i.e., *OA*, *OB*, and *OC* meet is a triple point as at this point three phases solid, liquid, and vapor coexist. It corresponds to a temperature of 0.0098°C and 4.58 mm pressure. The system is invariant at this point, i.e., degree of freedom is zero.

Sulfur System

It is a one-component four-phase system. The phases are two solid phases, rhombic and monoclinic, in addition to sulfur liquid and vapor.

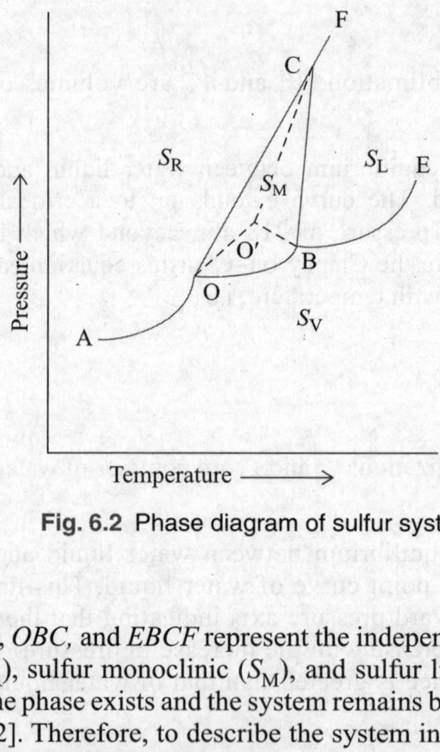

Fig. 6.2 Phase diagram of sulfur system

Area

The areas *AOBE*, *AOCF*, *OBC*, and *EBCF* represent the independent existence of sulfur vapour (S_V), sulfur rhombic (S_R), sulfur monoclinic (S_M), and sulfur liquid (S_L). Within any of these mentioned areas, only one phase exists and the system remains bivariant, i.e., degree of freedom is two [$F = 1 - 1 + 2 = 2$]. Therefore, to describe the system in any of these regions, only two variables temperature and pressure need to be defined.

Curves/Lines

The curve *AO* represents equilibrium between S_R and S_V. It is the sublimation curve of rhombic sulfur and it is univariant along the line [$F = 1 - 1 + 2 = 2$]. It is stable up to 96.5°C which is known as transition temperature. The curve *OB* represents the sublimation curve of S_M. It represents the equilibrium between S_M and S_V. The curve extends up to 120°C which is the melting point of S_M. The curve *BE* represents the equilibrium between

S_L and S_V. This is the vapor pressure curve of liquid sulfur and it extends up to a critical limit corresponding a temperature of 1040°C and a pressure of 116 atm. Here the liquid gets completely converted in to vapor. The line *OC* is the transition curve representing equilibrium between S_R and S_M. S_M is having less specific gravity (1.95 g cm^{-3}) than S_R (2.05 g cm^{-3}) and thus transformation is accompanied by the increase in volume. The result being the transition temperature increases with increase of pressure. The line *BC* represents the equilibrium between S_M and S_L. It is the melting point curve of monoclinic sulfur. The line is having positive slope indicating that melting point of monoclinic sulfur increases with the increase in pressure. It is stable up to a point corresponding to temperature 151°C and pressure 1288 atm. Along *CF* the phases in equilibrium are S_R and S_L. It is the melting point curve of S_R. It is having positive slope which indicates that the melting point of S_R increases with the increase in pressure. All these curves/lines are univariant [$F = 1 - 2 + 2 = 1$] as all of them represent equilibrium between two phases. The lines *OO′*, *BO′*, and *CO′* represent metastable equilibrium.

Triple Points

There are three stable triple points and one metastable triple point. At *O*, the three phases S_R, S_V, and S_M coexist. At *B*, the three phases S_M, S_V, and S_L coexist. At *C*, the three phases S_R, S_M, and S_L coexist. These triple points are characterized by temperature of 95.6°C, 120°C, and 151°C with pressure 0.006 mm, 0.04 mm, and 1288 atm, respectively. All such points are nonvariant [$F = 1 - 3 + 2 = 0$].

Two-Component System and Reduced Phase Rule

In two component systems, the degree of freedom, $F = 2 - P + 2 = 4 - P$. In such a case, the highest degree of freedom is 2, as the minimum number of phase is 1. Thus, three variables temperature, pressure, and composition are required to describe the system which is not feasible to present on pen and paper. For a two-component solid–liquid equilibrium, there is practically no gas phase and the effect of pressure is negligible. Then for simplifying the phase diagram, pressure is assumed to be constant and vapor phase is not considered. Now ultimate result being the degree of freedom is reduced by one and the corresponding phase rule is known as reduced or *condensed phase rule.*

$$F = 2 - P + 1 = 3 - P \qquad ...[6.7]$$

This relation [6.7] is known as reduced or condensed phase rule and is applicable to two-component solid–liquid equilibrium.

Eutectic System

Eutectic or “easy to melt” *system* is a binary system consisting of two different totally immiscible components in the solid state but is completely miscible in liquid state in all proportions without any chemical interaction. Such a solid solution of two components having the lowest freezing point of all the possible mixture of the components is known as *eutectic mixture* and the corresponding composition is known as *eutectic composition*. The minimum freezing point attainable corresponding to the eutectic mixture is termed as *eutectic point*. Some common eutectic systems along with their eutectic composition and eutectic point are summarized here.

Components (m.p. in °C)		Eutectic composition	Eutectic point (°C)
Bi (271)	Cd (321)	60% Bi; 40% Cd	144
Ag (960)	Cu (1083)	71.8% Ag; 28.2% Cu	778
Pb (327)	Ag (961)	97.4 % Pb; 2.6% Ag	303
Zn (419)	Al (659)	95.6%; 4.4% Al	381

Applications

1. Alloys that form eutectic mixtures are used as "fail safe" devices in boilers, similar to plugs in automobiles and other such safety devices.
2. Because of its low melting point, eutectic system is also used for joining two metal pieces together, e.g., lead–tin solder.

Note:

1. *Safety fuse* is a protective device carrying a low melting alloy that melts due to heat produced either by excess heating or by an excess current resulting in the circuit breaking. For example, pressure cooker is provided with a safety fuse made of an alloy with a definite composition. Below the eutectic temperature, the alloy exists in solid form, whereas above the eutectic temperature, it melts to liquid form. When cooker is heated above the eutectic temperature due to some reason, the safety fuse melts and thereby avoids chances of accident due to overheating of cooker. The important aspect to be taken care of is that the eutectic temperature of the fuse must be less than the safety limit temperature of the equipment.

   Fuses are also used for protecting cable in an electric circuit against damage from excessive current flow. The safety fuse in the form of wire can carry normal working current safely. Upon flow of excess current, the heat produced melts the fuse and the circuit breaks.
2. Example of safety fuse making alloys are Rose metal (Bi, 50%; Pb, 28%; Sn, 22%) with a melting point of 89°C, Wood metal (Bi, 50%; Pb, 25%; Sn, 12.5%; Cd, 12.5%) with a melting point of 70°C.
3. *Solders* are readily fusible alloys, which are applied between metal objects to unite them closely without heating the objects to the melting point. The selection of solder depends on the melting point of alloy at which the solder forms an intimate surface alloy with metals to be joined.
4. Example of some important solders are Brazing alloy (Sn, 92%; Sb, 5.5%; Ca, 2.5%), Tin man's solder (Sn, 66%; Pb, 34%).

Pb–Ag System

It is a two-component eutectic system, i.e., in molten state both the components are miscible in all proportions to form a homogeneous mixture. It consists of four phases, viz., Pb(s), Ag(s), (Pb + Ag) solution, and their vapor. The vapor amount is very small and does not have any significant role on equilibrium and is assumed to be constant. Thus, there are three phases, and condensed phase rule is used to explain the lines present in the phase diagram.

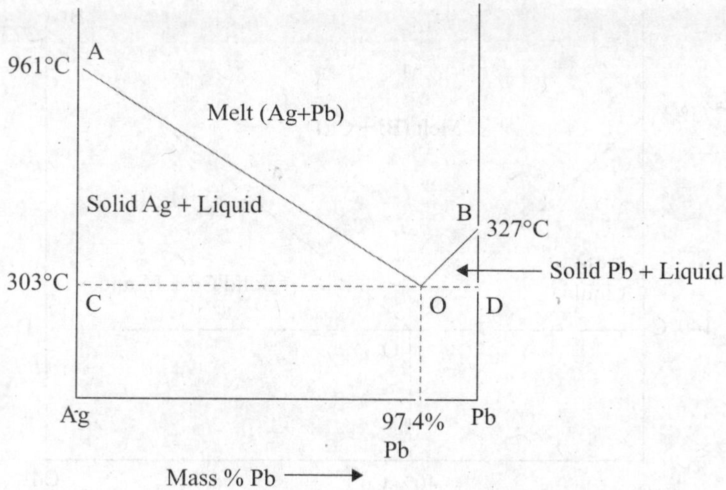

Fig. 6.3 Phase diagram for Ag–Pb system

Areas

Area *AOB* represents only liquid phase consisting of molten Ag and Pb. In this area, the system is bivariant, i.e., the degree of freedom is 2 ($F = 3 - 1 = 2$). Thus, both temperature and composition are required to explain it. The area *AOC* consists of two phases, viz., Ag(s) and solution of Ag and Pb. In this zone, the degree of freedom is 1 ($F = 3 - 2 = 1$), i.e., univariant. Area *BOD* again consists of two phases, viz., Pb(s) and solution of Pb and Ag. Here the degree of freedom is one. Area below the line *COD* consists of two phases, viz., Ag(s) and Pb(s). Here the degree of freedom is one and the system is univariant.

Lines

The line *AO* represents the equilibrium between solid Ag and liquid. It is the freezing point curve of pure Ag. The freezing point is 961°C which decreases gradually upon addition of Pb up to 303°C. The point "*O*" corresponds to the lowest freezing point and is the eutectic point. At the eutectic point, the degree of freedom is 0 ($F = 3 - 3 = 0$). Further addition of Pb results in its separation as solid. Along the line, the degree of freedom is 1 ($F = 3 - 2 = 1$). Line *BO* represents the equilibrium between solid Pb and liquid. It is the freezing point curve of pure Pb. The freezing point is 327°C which decreases gradually upon the addition of Ag up to the lowest value of 303°C. The freezing point does not fall below 303°C even on further addition of Bi. The system is univariant along the line.

Bi–Cd System

It is a two-component eutectic system, i.e., in molten state both the components are miscible in all proportions to form a homogeneous mixture. It consists of four phases, viz., $Bi_{(s)}$, $Cd_{(s)}$, (Bi + Cd) solution and their vapor. The vapor amount is very small and does not have any significant role on equilibrium and is assumed to be constant. Thus, there are three phases and condensed phase rule is used to explain the lines present in phase diagram.

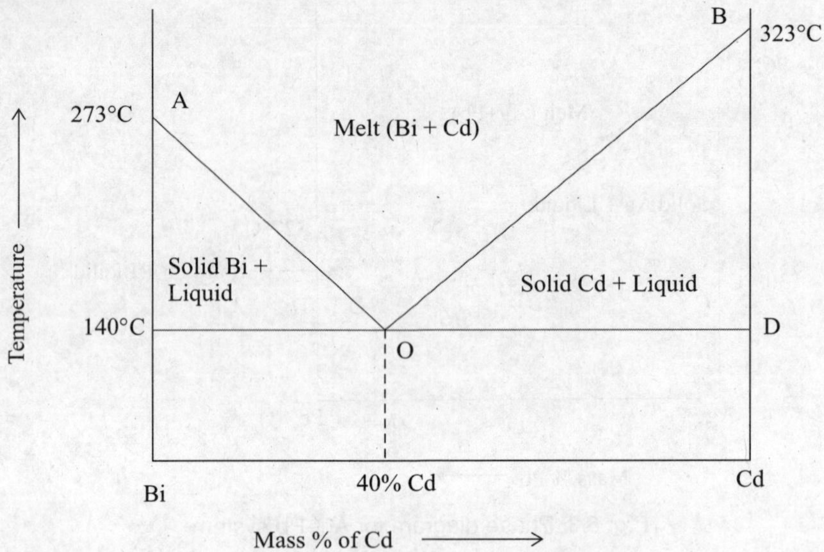

Fig. 6.4 Phase diagram for Bi-Cd system

Areas

Area *AOB* represents only liquid phase consisting of molten Bi and Cd. In this area the system is bivariant, i.e., degree of freedom is two $[F = 3 - 1 = 2]$. Thus, both temperature and composition are required to explain it. The area *AOC* consists of two phases, viz., $Bi_{(s)}$ and solution of Bi and Cd. In this zone, degree of freedom is one $[F = 3 - 2 = 1]$, i.e., univariant. Area *BOD* again consists of two phases, viz., $Cd_{(s)}$ and solution of Cd and Bi. Here degree of freedom is one. Area below the line *COD* consists of two phases, viz., $Bi_{(s)}$ and $Cd_{(s)}$. Here degree of freedom is one and the system is univariant.

Lines

The line *AO* represents the equilibrium between solid Bi and liquid. It is the freezing point curve of pure Bi. The freezing point is 273°C which decreases gradually upon addition of Cd up to 140°C. The point '*O*' corresponds to the lowest freezing point and is the eutectic point. At eutectic point, the degree of freedom is zero $[F = 3 - 3 = 0]$. Further addition of Cd results in its separation as solid. Along the line, the degree of freedom is one $[F = 3 - 2 = 1]$. The line *BO* represents the equilibrium between solid Cd and liquid. It is the freezing point curve of pure Cd. The freezing point is 323°C which decreases gradually upon the addition of Bi up to the lowest value of 140°C. The freezing point does not fall below 140°C even on further addition of Bi. The system is univariant along the line.

Fe–C System

Pure iron is a ductile metal. Molten pure iron freezes into δ-ferrite at 1537°C. Solid iron exists in three different states. δ-ferrite with bcc lattice in the temperature range 1537–1403°C, γ-ferrite (austenite) with fcc lattice in the temperature range 1403–910°C, and α-ferrite with again bcc structure below 910°C.

Phase diagram

There are two components in the system, viz., a metal iron and a non-metal carbon. The extreme left of the diagram is pure iron while extreme right is cementite (Fe_3C) which contains only 6.67% C. The equilibrium relationships among the alloys of Fe and C are given in Fig. 6.5.

The diagram consists of a number of fields, each occupied by either a single phase or a mixture of two phases.

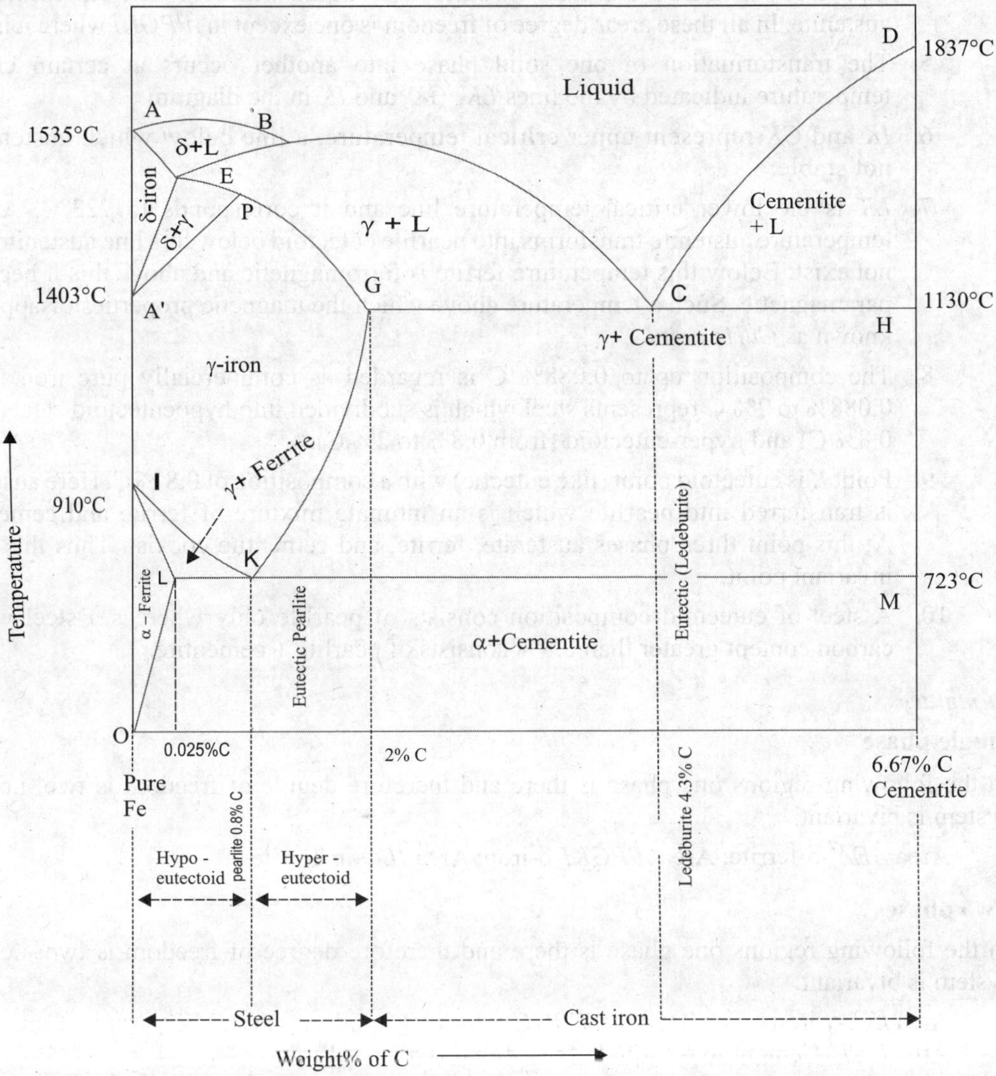

Fig. 6.5 Phase diagram for Fe–C system

1. The line *ABCD* is the liquidus line above which there is only one liquid phase consisting of dissolved carbon in molten iron.
2. The line *AEPGCH* is the solidus line, below which all compositions are solid. The compositions in between these two lines represent mixture of solids and liquids. With increase of carbon content, the melting point of the alloy is progressively depressed until it reaches point *C*.
3. Point *C* is the eutectic point where the carbon content is 4.3%. This corresponds to the lowest melting point of iron–carbon mixture corresponding to 1130°C. At eutectic composition the mixture solidifies to a eutectic solid known as *ledeburite* which is a eutectic mixture of austenite and cementite.

4. With further increase of carbon content the melting point further rises. In the area *AEB* the system exists as δ-iron + liquid. The area *DCH* consists of cementite + liquid. The area *EBGC* represents austenite + liquid while *A'PGKI* represents only austenite. In all these areas degree of freedom is one except in *A'PGKI* where it is two.
5. The transformation of one solid phase into another occurs at certain critical temperature indicated by the lines *LK, GK*, and *IK* in the diagram.
6. *IK* and *GK* represent upper critical temperature, a line below which austenite is not stable.
7. *LK* is the lower critical temperature line and it corresponds to 723°C. At this temperature austenite transforms into pearlite eutectoid below this line austenite does not exist. Below this temperature ferrite is ferromagnetic and above this it becomes paramagnetic. Such a temperature above which the magnetic properties disappear is known as *Curie point*.
8. The composition up to 0.088% C is regarded as commercially pure iron. From 0.088% to 2% C represents steel which is subdivided into hypoeutectoid steel (up to 0.8% C) and hyper-eutectoid (from 0.8% to 2% C).
9. Point *K* is eutectoid point (like eutectic) with a composition of 0.8 % C. Here austenite is transferred into pearlite which is an intimate mixture of ferrite and cementite. At this point three phases austenite, ferrite, and cementite coexist. Thus this is an invariant point.
10. A steel of eutectoid composition consists of pearlite only whereas a steel with a carbon content greater than 0.8% consists of pearlite + cementite.

Summary

Single phase

In the following regions one phase is there and therefore degree of freedom is two, i.e., the system is bivariant.

Area *AEA'*-δ-ferrite; Area *A'PGKI*-δ-iron; Area *ILO*- α-ferrite

Two phases

In the following regions one phase is there and therefore degree of freedom is two, i.e., the system is bivariant.

Area *IKL*-γ-iron + Ferrite; Area *EBGC*-γ-iron + Liquid; Area *GHMK*-γ-iron; + Cementite; Area *DCH*-Cementite + Liquid; Area *AEB*-δ-ferrite + Liquid

Points

All the points are invariant. *K* is the eutectoid point (pearlite phase); C is the eutectic point (ledeburite phase); and *P* is the peritectic point corresponds to a temperature of 1493°C.

Note:

Eutectic

It represents the following equilibrium

$$\text{Liquid} \underset{\text{Heating}}{\overset{\text{Cooling}}{\rightleftharpoons}} \text{Solid (1)} + \text{Solid (2)}$$

For example,

$$\text{Liquid} \underset{\text{Heating}}{\overset{\text{Cooling}}{\rightleftharpoons}} \underbrace{\text{Austentite} + \text{Cementite}}_{\text{Leduburite}}$$

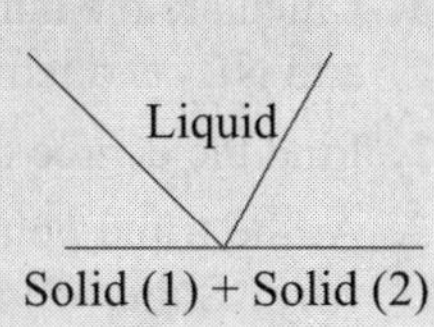

Eutectoid

Eutectoid represents like eutectic but here the equilibrium is

$$\text{Solid} \underset{\text{Heating}}{\overset{\text{Cooling}}{\rightleftharpoons}} \text{Solid (1)} + \text{Solid (2)}$$

For example,

$$\text{Austenite} \underset{\text{Heating}}{\overset{\text{Cooling}}{\rightleftharpoons}} \underbrace{\text{Ferrite} + \text{Cementite}}_{\text{Pearlite}}$$

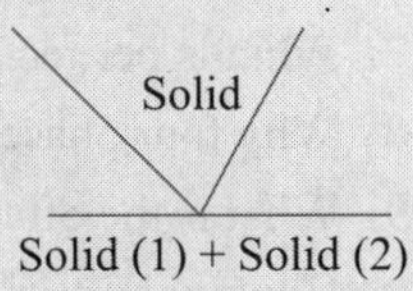

Peritectic

It represents the following equilibrium

$$\text{Liquid} + \text{Solid (1)} \underset{\text{Heating}}{\overset{\text{Cooling}}{\rightleftharpoons}} \text{Solid (2)}$$

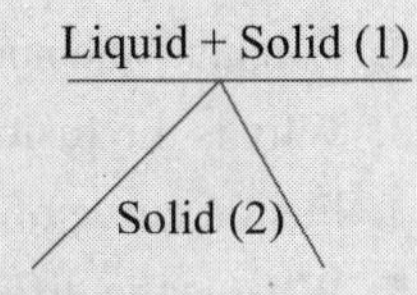

For example,

$$\text{Liquid} + \delta\text{-iron} \underset{\text{Heating}}{\overset{\text{Cooling}}{\rightleftharpoons}} \text{Austenite}$$

Peritectoid

A peritectoid transformation is the isothermal reversible reaction in which two solid phases react with each other upon cooling of a binary, ternary, ..., *n* alloy to create a completely different and single solid phase.

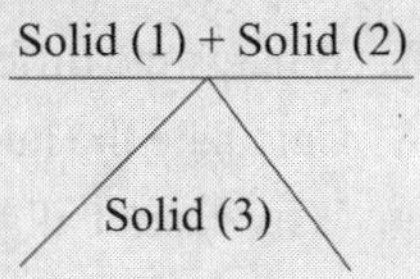

$$\underbrace{\text{Solid (1)} + \text{Solid (2)}} \underset{\text{Heating}}{\overset{\text{Cooling}}{\rightleftharpoons}} \text{Solid (3)}$$

QUESTIONS

1. Give statement of the phase rule.
2. What is condensed phase rule?
3. What is a triple point? Explain with respect to water system.
4. What is degree of freedom? Explain with suitable examples.
5. What is the degree of freedom for a pure substance under equilibrium?
6. What are the limitations of phase rule?
7. Transition curve of rhombic sulfur has positive slope. Explain.
8. Name the hardest and softest structures that appear in Fe–C equilibrium diagram.
9. The triple point of one component system is invariant. Explain.
10. Is it possible to observe four distinct phases for a binary alloy? Give reasons.

11. Calculate the number of phases, components, and degree of freedom for a mixture of N_2, H_2, and NH_3 at a temperature when the equilibrium $N_2(g) + H_2(g) \rightleftharpoons 2NH_3(g)$ is established.
12. Find the degree of freedom of a pure liquid at its critical point.
13. At the triple point of water, which component of the following curve has a larger slope and why? Solid → vapor, liquid → vapor.
14. What is the difference between critical point and triple point?
15. What do you mean by component? What is the maximum number of phases that can be in equilibrium at one-point of one-component system (T and P constants).
16. What is Curie temperature?
17. What is peritectic point?
18. Why four phases of sulfur system cannot coexist together?
19. What is the effect of pressure on transition temperature of sulfur?
20. How many triple points are there in the phase diagram of sulfur? Mention their temperature and pressure.
21. Differentiate between eutectic point and triple point of a thermodynamic system.
22. Calculate the number of components and degree of freedom for $N_2(g) + O_2(g) \rightleftharpoons 2NO\ (g)$.
23. Why is the fusion curve of ice in phase diagram slightly inclined towards the pressure axis?
24. Fusion curve of ice has a negative slope. Explain.
25. What is the difference between pearlite and ledeburite?
26. What is the difference between the one-component phase diagram and two-component phase diagram (condensed system)?
27. What is the difference between triple point and eutectic point?
28. Calculate the number of components and degree of freedom for $N_2(g) + O_2(g) \longrightarrow 2NO(g)$.
29. Why cannot all the phases of sulphur system co-exist at the same temperature and pressure?
30. Describe the phase diagram of water system.
31. Compare the terms triple point and eutectic points. Describe the phase diagram of bismuth-cadmium system.
32. Describe the terms phase, components, and degree of freedom.
33. Describe the phase diagram of sulfur system.
34. Draw the phase diagram of a one-component system which contains more than one solid phase and explain the following with the help of the diagram (i) Triple point, (ii) Metastable equilibrium, (iii) Univariant system.
35. Draw and explain the Fe–C phase diagram.
36. State and explain Gibb's phase rule. What is reduced phase rule? What are the limitations of phase rule?
37. Explain the use of Clapeyron–Clausius equation in explaining the lines and curves in a phase diagram for a one-component system.
38. What do you mean by metastable equilibrium? Explain the same with respect to water and sulfur systems.
39. Draw the phase diagram of Bi–Cd system and explain the eutectic point.
40. Draw schematic phase diagram of a water system and show triple point and critical temperature. Explain both the terms.

41. State Gibb's phase rule and derive the same.
42. Explain with suitable example and diagram the following terms used in the phase rule study of heterogeneous equilibrium: (a) triple point, (b) eutectic point, and (c) univariant point.
43. What do you mean by invariant points? Discuss invariant points in both water and sulfur system with diagram. (Mention temperature and pressure.)
44. What is the difference between Curie temperature, eutectic temperature, and transition temperature? Explain with examples.
45. What is the difference between the eutectic reaction, peritectic reaction, and eutectoid reaction and peritectoid reaction? Explain with examples.
46. Draw the phase diagram of Pb–Ag system.
47. What type of equilibrium exists between $H_2O_{(l)}$ and $H_2O_{(g)}$ at a temperature below 273 K?
48. Suggest an application of eutectics.
49. What is eutectic composition of Pb–Ag system?
50. What is the degree of freedom at the eutectic point?
51. Find the number of components, phases, and degree of freedom for following equilibrium:
    $NH_4Cl(s) \rightleftharpoons NH_3(g) + HCl(g)$; If $p(NH_3) = p(HCl)$ and if $p(NH_3) \neq p(HCl)$
52. Explain safety fuse with a suitable example.
53. Provide an example of safety fuse making alloy. Also provide the composition.
54. What is a solder? Explain with a suitable example.
55. What is the eutectic composition of Zn–Al system?
56. What is the composition of Brazing alloy?
57. What is the composition of Wood metal?

CHAPTER 7

Solid State Chemistry

Chapter Outline

- Types of Solids
- Crystal or Space Lattice
- Crystal System or Classes
- Bravais Lattice
- Close Packing in Solids
- Analysis of Cubic System
- Ionic Solids
- Laws of Crystallography
- Weiss and Miller Indices
- X-Ray Diffraction Studies of Crystals
- Defects in Solids

Solids are characterized by their definite shape, considerable mechanical strength, and rigidity. They include most of the materials that make modern technology to sustain such as wide varieties of steel and other alloys that are used in engineering and architecture, conductors and semiconductors used in power distribution and information technology, polymeric materials used in fabrication of many of the common objects in the modern world, glasses and ceramics find wide application in construction house and laboratory, etc.

Types of Solids

Solids are of two types: On the basis of relative arrangement of constituent particles in space, namely, crystalline solids, in which constituent particles have a definite orderly arrangement (e.g., sugar and salts) and amorphous in which the arrangement is rather haphazard (e.g., glass, ceramics, and rubber). A comparative analysis is as follows.

Crystalline Solids

1. They have sharp melting point.
2. They have characteristic heat of fusion.
3. They are anisotropic, i.e., their physical properties are different in different directions.
4. They have long-range order.
5. They give regular cut when cut with a sharp-edged utensil.
6. They are regarded as true solids.

Amorphous Solids

1. They melt in a range of temperature.

2. They have no characteristic heat of fusion.
3. They are isotropic, i.e., their physical properties are same in all directions.
4. They exhibit short-range order.
5. They give irregular cut when cut with a sharp-edged utensil.
6. They are regarded as pseudo solids or supercooled liquids.

Types of crystalline solids

Crystalline solids are of several types on the basis of the nature of constituent particles and the force that holds them together.

Ionic solids: In such solids, the electrostatic forces, i.e., ionic bonds hold the oppositely charged ions together.

Covalent solids: Here, the particles are atoms and the forces that hold them is the mutual sharing forces, i.e., covalent bonds.

Metallic solids: In such solids, electrostatic force holds Kernels and mobile electrons cloud together.

Molecular solids: Here, van der Waals forces hold the molecules together.

The different solids, their characteristic properties, and examples are as follows.

Type	Properties	Examples
Ionic solids	High melting point, brittle, bad conductor, soluble in polar solvents	ZnS, NaCl, CaF_2
Covalent solids	High melting point, hard, bad conductor, insoluble in most of the common solvents	Diamond, SiC
Metallic solids	Low to high melting point, soft to very hard, conductors, malleable, ductile	Li, Fe, Cu, Ag
Molecular solids	Low melting point, soft, volatile, bad conductor, soluble in nonpolar solvents	I_2, sugar, ice

Crystal or Space lattice

Crystal lattice is the three-dimensional definite orderly arrangement of structural motifs, which may be atoms, molecules or groups of atoms, molecules or ions. The lattice is depicted by the position of structural motifs in space. These positions are represented by similar dots and are referred to as lattice points or sites.

Unit Cell

Unit cell is the smallest portion of complete space lattice by repeating, which through translation or staking, it is possible to generate the complete space lattice. In other words, it is the fundamental building block of crystal lattice (see Fig. 7.1).

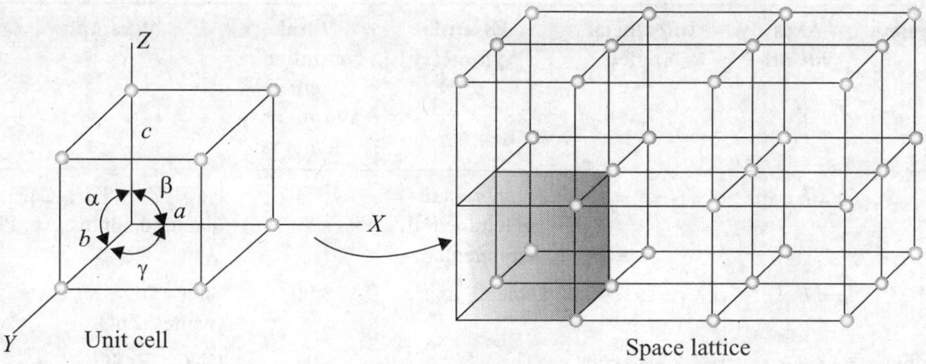

Fig. 7.1 Unit cell and space lattice

Types of unit cell

Unit cell can be classified on the basis of position of lattice points (see Fig. 7.2).

1. **Primitive (P):** Having lattice points only at the corners.
2. **Body-centered (I):** Having lattice points at the center of unit cell in addition to corners.
3. **Face-centered (F):** Having lattice points at the center of each face in addition to corners.
4. **Base- or end-centered (C):** Having lattice points at the centers of end faces in addition to corners.

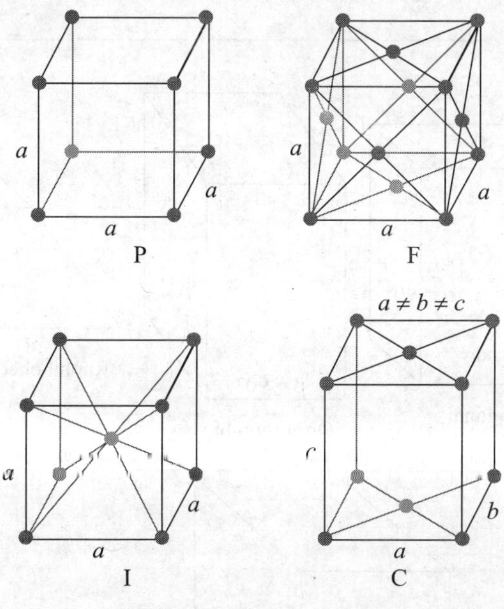

Fig. 7.2 Different unit cells

Crystal Systems or Classes

Different crystals can be grouped into seven basic categories on the basis of symmetry consideration, which are known as seven crystal systems or classes. The different classes along with their cut-offs along the crystallographic axes *a*, *b*, *c*, and three interfacial angles, essential symmetry elements, total number of symmetry elements, and examples, are summarized as follows.

Crystal system	Axes cut-off	Interfacial angles	Essential symmetry	Total number of symmetry elements	Examples
Cubic	$a = b = c$	$\alpha = \beta = \gamma = 90°$	Four C_3 axes in tetrahedral arrangement	23	NaCl, ZnS, KCl, CaF_2, diamond, alums, Ag, Pb
Tetragonal	$a = b \neq c$	$\alpha = \beta = \gamma = 90°$	One C_4 axis	11	SnO_2, TiO_2, Sn (white), ZnO_2
Orthorhombic	$a \neq b \neq c$	$\alpha = \beta = \gamma = 90°$	Three perpendicular C_2 axis	07	KNO_3, $BaSO_4$, $MgSO_4 \cdot 7H_2O$, Sulfur (orthorhombic)
Rhombohedral	$a = b = c$	$\alpha = \beta = \gamma \neq 90°$	One C_3 axis	15	$NaNO_3$, $CaSO_4$, calcite, quartz, As, Bi
Hexagonal	$a = b \neq c$	$\alpha = \beta = 90°$, $\gamma = 120°$	One C_6 axis	15	HgS, CdS, graphite, Zn, Mg, Ice
Monoclinic	$a \neq b \neq c$	$\alpha = \gamma = 90°$, $\beta \neq 90°$	One C_2 axis	03	$Na_2B_4O_7 \cdot 10H_2O$, Sulfur (monoclinic),
Triclinic	$a \neq b \neq c$	$\alpha \neq \beta \neq \gamma \neq 90°$	None	0	$K_2Cr_2O_7$, H_3BO_3, $CuSO_4 \cdot 10H_2O$

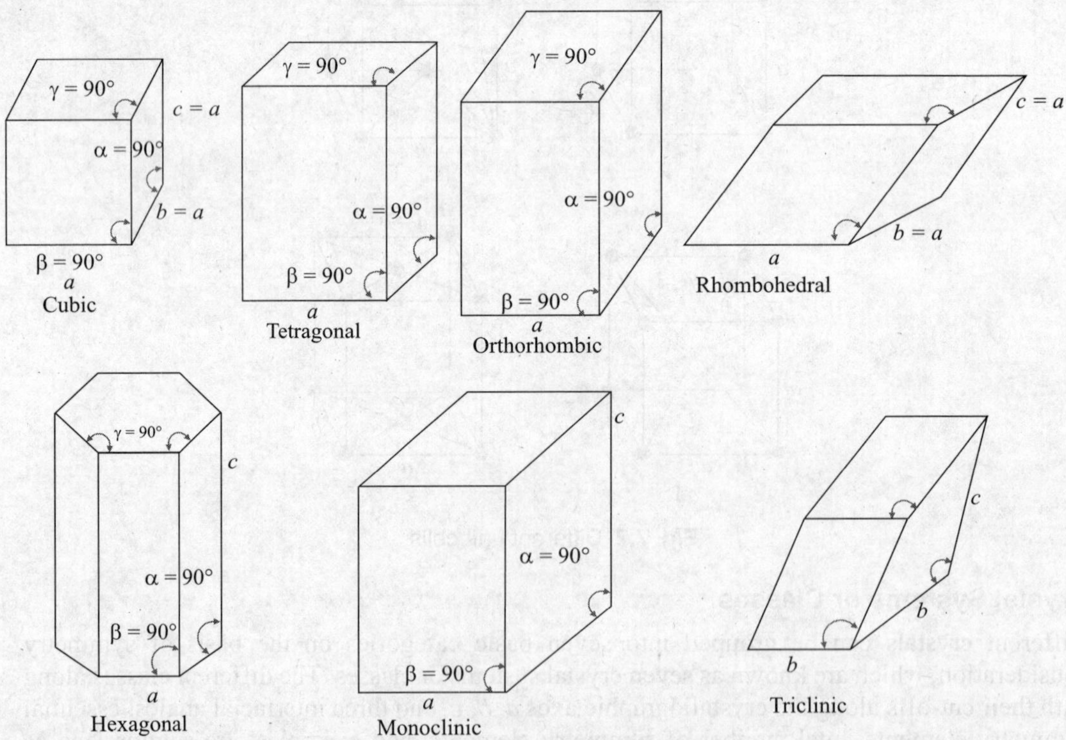

Fig. 7.3 Different crystal classes

Bravais Lattice

Bravais showed that there can be only 14 different ways in which similar points can be arranged in space that remain distributed over the seven crystal systems. These 14 space lattices are known as Bravais lattices, all of which are listed below.

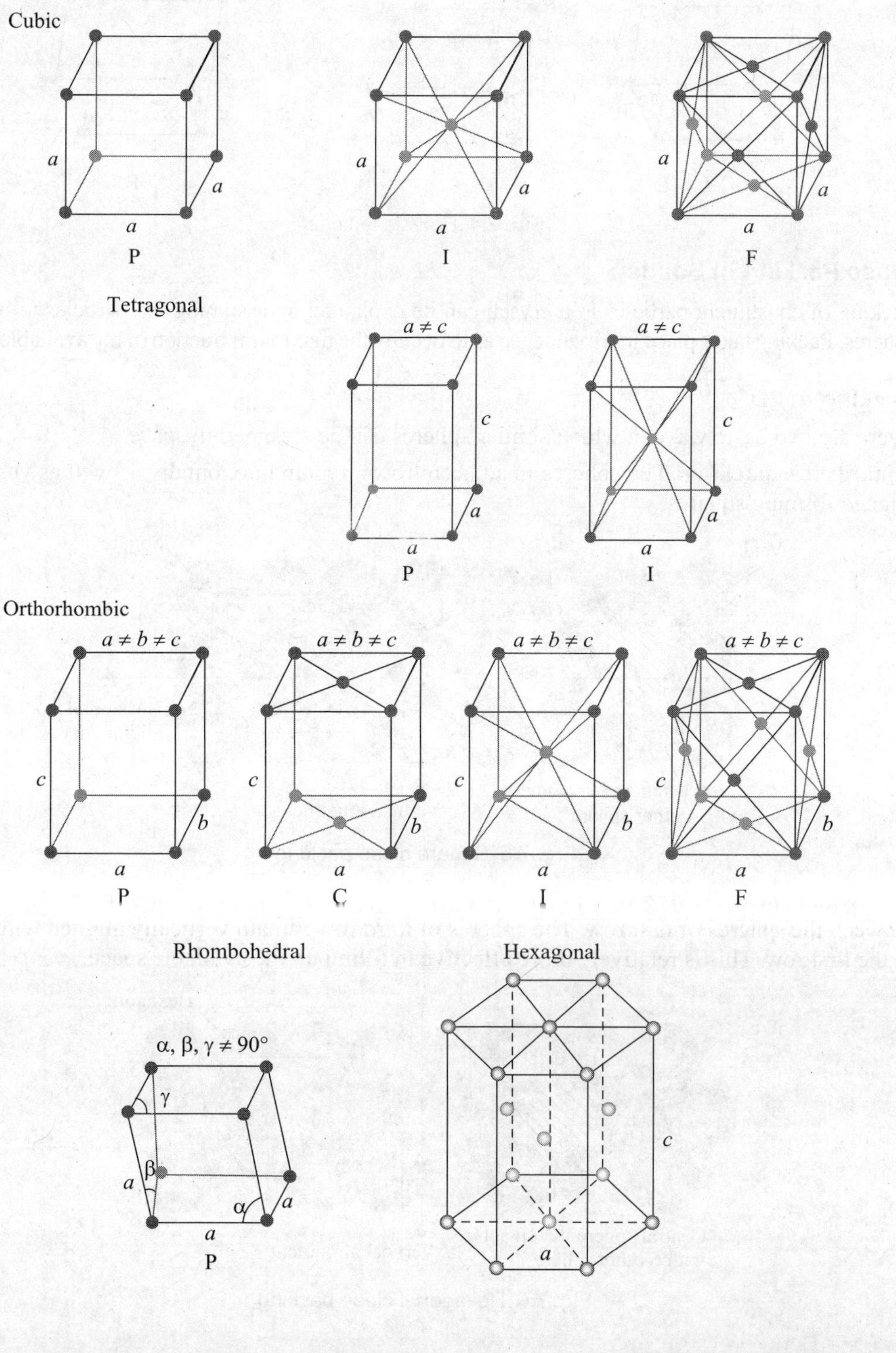

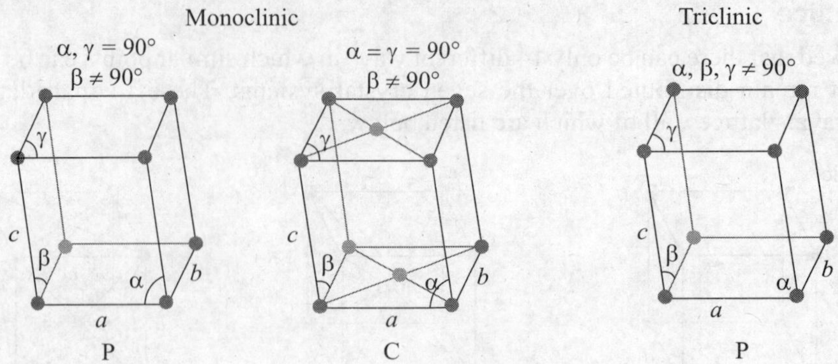

Fig. 7.4 Bravais lattices

Close Packing in Solids

Packing of constituent particles in a crystal can be explained by assuming the particles to be rigid spheres. Packing takes place in a manner so as to occupy the maximum fraction of the available space.

Packing in 2D

There are two basic ways in which similar spheres can be arranged in space.

Square close packing: The spheres in adjacent rows remain horizontally as well as vertically aligned forming squares.

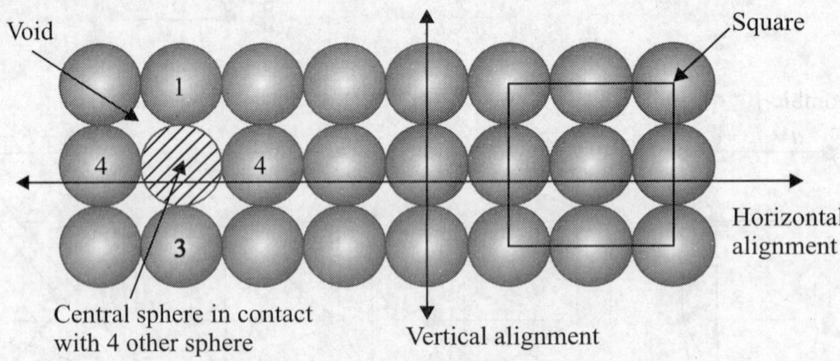

Fig. 7.5 Square close packing

Hexagonal close packing (hcp): The spheres in every second row remain in the depressions between the spheres of first row. The spheres of third row remain vertically aligned with those in the first row. This is relatively more effective in filling up the available space.

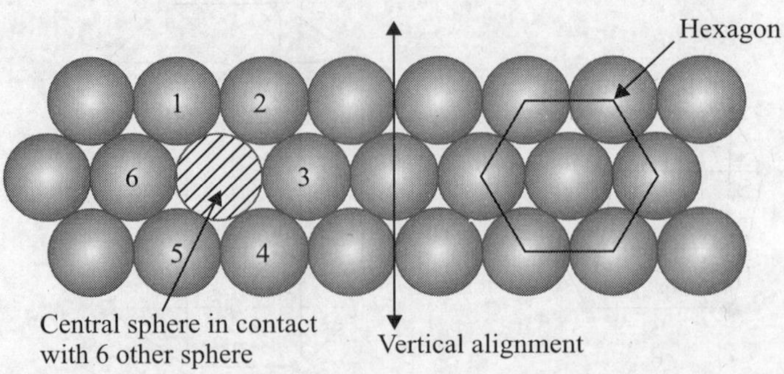

Fig. 7.6 Hexagonal close packing

Packing in 3D

In 3D packing, the hexagonal arrangement of spheres (being more effective in plane) is retained in different layers. In the base layer, two types of voids are marked as "*a*" and "*b*". The spheres of second layer are placed in the triangular voids of the first layer. In this way, only one type of void (say "*a*" type) can be filled at best. Now there are two types of voids in second layer. One type is a combination of four touching spheres from adjacent layers known as "Td" void and the other is a combination of two triangular voids of adjacent layer formed by six touching spheres which is known as octahedral ("Oh") void. The spheres of third layer can be placed in two different ways.

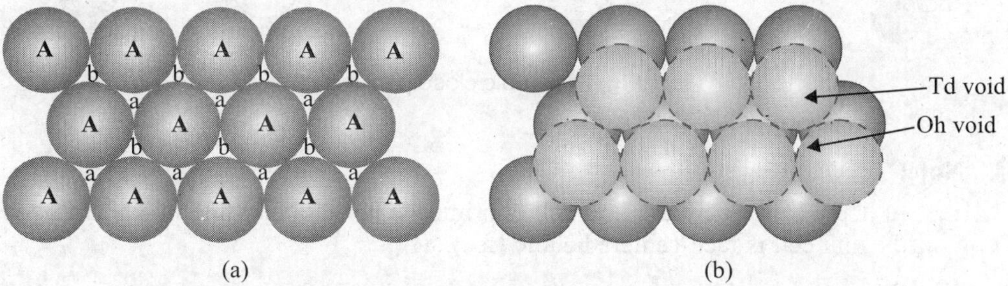

Fig. 7.7 (a) One layer; (b) Two layers

Case I: The spheres of third layer are placed on the second layer so that the "Td" voids remain covered. This results in a packing in which every alternate layer remains vertically aligned with each other. The arrangement is known as ABAB ... pattern or hcp. Such a packing is found in metals like Li, Cd, Mg, Zn, etc.

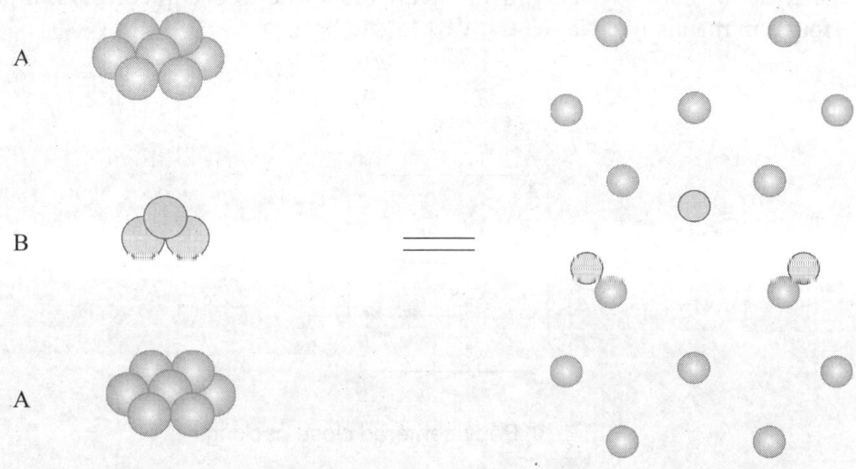

Fig. 7.8 Hexagonal close packing

Case II: The spheres of third layer are placed on the second layer so that the "Oh" voids remain covered. This results in a packing in which the third layer is different from the first two layers and the fourth layer remain vertically aligned with 1st layer. The arrangement is known as ABCABC... or cubic close packing (ccp). Such a packing is found in metals like Cu, Ag, Au, Pt, etc.

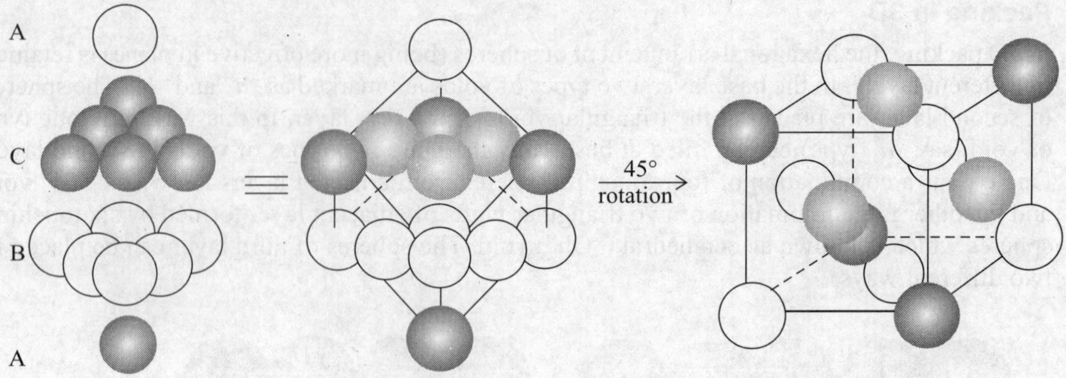

Fig. 7.9 Cubic close packing

Note:

1. In hcp arrangement the unit cell is primitive hexagonal while in ccp arrangement the unit cell is face-centered cubic (fcc).
2. Both these packings are equally efficient in filling up the available space. In both cases packing fraction is calculated to be 74% [refer to analysis of cubic system].
3. Other than hcp and ccp arrangements, another less packed arrangement of spheres is also possible which is known as body-centered cubic (bcc) packing. In bcc arrangement each sphere remains surrounded by eight nearest neighbors at the corners of a cube. The coordination number is eight. This is not close close-packed structure rather it is nearly close-packed structure in which only 68% [refer to analysis of cubic system] of the available space is occupied. Such a packing is found in metals like Na, K, Cs, W, Mo, etc.

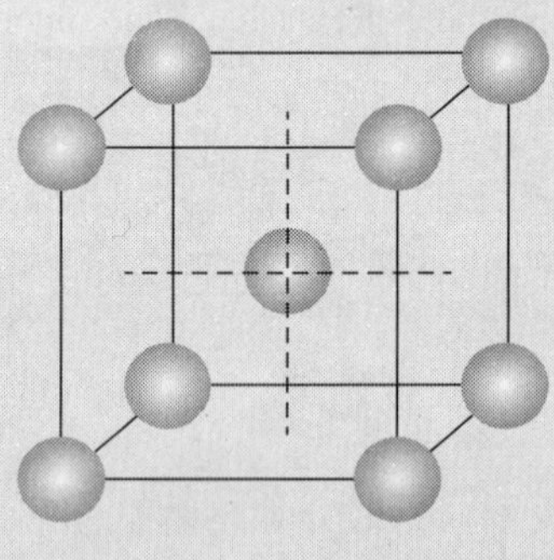

Fig. 7.10 Body-centered close packing

4. In a close-packed-structure there arises two types of voids, namely Td and Oh. A "Td" void is that which is formed by four touching spheres from two adjacent layers. The relative size is $r_{void}/r_{sphere} = 0.225$. On the other hand, an octahedral void is formed by six touching spheres from two adjacent layers. The relative size is $r_{void}/r_{sphere} = 0.414$ [refer to calculations made in the radius ratio rules].

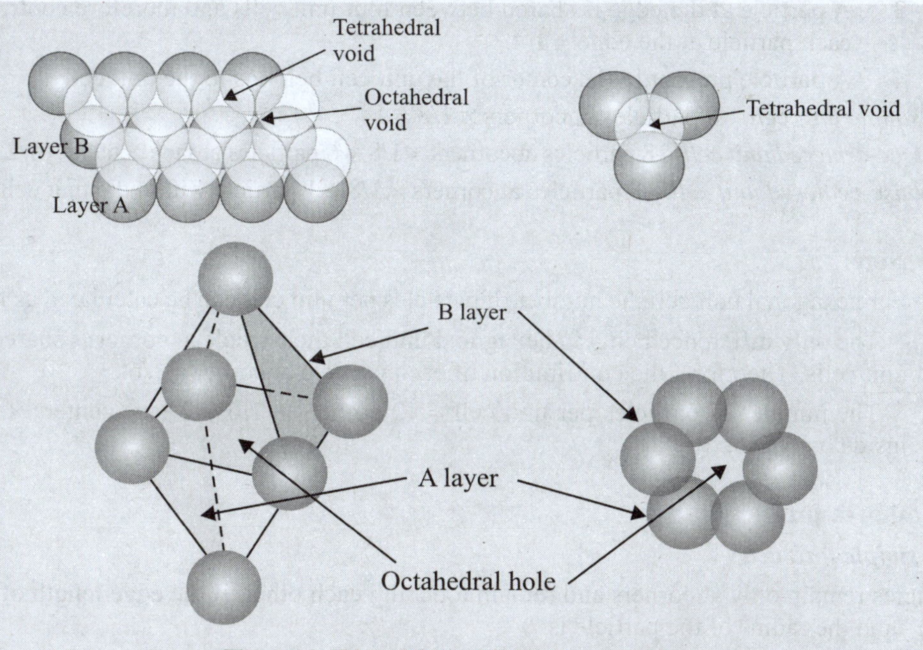

Fig. 7.11 Td and Oh voids in close packing

5. For every sphere in the close-packed arrangement there is one octahedral void and two tetrahedral voids.

Analysis of Cubic System

Number of Atoms per Unit Cell

The following points regarding contribution of individual particles should be remembered.

1. A particle at corners is shared by eight unit cells. Thus, contribution of each particle present at the corner = 1/8.

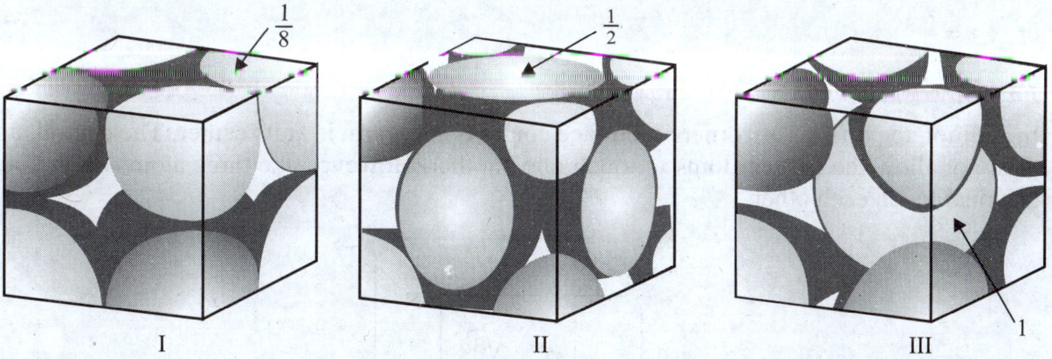

Fig. 7.12 (I) Simple cubic, (II) fcc, and (III) bcc

2. A particle on the face is shared between two unit cells and therefore contribution of each particle on the face = 1/2.

3. A particle at the edge is shared between four unit cells and therefore contribution of each particle at the edge = 1/4.
4. A particle present in the center of the unit cell belongs to the unit cell.

For simple unit cell—8 particles at corners × 1/8 = 1.

For face-centered unit cell—8 particles at corners × 1/8 + 6 particles at face centers × 1/2 = 4.

For base-centered unit cell—8 particles at corners × 1/8 + 1 particle within the unit cell = 2.

Note:

For hexagonal unit cell the number of particles per unit cell can be calculated as follows:

The only difference being in hexagonal unit cell the particle at corner is shared by six unit cells. Therefore, the contribution of each particle at corner = 1/6.

The number of particles per unit cell = 12 corners × 1/6 + 2 face centers × 1/2 + 3 inside body = 6.

Atomic Radius

For simple unit cell

Particles remain only at corners and remain touching each other, if the edge length of the cube is "*a*" and the radius of the particle is "*r*".

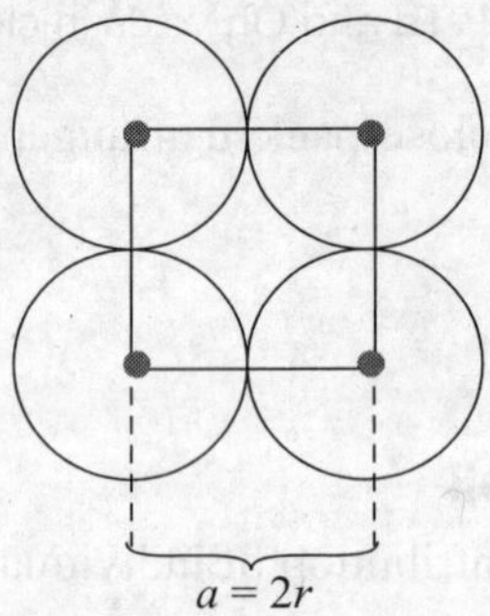

Fig. 7.13

Thus, $a = 2r$.

or $r = \dfrac{a}{2}$ ...[7.1]

For body-centered unit cell

In addition to particles at corners each face contains one particle at its center. The central atom does not allow the corner atoms to touch one another. However, the three atoms on the body diagonal touch each other.

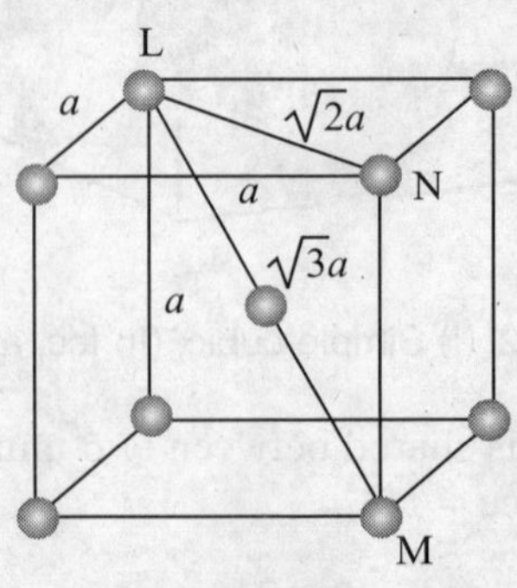

Fig. 7.14

Body diagonal = $\sqrt{3}a = 4r$

or $\quad r = \dfrac{\sqrt{3}a}{4}$ ...[7.2]

For face-centered unit cell

In this unit cell, three atoms on the face diagonal touch each other.

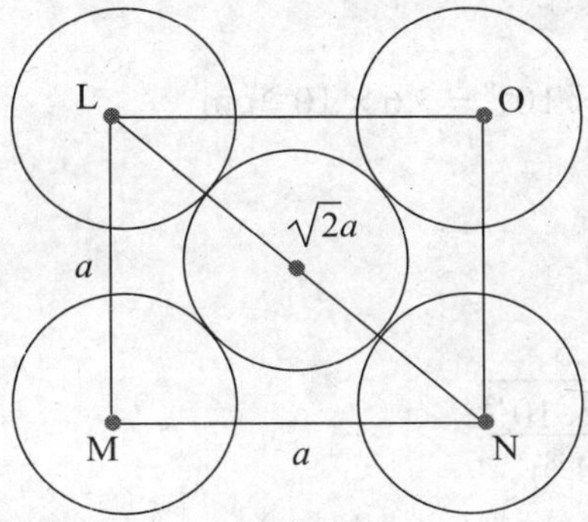

Fig. 7.15

Face diagonal = $\sqrt{2}a = 4r$

or $\quad r = \dfrac{\sqrt{2}a}{4}$

$\quad = \dfrac{a}{2\sqrt{2}}$ ...[7.3]

Example 7.1

Xenon crystallizes in fcc lattice. The edge length of the unit cell is 620 pm. Find the radius of xenon atom.

Solution

$$r = \frac{a}{2\sqrt{2}}$$

$$= \frac{620}{2 \times 1.414} = 219.25 \text{ pm}$$

The radius of the xenon atom is 219.25 pm.

Density of Unit Cell

$$\text{Density } (\rho) = \frac{\text{mass of the unit cell}}{\text{volume of the unit cell}}$$

$$= \frac{\text{number of particles per unit cell} \times \dfrac{\text{mass of the particle}}{\text{Avogadro's number}}}{\text{volume of the unit cell}}$$

$$= \frac{n \times \dfrac{M}{N}}{a^3} \text{ g cm}^{-3} \quad ...[7.4]$$

For simple, face-centered, and body-centered unit cells only "n" value is substituted with 1, 4, and 2, respectively.

Example 7.2

Copper has an fcc structure with atomic radius of 1.28 Å. Find the density.

Solution

For fcc, $r = \dfrac{a}{2\sqrt{2}}$

or $a = 2\sqrt{2}r = 2\sqrt{2} \times 1.28 \times 10^{-8} = 3.6 \times 10^{-8}$ cm

$$\text{Density } (\rho) = \frac{n \times \dfrac{M}{N}}{a^3}$$

$$= \frac{4 \times \dfrac{63.5}{6.023 \times 10^{23}}}{(3.6 \times 10^{-8})^3}$$

$$= 8.9 \text{ g cm}^{-3}$$

Example 7.3

Molybdenum has a density of 10.2 g cm^{-3} and lattice parameter of 3.15 Å. Find the number of atoms per unit cell and predict the type of crystal structure. The atomic mass of Mo is 95.94.

Solution

$$\text{Density } (\rho) = \frac{n \times \dfrac{M}{N}}{a^3}$$

or $n = \dfrac{\rho a^3 N}{M}$

or $n = \dfrac{10.2 \times (3.15 \times 10^{-8})^3 \times 6.023 \times 10^{23}}{95.94}$

or $n = 2.001 \cong 2$

$\Rightarrow$ Mo crystallizes in body-centered cubic fashion.

Example 7.4

Solid nitrogen has a density of 1.03 g/cm^3 at about 293 K. If solid nitrogen is known to have some cubic lattice with a length of 5.66 Å, what kind of cubic lattice does solid N_2 have?

Solution

Volume $= (5.66 \times 10^{-8})^3 = 181 \times 10^{-24}$ cm^3

Now, Mass per unit cell = Density × Volume

$$= \frac{1.03 \times 181 \times 10^{-24}}{1.66 \times 10^{-24}} \text{ amu}$$

$$= 112 \text{ amu}$$

Each N_2 molecule with two nitrogen atoms has a mass of 28 amu. Thus, the number of molecules per unit cell is 112/28 = 4 N_2 molecules per cell. As the number of molecules per unit cell is 4, the solid nitrogen has face-centered cubic lattice.

Edge Length

From relation [7.4],

$$a = \sqrt[3]{\frac{n \times M}{N \times \sigma}} \text{ cm} \qquad ...[7.5]$$

For simple, face-centered, and base-centered unit cells only "n" value is substituted with 1, 4, and 2 respectively.

Example 7.5

Fe has fcc structure with density 5.74 g cm^{-3}. Find the edge length of the unit cell.

Solution

$$a = \sqrt[3]{\frac{n \times M}{N \times \sigma}}$$

$$= \sqrt[3]{\frac{4 \times 56}{6.023 \times 10^{23} \times 5.75}}$$

$$= 2.15\text{Å}$$

Packing Fraction

Packing fraction refers to the fraction of the total volume of the unit cell which is occupied by the atoms, many often known as atomic packing factor (APF).

$$\text{APF} = \frac{\text{volume occupied by the atoms}}{\text{volume of unit cell}} \qquad ...[7.6]$$

For simple unit cell

$$\text{APF} = \frac{\frac{4}{3}\pi r^3}{(2r)^3} = 0.524, \text{ i.e., } 52.4\%$$

For body-centered unit cell

$$\text{APF} = \frac{2 \times \frac{4}{3}\pi r^3}{\left(\frac{4}{\sqrt{3}}\right)^3} = 0.68, \text{ i.e., } 68\%$$

For face-centered unit cell

$$\text{APF} = \frac{4 \times \frac{4}{3}\pi r^3}{(2\sqrt{2}r)^3} = 0.74, \text{ i.e., } 74\%$$

Note:

For hexagonal unit cell APF can be calculated as follows:

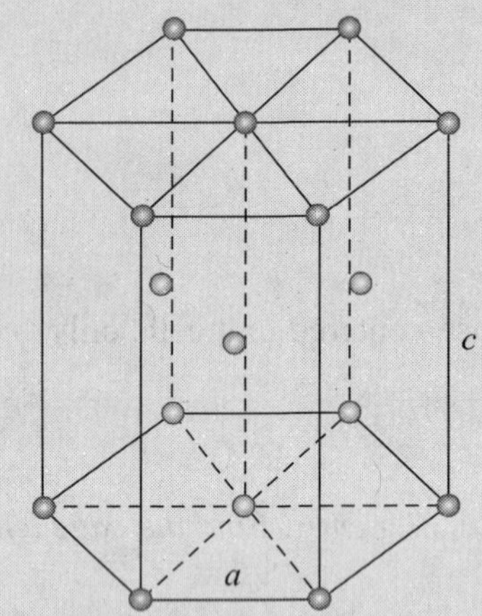

Fig. 7.16 Simple hexagonal unit cell

Number of particles per unit cell = 12 corners × 1/6 + 2 face centers × 1/2 + 3 inside body = 6

$$\text{Volume of spheres} = 6 \times \frac{4}{3}\pi r^3 = 8\pi r^3 \qquad \text{...[7.7]}$$

Volume of unit cell = base × axial height

Base area = area of a regular hexagon

= area of six equilateral triangles

$$= 6 \times \frac{1}{2} \times \text{base} \times \text{height}$$

$$= 6 \times \frac{1}{2} \times 2r \times 2r \sin 60°$$

$$= 6 \times \sqrt{3}r^2$$

Height (c) = 2 × (distance between closest packed layers)

= 2 × (1/3rd of body diagonal of "fcc" lattice with edge "a")

$$= 2 \times \frac{1}{3} \times \sqrt{3}a$$

$$= \frac{2 \times 2\sqrt{2}r}{\sqrt{3}}$$

$$= 4r\sqrt{\frac{2}{3}}$$

$$\text{Now, volume of the unit cell} = 6 \times \sqrt{3}r^2 \times 4r\,\frac{2}{3}$$

$$= 24\sqrt{2}r^3 \qquad \text{...[7.8]}$$

$$APF = \frac{\text{volume of spheres}}{\text{volume of the unit cell}}$$

$$= \frac{8\pi r^3}{24\sqrt{2}r^3}$$

$$= \frac{\pi}{3\sqrt{2}}$$

$$= \frac{3.143}{3 \times 1.414} = 0.74$$

that is, % of volume occupied is 74%.

Coordination Number

It refers to the number of neighboring atoms those remain directly surrounding a given atom.

Crystal structure	Coordination number
Primitive cubic	6
fcc	12
bcc	8

Ionic Solids

Ionic solids consist of cations and anions held together by electrostatic forces. These oppositely charged ions arrange themselves in a systematic pattern which extends throughout the crystal. In these solids each ion remains surrounded by the highest possible number of oppositely charged ions so as to maximize the attractive forces and minimize the potential energy. The number of ions surrounding any particular ion is called the coordination number. Positive and negative ions have same coordination number in solids having equal number of oppositely charged ions, e.g., NaCl and ZnS. On the other hand, coordination number of positive and negative ions are different in solids having unequal number of oppositely charged ions, e.g. CaF_2 and $ZnCl_2$.

Limiting Radius Ratios

The structure of ionic solids can be established by considering the relative sizes of the positive and negative ions, i.e., ratio of their radii.

$$\text{Radius ratio} = \frac{\text{radius of cation } (r_+)}{\text{radius of anion } (r_-)}$$

With simple geometric calculations it is possible to work out the number of ions of a given size those can remain in contact with some other ion. Thus, the coordination number can be predicted from the radius ratio.

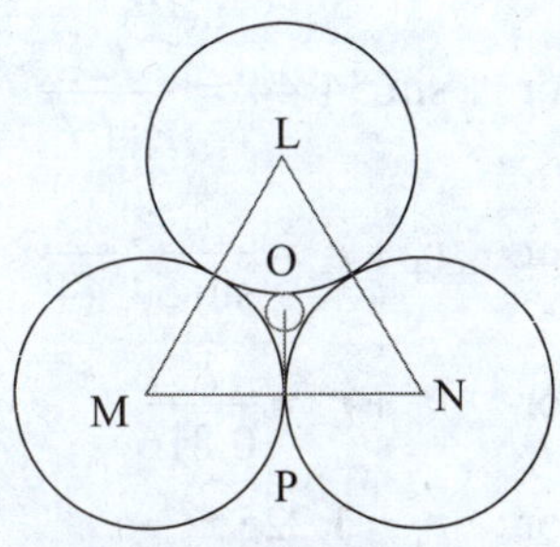

Fig. 7.17

Radius ratio for coordination number 3

Let us consider a hypothetical ionic compound AX, where three X^- ions are in contact with one A^+ ion. In the limiting case when A^- ions are also in contact with one another, it gives rise to an equilateral triangular arrangement.

As the angle LMN is 60°, the angle OMN is 30°.

$$\cos 30° = \frac{MP}{MO}$$

or $$\cos 30° = \frac{r_-}{r_+ + r_-}$$

or $$r_+ + r_- = \frac{r_-}{\cos 30°}$$

or $$r_+ + r_- = \frac{r_-}{0.866}$$

or $$r_+ = 1.155\, r_- - r_-$$

or $$\frac{r_+}{r_-} = 0.155$$

Now, if the radius ratio is <0.155 then the anions will no longer touch the central cation which will make the structure unstable. When the value exceeds 0.155 and reaches at 0.225 it is possible to fit fourth anion around the cation. Therefore, the limiting ratio for coordination number 3 is 0.155.

Radius ratio for coordination number 4

Figure 7.18 represents tetrahedral arrangement of four anions around a cation at the center of the cube. The angle LOM is the tetrahedral angle and thus the angle LON is 109° 28′/2 = 54°44′. Now, in the triangle LON,

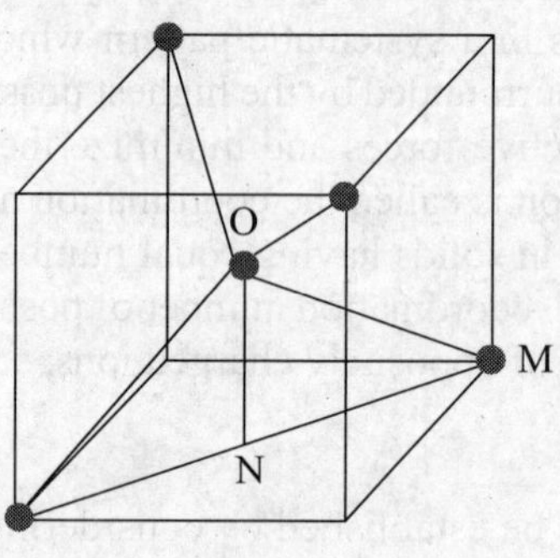

Fig. 7.18

$$\sin LON = \frac{ON}{OL}$$

or $$\sin 54°44' = \frac{r_-}{r_+ + r_-}$$

or $$r_+ + r_- = \frac{r_-}{\sin 54°44'}$$

or $$r_+ + r_- = \frac{r_-}{0.816}$$

or $$r_+ = 1.225\, r_- - r_-$$

or $$\frac{r_+}{r_-} = 0.225$$

Radius ratio for coordination number 6

Figure 7.19 represents square planar cross-section of an octahedron. The ions remain in contact along the face diagonal of the cube.

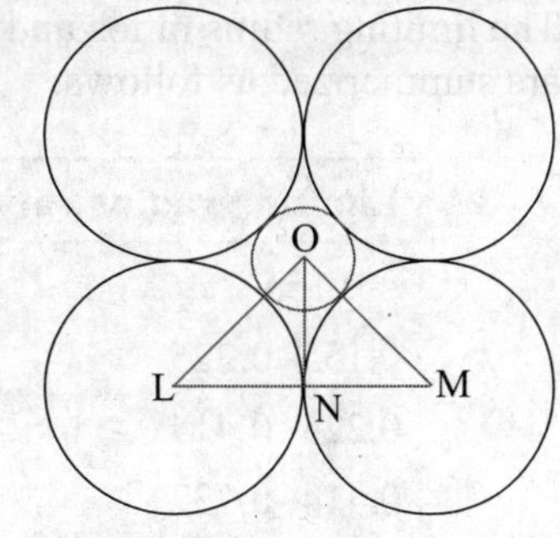

Fig. 7.19

In the triangle OLN,

$$\cos OLN = \frac{LN}{OL}$$

or $$\cos 45° = \frac{r_-}{r_+ + r_-}$$

or $$r_+ + r_- = \frac{r_-}{\cos 45°}$$

or $$r_+ + r_- = \frac{r_-}{0.707}$$

or $$r_+ = 1.414\, r_- - r_-$$

or $$\frac{r_+}{r_-} = 0.414$$

Radius ratio for coordination number 8

Figure 7.20 represents a bcc-type structure, where the coordination number is eight. In such a structure, the ions touch each other along the body diagonal of the cube, while anions are in contact with each other along the side of the cube.

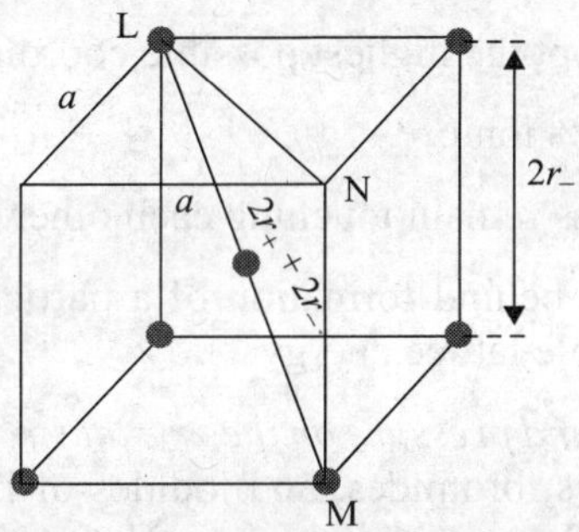

Fig. 7.20

The length of the body diagonal, $LM = 2r_+ + 2r_-$

The length of the face diagonal, $LN = 2\sqrt{2}r_-$

Edge length, $MN = 2r_+$

For a cube,

$$LM^2 = LN^2 + MN^2$$

or $$(2r_+ + 2r_-)^2 = (2\sqrt{2}r_-)^2 + (2r_+)^2$$

or $$\left(\frac{r_+}{r_-}\right)^2 + 2\left(\frac{r_+}{r_-}\right) - 2 = 0$$

or $$\frac{r_+}{r_-} = \frac{-2 \pm \sqrt{4-8}}{2} = 0.732$$

The limiting radius ratios and the coordination number along with the arrangement (structure) are summarized as follows.

Limiting radius ratio	Coordination number	Shape
< 0.155	2	Linear
0.155–0.225	3	Planar triangle
0.225–0.414	4	Tetrahedral
0.414–0.732	4	Square planar
0.414–0.732	6	Octahedral
>0.732	8	Body-centered cubic

Note:

1. Radius ratio helps to predict the correct structure in many cases but cannot be taken as a completely reliable method for predicting the actual structure. This is due to the fact that there are several factors other than geometrical ground which affect the structure. It is therefore, required to consider the validity of assumptions behind the radius ratio concepts.
   (a) Accurate ionic radii are known.
   (b) Ions behave as hard elastic spheres.
   (c) Ions always adopt the highest possible coordination number.
   (d) Bonding is 100% ionic.
   (e) +ve and –ve ions remain touching each other.
2. Ultimately the reason behind formation of a particular crystal structure is that it gives the most favorable lattice energy.
3. *Effect of temperature and pressure on the crystal structure*: At ordinary temperature and pressure, chlorides, bromides, and iodides of lithium, sodium, and rubidium along with some halides of silver possess NaCl structure with 6:6 coordination. On application of high pressure they transform to CsCl structure with 8:8 coordination. On the other hand, CsCl structure on heating transforms to the NaCl structure with 6:6 coordination.

AX Type

Zinc blende structure

This structure is named after the naturally occurring mineral form of zinc sulfide. The characteristic features of this structure are as follows:

1. The radius ratio $r_{Zn^{2+}}/r_{S^{2-}} = 0.40$, which suggests Td arrangement of anions around cation and vice versa.
2. The coordination number is 4:4.

3. The structure may be regarded as the cubic close-packed array of sulfide ions with Zn^{2+} ions occupying half of the Td voids in alternate fashion.

4. Number of "ZnS" units per unit cell

   Number of Zn^{2+} ions = 4

   Number of S^{2-} ions = 8 at corners $\times \frac{1}{8}$ + 6 at face centers $\frac{1}{2} = 4$

   Thus, the number of ZnS units per unit cell is 4.

5. Other examples being CdS, HgS, and copper halides.

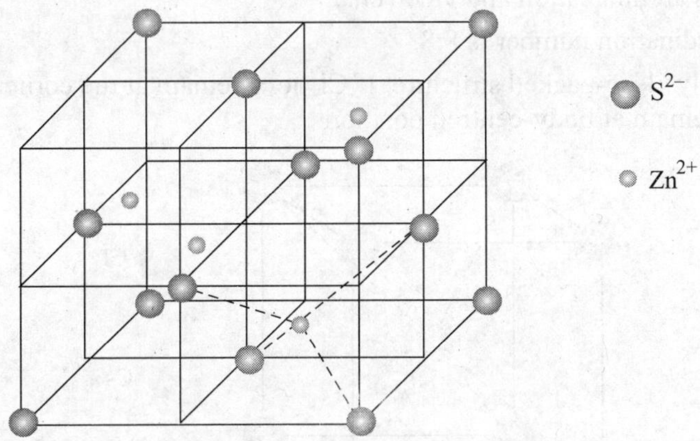

Fig. 7.21 Unit cell of ZnS

Rock salt structure

1. The radius ratio $r_{Na^+}/r_{Cl^-} = 0.52$, which suggests "Oh" arrangement of anions around cation and vice versa.
2. The coordination number is 6:6.
3. The structure may be regarded as the cubic close-packed array of chloride ions with Na^+ ions occupying all the "Oh" voids.

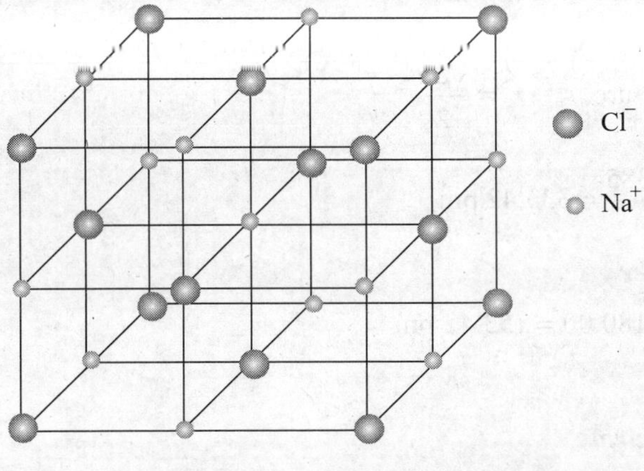

Fig. 7.22 Unit cell of NaCl

4. Number of NaCl units per unit cell

   Number of Na^+ ions = 4

   Number of Cl^- ions $= 8 \times \frac{1}{8} + 6 \times \frac{1}{2} = 4$

   Thus, there are four "NaCl" units per unit cell.
5. Other examples, are alkali metal halides, hydrides, and halides of silver (AgCl, AgF, AgBr).

Caesium chloride structure

1. The radius ratio $r_{Cs^+}/r_{Cl^-} = 0.93$, which suggests body-centered type of arrangement of anions around cation and vice versa.
2. The coordination number is 8:8.
3. It is nearly close-packed structure. If Cl^- ions remain at the corners of the cube then Cs^+ion remain at body-centred position.

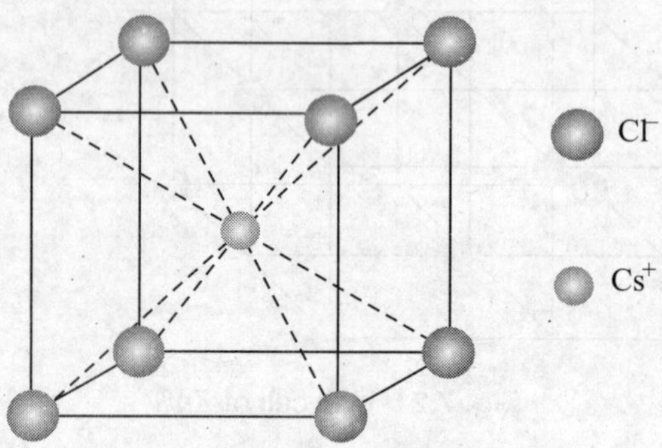

Fig. 7.23 Unit cell in unit cell

4. The number of CsCl units per unit cell is 1.
5. Other examples are CsBr, Csl, TlCl, TlBr, TlI, NH4Cl, etc.

Example 7.6

NH_4Cl crystallizes in BCC lattice with a unit distance of 385 pm. Find the inter-ionic distance and the radius of NH_4^+ ion if the radius of Cl^- ion is 180 pm.

Solution

For BCC structure, $r_+ + r_- = \frac{\sqrt{3}a}{2}$

or $\quad r_+ + r_- = \frac{\sqrt{3} \times 385}{2} = 333.42$ pm

Now, $\quad r_+ = (r_+ + r_-) - r_-$

or $\quad r_+ = 333.42 - 180.00 = 153.42$ pm

AX_2 Type

CaF2 (Fluorite structure)

It is named after mineral form of calcium fluoride (CaF_2).

1. The radius ratio is 0.73 or above.
2. The coordination number is 8:4.
3. Ca^{2+} ions form fcc arrangement. These ions are too small to touch each other, so that structure is not close-packed. However, the structure can be related to a close-packed arrangement, since Ca^{2+} occupy the same relative positions as for a cubic close-packed structure, and the F^- ions occupy all the tetrahedral holes.
4. Other examples are BaF_2, $BaCl_2$, SrF_2, $SrCl_2$, CdF_2, PbF_2, ThO_2, etc.

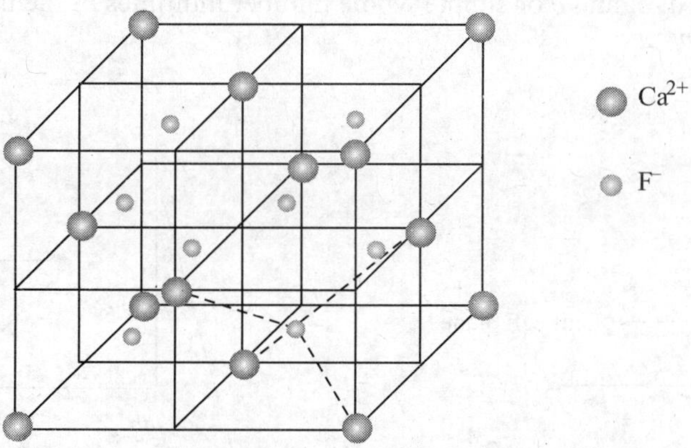

Fig. 7.24 Unit cell of CaF_2

Anti-fluorite structure

In such an arrangement the –ve ions occupy the same relative positions as for ccp structure and +ve ions occupy the 'Td' voids. The coordination number is 4:8. Examples are oxides and sulfides of alkali metals.

TiO_2 (rutile structure)

This is named after one mineral form of TiO_2.

1. The radius ratio is between 0.41 and 0.73.
2. Every Ti^{4+} is octahedrally surrounded by six O^{2-} ions and each O^{2-} ion has three Ti^{4+} ions around it in a plane triangular manner. Thus, the coordination number is 6:3.
3. The rutile structure is not close-packed. The unit cell is not cubic, since one of the axes is 30% shorter than the other two. It can be described as distorted body-centered cubic lattice of Ti^{4+} ions.

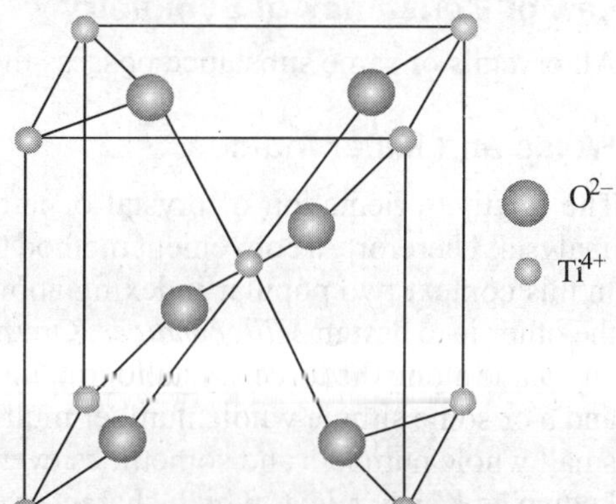

Fig. 7.25 Unit cell of TiO_2

Laws of Crystallography

There are three basic laws of crystallography.

Steno's Law of Constancy of Interfacial Angles

The angle between the corresponding faces or planes forming the external surface of a crystal remains constant for a particular substance irrespective of the shape, size, and formation of crystal.

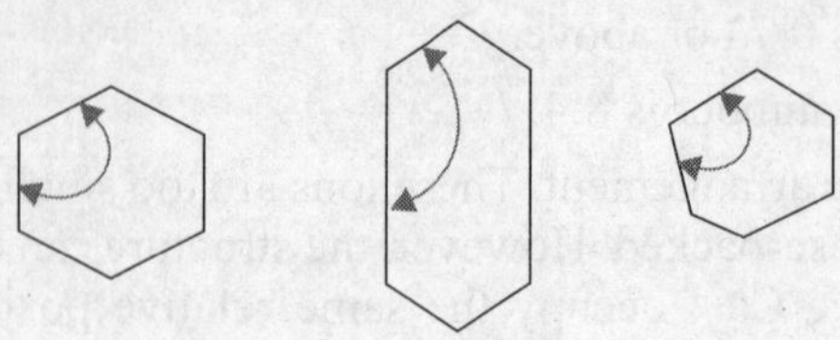

Hauy's Law

The intercepts or indices of any plane of a crystal along crystallographic axes are either equal to the unit intercepts *a*, *b*, and *c* or simple whole number multiples of them. Such a ratio at any plane is given by *la*:*mb*:*nc*.

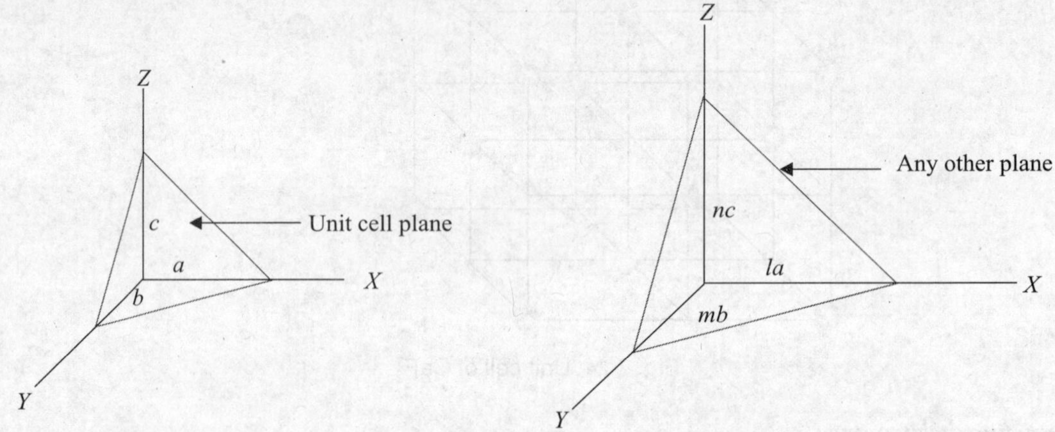

Fig. 7.26

Law of Constancy of Symmetry

All crystals of same substance possess the same elements of symmetry.

Weiss and Miller Indices

The relative orientation of crystal or lattice planes is an important aspect in crystal-structure analysis. Therefore, a convenient method to uniquely identify these surfaces or planes is required. In this context two popular indexing approaches are used. One is to assign *Weiss indices* while the other is to assign *Miller indices*. On the basis of the law of rational indices, the intercepts of any plane along the three crystallographic axes remain either equal to the unit cell intercepts *a*, *b*, and *c* or some simple whole number multiple of them, i.e., *la*, *mb* and *nc*. *l*, *m*, and *n* are usually small whole numbers and sometimes even fraction or infinity. The coefficients of *l*, *m*, and *n* are known as *Weiss indices* which characterize a given set of parallel and equidistant planes.

Miller indices (hkl)

The appearance of ∞ in Weiss indices is inconvenient. Therefore W. H. Miller developed a new approach for indexing the lattice planes. Miller Indices (*hkl*), a set of numbers which quantify the intercepts and thus may be used to uniquely identify the surface or plane. These are symbolic vector representation for the orientation of an atomic plane in a crystal lattice and are defined as the reciprocals of the fractional intercepts which the plane makes with the crystallographic axes.

Determination of Millar indices

Step 1: *Consider the intercepts along the three axes in crystallographic system.*

Step 2: *Specify the intercepts in fractional coordinates*: Coordinates are converted to fractional coordinates by dividing by the respective cell dimension—for example, a point (x, y, z) in a unit cell of dimensions $a \times b \times c$ has fractional coordinates of $(x/a, y/b, z/c)$. In the case of a cubic unit cell each coordinate will simply be divided by the cubic cell constant, a.

Step 3: *Take the reciprocals of the fractional intercepts*: This final manipulation generates the Miller indices. By convention these are then specified without being separated by any commas or other symbols. The Miller indices are also enclosed within standard brackets, e.g., let us find the Miller indices for the following planes in a cubic crystal.

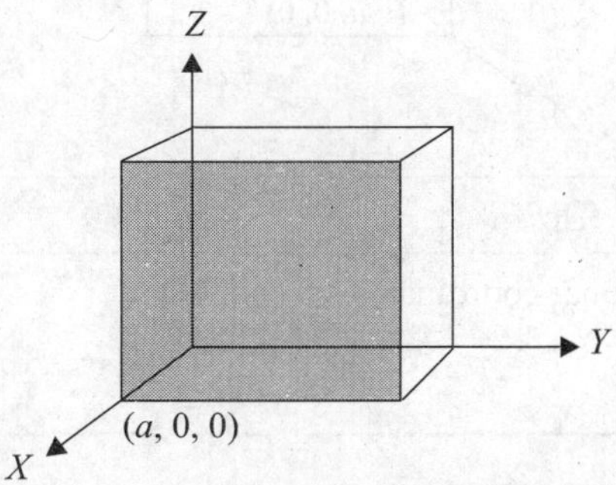

Intercepts	***a***	**0**	**0**
Intercept in fractional coordinates (Weiss indices)	$a/a = 1$	$0/a = \infty$	$0/a = \infty$
Reciprocal	$1/1 = 1$	$1/\infty = 0$	$1/\infty = 0$
Cleared fraction	1	0	0

Miller indices—(100)

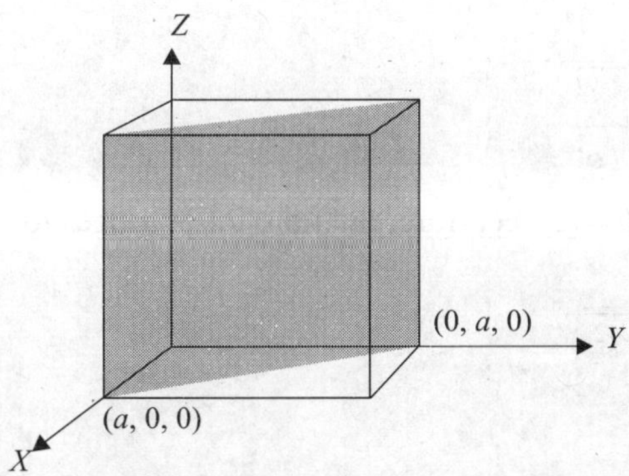

Intercepts	***a***	***a***	**0**
Intercept in fractional coordinates	$a/a = 1$	$a/a = 1$	$0/a = \infty$
Reciprocal	$1/1 = 1$	$1/1 = 1$	$1/\infty = 0$
Cleared fraction	1	1	0

Miller indices—(110)

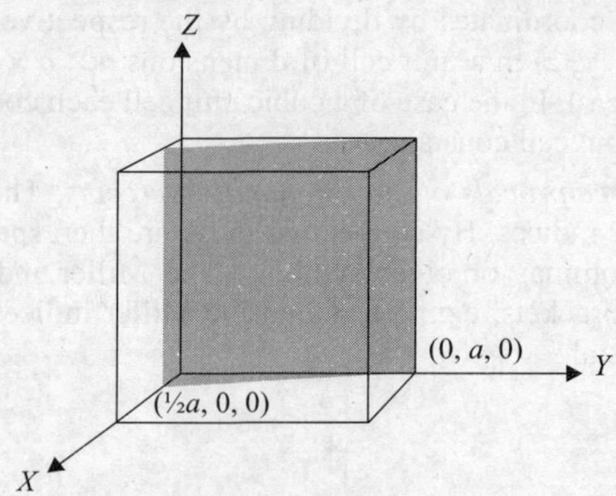

Intercepts	***a***	***a***	**0**
Intercept in fractional coordinates	1/2	1	∞
Reciprocal	2	1	0
Cleared fraction	2	1	0

Miller indices—(210)

Note:

If any of the intercepts are at negative values on the axes then the negative sign will carry through into the Miller indices. In such cases the negative sign is actually denoted by over striking the relevant number. For example, (0 0 –1) is denoted by $(0\,0\bar{1}1)$.

Interplanar spacing

The distance between adjacent planes of Millar indices (*hkl*) is

$$d_{hkl} = \frac{1}{\sqrt{\frac{h^2}{a^2} + \frac{k^2}{b^2} + \frac{l^2}{c^2}}} \quad ...[7.9]$$

For a cubic crystal $a = b = c$. Therefore, relation [7.9] reduces to

$$d_{\text{hkl}} = \frac{a}{\sqrt{h^2 + k^2 + l^2}} \quad ...[7.10]$$

Example 7.7

The planes in a crystalline solid intersect the crystal axes at (–a, b, ∞) and (a, 2b, 3c).

Solution

Intercepts	***a***	***b***	**∞**
Intercept in fractional coordinates	–1	1	∞
Reciprocal	–1	1	0
Cleared fraction	–1	1	0

Miller indices—$(\bar{1}10)$

Intercepts	$3a$	$2b$	c
Intercept in fractional coordinates	3	2	1
Reciprocal	1/3	1/2	1
Cleared fraction	2	3	6

Miller indices—(236)

Example 7.8

Potassium crystallizes in bcc lattice with unit cell length 5.34 Å. Calculate the distance of separation between the planes (110), (111), and (220).

Solution

$$d_{110} = \frac{5.34}{\sqrt{1^2+1^2+0^2}} = 3.77\ \text{Å}$$

$$d_{111} = \frac{5.34}{\sqrt{1^2+1^2+1^2}} = 3.08\ \text{Å}$$

$$d_{220} = \frac{5.34}{\sqrt{2^2+2^2+0^2}} = 1.88\ \text{Å}$$

Example 7.9

Calculate the separation between (123) planes in an orthorhombic lattice. Given a = 2.0, b = 2.5, and c = 1.8 Å.

Solution

$$d_{hkl} = \frac{1}{\sqrt{\dfrac{1^2}{2^2}+\dfrac{2^2}{(2.5)^2}+\dfrac{3^2}{(1.8)^2}}}$$

$$= 0.52\ \text{Å}$$

Example 7.10

Lead is having fcc structure with inter atomic distance 3.5 Å. Find the number of atoms per mm² in (110) plane.

Solution

$2r = 3.5$ Å

or $r = 1.75$ Å

Now,

$$a = \frac{4r}{\sqrt{2}} = \frac{4\times 1.75}{\sqrt{2}} = 4.95\ \text{Å}$$

Area of the plane $= \sqrt{2}(4.95\times 10^{-8})^2$

$= 24.5\times 10^{-16}\ \text{cm}^2$

$= 24.5\times 10^{-14}\ \text{mm}^2$

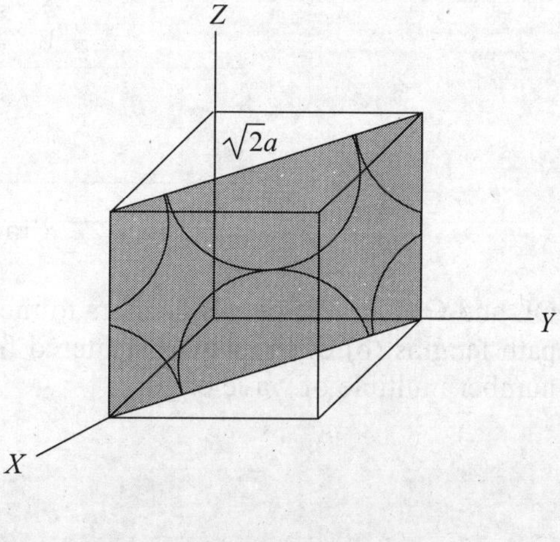

Number of atoms in the plane = 2(1/2) + 4 (1/4) = 2

Number of atoms per mm² in the plane (110) = $\dfrac{2}{24.5\times10^{-14}}=8.16\times10^{12}$

X-Ray Diffraction Studies of Crystals

The structure of crystals at the level of microscopic particles such as atom, molecule, or ion can be revealed by their interaction with X-rays. The wavelength of X-rays is comparable with inter-particle spacings of the crystal. Thus, crystals act as 3-D diffraction grating to X-rays. Upon striking on a crystal, X-rays form a definite diffraction pattern that can be collected on a photographic plate. From this pattern, it is possible to arrive at the shape size and the detailed information regarding the position of particles in the crystal.

Bragg's Equation

As per W.H. Bragg, scattering of X-rays by crystals can be considered as reflection from successive planes of atoms in the crystals. Scattering can only take place at certain angles that are determined by the wavelength of X-rays and the distance between the planes in the crystal. The empirical relation among the wavelength of X-rays, the inter-planner spacing, and the angle of scattering is known as Bragg's equation.

Derivation of Bragg's equation

The horizontal lines in Figure 7.27 represent parallel planes in the crystal structure separated by the distance *d*. Let X-rays strike on the crystal at glancing angle θ as shown. Some of the rays get scattered from the upper plane at the same angle, while some others will be absorbed and get scattered from the successive layers. The waves reflected by different layers remain in phase with one another only if the difference in path lengths of the waves reflected from the successive planes is equal to an integral number of wavelengths.

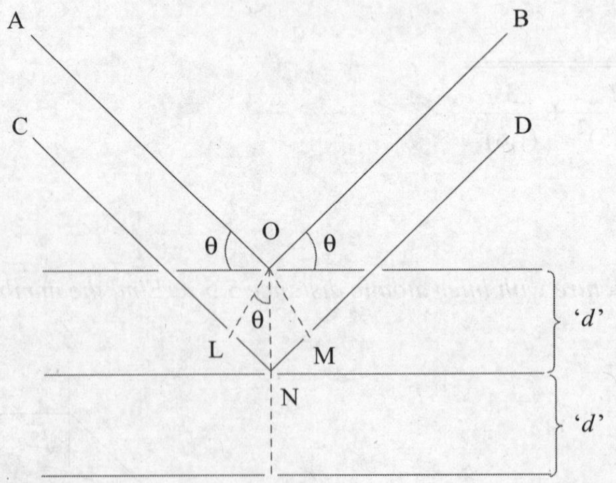

Fig. 7.27 X-ray reflections from a crystal

OL and OM are the perpendiculars to the incident and reflected X-rays. The difference in the path lengths (δ) of the waves scattered from the first two planes should be equal to a whole number multiple of wavelength.

$$LN + NM = \delta$$

or $$LN + NM = n\delta$$

or $$2LN = n\lambda, \text{ as } \Delta OLN \text{ and } \Delta OMN \text{ are congruent}$$

or $$2d \sin \theta = n\lambda \qquad [7.11]$$

where n is an integer, i.e., having values 1, 2, 3,… and is known as the order of diffraction. Relation [7.11] is known as Bragg's equation.

For a given set of lattice planes, d has a fixed value. Thus, the possibility of getting maximum diffraction, i.e., the possibility of getting diffracted waves in phase with one another, depends on θ. Upon gradual increase in θ, a number of positions will be there at which the diffractions will be maximum. At these positions, n will have values equal to 1,2,3, …, etc. In general n is set with 1.

Case I: If, $\lambda \geq 2d$, then there will be no solution for 'n' and hence there will be no diffraction i.e. X-rays will pass through the crystal without diffraction.

Case II: If $\lambda < 2d$, then X-rays will suffer diffraction through smaller angles.

Example 7.11

A simple cubic lattice has atoms that are spaced by 2.77 Å. If the diffraction is caused by the planes of atoms that are 2.77 Å apart, at what angle are X-rays diffracted in the first order if they have a wavelength of 1.82 Å?

Solution

For first-order diffraction, we have

$$\lambda = 2d \sin \theta$$

or $$1.82 = 2 \times 2.77 \times \sin \theta$$

or $$\sin \theta = 0.329$$

or $$\theta = 19.2°$$

The angle of diffraction is 19.2°.

Example 7.12

For Example 7.11, show that the angle of the second-order diffraction is not the double of the angle of the first-order diffraction.

Solution

For second-order diffraction, we have

$$2\lambda = 2d \sin \theta$$

or $$2 \times 1.82 = 2 \times 2.77 \times \sin \theta$$

or $$\sin \theta = 0.657$$

or $$\theta = 41.1°$$

The angle of diffraction is 41.1°.The angle for the first-order diffraction is 19.2° (from Example 7.11). It is quite clear from observation that the angle of the second-order diffraction is not the double of the angle of the first-order diffraction. This is because the order of diffraction is dependent on the "*sin*" of the angle, not on the angle itself.

Example 7.13

X-rays having wavelength 10 Å are diffracted at an angle of 30° by a crystal. Assuming the first-order diffraction, find the spacing between the crystal planes. Also find the angle for the second-order diffraction.

Solution

For first-order diffraction, we have

$$\lambda = 2d \sin \theta$$

or $10 = 2 \times d \times \sin 30°$

or $d = 10$ Å

For second-order diffraction,we have

$$2\lambda = 2d \sin \theta$$

or $2 \times 10 = 2 \times 10 \times \sin \theta$

or $\sin \theta = 1$

or $\theta = 90°$

The angle of diffraction is 90°.

Defects in Solids

A defect in crystal is deviation from perfectly ordered arrangement of the constituent ions, atoms, or molecules of the crystal thereby resulting in change in the properties. These defects may be at a lattice point along a line or over a surface. Accordingly the defects can be broadly classified into the following three types.

1. **Point defects** are places where an atom is missing or irregularly placed in the lattice structure. Point defects include stoichiometric, non stoichiometric, and impurity defects.
2. **Linear defects** are groups of atoms in irregular positions. Linear defects are commonly called dislocations.
3. **Planar defects** are interfaces between homogeneous regions of the material. Planar defects include grain boundaries, stacking faults, and external surfaces.

Here, the discussion is restricted only to point defects. As discussed in the classification point defects, the following verities are included.

Stoichiometric Defects

Stoichiometric compounds are those where the number of different type of atoms or ions present are exactly in the same ratios indicated by their formulae. Such compounds obey the law of constant composition and are also known as *Daltonide* compounds. Two types of defects are normally observed in such compounds, namely, *Schottky* and *Frenkel* defects.

Shottky defect

A Schottky defect consists of a pair of holes in the crystal lattice formed due to removal of a cation and an anion (Fig. 7.28). This sort of defect mainly occurs in ionic compounds where positive and negative ions are of similar size and the coordination number is high (usually 6 or 8), e.g., NaCl, KCl, and CsCl. Such a defect results in an overall decrease in density of crystal.

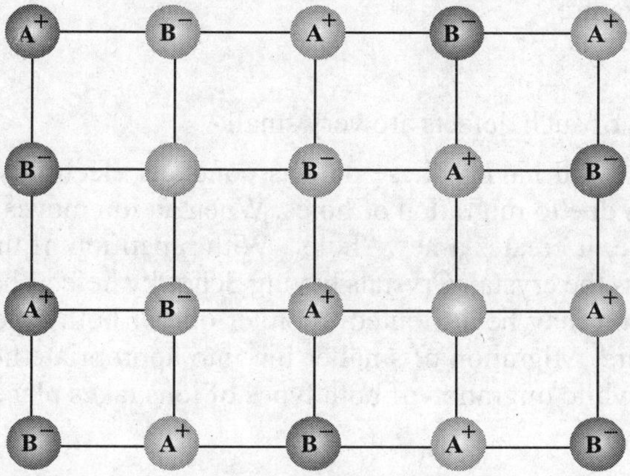

Fig. 7.28 Schottky defect

The number of Schottky defects formed per cm³ is

$$N\,e^{\left(-\frac{W_s}{2kT}\right)}$$

where N is the number of sites per cm³ that could be left vacant, W_s is the work necessary to form a Schottky defect, k is the gas constant, and T is the absolute temperature.

Frenkel defect

A Frenkel defect consists of a vacant lattice site, i.e., a hole and the ion which should have occupied the site now remains in the alternate interstitial position (Fig. 7.29). Mostly cations are relatively smaller in size and therefore it is easier to place cations in interstitial positions. Such a defect is found in ionic compounds where positive and negative ions differ widely in their sizes and the coordination number is low (usually 4 or 6), e.g., ZnS, AgCl, AgBr, AgI and CaF_2. There is no change in the overall density of crystal. As small positive ions are highly polarizing and large negative ions are readily polarizable (Fazan's rule), these compounds develop some covalent character. The distortion of electron cloud and proximity of like charges leads to a high dielectric constant.

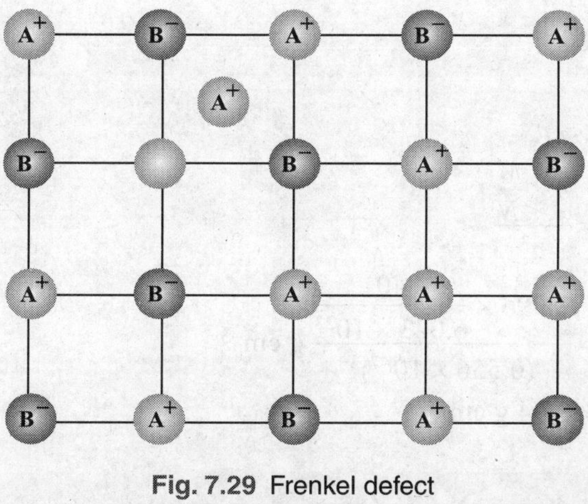

Fig. 7.29 Frenkel defect

The number of Frenkel defects formed per cm^3 is

$$\sqrt{NN'}\, e^{\left(-\frac{W_f}{2kT}\right)}$$

where N is the number of sites per cm^3 that could be left vacant, N' is the number of alternate interstitial position, W_f is the work necessary to form a Frenkel defect, k is the gas constant, and T is the absolute temperature.

Note:

1. The numbers of such defects are very small.
2. A crystalline solid having these defects conducts electricity to some extent. The conduction is due to migration of holes. When an ion moves from its lattice site to occupy a hole, it creates a new "hole". With repetition of the process a hole may migrate across the crystal. Crystals having Schottky defects have two types of holes and conduction may be attributed to either one or both types of holes depending on temperature. Migration of smaller ion into appropriate holes is favored at low temperature while migration of both types of ions takes place at high temperature.

Example 7.14

Calcium crystallizes in a face-centred cubic unit cell with a = 0.556 nm. Calculate the density if (a) It contained 0.1% Frenkel defects and (b) It contained 0.1% Schottky defects.

Solution

(a) Frankel defect does not change the density as the atom occupies interstitial position instead of lattice site. Thus, the "n" value remains as usual for fcc.

$$\text{Density } (\rho) = \frac{n \times \frac{M}{N}}{a^3}$$

$$= \frac{4 \times \frac{40}{6.023 \times 10^{23}}}{(0.556 \times 10^{-7})^3} \text{ g cm}^{-3}$$

$$= 1.55 \text{ g cm}^{-3}$$

(b) In Schottky defect atoms are missing. Thus, the value of "n" changes.

$$n = 4 - 4 \times \frac{0.1}{100}$$

$$= 4 - 0.004$$

$$= 3.996$$

Now,

$$\text{Density } (\rho) = \frac{n \times \frac{M}{N}}{a^3}$$

$$= \frac{3.996 \times \frac{40}{6.023 \times 10^{23}}}{(0.556 \times 10^{-7})^3} \text{ g cm}^{-3}$$

$$= 1.54 \text{ g cm}^{-3}$$

Nonstoichiometric Defects

Nonstoichiometric compounds are those where the number of different type of atoms or ions are not present exactly in the same ratios as indicated by their formulae, e.g., $Fe_{0.9}S$, $Fe_{0.84}O$, etc. Such compounds do not obey the law of constant composition and are also known as *Berthollide* compounds. Nonstoichiometric defects arise due to either metal excesses or metal deficiency.

Metal excess defect

This may occur in two ways.

F-centres

A negative ion remains absent from its lattice site and the hole created in the process remains occupied by an electron so as to maintain the electrical neutrality (Fig. 7.30). The compounds which are expected to show Schottky defect show this defects, e.g., NaCl, KCl, and LiH. The general representation of a compound with such defect is $AX_{1-\delta}$.

Note:

1. The anion site occupied by electron is called F-center (where F stand for Farbe, a German word meaning color). These F-centers are responsible for color, e.g., nonstoichiometric NaCl is yellow.
2. As the electron at F-center is unpaired, the substance having F-centers is paramagnetic.
3. Such substances also conduct to some extent. Conduction is due to transition of electron from F-center to conduction band. As electron is responsible for conduction this is known as an *n*-type semiconduction.

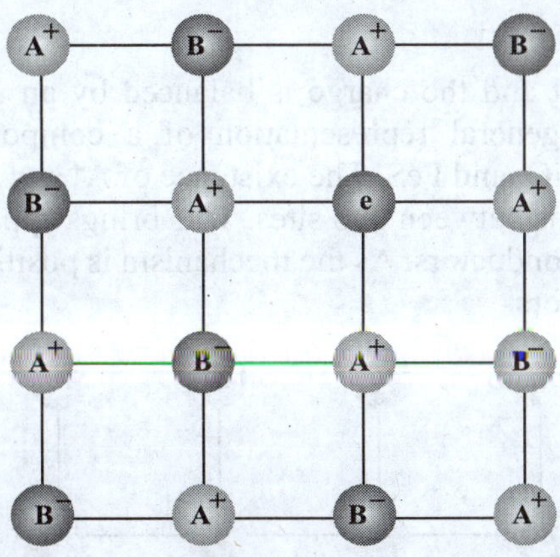

Fig. 7.30 F-centers

Interstitial ions and electrons

Here, an extra +ve ion occupies interstitial position in the lattice and neutrality is maintained by the inclusion of an interstitial electron (Fig. 7.31). The compounds which are expected to show Frankel defect show this defect, e.g., ZnO, CdO, and Fe_2O_3, etc. The general representation of a compound with such defect is $A_{1+\delta}X$.

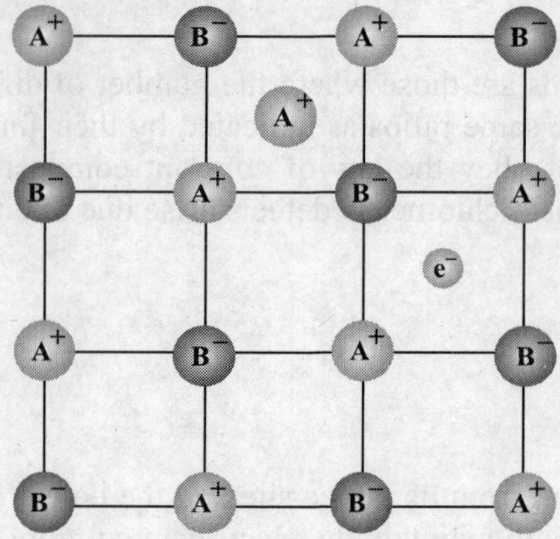

Fig. 7.31 Interstitial ion and electron

Note:

1. Crystals with metal excess defect carry free electrons and thereby behave as semiconductors. As the mechanism is normal electron conduction these are known as *n*-type semiconductors.
2. The free electrons often give absorption spectrum and thereby impart color to such compounds, e.g., nonstoichiometric NaCl is yellow; ZnO is white when cold but yellow when hot.

Metal deficient defect

This may also occur in two ways. Both these ways require variable valency of the metal and therefore mostly occurs in case of transition metals.

Positive ion absent

Here, a positive ion is absent and the charge is balanced by an adjacent metal ion with an extra positive charge. The general representation of a compound with such defects is $A_{1-\delta}X$. Examples are FeO, NiO, and FeS. The existence of A^+ and A^{2+} ions in close proximity results in exchange of electrons between two sites. This brings apparent movement of A^{2+} and such crystals operate as semiconductors. As the mechanism is positive hole migration these are known as *p*-type semiconductors.

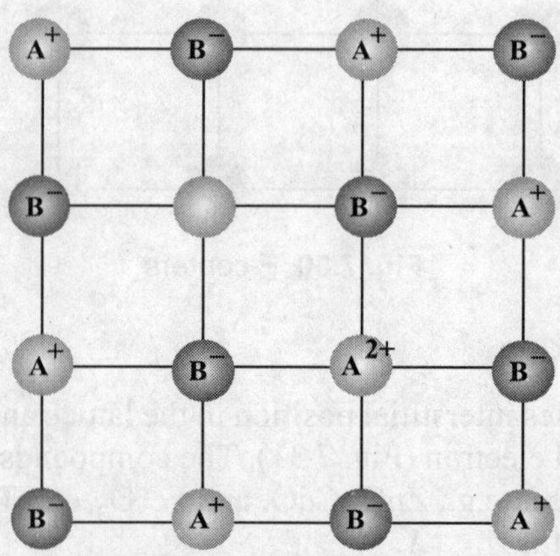

Fig. 7.32 Positive ion absent

Extra interstitial negative ions

Here, an extra –ve ion remains in an interstitial position and the charge is balanced by means of an extra +ve charge present on an adjacent metal ion. General representation is $AX_{1-\delta}$. Such a defect is not found in practice as it is difficult to accommodate large anions into interstitial positions.

Impurity Defects

Such defects arise when foreign atoms remain present at lattice in place of host atom or at the vacant interstitial sites. The former is known as substitutional impurity while the latter is known as interstitial impurity.

Substitutional impurity

A substitutional impurity is that in which an atom of a different type than the bulk atoms replaces one of the bulk atoms in the lattice. Substitutional impurity atoms are usually close in size (within approximately 15%) to the bulk atom, e.g., doping of Gr-13 or 15 elements of appropriate size in Gr-14 elements (mostly Ge and Si). When doped with Gr-13 elements +ve holes are created (Fig. 7.33). These holes can move across the crystal giving rise to electrical conductivity. On the other hand, when doped with Gr-15 elements, the crystals carry extra electrons for conduction. The former conduction is known as *p*-type semiconduction while the latter is known as *n*-type semiconduction.

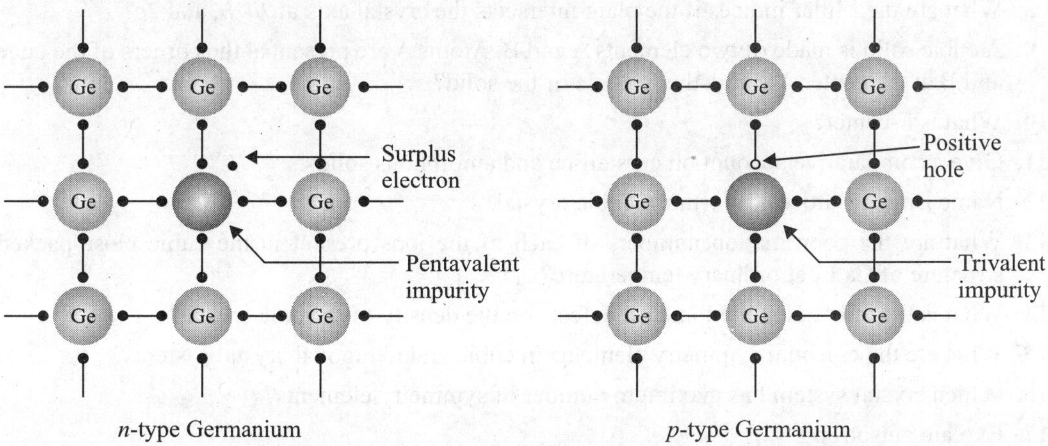

Fig. 7.33

Interstitial impurity

An interstitial impurity is that in which an atom of much smaller size than the atoms in the bulk matrix remains fitted in the open space between the bulk atoms of the lattice structure. An example of interstitial impurity atoms is the carbon atoms that are added to iron to make steel.

Note:

Defects affect primarily all properties of materials. To summarize:

	Properties	Defect type
1.	Electrical properties	All defects especially point defects.
2.	Optical properties	All defects especially point defects.

	Properties	Defect type
3.	Mechanical (e.g., strength, toughness, hardness, etc.)	All defects, especially dislocations.
4.	Magnetic	All defects.
5.	Kinetic (e.g., diffusion)	All defects, especially point defects.

QUESTIONS

1. The metal ion deficiency defect $MX_{1-\delta}$ is not possible, justify.
2. Define law of rational intercepts for a crystal.
3. Give one example each of solid where Frenkel and Schottky defects occur.
4. Calculate the number of atoms per unit cell of hexagonal cell.
5. What is the most probable structure for AB ionic solid if radius ratio is 0.863?
6. What is Schottky defect? In which type of crystals, this is encountered?
7. NaCl has fcc structure. How many Na^+ and Cl^- ions are there in the unit cell?
8. What are the Millar indices if the plain intersects the crystal axis at $2a$, b, and $2c$?
9. A cubic solid is made of two elements A and B. Atoms A are present at the corners of the cube and B at the center. What is the formula of the solid?
10. What is F-center?
11. Give a comparative account on crystalline and amorphous solids.
12. Name Bravais lattices for orthorhombic crystal.
13. What are the coordination numbers of each of the ions present in the cubic close-packed structure of CaF_2 at ordinary temperature?
14. What is the effect of stoichiometric defects on the density of an ionic crystal?
15. What are the essential symmetry elements in cubic and tetragonal crystal systems?
16. Which crystal system has maximum number of symmetry elements?
17. Explain anisotropy.
18. Arrange packing fraction of crystals crystallizing in ccp, fcc, and bcc in increasing order.
19. Doping of Ge with P produces which type of semiconductor?
20. What is the effect of temperature on conductivity of semiconductors?
21. Differentiate between intrinsic and extrinsic semiconductor.
22. Identify the crystal system in the following cases: (i) If $a = 4$ nm, $b = 7$ nm, $c = 9$ nm, and $\alpha = \beta = \gamma = 90°$ (ii) If $a = 6$ nm, $b = 6$ nm, $c = 6$ nm, and $\alpha = \beta = \gamma = 90°$.
23. In an ionic crystal if the general formula is AX and the coordination number is six, then the value of radius ratio is in the range: (i) 0.155–0.215, (ii) 0.215–0.414, (iii) 0.732–1, and (iv) 0.414–0.732. Make the correct choice.
24. Write down the difference between Frenkel defects and Schottky defects.
25. NaCl has FCC structure. How many Na^+ and Cl^- are there in the unit cell?
26. Discuss about common defects found in solids.

27. Discuss Schottky and Frenkel defects in case of ionic solids with example.
28. Calculate and compare atomic packing factor of fcc and bcc structures.
29. Name the types of Bravais lattices encountered in the cubic system. Also, assuming that the lattice points are occupied by atoms, find
    (a) The number of atoms in the unit cell of each lattice type.
    (b) The coordination number of each atom in such lattices.
30. Draw the (100), (110), and (111) planes of a simple cube. Also, calculate the number of atoms per unit cell for a simple cube.
31. What are close-packed structures? Compare the crystal parameters of these structures.
32. Name the Bravais lattices present in cubic system. Sketch their unit cells and find for each type of unit cell (a) the number of atoms per unit cell and (b) coordination number for each atom in the lattice.
33. Discuss different types of nonstoichiometric defects.
34. Discuss the radius ratio rule in establishing the structure of ionic solids.
35. Discuss important features of CCP structure. Give some examples of metal belonging to CCP structure.
36. What do you mean by atomic packing factor? Calculate the atomic packing factor of face-centered cubic lattice and simple cubic lattice.
37. If radius ratio lies between 0.414 and 0.732, then what is the expected coordination number?
38. Why germanium is preferred over silicon as a semiconductor material?
39. What type of semiconductor is obtained by doping Ge with Sb?

NUMERICAL PROBLEMS

1. Show that the radius ratio value for coordination number 3 of a solid is 0.155.
2. Determine the Miller indices for the plain with its intercepts along the axes are $2a$, $3b$, and $2c$ respectively.
3. A substance exists in two allotropic forms, i.e., α (fcc, radius = 0.3 nm) and β (bcc, radius = 0.37 nm). Find out the ratio of their densities (α/β).
4. Iron crystallizes in a body-centered cubic structure. Calculate the radius of iron atom if the edge length of unit cell is 286 pm
5. CsCl forms a body-centered cubic lattice. Cesium and chloride ions are in contact along the body diagonal of the cell. The length of the side of the unit cell is 412 pm and chloride has a radius of 181 pm. Calculate the radius of Cs^+ ion.
6. Silver crystallizes with fcc lattice with a unit cell length of 0.085 Å. Calculate the density and atomic radius of silver.
7. Silver has an atomic radius of 0.144 nm. Calculate the densities of silver if it crystallizes in (i) simple cube and (ii) fcc structure (atomic weight = 108 g).
8. A metal crystallizes into two cubic phases, fcc and bcc, whose unit cell lengths are 3.5 and 3.0 respectively. Calculate the ratio of densities of fcc and bcc.
9. A unit cell of NaCl has four formula units. The edge length of the unit cell is 0.564 nm. What is the density of the crystal?

10. Calculate the total number of cation vacancies if sodium chloride is doped with 0.01 mole% of $SrCl_2$.
11. KF has NaCl structure. What is the distance between K^+ and F^- ions in KF? Given density of KF is 2.5 g cm^{-3}.
12. The density of CaF_2 is 3.2 g cm^{-3} at 25°C. Calculate the dimension of the unit cell.
13. Three uni-univalent ionic solids AB, AC, and AD are composed of ions having following radii: $A^+ = 0.9$ nm, $B^- = 0.9$ nm, $C^- = 1.8$ nm $D^- = 2.7$ nm. Predict the structure and coordination of each solid.
14. At room temperature, sodium metal crystallizes in body-centered cubic cell with $a = 4.24$ Å. Calculate the theoretical density of sodium. Molar mass of sodium is 23.0 g/mol.
15. Metallic gold crystallizes in a face-centered cubic lattice. The length of the unit cell, $a = 4.07$ Å. Calculate the density and packing fraction. [Atomic mass of gold = 197 amu.]
16. Solid nitrogen has a density of 1.026 g/cm^3 at about 20 K. If it is known to have some cubic lattice with an edge length of 5.66 Å, what kind of cubic lattice does solid N_2 have?
17. Zinc selenide (ZnSe) is a bright-orange compound which is used as a transparent window for infrared spectroscopy has a cubic unit cell with $a = 5.7$ Å and a density of 5.26 g/cm^3. How many ionic formula units of ZnSe are in each unit cell? Which cubic unit cell does it have?
18. The unit cell of Ni is a face-centered cube of volume 0.0438 mm^3. Find the atomic radius of Ni.
19. What are the Miller indices, if the plane intersects the crystal lattice at 2a, b, 2c.
20. Silver has an atomic radius of 0.144 nm. Calculate the densities of silver if it crystallizes in (i) simple cubic and (ii) FCC structure (Atomic mass of Ag is 108 amu).
21. The ionic radii of Cs^+ and Br^- ions are 169 pm and 195 pm, respectively. What type of unit cell would be expected for CsBr crystals?
22. Find out the Miller indices of crystal planes with intercepts 2a, 3b, c and 6a, 3b, 3c.
23. Given that density of NaCl is 2.17 g/cm^3. Distance between Na^+ and Cl^- ions is 281 pm. Find Avogadro's number.
24. At what glancing angle would the first-order diffraction from 110 plane of KCl observed using X-rays of wavelength 140 pm? The dimension of the unit cell is 305 pm.
25. Potassium nitrate crystallizes in orthorhombic system with unit cell dimension, $a = 540$, $b = 910$, and $c = 640$ pm. Find the diffraction angle for the first-order X-ray diffraction from (010) and (111) planes using radiation with $\lambda = 154$ pm.
26. A face centered cubic crystal possess an atomic radius of 170 pm. Find the inter-planner spacingbetween (200) planes.
27. Find the angle at which first- and second-order diffraction will occur when X-rays of wavelength 1.54 Å are diffracted by the atoms of a crystal given that the inter-planer spacing 4.0 Å.

CHAPTER

8 Surface Chemistry

Chapter Outline

- Adsorption
- Adsorption Isotherms: Freundlich and Langmuir Isotherms
- Applications of Adsorption
- Ion-exchange Adsorption
- Surfactants
- Detergents

Adsorption at different interfaces such as liquid–gas, liquid–liquid, solid–liquid, and solid–gas has concerned scientists since the beginning of this century. The technological, environmental, and biological importance of adsorption was never a topic of debate. Its practical applications in industry and environmental protection are of paramount importance. The first stage in many catalytic processes is the adsorption of substrates. The method for separation of mixtures on a laboratory is based on utilizing the change in concentration of components at the interface. Moreover, vital problems such as purification of water, sewages, air, and soil also involve adsorption. During the last few years, new classes of solid adsorbents such as activated carbon fibers and carbon molecular sieves have been developed. In these adsorbents huge surface area can be achieved in a limited volume. Surface science is now generally considered to have become a well-defined branch of physical science representing an interdisciplinary area between chemistry, physics, biology, and engineering. This chapter presents a brief description of adsorption, factors affecting adsorption, applications on laboratory and industrial scale, as well as environmental protection. The chapter also provides a discussion on surfactants.

Adsorption

Adsorption is a process in which atoms, ions, or molecules from a gas, liquid, or dissolved solid are extracted from one phase and made to stick or adhere at the surface of a second phase, i.e., interface accumulation. This process creates a film of the *adsorbate* on the surface of the *adsorbent* (see Fig. 8.1). The phenomenon of adsorption is often confused with "absorption," which is the uniform distribution of particles of one phase with that of the second phase. A comparative account of adsorption and absorption is as follows.

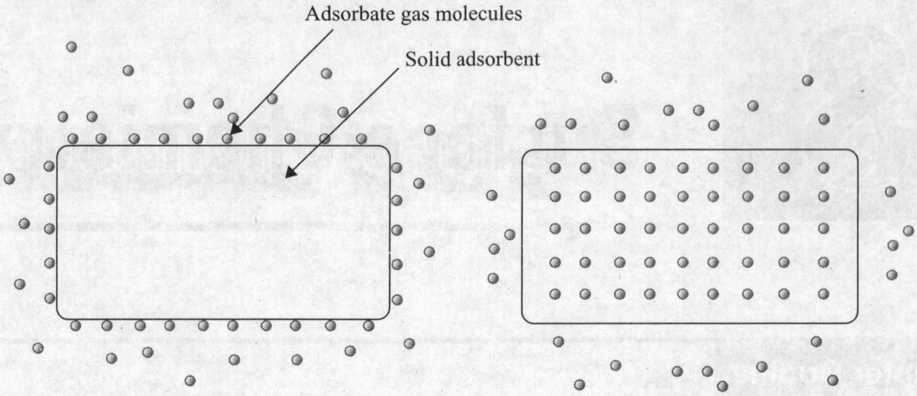

Fig. 8.1 The basic difference between adsorption and absorption

Adsorption	Absorption
Atoms, ions, or molecules from a gas, liquid, or dissolved solid are extracted from one phase and made to stick or adhere at the surface of a second phase	It refers to the uniform distribution of particles of one phase with that of the second phase
Surface phenomenon	Bulk phenomenon
Concentration of *adsorbate* is more at the surface	Concentration is uniform throughout
It is a fast process	It is a slow process
Quick equilibrium is achieved	Takes time to achieve equilibrium

Note:

1. Often both adsorption and absorption take place side by side. Hence, it becomes difficult to distinguish between the two processes. In such a case, the term *sorption* is used.
2. The basic requirements for adsorbents are that they must have high abrasion resistance, high thermal stability, and small pore diameters in addition to a distinct pore structure so as to enable fast transport of gaseous vapors.
3. Adsorbents are used in the form of spherical pellets, rods, moldings, or monoliths with hydrodynamic diameters between 0.5 and 10 mm.

Types of Adsorbents

Most of the adsorbents fall into one of following three classes:

1. **Oxygen-containing compounds**: These are typically hydrophilic and polar, e.g., silica gel and zeolites. Silica gel is a chemically inert, nontoxic, and dimensionally stable (up to 400°C). This is an amorphous form of SiO_2. It is used for drying of process air (e.g., oxygen and natural gas) and adsorption of heavy hydrocarbons from natural gas. Zeolites are natural or synthetic crystalline aluminosilicates, which have a repeating pore network and release water at high temperature. The channel diameter of zeolite cages usually ranges from 200 to 900 pm. These are applied

in drying of air, CO_2 removal from natural gas, CO removal from reforming gas, catalytic cracking, catalytic synthesis, and reforming.

2. **Carbon-based compounds:** These are typically hydrophobic and non-polar, e.g., activated carbon and graphite. Activated carbon is a highly porous, amorphous solid consisting of microcrystallites with a graphite lattice. It is the most widely used adsorbent, and its usefulness derives mainly from its large micropore volumes resulting in high surface area. Due to its high degree of microporosity, just one gram of activated carbon has a surface area in excess of 500 m^2. It is used in the form of small pellets or a powder. It is cheap. The main drawback is its combustible nature. It is used for the adsorption of organic substances and non-polar adsorbates. It is commonly used for waste water treatment. On the basis of their size and adsorption capacities, **activated carbon** is classified into two main classes: granular activated carbon (GAC) and powdered activated carbon (PAC).
3. **Polymer-based compounds:** These are polar or non-polar functional groups in a porous polymer matrix.

Mechanism of Adsorption

Let us explain the mechanism of adsorption by taking an example of adsorption of gases on a solid surface. The particles, i.e., atoms or molecules present in the bulk have their valencies completely satisfied. However, those at the surface are not surrounded by enough number of particles and such particles always have a tendency to satisfy their valencies. This results in the unbalanced or residual attractive forces on the surface as shown in Fig. 8.2. Any foreign particle that comes in close proximity of the surface can be held to these residual/free valency sites. This is a surface phenomenon where the concentration of foreign particles is more at the surface.

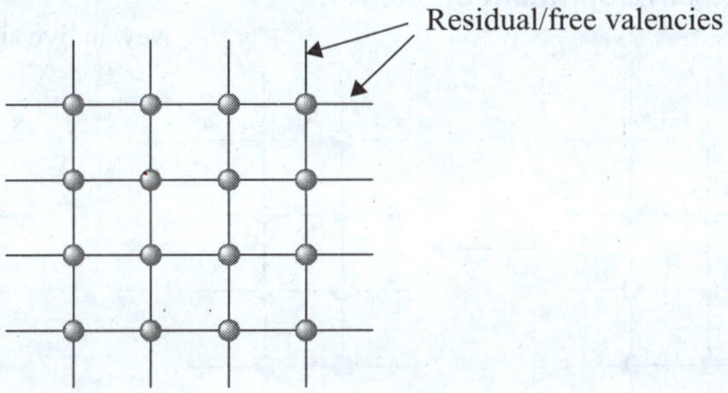

Fig. 8.2 Cross-sectional view of a solid adsorbent

Types of Adsorption

On the basis of the force that holds adsorbate and adsorbent, the adsorption can be classified into two basic categories: physical and chemical adsorption.

1. **Physical adsorption:** Here van der Waals' forces exist between adsorbate and adsorbent. The attraction is not site specific and the adsorbate particles are relatively free to move on the surface. This is relatively weak and reversible. Physical adsorption is a multilayer adsorption, e.g., adsorption of hydrogen on charcoal.
2. **Chemical adsorption**: Some degree of chemical bonding between adsorbate and adsorbent is characterized by strong attractiveness. Adsorbed molecules are not free to move on the surface. There is a high degree of specificity, and typically a monolayer is formed. The process is not reversible, e.g., chemical adsorption of hydrogen on the surface of nickel.

A comparative account of physical and chemical adsorptions is as follows:

Physical Adsorption	Chemical Adsorption
Attributed to intermolecular van der Waals' forces	Attributed to chemical bond formation
Easily liquefiable gases are adsorbed readily	Much more specific than physical adsorption
Heat of adsorption is relatively small (~5 kcal mol^{-1}).	Heat of adsorption is relatively large (20–100 kcal mol^{-1})
Reversible	Irreversible
Occurs rapidly at low temperature; decreases with increasing temperature	Increases with increase of temperature
Increase of pressure increases adsorption; decrease of pressure causes desorption	Change of pressure has no such effects
Forms multimolecular layers on the adsorbent surface	Forms unimolecular layer

Factors Affecting Adsorption

1. **Surface area of adsorbent:** In general, a large surface area favors greater adsorption. Surface area of a solid adsorbent can be increased by taking the adsorbent in the form of finely divided particles, in the form of a coating on an inert surface, or by scratching the surface of the adsorbent. All these practices generate new active sites (see Fig. 8.3) to facilitate adsorption. Nowadays materials such as zeolites and carbon molecular sieves (CMS) are in use as adsorbents that have a large internal surface area in a limited volume. These materials are designed with precise pore size distribution to have optimum efficiency.

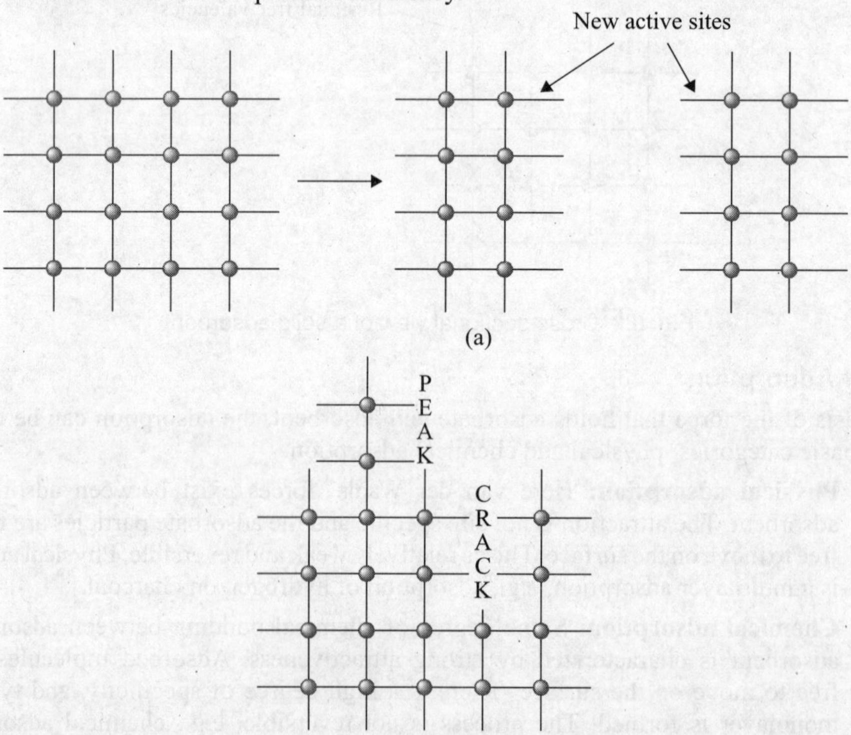

Fig. 8.3 (a) Subdivision increases active sites and (b) scratch results in formation of cracks and peaks

2. **Polarity of adsorbent:** Surface polarity is another important factor that affects the adsorption. Polar adsorbents such as zeolites and silica gel are hydrophilic, whereas non-polar adsorbents such as carbonaceous materials and polymer adsorbents are hydrophobic. The latter category has more affinity for oil or hydrocarbons than water.
3. **Nature of the adsorbate**
   (a) Easily liquefiable gases such as NH_3 and SO_2 are adsorbed to a greater extent than permanent gases such as H_2 and N_2 due to greater intermolecular forces in the adsorption process of the former. As liquefaction is related to critical temperature, higher critical temperature favors liquefaction and thereby the adsorption.
   (b) Any solute that lowers the surface tension is preferentially adsorbed over the solutes that increase the surface tension.
   (c) Adsorption of a solute is inversely proportional to its solubility in the solvent. The greater the solubility, the stronger the solute–solvent interaction and less is the extent of adsorption.
4. **Temperature:** Adsorption in general is an exothermic process. Therefore, it is expected that decrease in temperature should favor adsorption. The effect of temperature on the extent of adsorption (x/m, where x is the mass of adsorbate and m is the mass of adsorbent) can be presented as adsorption isobars. Analysis shows that for physical adsorption, the extent of adsorption decreases with increase in temperature which is as per Le Chatelier's principle. On the other hand, for chemical adsorption, the extent of adsorption increases with increase in temperature, approaches an optimum, and then decreases with further increase in temperature (see Fig. 8.4). The initial hike is attributed to the fact that the process needs some activation energy in the beginning. However, in the latter part, adsorption decreases due to exothermic nature of the process.

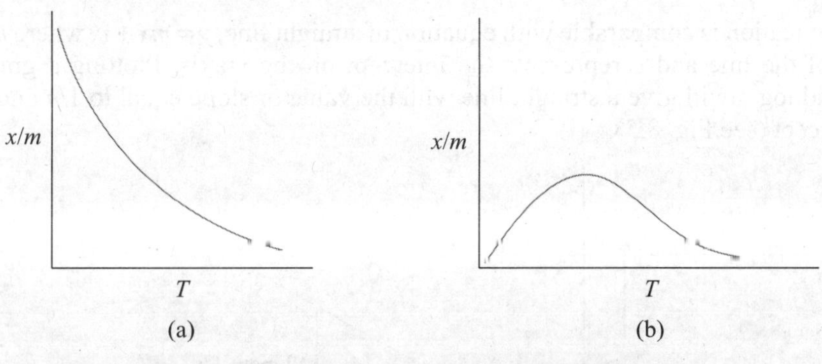

Fig. 8.4 (a) Physisorption isobar and (b) chemisorption isobar

5. **Effect of pressure:** In general, the extent of adsorption increases with increase in pressure until saturation. After saturation, the rates of adsorption become equal to that of desorption and the extent of adsorption will be independent of pressure.

Adsorption Isotherms

The adsorption of a gas on a solid adsorbent in a closed vessel is a reversible process where the amount of gas adsorbed depends on the equilibrium pressure and temperature. The relationship between the equilibrium pressure of a gas and its amount adsorbed on the solid adsorbent at any constant temperature is known as adsorption isotherm. Let us look into the important isotherms.

Freundlich Adsorption Isotherm

Freundlich (1909) gave an empirical expression representing the isothermal variation of adsorption of a quantity of gas adsorbed by unit mass of solid adsorbent with pressure which is known as the Freundlich adsorption isotherm.

$$\frac{x}{n} = kP^{1/n} \quad [8.1]$$

where x is the mass of the gas adsorbed, m is the mass of the adsorbent at pressure P, k and n are constants whose values depend on the adsorbent and the gas at a particular temperature.

Explanation

At low pressure, the extent of adsorption is directly proportional to the pressure, i.e., $x/m = kP^1$. At high pressure, the extent of adsorption is independent of pressure, i.e., $x/m = kP^0$. Therefore, at an intermediate value of pressure, adsorption is directly proportional to pressure raised to the power $1/n$. Here n is a variable whose value is greater than one.

$$\frac{x}{m} \propto P^{1/n} \text{ or } \frac{x}{m} = kP^{1/n}, \text{ where } k \text{ is constant of proportionality}$$

The above equation is known as the Freundlich adsorption equation.

Plotting of Freundlich Adsorption Isotherm

As per the Freundlich adsorption equation,

$$\frac{x}{m} = kP^{1/n}$$

Taking log on both sides of equation, we get

$$\log\left(\frac{x}{m}\right) = \log k + \frac{1}{n}\log P \quad [8.2]$$

The above equation is comparable with equation of straight line, $y = mx + c$, where m represents the slope of the line and c represents the intercept on the y-axis. Plotting a graph between $\log(x/m)$ and $\log p$ will give a straight line with the value of slope equal to $1/n$ and $\log k$ as the y-axis intercept (see Fig. 8.5).

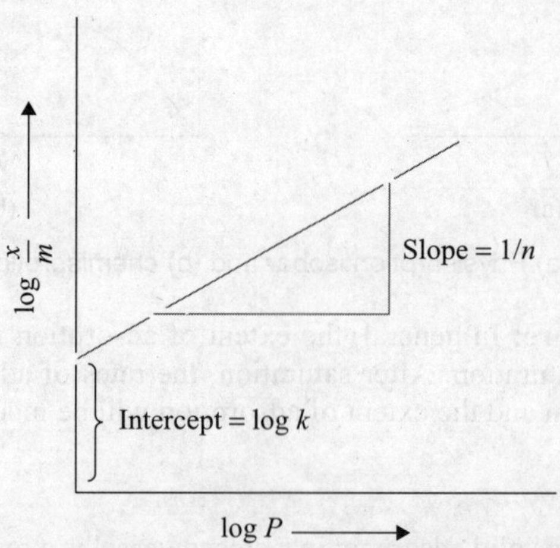

Fig. 8.5 Plot of log(*x*/*m*) as a function of log*P*

Limitation

Experimentally, it was determined that the extent of adsorption varies directly with pressure till saturation pressure P_s is reached. Beyond that point, the rate of adsorption saturates even after applying higher pressure. Thus, the Freundlich adsorption isotherm fails at higher pressure.

Langmuir Adsorption Isotherm

Langmuir (1916) derived an adsorption isotherm based on the assumptions that the layer of the gas adsorbed on the solid adsorbent is one-molecule thick, the adsorbed layer is uniform all over the adsorbent, and there is no interaction between the adjacent adsorbed molecules.

Derivation

Langmuir considered that the gas molecules strike a solid surface and are thus adsorbed. Some of these molecules then evaporate or "desorbed" fairly rapidly. A dynamic equilibrium is eventually established between the two opposing processes, adsorption and desorption (Fig. 8.6).

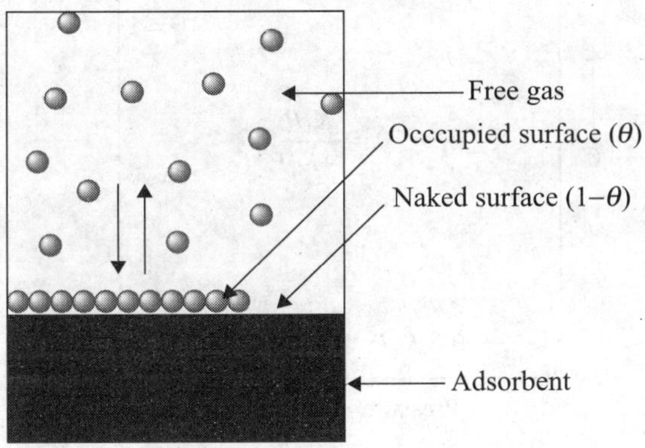

Fig. 8.6 Equilibrium between free molecules and those adsorbed on the adsorbent surface

$$\text{Reactants} + \text{Surface} \rightleftharpoons \text{Adsorbed Surface}$$

If θ is the fraction of the total surface covered by the adsorbed molecules, the fraction of the naked area is $(1 - \theta)$. Rate of adsorption $(R_a) \propto$ Fraction of unoccupied surface $(1 - \theta)$ and $R_a \propto P$. Thus,

$$R_a \propto P(1 - \theta)$$

$$= K_a P(1 - \theta) \qquad [8.3]$$

Rate of desorption $(R_d) \propto \theta$

$$= K_d \theta \qquad [8.4]$$

At equilibrium, $R_a = R_d$

or $K_a P(1 - \theta) = K_d \theta$

or $\theta[K_d + K_a] = K_a P$

$$\text{or} \quad \theta = \frac{K_aP}{K_d + K_aP}$$

$$= \frac{(K_a/K_d)P}{1 + \frac{K_aP}{K_d}}$$

$$= \frac{K_1P}{1 + K_1P}, \text{ where } K_1 = \frac{K_a}{K_d} \quad [8.5]$$

At low pressure

$K_1P \ll 1$, so that $\theta = K_1P$ [8.6]

This means the fraction of the surface covered remain directly proportional to the partial pressure of the gas molecules. This refers to the first-order reaction and is depicted by the initial steep rise of the isotherm (see Fig. 8.7).

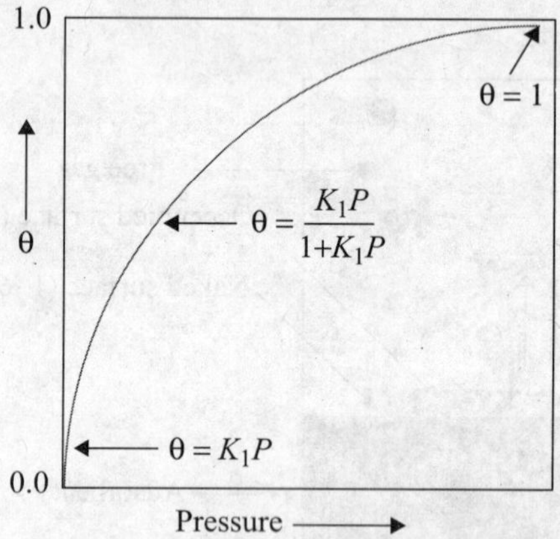

Fig. 8.7 Langmuir adsorption isotherm

At high pressure

$K_1P \ll 1$

Now from the basic relation, $\theta = \dfrac{K_1P}{1 + K_1P}$

$$\text{or} \quad \theta = \frac{K_1P}{K_1P} = 1 \quad [8.7]$$

Thus, at high pressure, the value of θ tends to become unity, i.e., the entire surface gets covered by a unimolecular layer of gas, thereby making the reaction rate independent of pressure which refers to zero-order reaction.

At intermediate pressure

From the relations [8.6] and [8.7], at intermediate pressure, the isotherm can be expressed as

$\theta = (K_1P)^n$ [8.8]

where n lies between 0 and 1.

Applications of Adsorption

Adsorption finds numerous applications both in laboratory and in industry. Some of these are as follows:

1. **Production of high vacuum:** High vacuum can be created by connecting a partially evacuated vessel to a container of activated charcoal cooled with liquid air. The charcoal adsorbs all the gas molecules in the vessel, resulting in a very high vacuum. This process is used in high vacuum equipment such as Dewar flask for storage of liquid air or liquid hydrogen.
2. **Gas mask:** All gas masks are devices containing an adsorbent (activated charcoal) or a series of adsorbents. These adsorbents remove poisonous gases by adsorption and thus purify the air for breathing.
3. **Heterogeneous catalysis:** In heterogeneous catalysis, the reactant molecules are adsorbed at the catalyst surface to form activated complex. The activated complex then decomposes to form the product molecules which subsequently take off from the surface, exposing it for further reaction (refer to Chapter 20 for details). Adsorption plays a major role in most of the industrial processes. Various manufacturing processes (Haber's process for manufacture of ammonia, Contact process for manufacture of sulfuric acid, hydrogenation of oil to fat, etc.) are heterogeneously catalyzed reactions.
4. **Removal of coloring matter from solutions:** Animal charcoal removes colors of solutions by adsorbing colored impurities. Thus, in the manufacture of cane sugar, the colored solution is clarified by treating with animal charcoal or activated charcoal.
5. **Froth flotation process:** The low-grade sulfide ores (PbS, ZnS, Cu_2S) are freed from silica and other earthy matter by *froth flotation process*. The finely divided ore mixed with oil (pine oil) is agitated with water containing a detergent which acts as a foaming agent. When air is bubbled into this mixture, the air bubbles are stabilized by the detergent. These adsorb mineral particles wetted with oil and rise to the surface. The earthy matter wetted by water settles down at the bottom (see Fig. 8.8).

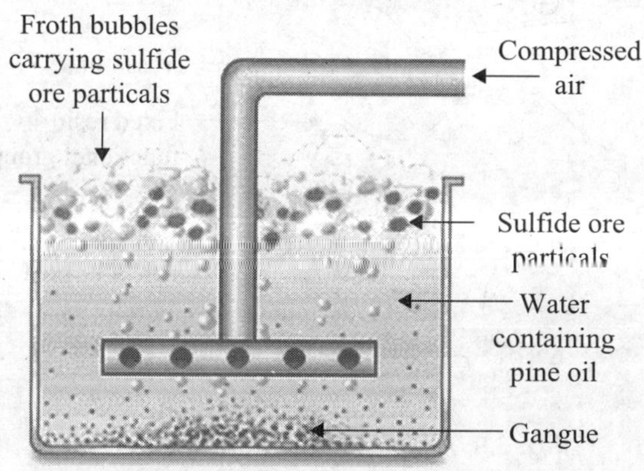

Fig. 8.8 Froth floatation process

6. **Chromatographic analysis:** Mixtures of small quantities of organic substances can be separated with the help of *chromatography*, which involves the principles of selective adsorption. The mixture is dissolved in a suitable solvent and poured through a tube containing the adsorbent (alumina). The component which is most readily adsorbed is removed in the upper part of the tube. The next most readily

adsorbed component is removed next, and so on. Thus, the material is separated into "bands" in different parts of the tube. Now pure solvent is poured through the tube. Each component dissolved in the solvent comes down by turn and is collected in a separate receiver. In a similar manner, mixtures of gases can be separated by selective adsorption of gases by liquids (*gas chromatography*).

7. **In waste water treatment**: Often waste water contains some compounds which are resistant to biodegradation and persist in water even after primary and secondary treatments. These impurities are toxic in nature. These compounds may be eliminated by passing over a bed of granulated activated carbon (GAC) which has an enormous surface area (about 500 m^2/g) and is commonly used as adsorbent. In the process, the contaminated water is allowed to trickle down through the GAC packed in a series of vessels. As the trickled waste water starts percolating downward through the granular activated carbon, the hazardous organics in polluted water are adsorbed on the porous GAC matrix. The GAC filter after sometime gets clogged with the adsorbed contaminates and hence must be replaced or regenerated for further use.

Ion-Exchange Adsorption

In recent years, many synthetic resins, which function as ion-exchangers, have been made. Ion exchange is an adsorption phenomenon where the mechanism of adsorption is electrostatic. Electrostatic forces hold ions to charged functional groups on the surface of the ion-exchange resin. The adsorbed ions replace ions that are on the resin surface on a 1:1 charge basis. The process is called *ion-exchange adsorption.* When cations are exchanged, the resin is known as *cation exchanger*. When anions are exchanged, it is referred to as *anion exchanger*. A typical cation exchanger is schematically presented in Fig. 8.9. The polymer chain has negative functional groups which are exchanged by their counter ions.

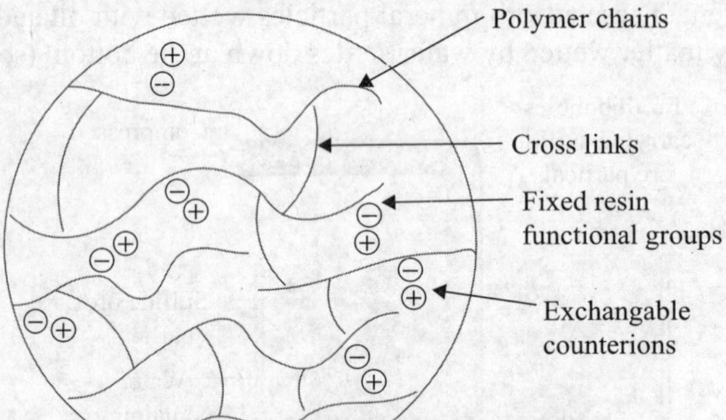

Fig. 8.9 A typical cation exchanger

Cationic Exchangers

These are high polymers with either strongly acidic functional groups derived from strong acids, e.g., R–SO_3H, or weakly acidic functional groups derived from weak acids, e.g., R–COOH. When solution of another cation is allowed to flow on it, H^+ ions are exchanged by the new cations. The process of cationic exchange is reversible. The resin can be regenerated upon treatment with an acid.

$$R^-H^+ + C^+ \rightleftharpoons R^-C^+ + H^+$$

Anionic Exchangers

These are high polymers with either strongly basic functional groups derived from quaternary ammonia compounds, $N^+R_3OH^-$ or weakly basic functional groups derived from primary and secondary amines, $R–NH_3OH$ or $RR'NH_2OH$. When solution of another anion is allowed to flow on it, OH^- ions are exchanged by the new anions. The resin can be regenerated upon treatment with a base.

$$R^+OH^- + A^- \rightleftharpoons R^+A^- + OH^-$$

Applications

It is used for water softening and deionization of water. The details have been discussed in Chapter 13, Water.

Surfactants

Surfactants or surface-active agents are molecules that contain a polar portion called head and a non-polar portion called tail. These are used to lower the surface or interfacial tension between two liquids or between a liquid and a solid. It can interact with both polar and non-polar molecules. Surfactants find wide application as detergents, wetting agents, emulsifiers, foaming agents, and dispersants. The general presentation of a surfactant is shown in Fig. 8.10.

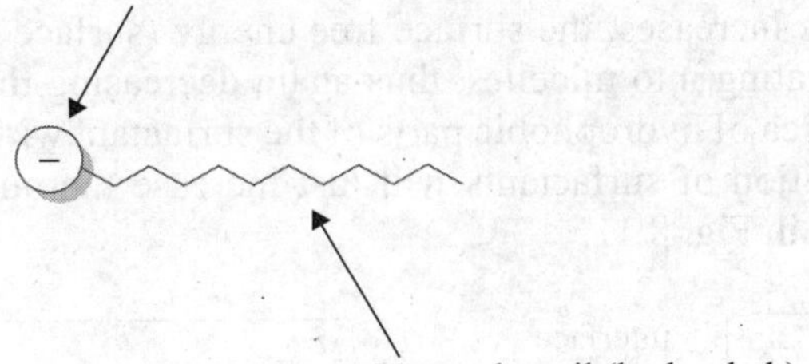

Fig. 8.10 Surfactant

Classification of Surfactants

On the basis of the polar head group, surfactants can be broadly classified as anionic, cationic, non-ionic, and amphoteric or zwitterionic.

Anionic surfactants: The head of such a surfactant carries net a negative charge, i.e., anionic functional groups. On the basis of anionic functional groups, these are classified into four categories such as *sulfates*: alkyl sulfates (e.g., ammonium lauryl sulfate and sodium lauryl sulfate), alkyl ether sulfates (e.g., sodium lauryl ether sulfate); *sulfonates*: alkyl benzene sulfonates (ABS), sulfonate fluorosurfactants; *phosphates*: alkyl ether phosphate, alkyl aryl ether phosphate; *carboxylates*: alkyl carboxylates (e.g., soaps such as sodium stearate), carboxylate fluorosurfactants such as perfluorooctanoate (PFO).

Cationic surfactants: The head of such a surfactant carries a net positive charge, i.e., cationic functional groups such as pH-dependent primary, secondary, and tertiary amines and permanently charged quaternary ammonium ions. Primary amines become positively charged at pH < 10, while secondary amines become charged at pH < 4. Some specific examples are cetyl trimethylammonium bromide (CTAB), cetyl trimethylammonium chloride (CTAC), cetylpyridinium chloride (CPC), benzethonium chloride (BZT), polyethoxylated tallow amine (POEA), cetrimonium bromide, dimethyldioctadecyl ammonium chloride, etc.

Non-ionic surfactants: These do not include any charged head. Some popular categories are fatty alcohols, polyoxypropylene glycol, glucoside, sorbitan alkyl esters, etc.

Amphoteric surfactants: These are characterized by the fact that these can carry both cationic and anionic centers attached to the same molecule. The charge of the molecule changes with pH, showing a zwitterionic form at an intermediate pH. Examples are amino acids, imino acids, betaines, lecithin, etc.

Critical Micelle Concentration

Critical micelle concentration (CMC) is defined as the concentration of the surfactants above which micelles form and all additional surfactants added to the system go to micelles. It is an important characteristic of a surfactant. Before reaching the CMC, the surface tension changes strongly with the concentration of the surfactant. After reaching the CMC, the surface tension remains relatively constant or changes with a lower slope. The value of the CMC for a given dispersant in a given medium depends on temperature, pressure, and sometimes on the presence and concentration of other surface-active agents. Micelles form above the CTC. For example, the value of CMC for sodium dodecyl sulfate in water in the absence of other additives at 25°C and atmospheric pressure is 8×10^{-3} mol/L.

Description

Upon introduction of surfactants into the system, they initially partition into the interface, reducing the system free energy by lowering the energy of the interface and removing the hydrophobic parts of the surfactant from contact with water. Subsequently, when the surface coverage by the surfactants increases, the surface free energy (surface tension) decreases and the surfactants start aggregating into micelles, thus again decreasing the system's free energy by decreasing the contact area of hydrophobic parts of the surfactant with water. Upon reaching the CMC, any further addition of surfactants will just increase the number of micelles. The different steps are depicted in Fig. 8.11.

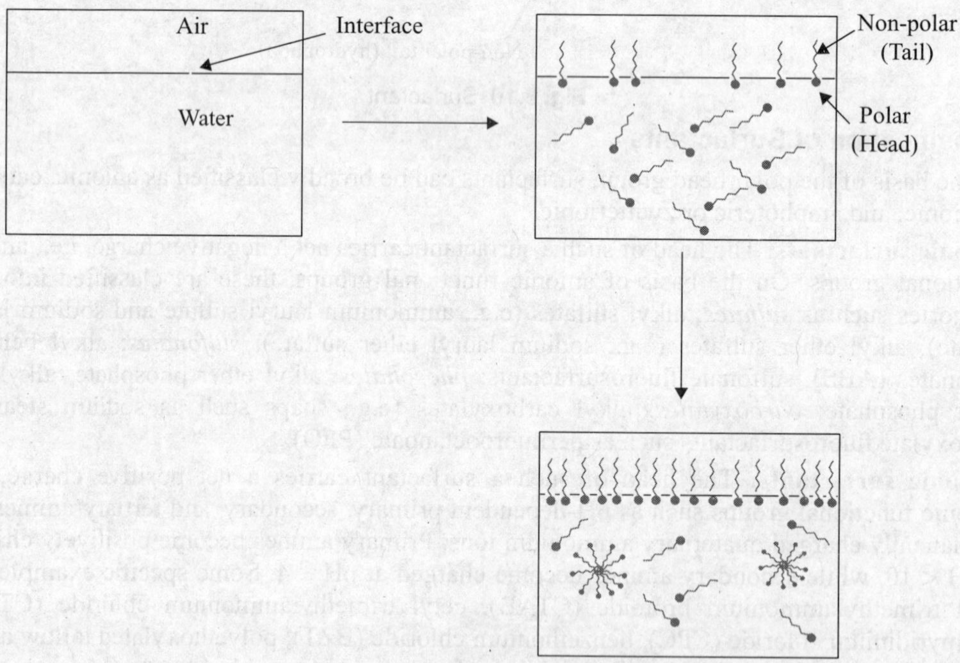

Fig. 8.11 Steps in the formation of micelles at or above the CMC

HLB Scale

The hydrophilic–lipophilic balance (HLB) of a surfactant reflects its partitioning behavior between a polar and a non-polar media. For non-ionic surfactants, Griffin suggested the following formula to calculate HLB:

$$\mathrm{HLB} = 20\left(\frac{M_\mathrm{h}}{M}\right)$$

where M_h is the molecular mass of the hydrophilic portion of the molecule and M is the molecular mass of the whole molecule.

HLB number ranging from 0 to 20 can be assigned to a surfactant based on emulsification data. It is semi-empirical only. An HLB value of 0 corresponds to a completely lipophilic or hydrophobic molecule, and a value of 20 corresponds to a completely hydrophilic or lipophobic molecule. The value of 10 is the midpoint. HLB value less than 10 indicates lipid soluble, whereas a value greater than 10 indicates water soluble. The HLB value can be used to predict the surfactant properties of a molecule as follows:

HLB value	Remark
0	No dispersibility in water
2	Antifoaming agent
6	W/O emulsifier
8	Wetting agent
10	Milky dispersion
12	O/W emulsifier
14	Clear solution
16	Detergent
16–20	Solubilizer/hydrotrope

Detergents

A ***detergent*** is a surfactant or a mixture of surfactants with cleaning properties in dilute solutions. These substances are usually linear alkylsulfonates (LAS) and alkylbenzenesulfonates (ABS), a family of compounds that are very similar to soap but are readily soluble in hard water. This is attributed to the fact that sulfonates of calcium, magnesium, and other ions responsible for hardness are soluble but in contrast carboxylates of the same are insoluble in water. Detergents are commonly available as powders or concentrated solutions. Like soaps detergents are amphiphilic, i.e., partly hydrophilic (polar) and partly hydrophobic (non-polar). This amphiphilic nature facilitates the mixing of hydrophobic compounds (such as oil and grease) with water. Detergents are classified into four categories as discussed earlier in this chapter under classification of surfactants.

Cleansing Action

Mostly the dirt is held to any surface such as cloth by the oil or grease which is present there. As oil or grease is not soluble in water, the dirt particles cannot be removed by simply washing clothes by water. When detergent is used, the non-polar hydrocarbon part of the detergent dissolves in oil droplets, while polar head remains attached to water. In this way, each oil droplet gets a surface negative charge. These oil droplets having surface negative charge cannot coalesce and a stable emulsion is formed (see Fig. 8.12). Now the oil droplets along with dart can be washed away with water. Thus, detergent cleans through emulsifying oil or grease. Not only it emulsifies oil or grease, but it also lowers the surface tension of water. The result being water wets things more effectively.

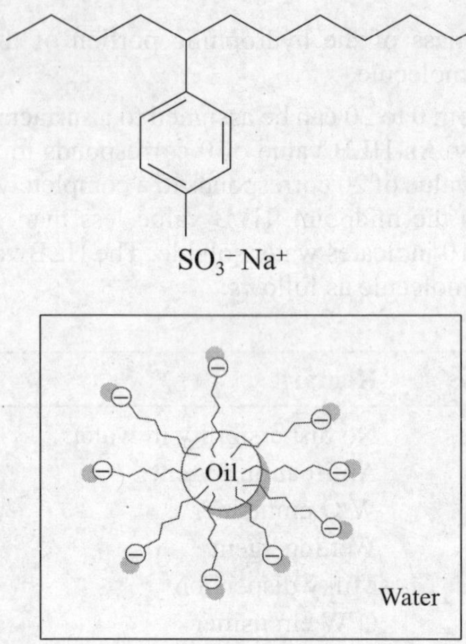

Fig. 8.12 A typical detergent and formation of oil in water emulsion

Advantages

1. Since detergents are the salts of strong acids, they do not decompose in acidic medium. Thus, detergents can effectively clean fabric even if the water is acidic.
2. Synthetic detergents are more soluble in water than soaps.
3. They have a stronger cleansing action than soaps.
4. As detergents are derived from petroleum, they save on natural vegetable oils, which are important as essential cooking medium.

Disadvantages

1. Many detergents are not biodegradable. Their elimination from municipal wastewaters by the usual treatments is not possible.
2. They have a tendency to produce stable foams in rivers which extend over several hundred meters of the river waters due to the effects of surfactants used in their preparation. Thus, they pose a danger to aquatic life.
3. They tend to inhibit oxidation of organic substances present in wastewaters by forming a sort of envelop around them.

QUESTIONS

1. What is adsorption and how it differs from absorption?
2. Differentiate between physical and chemical adsorption.
3. What is an adsorbent? Explain with examples.
4. Explain different types of adsorbent.
5. Explain carbon-based adsorbents with examples.
6. What do you mean by sorption?
7. Why platinized platinum is a better adsorbent than platinum?
8. Explain adsorption isotherm.
9. What is adsorption isobar?
10. Explain the regeneration process of exhausted resin in ion-exchange process.
11. Explain ion-exchange adsorption.
12. Explain Freundlich adsorption isotherm applicable to gaseous adsorption on solid surface.
13. What is the limitation of Freundlich adsorption isotherm?
14. Derive Langmuir adsorption isotherm for monolayer adsorption.
15. Explain under what condition Langmuir isotherm becomes identical with Freundlich adsorption isotherm.
16. Show that Freundlich isotherm is a special case of Langmuir adsorption isotherm.
17. Utilize Langmuir adsorption isotherm to explain "decomposition of PH_3 gas on tungsten surface is first order at low pressure and zeroth order at high pressure."
18. Explain froth floatation process.
19. "Finely divided substance is more effective adsorbent." Explain.
20. Give suggestions to increase the surface area of a solid adsorbent.
21. Easily liquefiable gases such as NH_3 and SO_2 are adsorbed to a greater extent than permanent gases such as H_2 and N_2. Explain.
22. What is the effect of temperature on the adsorption of gases on solid adsorbent?
23. Draw adsorption isobars for both physical and chemical adsorption.
24. Explain different factors that affect adsorption of a gas on a solid adsorbent.
25. Discuss two important applications of adsorption.
26. Explain how adsorption concept can be used to explain heterogeneous catalysis.
27. What are the advantages of detergents over soaps?
28. What are the disadvantages of detergents?
29. Explain HLB scale with examples.
30. What do you mean by HLB value 0?
31. What is critical micelle concentration (CMC)?
32. Explain different types of surfactants with suitable examples.
33. Explain amphoteric surfactant with suitable example.
34. Explain how ion-exchange adsorption can help in removing permanent hardness.

35. Explain how adsorption helps in the separation of a mixture of organic compounds in micro/semi-micro scale.
36. Explain how adsorption can help in waste water treatment.
37. What are anionic surfactants? Explain with examples.
38. What are amphoteric surfactants?
39. Explain the cleansing action of detergent.
40. Explain how adsorption is used in chromatographic separation.

CHAPTER

9 Photochemistry

Chapter Outline

- Light Sources
- Laws of Photochemistry
- Quantum Yield
- Photochemical Process (Primary, Secondary, Jablonski Diagram)
- Chemiluminescence
- Photosensitization
- Semiconductor Photochemistry
- Optical Sensors
- Supra-molecular Photochemistry

Photochemistry is the study of chemical reactions that proceed with the absorption of light (usually in the UV–vis region, i.e., 200 – 800 nm) by reacting atoms or molecules. One can find a number of examples in everyday life. *In nature*: photosynthesis; vision; phototropism, i.e., orientation of plants toward the direction of sunlight; the ozone layer; formation of vitamin in sunlight. *In medicine*: treatment of jaundice of newborn babies; photodynamic therapy for cancer treatment. *In industry*: photography; photopolymerization and degradation of polymers; photocopying; photochromism (sunglasses). Photochemical paths offer number of advantages over thermal methods, such as it helps in forming thermodynamically unfavored products as $\Delta G < 0$ is not the overall requirement of feasibility of photochemical reactions and it helps in overcoming large activation barriers in a short time span and allows to get reactivity otherwise inaccessible by thermal methods. In addition, one more typical advantage of photochemistry is that it talks in favor of green principles of chemistry, e.g., atom economy.

Light Sources

Photochemists typically work in a few sections of the electromagnetic spectrum, viz., UV: 100–400 nm, Vis: 400–700 nm, and near IR: 700–2500 nm. Typical light sources for preparative photochemistry are as follows:

1. The sun (300–1400 nm)
2. Low-pressure mercury (Hg at ~10^{-5} atm) lamp (Rayonet lamps): 185 nm (5%); 254 (95%)
3. Medium-pressure Hg (Hg at vapor pressure 5 atm) lamps (distinct lines between 250 and 600 nm)

4. High-pressure Hg lamps (Hg at vapor pressure approximately 100 atm; expensive, easily damaged) (emission 360–600 nm, broad)
5. Low- and high-pressure sodium lamps (emission around 600 nm)
6. High-power light-emitting diodes (available at low cost for 650–400 nm; very narrow and intensive emission, long lifetime) and UV–LED are currently still expensive.

Laws of Photochemistry

There are three basic and fundamental laws in photochemistry which explains the impact of radiation on chemical reactions.

Grotthuss–Draper Law

The law was first proposed in 1817 by T. Grotthuss and in 1842, independently, by J. W. Draper. As per the law, when light radiation is allowed to pass through a homogeneous reaction mixture, only that part of the light which is absorbed by reacting system can effectively produce chemical change. It is to be marked that the absorption of light leads to photochemical reaction but the same may not always lead to a chemical change. Sometimes the absorbed photon may get utilized only in increasing the thermal energy or may get re-emitted in the form of radiation of different frequency, i.e., fluorescence.

Einstein–Stark Law

Einstein-Stark law was independently formulated by German-born physicists J. Stark and A. Einstein between 1908 and 1913. It is also known as the photochemical equivalence law or photoequivalence law. As per the law, every photon that is absorbed by a reactant activates only one reactant in the primary step of photochemical process.

This law is concerned only with the primary absorption step. If every activated molecule in the primary absorption step decomposes, then the number of molecules suffering chemical change will be equal to the number of photons absorbed. But in some cases, the activated molecule from the primary step initiate a sequence of reactions so as to consume a number of molecules through a chain mechanism and in some cases a quick deactivation takes place so as to reduce the number of activated molecules from primary step suffering change. Therefore, the primary photon absorption step must be clearly distinguished from subsequent chemical change(s) and Einstein's law may be interpreted to mean that one quantum activates only one molecule but not that one molecule would react per quantum of light.

Lambert–Beer Law

When a beam of monochromatic light is passed through a pure homogeneous solution of a light-absorbing material, the decrease in the intensity of the light with the thickness of the solution ($-dI/dx$) is directly proportional to the intensity (I) of the light and to the concentration of the solution (c). This law is discussed in detail in Chapter 11.

Quantum Yield or Efficiency

As discussed earlier, sometimes photochemical reactions do not obey the law of photochemical equivalence and the number of reacting species is different from the number of photons absorbed in a specified time. To correlate the number of reacting species and the photons absorbed, a term "quantum yield" has been introduced which may be defined as "the number of reacting species undergoing reaction per photon of light absorbed." Mathematically, it can be expressed as

$$\text{Quantum yield }(\phi) = \frac{\text{Number of atoms/molecules reacting in a given time}}{\text{Number of photons absorbed in the same time}}$$

$$= \frac{\text{Number of mole reacting in a given time}}{\text{Number of Einsteins absorbed in the same time}}$$

$$= \frac{\text{Rate of chemical reaction}}{\text{Number of Einsteins absorbed in the same time}}$$

where "Einstein" is the energy of one mole of photons, i.e., $Nh\nu$.

If the law of photochemical equivalence is valid, then $\varphi = 1$, otherwise $\varphi \neq 1$. In many cases a single-activated reactant species initiate a series of secondary reactions consuming a large number of reactant species. Here φ exceeds unity. On the other hand, some reactions are there in which the number of reacting species undergoing change by absorption of photon is less than the number of photons absorbed. In such a case, the value of φ is less than unity.

High Quantum Yield

The photon absorbed in the primary reaction excites one reacting species causing its dissociation. The excited species so formed during dissociation initiate subsequent secondary reactions consuming further reactants.

$$AB \xrightarrow{h\nu} AB^* \longrightarrow A^* + B^* \quad \text{Primary}$$

$$\left.\begin{aligned} AB + A^* &\longrightarrow A_2 + B^* \\ B^* + B^* &\longrightarrow B_2 \end{aligned}\right\} \text{Secondary steps}$$

When the number of reactants is more than one, one of the reactant absorbs photon, gets excited, and decomposed. The excited fragments initiate secondary chain reaction consuming a large number of reacting species.

$$A_2 + h\nu \longrightarrow 2A^* \quad \text{Primary}$$

$$\left.\begin{aligned} A^* + B_2 &\longrightarrow AB + B^* \\ A_2 + B^* &\longrightarrow AB + \underbrace{A^*}_{\text{Used for initiating reaction again}} \end{aligned}\right\} \text{Secondary steps}$$

Low Quantum Yield

The excited reacting species formed in the primary excitation may get deactivated by collision with another inert particle or by fluorescence emission.

$$A + h\nu \longrightarrow A^*$$

$$\left.\begin{aligned} A^* &\longrightarrow A + h\nu \text{ (Fluorescence)} \\ A^* + A &\longrightarrow 2A \end{aligned}\right\} \text{Secondary steps}$$

The products of primary step may reunite to give back the original reactant.

$$A\text{–}B + h\nu \longrightarrow A^* + B^*$$

$$A^* + B^* \longrightarrow A\text{–}B$$

The product may undergo thermal reaction to yield the reactant molecules back.

$$2A \underset{\Delta}{\overset{h\nu}{\rightleftharpoons}} A_2$$

Some specific reactions along with their quantum yield as examples are as follows:

	Quantum Yield
$2NH_3 \longrightarrow N_2 + 3H_2$	0.2
$H_2 + Br_2 \longrightarrow 2HBr$	0.01
$3O_2 \longrightarrow 2O_3$	3
$CO + Cl_2 \longrightarrow COCl_2$	10^3

Example 9.1

When exposed to a radiation of 400 nm, 0.001 mol of a substance is decomposed. Calculate the number of photons absorbed during the reaction if the quantum efficiency is 10.

Solution

$$\text{Number of molecules decomposed} = 0.001 \times 6.023 \times 10^{23}$$

$$= 6.023 \times 10^{20}$$

$$\text{Quantum yield } (\phi) = \frac{\text{Number of molecules decomposed}}{\text{Number of photons absorbed}}$$

$$\text{or, Number of photonsabsorbed} = \frac{\text{Number of molecules decomposed}}{\phi}$$

$$= \frac{6.023}{10} \times 10^{20}$$

$$= 6.023 \times 10^{19}$$

Example 9.2

A radiation of 250 nm upon striking with hydrogen iodide results in the decomposition of 1.80×10^{-2} moles per 1000 cal of radiant energy. Calculate quantum efficiency.

Solution

$$\text{Energy per quantum of radiation} = \frac{hc}{\lambda}$$

$$= \frac{6.025 \times 10^{-34} \times 3 \times 10^{8}}{2.50 \times 10^{-7}}$$

$$= 7.23 \times 10^{-19}\ \text{J}$$

$$1 \text{ einstein} = 6.023 \times 10^{23} \times 7.23 \times 10^{-19}\ \text{J} = 4.35 \times 10^{5}$$

$$\text{Number of einsteins absorbed} = \frac{4184}{4.35 \times 10^{5}}\ 0.00962$$

Number of moles of HI decomposed per 1000 cals, i.e., 4184 J of radiation = 1.80×10^{-2}

$$\text{Quantum yield } (\phi) = \frac{\text{Number of moles decomposed}}{\text{Number of Einsteins absorbed}}$$

$$= \frac{1.80}{0.00962} \times 10^{-2} = 1.87$$

Photochemical Processes

Any photochemical process goes through two fundamental steps: excitation and de-excitation. To begin a photochemical reaction, the molecule must absorb a quantum of light energy from photon.

Photochemical Excitation

It is the first step of a photochemical reaction which involves the absorption of a quantum of radiation by a molecule leading to the formation of an excited species. This involves an electronic transition which is accompanied with changes in the vibrational and rotational quantum levels and is governed by Frank–Condon principle. There are four distinct possibilities of excitation of the reacting species.

Type-I

Such an excitation involves electronic transition from a stable ground state to a stable excited state without direct dissociation of the molecule. The spectrum consists of discontinuous bands with fine structures of closely spaced lines.

Type-II

This excitation involves electronic transition from a stable ground state to an unstable excited state. When the energy attained in the excited state exceeds the bond energy, the molecule dissociates into atoms or radicals immediately after the absorption of the energy quantum or photon. The dissociated fragments have different kinetic energies. A continuous spectrum is observed without any fine structure.

Type-III

This excitation involves electronic transition from a stable ground state to an excited state, which is quite unstable; therefore, the corresponding potential energy curve does not show any minimum. The molecule dissociates into atoms or radicals immediately after the absorption of the energy quantum or photon. A continuous spectrum is observed.

Type-IV

Sometimes a third electronic state exists, whose potential energy surface intersects the same of the stable excited state. Initially, during excitation, the electronic transition takes place from the stable ground state to the stable excited state. During vibration, there exists possibility of shifting from a stable excited state to an unstable excited state. In case of shifting, the molecule dissociates into atoms or radicals. Such a phenomenon is known as pre-dissociation. The spectrum is obtained as fine structure at a lower level followed by a continuum.

De-excitation Step

In the de-excitation step, the excited molecule may undergo directly through a number of physical processes or chemical reactions. All these processes fall under the category of primary photochemical processes. The photophysical processes are of three types: non-radiative processes between states, radiative processes between states, and loss of energy by intermolecular transfer (quenching). Secondary photochemical processes may occur upon completion of the primary step.

Primary Processes

1. **Photophysical processes:** The excited atoms or molecules that are unstable always have a tendency to dissipate energy. The fate of the excited species is discussed here. It may involve only one step or several steps. Sometimes it may involve a chain reaction. *Jablonski diagram* summarizes the different possible energy dissipating mechanisms (see Fig. 9.1).

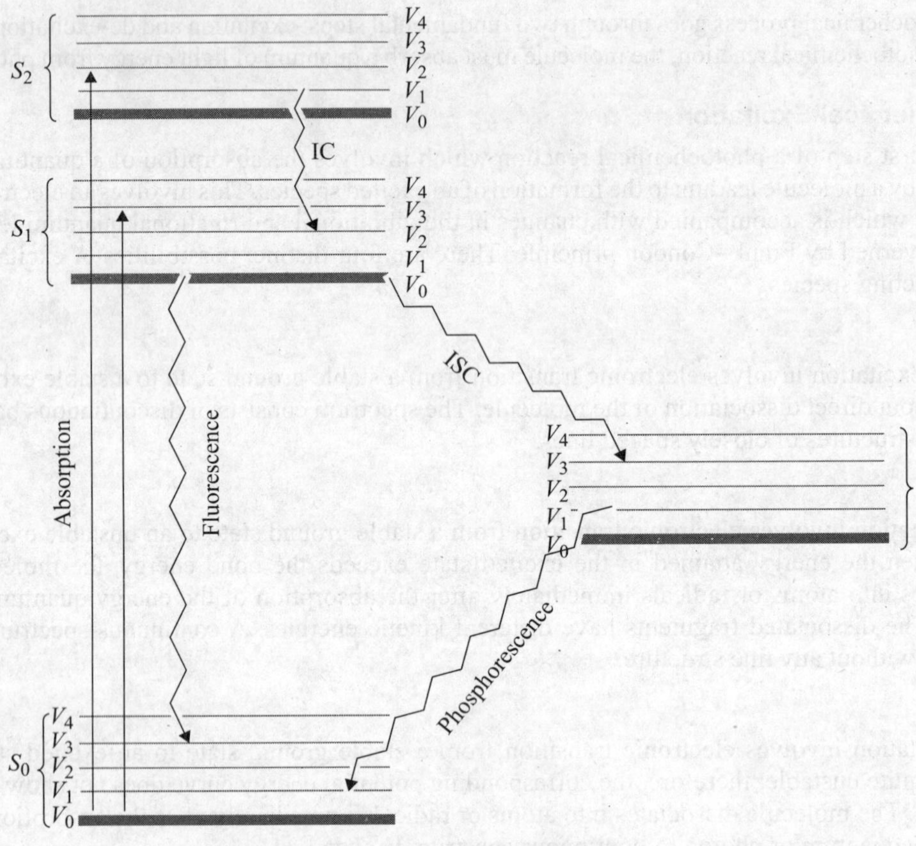

Fig. 9.1 Jablonski diagram

(a) *Non-radiative transitions:* Such transitions involve returning of excited species either from higher excited state to the first excited state or from the first excited state to the ground state without the emission of any radiation. During such a transition the energy of excited species gets dissipated through molecular collision in the form of heat. The transition among the electronic states of same multiplicity is described as internal conversion (IC) while among electronic states of different multiplicity is known as intersystem crossing (ISC). IC usually takes place within 10^{-11} s.

(b) *Radiative transitions:* Such transitions involve the returning of excited species from the first singlet excited state (S_1) or triplet state (T_1) to the ground state (S_0) along with the emission of radiation. There are two types of radiations, viz., fluorescence and phosphorescence. Fluorescence is because of the transition from singlet excited state (S_1) to the ground state (S_0) with the emission of radiation with lower energy (longer wavelength) than the incident radiation. This is an allowed transition and generally occurs within 10^{-9} to 10^{-6} s. On the other hand, phosphorescence involves transition from first triplet excited state (T_1) to the ground state (S_0) with the emission of radiation with lower energy than the incident radiation. This is a spin forbidden transition. The transition occurs due to partial relaxation of the selection rule which is in turn attributed to spin–orbit coupling. The life time is much longer than fluorescence which is of the order of 10^{-5} s.

In addition to radiative and non-radiative transitions, dissipation of energy is also possible through chemical reaction. The excited species may participate in a chemical reaction. As the life time of singlet excited state is much shorter than the triplet excited state, the latter gets more opportunity to undergo chemical reaction. The same has also been confirmed from experimental evidences.

Note:

Fluorescence	Phosphorescence
Fluorescence is because of the transition from singlet excited state (S_1) to the ground state (S_0) with the emission of radiation with lower energy than the incident radiation.	Phosphorescence involves transition from the first triplet excited state (T_1) to the ground state (S_0) with the emission of radiation with lower energy than the incident radiation.
This is an allowed transition.	This is a spin forbidden transition.
Generally occurs within 10^{-9} to 10^{-6} s.	The life time is much longer than fluorescence which is of the order of 10^{-5} s.
Life time is very short.	Life time is much longer.
Quantum efficiencies are much less.	Quantum efficiencies are much more than fluorescence.
It is shown by solids, liquids, and gases (at low pressure).	It is shown by only solids.
Examples of fluorescent materials: minerals such as CaF_2 and petroleum; organic dyes such as eosin and fluorescein; natural compounds such as chlorophyll and riboflavin.	Examples are minerals such as zinc sulfide and alkaline earth metal sulfides; many dyes; some fungi.

(c) *Intermolecular energy transfer:* Excited state of (S_1 or T_1) of donor molecule may transfer its large amount of energy to the acceptor molecule (A) and the acceptor molecule is promoted to excited sate while the donor species (D) return to the ground state. This is called quenching of excited state.

$$\text{D} \longrightarrow \text{D}^* \text{ (Excitation)}$$

$$\text{D}^* + \text{A} \longrightarrow \text{D} + \text{A}^* \text{ (Quenching)}$$

2. **Photochemical reactions:** Photochemical reactions are ones in which photons are absorbed by an atom or molecule called a chromophore. The chromophore transforms the light energy into high energy electron capable of conducting chemical work. In photochemical reactions, the number of molecules activated depends on the intensity of light; hence, the concentration of activated molecules will be proportional to the light intensity to which the reactant is exposed. There are various types of elementary photochemical processes which depend on the chemical structure of compounds and the nature of lower electronic excited states of molecules. A few important types of primary photochemical reactions are as follows:

(a) **Photo-induced electron transfer (PET)**

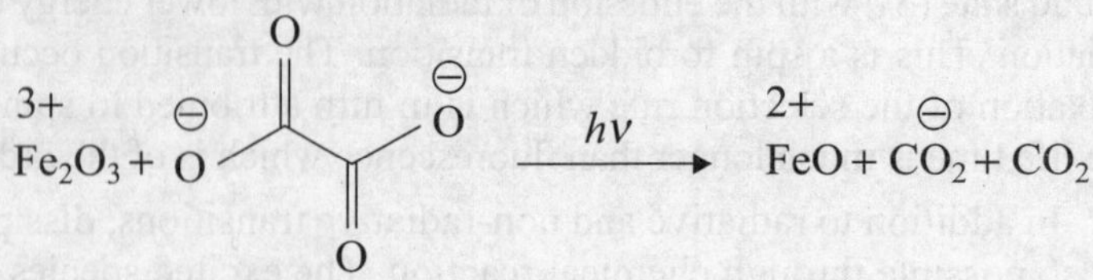

(b) **Photo-induced addition reaction:** Cyclic olefins are known to undergo addition reactions, on irradiation in methanol.

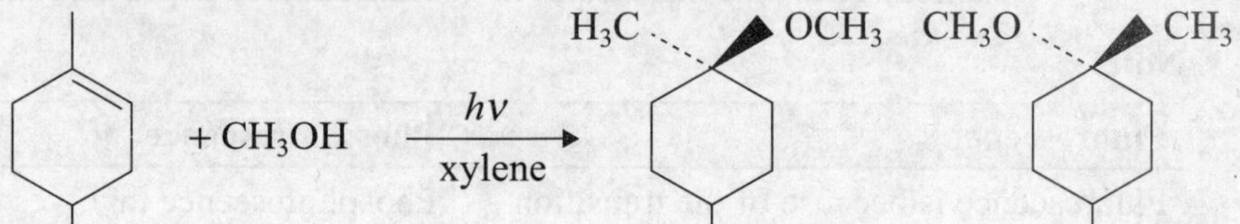

(c) **Hydrogen transfer**: Intramolecular hydrogen abstraction is a common photoreaction of carbonyl compounds with a hydrogen atom attached to the fourth carbon atom.

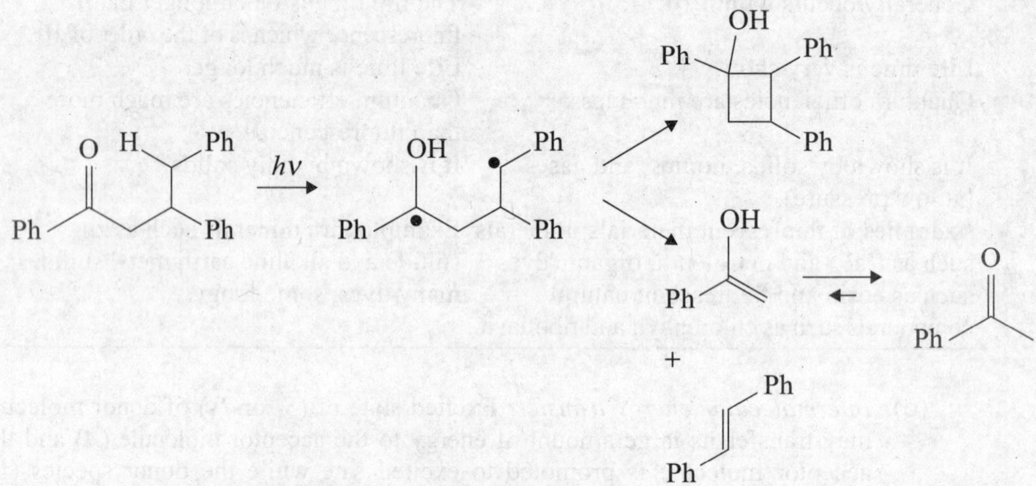

(d) **Photo-dissociation or Photolysis**

(i) ***Photolysis of hydrogen bromide***

$HBr \xrightarrow{h\nu} H + Br$ (Photochemical reaction)

$H + HBr \longrightarrow H_2 + Br$ } Dark reactions

$Br + Br \longrightarrow Br_2$

$2\,HBr \xrightarrow{h\nu} H_2 + Br$ Overall reaction

(ii) ***Photolysis of ketones***

Norrish type I: Ketones upon photochemical excitation undergo hemolytic fission at the C–C bond adjacent to carbonyl group. Such a reaction is known as α-cleavage or Norrish type I reaction.

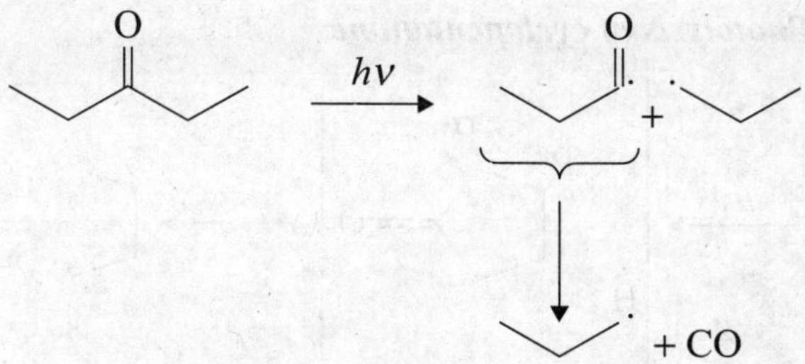

Norrish type II: Ketones with a γ-hydrogen undergo photochemical reaction which results in the formation of an olefin along with enol of a smaller ketone. Such a reaction is known as Norrish type II reaction.

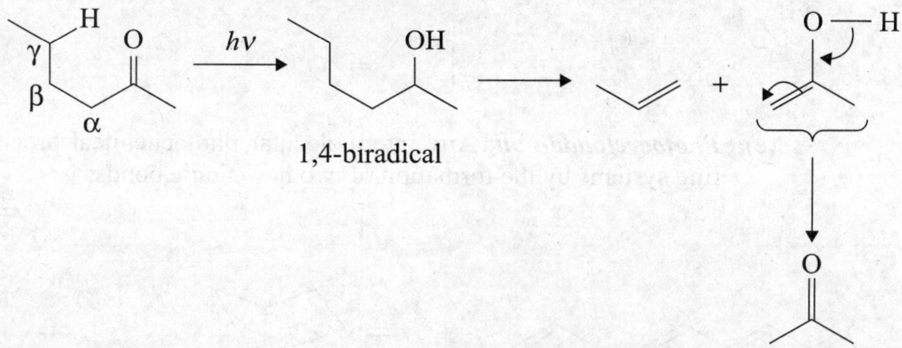

Note:
Norrish type II cleavage is often accompanied by type I split. For example, pentan-2-one upon irradiation yields the products hexane, acetone, butane-2,3-dione, and ethane.

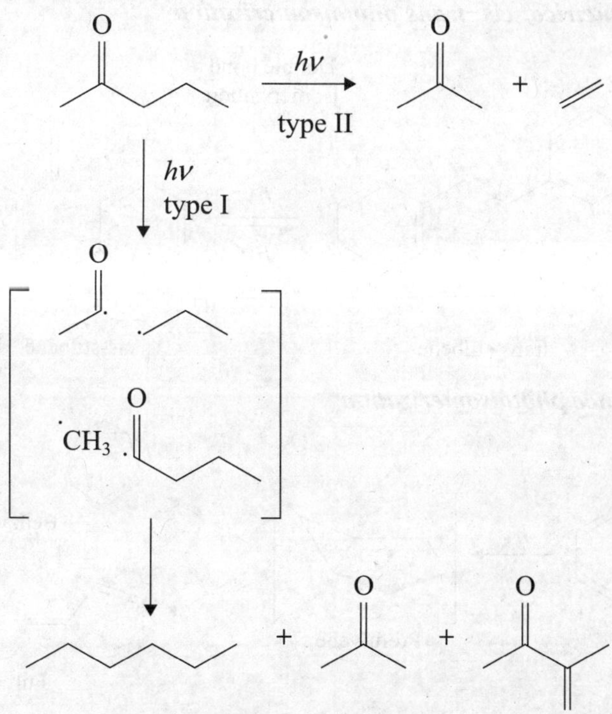

(iii) ***Photolysis of cyclopentanone***

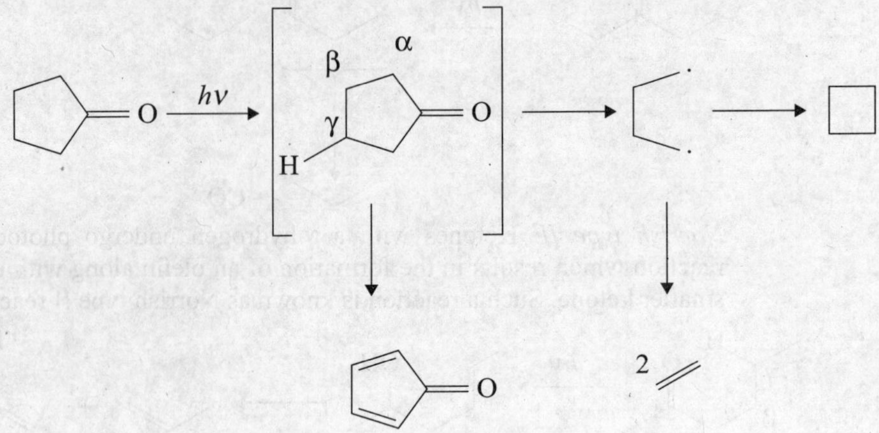

(e) ***Photocycloaddition***: Any intermolecular photochemical process leading to a ring systems by the formation of two new single bonds:

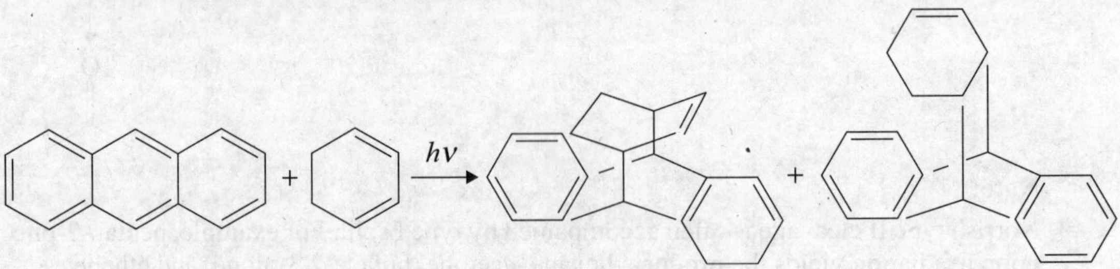

(f) ***Geometrical cis–trans photoisomerization***

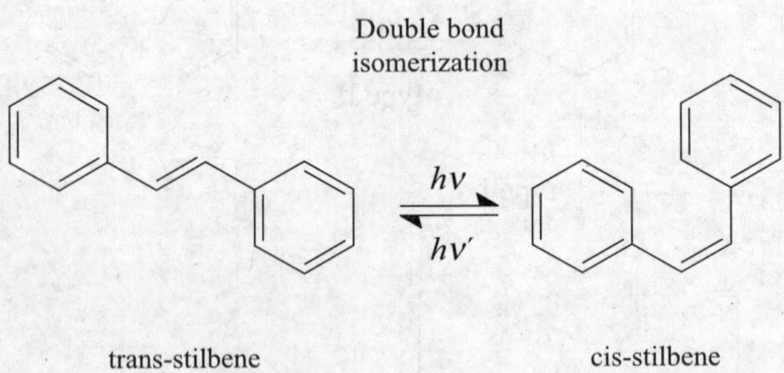

(g) ***Valence photoisomerization***

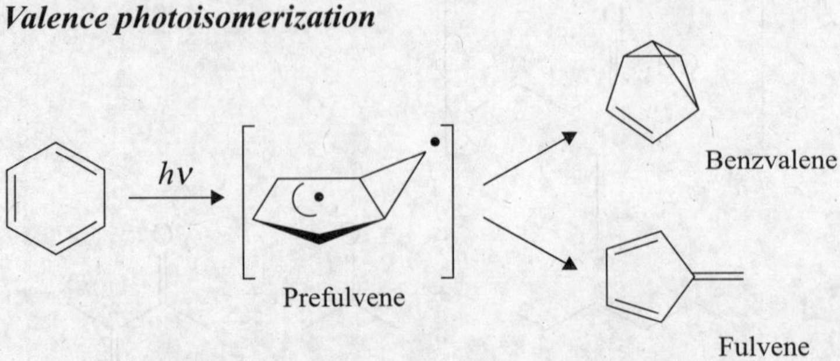

(h) ***Photosubstitution***

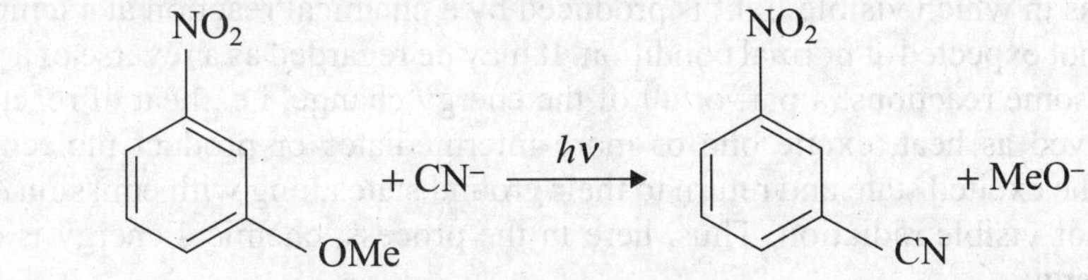

(i) ***Photo-induced rearrangement:*** It is a very common type of reaction in organic photochemistry. In most of the cases, these photo-rearrangement reactions are stereospecific in nature and goes through concerted reaction pathway. Sigmatropic reactions (a migration of a σ-bond across an adjacent π-system) are very common examples of photo-induced rearrangements.

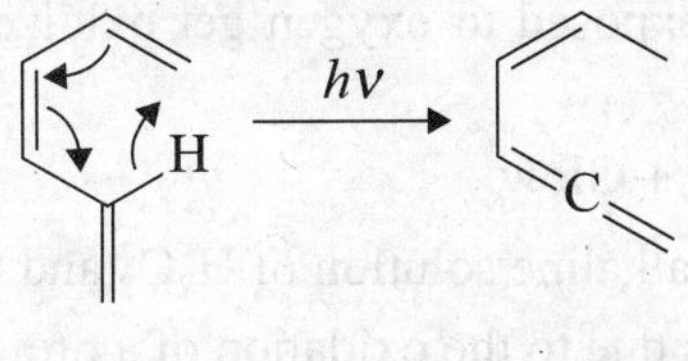

Secondary Processes

Secondary processes may occur upon completion of the primary step. Several examples of such processes are discussed here:

Formation of ozone: Ozone (O_3) is formed in the upper atmosphere from ordinary oxygen (O_2) gas molecules according to the reaction:

$O_2 \xrightarrow{h\nu} O_2^*$ (Excitation)

$O_2^* \longrightarrow O + O$ (Photo-dissociation, primary process)

$O + O_2 \longrightarrow O_3$ (Secondary photochemical reaction)

After a quantum of ultraviolet light is absorbed (step 1), the excited oxygen molecule dissociates into two oxygen atoms (step 2). An oxygen atom then reacts with O_2 to form ozone (step 3).

Chain reaction: The hydrogen–chlorine reaction is an example of a chain reaction. The overall reaction between hydrogen and chlorine gases in the presence of violet or ultraviolet light forms hydrogen chloride. It is given by

$H_2 + Cl_2 \xrightarrow{\text{light}} 2HCl$

This reaction actually proceeds according to the following series of steps:

$Cl_2 \xrightarrow{\text{light}} 2Cl$ (Photo-dissociation, primary process)

$$\left.\begin{array}{l} Cl^* + H_2 \longrightarrow HCl + H^* \\ H^* + Cl_2 \longrightarrow HCl + Cl^* \end{array}\right\} \text{(Secondary photochemical reaction)}$$

Chemiluminescence

It is a process in which visible light is produced by a chemical reaction at a temperature where radiation is not expected at normal condition. It may be regarded as a reverse of a photochemical reaction. In some reactions, a part or all of the energy change, i.e., heat of reaction, instead of getting evolved as heat, excite one or more intermediates or product molecules. These are unstable in the excited state and return to their ground state along with emission of extra energy in the form of visible radiation. Thus, here in the process, chemical energy is converted into radiation energy.

$$\text{Reactans} \longrightarrow \text{Product/s} \longrightarrow [\text{Product/s}]^{\#}$$

$$\downarrow$$

$$\text{Product/s} + h\nu$$

Let us look into some examples:

1. Yellow phosphorous exposed to oxygen get oxidized to P_2O_5 along with greenish white light.

   $$4P + 5O_2 \longrightarrow 2P_2O_5 + \text{Glow}$$

2. The reaction between alkaline solution of H_2O_2 and Cl_2 produces a red glow.
3. The glow of fireflies is due to the oxidation of a protein, luciferin, with the emission of luminescence.

Photosensitization

In many photochemical reactions, the reactants fail to absorb required energy directly. In these cases, the reactants absorb energy from some other light-absorbing foreign substances. The foreign substance is known as photosensitizer and the corresponding reactions are known as photosensitized reactions. A few examples are as follows:

1. Combination of CO and H_2 in the presence of Hg, a photosensitizer. The quantum yield for the process is 2. The primary process is the formation of hydrogen atom and then a chain reaction is followed.

   $$\left.\begin{array}{l} Hg + h\nu \longrightarrow Hg^* \\ Hg^* + H_2 \longrightarrow 2H + Hg \end{array}\right\} \text{Primary process}$$

   $$\left.\begin{array}{l} H + CO \longrightarrow HCO \\ HCO + H_2 \longrightarrow HCHO + H \\ 2HCO \longrightarrow HCHO + CO \\ 2HCO \longrightarrow (CHO)_2 \end{array}\right\} \text{Chain reaction}$$

2. It is an important photochemical reaction that takes place in green plants. During the process, CO_2 from the atmosphere combines with water in the presence of sunlight to form sugars. The sugars then get converted into complex carbohydrates. Chlorophyll, a magnesium-containing green pigment present in leaves, initiate the process. It absorbs ~680–700 nm and conveys the energy to chemical intermediates of the reaction. The process is an excellent example of photosensitization.

$$6CO_2 + 6H_2O \xrightarrow[h\nu]{\text{Chloropyll}} \underset{\text{Glucose}}{C_6H_{12}O_6} + 6CO_2$$

$$\Big\downarrow \text{Polymerize}$$

$$\underset{\text{Carbohydrate}}{(CH_2O)_n}$$

Note:

Importance of photochemical reactions

1. The excited states are rich in energy. Therefore, reactions may occur that are highly endothermic in the ground state. Using the equation $E = h\nu$, we can correlate light of a wavelength of 350 nm with an energy of 343 kJ/mol.
2. In the excited state, anti-bonding orbitals are occupied. This may allow reactions which are not possible for electronic reasons in the ground state.
3. Photochemical reaction can include singlet and triplet states. Thermal reactions usually only show singlet states. In photochemical reaction, intermediates may be formed which are not accessible at thermal conditions.
4. Photochemical synthesis has a high degree of stereoselectivity and stereospecificity. Therefore, it is used for the synthesis of many industrially important compounds. For example, synthesis of caprolactum, the monomer of nylon 6; synthesis of vitamin D_2 from ergosterol isolated from certain yeasts; and manufacture of halogenated aromatics.

Note:

Ergosterol is a sterol found in fungi. The name is derived from "ergot," a common name for the members of the fungal genus *Claviceps* from which it was first isolated. It is a component of fungal and yeast cell membranes. Ergosterol is a biological precursor (a provitamin) to vitamin D_2. It is turned into viosterol by UV light and is then converted into ergocalciferol, a form of vitamin D also known as D_2 or D_2. Ergosterol does not occur in plant or animal cells serving the same function as those of cholesterol in animal cells.

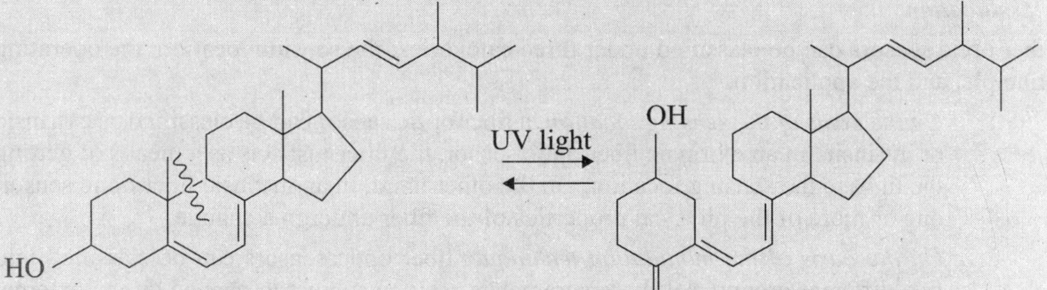

Ergosterol Ergocalciferol (Vitamin D_2)

Semiconductor Photochemistry

In a solid, the molecular orbitals interact strongly to form broad energy bands. The electronic structure of semiconductors (e.g. Si, TiO_2, ZnO, $SrTiO_3$, CdS, ZnS) is characterized by a fully filled *valence band* (VB) with electrons and a vacant *conduction band* (CB). Between the bands there is no energy level. The energy difference between the lowest energy level of the CB and the highest energy of the VB is known as the band-gap energy (E_g). Irradiation of the semiconductor with photons of energy equal to or exceeding the band-gap energy results in promotion of an electron from the VB to the CB, leaving an electron vacancy known as a *hole* behind in the VB. The photo-generated electrons and holes may recombine in the bulk of the semiconductor or on its surface within a very short time, releasing energy in the form of heat. However, electrons and holes those migrate to the surface of the semiconductor without recombination can respectively reduce and oxidize the reactants adsorbed by the semiconductor. Both surface adsorption and photochemical reaction rates can be enhanced by use of nanosized semiconductor particles, as it greatly enhances the available surface area. The generation of energy-rich electron–hole pairs can be utilized to

1. produce electricity in photovoltaic solar cells (discussed in chapter 14).
2. drive chemical reactions in which water is split into hydrogen and oxygen.
3. take part in photo-catalytic reactions.
4. change the surface of the semiconductor, resulting in the phenomenon of super-hydrophilicity.

Optical Sensor

Fiber Optic Sensors

Optical fibers have a major role not only in communication but also in the development of different types of sensors. Fiber optic sensors (FOS) successfully meet the requirements such as high sensitivity and quick response in sensing different chemical and physical variables. Using optical fiber sensing devices one can measure or monitor different physical and chemical parameters in terms of one of the principal parameters that describes the light beam. These principal parameters include light intensity, phase, polarization, and wavelength. Optical sensors are generally based either on measuring an intensity change in one or more light beams or on looking at phase changes in the light beams by causing them to interact or interfere with one another. The general structure of optical sensors consists of an optical source (laser, LED, laser diode, etc.), optical fiber, sensing or modulator element (which transduces the measurand to an optical signal), an optical detector and processing electronics (oscilloscope, optical spectrum analyzer etc.).

Classification

Fiber optic sensors can be classified under three categories: the sensing location, the operating principle, and the application.

1. *On the basis of the sensing location*, a fiber optic sensor can be classified as extrinsic or intrinsic. In an extrinsic fiber optic sensor, the fiber just acts as a means of getting the light to the sensing location. On the other hand, in an intrinsic fiber optic sensor, one or more of the physical properties of the fiber undergo a change.

2. *On the basis of the modulation technique*, fiber optic sensors can be classified into five different groups. All these parameters may be subject to change due to external perturbations. Thus, by detecting these parameters and their changes, the external perturbations can be sensed. The classification is as follows: (i) Intensity-modulated

fiber optic sensors, (ii) phase-modulated fiber optic sensors, (iii) polarization-modulated fiber optic sensors, (iv) frequency-modulated fiber optic sensors, and (v) wavelength-modulated fiber optic sensors. Among these modulation techniques, the first three modulation schemes are most commonly employed in a wide range of applications.

3. *On the basis of the application*, a fiber optic sensor can be classified as follows:
   (i) **Physical sensors**: These are used to measure physical properties such as temperature and stress.
   (ii) **Chemical sensors**: A fiber-optic chemical sensor is a device that can be used to measure the concentration or activity of a chemical species in a sample. Optical fiber based chemical sensors often use a reaction chamber within which a chemical reaction involving the sensing species occurs. A color change may result from this chemical reaction and, with light passing through the reaction chamber, the light intensity can be modulated by this color change. Consequently, this change in light intensity can be used to quantify the sensing species present.
   (iii) **Bio-medical sensors**: Biosensors are analytical devices that can detect chemical or biological species or a microorganism. Optical biosensors utilize optical techniques to detect and identify chemical or biological species. Mechanistically this sensor works in two phases: a bio-recognition element collects the chemical response from a biological species; secondly, it is converted into an optical signal through an optical probe (transduction) and conveyed to optical detection system. These are used in bio-medical applications such as measurement of blood flow and glucose content.

Applications

1. Measurement of physical properties such as strain, displacement, temperature, pressure, velocity, and acceleration in structures of any shape or size.
2. Foundation monitoring, joint expansion monitoring, spatial displacement measurement, leakage monitoring, and distributed temperature monitoring.
3. Detection of ions such as hydrogen. The simplest example of an ion selective FOCs is a fiber optic pH sensor with a fluorescent pH indicator dye immobilized at the distal end of a fiber optic probe.
4. Detection of gases such as oxygen, ammonia, carbon dioxide, hydrogen cyanide, and nitrogen dioxide. In case of oxygen, it uses fluorescence quenching of an immobilized fluorophore, whereas in case of acidic and basic gases, it monitors the change of a "pH-indicator dye" spectroscopically.
5. Detection of non-gaseous molecular species. It is based on direct spectroscopic detection.
6. Clinical diagnostics
7. Drug development
8. Environmental monitoring (air, water, and soil)
9. Food quality control

Advantages

Fiber optic sensors are excellent candidates for monitoring environmental changes, and they offer many advantages over conventional electronic sensors:

1. Greater sensitivity
2. Electrical passiveness

3. Freedom from electromagnetic interference
4. Wide dynamic range
5. Both point and distributed configurations
6. Multiplexing capabilities
7. Resistant to chemically aggressive
8. Intrinsically safe operation in explosive environments and potentially resistant nature to nuclear or ionizing radiations
9. Operation at very high temperature, pressure, or voltage.

Supramolecular Photochemistry

The section of photochemistry that studies electronic properties, structure, and photochemical transformations of supramolecular systems is called supramolecular photochemistry. Photochemically active components (chromophores), when introduced into supramolecular complexes, make it possible to use the light energy to carry out practical processes such as energy transfer, photo-induced electron transfer, and space division of charges, the change of redox potentials, and selective binding. Those effects can be used in light conversion devices, electronic switching, energy storage, photo-catalytic systems. Here, chromophores are typically polyaromatic molecules, e.g., metalloporphyrins, free porphyrins, bipyridyl and its analogues. Light makes those molecules experience electronic transition, which initiates a chain of physical or chemical processes in the whole supramolecular system. Examples are energy transfer in artificial photo antennae or electron transfer in supramolecular donor–acceptor systems.

Supramolecular photochemistry requires a guest–host complex model: a specific host binds the guest through non-covalent bonds and that these weak bonds control the pathways followed in a supramolecular photochemical reaction. The host–guest systems act as “nanocontainers” for the photochemical reaction. Carrying out photochemical reaction in organized media can lead to the product structure changing which can be exploited for the directional synthesis. For example, zeolites can be used as guest framework for supramolecular photochemistry. Zeolites are crystalline porous solids possessing an “open” or porous internal surface whose framework is constructed from SiO_4 and AlO_4 tetrahedra connected through oxygen bridges. The intersections are the likely “active sites” for reactions in zeolites, because they offer the greatest degree of void space for reacting molecules to interact. Thus, although zeolites as solids are formally “hard matter,” their internal void space is “soft.” As a result, zeolites can serve as hosts for guest molecules.

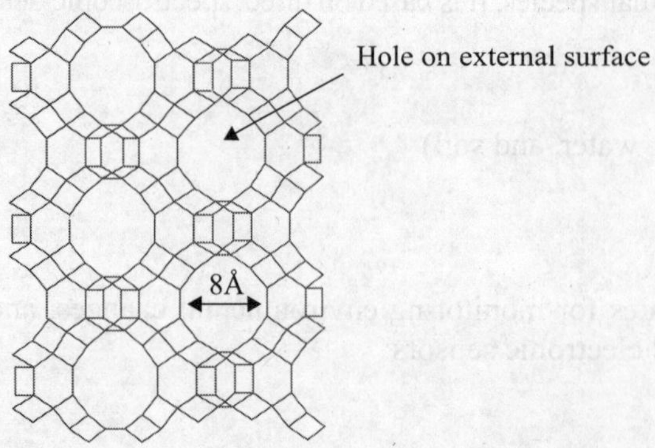

The supercages of the internal surface of zeolites provide nanoscopic reactors that control covalent bond formation of geminate radical pairs produced by photolysis of guest molecules adsorbed in the zeolite host. Within this guest framework, photochemistry of dibenzoyl ketones can be controlled (directional synthesis) based on the nature of the cation present in the zeolite architecture (MX, where M = metal cation and X = cation in the zeolite framework). The major product is the isomeric rearranged ketone.

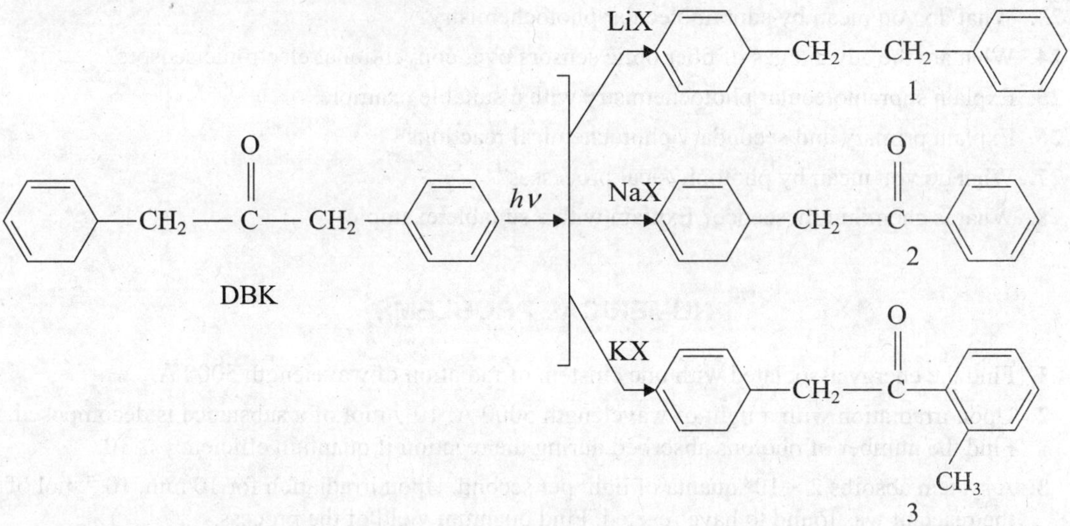

QUESTIONS

1. What are the typical light sources for preparative photochemistry?
2. State and explain Grotthuss–Draper law.
3. State and explain Einstein–Stark law.
4. Explain the term quantum yield or efficiency. In which conditions high quantum yield is obtained?
5. Give one example each for photochemical reactions with high and low quantum yields.
6. Explain fluorescence.
7. Define phosphorescence.
8. State the law of photochemical equivalence.
9. State and explain Lambert–Beer's law.
10. What do you mean by molar absorption coefficient?
11. Give a comparative account of "ΔG" of a thermochemical and a photochemical reaction.
12. Give a comparative account on thermochemical and photochemical reactions.
13. What are the importance of photochemical reactions?
14. What do you mean by radiative and non-radiative transitions?
15. Explain photosensitization with a suitable example.
16. What is radiative decay? Explain.
17. What are the applications of fiber optic sensor?

18. Show different possible energy dissipating mechanisms with the help of Jablonski diagram.
19. Explain photolysis reaction with a suitable example.
20. Explain the working principle of photovoltaic solar cells.
21. Explain biomedical sensors.
22. What is a chemical sensor? Explain with a suitable example.
23. What do you mean by supramolecular photochemistry?
24. What are the advantages of fiber optic sensors over conventional electronic sensors?
25. Explain supramolecular photochemistry with a suitable example.
26. Explain primary and secondary photochemical reactions.
27. What do you mean by photophysical processes?
28. What is chemiluminescence? Explain with a suitable example.

NUMERICAL PROBLEMS

1. Find the energy associated with one einstein of radiation of wavelength 5000 Å.
2. Upon irradiation with a light of wavelength 5000 Å, 10^{-4} mol of a substance is decomposed. Find the number of photons absorbed during the reaction if quantum efficiency is 10.
3. A system absorbs 2×10^8 quanta of light per second. Upon irradiation for 10 min, 10^{-3} mol of the reactant was found to have reacted. Find quantum yield of the process.
4. A certain substance in a cell of length "*l*" absorbs 10% of incident light. What percent of light will be absorbed in a cell which is four times as long?
5. Find the percentage of light transmitted through 10 mm length of a liquid having absorption coefficient 2.5.
6. A solution of 30 g/*l* of a dye in a 1.0 cm cell absorbs 40% of the light with wavelength 435 nm. Under the same condition, what percentage of light will be absorbed by a solution containing 15 g/*l* of the dye?
7. Ammonia is decomposed by a light of wavelength 200 nm with a quantum efficiency of 0.15. Find the number of calories of the light required to decompose 5 g of ammonia.
8. When HI gas is exposed to radiation of wavelength 250 nm, it is observed that 2×10^{-2} mol decomposes per 1000 cal of radiant energy absorbed. Find the quantum yield.

CHAPTER

10 Stereochemistry and Organic Reaction Mechanism

Chapter Outline

- Stereochemistry
- Optical Isomerism
- Geometrical Isomerism
- Conformational Isomerism
- Reaction Mechanism
- Substitution Reactions
- Addition Reactions
- Elimination Reactions
- Rearrangement Reactions
- Organometallics Compounds

Stereochemistry

The compounds having same molecular formula but different properties (physical, chemical, or both) are known as isomers, and the phenomenon is known as isomerism. Isomerism can be broadly classified as structural and stereoisomerism. Structural isomers differ in arrangement of atoms within the molecule without any reference to space, whereas stereoisomers differ in the spatial arrangement of atoms or groups (Greek: *stereo* means space, *meros* means parts). Stereoisomers can be classified into two types: configurational and conformational.

Configurational or Inversional Isomerism

The stereoisomers which are non-superimposible and non-interconvertible by rotational movement around single bonds are known as configurational isomers, and the phenomenon is known as configurational isomerism. The interconversion is possible only by breaking and making of bonds. Configurational isomerism involves *optical* and *geometrical* isomerism.

Optical isomerism

Plane polarized light: Ordinary light consists of waves vibrating in all planes perpendicular to the line propagation. When such a light is allowed to pass through NICOL prism, its vibrations in all planes are cut off except one plane. Such a light whose vibrations occur only in single plane is known as *plane polarized light* (Fig. 10.1).

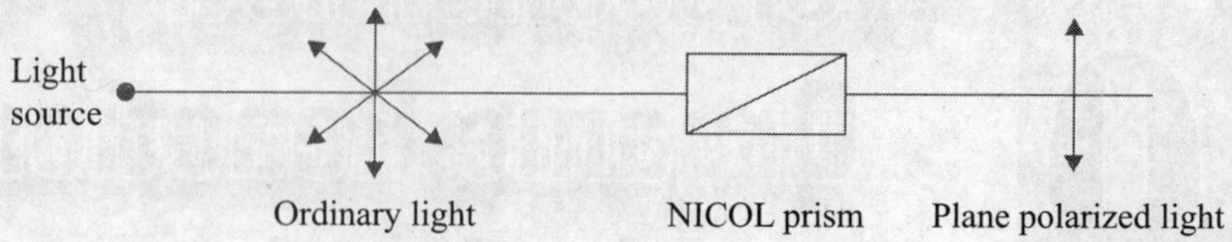

Fig. 10.1 Plane polarized light

Optical activity: The phenomenon by virtue of which certain substances exhibit remarkable ability to rotate plane polarized light is known as optical activity and the substances are known as optically active substances. Substances which rotate the plane of polarized light in clockwise direction are known as *dextrorotatory,* indicated by "d" or "+ve" form (Latin: *dextor* means right) and those which rotate the plane of polarized light in anticlockwise direction are known as *levorotatory* indicated by "ℓ" or "–ve" form (Latin: *leavous* means left).

Polarimeter: The instrument used for measuring the angle of rotation of plane polarized light is known as Polarimeter. It consists of two NICOL prisms which are placed by keeping their axes of polarization parallel to each other. The space in-between is used to keep the sample tube carrying the liquid or solution of the substance whose optical activity is to be studied. The schematic diagram of a Polarimeter is shown in Fig. 10.2.

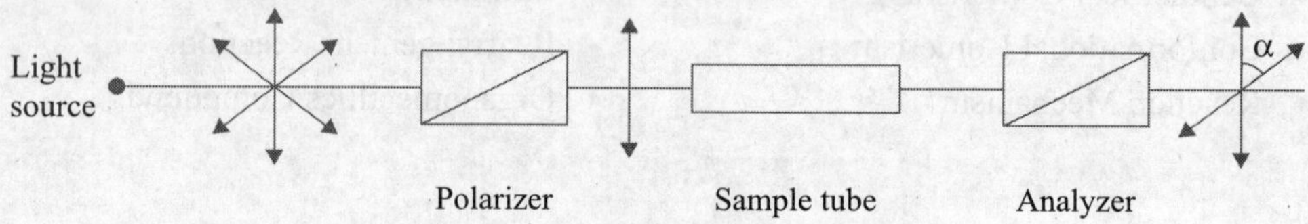

Fig. 10.2 Schematic diagram of a Polarimeter

The magnitude of rotation depends on the

1. nature of substance,
2. concentration of solution,
3. length of sample tube containing solution,
4. nature of solvent,
5. temperature of solution, and
6. wavelength of the light used (usually, D-lines of sodium having wavelength 589.3 nm is used).

Specific rotation: Optical activity is reported in terms of specific rotation which is characteristics of a particular compound. It is defined as the rotation in degrees observed when a plane polarized light is passed through 1 dm of solution having concentration of 1 g/ml at a specified temperature and wavelength. This is usually expressed as

$$[\alpha]_D^t = \frac{\alpha_{\text{Obs}}}{l \times c}$$

where D is the D-lines of sodium having wavelength 589.3 nm, t is the temperature (°C), l is the length of the Polarimeter tube, c is the concentration of solution (g/ml).

Requirement of optical activity: The only necessary, inflexible, and sufficient condition to exhibit optical activity is that the geometrical structure should not superimpose on its mirror image. Superimposibility can be verified with the help of symmetry elements such as plane, center, and axis. The molecule that lacks all the elements of symmetry, i.e., asymmetric, is capable of having non-superimposible mirror image and is optically active. Subsequently, it has been observed that the molecules which are devoid of only plane and center of symmetry are also optically active. Such molecules are known as dissymmetric molecules. Thus, all asymmetric molecules are dissymmetric but the reverse is not true. However, both of them are optically active. In recent practice, a new term has replaced the use of asymmetric and dissymmetric. The term simply relates optical activity to non-superimposibility of mirror images and not to the absence of elements of symmetry.

In reference to organic molecules, those molecules that contain at least one chiral carbon is optically active. Chiral carbon is that which remain attached to four different atoms or groups.

Note:

1. If a molecule has only one chiral center, it is always chiral. However, molecules with two or more chiral centers may be chiral or achiral.
2. There are some molecules which do not have any chiral center but are still chiral, e.g., allenes.

Allenes

Dienes containing double bonds between successive carbon atoms are known as allenes and can be represented by the following geometrical formula:

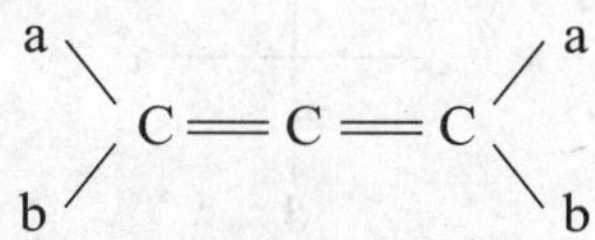

In this case, two terminal carbon atoms are in sp^2-hybridized state and the central one is sp-hybridized. The central atom remains linked to the adjacent carbon atoms by two collinear σ-bonds and two π-bonds. The π-bonds remain perpendicular to each other. Therefore, terminal groups which remain attached to the trigonal "C" atoms lie in planes perpendicular to each other. The result is that allenes neither possess plane nor a center of symmetry. However, they possess non-superimposible mirror image.

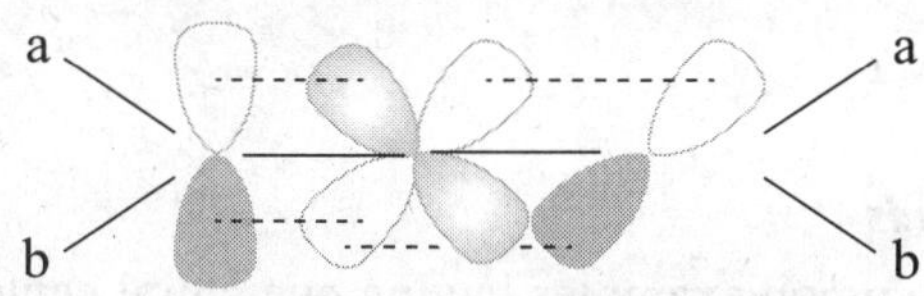

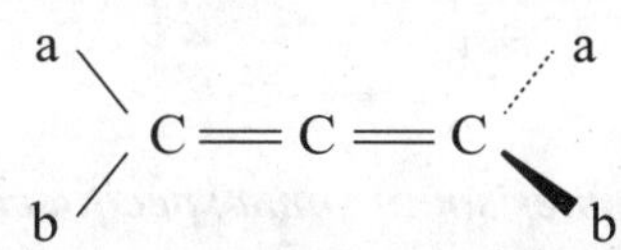

The same is true for allenes containing even number of double bonds. Therefore, they are optically active. In contrast, those contain odd number of double bonds that do not exhibit optical isomerism. This is because atoms or groups present on the terminal carbons lie in the same plane.

Fischer projections

Fischer projections, devised by Emil Fisher in 1891, are 2-D projection formulae of 3-D organic molecules. Following conventions are made for getting the Fischer projections.

1. The molecule having a chiral center is viewed such that two of the groups attached to the carbon remain horizontal and point toward the observer, while the other two are vertical and point away from the observer.
2. The different atoms or groups attached to the chiral carbon are then projected on the plane of the paper in the form of a cross. The chiral carbon lies at the intersection of horizontal and vertical bonds.
3. When the molecule contains two or more chiral carbon atoms, each carbon is viewed individually in similar manner.

4. Usually, the main carbon chain is written vertically with the most prior atom or group at the top. The chain is numbered as per the IUPAC system of nomenclature. The complete procedure is described as follows:

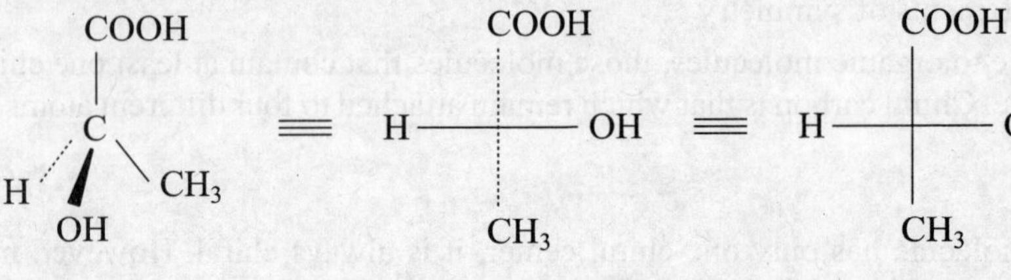

Lactic acid

Note:

1. A Fischer projection can be turned through 180° on the plane of the paper without affecting the configuration.

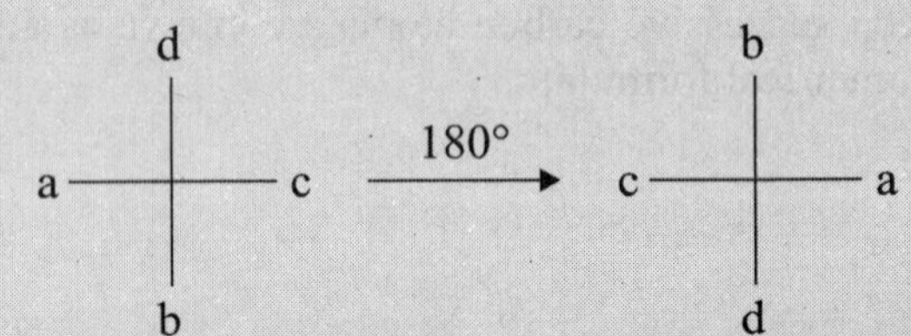

2. Even number of exchanges of pairs of atoms or groups attached to chiral carbon can be carried out without affecting the configuration.

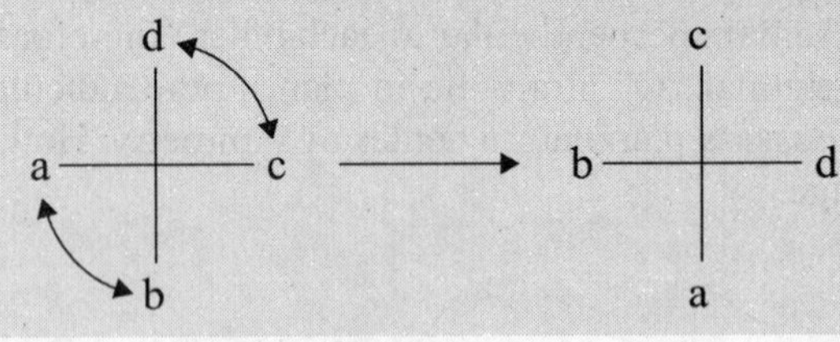

Optical isomerism in some specific compounds

Case I (Having one chiral center): Some common examples having one chiral center are as follows:

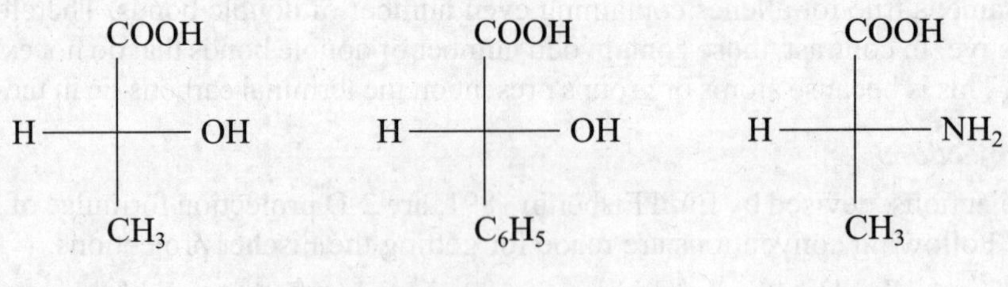

Lactic acid Mandelic acid Alanine

Lactic acid: Lactic acid exists in following isomeric forms:

1. *Enantiomers:* This exists as two optically active enantiomeric forms which are non-superimposible mirror images of each other and are known as enantiomers. One of these is known as the "d" form that rotates the plane of polarized light in clockwise

direction and the other is known as the "*l*" form that rotates the plane polarized light in anticlockwise direction.

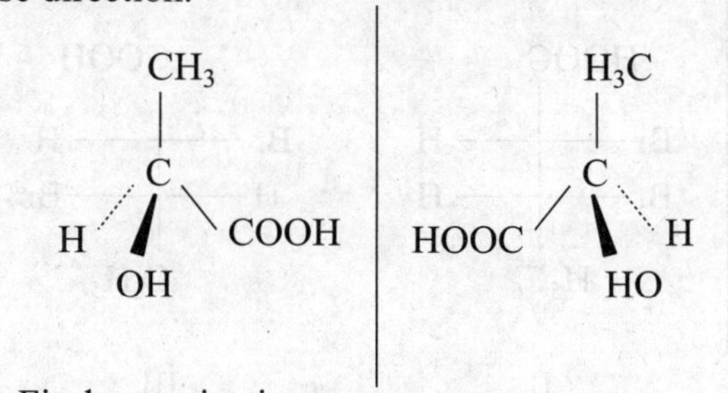

Fischer projection

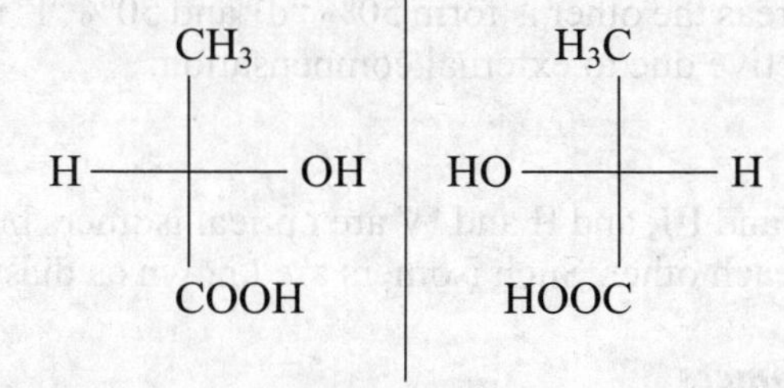

2. *Racemic form*: This is a mixture of 50% "d" and 50% "l" form. This is optically inactive due to external compensation.

Case II (Having two similar chiral centers): An example of such a compound is tartaric acid.

1. *Enantiomers*: It exists in two optically active forms which are non-superimposible mirror images of each other, i.e., enantiomers.

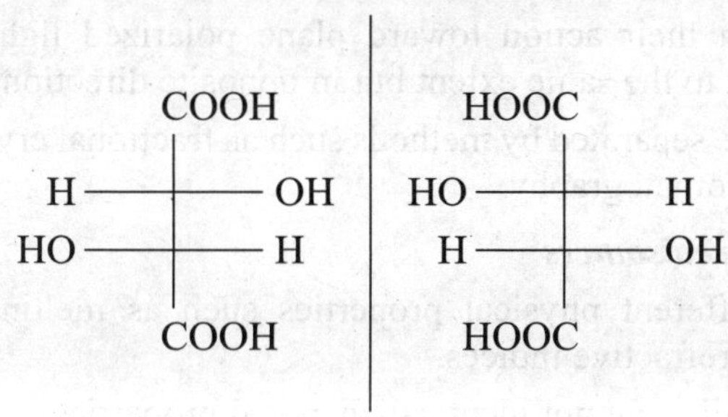

2. *Racemic form*. This is mixture of 50% "d" and 50% "l" form. This is optically inactive due to external compensation.
3. *Meso form*: This form caries a plane of symmetry. This is optically inactive due to internal compensation.

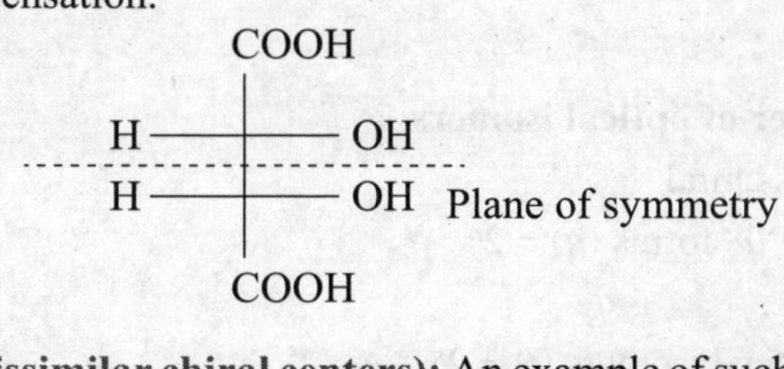

Case III (Having two dissimilar chiral centers): An example of such a compound is Cinnamic acid dibromide.

1. *Enantiomers*: It exists as two pairs of enantiomers.

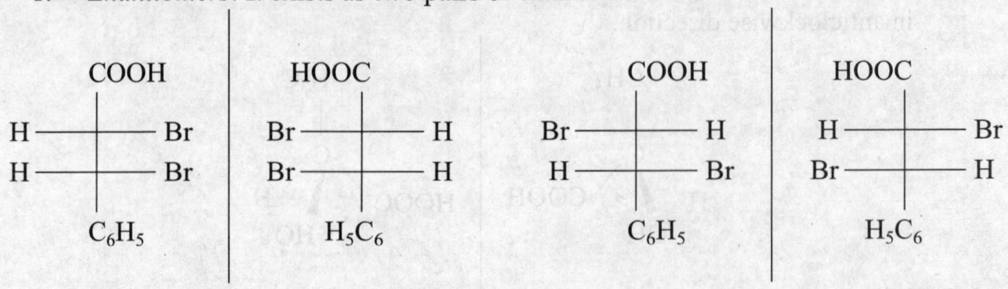

I II III IV

2. *Racemic form*: Two racemic forms exist. One form is 50% "d" and 50% "l" mixture of I and II, whereas the other is form 50% "d" and 50% "l" mixture of III and IV. This is optically inactive due to external compensation.

Note

I and III, I and IV, II and III, and II and IV are optical isomers but are not mirror images, i.e., enantiomers of each other. Such isomers are known as diastereoisomers.

Characteristics of enantiomers

1. They have identical physical properties such as melting points, boiling points, densities, and refractive indices.
2. They have identical chemical properties except their behavior toward optically active compounds.
3. Enantiomers have different biological properties.
4. They differ in their action toward plane polarized light. They rotate the plane polarized light to the same extent but in opposite directions.
5. They cannot be separated by methods such as fractional crystallization and fractional distillation chromatography.

Characteristics of diastereoisomers

1. They have different physical properties such as melting points, boiling points, densities, and refractive indices.
2. They have similar but not identical chemical properties.
3. They differ with respect to their specific rotations.
4. They can be separated by physical methods of separations such as fractional crystallization and fractional distillation chromatography.

Note

Finding the number of optical isomers

Case I: Molecule is chiral

Number of "d" and "l" forms $(a) = 2^n$

Meso form $(m) = 0$

Total number of optical isomers $(t) = 2^n$

where n is the number of chiral carbon atoms.

Case II: Molecule is symmetrical and has even number of chiral carbon atoms

$$a = 2^{n-1}$$

$$m = 2^{\left(\frac{n}{2}-1\right)}$$

$$t = 2^{n-1} + 2^{\left(\frac{n}{2}-1\right)}$$

Case III: Molecule is symmetrical and has odd number of chiral carbon atoms

$$a = 2^{n-1} - 2^{\left(\frac{n}{2}-\frac{1}{2}\right)}$$

$$m = 2^{\left(\frac{n}{2}-\frac{1}{2}\right)}$$

$$t = \left[2^{n-1} - 2^{\left(\frac{n}{2}-\frac{1}{2}\right)}\right] + 2^{\left(\frac{n}{2}-\frac{1}{2}\right)}$$

D, L nomenclature

Relative configuration to different optical isomers is assigned with reference to glyceraldehyde which is taken as an arbitrary standard by Rosanoff for its relationship with carbohydrates. (+)-glyceraldehyde which has the −OH group on the right and the hydrogen atom on the left is assigned with configurational symbol "D." The mirror image of the compound (−)-glyceraldehydes is assigned with configurational symbol "L."

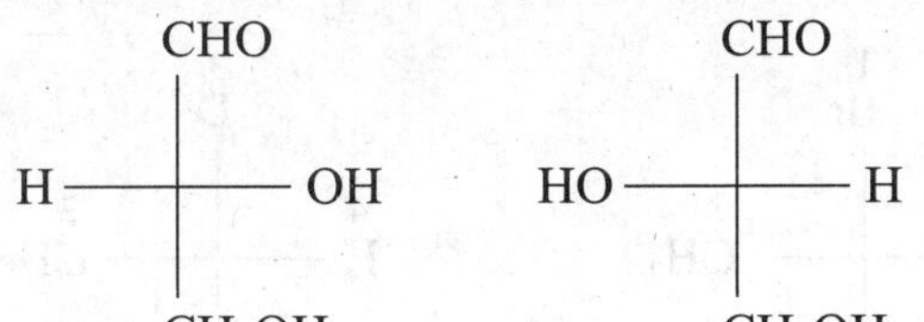

D(+)-glyceraldehyde L(−)-glyceraldehyde

How to assign?

1. Any compound that can be prepared from or converted into D(+)-glyceraldehyde is assigned with "D." Similarly, any compound that can be prepared from or converted into L(−)-glyceraldehyde is assigned with "L." For example, glyceric acid obtained from D(+)-glyceraldehyde belongs to D-series.

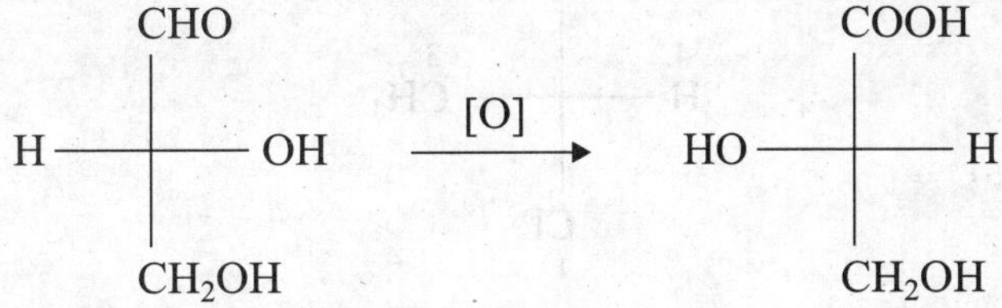

D(+)-glyceraldehyde D(+)-glyceric acid

2. When a molecule contains more than one asymmetric center, then each center is considered individually. In such a case, the carbon chain is numbered from the top and the various functional groups are assigned with "D" and "L" configurations depending upon whether they are attached to the right or left to the asymmetric center concerned.

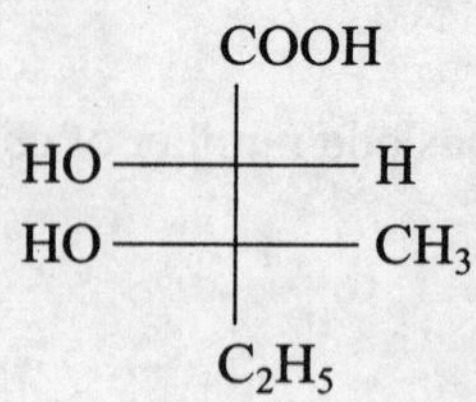

2-L-hydroxy-3-D-methyl-3-L-hydroxypentanoic acid

Absolute configuration

R, S nomenclature: Absolute configuration is assigned to different configurations by an unambiguous system developed by R. S. Cahn, Sir Christopher Ingold, and V. Prelog. It involves two steps:

Step I: Using a set of sequence rules, a sequence of priority is assigned to the four ligands which remain attached to the chiral center.

Rule 1: If four atoms attached to the chiral center are different, then priority depends on the atomic number, with the atom having higher atomic number getting higher priority. If two atoms are isotopes, then the one with higher mass number gets higher priority.

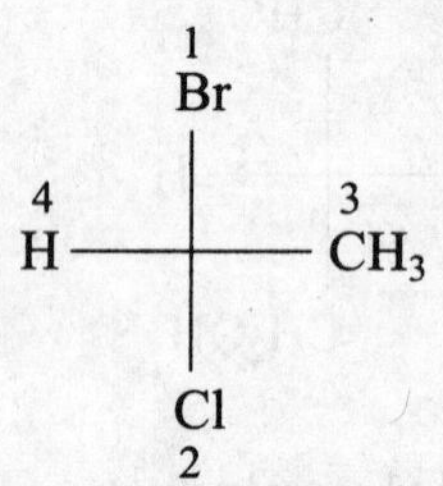

1-bromo-1-chloroethane

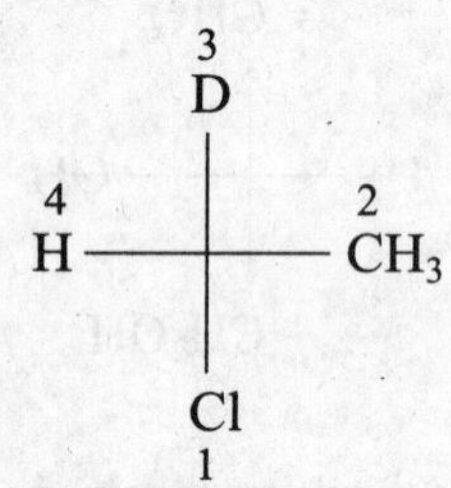

1-choloro-1-duteroethane

Rule 2: If two atoms directly attached to asymmetric centers have the same atomic number, priority is assigned by a similar comparison of the next atoms in the groups.

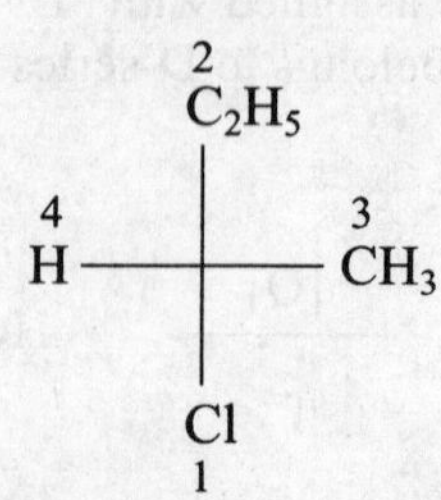

Rule 3: A doubly or triply bonded atom is equivalent to two or three such atoms.

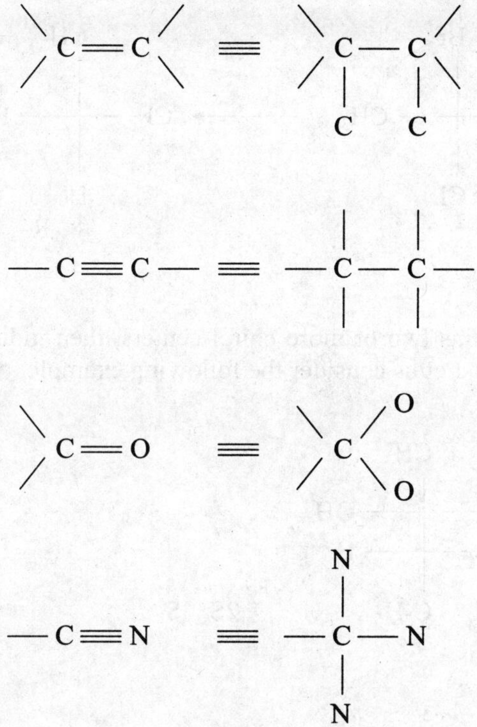

Example

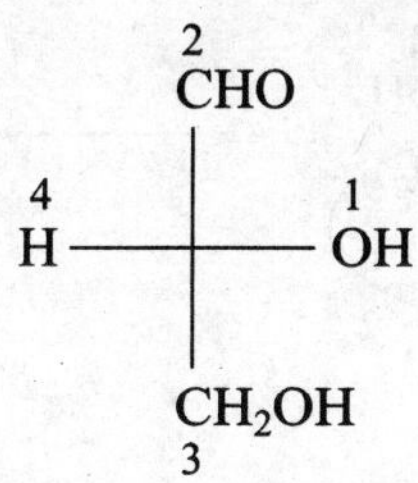

Step II: The molecule is oriented so that the ligand of the lowest priority remains away from the viewer or in vertical positions in case of Fischer projections. Now the arrangement of the rest three groups is viewed in decreasing order of their priority, i.e., 1 → 2 → 3. In doing so, if eye traces a clockwise orientation, the configuration is specified as "R" (Latin: *rectus* means right); if the orientation is counterclockwise, the configuration is specified as "S" (Latin: *sinister* means left).

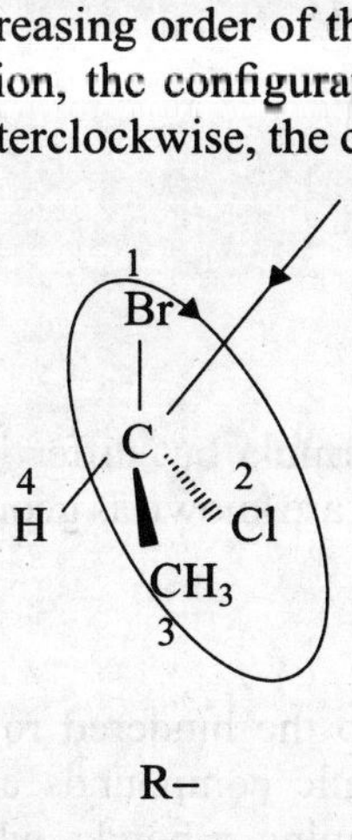

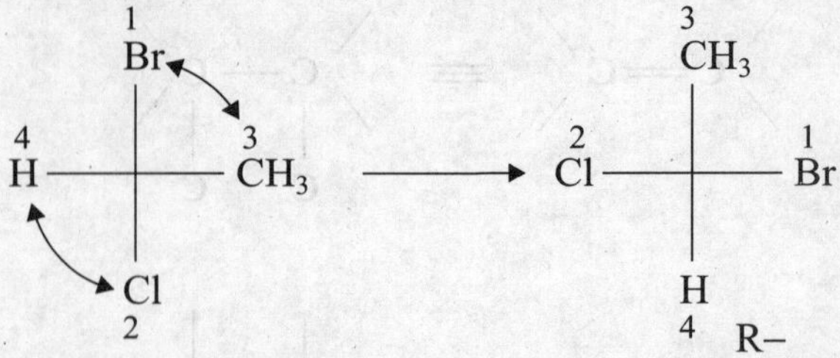

R–

> **Note**
>
> If the molecule contains two or more chiral centers, then individual centers are to be considered separately. Let us consider the following example:
>
> 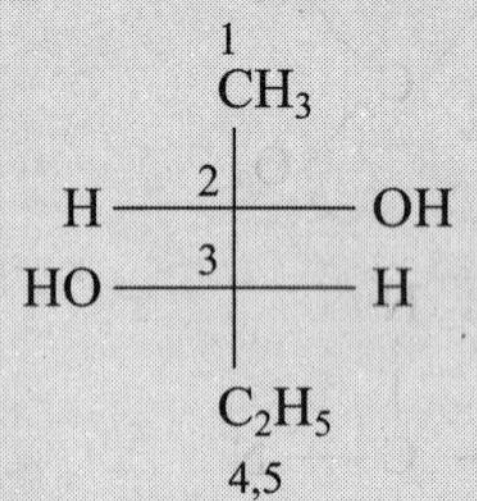
>
> 2S, 3S-
>
> 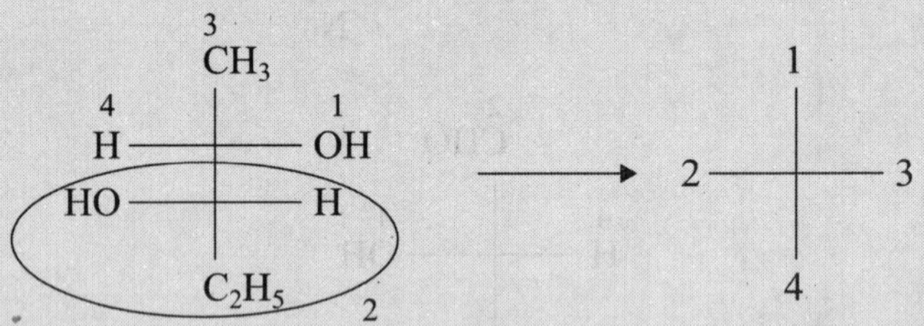
>
> S-
>
> 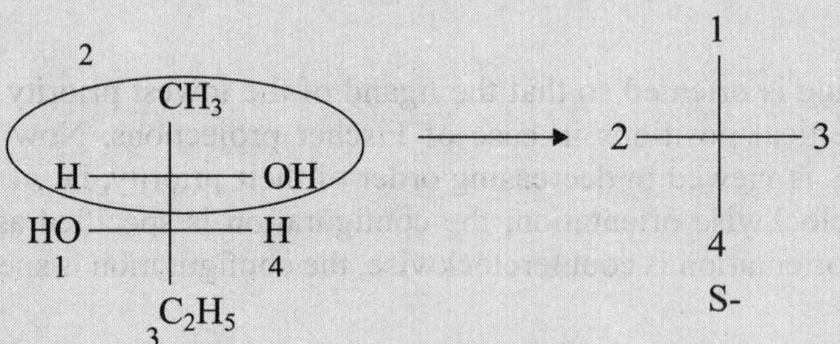
>
> S-

Geometrical Isomerism

Compounds having same structural formula but differ in the relative spatial arrangement of atoms or groups around the double bond are known as geometrical isomers, and the phenomenon is known as geometrical isomerism.

Why geometrical isomerism?

Geometrical isomerism is attributed to the hindered rotation around carbon–carbon double bond. The two carbon atoms in olefinic compounds are in the state of sp^2 hybridization. The hybrid orbitals get utilized in forming σ-bonds, while π-bonds are formed by sidewise overlapping of unhybridized p-orbitals. The essential condition to get effective overlap is the planer configuration of the molecule, as only in this configuration the p-orbitals remain parallel. Rotation of one carbon with respect to other disturbs coplanarity and does not facilitate the overlapping. Therefore, rotation requires sufficient energy (~50 kJ/mol) to break π-bonds.

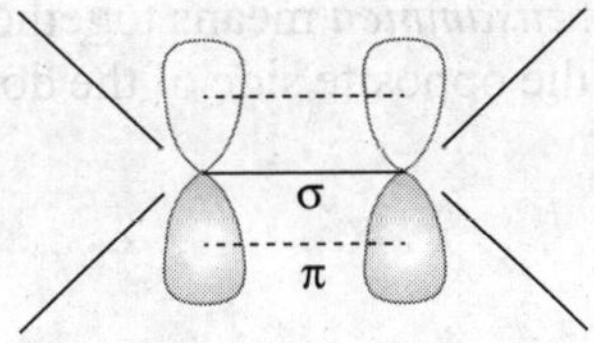

Conditions for geometrical isomerism

1. The molecule must contain a double bond.
2. Each of the two carbon atoms of double bond must remain attached to different substituent.

   Therefore, following alkenes exhibit geometrical isomerism.

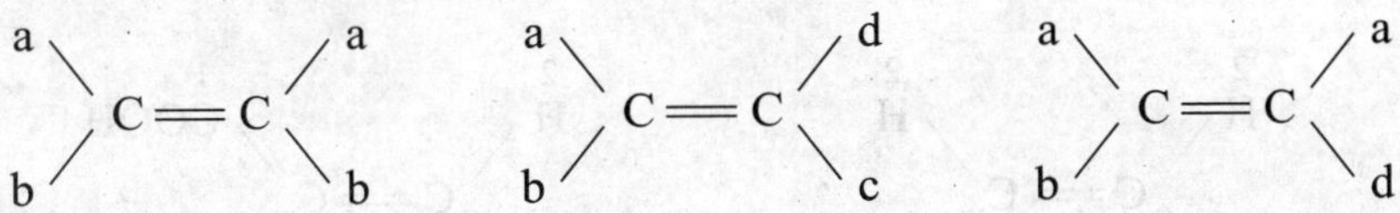

Nomenclature

***Cis–trans* system:** The isomer having the same groups on the same side of the double bond is known as *cis* form, whereas the one in which the same groups remain on the opposite side of the double bond is known as *trans* form.

Illustrations

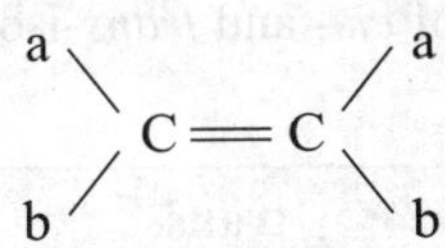

cis-

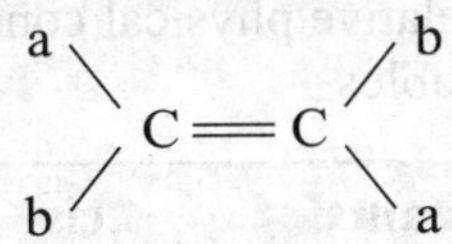

trans-

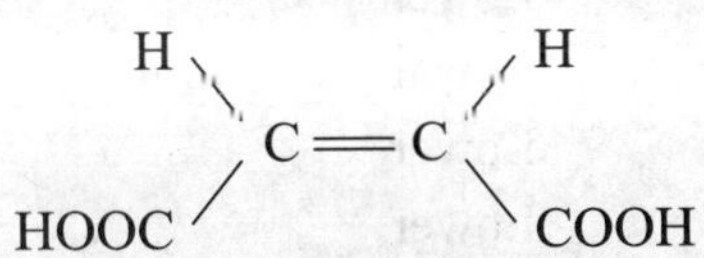

cis-but-2-ene-1,2-dioic acid
(maleic acid)

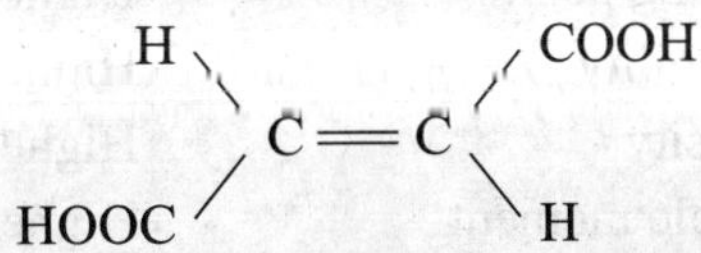

trans-but-2-ene-1,2-dioic acid
(fumaric acid)

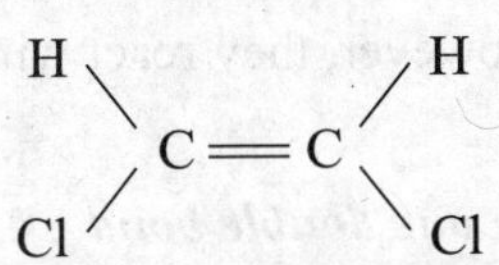

cis-1,2-dichloroethene

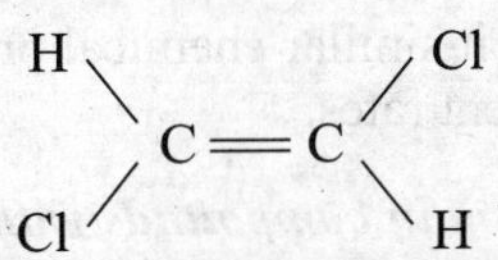

trans-1,2-dichloroethene

E–Z system: The following procedure is followed in specifying configuration.

Step 1: Assign the priority order to the two groups attached to individual "C" of the double bond by following sequence rules as described earlier in the R–S system of nomenclature.

Step 2: The configuration with atoms or groups of higher priority on the same side of the double bond is assigned with "Z" (German: *zusammen* means together). On the other hand, if atoms or groups of higher priority remain on the opposite side of the double bond, it is assigned with "E" (German: *entgegen* means against).

Illustration

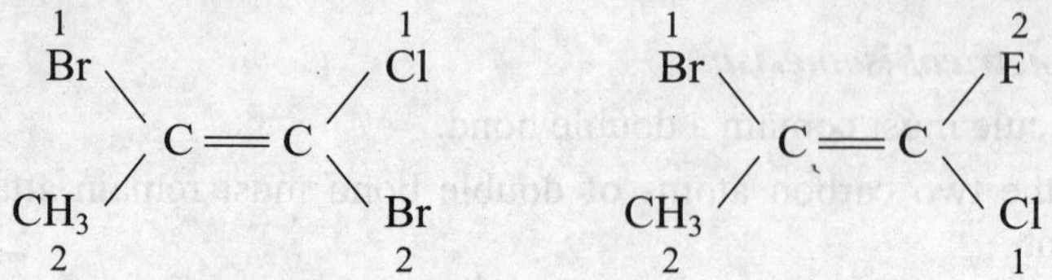

Z E

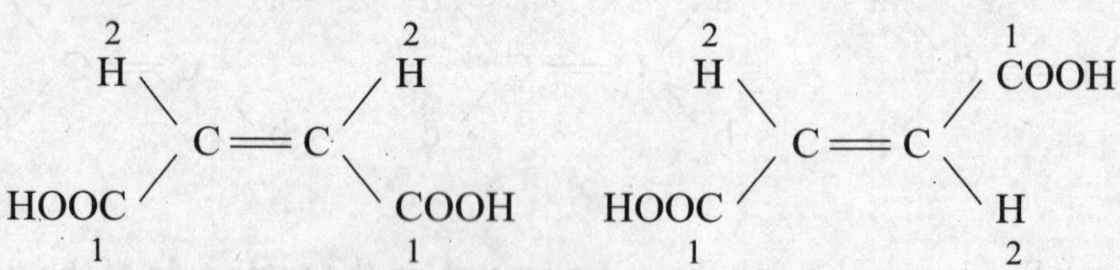

Z E

Characteristics of geometrical isomerism

1. They have different physical properties such as melting point, boiling point, solubility, and density. Relative physical constants of *cis*- and *trans*-isomers are mentioned in the following table:

Physical constants	cis-	trans-
Melting point	Lower	Higher
Boiling point	Higher	Lower
Solubility	Higher	Lower
Density	Higher	Lower
Dipole moment	Higher	Lower
Refractive index	Higher	Lower
Heat of combustion	Higher	Lower
Thermal stability	Lower	Higher

2. They exhibit similar chemical properties. However, they react with a given reagent with different rates.

Geometrical isomerism in compounds with more than one double bond

1. When a compound contains "n" number of dissimilarly substituted double bonds, then the number of geometrical isomers is 2^n. Examples are as follows:

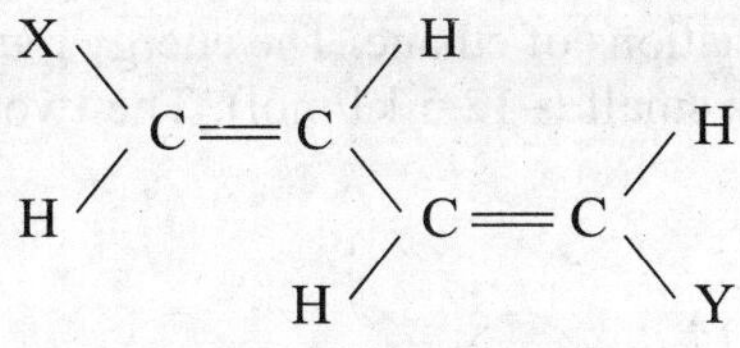

trans-trans

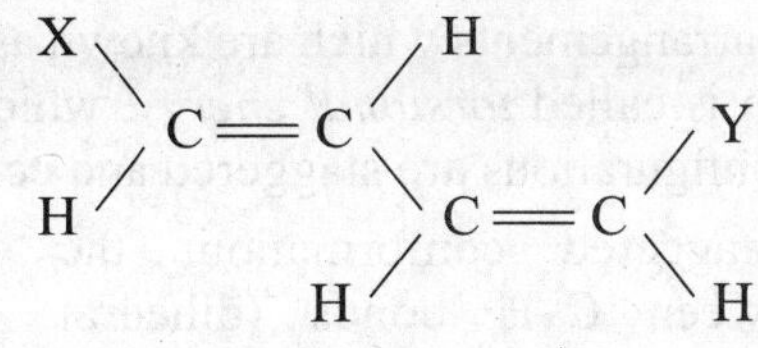

trans-cis

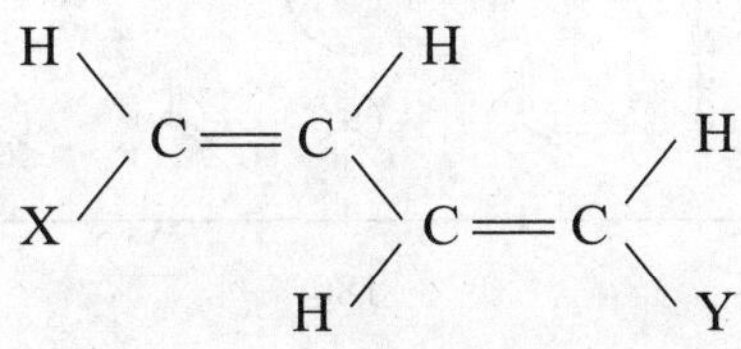

cis-trans

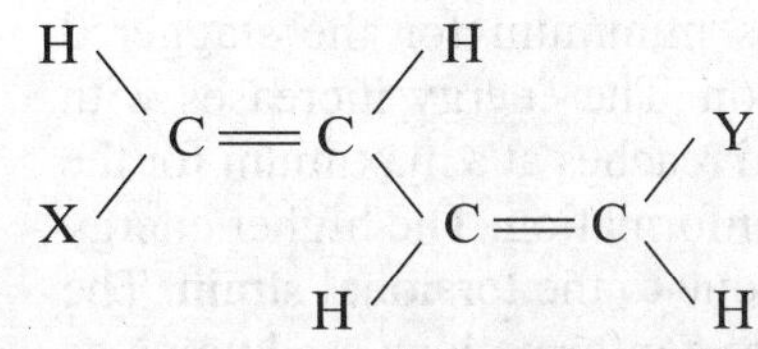

cis-cis

3. If some of the double bonds are identically substituted, the number of geometrical isomers is diminished. For example, in the above example when $x = y$, the number of geometrical isomers becomes 3.
4. Cumulenes possessing odd number of adjacent double bonds also exhibit geometrical isomerism.

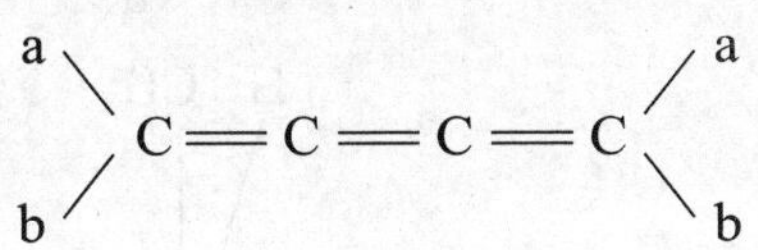

cis-

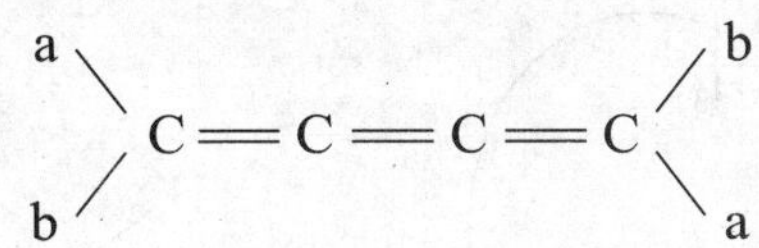

trans-

Conformational Isomerism

Conformational isomerism refers to any one of the infinite number of spatial arrangements of the atoms of a molecule that can arise from rotation about a single bond. The term should not be confused with configuration isomerism, which is the spatial arrangements of the atoms of a molecule that can be changed only by breaking and making of bonds.

Conformations of ethane

In ethane molecule, the two carbon atoms remain connected by a σ-bond. If one of the methyl groups of ethane is kept fixed and the other is rotated about the C–C bond, one can get a

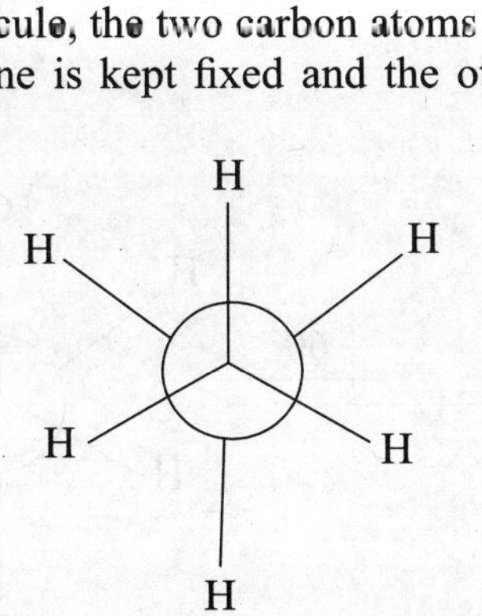

Staggered

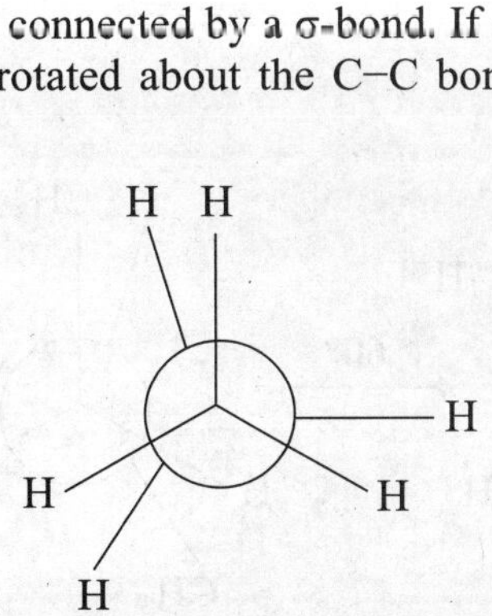

Eclipsed

number of arrangements which are known as conformations of ethane. The energy required for the rotation is called *torsional energy*, which is very small (~12.5 kJ/mol). The two extreme possible configurations are staggered and eclipsed.

In staggered conformation, the angle between C–H bonds (dihedral angle) as viewed along the C–C bond axis is 60°. In eclipsed conformation, dihedral angle is 0°. The potential energy of the molecule is minimum for the staggered conformation. The energy increases with rotation and reaches at a maximum for the eclipsed conformation. The higher energy of latter is due to the torsional strain. The intermediate conformations are known as skew conformations. The potential energy diagram is shown in Fig. 10.3.

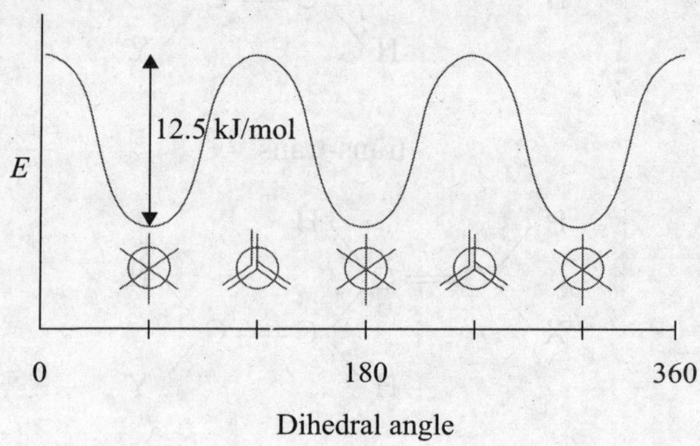

Fig. 10.3 Potential energy diagram of ethane

Conformations of n-butane

Conformations of *n*-butane can be discussed by considering *n*-butane as dimethyl ethane as shown here. By fixing one of the "C" atoms (say C_2 or C_3) and rotating the other around C_2–C_3 bond, one can get several conformations. The six important conformations are as follows:

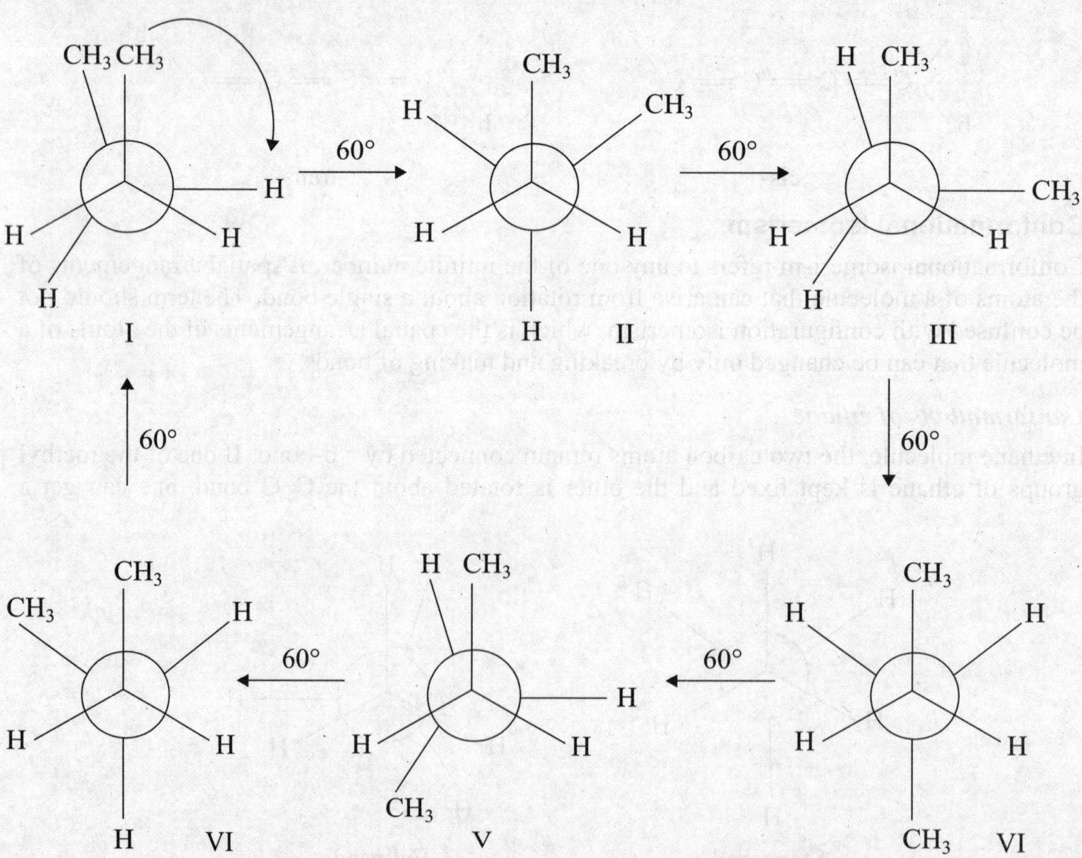

The conformation I in which two methyl groups are very much close is called fully eclipsed, and the conformation IV in which they are farthest apart is called fully staggered or anti-form. Conformations III and V are known as partially eclipsed, whereas II and VI are called partially staggered or gauche or skew. The relative stabilities of all these conformations are shown in the potential energy diagram (see Fig. 10.4).

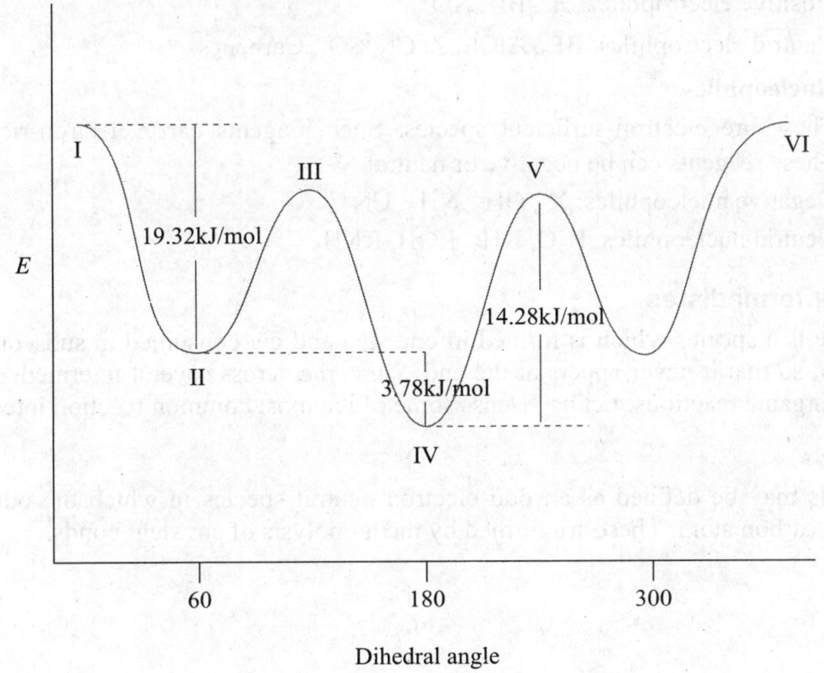

Fig. 10.4 Potential energy diagram of *n*-butane

Organic Reactions

It is a well known fact that vast number (in terms of millions) is one of the most important reasons for which organic compounds and their chemistry needs separate attention. In addition, organic compounds are mostly covalent. Because of these facts, we come across a huge number of reactions, and in many cases specific reaction conditions need to be maintained so as to facilitate them. Thus, dealing with all reactions individually seems to be almost impossible. To simplify the approach, it is essential to categorize and discuss the mechanisms involved in group-wise manner. A mechanism helps to predict three important aspects, such as the relative/absolute rate of the reaction, ragio-selectivity, i.e., selection of the prime product in cases where more than one possible products are pre sent and stereo selectivity, i.e., stereo chemical control during the reaction.

Organic reactions in general can be represented as

$$\textit{Substrate} + \textit{Attacking reagent} \longrightarrow \textit{Intermediate/s}$$
$$\downarrow$$
$$\textit{Product/s}$$

Attacking Reagents

Attacking reagents can be classified as follows:

1. **Electrophiles**

   These are electron seeking or loving species. Therefore, such reagents carry electron-deficient centers. These reagents can be positive or neutral.

   Positive electrophiles: H^+, Br^+, NO_2^+

   Neutral electrophiles: BF_3, $AlCl_3$, $ZnCl_2$, SO_3, Carbenes

2. **Nucleophiles**

   These are electron-sufficient species. Such reagents carry electron-rich centers. These reagents can be negative or neutral.

   Negative nucleophiles: X^-, OH^-, NH_2^-, CN^-

   Neutral nucleophiles: H_2O, NH_3, ROH, RNH_2

Reaction Intermediates

Intermediate is a species which is formed in one step and get consumed in subsequent step/s of a reaction so that it never appers at the end. We come across several intermediates during analysis of organic reactions. Let us discuss some of the most common reaction intermediates.

Free radicals

Free radicals may be defined as an odd electron neutral species in which the odd electron resides on a carbon atom. These are formed by the homolysis of covalent bonds.

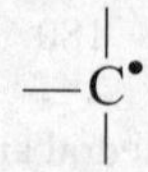

Shape

"C" atom that carries the odd electron is *sp*^{2} hybridized. The three sp^2 hybrid orbitals of carbon remain utilized in forming bonds with three other atoms or groups. The unhybridised *p*-orbital which remains perpendicular to plane of hybrid orbitals carries the odd electron.

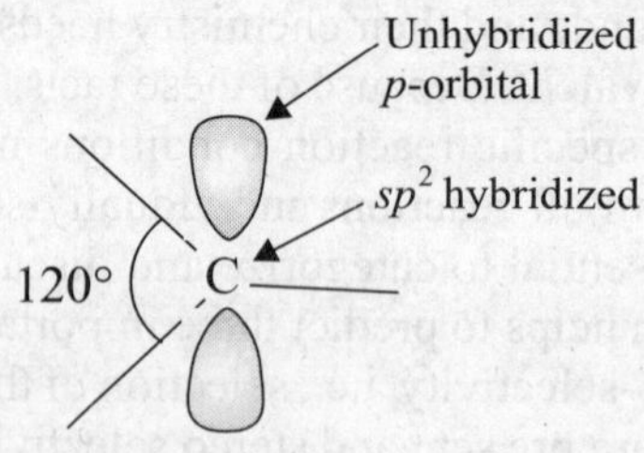

Fig. 10.5 Carbon free radical

Classification

Alkyl free radicals are classified into primary, secondary, and tertiary depending on nature of "C" atom that carries the odd electron. If odd electron lies on the 1°C, then the free radical is known as 1°/primary free radical, if it lies on a 2°C, then secondary free radical, and if lies on 3°C, then tertiary free radical.

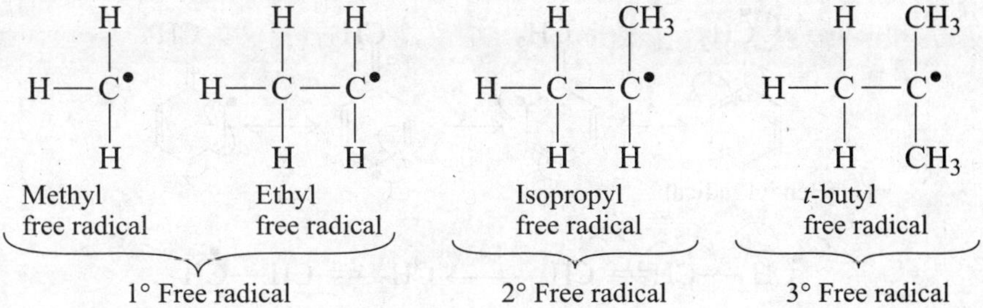

Stability

The presence of odd electron makes the radical unstable. Any electron displacement mechanism that helps in the delocalization or dispersal of the odd electron helps in increasing stability. The following electron displacement mechanisms may be considered.

Hyperconjugation

This explains stability of alkyl free radicals which follows the order 3° > 2° > 1° > methyl. More the number of possible hyperconjugative structures more is delocalization of odd electron and therefore more is the stability. In case of 3°, nine hyperconjugative structures are possible while in 2° and 1°, six and three structures are possible, respectively, as shown below. This explains the order of stability.

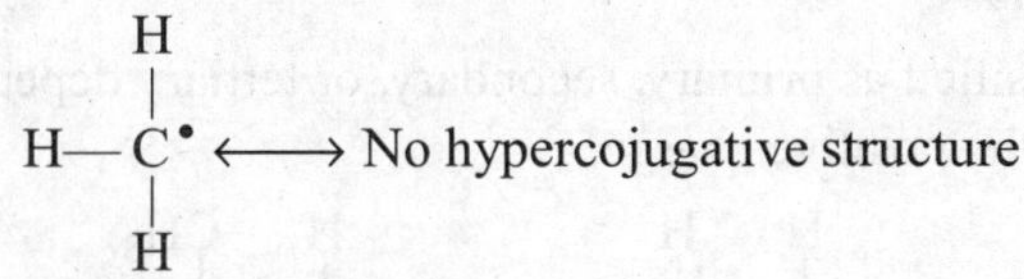

Methyl free radical

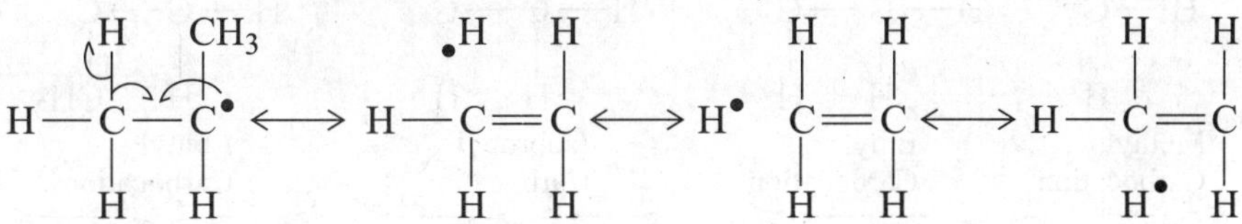

1° Free radical

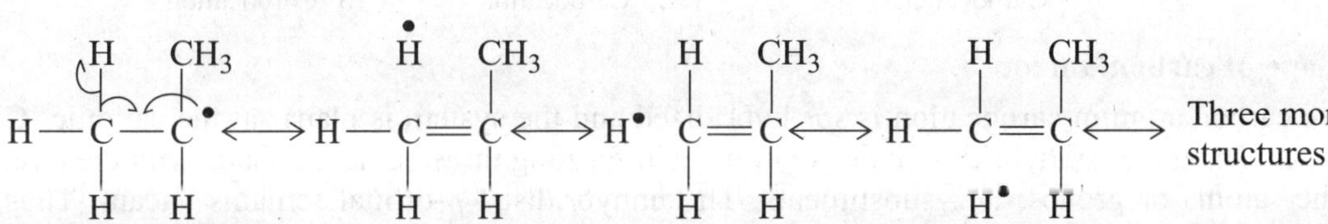

2° Free radical

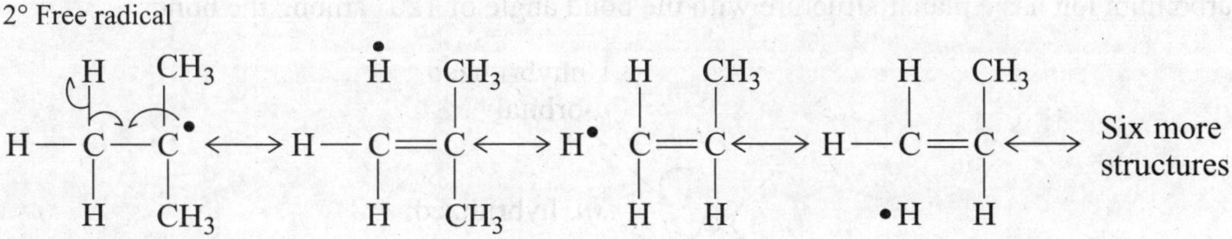

3° Free radical

Resonance

Resonance also helps in delocalizing the odd electron and thereby explains stability of radicals, e.g., in case of benzyl and allyl radicals.

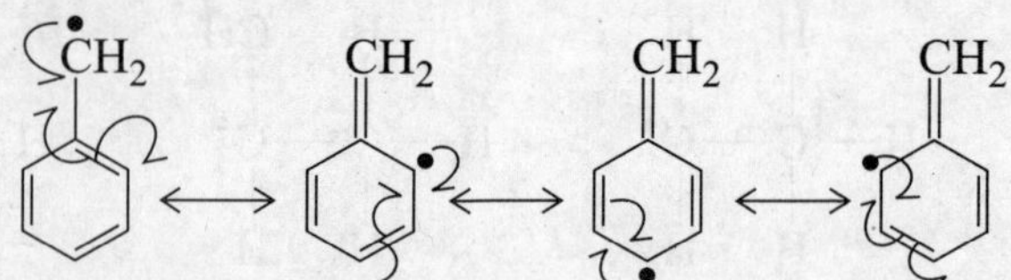

Benzyl radical

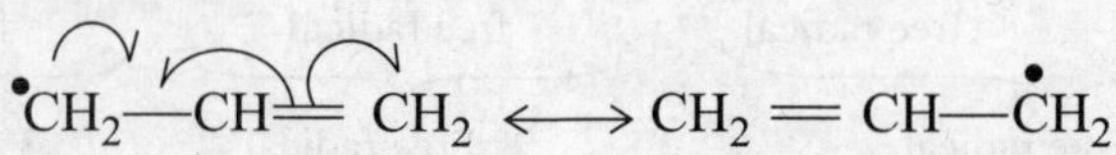

> **Note:**
> The overall order of stability of free radicals is as follows: benzyl > allyl > 3° > 2° > 1° > methyl.

Carbocations (*Carbonium ions*)

Carbocation is positively charged species containing a carbon atom having an incomplete octet, i.e., only six electrons in three covalent bonds. These are formed by heterolysis of covalent bonds.

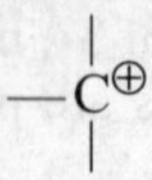

Types of carbocations

Carbocations are classified as primary, secondary, or tertiary depending upon the nature of the carbon atom bearing the positive charge.

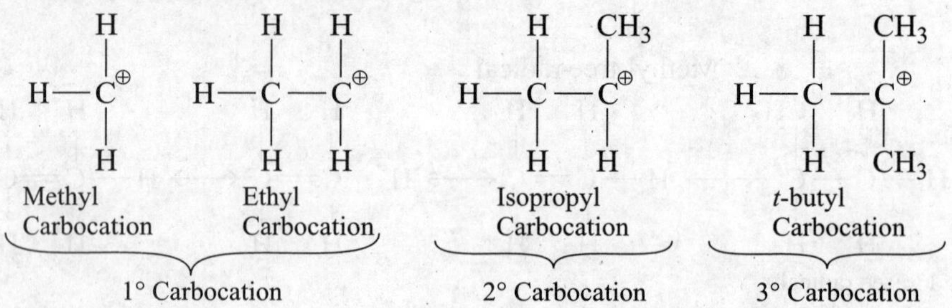

Shape of carbonium ion

The carbon atom in carbocation is sp^2 hybridized and the system is planar at the cationic 'C' center. The three sp^2 hybrid orbitals are utilized in forming three covalent bonds with the three other atoms or groups, i.e., substituents. The unhybridised *p*-orbital remains vacant. Thus, carbonium ion has a planar structure with the bond angle of 120° among the bonds.

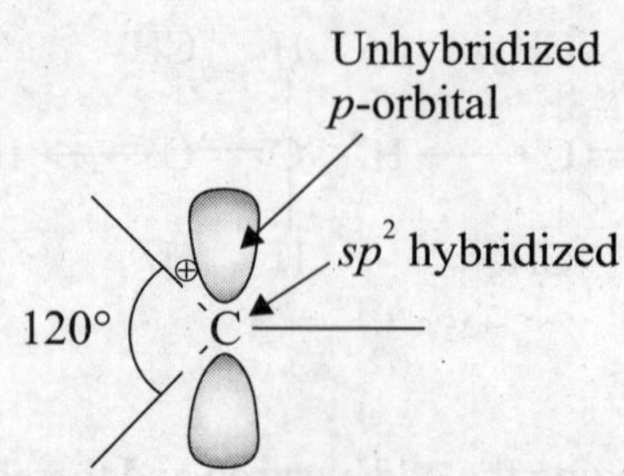

Fig. 10.6 Carbocation

Stability

The positive charge on carbocationic carbon always gets stabilized either through delocalization of positive charge or through electron pushing effect by the neighboring atom(s) and group(s). Delocalization of the charge is possible by two ways, viz., resonance effect and hyperconjugative effect. Electron pushing is through inductive effect. Sometimes aromaticity and structural effects may also stabilize carbocationic positive charge. The mechanisms mainly responsible for the dispersal of the charge here are resonance and hyperconjugation. The electron-releasing substituents tend to reduce the charge at the electron-deficient carbon (I) and thereby stabilize it. On the other hand, electron withdrawing groups tend to intensify the positive charge on the electron-deficient carbon (II) and hence makes the carbonium ion less stable.

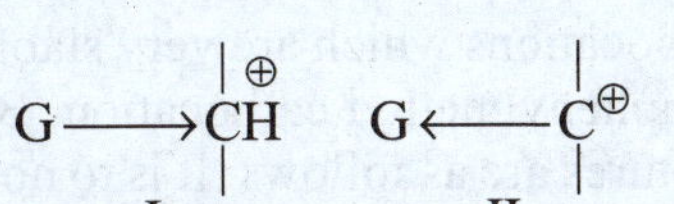

I II

Hyperconjugation

This explains stability of alkyl carbocations which follows the order 3° > 2° > 1° > methyl. More is the number of possible hyperconjugative structures, more is the delocalization of +ve charge and therefore more is the stability. In case of 3°, carbocation nine hyperconjugative structures are possible, while in 2° and 1°, carbocation six and three structures are possible, respectively, as shown below. Hence, this explans the order of stability.

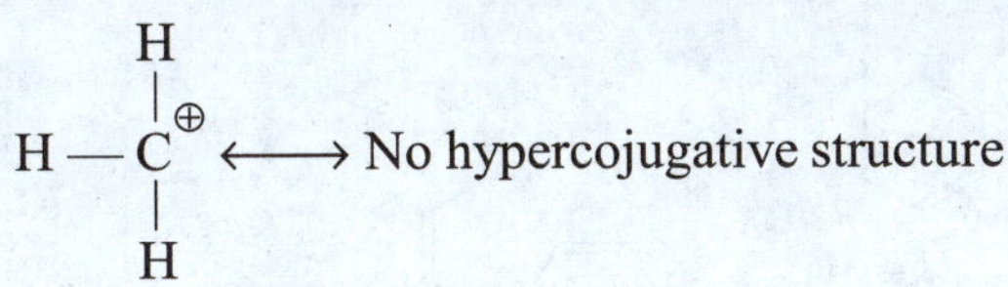

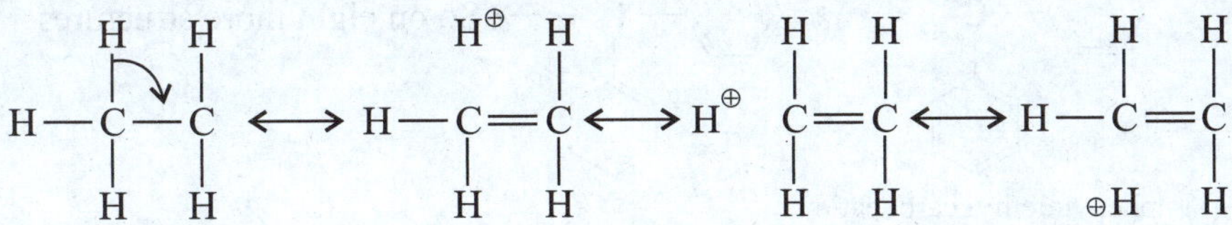

1° Carbocation

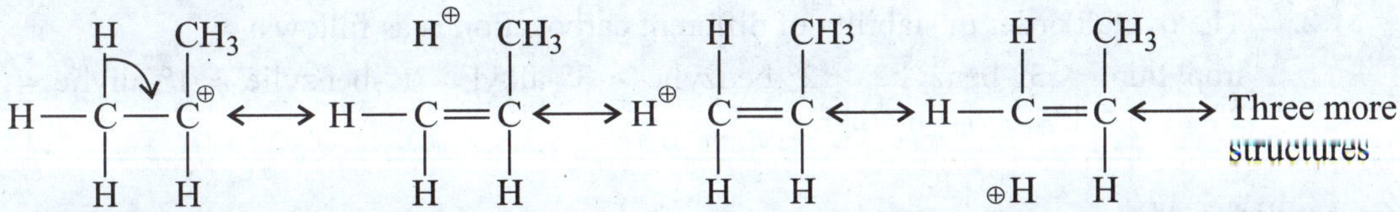

2° Carbocation

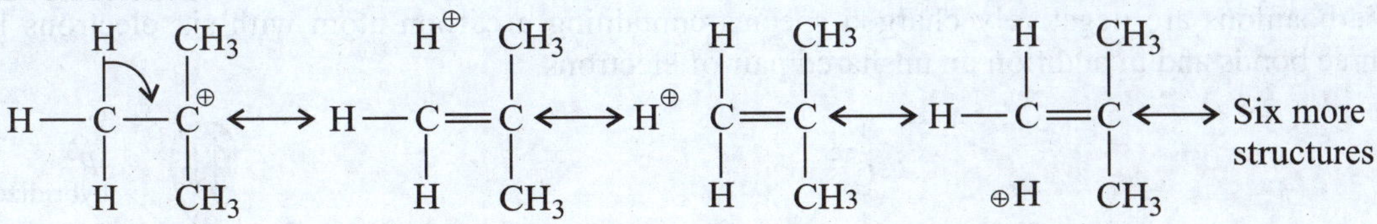

3° Carbocation

Resonance

Resonance also helps in delocalizing the +ve charge and thereby explains stability of carbocations, e.g., in case of benzyl and allyl carbocations.

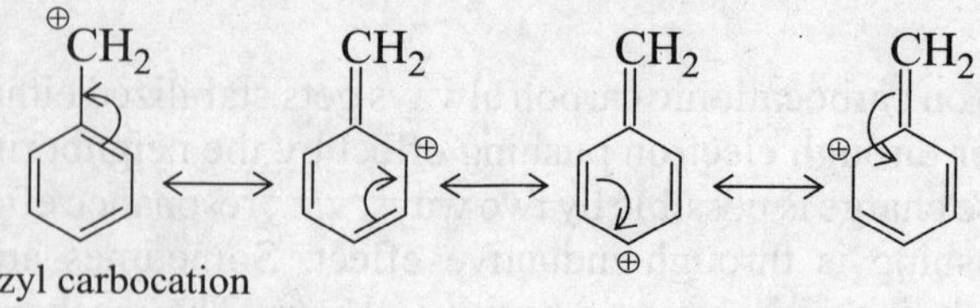

Benzyl carbocation

$$\overset{\oplus}{C}H_2-CH=CH_2 \longleftrightarrow CH_2=CH-\overset{\oplus}{C}H_2$$

Allyl carbocation

Note:

1. There are certain carbocations which are very stable and their solid salts are known e.g. tropylium and triphenylmethyl carbocation. Both the carbocations along with their resonating structures are as follows. It is to note that tropylium ion is so far the most stable carbocation known.

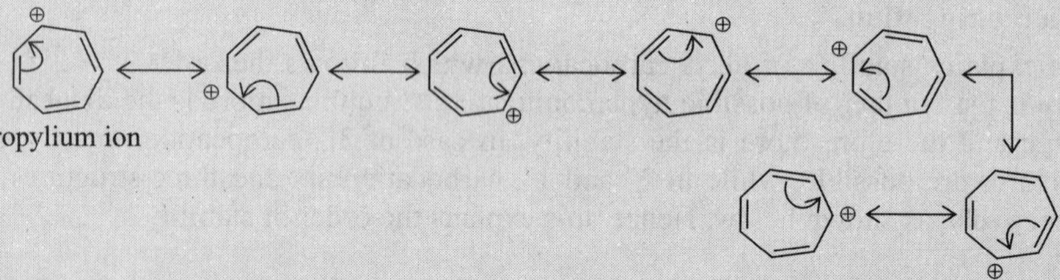

Tropylium ion

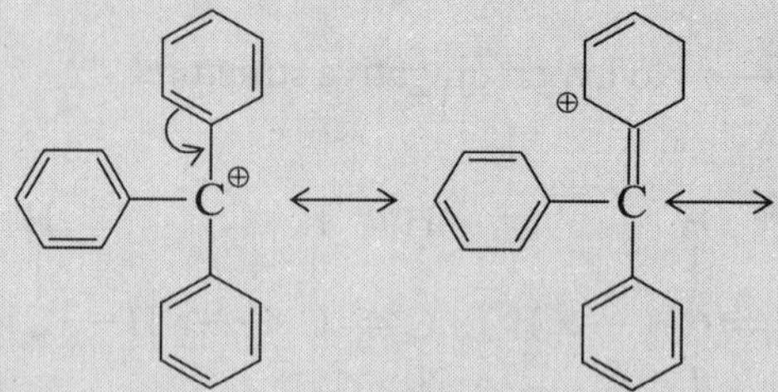

Triphenylmethyl carbocation

2. The overall order of stability of different carbocation is as follows:

tropylium > 3°-benzylie > 2°-benzylie > 3°-alkyl > 1°-benzylie ≈ 1°-allylie ≈ 2°-alkyl > 1°-alkyl > methyl.

Carboanions

Carboanions are negatively charged species containing a carbon atom with six electrons in three bonds and in addition an unshared pair of electrons.

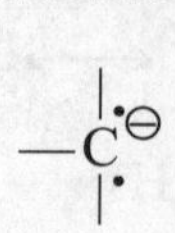

Shape

The carbon atom that carries the negative charge is sp^3 hybridized. Out of four sp^3 hybrid orbitals of carbons three remain utilized in forming bonds with three other atoms or groups. The fourth one carries the electron pair.

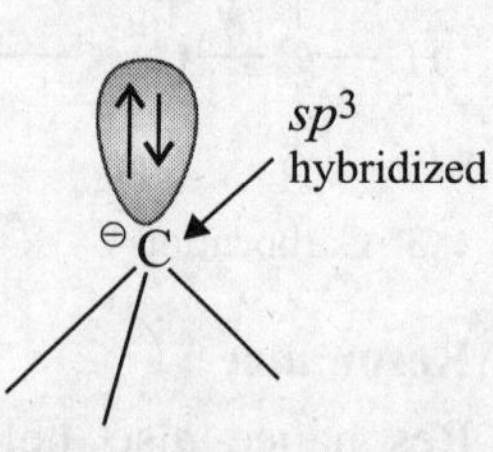

Fig. 10.7 Carboanion

Types

Carboanions are classified as primary, secondary, or tertiary depending upon the nature of the carbon atom bearing the negative charge.

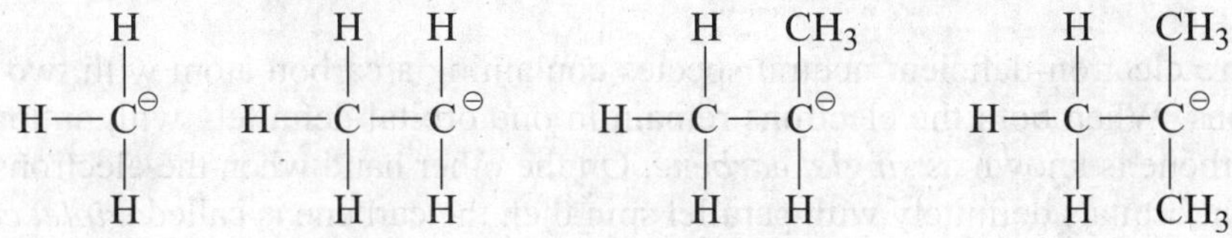

Methyl carboanion, Ethyl carboanion — 1° Carboanion; Isopropyl carboanion — 2° Carboanion; *t*-butyl carboanion — 3° Carboanion

Stability

Stability of a charged species increases by the dispersal of the charge. Therefore, any electron displacement mechanism that helps in spreading out the charge present on the electron rich carbon stabilizes the ion. The mechanisms mainly responsible for the dispersal of the charge are inductive effect and resonance. The electron-releasing substituents tend to intensify the charge at the electron rich carbon (I) and thereby making it less stable. On the other hand, electron-withdrawing groups tend to decrease the negative charge density on the electron-rich carbon (II) and hence stabilize it.

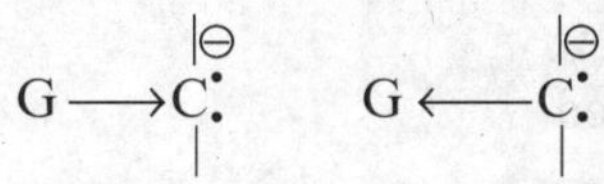

I II

Inductive effect

This explains stability of alkyl carboanions which follows the order: methyl > 1° > 2° > 3°. Increased number of alkyl groups at the carbon carrying the negative charge decreases the stability by intensifying the electron density through +I effect.

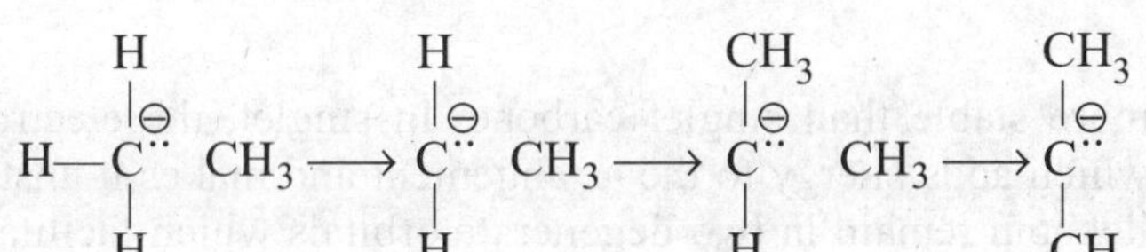

Resonance

Resonance also helps in delocalizing the –ve charge and thereby explains stability of carboanions, e.g., in case of benzyl and allyl carboanions.

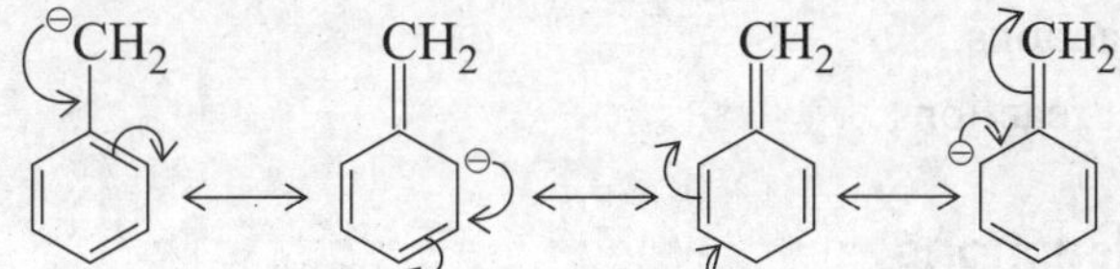

Benzyl carboanion

Allyl carboanion

Note: The overall order of stability of carboanions is as follows: benzyl- > allyl- > methyl- > 1° > 2° > 3°.

Carbene

Carbenes are electron-deficient neutral species containing a carbon atom with two bonds and two electrons. When both the electrons remain in one orbital definitely with antiparallel spin then the carbene is known as *singlet carbene*. On the other hand when the electrons remain in two different orbitals definitely with parallel spin then the carbene is called *triplet carbene.*

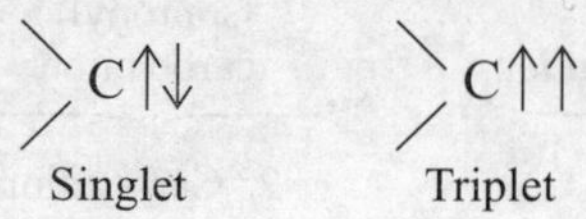

Shape

In singlet carbene the carbon is sp^2 hybridized. Out of the three hybrid orbitals so formed two remain utilized in forming bonds with other atoms or groups. The third hybrid orbital carries the two electrons with opposite spin. In contrast the carbon atom in triplet carbene is *sp* hybridized. The two hybrid orbitals remain utilized in forming bonds with other atoms/groups. The unhybridised *p*-orbitals which remain perpendicular to the internuclear axis carry one electron each with parallel spin.

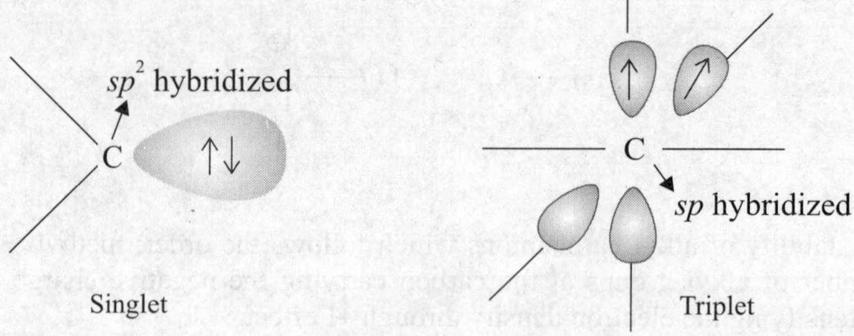

Stability

Triplet carbene is more stable than singlet carbene. In singlet, the electrons remain paired with opposite spin which adds energy to the arrangement and makes it unstable. In triplet the electrons with parallel spin remain in two degenerate orbitals which facilitate their exchange. The exchange lowers the energy of the arrangement and makes it relatively more stable.

Different organic reactions can be broadly classified into the following four types:

A. Substitution reactions
B. Addition reactions
C. Elimination reactions
D. Rearrangement reactions

A. Substitution Reactions

Nucleophilic Substitution (S_N) Reactions

In organic chemistry, nucleophilic substitution is a fundamental class of substitution reaction in which an electron-rich nucleophile initiates the process. A typical nucleophilic substitution reaction is shown as follows:

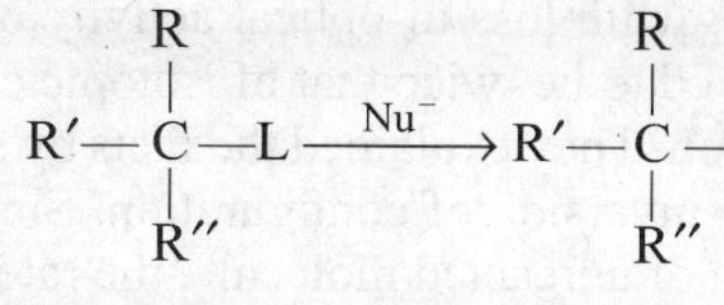

Edward D. Hughes and Sir Christopher Ingold in 1935 studied nucleophilic substitution reactions of alkyl halides and related compounds. According to them there are two main mechanisms at work and both of them competing with each other, viz., substitution nucleophilic unimolecular (S_N1) and substitution nucleophilic bimolecular (S_N2) mechanism. In addition rarely another mechanism is encountered which is known as substitution nucleophilic internal (S_Ni) mechanism.

Bimolecular nucleophilic substitution (S_N2) mechanism

Let us consider the nucleophilic substitution reaction of a typical alkyl halide say methyl bromide in aqueous NaOH solution.

$$\underset{\text{Substrate}}{CH_3Br} + \underset{\text{Nucleophile}}{\overset{\ominus}{O}H} \longrightarrow \underset{\text{Product}}{CH_3OH} + \underset{\text{Leaving group}}{Br^{\ominus}}$$

Mechanism

Kinetics data reveals that the rate depends on concentration of both substrate and nucleophile.

Rate $\propto$ $[CH_3Br]\,[OH^-]$

To fit into kinetic data Ingold suggested a concerted mechanism. In this path the nucleophile attacks the C atom from the side opposite to that of leaving group to form the transition state (TS). In TS, both nucleophile and leaving group, i.e., —OH and —Br carry partial negative charges as —OH has started to share its electrons, while —Br has started departing along with its shared pair. C is sp^2 hybridized in this state. Thus the three "H" atoms and carbon lie in one plane with "C—OH" and "C—Br" bonds lying perpendicular to the plane. The TS subsequently collapses to form the products. The energy required to break the "C—Br" bond is compensated by the energy released during the making of the "C—OH" bond.

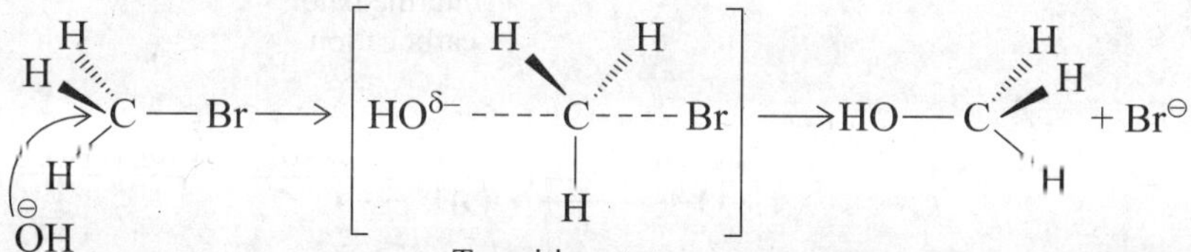

Transition state

Stereochemistry

S_N2 reactions always proceed with the inversion of configuration as nucleophile always attacks from the rear backside of the leaving group. This is popularly known as *Walden inversion configuration* which can be compared to the turning inside-out of an umbrella in strong wind. The experimental evidence can be gathered by carrying out substitution at an optically active carbon and measuring the specific rotation of both substrate and product.

However, one problem still persists that optical rotation and configuration of two different compounds are not necessarily related. Hughes and Ingold came with an innovative solution to establish the inversion of configuration. They allowed optically active 2-iodooctane to react with sodium iodide carrying isotopically labeled I* in dry acetone solution and observed exchange of I* with ordinary I along with loss of optical activity of substrate. Again the rate of loss of optical activity was observed to be twice that of isotopic exchange. The rate law had confirmed the S_N2 path for the reaction. They explained the facts by saying that the nucleophile attacked from backside bringing the inversion of configuration. Since the rotation of inverted molecule exactly cancels the rotation of unreacted molecule, the rate of loss of activity is twice the rate of isotopic exchange.

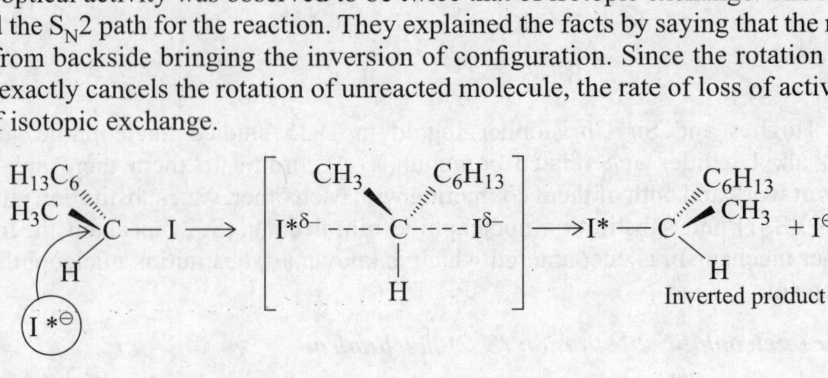

Unimolecular nucleophilic substitution (S_N1) mechanism

Let us consider the nucleophilic substitution reaction at a tertiary C center. To be precise, say substitution reaction of *t*-butyl bromide in aqueous NaOH.

$$(CH_3)_3C\,Br + OH^- \longrightarrow (CH_3)_3COH + Br^-$$

Mechanism

From Kinetics it has been found that rate is proportional to only substrate concentration.

$$\text{Rate} \propto [(CH_3)_3CBr]$$

To fit into kinetic data a two-step mechanism has been proposed. First step involves ionization of the substrate forming an intermediate carbocation. This is the slow step, i.e., rate-controlling step. The second step involves the attack of nucleophile to the electron-deficient carbon to form the product.

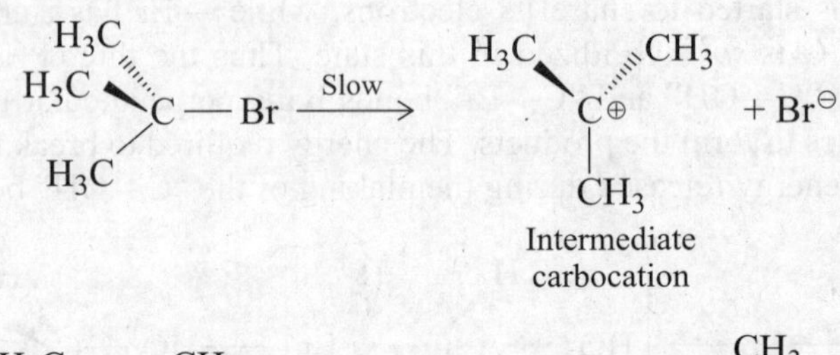

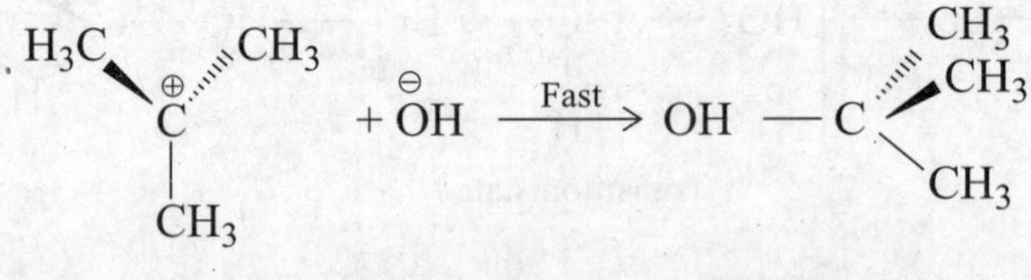

Stereochemistry

In the intermediate, the C atom is sp^2 hybridized. The three groups which remain attached to "C" lie in one plane while the unhybridised empty *p* orbital remains perpendicular to the plane. As both lobes seem to be equally available for the attack of nucleophile, the product is expected to be completely racemic. However, in real practice the product is partially racemized with higher percentage of inverted configuration. The reason being the leaving group after departure remains in close proximity of carbocation forming ion pair which remains as asymmetrically solvated carbocation (I). This ion pair prevents front side attack of Nu- and the result being nucleophilic attack takes place from back side forming inverted product. If carbocation (I) is stable enough then leaving group is replaced by solvent molecules forming symmetrically solvated carbocation (II) in which the nucleophile can attack from both sides forming an inverted as well as a retained product. Therefore, the stability of carbocation (I) decides the extent of racemization. More the stability more is the extent of racemization.

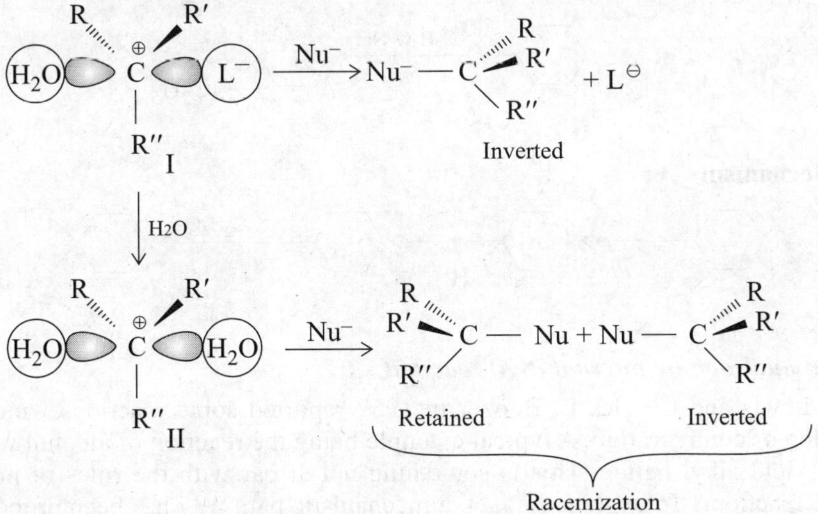

Regioselectivity

There is always a possibility of rearrangement in the carbocation intermediate before the attachment of nucleophile, e.g.

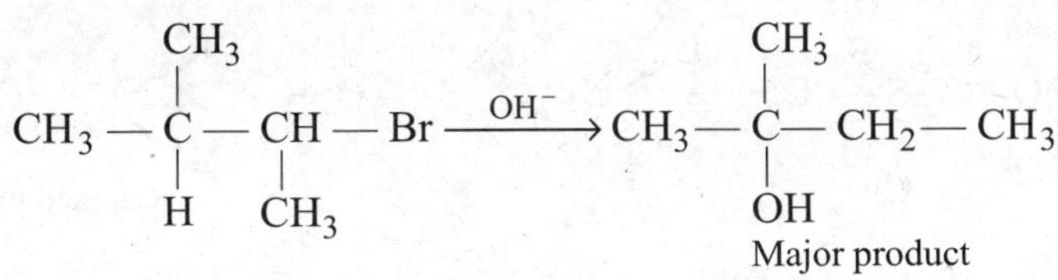

Mechanism

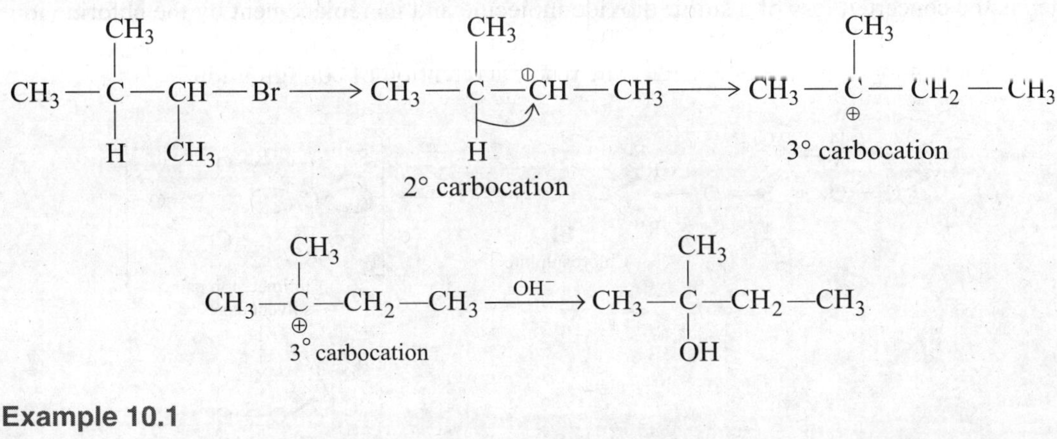

Example 10.1

Write the product and suggest the suitable mechanism.

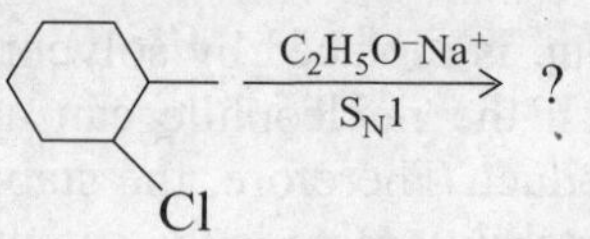

Solution

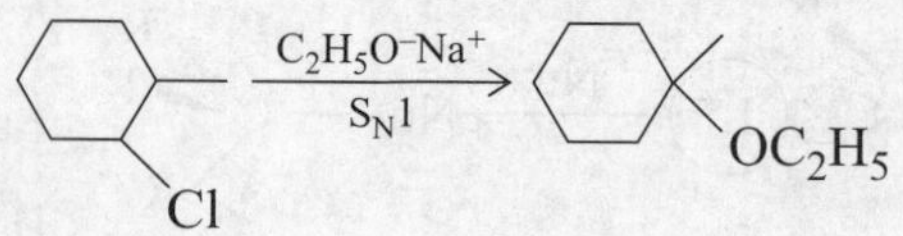

Mechanism

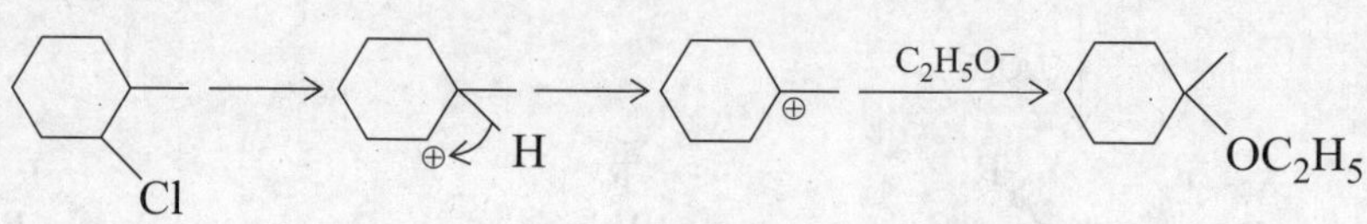

Substitution nucleophilic internal (S_Ni) reaction

Edward S. Lewis and Charles E. Boozer in 1952 reported some reactions which proceed with retention of configuration. A typical example being the reaction of alcohol with thionyl chloride to yield alkyl halide. This is something not at par with the rules of nucleophilic substitution reactions. To explain the fact, a mechanistic path way has been proposed which proceeds through a cyclic transition state facilitating the attack of nucleophile from front side of the leaving group. In the mechanism, both substrate and thionyl chloride remain in the rate-controlling step.

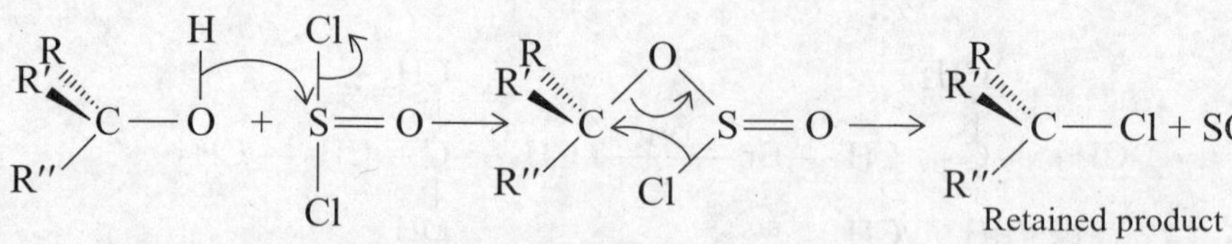

In recent years, a different approach to the mechanism has been established. In this path, the decomposition of chlrosulphite starts with the formation of an intimate ion pair. The second step is the concerted loss of a sulfur dioxide molecule and its replacement by the chloride ion, which was attached to the sulfite group. The Cl^- ion cannot get out of the solvent cage to attack the carbonium ion from the other side. The result is retention of configuration.

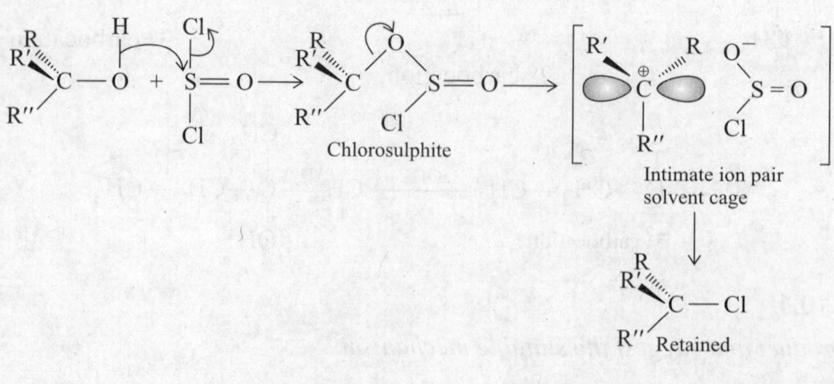

Note:

Addition of pyridine to the above reaction mixture yields alkyl halide with inverted configuration. This is due to the fact that pyridine being a strong base reacts with chlorosulfite intermediate to form free Cl^- ions which subsequently attack in S_N2 fashion from rear leading to inverted product. There is also an evidence for another mechanistic path where P_y reacts with HCl to form free Cl^- in the beginning.

mech-I

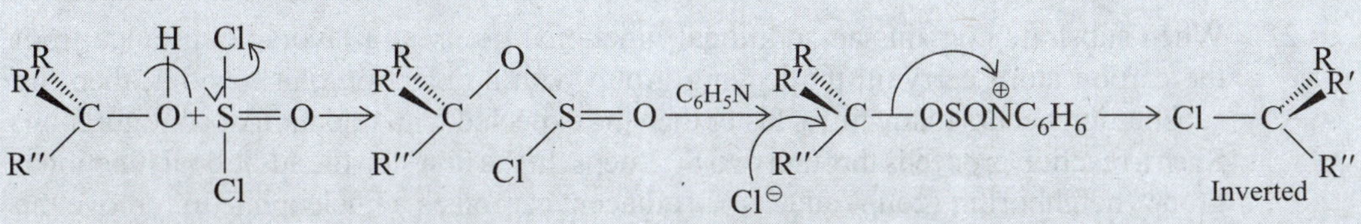

mech-II

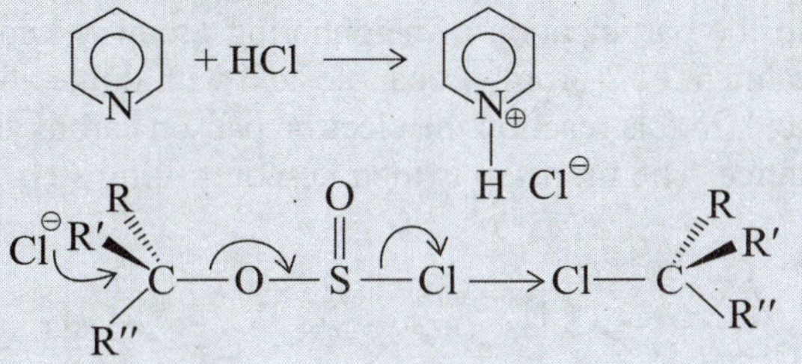

Factors influencing S_N reaction

1. **Nature of substrate**

S_N2: Here steric factor at the "C" center undergoing nucleophilic attack is very important. In this case Nu^- has to approach substrate from backside. When H atoms that remain attached to C atom undergoing substitution are replaced by bulky alkyl groups, Nu^- finds it increasingly difficult to approach from back side due to steric hindrance. Again bulky substituents make transition state over crowded resulting in significant nonbonding interactions. This increases the energy of transition state. The results being lowering of rate of substitution through S_N2 mechanism Thus relative ease of substitution through this mechanism follows the order: CH_2 > 1°- > 2°- > 3°-.

S_N1: In this mechanism stability of intermediate carbocation plays the important role. As stability of carbocation follows the order: 3° > 2° > 1° > —CH_3 the relative sate of substitution through the S_N1 mechanism follows the order: 3°- > 2°- > 1°- > -CH_2.

Note:

1. Molecules such as 1-bromobicyclo [2, 2, 1] heptane and 1-bromotriptycene having good leaving groups at bridge head position do not prefer to participate in substitution. This is because of the fact that due to steric hindrance Nu^- cannot approach from rear and lack of planarity at bridge head does not allow the formation of carbocation. Thus, S_N2 as well as S_N1 mechanisms cannot be operative efficiently to form any substituted product.

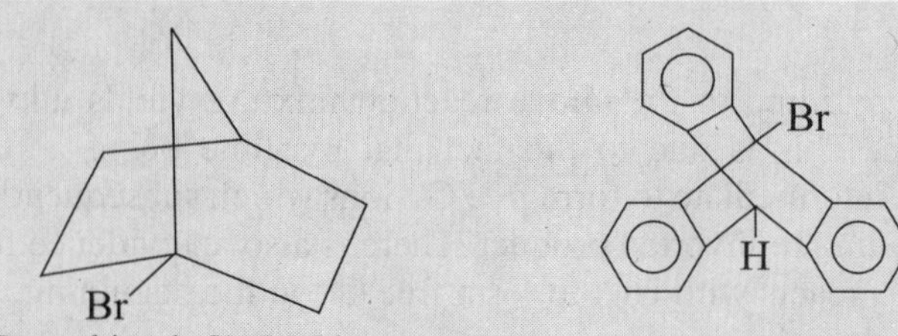

1-Bromobicyclo [2, 2, 1] heptane　　1-Bromotriptycene

2. When substrate contains an additional functional group at a favorable distance from the carbon atom carrying the leaving group with an electron pair to offer, then the substitution occurs many times faster than the expected with retention of configuration. Such a reaction proceeds through two S_N2 steps. In the first step the additional functional group (neighboring group) attacks the adjacent carbon as a nucleophile to remove the leaving group. In the second step the external nucleophile attaches itself to the site of leaving group. Due to two consecutive inversions the product obtained is a retained one. The rate enhancement due to the participation of neighboring group is known as *anchimeric assistance*, e.g., treatment of 2-bromopropanoic acid with dilute alkali results in the formation of lactic acid. In this reaction the electron pair on carboxylate anion provides anchimeric assistance. The first step is the rate-controlling step.

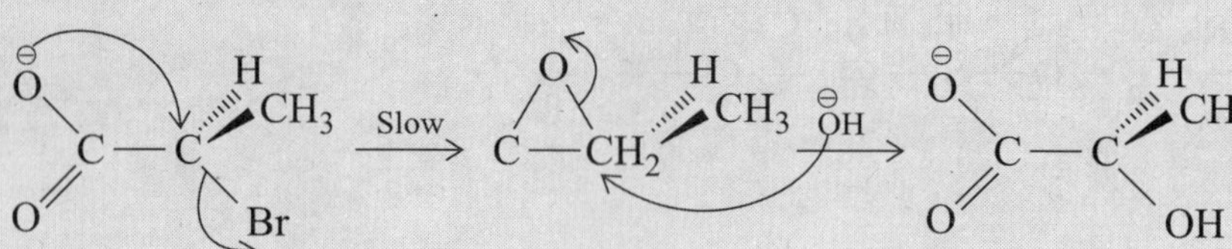

2-Bromopropanoate ion　　Lactate anion

However, in presence of strong alkali, hydroxide ion competes with carboxylate anion and the substrate undergoes normal S_N2 reaction to yield inverted product.

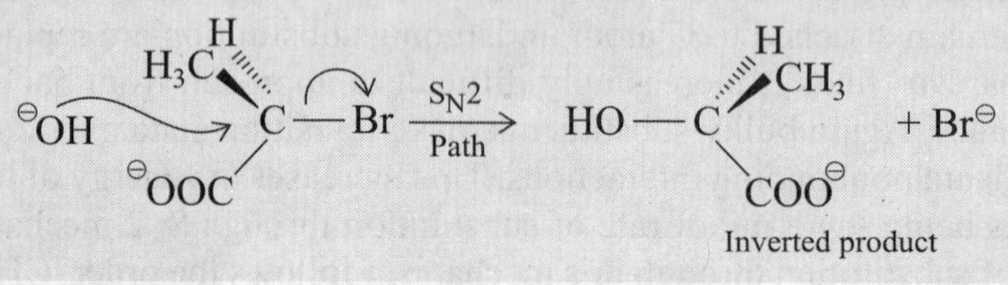

Inverted product

2. **Nature of solvent**

S_N2: In S_N2 mechanism rate significantly changes upon changing the solvent from polar protic to polar aprotic solvents such as dimethyl sulphoxide (DMSO) and dimethyl formamide (DMF). These solvents stabilize Nu^- through weak van der Waal's forces so that at the time of attack the solvent cage easily breaks which makes that a more powerful nucleophile. In contrast in polar protic solvents such as H_2O and MeOH the solvation occurs through much effective hydrogen bonding which reduces the nucleophilicity of the nucleophile to do S_N2 attack.

S_N1: In contrast to S_N2, S_N1 reaction occurs with the initial ionization of neutral molecule, and thus it is facilitated by good ionizing solvents. Cations are solvated by the solvent molecules through co-ordination with electron pairs whereas anions are solvated by solvent molecules through hydrogen bonding. The ionizing ability of different solvents can be compared with respect to their dielectric constants. The ionizing ability of some common polar solvents in decreasing order of dielectric constant values is as follows: $H_2O > HCOOH > CH_3OH > C_2H_5OH > CH_3COOH$

3. **Nature of nucleophile**

S_N2: Stronger nucleophiles cause faster rate. All nucleophiles are bases in a true sense but the nucleophilicity of a reagent, i.e., its ability to donate an electron pair to an electron-deficient carbon, may or may not remain parallel to its basicity which is defined as its ability to give an electron pair to proton, e.g., OH^- ion is strong base and also a good nucleophile but I^- ion is a very weak base but still a good nucleophile. The difference can be explained partly with respect to soft and hard bases. For a given degree of basicity, *softness* favours nucleophilicity which increases with polarizability. Some common nucleophiles in order of their relative nucleophilicity are: $CN^- > I^- > RS^- > OH^- \approx C_2H_5O^- > Br^- > Cl^- > NO_3^-$

Note:

1. **Soft and hard bases**

A soft base is that in which the donor atom is of low electronegativity, high polarisability, and easy to oxidise, e.g., RS^-, I^-, and CN^-. On the other hand, a hard base is that in which the donor atom is of high electronegativity, low polarisability, and difficult to oxidise e.g. OH^-, OR^- etc.

2. **Steric factor of nuecleophile**

Steric factors of nucleophile sometimes play significant role, e.g., quinuclidine reacts significantly faster than triethylamine, with isopropyl bromide. The reason being, in quinuclidine, the substituents are tied back by ring system, whereas freely rotating ethyl groups of triethylamine cover the unshared pair of electrons on nitrogen.

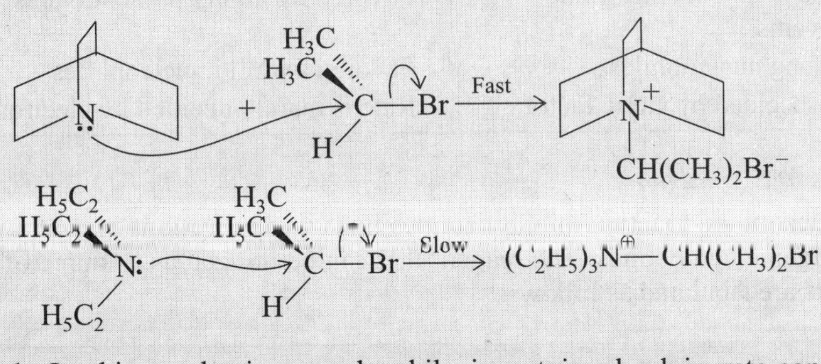

S_N1**:** In this mechanism, nucleophile is not involved in rate-controlling step. Therefore, the nucleophile does not affect the rate. However, if several nucleophiles are present, then the best one forms the major product.

3. **Nature of leaving group**

As leaving group breaks away with the shared pair of electron-weak bases are easier to be displaced in comparison to strong bases. Thus, the less basic is the substituent, more easily it can be displaced by an attacking nucleophile in S_N2 reactions and by the solvent in S_N1 reactions.

Note:

The stronger and harder is the base, less easily it can be displaced. Therefore, OH^- and NH_2^- are difficult to be displaced by other nucleophiles. However, displacement in such a case can be made effective by modifying the leaving group often through protonation, e.g., alcohols do not undergo substitution in neutral medium but readily do so in acidic medium, since their corresponding protonated forms (viz., H_2O and NH_3) are comparatively weak bases and hence better leaving groups.

$$R\text{—}OH + Br^{\ominus} \longrightarrow \text{No reaction}$$

$$\xrightarrow{H^+} R\text{—}Br + H_2O$$

Mechanism

$$R\text{—}OH + H^+ \longrightarrow R\text{—}\overset{\oplus}{O}H_2 \xrightarrow{\overset{\ominus}{Br}} R\text{—}Br + H_2O$$

Comparative account of S_N2 and S_N1

S_N2	S_N1
One-step mechanism	Two-step mechanism
Bimolecular reaction	Unimolecular reaction
Product is completely inverted	Partially racemized product with higher percent of inversion
No rearranged product is formed	The carbocation formed may undergo rearrangement
Favored by less polar solvents/polar non-protic solvents	Favored by highly polar solvents
Favored by strong nucleophiles	Favored by mild nucleophiles
Rate is mainly decided by steric factor	Rate is mainly decided by electronic factor

Some examples of S_N reactions

Nucleophilic substitution reaction of alkyl halides finds its applications in synthesis of almost all classes of organic compounds. The reagent that can be utilized as a source of nucleophile and the products are tabulated as follows:

S. No.	Source of nucleophile/ nucleophile	Product
1.	Aq. KOH/Ag_2O in boiled Water/OH^-	Alcohol
2.	RO^-Na^+ (Sodium alkoxide)/RO^-	Ether. The reaction is known as Williamson synthesis.
3.	Alc. NH_3 under pressure/itself	1° amines (in practice the reaction continues to form 20-amine, 30-amine, and finally a quaternary salt, i.e., tetralkyl ammonium halide)

S. No.	Source of nucleophile/ nucleophile	Product
4.	Alc. $RCOO^-Ag^+/RCOO^-$	Ester
5.	Alc. KCN/ NC^-	Alkyl cyanide (Nitrile). Here, cyanide is an ambident ion and attacks through C (form I). $\overset{\ominus}{:C} \equiv N: \longleftrightarrow \ddot{C} = \ddot{N}:^{\ominus}$ (I, II)
6.	AgCN/CN^-	Alkyl isocyanide. AgCN is predominantly covalent and attack takes place through nitrogen i.e. form II (shown in reaction 5)
7.	$NaNO_2$ / $:\overset{\ominus}{\ddot{O}} - \ddot{N} = \ddot{O}$	Alkyl nitrite. Here, $-NO_2$ is an ambident nucleophile. In this case, the attack takes place through nitrogen. $:\overset{\ominus}{\ddot{O}} - \ddot{N} = \ddot{O} \longleftrightarrow \ddot{O} = \ddot{N} - \overset{\ominus}{\ddot{O}}:$
8.	$AgNO_2$ / $:\overset{\ominus}{\ddot{O}} - \ddot{N} = \ddot{O}$	Nitroalkane. $AgNO_2$ is predominantly covalent and the attack takes place through oxygen.

Note:

Alkyl cyanides have a lot of applications in synthesis particularly as through this reaction one can increase the chain length.

$$R - CN + \begin{cases} \xrightarrow{H_2O-HCl} RCOOH \\ \xrightarrow{H_2O-Alk.H_2O_2} RCONH_2 \\ \xrightarrow{LiAlH_4} RCH_2NH_2 \end{cases}$$

Electrophilic Substitution Reactions (S_E)

Electrophilic substitution reactions are common in aromatic systems having extensively delocalized electron cloud. Such a reaction can be in general presented as:

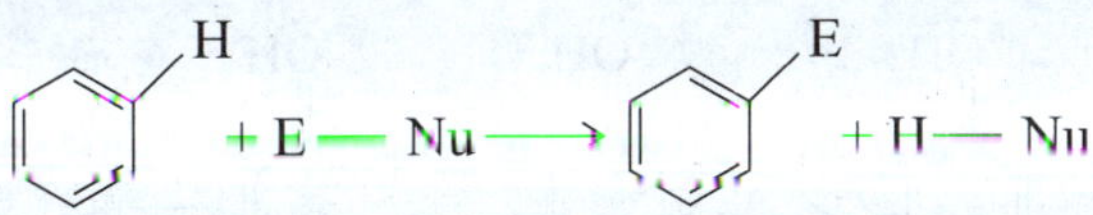

Mechanism

The reaction proceeds via three steps.

Step 1

Generation of electrophile either by spontaneous dissociation of the reagent or by acid catalyzed dissociation.

$$E—Nu \longrightarrow E^+ + Nu^-$$

or $\quad E—Nu + A \text{ (Lewis acid)} \longrightarrow E^+ + NuA^-$

Step 2

Formation of π-complex due to loose association of electrophile with aromatic ring which rearranges to give σ-complex. σ-Complex is resonance stabilized.

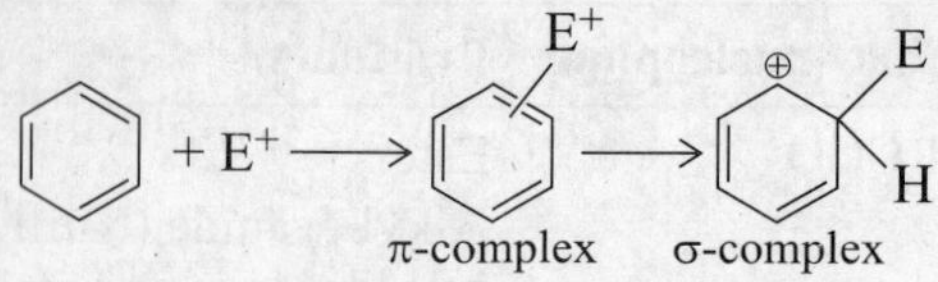

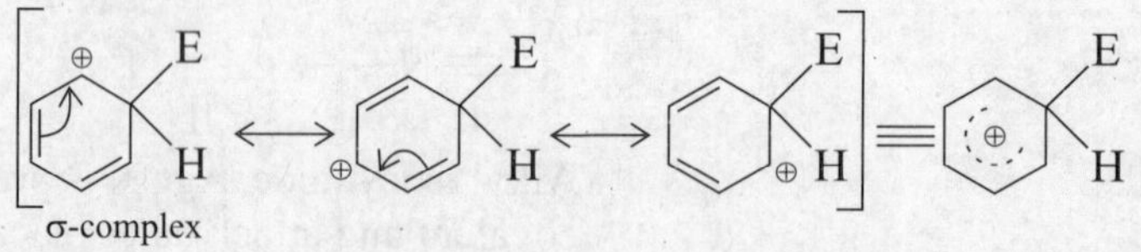

Step 3

Removal of proton form σ-complex and regain of aromaticity.

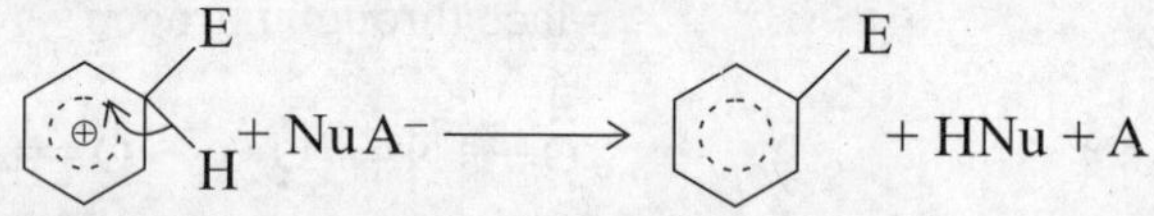

Effect of substituent in electrophilic substitution (orientation)

During electrophilic substitution, the group/s already present on the benzene ring directs / orient(s) the incoming electrophile either to ortho and para positions or only to meta position. This effect is known as directive influence of substituent or orientation effect.

***o*- and *p*-orientation**

Electron-releasing groups orient the incoming electrophile to *o*- and *p*-positions. Some common electron releasing groups in order of their ability to provide electrons are as follows:

$$—NH_2—NR_2 > —OH > —OR > —NHCOR > —OCOR > —C_6H_5 > —CH_3 > —X$$

Explanation: Such groups increases electron density at *o*- and *p*-positions through resonance (hyperconjugation in case of alkyl groups). This can be explained by analysis of resonating structures by taking a specific example where —OH is the substituent. Resonance hybrid clearly shows that *o*- and *p*-positions are relatively richer in electrons and therefore E^+ attacks preferably at *o*- and *p*-positions (indicated by arrow marks).

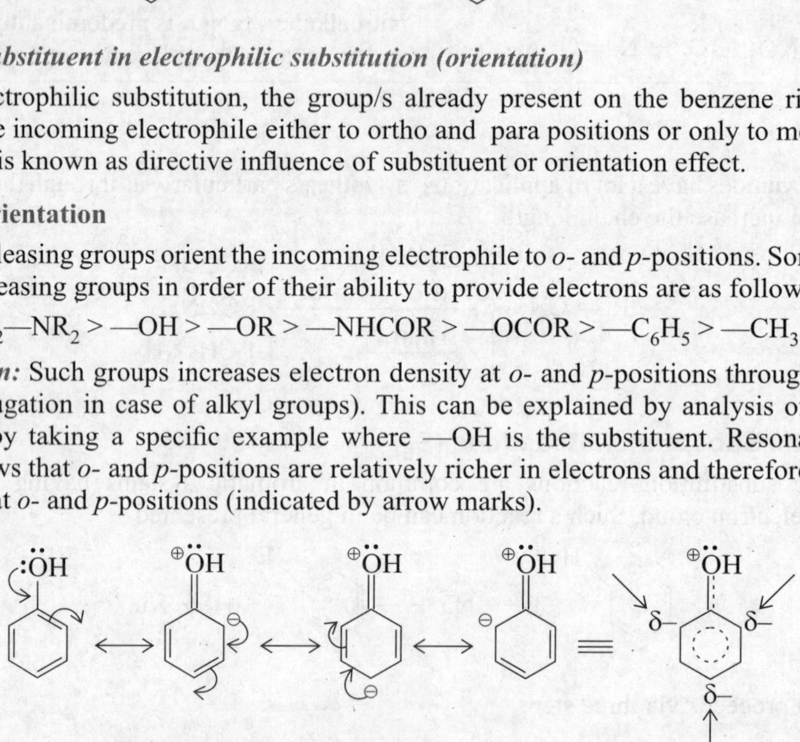

Resonance hybrid

***m*-orientation**

Electron-withdrawing groups orient the incoming electrophile to meta position. Some common electron-withdrawing groups in order of their ability to withdraw electrons are as follows:

$$—\overset{\oplus}{N}R_3 > —NO_2 > —CN > —SO_3H > —CHO > —COOH > —\overset{O}{\overset{\|}{C}}— OR > —\overset{O}{\overset{\|}{C}}— NH_2$$

Explanation: Such groups lower electron density at *o*- and *p*-positions through resonance. This can be explained by showing the resonating structures by taking a specific example where —NO_2 is the substituent. The resonance hybrid clearly shows that *o*- and *p*-positions are now electron deficient. As electron density is lowered at *o*- and *p*-positions, *m*-position remains relatively richer in electron. Thus, E^+ preferably attacks the *m*-position.

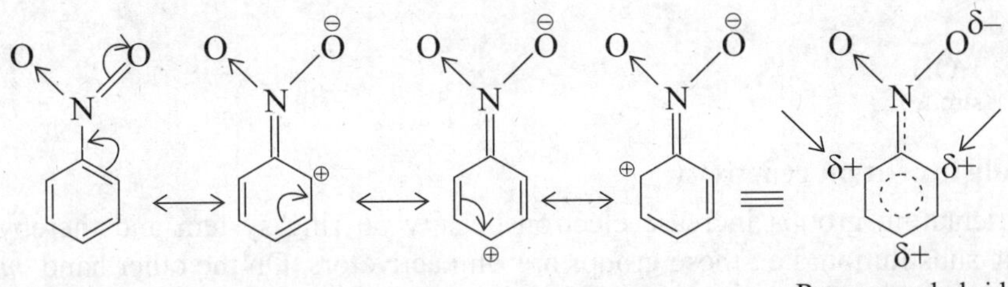

Competitive orientation in disubstituted rings

With the help of the principle that *during electrophilic substitution electron-releasing groups decide the further course of substitution,* it is possible to predict the orientation in disubstituted rings. Let us look into the following possibilities;

1. If two groups of similar or different orientation reinforce each other then it is easy to predict the position of the third group (indicated by arrow heads).

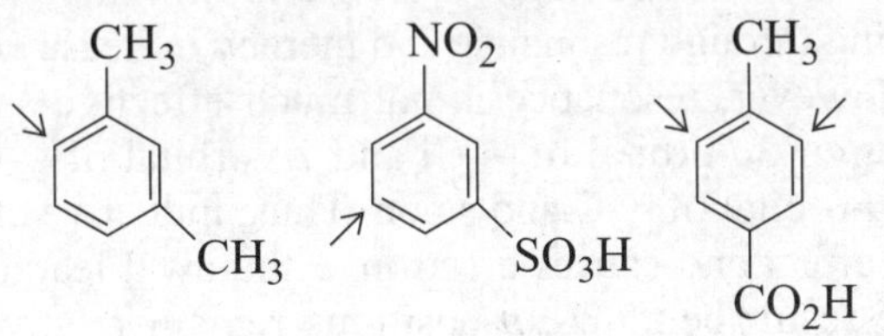

2. If the competition is there between an *o-/p*-orienting and an *m*-orienting group, the former overwhelms the effect of latter as it activates the ring by releasing electrons into it. When two such substituents are present meta to each other then the third substituent rarely enters into the position in between these groups due to steric hindrance and mostly it enters into ortho to *m*-orienting groups (Ortho effect).

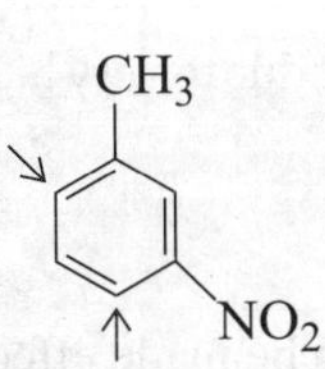

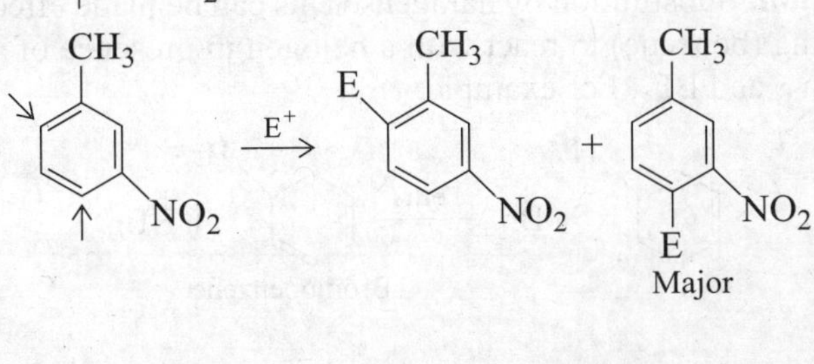

Major

3. If the competition is there between two *o*-, *p*-orienting groups then the group, having relatively more ability to release electron decides the orientation.

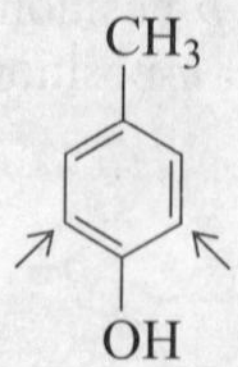

(strong)

Effect of substituent on reactivity

o- and *p*-orientating groups increase electron density on ring system and thereby facilitate electrophilic substitution, i.e., these groups are ring activators. On the other hand, *m*-orienting groups lower electron density on ring system and thereby decrease the rate of electrophilic substitution, i.e., these groups are ring deactivators.

Note:

1. *Halogens (Cl^-,Br^-, and I^-) are o- and p-orienting but at the same time are ring deactivators:*

   This anomalous behavior can be explained by considering the resultant of inductive and resonance effects. Halogens withdraw electrons through inductive effect causing deactivation of the ring. At the same time they also share their electron pair with the ring through resonance and thereby increase electron density at *o*- and *p*-positions. However, resonance is not much effective as it takes place through the overlapping of 3*p*-orbital of —Cl and 2*p*-orbital of —C or through 4*p*-orbital of —Br and 2*p*-orbital of —C and so on. Thus, inductive effect easily overwhelms the resonance effect and causes electron withdrawal leading to deactivation at all positions. The result being *o*-, *p*-positions remain relatively richer in electrons. Therefore, reactivity is controlled by inductive effect while orientation by resonance.
2. *Although oxygen is more electronegative than —Cl or —Br, yet the —OH group is an activating group while the latter are deactivating*:

   Here, in case of —OH group, the sharing of electron pair takes place through overlapping of 2*p*-orbital of —O and 2*p*-orbital of —C which is very effective as compared to 3*p*- and 2*p*-overlap in case of —Cl. Thus, resonance effect overwhelms the inductive effect and controls both reactivity and orientation.
3. In case of —F, inductive effect is relatively stronger due to very high electronegativity of F than resonance and control reactivity.

Some specific examples

1. **Halogenation:** Substitution by halogens. This can be made effective by allowing the aromatic ring (benzene) to react with a halogen in presence of a Lewis acid such as $FeCl_3$, $AlBr_3$, and BF_3. For example,

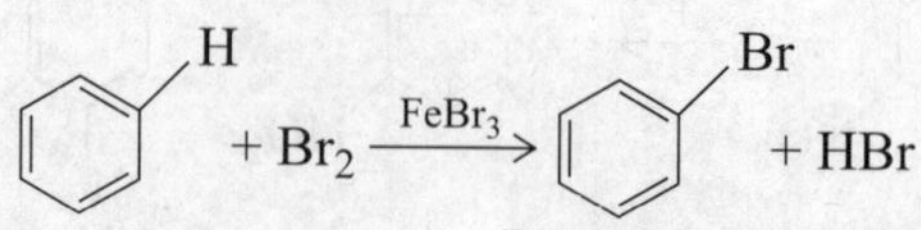

Mechanism

$$FeBr_3 + Br_2 \longrightarrow \underbrace{Br^+}_{\text{Electrophile}} + FeBr_4^-$$

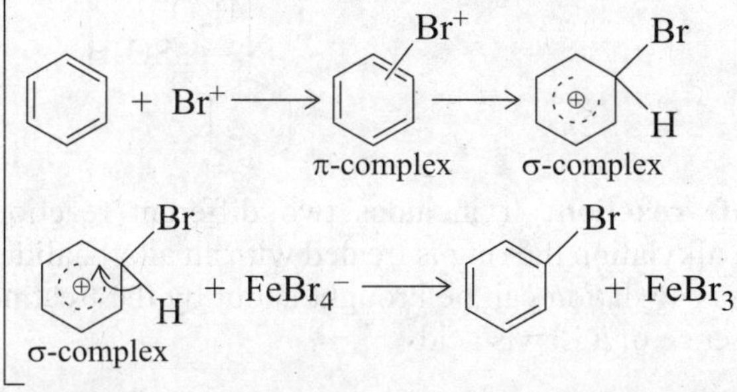

2. **Nitration:** Substitution by $-NO_2$ group. This can be made effective by allowing benzene to react with Conc. HNO_3 in presence of Conc. H_2SO_4.

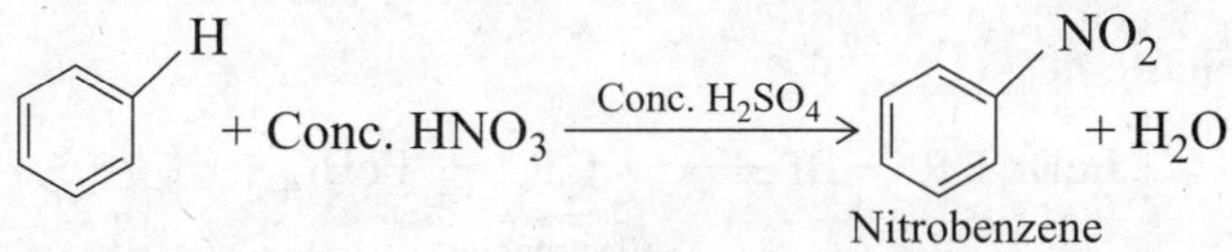

Mechanism

$$HNO_3 + H_2SO_4 \longrightarrow \underbrace{NO_2^+}_{\text{Electrophile}} + HSO_4^{\ominus} + H_2O$$

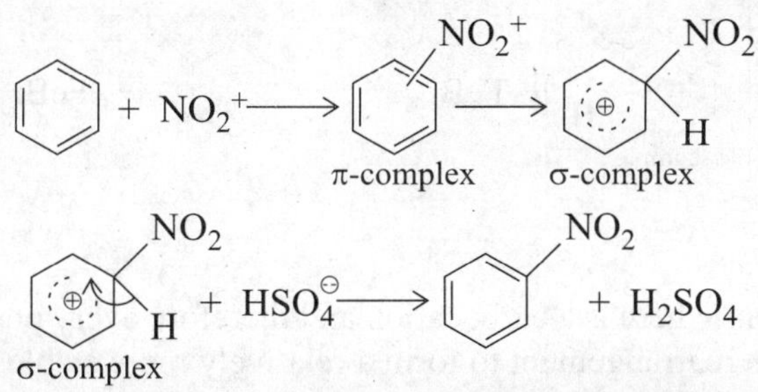

3. **Sulphonation:** Substitution by $-SO_3H$ group. This can be made effective by allowing benzene to react with fuming sulphuric acid ($H_2SO_4 \cdot SO_3$).

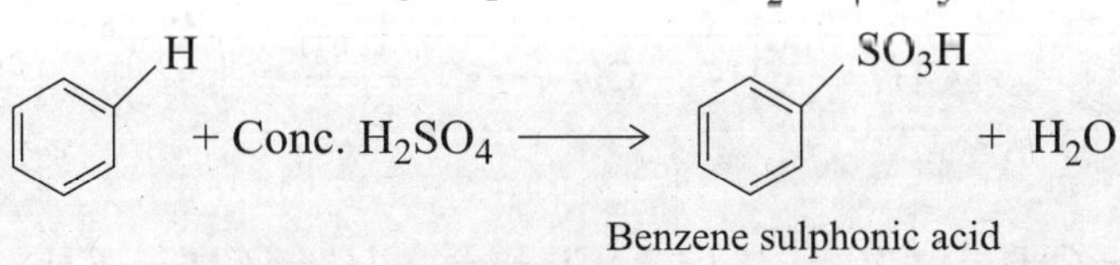

Mechanism

$$2H_2SO_4 \longrightarrow \underbrace{SO_3}_{\text{Electrophile}} + HSO_4^{\ominus} + H_3O^+$$

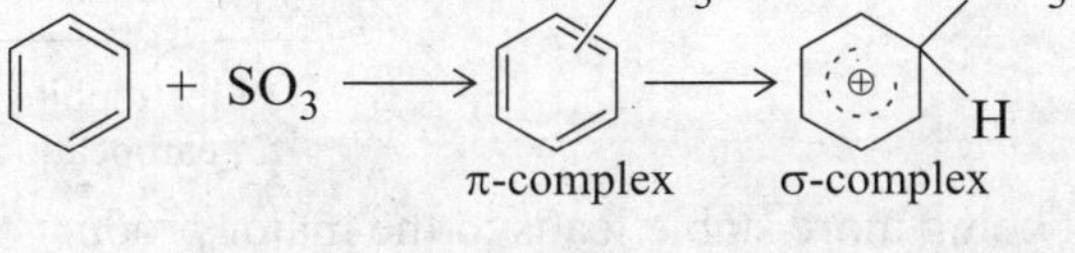

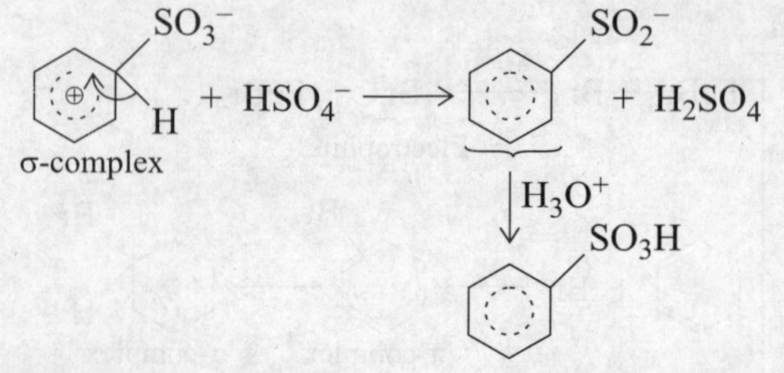

4. **Freidel-Craft reaction:** It includes two different reactions viz. *alkylation* and *acylation*. In alkylation the ring is treated with an alkyl halide in presence of a Lewis acid. Where as acylation can be brought about by the treatment with an acid halide again in presence of a Lewis acid.

(a) *Alkylation*

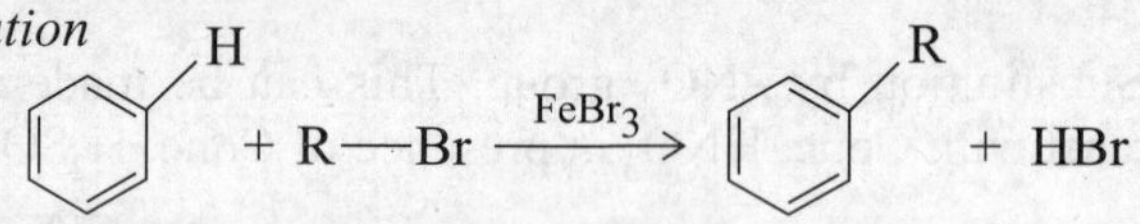

Mechanism

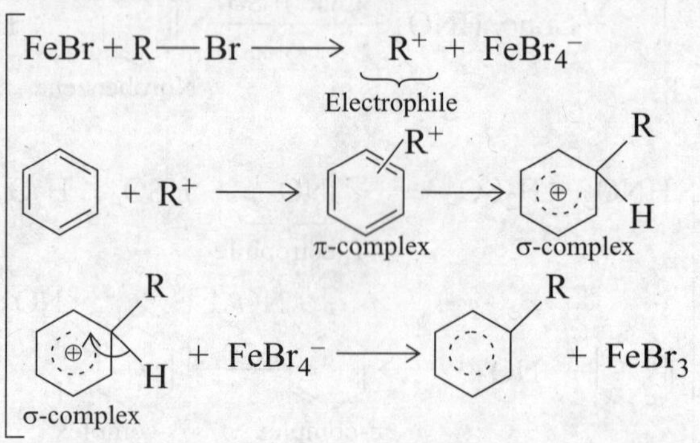

Note:

1. The electrophile here is a carbocation and therefore every possibility is there that it may undergo rearrangement to form a relatively more stable carbocation e.g.

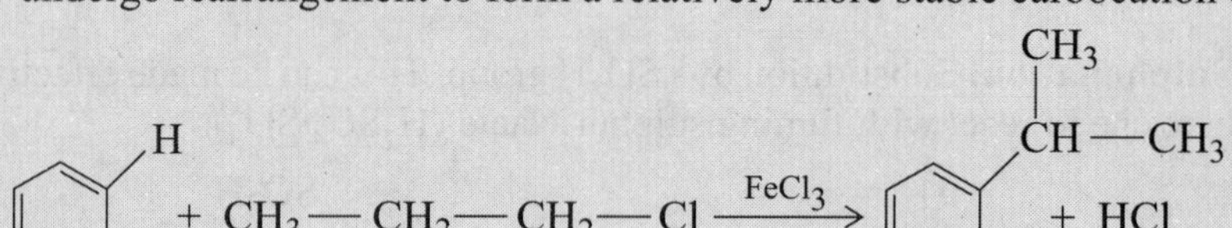

Mechanism

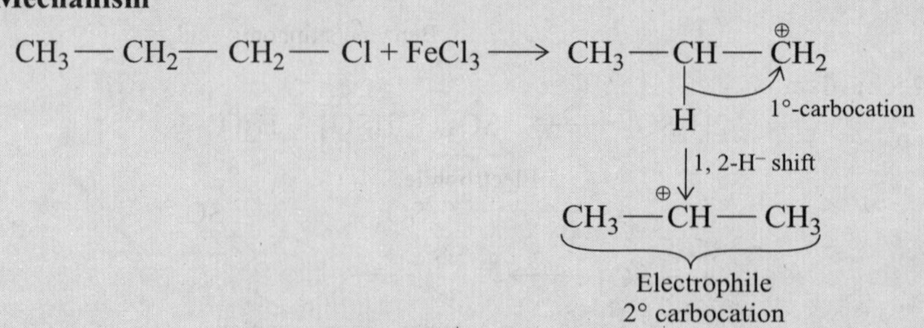

2° carbocation being more stable leads to the major product

2. Introduction of alkyl group activates the ring therefore in presence of excess alkyl halide disubstited products are formed.

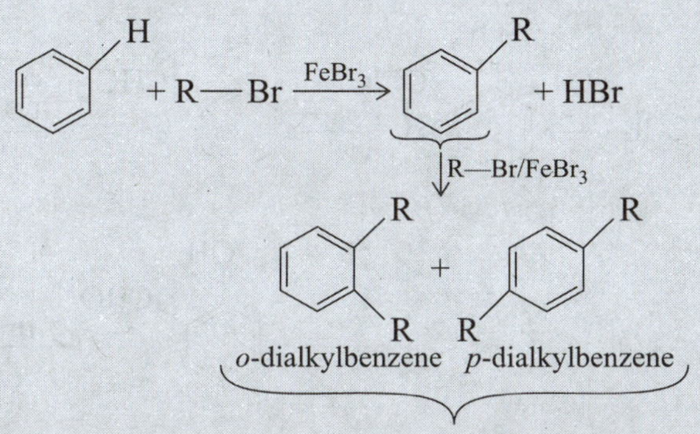

3. *m*-orienting groups present in the ring deactivate the ring and therefore does not favour Friedel-Craft reaction. This is why nitrobenzene does not respond to Friedel-Craft reaction.

(b) *Acylation*

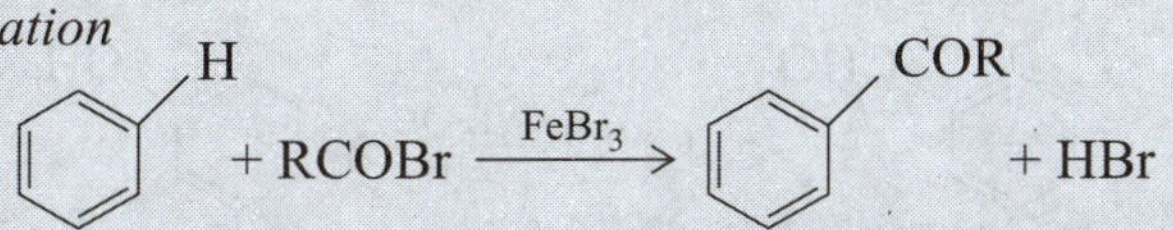

Mechanism

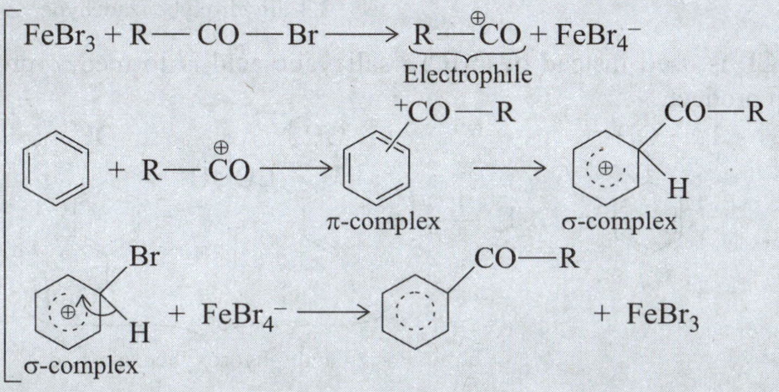

4. **Reimer-Tiemann reaction:** Phenol upon treatment with alkaline chloroform yields *o*- and *p*-hydroxybenzalde-hydes The reaction is known as Reimer-Tiemann reaction. This reaction is an example of electrophilic substitution reaction.

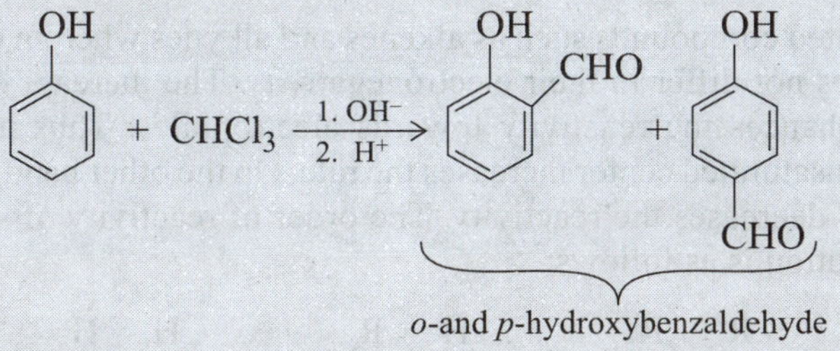

Mechanism

In the reaction dichlorocarbene is formed in the first step. In the subcequent step the phenoxide ion attacks the electron deficient dichlorocarbene to form benzal chloride which on hydrolysis followed by acidification gives the aldehyde.

$$CHCl_3 + OH^- \xrightarrow{-H_2O} {}^{\ominus}CCl_3 \xrightarrow{-Cl^-} :CCl_2$$

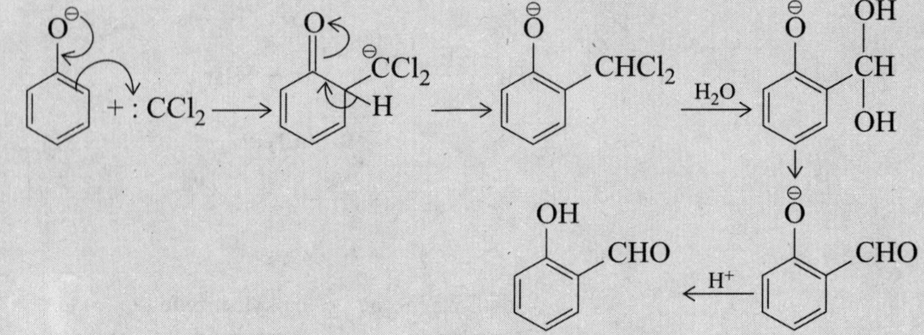

Note:

1. Though mixture of *o*- and *p*- products are formed, *o*-product predominates. If an *o*-position is occupied, then the aldehydes group is introduced at *p*-position.

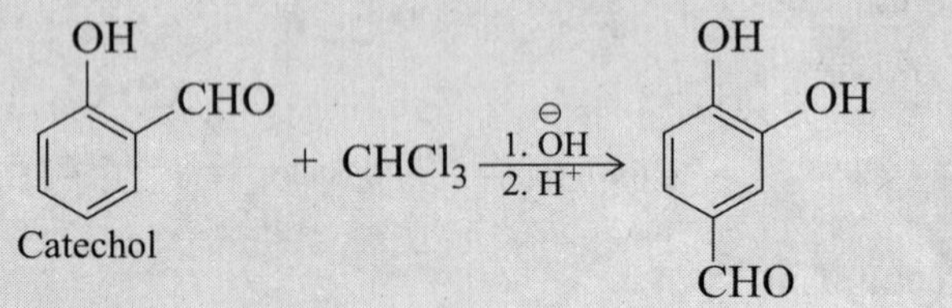

Catechol

3,4-dihydroxybenzadehyde

2. If CCl_4 is used instead of $CHCl_3$, salicyclic acid is formed, *o*-product being the main product.

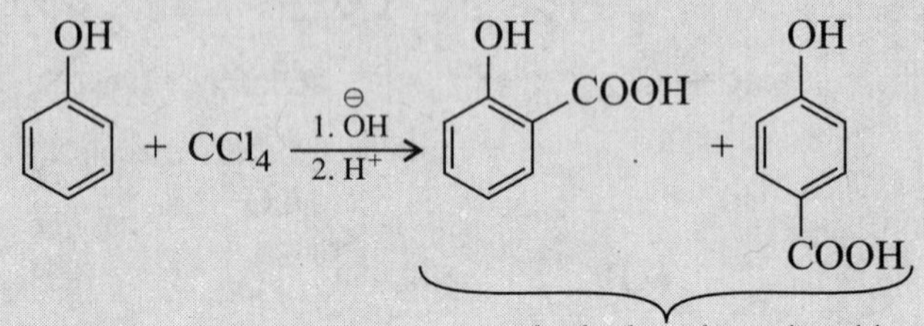

o- and *p*-hydroxybenzoic acid

B. Addition Reactions

Electrophilic Addition (Ad_E) Reactions

Addition to unsaturated compounds such as alkenes and alkynes wherein the atoms are carrying the unsaturation does not differ in their electronegativity. The increase of electron density on the double bond enhances the reactivity towards electrophiles. Thus, the electron-releasing groups attached to unsaturated center increases the rate. On the other hand, presence of electron-withdrawing groups decreases the reactivity. The order of reactivity of some alkenes towards electrophilic substitution is as follows:

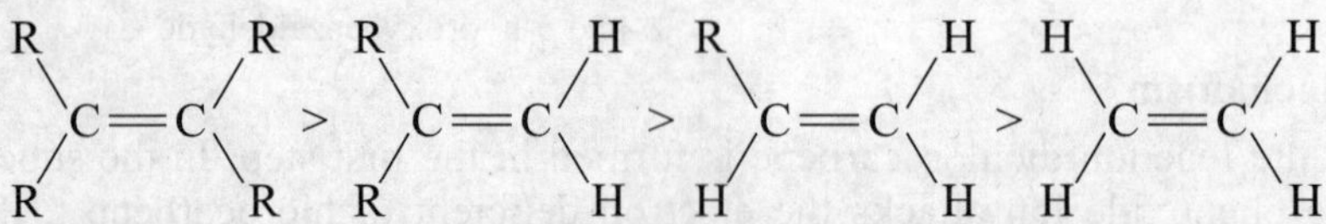

Let us discuss some electrophilic addition reactions along with their mechanism.

1. **Addition of halogens**

Addition of halogens to alkenes yields trans-1,2-dihalides. The mechanism being the diffused π-electron cloud of alkene induces polarity in the non-polar halogen molecule as it comes to close proximity. Then, a π-complex is formed which represents a loose association of halogen with π-electron cloud of alkene. Then the π-complex subsequently gets transformed into the intermediate *cyclic halonium ion* The halide ion then attacks the intermediate from rear to form trans-dihalide. The reaction is stereo selective.

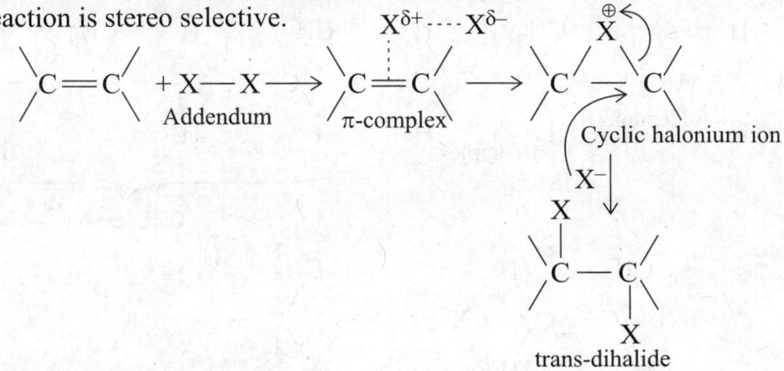

2. **Addition of halogen acids**

In this addition reaction, the addendum first associates itself to electron-rich π-center to form a π-complex. The π-complex subsequently gets transferred into the intermediate carbocation. In the next step, the nucleophile, i.e., the halide ion attaches itself to the intermediate to form the final addition product.

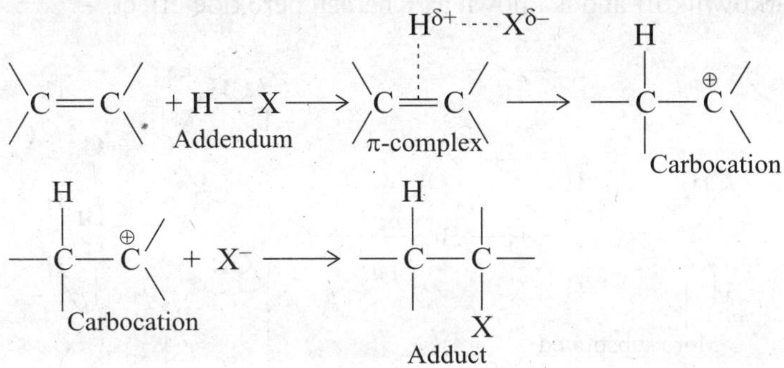

Ragioselectivity

In case of unsymmetrical alkenes the reaction leads to the formation of more than one product. The selection of major product can be done with respect to *Markownikoff rule*. As per the rule, the +ve part of the addendum goes to the least substituted carbon. For example,

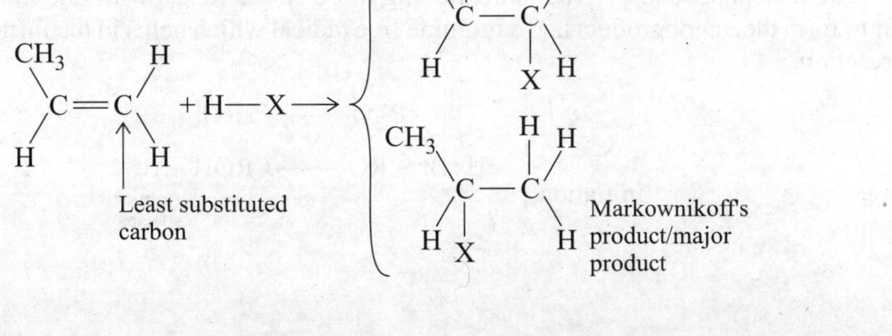

Explanation

During the addition, two different carbocations are formed as intermediate. The secondary (2°) carbocation being more stable leads to the formation of major product. This justifies the Markownikoff statement that +ve part of the addendum should go to the least substituted carbon so that a relatively more stable carbocation can be generated.

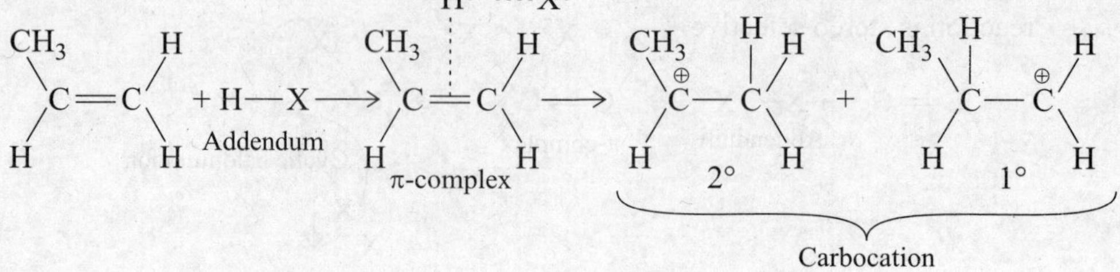

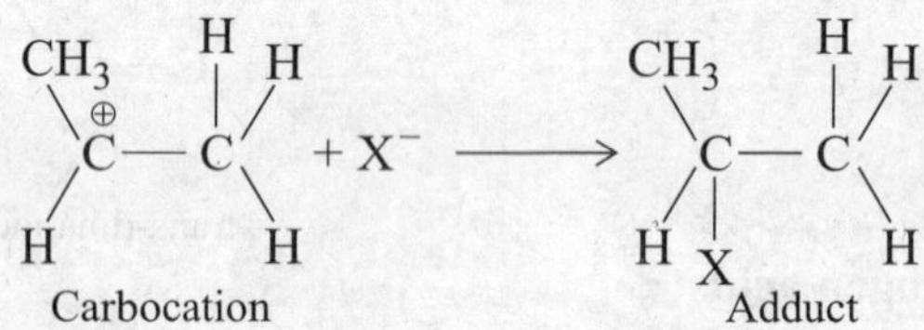

Anti-Markownikoff's addition (Kharash peroxide effect):

Addition of HBr to unsymmetrical alkene in presence of peroxide adopts a path opposite to that predicted by Markownikoff and is known as Kharash peroxide effect.

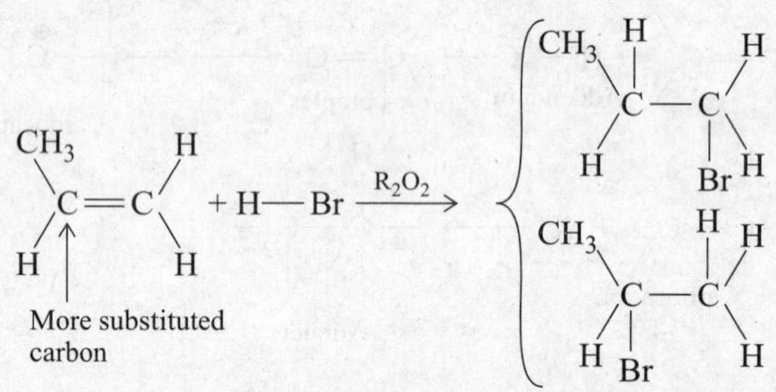

Explanation

The reaction follows free radical path instead of ionic. Here peroxides initiate the free radical path by generating bromine free radical. Out of the two carbon free radicals generated in the subsequent step, secondary free radical being more stable reacts with one more molecule of HBr to form the major product and a bromine free radical which helps in the further propagation of reaction.

Initiation

$$R_2O_2 \longrightarrow 2RO^{\bullet}$$

$$H:Br + RO^{\bullet} \longrightarrow ROH + \underset{\text{Active species}}{Br^{\bullet}}$$

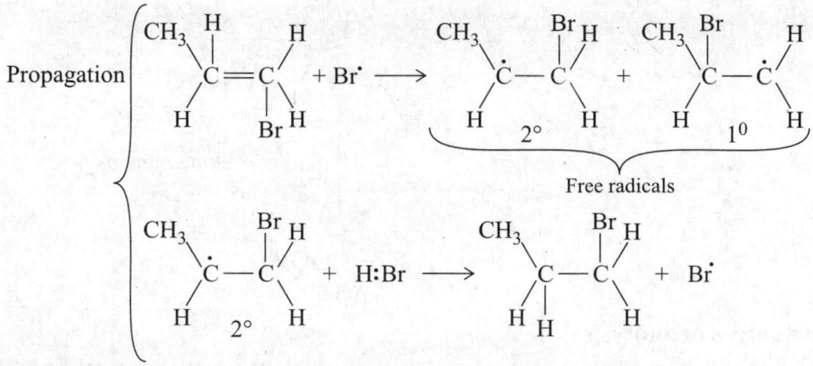

Note:

1. The peroxide effect is restricted only to the use of HBr. Other halogen acids such as HF and HCl do not participate in the process because of their high bond dissociation energy. In case of HI the iodine free radical generated is unstable and gets readily converted into iodine molecule.
2. Peroxide effect can be checked by the addition of sufficient amount of an inhibitor such as hydroquinone, diphenylamine, and diphenylsulphide, which arrest the free radicals.
3. **Addition of ozone**
   Addition of ozone across the double bond of alkene proceeds with the formation of an ozonide. Ozonide being unstable breaks down in the presence of an oxidizing or a reducing environment. The nature of products formed depends on the environment.

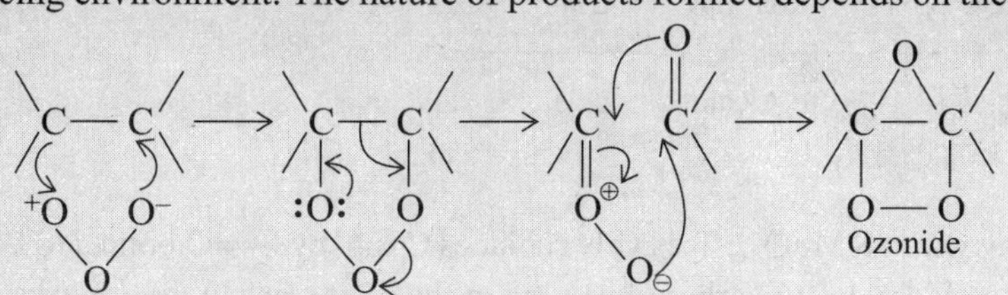

Oxidative ozonolysis

In oxidizing environment, i.e., in presence of silver oxide, hydrogen peroxide, or peracids, ozonide breaks down to form acids and/or ketones. This is because of the fact that an aldehyde formed readily gets oxidized into acid in oxidizing environment while a ketone remains as such (only gets oxidized in drastic condition with C—C bond cleavage to form mixture of acids, and the process is known as oxidative cleavage).

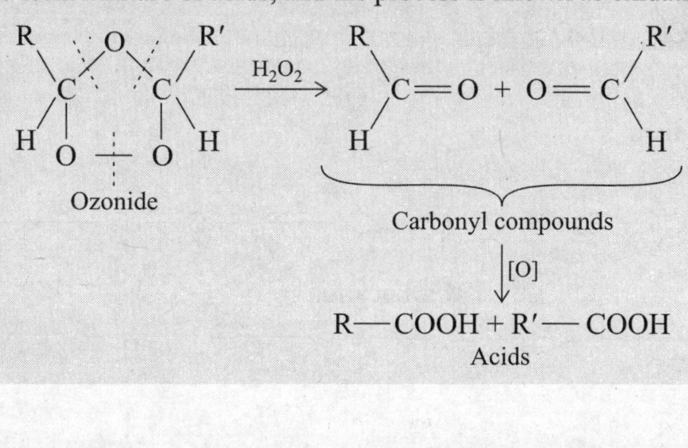

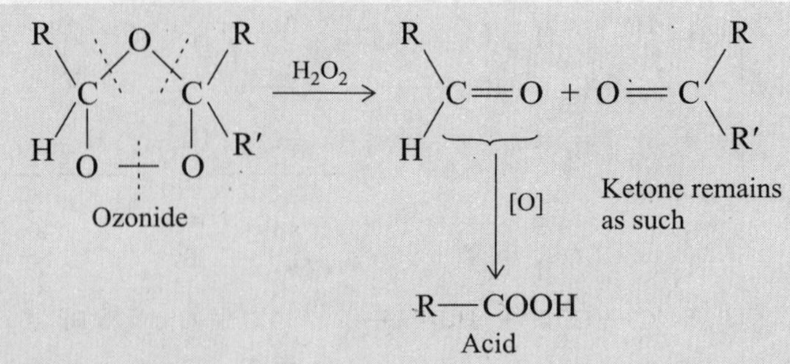

Reductive ozonolysis

In reducing environment, i.e., in presence of Zn–Acid and H_2–Raney nickel, ozonide breaks down to form aldehydes and/or ketones. Selective reducing agents such as $LiAlH_4$ or $NaBH_4$ form alcohols.

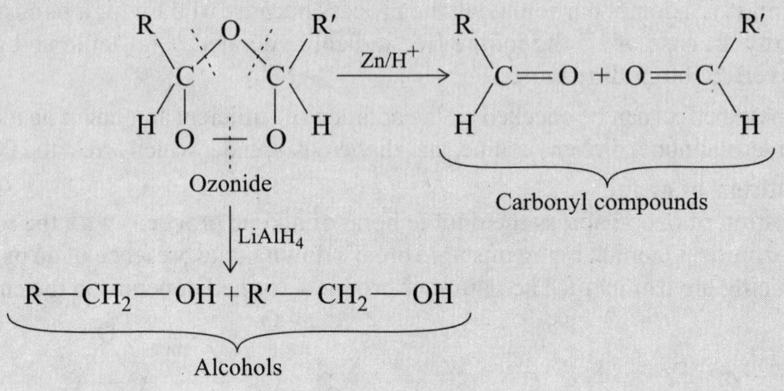

Note:

Cleavage by warm $KMnO_4$ effectively replaces C═C by C═O bond. However, $KMnO_4$ oxidizes the aldehydes to carboxylic acids in the next step. In other words use of warm $KMnO_4$ brings the same products as that of oxidative ozonolysis.

4. **Addition of water**

   Addition of water to alkenes is usually catalysed by acid and yields alcohols. The reaction takes place as per Markownikoff rule.

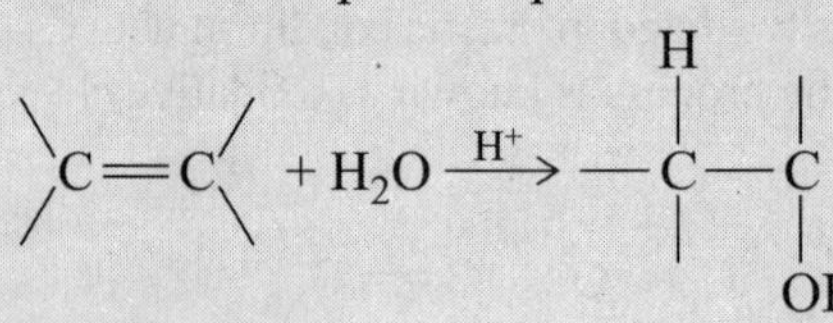

Mechanism

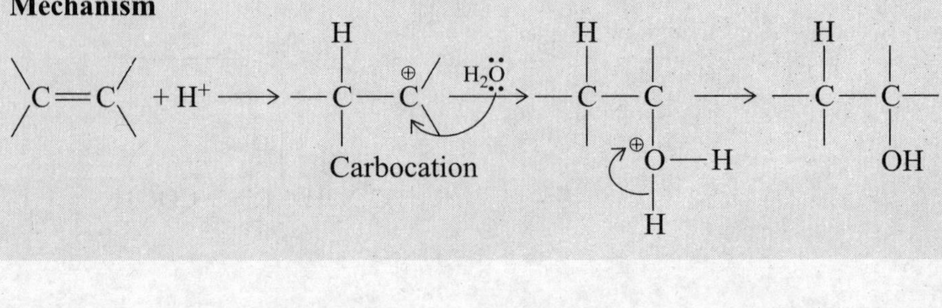

Note:

In case of alkynes the reaction rate with water is rather slow and therefore requires assistance of mercuric ions in addition to acid. Usually a mixture of sulphuric acid and mercuric sulphate is used to catalyse the process.

$$R-C=CH \xrightarrow{Hg^{2+},\ H^+} R-CH_2-\underset{\underset{O}{\|}}{CH}$$

Mechanism

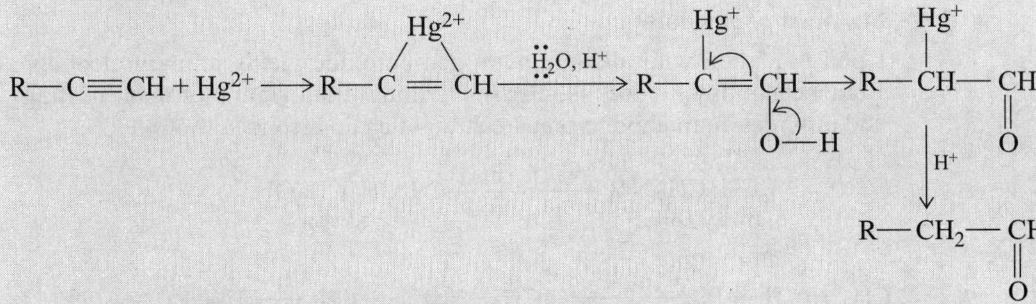

5. **Addition of diborane (hydroboration)**

   Diborane adds readily to alkenes as per Markownikoff's path (B atom adds to the least substituted carbon) at low temperature to form trialkyl boranes. The reaction proceeds in three steps but since the intermediates mono- and di-alkylboranes add more rapidly to alkenes they are not usually isolated. The reaction is exclusively *cis*-addition.

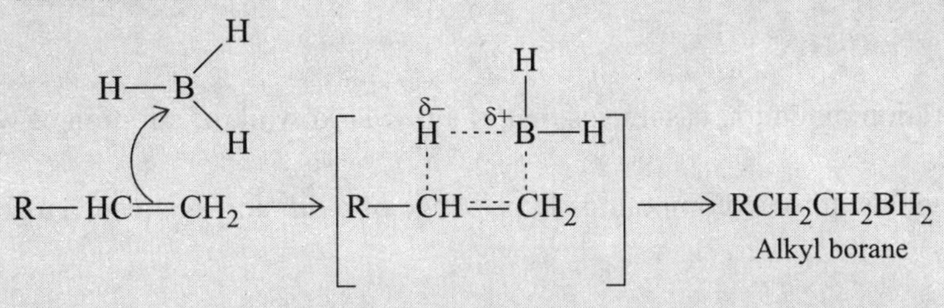

$$RCH_2CH_2BH_2 + R-CH=CH_2 \longrightarrow \underset{\text{Dialkyl borane}}{(RCH_2CH_2)_2BH} \xrightarrow{R-CH=CH_2} \underset{\text{Trialkyl borane}}{(RCH_2CH_2)_3B}$$

Note:

1. As diborane and alkyl boranes are spontaneously inflammable in air, the reaction is carried out in situ by action of $NaBH_4$ on BF_3 in ether or tetrahydrofuran (THF) medium.

$$2NaBH_4 + BF_3 \longrightarrow 2B_2H_6 + 3NaF$$

2. The reaction is stereo selective *cis*-addition.
3. Trialkylborane can be decomposed into variety of products in different conditions.

   (a) *Synthesis of alkane*

   Hydrolysis with weak aqueous acid yields alkanes. However, with alkaline silver, nitrate solution induces a coupling reaction forming higher alkanes.

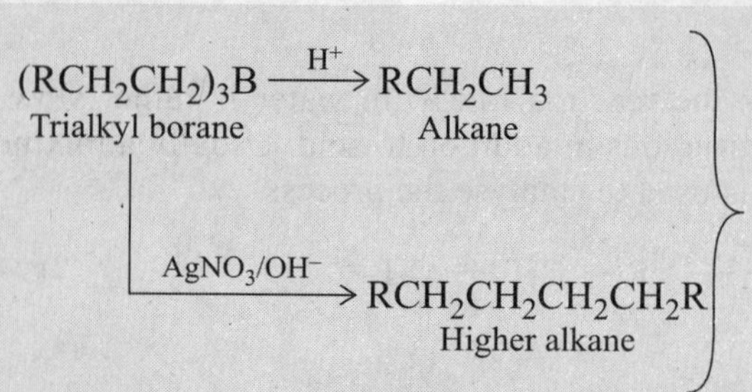

(b) *Synthesis of alcohols*

Upon oxidation with alkaline hydrogen peroxide yields primary alcohols. Branched trialkylboranes isomerises terminal trialkylboranes upon heating and provides an method to prepare straight chain alcohols.

$$\underset{\text{Trialkyl borane}}{(RCH_2CH_2)_3B} \xrightarrow{H_2O_2/OH^-} \underset{\text{Alcohol}}{3RCH_2CH_2OH}$$

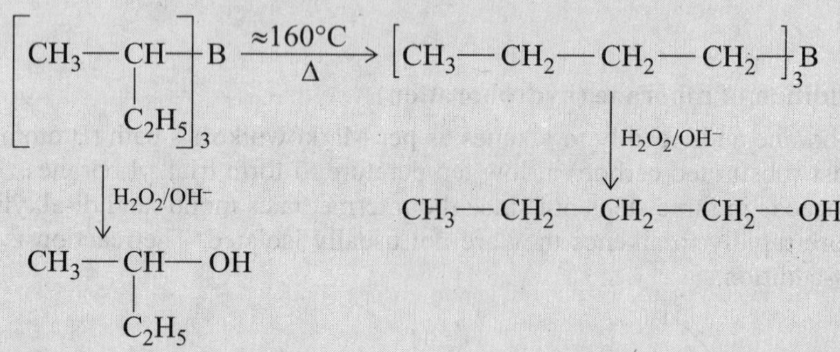

4. Hydroboration oxidation is same as that of anti-Markownikoff addition of water to alkene.
5. Alkynes yield carbonyl compounds in presence of oxidizing agent such as H_2O_2.

Example 10.2

Write the products in case of the following reaction:

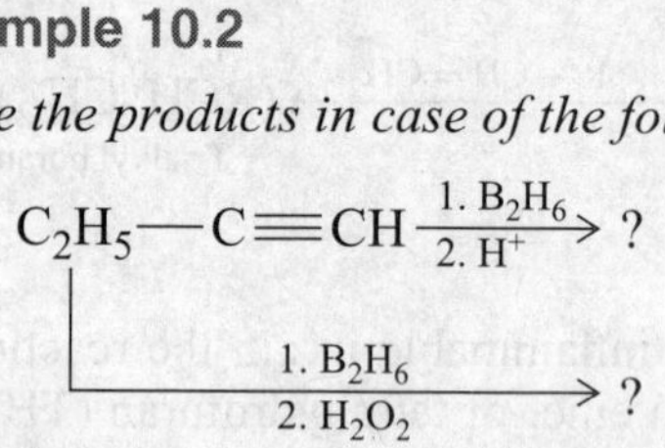

Solution

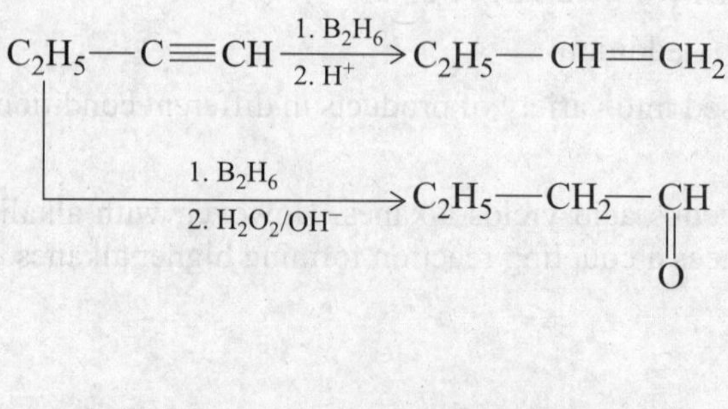

Scheme

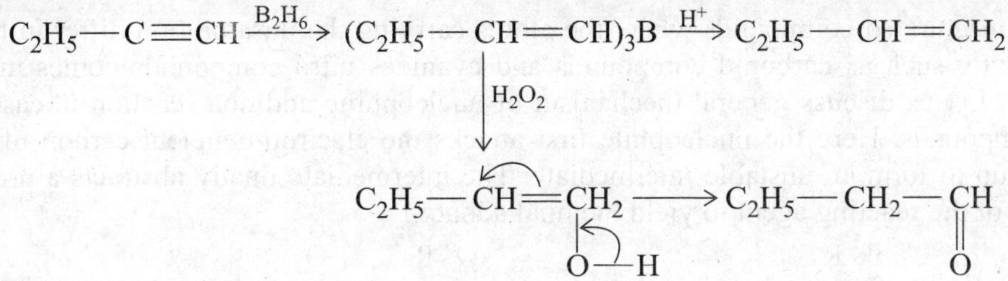

6. **cis-Dihydroxylation**

This is nothing but the reaction which involves the addition of two hydroxyl groups across the double bond. This can be brought about by using cold alkaline $KMnO_4$ (Bayer's reagent) or OsO_4. The reaction is stereo selective *cis*-addition, as it proceeds through cyclic intermediate.

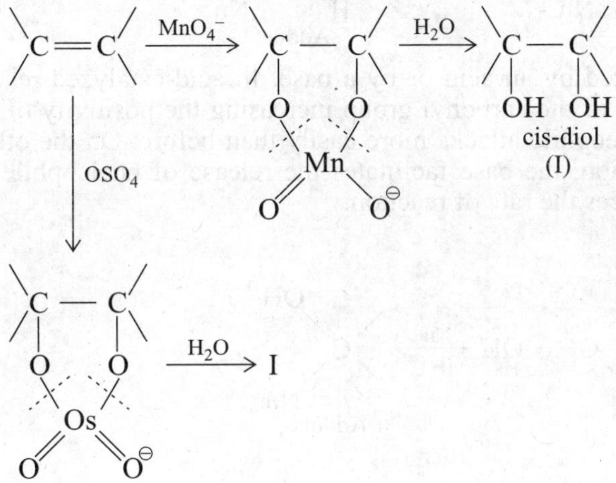

Note:

In presence of peracids hydroxylation leads to *trans-product* as it proceeds through formation of epoxides. Epoxide blocks one side of the double bond and thereby facilitate the rear attack of H_2O. Peracids are prepared in situ by mixing hydrogen peroxide on carboxylic acids in ether or chloroform medium.

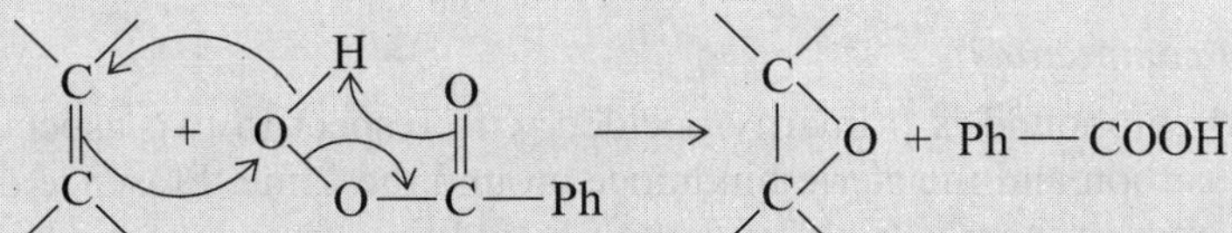

Perbenzoic acid Epoxide

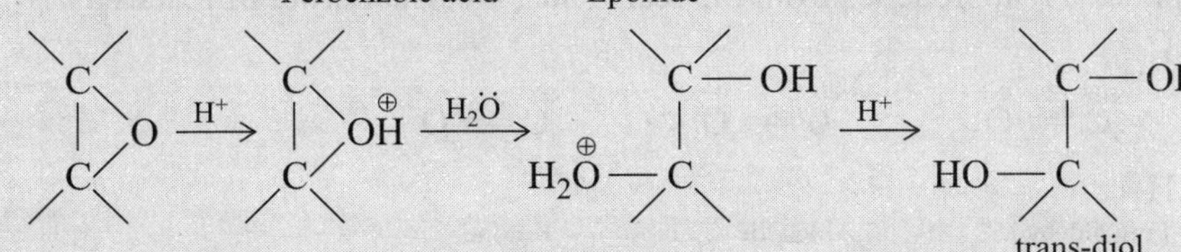

trans-diol

Nucleophilic Addition (Ad_N) Reactions

Addition to unsaturated compounds where the atoms carrying the unsaturation differ in their electronegativity such as carbonyl compounds and cyanides nitro compounds comes under this category. Let us discuss general mechanism of nucleophilic addition reaction in case of carbonyl compounds. Here the nucleophile first attacks the electron-deficient carbon of the carbonyl group to form an unstable intermediate. The intermediate finally abstracts a proton from solvent or the reacting agent to yield the final adduct.

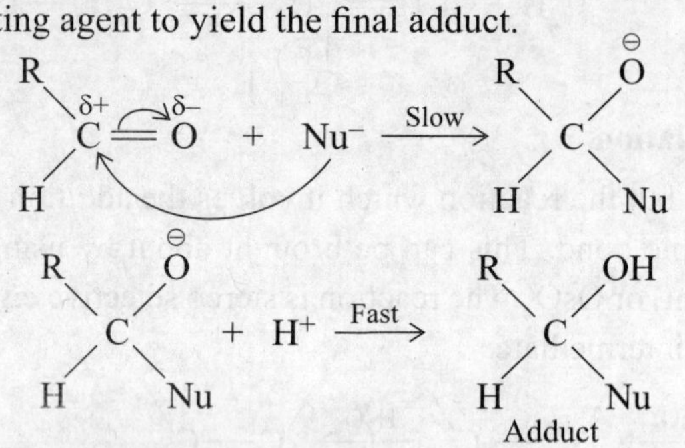

The reaction can be catalyzed by an acid or by a base. In acid-catalyzed reaction, H^+ ion helps in the easy polarization of the carbonyl group increasing the positivity of carbonyl carbon. The result being the nucleophile attacks more easily than before. On the other hand, in case of a base-catalyzed reaction, the base facilitates the release of nucleophile from its conjugate acid and thereby enhances the rate of reaction.

Acid-catalysed reaction

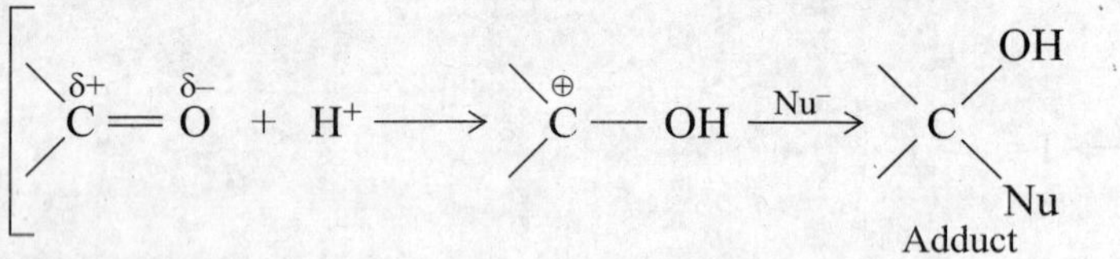

Base-catalysed reaction

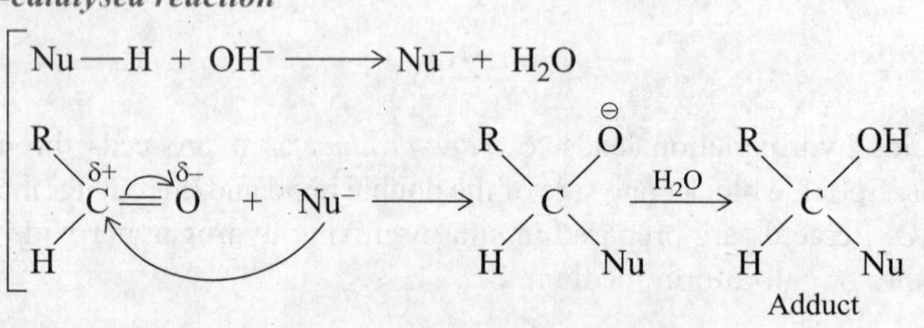

Reactivity of carbonyl compounds

Reactivity of carbonyl compound is primarily decided with respect to two aspects, viz., the positivity of carbonyl carbon and the steric hindrance around the same. Presence of electron-releasing alkyl groups reduce the positivity of carbon in addition provide steric hindrance for the nucleophile as it approaches from the rear. Thus, the usual order of reactivity is

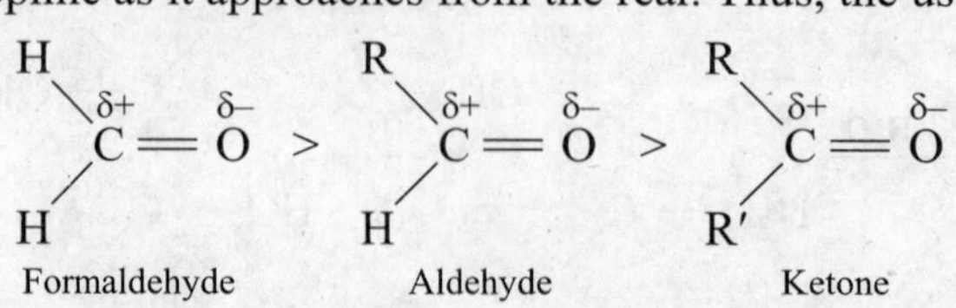

Let us discuss some specific nucleophilic addition reactions of carbonyl compounds.

1. **Addition of sodium bisulphate**

Upon treatment with aqueous sodium bisulphate, crystalline bisulphate addition products are formed.

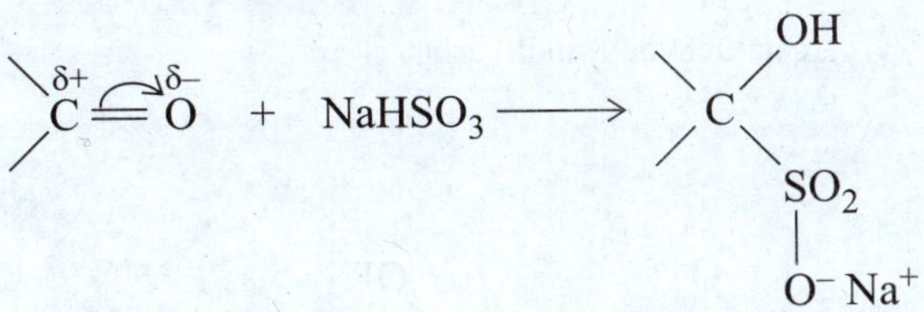

Bisulphite addition compound

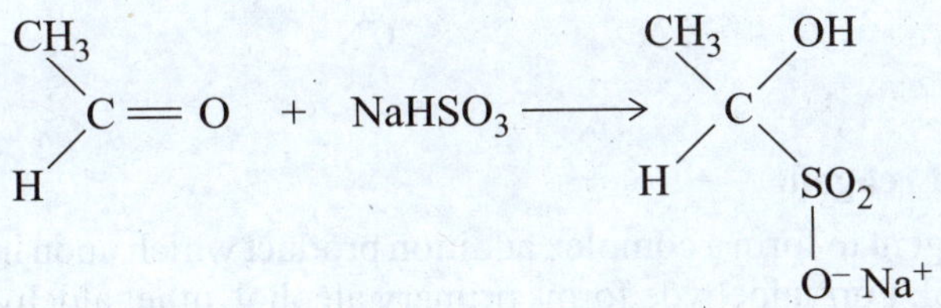

Bisulphite addition compound

Mechanism

$$HSO_3^{\ominus} + H_2O \rightleftharpoons H_3O^{\oplus} + SO_3^{2-}$$

Formation:

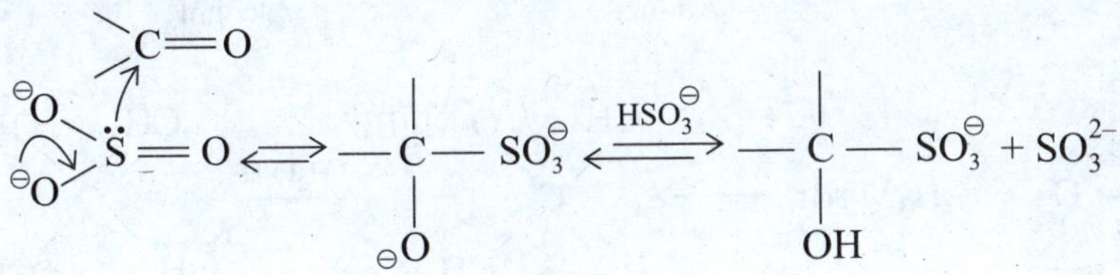

Decomposition:

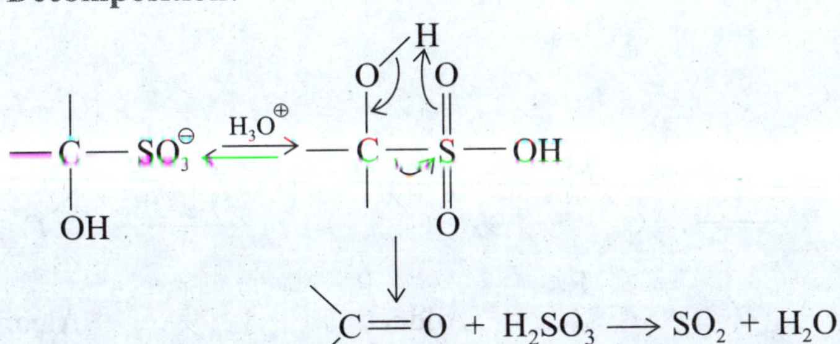

2. **Addition of HCN**

Addition of HCN yields cyanohydrins.

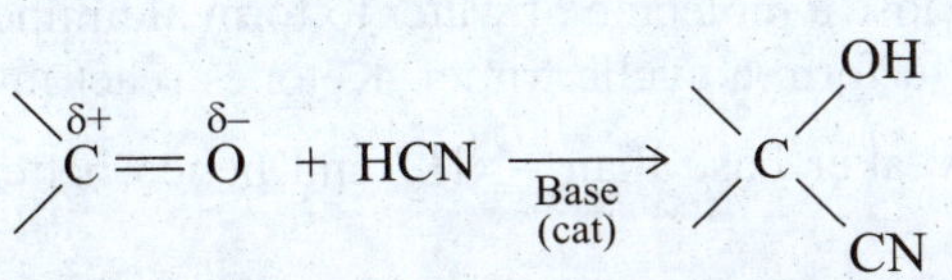

Cyanohydrin

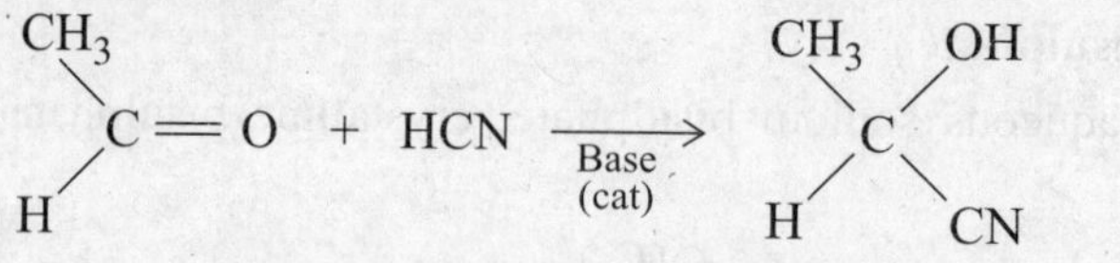

Mechanism

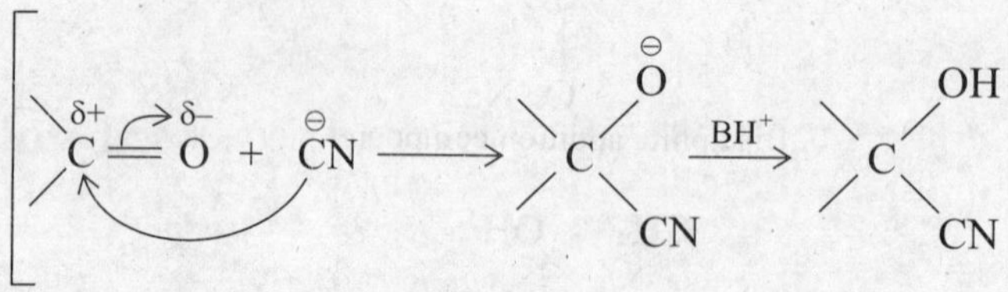

3. **Addition of Grignard reagent**

Add with Grignard reagent to form a complex addition product which upon hydrolysis with acid yields alcohol. Formaldehyde forms primary alcohol, other aldehydes form secondary alcohols and ketones form tertiary alcohols.

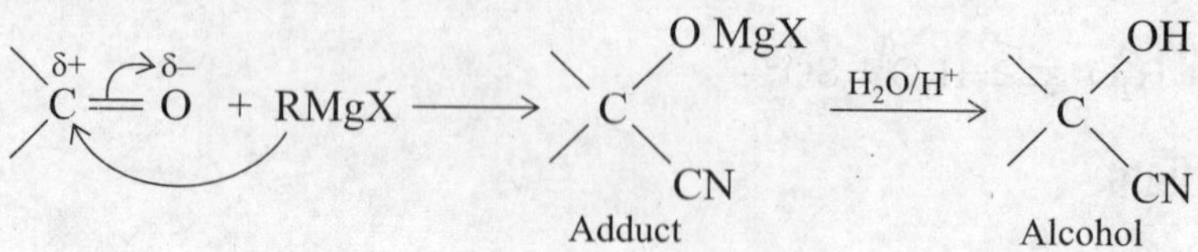

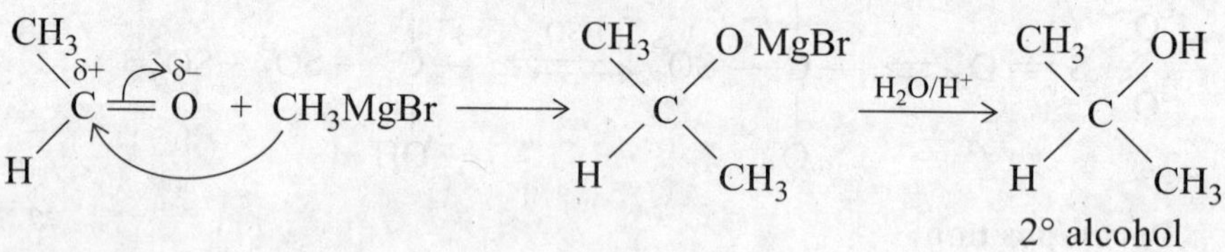

Mechanism

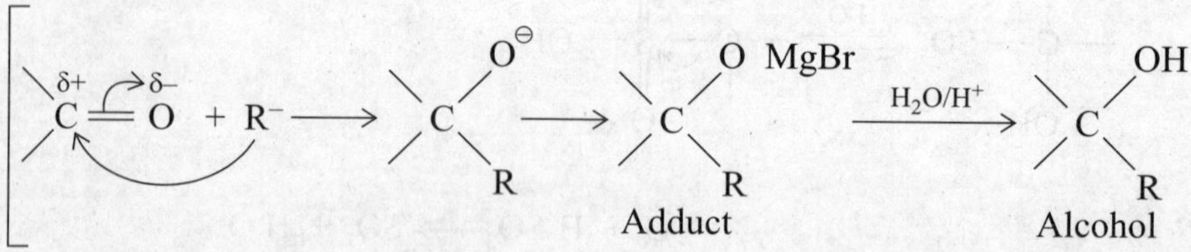

4. **Addition of NH_3**

Aldehydes except formaldehyde react with ammonia to form aldehyde ammonia. Aldehyde ammonia immediately lose a molecule of water to form aldimine. In most of the cases aldimine trimerises to form a cyclic trimer. Ketones react in a similar way to yield ketimine. $\overset{\ominus}{O}H$ is weaker base than $-NH_2^{\ominus}$ and hence better leaving group.

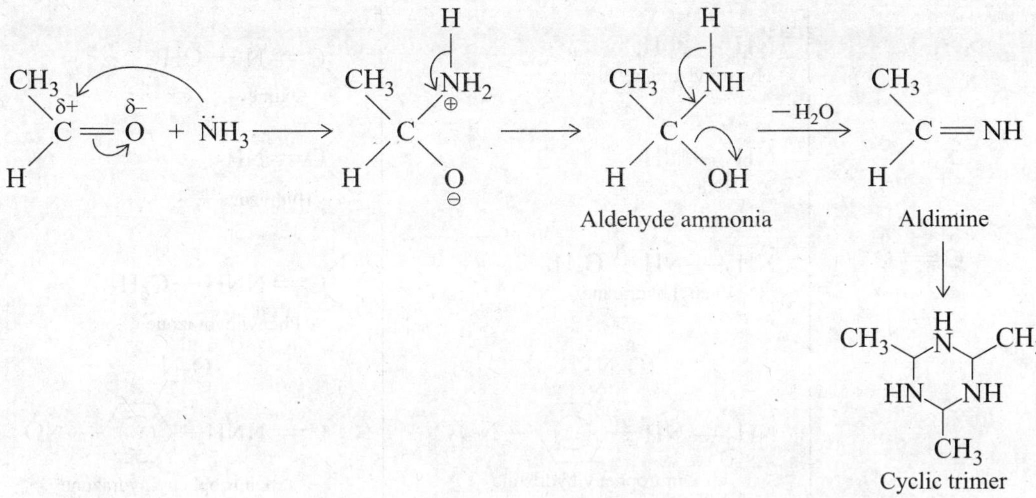

Note:

Formaldehyde reacts in a different manner to form hexamethylene tetrammine. The trade name of the compound is Urotropine.

$$6\left[\begin{matrix} H \\ \quad C=O \\ H \end{matrix}\right] + 4NH_3 \longrightarrow (CH_2)_6N_4$$

Urotropine

5. **Addition of ammonia derivatives**

Ammonia derivatives add on to carbonyl group to form unstable adducts which immediately lose a molecule of water to form condensation product.

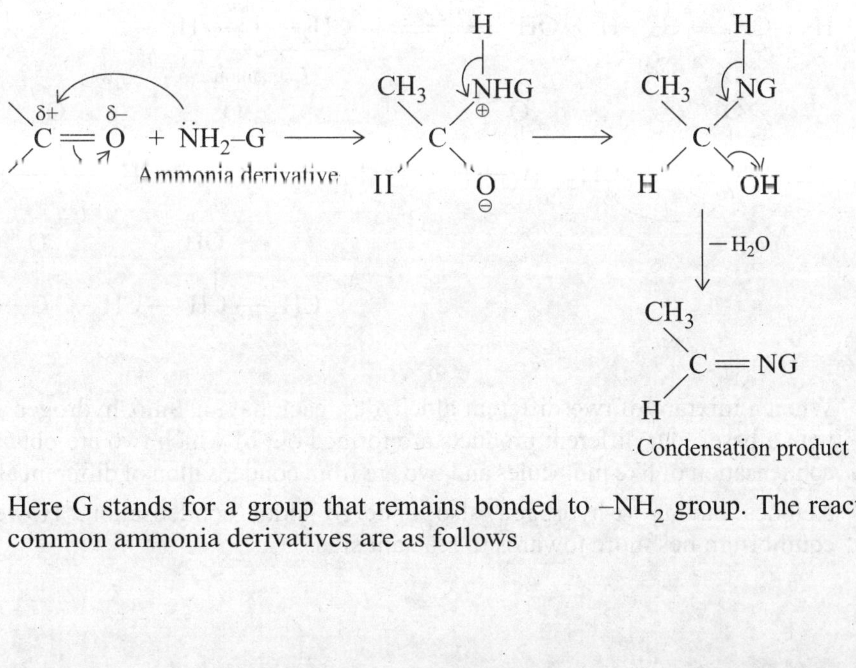

Here G stands for a group that remains bonded to $-NH_2$ group. The reaction with common ammonia derivatives are as follows

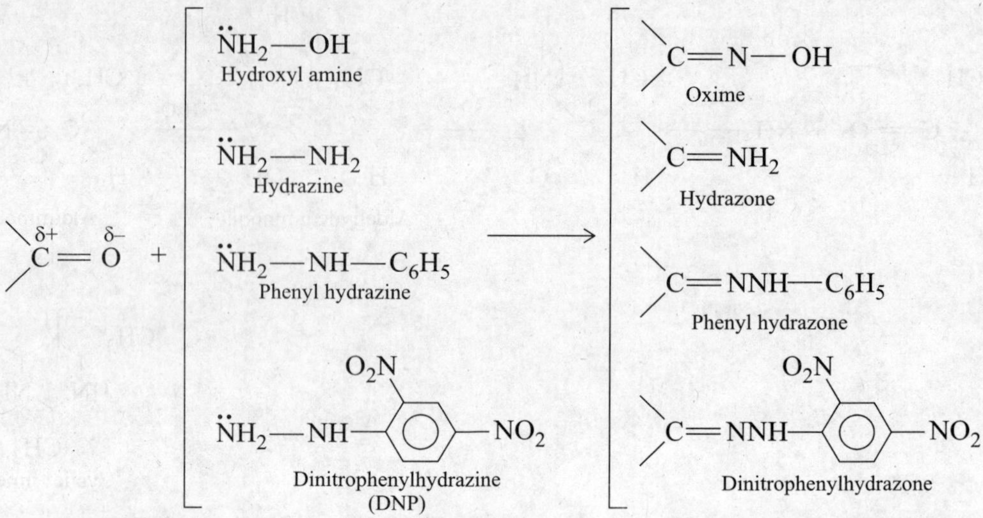

6. **Aldol condensation**

Aldehydes having at least one α-hydrogen undergo a reversible self addition reaction in presence of a dilute/weak base to give a product which carries both aldehyde and alcohol functional group known as aldol.

$$CH_3-\overset{\overset{\displaystyle O}{\|}}{C}-H + H-CH_2-\overset{\overset{\displaystyle O}{\|}}{C}-H \overset{OH^-}{\rightleftharpoons} \underset{\text{Aldol}}{CH_3-\overset{\overset{\displaystyle OH}{|}}{CH}-CH_2-\overset{\overset{\displaystyle O}{\|}}{C}-H}$$

Mechanism

The base abstracts the α-proton to form a carboanion. The nucleophile carboanion then attacks the carbonyl carbon to form the addition product.

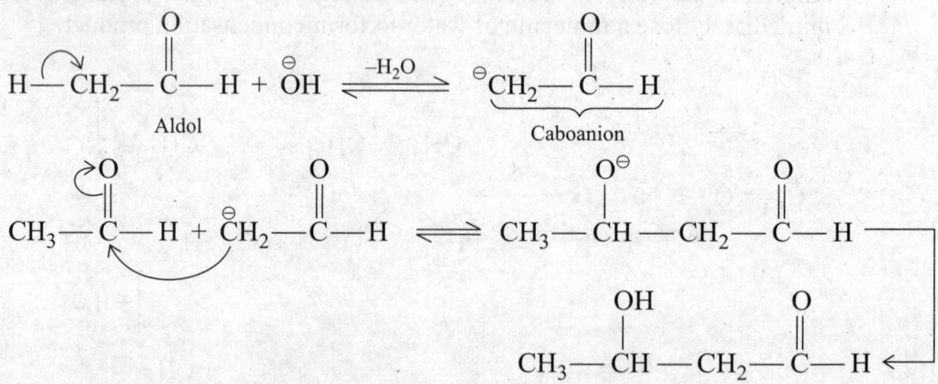

> **Note:**
>
> 1. When a mixture of two different aldehydes, each having an α-hydrogen is treated with a base, four different products are formed out of which two are obtained from condensation of like molecules and two are from condensation of different aldehydes.
> 2. Ketones having α-hydrogen also undergo aldol condensation. However, the equilibrium lies more towards to reactant side.

3. Aldol condensation can also take place between an aldehyde and a ketone provided one or both of them possess at least one α-hydrogen atom. Such a reaction is known as cross aldol condensation, e.g., acetaldehyde and acetone condense to form 4-hydroxypentan-2-one.

$$CH_3{-}\overset{\displaystyle O}{\overset{\|}{C}}{-}H + CH_3{-}\overset{\displaystyle O}{\overset{\|}{C}}{-}CH_3 \xrightleftharpoons{KOH} CH_3{-}\overset{\displaystyle OH}{\overset{|}{C}H}{-}CH_2{-}\overset{\displaystyle O}{\overset{\|}{C}}{-}CH_3$$

4. Aldehydes having α-hydrogen in presence of concentrated base undergo a series of aldol condensation to form a polymer.

7. **Cannizzaro's reaction**

Aldehydes lacking α-hydrogen upon treatment with strong base undergo a self-oxidation reduction reaction in which one molecule of the aldehydes is oxidized to acid while the other one is reduced to alcohol. The overall reaction involves two nucleophilic addition steps.

$$2\left[\begin{matrix}H \\ H\end{matrix}\!\!>C{=}O\right] + \text{Conc. NaOH} \longrightarrow H{-}\overset{\displaystyle O}{\overset{\|}{C}}{-}\overset{\ominus}{O} + CH_3OH$$

$$2\left[\begin{matrix}C_6H_5 \\ H\end{matrix}\!\!>C{=}O\right] + \text{Conc. NaOH} \longrightarrow C_6H_5{-}\overset{\displaystyle O}{\overset{\|}{C}}{-}\overset{\ominus}{O} + C_6H_5CH_2OH$$

Mechanism

Base attacks the carbonyl carbon of aldehyde molecule to produce an anion. In the rate-determining step, hydride ion attacks the carbonyl carbon of the second molecule.

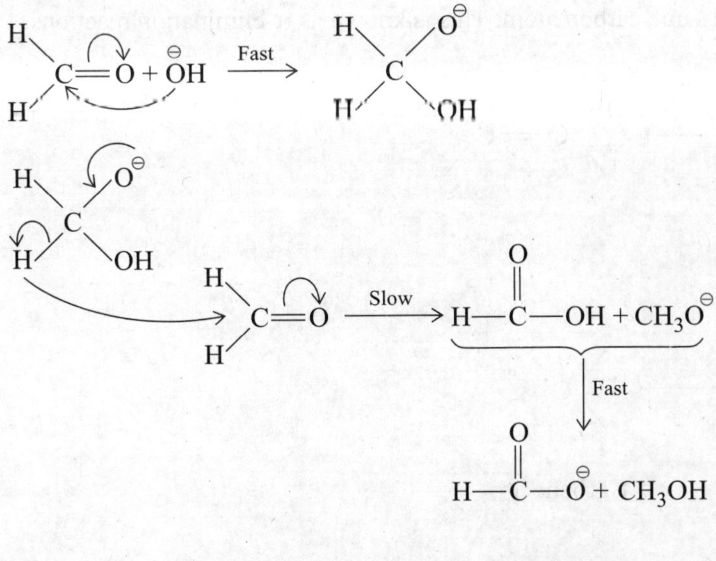

Note:

1. Compounds such as 1,2-dialdehydes and α-ketoaldehydes undergo *internal Cannizzaro reaction*. A widely studied example being conversion of phenylglyoxal to salt of mandelic acid.

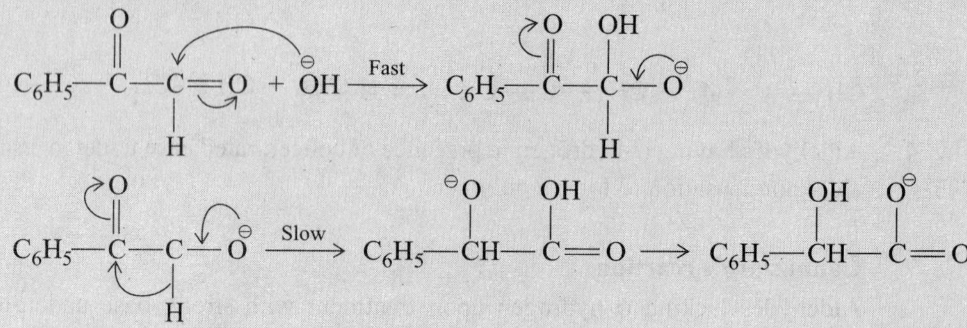

2. The reaction between two different aldehydes both of which are lacking of α-hydrogen is known as *crossed Canizzarro reaction*. Such a reaction leads to all possible products. However, if one of the aldehydes is formaldehyde the salt of formate ion and the alcohol of the other aldehydes are exclusively formed. This is due to the fact that formaldehyde is more reactive and is added in preference to the hydroxide ion.

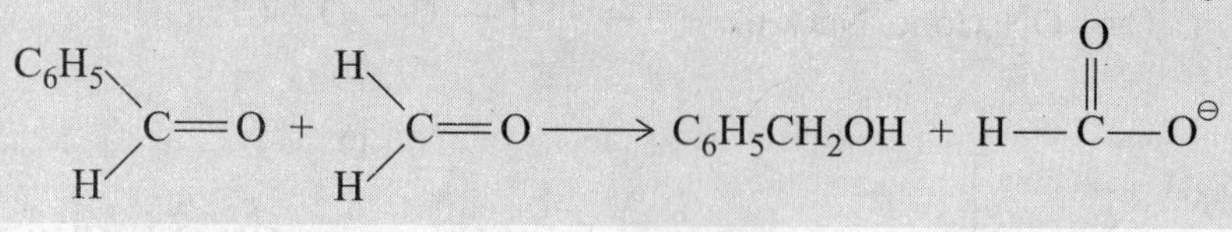

C. Elimination Reactions

Elimination reactions are identified as the reverse of addition reactions. Such reactions are broadly classified as β- or *1,2-elimination* and *α-elimination*. The first one involves loss of two atoms or groups from vicinal "C" atoms, resulting in the formation of a double or triple bond among them. Most commonly a proton is lost from one carbon, i.e., β-carbon, whereas a nucleophile from the adjacent carbon which is referred α-carbon. In the second category, both the atoms (or groups) are removed from the same carbon atom. This is known as α-elimination reactions.

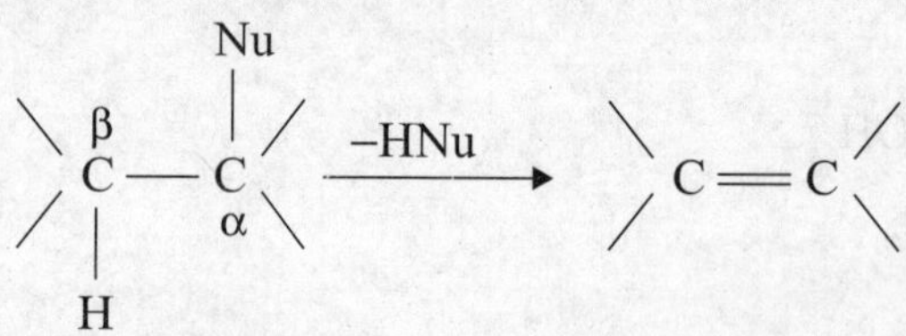

β-Elimination

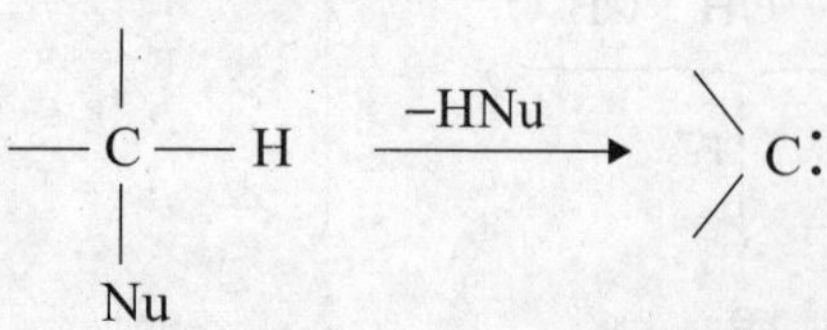

Carbene

α-Elimination

β- or 1, 2-elimination: Such a reaction may follow bimolecular (E_2) or unimolecular (E_1) path.

1. E_2 mechanism: Let us look into the elimination reaction of a primary alkyl halide, say ethyl bromide, by a strong base such as sodium ethoxide.

$$CH_3 - CH_2 - Br + C_2H_5ONa \longrightarrow CH_2 = CH_2 + C_2H_5OH + Br^-$$

Mechanism

The rate depends on the concentrations of both the substrate and the base. To fit into the kinetic data, a concerted mechanism has been proposed which involves the abstraction of proton by base from β-carbon and simultaneous release of nucleophile from the α-carbon along with the pair of bonding electrons.

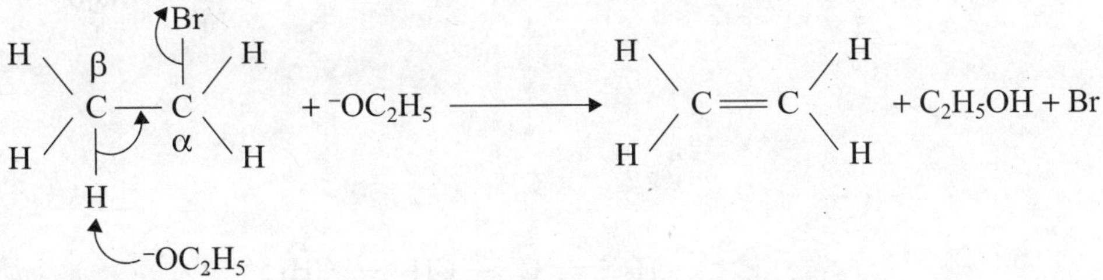

2. E_1 mechanism: Let us consider the elimination in *t*-butyl bromide. Here rate depends on the concentration of only substrate.

$$(CH_3)_3C - Br \xrightarrow{C_2H_5OH} (CH_3)_2C = CH_2 + C_2H_5OH$$

Mechanism

To fit into kinetic data, a two-step mechanism has been proposed. In the first step, under the influence of solvation, the nucleophile goes away along with the bonding electrons to form a carbocation. This is the rate controlling step. Subsequently, the carbocation loses a proton to solvent or some other proton acceptor.

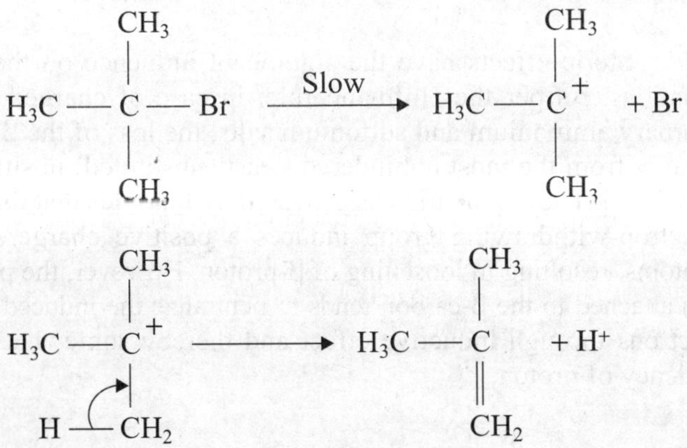

Orientation

The elimination reactions of unsymmetrical substrates usually yield a mixture of all possible products. There are two imperial rules to govern orientation.

(i) *Saytzeff rule:* It states that neutral substrates capable of forming double bond in either side of the chain prefer to yield most substituted alkene, i.e., the loss of the β-hydrogen occurs preferably from the most substituted position. This is valid for E_1 and most of the E_2 reactions. The reason is attributed to the relative stability of alkenes. It is a well established fact that the stability of double bond increases by alkyl substitution on the doubly bonded carbon atoms.

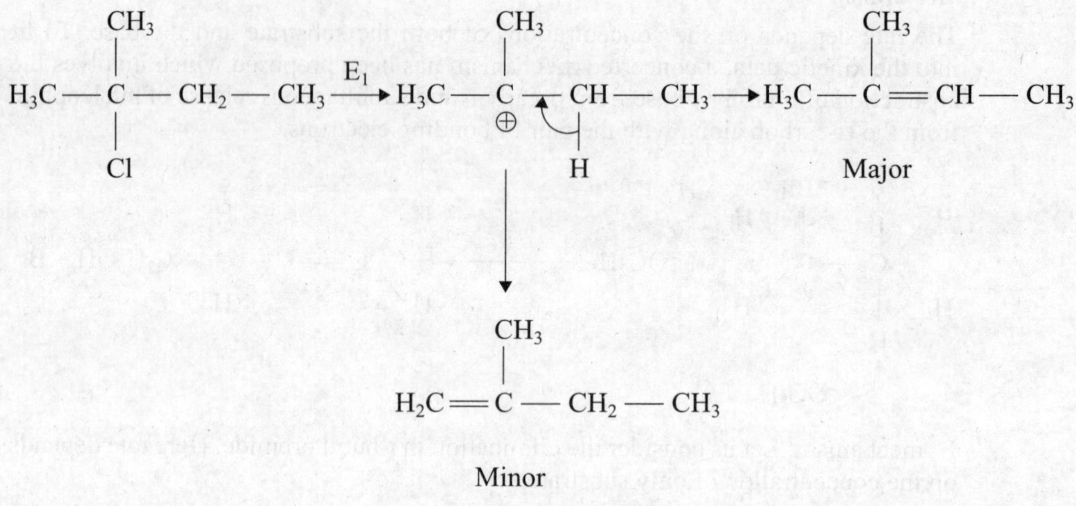

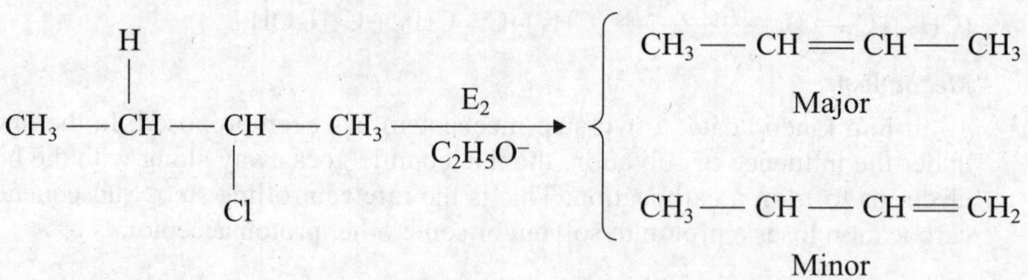

(ii) *Hofmann's rule:* Steric effects have the significant influence on the outcome of the eliminations. As per the Hofmann rule, in case of charged substrates such as quaternary ammonium and sulfonium salts, the loss of the β-hydrogen occurs preferably from the most unhindered (least substituted) position [$-CH_3 > -CH_2R > -CHR_2$]. The explanation as provided by Ingold is that the presence of strong electron-withdrawing group induces a positive charge on all the surrounding atoms, resulting in loosening of β-proton. However, the presence of alkyl group(s) attached to the β-carbon tends to neutralize the induced charge by releasing electrons through inductive effect and thereby somewhat arrest the releasing tendency of proton.

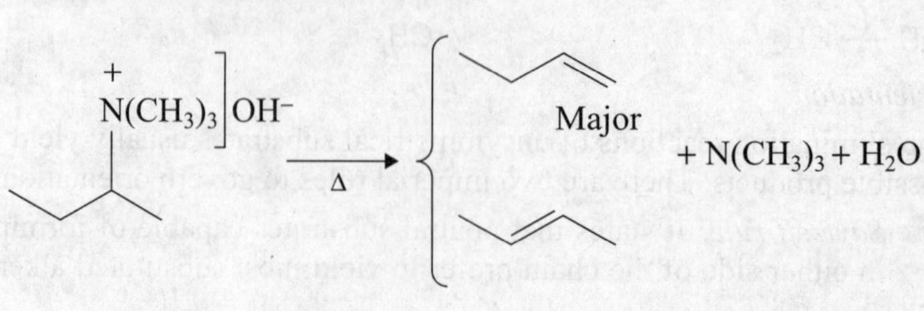

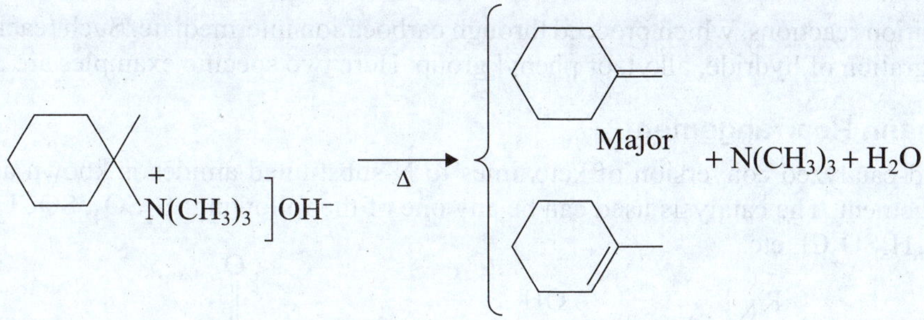

Elimination/Substitution

S_N1 and E_1 reactions, S_N2 and E_2 reactions occur simultaneously and compete with each other. If attacking reagent is a *good base*, i.e., electron pair donor to hydrogen, then it easily abstracts the β-carbon to cause elimination. However, at the same time if it is a *good nucleophile*, i.e., electron pair donor to electron deficient carbon, then it attacks the α-carbon to bring substitution. The following factors decide the ratio of elimination and substitution.

1. *Structure of reactant:* In general, proportion of elimination increases with increased chain branching of the reactant. The reason is two-fold. The reason may be attributed to the enhanced stability of highly substituted alkenes. In case of E_1 and S_N1 reactions, proceed through carbocation intermediate which has a planner structure with bond angle of 120°. With increase in branching, the intermediate hesitate to decrease the bond angle from 120° to 109.5° brought about by the substitution. However, elimination can easily be brought about as it does not involve any change in the bond angle.

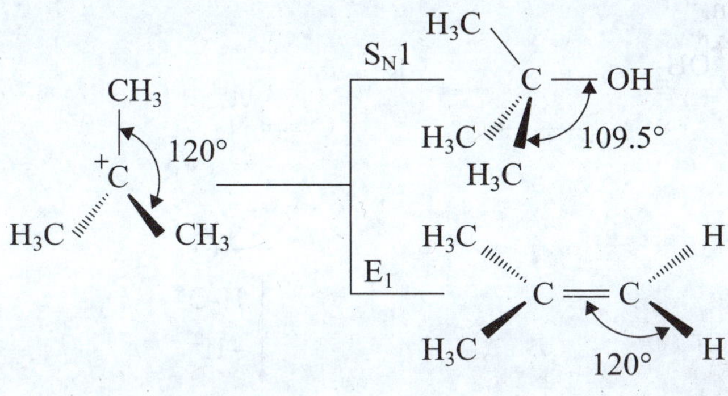

2. *Nature of base or nucleophile:* With the increase in the strength and concentration of base, unimolecular reactions tend to become bimolecular. This is more pronounced in elimination reaction than in substitution reaction, leading to higher proportion of the elimination reaction.
3. *Nature of solvent:* Bimolecular reactions are usually favored by decrease in polarity of the solvent. However, the effect is more pronounced in E_2 reactions. Therefore, less polar solvents favor bimolecular reactions as well as E_2 over S_N2 reactions.
4. *Temperature:* Activation energy of elimination reactions is usually higher than those for corresponding substitution reactions. Therefore, elevated temperature favors elimination.

D. Rearrangement Reactions

Rearrangement refers to the migration of a atom/group from one atom to another within the same molecule. We have already seen some rearrangement reactions during discussion of substitution and addition reactions, which proceed through carbocation intermediate. Such reactions involve 1, 2-migration of hydride, alkyl, or phenyl group. Here two specific examples are discussed.

Beckmann Rearrangement

The acid-catalyzed conversion of ketoximes to N-substituted amides is known as Beckmann rearrangement. The catalysis used can be any one of the following: H_2SO_4, $SOCl_2$, SO_3, P_2O_5, PCl_5, $C_6H_5SO_2Cl$, etc.

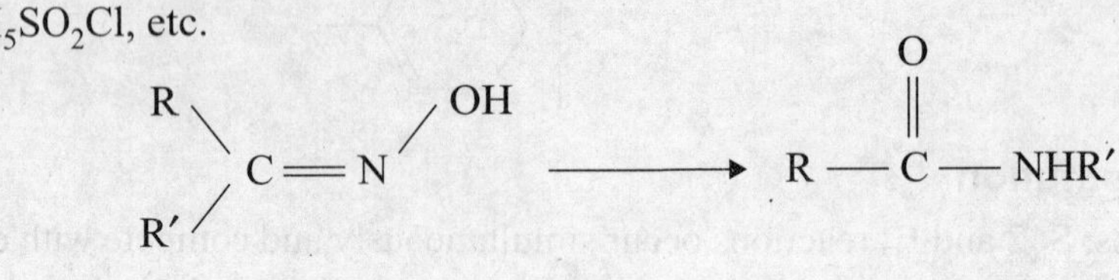

Ketoxime N-substitued amide

Mechanism

1. Conversion of –OH group to a better leaving group.

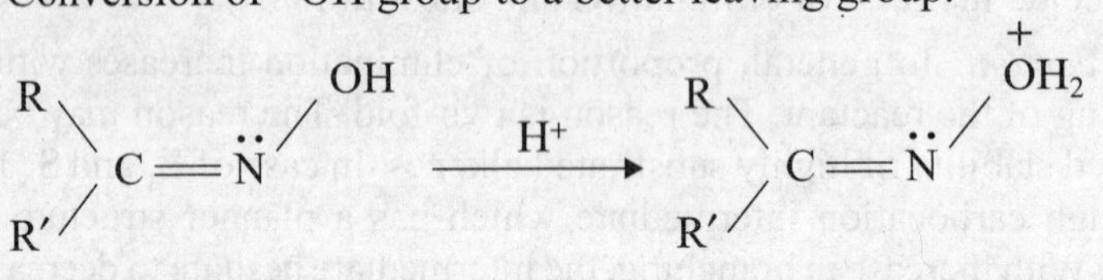

Ketoxime

2. (1, 2)-migration of group anti to hydroxyl group with its bonding electron pair from carbon to nitrogen.

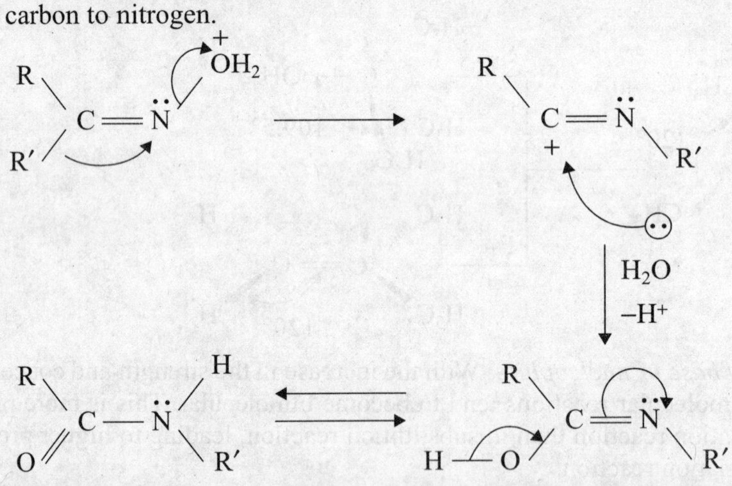

Important features

1. This rearrangement is intramolecular.
2. The reaction is stereospecific, i.e., migrating group is always anti (*trans*) to the hydroxyl group. This can be realized from the following example where (a) and (b) are geometrical isomers.

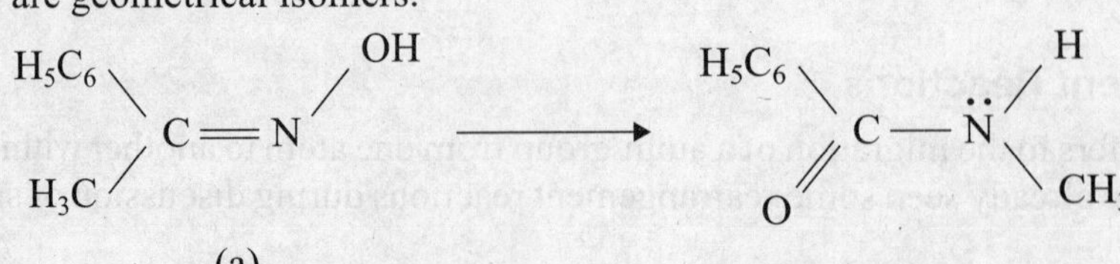

(a)

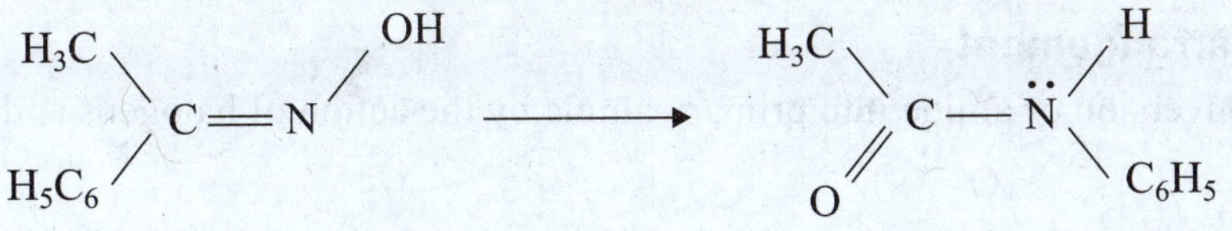

(b)

3. Catalyst converts –OH group into a better leaving group; therefore, the stronger is the acid used as catalyst, the faster is the rearrangement.
4. The migrating group retains its configuration. Therefore, migration and breaking of N–O bond are concerted.
5. Oximes of esters and ethers also undergo Beckmann rearrangement.
6. Some aldoximes undergo this rearrangement in the presence of polyphosphoric acid (PPA). However, the reaction is not a general one.

Applications

1. **In establishing configuration of ketoximes:** Let us consider the following reaction:

$$\text{RR'CNOH} \xrightarrow[\text{Rearrangement}]{\text{Beckmann}} \text{R'CONHR} \xrightarrow{\text{Hydrolysis}} \text{RNH}_2 + \text{RCOOH}$$

Formation of RNH_2 points toward the migration of group "R" to the nitrogen atom. Thus, groups "R" and "OH" are therefore anti to each other.

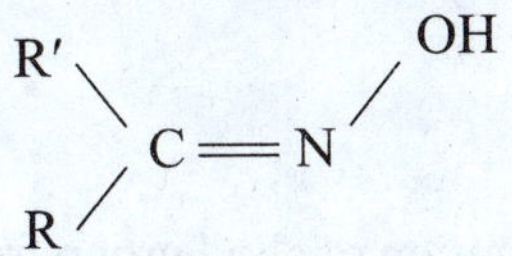

2. The reaction is utilized for ring expansion. An important example is the conversion of cyclohexanone oxime into caprolactam, which has considerable synthetic importance in manufacture of perlon (a textile polymer).

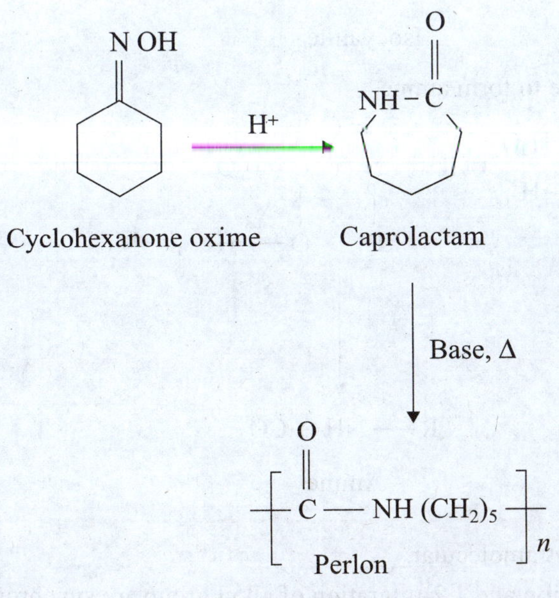

Hoffmann Rearrangement

It consists of conversion of amide into primary amine by the action of halogens and a base.

$$R-\overset{\overset{O}{\|}}{C}-NH_2 \xrightarrow[NaOH]{Br_2} R-NH_2 + CO_2$$

Mechanism

1. This involves the base-initiated bromination of amide.

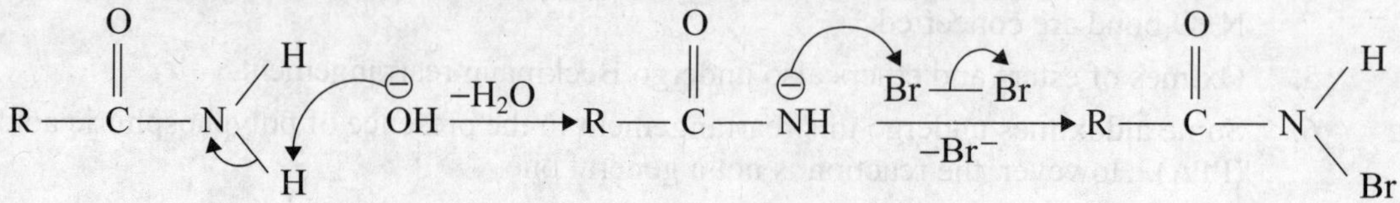

2. Base-initiated removal of proton from N-bromoamide.

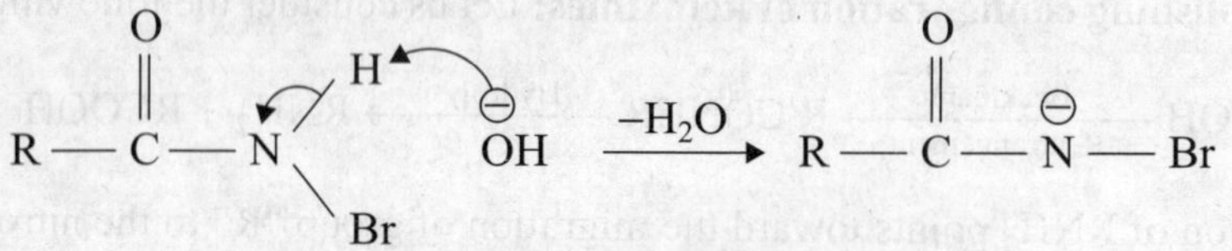

3. Removal of bromine to form the reactive nitrene intermediate.

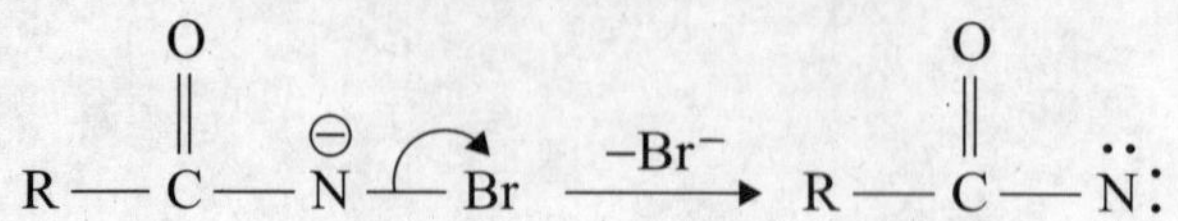

4. The nitrene spontaneously rearranges by the 1,2-migration of alkyl group from C to N.

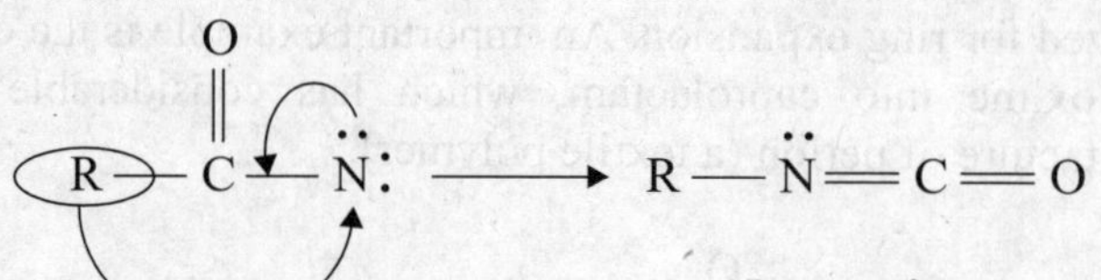

Isocyanite

5. Hydrolysis of isocyanate to form amine.

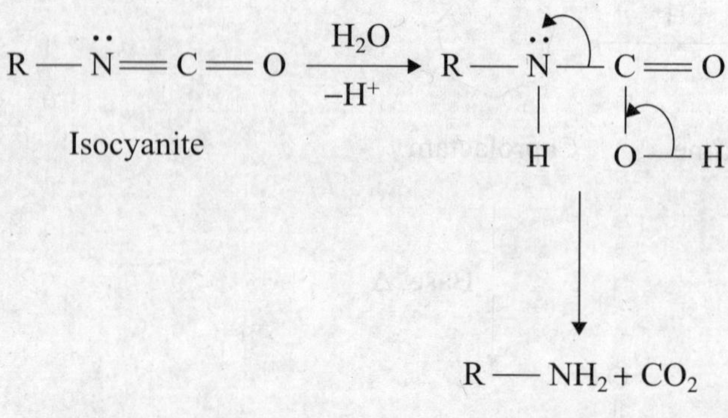

Amine

Important features

1. This rearrangement is intramolecular.
2. The departure of halide ion and 1,2-migration of alkyl group are synchronous.

3. The rearrangement proceeds with complete retention of configuration about the chiral center of the migrating group. Following example illustrates the fact.

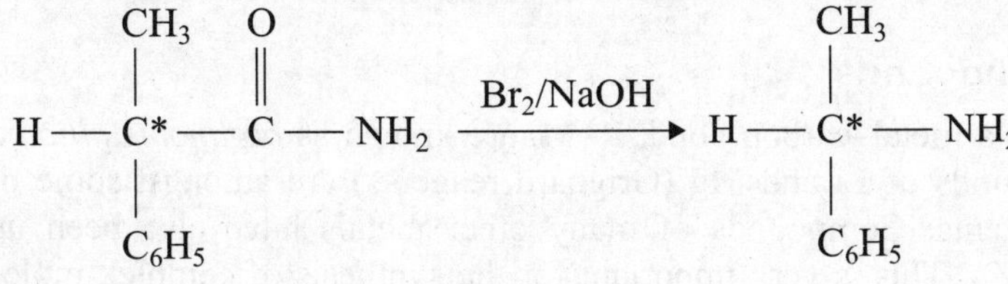

(+)-α-phenylpropionamide (+)-α-phenylethylamine

4. Increase in electron-releasing ability, i.e., nucleophilicity, facilitates the rearrangement.

Applications

1. The reaction is widely used for the preparation of amino acids, e.g., anthranilic acid and β-alanine.

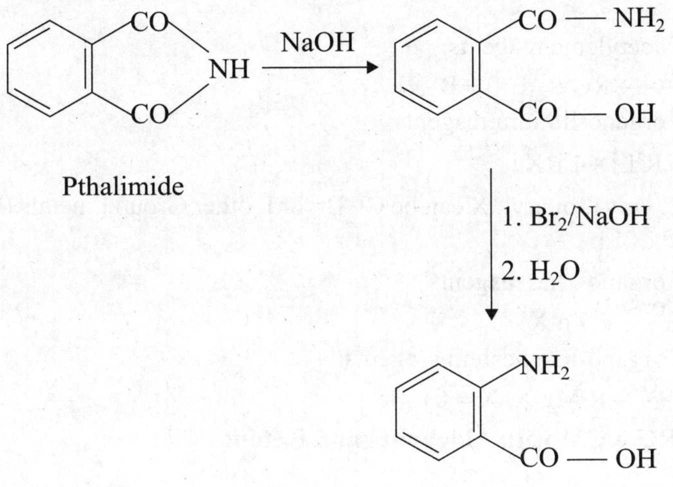

Pthalimide

Anthranilic acid

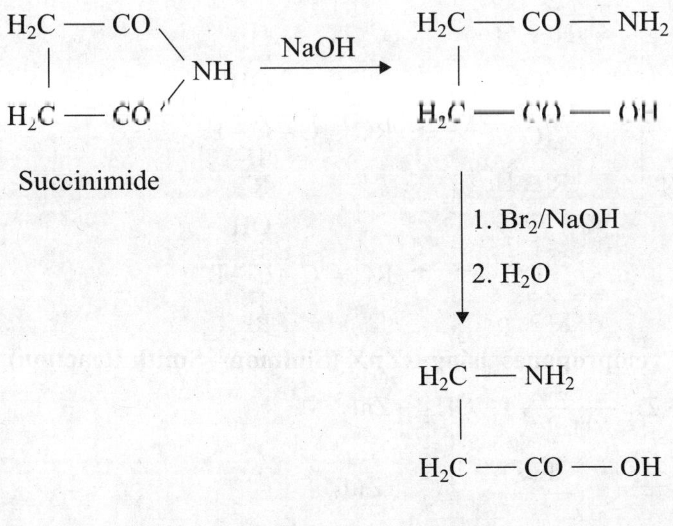

Succinimide

β-alanine

2. The reaction has wide importance in synthetic organic chemistry as it is utilized for degradation of carbon chain by one carbon atom.

Organometallic Compounds

Compounds containing a metal–carbon bond, R–M, are known as *organometallic* compounds. Organometallic compounds of Li and Mg (Grignard reagents) are amongst some of the most important organic reagents. Compounds of many other metals have also been utilized; for example, Na, Cu, and Zn. This is very important for the synthesis of complex molecules from simple starting materials. To rationalize the general reactivity of organometallics, it is convenient to view them as ionic, so $R–M = R^-M^+$. Organo-lithium and organo-magnesium compounds are strong bases since the negative charge is on carbon. Organometallic compounds also provide a source of nucleophilic carbon atoms which can react with electrophilic carbon to from a new carbon–carbon bond. Therefore, organometallic compounds react as electron rich or anionic carbon atoms, i.e., carboanions, which means they will function as either bases or nucleophiles.

Preparation

1. Preparation of acetylenic reagents:

$$RC \equiv CH \xrightarrow{B:^-} RC \equiv C:^- + B-H$$

2. Preparation of organo-lithium reagents

$$RX + 2\,Li \longrightarrow R\,Li + Li^+X^-$$

R can be alky1, viny1, or aryl. X can be Cl, Br, or I. other Group I metals (Na, K) can be used instead of Li.

3. Preparation of organo-zinc reagents

$$RX + Zn \xrightarrow{Et_2O} R\,Zn\,X$$

4. Preparation of organo-magnesium reagents:

$$RX + Mg \xrightarrow{Et_2O} R\,Mg\,X,\ X = Cl, Br, I$$

1. **Reactions of RC ≡ CM with Aldehydes and Ketones**

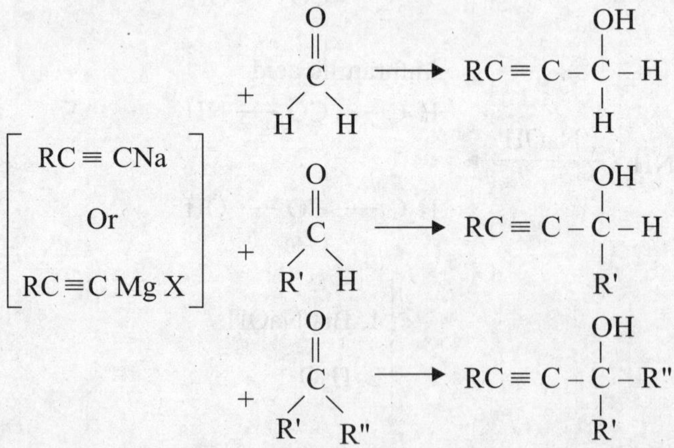

2. **Synthesis of Cyclopropanes using RZnX (Simmons–Smith Reaction)**

$$I-CH_2-I + Zn \xrightarrow[Et_2O]{Cu} I-CH_2-ZnI$$

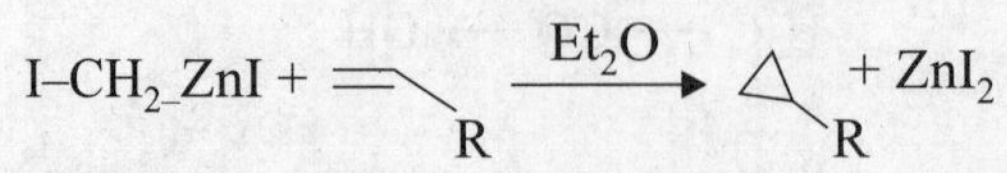

The reaction is stereospecific with respect to the alkene (mechanism is concerted). Substituents that are trans in the alkene are trans in the cyclopropane.

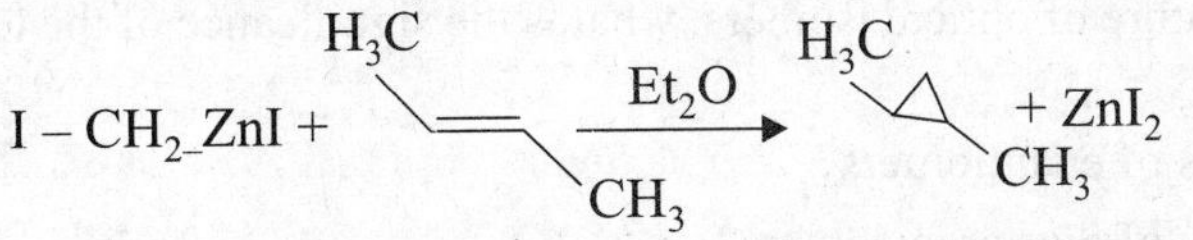

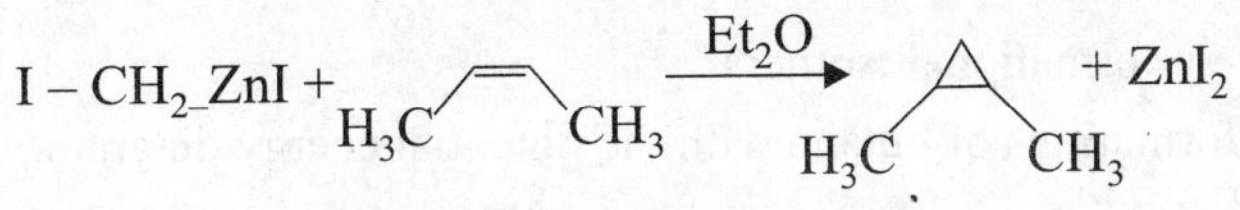

Mechanism of Simmons–Smith Reaction

A concerted reaction in which both the new C – C are formed simultaneously. Best viewed as the nucleophilic C = C causing loss of the iodide as leaving group and the electrons from the nucleophilic C–Zn being used to form the other C–C bond.

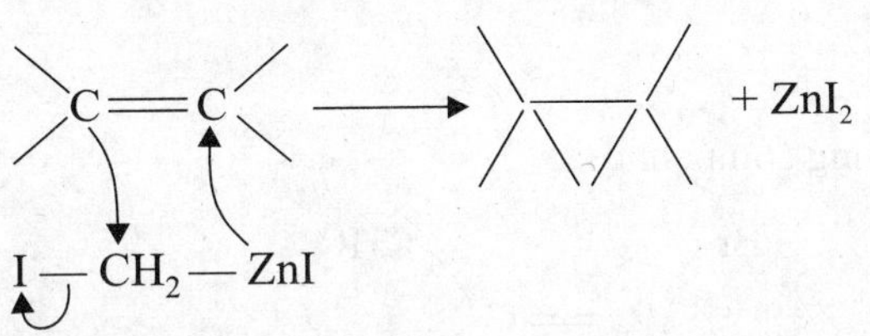

Metal–Organic Framework

Metal–organic frameworks (MOFs) are a new class of crystalline porous materials consisting of metal ions or clusters coordinated to rigid organic molecules, i.e., organic ligands to form one-, two-, or three-dimensional structures. These have high porosities and specific functionalities and find wide applications in catalysis, magnetism, separation, and gas adsorption. They not only offer high surface areas but also provide tunable pore shapes/sizes. As a consequence, they are allowed greater chemical alteration on a periodic scale and can be used as hosts for encapsulating other guest molecules to construct new multifunctional materials. Examples of some MOFs are Zn_4O (BTE) (BPDC), where BTE^{3-} = 4, 4′, 4″ – [benzene-1, 3, 5 – triyl-tris (ethyne π 2, 1– diyl)] tribenzoate and $BPDC^{2-}$ = biphenyl-4, 4′-dicarboxylate; $Zn_4O(BDC)_3$, where BDC^{2-} = 1, 4-benzenedicarboxylate; $Cu_3(BTC)_2$ $(H_2O)_3$, where H_3BTC = 1,3, 5-benzenetricarboxylic acid; and so on.

QUESTIONS

1. What are stereoisomers?
2. What is configurational isomerism?
3. What do you mean by plane polarized light?
4. What is optical activity?
5. What do you mean by specific rotation?
6. What is the only necessary, inflexible, and sufficient condition to exhibit optical activity?
7. Allenes do not contain any chiral center but still exhibit optical isomerism. Explain.
8. Explain Fischer projection with a suitable example.
9. What do you mean by enantiomers?

10. How enantiomers differ from diastereoisomers?
11. Discuss the optical isomers of tartaric acid.
12. In R, S system of nomenclature of optical isomers, what is the significance of the terms of "R" and "S"?
13. What are the characteristics of enantiomers?
14. What are the characteristics of diastereoisomers?
15. What is do you mean by conformational isomers?
16. Explain the different conformations of butane with the potential energy diagram.
17. Assign R, S rotation to the following compound:

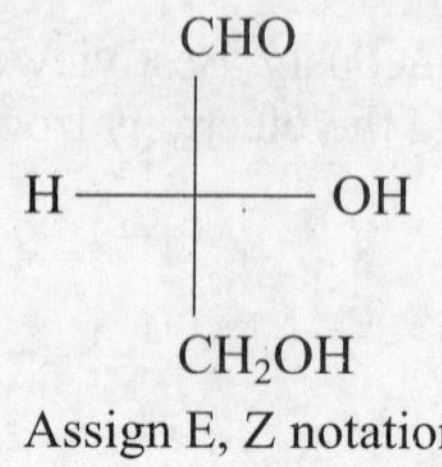

18. Assign E, Z notation to the following compounds:

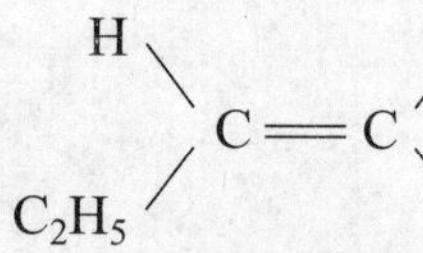

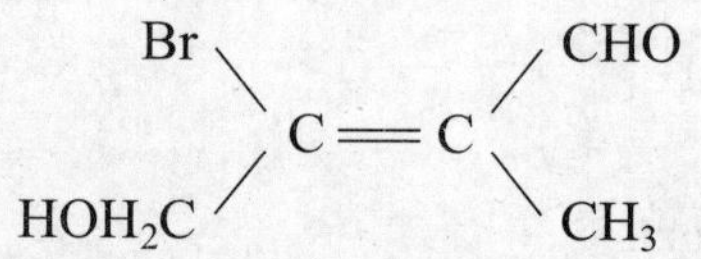

19. Discuss the optical isomers of lactic acid.
20. Assign R, S notation to the following compounds:

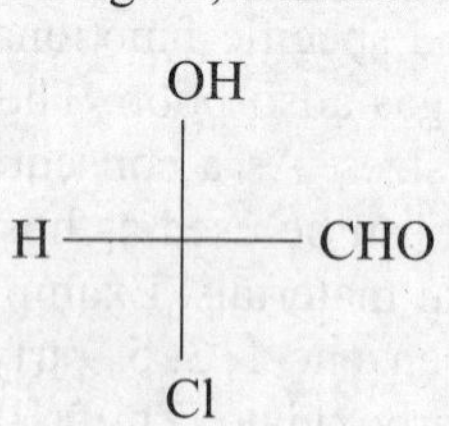

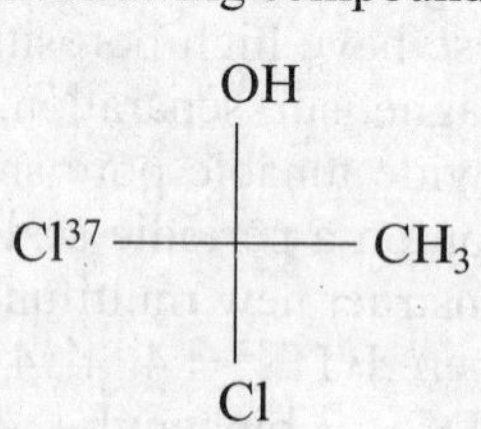

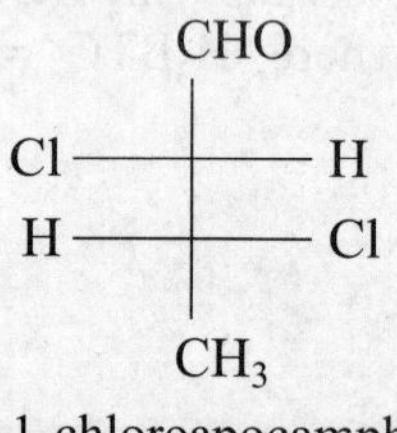

21. 1-chloroapocamphane does not hydrolyze upon being refluxed with alcoholic KOH for 24 h. Explain.
22. Explain internal Cannizzaro reaction with a suitable example.
23. What are reaction intermediates?
24. What is the shape of a carbocation? What is the state of hybridization of "C" in carbocation?
25. Arrange the following carbocations in order of their increasing stability: 3°, 1°-allylic, 2°-allylic, benzylic, and tropylium.
26. Name the intermediate formed in S_N1 mechanism.
27. What is peroxide effect?

28. What is Markownikoff rule?
29. Why peroxide effect is only confined to addition of only HBr?
30. Discuss the effect of solvent in S_N1 mechanism?
31. Polar aprotic solvents favour S_N2 mechanism. Explain.
32. S_N1 mechanism proceeds through partial racemization of the product. Explain.
33. What is the difference between basicity and nucleophilicity?
34. What are the requirements of a good nucleophile?
35. Nucleophilic substitution is not possible at bridge head carbon of a bicyclic system even in the presence of a potential leaving group at the location.
36. Why *o*-, *p*-orienting groups are ring activators?
37. Halogens (Cl—, Br—, and I—) are *o*- and *p*-orienting but at the same time are ring deactivators. Explain.
38. Although oxygen is more electronegative than —Cl or —Br, yet the —OH group is an activating group while the latter are deactivating. Explain.
39. What is ortho effect?
40. Differentiate between S_N1 and S_N2 reactions.
41. Why vinyl chloride does not undergo nucleophilic substitution reaction?
42. Why presence of α-hydrogen is essential for aldol condensation?
43. Why are ketones less reactive towards nucleophiles than aldehydes?
44. Identify the products:

(a) $CH_3—CH_2—CH{=}CH_2 \xrightarrow{OSO_4,\ H_2O_2} A$

$\quad \xrightarrow{RCO_3H,\ H_2O} B$

(b)

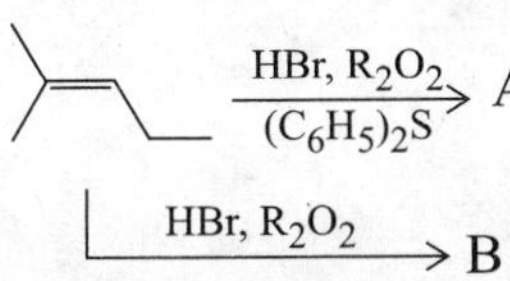

(c)

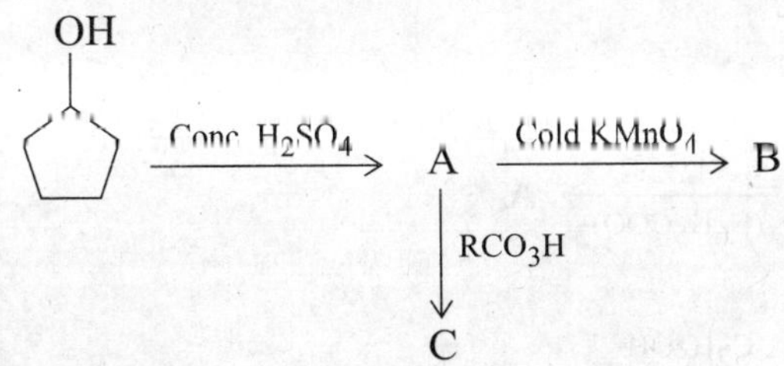

(d)

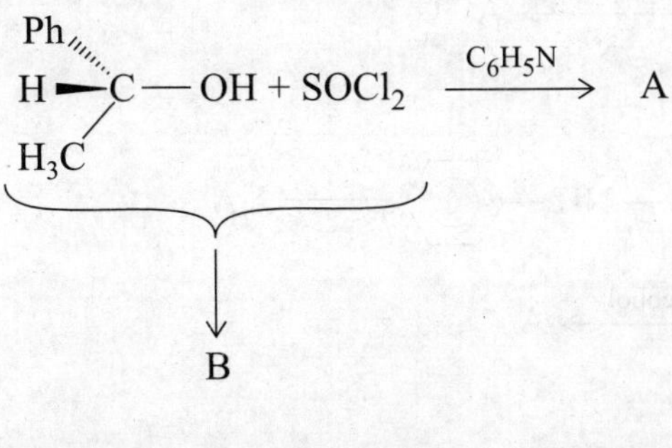

(e) $R{-}I + \text{Alc. KCN} \longrightarrow A \begin{cases} \xrightarrow{H_2O-HCl} B \\ \xrightarrow{H_2O-\text{Alk. } H_2O_2} C \\ \xrightarrow{LiAlH_4} D \end{cases}$

(f) 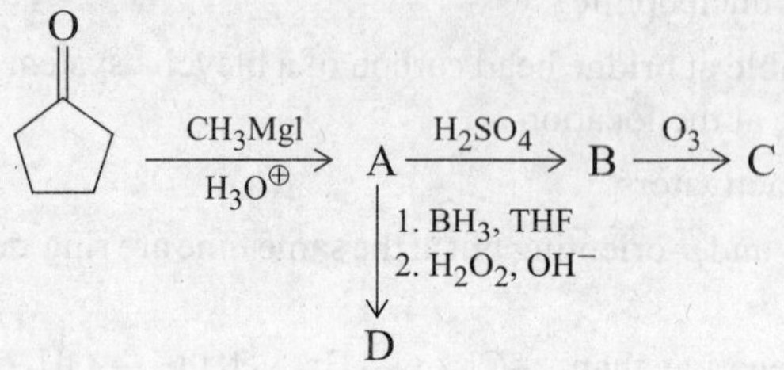

(g) 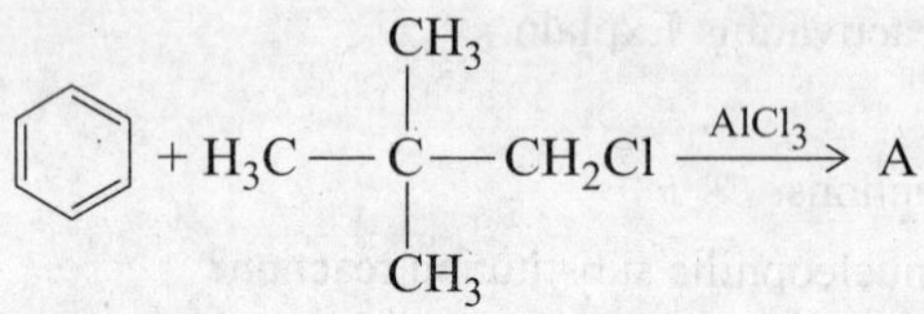

(h) 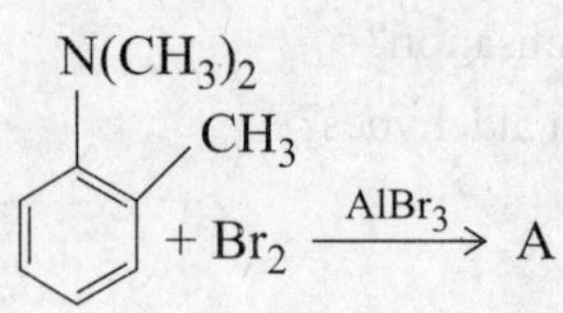

(i) $CH_3{-}CH_2{-}Cl \xrightarrow{\text{Aq. KOH}} A$

$\quad\quad \xrightarrow{\text{Alc. KOH}} B$

(j) $CH_3{-}CH{=}CH_2 \xrightarrow[2.\ H_2O_2,/OH^-]{1.\ B_2H_6,/THF} A$

$\quad\quad \xrightarrow{H_2O/H^+} B$

(k) $CH_2{=}CH{-}CH{=}CH_2 \xrightarrow[(C_6H_5COO)_2]{Cl_2} A$

(l) $CH_2{=}C(CH_3){-}CH(Cl){-}CH_3 \xrightarrow[S_N1]{C_2H_5OH} A$

(m) 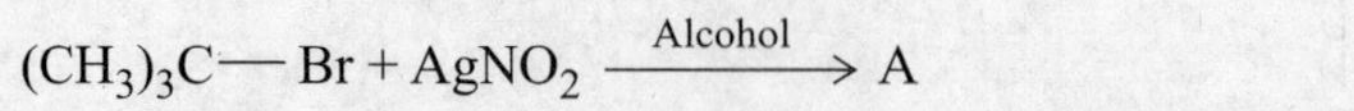

(n) $(CH_3)_3C{-}Br + AgNO_2 \xrightarrow{\text{Alcohol}} A$

45. Explain β-elimination reaction with a suitable example.
46. State and explain Saytzeff rule.
47. What do you mean by Hofmann's elimination?
48. Which factors decide the ratio of elimination and substitution?
49. In general, proportion of elimination increases with increased chain branching of the reactant. Explain.
50. The Beckmann rearrangement is stereospecific. Explain with a suitable example.
51. Write the major product and suggest a suitable mechanism.

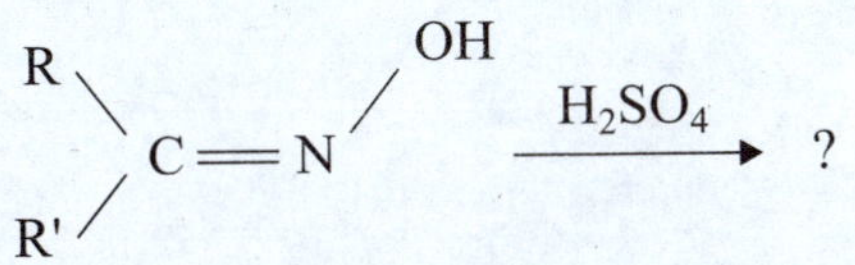

52. Explain the mechanism of Hoffmann rearrangement.
53. Explain with an example how Beckmann rearrangement can be utilized for ring expansion.
54. The Hoffmann rearrangement proceeds with complete retention of configuration about the chiral center of the migrating group. Explain with a suitable example.
55. Provide the mechanism in following transformation:

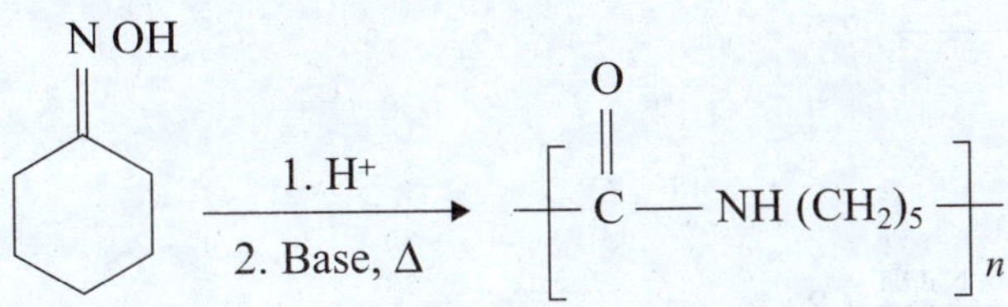

56. Discuss one application of Hoffmann rearrangement.
57. What is the intermediate in Hoffmann rearrangement?
58. Relative higher strength and concentration of base facilitates which elimination mechanism.
59. Explain the stereo chemical aspects of S_N1 and S_N2 reactions.
60. What are the different factors that affect a nucleophilic substitution reaction?
61. State and explain Markownikoff's rule. Why does the rule fail during addition of HBr in presence of peroxide?
62. Provide the mechanism of ozonolysis by taking a suitable alkene. Show how the products differ when you carry out ozonolysis in oxidizing and reducing environments.
63. What is anchimeric assistances? Explain with a suitable example. What are the requirements? Also provide the result.
64. What are singlet and triplet carbenes? Which form is more stable and why? Also provide their shapes.
65. Discuss cross aldol condensation involving equimolar quantities of acetaldehyde and formaldehyde. Also write the different side products of the reaction?
66. What is cross cannizzaro reaction? Explain with a suitable example.
67. What is Reimer–Tiemann reaction? Provide the mechanism.
68. For the following reactions, write the major product and suggest a suitable mechanism for its formation.

(a) 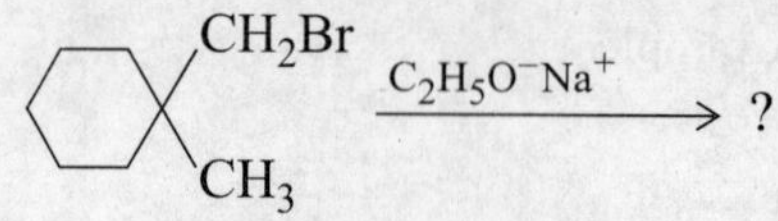

(b) 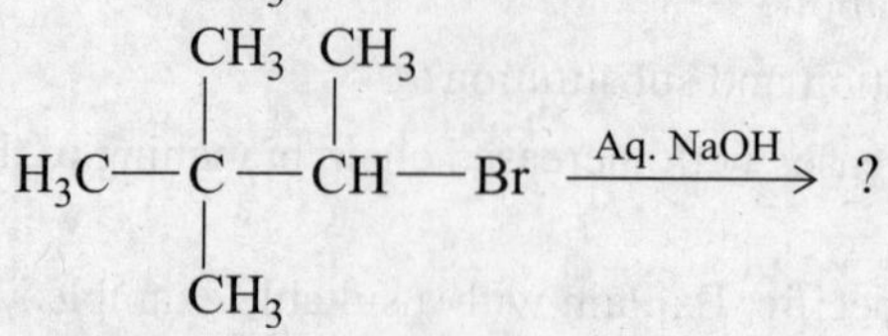

(c) 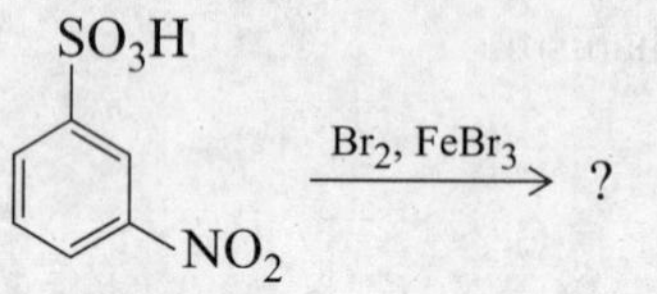

(d) 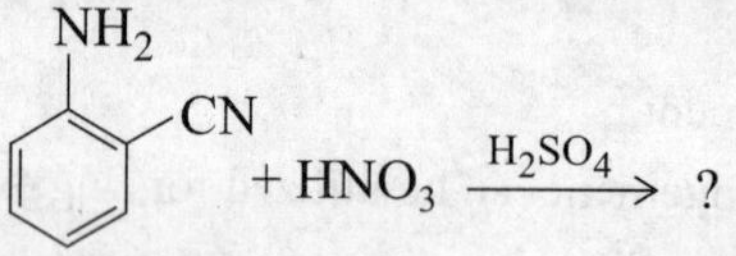

(e) 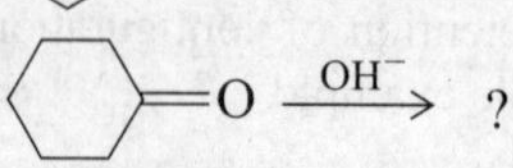

(f) 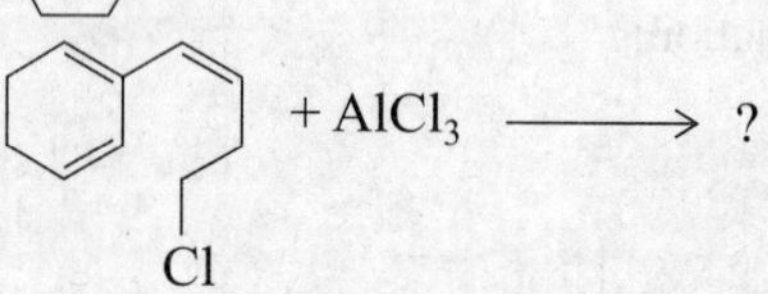

(g) 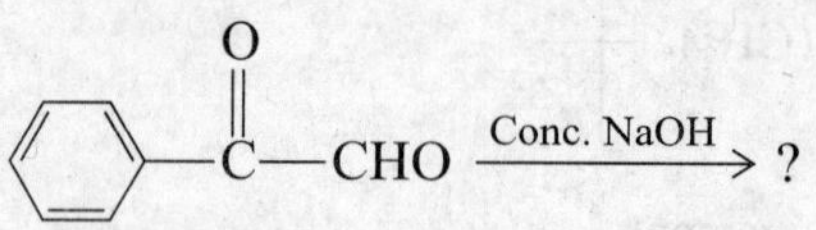

(h) 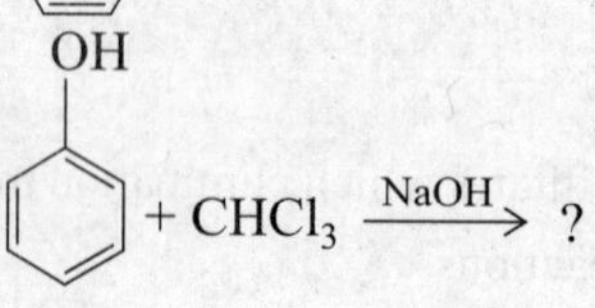

CHAPTER

11 Analytical Chemistry

Chapter Outline

- UV-Vis Spectroscopy
- IR Spectroscopy
- Flame Photometry
- Atomic Absorption Spectroscopy
- Thermal Analysis (TGA, DTA, and DSC)
- Chromatography (Column, Gas, HPLC)

Spectroscopy is the study of the interaction between matter and electromagnetic radiation with specified wavelengths. Spectrometry is the measurement of these responses, and the instrument that performs such measurements is known as a spectrometer or spectrograph. If the matter is a molecule, specifically the term *molecular spectroscopy* is used. The nature of the interaction between electromagnetic radiation and the matter is of different types. The most common interactions are as follows:

1. Absorption—Energy is absorbed by the matter, as a result of which molecules are excited and promoted to higher energy levels.
2. Emission—Energy is radiated from the matter, as result of which molecules are de-excited and accordingly get demoted to the lower energy levels.

The energy levels associated with a molecule may be electronic (related to the distribution of constituent electrons), vibrational (related to different types of vibrational motions of the molecules), rotational (related to different types of rotational motions of the molecules), and nuclear (related to the distribution of constituent nuclei within the molecule). Depending on the different types of energy levels, molecular spectroscopy can be discussed under the following headings:

1. *UV-Vis spectroscopy* corresponds to the excitation of the outer shell electrons between the energy levels that correspond to the molecular orbital of the systems. In this spectroscopy, molecule is excited from the lower electronic state to the upper one. This spectroscopy is used to detect chromophoric (color generating) groups in a molecule.
2. *IR spectroscopy* corresponds to the transition of molecules between vibrational energy levels. It measures the bond vibration frequencies in a molecule and is used to determine the functional group.

3. *Rotational* for transition between rotational energy levels.
4. *NMR* (nuclear magnetic resonance) for transition between nuclear energy levels. This spectroscopy is used to detect carbon–hydrogen framework of the compound.

UV-Vis Spectroscopy (Electronic Spectroscopy)

UV-Vis region of the complete electromagnetic spectrum extends from 150 to 800 nm or mμ. In practice, 200–800 mμ is considered for analysis. In the region below 200 mμ, oxygen and nitrogen present in air absorb strongly. Therefore, this region can be considered only after the evacuation of the complete path length and is known as far/vaccum UV-region.

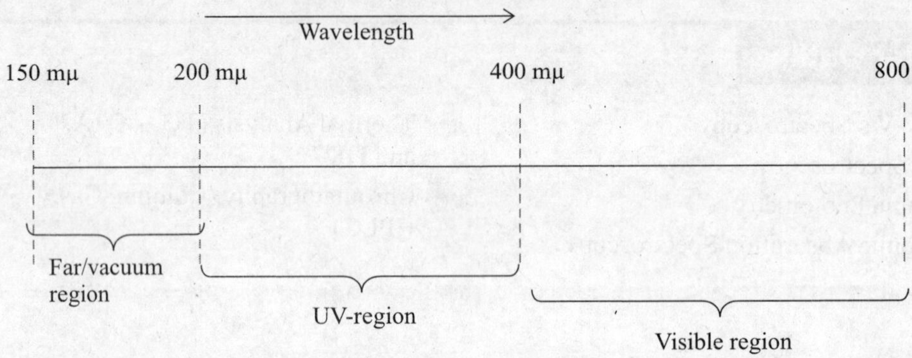

Absorption Law (Beer–Lambert Law)

When a beam of monochromatic light is passed through a pure homogeneous solution of a light-absorbing material, the decrease in the intensity of the light with the thickness of the solution ($-\mathrm{d}I/\mathrm{d}x$) is directly proportional to the intensity (I) of the light and to the concentration of the solution (c) (Fig. 11.1).

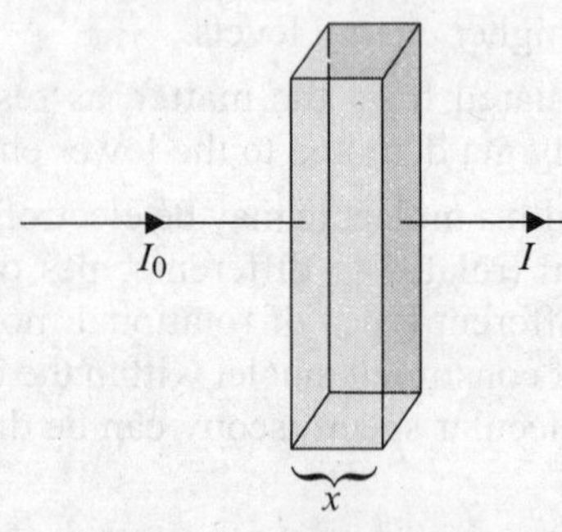

Fig. 11.1

Thus, $-\dfrac{\mathrm{d}I}{\mathrm{d}x} \propto Ic$

or $\dfrac{\mathrm{d}I}{\mathrm{d}x} = \in' Ic$ (where $\in'$ is the proportionality constant known as molar absorption coefficient)

or $\displaystyle\int_{I_0}^{I} \frac{\mathrm{d}I}{\mathrm{d}x} = \int_0^x \in' c\,\mathrm{d}x$

or $\ln \frac{I}{I_0} = -\in' cx$

or $\frac{I}{I_0} = e^{-\in' cx}$

or $I = I_0 e^{-\in' cx}$ ...[11.1]

Again,

$$\log \frac{I}{I_0} = -\frac{\in'}{2.303} cx$$

or $\log \frac{I}{I_0} = -\in cx$ ...[11.2]

or $I = I_0 10^{-\in cx}$ ...[11.3]

where $\in$ is the molar extinction coefficient or simply absorptivity which is nothing but $\in'/2.303$, I_0 is the intensity before transmission, I is the intensity after transmission through a thickness x of the medium, x is the total path length, and c is the concentration of the solution. Obviously, $I_0 > I$.

Alternative expression

Relation [11.2] can be expressed as

$\log \frac{I_0}{I} = \in cx$ ...[11.4]

or $A = \in cx$ ...[11.5]

Here it is to be marked that $(I/I_0) = T$ (trasmittance). Thus, $A = -\log_{10} T = -\log_{10}(I/I_0)$. It is observed that a plot of absorbance against concentration is linear. It is therefore more convenient to express results in absorbance rather than transmittance when measuring unknown concentrations, as the former allows linear calibration plots. The nature of both the plots are shown in Fig. 11.2.

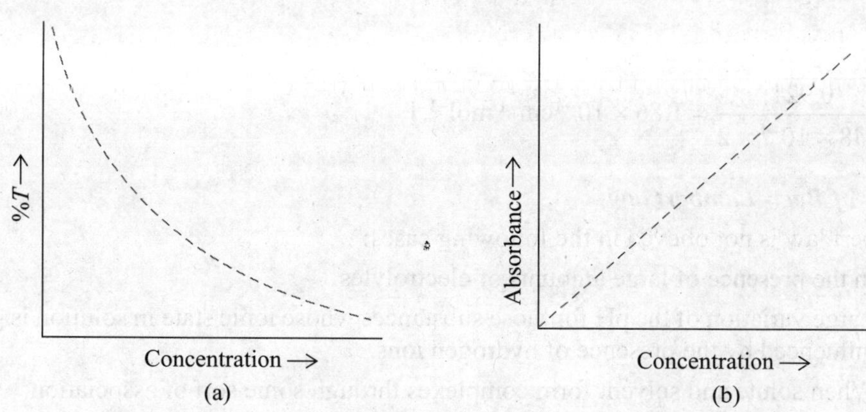

Fig. 11.2 (a) plot of transmittance against concentration and (b) plot of absorbance against concentration

Physical significance of ∈

We know,

$$\in = \frac{A}{cx}$$

So the molar absorptivity ∈ is the absorbance per centimeter when the concentration of absorbing material is 1M. The molar absorptivity is a measure of the ability of an analyte to absorb light at a specified wavelength or, in other words, the molar absorptivity of a compound is a constant that is characteristic of the compound at a particular wavelength.

Example 11.1

The molar absorptivity of a substance is 2.0×10^4 cm^{-1} mol^{-1} l. Calculate the transmittance through a cuvette of path length 5.0 cm containing 2.0×10^{-6} mol l^{-3} solution of the substance.

Solution

As per the Beer–Lambert law, $A = \in cx$

or $A = 2.0 \times 10^4 \times 2.0 \times 10^{-6} \times 5.0$

$= 0.2$

or $\log \frac{1}{T} = 0.2$

or $T = 0.63$

Example 11.2

A solution containing 36.5 g of $K_2Cr_2O_7$ per 500 cm^3 was taken in a cuvette having a path length of 2 cm and its transmittance was measured at 455 nm. If the percentage transmittance is found to be 12, calculate the molar absorptivity of $K_2Cr_2O_7$.

Solution

$$\text{Molarity of } K_2Cr_2O_7 = \frac{0.0365}{294} \times \frac{1000}{500} = 2.48 \times 10^{-4} \text{ mol l}^{-1}$$

$T = 0.12$, thus $A = \log (1/T) = 0.921$

Substituting in Beer–Lambert law, $A = \in cx$

or $$\in = \frac{A}{cx}$$

$$= \frac{0.921}{2.48 \times 10^{-4} \times 2} = 1.86 \times 10^{-3} \text{ cm}^{-1} \text{ mol}^{-1} \text{ l}$$

Limitations of Beer–Lambert law

Beer–Lambert law is not obeyed in the following cases:

1. In the presence of large amounts of electrolytes.
2. Large variation of the pH for those substances whose ionic state in solution is greatly influenced by the presence of hydrogen ions.
3. When solute and solvent form complexes through some sort of association.
4. The radiation is non-monochromatic, that is, polychromatic.
5. Applicable only for diluted solution.

Theory of UV-Vis Spectroscopy

According to Planck's law, an energy level associated with electron(s) is energetically always quantized. So, at a specific wavelength, when the radiation energy perfectly matches with the energy gap between two quantized energy levels, only electron undergoes transition from the lower level to the upper level. That means, any electronic transition is also *quantized in nature*, by default, even if the interacting energy is continuum in nature. Electronic transition resulting in UV-Vis spectroscopy always follows Franck–Condon principle: "At the instant of excitation, only electrons are reorganized, the heavier nuclei retain the ground state geometry." Because of this electronic transitions always take place vertically with respect to nuclear coordinate (Fig. 11.3).

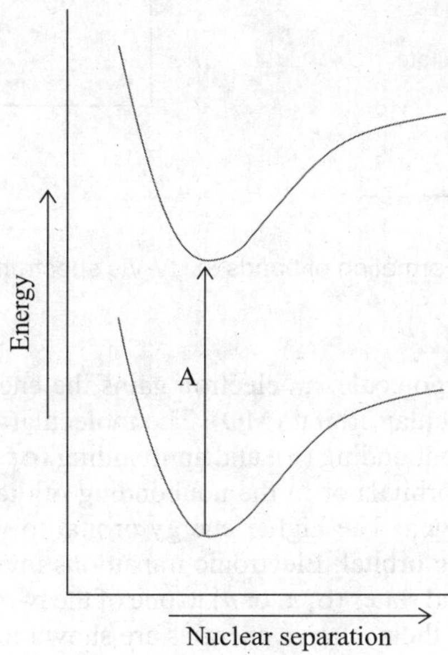

Fig. 11.3

Why broad band, not line spectra?

For ultraviolet and visible wavelengths, one should expect that the absorption spectrum of a molecule should show a collection of few very sharp lines. Each line should occur at a wavelength where the energy of an incident photon exactly matches the energy required to bring an electronic transition. In practice, it is found that the ultraviolet and visible spectra of most of the molecules consist of a few humps rather than sharp lines. These humps show that the molecule is absorbing radiation over a band of wavelengths. One reason for this band, rather than line absorption, is that an electronic level transition is usually accompanied by a simultaneous change between the more numerous vibrational levels. Furthermore, each of the many vibrational levels associated with the electronic states also has a large number of rotational levels associated with it. Thus, a transition can consist of a large electronic component, a smaller vibrational element, and an even smaller rotational change. The rotational contribution to the transition has the effect of filling in the gaps in the vibrational fine structure. "To be specific, an electronic band coupled with vibrational and rotational fine structures in superimposed fashion is the answer of this query. In addition, when molecules are closely packed together as they normally are in solution, they exert influences on each other which slightly disturb the already numerous, and almost infinite energy levels and blur the sharp spectral lines into bands" (Fig. 11.4).

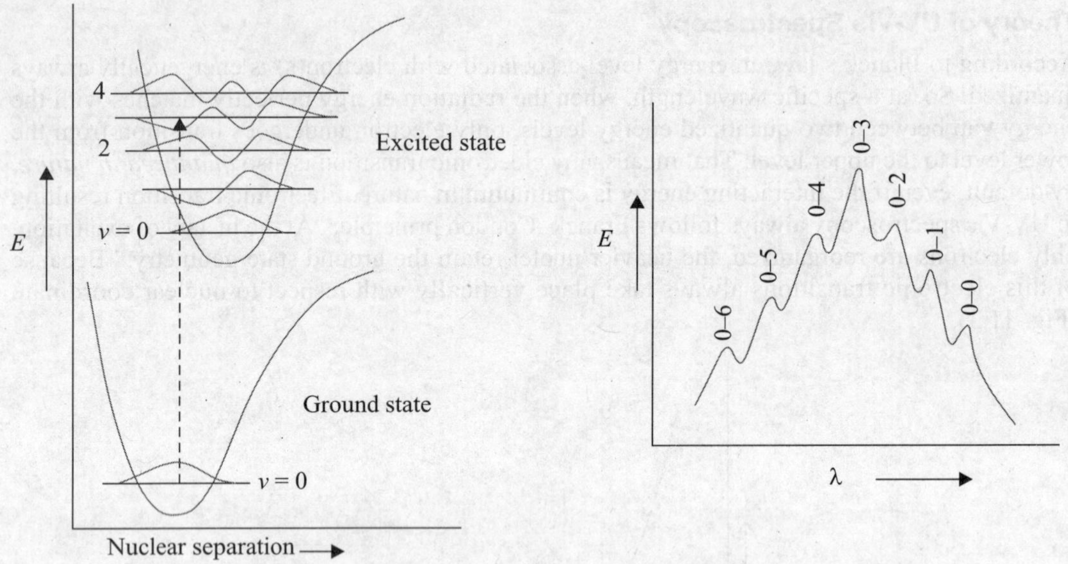

Fig. 11.4 Formation of bands in UV-Vis spectrum

Different electronic transitions

When a photon is absorbed by a molecule, an electron gains the energy of the photon and is promoted to a higher energy molecular orbital (MO). The molecular orbitals in molecules are of three types, bonding (σ or π), nonbonding (*n*), and antibonding (σ* or π*). The electrons are normally resident in the bonding orbitals or in the nonbonding orbitals if there are lone pairs on atoms such as nitrogen or oxygen. The higher energy orbital to which they are promoted is almost invariably an antibonding orbital. Electronic transitions involve the promotion of an electron from one of the three ground states (σ, π, or *n*) to one of the two excited states (σ* or π*). The four important transitions and their relative energies are shown in Fig. 11.5.

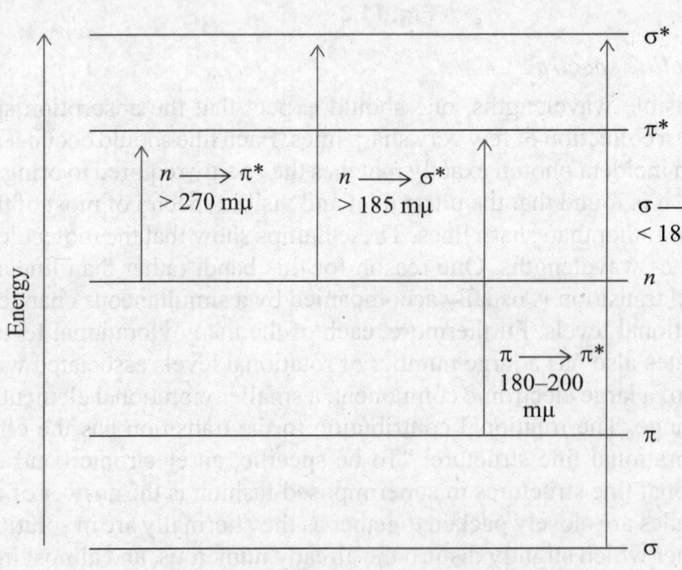

Fig. 11.5 Different possible transitions

The energy order for different transitions is $n \rightarrow \pi^* < \pi \rightarrow \pi^* < n \rightarrow \sigma^* < \sigma \rightarrow \sigma^*$. The lower the energy gap, the longer is the wavelength of EM radiation required to have the same energy gap. Thus, transitions of $\pi \rightarrow \pi^*$, $n \rightarrow \pi^*$ and $n \rightarrow \sigma^*$ normally produce absorption in the UV/visible region (200–700 mμ), that is, only molecules with n or π electrons give characteristic UV/Vis spectra. From the molecular orbital diagram it is clear that in all compounds other than alkanes there are several possible electronic transitions that can occur with different energies. Let us look into these transitions in detail.

Types of electronic transitions

1. $\sigma \rightarrow \sigma^*$ ***transitions:*** Compounds with only σ bond are required to have such transitions. It appears in saturated hydrocarbons where all valence electrons are utilized in the formation of σ-bonds. Such transitions require short wavelength (< 200 mμ) and mostly occur in far/vacuum UV region. For example, cycloalkane: λ_{max} = 135 mμ.

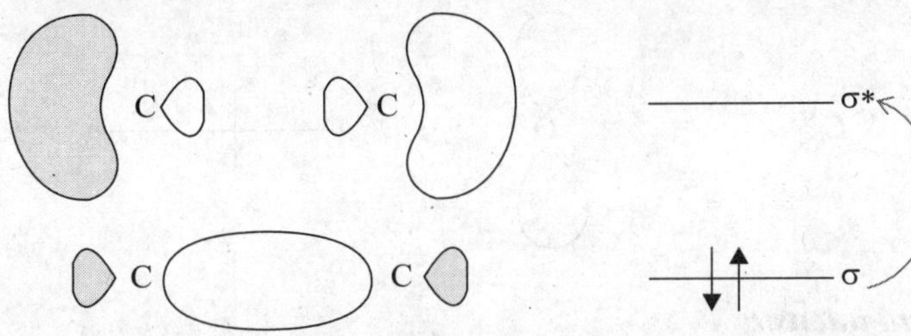

2. $n \rightarrow \sigma^*$ ***transitions:*** Excitation takes place from a nonbonding orbital to an antibonding σ* orbital. This is a symmetry forbidden and low-intensity transition. This is found in saturated compounds containing a hetero atom with unshared pair of electron. For example, saturated halides, alcohols, ethers, amines, and carbonyl compounds. Let us see some specific examples: CH_3OH (174 mμ), MeCl (169 mμ), MeI (258 mμ).

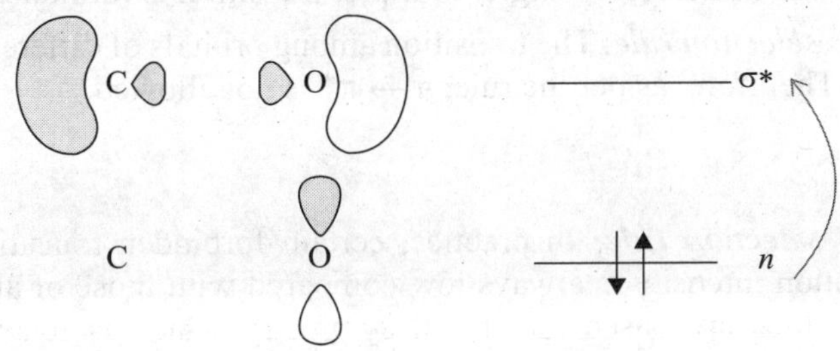

3. $\pi \rightarrow \pi^*$ ***transitions:*** Found in compounds containing double, triple bonds, or aromatic rings. Here a π electron is excited to an antibonding π* orbital. This is usually a symmetry allowed and high intensity transition. For example, unconjugated alkenes absorb

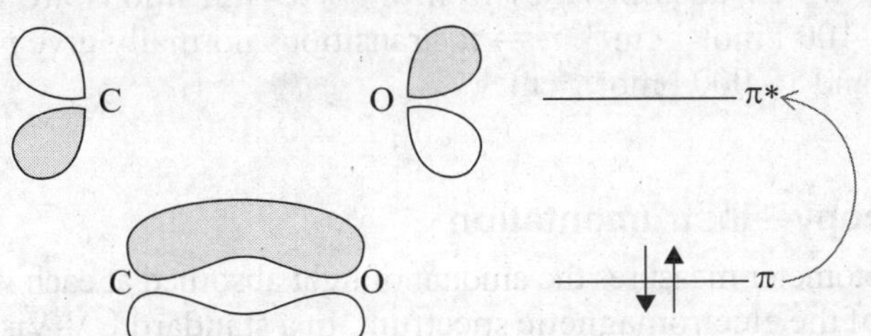

around 170–190 mμ and carbonyl compounds absorbs around 180 mμ. Extention in conjugation lowers energy gap and brings a hike in λ_{max}.

4. ***n → π* transitions:*** Found in unsaturated compounds containing a hetero atom with unshared pair of electron, such as carbonyl compounds and nitriles. Here the excitation of an electron from a nonbonding orbital to an antibonding π* orbital takes place. Extended conjugation lowers energy gap and increases λ_{max}. This is a symmetry forbidden and low-intensity transition. For example, in case of saturated aldehydes and ketones, λ_{max} remains around 185–300 mμ.

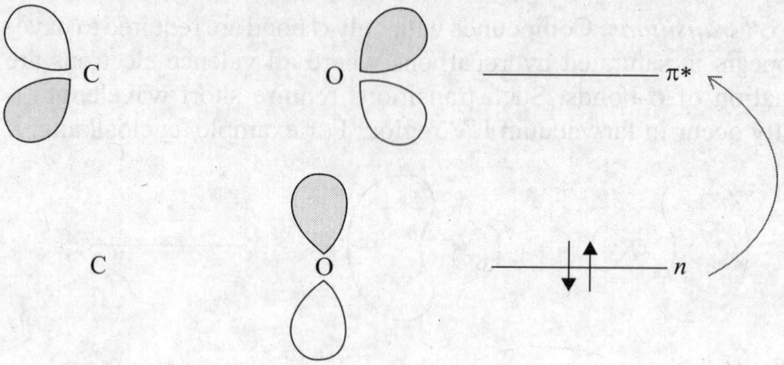

Selection rules and intensity

All possible transitions are not allowed. There are certain selection rules that quantum theory imposes on electronic transitions to determine which are allowed and which are forbidden. The point to be highlighted is that the intensity of transition is directly proportional to the probability of transition.

1. *Spin selection rule*: Transition involving change in spin quantum number of electron is not allowed. Therefore, singlet to triplet transition is forbidden.
2. *Symmetry selection rule*: The transition among orbitals of different symmetries is not allowed. Therefore, as per the rule, $n \rightarrow \pi^*$ is not allowed.

Note:

Relaxation of selection rule: In practice, certain forbidden transitions are observed, but the absorption intensity is always low compared with those of allowed transitions. The selection rules are based on orbital symmetry which is relaxed by vibrational components of the transition, thus allowing "forbidden" transitions to occur (although with low probability). Most absorption spectroscopy of organic compounds is based on transitions of *n* or π electrons to the π* excited state. This is because the absorption peaks for these transitions fall in an experimentally convenient region of the spectrum (200–700 nm). Molar absorptivities from $n \rightarrow \pi^*$ transitions are relatively low, and range from 10–100 l mol^{-1} cm^{-1}. $\pi \rightarrow \pi^*$ transitions normally give molar absorptivities between 1000 and 10,000 l mol^{-1} cm^{-1}.

UV-Vis Spectroscopy—Instrumentation

A UV-Vis spectrophotometer measures the amount of light absorbed at each wavelength of the UV and visible regions of the electromagnetic spectrum. In a standard UV-Vis spectrophotometer, a beam of light is splited and half of the beam (the sample beam) is directed through a transparent cell containing a solution of the compound being analyzed, and the other half (the reference beam) is directed through an identical cell that does not contain the compound but contains the solvent. Figure 11.6 shows the schematic representation of a typical UV-Vis spectro meter.

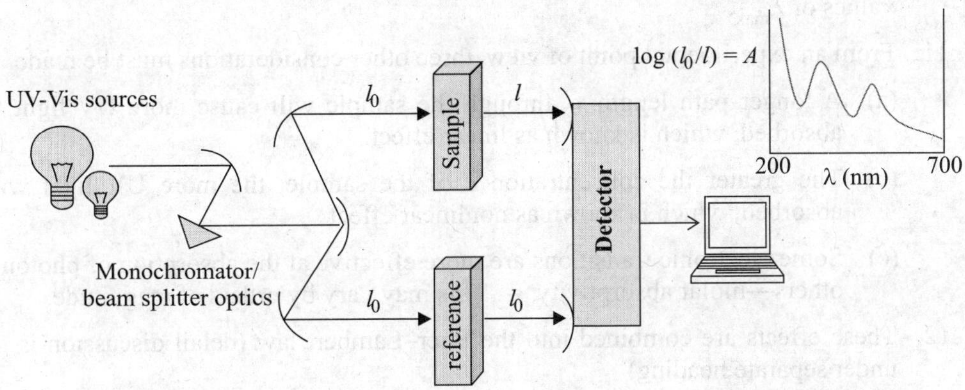

Fig. 11.6 Schematic representation of a typical UV-Vis spectrometer

Important features of UV-Vis spectroscopy

1. Two sources are required to scan the entire UV-Vis band: Deuterium lamp covers the UV region (–200 to 330) mμ, while tungsten lamp covers the visible region (330–700 mμ).
2. The beam splitter sends a separate band to a cell containing the sample solution and a reference solution.
3. The detector measures the difference between the transmitted light through the sample (I) and the incident light (I_0) and sends this information to the recorder.
4. Virtually all UV spectra are recorded in solution phase.
5. Cells can be made of plastic glass, or quartz. A typical sample cell commonly called a *cuvette*.
6. Only quartz is transparent in the full 200–700 mμ range, while plastic and glass are only suitable for visible spectra.
7. Solvents must be transparent in the region to be observed and the wavelength where a solvent is no longer transparent is referred to as the cutoff.
8. Since spectra are only obtained up to 200 nm, solvents typically only need to lack conjugated systems or carbonyls. Common solvents and their cutoffs in terms of millimicron (mμ) are as follows.

Solvent	Cutoff (λ) in mμ	Solvent	Cutoff (λ) in mμ
Acetonitrile	190	95% Ethanol	205
Chloroform	240	*n*-Hexane	201
Cyclohexane	195	Methanol	205
1,4-Dioxane	215	Isooctane	195
Water	190		

9. The x-axis of the spectrum is in wavelength and the y-axis of the spectrum is in absorbance, A. Here $A \log_{10} (I_0/I)$ and it is the inverse of transmittance.
10. Due to the lack of any fine structure, spectra are rarely shown in their raw form, rather the peak maxima are simply reported as a numerical list of "lambada max" values or λ_{max}.
11. From an experimental point of view, three other considerations must be made.
    (a) A longer path length x through the sample will cause more UV light to be absorbed, which is known as linear effect.
    (b) The greater the concentration c of the sample, the more UV light will be absorbed, which is known as nonlinear effect.
    (c) Some electronic transitions are more effective at the absorption of photon than others—molar absorptivity, $\in$. This may vary by orders of magnitude.
12. These effects are combined into the Beer–Lambert law (detail discussion is given under separate heading)
    (a) For most of the UV spectrometers, x remains constant (standard cells are typically 1 cm in path length).
    (b) Concentration is typically varied depending on the strength of absorption observed or expected.
    (c) Molar absorptivities vary by orders of magnitude:
        (i) Values of 10^4–10^6 are termed high-intensity absorptions
        (ii) Values of 10^3–10^4 are termed low-intensity absorption
        (iii) Values of 0–10^3 are the absorptions of forbidden transitions
13. Absorbance "A" is unitless, so the unit for $\in$ is litre/(mol × cm) or cm^2/mol.
14. Since path length and concentration effects can be easily factored out, absorbance (A) simply becomes proportional to $\in$ and the y-axis is expressed as $\in$ directly or as the logarithm of $\in$.
15. Three types of plots are generally drawn during measurement in UV-Vis spectroscopy, which are shown in Fig. 11.7.

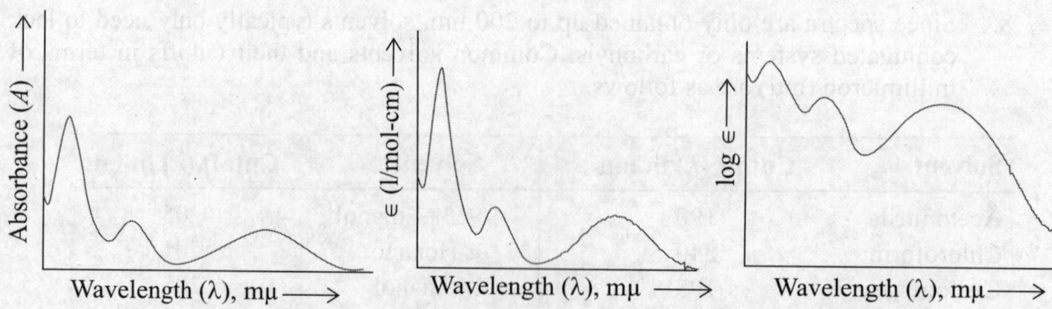

Fig. 11.7 Different modes of representing UV-Vis spectrum

Concept of Chrompohore and Auxochrome

Any isolated covalently bonded group that shows a characteristic absorption in the UV-Vis region is known as *chromphore.* Let us tabulate some of the imporatant chromophores along with the possible modes of transitions and their corresponding wavelengths.

Chromophore	Example	Excitation	λmax in mμ	∈	Solvent
C=C	Ethene	$\pi \rightarrow \pi^*$	171	15000	Hexane
C≡C	1-Hexyne	$\pi \rightarrow \pi^*$	180	10000	Hexane
C=O	Ethanal	$n \rightarrow \pi^*$	290	15	Hexane
		$\pi \rightarrow \pi^*$	180	10000	
N=O	Nitromethane	$n \rightarrow \pi^*$	275	17	Ethanol
		$\pi \rightarrow \pi^*$	200	5000	
C—X; X: Br, I	Methyl bromide/	$n \rightarrow \sigma^*$	205	200	Hexane
	methyl iodide	$n \rightarrow \sigma^*$	255	360	

Note:

The presence of chromophores in a molecule is detected by UV-visible spectroscopy. It is quite problematic to detect isolated chromophores because they generally absorb below 200 nm. Fortunately, conjugation generally moves the absorption maxima to longer wavelengths.

An *auxochrome* is an auxillary group which interacts with chromophore and causes a shift in the UV or visible absorption maximum to a longer wavelength. However, by itself it does not absorb in UV-Vis zone. The effect of chromophore is due to its ability to extend conjugation of a chrophore by the sharing of nonbonding electrons. For example,

—NH_2, —NHR, —NR_2, —OH, —OR, —X groups.

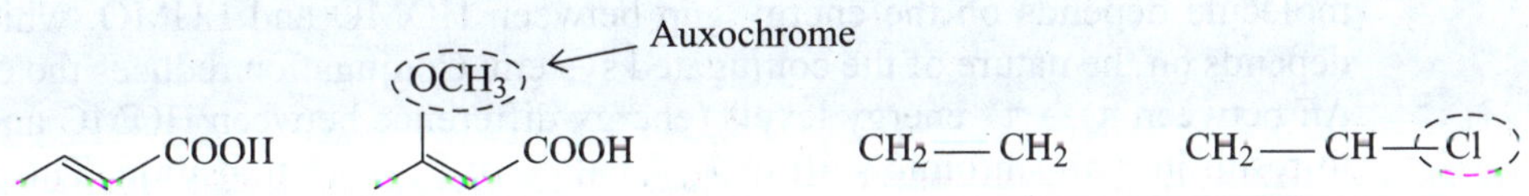

$\pi \rightarrow \pi^*$: $\lambda_{max} = 204$ mμ $\lambda_{max} = 234$ mμ $\lambda_{max} = 171$ mμ $\lambda_{max} = 185$ mμ

Different shifts in absorbance and intensity in shown in Fig. 11.8.

Bathochromic shift (red shift): It is the shift of λ_{max} to the longer wavelength. Shift of an absorption maximum to the longer wavelength is called bathochromic shift. It occurs due to substituent and solvent effects (detail is discussed in factors affecting absorbance and intensity).

Hypsochromic shift (blue shift): It is the shift of λ_{max} to shorter wavelength. Shift of absorption maximum to the shorter wavelength is known as hypsochromic shift. It also occurs due to substituent and solvent effects.

Hyperchromic effect: It is the effect leading to increased absorption intensity; that is, $\in$.

Hypochromic effect: It is the effect leading to decreased absorption intensity; that is, $\in$.

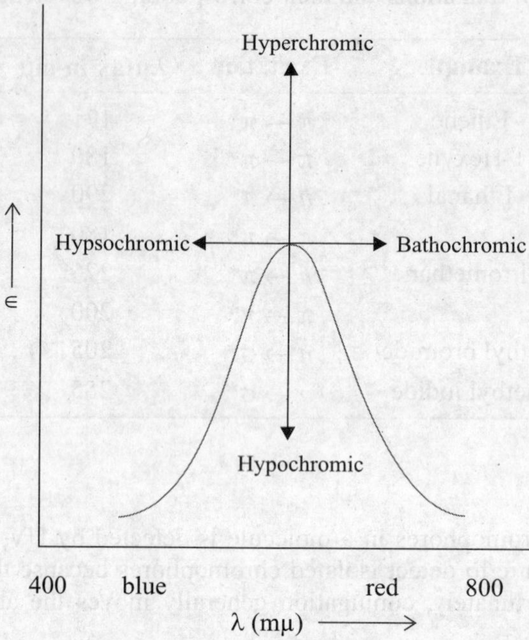

Fig. 11.8 Different shifts in absorbance and Intensity

Factors Affecting Absorbance and Intensity

Effect of Substituents

1. **Conjugation**

   For "ene" system: Wavelength necessary to effect $\pi \rightarrow \pi^*$ transition in a conjugated molecule depends on the energy gap between HOMO and LUMO, which in turn depends on the nature of the conjugated system. Conjugation reduces the energy gap ΔE between $\pi \rightarrow \pi^*$ energy levels (energy difference between HOMO and LUMO) to result in bathochromic shift of λ_{max} value for $\pi \rightarrow \pi^*$ transition. This is evident from the MO diagram shown in Fig. (11.9).

   Extending this effect out to longer conjugated systems the energy gap becomes progressively smaller. Each additional double bond in the conjugated electron system shifts the absorption maximum about 30 nm in the same direction. Also, the molar absorptivity ($\in$) roughly doubles with each new conjugated double bond. Thus, extending conjugation generally results in *bathochromic* and *hyperchromic* shifts in absorption. The appearance of several absorption peaks or shoulders for a given chromophore indicates the presence of different conformations of such systems as well as electronic transitions between the different vibrational energy levels possible for each electronic state. The λ_{max} and $\in$ values for ethylene and conjugated dienes are tabulated below to realize physically the effect of conjugation.

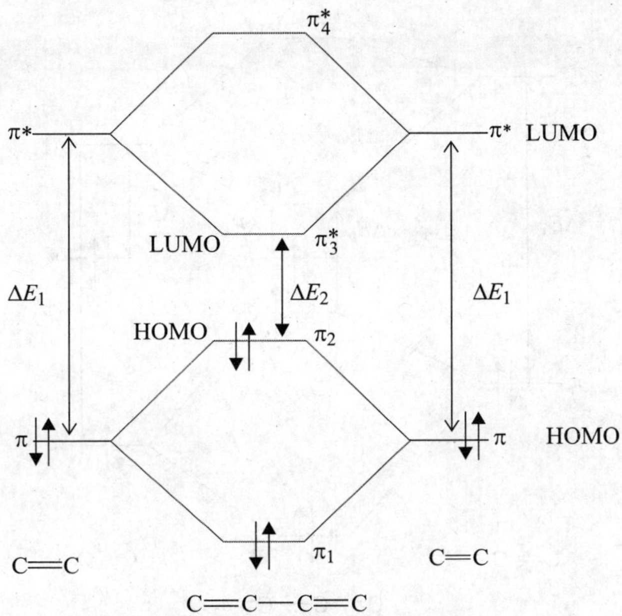

Fig. 11.9 Molecular orbital diagram illustrating the effect of conjugation on the $\pi \rightarrow \pi^*$ absorption maximum

Compound	λ_{max} in mμ	∈ in cm² mol⁻¹
$CH_2{=}CH_2$	171	15000
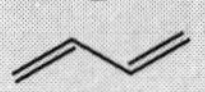	217	21000
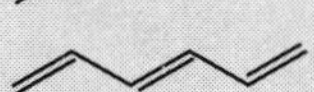	256	50000
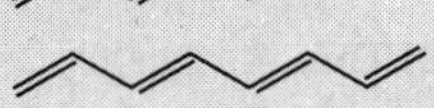	290	85000
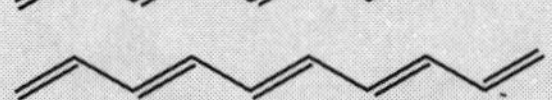	334	125000
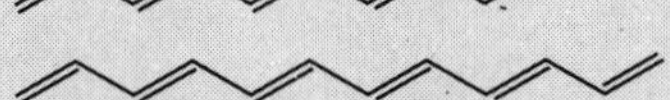	364	138000

For carbonyl compounds: Simple ketones, acids, esters, amides, and other compounds containing both π systems and unshared electron pairs show two absorptions, viz., an $n \rightarrow \pi^*$ transition at longer wavelengths (>300 mμ, low intensity, symmetry forbidden transition) and $\pi \rightarrow \pi^*$ transition at shorter wavelengths (<250 mμ, high intensity, symmetry allowed transition) (Fig. 11.10). With conjugation (enones), the λ_{max} of the $\pi \rightarrow \pi^*$ band moves to longer wavelengths and can be predicted by Woodward's rules. The value usually rises nearly 10000 with conjugation, and as it is very intense, it may obscure or bury the weaker $n \rightarrow \pi^*$ transition. Due to increase in conjugation both $n \rightarrow \pi^*$ and $\pi \rightarrow \pi^*$ energy gap decrease ($\Delta E_2 > \Delta E_5$ and $\Delta E_3 > \Delta E_4$, respectively); hence *red shift* occurs for both these transitions.

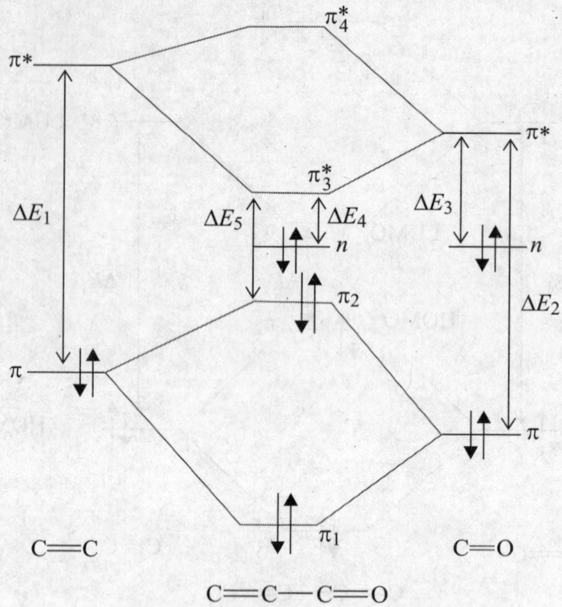

Fig. 11.10 Molecular orbital diagram illustrating the effect of conjugation on both $\pi \rightarrow \pi^*$ and $n \rightarrow \pi^*$ absorption maximum

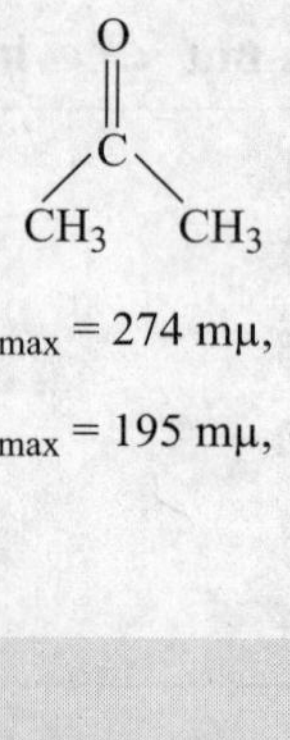

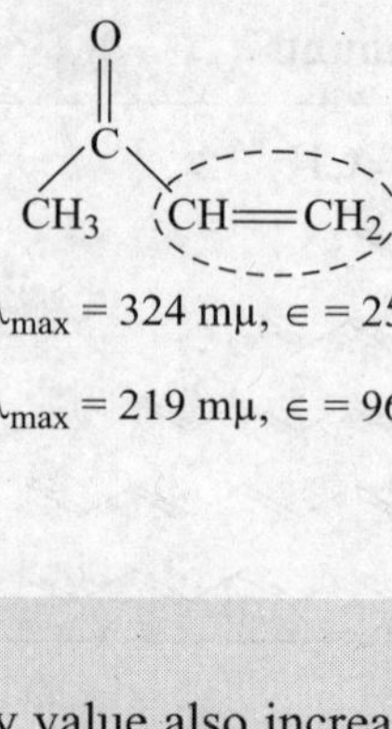

$n \rightarrow \pi^*$	$\lambda_{max} = 274$ mμ, $\in = 14$	$\lambda_{max} = 324$ mμ, $\in = 25$
$n \rightarrow \pi^*$	$\lambda_{max} = 195$ mμ, $\in = 9000$	$\lambda_{max} = 219$ mμ, $\in = 9600$

Note:

With an increase in conjugation molar absorptivity value also increases (hyperchromic shift). Molar absorptivity is related to the probability of transition which is, in turn, proportional to the square of transition dipole moment. With increase in conjugation transition, dipole moment increases (as the distance between positive end and negative end increases) and therefore $\in$ value also increases.

2. **Auxochrome**

For "ene" system: Substitution with an atom containing nonbonding electrons (auxochrome, i.e., —OH, —OR, —NH_2, —NHR, —SH, —SR, —X) results in a bathochromic shift of $\pi \rightarrow \pi^*$ transition due to conjugative interaction between filled "n" orbital and π-bond of ethylenic system. Such interaction reduces $\pi \rightarrow \pi^*$ energy gap and *red shift* occurs (Fig. 11.11).

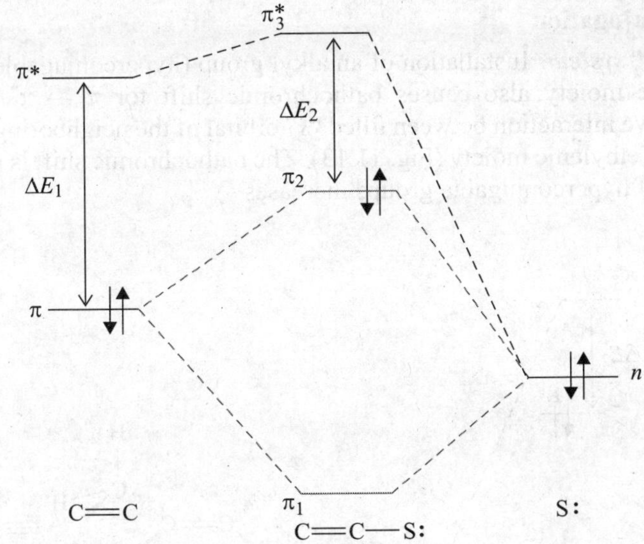

Fig. 11.11 Molecular orbital diagram illustrating the effect of auxochrome on the $n \rightarrow \pi^*$ absorption maximum

For carbonyl compounds: In case of carbonyl compounds, due to conjugative interaction, the $n \rightarrow \pi^*$ transitions are shifted to higher energy (shorter wavelength, $\Delta E_4 > \Delta E_2$). As a result pronounced *hypsochromic shifts* are observed for the $n \rightarrow \pi^*$ transition. It is important to note that this is different from the auxochromic effect on $\pi \rightarrow \pi^*$ which extends conjugation (like in the case of "ene" system discussed above) and causes a *bathochromic shift* ($\Delta E_3 < \Delta E_1$). In most of the cases, this bathochromic shift is not enough to bring the $\pi \rightarrow \pi^*$ transition into the observed range (Fig. 11.12).

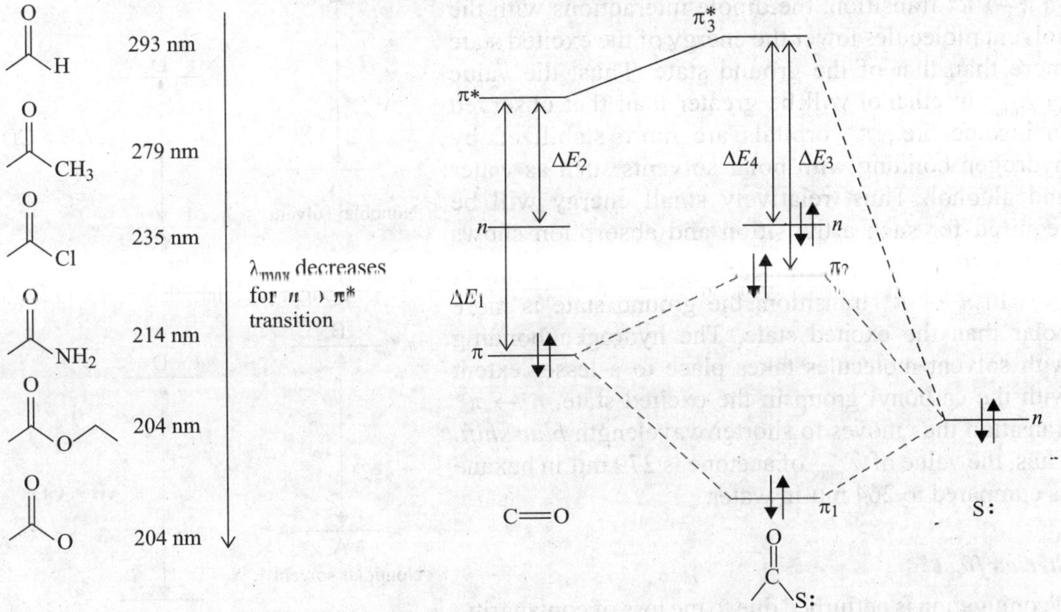

Fig. 11.12 Molecular orbital diagram illustrating the effect of auxochrome on the $n \rightarrow \pi^*$ absorption maximum

3. **Hyperconjugation**

For "ene" system: Installation of an alkyl group (hyperconjugable) as a substituent on alkene moiety also causes bathochromic shift for $\pi \rightarrow \pi^*$ transition due to conjugative interaction between filled "*s*" orbital of the neighboring C—H bond and π bond of ethylenic moiety (Fig. 11.13). The bathochromic shift is progressive as the number of hyperconjugable groups increases.

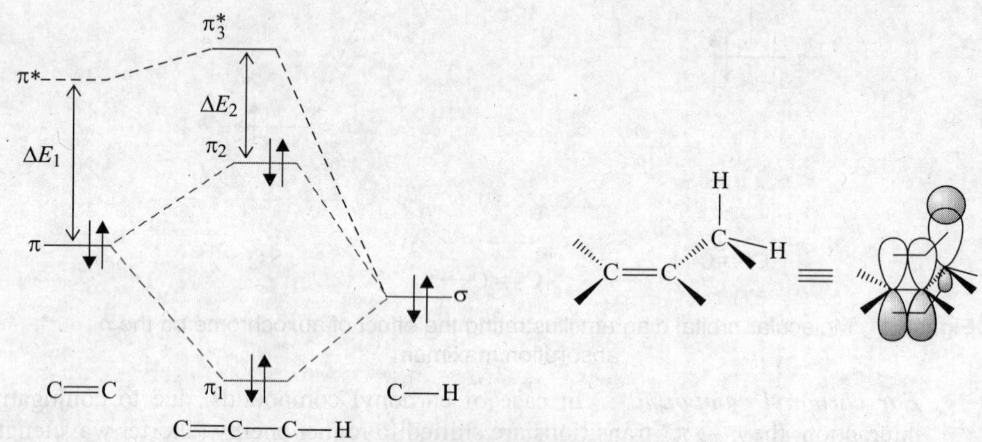

Fig. 11.13 Molecular orbital diagram illustrating the effect of hyperconjugation on the $\pi \rightarrow \pi^*$ absorption maximum

Effect of solvent

In $\pi \rightarrow \pi^*$ transition, the dipole interactions with the solvent molecules lower the energy of the excited state more than that of the ground state. Thus, the value of λ_{max} in ethanol will be greater than that observed in hexane, i.e., π^* orbitals are more stabilized by hydrogen bonding with polar solvents such as water and alcohol. Thus, relatively small energy will be required for such a transition and absorption shows a *red shift.*

In $n \rightarrow \pi^*$ transition, the ground state is more polar than the excited state. The hydrogen bonding with solvent molecules takes place to a lesser extent with the carbonyl group in the excited state. $n \rightarrow \pi^*$ transition thus moves to shorter wavelength *blue shift.* Thus, the value of λ_{max} of acetone is 279 mμ in hexane as compared to 264 mμ in water.

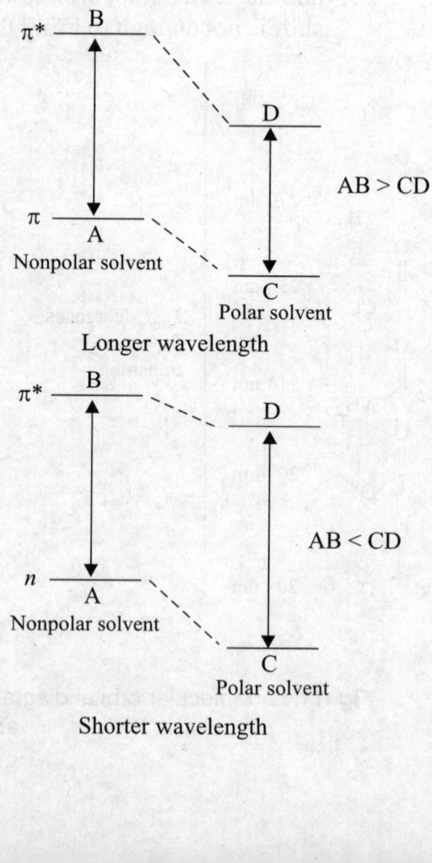

Steric effect

If conjugation is perturbed due to the loss of coplanarity, there remains a fair chance that energy gap between HOMO and LUMO increases resulting in blue shift of

λ_{max}. For example, in *cis*-stilbene due to steric interaction between o-hydrogen atoms, planarity throughout the π–π conjugated system is hampered (steric inhibition of resonance) and blue shift occurs by an amount 16 mμ in comparison to its *trans*-counterpart where extended conjugation remains intact.

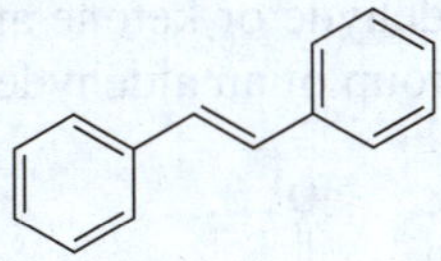

trans-Stilbene
λ_{max} = 296 mμ, ∈ = 2900

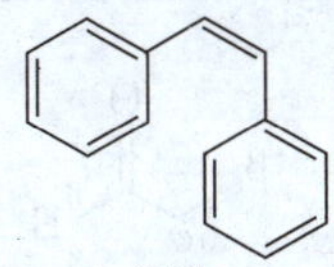

cis-Stilbene
λ_{max} = 280 mμ, ∈ = 10500

Woodward–Fieser Rules

R.B. Woodward studied the UV spectra of conjugated dienes and developed a set of empirical rules for predicting the wavelength of maximum UV absorption. Later L.M. Fieser extended the rules to conjugated aldehydes and ketones. In order to apply the rules it is essential to know the following structures.

Conjugated dienes: Conjugated dienes are available in two fundamental conformations, viz., *s*-cis and *s*-trans conformations. *s*-cis conformation is one in which both double bonds lie on the same side of the single bond that joins them, and *s*-trans conjugated diene is one in which the two double bonds lie on opposite sides of the single bond that joins them (*s* stands for the single bond that connects the two double bonds).

s-cis

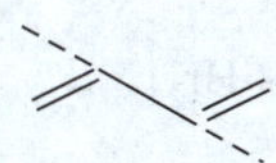

s-trans

Endocyclic vs exocyclic double bonds: An interesting feature of double bond is that it may be part of a ring system, when it is called endocyclic double bond because the bond lies within the ring. Double bond may remain projected from a ring, when it is called exocyclic double bond because the bond lies outside the ring. If a compound is bicyclic, a double bond might be endocylic with respect to one ring and exocyclic with respect to the other one.

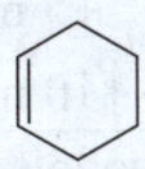

Endocyclic

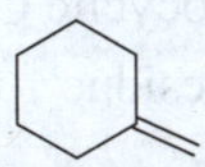

Exocyclic

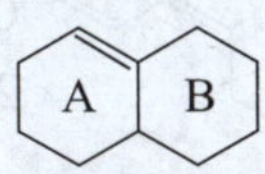

Endo to A
Exo to B

Extended conjugated double bonds: Two double bonds separated by a single bond are conjugated. If a third double bond is separated from one of the original pair of double bonds by a single bond, the three double bonds represent an extended conjugated system.

s-cis

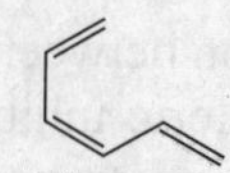

s-cis extended

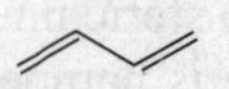

s-trans

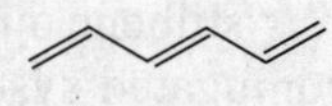

s-trans extended

Conjugated aldehydes and ketones: A conjugated aldehyde or ketone arises when a double bond is separated by a single bond from the carbonyl group of an aldehyde or ketone.

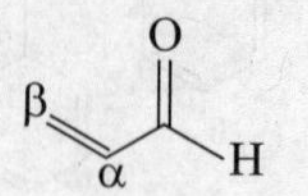

Conjugated aldehyde

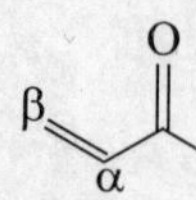

Conjugated ketone

1. ***Acylic dienes***

   Base value acyclic butadiene = 217 mμ

   The incremental contribution of substituents is added to this base value from the following table.

Group	Increment
Extended conjugation	+30
Each exo-cyclic C=C	+5
Alkyl	+5
—$OCOCH_3$	+0
—OR	+6
—SR	+30
—Cl, —Br	+5
—NR_2	+60

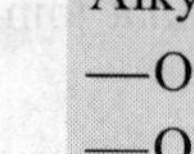

Isoprene	
Acyclic butadiene	217 mμ
One alkyl substituion	+5 mμ
	222 mμ
Experimental value	220 mμ

Allylidenecyclohexane	
Acyclic butadiene	217 mμ
One exocyclic C=C	+5 mμ
2 ring residue	+10 mμ
	232 mμ
Experimental value	237 nm

2. ***Cyclic Dienes***: There are two major types of cyclic dienes, with two different base values. The increment table is the same as for acyclic butadienes with a couple of additions.

Heteroannular (transoid):

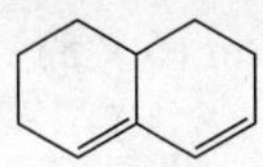

Base value λ_{max} = 214 mμ
∈ = 5.000 – 15.000

Homoannular (cisoid):

Base value λ_{max} = 253 mμ
∈ = 12.000 – 28.000

Group	Increment
Additional homoannular	+39
Ring residue/Alkyl substituent	+5
Where both types of diene are present, the one with the longer λ becomes the base	

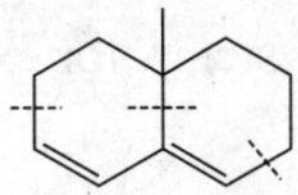

Heteroannular diene	214 mμ
3 ring residue (3 × 5)	+15 mμ
1 exocyclic C=C	+ 5 mμ
	234 mμ
Experimental value	235 mμ

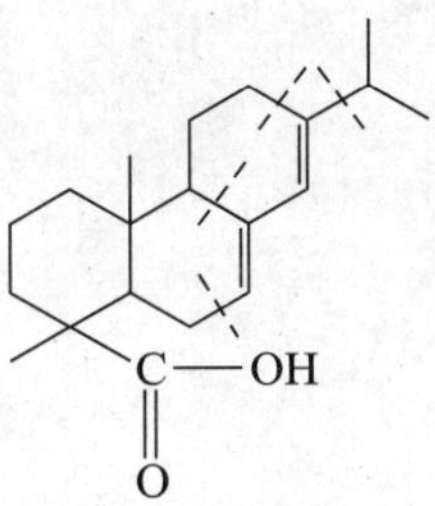

Heteroannular diene	214 mμ
4 ring residue/alkyl substitution (4 × 5)	+20 mμ
1 exocyclic C=C	+ 5 mμ
	239 mμ

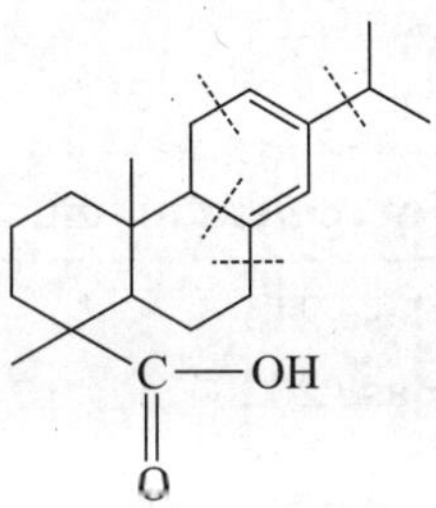

Homoannular diene	253 mμ
4 ring residue/alkyl substitution (4 × 5)	+20 mμ
1 exocyclic C=C	+ 5 mμ
	278 mμ

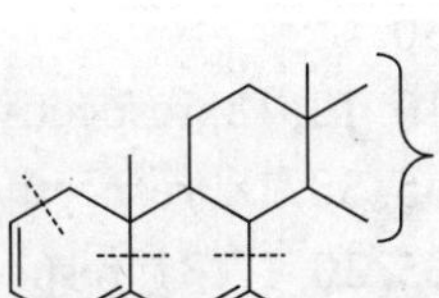

Homoannular diene	253 mμ
4 ring residue/alkyl substitution (4 × 5)	+ 20 mμ
Extra conjugation	+30 mμ
1 exocyclic C=C	+ 5 mμ
	308 mμ

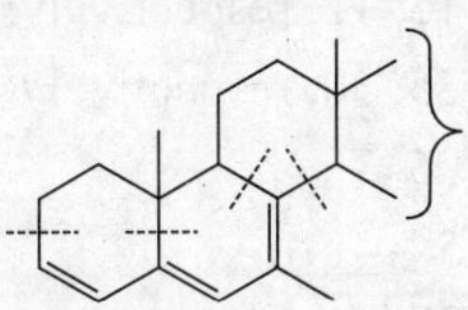

Homoannular diene	253 mμ
5 ring residue/alkyl substitution (5 × 5)	+ 25 mμ
Extra conjugation	+30 mμ
2 exocyclic C=C	+10 mμ
	318 mμ

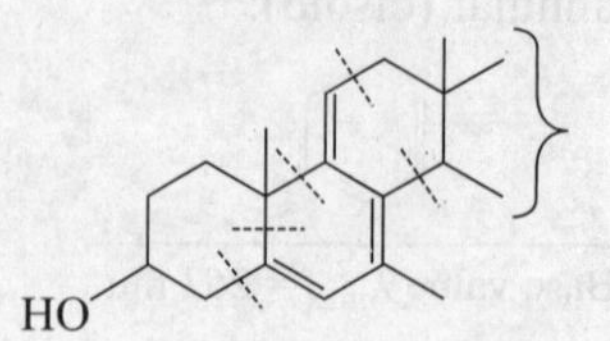

Homoannular diene	253 mμ
6 ring residue/alkyl substitution (6 × 5)	+ 30 mμ
Extra conjugation	+30 mμ
3 exocyclic C=C	+ 15 mμ
	328 mμ

Note:

Some common errors while dealing with cyclic dienes:

The following compound has three exocyclic double bonds. The indicated bond is exocyclic to *two* rings.

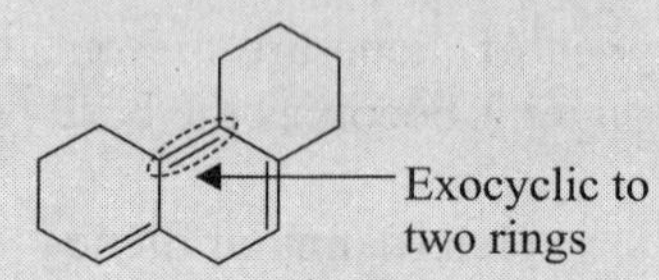

These are some cases which are to be considered as acyclic systems, for example

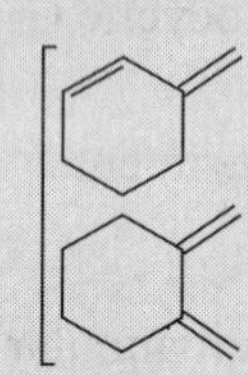

3. ***Enones (cyclic and acyclic)***

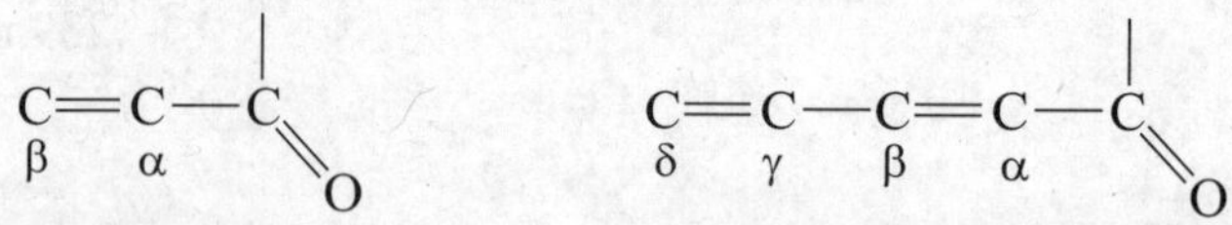

Group		Increment in mμ
6-membered ring or acyclic enone		Base 215
5-membered ring parent enone		Base 202
Acyclic dienone		Base 245
Double bond extending conjugation		30
Alkyl group or ring residue	α, β, γ and higher	10, 12, 18, respectively
—OH	α, β, γ and higher	35, 30, 18, respectively
—OR	α, β, γ, δ	35, 30, 17, 31, respectively
—O(C=O)R	α, β, δ	6
—Cl	α, β	15, 12, respectively
—Br	α, β	25, 30, respectively
—NR_2	β	95
Exocyclic double bond		5
Homocyclic diene component		39

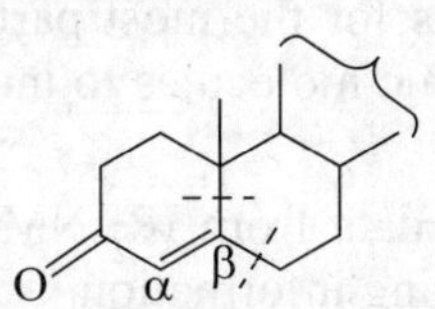

Parent value	215
α-alkyl (0)	+0
β-alkyl (2)	+24
γ, δ, etc. (0)	+ 0
Extra conjugation	+0
1 exocyclic C=C	+ 5
Homoannular	+ 0
	244 mμ

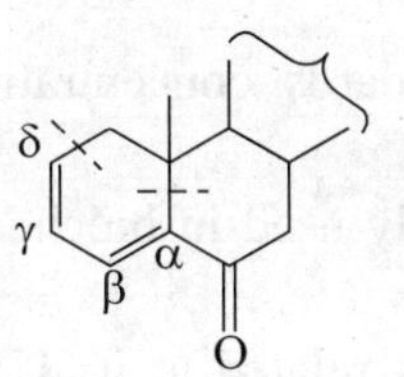

Parent value	215
α-alkyl (1)	+10
β-alkyl (0)	+0
γ, δ, etc. (1)	+18
Extra conjugation	+30
1 exocyclic C=C	+5
Homoannular	+ 39
	317 m

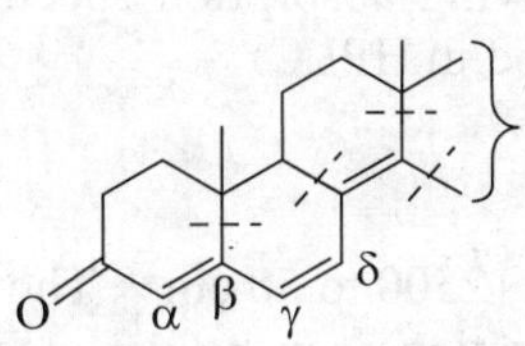

Parent value	215
α-alkyl (0)	+0
β-alkyl (1)	+12
γ, δ, etc. (3)	+54
Extra conjugation (2)	+60
3 exocyclic C=C	+15
Homoannular	+ 0
	356 m

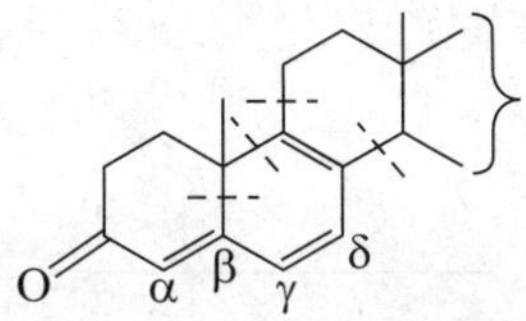

Parent value	215
α-alkyl (1)	+0
β-alkyl (1)	+12
γ, δ, etc. (3)	+54
Extra conjugation (2)	+60
1 exocyclic C=C	+5
Homoannular	+ 39
	385 m

Note:

Unlike conjugated alkenes, solvent does have an effect on λ_{max}.

Solvent correction	Increment in mμ
Water	+8
Ethanol, methanol	0
Chloroform	–1
Dioxane	–5
Ether	–7
Hydrocarbon	–11

Analytical Uses of UV-Vis Spectroscopy

In practice, ultraviolet spectrometry is limited to conjugated systems for the most part, and UV-Vis spectroscopy can be used in the structure elucidation of organic molecules to indicate whether conjugation is present in a given sample.

1. Although conjugation in a molecule may be indicated by data from IR, NMR, or mass spectrometry, UV-Vis analysis can provide corroborating information.
2. A more widespread use of UV-Vis spectroscopy, however, has to do with determining concentration of an unknown sample.
3. The relationship $A = \in C\,l$, "C l" indicates that the amount of absorption by a sample at a certain wavelength is dependent on its concentration.
4. Using calibration curve of λ_{max} versus concentration of standards, concentration of an unknown sample could be determined.
5. Quantitative analysis using UV-Vis spectroscopy is routinely used in biochemical studies to measure the rates of enzymatic reactions (kinetics).
6. The concentration of a species involved in the reaction (as related to its UV-Vis absorbance) is plotted versus time to determine the rate of reaction.
7. UV-Vis spectroscopy is also used in environmental chemistry to determine the concentration of various metal ions (sometimes involving absorption spectra for organic complexes with the metal), as a selection method in HPLC.

IR Spectroscopy

IR region of the complete electromagnetic spectrum extends from 12500 to 50 cm^{-1}. The most important region being 4000–667 cm^{-1} in which molecular vibrations can be detected and measured. The region from 4000 to 12500 cm^{-1} is called near IR region and from 667 to 50 cm^{-1} is called far IR region.

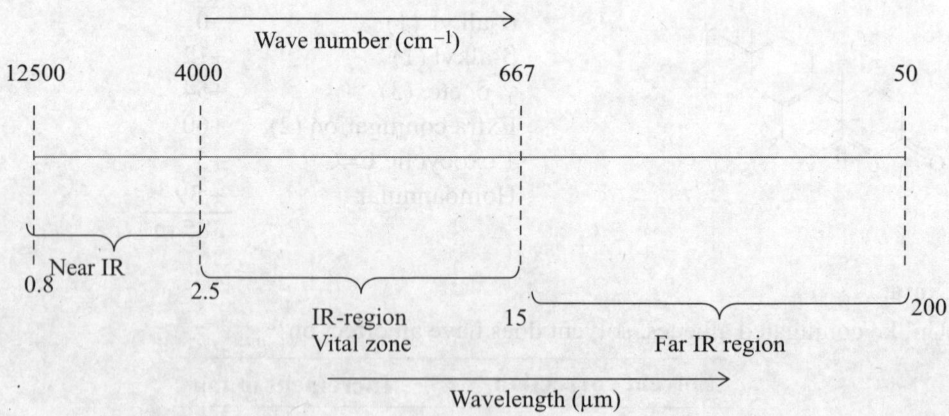

Theory of IR Spectroscopy

IR radiation does not have enough energy to induce electronic transitions as seen with UV. Absorption of IR is restricted to compounds with small energy differences in the possible vibrational and rotational states. In IR spectroscopy, an organic molecule is exposed to infrared radiation. When the radiant energy matches the energy of a specific molecular vibration, absorption occurs. For a molecule to absorb IR, the vibrations or rotations within a molecule must cause a net change in the dipole moment of the molecule. The alternating electrical field of the radiation (remember that electromagnetic radiation consists of an oscillating electrical field and an oscillating magnetic field, perpendicular to each other) interacts with fluctuations in the dipole moment of the molecule. If the frequency of the radiation matches the vibrational frequency of the molecule, then radiation will be absorbed, causing a change in the amplitude of molecular vibration.

Molecular rotations: Rotational transitions are of little use to the spectroscopist. Rotational levels are quantized, and absorption of IR by gases yields line spectra. However, in liquids or solids, these lines broaden into a continuum due to molecular collisions and other interactions.

Molecular vibrations: The positions of atoms in a molecule are not fixed and they are subjected to a number of different vibrations. Vibrations fall into the two main categories, viz., *stretching* and *bending*.

Stretching: In this type of vibration there occurs a change in inter-atomic distance along the bond axis. It is again of two types, viz., symmetrical and asymmetrical stretching. In the former, the movement of atoms occurs in the same direction with respect to the central atom in a molecule, whereas in the latter, one atom moves towards and the other moves away from the central atom. Both these vibrations are shown in Fig. 11.14.

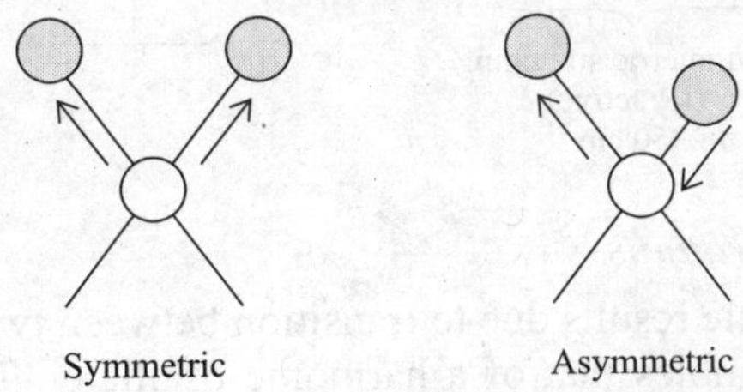

Fig. 11.14 Stretching vibrations

Bending: In this type of vibration, the position of atoms changes with respect to the original bond axis. This can further be classified into four types (Fig. 11.15):

1. Rocking: Movement of atoms takes place in the same direction.
2. Scissoring: Two atoms approach each other.
3. Wagging: Two atoms move up and down the plane with respect to the central atom.
4. Twisting: One of the atom moves up the plane, whereas the other moves down the plane with respect to the central atom.

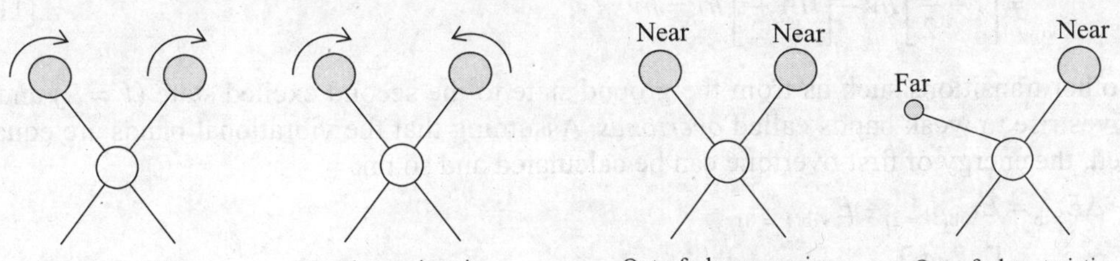

Fig.11.15 Different bending modes of vibrations

Note:

1. Bending vibrations require less energy and therefore take place at lower wave number, i.e., vibrational frequency than stretching.
2. Usually bending vibrations occur at frequencies below 1500 cm^{-1}. These are not useful for structural elucidation as the numbers of bands are large and often bands are obscured due to overtones and combination bands.

Selection rule

The most fundamental requirement for infrared activity is that a vibration must cause a change in the dipole moment of the molecule, for example,

1. HCl, CO: Polar (IR active)
2. H_2, N_2: Nonpolar (IR inactive)
3. Exception: CO_2 is nonpolar still IR active. This is due to the fact that in asymmetric stretching of CO_2, there occurs a change on dipole moment and is active. Both possible bending modes are active and occur at the same frequency.

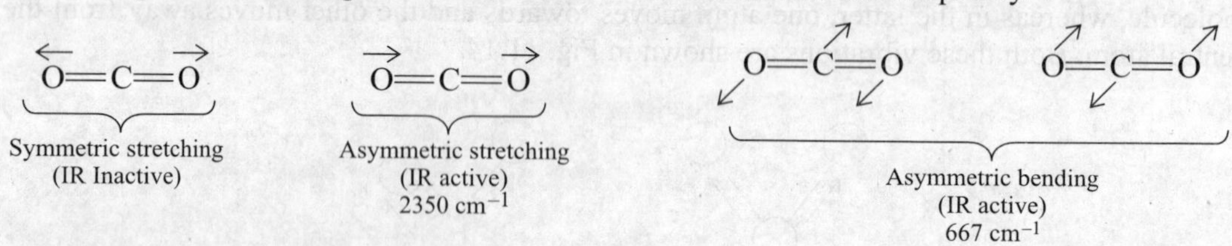

Number of fundamental vibrations

The IR spectrum of a molecule results due to transition between two vibrational energy levels. The vibrational motion resembles that of a harmonic oscillator. The vibrational energy of a chemical bond is quantized and can have values

$$E_{\text{Vib}} = \left[V + \frac{1}{2}\right]h\nu \qquad \text{...[11.6]}$$

where V is the number of vibrational level and can have values 0, 1, 2, 3, and so on, h is Planck's constant, and ν is the vibrational frequency of the band.

Transition from the ground state ($V = 0$) to the first excited state ($V = 1$) absorbs radiation strongly and gives rise to intense band called *fundamental band*. From the energy of the fundamental band the frequency can be calculated.

$$\Delta E_{\text{Vib}} = E_{\text{Vib}(V=1)} - E_{\text{Vib}(V=0)}$$

$$= \left[1 + \frac{1}{2}\right]h\nu - \left[0 + \frac{1}{2}\right]h\nu = h\nu \qquad \text{...[11.7]}$$

The other transitions such as from the ground state to the second excited state ($V = 2$) and so on gives rise to weak bands called *overtones*. Assuming that the vibrational bands are equally spaced, the energy of first overtone can be calculated and so on.

$$\Delta E_{\text{Vib}} = E_{\text{Vib}(V=2)} - E_{\text{Vib}(V=0)}$$

$$= \left[2 + \frac{1}{2}\right]h\nu - \left[0 + \frac{1}{2}\right]h\nu = 2h\nu \qquad \text{...[11.8]}$$

Polyatomic molecules may exhibit more than one fundamental vibrational absorption bands. The number of these fundamental bands is related to the degrees of freedom in a molecule. The number of degrees of freedom is equal to the sum of coordinates necessary to locate all the atoms of a molecule in space. For each atom 3 degrees of freedom are there corresponding to Cartesian coordinates required to describe its position in space. In a molecule the total number of degrees of freedom is equal to $3n$, where n is the number of atoms in a molecule. Now these $3n$ degrees of freedom are the sum of translational, vibrational, and rotational degrees of freedom. Thus,

Translational + rotational + vibrational degrees of freedom = $3n$

Linear molecule

Here translational degrees of freedom = 3

Rotational degrees of freedom = 2, as the rotation of such a molecule about its parent axis do not bring any change in the position of atoms. Thus,

$$\text{Vibrational degrees of freedom} = 3n - 5 \quad \text{...[11.9]}$$

Nonlinear molecule

Here translational degrees of freedom = 3

Rotational degrees of freedom = 3, as the rotation of such a molecule about all the three axes bring change in the position of atoms. Thus,

$$\text{Vibrational degrees of freedom} = 3n - 6 \quad \text{...[11.10]}$$

Example 11.3

Find the number of vibrational degrees of freedom for CO_2 and CH_4.

Solution

In case of CO_2 which is a linear molecule, the vibrational degrees of freedom $= 3n - 5 = 3 \times 3 - 5 = 4$

In case of CH_4 which is a nonlinear molecule, the vibrational degrees of freedom $= 3n - 6 = 3 \times 4 - 6 = 6$

Note:

It has been observed that the theoretically calculated numbers of fundamental vibrations are usually more than found in an IR spectrum. The reason for the smaller number of fundamental vibrations than expected number are as follows:

1. Several of the vibrations are redundant or degenerate, i.e., energies of two or more vibrations are identical or nearly identical.
2. Symmetry of the molecule.
3. Undetectable low absorption intensity.
4. Out of the instrumental detection range.

Vibrational Frequency

In a true sense interaction between IR radiation and a molecule occurs in a discrete manner following the Planck's quantum theory, but most of us live in a world that appears continuous to us and we do not have much experience discussing phenomena that occur in discrete steps. The model used here is based as much as possible on classical physics. The stretching frequency of a bond can be approximated by Hooke's law. In this approximation, two atoms and the connecting bond are treated as a simple harmonic oscillator composed of 2 masses (atoms) joined by a spring as shown in Fig. 11.16.

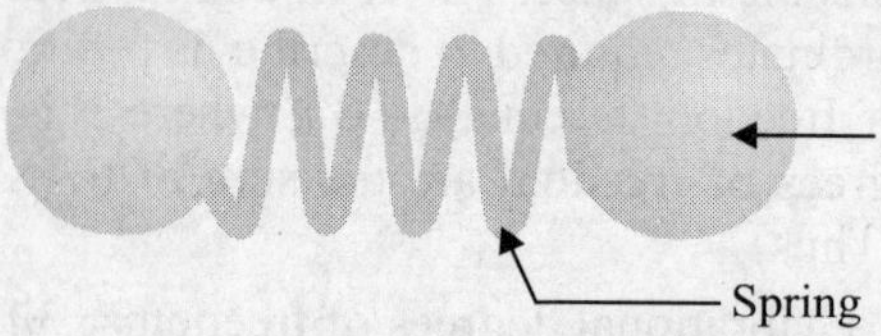

Fig. 11.16 Ball and spring model

According to Hooke's law, the frequency of the vibration of the spring is related to the mass and the force constant of the spring by the following formula:

$$\bar{\nu} = \frac{1}{2\pi c}\sqrt{\frac{k}{\mu}} \qquad \text{...[11.11]}$$

where, $\bar{\nu}$ is the frequency of vibration in cm^{-1}, k is the force constant, and μ is the reduced mass and is equal to $m_1 m_2/m_1 + m_2$; (m_1 and m_2 being atomic masses).

The above equation shows the relationship of bond strength and atomic mass to the wave number at which a molecule is going to absorb IR radiation. As the force constant increases, the vibrational frequency (wave number) also increases. Force constant depends on the number of bonds present between two atoms. With the increase of number of bonds the bond strength increases which makes it harder to stretch.

Bond	Wave number (cm^{-1})	
C—X	~1200	
C═X	~1600	where X = C, N, etc.
C≡X	~2200	

Note:

The following table shows where absorption by single, double, and triple bonds are observed in an IR spectrum.

Bonds	Range	Bonds	Range	Bonds	Range	Bonds	Range
C—H, N—H, O—H	2700 – 3800 cm^{-1}	C—C, C—O, C—N	800 – 1300 cm^{-1}	C═C, C═O, C═N, N═O	1500 – 1900 cm^{-1}	C≡C, C≡N	2000 – 2300 cm^{-1}

1. Conjugation also lowers the stretching frequency. With increase in conjugation multiple bond character is reduced which reduces bond strength. The following example is illustrating the drop in stretching frequency value for C═C bond due to conjugation arising out of resonance.

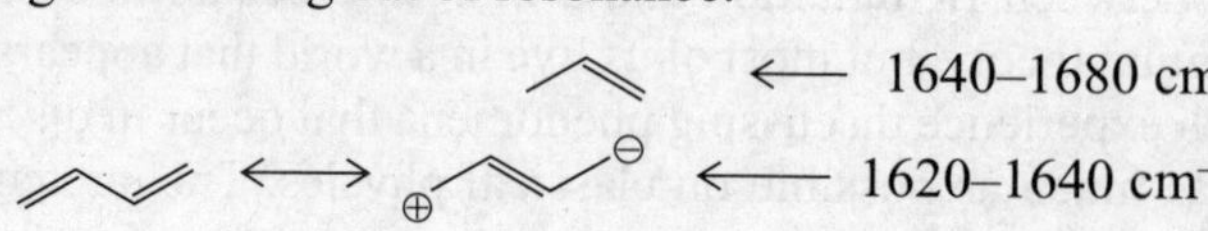

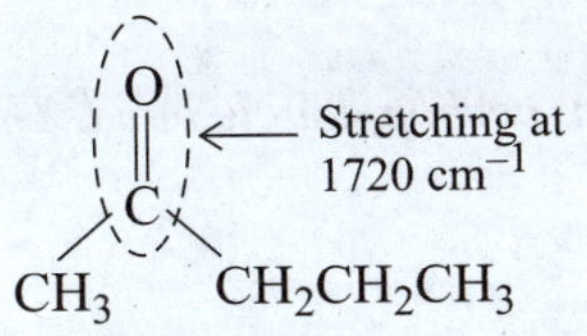

pentan-2-one

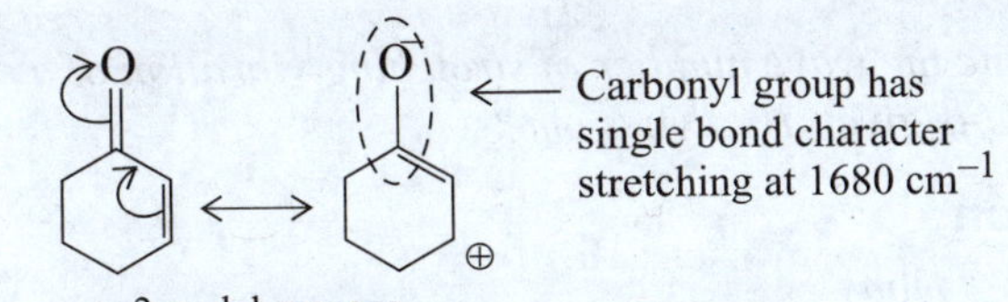

2-cyclohexanone

2. As the "*s*" character increases in a bond, the bond becomes stiffer. We already have seen that *sp* hybridized C—C bonds are stiffer than sp^3 hybridized C—C bonds. The same is also true for carbon–hydrogen bonds.

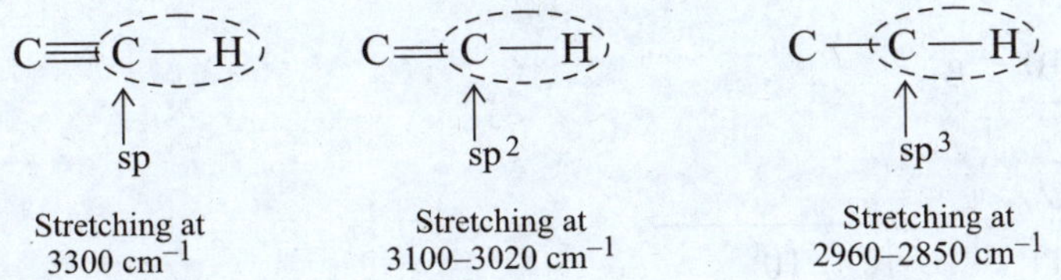

3. The competition between I-effect and R-effect sometimes becomes important in deciding the magnitude of stretching frequency. For example, stretching frequency for C—O bond in ester is more than that for amide.

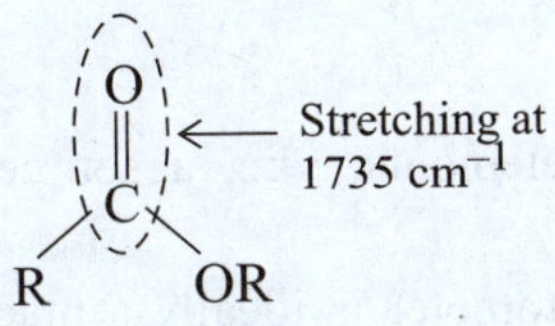

–I effect is important

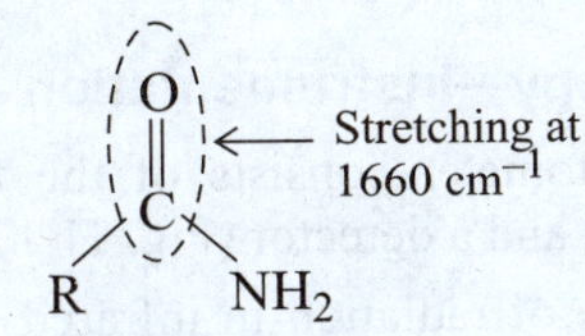

+R effect is important

In ester, –I effect is predominant over +R effect of the —OR group. Due to –I effect the nonbonding "lp" of electron cloud is drifted to bonding orbital of C=O bond as a result of which the C—O bond order increases and $n_{C=O}$ becomes higher in value. On the other hand, for amide class of compounds, +R effect is predominant over –I effect of the —NH_2 group due to less electronegativity of N atom in comparison to O atom. This +R effect effect reduces "C=O" double bond character by an appreciable amount and as a result of which $n_{C=O}$ becomes lower in value for amides in comparison to esters.

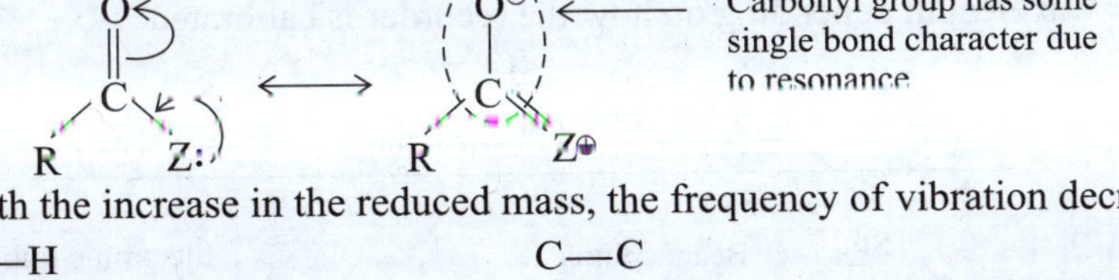

4. With the increase in the reduced mass, the frequency of vibration decreases.

C—H	C—C
$\mu = 1.53 \times 10^{-24}$ g	$\mu = 9.97 \times 10^{-24}$ g
$\bar{\nu} = 2800 - 3000\ cm^{-1}$	$\bar{\nu} = 1200\ cm^{-1}$

5. In many cases, the frequency of vibration increases inspite of slight increase in the reduced mass. In those cases, rigidity of the bond in terms of the force constant becomes the major guiding factor.

C—H	O—H
$\mu = 1.53 \times 10^{-24}$ g	$\mu = 1.56 \times 10^{-24}$ g
$\bar{\nu} = 2800 - 3000\ cm^{-1}$	$\bar{\nu} = 3300\ cm^{-1}$

Example 11.4

Calculate the wave number of stretching vibration of a carbon–carbon double bond. The force constant is given 10^6 dynes cm^{-1}.

Solution

$$\mu = \frac{m_1 m_2}{m_1 m_2}$$

$$= \frac{12 \times 12}{12 + 12} = 6 \text{ amu}$$

$$= 9.97 \times 10^{-24} \text{ g}$$

$$\bar{\nu} = \frac{1}{2\pi c}\sqrt{\frac{k}{\mu}}$$

$$= \frac{1}{2 \times 3.14 \times 10^{10}}\sqrt{\frac{10^6}{9.97 \times 10^{-24}}}$$

$$= 1680 \text{ cm}^{-1}$$

IR Spectroscopy—Instrumentation

The spectrophotometer consists of the following elements, viz., a source of radiation; a monochromator, and a detector (Fig. 11.17).

The source of radiation in infrared spectrophotometer is ideally a black body radiator. The *source* generates light across the spectrum of interest. A *monochromater* (in IR this can be either a salt prism or a grating with finely spaced etched lines) separates the source radiation into its different wavelengths. A *slit* selects the collection of wavelengths that shine through the sample at any given time. In double beam operation, a *beam splitter* separates the incident beam in two: one half goes to the sample and the other to a reference. The *sample* absorbs light according to its chemical properties. A *detector* collects the radiation that passes through the sample, and in double-beam operation, compares its energy to that going through the reference. The detector puts out an electrical signal, which is normally sent directly to an analog *recorder*. A link between the monochromater and the recorder allows you to record energy as a function of frequency or wavelength depending on how the recorder is calibrated.

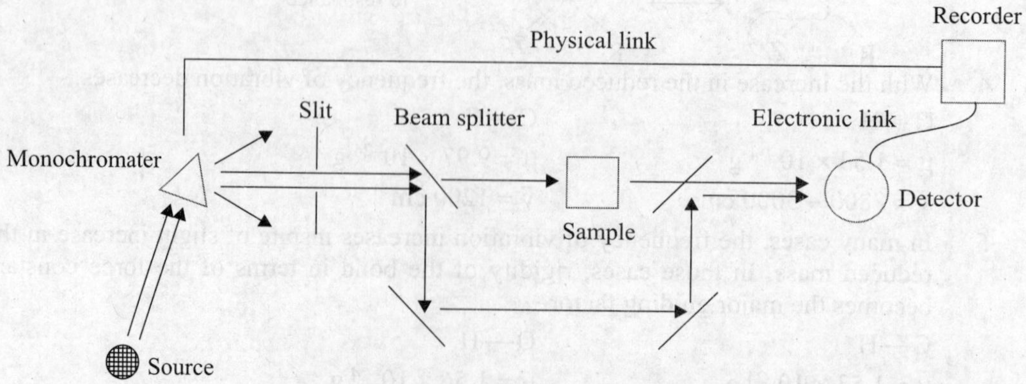

Fig. 11.17 Schematic diagram of a typical IR spectrometer

1. Through infrared spectrometer one can study how molecules absorb infrared radiation and ultimately convert it to heat.
2. The infrared radiation extends from 0.8 to 200 μm.
3. The common practical infrared sources are Globar rod, Nernst filament, and Nichrome wire.
4. The energy emitted by a black body radiator varies with wavelength and temperature.
5. The light from the mirrors pass through the grating so that only a relatively narrow band of wavelength is allowed.
6. For high resolution, prisms made of SiO_2, NaCl, and KBr are used.
7. Entrance and exit slits are used to produce narrow bandwidth with a better spectral definition.
8. Detectors used in infrared spectrophotometers usually convert the thermal radiant energy into electrical energy. The detector converts the infrared radiation into its equivalent voltage signal. This voltage signal is applied to a high-speed plotter.
9. The detectors used are thermocouple, bolometer, and golay cells.
10. A typical IR spectrum is shown in Fig. 11.18. The wave number, plotted on the x-axis, is proportional to energy; therefore, the highest energy vibrations are on the left. The percent transmittance (% T) is plotted on the y-axis. The absorption of radiant energy is therefore represented by a "trough" in the curve: zero transmittance corresponds to 100% absorption of light at that wavelength. The percentage transmittance is the percent of incident light (I_0) that passes through the sample [% $T = 100 \times (I/I_0)$. Unlike absorbance, percentage transmittance is not additive, and thus the contributions due to impurities or solvent cannot be subtracted out. Thus, these spectra cannot be used to determine the concentration of the material.

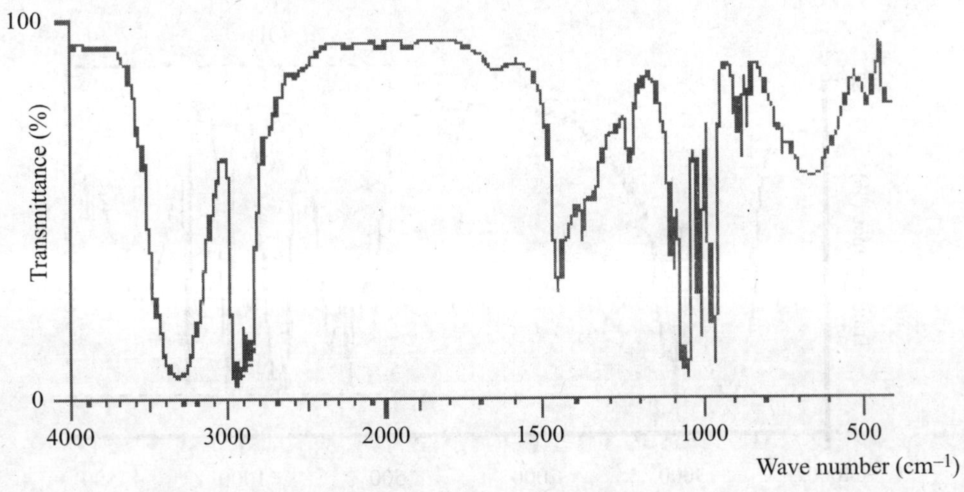

Fig. 11.18 A typical IR spectrum

11. The region from about 1500 to 500 cm^{-1} usually contains a very complicated series of absorptions. These are mainly due to all manner of bending vibrations within the molecule. This is called the *fingerprint region* (Fig. 11.19). It is much more difficult to pick out individual bands in this region than the "cleaner" region at higher wave

numbers. The importance of the fingerprint region is that each different compound produces a different pattern of troughs in this part of the spectrum and therefore used for comparing the identity of two compounds. To have an illustration let us consider the example of two isomeric compounds propan-1-ol and propan-2-ol. Both compounds have very similar troughs in the area around 3000 cm^{-1}, but completely different pattern in the fingerprint region between 1500 and 500 cm^{-1}.

Infrared of propan-1-ol, $CH_3CH_2CH_2OH$

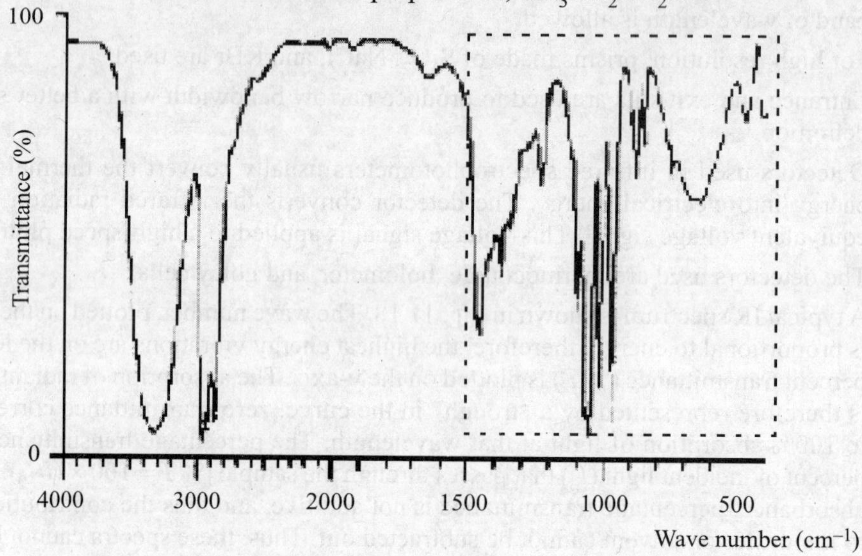

Infrared spectrum of propan-2-ol, $CH_3CH(OH)CH_3$

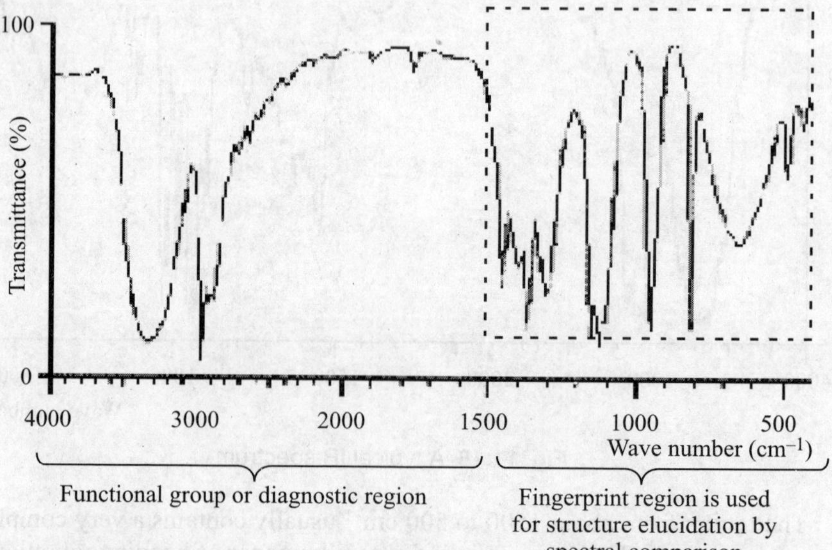

Fig. 11.19 Functional group or diagnostic region and fingerprint region

Analyzing Infrared Spectra

1. The position, intensity, and shape of an absorption band are helpful in identifying functional groups.
2. The absence of absorption bands can be useful in identifying a compound in IR spectroscopy.
3. Bonds in molecules lacking dipole moments cannot be detected.

Examples

An alkane IR spectrum

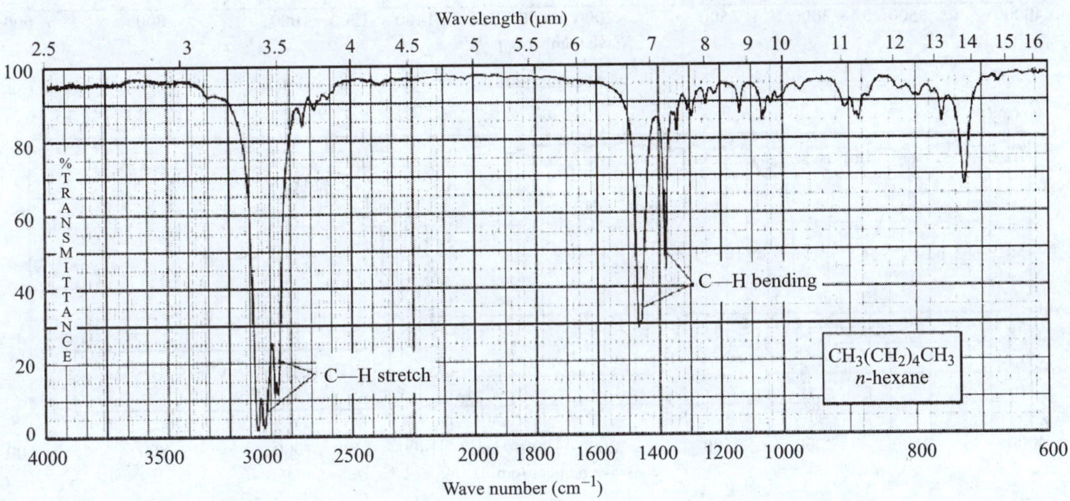

An alkene IR spectrum

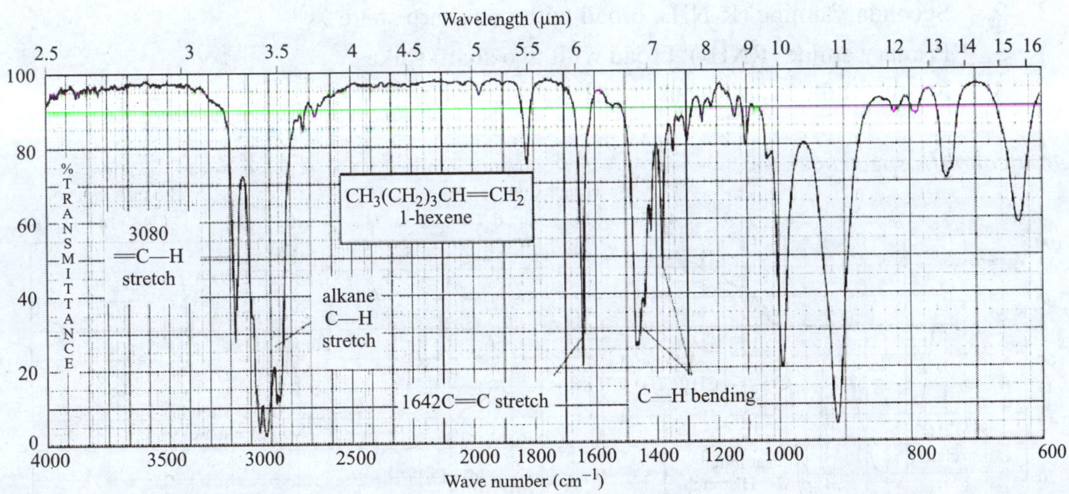

Some alkyne IR spectra

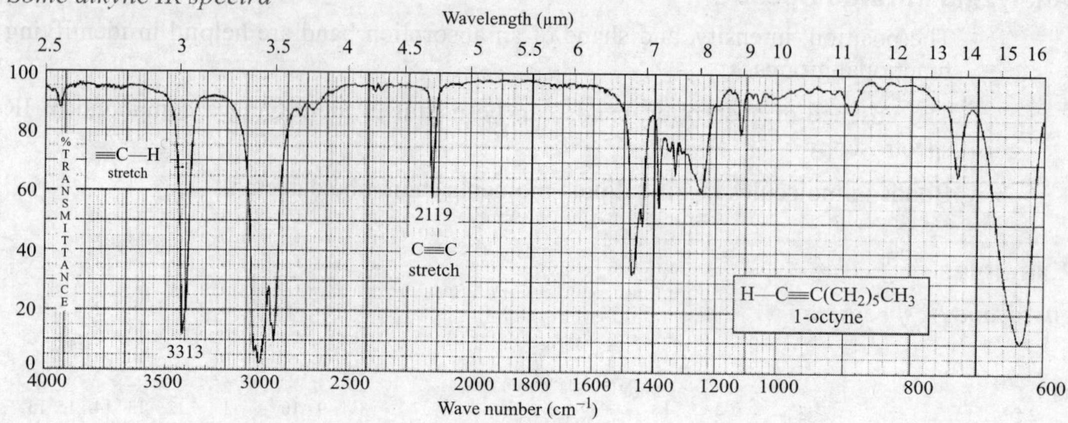

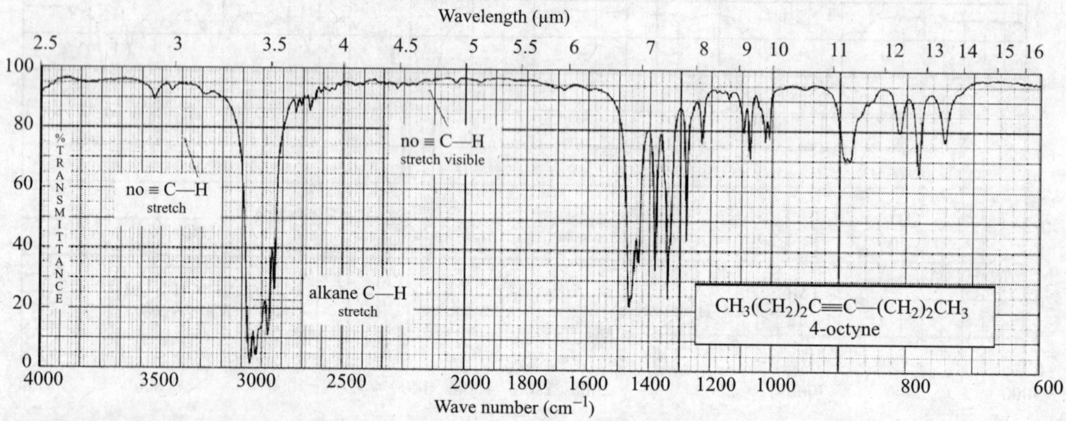

Note:

O—H and N—H stretching: Both of these occur around 3300 cm^{-1}, but they look different

1. Alcohol O—H: broad with rounded tip
2. Secondary amine (R_2NH): broad with one sharp spike
3. Primary amine (RNH_2): broad with two sharp spikes
4. No signal for a tertiary amine (R_3N)

An alcohol IR spectrum

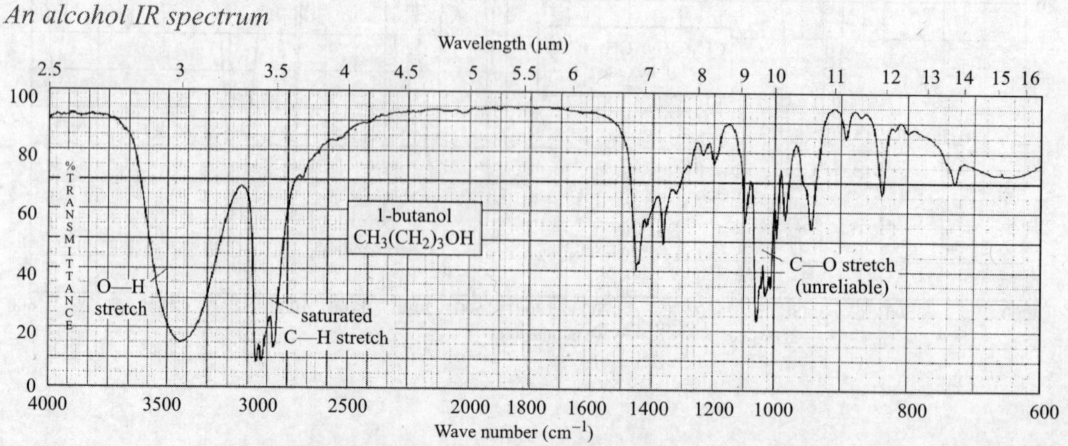

An amine IR spectrum

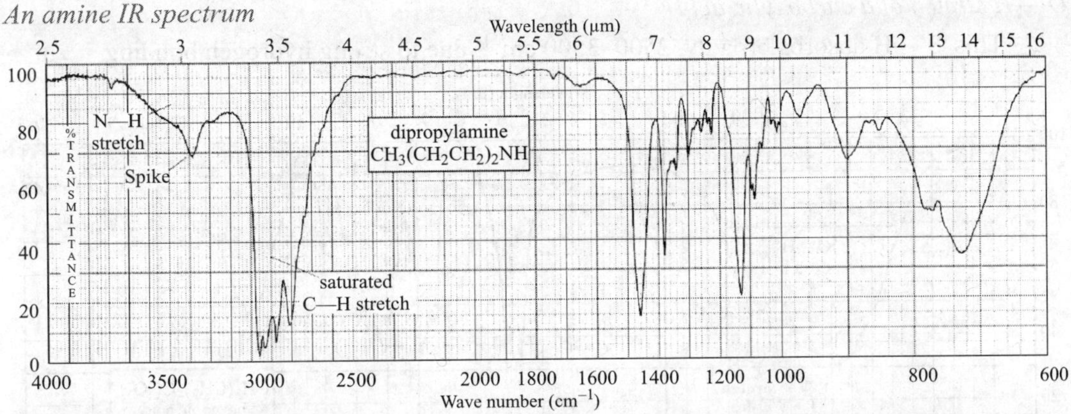

Note:

Carbonyl stretching

1. The C═O bond of simple ketones, aldehydes, and carboxylic acids absorbs around 1710 cm^{-1}.
2. Usually, it is the strongest IR signal.
3. Carboxylic acids will have O—H stretch also.
4. Aldehydes have two C—H signals around 2700 and 2800 cm^{-1}.

A ketone IR spectrum

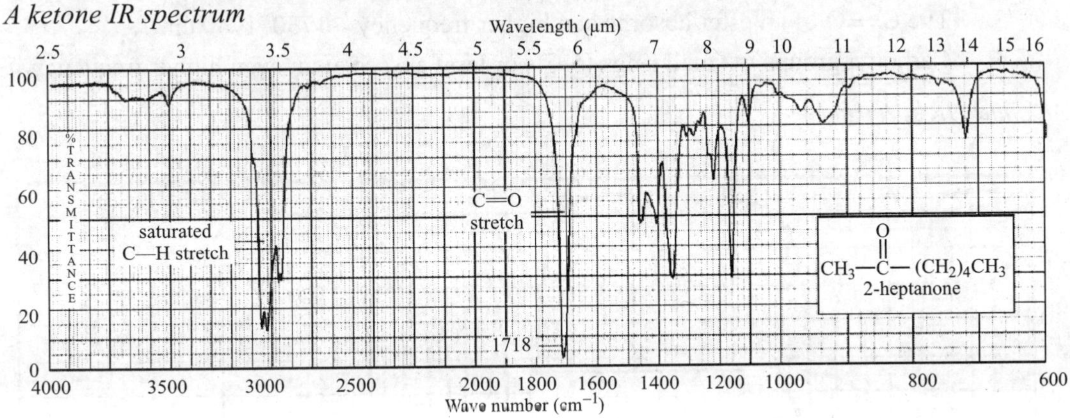

An aldehyde IR spectrum

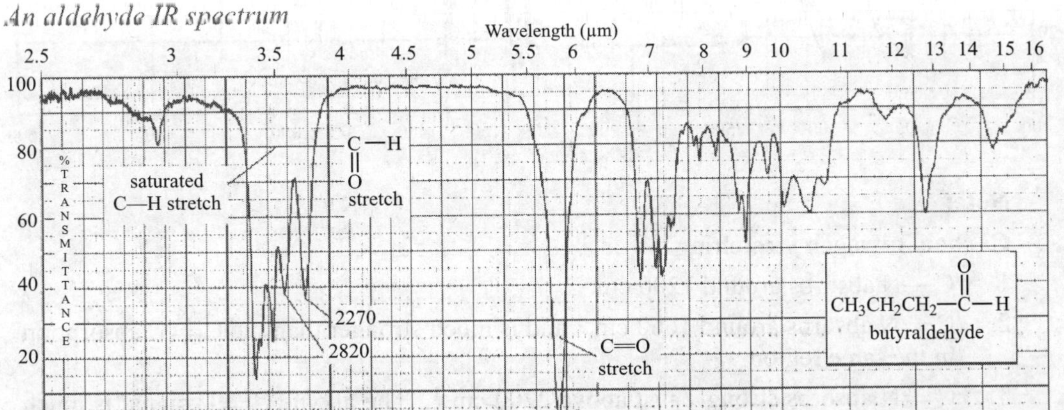

O—H stretch of a carboxylic acid

This O—H absorbs broadly, 2500–3500 cm^{-1}, due to strong hydrogen bonding

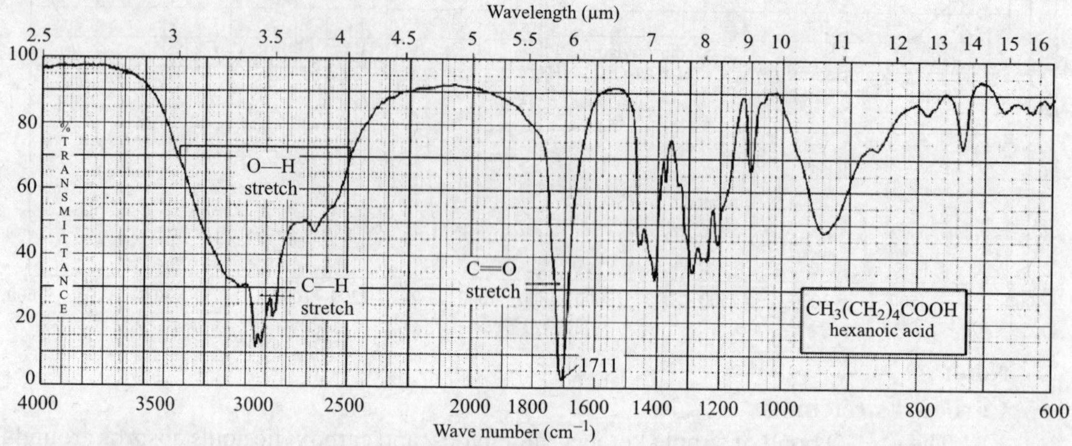

Note:

Variations in C=O Absorption

1. Conjugation of C=O with C=C lowers the stretching frequency to ~1680 cm^{-1}.
2. The C=O group of an amide absorbs at an even lower frequency, 1640–1680 cm^{-1}.
3. The C=O of an ester absorbs at a higher frequency, ~1730–1740 cm^{-1}.
4. Carbonyl groups in small rings (5 C's or less) absorb at an even higher frequency.

An amide IR spectrum

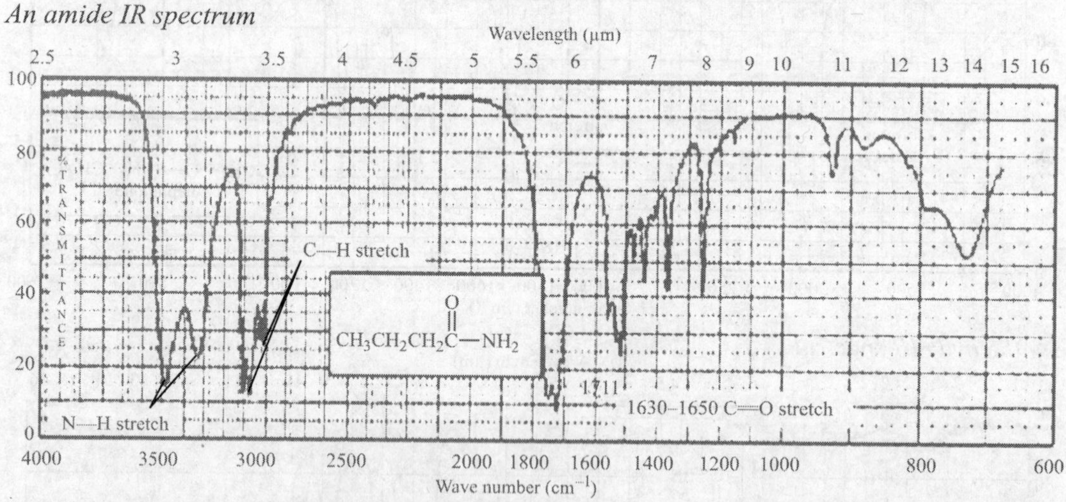

Note:

Carbon–nitrogen stretching

1. C—N absorbs around 1200 cm^{-1}
2. C=N absorbs around 1660 cm^{-1} and is much stronger than the C=C absorption in the same region.
3. C≡N absorbs strongly just above 2200 cm^{-1}. The alkyne C≡C signal is much weaker and is just below 2200 cm^{-1}.

A nitrile IR spectrum

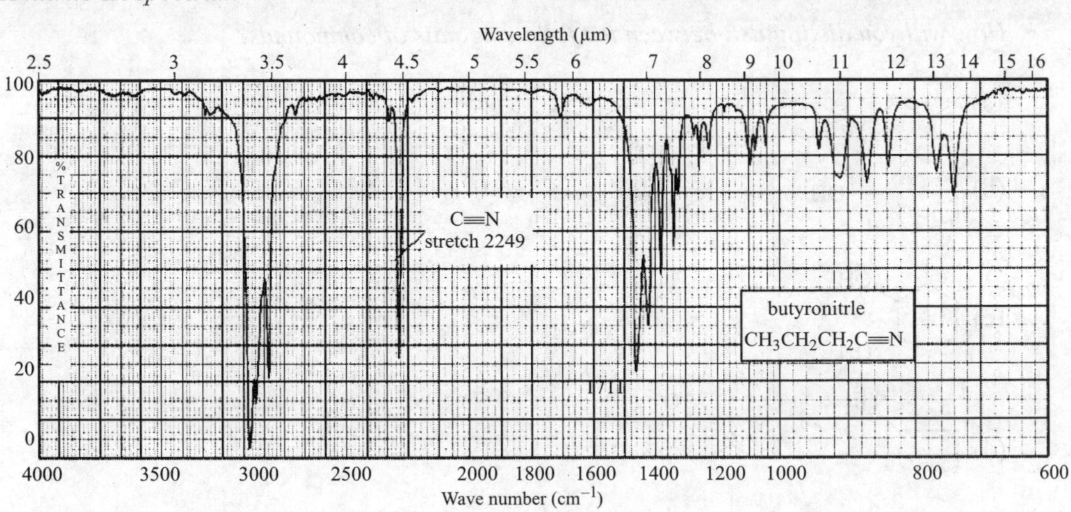

Summary of IR Absorptions

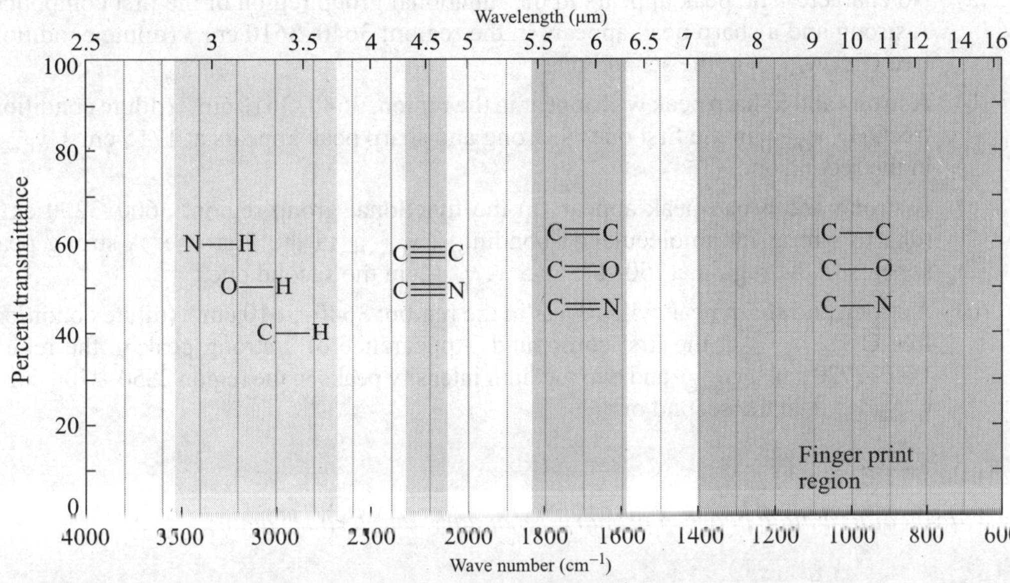

Applications of IR Spectroscopy

1. Widely used to detect functional groups in a chemical substance.
2. A potential tool to discriminate between a set of geometrical isomers (cis–trans) in many cases.
3. A well-known tool to analyze surfaces. The spectra from surfaces appears as bands because the density of the molecules on the surface is high and the wave functions of the molecules overlap. From this band spectrum, we can get information about the chemical structure of the surface molecules.
4. In biology, IR spectroscopy is most commonly employed to quantitate secondary structure or to determine changes in these structures.

Examples 11.5

How will you distinguish between the following pair of compounds?

(a) 

(b) 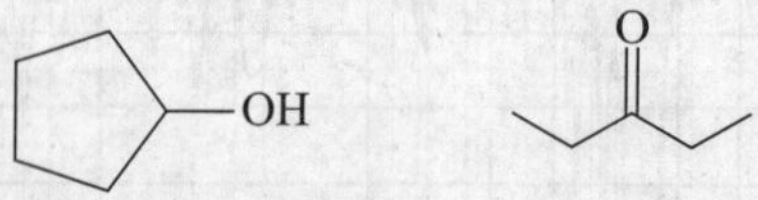

(c) 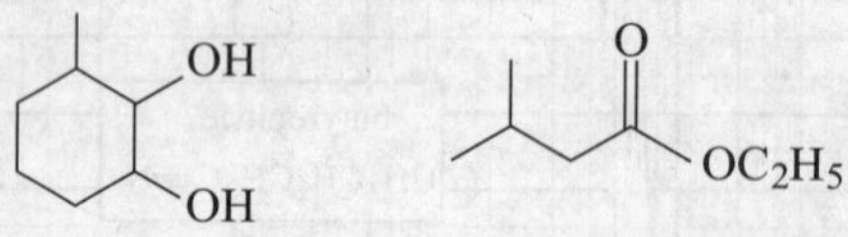

(d) 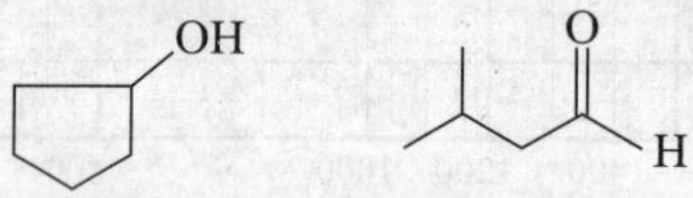

Solution

(a) No characteristic peak appears in the functional group region of the first compound. A strong and a sharp peak appears in the region: 3640–3610 cm^{-1} (dilute condition, free OH), ν_{O-H} in the second one.

(b) A strong and a sharp peak will appear in the region: 3640–3610 cm^{-1} (dilute condition, freeOH), ν_{O-H} in the first one. A strong and sharp peak appears at 1715 cm^{-1}, $\nu_{C=O}$ in the second one.

(c) A strong and broad peak appears in the functional group region: 3600–3200 cm^{-1} (due to strong intramolecular H-bonding) , ν_{O-H} in the first one. A strong peak appears in the region: 1750–1735cm^{-1} , $\nu_{C=O}$ in the second one.

(d) A strong and sharp peak will appear in the region: 3640–3610 cm^{-1} (dilute condition, free OH), ν_{O-H} in the first compound. Appearance of a strong peak in the region 1740–1720 cm^{-1}, $\nu_{C=O}$ and two medium intensity peaks in the region 2850–2700 cm^{-1}, $\nu_{(O=C)-H}$ in the second one.

Examples 11.6

How will you differentiate between primary, secondary, and tertiary amine?

Solution

The N—H stretches (ν_{N-H}) of amines are in the region 3300–3000 cm^{-1}. These bands are weaker and sharper than those of the alcohol O—H stretches which appear in the same region. In primary amines (RNH_2), there are two bands in this region, the asymmetrical N—H stretch and the symmetrical N—H stretch.

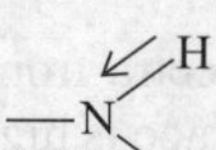

Asymetric N—H stretching
higher wave number

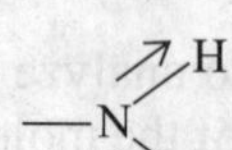

Symmetric N—H stretching
lower wave number

Secondary amines (R_2NH) show only a single weak band in 3300–3000 cm^{-1} region, since they have only one N—H bond. Tertiary amines (R_3N) do not show any band in this region, since they do not have a N—H bond.

The N—H bending vibration ($\delta_{N—H}$) of primary amines is observed in the region 1650–1580 cm^{-1}. Usually, secondary amines do not show a band in this region and tertiary amines never show a band in this region.

Another band attributed to amines is observed in the region 910–665 cm^{-1}. This strong, broad band is due to N—H wag and observed only for primary and secondary amines. The C—N stretching vibration of aliphatic amines is observed as medium or weak bands in the region 1250–1020 cm^{-1}. In aromatic amines, the band is usually strong and in the region 1335–1250 cm^{-1}.

Summary

1. N—H stretch 3400–3250 cm^{-1}
   (a) 1° amine: two bands from 3400 to 3300 and from 3330 to 3250 cm^{-1}
   (b) 2° amine: one band from 3350 to 3310 cm^{-1}
   (c) 3° amine: no bands in this region
2. N—H band (primary amines only) from 1650 to 1580 cm^{-1}
3. C—N stretch (aromatic amines) from 1335 to 1250 cm^{-1}
4. C—N stretch (aliphatic amines) from 1250 to 1020 cm^{-1}
5. N—H wag (primary and secondary amines only) from 910 to 665 cm^{-1}

Example 11.7

How will you differentiate between primary, secondary and tertiary alcohols?

Solution

You have to look for the peak of the C—C—O assymetric stretch (usually, simply called C—O stretch). For primairy alcohols it appears between 1075 and 1000 cm^{-1}, for secondary it appears between 1150 and 1075 cm^{-1}, for tertiary it appears between 1210 and 1100 cm^{-1}.

Example 11.8

How IR spectroscopy remains useful in predicting substitution of alkenes?

Solution

C═C stretch frequency can be used to determine the type of substitution: tetra substituted alkene does not absorb at all. A *cis* isomer absorbs more strongly than a *trans* isomer (*cis* is less symmetrical than *trans*). Simple monosubstituted alkenes absorb at 1640 cm^{-1}, $\nu_{C=C}$. Similarly, C—H out of plane bending vibration is also a very potential tool to determine the type of alkene substitution: simple 1,1-disubstituted alkene absorbs at 1650 cm^{-1}, $\delta_{C—H}$, while monosubstituted alkene gives two peaks near 990 and 910 cm^{-1}, $\delta_{C—H}$. 1,2-disubstituted (*cis*) gives one strong band near 700 cm^{-1}, $\delta_{C—H}$; 1,2-disubstitued (*trans*) gives one band near 970 cm^{-1}, $\delta_{C—H}$; 1,1-disubstituted gives one strong band near 890 cm^{-1}, $\delta_{C—H}$; a tri-substituted double bond absorbs near 815 cm^{-1}, $\delta_{C—H}$; a tetra-substituted double bond does not absorb at all.

Example 11.9

How IR spectroscopy becomes useful to understand the nature of ether?

Solution

C—O stretch is the most important, which occurs at 1300–1000 cm^{-1}.

1. In dialkyl ethers, stretching occurs as a strong band at 1120 cm^{-1}.
2. Aryl alkyl ethers give two peaks: an asymmetric C—O—C stretch near 1250 cm^{-1} and a symmetric stretch near 1040 cm^{-1}.
3. Vinyl alkyl ethers give two peaks: a strong asymmetric stretch at 1220 cm^{-1} and a weak symmetric stretch near 850 cm^{-1}.

Example 11.10

How IR spectroscopy becomes useful to differentiate between a normal double bond conjugated aldehyde/ketone/ester and an aromatic aldehyde/ketone/ester?

Solution

$\nu_{C=O}$ for aldehyde

1. 1740–1725 cm^{-1} for normal aliphatic aldehyde.
2. 1700–1680 cm^{-1} for conjugation with double bond.
3. 1700–1660 cm^{-1} for conjugation with phenyl group.

$\nu_{C=O}$ for ketone

1. 1700–1675 cm^{-1} for conjugation with double bond.
2. 1700– 680 cm^{-1} for conjugation with one phenyl group.
3. 1670–1600 cm^{-1} for conjugation with two phenyl groups.

$\nu_{C=O}$ for ester

1. 1750–1735 cm^{-1} for normal aliphatic esters (for example, ethyl butyrate, 1738 cm^{-1}).
2. 1740–1750 cm^{-1} if carbonyl carbon conjugated with an alkene (for example, methyl methacrylate, 1725 cm^{-1}).
3. 1740–1715 cm^{-1} if carbonyl carbon conjugated with aromatic (for example, methyl benzoate, 1724 cm^{-1}).
4. 1765–1762 cm^{-1} if oxygen atom conjugated with alkene or aromatic (note that this is a shift to higher frequency). For example, phenyl acetate, 1765 cm^{-1}; vinyl acetate, 1762 cm^{-1}.

Flame Photometry

The flame photometry or flame emission photometry is a type of emission spectroscopy, and the main principle involved is the measurement of emission radiation. The sample metal atoms are brought to excitation state by using thermal energy. The excited atoms subsequently come back to the ground state by the emission of radiant energy which is characteristic to the metal under investigation. It is suitable for qualitative and quantitative determination of several cations, especially for metals that are easily excited to higher energy levels at a relatively low flame temperature and have flame spectrum of significant intensity for detection by a photocell such as groups 1 and 2 elements (Li, Na, K, Ca, etc.).

Instrument

The basic components of a typical flame photometer are flame atomizer, filter, detector, amplifier, and readout device.

Flame atomizer: It consists of a nebulizer and a burner. Nebulizer helps in aspirating a homogeneous solution containing the relevant substance to be analyzed into the flame at a steady rate. In the burner, the fuel and the oxidant burn to give a flame that can be maintained in a constant form and at a constant temperature. The temperature of burner can be controlled by monitoring fuel-to-air ratio, type of solvent used in preparing the sample solution, the amount of solvent entering into flame, and the type of burner used. Two types of burners are popularly used, viz., (i) Pre-mix burner in which the aspirated sample, fuel, and oxidant are thoroughly mixed before combustion. In this burner, there is a loss of sample (95%) as large droplets which drain out. (ii) Total consumption burner in which the air and fuel are mixed in a chamber which is delivered through nozzle, where the sample is aspirated. Here the sample is completely consumed.

Monochromator (or filter): The work of monochromator is to isolate the light of the wavelength to be measured from that of extraneous emissions. Generally, a grating or a prism monochromator is employed.

Detector: It helps in measuring the intensity of radiation emitted by the flame. Photoemissive cells or photomultiplier tubes are commonly employed for the purpose.

Amplifier and readout device: It is used to amplify the signal and provide a suitable output. The instrument has microprocessor-controlled electronics that provides outputs compatible with the printers and computers, thereby minimizing the possibility of operator error in transferring data.

A typical flame photometer is shown in Fig. 11.20.

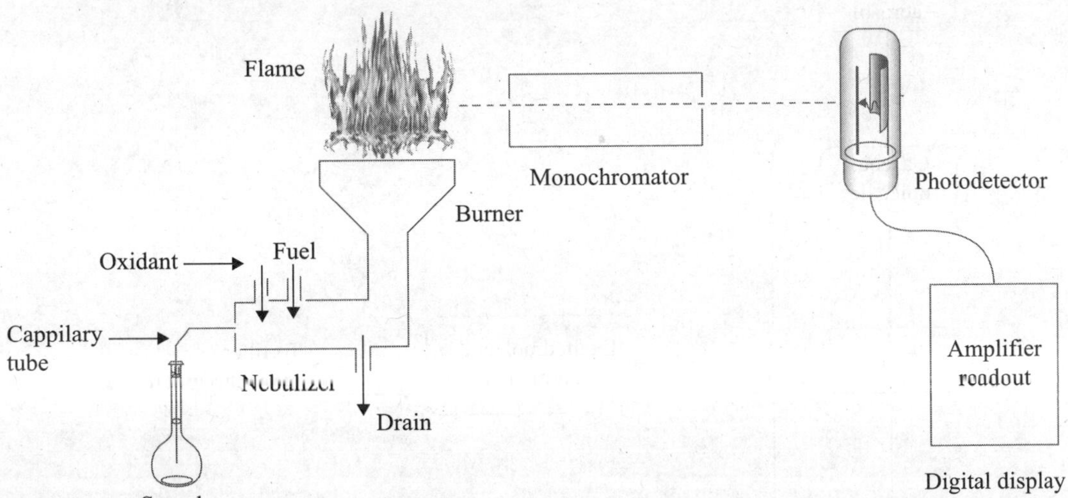

Fig. 11.20 A typical flame photometer

Working Principle

A solution containing the relevant substance to be analyzed is aspirated into the burner and dispersed into the flame as a fine spray. This process is called nebulization. The heat of the flame vaporizes the sample constituents without any chemical change. Subsequently, the molecules and ions of the sample species get decomposed and reduced to atoms by heat of the flame and action of the reducing gas, i.e., fuel. The atoms at this stage absorb energy from the heat of the flame which brings excitation of electrons to higher energy levels. Electrons in the excited state are very unstable and get back to the ground state or lower energy state through relaxation. As they do so, they emit the energy in the form of radiation of characteristic wavelength, which is measured by a detector. For some metals, this radiation corresponds to wavelengths of light in the visible region of the electromagnetic spectrum and is observed as a characteristic color of the flame. As electrons from different energy levels are able to emit light as they relax, the flame color observed will be a mixture of all the different wavelengths emitted by the different electrons in the metal atom under investigation. Flame photometers use optical filters to monitor for the selected emission wavelength produced by the analyte species. Comparison of emission intensities of unknowns to either that of standard solutions (plotting calibration curve) or to those of an internal standard (standard addition method) allows quantitative analysis of the analyte metal in the sample solution. The complete principle is presented in Fig. 11.21.

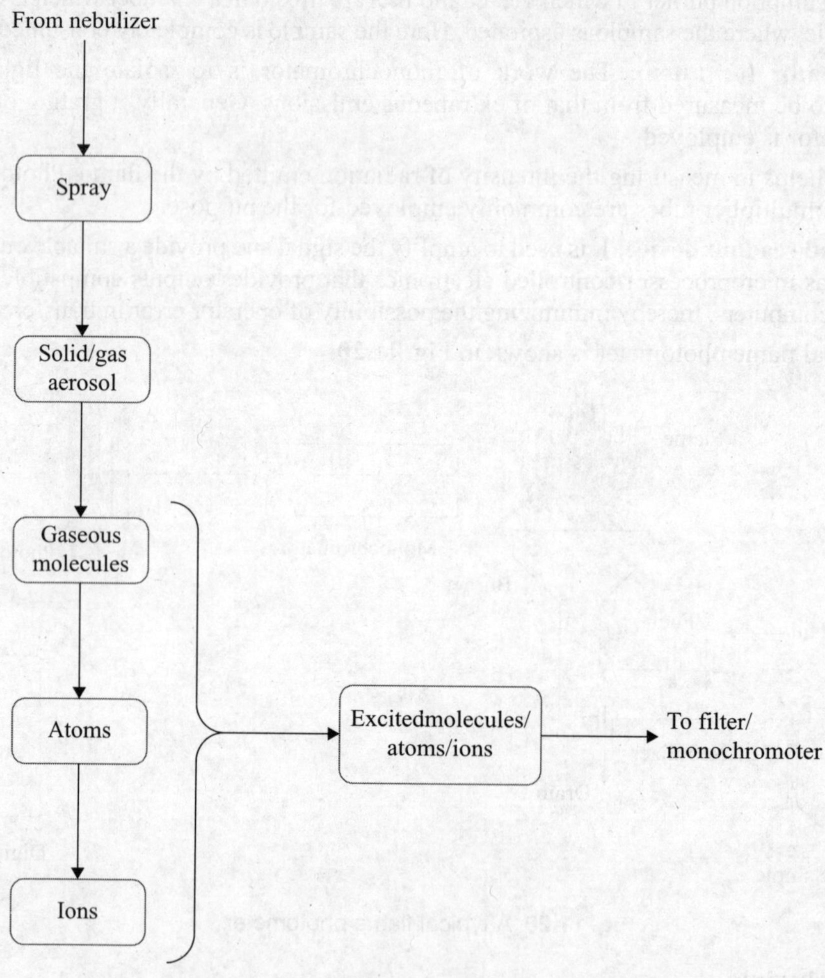

Fig. 11.21 Schematic representation of working of a photometer

Quantitative Applications

1. In clinical chemistry for the determination of Na and K in body fluids such as blood serum. This is achieved by diluting the blood serum followed by aspiration in to the flame.

2. In agriculture industry, it is used to determine the concentration of various soil components.
3. Analysis of food and drinks for alkali metals.
4. For quantitative estimation of alkali and alkaline earth metals in mineral extraction and pharmaceuticals.
5. In cement and petroleum industries.

Note:

1. Flame temperature greater than 2000 K is maintained by burning the fuel gas in an oxidant gas such as air or nitrous oxide or oxygen diluted with nitrogen or argon. Temperature attended by some common fuel gases is as follows.

Fuel gas	Temperature (in K)	
	Air	Nitrous oxide
Acetylene	2400	3200
Hydrogen	2300	2900
Propane	2200	3000

2. A major problem is self-absorption. This becomes important because there is a lower population of excited atoms in the outer region of the flame than in the central hotter region of the flame which allows the absorption of emitted radiation by the hot central part by the relatively cooler outer region. For high analyte concentrations, the result is self-absorption which leads to a negative non-linear curve that limits the operating range of the instrument.

Atomic Absorption Spectroscopy

Atomic absorption spectroscopy (AAS) is a technique for the determination of the concentration of trace metals in a sample taken in the solution form. The technique can be used to analyze the concentration of over 62 different metals including common rare earths. The technique basically makes use of a flame to atomize the sample. The atomic vapor so formed is then allowed to absorb radiation of a selected wavelength which is characteristic of the individual element. The absorbance is then measured that remain proportional to the concentration of the metal. Here in this technique the estimation of one element can be made in the presence of many other elements without interference. Sample preparation can also be made in non-aqueous solvents in addition to aqueous solvent.

Instrument

The basic components of a typical AAS are same as that of a flame photometer: flame atomizer, filter, detector, amplifier, and readout device. In addition, there is a light source. The light source is a hollow cathode lamp which is a metal vapor lamp that emits light at the characteristic wavelength(s) of the metal in the cathode. Inside the lamp, there is a cylindrical metal cathode containing the metal for excitation and an anode. When a high voltage is applied across the electrodes, the metal atoms in the cathode get excited into producing light with a certain emission spectrum. A typical AAS is shown in Fig. 11.22.

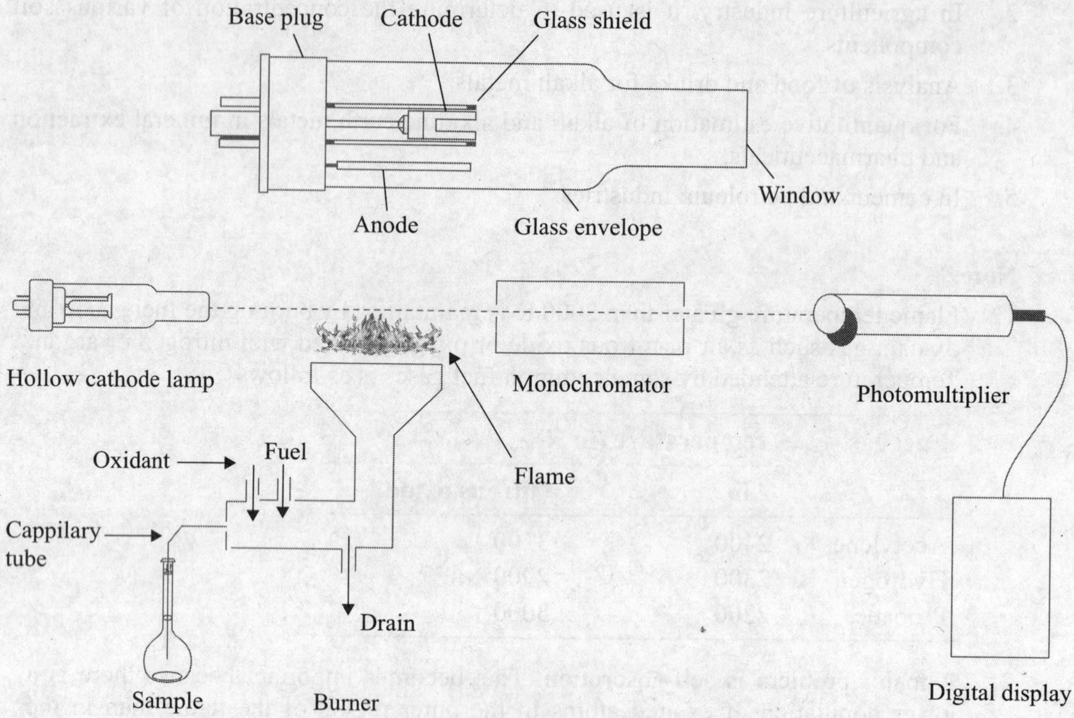

Fig. 11.22 Atomic absorption spectroscopy

Working Principle

A solution containing the relevant substance to be analyzed is aspirated into the burner and dispersed into the flame as a fine spray. The flame is arranged such that it is laterally long (usually 10 cm) and not deep. The height of the flame must also be monitored by controlling the flow of the fuel mixture. The heat of the flame vaporizes the sample constituents without any chemical change. Subsequently, the molecules and ions of the sample species get decomposed and reduced to atoms by heat of the flame and action of the reducing gas, i.e., fuel. At this point of time, characteristic radiation obtained from a hollow cathode lamp is focused into the flame containing the atomic vapors. The electrons of the atoms in the flame get promoted to higher orbitals for an instant by absorbing a set quantity of radiant energy (a quantum). This amount of radiant energy is specific to a particular electron transition in a particular element. As the quantity of energy put into the flame is known and the quantity remaining at the other side (at the detector) can be measured, it is possible to calculate how many of these transitions took place, and thus get a signal that is proportional to the concentration of the element being measured as per Beer–Lambert's law.

Note:

1. Some elements such as As, Se, Ge, Te, Sb, and Sn can be estimated by converting them to their hydrides in a hydride generator and subsequent aspiration into the argon–hydrogen flame. The reaction taking place in hydride generator for an element say arsenic can be expressed as

$$\text{As (V) Solution} \xrightarrow[H^+]{NaBH_4} AsH_3 \xrightarrow[\text{Heat}]{} As^0 + H_2$$

2. Mercury (Hg) can be determined by flame-less (cold vapor) atomic absorption technique. This is due to the fact that Hg has enough vapor pressure to generate appreciable atomic species without any special condition. In this technique, Hg^{2+} ions are reduced to elemental Hg^0 by $NaBH_4$ or $SnCl_2$. The resultant vapor is swept into an absorption cell with air, where it is exposed as a radiation coming from Hg vapor lamp.
3. In order to increase the detection limit, electrothermal atomization may be adopted in place of flame atomization using a graphite furnace. The graphite furnace is a hollow cylinder which is directly placed in the path of the light beam. Sample is taken in the cylinder through a hole in the tip. An electrical current is allowed to pass through the cylinder for heating it to incandescence. The sample gets volatilized in the cylinder and the atoms are then exposed to characteristic radiation coming from hollow cathode lamp. This technique offers better sensitivity due to improved atomization efficiency and higher attainable temperature.

Applications

This is very sensitive instrument used for the detection of trace metals in environmental samples, biological materials, food stuffs, etc. It can also be utilized for the determination of lead in alloys and petrol, vanadium in lubricating oil, etc.

Disadvantages

1. A separate lamp for each element is required.
2. This technique cannot be used for the estimation of elements such as Al, Ti, W, Mo, Si, etc., as these elements form stable oxides in the flame.

Thermal Methods of Analysis

These methods are based upon the measurement of the dynamic relationship between temperature and one of the properties of the system such as mass, mass change, and heat of reaction. Most important techniques of thermal methods are thermogravimetric analysis (TGA), differential thermal analysis (DTA), and differential scanning calorimetry (DSC).

Thermogravimetric Analysis

Thermogravimetry is a technique in which the mass of a sample is recorded continuously with linear increase in temperature from room temperature to as high as 1200 K. Thermogravimetric analysis (TGA) is useful for determining sample purity as well as to find water, carbonate, and organic content in the sample. It is also used for studying decomposition reactions. The main components of TGA instrument are analytical thermo balance, furnace, and recorder. Analytical balance is used to measure the mass with reproducibility in the order of ±10 μg. Furnace linked with microprocessor-controlled power source is programmed to increase temperature linearly at a predetermined rate of 0.5–25°C/min. Arrangement is made for providing inert atmosphere for the sample as and when required. Recorder provides a plot of mass (m) or (dm/dt) as a function of temperature which is known as *thermogram* or *differential thermogram*, respectively. The block diagram of a typical TGA instrument is shown Fig. 11.23.

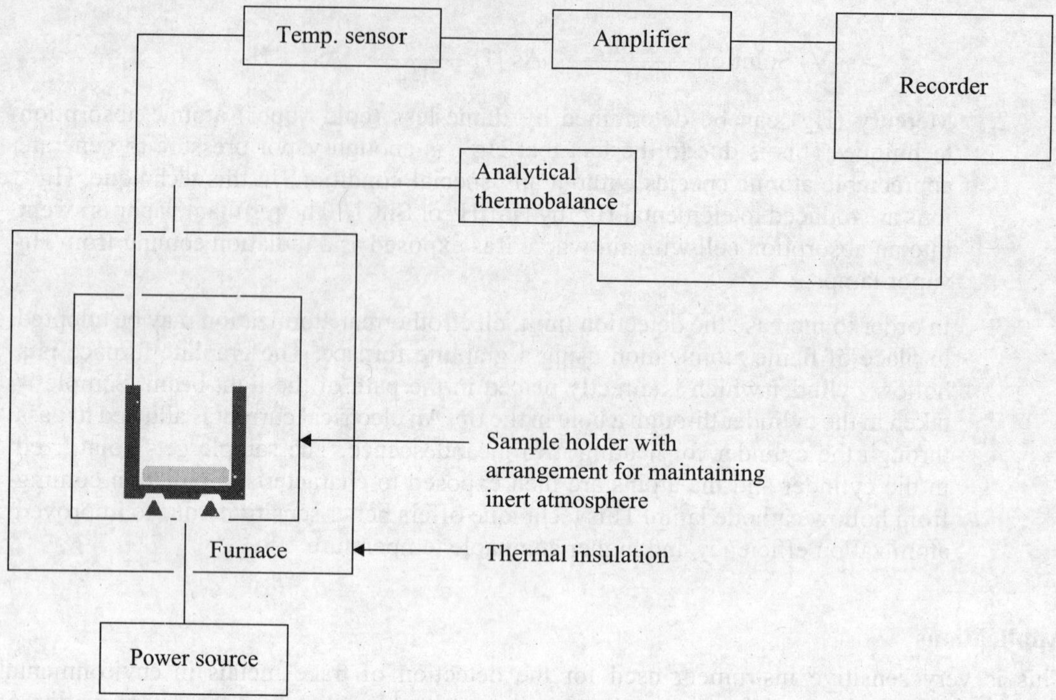

Fig. 11.23 TGA instrument

Analysis of TGA plot

A thermogram basically consists of two portions, viz., a horizontal and a slanting portion. A typical thermogram is shown in Fig. 11.24. Horizontal portion (I) indicates the no mass change from which one can get idea about the thermal stability of the material. The slanting downward portion (II) indicates mass loss which may be attributed to dehydration, dissociation, formation of volatile products, etc.

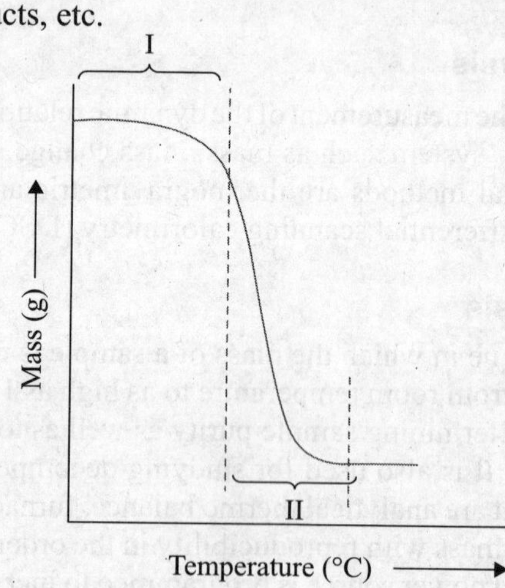

Fig. 11.24 A typical TGA curve

Factors affecting TGA results

There are various factors that affect TGA results:

1. **Heating rate**: A faster heating rate lead to higher decomposition temperature.

2. **Furnace atmosphere**: The function of atmosphere is to remove the gaseous products released during thermogravimetry so as to ensure the constancy of the surrounding gas as far as possible. It has a remarkable effect sometimes, e.g., there occurs a significant hike in the decomposition temperature of $CaCO_3$ in CO_2 atmosphere as compared to that in N_2 atmosphere.
3. **Crucible geometry**: The geometry may change the slope of thermogram. A flat plate-shaped crucible is always preferred as it facilitates the diffusion of any evolved gases.
4. **Sample characteristics**: The weight, particle size, and mode of preparation guide the thermogravimetric result. A large sample often creates a deviation from linearity in the temperature rise. In practice, a small sample weight in addition with particle size as small as possible is used.

Applications

Applications of TGA are as follows:

1. **In qualitative analysis:** TG thermogram provides valuable information for qualitative analysis of a sample such as stability of the substance at elevated temperature, identification of substances, and decomposition mechanism of polymers.
2. **In study of polymers:** It is used to measure thermal stability of polymers. As each polymer follows a characteristic TG thermogram pattern, it can be used for identification purposes. The amount of filler in polymeric sample can be estimated. For example, the determination of $CaCO_3$ in polyester can be measured from the thermogram shown in Fig. 11.25. The loss of weight in region 1 is attributed to decomposition of polyester and removal of volatilities. On the other hand, the weight loss in region 2 is attributed to decomposition of $CaCO_3$ and loss of CO_2. Now, the amount of filler can be calculated by using the following formula:

$$\% \text{ of } CaCO_3 = \% \text{ of } CO_2 \times \frac{\text{Molecular weight of } CaCO_3}{\text{Molecular weight of } CO_2}$$

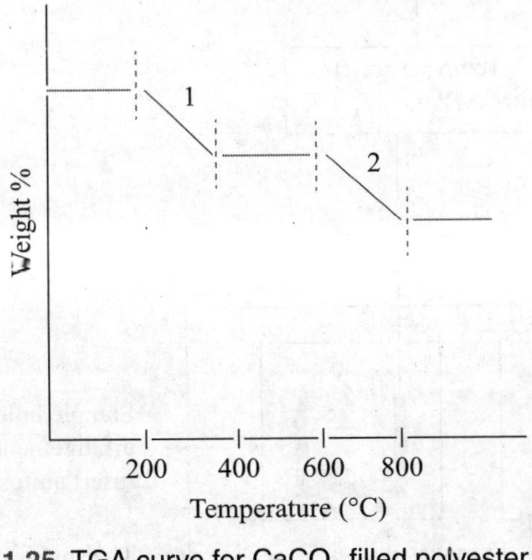

Fig. 11.25 TGA curve for $CaCO_3$ filled polyester resin

3. **Determination of composition of mixtures and alloys:** Composition of mixtures and alloys can be established from the TG thermogram provided each component in the mixture possesses a unique pyrolysis curve. For example, let us look into the determination of a mixture of calcium and strontium as their carbonates. Both the carbonates decompose to their oxides with evolution of CO_2. $CaCO_3$ decomposes

in the temperature range 600–850°C $SrCO_3$ in the range 950–1150°C. Now the amount of Ca and Sr can be calculated from the weight losses at lower and higher temperature range, respectively.

Limitations

1. For TGA to be useful, temperature variation must bring about a change in the mass of the analyte. Therefore, it is limited to decomposition and oxidation reactions along with physical process such as vaporization, sublimation, and desorption.
2. It cannot be utilized for pure fusion reactions, crystalline transitions, solid state reactions without any volatile product(s), etc.
3. It cannot be utilized for the determination of glass transition temperature of polymers.

Differential Thermal Analysis

In differential thermal analysis (DTA), the temperature difference that develops between a sample and an inert reference material is measured, when both are subjected to identical heat treatments as a function of temperature or time. The instrumental set up is more or less same as that of TGA. However, the furnace in DTA contains two chambers which are identical and symmetrically located and are connected with temperature sensors, i.e., thermocouple. The block diagram for a typical DTA setup is shown in Fig. 11.26.

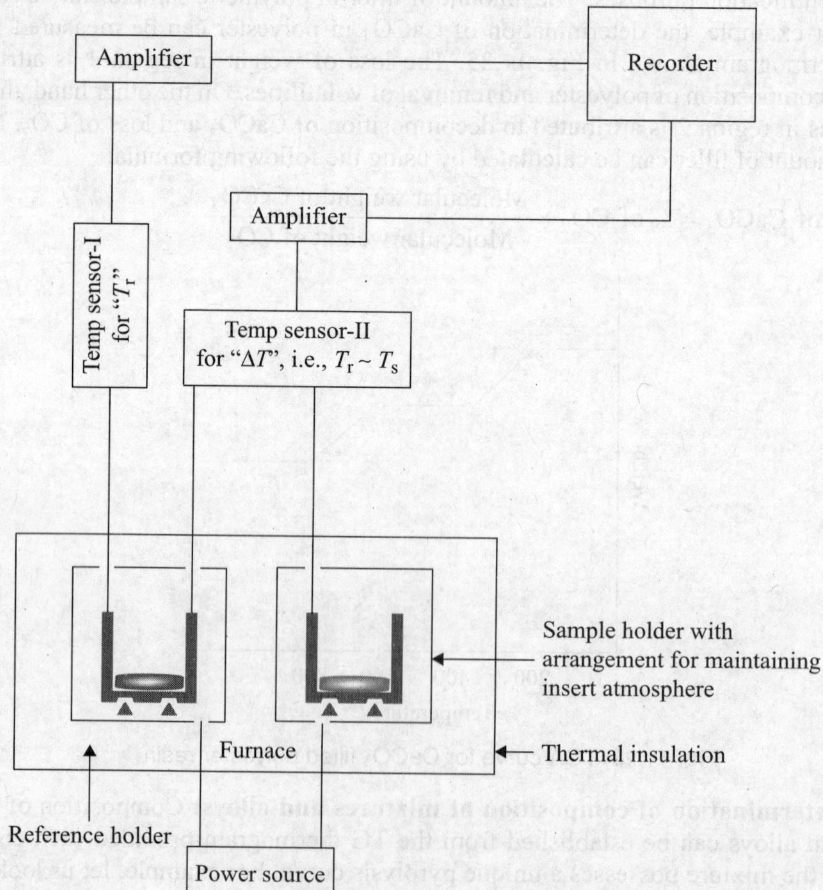

Fig. 11.26 A typical DTA setup

The sample and the reference are placed symmetrically in the furnace. Matters that do not change in the measurement temperature range (usually α-alumina) are used as reference. The temperature of the furnace and both the chambers are allowed to increase linearly at a rate of 5–12°C/min. During this process, a differential thermocouple is set up to continuously detect the temperature difference between the sample (T_s) and the reference (T_r), i.e., ΔT, as a function of reference temperature. For temperature measurement, the temperature sensor is directly placed in the sample or attached to the chamber. As the sample undergoes transition with liberation or absorption of energy, the deviation of sample temperature from that of reference reveals information regarding the exothermic or endothermic nature of transition as well as the transition temperature. The plot of ΔT as the function of reference temperature is known as differential thermogram.

Analysis of differential thermogram

A typical ***differential thermogram*** is shown in Fig. 11.27. For exothermic changes such as oxidation and adsorption, the peaks appear above zero in thermogram. On the other hand, for endothermic changes such as desorption, sublimation, and fusion, the peaks appear below zero. In general, sharp endothermic changes give idea of change in crystallinity or fusion processes, while broad endothermic peaks to dehydration reaction.

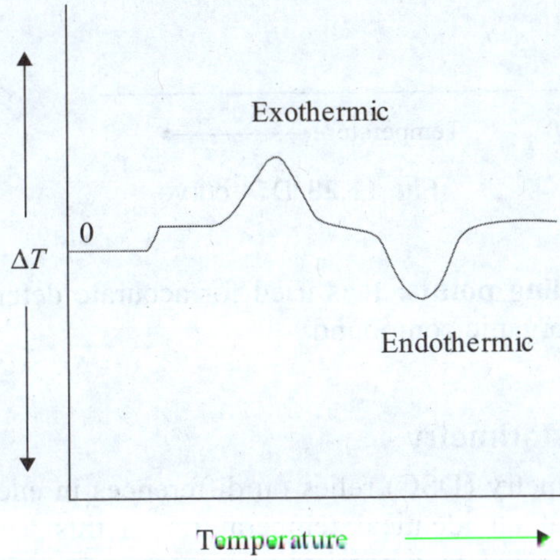

Fig.11.27 A typical differential thermogram

> **Note:**
> The shape of a DTA peak also depends on the sample weight and heating rate. Fewer amounts of sample and slow heating rate lead to sharp peaks with improved resolution.

Applications

1. **In qualitative analysis:** DTA is used for qualitative analysis of materials. It serves as a rapid method for identifying minerals and polymeric materials, e.g., white asbestos

(chrysolite) shows a de-hydroxylation endotherm at 650°C and a crystallization exotherm at 845°C. Each component polymer in a polymer blend can be identified by using DTA.

2. **Phase diagram:** It helps in the generation of phase diagrams and the study of phase transitions.

3. **Polymer characterization**: Widely used to study characterization of polymers. An idealized DTA curve (Fig. 11.28) illustrates the different type of transitions that can be encountered during heating of a polymer.

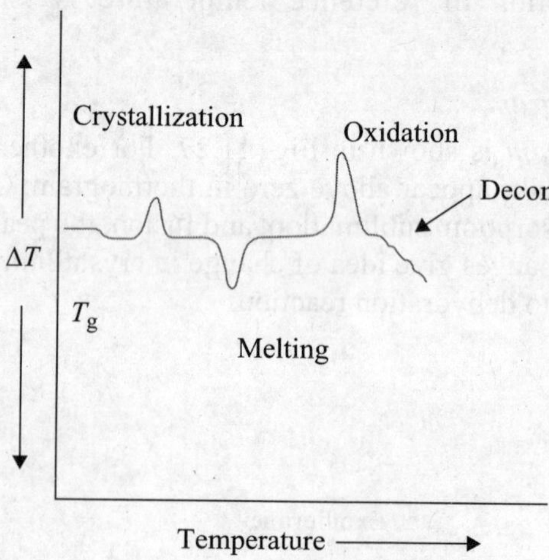

Fig. 11.28 DTA curve

4. **Melting and boiling points:** It is used for accurate determination of melting and boiling points of organic compound.

Differential Scanning Calorimetry

Differential scanning calorimetry (DSC) relies on differences in energy required to maintain the sample and reference at an identical temperature. In this technique, the sample and reference materials are subjected to a precisely programmed temperature change. When a thermal transition occurs in the sample, thermal energy is added to either the sample or the reference in order to maintain both the sample and the reference at the temperature. Because the energy transferred is exactly equivalent in magnitude to the energy absorbed or evolved in the transition, direct calorimetric measurement of the transition energy is obtained from this balancing energy. On the DSC chart, the abscissa indicates the transition temperature and the peak area measures the total energy transfer to or from the sample. The block diagram for a typical DSC setup is shown in Fig. 11.29.

DSC curve

DSC curves (Fig. 11.30) typically consist of the heat flow plotted versus the temperature. These curves can be used to calculate the enthalpies of transitions (ΔH) by integrating the peak of the state transition.

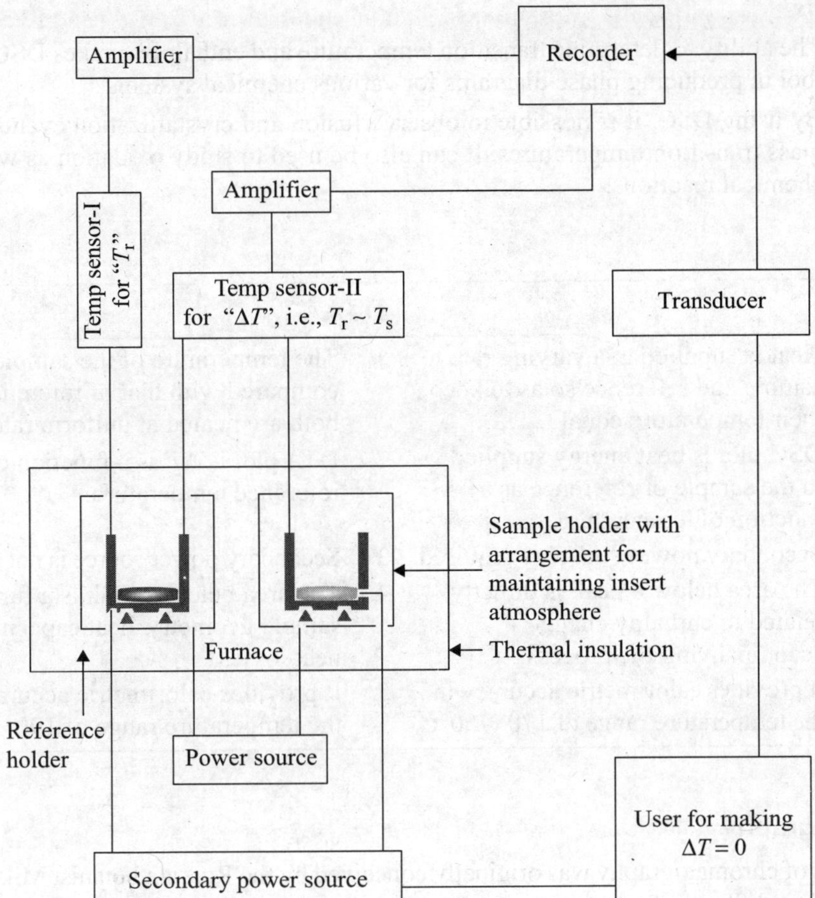

Fig. 11.29 Block diagram for a DSC setup

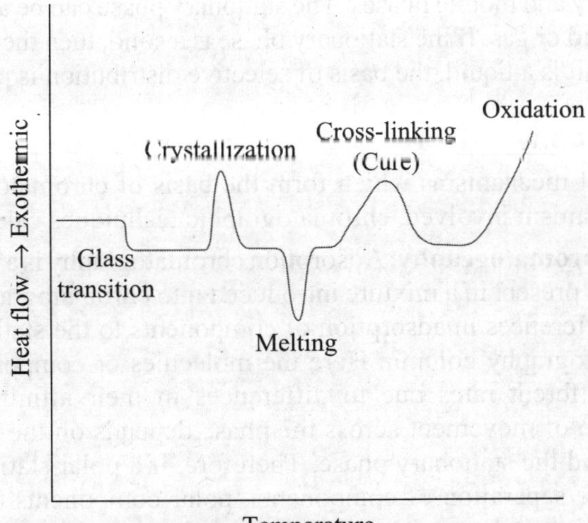

Fig. 11.30 DSC curve

Applications

1. The ability to determine transition temperature and enthalpies makes DSC a valuable tool in producing phase diagrams for various chemical systems.
2. By using DSC, it is possible to observe fusion and crystallization events as well as glass transition temperatures. It can also be used to study oxidation as well as other chemical reactions.

Note:

DSC	DTA
1. Heat is supplied at a varying rate to sample and reference so as to keep their temperature equal.	1. The temperature of the sample is compared with that of reference as both are heated at uniform rate.
2. DSC plot is heat energy supplied to the sample or reference as a function of temperature.	2. DTA plot is ΔT as a function of reference temperature.
3. Secondary power source is required.	3. Secondary power source is not required.
4. The area below a peak is directly related to enthalpy change accompanying the process.	4. The area below a peak is a function of sample geometry, heat capacity, and heat losses.
5. It provides calorimetric accuracy in the temperature range of 170–750°C.	5. It provides calorimetric accuracy in the temperature range of 190–1600°C.

Chromatography

The concept of chromatography was originally conceived by the Russian botanist Mikhail Tswett in 1903. He used this method to separate plant pigments into colored components for which he named this separation technique as *chromatography* (Greek: "written in color"). Chromatography is based on the principle of selective distribution of the different components of a mixture between two phases, viz., stationary and mobile phases. The stationary phase can be a solid or liquid, while the mobile phase is a liquid or gas. If the stationary phase is a solid, then the selective distribution is based on adsorption; if it is a liquid, the basis of selective distribution is partition.

Types of Chromatography

There exist four different mechanisms which form the basis of chromatographic separations. On the basis of the mechanism involved, chromatographic techniques can be classified as

1. **Adsorption chromatography:** Adsorption chromatography is a process of separation of components present in a mixture introduced into chromatography system based on the relative differences in adsorption of components to the stationary phase present in the chromatography column. Here the molecules or components of the mixture travel with different rates due to differences in their affinity toward stationary phase. The rate of movement across the phase depends on the relative polarities of components and the stationary phase. Therefore, if a polar stationary phase is used, then during the separation of components, polar components elute out late due to greater adsorption and non-polar components elute out first. This is exactly reverse on using a non-polar stationary phase. As adsorption phenomenon is an inherent property of solid, it is used with only solid stationary phase.

2. **Partition chromatography:** Partition chromatography is the process of separation by which the components of a mixture get distributed into two immiscible liquid phases due to differences in partition coefficients during the flow of mobile phase in the chromatography column. Here both stationary and mobile phases are liquid in nature. Polar molecules get partitioned into polar phase and vice verse. This mode of *partition chromatography* applies to liquid–liquid and liquid–gas chromatographies and not to solid–gas chromatography. This is due to the fact that partition is the phenomenon in between a liquid and liquid or liquid and gas or gas and gas. Different distribution coefficient values ensure different rate of movement and separation of the components of the mixture. The coefficient of distribution (K_D) of substances between two immiscible liquids is the ratio of the concentration of the substance in one liquid, i.e., mobile solvent, to the concentration of the same substance in another liquid, i.e., stationary liquid.

$$K_D = \frac{C_{\text{Mobile solvent}}}{C_{\text{Staionary liquid}}}$$

Note

In column chromatography and thin layer chromatography, *adsorption chromatography* is used. However, in high performance liquid chromatography (HPLC), paper chromatography, and gas chromatography, *partition chromatography* is the principle of separation.

3. **Ion-exchange chromatography:** It is a process that allows the separation of ions and polar molecules based on their affinity to the ion exchanger. It can be used for almost any kind of charged molecule including large proteins, small nucleotides, and amino acids. Ion-exchangers are water-insoluble polymer beads which consist of a polymeric C chain to which a number of acidic functional groups such as $-SO_2$, $-OH$, $-COOH$ or anionic groups such as $-NH_3^+Cl^-$ are attached. Ion-exchangers with fixed negative charges can bind to mobile cations and are called cation exchangers (e.g., carboxy methyl cellulose and sulfonated polystyrene), whereas the ion-exchangers with fixed positive charges can bind mobile anions and are called anion exchangers (e.g., dimethylaminoethyl cellulose and triethyl-amino polystyrene). A typical cation exchanger is shown in Fig. 11.31. The ion exchanger acts as the stationary phase.

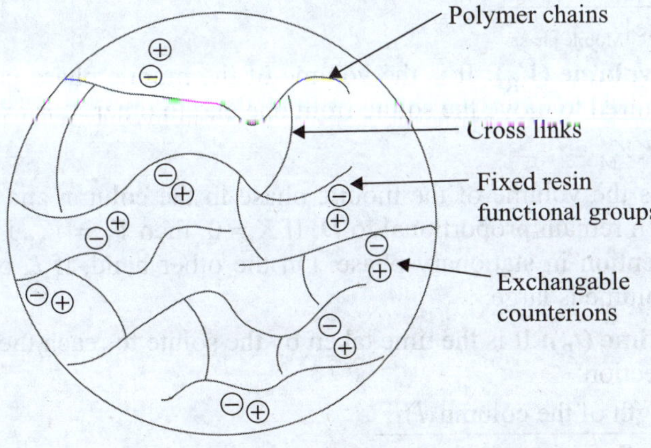

Fig. 11.31 A cation exchanger

An important application of ion-exchange chromatography is separation of the lanthanides. All the lanthanides form ions with +3 oxidation state, i.e., M^{3+}, whose ionic radii decrease progressively with increasing atomic number from La^{3+} with radius 0.125 nm to Lu^{3+} with 0.099 nm. As the ionic radii decrease along the series of elements, the ability to form complex ions increases which forms the basis of their separation on an ion-exchange column. A solution containing +3 lanthanide ions is placed at the top of a cation-exchange column and the lanthanide ions release an equivalent amount of hydrogen ions from the column. A solution of ammonium 1-hydroxy-l-methyl propanoate is slowly run down the column and the cations partition themselves between the ion-exchanger and the eluting solution (with which they form complexes). Since the smaller ions show a greater preference for the complexing solution, these ions are the first to emerge from the column.

4. **Molecular exclusion chromatography:** This chromatographic method depends on the particle sizes or molecular weights of the solutes for isolating them from a mixture and is extensively used in the separation of macro-biomolecules such as proteins and nucleic acids, and even viruses and ribosomal particles. A buffered solution of the mixture is allowed to flow under gravity through a column of hydrated beads of an inert and cross-linked polymeric material such as the poly-saccharides (agarose, dextran, and Sephadex) or poly-acrylamides. Solute particles move down the column at different rates as per their sizes. Large molecules flow at a faster rate down the column, but small molecules penetrate into the beads through their pores and the movement is considerably retarded—the degree of retardation being inversely proportional to their particle sizes. On passing suitable solvents through the column for elution, molecules or particles of different sizes can, therefore, be collected in different fractions of the eluate. Such column of polysaccharide or polyacrylamide gels, therefore, serve as molecular sieves and the method is also known as gel-filtration or molecular-sieve chromatography. By using such molecular sieves formed of hydrated polymer beads with specific pore diameters, considerable purification of specific solutes can be achieved.

Terminologies in Chromatography

1. **Distribution ratio:** The ratio of concentration of solute in stationary phase to that in the mobile phase. It decides the rate of flow of solute. The smaller is the D value, the faster will be the flow of solute through the mobile phase.

$$D = \frac{[\text{Solute}]_{\text{Stationary phase}}}{[\text{Solute}]_{\text{Mobile phase}}}$$

2. **Retention volume (V_R):** It is the volume of the mobile phase passing through the column required to move the solute from one end to other. It is expressed as

$$V_R = V_M + KV_M$$

where V_M is the volume of the mobile phase in the column and K is the retention factor, which remain proportional to D. If $K = 0$, then $V_R = V_M$, i.e., solute is eluted without retention in stationary phase. On the other hand, if K or D is large, then retention volume is large.

3. **Retention time (t_R):** It is the time taken by the solute to reach the detector from the point of injection.

$$t_R = \frac{\text{Length of the column } (l)}{\text{Length flow rate of solute } (v)}$$

Note

$V_R = F \times t_R$

where V_R is the retention volume and F is the constant flow rate of mobile phase.

4. **Retention factor (R_f):** It is the ration of the distance traveled by a solute to that traveled by the mobile phase.

$$R_f = \frac{\text{Distance traveled to the center of the solute spot}}{\text{Distance traveled by the mobile phase front}}$$

Note

R_f is inversely related to D and its value is ≤ 1.

Let us discuss some important chromatographic techniques popularly used now days.

Column Chromatography

The stationary phase or adsorbent in column chromatography is a solid which is mostly silica gel and alumina. It is usually taken in the form of finely ground powders or gels and/or microporous for a substantially enhanced surface area. There is a ratio between the stationary phase weight and the dry weight of the analyte mixture that can be applied onto the column. For silica column chromatography, this ratio lies within 20:1 to 100:1, depending on how close to each other the analyte components are being eluted. The mobile phase or eluent is either a pure solvent or a mixture of different solvents. It is chosen so that the retention factor value of the compound of interest is roughly around 0.2–0.3 in order to minimize the time and the amount of eluent to run the chromatography. The eluent has also been chosen so that the different compounds can be separated effectively. A simple laboratory column runs by gravity flow. The flow rate of such a column can be increased by using a pump or by using compressed gas, e.g., air, nitrogen, or argon to push the solvent through the column. In such a case, the chromatography is known as flash column chromatography. A faster flow rate of the eluent minimizes the time required to run a column and thereby minimizes diffusion, resulting in a better separation. The particle size of the stationary phase is generally finer (63–200 μm) in flash column chromatography than in gravity column chromatography (40–63 μm). A typical setup is shown in Fig. 11.32.

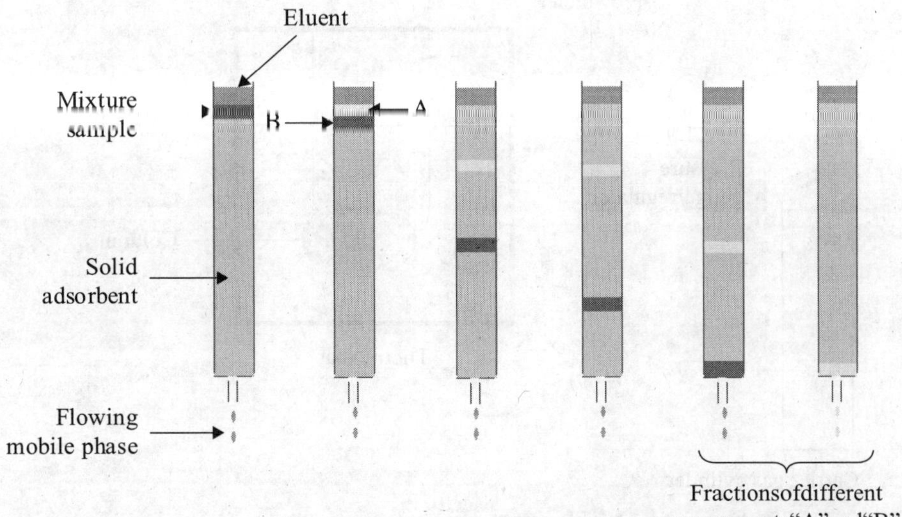

Fig. 11.32 Column chromatography

Gas Chromatography

Gas chromatography is named so because the mobile phase in this chromatography is an inert gas. The stationary adsorbent phase can be either liquid or solid. Accordingly gas chromatography is of two types, viz., gas–liquid chromatography (GLC) and gas–solid chromatography (GSC). In GLC, the column is packed with a porous solid with a large surface area coated with a thin-layer of a non-volatile liquid which acts as stationary phase. Separation takes place due to difference in partitioning of sample between the mobile gas phase and thin-layer of coated liquid on inert support (Fig. 11.33). In GSC, the column is packed with an active solid stationary phase and the components of the mixture are distributed between the gas phase and the solid phase. Due to differences in adsorption behavior of components of mixture, the separation is achieved.

Instrument

Gas supply: Mobile phases are generally inert gases such as helium, argon, or nitrogen. The gas is supplied from a high pressure cylinder having a pressure regulator and flow meters.

Injection port: The injection port consists of a rubber septum through which a syringe needle is inserted to inject the sample. The injection port is maintained at a higher temperature than the boiling point of the least volatile component in the sample mixture.

Column: The column is usually 1/8″ or 1/4″ × 6–50′ tubing. In GLC, the column is packed with a porous solid such as glass beads, finely divided celite, and polymers such as tenax GC with a large surface area coated with a thin layer of a non-volatile liquid such as silicone oil

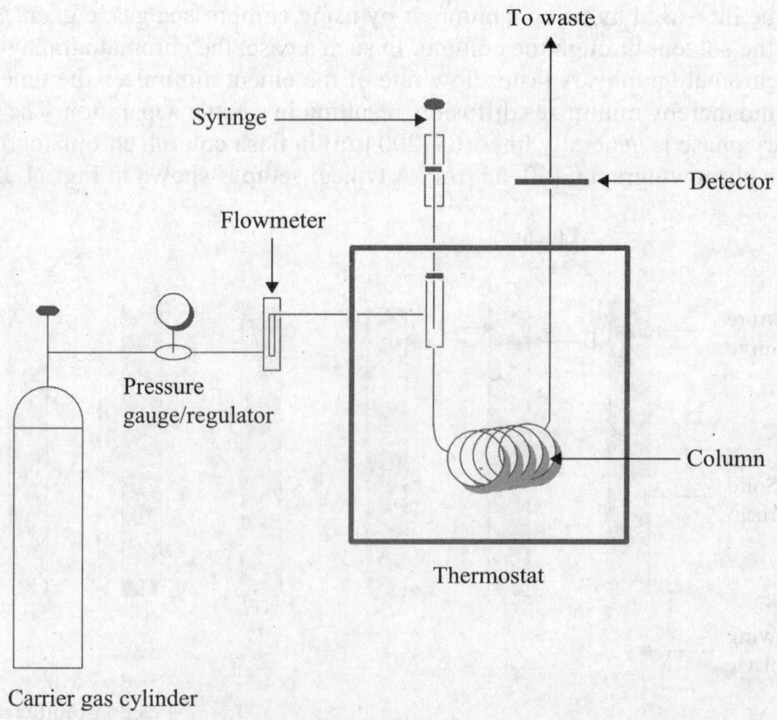

Fig. 11.33 Schematic diagram of a gas chromatograph

and polyethylene glycol which acts as stationary phase. Separation takes place due to difference in partitioning of sample between the mobile gas phase and thin layer of coated liquid on inert support. In GSC, the column is packed with an active solid stationary phase such as silica or alumina. Since the partitioning behavior is dependent on temperature, the separation column is usually kept in a thermostat-controlled oven. Separating components with a wide range of boiling points is accomplished by starting at a low oven temperature and increasing the temperature over time to elute the high-boiling point components.

Detector: After the components of a mixture are separated using gas chromatography, they must be detected as they exit the GC column. Thermal conductivity detector (TCD) and flame ionization detector (FID) are the two most common detectors on commercial GCs. The others are atomic-emmision detector (AED), chemiluminescence detector, electron-capture detector (ECD), flame-photometric detector (FPD), mass spectrometer (MS), and photoionization detector (PID).

Theory

The vapor of a mixture of volatile samples which are thermally stable at the operating temperature is introduced into a chemically inert carrier gas (such as N_2, He, and Ar) via an injection port. The mixture is then swept along GLC or GSC column. During the passage, different constituents migrate at different rate through the column due to their different distribution ratios between the mobile and stationary phases. A continuous flow of gas elutes the components from the column in order of increasing distribution ratio. As the component leaves the column, it is detected by instrumental means. A strip chart recorder, attached to the detector, shows separate peaks for each component. The size of the peaks indicates the amount of that particular component in the mixture, and the location on the chart indicates its nature. The series of peaks obtained is called *chromatogram*.

Applications

Gas chromatography has been used in the analysis of (i) natural gases, (ii) gasoline plant samples, (iii) refinery gases, (iv) synthetic rubber and plastic intermediates, (v) steroidal hormones, and (vi) trace atmospheric constituents. Actually, it has almost unlimited applications. Some of these are as follows:

1. Separation of close boiling benzene (b.p. 80.1°C) and cyclohexane (b.p. 80.8°C) mixture is virtually impossible by distillation process, but it is achieved easily by gas chromatography (GC).
2. By using GC, the ethyl alcohol content in blood can be determined with high accuracy by using glycol column.
3. Multicomponent analysis can be carried out in a relatively short time.

Comparative account of GSC and GLC

GSC	GLC
Stationary phase is solid	Stationary phase is liquid
Mobile phase is gas	Mobile phase is gas
Basis of separation is adsorption on the solid surface.	Basis of separation is partition between the gas and liquid phase.

GSC	GLC
Adsorbents are packed in the form of fine size graded powder.	Liquids are either coated as a fine film on the column wall or coated as a fine film on the inert support.
Column length is 0.7–2 m.	Column length is 3–300 m.
Thermal stability of the stationary phase is usually good.	Only a few stationary phases are known to be stable above 300°C.
Packing may catalyze to produce some chemical change.	Vary rarely with the stationary liquid, but may occur due to interaction with solid support.
Limited applicability due to difficulty in reproducing surface conditions or due to surface catalysis.	Vast applicability, since large number of liquids of specific separation is available.
Useful in the separation of permanent gases and low boiling substances.	Useful in the separation of all volatile materials, except the permanent gases.

High-Performance Liquid Chromatography

HPLC stands for high-performance liquid chromatography (also known as high-pressure liquid chromatography). It is a modified version of gas chromatography that uses liquid rather than gas as the eluant. The principle is much the same as in GLC. However, because liquid is more viscous than a gas, the pressure used to make them pass through a column is greater than that in GLC which usually remains between 20 and 200 atm. Such high pressures require a strong column, which is often ~25 cm in length packed with silica or polymer gels. The eluent used for LC analysis may contain gases which appear as a noise during detection and causes unstable baseline. The gases are removed by the special polymer membrane tubing in the filter. The separation is often largely influenced by the column temperature. In order to obtain repeatable results, it is important to keep the consistent temperature conditions. Also for some analysis such as sugar and organic acid, better resolutions can be obtained at elevated temperature (50~80°C). There are possibilities that small difference of temperature may cause different separation results. Thus, columns are generally kept inside a thermostat. The molecules coming off the column are detected by an ultraviolet spectrophotometer, and the output appears as a series of peaks very much like the GLC charts as shown in Fig. 11.34, where each peak corresponds to one component. Owing to its accuracy, HPLC has become very widely used in analysis and research. The outline of a typical HPLC apparatus is shown in Fig. 11.34.

Note:

1. Complementary to GC, it is used widely for the separation of non-volatile substances including ionic and polymeric samples.
2. **Advantages and limitations**: The technique has lot of advantages such as amenable to diverse analyte or sample types, precise and highly reproducible quantitative analysis, flexible, customizable, automated operation. The only limitation seems to be lack of an ideal universal detector.

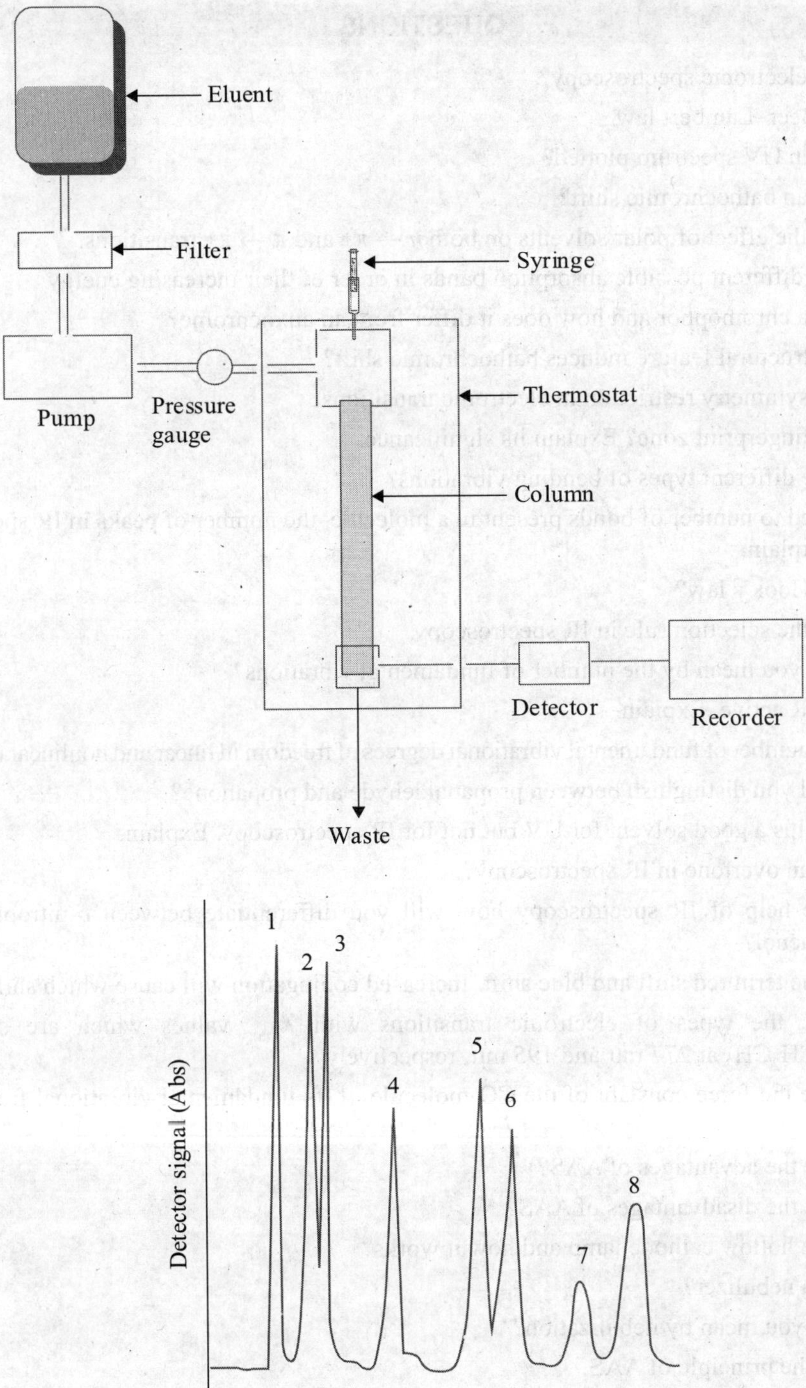

Fig. 11.34 Outline of an HPLC apparatus

QUESTIONS

1. What is electronic spectroscopy?
2. Define Beer–Lambert law.
3. How is an UV spectrum plotted?
4. What is an bathochromic shift?
5. Explain the effect of polar solvents on both $n \rightarrow \pi^*$ and $\pi \rightarrow \pi^*$ transitions.
6. Arrange different possible absorption bands in order of their increasing energy.
7. What is a chromophor and how does it differ from an auxochrome?
8. Which structural feature induces bathochromic shift?
9. What is symmetry restriction in electronic transitions?
10. What is fingerprint zone? Explain its significance.
11. What are different types of bending vibrations?
12. Compared to number of bonds present in a molecule, the number of peaks in IR spectrum are more. Explain.
13. What is Hook's law?
14. Provide the selection rule in IR spectroscopy.
15. What do you mean by the number of fundamental vibrations?
16. CO_2 is IR active. Explain.
17. Find the number of fundamental vibrational degrees of freedom in linear and nonlinear molecules.
18. How will you distinguish between propanaldehyde and propanone?
19. Methanol is a good solvent for UV but not for IR spectroscopy. Explain.
20. What is an overtone in IR spectroscopy?
21. With the help of IR spectroscopy how will you differentiate between *o*-nitrophenol and *p*-nitrophenol?
22. Define the term red shift and blue shift. Increased conjugation will cause which shift?
23. Correlate the types of electronic transitions with λ_{max} values which are shown by $CH_3COCH_2CH_3$ at 277 mμ and 195 mμ, respectively.
24. Calculate the force constant of the CO molecule, if its fundamental vibrational frequency is 2140 cm^{-1}.
25. What are the advantages of AAS?
26. What are the disadvantages of AAS?
27. What is a hollow cathode lamp and how it works?
28. What is a nebulizer?
29. What do you mean by nebulization?
30. Discuss the principle of AAS.
31. What is the difference between atomic emission and atomic absorption spectroscopy?
32. Discuss the application of AAS.
33. What is flame-less or cold vapor atomic absorption spectroscopy?
34. What are the atomization techniques other than by using flame?
35. What for graphite furnace is used in AAS?

36. Suggest a technique adopted for enhancing detection limits of metals in AAS.
37. Discuss the principle of flame photometry.
38. What do you mean by hydride generator? For which elements this is used.
39. Discuss the application of flame photometry.
40. What is the limitation of flame photometry?
41. Provide a few applications of flame emission photometry.
42. Which type of detector is used in flame photometry?
43. Describe different components of a flame photometer. Also discuss the function of individual components.
44. Describe different steps when a sample is aspirated into the flame.
45. What are different thermal methods of analysis?
46. What is flash column chromatography?
47. Explain the working principle of HPLC.
48. Differentiate between GLC and GSC.
49. Explain column chromatography.
50. Explain the working principle of GC in detail with a schematic presentation of the same.
51. Briefly explain retention volume and time.
52. Discuss the applications of gas chromatography.
53. What is ion-exchange chromatography?
54. What is molecular exclusion chromatography?
55. Explain the four different mechanisms which form the basis of chromatographic separations.
56. Discuss the working of TGA with the help of a block diagram.
57. What information one can draw from a DTA thermogram? Explain with the help of a suitable example.
58. Give a comparison of DTA and DSC techniques.
59. Discuss the principle and working of DTA. How is it different from TGA?
60. What is the principle of thermogravimetric analysis?
61. Discuss two applications of DTA.
62. What type of transitions are observed in α, β-unsaturated compounds? How absorption maximum and intensity are shifted when carbonyl group is not conjugated?
63. Discuss the various types of electronic transitions with suitable examples in each category. Provide the effect of polarity of solvent on each type of transition.
64. Discuss how conjugation, solvent, and hyperconjugation affects the intensity of absorption bands.
65. Discuss the instrumentation in UV-Vis spectroscopy. What are the applications of UV-Vis spectroscopy?
66. Apply Woodward–Fieser rule to find λ_{max} for the following compounds:

(a) 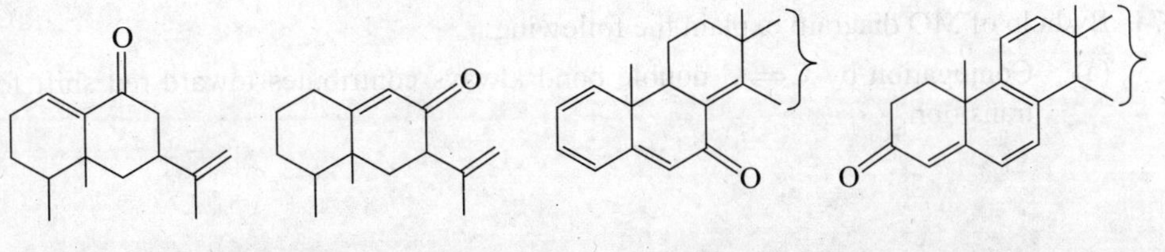

(b) 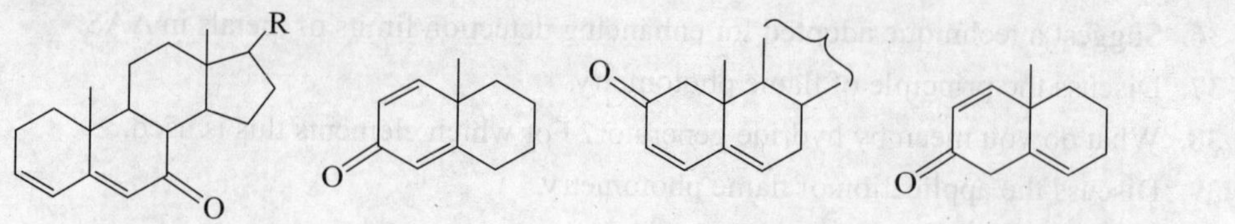

(c) 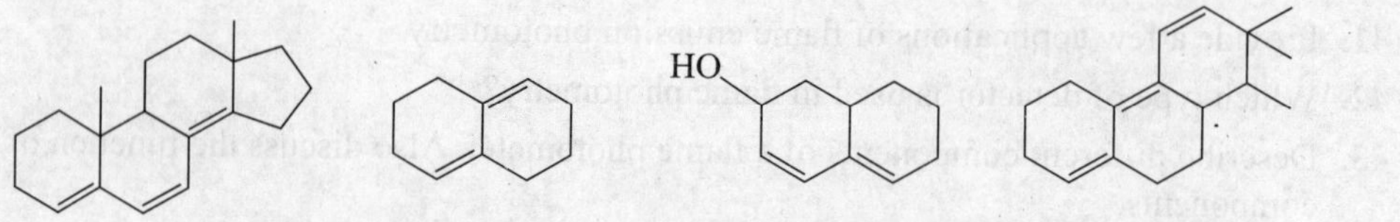

67. Hydrogenation of triene "A" with one equivalent of H_2 could give three isomers of $C_{10}H_{14}$. Show how the expected λ_{max} values could distinguish among these isomers.

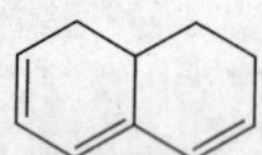

A

68. Calculate the wave number (cm^{-1}) of the fundamental peak due to the stretching vibrations of a CO group ($K = 10^6$ dyne cm^{-1}).

69. How can you distinguish the two different structural isomers "A" and "B" bearing molecular formula $C_{10}H_{16}$ by using UV-Vis spectroscopy.

70. Discuss the instrumentation in IR spectroscopy.

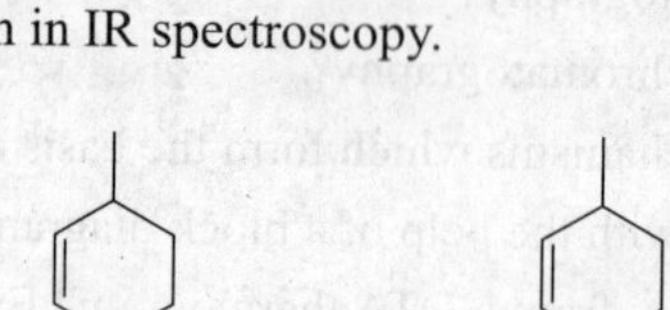

A B

71. Discuss the theory of IR spectroscopy.

72. (a) What is Beer–Lambert law? Show that absorption is linearly proportional to concentration of the solution.
    (b) During the measurement of absorption, the concentration of the solution should be within the limit of dilution. Why?
    (c) Discuss the limitations of Beer–Lambert law.

73. (a) Schematically represent and discuss different types of electronic transitions and hence show that $n \rightarrow \pi^*$ transition is of the lowest energy demanding among all of them.
    (b) According to quantum theory UV-Vis spectrum should be a collection of few spectral lines. But, in practice, during recording spectrum we get an appearance of band type. Can you justify it?

74. By help of MO diagram explain the following:
    (a) Conjugation by C=C double bond always contributes toward red shift for $\pi \rightarrow \pi^*$ transition.

(b) Installation of an auxochrome (usually more electronegative than carbon) at the α-position of a keto-group will have opposite effect on $\pi \rightarrow \pi^*$ and $n \rightarrow \pi^*$ λ_{max} absorption values compared to the parent keto compound with no auxochrome as such.

(c) Hyperconjugation is noted by red shift of $\pi \rightarrow \pi^*$ absorption.

75. 4-Methyl acetophenone shows an intense absorption at λ_{max} 252 nm ($\in$ = 15000). Indicate the nature of electronic transition for this absorption. This absorption value is blue shifted by an amount 16 nm for the compound 2,4,6-trimethyl acetophenone. Explain.

76. (a) Auxochrome itself does not absorb any light in the UV-Vis region, but it shows immense effect on the UV-Vis spectra of any compound.

(b) $\pi \rightarrow \pi^*$ and $n \rightarrow \pi^*$ absorption values show opposite trend on changing from nonpolar solvent to polar solvent.

(c) *trans*-Stilbene not only shows red shift for $\pi \rightarrow \pi^*$ transition in comparison to its *cis* counterpart, but it also shows hyperchromic shift in terms of $\in$ values: *trans*-stilbene (λ_{max} = 296 nm, $\in$ = 29000), *cis*-stilbene (λ_{max} = 280 nm, $\in$ 10500).

77. In the following compound although the keto group is nonconjugated, yet it shows the characteristic absorption value for conjugated ketone. Justify.

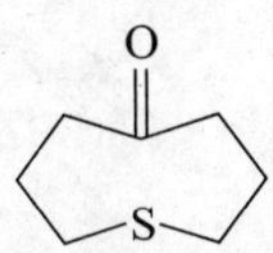

λ_{max} = 238 mμ ($\in$ = 2535)

78. (a) *p*-Nitrophenol turns deep yellow colored when treated with aqueous solution of NaOH. Why?

(b) UV-Vis spectrum of aniline behaves like that of benzene in acidic solution. Justify.

79. Calculate λ_{max} value for the following compounds:

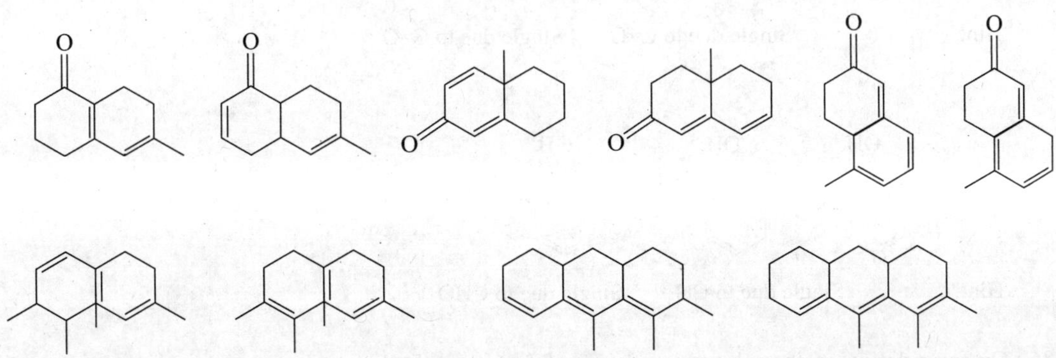

80. How will you monitor the following reaction with the help of UV-Vis spectroscopy:

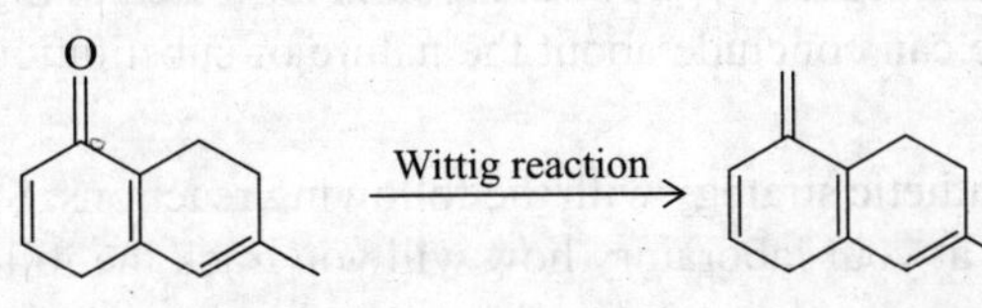

81. Deduce the structure of the isomeric compounds (A) and (B) having molecular formula C_3H_6O and the following IR spectral data

(a) 1710 cm^{-1} and (b) ~3300 cm^{-1} and 1640 cm^{-1}

82. For the following two sets of conversions, in one case ν_{co} absorption value will increase on going from reactant to product, while in other case, it will decrease. Justify your answer.

$CH_3CO_2Et \longrightarrow CH_3CO_2Ph$

$CH_3CO_2Et \longrightarrow CH_2{=}CH{-}CO_2Et$

83. How will you monitor the following conversions by IR spectroscopy?

$CH_3CO_2Me \longrightarrow PhCO_2Me$

$PhCOPh \longrightarrow PhCH(OH)Ph$

$CH_3CH_2CN \longrightarrow CH_3CH_2CO_2H$

84. For the following set of reactions some characteristics picks (IR absorption) will appear and some will disappear. Which will appear and which will disappear?

$CH_3CO_2Me \longrightarrow PhCO_2Me$

$PhCOPh \longrightarrow PhCH(OH)Ph$

$CH_3CH_2CN \longrightarrow CH_3CH_2CO_2H$

85. How will you monitor the following reactions simply by IR spectroscopy?

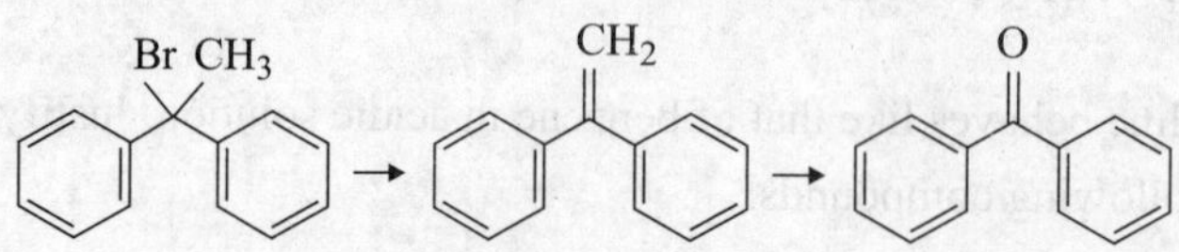

Hint: Single due to C=C Single due to C=O

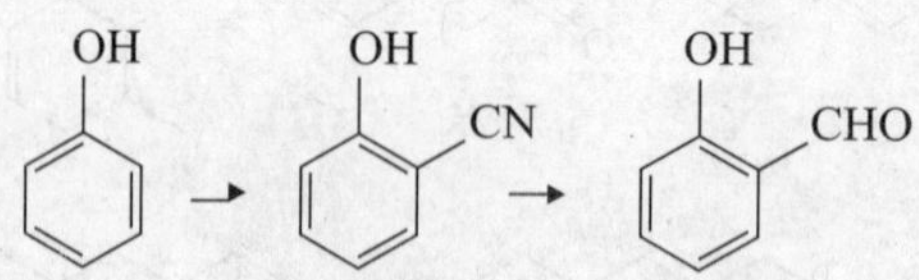

Hint: Single due to CN Single due to CHO

86. On formylation of phenol, two products are formed: *o*-hydroxy phenol and *p*-hydroxy phenol. Both these compounds show intense IR absorption peak due to ν_{O-H} in $CHCl_3$ solution. But on dilution the IR absorption signal (ν_{O-H}) of compound is shifted to higher value. Based on this simple observation one can conclude about the nature of substitution in the said compounds. Explain with reason.

87. Here is a traditional synthetic strategy with the following reactions. Simply with the help of IR spectroscopy available at your laboratory how will you track the following steps?

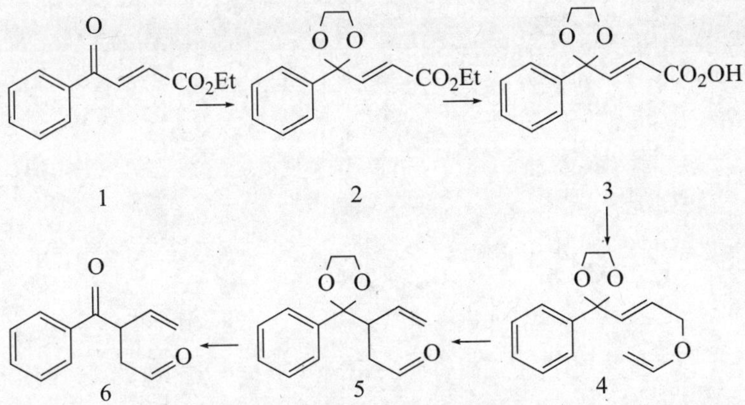

Hint:	**1** ⟶	**2** ⟶	**3** ⟶	**4** ⟶	**5** ⟶	**6**
Signal ⇨	C = O due to keto and ester	C = O due to ester	OH	~~OH~~	C = O due to aldehyde	C = O due to ketone and aldehyde

CHAPTER

12 Electrochemistry

Chapter Outline

- Conductance
- Kohlrausch's Law
- Conductometric Titrations
- Ionic Mobility
- Transport Number
- Electrochemical Cells
- Electrode Potential (E)
- Cell Potential (emf of the Cell)
- Standard Cell
- Measurement of Cell Potential
- Measurement of Electrode Potential
- Electrochemical Series
- Nernst Equation
- Thermodynamics of Cell

Electrochemistry serves as an interface between chemistry and everyday life. When we switch on a calculator, a computer, a radio, start a car, use a mobile phone, use a digital watch, and so on we are depending upon the electrochemical reactions occurring in the cells or batteries. It also finds a lot of applications in getting pure metals in metallurgy. A number of industrially important materials can be prepared by electrolytic processes. In analytical chemistry, membrane sensitive electrodes are used to measure dissolved ions in water. Corrosion, a process responsible for the destruction of metals and metallic structures, also involves electrochemical reactions.

Electrochemistry is a part of physical chemistry that deals with the study of interchange of chemical and electrical energy. It mainly concerns itself with two processes that involve oxidation and reduction, viz., generation of current at the cost of a chemical reaction and utilization of current to bring about a chemical change. Here, in this chapter, greater emphasis has been given to generation of current. This chapter also deals with some fundamental aspects of conductance. Commercial cells or batteries and mechanism of corrosion have been discussed under separate chapters.

Conductance

Conductance refers to the ease with which current can flow through a conductor. It is inversely related to resistance and has a unit ohm^{-1} or mho or siemen. Thus,

$$\text{Conductance } (C) = \frac{1}{R} \qquad [12.1]$$

Specific conductance

Specific conductance (κ) is the reciprocal of specific resistance. Mathematically,

$$\kappa = \frac{1}{\rho}$$

or
$$\kappa = \frac{1}{Ra/\iota}$$

$$= \frac{1}{R} \times \frac{\iota}{a} \quad [12.2]$$

$$= C \times \text{Cell constant}$$

Unit: ohm^{-1} cm^{-1} or S cm^{-1}

If l is 1 cm and a is 1 cm^2, then $\kappa = C$.

Thus, specific conductance is nothing but the conductance of unit volume, i.e., 1 cm^3 of the electrolyte.

Molar conductance

Molar conductance (Λ_M) is the conductance of all the ions present in a certain volume of solution containing one gram mole of electrolyte.

Let us consider V cm^3 of electrolyte having 1 mol of electrolyte. Then

$$\text{Total conductance of the electrolyte} = \Lambda_M \quad [12.3]$$

Again, conductance of 1 cm^3 of solution is κ. Thus,

$$\text{Conductance of } V \text{ cm}^3 \text{ of solution} = \kappa \times V \quad [12.4]$$

Comparing relations [12.3] and [12.4],

$$\Lambda_M = \kappa \times V \quad [12.5]$$

If M moles of electrolyte remain present in 1000 cm^3 of electrolyte, then V in relation [12.5] can be replaced by $\frac{1000}{M}$ and relation [12.5] can be expressed in more general form,

$$\Lambda_M = \kappa \times \frac{1000}{M} \quad [12.6]$$

Remember M is the molarity of the electrolyte.

Unit: ohm^{-1} cm^2 mol^{-1}

Equivalent conductance

Equivalent conductance (Λ_{Eq}) is the conductance of all the ions present in a certain volume of solution containing one gram equivalent of electrolyte. In a very similar manner, as described above, a relation for equivalent conductance can be developed.

$$\Lambda_{Eq} = \kappa \times \frac{1000}{N} \quad [12.7]$$

Remember N is normality of the electrolyte.

Unit: ohm^{-1} cm^2 $equivalent^{-1}$

Effect of Temperature

Increase in temperature reduces the resistance by reducing the extent of solvation of ions, inter-ionic forces, and viscosity of the medium. The ultimate result is the conductance, specific or molar or equivalent, increases with increase in temperature.

Effect of Concentration on Λ_M or Λ_{Eq}

To analyze the effect of concentration on molar conductance, let us consider the following plot that has been plotted by taking molar conductance as a function of concentration (Fig. 12.1). The analysis of the plot reveals following facts:

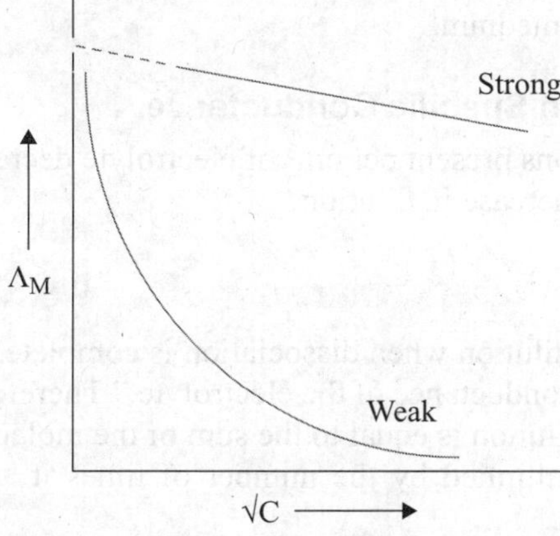

Fig. 12.1 Variation of molar conductance with concentration

1. For both strong and weak electrolytes, Λ_M increases with decrease in concentration.
2. The magnitude of rise in Λ_M with decrease in concentration is quite significant for weak electrolyte.
3. For strong electrolyte, Λ_M has a tendency to touch the axis as concentration tends to zero, i.e., at infinite dilution. The value of molar conductance at zero concentration is the optimum conductance and is denoted as Λ^0_M, i.e., molar conductance at zero concentration.
4. For strong electrolyte, optimum molar conductance, i.e., Λ^0_M, can be obtained by extrapolation of the curve as shown by dotted line.
5. For weak electrolyte, the curve has no tendency to touch the axis as concentration tends to zero. Here, $\Lambda^0{}_M$ cannot be obtained straight way by using extrapolation method.

Explanation

The significant variation for weak electrolyte can be explained with respect to Ostwald's dilution law. As per the law, the degree of dissociation (α) increases with decrease in concentration. Therefore, the same amount of electrolyte furnishes more and more number of ions with decrease in concentration. This ultimately results in the rise in molar conductance. In case of strong electrolyte, the number of ions remains the same independent of concentration.

In a concentrated solution, the ions are closely spaced. With increase in dilution the inter-ionic spacing increases which results in an increase in mobility of the charge carriers. For strong electrolyte, the relation is expressed in terms of Debye–Huckel–Onsager equation, which is the equation of a straight line.

$$\Lambda_m = \Lambda_M^0 - (A + B)\Lambda_M^0 \sqrt{c} \quad [12.8]$$

where A and B are constants whose value depends on the nature of solvent and the temperature. The values being,

$$A = \frac{82.4}{(DT)^{1/2}\eta}; \; B = \frac{8.20 \times 10^5}{(DT)^{3/2}}$$

In the above two relations, c is the concentration in mol/l, D is the dielectric constant, η is the coefficient of viscosity of the medium.

Effect of Concentration on Specific Conductance

With dilution the number of ions present per cm^3 of electrolyte decreases. The result is specific conductance decreases with increase in dilution.

Kohlrausch's Law

The statement is "At infinite dilution when dissociation is complete, each ion makes a definite contribution toward the total conductance of the electrolyte." Therefore, the molar conductance of any electrolyte at infinite dilution is equal to the sum of the molar conductance of the cation and anion with each term multiplied by the number of times it appears in the dissociation expression.

For a hypothetical electrolyte A_xB_y,

$$A_xB_y \rightleftharpoons xA^{y+} + yB^{x-}$$

$$\Lambda^0(A_xB_y) = x\lambda_+^0 + y\lambda_-^0 \quad [12.9]$$

For AgCl, Λ^0 (AgCl) = λ^0 (Ag^+) + λ^0 (Cl^-)

For Na_2SO_4, Λ^0 (Na_2SO_4) = 2λ^0 (Na^+) + λ^0 (SO_4^{2-})

Applications

1. **To find Λ_M^0 of weak electrolyte:** The optimum molar concentration of weak electrolytes cannot be obtained by direct extrapolation method. However, the same can be obtained indirectly by applying Kohlrausch's law. Let us find the optimum conductance of acetic acid.

$$\begin{aligned}\Lambda^0(CH_3COOH) &= \lambda^0(CH_3COO^-) + \lambda^0(H^+)\\ &= \lambda^0(CH_3COO^-) + \lambda^0(Na^+) + \lambda^0(H^+) + \lambda^0(Cl^-) - [\lambda^0(Na^+) + \lambda^0(Cl^-)]\\ &= \Lambda^0(CH_3COONa) + \Lambda^0(HCl) - \Lambda^0(NaCl)\end{aligned}$$

Knowing the optimum conductance of CH_3 COONa, HCl, and NaCl, the same for CH_3 COOH can be calculated.

Example 12.1

Find the optimum conductance of NH_4OH. Given the optimum conductance of $Ba(OH)_2$, NH_4Cl, and $BaCl_2$ are 523, 130, and 280 S cm^2 mol^{-1}, respectively.

Solution

$$\Lambda^0(NH_4OH) = \lambda^0(NH_4^+) + \lambda^0(OH^-)$$
$$= \lambda^0(NH_4^+) + \lambda^0(Cl^-) + \lambda^0(OH^-) + \frac{1}{2}\lambda^0(Ba^{2+}) - \left[\frac{1}{2}\lambda^0(Ba^{2+}) + \lambda^0(Cl^-)\right]$$
$$= \Lambda^0(NH_4Cl) + \frac{1}{2}\Lambda^0[Ba(OH)_2] - \frac{1}{2}\Lambda^0(BaCl_2)$$
$$= 130 + \frac{1}{2}\times 523 - \frac{1}{2}\times 280$$
$$= 251.5\ \text{S cm}^2\ \text{mol}^{-1}$$

2. **To find degree of dissociation of weak electrolyte:** The degree of dissociation can be calculated by the following equation:

$$\alpha = \frac{\Lambda_C}{\Lambda^0}$$

where Λ_C is the conductance of the electrolyte having concentration C and Λ^0 is the same at infinite dilution.

Example 12.2

The molar conductivities of sodium acetate, hydrochloric acid, and sodium chloride at infinite dilutions are 91.5, 425, and 128 S cm^2 mol^{-1}, respectively. Find the degree of dissociation of 0.1M acetic acid if the molar conductivity in this concentration is 0.388 S cm^2 mol^{-1} at the same temperature.

Solution

$$\Lambda^0(CH_3COOH) = \lambda^0(CH_3COO^-) + \lambda^0(H^+)$$
$$= \lambda^0(CH_3COO^-) + \lambda^0(Na^+) + \lambda^0(H^+) + \lambda^0(Cl^-) - [\lambda^0(Na^+) + \lambda^0(Cl^-)]$$
$$= \Lambda^0(CH_3COONa) + \Lambda^0(HCl) - \Lambda^0(NaCl)$$
$$= 91.5 + 425 - 128$$
$$= 388.5\ \text{S cm}^2\ \text{mol}^{-1}$$

The degree of dissociation can be calculated by the following equation:

$$\alpha = \frac{\Lambda_C}{\Lambda^0}$$
$$= \frac{0388}{388.5} = 0.001$$

3. **To find solubility product:** The solubility can be obtained by the relation [12.6].

$$\Lambda_M = \kappa \times \frac{1000}{S}$$

where S is the solubility in mol/l.

Example 12.3

At a given temperature, the saturated solution of AgCl has conductivity 1.12×10^{-6} S cm^{-1}. The ionic conductance of Ag^+ and Cl^- ions at infinite dilution are 54 and 65.5 S cm^2 eq^{-1} at the same temperature. Calculate the solubility and solubility product at the same temperature.

Solution

$$\Lambda^0 = \lambda_+^0 + \lambda_-^0 = 54 + 65.5 = 119.5 \text{ S cm}^2 \text{ eq}^{-1}$$

$$\text{Again, } \Lambda^0 = \kappa \times \frac{1000}{S} = 1.12 \times 10^{-6} \times \frac{1000}{S}$$

$$\text{or} \quad S = 1.12 \times 10^{-6} \times \frac{1000}{\Lambda^0}$$

$$= 1.12 \times 10^{-6} \times \frac{1000}{119.5} \text{ eq/l}$$

$$= 1.12 \times 10^{-6} \times \frac{1000}{119.5} \times 143.5 \text{ g/l}$$

$$= 1.345 \times 10^{-3} \text{ g/l}$$

Now, $K_{sp} = S^2 = 1.809 \times 10^{-6}$

Conductometric Titrations

Conductometric titration is a volumetric analysis method in which change in conductance of a solution at the end point during a titration is measured. During the course of titration, the number of free ions as well as their mobility changes which brings a change in the conductance. For the purpose, the titrant is added from the burette into a definite volume of solution to be titrated which is taken in a conductance cell. The conductance readings corresponding to different lots of additions are plotted as a function of volume of titrant which results in two linear curves. The point of intersection of the curves is the end point. Here acid–base and precipitation reactions are taken into account.

Acid–Base Titrations

Strong acid–strong base titration

Let us look into a titration of a strong acid, say HCl, with a strong base, say NaOH. At the commencement, the conductivity of acid solution is high due to highly mobile H^+ ions. Upon addition of base, the OH^- ions remove H^+ ions from solution by forming feebly ionisable H_2O. Therefore, the conductance of the solution decreases progressively, till the end point "O." On further addition of base, the conductivity of the solution again rises due to addition of highly mobile OH^- ions (Fig. 12.2).

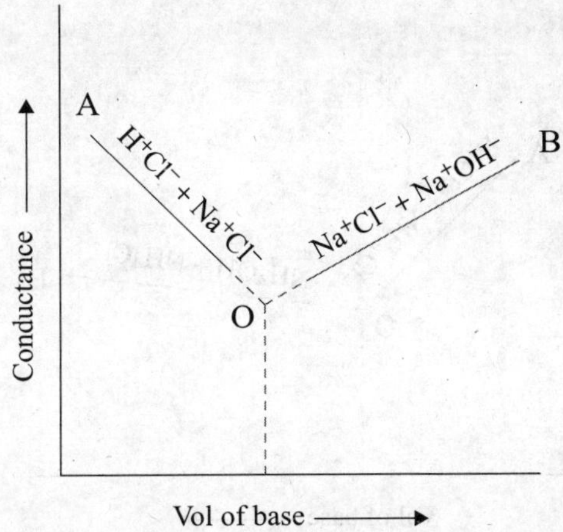

Fig. 12.2 Strong acid–strong base titration

Weak acid–strong base titration

Let us consider the titration between a weak acid, say acetic acid, and a strong base, say sodium hydroxide. The initial conductance is low due to feebly ionized weak acid. Upon addition of sodium hydroxide, highly ionized sodium acetate is formed. The Ac^- ions at first tend to suppress the ionization of acetic acid due to common ion effect but after a while the conductance begins to increase because the conducting power of salt exceeds that of weak acid. Immediately after the end point, further addition of sodium hydroxide introduces the first moving OH^- ions which lead to sharp increase along OB (Fig. 12.3).

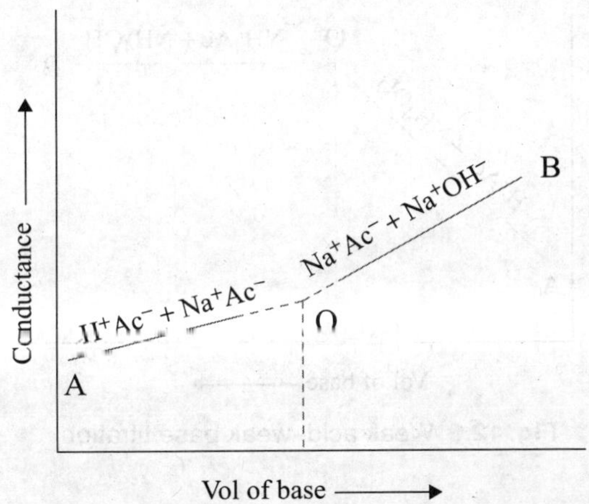

Fig. 12.3 Weak acid–strong base titration

Strong acid–weak base titration

Let us consider the titration between HCl and NH_4OH. In the beginning of the titration, conductance decreases sharply due to removal of highly mobile H^+ ions from solution and their replacement by slow moving NH_4^+ ions. After the end point, the conductance increases slowly due to introduction of feebly ionizable NH_4OH (Fig. 12.4).

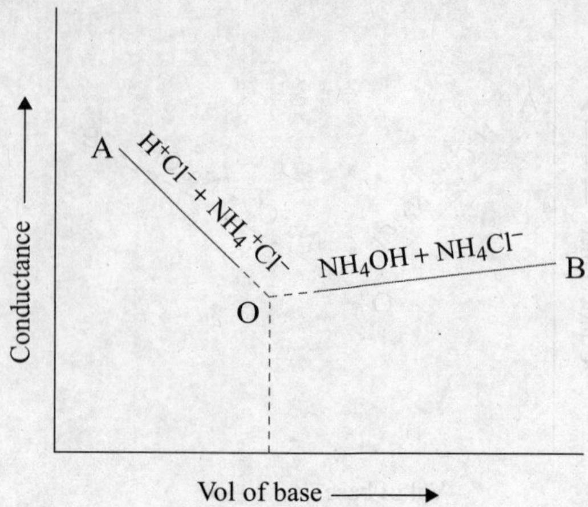

Fig. 12.4 Strong acid–weak base titration

Weak acid–weak base titration

Let us consider the titration between acetic acid and ammonium hydroxide. In the beginning, the conductance is low due to the poor dissociation of weak acid. However, it starts increasing along OA as the highly ionizable salt is formed. After the end point, the conductance remains almost constant as the free base NH_4OH is a weak electrolyte (Fig. 12.5).

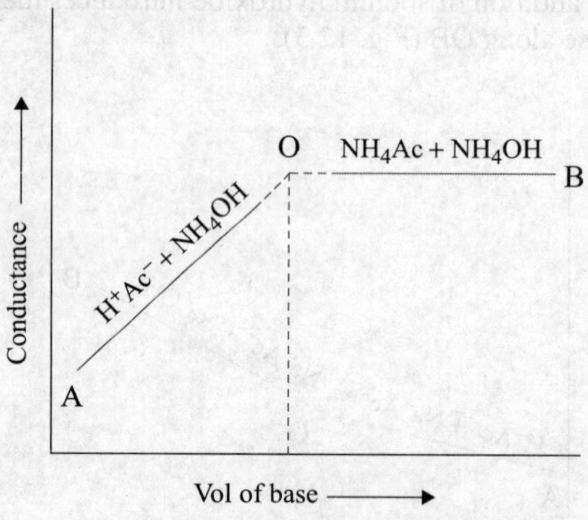

Fig. 12.5 Weak acid–weak base titration

Precipitation Titrations

Illustration I

Let us consider titration between KCl and $AgNO_3$ solutions. In the reaction, AgCl gets precipitated. Thus, Cl^- ions are replaced by free NO_3^- ions. As the mobility of Cl^- and NO_3^- are almost same, the conductance of the solution does not change appreciably with the addition of $AgNO_3$. After equivalence point, further addition of $AgNO_3$, i.e., free Ag^+ and NO_3^- to the solution brings a steep rise in the conductance of the solution (Fig. 12.6).

$$K^+Cl^- + Ag^+NO_3^- \rightarrow AgCl\downarrow + K^+NO_3^-$$

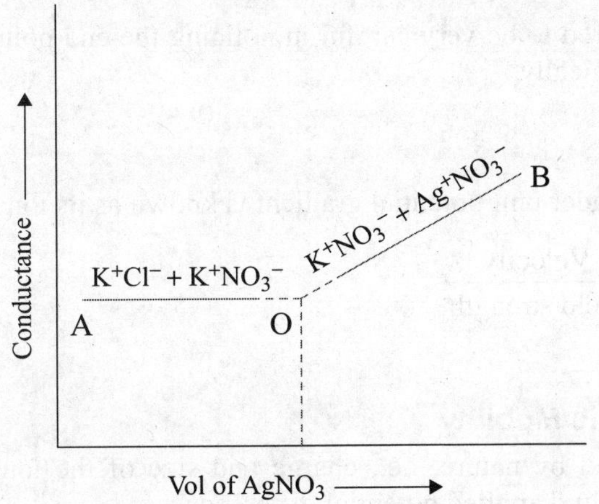

Fig. 12.6 Precipitation titration between KCl and $AgNO_3$ solutions

Illustration II

Precipitation titration between $BaCl_2$ and $NaSO_4$ solutions. In the reaction, barium sulphate gets precipitated. Thus, Ba^{2+} ions are replaced by free Na^+ ions. As the mobility of Na^+ is less than Ba^{2+} ions, the conductance of the solution decreases with the addition of Na_2SO_4. After equivalence point, further addition Na_2SO_4 of, i.e., free Na^+ and $SO_4{}^{2-}$, to the solution brings a steep rise in the conductance of the solution (Fig. 12.7).

$$[Ba^{2+} + 2Cl^-] + [2Na^+ + SO_4^{2-}] \rightarrow BaSO_4\downarrow + [2Na^+ + 2Cl^-]$$

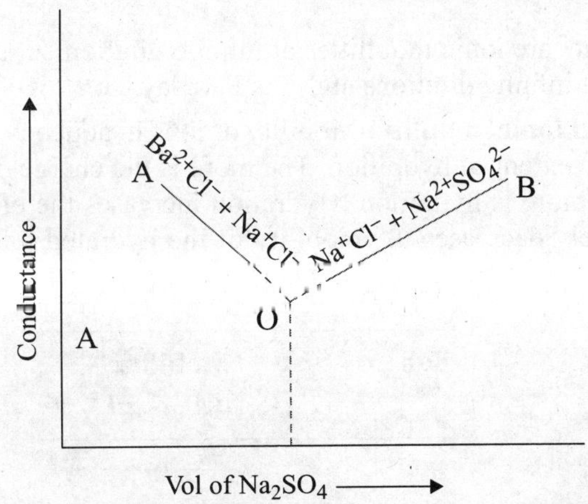

Fig. 12.7 Precipitation titration between $BaCl_2$ and $NaSO_4$ solutions

Advantages of Conductometric Titrations

1. Useful in dilute solutions.
2. Useful in colored solutions where color change of indicator is difficult to notice.

3. Can be used for detection of end point during weak acid and weak base titration which usually does not give sharp end point.
4. It is not required to be very careful in noticing the end point as in this method it is detected graphically.

Ionic Mobility

The velocity of an ion under unit potential gradient is known as its ionic mobility. Thus,

$$\text{Ionic mobility} = \frac{\text{Velocity}}{\text{Field strength}} \qquad [12.10]$$

Unit: $m^2\ s^{-1}\ V^{-1}$

Factors Affecting Ionic Mobility

Ionic mobility is affected by nature, i.e., charge and size of the ions, concentration of the electrolyte, temperature, and applied potential difference.

Note:

1. At infinite dilution,

$$\lambda_+^0 = u_+^0 F$$

or $$u_+^0 = \frac{\lambda_+^0}{F}$$

Similarly, $$u_-^0 = \frac{\lambda_-^0}{F}$$

where u_+^0 and u_-^0 are ionic mobilities at infinite dilution, λ_+^0 and λ_-^0 are molar ionic conductance at infinite dilutions and F is Faraday, i.e., 96500 C.

2. **Hydration and ionic mobility:** Mobility of ions in aqueous solutions significantly depends on the extent of hydration. The more is the charge density, i.e., charge-to-size ratio, the more is hydration. Hydration increases the effective size of the ion which ultimately decreases the mobility of the hydrated ion. Let us look into the ionic mobilities of some cations and anions.

Ion	Mobility $U \times 10^8\ m^2\ s^{-1}\ V^{-1}$
F^-	5.70
Cl^-	7.90
Br^-	8.13
Li^+	4.01
Na^+	5.20
K^+	7.62

Transport Number

The transport number of an ion is the fraction of the total charge carried by the ion in an electrolyte. Mathematically, it can be expressed as

$$\text{Transport number of cation } (t_+) = \frac{\text{Charge carried by cation}}{\text{Total charge carried by cation and anion together}}$$

$$= \frac{u_+}{u_+ + u_-} \qquad [12.11]$$

$$\text{Transport number of anion } (t_-) = \frac{\text{Charge carried by anion}}{\text{Total charge carried by cation and anion together}}$$

$$= \frac{u_-}{u_+ + u_-} \qquad [12.12]$$

where u_+ and u_- are the mobilities of cation and anion, respectively.

Again, limiting ionic conductance at infinite dilution is proportional to absolute ionic mobility, i.e., for cation,

$$\lambda_+^0 \propto u_+^0$$

or $\lambda_+^0 = Fu_+^0$

Similarly for anion, $\lambda_-^0 = Fu_-^0$

Therefore, at infinite dilution, $t_+ = \dfrac{u_+^0}{u_+^0 + u_-^0} = \dfrac{\lambda_+^0}{\lambda_+^0 + \lambda_-^0}$ [12.13]

Similarly, $t_+ = \dfrac{u_-^0}{u_+^0 + u_-^0} = \dfrac{\lambda_-^0}{\lambda_+^0 + \lambda_-^0}$ [12.14]

Here, F stands for Faraday, i.e., 96500 C.

Note:

1. $t_+ + t_- = 1$
2. $\dfrac{t_+}{t_-} = \dfrac{u_+}{u_-}$

Example 12.4

The equivalent conductivity of KCl at infinite dilution is 120 S cm² eq⁻¹. The transport number of chloride ion in KCl at the same temperature is 0.505. Find the limiting ionic mobility and ionic conductance of K^+ ion.

Solution

$$t_+ = 1 - t_-$$

$$= 1 - 0.505$$

$$= 0.495$$

$$\lambda_+^0 = \Lambda^0 \times t_+ = 120 \times 0.495 = 59.4 \text{ S cm}^2 \text{ eq}^{-1}$$

Now, limiting ionic mobility, $u_+^0 = \dfrac{\lambda_+^0}{F} = \dfrac{59.4}{96500} = 6.15 \times 10^{-4} \text{ cm}^2 \text{ s}^{-1} \text{ V}^{-1}$

Example 12.5

A dilute solution of NaCl is placed between two inert electrodes 10 cm apart, across which a potential difference of 5 V is applied. Find the distance covered by the Na^+ ion in 1 h at 298 K. Limiting ionic conductivity of Na^+ is 70.5 S cm^2 eq^{-1} at the same temperature.

Solution

$$u_+^0 = \frac{\lambda_+^0}{F} = \frac{70.5}{96500} = 7.306 \times 10^{-4} \text{ cm}^2 \text{ s}^{-1} \text{ V}^{-1}$$

Velocity of Na^+ ion = Ionic mobility × Potential gradient

$= 7.306 \times 10^{-4} \times 0.5$

$= 3.65 \times 10^{-4}$ cm/s

Now, the distance traveled by Na^+ ion in 1 h = $3.65 \times 10^{-4} \times 3600 = 1.32$ cm.

Electrochemical Cells

A setup in which decrease in free energy accompanying a selective indirect redox reaction is converted into electrical energy is known as electrochemical cell or sometimes galvanic/voltaic cell after the names of L. Galvani and A. Volta, who were among the first to work on conversion of chemical energy to electrical energy.

Construction

Every cell is made of two half cells or electrodes. The electrode used for oxidation is called anode while that used for reduction is called cathode. By convention anode is placed at the left side and cathode at the right side of the setup. Connection is made through a conducting wire in the outer circuit while by a salt bridge on the solution side. For example, Zn–$CuSO_4$ cell.

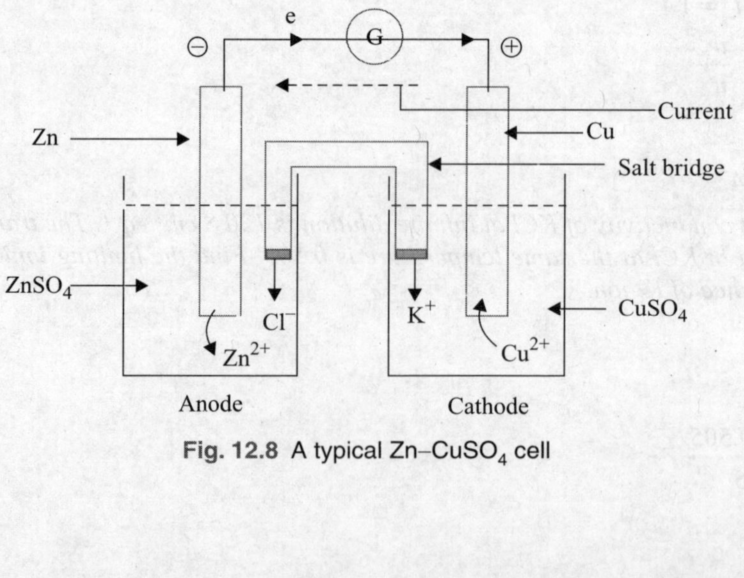

Fig. 12.8 A typical Zn–$CuSO_4$ cell

Working

Let us try to explain the working of an electrochemical cell with respect to the specific example of Zn–$CuSO_4$ cell. Upon completion of circuit the Zn-electrode gets oxidized to Zn^{2+} ions and the electrons lost in the process are pushed through the outer metallic wire towards cathode. At cathode Cu^{2+} ions accept the electrons and get reduced to Cu-metal. The whole process results in the migration of electrons from anode to cathode and therefore conventional current flows from cathode to anode which is confirmed from the deflection in the galvanometer.

Anode $\quad Zn_{(s)} \longrightarrow Zn^{2+}_{(aq)} + \underset{\text{Migrate to cathode}}{2e}$

Cathode $\quad Cu^{2+}_{(aq)} + \underset{\text{From anode}}{2e} \longrightarrow Cu_{(s)}$

Cell $\quad Zn_{(s)} + Cu^{2+}_{(aq)} \longrightarrow Zn^{2+}_{(aq)} + Cu_{(s)}$

It is evident that during cell operation anode acquires progressively positive charge while cathode negative charge. As a result, anode does not further allow the movement of electrons away from it and similarly cathode does not allow the movement of electrons into it and the cell operation comes to an end. Therefore charge neutrality in both the compartments is an essential requirement for cell operation. The purpose is satisfied by the use of salt bridge. It provides –ve ions to anode and +ve ions to cathode through selective desorption.

Sign Convention

Anode provides electrons during the cell operation and is electron rich while cathode always has a demand for the electrons. Therefore anode is always assigned with –ve sign while cathode with a positive sign and current always flows from +ve terminal to –ve terminal. It should be noted that *anode* represents an electrode through which electron goes out from the electrolyte (Greek *ana hodos*—away flow) and *cathode* represents the one through which electron enters into the electrolyte (Greek *cata hodos*—towards flow).

Salt Bridge

It is a U-shaped glass tube filled with saturated solution of some selective electrolyte mixed with agar-agar powder or gelatin to impart gel like characteristics. The mouths of the tube are blocked with cotton plugs. All these precautions are taken to ensure that the contents of the salt bridge should not undergo mechanical mixing with the contents of the electrode.

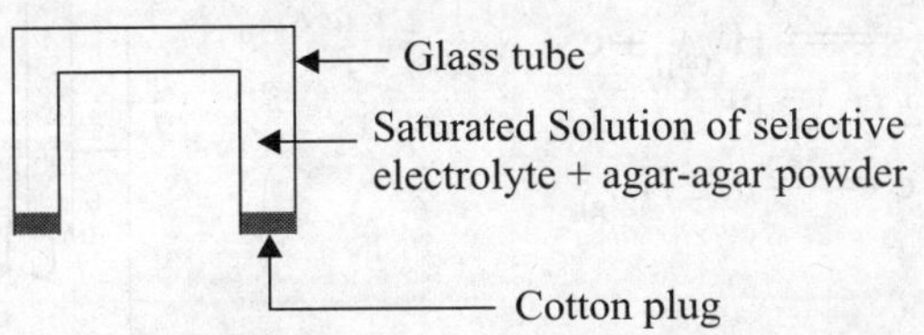

Selection of electrolyte

Both cation and anion of the electrolyte should have same transport number. Common electrolytes used for the purpose are KCl, KNO_3, NH_4Cl, etc.

Functions

The functions of salt bridge are as follows:

1. It completes the circuit by connecting the electrodes at the solution side.
2. It maintains electrical charge neutrality in both the compartments during cell operation by selectively providing anions to anode and cations to cathode.

Types of Electrodes

The different electrodes can be grouped into the following basic categories:

Type I

These electrodes are reversible with respect to the electrode material. Metal–metal ion electrodes, gas electrodes, and amalgam electrodes fall in this category. Metal–metal ion electrode consists of a metal immersed in a solution containing its own ions such as Zn electrode (Fig. 12.9). In a gas electrode, a gas is brought in contact with its own ions in the solution such as hydrogen electrode (Fig. 12.10). In amalgam electrode, a coating of mercury is given over the metal in order to control its reactivity. This coated metal is then dispersed in a solution of its own ions. Cadmium amalgam electrode is shown in Fig. 12.11.

Zinc electrode

Anode: $Zn_{(s)}/Zn^{2+}_{(aq)}$

Reaction: $Zn_{(s)} \rightleftharpoons Zn^{2+}_{(aq)} + 2e$

Cathode: $Zn^{2+}_{(aq)}/Zn_{(s)}$

Reaction: $Zn^{2+}_{(aq)} + 2e \rightleftharpoons Zn_{(s)}$

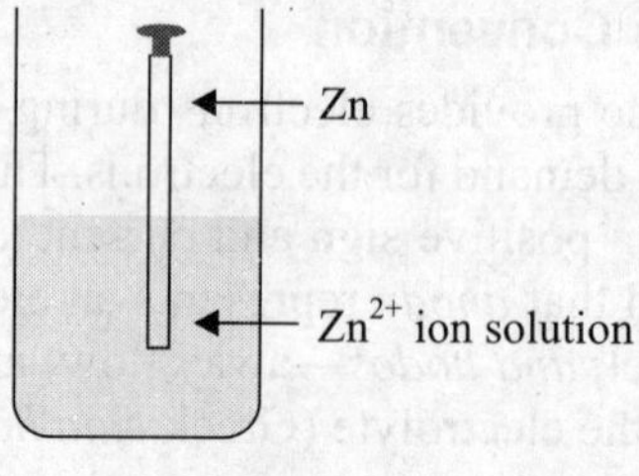

Fig. 12.9

Hydrogen electrode

Anode: Pt, $1/2\ H_{2(g)}/H^+_{(aq)}$

Reaction: $1/2\ H_{2(g)} \rightleftharpoons H^+_{(aq)} + e$

Cathode: $H^+_{(aq)}/1/2\ H_{2(g)}$, Pt

Reaction: $H^+_{(aq)} + e \rightleftharpoons 1/2\ H_{2(g)}$

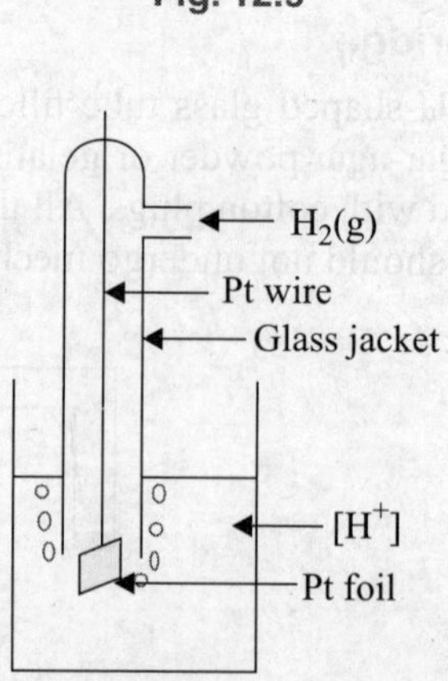

Fig. 12.10

Cadmium amalgam electrode

Anode: Cd–Hg / $Cd^{2+}_{(aq)}$

Reaction: $Cd_{(s)} \rightleftharpoons Cd^{2+}_{(aq)} + 2e$

Cathode: $Cd^{2+}_{(aq)}$/Cd–Hg

Reaction: $Cd^{2+}_{(aq)} + 2e \rightleftharpoons Cd_{(s)}$

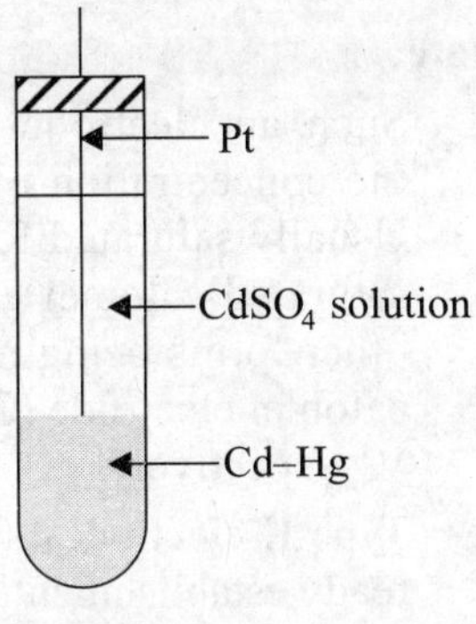

Fig. 12.11

Type II

These types of electrodes consist of a metal, an insoluble salt of the same metal, and a solution of a soluble salt with common anion. These electrodes behave as if they are reversible with respect to the common anion; for example, calomel electrode and silver–silver chloride electrode.

Calomel electrode

Anode: $Hg_{(l)}/Hg_2Cl_{2(s)}$, $KCl_{(aq)}$

Reaction:

$$2Hg_{(l)} \rightleftharpoons Hg_2{}^{2+}{}_{(aq)} + 2e$$

$$Hg_2{}^{2+}{}_{(aq)} + 2Cl^-{}_{(aq)} \rightleftharpoons Hg_2Cl_{2(s)}$$

$$2Hg_{(l)} + 2Cl^-{}_{(aq)} \rightleftharpoons Hg_2Cl_{2(s)} + 2e$$

Cathode: $KCl_{(aq)}$, $Hg_2Cl_{2(s)}/Hg_{(l)}$

Reaction:

$$Hg_2Cl_{2(s)} \rightleftharpoons Hg_2{}^{2+}{}_{(aq)} + 2Cl^-{}_{(aq)}$$

$$Hg_2{}^{2+}{}_{(aq)} + 2e \rightleftharpoons 2Hg_{(l)}$$

$$Hg_2Cl_{2(s)} + 2e \rightleftharpoons 2Hg_{(l)} + 2Cl^-{}_{(aq)}$$

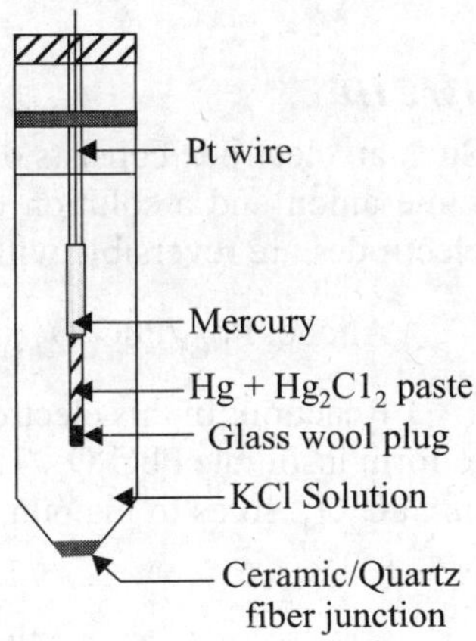

Fig. 12.12 Calomel electrode

Silver–silver chloride electrode

Anode: $Ag_{(s)}/AgCl_{(s)}$, $KCl_{(aq)}$

Reaction:

$$Ag_{(s)} \rightleftharpoons Ag^+{}_{(aq)} + e$$

$$Ag^+{}_{(aq)} + Cl^-{}_{(aq)} \rightleftharpoons AgCl_{(s)}$$

$$Ag_{(s)} + Cl^-{}_{(aq)} \rightleftharpoons AgCl_{(s)} + e$$

Cathode: $KCl_{(aq)}$, $AgCl_{(s)}/Ag_{(s)}$

Reaction:

$$AgCl_{(s)} \rightleftharpoons Ag^+{}_{(aq)} + Cl^-{}_{(aq)}$$

$$Ag^+{}_{(aq)} + e \rightleftharpoons Ag_{(s)}$$

$$AgCl_{(s)} + e \rightleftharpoons Ag_{(s)} + Cl^-{}_{(aq)}$$

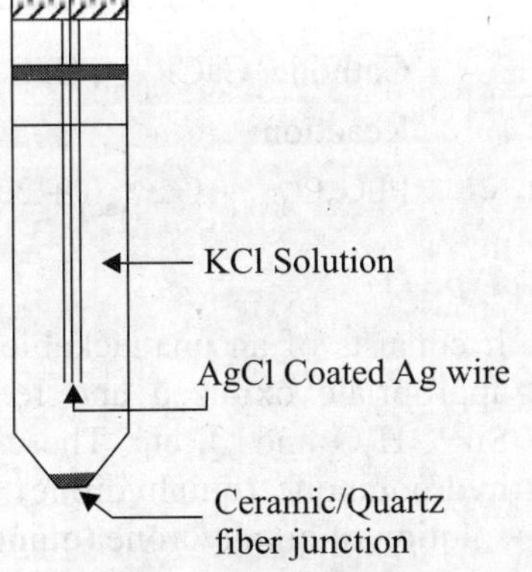

Fig. 12.13 Silver–silver chloride electrode

Note:

1. Such an electrode is reversible with respect to anion. In calomel electrode, the concentration of Cl^- ions plays an important role in deciding the potential. Usually saturated KCl is used when the corresponding name of the electrode is saturated calomel electrode with standard potential of 0.2422 V at 298K. The other forms being normal calomel electrode (1 N KCl is used) and decinormal calomel electrode (0.1 N KCl is used) when the potentials are 0.2810 and 0.3335 V, respectively.
2. Type-II electrodes are of great importance in electrochemistry as they permit the ready establishment of an electrode reversible with respect to anions like sulphate, oxalate, etc.
3. These electrodes are used as secondary reference electrodes. Secondary in the sense that the potential of these electrodes is established with respect to primary reference, i.e., standard hydrogen electrode (SHE) whose potential is arbitrarily assigned as zero.

Type III

Such an electrode consists of a metal, one of its insoluble salts, another insoluble salt carrying same anion and a solution of a soluble salt having the same cation as the latter salt. These electrodes are reversible with respect to cation.

Anode: $Pb_{(s)}/PbC_2O_{4(s)}, CaC_2O_{4(s)}, CaCl_{2(aq)}$

Reaction: In this electrode Pb oxidizes to Pb^{2+} ions which then combine with $C_2O_4^{2-}$ ions to form insoluble PbC_2O_4. The removal of oxalate ions from the solution causes the dissolution of CaC_2O_4 so as to maintain its solubility product. The electrode is reversible with respect to Ca^{2+} ions.

$$Pb_{(s)} \rightleftharpoons Pb^{2+}_{(aq)} + 2e$$
$$Pb^{2+}_{(aq)} + C_2O_4^{2-}{}_{(aq)} \rightleftharpoons PbC_2O_{4(s)}$$
$$CaC_2O_{4(s)} \rightleftharpoons Ca^{2+}_{(aq)} + C_2O_4^{2-}{}_{(aq)}$$
$$Pb_{(s)} + CaC_2O_{4(s)} \rightleftharpoons PbC_2O_{4(s)} + Ca^{2+}_{(aq)} + 2e$$

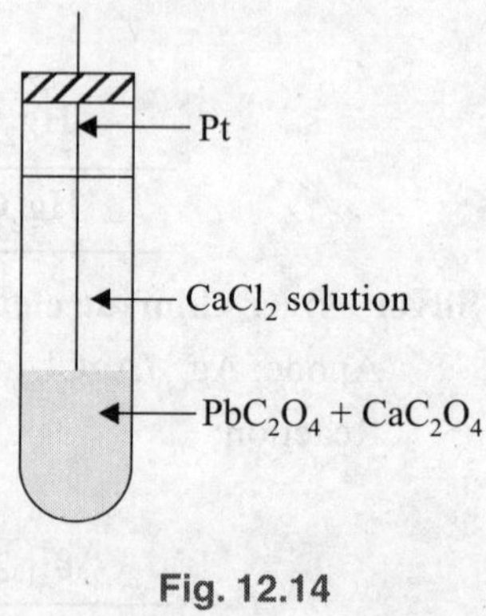

Fig. 12.14

Cathode: $CaCl_{2(aq)}, CaC_2O_{4(s)}, PbC_2O_{4(s)}/Pb_{(s)}$

Reaction:

$$PbC_2O_{4(s)} + Ca^{2+}_{(aq)} + 2e \rightleftharpoons Pb_{(s)} + CaC_2O_{4(s)}$$

Type IV

It consists of an unattackable metal such as Au or Pt immersed in a solution containing an appropriate oxidized and reduced form of an oxidation reduction system like Sn^{4+} and Sn^{2+}, H_2Q and Q, etc. These electrodes are also known as redox electrodes, e.g., quinone-hydroquinone (quinhydrone) electrode. It consists of a 'Pt' strip immersed in a saturated solution of quinhydrone (quinone and hydroquinone in 1:1 ratio) in a buffered solution.

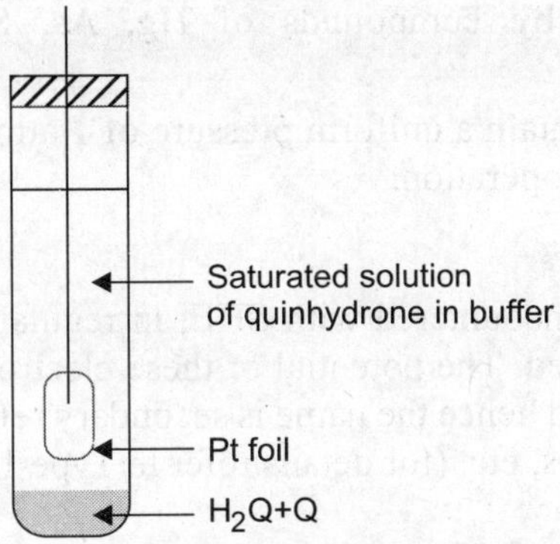

Fig. 12.15 Quinhydrone electrode

Anode: $Pt/H_2Q_{(s)}, Q_{(s)}$

Reaction:

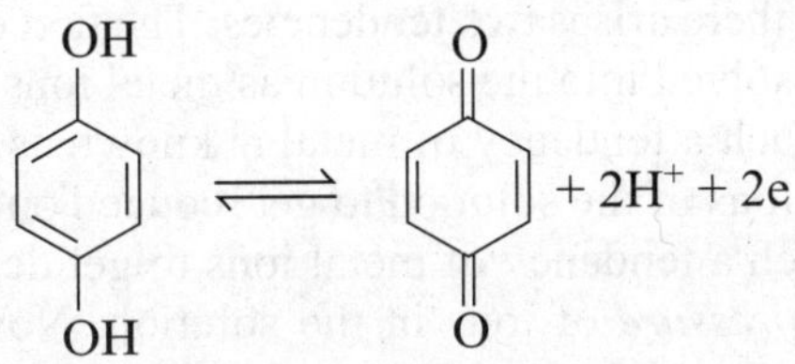

or

$$H_2Q \rightleftharpoons Q + 2H^+ + 2e$$

Cathode: $Pt/Q_{(aq)}, H_2Q_{(aq)}$

Reaction:

$$Q + 2H^+ + 2e \rightleftharpoons H_2Q$$

Reference Electrodes

A reference electrode is an electrode with standard potential. Reference electrodes are of two types.

Primary reference electrode

Standard hydrogen electrode (SHE) is used as primary reference electrode. The representation of the electrode is Pt, $\frac{1}{2}H_2$ (1 atm)/H^+ (1 M); 298 K as anode and the schematic presentation is given below. Here Pt-wire is used for the conduction purpose and is mentioned always on the gas side as gases are poor conductors due to lack of charge carriers. Pt-foil coated with platinum black facilitates electrode reaction by only providing the surface with active sites. The potential of SHE is arbitrarily fixed as 0.00 V at all temperatures.

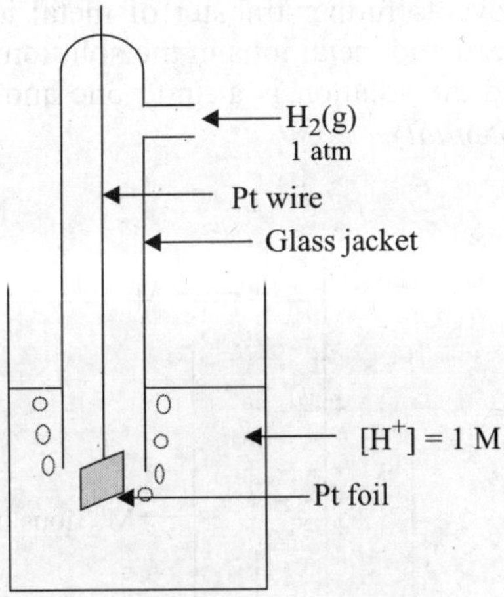

Fig. 12.16 Standard hydrogen electrode

Limitations

- Difficulty in handling, i.e., it is not portable.

- Readily poisoned by compounds of Hg, As, S and oxidizing agents like MnO_4^-, $Cr_2O_7^{2-}$, etc.
- It is difficult to maintain a uniform pressure of 1 atm and unity concentration of H^+ ions throughout the operation.

Secondary reference electrodes

Looking into the difficulties encountered with SHE, in regular practice the use of secondary reference electrodes is promoted. The potential of these electrodes is obtained with respect to primary reference electrode and hence the name is secondary reference, e.g., calomel electrode, silver–silver chloride electrodes, etc. (for details refer to Type-II electrodes).

Electrode Potential (*E*)

Here the discussion is done with respect to metal–metal ion electrodes. However, the same concept can be extended to other varieties of electrodes. The development of electrode potential was originally explained by Nernst. According to him, when a metal strip is brought in contact with its own ions in solution, there arises two tendencies. The first one being the tendency of the metal to get oxidized and dissolved into the solution as metal ions leaving behind the electrons on the surface of the strip. Such a tendency of metal is known as *solution pressure*. The other tendency is that of the metal ions of the solution to get reduced on the metal surface by gaining electrons from the metal. Such a tendency of metal ions to get deposited on the surface of the metal is known as *osmotic pressure* of ions in the solution. Now there arise three different possibilities.

Case I: *Solution pressure is higher than osmotic pressure*

In such a case metal preferentially dissolves into the solution as corresponding metal ions leaving behind the electrons on the metal strip. Thus the strip becomes negatively charged. Now the excess positive ions from the solution cluster around the negatively charged strip forming an electrical double layer at the junction of the two phases. This electrical double layer prevents further transfer of metal ions into the solution and equilibrium is reached between metal and metal ions in the solution. At equilibrium, the potential difference between the strip and the solution is a finite one and is known as electrode potential (*to be specific oxidation potential*).

$$M_{(s)} \rightleftharpoons M^{n+}_{(aq)} + ne$$

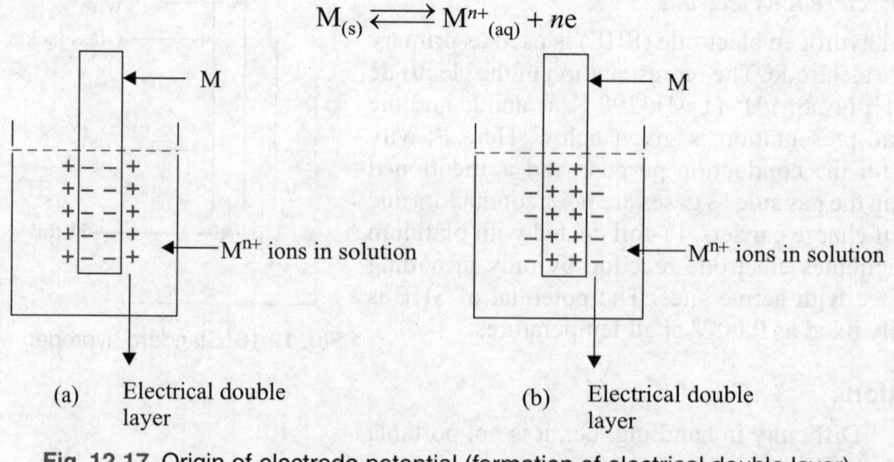

Fig. 12.17 Origin of electrode potential (formation of electrical double layer)

Case II: *Osmotic pressure is higher than solution pressure*

In such a case metal ions preferentially get reduced at the surface of the metal strip by gaining electrons from the strip, making it positively charged. Now the excess negative ions from the solution cluster around the positively charged strip forming an electrical double layer at the junction of the two phases. This electrical double layer prevents further transfer of metal ions and equilibrium is reached between the metal ions in the solution and the metal. At equilibrium, the potential difference between the solution and the strip is a finite one and is known as electrode potential (*to be specific reduction potential*).

$$M^{n+}{}_{(aq)} + ne \rightleftharpoons M_{(s)}$$

Case III: *Solution pressure is equal to osmotic pressure*

In such a case electrical double layer is not formed and there develops no potential. Such an electrode is known as *null electrode*.

Definition

The potential difference between a metal strip and a solution containing its own ions in equilibrium at the junction of the two phases is known as electrode potential.

Physical significance

Oxidation potential is the ability of an element to lose electron, i.e., to get oxidized in the presence of a solvent, while reduction potential is the ability of an element to accept electron, i.e., to get reduced in the presence of a solvent.

Factors Affecting Electrode Potential

1. **Nature:** The ability of an element to lose or gain an electron depends largely on its nature. For this, periodic properties such as size, ionisation energy, electron affinity, screening factor, etc. may be taken as guiding factors. However many periodic properties often fail to account for the relative tendencies of elements to lose or gain electrons. This is because of the fact that periodic properties are concerned with isolated gaseous atoms, while electrode potential is considered as the ability of an element to lose or gain electron in the presence of a solvent. Therefore solvation energy comes into play which has a significant contribution in deciding the electrode potential. For example, among alkali metals Li has more ionisation energy than Na and therefore is expected to have less oxidation potential. However the oxidation potential of Li (+3.05 V) is found to be more than Na (+2.71 V). The reason lies in the fact that Li^+ ion being smaller as compared to Na^+ is extensively solvated (hydrated) leading to the release of substantial amount of solvation energy which overwhelms the ionisation energy.

$$Li + xH_2O \longrightarrow [Li(H_2O)_x]^+ + \text{Solvation energy}$$

2. **Concentration of active ions:** Concentration of active ions can disturb the equilibrium between metal and metal ions and therefore is capable of changing the electrode potential. The effect can be analysed through simple application of Le-chatelier's principle but the exact quantitative relation is given by Nernst expression. For example, an increase in the concentration of ions shifts the equilibrium $M(s) \rightleftharpoons M^{n+} + ne_{(aq)}$ towards the metal side and thereby lowers the tendency of an element to lose electron, i.e., oxidation potential.

3. **Temperature:** Temperature has a significant effect. The quantitative relation between temperature and potential is discussed in Nernst equation.
4. **Pressure:** This is only important for gas electrodes.

Standard electrode potential ($E°$): The electrode potential when a pure metal strip is brought in contact with a solution containing its own ions having unity activity (in ideal case 1M) at 298 K and under 1 atm pressure is known as the standard electrode potential.

Cell Potential (EMF of the Cell)

In an electrochemical cell the potential difference across the electrodes operates as a driving force for the flow of electrons and thereby current and is known as cell potential/ electromotive force (emf). It can be expressed in terms of both reduction potential and oxidation potential. In terms of tendency to gain electron, i.e., reduction potential cathode remains at higher potential. On the other hand, with respect to tendency to lose electron i.e. oxidation potential anode remains at higher potential. When both electrodes are taken in their respective standard states, the cell potential is known as standard cell potential ($E°_{Cell}$).

In terms of reduction potential,

$$E°_{cell} = E°_{cathode} - E°_{anode}$$

In terms of oxidation potential,

$$E°_{cell} = E°_{anode} - E°_{cathode}$$

Standard Cell

An electrochemical cell that provides a constant output voltage over a wide range of temperature is known as standard cell. In other words, a standard cell is that which has a very small temperature coefficient, e.g., *Weston standard cadmium cell.*

Setup

It is made of a H-shaped glass tube sealed with platinum wires at the lower ends. Anode consists of cadmium amalgam with $CdSO_4$ solution while cathode is made of Hg, a sparingly soluble salt of Hg, i.e., $HgSO_4$ and a highly soluble salt solution of $CdSO_4$. The voltage output is 1.018 V at 298 K with temperature coefficient of -5×10^{-5} V K^{-1}. The schematic presentation of the cell is as follows.

Cd–Hg/$CdSO_4$ (Solution)/$HgSO_4$/Hg

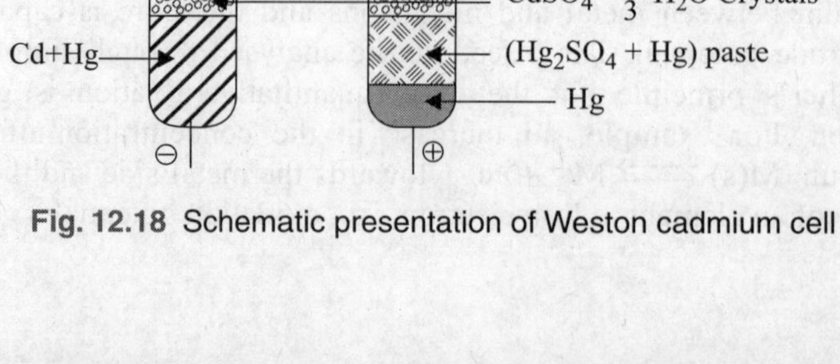

Fig. 12.18 Schematic presentation of Weston cadmium cell

Reaction:

Anode: $Cd_{(s)} \longrightarrow Cd^{2+}_{(aq)} + 2e$

Cathode: $HgSO_{4(s)} \longrightarrow Hg_2^{2+}{}_{(aq)} + SO_4^{2-}{}_{(aq)}$

$Hg_2^{2+}{}_{(aq)} + 2e \longrightarrow 2Hg_{(l)}$

$$Cd_{(s)} + HgSO_{4(s)} \longrightarrow Cd^{2+}_{(aq)} + 2Hg_{(l)} + SO_4^{2-}{}_{(aq)}$$

Measurement of Cell Potential

Electrode potential can be measured by using a voltmeter across the electrodes. However, voltmeter always provides a voltage less than the optimum output voltage. The reason being voltmeter can give potential difference only when cell is sending current in the circuit and some current loss is there in overcoming the internal resistance of the cell. This problem can be solved by using potentiometer. The circuit diagram for a typical potentiometer keeping only the essential components to understand its working is shown below.

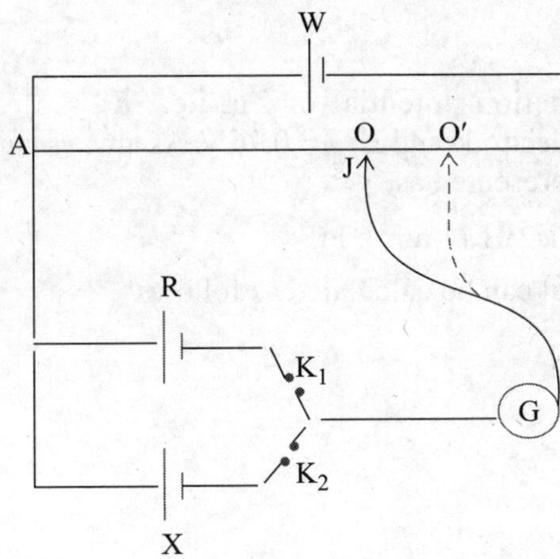

Fig. 12.19 Circuit diagram of a typical potentiometer

where AB is the high resistance wire, W is the working cell whose emf can be varied with adjustment of length of the resistance wire AB, R is the standard reference cell, X is the cell with unknown potential, K_1 and K_2 are the keys, G is the galvanometer, and J is the jockey.

The measurement using potentiometer involves two steps.

Step I: Key K_1 is closed keeping K_2 open. The purpose is to bring only the reference cell into the circuit. Now adjust the position of jockey on the high resistance wire so as to make the working cell emf equal to that of the reference cell. This can be confirmed with null deflection in the galvanometer. Such a point on the resistance wire is known as null deflection point, say *O*.

Step II: The process is repeated by keeping the cell with unknown potential in the circuit to get another null deflection point, say *O′*.

Calculation:

$E_R \propto AO$

$E_X \propto AO'$

Now, $E_X = \dfrac{AO'}{AO}$

or $$E_X = \frac{AO'}{AO} \times E_R \qquad ...[12.11]$$

Measurement of Electrode Potential

Potential of single electrode can be measured by using the following steps:

Step I: The electrode with unknown potential is coupled with the reference electrode (SHE) to construct a cell.

Step II: A galvanometer is used in the circuit across the electrodes to decide the direction of flow of current, i.e., cathode and anode.

Step III: The galvanometer is replaced with a potentiometer to find the cell potential.

Step IV: Finally the basic empirical relation of cell potential is utilized to find the potential.

Illustration 1

Let us find the standard reduction potential of Zn, i.e., $E^\circ_{Zn^{2+}/Zn}$. From the experiment current flows from SHE to Zn-electrode and $E^\circ_{cell} = 0.76$ V. As always current flows from cathode to anode and the cell can be represented as,

$Zn/Zn^{2+}(1\ M)//H^+(1\ M)/(1/2)H_2(1\ atm)$, Pt.

Now the required potential can be calculated as follows

$$E^\circ_{Cell} = E^\circ_{H^+/\frac{1}{2}H_2} - E^\circ_{Zn^{2+}/Zn}$$

or $$E^\circ_{Zn^{2+}/Zn} = -0.76V$$

Illustration 2

Let us find the standard reduction potential of Ag, i.e., $E^\circ_{Ag^+/Ag}$. From the experiment current flows from Ag-electrode to SHE and $E^\circ_{Cell} = 0.80$ V. As always current flows from cathode to anode and the cell can be represented as,

Pt, $\frac{1}{2}H_2$ (1 atom)/H^+ (1 M)//Ag^+(1 M)/Ag

Now the required potential can be calculated as follows:

$$E^\circ_{Cell} = E^\circ_{Ag^+/Ag} - E^\circ_{H^+/(1/2)H_2}$$

or $$E^\circ_{Ag/Ag} = 0.80\ V$$

Electrochemical Series

Different elements can be arranged as per the increasing or decreasing order of their potentials. The array so obtained is known as electrochemical series. The most popular representation is the arrangement of elements in the increasing order of their reduction potentials. Some common elements (in the form of reduction electrode) and their standard potentials are given as follows:

Electropositive ↑

Electrode	Standard potential in volts
Li^+/Li	−3.05
K^+/K	−2.93
Ca^{2+}/Ca	−2.87
Na^+/Na	−2.71
Mg^{2+}/Mg	−2.37
Al^{3+}/Al	−1.66
Mn^{2+}/Mn	−1.18
Zn^{2+}/Zn	−0.76
Cr^{3+}/Cr	−0.74
Fe^{2+}/Fe	−0.44
Ni^{2+}/Ni	−0.25
Pb^{2+}/Pb	−0.13
$H^+/(1/2)H_2$	0.00
Cu^{2+}/Cu	+0.34
Ag^+/Ag	+0.80
$(1/2)Br_2/Br^-$	+1.08
$(1/2)F_2/F^-$	+2.87

↓ Electronegative

Nernst Equation

Let us consider a hypothetical cell reaction

$$aA + bB \rightleftharpoons lL + mM$$

Applying Van't Hoff reaction isotherm,

$\Delta G = \Delta G^\circ + RT \ln Q$ (Q is the reaction co-efficient)

or $$-nFE = -nFE^\circ + RT \ln \frac{[L]^l [M]^m}{[A]^a [B]^b} \qquad \{\because -\Delta G = nFE\}$$

Dividing both sides by $-nF$,

or $$E = E^\circ - \frac{RT}{nF} \ln \frac{[L]^l [M]^m}{[A]^a [B]^b} \qquad ...[12.12]$$

$$= E^\circ + \frac{RT}{nF} \ln \frac{[A]^a [B]^b}{[L]^l [M]^m} \qquad ...[12.13]$$

$$= E^\circ + \frac{2.303\, RT}{nF} \log \frac{[A]^a [B]^b}{[L]^l [M]^m} \qquad ...[12.14]$$

At 298 K a simpler form can be obtained by substituting

R: 8.314 J K^{-1} mol^{-1}

F: 96500 C

T: 298 K

Now the above equation takes the form

$$E = E^\circ + \frac{0.059}{n}\log\frac{[A]^a\,[B]^b}{[L]^l\,[B]^m} \qquad ...[12.15]$$

Equations [12.12] – [12.15] are different forms of Nernst equation.

Applications

1. **To find the electrode and cell potentials**: Electrode and cell potentials can be calculated under a given set of conditions by using Nernst equation.

Example 12.6

Find the potential of the following half cells at 298 K

(*a*) *$FeSO_4$ (0.1 M)/Fe. Standard potential being –0.44 V*

(*b*) *Pt, H_2 (2 atm)/HCl (0.02M)*

(*c*) *$ZnSO_4$ (0.1 M)/Zn. Assuming 80% dissociation of the salt and the standard potential being –0.76 V*

(*d*) *A solution containing 0.0045 M of $Cr_2O_7^{2-}$ and 0.015 M of Cr^{3+} shows a pH of 2.0. Calculate the potential of half reaction. Given standard potential of the reaction $Cr_2O_7^{2-} \longrightarrow Cr^{3+}$ is 1.33 V.*

Solution

(a) $Fe^{2+} + 2e \longrightarrow Fe$

$$E = E^\circ + \frac{0.059}{n}\log[Fe^{2+}]$$

$$= -0.44 + \frac{0.059}{n}\log[Fe^{2+}]$$

$$= -0.44 - 0.0295$$

$$= -\,0.4695\ V$$

(b) $(1/2)H_2 \longrightarrow H^+ + e^-$

$$E = E^\circ + \frac{0.059}{n}\log\frac{\sqrt{P_{H_2}}}{[H^+]}$$

$$= 0 + \frac{0.059}{n}\log\frac{\sqrt{P_{H_2}}}{[H^+]}$$

$$= \frac{0.059}{1}\log\frac{\sqrt{2}}{(0.02)}$$

$$= 0.109\ V$$

(c) $[Zn^{2+}] = 0.1\times\frac{80}{100} = 8\times10^{-2}\ M$

The reaction is $Zn^{2+} + 2e \longrightarrow Zn$

$$E = E^\circ + \frac{0.059}{n}\log[Zn^{2+}]$$

$$= -0.76 + \frac{0.059}{2}\log(8\times10^{-2})$$

$$= -0.76 + 0.00027$$

$$= -0.7597\ V$$

(d) $Cr_2O_7^{2-} + 14H^+ + 6e \longrightarrow 2Cr^{3+} + 7H_2O$

$$E = E^\circ + \frac{0.059}{n}\log\frac{[Cr_2O_7^{2-}][H^+]^{14}}{[Cr^{3+}]^2}$$

$$= 1.33 + \frac{0.059}{6}\log\frac{0.0045\times(10^{-2})^{14}}{[0.015]^2}$$

$$= 1.33 - 0.26$$

$$= 1.07\ V$$

Example 12.7

Represent the cell in which the following reaction takes place.

$$Mg_{(s)} + 2Ag^+_{(aq)} \longrightarrow Mg^{2+}_{(aq)} + 2Ag_{(s)}$$

Calculate the cell potential. Given that $E^\circ_{Mg^{2+}/Mg}$ and $E^\circ_{Ag^+/Ag}$ are −2.37 V and +0.80 V. The concentrations of Ag^+ and Mg^{2+} ions are 0.02 and 0.001 M, respectively.

Solution

Cell representation: $Mg/Mg^{2+}//Ag^+/Ag$

Reaction:

Anode:	$Mg_{(s)} \longrightarrow Mg^{2+}_{(aq)} + 2e$
Cathode:	$Ag^+_{(aq)} + e \longrightarrow Ag_{(s)} \times 2$
Cell:	$Mg_{(s)} + 2Ag^+_{(aq)} \longrightarrow Mg^{2+}_{(aq)} + 2Ag_{(s)}$

Calculation:

$$E = E^\circ + \frac{0.059}{n}\log\frac{[Ag^+]^2}{[Mg^{2+}]}$$

$$= E^\circ_{Ag^+/Ag} - E^\circ_{Mg^{2+}/Mg} + \frac{0.059}{2}\log\frac{(0.02)^2}{(0.001)}$$

$$= 0.80 - (-2.37) - 0.01174$$

$$= 3.1583$$

2. **To find the equilibrium constant:** From Nernst equation (refer relation [12.12]),

$$E = E^\circ - \frac{2.303\,RT}{nF}\log Q$$

At equilibrium, $E = 0$ and $Q = K$

$$\text{or} \quad E^\circ - \frac{2.303\,RT}{nF}\log K = 0$$

$$\text{or} \quad \log K = \frac{nFE^\circ}{2.303\,RT} \quad \text{...[12.16]}$$

$$\text{At 298 K, } \log K = \frac{nE^\circ}{0.059} \quad \text{...[12.17]}$$

Example 12.8

Calculate the equilibrium constant for the reaction, $Fe^{3+} + 3I^- \rightleftharpoons Fe^{2+} + I_3^-$. The standard reduction potentials for Fe^{3+}/Fe^{2+} and I_3^-/I^- are 0.77 and 0.54 V, respectively.

Solution

$$E^\circ = E_{Fe^{3+}/Fe^{2+}} - E_{I_3^-/I^-}$$

$$= 0.77 - 0.54$$

$$= 0.23 \text{ V}$$

$$\log K = \frac{nE^\circ}{0.059}$$

$$= \frac{0.23}{0.059} = 3.898$$

$$\text{or} \quad K = 7.91 \times 10^3$$

Example 12.9

Calculate the equilibrium constant for the reaction, $In^{2+} + Cu^{2+} \rightleftharpoons In^{3+} + Cu^+$. Given the standard reduction potentials for Cu^{2+}/Cu^+, In^{3+}/In^+ and In^{2+}/In^+ are 0.15, −0.42 and −0.40 V, respectively.

Solution

$$E^\circ_{In^{3+}/In^{2+}} = ?$$

$$In^{3+} + 2e \longrightarrow In^+;\ E^\circ_1 = -0.42 \text{ V}$$

$$In^{2+} + e \longrightarrow In^+;\ E^\circ_2 = -0.40 \text{ V}$$

$\ominus$

$$In^{3+} + e \longrightarrow In^{2+};\ E^\circ_3 = ?$$

$$\Delta G^\circ_3 = \Delta G^\circ_1 + \Delta G^\circ_2$$

$$\text{or} \quad 1 \times F \times E^\circ_{In^{3+}/In^{2+}} = 2 \times F \times E^\circ_{In^{3+}/In^+} - 1 \times F \times E^\circ_{In^{2+}/In^+}$$

$$\text{or} \quad E^\circ_{In^{3+}/In^{2+}} = 2 \times E^\circ_{In^{3+}/In^+} - E^\circ_{In^{2+}/In^+}$$

$$\text{or} \quad E^\circ_{In^{3+}/In^{2+}} = 2 \times (-0.42) - (-0.40) = -0.44 \text{ V}$$

$$E^\circ = E_{Cu^{2+}/Cu^+} - E_{In^{3+}/In^{2+}}$$

$$= 0.15 - (-0.44) = 0.59 \text{ V}$$

$$\log K = \frac{0.59}{0.059}$$

$K = 10$

or $K = 10^{10}$

3. **To find emf of concentration cell:** A concentration cell is that in which potential difference across the electrodes arises due to the difference in the concentration of electrode material or the active ions of the electrolyte. Therefore concentration cells are of two types, viz. *electrode concentration cell* and *electrolyte concentration cell.* In electrode concentration cell difference is there in concentration of electrode material. For example, gas electrodes operating at different pressures or amalgam electrodes with different metal to mercury ratio. Such cells do not have liquid junction potential. In electrolyte concentration cell, the electrodes differ only with respect to the concentration of active ions. In general, it can be represented as

$$\underbrace{M/M^{n+}(C_1)}_{\text{Anode}}//\underbrace{M^{n+}(C_2)/M}_{\text{Cathode}};\ C_2 > C_1$$

C_2 and C_1 are the concentration of metal ions in mol l^{-1} at anode and cathode, respectively with $C_2 > C_1$.

Reaction:

Anode:	M	$\longrightarrow$	$M^{n+}(C_1) + ne$
Cathode:	$M^{n+}(C_2) + ne$	$\longrightarrow$	M
Cell:	$M^{n+}(C_2)$	$\longrightarrow$	$M^{n+}(C_1)$

Calculation:

$$E = E^\circ + \frac{2.303\,RT}{nF}\log\frac{C_2}{C_1}$$

$$= 0 + \frac{2.303\,RT}{nF}\log\frac{C_2}{C_1}$$

$$= \frac{2.303\,RT}{nF}\log\frac{C_2}{C_1}$$

$$\text{At 298 K, } E = \frac{0.059}{n}\log\frac{C_2}{C_1} \qquad \text{...[12.18]}$$

Example 12.10

Two silver rods are placed in silver nitrate solutions of concentrations 0.1 M and 0.01 M in a cell. Calculate the cell emf.

Solution

The given cell can be represented as:

$$\underbrace{Ag/Ag^+(0.01M)}_{\text{Anode}}//\underbrace{Ag^+(0.1M)Ag}_{\text{Cathode}}$$

$$E = \frac{0.059}{n}\log\frac{C_2}{C_1}$$

$$= \frac{0.059}{1}\log\frac{0.1}{0.01}$$

$$= 0.059\ \text{V}$$

Example 12.11

A cell is made of two hydrogen electrodes. Anode is in contact with a solution of 10^{-5}M H^+ ion. Find the concentration of H^+ ions at cathode if the emf of the cell is 0.2 V.

Solution

The cell can be represented as

$$\underbrace{Pt, H_2/H^+(10^{-5}M)}_{\text{Anode}} // \underbrace{H^+(?)/H_2, Pt}_{\text{Cathode}}$$

$$E = \frac{0.059}{n} \log \frac{C_2}{C_1}$$

or $$0.2 = \frac{0.059}{1} \log \frac{C_2}{10^{-5}}$$

or $$C_2 = 2.456 \times 10^{-2}\ M$$

Thus, $[H^+] = 2.456 \times 10^{-2}$ M at cathode

Note

1. **Liquid junction potential:** When two different electrolyte solutions are placed in contact a potential difference develops at their interface which is known as liquid junction potential. Liquid junction potential is mainly due to unequal mobility of ions. This can be explained by taking an example of a solution of common salt in contact with distilled water. Due to higher mobility of Cl^- ions than Na^+ ions, the former diffuse faster than the latter. The result is that an electrical double layer is developed at the junction of salt and water which leads to the development of a potential difference among them.

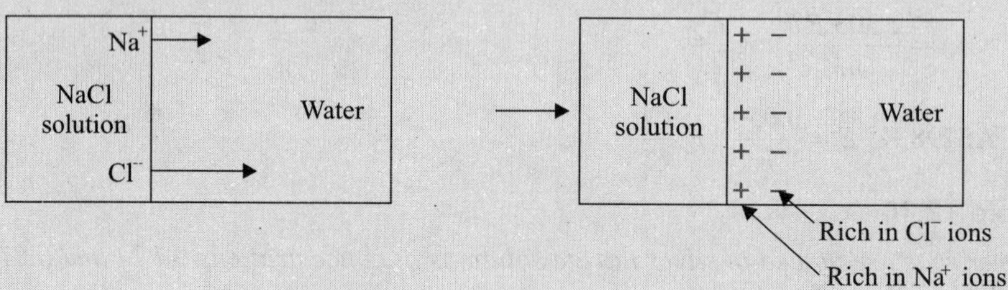

Fig. 12.20 Formation of liquid junction potential

2. **Concentration cell with transference:** When concentration cell is made by connecting two solutions having different concentrations of active ions through a salt bridge, then it involves liquid junction potential. Liquid junction potential drives the transport of ion from one solution to other. Such a cell is known as concentration cell with transport or transference.

   $Zn / Zn^{2+} (C_1) // Zn^{2+} (C_2) / Zn$

3. **Concentration cell without transference:** When two half cells are connected through a common solution then liquid junction potential is absent. In such a case,

the transport of ion is not possible due to the absence of driving force. Such a cell is known as concentration cell without transport or transference; for example, cadmium amalgam cell in which different quantities of cadmium are dissolved in mercury.

$Cd{-}Hg\ (a_1)\ /\ CdSO_{4(aq)}\ /\ Cd{-}Hg(a_2)$

4. **To find the solubility/solubility product of a sparingly soluble salt:** In case of a sparingly soluble salt, ionisation is complete even in saturated solution. Therefore ionic concentration is proportional to the solubility of the salt. For a hypothetical electrolyte A_xB_y the relation between solubility and solubility product is as follows:

$K_{SP} = x^x y^y S^{x+y}$

Example 12.12

The emf of the cell Ag /AgI (s), 0.05M KI // 0.05M AgNO$_3$ / Ag is 0.80 V. Calculate the solubility product and solubility of AgI.

Solution

$$E_{cell} = E_{Ag^+/Ag} - E_{Ag\ I/Ag}$$
$$= E^\circ_{Ag^+/Ag} + 0.059 \log [Ag^+]_{RHE} - \{E^\circ_{Ag^+/Ag} + 0.059 \log K_{SP}\ (Ag\ I) - 0.059 \log [I^-]\}$$
$$= 0.059 \log [Ag^+]_{RHE} + 0.059 \log [I^-] - 0.059 \log K_{SP}\ (AgI)$$
$$= 0.059 \log (0.05) + 0.059 \log (0.05) - 0.059 \log K_{SP}\ (Ag\ I)$$

$$\log\ K_{SP}\ (Ag\ I) = -16.10$$
$$K_{SP}\ (Ag\ I) = 7.91 \times 10^{-17}$$
$$S = \sqrt{K_{sp}} = 8.89 \times 10^{-9}$$

5. **To find the pH of an unknown aqueous solution:** pH of an aqueous solution can be measured by using different electrodes such as hydrogen electrode, quinhydrone or glass electrode.

Type I: Using hydrogen electrode

Let us put a hydrogen electrode in a solution of unknown pH which can be represented as, $H^+(?)/\frac{1}{2}H_2(1\ atm)$, Pt. Now the reaction is

$H^+ + e \rightleftharpoons (1/2)H_2$

Applying Nernst expression

$$E_{H^+/\frac{1}{2}H_2} = E^\circ_{H^+/(1/2)H_2} + \frac{0.059}{1} \log [H^+]$$

or $$E_{H^+/(1/2)H_2} = -0.059\ pH \quad ...[12.19]$$

Case 1: *By coupling with primary reference electrode*

Pt, $(1/2)H_2(1\ atm)/H^+(?)//H^+(1M)/(1/2)H_2(1\ atm)$, Pt

$$E_{Cell} = E^\circ_{H^+/(1/2)H_2} - E_{H^+/(1/2)H_2}$$

or $E_{cell} = 0 - (-0.059\ pH)$

or $$pH = \frac{E_{Cell}}{0.059} \quad ...[12.20]$$

Case 2: ***By coupling with secondary reference electrode, say saturated calomel electrode***

Pt, ½H_2(1 atm)/H^+(?)//KCl(sat.), Hg_2Cl_2/Hg

$$E_{Cell} = E^\circ_{Calomel} - E_{H^+/(1/2)H_2}$$

or $E_{Cell} = 0.2422 - (-0.059\ pH)$

or $$pH = \frac{E_{Cell} - 0.2422}{0.059} \quad ...[12.21]$$

Note:

SHE has the following limitations:

1. It is not portable.
2. It requires considerable volume of test solution.
3. The test solution often poisons the Pt surface.
4. It is difficult to maintain uniform pressure.

Type II: Using quinhydrone electrode

The representation for the quinhydrone electrode is Q, H_2Q/Pt

Reaction:

$$Q + 2H^+ + 2e \rightleftharpoons H_2Q$$

Applying Nernst equation,

$$E_{Q/H_2Q} = E^\circ_{Q/H_2Q} + \frac{0.059}{2} \log [H^+]^2$$

or $$E_{Q/H_2Q} = 0.6996 + \frac{0.059}{2} \times 2 \log [H^+]$$

or $$E_{Q/H_2Q} = 0.6996 - 0.059\ pH \quad ...[12.22]$$

To find the pH this electrode is to be connected with a reference electrode. Let's try to describe the process by coupling this electrode with a saturated calomel electrode. Now the cell becomes

Hg/Hg_2Cl_2, KCl(sat.)//H^+(?)/Q, H_2Q/Pt

Now,

$$E_{Cell} = E_{H_2Q/Q} - E^\circ_{Calomel}$$

or $E_{cell} = 0.6996 - 0.059\ pH - 0.2422$

or $$pH = \frac{0.06996 - 0.2422 - E_{Cell}}{0.059} \quad ...[12.23]$$

Note:

Quinhydrone electrode does not give satisfactory results in strongly alkaline solutions where pH > 8.5. This is due to the fact that hydroquinone ionizes as an acid and gets oxidized by atmospheric oxygen after normal equilibrium between hydroquinone and quinone.

Type III: Using membrane sensitive electrode (glass electrode)

Construction

The glass electrode is made of a special soda silicate glass with high electrical conductivity The thin glass bulb remains filled with 0.1 M HCl and a silver wire coated with silver chloride is kept immersed in it. The Ag/AgCl acts as an internal reference electrode. The electrode can be represented as,

Ag/AgCl/0.1 M HCl/Glass

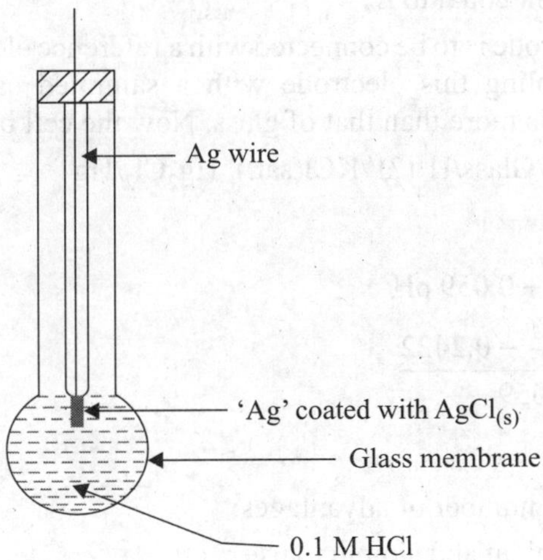

Fig. 12.21

Here the thin glass membrane keeps two solutions of different pH separated from each other. The membrane acts as an ion-exchange resin and establishes equilibrium between the Na^+ ions of glass and H^+ ions of the solution. The potential difference developed across the membrane is proportional to the difference in pH.

$$\underbrace{Na^+GL}_{\text{Membrane}} + H^+ \rightleftharpoons \underbrace{H^+GL}_{\text{Membrane}} + Na^+$$

The potential difference across the glass membrane arises due to the difference in H^+ ion concentrations inside (C_1) and outside (C_2) the glass bulb.

$$E_b = \frac{2.303\,RT}{nF}\log\frac{C_2}{C_1} \qquad \text{...[12.24]}$$

As C_1 is 0.1 M and is constant,

$$E_b = \frac{2.303\,RT}{nF}\log C_2 - C$$

$$= \frac{2.303\,RT}{1 \times F}\log[\mathrm{H}^+] - C$$

$$= -\frac{2.303\,RT}{F}\,\mathrm{pH} - C \qquad \text{...[12.25]}$$

At 298 K, $E_b = -0.059\ \mathrm{pH} - C$ ...[12.26]

C is a constant depending on the pH of the solution taken inside the glass bulb.

Theoretically, $E_b = 0$ when $C_1 = C_2$. However, a small potential contribution exists even if $C_1 = C_2$, this is known as asymmetric potential. The potential of the glass electrode thus is given as

$$E_G = E_b + E_{Ag/AgCl} + E_{assy}$$

$$= -\,0.059\ \mathrm{pH} - C + E_{Ag/AgCl} + E_{assy}$$

$$= E_G^{\circ} - 0.059\ \mathrm{pH} \qquad \text{...[12.27]}$$

where E_G° is a constant equal to $E_{Ag/AgCl} + E_{assy} - C$

To find pH, this electrode is to be connected with a reference electrode. Let's try to describe the process by coupling this electrode with a saturated calomel electrode assuming potential of calomel is more than that of glass. Now the cell becomes

Ag/AgCl/0.1 M HCl/Glass/H^+(?)//KCl(sat.), Hg_2Cl_2/Hg

$$E_{Cell} = E^{\circ}_{Calomel} - E_G$$

$$= 0.2422 - E_G^{\circ} + 0.059\ \mathrm{pH}$$

or $$\mathrm{pH} = \frac{E_{Cell} + E_G^{\circ} - 0.2422}{0.059} \qquad \text{...[12.28]}$$

Note:

Glass electrode has a number of advantages:

1. It is very convenient and simple to use.
2. It is not easily poisoned.
3. Its activity is not affected by strong oxidizing and reducing agents.
4. It provides accurate results.
5. It can be used in turbid, colored and colloidal solutions.

Example 12.13

The emf of the cell Pt, H_2 (1 atm)/H^+ (?) // KCl (1 M)/Hg_2Cl_2(s), Hg is 0.52 V at 298 K. Calculate the pH of the unknown solution. Given $E^{\circ}_{Calomel} = 0.28$ V.

Solution

$$E_{Cell} = E^{\circ}_{Calomel} - E_{H^+/H_2}$$

or $$0.52 = 0.28 - (-\,0.059\ \mathrm{pH})$$

or $$\mathrm{pH} = \frac{0.52 - 0.28}{0.059}$$

$$= 4.06$$

Example 12.14

Calculate the pH of a solution placed in a quinhydrone half cell coupled with a standard calomel half cell. The emf of the cell is 0.15 V at 298 K. Given $E^\circ_{Calomel} = 0.2415$ V and $E^\circ_Q = 0.6996$ V.

Solution

$$Hg/Hg_2Cl_2, KCl//H^+(?)/Q, H_2Q/Pt$$

or $E_{Cell} = E_{H_2Q/Q} - E^0_{Calomel}$

or $0.15 = 0.6996 - 0.059\ pH - 0.2415$

or $pH = \dfrac{0.6996 - 0.2415 - 0.15}{0.059}$

$= 5.22$

Thermodynamics of Cell

Thermodynamic parameters accompanying a cell operation are enthalpy, entropy, and free energy change. The details of finding the above parameters as described in Chapter 3, "Thermodynamics". During cell operation, decrease in free energy appears as electrical energy. Therefore, $-\Delta G = nFE$ ...[12.29]

Again, from Gibb's Helmholtz equation, $\Delta G = \Delta H + T\left[\dfrac{\partial(\Delta G)}{\partial T}\right]_P$

Now, substituting ΔG in the above relation, we get

$$-nFE = \Delta H + T\left[\frac{\partial(-nFE)}{\partial T}\right]_P$$

$$\text{Or,}\quad \Delta H = nF\left[T\left[\frac{\partial(E)}{\partial T}\right]_P - E\right] \qquad ...[12.30]$$

Comparing the relation with, $\Delta H = \Delta G + T\Delta S$, we get

$$\Delta S = nF\left[\frac{\partial(E)}{\partial T}\right]_P \qquad ...[12.31]$$

Relations [12.29], [12.30], and [12.31] can be utilized to find free energy change, enthalpy change and entropy change during the cell operation.

Example 12.15

The galvanic cell Ag(s)/AgCl(s)/KCl(1.0 M)/Hg_2Cl_2(s)/Hg(l) is an example of cell without a liquid junction since the two electrodes dip into the same electrolyte. The emf of the cell is 0.058 V at 298 K and 0.0614 V at 308 K.

(a) Write down the cell reaction.

(b) Calculate ΔS°, ΔG°, and ΔH° at 298 K.

Solution

$$2Ag_{(s)} + 2Cl^-_{(aq)} \longrightarrow 2AgCl_{(s)} + 2e$$

$$Hg_2Cl_{2(s)} + 2e \longrightarrow 2Hg_{(l)} + 2Cl^-_{(aq)}$$

$$2Ag_{(s)} + Hg_2Cl_{2(s)} \longrightarrow 2Hg_{(l)} + 2AgCl_{(s)}$$

Now, temperature coefficient, $\left(\frac{\partial E}{\partial T}\right)_P = \frac{0.0614 - 0.058}{10} = 3.4 \times 10^{-4}\ \text{V K}^{-1}$

$\Delta G° = -nFE° = -2 \times 96500 \times 0.058 = -11.194\ \text{kJ K}^{-1}$

$$\Delta S° = nF\left(\frac{\partial E}{\partial T}\right)_P = 2 \times 96500 \times 3.4 \times 10^{-4} = 65.62\ \text{J K}^{-1}\ \text{mol}^{-1}$$

$$\Delta H° = nF\left[T\left(\frac{\partial E}{\partial T}\right)_P - E\right]$$

$$= 2 \times 96500[298 \times 3.4 \times 10^{-4} - 0.058]$$

$$= 8.361\ \text{kJ}$$

QUESTIONS

1. What is a reference electrode?
2. Why the use of primary SHE is not promoted in regular practice?
3. What is a standard cell?
4. What is the basis on which an electrolyte is selected for making salt bridge?
5. What do you mean by a salt bridge? Why is it used?
6. Explain redox electrode with a suitable example.
7. What is a secondary reference electrode?
8. A salt bridge or porous partition is not required in a lead acid storage cell. Explain.
9. Write down the emf expression by representing the cell in which the following reaction persists $AgCl_{(s)} + \frac{1}{2}H_{2(g)} \rightleftharpoons Ag_{(s)} + HCl_{(aq)}$.
10. What are the disadvantages of use of hydrogen electrode for pH determination?
11. Why is quinhydrone electrode not suitable for pH measurement in strongly alkaline solution?
12. Write down electrode reaction of calomel electrode and oxygen gas electrode.
13. Why is coating of zinc on iron called sacrificial anode?
14. What is an electrochemical cell? Explain the construction and working with a suitable example.
15. Explain different types of electrodes with suitable examples.
16. What do you mean by single electrode potential? Discuss electrode reaction in case of metal–sparingly soluble metal salt electrode and oxidation–reduction electrode with reference to two suitable examples for each with respective electrode reaction.
17. How can you determine the pH of an unknown solution by using quinone–hydroquinone electrode?
18. Design a cell to determine the pH of an aqueous acidic unknown solution by using a calomel electrode.
19. Discuss the limitation of voltmeter in measuring the cell potential. Also discuss how potentiometer helps in overcoming the limitation.
20. What is a glass electrode? Explain how can you determine the pH of an unknown solution by using glass electrode?

21. Derive Nernst equation. Explain how can it be utilised to find the emf of an electrolyte concentration cell.

22. What do you mean by thermodynamics of a cell? Derive the empirical relations to find the thermodynamic parameters during cell operation.

23. What do you mean by thermodynamics of a cell? Derive the empirical relations to find the thermodynamic parameters during cell operation.

24. What is specific conductance?

25. What is cell constant?

26. How molar conductance is related with specific conductance?

27. What is the unit of equivalent conductance?

28. Explain the variation of molar conductance of NH_4OH with dilution.

29. Explain the nature of the curve during conductometric titration of a strong acid with a strong base.

30. Can conductometric titration be utilized for studying precipitation titration?

31. Explain how conductance measurement can be utilized for the degree of dissociation of a weak electrolyte.

32. Why Λ_∞ for a weak electrolyte solution cannot be directly determined experimentally?

33. What is the effect of temperature on molar conductivity?

NUMERICAL PROBLEMS

1. The emf of Zn/$ZnSO_4$//$CuSO_4$/Cu cell at 25°C is 0.03 V and the temperature coefficient of emf is 1.4×10^{-4} V per degree. Calculate the heat of reaction and change in entropy taking place in the cell.

2. Calculate the emf of a concentration cell at 25°C consisting of two Zn- electrodes immersed in solutions of Zn^{2+} ions of 0.1 M and 0.01 M concentrations.

3. Calculate $\Delta E°$ and $\Delta G°$ for $Fe^{3+} + e \longrightarrow Fe^{2+}$ at 298 K. Given $Fe^{3+} + 3e \longrightarrow Fe$, $E° = -0.441$ V; $Fe^{2+} + 2e \longrightarrow Fe$, $E° = 0.771$ V.

4. The emf of the cell SCE//KCl (0.1 M), AgCl(s)/Ag is 0.26 V at 25°C. Find out the solubility of AgCl. ($E°$: SCE = 0.2415, $Ag^+ / Ag = 0.80$ V)

5. A quinhydrone electrode was coupled with another electrode in a solution of pH 5.6. Find the potential of the unknown electrode. (E: Cell = 0.123V, Quinhydrone = 0.699 V)

6. A silver electrode is placed in saturated aqueous Ag_2SO_4 solution. The potential difference between Ag and SHE is found to be 0.72V. Determine the solubility product of Ag_2SO_4. Given $E°_{Ag/Ag^+} = 0.80$V.

7. Construct a cell in which the following disproportionation reaction takes place.

   $2CuCl \longrightarrow CuCl_2 + Cu$

   Also calculate the equilibrium constant for the reaction if Cu^{2+}/Cu^+ and Cu^+/Cu are 0.15 and 0.52 V, respectively.

8. For the galvanic cell Ag/AgCl(s), KCl (0.1M)//KBr (0.001 M), AgBr(s)/Ag, calculate the emf generated and assign correct polarity to each electrode for a spontaneous process after the analysis of cell reaction at 25°C. Given K_{SP} for AgCl and AgBr are 2.8×10^{-10} and 3.3×10^{-13}, respectively.

9. For the cell $Mg(s)/Mg^{2+}(aq)//Ag^{+}(aq)/Ag(s)$, calculate the equilibrium constant and the maximum work that can be obtained during cell operation at 298 K. Given standard reduction potentials of magnesium and silver electrodes are – 2.37 and + 0.80 V, respectively.
10. Calculate the standard potential of Ni^{2+}/Ni electrode. If the cell potential of the cell Ni/Ni^{2+} (0.01M)//Cu^{2+} (0.1M)/Cu is 0.59 V. $E°$ of $Cu^{2+}/Cu = 0.34$ V.
11. Calculate the equilibrium constant for the following reaction at 298 K. $Cu_{(s)} + Cl_{2(g)} \rightarrow CuCl_{2(aq)}$
$E°_{Cu^{2+}/Cu} = 0.34$ V and $E°_{\frac{1}{2}Cl_2/Cl^-} = 1.36$ V.
12. Zinc granules are added in excess to 500 ml of 1 M $Ni(NO_3)_2$ solution at 25°C until the equilibrium is reached. If $E°_{Zn^{2+}/Zn}$ and $E°_{Ni^{2+}/Ni}$ are – 0.75 and – 0.24 V, respectively, find out $[Ni^{2+}]$ at equilibrium.
13. The standard reduction potential of $Cu(OH)_2/Cu$ is + 0.34 V. Calculate the reduction potential at pH = 12 for the above couple. K_{SP} of $Cu(OH)_2$ is 1×10^{-19}.
14. Find the solubility product of a saturated solution of Ag_2CrO_4 in water at 298 K if the emf of the cell Ag /Ag^+ (satd. Ag_2CrO_4 sol.)//Ag^+ (0.1 M)/ Ag is 0.164 V at the same temperature.
15. The standard emf of the cell $Cd_{(s)}/CdCl_2$ (0.1 M) // $AgCl_{(s)}/Ag_{(s)}$ with cell reaction $Cd_{(s)} + 2AgCl_{(s)} \rightarrow 2Ag_{(s)} + Cd^{2+}_{(aq)} + 2\,Cl^-_{(aq)}$ is 0.6915 V at 0°C and 0.6753 V at 25°C. Find the enthalpy change of the reaction at 25°C.
16. An alloy of Pb–Ag weighing 1.08 g was dissolved in dilute HNO_3 and the volume made to 100 ml. A silver electrode was dipped in the solution and the emf of the cell Pt, $H_{2(g)}$ / H^+ (1 M) // $Ag^+_{(aq)}$ / $Ag_{(s)}$ was 0.62 V. If $E°_{Cell} = 0.80$ V, what is the percentage of Ag in the alloy.
17. The following cell is found to have an emf equal to zero. Pt, H_2 (x atm) / 0.01 M H^+ // 0.1 M H^+ / H_2 (y atm), Pt. Find the ratio x/y.
18. A Daniell cell is set up by dipping a Zn rod weighing 100 g in 1 liter of 1.0 M $CuSO_4$ solution. How long would the cell run if it delivers a steady current of 1.0 A?
19. Standard free energies of the formation of $H_2O_{(l)}$, $CO_{2(g)}$, and $C_5H_{12(g)}$ at 298 K are –237.2, –394.4, and –8.2 kJ /mol, respectively. Find standard cell potential for pentane–oxygen fuel cell.
20. A dilute solution of KCl was placed between two Pt electrodes 10 cm apart, across which a potential difference of 6.0 V was applied. How far would K^+ ions move in 15 min at 298 K? Ionic conductivity of K^+ at infinite dilution is 73.52 S cm^2 eq^{-1} at the same temperature.
21. The emf of a cell corresponding to the reaction $Zn_{(s)} + 2H^+_{(aq)} \rightarrow Zn^{2+}$ (0.1 M) + $H_{2(g)}$, 1 atm is 0.28 V at 25°C. Find the pH of the solution at the hydrogen electrode. Given $E°_{Zn^{2+}/Zn} = -0.76$ V.
22. Calculate the equilibrium constant of a cell reaction involving one electron transfer with standard potential of 0.196 V at 25°C.
23. How much maximum work would be obtained by operation of H_2–O_2 fuel cell in which following reactions occur?

$$O_2 + 4H^+ + 4e \rightarrow 2\,H_2O \qquad (E° = 1.229\text{ V})$$
$$H_2 \rightarrow 2H^+ + 2e \qquad (E° = 0.000\text{ V})$$

24. The standard electrode potentials of the electrodes $Ag^+(aq)/Ag(s)$, and $Fe^{3+}(aq)/Fe^{2+}(aq)$, are 0.799 V and 0.771 V at 298 K, respectively. Write down the electrode reactions and designate the cell. Calculate the equilibrium constant for the cell reaction at 298 K.
25. Calculate the change in emf with temperature of the fully charged lead acid storage cell, if ΔS = 2.72 kJ mol^{-1} for the cell reaction:

$$PbO_2(s) + Pb(s) + 2H_2SO_4 \rightarrow 2PbSO_4(s) + 2H_2O\ (l)$$

26. A hydrogen electrode and normal calomel electrode ($E^0 = 0.28V$) had a voltage of 0.435V when placed in a solution at 298K. Calculate the pH of the solution.

27. The equivalent conductance of 1.02×10^{-3} M acetic acid is 48 Ω^{-1} eq^{-1} cm^2 at 298 K. At infinite dilution, the same is 390 Ω^{-1} eq^{-1} cm^2 at the same temperature. Find the degree of dissociation of acetic acid.

28. A 0.01 M KCl solution shows a resistance of 200 Ω in a conductivity cell. The specific conductivity of the same solution at the experimental temperature is 0.0014 mho/cm. If a 0.02 M solution of an acid shows a resistance of 70 Ω in the same cell, find specific and equivalent conductance of the acid.

29. At 18°C, the velocity of migration of Ag^+ ion is 0.00057 cm s^{-1} and the NO_3^- ion is 0.00065 cm s^{-1} at infinite dilutions. What is the equivalent conductivity of $AgNO_3$ at infinite dilution?

30. A 0.02 M solution of weak acid has a conductivity 4.2×10^{-4} S cm^{-1}. The degree of dissociation of the acid at the same dilution is 0.06. Find the equivalent conductivity of the acid at infinite dilution.

31. The equivalent conductivity of KCl at infinite dilution is 130 cm^2 eq^{-1}. The transport number of Cl^- ion in KCl at the same temperature is 0.50. What is the limiting ionic mobility and ionic conductance of K^+ ion?

32. At a certain temperature, the saturated solution of silver chloride has conductivity 10^{-6} S cm^{-1}. The ionic conductance of Ag^+ and Cl^- ions at infinite dilution are 54 and 65 S $cm^2 eq^{-1}$ at the same temperature. Find the solubility of AgCl at this temperature.

33. A salt solution of 0.25 N placed in a cell whose electrodes are 2 cm apart and 3.5 cm^2 in area offers a resistance of 25 Ω. Find equivalent conductivity of solution.

34. At 298 K, the equivalent conductivity of Ag^+ and NO_3^- are 54 and 61, respectively, at infinite dilution. Calculate ionic mobilities and transport number of the ions at infinite dilution.

CHAPTER

13 Water

Chapter Outline

Water is considered to be the most common and abundant (in the solid form as ice; in the liquid form, it covers about 70% of the Earth's surface) liquid on our planet, which is vital to all life forms. In atmosphere, it remains in varying amounts. Most of the living tissues are made up of water. It acts as the dispersion medium for all biochemical reactions occurring in living organisms and at the same time also takes part in many of these reactions. Water is not only vital to different life forms but is also an important requirement for industries. The most important use of water as an engineering material is in *steam generation*, an essential component for power generation from fossil fuel. It is also used as a coolant in power plants. Other wide uses of water are irrigation, drinking, sanitary, washings, air-conditioning, firefighting, etc.

Chemically, water is a compound of hydrogen and oxygen, having the formula H_2O. It reacts with metals and metal oxides to form bases, while with non-metallic oxides it forms acids. It is a polar compound and acts as a good solvent. In fact, it is considered to be the universal solvent. Pure water feebly conducts current because of its self-ionization. Both its polarity and ionization are attributed to the high dielectric constant. Water has interesting thermal properties. When heated from 0°C (the melting point) to 4°C, it contracts and becomes denser. However, most of the other substances expand and become less dense when heated. The molecular association is through hydrogen bonding, which is stronger than the other van der Walls' forces. Because of this hydrogen bonding, the latent heats of fusion and of evaporation and the heat capacity of water are unusually high.

Sources of Water

The main sources of water are as follows:

1. **Surface water**: It includes both flowing (streams and rivers) and still (lakes, ponds, and reservoirs) water.
2. **Underground water**: It includes water from wells and springs.
3. **Rainwater**
4. **Seawater**

Impurities in Water

Impurities in water can be broadly classified into the following types:

1. **Dissolved impurities**: These include dissolved salts such as carbonates, bicarbonates, chlorides, and sulfates of sodium, calcium, magnesium, and iron. Dissolved gases such as O_2 and CO_2 also come under this category.
2. **Suspended impurities**: These may be inorganic impurities such as clay and sand or organic impurities such as oil globules, animal matter, and vegetables.
3. **Colloidal impurities**: These include products from organic waste, finely divided silica, and clay.
4. **Microorganisms**: These include bacteria, fungi, and algae.

Hardness of Water

Hardness is the property of water by virtue of which it fails to form lather with soap. This is due to the presence of certain dissolved salts of calcium, magnesium, and other heavy metals such as iron, aluminum, and manganese in it. These metal ions react with the carboxylate ions of soap to form insoluble carboxylates which precipitate out as a brown sticky material known as *scum*. Carboxylate ion in soap is mainly responsible for its cleansing action. It does so by acting as a surfactant which stabilizes oil-in-water emulsion.

$$Ca^{2+} + RCOO^- \longrightarrow \underset{\text{Calcium carboxylate}}{(RCOO)_2\,Ca\downarrow}$$

$$Mg^{2+} + RCOO^- \longrightarrow \underset{\text{Magnesium carboxylate}}{(RCOO)_2\,Mg\downarrow}$$

Water hardness may be of two types: temporary and permanent.

1. **Temporary:** It is attributed to the presence of dissolved bicarbonates of calcium, magnesium, and other heavy metals. As the name suggests, such hardness can be removed simply by boiling the water. In the process, the bicarbonates decompose to insoluble carbonates or hydroxides which subsequently settle down as a crust at the bottom of the vessel. Such hardness is also known as *carbonate hardness*.

$$Ca(HCO_3)_2 \longrightarrow \underset{\text{Insoluble}}{CaCO_3\downarrow} + H_2O + CO_2$$

$$Ca(HCO_3)_2 \longrightarrow \underset{\text{Insoluble}}{Ca(OH)_2\downarrow} + 2CO_2$$

2. **Permanent**: It is attributed to the presence of chlorides and sulfates of calcium, magnesium, and other heavy metals. It cannot be removed merely by boiling the water. This type of hardness is also known as *noncarbonate hardness*.

Note:

1. **Calcium carbonate equivalent:** The concentrations of hardness producing ions and also sometimes non-hardness producing ions are expressed in terms of calcium carbonate equivalents as this mode permits easy multiplication/division of concentrations as and when required. The choice of calcium carbonate is because its molecular mass is 100 and it is the most insoluble salt that can be precipitated in water treatment.

$$\text{Calcium carbonate equivalent} = \begin{matrix}\text{Mass of hardness}\\ \text{imparting substance}\\ \text{(mg/l)}\end{matrix} \times \left[\frac{\begin{matrix}\text{Equivalent mass}\\ \text{of CaCO}_3\end{matrix}}{\begin{matrix}\text{Equivalent mass of hardness}\\ \text{importing substance}\end{matrix}}\right]$$

$$= \left[\begin{matrix}\text{Mass of hardness}\\ \text{imparting substance}\\ \text{(mg/l)}\end{matrix} \times \text{Multiplication factor}\right] \text{mg/l or ppm}$$

For example,

$$\text{Calcium carbonate equivalent of } HCO_3^- = \left[\begin{matrix}\text{Mass of } HCO_3^-\\ \text{(mg/l)}\end{matrix} \times \frac{50}{61}\right] \text{mg/l}$$

$$\text{Calicum carbonate equivalent of } CaSO_4 = \left[\begin{matrix}\text{Mass of } CaSO_4\\ \text{(mg/l)}\end{matrix} \times \frac{50}{68}\right] \text{mg/l}$$

2. **Units of hardness**: It is usually expressed in milligram per liter (mg/l) or parts per million (ppm) of calcium carbonate equivalent. It is also expressed in units such as Degree French (°Fr) and Degree Clarke (°Cl). For such units, we use the following conversion formulas: 1°Fr = 10 mg/l and 1°Cl = 0.07 mg/l.

Example 13.1

A water sample contains 280 mg of $CaSO_4$ per liter. Calculate the hardness in terms of $CaCO_3$ equivalent.

Solution

$$\text{Hardness} = \text{Mass of } CaSO_4 \text{ (mg/l)} \times \left[\frac{\text{Equivalent mass of } CaCO_3}{\text{Equivalent mass of } CaCO_4}\right]$$

$$= \left[280 \times \frac{50}{68}\right] \text{mg/l}$$

$$= 205.88 \text{ mg/l}$$

Example 13.2

How many grams of $MgCl_2$ dissolved per liter gives 60 ppm of hardness?

Solution

$$\text{Hardness} = \text{Mass of } MgCl_2 \text{ (mg/l)} \times \left[\frac{\text{Equivalent mass of } CaCO_3}{\text{Equivalent mass of } MgCO_2}\right]$$

$$\text{Mass of } MgCl_2 = \frac{\text{Hardness} \times \text{Equivalent mass of } MgCl_2}{\text{Equivalent mass of } CaCO_3}$$

$$= \left[60 \times \frac{47.5}{50}\right] \text{mg/l}$$

$$= 57 \text{ mg/l}$$

Example 13.3

A sample of water on analysis is found to contain 4 mg/l $Ca(HCO_3)_2$, 8 mg/l $CaSO_4$, and 12 mg/l of $MgCl_2$. Calculate temporary, permanent, and total hardness of water.

Solution

$$\text{Hardness due to } Ca(HCO_3)_2 = \left[4 \times \frac{50}{81}\right] \text{mg/l} = 2.47 \text{ mg/l}$$

$$\text{Hardness due to } CaSO_4 = \left[8 \times \frac{50}{68}\right] \text{mg/l} = 5.88 \text{ mg/l}$$

$$\text{Hardness due to } MgCl_2 = \left[12 \times \frac{50}{47.5}\right] \text{mg/l} = 12.63 \text{ mg/l}$$

Temporary hardness is due to the presence bicarbonate of calcium and is equal to 2.47 mg/l. Permanent hardness is due to the presence of sulfate of calcium (5.88 mg/l) and chloride of magnesium (12.63 mg/l) and is equal to 18.51 mg/l (i.e., 5.88 + 12.63).

Softening Methods

The process of removal of hardness producing ions/salts from water is known as softening of water. We will discuss here some important methods for water softening.

Lime–soda process

In lime–soda (LS) process, the dissolved hardness-causing salts are converted into insoluble carbonates and hydroxides by the adding a calculated quantity of lime [$Ca(OH)_2$] and soda (Na_2CO_3). The insoluble compounds so precipitated are then filtered off. The LS process can again be applied either at the room temperature or at an elevated temperature.

1. **Cold LS process**

   Principle: In this process, calculated quantity of lime and soda are mixed with water at room temperature. The insoluble carbonates and hydroxides so formed are very fine and cannot be filtered easily. To facilitate filtration, a small amount of coagulant such as alum, aluminum sulfate, sodium aluminate, or ferrous sulfate is added. The coagulant hydrolyses to aluminum hydroxide which entraps the fine particles, thus facilitating the easy filtering of the sludge. This process produces water containing residual hardness of ~50 ppm.

$NaAlO_2 + 2H_2O \longrightarrow NaOH + Al(OH)_3$

Method: Raw water and calculated quantities of lime, soda, and coagulant are introduced from the top into the inner cylindrical chamber fitted with a vertical rotating shaft attached with paddles as shown in Fig. 13.1. As the water comes down, it gets softened which then flows into the outer coaxial chamber and rises in the upward direction. Sludge or floc with relatively higher specific gravity settles down. The softened water is then allowed to pass through a filtering medium made of wood fibers to confirm the complete removal of the sludge. Finally, the soft water comes out through the outlet at the top, while the sludge is removed from the bottom periodically.

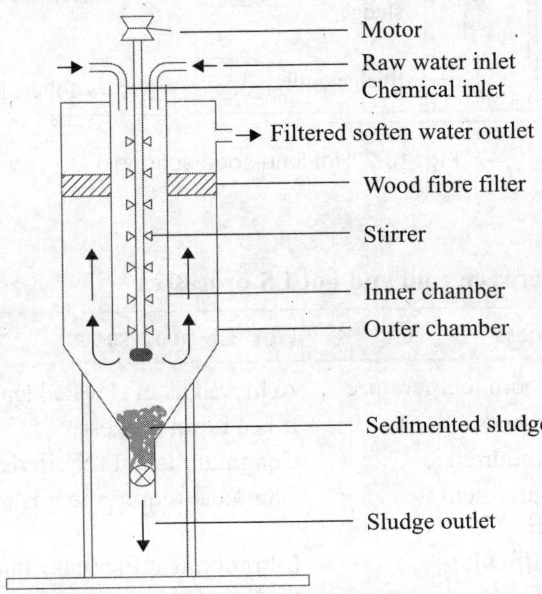

Fig. 13.1 Cold lime–soda softener

2. **Hot LS method**

The softening process is carried out at a temperature close to the boiling point of water. Here all the reactions are boosted up, increasing the softening process to manyfold. In the process, the sludge quickly settles down without the help of coagulant. The dissolved gases such as carbon dioxide and air are driven out easily. The filtration becomes much easier due to lower viscosity of the water. This process produces water containing residual hardness of ~15 ppm. In this process, the raw water mixed with chemicals is sprayed into superheated steam in a reaction tank as shown in Fig. 13.2. Here the plant consists of three parts:

(i) A reaction tank in which raw water, chemicals, and steam are thoroughly mixed.

(ii) A sedimentation tank where sludge settles down.

(iii) A sand filter which ensures the complete removal of sludge.

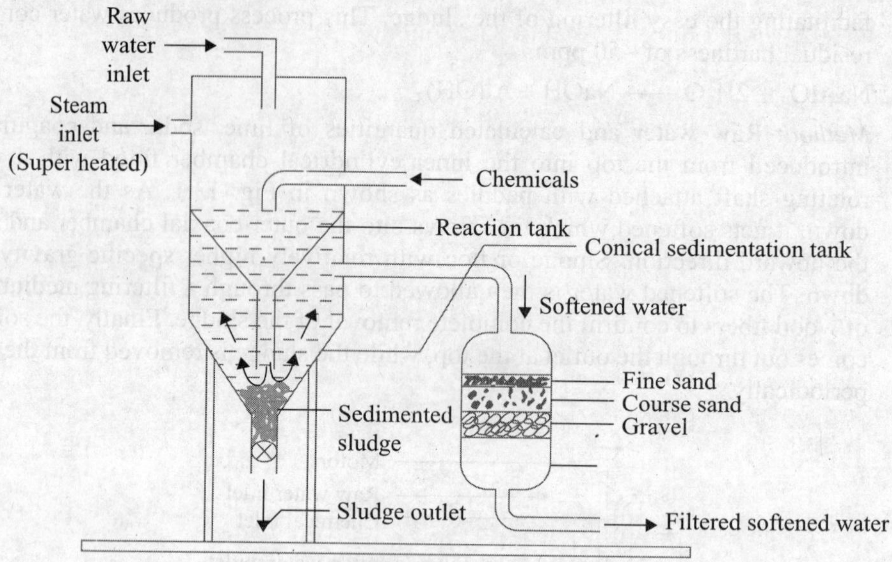

Fig. 13.2 Hot lime-soda softener

Note

1. **Differences between cold and hot LS processes**

Cold LS process	Hot LS process
Achieved at room temperature	Achieved at an elevated temperature of ~100°C.
It is a slow process	It is a rapid process
Coagulant is required	Coagulant is not required
Chemical requirement is relatively high	Chemical requirement is relatively less
Filtration is difficult	Filtration is rather easy due to decrease in viscosity at elevated temperature
Residual hardness ~50 ppm (relatively high)	Residual hardness ~15 ppm (relatively small)
Dissolved gases are not removed	Dissolved gases are removed

2. **Advantages of LS process**
   - It is economical.
   - After treatment, water remains alkaline; hence, it has less corrosion tendency.
   - Pathogenic bacteria are considerably reduced owing to its alkaline nature.
   - Iron and manganese are also removed to some extent.
3. **Disadvantages of LS process**
   - It needs careful operation and skilled supervision.
   - Disposal of sludge is a problem.
   - Softened water still contains a lot of soluble salts such as sodium sulfate which cannot be used in high pressure boilers.

4. **Calculation of lime and soda requirement**

A given hard water sample may contain any combination of different salts or ions. Therefore, it requires different quantities of lime and soda for effective softening. The reaction of different constituents with lime and soda is as follows.

Constituent	Reaction	Need
Temporary [Ca^{2+}/$Ca(HCO_3)_2$]	$Ca(HCO_3)_2 + Ca(OH)_2 \rightarrow 2CaCO_3 + H_2O$	L
Temporary [Mg^{2+}/ $Mg(HCO_3)_2$]	$Mg(HCO_3)_2 + 2Ca(OH)_2 \rightarrow 2CaCO_3 + Mg(OH)_2 + H_2O$	2L
Permanent [Ca^{2+} and Mg^{2+}] from corresponding chlorides/ sulfates	$Ca^{2+} + Na_2CO_3 \rightarrow Ca(CO_3)_2 \cdot{:}\, Na^+$	S
	$Mg^{2+} + Ca(OH)_2 \rightarrow Mg(OH)_2 + Ca^{2+}$	L
HCO_3^- from say $NaHCO_3$	$2HCO_3^- + Ca(OH)_2 \rightarrow CaCO_3 + CO_3^{2-} + H_2O$	L–S
CO_2	$CO_2 + Ca(OH)_2 \rightarrow CaCO_3 + H_2O$	L
H^+ [free acids like HCl, H_2SO_4 etc.]	$2H^+ + Ca(OH)_2 \rightarrow Ca^{2+} + H_2O$ $Ca^{2+} + Na_2CO_3 \rightarrow Ca(CO_3)_2 + Na^+$	L + S
$FeSO_4$ [Coagulant]	$Fe^{2+} + Ca(OH)_2 \rightarrow Fe(OH)_2 + Ca^{2+}$ $Ca^{2+} + Na_2CO_3 \rightarrow CaCO_3 + 2Na^+$	L + S
$Al_2(SO_4)_3$ [Coagulant]	$2Al^{3+} + 3Ca(OH)_3 \rightarrow 2Al(OH)_3 + 3Ca^{2+}$ $3Ca^{2+} + 2Na_2CO_3 \rightarrow 3CaCO_3 + 2Na^+$	L +S
$NaAlO_2$ [Coagulant]	$NaAl_2O + 2H_2O \rightarrow Al(OH)_3 + NaOH$	–L

Now, following formulas can be utilized to find the lime and soda required for softening of hard water. Remember, all values should be in $CaCO_3$ equivalent. The substances, such as NaCl, Na_2SO_4, KCl, SiO_2, and Fe_2O_3, that do not consume lime and soda need not be considered.

Lime requirement for sofening (mg/l)

$$= \frac{74}{100}\left[\text{Temp.}\left\{Ca^{2+} + 2\times Mg^{2+}\right\} + \text{Perm.}\left\{Mg^{2+} + Fe^{2+}\, Al^{3+}\right\} + CO_2 + H^+ + HCO_3^- - NaAlO_2 \atop \text{all in tems of } CaCO_3 \text{ equivalents}\right]$$

Soda requirement for sofening (mg/l)

$$= \frac{106}{100}\left[\text{Perm.}\left\{Ca^{2+} + Mg^{2+} + Fe^{2+} \times Al^{3+}\right\} + H^+ - HCO_3^- \atop \text{all in tems of } CaCO_3 \text{ equivalents}\right]$$

Example 13.4

A water sample contains the following impurities: Ca^{2+} = *20 ppm,* Mg^{2+} = *18 ppm,* HCO_3^- = *180 ppm, and* SO_4^{2-} = *24 ppm. Calculate the amount of lime and soda needed for softening.*

Solution

$$CaCO_3 \text{ equivalent of } Ca^{2+} = \left[20 \times \frac{50}{20}\right] \text{ mg/l} = 50 \text{ ppm}$$

$$CaCO_3 \text{ equivalent of } Mg^{2+} = \left[18 \times \frac{50}{12}\right] \text{ mg/l} = 75 \text{ ppm}$$

$$CaCO_3 \text{ equivalent of } HCO_3^- = \left[180 \times \frac{50}{61}\right] \text{ mg/l} = 147.54 \text{ ppm}$$

$$\text{Lime requirement for sofening} = \frac{74}{100} [\text{Prem. } Mg^{2+} + HCO_3^-]$$

$$= \frac{74}{100} (75 + 147.54)$$

$$= 164.68 \text{ mg/l}$$

$$\text{Soda requirement for sofening} = \frac{106}{100} [\text{Prem. } \{Ca^{2+} + Mg^{2+}\} - HCO_3^-]$$

$$= \frac{106}{100} (50 + 75 - 147.54)$$

$$= -22.54 \text{ mg/l}$$

The value is negative. This implies that soda requirement is nil.

Example 13.5

Calculate the amount of lime and soda needed for softening 50000 l of water containing following salts per liter: $Ca(HCO_3)_2$ = 10 mg, $Mg(HCO_3)_2$ = 15 mg, $MgSO_4$ = 20 mg, $CaSO_4$ = 18 mg, $CaCl_2$ = 8 mg, and NaCl = 4 mg.

Solution

Lime requirement for sofening

$$= \frac{74}{100} [\text{Temp. } \{Ca^{2+} + 2 \times Mg^{2+}\} + \text{Perm. } (Mg^{2+})] \times \text{Volume of water}$$

$$= \frac{74}{100} \left[10 \times \frac{50}{81} + 2 \times 15 \times \frac{50}{73} + 20 \times \frac{50}{60}\right] \times 50000 \text{ mg}$$

$$= 1605430 \text{ mg} = 1.605 \text{ kg}$$

$$\text{Soda requirement for sofening} = \frac{106}{100} [\text{Temp. } \{Ca^{2+} + Mg^{2+}\} \times H^+)] \times \text{Volume of water}$$

$$= \frac{106}{100} \left[20 \times \frac{50}{60} + 18 \times \frac{50}{68} + 8 \times \frac{50}{55.5}\right] \times 50{,}000 \text{ mg}$$

$$= 1967360 \text{ mg} = 1.967 \text{ kg}$$

Example 13.6

Calculate the amount of lime and soda needed for softening 50000 l of water with the following analysis using 10 ppm of sodium aluminate as coagulant. Analysis result: $Ca^{2+} = 100$, $Mg^{2+} = 35$, $CO_2 = 50$, $HCO_3^- = 250$, $H^+ = 2$ ppm.

Solution

$$\text{Lime requirment for sofening (mg/l)} = \frac{74}{100}[Mg^{2+} + CO_2 + H^+ + HCO_3^- - NaAlO_2]$$

$$\text{Soda requirment for sofening (mg/l)} = \frac{106}{100}[Ca^{2+} + Mg^{2+} + H^+ - HCO_3^-]$$

Substitute the values after converting into $CaCO_3$ equivalent as per Example 13.5.

Zeolite/permutit process

Zeolite or permutit process involves a reversible exchange of ions between the stationary ion-exchange phase, i.e., zeolite, and the external mobile liquid phase. Zeolite is hydrated sodium aluminosilicate, $Na_2O{\cdot}Al_2O_3{\cdot}xSiO_2{\cdot}yH_2O$, where $x = 2$ to 10 and $y = 2$ to 6 [e.g., natralite, $Na_2O{\cdot}Al_2O_3{\cdot}3SiO_2{\cdot}2H_2O$; thomsonite $(Na_2O{\cdot}CaO)Al_2O_3{\cdot}2SiO_2{\cdot}2.5H_2O$]. Zeolites are the substances insoluble in water and can act as cation exchangers. These are commercially known as permutits and are basically classified as natural zeolites (derived from green sands by washing, heating, and then treating with NaOH) and synthetic zeolites (derived directly from a combination of silicate and sodium aluminate).

Process: In this process, raw water is introduced from the top of a steel tank packed with a thick layer of loosely packed zeolite over a layer of coarse sand and gravel (see Fig. 13.3). Zeolite can be represented by Na_2Z, where Z: $Al_2Si_2O_6{\cdot}xH_2O$. The following reactions take

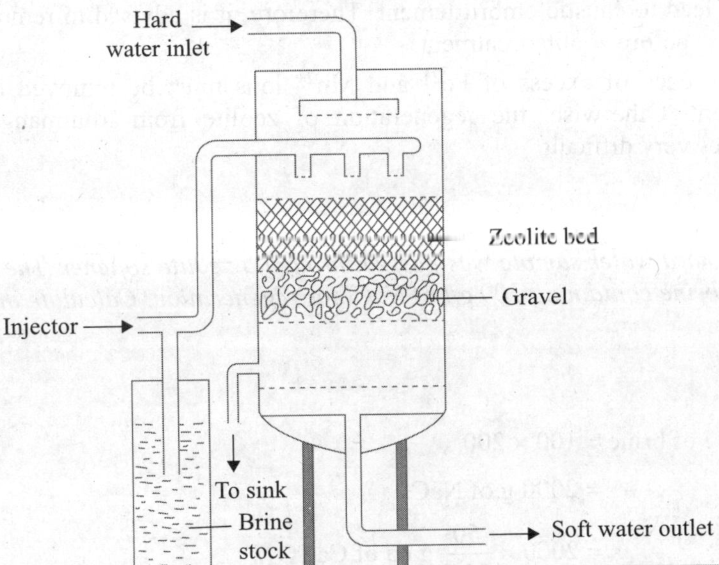

Fig. 13.3 Zeolite softener

place. The hardness causing ions are retained by zeolite as CaZ and MgZ, and the outgoing water remains rich in Na^+ ions.

$$Na_2Z + Ca(HCO_3)_2 \longrightarrow CaZ + 2NaHCO_3$$

$$Na_2Z + Mg(HCO_3)_2 \longrightarrow CaZ + 2NaHCO_3$$

$$Na_2Z + CaCl_2 \longrightarrow CaZ + 2NaCl$$

$$Na_2Z + MgCl_2 \longrightarrow MgZ + 2NaCl$$

$$Na_2Z + CaSO_4 \longrightarrow CaZ + 2Na_2SO_4$$

This process removes both temporary and permanent hardness. The advantage of the process is that after the exhaustion of the zeolite bed, the same can be regenerated by simply passing 10% solution of sodium chloride or brine through it.

$$CaZ/MgZ + 2NaCl \longrightarrow Na_2Z + CaCl_2/MgCl_2$$

Limitations

1. Suspended particulates present in raw water many at times clog the pores of the zeolite bed.
2. Softened water contains about 25% more dissolved solids as compared to LS process.
3. The presence of acid in water destroys zeolite; for this raw water must be neutralized before treatment.
4. Water should not be hot because zeolite tends to dissolve in it.
5. Anions are not removed in this process. Thus, bicarbonates present in hard water get converted into $NaHCO_3$ which goes to soft water. When such water is used in boiler, it may lead to caustic embrittlement. Therefore, it is advised to remove temporary hardness before zeolite treatment.
6. The presence of excess of Fe^{2+} and Mn^{2+} ions must be removed before zeolite treatment. Otherwise, the regeneration of zeolite from iron/manganese zeolite becomes very difficult.

Example 13.7

About 10000 l of hard water sample was passed through a zeolite softener. The softener then required 200 l of brine containing 100 g/l of NaCl for regeneration. Calculate the hardness of the water sample.

Solution

$$\text{NaCl in 200 l of brine} = 100 \times 200$$

$$= 2000 \text{ g of NaCl}$$

$$= 2000 \times \frac{50}{58.5} \text{ g eq of } CaCO_3$$

$$= 17094 \text{ g eq of } CaCO_3$$

10000 l of water contains 17094 g eq of $CaCO_3$

$$\text{Now, 1 l contains} = \frac{17094}{10000} \times 10^3$$

$$= 1709 \text{ mg}$$

Thus, hardness of water is 1709 mg/l.

Example 13.8

An exhausted zeolite softener was regenerated by passing 100 l of NaCl solution, having strength of 150 g/l of NaCl. Find the total volume of water that can be softened by the same softener, if hardness of water is 500 ppm.

Solution

$$100 \text{ l of NaCl} = 100 \times 150 \text{ g/l}$$

$$= 15000 \text{ g/l of NaCl}$$

$$= 15000 \times \frac{50}{58.5} \text{ g eq of } CaCO_3$$

$$= 1.29 \times 10^4 \text{ g eq of } CaCO_3$$

$$= 1.29 \times 10^7 \text{ mg eq of } CaCO_3$$

Now, 500 mg hardness is there in 1 l water. Therefore,

$$1.29 \times 10^7 \text{ mg hardness} = \frac{1.29 \times 10^7}{500} \text{ l of water}$$

$$= 25800 \text{ l of water}$$

Ion-exchange resin

Ion-exchange resin method involves a reversible exchange of ions between the stationary ion-exchange resin and the external mobile liquid phase. Ion-exchange resins are insoluble, cross-linked, long-chain organic polymers with a micro-porous structure. The functional groups attached to them are responsible for their ion-exchange properties. Resins having acidic functional groups are capable of exchanging their H^+ ions with the cations responsible for hardness, while those having basic functional groups are capable of exchanging their anions with other hardness-producing anions.

Note:

1. **Cation-exchange resins:** These are mainly styrene-divinyl benzene copolymers which upon sulfonation or carboxylation is capable of exchanging their hydrogen ions with hardness-producing ions of water (see Fig. 13.4). Dowex-50 and Amberlite IR-120 are examples of commercially available cation exchangers.

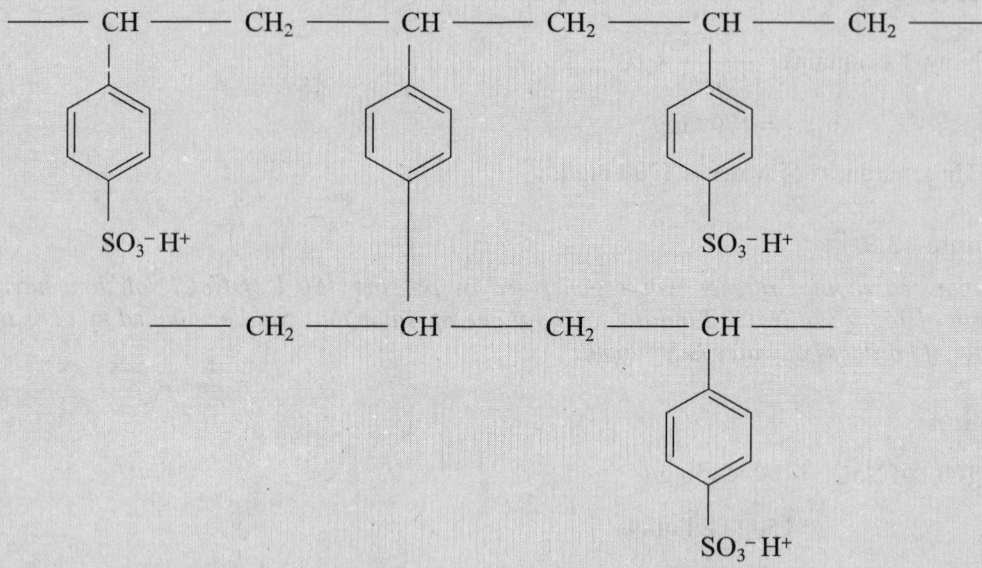

Fig. 13.4 Sulfonate form of cation exchanger

2. **Anion-exchange resins**: These are mainly styrene-divinyl benzene or amine–formaldehyde copolymers containing basic functional groups such as amino/quaternary ammonium/quaternary sulfonium/tertiary sulfonium groups as an integral part of the resin matrix (see Fig. 13.5). After treatment with NaOH, these resins become capable to exchange their OH^- ions with hardness imparting negative ions.

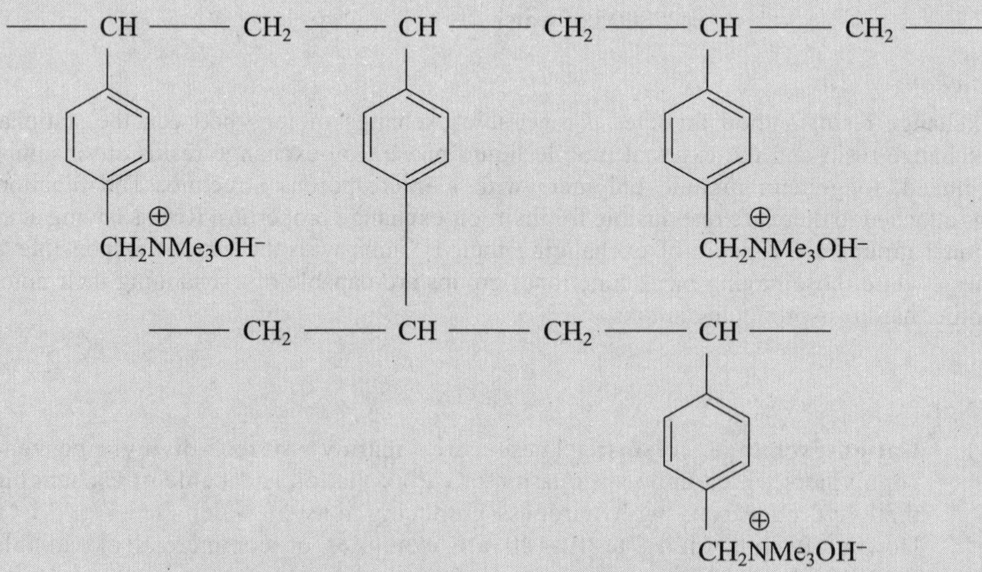

Fig. 13.5 Hydroxide form of anion exchanger

Process: The hard water is first passed through the cation-exchange column as shown in Fig. 13.6. The hardness-producing cations such as Ca^{2+} and Mg^{2+} are taken up by the resin and an equivalent amount of H^+ ions are released into water. Water is subsequently allowed to pass through the anion-exchange column where hardness-producing anions such as Cl^- and SO_4^{2-} are taken up by the resin and an equivalent quantity of OH^- ions are released by the resin into water. H^+ and OH^- ions released from the exchange columns combine to produce water. Finally, the water is allowed to pass through a degasifier. It is a tower which is kept at a higher temperature by using a steam jacket and at the same time low pressure is maintained by using a vacuum pump. A high temperature and low pressure reduces the dissolved gases such as CO_2 and O_2 in water. The reactions occurring in exchange columns are as follows:

$$xRSO_3^-H^+ + M^{x+} \longrightarrow (RSO_3)_x M^{x+} + xH^+$$

$$\underbrace{x[\overset{\oplus}{R}N(Me)_3]\,OH^-}_{\text{Solid}} + \underbrace{A^{x-}}_{\text{Solution}} \longrightarrow \underbrace{[RN(Me)_3]_x A^{x-}}_{\text{Solid}} + \underbrace{xOH^-}_{\text{Solution}}$$

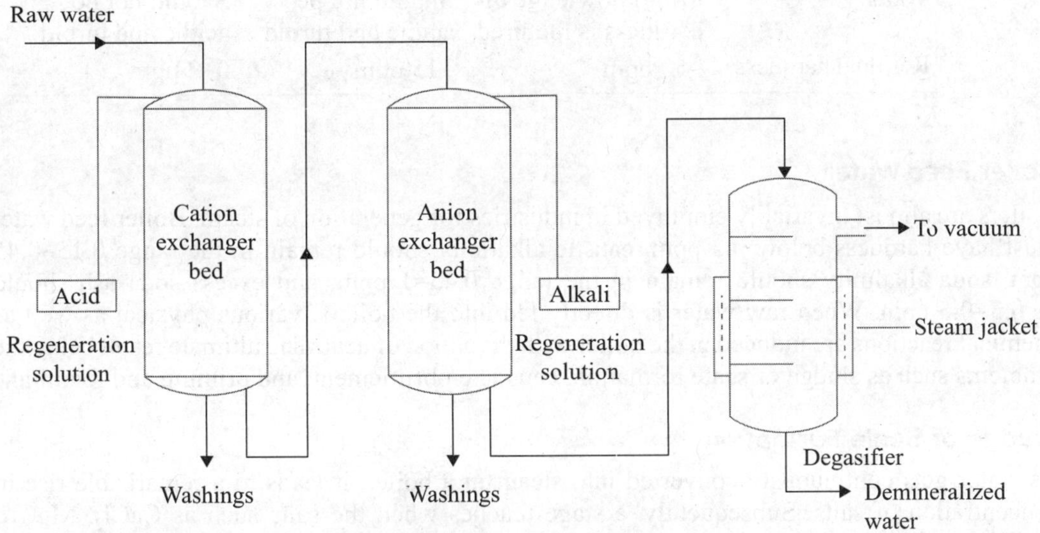

Fig. 13.6 Demineralization of water

The regeneration of exhausted cation-exchange column is possible by passing a solution of dil. HCl/dil. H_2SO_4, while the regeneration of anion-exchange column is possible by passing a solution of dil. NaOH. After the treatment, the columns are washed by de-ionized water.

Advantages

1. The process can be utilized to soften highly acidic/alkaline water.
2. It produces water of very low hardness, say up to a residual hardness 2 ppm.

Disadvantages

1. The equipment and chemicals are costly.
2. If turbidity is >10 ppm, then efficiency is reduced substantially. Therefore, pretreatment such as coagulation and filtration must be done before this treatment.

Note:

1. **Mixed bed deionizer:** This consists of a single ion-exchange column containing an intimate mixture of strongly acidic and basic ion exchangers. The operation principle is same as discussed above. To regenerate such a bed deionizer, at first it is necessary to separate the two resins. These resins are then regenerated separately. Such a mixed bed deionizer is convenient to use but comparatively more expensive.
2. **A comparative account of different processes**

Characteristic	Lime–Soda	Zeolite	Ion-exchange
Requirements	Lime, soda, coagulant	Zeolite	Cation- and anion-exchange resins
Exchange of ions	No exchange of ions	Exchange of only cations	Exchange of both cation and anion
Capital cost	Low	High	Very high
Water	Prior knowledge of hardness is required	Should not be acidic and turbid	Should not be acidic and turbid
Residual hardness	~50 ppm	~15 ppm	0–2 ppm

Boiler Feed Water

Boilers are almost invariably employed in industries for generation of steam. Boiler feed water must have hardness below 0.2 ppm, caustic alkalinity should remain in the range 0.15–0.45 ppm, soda alkalinity should remain in the range 0.45–1 ppm, and excess soda ash should be 0.3–0.5 ppm. When raw water is directly fed into the boilers, various physical as well as chemical reactions are induced in the boiler with the action of heat. The ultimate result being the problems such as sludge or scale formation, caustic embrittlement, and priming and foaming.

Sludge or Scale Formation

As water gets continuously converted into steam in a boiler, it leads to a remarkable rise in concentration of salts. Subsequently, a stage reaches when the salts such as $CaCl_2$, $MgCl_2$, $MgCO_3$, and $MgSO_4$, which have greater solubility in hot water than in cold water, change into a loose and slimy precipitate called *sludge*. It is formed at the relatively colder region of the boiler and gets deposited in the bends and tubes of the boiler where the flow rate of water is low.

If the precipitated matter forms a hard, adhering coating on the inner walls and at the bottom of the boiler, it is known as *scale*. These are formed on relatively hot surface of the boiler by salts such as $CaSO_4$, $CaCO_3$, $Mg(OH)_2$, and $Ca/MgSiO_3$, which have negative temperature coefficient of solubility. $CaCO_3$ is mainly formed by decomposition of corresponding bicarbonate and is a problem in low-pressure boilers. In high-pressure boilers, it is soluble because of the formation of $Ca(OH)_2 \cdot CaSO_4$ creates problem mainly in high-pressure boilers. $Mg(OH)_2$ is formed by the hydrolysis of dissolved magnesium salts. The reactions are as follows:

$$Ca(HCO_3)_2 \longrightarrow \underbrace{CaCO_3\downarrow}_{\text{Insoluble (cold)}} + CO_2 + H_2O$$

$$CaCO_3 + H_2O \longrightarrow \underbrace{Ca(OH)_2}_{\text{Soluble}} + CO_2$$

$$MgCl_2 + H_2O \longrightarrow \underbrace{Mg(OH)_2}_{\text{Scale}} + CO_2$$

Disadvantages

1. Excessive sludge settles in the region of poor water circulation such as pipe connections, plug openings and gauge-glass connections thereby causing chocking of the pipes.
2. Sludge and scale are poor conductors of heat and therefore prevent the effective transfer of heat to water.
3. In order to provide a steady supply of heat to water, excessive or overheating is often required which increases fuel consumption. In addition, overheating also softens and weakens the boiler material and causes distortion of boiler tube. It may also result in burning out of superheated metal plates and tubes and breakdown of joints making the boiler unsafe, particularly at a high pressure.
4. Scales often crack due to their uneven expansion allowing the water to come immediately in contact with overheated metal. This suddenly results in the formation of a large quantity of steam which in turn leads to excess pressure and then to explosion.

Prevention

1. Sludge formation can be prevented by *blow down operation.* It is nothing but the removal of concentrated water through an outlet at the bottom of boiler as the hardness becomes extremely high inside it. After blow down operation, *make-up* is done by the addition of fresh water.
2. It can be prevented by using softened water, i.e., treatment of water before entering into the boiler for reducing the concentration of hardness-producing ions. This process is also known as *external treatment*.
3. Scale formation can be prevented by internal treatment or conditioning that involves addition of some suitable chemicals to the boiler water either to precipitate the scale-forming impurities in the form of sludge so that they can be removed by blow down operation or to convert them into soluble compounds, which can remain in the dissolved form in water. Let us look into some of the *internal conditioning methods* which are commonly in practice.

   (a) **Phosphate conditioning**: It is widely used in high-pressure boilers. It involves addition of sodium phosphate that reacts with calcium or magnesium salts to form soft sludge of calcium or magnesium phosphate, which can be easily removed by blow down operation. The choice of phosphate salt depends on the alkalinity of water. Na_3PO_4 is used for alkaline water, whereas Na_2HPO_4 is used in highly alkaline water, and NaH_2PO_4 is used in acidic water.

   $$3MCl_2 + 2Na_3PO_4 \longrightarrow M_3(PO_4)_2\downarrow + 6NaCl$$

   $$3MSO_4 + 2Na_3PO_4 \longrightarrow M_3(PO_4)_2\downarrow + 3Na_2SO_4$$

   M : Ca^{2+}/Mg^{2+}

   (b) **Calgon conditioning**: Calgon is sodium hexametaphosphte, which can be used to convert $CaSO_4$ into a soluble complex.

   $$\underbrace{Na_2[Na_4(PO_3)_6]}_{\text{Calgon}} + CaSO_4 \longrightarrow \underbrace{Na_2[Ca_2(PO_3)_6]}_{\text{Soluble}} + 2Na_2SO_4$$

(c) **Carbonate conditioning**: In low-pressure boilers, sodium carbonate can be used to convert calcium sulfate into calcium carbonate, which precipitate as loose sludge and can be removed by the blow down process.

$$Na_2CO_3 + CaSO_4 \rightleftharpoons CaCO_3 + Na_2SO_4$$

(d) **Colloidal conditioning**: In low-pressure boilers, it is achieved by the addition of some organic substances such as kerosene, agar-agar, and tannin, which form a coating on scale-forming precipitates, thereby making them non-sticky and loose. The loose precipitates can be easily removed.

Removal of scale

Scale can be removed by either mechanical or chemical methods. In mechanical method, it is removed by using a scraper or a wire brush. It can also be removed by giving thermal shock, i.e., heating and subsequent sudden cooling. In chemical method, it is made soluble by adding suitable chemical. For example, $CaCO_3$ can be removed by adding ~10% HCl.

Difference between sludge and scale

Sludge	Scale
Sludge forms soft, loose, and slimy precipitate	Scales are hard deposits
These are non-adherent deposits	These firmly stick to the inner surface of the boiler
Formed by substances such as $CaCl_2$, $MgCl_2$, $MgCO_3$, and $MgSO_4$.	Formed by substances such as $CaSO_4$, $CaCO_3$, $Mg(OH)_2$, and $Ca/MgSiO_3$.
Formed on comparatively colder portion of the boiler.	Formed on comparatively hot portion of the boiler.
They decrease the efficiency of boiler, but are less dangerous	They decrease the efficiency of boiler and chances of explosion are also there
Can be removed by blow down operation	Cannot be removed by blow down operation

Caustic Embrittlement

Caustic embrittlement is the phenomenon in which the boiler material becomes brittle due to the accumulation of caustic substances. With evaporation of water, concentration of Na_2CO_3 increases in the boiler, which is used as a water softener in the lime–soda process. Sodium carbonate upon hydrolysis yields NaOH which makes the water alkaline. This alkaline water subsequently enters into the fine cracks present in the inner walls of the boiler by capillary action. The water evaporates inside the cracks and concentration of hydroxide keeps on increasing progressively. This concentrated alkali attacks the boiler material and the iron of the boiler dissolves as sodium ferrate. This causes embrittlement of boiler parts such as rivets, bends, and joints, which remain under stress. Sodium ferrate then decomposes to magnetite, regenerating caustic soda which further enhances corrosion. The reactions are as follows:

$$Na_2CO_3 + H_2O \longrightarrow 2NaOH + CO_2$$

$$Fe + NaOH \longrightarrow \underset{\text{Sodium ferroate}}{Na_2FeO_2}$$

$$3Na_2FeO_2 + 4H_2O \longrightarrow 6NaOH + \underset{\text{Megnetite}}{Fe_3O_4} + H_2$$

The whole process can also be explained by taking into consideration the following concentration cell. In the cell, iron surrounded by dilute NaOH behawwves anodic with respect to the iron that remains in contact with concentrated NaOH.

Fe (under stress) / Conc. NaOH/dil. NaOH / Fe (stress free)
Anode Cathode

Prevention

Caustic embrittlement can be prevented as follows:

1. By using sodium sulfate as softening reagent instead of sodium carbonate. It also prevents infiltration of caustic soda, i.e., NaOH, by blocking the hairline cracks.
2. By adding tannin or lignin to the boiler water which can block the hairline cracks and prevent infiltration of NaOH into these areas.

Priming and Foaming

Priming refers to the carryover of varying amounts of water droplets along with the steam. This results in a lowering of the energy efficiency of the steam and leads to the deposit of salt crystals on the super heaters and in the turbines. It is caused by improper construction of boiler, excessive ratings, and sudden fluctuations in steam demand. Sometimes the presence of impurities in the boiler water also aggravates priming. When this boiler water carryover is excessive, steam-carried solids produce deposits on the turbine blades. Priming is a common cause of high levels of boiler water carryover. These conditions often lead to super heater tube failures as well. Priming is related to the viscosity of the water and its tendency to foam. These properties are governed by alkalinity, the presence of certain organic substances, and by total salinity or total dissolved solids (TDS). The degree of priming also depends on the design of the boiler and its steaming rate.

Build-up of bubbles or froth on the surface of the boiler water is known as *foaming*. It is believed that the presence of some specific substances such as alkalies, oils, fats, greases, certain types of organic matter, and fine suspended solids are particularly responsible for foaming. The suspended solids which remain collected in the surface film surrounding a bubble make it tough. The steam bubble therefore resists breaking and builds up foam. It is believed that the finer the suspended particles, the greater is their collection in the bubble.

Prevention

1. Priming can be prevented by fitting mechanical steam purifiers, low water level in boiler, ensuring softening, and timely blow down operation.
2. Foaming can be avoided by adding antifoaming chemicals such as castor oil which act by counteracting the reduction in surface tension and by removing foaming agent, i.e., oil from boiler water by addition of sodium aluminate or aluminum sulfate.

Boiler Corrosion

Boiler corrosion is decay of boiler material by a chemical or electrochemical attack by its environment. It reduces the boiler life, causes leakage in joints and rivets, and thus increases the cost of maintenance. Corrosion is attributed to the presence of dissolved oxygen, carbon dioxide, and mineral acids which are generated by the hydrolysis of dissolved salts.

1. **By dissolved oxygen**: The concentration of oxygen in water is about 8 mg/l at the room temperature. At elevated temperature, dissolved oxygen attacks the boiler material, i.e., iron.

$$4Fe + 2H_2O + O_2 \longrightarrow 4Fe(OH)_2 \xrightarrow{O_2} \underbrace{2[Fe_2O_3 \cdot 2H_2O]}_{\text{Rust}}$$

2. **By carbon dioxide**: Carbon dioxide in water comes from atmosphere and decomposition of bicarbonates. CO_2 with water forms carbonic acid, which has a slow corrosive effect on the boiler material.
3. **By mineral acids**: Mineral acids are generated through the hydrolysis of dissolved acidic salts. The liberated acid reacts with iron of boiler to form ferrous hydroxide which subsequently gets converted into rust.

$$MgCl_2 + H_2O \longrightarrow Mg(OH)_2 \downarrow + 2HCl$$

$$2HCl + Fe \longrightarrow FeCl_2 + H_2 \uparrow$$

$$FeCl_2 + 2H_2O \longrightarrow \underbrace{Fe(OH)_2} + HCl$$

$$Fe(OH)_2 \xrightarrow{O_2} \underbrace{Fe_2O_3 \cdot 2H_2O}_{\text{Rust}}$$

Prevention

Following techniques are usually employed to prevent the boiler corrosion:

1. Dissolved oxygen can be removed by adding calculated quantity of hydrazine, sodium sulfite, or sodium sulfide. Hydrazine is the best choice as nitrogen formed in the process is harmless. It removes oxygen without increasing the load of dissolved solids in water. On the other hand, the other salts form sodium sulfate which decomposes to yield SO_2. In steam pipes, SO_2 appears as sulfurous acid, which is corrosive.

$$N_2H_4 + O_2 \longrightarrow N_2 + 2H_2O$$

$$2Na_2SO_3 + O_2 \longrightarrow 2Na_2SO_4$$

$$Na_2S + O_2 \longrightarrow Na_2SO_4$$

Note:

About 40% aqueous solution of hydrazine is used because pure hydrazine is an explosive inflammable liquid. In addition, excess of hydrazine is avoided as it may decompose to ammonia, which is capable of corroding some alloys such as brass used in condenser tubes.

$$3N_2H_4 \longrightarrow 4NH_3 + N_2$$

2. Dissolved oxygen can be removed by using mechanical de-aeration. In this process, water is sprayed over preheated perforated plates arranged in a stalk under low pressure.
3. CO_2 can be removed by mechanical de-aeration along with oxygen or by adding calculated quantity of ammonia solution which converts CO_2 into carbonate.

$$NH_4OH + CO_2 \longrightarrow (NH_4)_2CO_3 + H_2O$$

4. Boiler water is usually alkaline. However, a calculated quantity of alkali may be added from outside to neutralize excess acid present, if any.

Desalination of Brackish Water

Desalination is the process of removal of dissolved salts (mostly sodium chloride) from water. Water having dissolved salts with an average of 3.5% is known as brackish water. Such water is unfit for drinking purpose. For desalination, i.e., removal of these dissolved salts, methods such as electrodialysis and reverse osmosis can be used. Let us look into these methods in detail.

Electrodialysis

It is a process used to transport ions of salts from one solution to another through a semipermeable membrane, under the influence of an electric potential difference. The membranes are ion selective, i.e., allow the passage of either cation or anion through them. Cation-selective membrane allows the passage of cations only, while anion-selective membrane allows the passage of negative ions. This is achieved in a set up called electrodialysis cell (see Fig. 13.7). The electrodialysis unit consists of compartments formed by alternate cationic and anionic exchange membranes arranged in a row. The cathode is placed adjacent to the cation-exchange membrane, and the anode is placed adjacent to the anion-exchange membrane. Water is allowed to enter from the top. On application of electric field perpendicular to the direction of water flow, the ions of salts move toward oppositely charged electrodes. The membranes alternately allow positively or negatively charged ions to flow through (as shown in Fig. 13.7). This result in some compartments rich in ions while others free of ions.

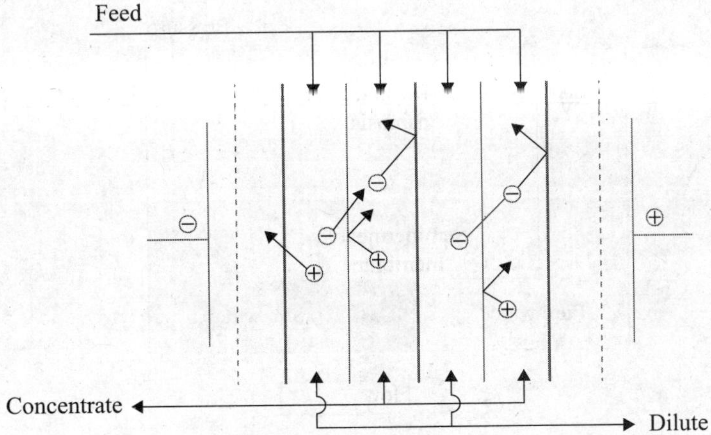

Fig. 13.7 Electrodialysis cell

Note:

1. Sometimes pretreatment is necessary before the electrodialysis. Suspended solids with a diameter ≥10 μm need to be removed as they may plug the pores of membrane. Certain substances such as large organic anions, colloids, iron oxides, and manganese oxide are able to neutralize a membrane. These disturb the selective effect of the membrane.
2. Pretreatment methods, which aid the prevention of the above effects, are active carbon filtration (for organic matter), flocculation (for colloids), and filtration techniques.
3. Cation-selective membranes consist of sulfonated polystyrene, while anion-selective membranes consist of polystyrene with quaternary ammonia.

Reverse Osmosis

When two solutions of unequal concentrations are kept separated by a semi-permeable membrane, solvent molecules spontaneously flow from dilute to concentrated solution through the membrane. This phenomenon is called osmosis. Osmotic pressure is the pressure required to be applied on the dilute solution side to stop this spontaneous flow of solvent molecules so as to maintain equilibrium with no net flow of solvent. The solvent flow can be reversed by applying hydrostatic pressure in excess of osmotic pressure on the concentrated solution side. This is the principle behind reverse osmosis (RO). In this method, pure solvent, i.e., water, is separated from contaminants (ionic/non-ionic) rather than contaminants from solvent. In practice, tap water is pushed through the semipermeable membrane so that pure water comes out leaving behind impurities (see Fig. 13.8). A RO membrane is capable of removing impurities and particles larger than 0.001 μm. The membrane is the heart of water purification system that is based on the principle of reverse osmosis. The most commonly used membranes are the CTA (cellulose triacetate), which is chlorine tolerant, and the thin film composite membrane (TFC/TFM), which is not chlorine tolerant.

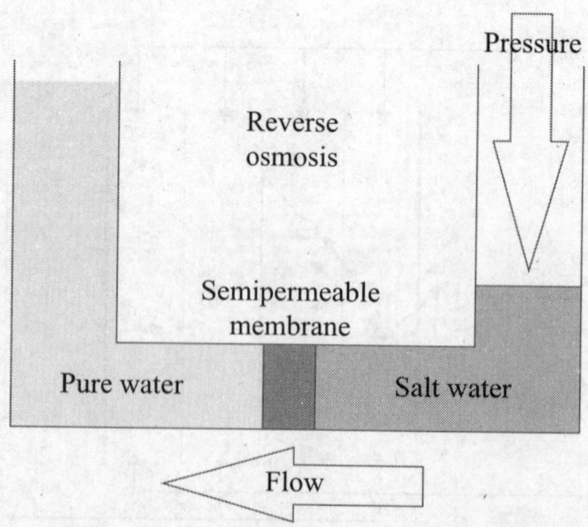

Fig. 13.8 Reverse osmosis (RO) cell

Note:

1. The main advantages of RO technique are as follows:
   (a) It can remove ionic and non-ionic inorganic stuffs and also colloidal and high molecular weight organic matters.
   (b) The life time of membrane is quite high, which is in average more than a year.
   (c) The maintenance cost is only the replacement of membrane.
2. Reverse osmosis is the final category of membrane filtration and is also known as *hyper-filtration/super-filtration*. It removes particles with size larger than 0.1 nm.

Water for Domestic Use

Drinking or potable water is fit for human consumption. The standard prescribed by ISI, USPH, and WHO for drinking water are summarized in Table 13.1.

Table 13.1 ISI, USPH, and WHO standards for drinking water

Sl. no.	Parameter	ISI (mg/l)	USPH (mg/l)	WHO (mg/l)
1	pH	6.5–8.5	6.0–8.5	6.5–9.2
2	Total hardness	300		500
3	Chlorides	250	250	
4	Sulfates	150	250	
5	Nitrates	45		
6	Fluoride	0.6–1.2	1.5	
7	TDS	500		500
8	Iron	0.3	<0.3	1.0
9	Zinc		5.5	
10	Lead	0.1	<0.05	0.1
11	Mercury	0.001	0.001	
12	Arsenic	0.05	0.05	0.05
	Cadmium		0.01	0.01
13	Chromium (Cr^{+6})	0.05		0.05
14	Polycyclic aromatic hydrocarbon (PAH)	–	0.002	–
15	Pesticides (total)	Absent	0.005	–
16	Phenol	0.001	0.001	0.002
17	COD	4.0	4.0	10.0
18	BOD		5.0	6.0

Water purification is the process by virtue of which undesirable chemicals, biological contaminants, suspended solids, and gases are removed from the contaminated water. The requirement is to produce water fit for a specific purpose. Mostly water is purified for human consumption, i.e., drinking water, but water purification may also be designed for a variety of other purposes including meeting the requirements of medical, pharmacological, chemical, and industrial applications. A few methods that are generally used are as follows: physical methods such as filtration and distillation, biological processes such as slow sand filtration, chemical processes such as chlorination and flocculation, and the use of electromagnetic radiation such as UV.

Chlorination

Chlorination of water is the process of adding chlorine to water so as to make it fit for human consumption as drinking water. Among halogens, chlorine is the most efficient disinfectant and is added to public water supplies to kill disease-causing pathogens such as bacteria, viruses, and protozoans that commonly grow in water supply reservoirs. Chlorine is a gas at atmospheric pressures but liquefies under pressure. The liquefied gas is transported and used as such. As a strong oxidizing agent, it kills pathogens via the oxidation of organic molecules. Chlorine and its hydrolysis product hypochlorous acid readily penetrate the negatively charged surface of pathogens and are able to disintegrate the lipids that compose the cell wall and react with intracellular enzymes and proteins, making them nonfunctional. As a result microorganisms either die or no longer able to multiply. Hypochlorous acid is a weak acid and dissociates at higher pH (above 6.5) to form H^+ and hypochlorite (OCl^-) ions which cannot combine with enzymes inside the cells of microorganisms. Thus, chlorine acts at its optimum efficiency at a pH below 6.5. In pH range 6.5–8.5, both these species HOCl and OCl^- remain present in water and are commonly referred to as free or available chlorine.

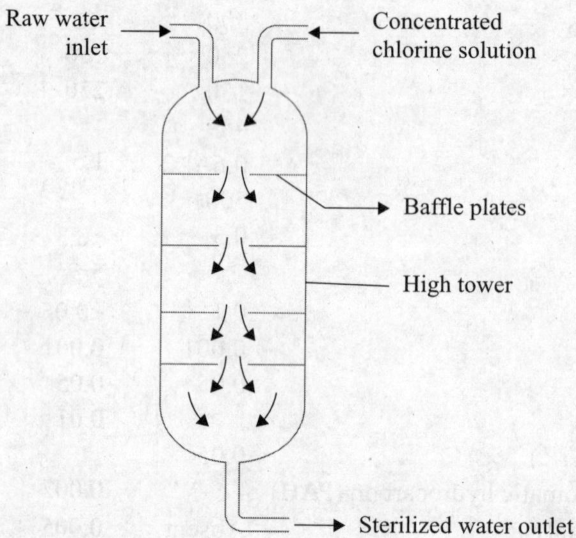

Fig. 13.9 Chlorinator

$$Cl_2 + H_2O \longrightarrow HOCl + HCl$$

$$HCl \xrightarrow{pH > 6.5} H^+ + \underbrace{OCl^-}_{\text{Inefficient}}$$

Break point chlorination

It is a process which involves addition of excess chlorine so as to oxidize organic matter, reducing substances and free ammonia in raw water and leaving behind free chlorine that imparts disinfecting action against disease-causing bacteria. The results of increasing dosage of chlorine can be depicted in the form of plot that has been plotted by taking residual chlorine as a function chlorine dosage applied (see Fig. 13.10).

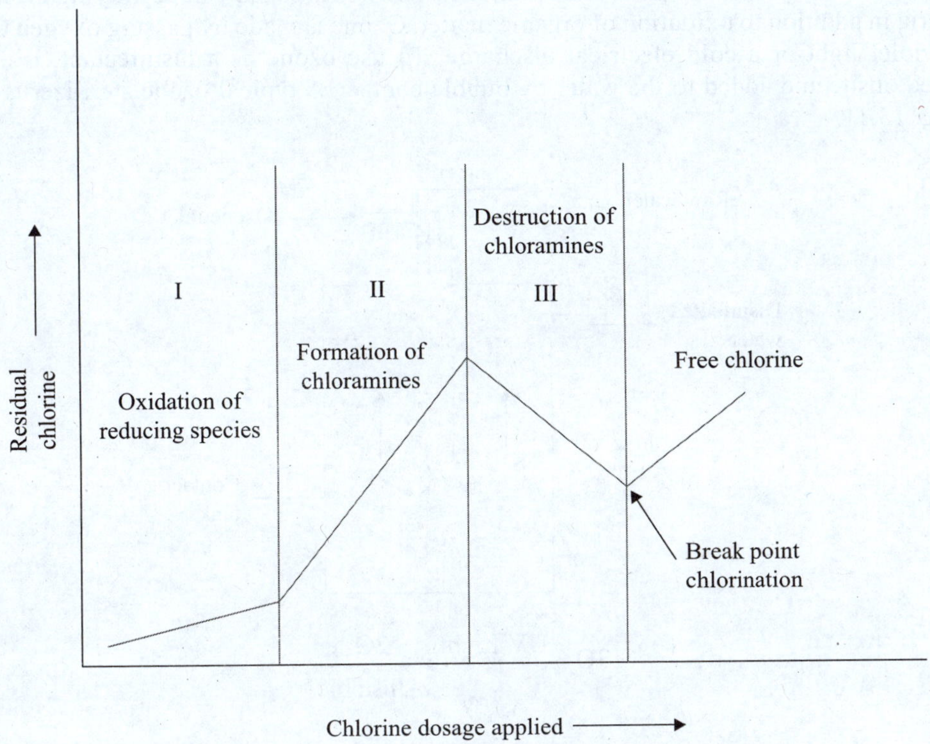

Fig. 13.10 Plot for residual chlorine vs chlorine dosage applied

In phase I, chlorine is reduced to chlorides by easily oxidizable stuff (H_2S, Fe^{2+}, Mn^{2+}, etc.). In phase II, Cl_2 is consumed by reaction with organic matter and if NH_3 is present, chloramine formation begins. In phase III, chloramines are broken down and converted into nitrogen gas, which leaves the system (break point). After this point, oxidant demand has been destroyed and disinfection can proceed. The addition of chlorine at the dip or break is called break point chlorination. At this point, free residual chlorine begins to appear.

Actually, tastes and odors of chlorine disappear at the break point. In addition, disinfection by free chlorine makes the water free from all pathogens.

Note:

1. Break point chlorination confirms the complete oxidation of reducing stuff, removal of color due to the presence of organic compound, complete destruction of pathogens, and also removal of odor and taste.
2. Over-chlorination after break point may lead to unpleasant odor and taste in water. This can be taken care of by filtering the water through a bed of molecular carbon. This can also be made effective by adding activated carbon directly or by adding a small quantity of SO_2, Na_2SO_3, or $Na_2S_2O_3$.

   $Cl_2 + Na_2SO_3 \longrightarrow NaSO_4 + 2HCl$

Ozonization

Ozone is an unstable molecule which readily breaks down, liberating one atom of oxygen. This nascent oxygen is very powerful oxidizing agent and is capable of destroying the harmful bacteria in addition to oxidation of organic matter. Ozone is made by passing oxygen through ultraviolet light or a cold electrical discharge. To use ozone as a disinfectant, it must be created onsite and added to the water by bubble contact. A typical ozone sterilizer is shown in Fig. 13.11.

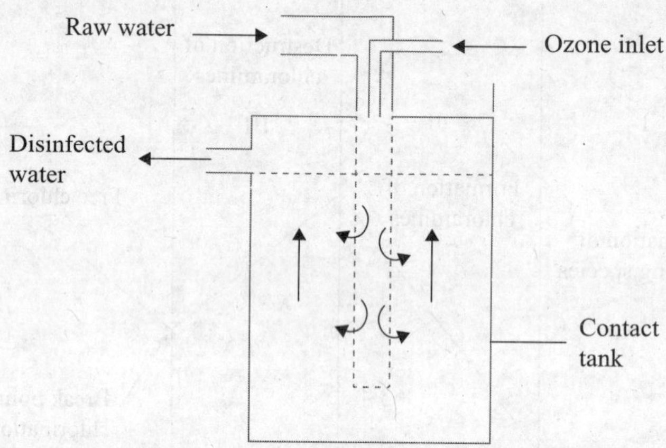

$$3O_2 \xrightarrow{\text{UV Light}} \underbrace{2O_3}_{\text{Unstable}} \rightarrow \underbrace{O_2 + [O]}_{\text{Nascent oxygen}}$$

Fig. 13.11 Ozone sterilizer

> **Note:**
>
> Some of the advantages of ozone include the removal of color, odor, and taste. Another advantage of ozone is that it leaves no residual disinfectant in the water. The only disadvantage is that the method is not economical one and is quite expensive.

UV Treatment

Ultraviolet (UV) light is very effective at inactivating cysts, in low turbidity water. UV light's disinfection effectiveness decreases as turbidity increases. This is due to the absorption, scattering, and shadowing caused by the suspended solids. The main disadvantage of the use of UV radiation is that it leaves no residual disinfectant in water, as is the case in ozone treatment. Therefore, it is sometimes necessary to add a residual disinfectant after the primary disinfection process. This is often done through the addition of chloramines, as a primary disinfectant. When used in this manner, chloramines provide an effective residual disinfectant with very few of the negative effects of chlorination.

Analysis of Water

Alkalinity

Alkalinity of water is a measure of its ability to neutralize acid. It is attributed to the presence of hydroxides, carbonates, and bicarbonates. The presence of some other bases such as borates, silicates, and phosphates can also contribute to the total alkalinity, though to a small extent. Depending on the ions responsible for alkalinity, it can be classified as *caustic alkalinity* (due to the presence of OH^- and CO_3^{2-} ions) and *bicarbonate alkalinity* (due to the presence of HCO_3^- ions).

Principle

Alkalinity can be estimated by titration against a standard acid, using phenolphthalein and methyl orange as indicators. The titration up to phenolphthalein end point marks the complete neutralization of hydroxide ions and CO_3^{2-} up to HCO_3^- ions, i.e., half neutralization of carbonate ions—resulting in completion of reactions 1 and 2. On the other hand, the titration up to methyl orange end point indicates the completion of reactions 1, 2, and 3, i.e., complete neutralization of OH^-, CO_3^{2-}, and HCO_3^- ions. Thus, acid used after the phenolphthalein end point corresponds to the one-half of the normal carbonate and all bicarbonates.

$$\left.\begin{array}{l}\left.\begin{array}{l} OH^- + H^+ \longrightarrow H_2O \text{ — } 1 \\ CO_3^{2-} + H^+ \longrightarrow HCO_3^- \text{ — } 2 \end{array}\right] P \\ HCO_3^- + H^+ \longrightarrow H_2O + CO_2 \text{ — } 3 \end{array}\right] M$$

From the measurement of both end points, i.e., phenolphthalein and methyl orange end points, it is possible to find corresponding alkalinity.

Procedure

Step 1: Pipette out a specific volume of water sample into a conical vessel and add 2–3 drops of phenolphthalein indicator.

Step 2: Titrate the sample with a standard acid by adding the same from a burette till the end point which can be marked by the disappearance of pink color.

Step 3: Continue titration by adding the same standard acid after adding 2–3 drops of methyl orange.

Step 4: Titrate till the end point, which can be marked from the appearance of red color.

Calculation

Let the volume and normality of acid used be V_1 and N_1, respectively. Again, let V_2 be the volume of water sample taken in the conical flask and N_2 be the normality. Now,

$$\underbrace{N_1V_1}_{\text{Acid}} = \underbrace{N_2V_2}_{\text{Water}}$$

$$\text{or} \quad N_2 = \frac{N_1V_1}{V_2} = x\,(\text{say})$$

$$\begin{aligned}\text{Strength in terms of calcium carbonate equivalent} &= N_2 \times \text{Equivalent weight of } CaCO_3 \\ &= x \times 50 \text{ g/l} \\ &= x \times 50 \times 1000 \text{ mg/l or ppm}\end{aligned}$$

Thus, Phenolphthalein alkalinity $(P) = x \times 50 \times 1000$ ppm

In a very similar manner, methyl orange alkalinity (M) can be calculated and can be expressed as

$$M = y \times 50 \times 1000 \text{ ppm}$$

where y is the normality.

Note:

Alkalinity due to individual ions can also be calculated from the values of P and M. Let us look into the following cases:

Case I ($P = 0$): Here the volume of acid used until the phenolphthalein end point is zero. This can happen only when both OH^- and CO_3^{2-} are absent. The alkalinity here is attributed only to HCO_3^- ions present and can be determined by using the methyl orange indicator.

Bicarbonate alkalinity in terms of $CaCO_3$ equivalent = M

Now, the concentration of bicarbonate ions is given by

$$[HCO_3^-] = \frac{M \times 61}{50} \text{ mg/l}$$

Case II ($P = \frac{1}{2} M$): This can happen when only CO_3^{2-} ions are present. Half of the CO_3^{2-} present will be neutralized in the presence of phenolphthalein and the other half, i.e., from bicarbonate to carbon dioxide and water, will be neutralized in the presence of methyl orange. Here carbonate alkalinity will be $2P$ or M.

Now, the concentration of carbonate ions is given by

$$[CO_3^{2-}] = \frac{2P \times 30}{50} \text{ mg/l}$$

Case III ($P < \frac{1}{2} M$): This can happen when HCO_3^- ions are present in addition to CO_3^{2-} ions. The acid used till phenolphthalein end point corresponds to neutralization of half of CO_3^{2-}. Further titration using methyl orange corresponds to neutralization of HCO_3^- obtained from CO_3^{2-} and HCO_3^- originally present in the reaction mixture. Here alkalinity due to CO_3^{2-} is $2P$ and alkalinity due to HCO_3^- is "$M - 2P$."

Now, the concentration of carbonate ions is given by

$$[CO_3^{2-}] = \frac{2P \times 30}{50} \text{ mg/l}$$

And, the concentration of bicarbonate ions is given by

$$[HCO_3^-] = \frac{(M - 2P) \times 61}{50} \text{ mg/l}$$

Case IV ($P > \frac{1}{2} M$): This can happen due to the presence of OH^- ions in addition to CO_3^{2-} ions. The acid used till phenolphthalein end point corresponds to half neutralization of CO_3^{2-} and complete neutralization of OH^-. Further titration using methyl orange corresponds to neutralization of HCO_3^-. Here alkalinity due to CO_3^{2-} is $2(M - P)$ and alkalinity due to OH^- is "$M - 2(M - P)$."

Now, the concentration of carbonate ions is given by

$$[HCO_3^-] = \frac{2(M - P) \times 30}{50} \text{ mg/l}$$

Now, the concentration of carbonate ions is given by

$$[OH^-] = \frac{2(P - M) \times 17}{50} \text{ mg/l}$$

Case V ($P = M$): This can happen when only OH^- ions are present. Here alkalinity due to OH^- ions is $P = M$.

Now, the concentration of carbonate ions is given by

$$[OH^-] = \frac{P \times 17}{50} \text{ mg/l}$$

Example 13.9

About 50 ml of a water sample required 10 ml of N/50 sulfuric acid using methyl orange as indicator but failed to develop any color with phenolphthalein. What is the type of alkalinity present?

Solution

As $P = 0$, only HCO_3^- ions are present.

$$\underbrace{N_1V_1}_{\text{Acid}} = \underbrace{N_2V_2}_{\text{Water}}$$

$$\text{or} \quad N_2 = \frac{\frac{1}{50} \times 50}{50} = \frac{1}{250}$$

Strength in terms of calcium carbonate equivalent = $N_2 \times$ Equivalent weight of $CaCO_3$

$$= \frac{1}{250} \times 50 \text{ g/l}$$

$$= 200 \text{ mg/l or ppm}$$

Thus, alkalinity due to bicarbonate is 200 ppm.

Example 13.10

100 ml water sample on titration with N/50 sulfuric acid consumed 20 ml up to phenolphthalein end point. On continuation of titration in presence of methyl orange 40 ml of acid is consumed. Find the alkalinity of water sample in terms of $CaCO_3$. Also comment on the type of alkalinity.

Solution

$$\underbrace{N_1V_1}_{\text{Acid}} = \underbrace{N_2V_2}_{\text{Water}}$$

$$\text{or} \quad N_2 = \frac{\frac{1}{50} \times 20}{100} = \frac{1}{250}$$

Strength in terms of calcium carbonate equivalent = $N_2 \times$ Equivalent weight of $CaCO_3$

$$= \frac{1}{250} \times 50 \text{ g/l}$$

$$= 200 \text{ mg/l or ppm}$$

Thus, Phenolphthalein alkalinity (P) = 200 ppm

Similarly, the alkalinity of methyl orange can be calculated as follows:

$$\underbrace{N_1V_1}_{\text{Acid}} = \underbrace{N_2V_2}_{\text{Water}}$$

$$\text{or} \quad N_2 = \frac{\frac{1}{50} \times 40}{50} = 0.008$$

Strength in terms of calcium carbonate equivalent = N_2 × Equivalent weight of $CaCO_3$

= 0.008 × 50 g/l

= 400 mg/l or ppm

Thus, Methyl orange alkalinity (M) = 400 ppm

As $P = ½ M$, only carbonate ions are present.

Thus, Carbonate alkalinity = 400 mg/l

Hardness

Principle

Estimation of total hardness in a given water sample is carried out by titrating against EDTA solution (solution of disodium salt of ethylenediaminetetraacetic acid) using suitable indicators in different mediums. Both Ca and Mg content are determined by titrating against EDTA solution using Eriochrome Black-T (EBT) indicator in the presence of buffer solution of pH 10. EBT behaves as a weak acid which dissociates as follows:

$$\underbrace{H_2In^-}_{\text{Wine red}} + H_2O \rightleftharpoons \underbrace{HIn^{2-}}_{\text{Blue}} + H_3O^+$$

The acid and the conjugate base have different colors. For metal ion detection, the pH is maintained on the basic side so that HIn^{2-} form predominates in the absence of metal ions. EBT forms complexes with calcium and magnesium ions which are wine red. When EDTA solution is added, both Ca and Mg–EDTA complexes are formed, which are comparatively stable displacing indicator in the form of HIn^{2-}. Until the equivalence point in a titration, the indicator complexes with the excess metal ion so that the solution is wine red. With the slight excess of EDTA, the solution turns blue as a consequence of the reaction buffered at pH 10. The reaction is as follows:

$$\underbrace{MIn^-}_{\text{Wine red}} + \underbrace{H_2Y^{2-}}_{\text{EDTA}} \xrightleftharpoons{pH = 10} \underbrace{HIn^{2-}}_{\text{Light Blue}} + MY^{2-}$$

This method determines the total hardness. For the determination of permanent hardness, temporary hardness is removed by boiling. After the removal of precipitate by filteration, permanent hardness in the filtrate is determined by titration with EDTA as before.

Procedure

1. Pipette out 50 ml of standard hard water that contains 1 mg of $CaCO_3$ per ml into a 250 ml conical flask. Add 10 ml of buffer and 2–3 drops of indicator.
2. Titrate the solution against EDTA solution until wine-red color changes to blue. Let the volume consumed be V_1 ml.

3. Follow the same procedure by taking 50 ml of unknown water sample. Let the volume of EDTA consumed be V_2 ml.

Calculation

Standardization of EDTA

V_1 ml EDTA = 50 ml of standard hard water

= 50 mg of $CaCO_3$

Now, 1 ml EDTA $= \frac{50}{V_1}$ mg of $CaCO_3$ equivalent hardness

Calculation of total hardness

50 of unknown hard water sample = V_2 ml of EDTA

$= V_2 \times \frac{50}{V_1}$ mg of $CaCO_3$ equivalent

Now, 1000 ml contains $= V_2 \times \frac{50}{V_1} \times \frac{1}{50} \times 1000$

$= 1000 \times \frac{V_2}{V_1}$ mg/l

Example 13.11

About 0.25 g of calcium carbonate was dissolved in HCl and the solution was made up to one liter. About 100 ml of hard water sample required 30 ml of same EDTA solution during titration. After boiling 100 ml of the same water, cooling, filtering, and then titration required 10 ml of EDTA solution. Find temporary and permanent hardness.

Solution

1 ml of standard hard water contains 0.25 mg $CaCO_3$

Now, 30 ml of EDTA = 100 ml of standard hard water

$= 100 \times 0.25$

= 25 mg $CaCO_3$

or 1 ml EDTA = 25/30 = 0.83 mg $CaCO_3$

Total hardness

100 ml of unknown hard water sample = 30 ml of EDTA

$= 30 \times 0.83$

= 24.9 mg $CaCO_3$

Now, 1000 ml of sample contains $= \frac{24.9}{100} \times 1000 = 249$ mg of $CaCO_3$ eq. hardness

Thus, Total hardness = 249 mg/l or ppm

Permanent hardness

100 ml of boiled hard water sample = 10 ml of EDTA

$= 10 \times 0.83$

= 8.3 mg $CaCO_3$

Now, 1000 ml of sample contains $= \frac{8.3}{100} \times 1000 = 83$ mg of $CaCO_3$ eq. hardness

Thus, Permanent hardness = 83 mg/l or ppm

Temporary hardness

Temporary hardness = 249 – 83 = 166 mg/l

Dissolved Oxygen

Dissolved oxygen (DO) can be determined by Winkler's method, which is nothing but iodometric titration. In this method, the dissolved oxygen present in water is utilized to oxidize KI so as to liberate equivalent amount of iodine. The iodine liberated is estimated by titrating against standard hypo solution using starch as indicator. Again as the molecular oxygen itself cannot react with KI, an oxygen carrier such as manganese hydroxide is used. The basic reactions involved are as follows.

$$MnSO_4 + KOH \longrightarrow Mn(OH)_2 + K_2SO_4$$

$$\underbrace{Mn(OH)_2}_{\text{Oxygen carrier}} + O_2 \longrightarrow \underbrace{Mn(OH)_2}_{\text{Basic manganic oxide}}$$

$$MnO(OH)_2 + H_2SO_4 \longrightarrow MnSO_4 + 2H_2O + \underbrace{O}_{\text{Nascent oxygen}}$$

$$2KI + H_2SO_4 + [O] \longrightarrow K_2SO_4 + H_2O_4 + I_2$$

$$I_2 + Na_2S_2O_3 \longrightarrow Na_2S_2O_4 + 2NaI$$

Note:

Sometimes water contains nitrates, sulfites, etc., which themselves can liberate oxygen from KI. In such cases to avoid interference, sodium azide is used in alkaline medium.

Procedure

Step 1: Collect a specific amount of water sample (say 250 ml) in a stoppered bottle avoiding any contact with air.

Step 2: Add 2 ml each of manganous sulfate and alkaline KI solution to the sample. Stopper the bottle, shake it properly, and allow the precipitate to settle down.

Step 3: Add sulfuric acid to dissolve the precipitate.

Step 4: Pipette a specific amount of the yellow solution and titrate against standard sodium thiosulfate (hypo) solution using starch as indicator. The end point of titration can be noticed by just disappearance of blue color.

Calculation

Let the volume and normality of thiosulfate solution used be V_1 and N_1, respectively. Again, let V_2 be the volume of water sample taken in the conical flask and N_2 be the normality. Now,

or $N_2 = \frac{V_1 V_1}{V_2} = x(\text{say})$

Now, I_2 liberated is equivalent to the amount of oxygen present in the original sample of water. Thus,

Strength of dissolved oxygen = $x \times$ Equivalent weight of oxygen

$$= x \times 8 \text{ g/l}$$

$$= x \times 8 \times 1000 \text{ mg/l or ppm}$$

Chloride

Chloride can be estimated by titrating with standard silver nitrate solution using K_2CrO_4 as indicator. This method is known as Mohr's method. K_{sp} of AgCl is less than that of Ag_2CrO_4. Therefore, as long as Cl^- ions remain in the solution, AgCl continue to precipitate. After complete removal of chloride ions, even addition of a drop of $AgNO_3$ leads to precipitation of Ag_2CrO_4, which is red in color.

Procedure

Step 1: Pipette out 100 ml of water sample into a conical flask. Add 1 ml of K_2CrO_4 indicator.

Step 2: Titrate with *N*/50 $AgNO_3$. Initially, white precipitate is obtained. The end point is noticed by the formation of permanent reddish-brown color.

Calculation

$$\underbrace{N_1 V_1}_{\text{Chloride}} = \underbrace{N_2 V_2}_{\text{AgNO}_3}$$

or $$100 \times N_1 = \frac{V_2}{50}$$

or $$N_1 = \frac{V_2}{5000}$$

Strength of chloride ions = $N_1 \times 35.5$ g/l

$$= N_1 \times 35.5 \times 1000 \text{ mg/l}$$

$$= \frac{V_2}{5000} \times 35.5 \times 1000 \text{ mg/l}$$

$$= 7.1\, V_2 \text{ mg/l}$$

Fluoride

The recommended limit of fluoride in drinking water is 1 mg/l. Fluoride in high concentration causes dental fluorosis. The anthropogenic sources of fluoride in water are effluents of steel, aluminum and electroplating industries, effluents of pesticides and fertilizers industries, agricultural washings, etc. The popular method for the estimation of fluoride is colorimetric method or *SPADNS Zirconium Lake method.*

Principle

The fluoride present in water reacts with zirconium SPADNS [sodium 2-(parasulfophenylazo)-1,8-dihydroxy-3,6-napthalene disulfonate] solution to form a colored lake, which is influenced by acidity of the reaction mixture. By increasing the proportion of acid in the reagent, the reaction can be made practically instantaneously.

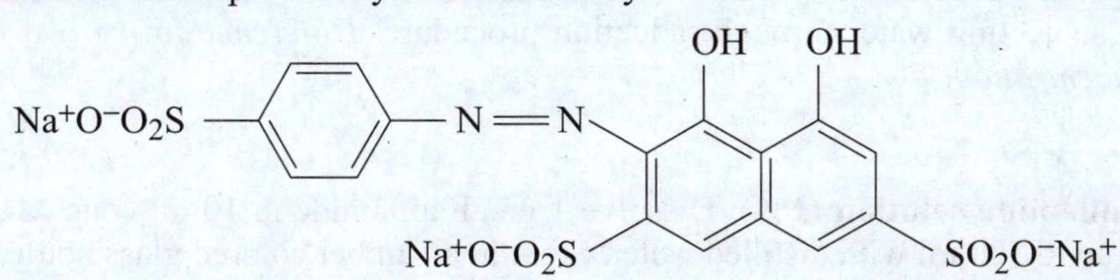

SPADNS

Reagents

1. **Zirconyl acid SPADNS reagent**: About 958 mg of SPADNS is dissolved in distilled water and diluted to 500 ml. About 133 mg of zirconyl chloride octahydrate ($ZrCl_2 \cdot 8H_2O$) is dissolved in 25 ml distilled water and 350 ml of conc. HCl is added and diluted to 500 ml with distilled water. Equal volumes of SPADNS solution and zirconyl acid are mixed.
2. **Standard fluoride solution**: About 0.221 g of anhydrous sodium fluoride is dissolved in water and diluted up to one liter. The stock solution is further diluted to get standard solution having 10 mg/l of fluoride.

Procedure

1. For the preparation of calibration curve, 1, 2, 3, 4, 5, and 6 ml of the stock solution is pipetted out into 50 ml flasks. About 10 ml of zirconyl-SPADNS reagent and one drop of $NaAsO_2$ are added to each of the solutions. $NaAsO_2$ is used to remove residual chlorine which interferes with the test. It is diluted up to the mark and mixed well. The absorbance of the solutions are measured at 570 nm against a reagent blank and a calibration plot is constructed by plotting absorbance against concentrations.
2. A suitable aliquot of water sample is taken and the steps are repeated. Using the calibration curve, the concentration of fluoride is calculated in milligram per liter.

Nitrate

Nitrate is a form of nitrogen, which is found in several different forms such as ammonia, nitrates, and nitrites in terrestrial and aquatic ecosystems. It is an essential plant nutrient. However, in excess amounts it can cause significant water quality problems. Nitrate in excess amounts accelerates eutrophication, causing natural aging of aquatic ecosystem. This affects dissolved oxygen, temperature, and other indicators. Excess nitrates can cause hypoxia (low levels of dissolved oxygen) and can become toxic to even warm-blooded animals at higher concentrations $\geq$10 mg/l. The natural level nitrate in surface water is typically low (less than 1 mg/l). Sources of nitrate include wastewater treatment plants, runoff from fertilized cropland, failing on-site septic systems, runoff from animal manure storage areas, and industrial discharges that contain corrosion inhibitors. It can be estimated by colorimetric method.

Principle

The method of nitrite determination depends on reaction with sulfanilamide to form a diazonium compound, which is then coupled with *N*-(1-napthyl)-ethylenediamine to form an azo dye. The absorbance of the dye is measured spectrophotometrically at 540 nm. The nitrate in the water is reduced, almost quantitatively to nitrite, by passing through a column containing copperized cadmium granules. The nitrite thus produced is determined by making azo dye as mentioned above. Here nitrite originally present in the sample passes through the column without change. Therefore, this method estimates total nitrate plus nitrite. Nitrite can be measured by the same process without subjecting water through reduction procedure. *Difference in the two values gives nitrate concentration.*

Reagents

1. **Sulfanilamide solution (1%)**: Dissolve 1 g sulfanilamide in 10 ml conc. HCl and make up to 100 ml with distilled water. Store in an amber colored glass bottle.

2. **N-(1-Naphthyl)ethylenediamine dihydrochloride (1%):** Dissolve 0.1 g in 100 ml double distilled water and store in an amber colored glass bottle.
3. **Nitrite standard solution**: Dissolve 0.069 g anhydrous sodium nitrite (dried at 100°C for 1 h) in 100 ml distilled water in a volumetric flask. The solution contains 10 mμ or 10000 μmol NO_2-N/l. Prepare some standard solutions such as 1, 2, 3 mμ/l from the stock solution by proper dilution.

Procedure

1. For the preparation of calibration curve, take 25 ml each of the working standard solutions in glass tubes. To each tube add 1 ml of sulfanilamide, mix, and keep for 4 min. Add 1 ml of NEDA solution and allow the reaction to proceed for 10 min after mixing the contents. The absorbance of the solutions is measured at 540 nm against a reagent blank and a calibration plot is constructed by plotting absorbance as a function of concentration.
2. Suitable aliquot of water sample is taken and the steps are repeated. Using the calibration curve, the concentration of nitrite is calculated in milligram per liter.

Sulfate

Sulfate can be estimated by gravimetric method. Sulfate is precipitated as $BaSO_4$ by the addition of $BaCl_2$ in HCl medium. The precipitation is carried out near the boiling temperature and after a period of digestion, the precipitate is filtered, washed with water until free from chloride, ignited, and weighed as $BaSO_4$.

Wastewater or Sewage Treatment

The primary objective is to remove the contaminants from water so that the treated water can meet the acceptable quality standards. The quality standards usually depend on whether water will be reused or discharged into a receiving stream. Advance wastewater treatment involves physical, chemical, or biological processes or their various combinations depending on the impurities to be removed.

Primary Treatment

It comprises pretreatment and sedimentation step.

1. **Pretreatment**: It removes the large and coarse solids and inorganic suspended matter. The waste water is passed through the mesh screens to remove gravels, coarse solids, silt, etc. For removal of large suspended floating matter, the waste water is passed through bar screens.
2. **Sedimentation**: Suspended inorganic and organic solids are removed by settling process using continuous flow type sedimentation tanks. Often chemical treatment/conditioning is done for rapid and complete removal of suspended matter. Coagulants such as alum, lime, and ferrous sulfate are commonly used for the purpose. The material that floats in the settling basin is collectively called grease which can be removed by skimming.

Secondary Treatment

Secondary treatment is also known as biological treatment. It is an aeration process in the presence of microbial population so as to oxidize organic matter present in waste water. It is achieved by the use of biological film system and activated sludge system. In the process, carbon of organic matter is converted to CO_2, nitrogen is converted to $NH_4^+ + NH_3$, which is finally converted into nitrites and nitrates. The dissolved bases present in waste water subsequently form respective nitrites and nitrates.

$$\underset{(C,\,H,\,O,\,N)}{\text{Organic Waste}} + O_2 \longrightarrow CO_2 + H_2O + \underbrace{NH_4^+ + NH_3}_{\displaystyle\downarrow \atop \displaystyle NO_3^- + NO_2^-}$$

Biological film system (trickling filter)

In this process, the wastewater is brought in contact with a mixed microbial population in the form of a film of slime attached to the surface of a solid support medium. Trickling filter consists of a rock bed made of furnace slag/crushed rock/anthracite coal/broken bricks with loose packing so as to facilitate circulation of air. The bed is covered with a biological slime consisting of bacteria. The water is sprayed over the bed. As it trickles down, the microorganisms utilize oxygen to decompose the dissolved organic load. Purified water is removed at the bottom. A typical trickling filter is shown in Fig. 13.12.

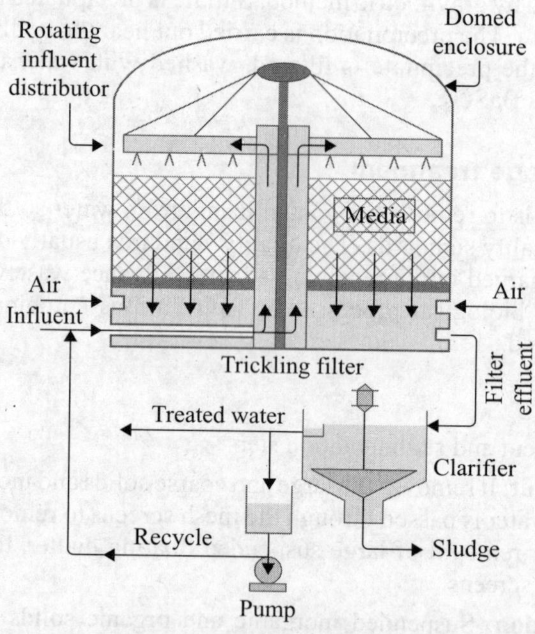

Fig. 13.12 Trickling filter

Activated sludge process

The principle is to provide excess oxygen or air through the wastewater containing aerobes. Here aeration is carried out in the presence of a part of the sludge taken from the previous oxidation process which is known as activated sludge. The name is so because it contains numerous microorganisms. In the process, the wastewater is mixed with proper quantity of activated sludge. This mixture is then sent to the aeration tank in which the mixture is continuously aerated and agitated. Here oxidation of organic matter takes place. Then the effluent is sent to sedimentation tank. In the tank sludge is deposited and the clean water is drawn off. For seeding fresh batch of sewage, a part of the settled sludge is sent back, while the rest is disposed of. The block diagram of a typical activated sludge plant is shown in Fig. 13.13.

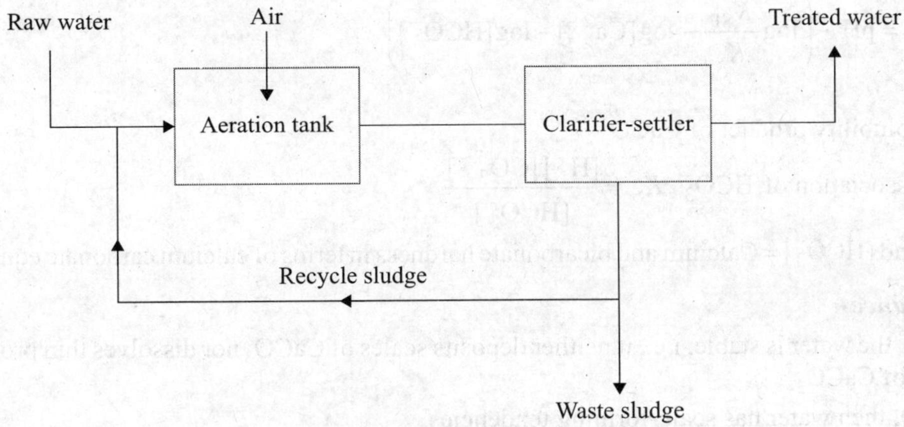

Fig. 13.13 Activated sludge treatment

Advanced waste treatment

The effluent from secondary treatment plant still contains typically 20–30 mg/l of BOD. In addition, it may also contain significant amount of plant nutrients, dissolved solids, and pathogens. Wastewater from industries may also contain heavy metals and other contaminants. Depending on the contaminants, different advanced methods are used in the treatment. For example, to remove dissolved solids, methods such as distillation, electrodialysis and reverse osmosis can be used; to remove pathogens, disinfection is brought about by chlorination, ozonization, or UV treatment; to remove dissolved solids, specific coagulants are used. Some of these methods have been separately discussed in the chapter.

The complete wastewater treatment process can be schematically shown in Fig. 13.14.

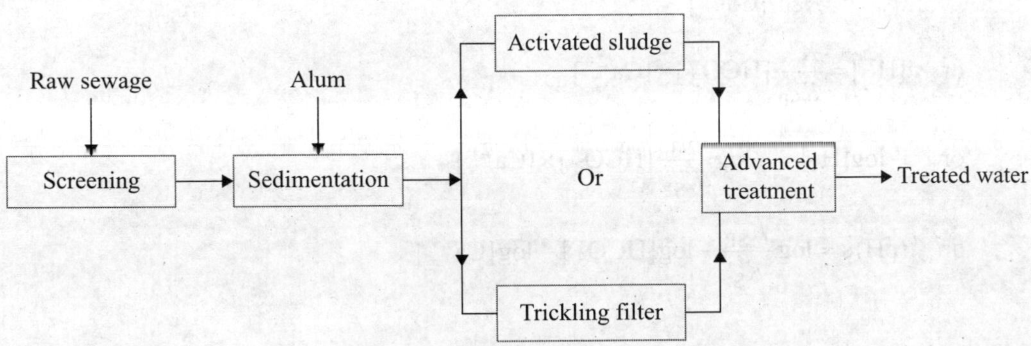

Fig. 13.14 Wastewater treatment process

Cooling Water

One important use of water is as coolant. The requirements for cooling water are that it should be non-corrosive, non-scaling, and non-staining. The scaling or corrosive nature of water is expressed in terms of *Langelier index* (LI) or $CaCO_3$ *saturation index*. It is the difference between the actual pH and the saturation pH, i.e., (pH)s.

$$LI = pH - (pH)s$$

$$\text{or} \quad LI = pH - \left(\log \frac{K_{SP}}{K_S} - \log[Ca^{2+}] - \log[HCO_3^-] \right)$$

where

K_{SP} = Solubility product of $CaCO_3$

K_S = Dissociation of HCO_3^-, $K_S = \dfrac{[H^+][CO_3^{2-}]}{[HCO_3^-]}$

$[Ca^{2+}]$ and $[HCO_3^-]$ = Calcium and bicarbonate hardness in terms of calcium carbonate equivalent

Significance

If LI = 0, the water is stable, i.e., it neither deposits scales of $CaCO_3$ nor dissolves thin protective coating of $CaCO_3$.

If LI > 0, then water has scale-forming tendencies.

If LI < 0, then water has corrosive tendencies.

Note:

1. For cooling, normally water LI is adjusted between 0.6 and 1.0.
2. Let us see how to find (pH)s:

$$K_S = \frac{[H^+][CO_3^{2-}]}{[HCO_3^-]}$$

$$\text{or} \quad [H^+] = \frac{K_S\,[HCO_3^-]}{[CO_3^{2-}]}$$

$$\text{or} \quad [H^+] = \frac{K_S\,[HCO_3^-]}{K_{SP}/[Ca^{2+}]}$$

$$\text{or} \quad [H^+] = \frac{K_S}{K_{SP}}[HCO_3^-] \times [Ca^{2+}]$$

$$\text{or} \quad -\log[H^+] = -\log \frac{K_S}{K_{SP}}[HCO_3^-] \times [Ca^{2+}]$$

$$\text{or} \quad (pH)s = \log \frac{K_{SP}}{K_S} - \log[HCO_3^-] - \log[Ca^{2+}]$$

QUESTIONS

1. What are the major sources of water?
2. What is coagulant? Provide two examples.
3. Provide the name of the dissolved gases in water that cause corrosion.

4. What is the principle of lime–soda process of water softening?
5. Why coagulants are not used in hot lime–soda process?
6. How can one recover exhausted ion-exchange resins?
7. How can you remove temporary hardness?
8. Differentiate between scale and sludge.
9. What is the role of buffer during titration of hard water with EDTA solution?
10. Explain desalination.
11. Why water softened by zeolite process is unfit for boiler use?
12. The presence of CO_2 in boiler feed water is avoided. Explain.
13. Why hardness is expressed in terms of calcium carbonate equivalent?
14. Which salts are responsible for temporary and permanent hardness of water?
15. What is the advantage of hot lime–soda process over cold lime–soda process?
16. What is break point chlorination?
17. Why calgon conditioning is better than phosphate conditioning?
18. Calgon treatment prevents scale formation in boilers. Explain.
19. What is meant by RO as applied to water chemistry?
20. Why magnesium bicarbonate does require double amount of lime for softening?
21. What do you mean by priming and foaming?
22. What are Zeolites? Explain with one example.
23. How can you prevent caustic embrittlement?
24. Why is hot LS process better than cold LS process?
25. Why water softened by lime–soda process is not suitable for boilers?
26. Name two coagulants used in lime–soda process.
27. What is the harmful effect of silica in water?
28. Explain why alkalinity of water cannot be due to the simultaneous presence of OH^-, CO_3^{2-}, and HCO_3^-.
29. What causes alkalinity in natural water?
30. What do you mean by blow down process?
31. What is the role of coagulant in lime–soda process?
32. Explain why hard water consumes a lot of soap.
33. Explain carbonate conditioning.
34. Why use of coagulant is not recommended in hot lime–soda process?
35. What is the main advantage of reverse osmosis over ion-exchange process?
36. Give specifications of boiler feed water.
37. What do you mean by mixed bed demineralization?
38. Why boiled water is not always suitable for drinking purpose?
39. Discuss the ion-exchange process of softening hard water.
40. Explain the regeneration process of exhausted ion-exchange resin.
41. How is boiler scale formed? Discuss the disadvantages of scale formation.

42. What is caustic embrittlement?
43. Zeolite softened water avoids caustic embrittlement in boilers. Expalin.
44. Differentiate between scale and sludge.
45. What is the advantage of break point chlorination?
46. Discuss the alkalinity of water in condition $P < \frac{1}{2} M$.
47. What is phosphate conditioning?
48. Why water softened by zeolite process is unfit for use in boilers?
49. What are primary and secondary treatments of wastewater?
50. Explain secondary treatment of wastewater in detail.
51. What is activated sludge process?
52. Explain biological treatment of wastewater using trickling filter.
53. Provide the principle of Winkler's method for the determination of dissolved oxygen.
54. Explain in detail the determination of nitrate in water.
55. What is Langelier index?
56. Discuss the significance of Langelier index.

NUMERICAL PROBLEMS

1. A water sample on analysis gives the following data: $Ca(HCO_3)_2$ = 40 ppm, $Mg(HCO_3)_2$ = 35 ppm, $MgSO_4$= 30 ppm, $CaSO_4$ = 32 ppm, $CaCl_2$ = 25 ppm, and NaCl = 10 ppm. Find the lime and soda (each of 90% purity) required per liter for treatment. Also find carbonate and non-carbonate hardness.
2. How many grams of ferrous sulfate dissolved per liter of water will impart hardness of 150 ppm of hardness?
3. About 100 ml of water sample has a hardness equivalent to 15 ml of 0.05 N $MgSO_4$. What is the hardness in ppm?
4. Standard hard water contains 20 g of $CaCO_3$ per liter. About 10 ml of this required 12.5 ml of EDTA solution, and 100 ml of the sample water required 15 ml EDTA solution. The same sample after boiling required 10 ml of EDTA solution. Calculate the temporary hardness of the given sample of water in terms of ppm.
5. If 10 ml of a sample of hard water consumes 15 ml of 0.01 M EDTA, find the hardness of water sample.
6. About 100 ml of water sample consumed 20 ml of 0.01 M EDTA before boiling and 12 ml of the same EDTA after boiling. Find temporary and permanent hardness.
7. Calculate the quantity of lime (74% pure) and soda (90% pure) required for softening 5000 l of water containing 75 mg/l of Mg $(HCO_3)_2$, 200 mg/l of $CaCl_2$, 120 mg/l of $MgSO_4$, and 150 mg/l of $Ca(NO_3)_2$.
8. Find the amount of lime and soda required to soften 10,000 l of water having 25 ppm temporary hardness and 10 ppm permanent hardness.
9. Find the amount of lime and soda required to soften 10000 l of water having 4.86 ppm $Ca(HCO_3)_2$, 7.3 ppm of $Mg(HCO_3)_2$, 6.5 ppm $CaSO_4$, 5.0 ppm $MgCl_2$, 9.0 ppm $MgSO_4$, 3.5 ppm SiO_2, and 5.0 ppm NaCl.

10. A water sample on analysis gives the following data: $Ca^{2+} = 20$ ppm, $Mg^{2+} = 25$ ppm, $K^{+} = 10$ ppm, $HCO_3^- = 120$ ppm, and $CO_2 = 20$ ppm. Find the lime (90%) and soda (85%) required to soften 25000 l of water sample.
11. A zeolite softener is 80% exhausted when 10000 l of hard water was passed through it. The softener required 150 l of NaCl solution of strength 50 g/l of solution. Find the hardness of water.
12. About 100 ml of a raw water sample on titration with N/50 sulfuric acid required 12 ml of the acid up to phenolphthalein end point and 15 ml of the acid up to methyl orange end point. Find the type and magnitude of alkalinity present in the water sample.
13. A water sample is not alkaline to phenolphthalein. However, 100 ml of the sample water on titration with N/50 HCl required 15 ml to obtain the end point using methyl orange as indicator. What are the types and the amounts of alkalinity present in the sample?
14. About 100 ml of a sample of water required 10 ml of N/50 H_2SO_4 using methyl orange as indicator but did not give any coloration with phenolphthalein. What type of alkalinity is present? Express the same in mg/l.
15. About 100 ml of water sample on titration with N/50 sulfuric acid using phenolphthalein as indicator gave the end point when 10 ml acid was run down. Another lot of 100 ml of the sample also required 10 ml of the acid to obtain methyl orange end point. What type of alkalinity is present in the sample? Express this in ppm.

CHAPTER

14 Fuel and Combustion

Chapter Outline

- Classification of Fuel
- Calorific Values
- Classification of Coal
- Analysis of Coal
- Carbonization
- Petroleum
- Cracking
- Synthetic Petrol
- Refining of Petroleum
- Reforming
- Fuel for IC Engines
- Aviation Fuel
- Biodiesel
- Power Alcohol
- Gaseous Fuel
- Non-conventional Sources

In recent years man's dependence on energy has increased substantially due to technological advances and rapid industrial growth. Nowadays energy chiefly comes from fossil fuels, i.e., from wood, charcoal, coal, kerosene, petrol, diesel, CNG, LPG, etc. However, these sources will not last forever. Therefore, proper understanding is necessary for their proper utilization and conservation for future use. This chapter will try to develop basic understanding of different types of fuels including the alternatives of fossil fuel.

Fuels and Their Cassification

Fuel is a combustible substance containing carbon as the main constituent, which on combustion gives a large amount of heat that can be used economically for domestic and industrial purposes. Fuels can be classified as per their occurrence as ***natural or primary fuels***. These are available in nature as such; for example, wood, peat, coal, petroleum, and natural gas. ***Artificial or secondary fuels*** are those which are prepared from the primary fuels, for example, charcoal, coke, kerosene oil, diesel oil, petrol, coal gas, oil gas, producer gas, and blast furnace gas. In each category, fuels can be further classified on the basis of their physical state of aggregation as solid, liquid, and gas (see Fig. 14.1).

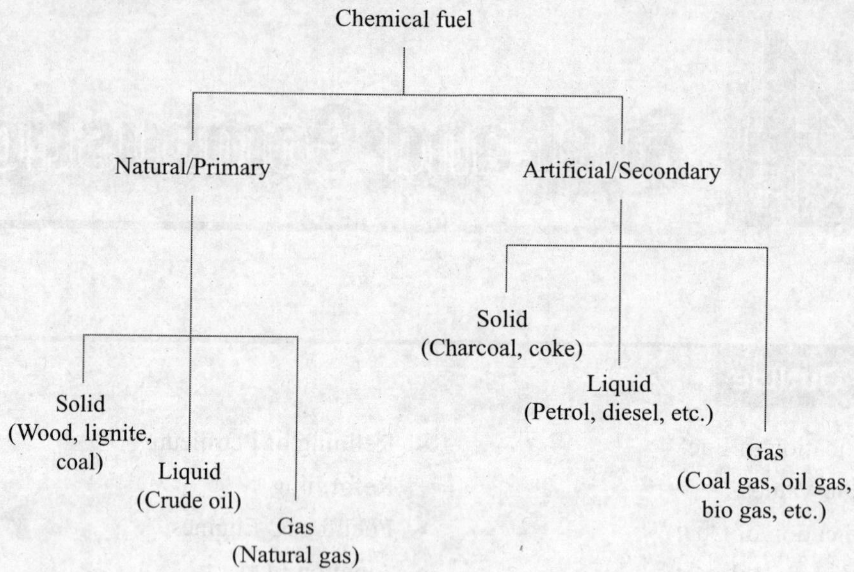

Fig. 14.1 Classification of fuel

Characteristics of a Good Fuel

1. **Calorific value:** Calorific value of a fuel is the heat liberated during the complete combustion of unit mass/volume of a fuel in excess oxygen. A good fuel has a high calorific value, because the amount of heat liberated and temperature attained thereby depend on it.
2. **Ignition temperature:** Ignition temperature is the lowest temperature to which the fuel must be pre-heated so that it starts burning smoothly. Low ignition temperature is dangerous for storage and transport of fuel, because it can cause fire hazards. On the other hand, high ignition temperature causes difficulty in igniting the fuel; however, the fuel is safe during storage, handling, and transport. Therefore, an ideal fuel should have "moderate" ignition temperature.
3. **Moisture content:** The moisture content of a fuel reduces its heating value. Therefore, fuel should have low moisture content.
4. **Non-combustible matter content:** The non-combustible matter also reduces the heating value, besides additional cost of storage, handling, and disposal of the waste products produced which mostly appears as ash/clinker after combustion. Hence, a fuel should have low content of non-combustible matter.
5. **Velocity/rate of combustion:** If the rate of combustion is low, then the required temperature may not be achieved because a part of the heat liberated may get radiated, instead of utilized in raising the temperature. On the other hand, too high rate may lead to explosion. Therefore, moderate rate of combustion is required.
6. **Product characteristics:** Fuel on combustion should not give rise to objectionable products such as harmful gases like CO and SO_2.
7. **Cost:** A good fuel should be readily available in bulk at a cheap rate.

8. **Easy to transport:** Fuel must be easy to handle, store, and transport at a low cost.
9. **Combustion should be easily controllable:** Combustion of the fuel should be easy to start or stop as and when required.
10. **Should not undergo spontaneous combustion:** Spontaneous ignition can cause fire hazards.
11. **Efficiency:** Should burn in air efficiently, without much smoke.

Relative Merits of Different Types of Fuels

Characteristics	Solid	Liquid	Gas
Cost	Cheap	More costly	Most costly
Storage	Easy	Can be stored in closed containers	Can be stored in leakproof large storage tanks
Risk of Hazard	Least	Relatively more	Very high
Handling cost	High	Low	Low
Combustion rate	Slow	Quick	Very rapid
Combustion control	Not easy	Can be controlled	Possible by controlling air supply
Ash	Ash disposal is a problem	No ash problem	No ash problem
Smoke	Invariably produced	High carbon/aromatic fuels may produce smoke	Not produced
Calorific value	Least	Higher	Highest
Use in IC engines	Not possible	Possible	Possible
Thermal efficiency	Least	Higher	Highest

Caloric Value

Calorific value of a fuel is the heat liberated during the complete combustion of unit mass/volume of a fuel in excess oxygen.

Units of heat

1. **Calorie:** It is the amount of heat required to raise the temperature of one gram of water through one degree centigrade. Kilocalorie is the larger unit which is equal to 1000 calories.
2. **British Thermal Unit (B.Th.U.):** It is defined as the quantity of heat required to raise the temperature of one pound of water through one degree Fahrenheit. This is the English system unit. Thus,

   1 B.Th.U = 252 cal = 0.252 kcal or 1 kcal = 3.968 B.Th.U.

3. **Centigrade Heat Unit (C.H.U.):** It is the quantity of heat required to raise the temperature of one pound of water through one degree centigrade. Thus,

   1 kcal = 3.968 B.Th.U. = 2.2 C.H.U.

Note:

1. **Higher or gross calorific value**: Hydrogen is found in all fuels. During experimental determination of calorific value of hydrogen-containing fuel, the hydrogen is converted into steam. Now, if the products of combustion are condensed to the room temperature, the latent heat of condensation of steam also gets included in the measured heat, which is then called *higher or gross calorific value* (HCV). Thus, HCV may be defined as the total amount of heat produced during the complete combustion of unit mass/volume of the fuel and the products of combustion have been cooled to room temperature.
2. **Lower or net calorific value:** In the actual use of any fuel, the water vapor and moisture escape as such along with hot combustion gases. Hence, a lesser amount of heat is available. Thus, net or lower calorific value (LCV) may be defined as the total amount of heat produced during the complete combustion of unit mass/volume of the fuel and the products are permitted to escape.

   $$\begin{aligned} \text{LCV} &= \text{HCV} - \text{Latent heat of water vapor} \\ &= \text{HCV} - \text{Mass of hydrogen} \times 9 \times \text{Latent heat of steam [as 1 part by mass of hydrogen produces 9 parts by mass of water]} \end{aligned}$$

   Latent heat of steam is 587 kcal/kg or 1060 B.Th.U./lb of water vapor formed at room temperature (i.e., 15°C).
3. **Units of calorific value:** For solid/liquid fuel, the calorific value is, generally, expressed in calorie/gram (cal/g) or kilocalorie/kg (kcal/kg) or British thermal unit/lb (B.Th.U/lb). In case of gaseous fuels, the units used are kilocalorie/cubic meter (kcal/m^3) or B.Th.U./cubic feet (B.Th.U./ft^3).

   $$\begin{cases} 1 \text{ kcal/kg} = 1.8 \text{ B.Th.U./lb} \\ 1 \text{ kcal/m}^3 = 0.1077 \text{ B.Th.U./ft}^3 \\ 1 \text{ B.Th.U./ft}^3 = 9.3 \text{ kcal/m}^3 \end{cases}$$

Determination of Calorific Value

Bomb calorimeter

Bomb calorimeter is used to find the calorific value of solid and non-volatile liquid fuels. A typical bomb calorimeter is shown in Fig. 14.2. It consists of a strong cylindrical stainless steel bomb which can withstand a pressure of at least 50 atm. Here the combustion of fuel is made to take place. A screw cap is used to make it a perfect gas-tight seal. The cap is fitted with two stainless steel electrodes and an oxygen inlet valve. To one of the electrodes, a small ring is attached. In this ring a nickel or stainless steel crucible can be supported. The bomb is placed in a copper calorimeter, which is surrounded by air and water jacket to prevent heat loss due to radiation. The calorimeter is provided with an electrically operated stirrer and Beckmann's thermometer, which can accurately read temperature difference up to 1/100th of degree.

Principle: A known mass of fuel is allowed to completely burn. The quantity of heat produced is absorbed in water and measured.

Working: A known mass (about 0.5–1.0 g) of the given fuel is taken in a clean crucible. The crucible is then supported over the ring. A fine magnesium wire, touching the fuel sample,

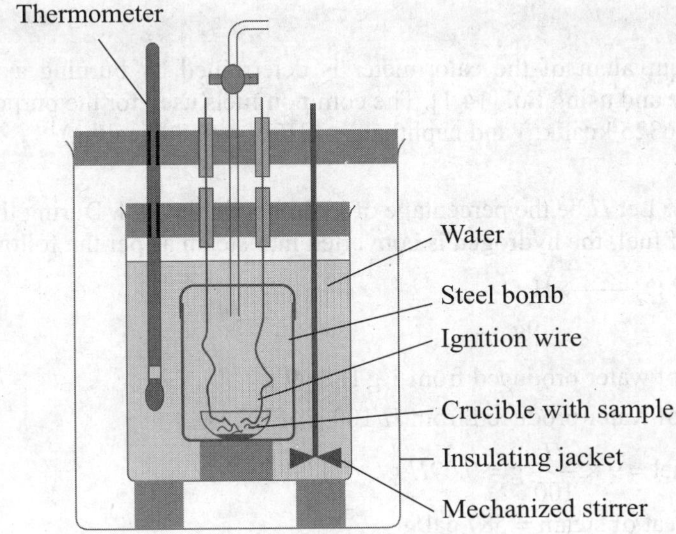

Fig. 14.2 Bomb calorimeter

is then stretched across the electrodes. The bomb lid is tightly screwed and kept filled with oxygen at ~25 atm pressure. The bomb is then lowered into the calorimeter, containing a known weight of water. The initial temperature of the water is noted after stirring. The electrodes are then connected to 6–12 V battery source so as to complete the circuit. The sample burns and heat is liberated. Uniform stirring of water is continued and the maximum temperature attained is recorded.

Calculation:

Let x = Weight (in grams) of fuel sample taken in a crucible

W = Weight of water in the calorimeter

w = Water equivalent (in grams) of calorimeter, thermometer, bomb, etc.

t_1°C = Initial temperature of the water in calorimeter

t_2°C = Final temperature of water in calorimeter

L = Higher calorific value in fuel (in cal/g)

Now, Heat liberated by burning of fuel = xL

Again, Heat absorbed by water = $W \times S \times (t_2 - t_1)$

Heat absorbed by apparatus = $w \times (t_2 - t_1)$

Here specific heat of water is 1 cal/g°C

Total heat absorbed = $(W + w)\,(t_2 - t_1)$

But, Heat absorbed by fuel = Heat absorbed by water, apparatus, etc.

or $xL = (W + w)(t_2 - t_1)$

or $$\text{HCV of fuel } (L) = \frac{(W + w)\,(t_2 - t_1)}{x} \text{ cal/g} \qquad [14.1]$$

Note:
The water equivalent of the calorimeter is determined by burning a fuel of known calorific value and using Eq. [14.1]. The common fuels used for the purpose are benzoic acid (HCV = 6325 kcal/kg) and naphthalene (HCV = 9688 kcal/kg).

Evaluation of LCV: Let H be the percentage of hydrogen in the fuel. During the determination of calorific value of fuel, the hydrogen is converted into steam as per the following equation:

$$\underset{1\text{g}}{H_2} + 1/2\ O_2 \longrightarrow \underset{9\text{g}}{H_2O}$$

Weight of water produced from 1 g H_2 = 9 g

Weight of water produced from H/100 g of H_2, i.e.,

$$1 \text{ g of fuel} = 9 \times \frac{H}{100} \text{ g} = 0.09H \text{ g}$$

Again, Latent heat of steam = 587 cal/g

Now, Heat taken by water in forming steam = $0.09H \times 587$ cal/g

LCV = HCV – Latent heat of water formed

$= (L - 0.09H \times 587)$ cal/g (or kcal/kg)

Corrections: To get more accurate results, the following corrections are applied:

1. **Fuse wire connection (t_F):** Correction has to be made for the heat liberated, by ignition of the fuse wire used.
2. **Acid correction (t_A):** Fuels containing "S" and "N" are oxidized, under high pressure and temperature of ignition, to H_2SO_4 and HNO_3, respectively, in the calorimeter.

$$S + 2H + 2O_2 \rightarrow H_2SO_4 + \text{Heat}$$

$$2N + 2H + 3O_2 \rightarrow 2HNO_3 + \text{Heat}$$

Formation of these acids is exothermic and therefore the measured heat also includes the heat given out during the acid formation. However, the heat liberated is not obtained during the practical use of coal as the gases so formed pass off into the atmosphere. The amount of nitric acid is analyzed from washings of bomb by titration. H_2SO_4 alone is determined by precipitation as $BaSO_4$. The correction for 1 mg of S is 2.25 cal; however, for 1 ml of N/10 HNO_3 formed, it is 1.43 cal.

3. **Cooling correction (t_C):** If time taken to cool the water in calorimeter from the maximum to room temperature is "t" minutes and the rate of cooling is dt°C/min, then the cooling correction of "d$t \times t$" is to be added to the rise in temperature.

After the corrections, Eq. [14.1] becomes

$$\text{HCV of fuel } (L) = \frac{(W + w)\,(t_2 - t_1 + t_C) - (t_A + t_F)}{x} \text{ cal/g} \qquad [14.2]$$

Boy's gas calorimeter

Boy's gas calorimeter is the standard apparatus used for measuring the calorific values of gaseous and volatile liquid fuels. The apparatus consists of a suitable gas burner in which a known volume of gas can be burnt at a known pressure and at a uniform rate of 3–4 l/min.

Around the burner, there is a combustion chamber, which has copper tubing coiled inside as well as outside it. Water at a constant rate is passed through the coil. Water enters at the top through the outer coil and then through the inner coil it goes up and exit at the top. The attached thermometers give the temperature of incoming and outgoing water. The circulated water takes away practically whole of the heat of burner and the steam formed during combustion gets condensed as water, which can then be collected. The whole assembly is kept enclosed in an insulated chamber.

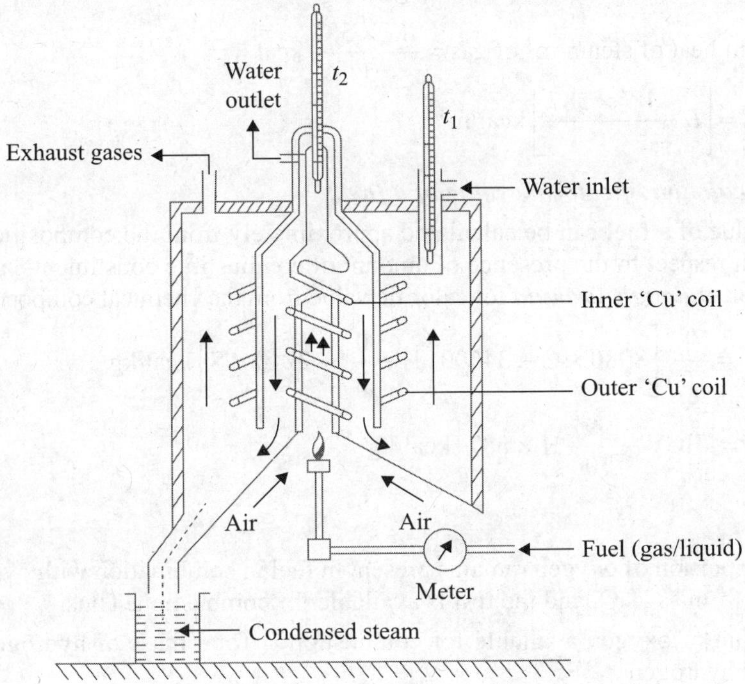

Fig. 14.3 Boy's gas calorimeter

Working: Circulation of water and burning of gaseous fuel are continued for about 15 min to warm up the calorimeter. After warming up of the calorimeter, the rates of fuel burning and water circulation are adjusted so that water leaves the apparatus nearly at the atmospheric pressure. After establishment of steady conditions, the volume of fuel burnt at a given temperature and pressure in a certain time period, the quantity of water flowing through the coil in the same time, the rise in temperature, i.e., $t_2 - t_1$, and weight of water condensed during this time are calculated.

Calculation:

Let V m^3 = Volume of gas burnt at STP

W kg = Weight of water passed through the coil in time "t"

t_1°C and t_2°C = Temperature of incoming and outgoing water

L = Higher calorific value of fuel (HCV)

W' kg = Weight of condensed water

Heat absorbed by circulating water = $W(t_2 - t_1)$

Heat produced by combustion of fuel = VL

Now, Heat loss = Heat gain

or $VL = W(t_2 - t_1)$

or $$L = \frac{W(t_2 - t_1)}{V} \quad [14.3]$$

Determination of LCV

Weight of water condensed/m³ of gas = W'/V kg

Thus, $$\text{Latent heat of steam/m}^3 \text{ of gas} = \frac{W' \times 587}{V} \text{ kcal}$$

$$\text{LCV} = \left[L - \frac{W' \times 587}{V}\right] \text{kcal/m}^3 \quad [14.4]$$

Theoretical calculation of calorific value of a fuel

The calorific value of a fuel can be calculated approximately from the composition of the fuel particularly with respect to the presence of amount of combustible constituents, i.e., hydrogen carbon and sulfur. ***Dulong's formula*** for calorific value from the chemical composition of fuel is

$$\text{HCV} = \frac{1}{100}\left[8080 \times \text{C} + 34500\left(\text{H} - \frac{0}{8}\right) + 2240 \times \text{S}\right] \text{kcal/kg} \quad [14.5]$$

$$\text{LCV} = \left[\text{HCV} - \frac{9}{100}\text{H} \times 587\right] \text{kcal/kg} \quad [14.6]$$

Note:

1. Some portion of oxygen remains present in fuel in combination with hydrogen, i.e., fixed form as H_2O, and the rest is available for combustion. Thus,

   Amount of oxygen available for combustion = Total mass of hydrogen in fuel – Fixed hydrogen

   $= \text{H} - \frac{0}{8}$ (as 8 parts of oxygen combine with one part of hydrogen to form water)

2. Calorific values of carbon, hydrogen, and sulfur are 8080, 34500, and 2240 kcal/kg, respectively.

Example 14.1

Find the gross and net calorific value of coal having the following composition: Carbon = 80%, Hydrogen = 10%, Nitrogen = 2%, Sulfur = 1%, and Ash = 7%. Given latent heat of steam is 587 cal/g.

Solution

$$\text{GCV} = \frac{1}{100}\left[8080 \times \text{C} + 34500\left(\text{H} - \frac{0}{8}\right) + 2240 \times \text{S}\right] \text{kcal/kg}$$

$$= \frac{1}{100}\left[8080 \times 80 + 34500\left(10 - \frac{0}{8}\right) + 2240 \times 1\right] \text{kcal/kg}$$

$$= \frac{1}{100}[646400 + 345000 + 2240] \text{ kcal/kg}$$

$$= 9936.4 \text{ kcal/kg}$$

$$\begin{aligned}\text{NCV} &= (\text{GCV} - 0.09 \times \text{H} \times 587)\ \text{kcal/g} \\ &= (9936.4 - 0.09 \times 10 \times 587)\ \text{kcal/g} \\ &= 9408.3\ \text{kcal/g}\end{aligned}$$

Example 14.2

About 0.7 g of a fuel containing 80% carbon, when burnt in a bomb calorimeter, increased the temperature of water from 27°C to 29°C. If the calorimeter contains 250 g of water and the water equivalent is 150 g, calculate the HCV of the fuel in kJ/kg.

Solution

$$\begin{aligned}\text{HCV of fuel } (L) &= \frac{(W + w)\,(t_2 - t_1)}{x}\ \text{cal/g} \\ &= \frac{(250 + 150)\,(29 - 27)}{0.7}\ \text{cal/g} \\ &= 1142.86\ \text{cal/g} \\ &= 4800\ \text{J/g} = 4800\ \text{kJ/kg}\end{aligned}$$

Example 14.3

About 0.8 g coal sample contains 90% C, 6% H, and 4% ash. On testing with bomb calorimeter, following data were recorded: Weight of water = 500 g, water equivalent of calorimeter = 2200 g, rise in temperature = 2.4°C, fuse wire correction = 8 cal, and acid correction = 50 cal. Find gross and net calorific value of coal assuming the latent heat of condensation of steam as 587 cal/g.

Solution

$$\begin{aligned}\text{HCV of fuel } (L) &= \frac{(W + w)\,(t_2 - t_1) - (t_A + t_F)}{x}\ \text{cal/g} \\ &= \frac{(500 + 2200)\,(2.4) - (50 + 8)}{0.8} \\ &= 10034.4\ \text{cal/g}\end{aligned}$$

$$\begin{aligned}\text{NCV} &= (\text{GCV} - 0.09 \times \text{H} \times 587)\ \text{cal/g} \\ &= (10034.4 - 0.09 \times 4 \times 587)\ \text{cal/g} \\ &= 9823.1\ \text{cal/g}\end{aligned}$$

Example 14.4

In Boy's gas calorimeter, following data were recorded: volume of gas used = 0.1 m^3 at STP, weight of water heated = 20 kg, inlet water temperature = 20°C, outlet water temperature = 35°C, and weight of steam condensed = 0.02 kg. Find the higher and lower calorific values per cubic meter at STP considering that the heat liberated in condensing water vapor and cooling the condensate is 580 kcal/kg.

Solution

$$\begin{aligned}\text{HCV } (L) &= \frac{W(t_2 - t_1)}{V} \\ &= \frac{20\,(35 - 20)}{0.1} = 3000\ \text{kcal/m}^3\end{aligned}$$

$$LCV = HCV - \frac{m}{V} \times 580$$

$$= 3000 - \frac{0.02}{0.1} \times 580 = 3000 - 116$$

$$= 2884 \text{ kcal/m}^3$$

Classification of Coal

Various types of coal are commonly recognized on the basis of rank or degree of alternation or coalification from the parent material, i.e., wood. The progressive transformation of wood to anthracite is shown in Fig. 14.4. This transformation of wood to anthracite results in decrease in the moisture content, hydrogen, oxygen, nitrogen, sulfur, and volatile matter content, with a corresponding rise in carbon content and increase in the calorific value and hardness.

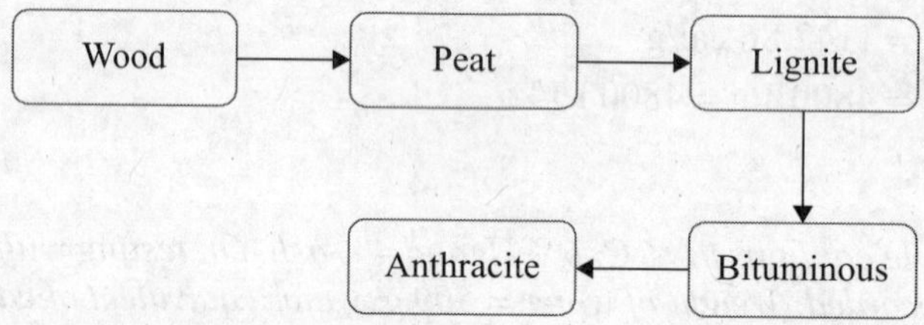

Fig. 14.4 Transformation of wood to anthracite

Peat: It is brown fibrous jelly-like mass which is generated at the first stage in the coalification of wood. It may contain as much as 80–90% water, but on air drying (after 1–2 months drying), it burns freely. It is not economical because of very high percentage of water content. The average composition of air-dried peat is C = 57%, H = 6%, O = 35%, ash content = 2.5–6%. Its calorific value is about 5400 kcal/kg (on air-dry basis).

Lignite: This is soft, brown colored variety of lowest rank coals, which consists of vegetable matter decomposed more than that in peat. Lignite is compact in texture, containing 20–60% moisture. On air-drying, it breaks up into small pieces. Air-dried lignite contains C = 60–70% and O = 20%. Lignite burns with long smoky flame. The calorific value is about 6500–7100 kcal/kg (on air-dry basis). Lignite is used as household fuel and boiler fuel. It is also used in the manufacture of producer gas.

Bituminous coals (common coals): These are pitch-black to dark-grey in color. They show a laminated structure of alternate very bright and dull layers. The bituminous coals are sub-classified on the basis of carbon content as sub-bituminous, bituminous, and semi-bituminous coals.

(i) Sub-bituminous coals are black in color and are more homogeneous and smooth in appearance. Carbon content varies from 75% to 83% with calorific value ~7000 kcal/kg. Their moisture and volatile contents are high and on exposure in air, these crumble into small pieces.

(ii) Bituminous coals show a typically banded appearance and C content ranges from 78% to 90% and volatile matter from 20% to 45%. Their calorific value on ash-free basis is about 8000 to 8500 kcal/kg. Coal of this class is used in the large quantities in industries for making metallurgical coke, coal gas, and for steam raising.

(iii) Semi-bituminous coals are rich in carbon (90–95%) and have low volatile matter. These are used for *coke manufacture*. Their calorific value is about 8500–8600 kcal/kg.

Anthracite: It is the highest rank coal containing highest percentage of carbon, i.e., 92–98%, and has lowest volatile matter and moisture contents. Because of low volatile matter content, they ignite with difficulty, but burn without any smoke and give intense local heating. These are the hardest kind of coal, having dense structure and lustrous in appearance. They possess no caking power. The calorific value is about 8650–8700 kcal/kg and ash content is very small (about 3%).They are used for steam raising, for household purpose, and in metallurgical processes where no smoke and high local heat are desired.

Analysis of Coal

In order to assess *the quality of coal*, it is subjected to two types of analysis: proximate and ultimate analysis.

Proximate Analysis

It involves determinations of moisture, volatile matter, ash, and fixed carbon.

Moisture: A known amount of finely powered air-dried coal sample is taken in a crucible. The crucible is placed inside an electric hot air oven, maintained at 105–110°C for about an hour. Then the crucible is cooled in a desiccator and weighed. The process of heating, cooling, and weighing of the crucible is repeated till the weight becomes constant. Loss in weight is reported as moisture on percentage basis.

$$\% \text{ of moisture} = \frac{\text{Loss of weight}}{\text{Weight of coal taken}} \times 100 \qquad [14.7]$$

Volatile matter: The volatile matter present in the coal may be combustible gases such as H_2, CH_4, CO, and other lower hydrocarbons and non-combustible gases such as CO_2 and N_2. For the determination of volatile matter, moisture-free coal is taken in a silica crucible covered with a lid and placed in an electric furnace (muffle furnace), maintained at 925°C + 20°C for ~10 min. The crucible is taken out and cooled first in air, then inside a desiccator and weighed again. Loss in weight is reported as volatile matter on the percentage basis.

$$\% \text{ of volatile matter} = \frac{\text{Loss of weight}}{\text{Weight of coal taken}} \times 100 \qquad [14.8]$$

Ash: Ash is non-combustible useless matter left behind after the complete combustion of coal. The residual coal is then heated without lid in a muffle furnace at 700 ± 50°C for half an hour. The crucible is then taken out, cooled first in air, then in desiccator and weighed. Heating, cooling, and weighing are repeated, till a constant weight is obtained. The residue is reported as ash on the percentage basis.

$$\% \text{ of ash} = \frac{\text{Weight of ash formed}}{\text{Weight of dry coal taken}} \times 100 \qquad [14.9]$$

Fixed carbon: After the determination of moisture, volatile matter, and ash content, the remaining material is known as a fixed carbon. It also represents the quantity of carbon (coal) that can be burnt by a primary current of air drawn through the hot bed of a fuel. The higher is the percentage of fixed carbon, the greater is the calorific value. Thus, high percentage of fixed carbon is desirable.

$$\text{Percentage of fixed carbon} = 100 - \% \text{ of (moisture + volatile matter + ash)} \qquad [14.10]$$

Ultimate Analysis

Ultimate analysis involves the measurement of C, H, N, S, O, and ash.

Carbon and hydrogen: Higher percentage of carbon and hydrogen makes a rise in calorific value of coal. In addition, the presence of higher percentage of carbon in coal reduces the size of the required chamber for combustion. However, hydrogen is mostly associated with the volatile matter; hence, it affects the use to which the coal is put. For the measurement, a known weight of coal sample say 1–2 g is burnt in a current of dry oxygen in a combustion tube so as to convert C and H to CO_2 and H_2O, respectively (see Fig. 14.5). The gaseous products so formed are absorbed in known weights of KOH and $CaCl_2$, respectively, as per the equations discussed here. The increase in weights of KOH and $CaCl_2$ are then determined to further calculate the weight of CO_2 and H_2O formed.

$$2KOH + CO_2 \longrightarrow K_2CO_3 + H_2O$$

$$CaCl_2 + 7H_2O \longrightarrow CaCl_2{\cdot}7H_2O$$

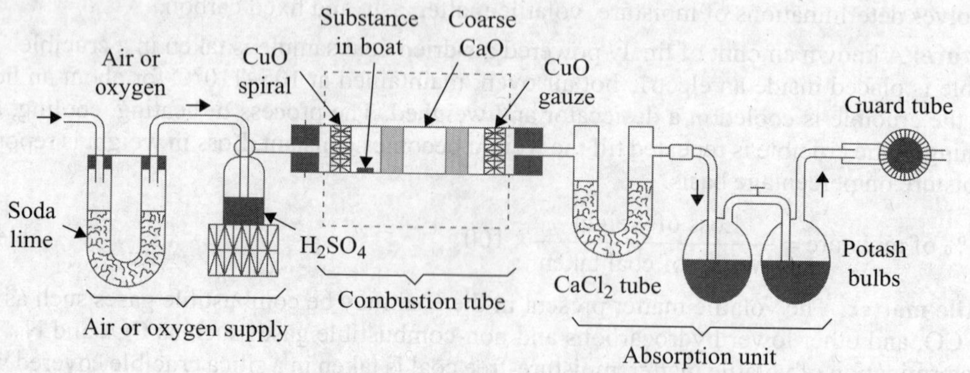

Fig. 14.5 Setup for determination of C and H

$$\underbrace{C}_{12} + O_2 \longrightarrow \underbrace{CO_2}_{44}$$

$$\text{Now, } \frac{\text{Weight of C}}{\text{Weight of } CO_2} = \frac{\text{Atomic weight of C}}{\text{Molecular weight } CO_2}$$

$$\text{or Weight of C} = \frac{\text{Atomic weight of C}}{\text{Molecular weight } CO_2} \times \text{Weight of } CO_2$$

$$\text{or Weight of C} = \frac{12 \times \text{Weight of C}}{44} \times 100$$

$$\text{Now, \% of C} = \frac{\text{Weight of C}}{\text{Weight of coal sample}} \times 100 \qquad [14.11]$$

Again,

$$\underbrace{H_2}_{2} + 1/2O_2 \longrightarrow \underbrace{H_2O}_{18}$$

$$\text{Now,} \quad \frac{\text{Weight of } H_2}{\text{Weight of } H_2O} = \frac{\text{Molecular weight of } H_2}{\text{Molecular weight } H_2O}$$

$$\text{or Weight of } H_2 = \frac{\text{Molecular weight of } H_2}{\text{Molecular weight } H_2O} \times \text{Weight of } H_2O$$

$$\text{or Weight of } H_2 = \frac{2 \times \text{Weight of } H_2O}{18} \times 100$$

$$\text{Now, \% of } H_2 = \frac{\text{Weight of } H_2}{\text{Weight of coal sample}} \times 100 \quad [14.12]$$

Nitrogen: This is an undesirable component in coal as it has no calorific value. Thus, a good quality coal should have very little nitrogen content. For the estimation of nitrogen, about 1 g of accurately weighed powdered coal is heated with concentrated H_2SO_4 along with K_2SO_4 (catalyst) in a long-necked flask (known as Kjeldahl flask). After the solution becomes clear, it is treated with excess of NaOH and the liberated ammonia is distilled over and absorbed in a known volume of standard acid solution. The residual acid is then determined by back titration with standard NaOH solution. From the volume of acid used by ammonia liberated, the percentage of N in coal can be calculated using the equations discussed here. The reactions occurring in the Kjeldahl flask and during absorption of NH_3 in acid are as follows:

$$N_2 + H_2SO_4 \longrightarrow (NH_4)_2SO_4 \xrightarrow{\text{NaOH}} 2Na_2SO_4 + \underbrace{2NH_3}_{} + 2H_2O$$

$$2NH_3 \xrightarrow{H_2SO_4} (NH_4)_2SO_4$$

Let V_1 be the volume of standard H_2SO_4 solution ($N/10$) and V_2 be the volume of standard NaOH solution ($N/10$).

Now, the amount of acid required to neutralize ammonia evolved from coal is calculated as follows:

$$\text{Amount of acid} = \frac{N}{10} \times V_1 - \frac{N}{10} \times V_2$$

$$= 0.1\,(V_1 - V_2) \text{ Meq}$$

$$= \frac{0.1\,(V_1 - V_2)}{1000} \text{ eq}$$

$$\text{Thus,} \quad \text{Weight of nitrogen} = \frac{0.1\,(V_1 - V_2)}{1000} \times 14$$

$$\text{Now,} \quad \text{\% of nitrogen} = \frac{\text{Weight of nitrogen}}{\text{Weight of coal sample}} \times 100$$

$$= \frac{\frac{0.1\,(V_1 - V_2)}{1000} \times 14}{1} \times 100 = 0.1\,(V_1 - V_2) \times 14 \quad [14.13]$$

Sulfur: Although sulfur contributes to the heating value of coal, on combustion it produces acidic oxides such as SO_2 and SO_3, which have harmful effects of corroding the equipment and also cause atmospheric pollution in the form of acid rain. The presence of sulfur is highly undesirable in coal used in making coke for iron industry, because it is transferred to the iron metal and badly affects the quality and properties of steel. Sulfur is determined from the washings obtained from the known mass of coal used in a bomb calorimeter for the determination of a calorific value. During this determination, S is converted into sulfate. The washings are treated with barium chloride solution, when barium sulfate is precipitated. This precipitate is filtered, washed, and heated to constant weight.

$$\underset{32}{S} \xrightarrow{O_2} SO^{2-} \xrightarrow{BaCl_2} \underset{233}{BaSO_4}$$

$$\text{Now, } \frac{\text{Weight of S}}{\text{Weight of } BaSO_4(W_2)} = \frac{\text{Atomic weight of S}}{\text{Molecular weight } BaSO_4}$$

$$\text{or Weight of S} = \frac{32}{233} \times W_2 \text{ g}$$

Let weight of coal taken = W_1 g

$$\text{Now, \% of S} = \frac{\frac{32}{233} \times W_2 \text{g}}{W_1} \times 100 \qquad [14.14]$$

Oxygen: Oxygen content decreases the calorific value of coal. High oxygen content in coals is characterized by high inherent moisture, low calorific value, and low caking power. Moreover, oxygen is present in combined form with hydrogen in coal; thus, hydrogen available for combustion is lesser than the actual one. An increase in 1% oxygen content decreases the calorific value by about 1.7%; hence, oxygen is undesirable. Thus, a good quality coal should have low percentage of oxygen.

It is obtained by difference.

$$\text{Percentage of O} = 100 - \text{\% of } (C + H + S + N + \text{ash}) \qquad [14.15]$$

Example 14.5

About 2.5 g of a coal sample was taken in a silica crucible. After one hour heating at 110°C, the residual weight is 2.4 g. After strong heating at ~950°C for 7 min, the residual weight is 1.5 g. Subsequent heating was done without lid till constant weight. The final weight was found to be 0.3 g. Find the results of proximate analysis.

Solution

Weight of moisture = 2.5 – 2.4 = 0.1 g

Weight of volatile matter = 2.4 – 1.5 = 0.9 g

Weight of ash = 0.3 g

$$\text{\% of moisture} = \frac{0.1}{2.5} \times 100 = 4$$

$$\text{\% of volatile matter} = \frac{0.9}{2.5} \times 100 = 36$$

$$\text{\% of ash} = \frac{0.3}{2.5} \times 100 = 12$$

$$\text{\% of fixed carbon} = 100 - (4 + 36 + 12) = 48$$

Example 14.6

About 0.5 g of a coal sample was used in a bomb calorimeter for the determination of calorific value. The ash formed in the calorimeter was extracted with acid and the acid extract was heated with barium chloride solution to form the precipitate of barium sulfate. The weight of dried precipitate was fond to be 0.05 g. Find the percentage of sulfur in the coal sample.

Solution

$$\text{Now, \% of S} = \frac{\frac{32}{233} \times W_2\text{g}}{W_1} \times 100$$

$$= \frac{32 \times 0.5 \times 100}{233 \times 0.5}$$

$$= 1.37\%$$

Example 14.7

About 2 g sample of coal was subjected to Kjeldahl digestion. The ammonia liberated was collected by absorbing in 25 ml N/10 sulfuric acid. The excess acid was neutralized by 15 ml of 0.1 N NaOH. Find the percentage of nitrogen in the coal sample.

Solution

Now, the amount of acid required to neutralize the ammonia evolved from coal is given by

$$\text{Required amount of acid} = \frac{1}{10} \times 25 - \frac{0.1}{10} \times 15$$

$$= 0.1 \text{ Meq}$$

$$= \frac{0.1}{1000} \text{ eq}$$

$$\text{Thus, Weight of nitrogen} = \frac{0.1}{1000} \times 14 = 0.02 \text{ g}$$

$$\text{Now, \% of nitrogen} = \frac{\text{Weight of nitrogen}}{\text{Weight of coal sample}} \times 100$$

$$= \frac{0.02}{2} \times 100 = 1\%$$

Carbonization of Coal

The process of converting coal into coke is called carbonization. Coke is the porous, hard, and strong residue left after the heating of coal in the absence of air. On the basis of the behavior of coal upon heating, it is classified as *non-coking* and *coking* coals. The first category of coal undergoes practically no fusing effect and is also known as free-burning coal. The second category of coal gives porous, hard, and strong residue after heating in the absence of air. It is used for metallurgical proposes.

It is important to note that only caking coals which become soft, plastic, and fuse together to form a large coherent mass upon heating in the absence of air can be converted into coke. Such property is found in *bituminous* type of coal; thus, only bituminous coal can be converted into coke. Caking coal with high volatile matter content are used for gas manufacture while with lower volatile matter content are used for manufacture of metallurgical coke and are known as coking coal (see Fig. 14.6).

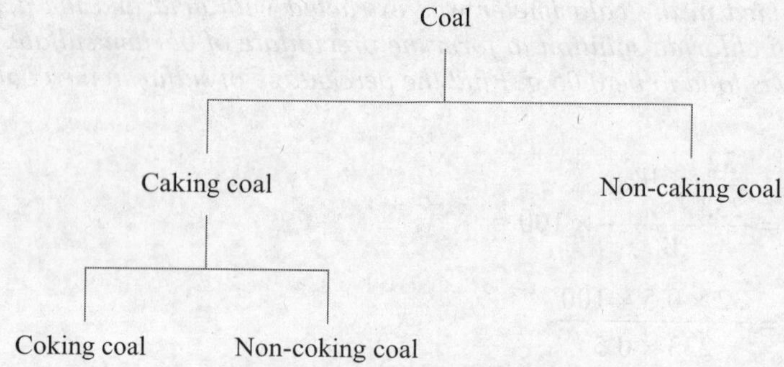

Fig. 14.6 Classification of coal

Requirements of metallurgical coke

Following are the requirements of a good metallurgical coke:

1. Coke should burn easily. However, it should not be very reactive.
2. It should possess high calorific value.
3. The mechanical strength of coke should be very high so that it is able to withstand the abrasion and overburden of the ore, fuel, and the flux in the furnace.
4. Porosity of the coke should be very high so as to facilitate the contact of oxygen with carbon, and thereby the complete combustion.
5. It must contain the lowest possible percentages of moisture, ash, sulfur, and phosphorous.
6. The calorific intensity of coke should be high enough to melt the metal.

Types of Carbonization

There are two types of carbonizations of coal.

1. **Low temperature carbonization:** In this process, the heating of coal is carried out at 500–700°C. The coke so produced is mainly suitable for domestic purpose.
2. **High temperature carbonization:** In this process, the heating of coal is carried out at 900–1200°C. The coke so produced is of the right porosity, hardness, purity, and strength. Such coke is mainly suitable for metallurgy.

A detailed comparative account of both processes are summarized as follows:

Characteristics	Low temperature carbonization	High temperature carbonization
Heating temperature	500–700°C	900–1200°C
% yield of coke	75–80%	65–75%
% of volatile matter in coke	5–15%	1–3%
Mechanical strength	Not mechanically strong	Good mechanical strength
Quantity of byproduct gas produced	130–150 m^3/ton	300–390 m^3/ton

Characteristics	Low temperature carbonization	High temperature carbonization
Calorific value of byproduct gas	6500–9500 kcal/m^3	5400–6000 kcal/m^3
Hardness of coke	Soft	Hard
Smoke produced on burning	Smokeless	Smoky
% of aromatic hydrocarbon in tar	Smaller	Higher
In gas		
(a) % of straight chain hydrocarbon	Higher	Lower
(b) % of aromatic hydrocarbon	Lower	Higher
Use of coke	For domestic purpose	For metallurgical process

Petroleum

Petroleum or crude oil (Latin: *petra*, rock; *oleum*, oil) is dark greenish-brown, viscous oil found deep in the Earth's crust. It is a complex mixture of various hydrocarbons such as straight-chain paraffinic, olefinic, and aromatic hydrocarbons together with small amounts of organic compounds containing oxygen, nitrogen, and sulfur. The average composition of crude petroleum is C = 80–87%, H = 11–15%, S = 0.1–3.5%, N = 0.4–0.9%, and O = 0.1–0.9%.

Classification of Petroleum

The chemical nature of the crude petroleum varies with the part of the world in which it is found. There are three classes of petroleum as follows:

1. **Paraffinic-base** type crude is mainly composed of the saturated hydrocarbons from CH_4 to $C_{35}H_{72}$ and a little of the naphthalenes and aromatics. The hydrocarbons from $C_{18}H_{38}$ to $C_{35}H_{72}$ are semi-solids, called waxes.
2. **Asphaltic-base** type crude mainly contains cycloparaffins or naphthalens with smaller amount of Paraffins and aromatic hydrocarbons.
3. **Mixed-base** type crude contains both paraffinic and asphaltic hydrocarbons and are, generally, rich in semi-soild waxes.

Origin of Petroleum

According to modern theory, petroleum has resulted from the partial decomposition of marine animals and vegetable organisms of pre-historic forests. Changes to the Earth's surface caused by volcanos and earthquakes had buried these materials underground, where they have been subjected to intense pressure and heat, during the ages of time. The conversion of these materials into various hydrocarbons has been going on either under the influence of radioactive substances such as uranium or by the bacterial decomposition under the anaerobic and strongly reducing conditions and temperature under high pressure. Mining of petroleum is done by drilling holes in the Earth's crust and sinking pipes up to the oil-bearing porous rocks. Oil, usually, comes out itself due to hydrostatic pressure of natural gas. Alternatively, it may be mechanically pumped up by using either lift pump or air-lift pump. The latter consists of two co-axial pipes, lowered into the base of oil bed. Compressed air is forced through the outer pipe, whereby oil comes out through the inner pipe (see Fig. 14.7). The oil is conveyed to refinery by a system of pipelines.

Refining of Crude Oil

Crude oil is separated into various useful fractions having different boiling points by fractional distillation. These fractions are finally converted into desired specific products. The process is called *refining of crude oil*, and the plants set up for the purpose are called the *oil refineries*. The process of refining involves the following stages:

1. **Separation of water (Cottrell's process):** The crude oil from the oil well is an extremely stable emulsion of oil and salt water. The crude oil is allowed to flow between two highly charged electrodes. The colloidal water-droplets coalesce to form large props, which separate out from the oil.
2. **Removal of harmful sulfur compounds:** It is achieved by treating oil with copper oxide. A reaction occurs with sulfur compounds, which result in the formation of copper sulfate, which is then removed by filtration.
3. **Fractional distillation:** The crude oil is then heated to about 400°C in an iron retort, whereby all volatile constituents, except the residue (asphalt or coke), are evaporated. The hot vapors are then passed through a cylindrical tower known as *fractionating column*, containing a number of horizontal stainless steel trays at short distances (see Fig. 14.7). Each tray is provided with small chimney, covered with a loose cap. As vapors go up, fractional condensation takes place at different heights of column. Higher boiling fraction condenses first, while the lower boiling fractions condense later as shown in the figure. Various principal fractionation products thus obtained are mentioned in the following table.

Fraction	Boiling range	Approx. composition (hydrocarbon containing C)	Uses
Uncondensed gas	<30°C	C_1–C_4	Domestic/industrial fuel under the name LPG
Petroleum ether	30–70°C	C_5–C_7	As solvent
Gasoline/petrol	40–120°C	C_5–C_9	As motor fuel, solvent and dry cleaning
Naphtha/solvent spirit	120–180°C	C_9–C_{10}	Solvent and dry cleaning
Kerosene oil	180–250°C	C_{10}–C_{16}	Jet engine fuel, preparing lab gas
Diesel/fuel/gas oil	250–320°C	C_{10}–C_{18}	Diesel engine fuel
Heavy oil	320–400°C	C_{17}–C_{30}	For getting gasoline by cracking
This on re-fractionation gives			
(a) Lubricating oil			As lubricant
(b) Petroleum jelly			In cosmetics and medicines
(c) Grease			As lubricant
(d) Paraffin wax			In candles, boot polish, wax paper, tarapaulin cloth, etc.
Residue which may be asphalt or petroleum coke	>400°C	C_{30} and above	Road makings, water proofing of roof, as a fuel in molding arc light rods

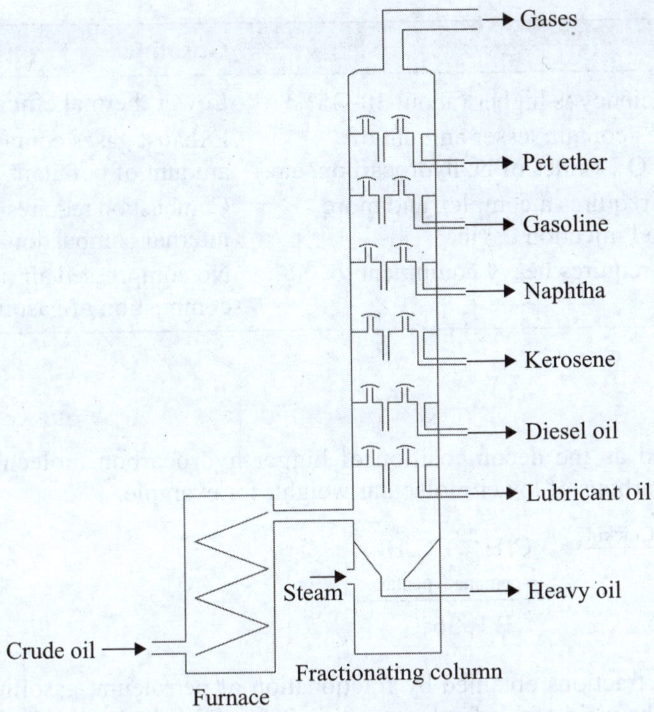

Fig. 14.7 Fractionating column

A brief description of three most important liquid fuels derived from petroleum is as follows:

1. **Gasoline or petrol** is obtained between 40°C and 120°C and is a mixture of hydrocarbons from pentane to octane. The approximate composition is C = 84%, H = 15%, N + S + O = 1%. Its calorific value is about 11250 kcal/kg. It is highly volatile, inflammable, and used as fuel for internal combustion engines of automobiles and aeroplanes.
2. **Kerosene oil** is a fraction obtained between 180°C and 250°C and is a mixture of hydrocarbons from decane to hexadecane. Its approximate composition is C = 84%, H = 16% with less than 0.1% S. Its specific gravity is 0.75–0.85. Its calorific value is 11100 kcal/kg. Kerosene does not vaporize easily because of its high boiling point range. It is used as domestic fuel in stoves, as jet engine fuel, and for making oil gas.
3. **Diesel oil** is a fraction obtained between 250°C and 320°C and is a mixture of hydrocarbons from $C_{15}H_{32}$ to $C_{18}H_{38}$. Its density is 0.86 to 0.95. Its calorific value is about 11000 kcal/kg. It is used as a diesel engine fuel.

Note:

Comparison of diesel fuel with gasoline fuel.

Diesel	Gasoline
Cheaper than gasoline	Costlier
Consumption per unit of power produced is less	More consumption

Diesel	Gasoline
Thermal efficiency is higher (about 30–35%)	Lower thermal efficiency
Exhaust gases contain lesser amount of pollutants (CO_2, oxides of N, hydrocarbon, etc.)	Exhaust gases contain higher amount of pollutant gases
Combustion requires a complex and more expensive fuel injection device	Combustion requires a rather simple internal combustion of engine
Combustion requires heavy equipment to compress air	No compressed air needed during combustion of gasoline

Cracking

Cracking is defined as the decomposition of bigger hydrocarbon molecules into simpler, low-boiling hydrocarbons of lower molecular weight; for example,

$$\underbrace{\underset{\text{Decane}}{C_{10}H_{22}}}_{\text{B.P. } 174^\circ\text{C}} \xrightarrow{\text{Cracking}} \underbrace{\underset{n\text{-pentane}}{C_5H_{12}} + \underset{\text{pentane}}{C_5H_{10}}}_{\text{B.P. } 36^\circ\text{C}}$$

Out of all the fractions obtained by fractionation of petroleum, gasoline has the largest demand; however, the yield of this fractions is only 20% of the crude oil. Also the quality of so-called gasoline is not high. Therefore, before use it has to be properly blended. At the same time major portion is heavier petroleum fractions. This middle and heavy fractions can be cracked to get gasoline and petrol. The petrol made by cracking has better characteristics (as for as the IC engine is concerned) than the *straight-run* petrol. There are two popular methods of cracking, viz., thermal and catalytic (see Fig. 14.8).

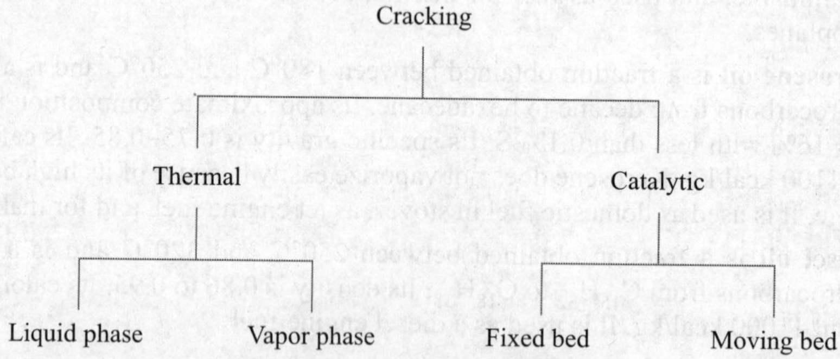

Fig. 14.8 Methods of cracking

1. **Thermal cracking:** Heavy oils are subjected to high temperature and pressure in the absence of catalyst. In the process, the bigger hydrocarbon molecules break down to give smaller molecules of the paraffins, olefins, and some hydrogen. This process may be carried out either in liquid phase or vapor phase. The comparative account of these two processes is as follows:

Characteristics	Liquid-phase cracking	Vapor-phase cracking
Temperature	475–530°C	600–650°C
Pressure	100 kg/cm^2	10–20 kg/cm^2
Yield of petrol	50–60%	–
Octane rating	65–70	>70
Criteria	Any heavy oil can be utilized	Oil should be readily vaporized
Time required	More	Less

2. **Catalytic cracking:** The quality and quantity of gasoline produced by cracking can be greatly improved by using a suitable catalyst such as aluminum silicate [$Al_2(SiO_3)_3$] or alumina (Al_2O_3). There are two methods of catalytic cracking: fixed-bed and moving-bed catalytic cracking.

   (a) *Fixed-bed catalytic cracking*: The heavy oil charge is passed through a pre-heater where it is heated to the cracking temperatures, i.e., 420–450°C. The hot vapor is then forced through a catalytic chamber containing artificial clay mixed with zirconium oxide maintained at 425–450°C and 1.5 kg/cm^2 pressure. In the process, ~40% of the charge is converted into gasoline and about 2–4% carbon is formed which gets adsorbed on the catalyst bed. The bed is recharged in every 8–10 h by burning off the deposited carbon. Vapors produced are then subjected to fractionation, where heavy oil fractions condense. Vapors are then led through a cooler, where some of the gases are condensed along with gasoline and uncondensed gases move on (see Fig. 14.9). The gasoline containing some dissolved gases is then sent to a stabilizer, where the dissolved gases are removed and pure gasoline is obtained.

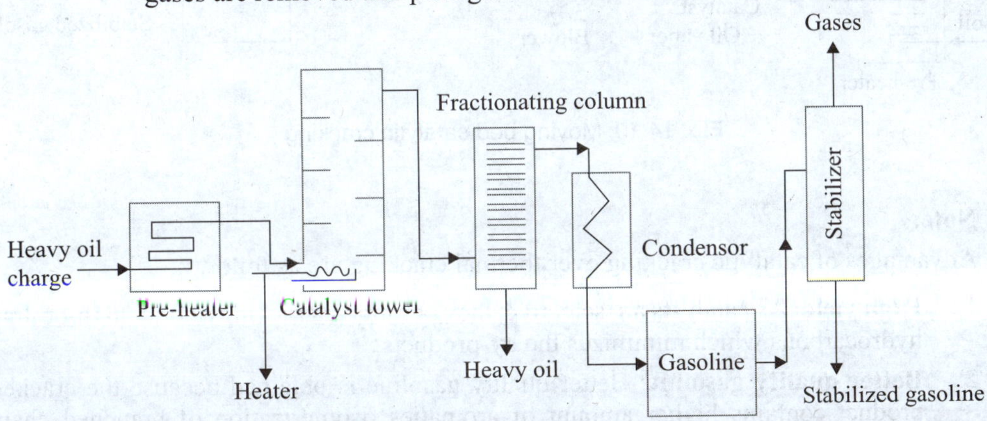

Fig. 14.9 Fixed-bed catalytic cracking

Note:
During the re-activation interval, vapors are diverted through another catalyst chamber.

   (b) *Moving-bed catalytic.cracking*: The solid catalyst is taken in a very finely powdered form, so that it behaves almost as fluid, which can be circulated in a gas stream. Vapors of cracking charge, i.e., heavy oil mixed with fluidized catalyst is forced up into a large reactor bed maintained at a temperature of ~500°C in which cracking of the heavier into lighter molecules occurs (Fig. 14.10). Near the top of the reactor there is a centrifugal separator (cyclone), which allows only the cracked oil vapors to pass on to the fractionating column. The powdered catalyst gradually becomes heavier as a result of coating with carbon and settles to the bottom, from where it is forced by an air blast to regenerator maintained at 600°C. In regenerator, carbon is burnt and the regenerated catalyst is made ready for mixing with fresh batch of incoming cracking oil. At the top of the regenerator, there is a separator, which permits only gases to pass out, but holds back catalyst particles.

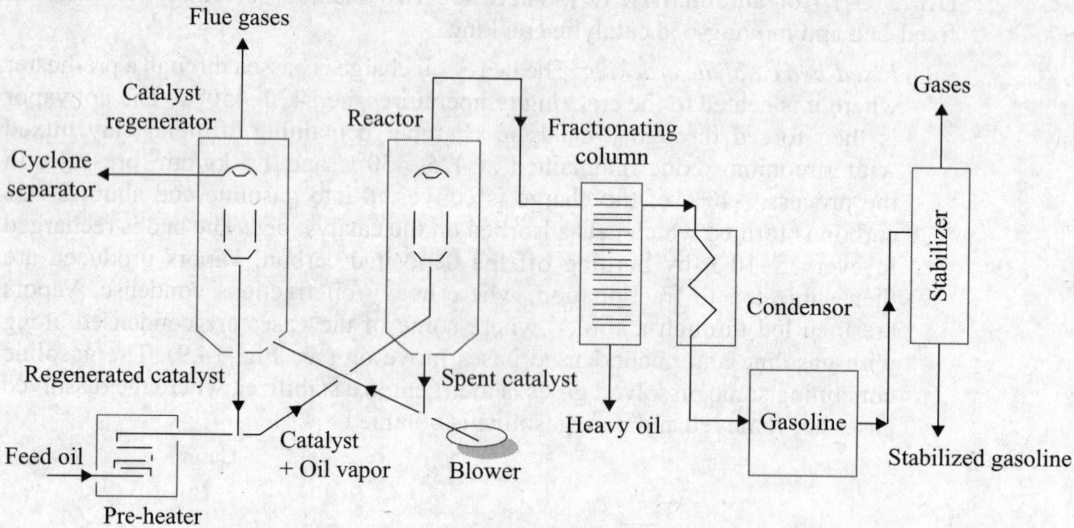

Fig. 14.10 Moving bed catalytic cracking

Note:

Advantages of catalytic cracking over thermal cracking are as follows:

1. **High yield**: As catalysts are selective, they permit the cracking of only high-boiling hydrocarbons which minimizes the by-products.
2. **Better quality gasoline**: Better quality gasoline is obtained because the cracked product contains higher amount of aromatics, isomerization of branched chain compounds occur, contains relatively less sulfur.
3. No external fuel is necessary for cracking.
4. A much lower pressure of about 1–5 kg/cm^2 is needed.
5. The process of cracking can be controlled.
6. The percentage of gum forming compounds (unsaturated straight chain compounds) is very low.
7. The production cost is very low.

Synthetic Petrol

Petrol can be synthesized by any of the following three methods.

1. **Polymerization:** The gases obtained as a by-product from cracking of heavy oils contain olefins (such as ethylene, propene, and butene) and alkanes (such as methane, ethane, propane, and butane). When this gaseous mixture is subjected to high temperature and pressure, with or without the presence of catalyst, it polymerizes to form higher hydrocarbons, resembling gasoline which is called polymer gasoline. Polymerization can be thermal or catalytic. In thermal polymerization, a temperature of 500–600°C and a pressure of 70–350 kg/cm^2 are used. Catalytic polymerization is carried out in the presence of a catalyst such as phosphoric acid at lower temperature of 150–200°C and pressure.

$$CH_3-CH=CH_2+CH_3-CH_2-CH=CH_2 \xrightarrow[\text{and/or catalyst}]{\text{Pressure, heat}} CH_2=CH-CH_2-CH_2-CH(CH_3)_2$$

2. **Fischer–Tropsch method:** This process can effectively be viewed as a method to transform any available carbon source into hydrocarbon chains. This process is a collection of chemical reactions that converts a mixture of CO and H_2, which is known as synthesis gas or syngas, into liquid hydrocarbons in the presence of suitable catalysts. It was first developed by Franz Fischer and Hans Tropsch in 1925. In the process, carbon containing feedstock, i.e., coal, natural gas, and biomass are processed into a mixture of CO and H_2, which is termed as gasification. Gasification of coal can be done by passing steam over heated coal. The gas is then purified by passing through Fe_2O_3 so as to remove H_2S and then into a mixture of Fe_2O_3 and Na_2CO_3 so as to remove organic sulfur compounds. The purified gas is compressed and led through a convertor containing a catalyst maintained at about 200–300°C. A variety of catalysts can be used, but the most common are the transition metals cobalt, iron, and ruthenium supported on high-surface-area binders or supports such as silica, alumina, or Zeolites. The process results in a mixture of saturated and unsaturated hydrocarbons.

$$\begin{cases} nCO + 2nH_2 \longrightarrow C_nH_{2n} + nH_2O \\ nCO + (2n+1)\,H_2 \longrightarrow C_nH_{2n+2} + nH_2O \end{cases}$$

The reaction is exothermic; hence out coming hot gaseous mixture is led to a cooler, where crude oil is obtained. The crude oil thus obtained is then fractionated to yield gasoline and high-boiling heavy oil. The heavy oil is subjected to cracking so as to get more gasoline (see Fig. 14.11).

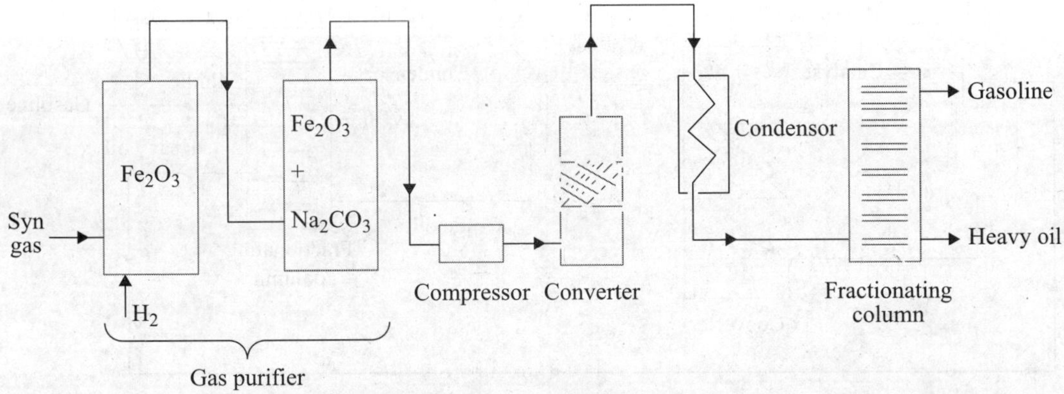

Fig. 14.11 Setup of Fischer–Tropsch process

Note:

1. Cobalt catalysts are more active for Fischer–Tropsch synthesis when the feedstock is natural gas in which hydrogen-to-carbon ratio is high.
2. Iron may be more suitable for low-hydrogen-content synthesis gases such as those derived from coal.
3. Unlike Co, Ni, and Ru which remain in the metallic state during synthesis, iron catalysts tend to form a number of phases, including various oxides and carbides during the reaction. Control of these phase transformations plays an important role in maintaining catalytic activity and preventing breakdown of the catalyst particles.
4. Promoters also have an important influence on activity. Alkali metal oxides and copper are common promoters used in the processes.

3. **Bergius process:** This is a method of production of liquid hydrocarbon for use as synthetic fuel by hydrogenation of highly volatile bituminous coal at high temperature and pressure. It was first developed by Friedrich Bergius in 1913. In the process, coal is finely powdered and made into a paste with heavy oil and then a catalyst is incorporated. Several catalysts are in use such as tungsten or molybdenum sulfides, tin or nickel oleate, etc. The mixture is pumped into a reactor and is heated with hydrogen at ~450°C under a pressure of 200–250 atm. In the reactor, hydrogen combines with coal to form saturated hydrocarbons, which decompose at prevailing high temperature and pressure to yield low-boiling liquid hydrocarbons. The issuing gases from the reaction vessel are led to condenser, where the crude oil is obtained. The obtained crude oil is then fractionated to gasoline, middle oil, and heavy oil. The latter is recycled again for making paste with fresh coal dust. The middle oil is hydrogenated in the presence of a solid catalyst to yields more gasoline. The yield of gasoline is ~60% of the coal dust used. The overall reaction in the reactor is as follows:

$$nC + (n - x + 1)\, H_2 \longrightarrow C_nH_{2n-2x+2}, \text{ where } x \text{ is degree of unsatuation}$$

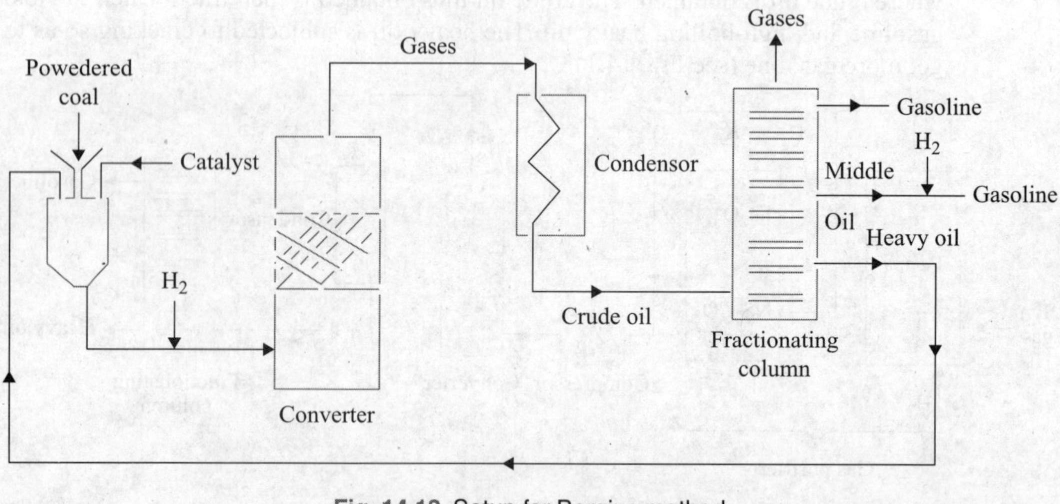

Fig. 14.12 Setup for Bergius method

Note:

Iron sulfides present in the coal may have sufficient catalytic activity for carrying out the original Bergius process.

Refining of Gasoline

The straight-run gasoline (obtained either from fractionation of crude petroleum or by synthesis) contains some undesirable unsaturated straight-chain hydrocarbons and sulfur compounds. The former gets oxidized and polymerized, thereby causing gum and sludge formation on storing. Sulfur compounds lead to corrosion of internal combustion engine. Refining of straight-run petrol is achieved as follows:

1. **Removal of impurities**

   (a) The sulfur compounds are removed by the treatment of gasoline with an alkaline solution of sodium plumbite with controlled addition of S. This refining process is known as *sweetening*, which converts sulfur compounds into disulfides (*Doctor's process*). The solid PbS is removed by filtration. The disulfides in gasoline are also objectionable; hence, these are extracted with a suitable solvent.

$$\left\{\begin{array}{l} \underset{\text{Meracptans}}{2\,RSH} + \underset{\text{Sodium plumbite}}{Na_2PbO_2} \longrightarrow \underset{\text{Lead meracptide}}{Pb(SR)_2} + 2NaOH \\ Pb(SR)_2 + S \longrightarrow PbS_{(s)}\downarrow + RSSR \end{array}\right.$$

   (b) Olefines and coloring matter of gasoline are, usually, removed by percolating gasoline through *fuller's earth*, which adsorbs preferentially only the colors and olefines.

2. **Reforming:** The primary objective of reforming is to improve the anti-knock characteristics of straight-run gasoline (see section on "Reforming").
3. **Addition of inhibitors:** After the refining of gasoline, some inhibitors such as aromatic amines and amino phenols are added to retard the oxidation reactions, thereby improving storing qualities of gasoline.
4. **Blending:** Even after refining, the gasoline does not have good combustion qualities, and it is, generally, blended suitably with other high octane number fractions produced by catalytic cracking processes to meet the required specifications.

Note:

1. **Sweetening:** The processes which oxidize mercaptans into more innocuous disulfides that remain in the fuels are called sweetening. The doctor's process employs sodium plumbite as a sweetening agent. Sweetening can also be achieved by the treatment with sodium hypochlorite, activated bauxite, sodium phenolate, sodium isobutyrate, sodium naphthenate, *p*-phenylene diamine etc.
2. **Characteristics of an ideal gasoline**

   (a) It must be cheap and readily available.

   (b) It must burn clean and produce no corrosion on combustion.

(c) It should mix readily with air and afford uniform manifold distribution, i.e., it should easily vaporize.

(d) It must be knock-resistant.

(e) It should not reignite easily.

(f) It should not tend to decrease the volumetric efficiency of the engine.

(g) It must have a high calorific value.

Reforming

Reforming is a process of bringing about structural modifications in the components of straight-run gasoline prepared by the fractional distillation of the crude oil, with the primary objective of improving its anti-knock characteristics. It is carried out either thermally or in the presence of a catalyst.

1. **Thermal reforming**: The straight-run gasoline is heated in a reactor (Fig. 14.13) at 500–600°C at ~85 atm pressure in the absence of catalyst. The conditions are controlled carefully by quenching, i.e., rapid cooling the products by spray of cold oil to avoid the formation of gas. The reformed products are then fractionated to remove residual gas. During thermal reforming, some cracking also occurs to yield saturated and unsaturated hydrocarbons. The hydrocarbons might undergo dehydrogenation, followed by cyclization to yield naphthalenes (aromatization). The conversion of *n*-alkenes to branched-chain alkenes also takes place during thermal reforming.

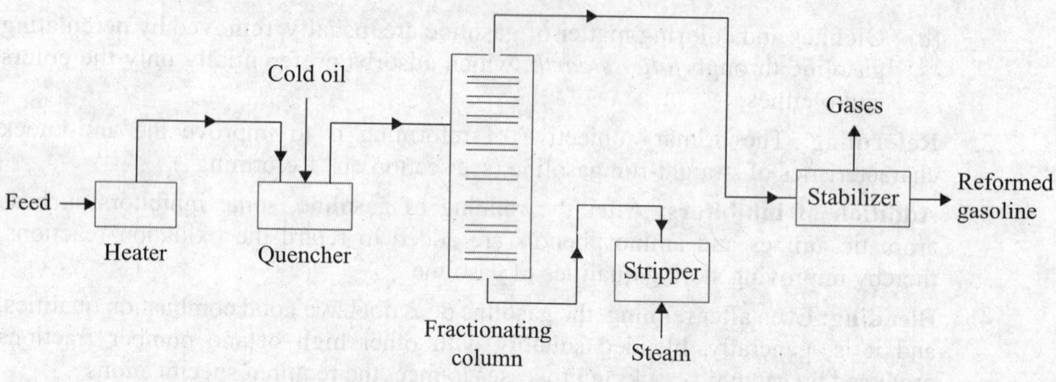

Fig. 14.13 Setup for thermal reforming

2. **Catalytic reforming:** To get a better grade and yield of gasoline, catalytic reforming is carried out by using either a fixed bed or a fluidized bed at 460–350°C and 35–50 atm pressure in the presence of a catalyst Pt supported on alumina. The flow diagram for a fixed-bed catalytic reforming is shown in Fig. 14.14.

The feedstock is heated and fractionated to remove low boiling vapors, water, and oxygen so as to avoid any explosive reaction with hydrogen. The fraction with boiling point 100–190°C is selected and mixed with compressed hydrogen and heated up to 500°C by passing through a heater. After compressing to ~25 atm, the mixture is passed through a series of reactors having catalyst bed. The mixture is to be preheated before passing from one reactor to another as the process of reforming is endothermic. The products are then separated into liquid and gas phase

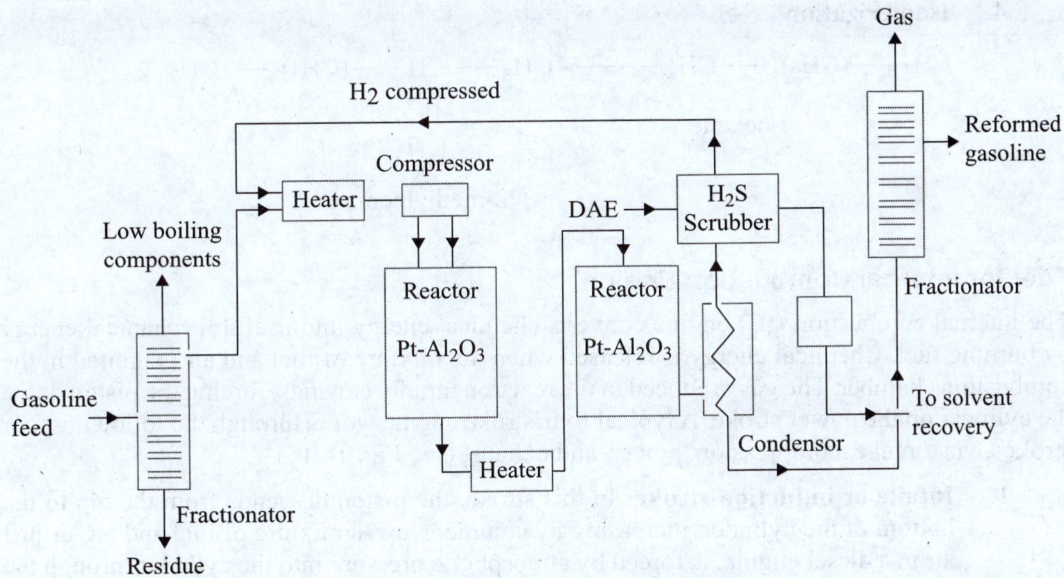

Fig. 14.14 Catalytic reformer setup

(H_2 and H_2S). H_2S is removed by absorbing in diethanolamine (DEA) in H_2S scrubber. Some portion of H_2 is recycled for removing sulfur, while the rest is used for hydrogenation of alkene and hydro-cracking. The residue from condenser is fractionated to remove gases and higher boiling fractions.

The main reactions during catalytic reforming process are as follows:

1. **Dehydrogenation**

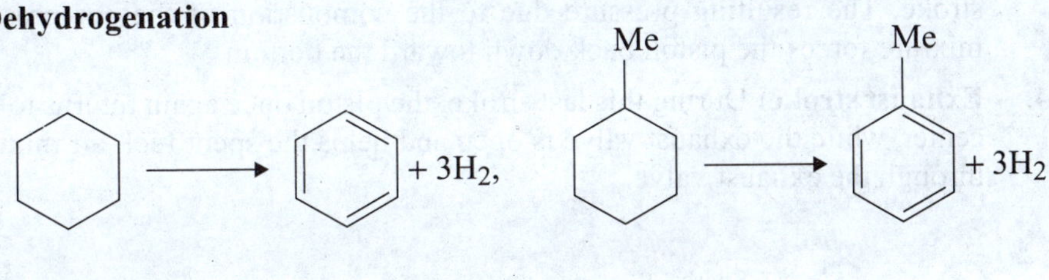

Cyclohexane Benzene Methyl cyclohexane Toluene

2. **Dehydrocyclization**

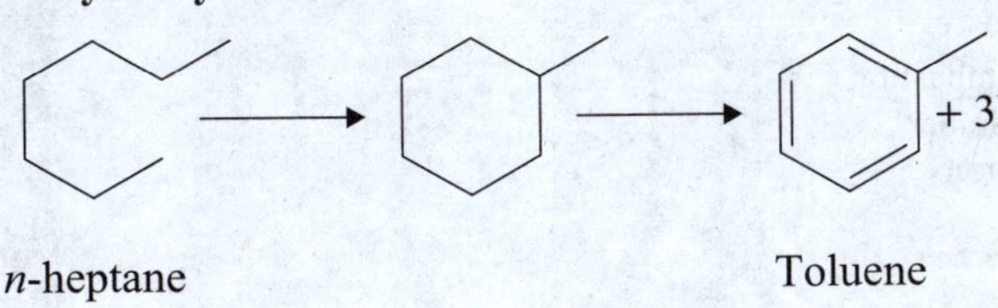

n-heptane Toluene

3. **Hydro-cracking**

$$\underset{n\text{-decane}}{CH_3 — (CH_2)_8 — CH_3} + H_2 \xrightarrow{Pt} 2\underset{n\text{-pentane}}{CH_3 — (CH_2)_3 — CH_3}$$

4. **Isomerization**

$$CH_3 - (CH_2)_4 - CH_3 \longrightarrow CH_3 - \underset{\displaystyle CH_3}{\underset{|}{CH}} - (CH_2)_2 - CH_3$$

n-hexane → 2-methylpentane

Fuel for Internal Combustion Engine

The internal combustion (IC) engine converts chemical energy into useful mechanical energy by burning fuel. Chemical energy is released when the mixture of fuel and air is ignited in the combustion chamber. The gas produced in the reaction rapidly expands, forcing the piston down the cylinder on the power stroke. A typical four-stroke engine works through the following four strokes, viz., intake, compression, power, and exhaust (see Fig. 14.15).

1. **Intake or induction stroke:** In this stroke, the piston descends from the top to the bottom of the cylinder, increasing its volume. Now, a mixture of fuel and air, or just air in a diesel engine, is forced by atmospheric pressure into the cylinder through the intake port. The intake valve then closes.
2. **Compression stroke:** In this stroke, with both intake and exhaust valves closed, the piston returns to the top of the cylinder compressing the fuel–air mixture or air into the combustion chamber of the cylinder head. In this stroke, the temperature of the air or fuel–air mixture rises by several hundred degrees.
3. **Power stroke:** In this stroke, the compressed air–fuel mixture in a gasoline engine is ignited by a spark plug at top dead center, or fuel is injected into a diesel engine, which ignites as the result of the heat generated in the air during the compression stroke. The resulting pressure due to the combustion of the compressed fuel–air mixture forces the piston back down toward the bottom.
4. **Exhaust stroke:** During this last stroke, the piston once again returns to the top dead center, while the exhaust valve is open and helps the spent fuel–air mixture to expel through the exhaust valve.

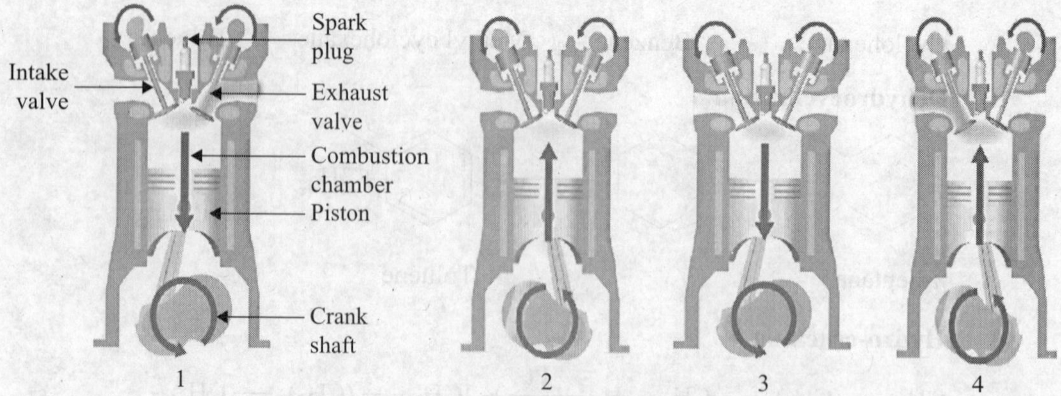

Fig. 14.15 A four-stroke internal combustion engine

Knocking

In an internal combustion petrol engine, a mixture of vapor of gasoline and air is used as a fuel. After the initiation of the combustion reaction by spark in the cylinder, the flame should spread rapidly and smoothly through the gaseous mixture so that the expanding gas can drive the piston down the cylinder. The ratio of the gaseous volume in the cylinder at the end of the suction stroke to the volume at the end of compression stroke of the piston is known the *compression ratio* (CR). The efficiency of an IC engine increases with the increases in the compression ratio. At a high CR, in some circumstances depending on composition of fuel, the rate of oxidation becomes so great that the last portion of the fuel–air mixture gets ignited instantaneously, producing a shock wave which dessipates its energy by hitting the cylinder walls and piston. The result being a characteristic rattling sound is emitted which is known as *knocking*. The CR at which fuel leads to knocking is called *critical compression ratio*. The knocking results in loss of efficiency, i.e., power output and mechanical damage of cylinder components by overheating.

Factors affecting knocking

Knocking depends on three factors: design of engine, operating conditions, and chemical structure of the hydrocarbon in fuel. The tendency of fuel constituents to knock follows the order: straight-chain paraffins > branched-chain paraffins (i.e., iso-paraffins) > olefins > cyclo-paraffins (i.e., naphthalenes) > aromatics. Thus, olefins of the same carbon chain length possess better anti-knock properties than the corresponding paraffins and so on.

Octane Rating

The resistance offered by gasoline to knock cannot be expressed in absolute term. Therefore, it is expressed in terms of a relative scale introduced by *Edger* in 1926. It has been found that *n*-heptane knocks very badly; hence, its anti-knock value has arbitrarily been given as zero. On the other hand, isooctane i.e., 2,2,4-trimethyl pentane, gives very little knocking, so its anti-knock value has been given as 100. Thus, octane number or rating of a gasoline IC engine fuel is the percentage of isooctane in a mixture of isooctane and *n*-heptane, which matches the fuel under test in knocking characteristics. In this way, an "80-ocatne" fuel is one which has the same combustion characteristics as an 80:20 mixture of isooctane and *n*-heptane.

Improvement of anti-knock characteristics of a fuel

The octane number of IC engine fuels can be raised by the addition of materials such as tetraethyllead [TEL; $(C_2H_5)_4Pb$] and diethyl telluride [$Te(C_2H_5)_2$]. In motor spirit (or motor fuel), about 0.5 ml and in aviation fuels, about 1.0–1.5 ml of TEL is added per liter of petrol. According to the most accepted theory, TEL is converted into a cloud of finely divided lead oxide particles in the cylinder. These particles react with any hydrocarbon peroxide molecules formed, thereby slowing down the chain oxidation reaction decreasing the chances of any early detonation. To remove the deposit of lead oxide formed from the engine, a small amount of ethylene dibromide is also added to petrol. Ethylene dibromide removes lead oxide as volatile lead bromide along with the exhaust gases.

$$Pb + CH_2Br - CH_2Br \longrightarrow PbBr_2 + CH_2 = CH_2$$

Note

1. The presence of sulfur compounds in petrol reduces the effectiveness of the TEL.
2. **Unleaded petrol:** Unleaded petrol is one where in the enhancement of octane rating is accomplished without the addition of lead compounds. Combustion of leaded petrol leads to formation of litharge (PbO), which deposits on the inner wall of cylinder and jams the piston. Lead present in exhaust gas poisons the catalyst used in catalytic converters fitted to exhaust system. In addition, it also contaminates the environment. An alternative method of increasing octane number of petrol is to add high octane compounds such as isopentane, isooctane, ethyl benzene, and methyl tert-butyl ether (MTBE). Out of these, MTBE is preferred as it contains oxygen in the form of ether group and supplies oxygen for the combustion of petrol in IC engines, thereby reducing the extent of peroxy compound formation.
3. A catalytic converter in exhaust system contains a catalyst which converts the toxic gases such as CO and NO to harmless gases CO_2 and N_2, respectively. Moreover, it oxidizes unburnt hydrocarbons into CO_2 and H_2O.

Diesel Engine Fuels

In a diesel engine, air is first drawn into the cylinder and compressed to a high pressure of ~10^5 kg/m^2 which is accompanied by a rise in temperature to about 500°C. Towards the end of compression stroke, diesel is injected in the form of finely divided spray into the cylinder. The fuel absorbs the heat and ignites spontaneously as it attains the ignition temperature. The rise in pressure due to expanding gases pushes the piston in the power stroke (see Fig. 14.16).

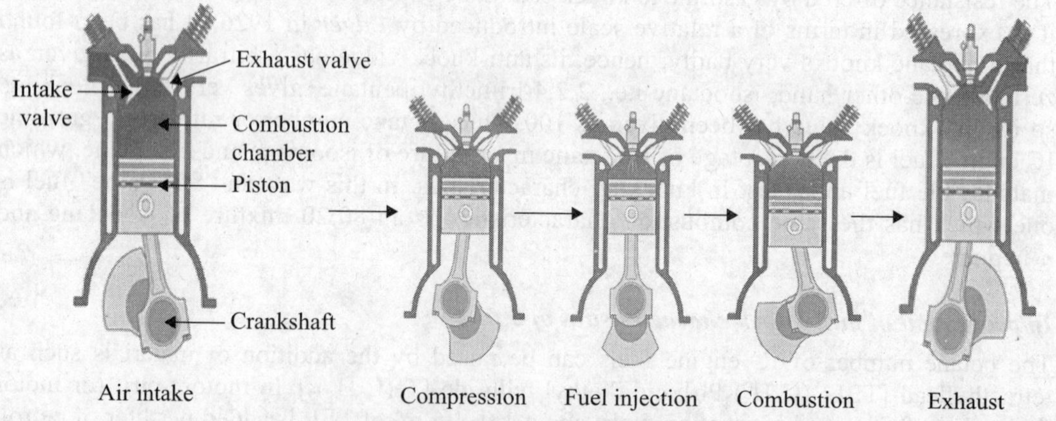

Fig. 14.16 A five-stroke diesel engine

Unlike gasoline engine, the combustion of fuel in a diesel engine is not instantaneous. The interval between fuel injection and ignition is called *ignition delay*. The ignition delay depends on the engine design, efficiency of mixing of spray and air, injector design, and the most important chemical nature of the fuel. If ignition delay is long, then it leads to accumulation of fuel in the engine. Now upon ignition, explosion may result causing *diesel knock*. The main characteristics of diesel engine fuel is that is should easily ignite below compression temperature, and there should be as short an ignition delay as possible.

Cetane Rating

The suitability of a diesel fuel is determined by its cetane value, which is a measure of the ease with which the fuel ignites under compression. It is the percentage of hexadecane in a mixture of hexadecane and 2-methyl naphthalene, which has the same ignition characteristics as that of the diesel fuel. The cetane number of diesel fuel can be raised by the addition of a small quantity of certain "pre-ignition dopes" such as ethyl nitrite and isoamyl nitrite. Ignition quality order among hydrocarbon constituents of a diesel fuel is *n*-alkanes > naphthalenes > alkenes > branched alkanes > aromatics. Therefore, hydrocarbons which are poor gasoline fuels are quite good diesel fuels.

Note

1. **High-speed and low-speed diesels:** In a high-speed diesel engine, the time lag in getting the diesel droplets heated to ignition point is very short, about 1/500th of a second. Such diesel engines require diesel with cetane number in excess of 45 (up to 60). On the other hand, a low-speed diesel requires cetane number about 25. Cetane number of medium speed diesel is about 35.
2. **Difference between octane and cetane ratings**

Octane rating	Cetane rating
Octane number or rating of a gasoline IC engine fuel is the percentage of isooctane in a mixture of isooctane and *n*-heptane, which matches the fuel under test in knocking characteristics.	It is the percentage of hexadecane in a mixture of hexadecane and 2-methy naphthalene, which has the same ignition characteristics as that of the diesel fuel.
It is used for the determination of suitability of fuel for gasoline IC engine.	It is used for the determination of suitability of diesel fuel.
Straight-chain hydrocarbons are worst fuels due to low octane number.	Straight-chain hydrocarbons are best fuels due to high cetane number.
Octane rating can be increased by the addition of tetraethyl lead and diethyl telluride	Cetane rating can be increased by the addition of ethyl nitrite, isoamyl nitrite, acetone peroxide, etc.

3. **Difference between gasoline and diesel engines**

Description	Gasoline engine	Diesel engine
Fuel	Gasoline + Air	Diesel + Air
Ignition	Spark plug	Compression of air
Knocking is attributed to	Pre- ignition	Delayed ignition
Fuel characteristic expressed in	Octane rating	Cetane rating
Additives to reduce knocking	Tetraethyl lead and diethyl telluride	Ethyl nitrite, isoamyl nitrite, acetone peroxide, etc.

Aviation Fuel

Aviation Gasoline (Avgas)

Avgas is a gasoline fuel used for small aircrafts with piston engines. Piston engine operates using the same basic principle as that used in spark ignition engines of cars, but they have a much higher performance requirement. Avgas is very volatile and is extremely flammable at normal operating temperatures. It is prepared by mixing alkylated branched paraffins with cracked gasoline containing unsaturated open-chain hydrocarbons.

Avgas grades are defined primarily by their octane rating. Two ratings are applied to aviation gasolines, viz., the lean mixture rating and the rich mixture rating, which results in a multiple numbering system; for example, avgas 100/130 means the lean mixture performance rating is 100 and the rich mixture rating is 130. In the past, there were many different grades of aviation gasoline in general use, e.g., 80/87, 91/96, 100/130, 108/135, and 115/145. However, with decreasing demand these have been rationalized down to one grade, Avgas 100/130. Again to avoid confusion in handling aviation gasoline, it is a common practice to designate the grade by just the lean mixture performance, i.e., Avgas 100. Currently, two major grades are in use internationally, viz., Avgas 100LL and Avgas 100. In the former, "LL" stands for *low lead* and it is the low lead version of Avgas 100. Low lead is a relative term. There is still up to 0.56 g/l of lead in Avgas 100LL. For easy identification the fuels are dyed. Avgas 100LL is colored blue, while Avgas 100 is colored green. Very recently a new Avgas grade 82UL (UL standing for unleaded) has been introduced. This is a low octane grade suitable for low compression ratio engines. It has a higher vapor pressure and can be manufactured from motor gasoline components.

Jet fuel or aviation turbine fuel

It is colorless to straw-colored aviation fuel designed for use in aircrafts powered by gas-turbine engines. The most commonly used fuels for commercial aviation are "Jet A" and "Jet A-1." The only other jet fuel commonly used in civilian turbine-engine powered aviation is "Jet B" which is used for its enhanced cold-weather performance. Jet fuel or aviation turbine fuel (ATF) is a mixture of a large number of different hydrocarbons. The range of their sizes, i.e., carbon numbers, is restricted by the requirements for the product, e.g., the freezing point or smoke point. Kerosene-type jet fuel including Jet A and Jet A-1 has a carbon number distribution between 8 and 16 carbon atoms per molecule while wide-cut or naphtha-type jet fuel including Jet B has a carbon number distribution between about 5 and 15 carbon atoms per molecule. Jet A specification fuel has been used in the United States since the 1950s and is usually not available outside the United States, whereas Jet A-1 is the standard specification fuel used in the rest of the world. Both Jet A and Jet A-1 have a flash point higher than 38°C (100°F), with an auto-ignition temperature of 210°C (410°F).

Jet B is a fuel in the naphtha–kerosene region that is used for its enhanced cold-weather performance. However, Jet B's lighter composition makes it more dangerous to handle. For this reason it is rarely used, except in very cold climates. A blend of approximately 30% kerosene and 70% gasoline is known as wide-cut fuel. It has a very low freezing point of −60°C (−76°F) in addition to a low flash point.

Biodiesel

Biodiesel refers to a vegetable oil or animal fat based diesel fuels consisting of alkyl esters. It is used in standard diesel engines. It can be used alone or blended with petrodiesel in any proportions. For identification of blends of biodiesel and conventional hydrocarbon based diesel, a system known as the "B" factor is often used. 100% biodiesel is referred to as "B100";

20% biodiesel, 80% petrodiesel is labeled "B20"; 5% biodiesel, 95% petrodiesel is labeled "B5"; and so on. Blends of 20% or less can be used in diesel equipment with no or only minor modifications. Blends of 20% biodiesel and lower can be used in diesel equipment with no, or only minor modifications. The pure form "B100" can be used only after engine modifications to avoid maintenance and performance problems. Biodiesel can also be used as a low carbon alternative to heating oil.

Production

Biodiesel is produced through the base catalyzed trans-esterification of vegetable oil or animal fat with short-chain alcohols such as methanol or ethanol. Alcohol reacts with the fatty acids to form the mono-alkyl ester (biodiesel) and crude glycerol. The reaction is reversible for which excess alcohol must be added to ensure complete conversion. The basic reaction is as follows:

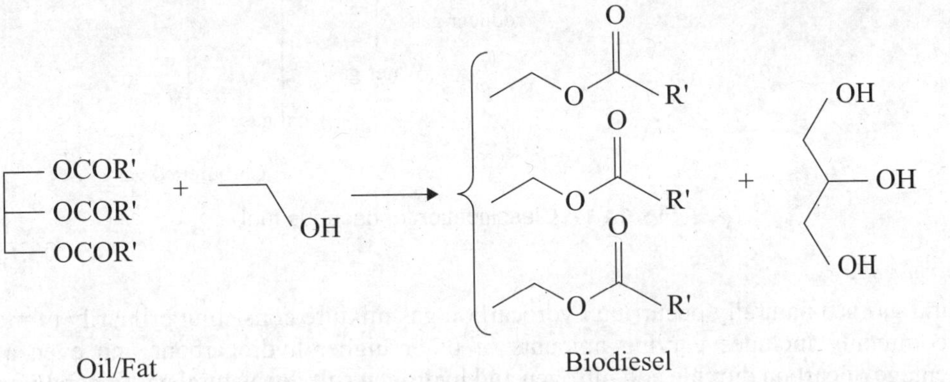

> **Note:**
> 1. Under normal conditions, this reaction occurs either extremely slowly or not at all. Therefore, elevated temperature as well as catalysts is used to make the reaction proceed at an appreciable rate.
> 2. Almost all biodiesel is produced from virgin vegetable oils using the base-catalyzed technique which is the most economical process for treating virgin vegetable oils.
> 3. Vegetable oils require only low temperatures and pressures and produce over 98% conversion provided the starting oil is low in moisture and free fatty acids.
> 4. Other catalyst free methods such as supercritical process and ultrasonic reactor method can also be used.

Power Alcohol

Petrol blended with 20–25% ethyl alcohol is known as power alcohol for IC engines. Gasohol is a mixture of 90% unleaded petrol and 10% ethyl alcohol. Its performance is comparable with 100% unleaded petrol with an additional advantage of superior anti-knocking properties. It has gained attention as an alternative to pure gasoline in recent years as its use does not require any engine modification.

> **Note:**
> The main disadvantages are that it lowers the calorific values of petrol and may cause corrosion as alcohol is easily oxidized to acids.

Gaseous Fuels

The basic classification scheme of classification of gaseous fuel is shown in Fig. 14.17:

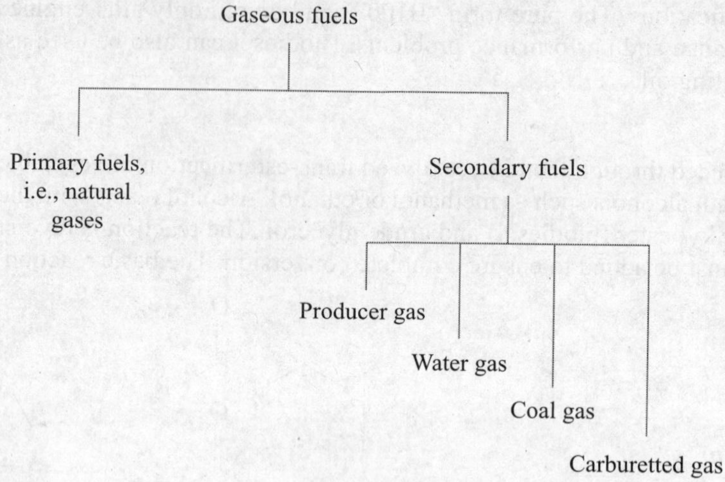

Fig. 14.17 Classification of gaseous fuel

Natural gas

Natural gas is a naturally occurring hydrocarbon gas mixture consisting primarily of methane, but commonly includes varying amounts of other higher hydrocarbons and even a lesser percentage of carbon dioxide and nitrogen and hydrogen sulfide. Natural gas generally remains associated with petroleum deposits and is obtained from wells dug in the oil-bearing regions. When natural gas occurs along with petroleum in oil wells, it is called "wet gas." On the other hand, when the gas is associated with crude oil, it is called "dry gas." Before use, the natural gas is purified to remove objectionable ingredients such as water, dust, grit, H_2S, CO_2, N_2, and heavier liquefiable hydrocarbons. The approximate composition of natural gas is CH_4 = 70–90%, C_2H_6 = 5–10%, H_2 = 3%, $CO + CO_2$ = rest. The calorific value varies from 12000 to 14000 kcal/m^3.

Uses

1. It is an excellent domestic fuel and can be conveyed over very large distance in pipelines.
2. It is used in the manufacture of a number of chemicals by synthetic processes.
3. It is used as a raw material for the manufacture of carbon black, which is used as filler for rubber, and hydrogen, which is used in ammonia synthesis.
4. Synthetic proteins which are used as animal feed are obtained by microbiological fermentation of methane.

Note:

H_2S gas present in natural gas is removed by scrubbing with monoethanolamine ($NH_2–CH_2–CH_2–OH$). H_2S is removed upon heating.

$$2HO–CH_2–CH_2–OH + H_2S \longrightarrow (HO–CH_2–CH_2–OH)_2 \cdot H_2S$$

Compressed natural gas

Compressed natural gas (CNG) is nothing but natural gas mainly composed of methane compressed to a high pressure of about 1000 atm. A steel cylinder containing 15 kg of CNG contains about 2×10^4 L or 20 m^3 of natural gas at 1 atmospheric pressure. CNG is a fossil fuel substitute for gasoline, diesel fuel, and LPG. Although CNG's combustion does produce greenhouse gases, it is widely considered a more environmentally clean alternative to conventional fuels. It is much safer than other fuels in the event of a spill, because natural gas is lighter than air and disperses quickly when released. The main disadvantage is that CNG vehicles require a greater amount of space for fuel storage than conventional gasoline powered vehicles. The main advantages of CNG are as follows:

1. Due to its high auto-ignition temperature (540°C) than gasoline and diesel, CNG is considered as a much safer fuel.
2. The conversion of gasoline operated automobiles into CNG operated vehicle is very easy.
3. The operating cost of CNG fuel is much lower compared to gasoline operation.
4. CNG fuel systems are sealed, preventing losses due to spills and evaporation.
5. Combustion of CNG leads to lesser CO_2 and CO emissions than gasoline. For release of same amount of energy, CNG produces nearly 40% less CO_2 than petrol. The CO release is reduced even further.
6. CNG mixes better with air than liquid fuels.
7. Emission from CNG operated vehicle contains no unregulated pollutants (e.g., smoke, SO_2, SO_3, C_6H_6, HCHO).

Producer gas

Producer gas is a mixture of combustible gases such as CO and H_2 along with a large percent of non-combustible gases such as N_2 and CO_2. The average composition is CO (22–30%), H_2 (8–12%), N_2 (52–55%), and CO_2 (3%). It is insoluble in water and is poisonous in nature with a calorific value 900–1300 kcal/m^3.

Preparation

It is prepared by passing air mixed with a little steam (about 0.35 kg/kg of coal) over a red hot coal/coke bed maintained at about 1100°C in a special reactor called *gas producer* (Fig. 14.18). It consists of a steel vessel which is lined inside with refractory bricks. It is provided with a cup and cone feeder at the top and a side outlet for the producer gas. It has an inlet for passing air and steam in addition to an exit at the base for the removal of ash. The changes at different reaction zones are as follows.

Ash zone: It is the lowest zone consisting mainly of ash. The ash protects the grate of the producer plant from intense heat of combustion. The temperature of supplied air and steam is increased as they pass through this zone.

Combustion zone: It is the zone next to the ash zone. It is known as the oxidation zone. Here the carbon burns and forms CO and CO_2. The temperature of this zone is about 1100°C.

$$\begin{cases} C + 1/2O_2 \longrightarrow CO + 53 \text{ kcal} \\ C + O_2 \longrightarrow CO_2 + 97 \text{ kcal} \end{cases}$$

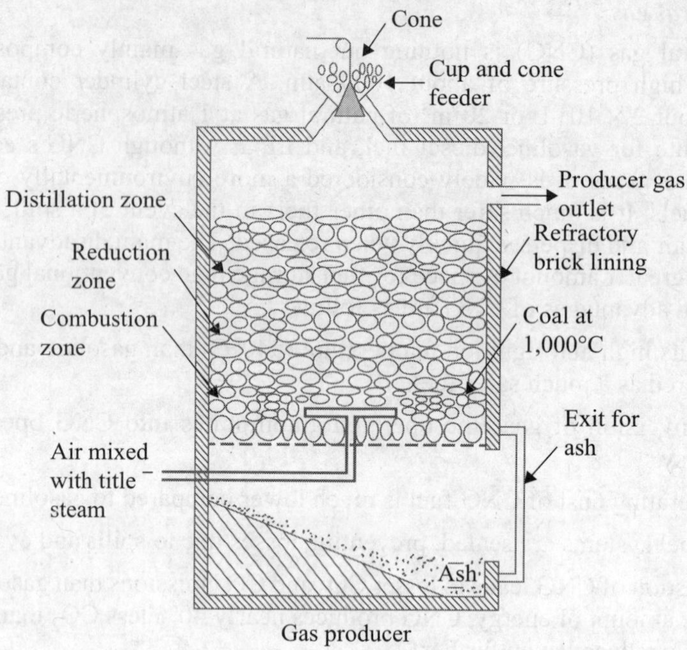

Fig. 14.18 Gas producer for manufacturing producer gas

Reduction zone: Here carbon dioxide and steam combines moves up through the red-hot coke and liberates free hydrogen and carbon monoxide. All these reduction reactions are endothermic, so the temperature in the reduction zone is about 1000°C. If no steam is supplied, the temperature of the producer further rises and this may fuse the ash and refractory lining. To avoid these troubles and to produce richer gas, a little steam admixed with air is used. A balance between the air and steam supply is struck so as to maintain proper temperature of ~1100°C.

$$\begin{cases} CO_2 + C \longrightarrow 2CO - 36 \text{ kcal} \\ C + H_2O \longrightarrow CO + H_2 - 29 \text{ kcal} \\ C + 2H_2O \longrightarrow CO_2 + 2H_2 - 19 \text{ kcal} \end{cases}$$

Distillation zone: This is the uppermost part of the fuel bed. The heat given by the gases and the heat radiated from the reduction zone help to distil the fuel, thereby adding volatile matter of coal to the outgoing gas.

Uses

1. It is used in heating open-hearth furnaces, muffle furnaces, retorts used in coke and coal gas manufacture.
2. It is used as a reducing agent in metallurgical operations.

Water gas

It is a mixture of combustible gases, viz., CO and H_2, with a little non-combustible gases such as CO_2 and N_2. It is non-luminous and burns with a blue flame often known as *blue gas*.

Its calorific value is ~2800 kcal/m^3. The average composition is CO (41%), H_2 (51%), N_2 (4%), and CO_2 (4%).

Production

It is made by passing alternatively steam and little air through a bed of red hot coal or coke maintained at about 900–1000°C in a reactor. The reactor consists of a steel vessel which is lined inside with refractory bricks. It has a cup and cone feeder at the top and an opening near the top for the exit of water gas. It is provided with separate inlet pipes for passing air and steam. At the bottom, it is provided with an exit for ash formed (Fig. 14.19). Supplied steam reacts with red hot coal or coke at 900–1000°C to from carbon monoxide and hydrogen. The reaction is endothermic and tends to decrease the temperature of bed. The temperature of the bed is raised and maintained by cutting off the steam supply and blowing air when the exothermic reactions take place.

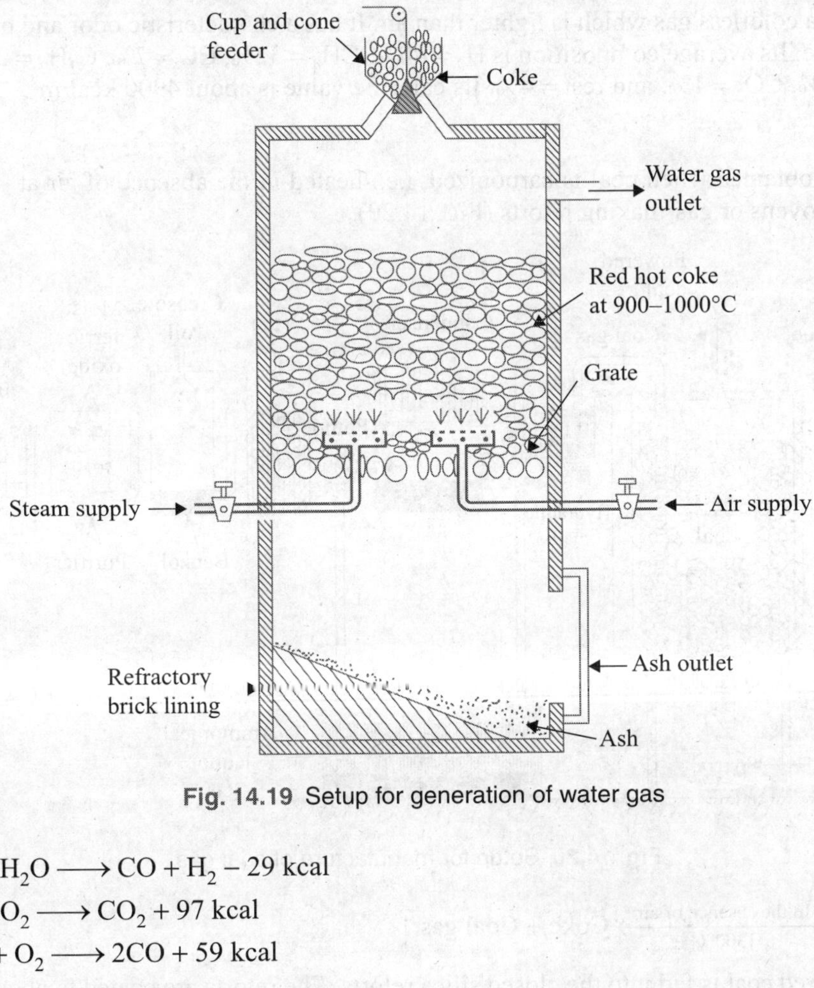

Fig. 14.19 Setup for generation of water gas

$$C + H_2O \longrightarrow CO + H_2 - 29 \text{ kcal}$$

$$C + O_2 \longrightarrow CO_2 + 97 \text{ kcal}$$

$$2C + O_2 \longrightarrow 2CO + 59 \text{ kcal}$$

Uses

It is used as (i) a source of hydrogen gas, (ii) an illuminating gas, and (iii) a fuel gas.

Note:

1. Calorific value of water gas can be improved by adding gaseous hydrocarbons obtained by cracking crude oils. This gaseous mixture is called *carbureted water gas* which contains about 35% H_2, 25% CO, 35% hydrocarbons (saturated and unsaturated), and 5% $N_2 + CO_2$. Its calorific value is ~4500 kcal/m^3. It is used for heating and illumination purposes.
2. ***Semi-water gas*** is obtained by passing a properly adjusted air and steam mixture continuously through a bed of red-hot coke so that the endothermic reaction just balances the exothermic reaction. Its average composition is $H_2 = 12\%$, $CH_4 = 3\%$, $CO = 30\%$, $CO_2 = 2\%$, and $N_2 = 53\%$. Their calorific value is ~1700 kcal/m^3. It is used as (i) a fuel and (ii) a source of N_2 and H_2 in the manufacture of NH_3.

Coal gas

Coal gas is a colorless gas which is lighter than air. It has a characteristic odor and burns with a smoky flame. Its average composition is $H_2 = 40\%$, $CH_4 = 32\%$, $CO = 7\%$, $C_2H_2 = 2\%$, $C_2H_2 = 3\%$, $N_2 = 4\%$, $CO_2 = 1\%$, and rest = 4%. Its calorific value is about 4900 kcal/m^3.

Production

Coal gas is obtained when coal is carbonized, i.e., heated in the absence of air at ~1300°C in either coke ovens or gas-making retorts (Fig. 14.20).

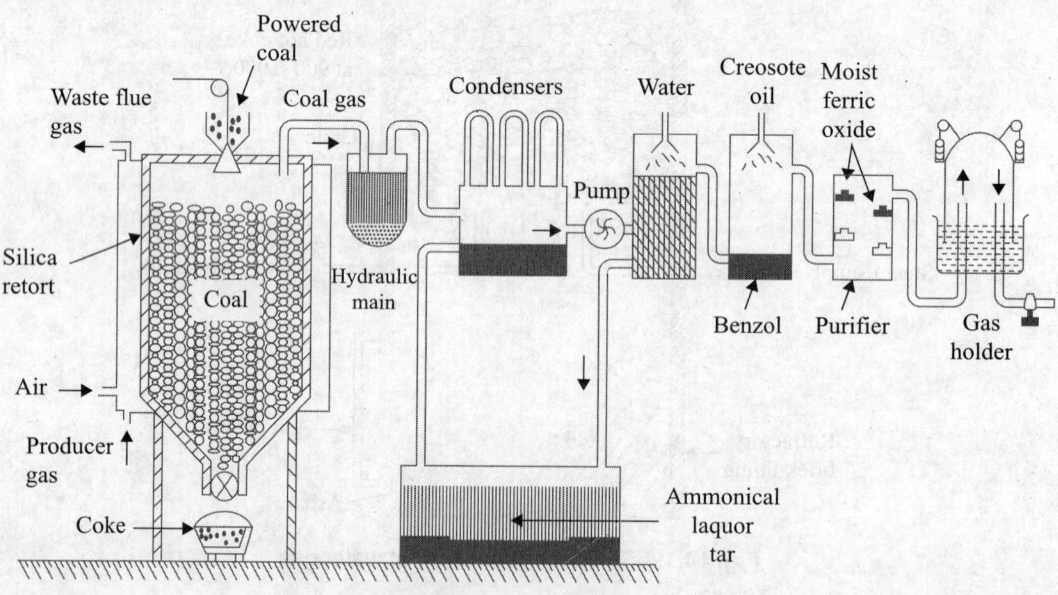

Fig. 14.20 Setup for manufacture of coal gas

$$\text{Coal} \xrightarrow[\text{1300°C}]{\text{In the absence of air}} \text{Coke} + \text{Coal gas}\uparrow$$

Powdered coal is fed into the closed silica retorts. The retorts are heated to about 1300°C. The gas coming out from the retort is first scrubbed by passing through a hydraulic main. Major portion of the tar is then removed by cooling the gas in a condenser. The remaining tar and ammonia present in the gas are removed by scrubbing with water in a scrubber. The cooled gas is then passed through creosote oil to dissolve benzol, naphthalene, etc. The gas is then freed from H_2S by passing over moist Fe_2O_3. The purified coal gas is finally stored over water in gas holders. The exhausted iron oxide purifier can be recharged by simply exposing to air. Exposure to simply oxidizes Fe(II) to Fe(III).

$$2Fe(OH)_{3(s)} + 3H_2S(g) \longrightarrow Fe_2S_{3(s)} + 6H_2O_{(l)}$$

$$2\overset{2+}{Fe}_2S_{3(s)} + 3O_2(g) \longrightarrow 2\overset{3+}{Fe}_2O_{3(s)} + 6H_2S(g)$$

Uses

It is used (i) as an illuminant in cities and towns, (ii) as a fuel, and (iii) in metallurgical operations for providing reducing atmosphere.

Oil gas

It is golden color gas with an average composition of CH_4 = 25–30%, H_2 = 50–55%, CO = 10–12%, and CO_2 = 3%. Its calorific value remains in the range 4500–5400 kcal/m^3.

Production

It is obtained by cracking of kerosene oil. The plant used consists of a strong cast iron retort, enclosed in a coal-fired furnace. A bonnet is fitted at the mouth of retort, through a molten lead seal. The other end of the bonnet is connected to a hydraulic main, i.e., a tank containing water, through a water seal. A pipe from the hydraulic main leads to the gas holder. The retort is heated to red heat and oil is continuously allowed to fall in the red hot bottom of the retort. The oil coming in contact with red hot bottom, immediately gets cracked into a number of lower gaseous hydrocarbons. The resulting gaseous mixture goes out through the bonnet to a hydraulic main to condense tar. The proper cracking of the oil is estimated from the color of the gas at testing cap. The gas is finally stored over water in gas holders (Fig. 14.21). The yield of gas usually remains in the range 40–50%.

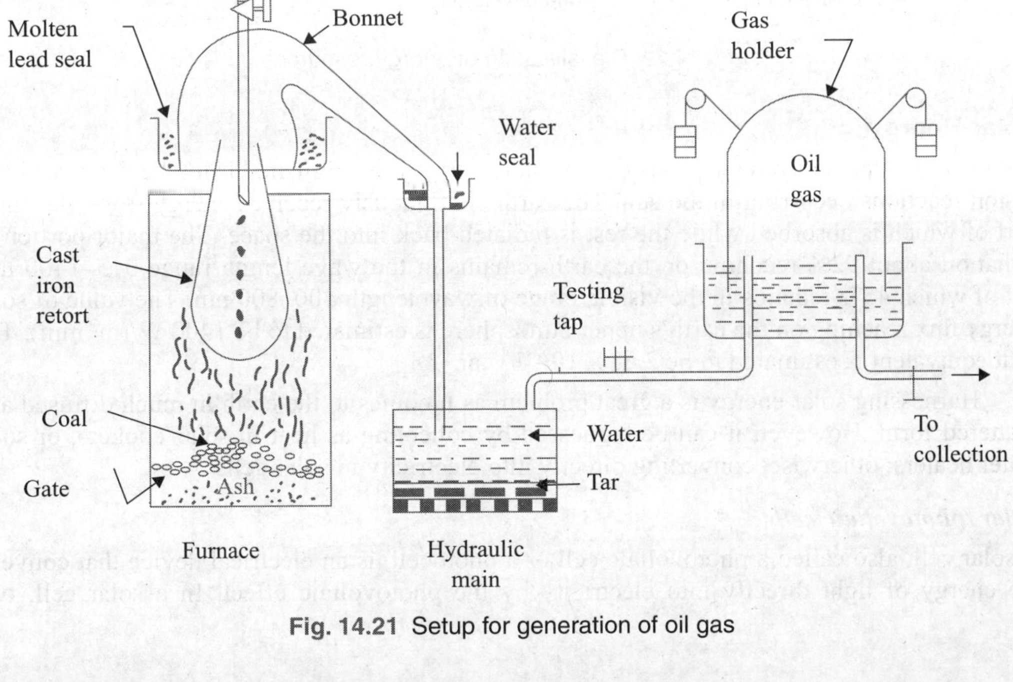

Fig. 14.21 Setup for generation of oil gas

$$\underbrace{C_{12}H_{26}}_{\text{Kerosene oil}} \longrightarrow \underbrace{CH_4 + C_2H_6 + C_2H_4 + C_2H_2 + C_2H_2 + C_3H_8 + C_3H_6}_{\text{Mixture of lower hydrocarbons}} + \underbrace{C}_{\text{Tar}}$$

Uses

Primarily used as a laboratory gas and also used to improve the calorific value of water gas. The mixture of the two gases is known as carbureted water gas.

Non-conventional Sources

Energy sources can be broadly classified as primary and secondary sources. Primary energy sources are mined or otherwise obtained from the environment such as *fossil fuel, hydro, geo-thermal, solar, wind, tidal energies,* etc. On the other hand, secondary energy sources are those which do not occur in nature but are derived from primary energy resources such as *gasoline from crude oil, electrical energy from coal burning, hydrogen from electrolysis of water,* etc. Primary energy sources can further be classified as conventional and non-conventional sources. Conventional sources are those which are finite and exhaustible, e.g., fossil fuels and nuclear fuels, while non-conventional energy sources are those which are being continuously produced in nature and non-exhaustible, e.g., solar energy, geo-thermal energy, and wind energy. The classification scheme is shown in Fig. 14.22.

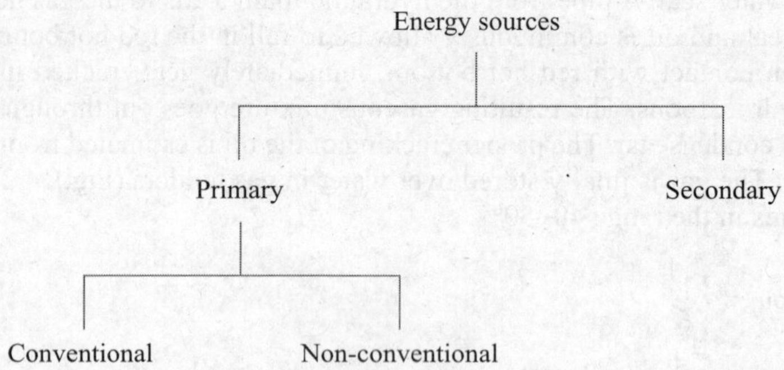

Fig. 14.22 Classification of energy resources

Solar Energy

The energy obtained from the sun is called solar energy. It is originated from the thermonuclear fusion reactions occurring in the sun. The earth continuously receives energy from the sun, a part of which is absorbed while the rest is radiated back into the space. The major portion of radiation about 92% reaching on the earth remains in the wave length range 315–1400 nm, out of which 45% remains in the visible range of wavelength 400–800 nm. The value of solar energy flux reaching on the earth's upper atmosphere is estimated to be 1400 W/(m^2 min). The heat equivalent is estimated to be 2.68×10^{24} J/year.

Harnessing solar energy is a great problem as it comes to the earth in much diffused and scattered form. However, it can be harnessed by collecting as heat in solar cookers, or solar water heaters; otherwise, converting directly into electricity in solar cells.

Solar /photovoltaic cell

A solar cell, also called a photovoltaic cell or a photocell, is an electrical device that converts the energy of light directly into electricity by the photovoltaic effect. In a solar cell, two types (*n*-type and *p*-type) of semiconductors are used. These semiconductor materials are so arranged that one region is the *n*-type while the adjacent one is the *p*-type. The boundary between these two reasons within a single crystal is known as *p–n junction*. As light falls on the *p–n* junction, electrons from the valence band are promoted to the conduction band, thereby generating electron–hole pairs on both sides of the junction. In other words, an electron pair bond is dissociated into an electron and a hole. Since the *p–n* junction is a barrier for both types of charge carriers, concentration of holes builds up on the *p*-side of the junction while that of electrons builds up on the *n*-side. When these concentrations exceed the equilibrium concentration of the carriers in the corresponding parts of the semiconductor, a drift of holes toward A and that of electrons towards B takes place. The result being a potential difference, the generated current flows from A to B. The mechanism is schematically shown in Fig. 14.23. In an actual practice, a large number of solar cells are joined together in a definite pattern to get solar cell panel, which is capable of providing required electric power.

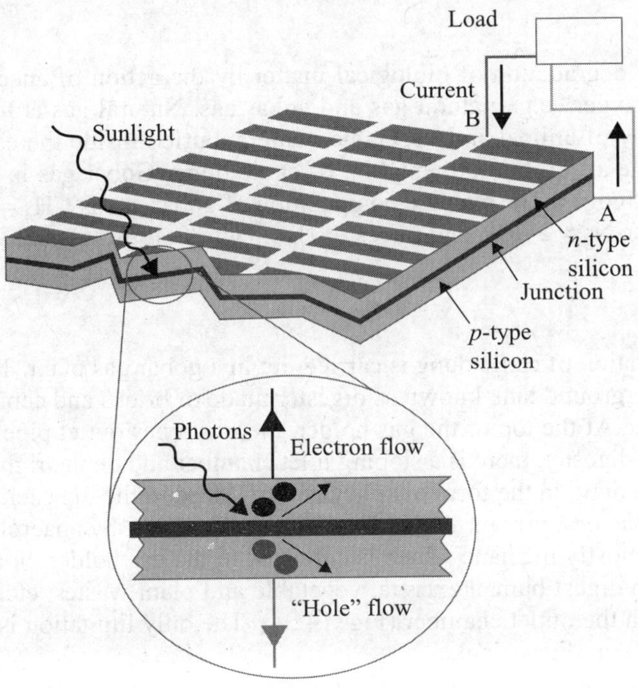

Fig. 14.23 Mechanism of current generation in a photovoltaic cell

Uses

1. For producing electricity on artificial satellites and space probes.
2. For providing electricity for street lighting, water pump operations, and running radio, and TV sets in remote areas.
3. For operating electronic gazettes such as watches and calculators.

Biomass

Biomass is the waste organic matter obtained from the dead plants and animals. Biomass can either be used directly through combustion to produce heat or indirectly after converting it to various forms of bio-fuel which is achieved by different methods such as *thermal*, *chemical*, and *biochemical* methods, e.g., wood, cattle dung, bagasse, poultry wastes, vegetable wastes, waste paper, waste cotton clothes, plant wastes like grass, husk, leaves, weeds, etc., human excreta, animal/bird excreta, dead animals, sewage, etc.

Note:

Advantages of converting biomass into biogas:

1. Biogas production is cheap.
2. The gas has all advantage of gaseous fuel such as cleanliness is the absence of smoke, flexibility, etc.
3. It does not contain poisonous gas such as carbon monoxide as an ingredient.
4. It provides simultaneously excellent yield of good manure.

Biogas

It is produced by the degradation of biological matter by the action of anaerobic bacteria in the absence of free oxygen, e.g., natural gas and gobar gas. Natural gas is formed as a result of a long period decay of animal and vegetable matters, buried inside the earth, while gober gas is produced by the anaerobic fermentation of cattle dung. Gobar gas is the cheapest and most easily available biogas. The average composition of gobar gas is CH_4 = 50–60%, CO_2 = 30–40%, H_2 = 5–10%, N_2 = 2–6%, and traces of H_2S. Out of all these, methane makes biogas an excellent fuel.

Production

The anaerobic degradation of cattle dung is carried out in a gobar gas plant. The plant consists of a well-shaped underground tank known as digester made of bricks and cement. It is covered with a steel gas holder. At the top of the gas holder, there is a gas outlet pipe and a gas valve. On the left side of the digester, there is a sloping inlet chamber and on the right side, there is an outlet chamber. Cattle dung in the form of slurry is introduced to the digester through the inlet chamber. Anaerobic bacteria present in the dung digest this slurry by anaerobic fermentation. The gas generated is mostly methane which is collected in the gas holder. In addition to cattle dung, the digester can digest human excreta, vegetable and plant wastes, etc. The spent dung slurry gets collected in the outlet chamber (Fig. 14.24). The only limitation is that the gas can be used only within 10 m of gas plant.

Advantages of biogas

1. Biogas or gobar gas production is economical. It has been found that 1 kg of dry cattle dung gives about 160 L of gobar gas, which can supply 188 kcal of heat. On the other hand, 1 kg of dry dung gives only 23.4 kcal of effective heat.
2. The gas has all advantages of gaseous fuel such as cleanliness, absence of smoke, dust, and dirt.
3. It does not contain poisonous gas CO as an ingredient.
4. It involves no storage problem, since biogas can be supplied through pipes directly from the biogas plant.
5. Production cost is very low.
6. It provides simultaneously excellent yield of good manure.

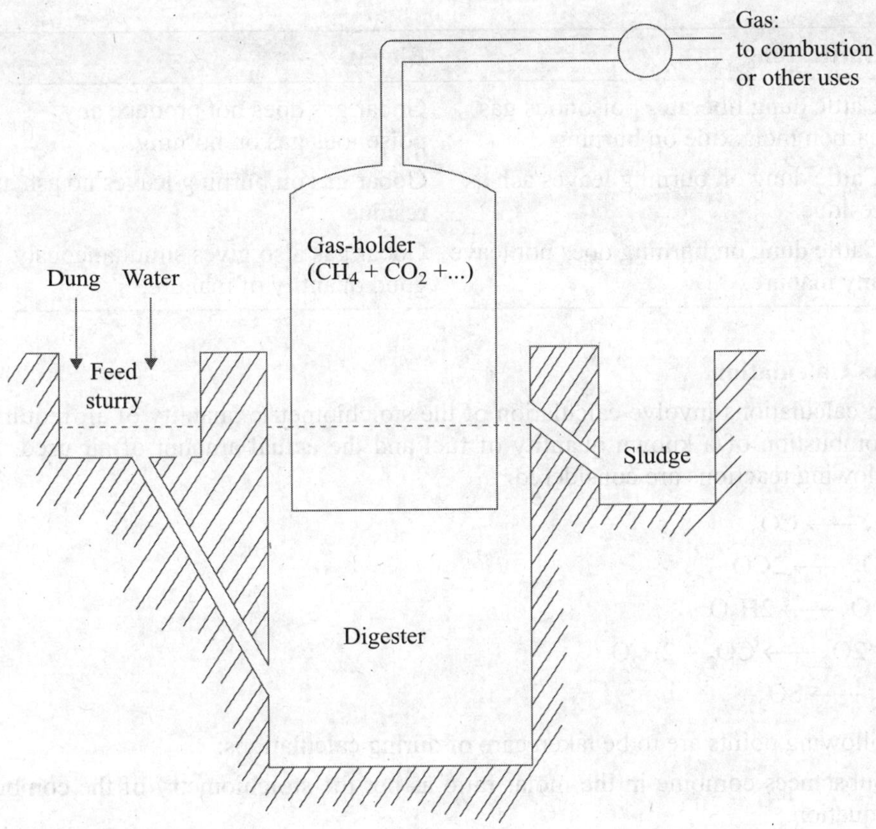

Fig. 14.24 Gobar gas plant

Uses

It is used as a domestic fuel. It can also be used for lighting and power purposes. It also gives simultaneously excellent yield of good manure which has 2–6% of nitrogen.

Note:

A comparative account of cattle dung and biogas obtained from it is as follows:

	Cattle dung	Biogas
1.	Lower amount of heat is liberated which is 23.4 kcal/kg of dry dung on direct burning.	Higher amount of heat (188 kcal/kg) is liberated by burning biogas obtained from the same mass of cattle dung.
2.	Cattle dung on burning liberates smoke, dust, dirt, etc., and causes blackening of utensils and houses.	Gobar gas has all the advantages of gaseous fuels such as cleanliness of utensils, flexibility, and absence of smoke, dust, and dirt.
3.	Cattle dung flame can provide temperature only up to 300°C.	Flame of biogas can provides temperature of 540°C.

	Cattle dung	Biogas
4.	Cattle dung liberates poisonous gas carbon monoxide on burning.	Gobar gas does not produce any poisonous gas on burning.
5.	Cattle dung on burning leaves ash as residue.	Gobar gas on burning leaves no ash as residue.
6.	Cattle dung on burning does not leave any manure.	Gobar gas also gives simultaneously good quantity of manure.

Combustion Calculation

Combustion calculations involve calculation of the stoichiometric quantity of air required for complete combustion of a known quantity of fuel and the actual amount of air used. In the process, following reactions are considered:

$$\left\{\begin{array}{l} C + O_2 \longrightarrow CO_2 \\ 2C + O_2 \longrightarrow 2CO \\ 2H_2 + O_2 \longrightarrow 2H_2O \\ CH_4 + 2O_2 \longrightarrow CO_2 + 2H_2O \\ S + O_2 \longrightarrow SO_2 \end{array}\right.$$

The following points are to be taken care of during calculations:

1. Substances combine in the molar ratio as per the stoichiometry of the combustion equation.
2. The composition of air is taken as 21% O_2 and 79% N_2 (by volume); 23% O_2 and 77% N_2 (by weight). The average molecular weight of air is taken as 28.952.
3. 1 kmol of a gas occupies 22.4 m^3 at NTP.
4. Analysis of solids is reported on weight basis. In order to convert them into moles, it is required to divide each of them by their molecular weight.
5. Analysis of gases is reported on the basis of volume and therefore directly provides their number of moles present per 100 mol of mixture.
6. Minimum oxygen required is calculated on the basis of complete combustion.

Example 14.8

Find the minimum amount of air required for the complete combustion of 10 kg of a sample fuel containing 75% C, 5% H_2, 8% O_2, 3% S, and the rest N_2 by weight. Also find the volume of air in m^3 at NTP and percentage composition by weight and volume of the dry products of combustion.

Solution

$$\left\{\begin{array}{llll} C & + \; O_2 & \longrightarrow & CO_2 \\ 12\text{ kg} & 32\text{ kg} & & 44\text{ kg} \\ H_2 & + \; 1/2O_2 & \longrightarrow & H_2O \\ 2\text{ kg} & 16\text{ kg} & & 18\text{ kg} \\ S & + \; O_2 & \longrightarrow & SO_2 \\ 32\text{ kg} & 32\text{ kg} & & 64\text{ kg} \end{array}\right.$$

Constituents	Weight (kg)	Weight of O_2 (kg)	Weight of dry air of products (kg)
C	75	$\frac{32}{12} \times 75 = 200$	$\frac{75}{12} \times 44 = 271.33$
H_2	5	$\frac{16}{2} \times 5 = 40$	–
O_2	8	–8	–
S	3	$\frac{32}{32} \times 3 = 3$	$\frac{3}{32} \times 64 = 6$
N_2	9	–	9

Total weight of oxygen required 235 kg
for combustion of 100 kg coal

Total weight of oxygen required for combustion of 100 kg coal = 235 kg

Oxygen required for combustion of 1 kg of coal = 2.35 kg

Thus, oxygen required for combustion of 10 kg of coal = 2.35 × 10 = 23.5 kg

Now, air required for combustion of 10 kg of coal = $23.5 \times \frac{100}{23} = 73.4$ kg

NTP volume

32 kg of O_2 occupies 22.4 m^3 volume at NTP

Thus, 23.5 kg of O_2 occupies = $\frac{22.4}{32} \times 23.5 = 16.45$ m^3

Now, 21 m^3 of O_2 is present in 100 m^3 of air at NTP

Thus, 16.45 m^3 of O_2 is present in $\frac{100}{21} \times 16.45 = 78.33$ m^3

So, volume of air required at NTP = 78.33 m^3.

By weight

The dry products of combustion formed from 1 kg of coal are

$CO_2 = 2.71$ kg

$SO_2 = 0.06$ kg

$N_2 = 0.09$ (from fuel) + (7.34 – 2.35) = 5.08 kg

Total weight of dry products = 2.71 + 0.06 + 5.08 = 7.85 kg

Now, gravimetric composition of dry products is

$$CO_2 = \frac{2.71}{7.85} \times 100 = 34.52\%$$

$$SO_2 = \frac{0.06}{7.85} \times 100 = 0.76\%$$

And, $N_2 = \frac{5.08}{7.85} \times 100 = 64.71\%$

By volume

$$CO_2 = \frac{2.71}{44} = 0.062 \text{ kmol}$$

$$SO_2 = \frac{0.06}{64} = 0.00094 \text{ kmol}$$

$$N_2 = \frac{5.08}{28} = 0.181 \text{ kmol}$$

Total volume = 0.062 + 0.00094 + 0.181 = 0.244 kmol

Now, volumetric composition of dry products is

$$CO_2 = \frac{0.062}{0.244} \times 100 = 25.41\%$$

$$SO_2 = \frac{0.00094}{0.244} \times 100 = 0.39\%$$

$$\text{And, } N_2 = \frac{0.181}{0.244} \times 100 = 74.18\%$$

Example 14.9

A sample of a solid fuel contains 60% C, 4% H_2, 6% O_2, 2% N_2, and 28% ash. Find percentage composition of the dry products of combustion, assuming that 40% excess air is used.

Solution

Constituents	Weight (kg)	Weight of O_2 (kg)	Weight of dry air of products (kg)
C	60	$\frac{32}{12} \times 60 = 160$	$\frac{60}{12} \times 44 = 220$
H_2	4	$\frac{16}{2} \times 4 = 32$	–
O_2	6	–6	–
N_2	2	–	2
Ash	28	–	–

Total weight of oxygen required 186 kg
for combustion of 100 kg coal

Thus weight of oxygen required for 1 kg of coal = 1.86 kg

$$\text{Now, air required is} = 1.86 \times \frac{100}{23} = 8.087 \text{ kg}$$

$$\text{Weight of air actually used} = 8.087 \times \frac{140}{100} = 11.322 \text{ kg}$$

The dry products of combustion formed from 1 kg of coal are,

$CO_2 = 2.2$ kg

$$O_2 = \text{Excess air} \times \frac{23}{100} = (11.322 - 8.087) \times 0.23 = 0.744 \text{ kg}$$

$$N_2 = 0.02 \text{ (from fuel)} + 11.322 \times \frac{77}{100} \text{ (from air)} = 8.738 \text{ kg}$$

Total weight of dry products = 2.2 + 0.744 + 8.738 = 11.682 kg

Now, gravimetric composition of dry products is,

$$CO_2 = \frac{2.2}{11.682} \times 100 = 18.83\%$$

$$SO_2 = \frac{0.744}{11.682} \times 100 = 6.37\%$$

$$\text{And, } N_2 = \frac{8.738}{11.682} \times 100 = 74.79\%$$

Example 14.10

A gas the following composition by volume: $H_2 = 22\%$, $CH_4 = 4\%$, $CO = 20\%$, $CO_2 = 6\%$, $O_2 = 3\%$, and $N_2 = 45\%$. If 25% excess air is used, find the actual weight of air supplied per m³ of this gas.

Solution

Constituents	% mol	Moles of O_2 required
H_2	22	11
CH_4	4	8
CO	20	10
CO_2	6	–
O_2	3	–3
N_2	45	–
	Total O_2 required	26

$$\text{Air required for 100 mols of fuel gas} = 26 \times \frac{100}{21} = 123.8 \text{ mol}$$

$$\text{Air supplied} = 123.8 \times \frac{125}{100} = 154.75 \text{ mol}$$

$$\text{Now, air supplied for 1 mol of gas} = \frac{154.75}{100} = 1.547 \text{ mol}$$

$$\text{Air supplied per m}^3 \text{ of gas} = 1.547 \text{ m}^3 = \frac{1.547 \times 28.97}{22.4} = 2 \text{ kg}$$

(as 22.4 m³ of air, i.e., 1 kmol at NTP weighs 28.95 kg)

QUESTIONS

1. What are primary and secondary fuels? Explain with examples.
2. Give a comparative account of different types of fuels.
3. What is calorific value of a fuel?
4. What are the characteristics of a good fuel?

5. What is the difference between gross and net calorific value of a fuel?
6. How is the calorific value of a solid fuel determined by using bomb calorimeter?
7. How is the calorific value of gaseous and volatile liquid fuels calculated by using Boy's gas calorimeter?
8. Discuss the necessary corrections required during the estimation of calorific value of a solid fuel in bomb calorimeter. Provide the final equation for HCV after correction.
9. Arrange different types of coals in the increasing order of their calorific values.
10. What is proximate analysis?
11. Why coke is preferred over coal in industrial applications?
12. What do you mean by reforming?
13. What is knocking?
14. Discuss methods to improve anti-knock characteristics of a fuel.
15. What is meant by octane number of a gasoline?
16. Why a small quantity of ethylene dibromide is added to petrol along with anti-knocking agent TEL?
17. Give name of some compounds those are added to petrol to improve octane rating.
18. Arrange the following compounds in increasing order of their octane number: 3-ethylpentane; 2,2-dimethylpentane; 2,2,3-trimethylbutane; and 3,3-dimethylpentane.
19. What are the different steps in the working of a typical four-stroke engine?
20. Explain the working of a diesel engine.
21. What do you mean by compression ratio of IC engine?
22. What is power alcohol?
23. What is biodiesel?
24. What is CNG? Why it is preferred over LPG?
25. What is the importance of measuring fixed carbon in coal?
26. What is cetane number of diesel fuel?
27. Differentiate between octane number and cetane number.
28. What are high-speed and low-speed diesels?
29. Explain knocking in a diesel engine.
30. What are the limitations of alcohol–gasoline blends in IC engines?
31. What is sweetening of petrol?
32. Explain Doctor's process in refining of gasoline.
33. How is water gas superior to producer gas?
34. Why air saturated with steam is used in the production of producer gas?
35. Why caloric value of coal gas is higher than that of producer gas?
36. Why in a catalytic cracking process, catalyst requires regeneration?
37. What do you mean by carbureted water gas?
38. What is semi-water gas? Provide its average chemical composition.
39. Differentiate proximate and ultimate analysis of coal.
40. What is the importance of ultimate analysis of coal?

41. Explain determination of nitrogen in ultimate analysis.
42. How sulfur is determined in ultimate analysis?
43. Which parameters are determined in proximate analysis?
44. Explain proximate analysis of coal and its significance.
45. Explain briefly ultimate analysis of coal and its significance.
46. Explain carbonization of coal.
47. Explain knocking in IC engines.
48. Explain fluidized bed catalytic method for obtaining gasoline with the mechanism involved.
49. Describe the determination of calorific value of a solid fuel by bomb calorimeter.
50. Explain proximate analysis in detail. What is the significance?
51. What are the requirements of metallurgical coke?
52. How is metallurgical coke prepared?
53. Describe fractional distillation of petroleum.
54. What is synthetic petrol? Discuss any one method to prepare synthetic fuel.
55. Explain the Bergius process for production of liquid hydrocarbon.
56. Describe the production of gobar gas. What is the advantage of gobar gas to the raw cattle dung?
57. Give a comparative account of cattle dung and biogas.
58. What is oil gas? Discuss its production.
59. What is the average chemical composition of oil gas? Provide its use.
60. Discuss the details of the preparation of producer gas.
61. Discuss Fischer–Tropsch method for preparation of synthetic petrol.
62. Explain the generation of current in a photovoltaic cell.
63. What do you mean by avgas 100/130?
64. What is aviation turbine fuel (ATF)?
65. Differentiate between liquid and vapor phase cracking of hydrocarbons.
66. Explain primary and secondary gaseous fuels with suitable examples.
67. What are non-conventional sources of energy?
68. What is photo voltaic cell? Explain its principle of working.
69. What for inhibitor is added during refining of gasoline?
70. Describe different fractions obtained during fractional distillation of petroleum along with their applications.

NUMERICAL PROBLEMS

1. 0.9 g of a fuel upon complete combustion in excess oxygen increases the temperature of water in a calorimeter containing 1250 g of water by 2.5°C. Find the higher calorific value of fuel. Given water equivalent of calorimeter is 135 g.
2. Find HCL and LCV of a coal sample 75% carbon, 7.5% hydrogen, 9% oxygen, 2.5% sulfur, and 6% nitrogen.

3. During an experiment in Boy's calorimeter some results have been obtained. 0.1 m^3 volume at STP, temperatures of inlet and outlet for water are 20°C and 33°C, respectively, weight of water heated is 25 kg, and weight of steam condensed is 0.025 kg. Find the higher and lower calorific values per m^3 at STP. Given the heat released during condensation of water vapor is 580 kcal/kg.
4. The temperature of 950 g of water increased from 250 to 280°C on burning 0.7 g of solid fuel in a bomb calorimeter. Water equivalent of calorimeter and latent heat of steam are 400 g and 587 cal/g, respectively. Assuming that the fuel contains 0.6% of hydrogen, find the net calorific value.
5. 0.9 g of a liquid fuel containing 90% carbon, 6% hydrogen gave the following results in bomb calorimeter experiment: Amount of water in calorimeter is 1400 g, water equivalent of calorimeter is 400 g, and rise in temperature is 1.5°C. If the latent heat of steam is 587 cal/g, calculate the gross and net calorific values.
6. Find the weight and volume of air required for the combustion of 2 kg of C.
7. Calculate the volume of air required for the complete combustion of 5 l of CO.
8. Estimate the weight of air needed for complete combustion of 2 kg of coal containing 75% C, 20% H_2, and rest oxygen.
9. A sample of coal is found to have 70% carbon, 6% hydrogen, 12% oxygen, 1.5% sulfur, 3.5% nitrogen, and rest ash. Find the minimum amount of air required for complete combustion of 5 kg of such coal.
10. A gaseous fuel has the following composition by volume: methane, 5%; hydrogen, 20%; carbon monoxide, 25%; carbon dioxide, 6%; and the rest nitrogen. If 10% excess air is used for combustion, then find the volume of air supplied per m^3 of fuel and composition of dry flue gas.
11. The percentage composition of bituminous coal is found to be C = 75%, H = 5%, O = 12.5%, N = 3.2%, S = 2%, and rest ash. Find the minimum weight of air required for complete combustion of 2 kg of coal and also find the percentage composition of dry products of combustion by weight.
12. The composition of a producer gas is found to be H_2 = 15%, CH_4 = 3%, CO = 20%, CO_2 = 5%, N_2 = 55%, O_2 =2% by volume. Find the air required for complete combustion of 1 m^3 of this gas. If 40% excess air is used, find the volume analysis of the dry combustion products.
13. A hydrocarbon fuel on burning gave a flue gas having 3.5% O_2, 13.5% CO_2, 82.9% N_2. What is the composition of the fuel by weight and the percentage excess of air used?
14. A fuel containing 90% C and 6% H by mass was burnt 90% of air of that required for complete combustion. Find out the percentage of dry products of combustion by mass, if H is burnt completely and no C is left behind.
15. 1.6 g of coal was digested in Kjeldahl flask and ammonia evolved was absorbed in 50 ml of 0.1N sulfuric acid. The excess acid required 6 ml of 0.1N NaOH for neutralization. Find the percentage of N.
16. 0.2 g of a coal sample was used in a bomb calorimeter for determination of calorific value. The ash formed in the calorimeter was extracted with acid and the acid extract was heated with barium chloride solution to form the precipitate of barium sulfate. The weight of dried precipitate was found to be 0.02 g. Find the percentage of S in the coal sample.

17. 1.5 g of a coal sample was taken in a silica crucible. After one hour heating at 110°C, the residual weight is 1.2 g. After strong heating at ~950°C for 7 min, the residual weight is 0.45 g. Subsequent heating was done without lid till constant weight. Final weight is found to be 0.15 g. Find the results of proximate analysis.
18. A liquid hydrocarbon fuel contains 90% carbon and 10% hydrogen by weight. If 50 kg of the fuel is burnt, find the theoretical amount of air required and the volumetric composition of the combustion products if 20% excess air is used.
19. A gas used in the IC engine has the following composition by volume: $H_2 = 45\%$, $CH_4 = 35\%$, $CO = 15\%$, and rest N_2. Find volume of air required for the combustion of 1 m^3 of the gas.
20. A gaseous fuel has the following composition: $H_2 = 50\%$, $CH_4 = 30\%$, $C_2H_6 = 5\%$, $CO = 6\%$, and rest N_2. Find the volume of air required per cubic meter of gas if 25% excess air is supplied for combustion. Also find percentage composition by volume of dry products of combustion. (Assume air to be a mixture of 80% N_2 and 20% O_2 by volume).

CHAPTER 15

Inorganic Engineering Materials

Chapter Outline

- Abrasives
- Refractories
- Cement
- Superconductors
- Lubricants

Inorganic engineering materials play vital role in the fields of civil and mechanical engineering. In this chapter, an attempt has been made to discuss some important materials such as abrasives, refractory materials, cement, superconductors, and lubricants.

Abrasives

An abrasive is a material, often a mineral, that is used to shape or finish a work piece through rubbing. Finishing a material often means polishing it to gain a smooth, reflective surface or may also involve roughening the material as in satin, matte, or beaded finishes. Abrasives are used very extensively in variety of industrial, domestic, and technological applications. Thus, there exists a large variation in the physical and chemical composition of abrasives as well as their shape. Common uses for abrasives include grinding, polishing, cutting, drilling, sharpening, etc.

Hardness is the primary property of abrasive. It is a measure of how resistant solid matter is to different kinds of permanent shape change upon application of force. It is a common practice to measure and express hardness in terms of an arbitrary scale known as Mohs scale (as given below) in which diamond is assigned with the highest value 10, while talc the lowest value of 1.

Note:

The behavior of solid materials under force is complex, for which there are different measurements of hardness such as *scratch hardness*, which is the measure of how resistant a sample is to fracture or permanent plastic deformation due to friction from a sharp object, *indentation hardness* that measures the resistance of a material toward deformation due to a constant compression load from a sharp object, and *rebound hardness*or *dynamic hardness* that measures the height of the bounce of a diamond-tipped hammer dropped from a fixed height onto a material.

Mohs scale
- 1 (Talc)
- 2 (Gypsum)
- 3 (Calcite)
- 4 (Fluorite)
- 5 (Apatite)
- 6 (Feldspar)
- 7 (Quartz)
- 8 (Topaz)
- 9 (Corundum)
- 10 (Diamond)

Classification

Abrasives may be classified as either natural or synthetic. Some naturally occurring abrasives are calcite (calcium carbonate), Emery (impure corundum), diamond dust, novacutile (it is a form of micro crystalline or cryptocrystalline quartz), Pumice dust, sand, etc. Some abrasive minerals (such as zirconia, alumina) occur naturally, but due to rare abundance or cost involved in extraction, synthetic stone is preferred industrially. The other artificial abrasives include borazone (cubic boron nitride or CBN), ceramic, ceramic aluminum oxide, ceramic iron oxide, corundum (alumina), dry ice, glass powder, silicon carbide (carborundum), etc. Let us discuss some important abrasives in detail.

1. **Quartz:** SiO_2 exists in at least 12 different forms. The principal forms are quartz, tridymite, and cristobalite, each of which has different structures at low and high temperature. α-Quartz is the most common one which is stable at room temperature. It is a major constituent of granite and sandstone. In this form, Si is tetrahedrally surrounded by four oxygen atoms. Each corner is shared by another tetrahedron, thus leading to an infinite array. These tetrahedra form helical chains which remain interlinked. The natural abundance of high-purity quartz is low, and it is synthesized by hydrothermal growth of seed crystals from aqueous NaOH and vitreous silica at 400°C under pressure.

   Uses

   (i) Used as grinding and sharpening stones.

   (ii) The rock consisting of quartz particles cemented together with feldspars, clays, carbonates, and other minerals are used for grinding floor, pigments, ores, etc.

   (iii) It is an important piezoelectric material for crystals in gramophone pickups, gas lighters, etc.

2. **Garnets:** Garnets are nesosilicates having general formula $X_3Y_2(SiO_4)_3$. The X site is usually occupied by divalent cations (Ca^{2+}, Mg^{2+}, Fe^{2+}) and the *Y* site by trivalent

cations (Al^{3+}, Fe^{3+}, Cr^{3+}) in an octahedral or tetrahedral framework with $[SiO_4]^{4-}$ occupying the tetrahedra. Hardness ranges from 6 to 7.5 on Mohs scale.

Uses

(i) Garnet sand is a good abrasive and a common replacement for silica sand in sand blasting.

(ii) Mixed with very high pressure water, garnet is used to cut steel and other materials in water jets.

(iii) Used as gemstone.

3. **Corundum:** Corundum is a crystalline mineral form of aluminum oxide (α-Al_2O_3) with traces of iron, titanium, and chromium. It is available as a mineral and is also prepared by heating $Al(OH)_3$ or γ-Al_2O_3 above 1000°C. Hardness of pure corundum is 9.0 on Mohs scale. It is not affected by acids. It has a high melting point of over 2000°C. Corundum is unusual for its specific gravity of 4.02 g/cm^3, which is very high for a transparent mineral composed of elements with the low atomic mass.

Uses

(i) It is commonly used as an abrasive on everything from sandpaper to large machines used in machining metals, plastics, and wood.

(ii) It is also used in a refractory to line furnaces.

(iii) *Emery* is an impure form of corundum, which is a mixture of corundum and other substances such as iron spinel, magnetite, and rutile. This mixture is less abrasive with an average hardness near 8.0.

4. **Emery:** It is a naturally occurring odorless mineral. It is an impure fine grained variety of natural corundum containing 25–45% of iron oxide. The average composition is Al_2O_3, 58%; Fe_2O_3, 24%; SiO_2, 4%; TiO_2, 3%; and CaO, 2%.

Characteristics

(i) Mohs hardness is 8.

(ii) Specific gravity is 3.5–3.8.

(iii) Its crystallography is crystalline.

(iv) Its abrasive particles have much smoother surfaces than SiC and Al_2O_3 abrasive particles. Thus, its cutting rate is inferior to the other two abrasives.

Uses

Mostly used for polishing applications. Tumbling and de burring media, lens grinding, barrel finishing, etc.

5. **Diamond:** Diamond is the natural isotope of carbon. It is the hardest occurring natural substance. There exist covalent bond networks among the carbon atoms, leading to a giant structure of diamond and provide the stone its hardness.

Characteristics

(i) These are colorless, though industrial diamonds are black. Most naturally occurring diamonds contain traces of nitrogen except blue diamond that contains traces of aluminum.

(ii) Its hardness is 10 on Mohs scale.

(iii) Crystal habits include isomeric forms such as cubes and octahedrons.

(iv) Its specific gravity is 3.5.

(v) It has very good thermal conductor, which is 5 times better than silver.

(vi) Possess very high melting point of 3930°C.

(vii) Chemically inert and not attacked by acids or alkalis.

Uses

(i) Off-color diamonds (borts) are used in drill points, as saw teeth for cutting rocks, stones, or grinding wheels.

(ii) As abrasive powder for cutting and polishing.

(iii) Large diamonds are cut as gemstones. The size of gemstones are expressed as carats (1 g = 5 carat).

6. **Silicon carbide (SiC) or Carborundum:** It is a bluish-black crystalline mineral and a very popular abrasive. It occurs in nature as the extremely rare mineral *moissanite*. However, virtually all the silicon carbide sold in the world is synthetic. It is synthesized by subjecting a mixture of silica and carbon, i.e., coke, to a very high temperature of ~2000°C in an electric furnace. The basic equation is as follows:

$$SiO_2 + 3C \longrightarrow SiC + 2\,CO$$

Characteristics

(i) Silicon carbide exists in about 250 crystalline forms. α-SiC is the most commonly encountered polymorph, which is formed at temperatures greater than 1700°C. It has a hexagonal crystal structure similar to that of wurtzite. β-SiC is a zinc blende crystal structure similar to that of diamond which is formed at temperatures below 1700°C.

(ii) It is very hard with hardness of 9.3 on Mohs scale.

(iii) Withstand a very high temperature without damage but at the same time somewhat brittle.

(iv) Highly chemically un-reactive.

(v) Silicon carbide is a semiconductor, which can be doped by both electron-excess nitrogen or phosphorous and electron-deficientaluminum, boron, or gallium to form *n*- and *p*-type extrinsic semiconductors, respectively.

(vi) SiC also has a very low coefficient of thermal expansion (4.0×10^{-6} m/K) and experiences no phase transitions that would cause discontinuities in thermal expansion.

Uses

(i) Widely used in cutting wheels, abrasive papers, and clothes.

(ii) Also used for grinding of materials of low tensile strengths such as cast iron, brass, porcelain, glass, and optical grinding of lenses.

(iii) Grains of silicon carbide can be bonded together by sintering to form very hard ceramics that are widely used in applications requiring high endurance, such as car brakes, car clutches, and ceramic plates in bulletproof vests.

(iv) It is also used in high-temperature or high-voltage semiconductor electronics.

(v) Silicon carbide is an important material in TRISO-coated fuel particles, a type of nuclear fuel found in high temperature gas cooled reactors. The coating gives the fuel particles structural support and is the main diffusion barrier to the release of fission products.

7. **Boron carbide:** Boron carbide with chemical formula approximately B_4C is an extremely hard boron–carbon ceramic material. It is prepared by heating boron oxide with coke in an electric furnace at ~2500°C. The basic reaction is as follows:

$$2B_2O_3 + 7C \longrightarrow B_4C + 6\,CO$$

Characteristics

(i) Boron carbide has a complex crystal structure typical of icosahedrons-based borides. The B_{12} icosahedra form a rhombohedral lattice unit surrounding a C–B–C chain that resides at the center of the unit cell (Fig. 15.1).

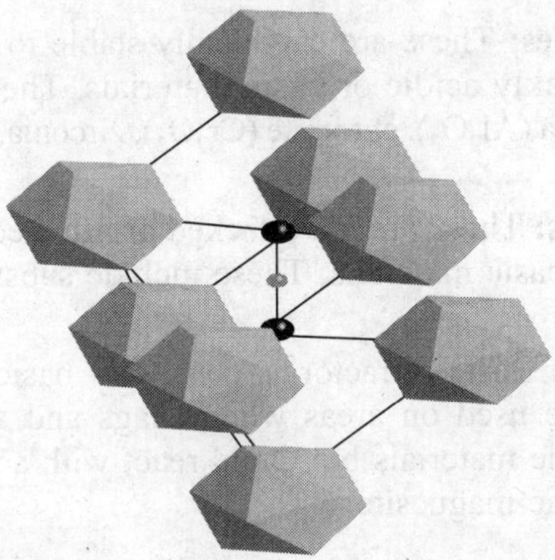

Fig. 15.1 Unit cell of B_4C. The blue sphere and icosahedra consist of boron atoms, and black spheres are carbon atoms

(ii) Because of the B_{12} structural unit, the chemical formula of ideal boron carbide is written as $B_{12}C_3$ instead of B_4C, and the carbon deficiency of boron carbide is described in terms of a combination of the $B_{12}C_3$ and $B_{12}C_2$ units.

(iii) It is one of the hardest materials known, with a Mohs hardness of about 9.5.

(iv) Withstand a very high temperature (melting point 3036 K) without damage.

Uses

(i) Used in tank armor, bulletproof vests, etc.

(ii) Used as an absorbent for neutrons in nuclear power plants in the form of control rods.

(iii) For making grinding dies and for cutting sharpening hard high-speed tools.

(iv) Used in brake linings of vehicles.

Refractories

Refractories are inorganic materials which withstand high temperature as well as abrasive and corrosive action of molten metals, slags, and gases without suffering a deformation in shape. The primary function of a refractory is to serve as structural material and maintain its mechanical functions at high temperatures under the service conditions. Refractories can be broadly classified into three types on the basis of their chemical composition (Fig. 15.2).

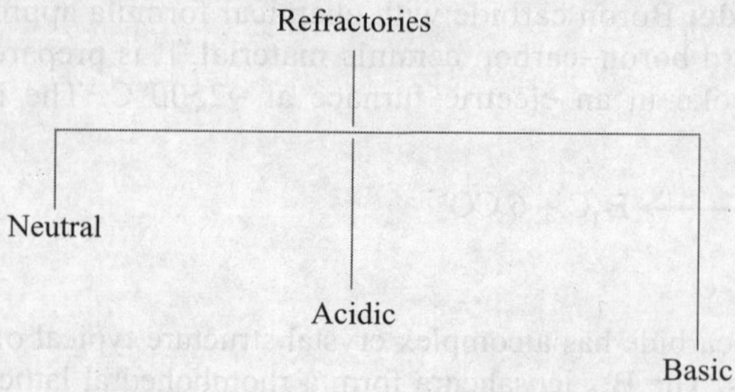

Fig. 15.2 Classification of refractories

1. **Neutral refractories:** These are chemically stable to both acids and bases. These are made from weakly acidic or basic materials. The common examples of these materials are alumina (Al_2O_3), chromite (Cr_2O_3), zirconia, zircon, spinel, mullite, silicon carbide, etc.
2. **Acidic refractories:** These are not attacked or affected by acidic materials, but are easily affected by basic materials. These include substances such as silica and fire clay refractories.
3. **Basic refractories:** Basic refractories consist of basic materials such as CaO and MgO and these are used on areas where slags and atmosphere are basic. These are stable to alkaline materials but could react with acids. Other examples include dolomite and chrome-magnesite.

Properties

Selection of refractory is made keeping in view the facts like working temperature of the furnace, nature of material to be handled, magnitude of temperature fluctuation and their frequency, load to be applied, and chemical reactions likely to be encountered. Thus, in construction of furnace, several types of refractories are required so as to withstand different conditions prevailing in different parts of the furnace. Let us look into the important properties of refractories.

1. **Refractoriness:** It is the ability of a refractory material to withstand the heat without appreciable softening under the service condition. It is normally expressed in terms of softening or fusion temperature. Softening temperature of the refractory material should be higher than the operating temperature of the furnace in which it is to be used. Most of the commercial refractory materials donot exhibit sharp melting points and gradually soften over a range of temperature. This may be attributed to the fact that they are composed of both crystalline and amorphous minerals. Fusion temperatures of some pure and commercial refractories are as follows:

Refractory material	Fusion temperature (°C)
Silica (SiO_2)	1710
Fire clay bricks	1600–1750
Kaolinite ($Al_2O_3 \cdot 2SiO_2 \cdot 2H_2O$)	1785
Bauxite brick	1732–1850
Alumina (Al_2O_3)	2050
Magnesia brick	2200

Refractory material	Fusion temperature (°C)
Zirconia (ZrO_2)	2710
Silicon carbide (SiC)	2700
Boron carbide (B_4C)	2450
Silicon nitride (Si_3N_4)	1900
Carbon (C)	3500

Measurement

Softening temperature is measured by *Seger* or *pyrometriccone test.* In this test, the refractory material is finely ground and molded into the small pyramidshaped cones with triangular base of standard dimensions. These cones along with some standard pyrometric cones of same dimension are then placed on a plaque and are heated at a prescribed heating rate usually 10°C/min. The fusion temperature of a test cone is the temperature at which its tip touches the base. The *pyrometric cone equivalent* (PCE) value of a refractory is taken as the number of the standard cone which fuses along with the test cone. If the test cone softens earlier than one standard cone, but latter than the previous one, the PCE value of the test sample is taken as the average of the two values. Seger cone number and fusion temperatures of Seger cones at heating rate 10°C/min are given here for reference.

Seger cone number	Temperature (°C)
1	1110
5	1180
10	1300
15	1435
20	1530
30	1670
35	1770

2. **Refractoriness under load or strength:** Load bearing capacity is another essential quality of refractory in addition to the temperature resistance. Commercial refractories are expected to withstand varying loads of the charge at the operating temperature.

   Measurement

   Refractoriness under load (RUL) test is usually performed by applying a load to the refractory specimen of standard size, which is kept in a carbon-resistance furnace. The heating rate is maintained at 10°C/min. The height of the specimen is plotted at a function of temperature and RUL is expressed as the temperature at which 10% deformation takes place.

Note:

1. Based on RUL test, the refractory material are classified into three categories:
   (i) *High heat-duty brick*: materials that donot deform more than 10% at 1350°C.
   (ii) *Intermediate heat-duty brick*: materials that donot deform more than 10% at 1300°C.

(iii) *Moderate heat-duty brick*: materials that do not deform more than 10% at 1100°C.

2. Seger cone strength is not useful for strength. This is because some refractories such as high alumina bricks and fire clays that melt over a wide range of temperature collapse far below true fusion temperature under appreciable load. At the same time, some refractories such as silica bear excellent load bearing capacity up to its fusion temperature as they soften over a relatively narrow range of temperature.

3. **Dimensional stability:** It is the resistance of the material to any change in volume under exposure to high temperature over a prolonged time. These changes may be permanent or irreversible and temporary or reversible. Irreversible change may result in contraction or expansion of refractory. Contraction is due to the formation of increasing amount of liquid from the low fusible constituent which gradually fills the pores of the refractory body, causing a high degree of vitrification and shrinkage. Fire clay furnishes a very good example of this category. Shrinkage is also possible by the transformation of one crystalline form into another relatively more dense form, e.g., magnesite brick (amorphous MgO). In this case, amorphous *magnesite brick* (specific gravity 2. 65) when subjected to high temperature for a long time changes to crystalline *periclase* (specific gravity 3. 54). Expansion occurs when one crystalline form of refractory changes into another relatively less dense form, e.g., silica brick. The changes for silica brick is shown here.

$$\underset{\text{Sp. gravity 2.65}}{\text{Quartz}} \longrightarrow \underset{\text{Sp. gravity 2.26}}{\text{Tridymite}} \longrightarrow \underset{\text{Sp. gravity 2.32}}{\text{Crystobalite}}$$

4. **Porosity:** Porosity is the ratio of volume of pores to that of the bulk and can be expressed as

$$P = \frac{W - D}{W - A} \times 100$$

where W is the weight of saturated specimen, D is the weight of dry specimen, and A is the weight of saturated specimen submersed in water.

It is important for refractories as it affects many characteristics such as chemical stability, abrasion resistance, strength, and thermal conductivity. It decreases strength, resistance to abrasion, and at the same time increases thermal spalling, i.e., thermal shock resistance. In addition, air gets entrapped in the pores and increases the insulation characteristics of porous bricks. A good refractory in general should have low porosity.

5. **Thermal spalling:** High temperature as well as its fluctuations induces uneven expansion and contraction of refractory material which ultimately leads to cracking and fracturing of refractory bricks. This phenomenon is known as thermal spalling. Thermal spalling can also be caused by the variation in the coefficient of expansion due to slag penetration in the refractory bricks. Thermal spalling can be lowered by

(i) using a refractory with high porosity, good thermal conductivity, and low coefficient of expansion.

(ii) avoiding sudden change in temperature.

(iii) proper furnace design.

(iv) over-firing the refractories at a high temperature for a sufficiently long time during manufacture.

6. **Chemical properties:** The acceptability of a refractory should be determined on the basis of its chemical nature. It should not easily form fusible products with slags, fuel ashes, and furnace gases. It is advisable not to use an acidic refractory in a basic environment and vice versa, though in many cases a sharp distinction cannot be made among acidic, basic, and neutral refractories.

7. **Thermal conductivity:** It is important in view of the fact that it determines the amount of heat that flows through a furnace wall under given service conditions. Refractories with low thermal conductivity is used in blast furnace and open hearth furnace to reduce the heat losses due to radiation and maintain high temperature inside the furnace. At the same time, refractories with high thermal conductivity is used in muffle walls and retorts where charge is separated from the flame and efficient heat transfer from outer surface to the charge is required.

Note:

1. Densest and least porous bricks are good thermal conductors due to the absence of air voids. In contrary in porous bricks, the entrapped air in pores provides an insulating effect.
2. Porous bricks are prepared by mixing carbonaceous materials such as saw dust with refractory mix before molding. During burning the carbonaceous materials burns off, leaving behind voids.

8. **Electrical conductivity:** Selection of refractory material should be done in keeping in view that conductivity increases with rise in temperature. In general, all refractory materials except graphite are poor conductors of electricity.

9. **Heat capacity:** The dense and heavy fire clay bricks possess high heat capacity and are suitable for regenerators, blast furnaces, coke ovens, glass furnaces, etc. In contrast, refractory materials of low heat capacity are required in intermittently operated furnaces where the working temperature can be achieved in less time with less consumption of fuel. Heat capacity of refractories depends on their thermal conductivity, specific heat, and specific gravity.

10. **Texture:** Texture can be course or fine. Course textured bricks have higher porosity than fine textured ones. Therefore, former have good resistance to thermal spalling and the same time have low strength, low abrasion, and corrosion resistance.

11. **Permeability:** It is a measure of rate of diffusion of molten solids, liquids, and gases through the connected pores of refractory. A good refractory material should have low permeability.

12. **Resistance to abrasion or erosion:** Erosion is gradual wearing away of a material from its surface due to mechanical action of flue gases escaping at high velocities, particles of carbon and grit, etc. Therefore, during the selection of refractory care must be taken to use abrasion-resistant refractory.

Manufacture of Refractories

Manufacture of refractories involves several physical operations and chemical conversions which are essentially same for different products though the raw materials are different. The basic steps are described in the following flow diagram.

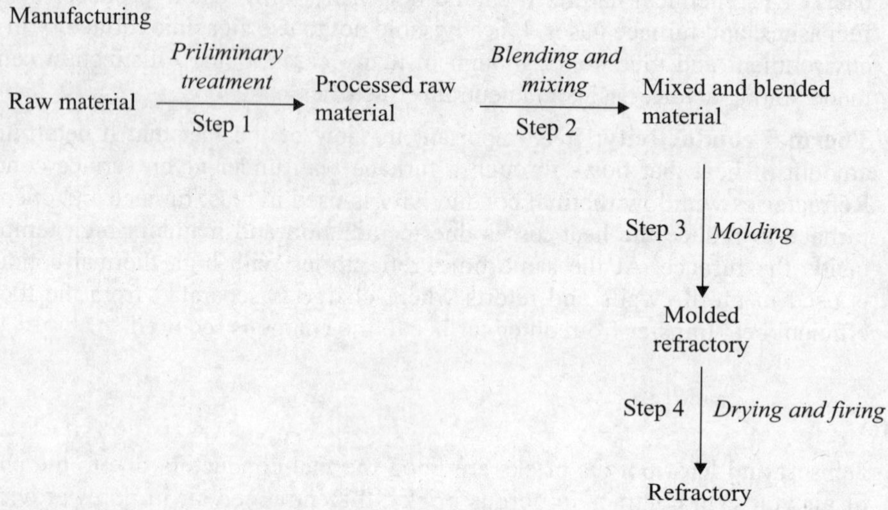

Preliminary treatment

This process involves crushing and grinding of raw materials by using ball mill or stamp mill. This also involves beneficiation process used to remove the undesirable impurities by using one or more methods collectively such as gravity separation, magnetic separation, froth floatation, and chemical treatments.

Blending and mixing

In this step, the raw materials of the correct size are blended with bond addition and water. This is done with the aim to control porosity by removal of entrapped air, producing a homogeneous mixture and thorough distribution of plastic material with non-plastic constituents. The quantity of water to be used depends on the molding technique to be followed at subsequent stages: for dry pressing, 3–7%; for extrusion molding, 10–15%; and for hand molding, 10–20% of water. Blending is done usually with paddle mills, Pug/Pan mills.

Molding

Molding is done either manually or mechanically by the application of high pressure. Mechanical molding produces refractories of high density and strength as compared to hand molding.

Drying and firing

Drying is done to remove moisture. It is usually done very slowly under well set-conditions of humidity and temperature depending on the type of refractory. This is achieved in tunnel driers or hot floor driers. Firing is done to stabilize and strengthen their structure. This is achieved in tunnel kilns, shaft kilns, or rotary kilns.

Common Refractory Bricks

1. **Fire clay bricks:** Fire clay refractories are made of raw and calcinated aluminosilicate known as fire clay as they can withstand high temperature. Calcinated fire clay known

as *grog* accounts for 50% or more of the batch mix. Grog is prepared by calcinating fire clay at ~1400°C in rotary kilns followed by crushing, sieving, and grading. The graded fraction is suitably blended using plastic clay as bonding material. For high grog bricks, additional bonding material such as molasses or dextrin is used. Molding is done by hand or machine. The bricks are dried and subsequently fired at 1100–1400°C depending on the use. General composition of fire clay bricks ranges from 55% SiO_2 and 35% Al_2O_3 (feebly acidic) to 40% SiO_2 and 55% Al_2O_3 (nearly neutral). The rest is the accessory oxides present in the clay, i.e., K_2O, CaO, MgO, and FeO.

Properties

(i) These bricks are light yellow to reddish brown in color depending on the percentage of iron oxide present.

(ii) These bricks are slightly acidic and the extent of acidic character depends on the SiO_2 content.

(iii) These bricks possess less porosity, less refractiveness, and higher resistance for thermal spalling than silica bricks. The higher is the percentage of grog in the brick, the more is the resistance to thermal spalling.

(iv) These have high crushing strength of ~200 kg/cm^2.

(v) The softening temperature is 1350°C under a load of 2 kg/cm^2.

Uses

Used for lining blast furnace, open hearths, ovens, crucible furnaces, regenerators, ceramic and metallurgical kilns, etc.

2. **Silica bricks:** Silica bricks are made of siliceous rocks such as quartz, quartzite, sand, and sandstone. During manufacture of bricks, the rock is first crushed and ground with 2% lime and water. The paste is then molded into bricks by machine pressing. The bricks are then air dried followed by heating in kilns. The temperature is raised slowly up to 1500°C in a time span of 24 h and the temperature is maintained for about 12 h. During the process, quartzite is converted into cristobalite, which is an allotropic modification. Then cooling is done carefully during which cristobalite slowly changes to tridymite which is reverse allotropic transformation. Thus, the final bricks contain a mixture of tridymite and cristobalite.

$$\underset{\text{Sp. gravity 2.65}}{\text{Quartzite}} \longrightarrow \underset{\substack{(\alpha\text{-silica})\\ \text{Sp. gravity 2.26}}}{\text{Tridymite}} \rightleftharpoons \underset{\substack{(\beta\text{-silica})\\ \text{Sp. gravity 2.32}}}{\text{Cristobalite}}$$

Properties

(i) These bricks are yellowish in color with brown specks throughout the body.

(ii) These have homogeneous texture, free from air pockets and molding defects that possess low porosity (17–25%).

(iii) These have remarkable load bearing capacity of 3.5 kg/cm^2 up to about 1600°C temperature.

(iv) The bricks are light and at the same time possess high rigidity and mechanical strength.

(v) These bricks are not susceptible to thermal spalling below 800°C.

(vi) Silica bricks are suitable for acidic furnace charges.

Uses

These are used in lining roofs of openhearth and reverberatory furnaces, lining of acid converters, etc.

3. **High alumina bricks:** Alumina content in these bricks is above 47.5%. These are made by mixing calcinated bauxite (Al_2O_3) with clay bind.

Properties

(i) They possess very low coefficient of expansion.

(ii) These have more refractoriness and slag resistance property as compared to fireclay and silica bricks.

(iii) Up to 1000°C, these are inert to the action of gases such as CO and natural gases.

Uses

Used in linings of cement rotary kilns, glass furnaces, oil-fired furnaces, lead dressing reverberatory furnaces, etc.

4. **Magnesite refractories:** It is prepared by mixing calcinated magnesite powder (MgO) of proper particle size with sulfite lye or molasses as binder and 2–6% alumina as an ingredient for improving shock resistance. The mixture is blended by adding water and then molded into bricks. The bricks are then dried and heated to 1500°C for about 8 h which is then slowly cooled.

Properties

(i) These refractories are resistant to basic slag.

(ii) These refractories can be used upto 2000°C without load. And up to 1500°C under a load of 3.5 kg/cm^2.

(iii) Poor resistant to abrasion and spalling.

Uses

Mainly used for lining of basic converters and open hearth furnaces. It is also used for lining reverberatory furnace used for smelting lead, copper, and tin ores.

5. **Zirconia bricks:** These are prepared by mixing powdered zirconite mineral (ZrO_2) and colloidal zirconia or alumina as binder. The mixture is then molded into bricks. The bricks are then heated at 1700°C. A zirconite changes volume on heating and cooling, and hence some MgO or CaO is added to stabilize it.

Properties

(i) These are neutral refractories.

(ii) Survive up to 1900°C under a load of 3. 5 kg/cm^2.

Uses

Zirconia bricks are highly costly and are used only where high temperature is maintained, e.g., high frequency electric furnace.

Cement

Nowadays concrete is the most widely used non-metallic material for construction. The essential bonding material that binds sand and rock upon mixing with water in concrete is the cement. Cement is a material that possesses adhesive and cohesive properties and is capable of binding materials such as sand, stones, and bricks. There are four different types of cements, viz., natural, puzzolana, slag, and Portland cement.

1. **Natural cement:** It is made by calcinating a naturally occurring argillaceous limestone, i.e., 20–40% clay containing limestone, at a high temperature and subsequent pulverization of the calcinated mass. During calcination, silica and alumina present combine with calcium oxide to form corresponding calcium silicates and aluminates. This cement has hydraulic properties but is quick setting and of relatively low strength.
2. **Puzzolana cement:** It is prepared by simply mixing and grinding natural puzzolana, which is deposits of volcanic ash produced by rapid cooling of lava, a mixture of calcium, iron, aluminum silicates, and slaked lime. It is among the oldest cementing materials. These cements have hydraulic properties. It is used mixed with Portland cement.
3. **Slag cement:** It is made by mixing blast furnace slag and hydrated lime. In the manufacturing process, blast furnace slag which is a mixture of calcium and aluminum silicates is granulated by adding water. The mixture of dried granulated slag and hydrated lime is then pulverized. Setting of this cement is relatively slower than the Portland cement; therefore, accelerators such as clay, silt, or caustic soda is sometimes added. These cements have lower strength and poor abrasion resistance.
4. **Portland cement:** A finely ground product obtained by calcinating together an intimate mixture of argillaceous and calcareous materials in proper proportion at ~1500°C followed by subsequent addition of gypsum as retarder. It was discovered by Joseph Aspidin in 1924.

Manufacture of Portland cement: The raw materials as mentioned above are

(i) argillaceous materials, which supply silica, alumina, and iron oxide. For example, clay, shale, fly ash, and blast furnace slag.

(ii) calcareous materials, which supply lime. For example, calcite, aragonite, marine shells, limestone, and chalk.

(iii) gypsum, i.e., $CaSO_4 - 2H_2O$

The basic steps involved in the manufacturing are discussed as follows.

Crushing: This is done before mixing the components. In this step, the raw materials are crushed into 2 or 3 inch size particles in gyratory crushers. The small pieces are then ground to fine powder by ball mill

Mixing: This is done either by dry or wet process. In the dry process, the powdered ingredients are mixed in the required proportions to get dry raw mix which is then stored in storage bins called silos. On the other hand, in the wet process, the ingredients are mixed in the right proportions in the presence of water to form slurry. The slurry is then stored in storage tanks.

Dry process	Wet process
This process is adopted when raw materials are hard.	This process is adopted for any type of raw material, i.e., both hard and soft.
Suitable for raw materials with inherent moisture content of 15% or less.	Suitable for raw materials with inherent moisture content of more than 15%.

Dry process	Wet process
The quality of cement produced is inferior.	The quality of cement produced is superior as in this process accurate control of composition can be achieved.
It is a slow process.	It is a comparatively faster process.
As a whole, the process is costly.	As a whole, the process is cheap.

Burning: Both dry and wet processes feed rotary kilns where burning is achieved. The rotary kiln is a long steel cylinder with length 30–160 m and a diameter of 2–4 m with the inner surface lined with fire brick refractory. The kiln is kept mounted on rollers so as to facilitate rotation about its longitudinal axis and kept inclined downward toward the exit end. Material is fed from the upper end of the kiln which slowly passes toward the lower end at a rate which is controlled by slope and rotation speed. Burning fuel (powdered coal or oil) mixed with air is injected at the lower end which increases the interior temperature to ~1750°C. There exist different temperature zones in the kiln (Fig. 15.3).

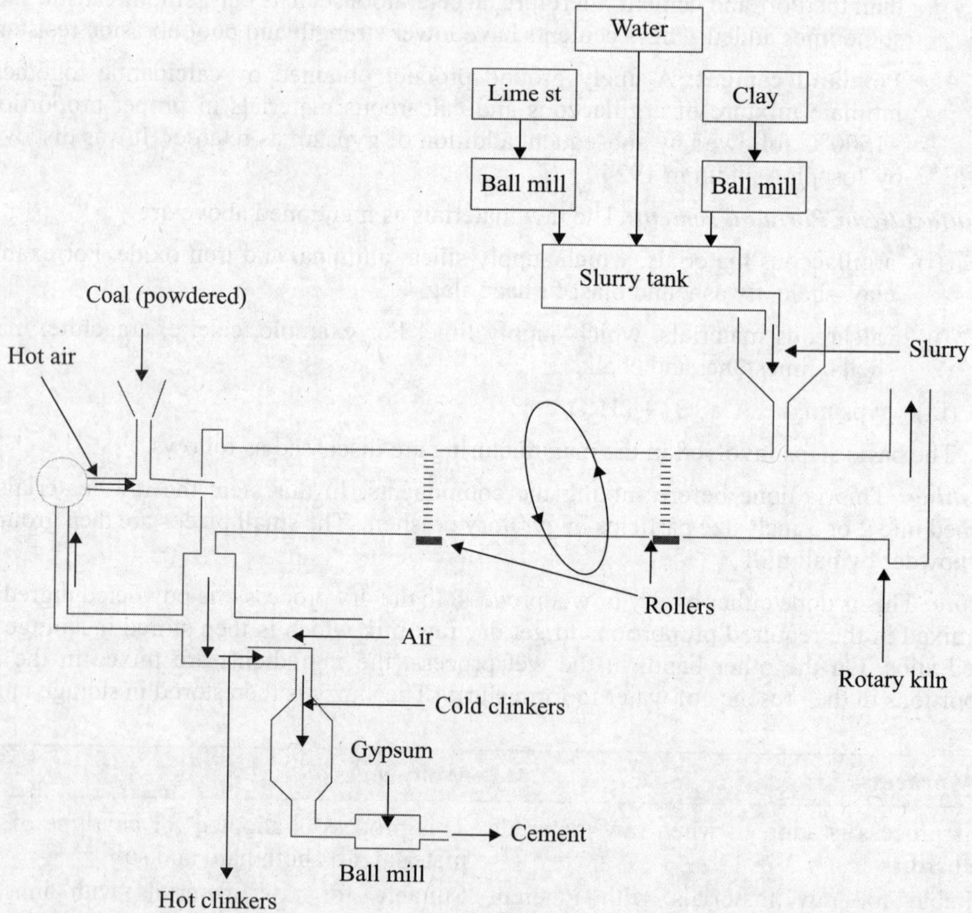

Fig. 15.3 Rotary kiln

(i) **Drying zone:** This is the upper zone of the kiln where temperature is 100–500°C. This is known as drying zone, as moisture is driven out at this zone and materials get heated.

(ii) **Calcination zone:** It is the middle portion of the kiln where temperature is ~1000°C. Here, $CO_2$is expelled from lime stone to form small lumps of quick lime known as nodules.

$$CaCO_3 \rightleftharpoons CaO + CO_2\uparrow$$

(iii) **Burning zone**: It is the lowest portion of the kiln where temperature is ranged from 1500°C to 1700°C. In this zone, mixture fuses to form calcium aluminates and silicates which subsequently get transformed into small rounded hard grayish stones called *clinkers*. The clinkers are very hot and therefore are cooled by administering cool air from the opposite direction in a small rotary kiln placed below as shown in the figure. The hot air released in the cooling process is utilized further for burning of fuel.

$$2CaO + SiO_2 \longrightarrow \underset{\text{Disodium silicate } (C_2S)}{2CaO \cdot SiO_2}$$

$$3CaO + SiO_2 \longrightarrow \underset{\text{Trisodium silicate } (C_3S)}{3CaO \cdot SiO_2}$$

$$3CaO + Al_2O_3 \longrightarrow \underset{\text{Trisodium alumiate } (C_3A)}{3CaO \cdot Al_2O_3}$$

$$4CaO + Al_2O_3 + Fe_2O_3 \longrightarrow \underset{\text{Tetracalcium aluminoferrite } (C_4AF)}{4CaO \cdot Al_2O_3 \cdot Fe_2O_3}$$

Grinding: The cold clinkers are then subjected to final grinding in ball or tube mills. During the final grinding, 2–3% of powdered gypsum ($CaSO_4 \cdot 2H_2O$) is added, which acts as a retarding agent for early setting of cement. It retards the rate of initial setting by reacting with C_3A which is the first component to hydrate to form tricalcium sulfoaluminate. The powder so obtained is Portland cement which is then stored in silos from which it fed to automatic packing machines.

$$\underset{C_3A}{3CaO \cdot Al_2O_3} + x\, CaSO_4 \cdot 2H_2O \longrightarrow \underset{\text{Tricalcium sulphoaluminate}}{3CaO \cdot Al_2O_3 \cdot x\, CaSO_4 \cdot 2H_2O}$$

Note:

IS 269-1975 specification of Portland cement

As per the specification, the composition of ordinary Portland cement should satisfy the following requirements:

(a) Lime saturation factor $\left[\dfrac{CaO\text{–}0.7\, SO_3}{2.8\, SiO_2 + 1.2\, Al_2O_3 + 0.65\, Fe_2O_3}\right]$ should lie from 0.66 to 1.02.

(b) The ratio of alumina to iron oxide (Al_2O_3/Fe_2O_3) should not be less than 0.66.

(c) Insoluble residue should not exceed 2%.

(d) Total loss on ignition should not exceed 4%.

(e) Total sulfur content calculated as sulfuric anhydride (SO_3) should not be more than 2.75%.

(f) Weight of magnesia should not be more than 6%.

(g) Fineness not to exceed 10%, i.e., after sieving the residue by weight on B.S. 170 mesh test sieve.

(h) Settling time: Initial, Not less than 10 min; Final, Not more than 10 h.

(i) Heat of hydration: After 07 days $\leq$ 65 cal/g.

(j) Compressive strength: After 07 days $\geq$ 2500 lb/in^2.

(k) Tensile strength: After 07 days $\geq$ 375 lb/in^2.

Chemical composition

Portland cements are composed of four basic compounds, viz., dicalcium silicate (C_2S), tricalcium silicate (C_3S), tricalcium aluminate (C_3A), and tetracalcium alminoferrite (C_4AF). In addition, calcium sulfate, free calcium oxide, and magnesium oxide together add up to 10%. Each of these components serves specific purpose. The behavior of cement can be altered by adjusting the relative percentages of these compounds.

Setting and hardening

When water is mixed with cement to form cement paste, hydration reactions begin resulting in the formation of gel and crystalline products. The interlocking of crystals finally binds the inert particles of the aggregates into a compact rock such as material. The complete process comprises setting and then hardening. Setting is the stiffening of the original plastic mass while hardening refers to development of strength due to crystallization. In initial setting of cement, paste is mainly attributed to hydration of C_3A and gel formation of $C_4AF \cdot C_2S$ also hydrolyzes to tobermonite gel which significantly contributes to the setting due to very high surface area.

$$C_3A + 6H_2O \longrightarrow \underset{\text{Crystalline}}{C_3A \cdot 6H_2O} + 880 \text{ kJ/kg}$$

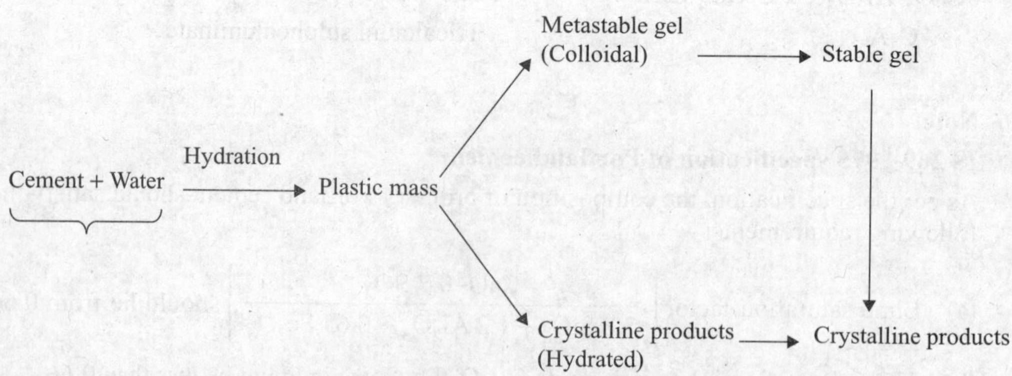

Fig. 15.4 Physical changes during setting and hardening

$$\underset{}{C_4AF + 7H_2O} \longrightarrow \underset{\text{Crystalline}}{C_3A \cdot 6H_2O} + \underset{\text{Gel}}{CF \cdot H_2O} + 420 \text{ kJ/kg}$$

$$2C_2S + 4H_2O \longrightarrow \underbrace{C_3S_2 \cdot 6H_2O}_{\text{Tobermonite gel}} + \underset{\text{Crystalline}}{Ca(OH)_2} + 250 \text{ kJ/kg}$$

The physical changes occurring in the process of setting and hardening can be summarized in Fig. 15.4.

Effect of Different Chemicals on Cement Concrete

Degradation of concretetakes place through physical and chemical damages. Chemical damage may result from exposure to carbonates, chlorides, sulfates, etc. Let us see in detail the effect of some important chemicals on cement concrete.

Effect of CO_2

Carbon dioxide present in air may react with the calcium hydroxide in concrete to form calcium carbonate. This process is called *carbonatation*, which is the reverseprocess of calcination of lime that takes place in a cement kiln. It is a continuous process propagating from the outer surface toward the core. The rate slows down with increasing diffusion depth. It decreases alkalinity, which is essential for corrosion prevention of the reinforcement steel. It has been observed that at a pH < 10, corrosion of steel is promoted.

Effect of chloride

Chlorides, particularly calcium chloride, have been used to shorten the setting time of concrete. However, calcium chloride and, to a lesser extent, sodium chloride have been shown to leach calcium hydroxide and cause chemical changes in Portland cement, leading to loss of strength, as well as attacking of the steel reinforcement present in most concrete.

Effect of sulfates

Most sulfates are slightly to highly soluble in water with the exception of barium sulfate. Sulfates are ubiquitous in the natural environment and are present from many sources which include(i) gypsum (*calcium sulfate*) often present as an additive in "blended"cements, (ii) rain watercontaining sulfurous and sulfuric acids formed by the interaction of "SO_x" with moisture present in atmosphere, and (iii) oxidation of sulfide in the presence of bacteria, e.g., bacteria present in sewer mainsreduce the ever present hydrogen sulfide gas to a film of sulfide/bisulfide ions, both of which readily oxidizes on exposure to air or oxygenated stormwater, to produce sulfate ions and hydrogen ions (as shown in the reaction). Sulfates in solution cause significant microstructural effects, leading to the weakening of the cement binder. Sulfate solutions can also cause damage to porous cementitious materials through crystallization and re-crystallization which is known as salt attack. The corrosion often present in the crown (top) of concrete sewers is attributed to this process and is known as *crown corrosion*.

$$HS^- + H_2O + O_2 \longrightarrow 2H^+ + SO_4^{2-}$$

Superconductors

Superconductor is the material that offers no resistance to the flow of electricity. It was first observed by Dutch physicist Heike Kamerlingh Onnes in 1911. He found that when mercury was cooled to the temperature of liquid helium, i.e., 4 K (–269°C), the resistance suddenly disappeared. This phenomenon of disappearance of electrical resistance of a material below a certain temperature is known as superconductivity. The temperature below which the electrical resistance becomes zero, i.e., a material of normal conducting state changes to superconducting state is called critical temperature (T_C).

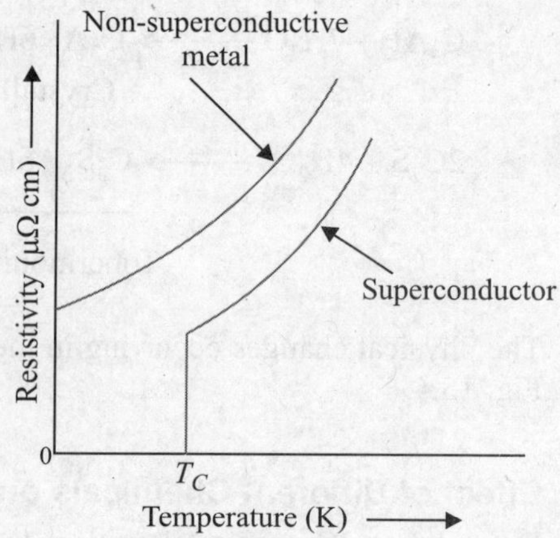

Fig. 15.5

Superconductors can be classified with respect to their magnetization behavior and superconducting transition temperatures.

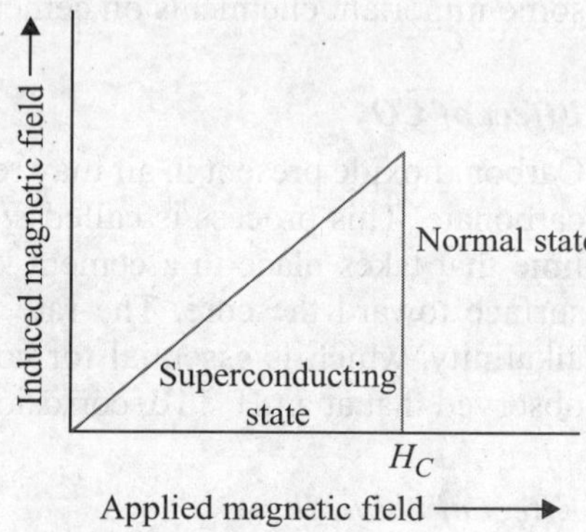

Fig. 15.6

1. Based on the magnetization behavior of superconductors in an external magnetic field, they are classified into the following two types:

   Type-I superconductors: In these superconductors, the magnetic field is totally expelled from the interior of the material below a certain magnetizing field H_C. At H_C, the material loses its superconductivity abruptly and the magnetic field penetrates fully. Very pure samples of lead, mercury, and tin are in this group.

   Characteristics

   (i) It loses its magnetization suddenly.

   (ii) It exhibits complete *Meissner effect*. The Meissner effect is an expulsion of a magnetic field from a superconductor during its transition to the superconducting state. Below the transition temperature, the samples cancel nearly all the magnetic field inside.

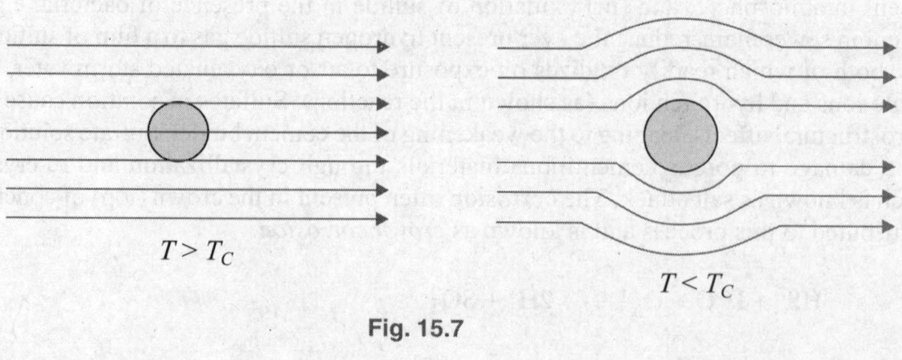

Fig. 15.7

(iii) There is only one critical magnetic field.
(iv) No mixed state exists.
(v) These are also called soft superconductors.

Type-II superconductors: Such materials lose their magnetization gradually rather than suddenly. Figure 15.8 shows a Type-II superconductor in an increasing magnetic field. There are two critical magnetic fields: lower critical field (H_{C1}) and upper critical field (H_{C2}). Below H_{C1}, the superconductor excludes all magnetic field lines. At field strengths between H_{C1} and H_{C2}, the field begins to enter into the material. When this occurs, the material is said to be in the mixed state. However, Type-II superconductors have much larger H_C values than Type-I superconductors. A few examples in this category are Nb–Sn, Nb–Zr, Nb–Ti, etc.

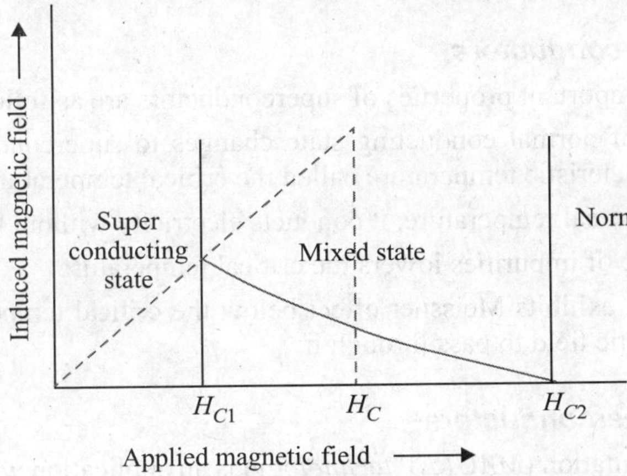

Fig. 15.8

Characteristics

(i) It loses its magnetization gradually.
(ii) It does not exhibit complete Meissner effect.
(iii) There are two critical fields.
(iv) Mixed state is present.
(v) These are also called hard superconductors.

2. Again, based on the superconducting transition temperatures, the superconductors are classified into the following two types:

Low-temperature superconductors: Superconductors with low T_C (less than 20 K) are known as low-temperature superconductors. They are also known as elemental superconductors. They are not in practical use due to ultra-low transition temperatures. Pure metals come under this category, e.g., lead with T_C = 7.2 K, mercury with T_C = 4.15 K, lanthanum with T_C = 4.88 K, etc.

High-temperature superconductors: In a superconductor, if the transition temperature is high, i.e., greater than 20 K, then it is known as high-temperature superconductor. This category of superconductors is comprised of metallic compounds and alloys. In 1986, Muller and Bednorz discovered high-temperature superconductor ceramics. Some of the high T_C materials along with their T_C values are listed below. $La_{1.85}Ba_{0.15}CuO_4$ with T_C of 36 K, $YBa_2Cu_3O_{6.9}$ with T_C of 90 K, $HgBa_2CaCu_2O_6$ with T_C of 133 K, etc.

Note:

BCS theory: J. Bardeen, L. N. Copper, and J. R. Schriffer in 1957 successfully explained the concept of zero resistance. The theory is popularly known as BCS theory. BCS theory suggests that electrons team up in pairs known as "Cooper pairs" in order to help each other overcome molecular obstacles. Scientists call this process phonon-mediated coupling because of the sound packets generated by the flexing of crystal lattice. This theory successfully explains the conductance in low-temperature superconductors. However, it fails to explain the conductance in high-temperature superconductors.

Properties of Superconductors

To consolidate, some important properties of superconductors are as follows:

1. A material of normal conducting state changes to superconducting state below a certain characteristic temperature called the critical temperature (T_C).
2. Below the critical temperature, it conducts electricity without the change of energy.
3. The presence of impurities lowers the critical temperature.
4. The material exhibits Meissner effect below the critical temperature, i.e., does not allow magnetic field to pass through it.

Applications of Superconductors

1. Magnetic-levitation (*MAGLEV technology*) is an application where superconductors play an important role. Transport vehicles such as trains can be made to "float" on strong superconducting magnets, virtually eliminating friction between the train and its tracks.
2. An area where superconductors can perform a life-saving function is in the field of biomagnetism used for medical diagnosis. Magnetic resonance imaging (MRI) was actually discovered in the mid 1940s, the principle being impinging a strong superconductor-derived magnetic field into the body; the hydrogen atoms that exist in the body's water and fat molecules are forced to accept the energy from the magnetic field. They then release this energy at a frequency that can be detected and displayed graphically by a computer.
3. Type-II superconductors can be used for storing and retrieving digital information. Scientists dream for "petaflop" computers in the next generation with the help of superconductors. A petaflop is a thousand-trillion floating point operations per second. Today's fastest computers have only recently reached "petaflop" speeds—quadrillions of operations per second. Currently, the fastest is China's Tianhe-1A, operating at 2.67 petaflops per second.
4. Power generation and transmission is another field where superconductors find wide application. Electric generators made with superconducting wire are far more efficient than conventional generators wound with copper wire. In fact, their efficiency is above 99% and their size about half that of conventional generators.

5. In the electronics industry, ultra-high-performance filters are now being built with superconducting materials. These filters have an ability to pass desired frequencies and block undesirable frequencies in high-congestion radio frequency applications such as cellular telephone systems.
6. Superconductors have also found widespread applications in the military. High-temperature SQUIDs (superconducting quantum interference devices) are being used by NAVY to detect mines and submarines. SQUIDs are capable of sensing a change in a magnetic field over a billion times weaker than the force that moves the needle on a compass.
7. Now scientists are thinking of "E-bombs". These are devices that make use of strong, superconductor-derived magnetic fields to create a fast, high-intensity electromagnetic pulse (EMP) to disable an enemy's electronic equipment.

Lubricants

A *lubricant* is a substance used to reduce friction betweentwo moving, rolling, or sliding surfaces. *Lubrication* is the phenomenon by virtue of which the frictional resistance between moving surfaces is reduced by using lubricant in between them.

In addition to the primary function of reducing friction, lubricants reducewear, tear, and surface deformation, act as coolant to carry away heat from machines, increases efficiency of machines by reducing waste of energy, reduces maintenance and running cost of the machines, prevent foreign matter to enter a bearing damaging the smooth surface of the journal and bearing and sometimes acts as a seal.

Classification of Lubricants

Lubricants are broadly divided into three basic classes.

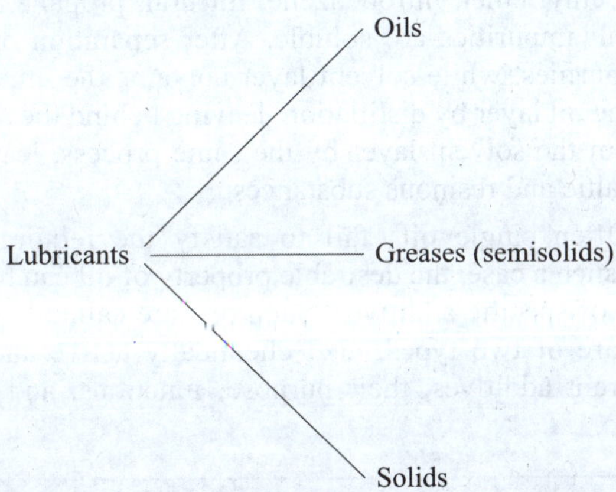

Lubricating Oils

A general term used to cover all liquid lubricants. These include three basic categories such as animal and vegetable oils, mineral or petroleum oils, and blended oils.

1. **Animal and vegetable oil**: Oils of animal and vegetable origin contain glycerides of higher fatty acids. These oils donot distil, rather decompose on heating. Hence, these are known as *fixed oils*. Fixed oils are expensive and their abundance is also low. They easily hydrolyze in the presence of water. For all these limitations, their

use as such are not promoted, rather they are used for blending with mineral oils to incorporate desired properties such as oiliness. Examples of animal oil are lard oil, tallow oil, and fish oil, whereas olive oil, castor oil, palm oil, cotton seed oil, and rapeseed oil come under vegetable oil category.

2. **Mineral oil:** These are low-molecular-weight hydrocarbons with 12–50 carbon atoms. Viscosity for these oils directly depends on their chain length. As these are obtained by distillation of petroleum, these are also known as petroleum oils. The oiliness of these oils is less as compared to animal or vegetable oil which can be increased by adding high-molecular-weight organic compounds such as oleic or stearic acid. Crude petroleum oil carries impurities such as wax which increases the pour point, asphalt which decomposes at high temperature causing deposition of carbon and sludge formation, and some easily oxidizable constituents which also leads to sludge formation. These impurities must be removed before using it as lubricant.

   Purification: Methods such as dewaxing, acid refining, and solvent refining are used for the purification of petroleum oil.

   Dewaxing is the process in which oil is mixed with suitable solvent such as propane and trichloroethylene followed by cooling. In the process, wax precipitates, which can be removed by filtration or centrifugation. Finally, the solvent is removed by distillation.

   Acid refining is the process in which oil is treated with conc. H_2SO_4 to remove asphaltic and other impurities from dewaxed oil. The impurities either get dissolved in the acid or get converted into tarry sludge. Sludge is removed by filtration. The filtrate is neutralized by calculated quantity of caustic soda for neutralizing excess acid present. Finally, the oil is decolorized by the passage through fuller's earth maintained at 100–140°C.

   Solvent refining is the process in which the oil is mixed with a suitable solvent such as dichloroethyl ether, nitrobenzene, furfural, propane and cresol in which it is immiscible but impurities are soluble. After separation of layers, the oil layer is free from impurities, while solvent layer contains the impurities. The solvent is removed from the oil layer by distillation, leaving behind the refined oil. The solvent is recovered from the solvent layer by the same process, leaving behind a residue containing asphaltic and resinous substances.

3. **Blended oil:** Often single oils fail to satisfy the requirement of the modern machineries. In such a case, the desirable property of oil can be improved by adding small quantities of specific additives. Such oils are called blended or compounded oils. Additives are of two types, viz., chemically active and chemically inactive additives. Different additives, their purpose, functions, and typical examples are summarized here.

Name of additive	Chemical used	Functions
Antioxidant	Aromatic amines, phenols, organic sulfides, and phosphides	Retard the oxidative decomposition of oil by terminating free radical chain reactions and decomposing peroxides
Metal deactivator	Sulfur compounds, diammines, triarylphosphites, etc.	They form inactive layer on metal surfaces by complexing with metal ions and thereby reducing the catalytic effect of metals during oxidation and corrosion

Name of additive	Chemical used	Functions
Anti-wear	Zinc dialkyldithiophosphate, organic phosphates, etc.	Prevent metal–metal contact by chemical reaction with metal surface to form a film with lower shear strength than the metal
Anti-foamant	Silicon polymers, oil insoluble liquids such as glycerol	Prevent persistent foam formation
Viscosity index improvers	Long-chain alkyl acrylates and polyesters, polystyrene, etc.	Reduce viscosity index by preferential adsorption of surface-active materials
Corrosion inhibitors	Organometallic compounds, zinc dithiophosphates, sulfurized terpenes, etc.	Prevent corrosion of metal parts by neutralization of corrosive acids and/ or preferential adsorption of polar constituents on metal surface to provide a protective film
Emulsifiers	Sodium salts of sulfonic acids, fatty amine salts, monoesters of polyhydric alcohols, etc.	Help the formation of lubricating oils with water by making mineral oil miscible with water
Dispersants	Alkyl succinimides, nitrogen-containing polymethacrylates, etc.	Prevent agglomeration of contaminants by polar attraction to dispersant molecules
Pour-point depressant	Polymethacrylates, phenolic polymers, and alkylated naphthalene	Lower the pour point of the oil by wax crystal formation and thereby reducing interlocking
Deposit inhibitors	Magnesium phenolates, phosphates and sulfonates	Reduce deposits by neutralizing the sludge precursors

Greases

Technically, these are oils that contain a thickening agent to make them semi-solid. Oil is the principal component which may be petroleum oil and the thickening agents are usually special soaps of Li, Na, Ca, Ba, etc. Non-soap thickeners can also be used which include silica gel, carbon black, polyureas, bentonite clays, etc. The fibrous structure of thickeners helps in trapping the oil and thereby enable the lubricants to cling to the moving parts. Grease flows only under pressure (non-Newtonian flow). The shear or frictional resistance of greases is much higher than oils for which they support much heavier load at lower speed. Unlike lubricating oils, greases fail to effectively dissipate heat from bearings. Therefore, these are preferred for low-temperature operations.

Preparation

Greases are prepared by saponification of fat with alkali followed by adding hot lubricating oils with constant mixing.

Classification

1. **Soda based**: In these greases, sodium soaps are used as thickening agent in petroleum oils. As sodium salt content is soluble in water, these greases are not water resistant. These greases can be used up to 175°C. Thesegreases are used in ball bearings.
2. **Lithium based**: In these greases, lithium soaps are used as thickening agent in petroleum oils. These greases are water resistant and can be used up to 150°C.

These have high mechanical and oxidation stability. These are suitable for use at low temperatures, e.g., for aircraft applications where temperature goes to as low as −55°C at extreme altitudes.

3. **Calcium based**: In these greases, calcium soaps are used as thickening agent in petroleum oils. These are also known as *cap greases*. These water resistant can be used up to 80°C. These are the cheapest and most common verity.
4. **Axle greases**: These are prepared by adding lime to resin and fatty oils along with some fillers such as talc and mica. These are water resistant and are used for equipment working under high load and at low speed.

Solid lubricants

These include lubricants that are used in solid formand may be bulky solids, paint-like coatings, or loose powders. The important solid lubricants are graphite, molybdenum sulfide, talc, mica, etc.

1. **Graphite**: It is the most widely used solid lubricant. Graphite is structurally composed of flat plates, each made up of network of hexagons in which each carbon is sp^2 hybridized as in Fig. 15.9. The distance of carbon atoms between planes is relatively longer (3.4 Å) than the same between carbon atoms belonging to the same plane (1.42 Å). Therefore, the plates are held by only weak vander Walls' forces of attraction which facilitates the easy sliding of one layer on the other. It is used either in powdered form or as suspension form in oil or water. The emulsion is stabilized by the addition of emulsifying agent such as tannin. When graphite is dispersed in water, it is called *oildag*, while dispersed in water is known as *aquadag*. Oildag is particularly important in internal combustion engines as it forms a film between the piston rings and the cylinder so as to give better compression. On the other hand, aquadag is useful where a lubricant free from oil is needed, e.g., foodstuff industry. In an oxidative atmosphere, graphite is effective at high temperatures up to 450°C. The thermal conductivity of graphite is low, whichis approximately 1.3 W/mK at 40°C. Graphite is classified into two main groups:natural and synthetic. Synthetic graphite is a high temperature sintered product and is characterized by its high purity

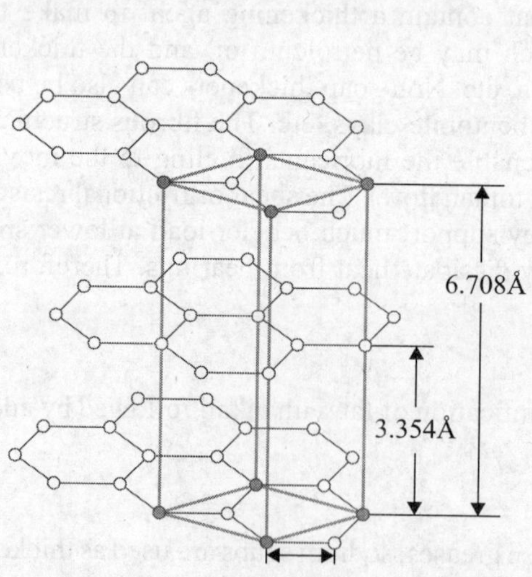

Fig. 15.9 Layered structure of graphite

of carbon (99.5–99.9%). Natural graphite is derived from mining whose quality varies with quality of ore and post-mining processing of the ore. The end product is graphite with a content of carbon (96–98% carbon), sulfur, SiO_2, and ash. The higher the carbon content and the degree of graphitization, i.e., crystallinity, the better is the lubricity and resistance to oxidation.

Uses

(i) Graphite is mixed with greases to form graphite-greases, which are used at higher temperature.

(ii) Used as lubricant in air-compressors, foodstuff industry, cast iron bearings, railway track joints, internal combustion engine, etc.

2. **Molybdenum sulfide (MoS_2):** It has a sandwich-like structure (Fig. 15.10) in which a layer of "Mo" atoms lies between two layers of "S"atoms. The distance between Mo and S layers is 3. 13 Å. It has lower shear strength in a direction parallel to the layers due to poor inter-laminar attraction. This is why it is used as lubricant. It is stable up to 400°C. The uses of MoS_2 are same as that of graphite.

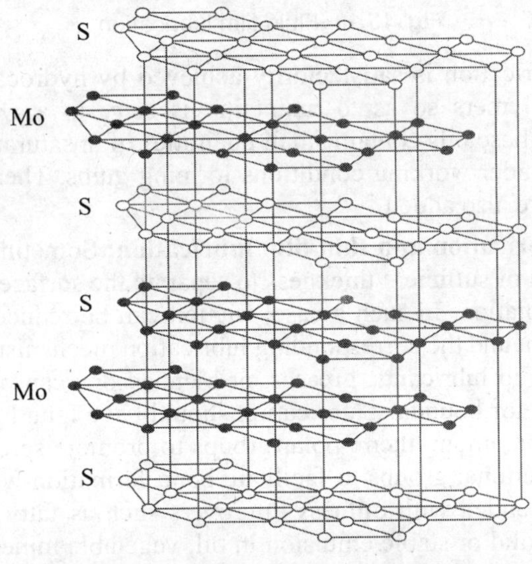

Fig. 15.10 Sandwich structure of MoS_2

Mechanism of Lubrication

Lubrication mechanism can be classified into following three basic types:

1. **Hydrodynamic lubrication or fluid film lubrication:** In this lubrication, sliding surfaces remain separated from each other by a thick lubricating film of at least 1000 Å thickness. This lubricating film prevents direct surface-to-surface contact and thereby prevent the interlocking of irregularities of sliding surfaces. This ultimately reduces friction. Now, the friction present is only attributed to the internal resistance between the particles of the lubricant moving over each other as shown in Fig. 15.11. Here friction depends on the viscosity and thickness of the lubricant, relative velocity of the layers, and area of the sliding surfaces. The coefficient of friction (f/w) in this case is as low as 0.001–0.03, where f is the force required to cause motion and w is the applied load.

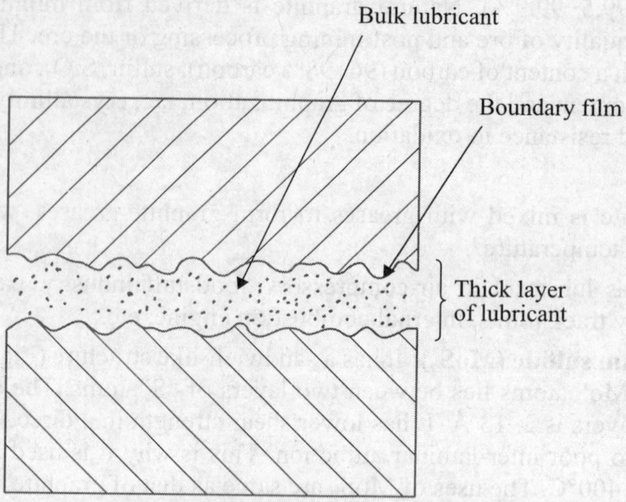

Fig. 15.11 Fluid film lubrication

Fluid film lubrication is satisfactorily achieved by hydrocarbon oils blended with long-chain polymers so as to maintain viscosity in a wide range of operating temperature. These oils contain small quantities of unsaturated hydrocarbons which get oxidized under working conditions forming gums. Therefore, during blending, antioxidants are also added.

2. **Boundary lubrication and thin film lubrication:** Sometimes the lubricant fails to generate a film of sufficient thickness to separate the surfaces due to heavy load and slow rate of rotation. In such a case, friction can be reduced with the selection of proper lubricant and the corresponding lubrication mechanism is known as boundary lubrication. Solid lubricants, greases, or blended oils can be used for the purpose. The lubricants for boundary lubrication should have long hydrocarbon chains with lateral attraction among them, polar groups to promote spreading over the surface, and active functional groups to facilitate bond formation with metal surfaces, e.g., mineral oils blended with oiliness improvers such as fatty acids or oils, graphite, and MoS_2 as solid or stable emulsion in oil, vegetable/mineral oils and their soaps. Here, a thin lubricating layer is formed at the surface due to adsorption of lubricant

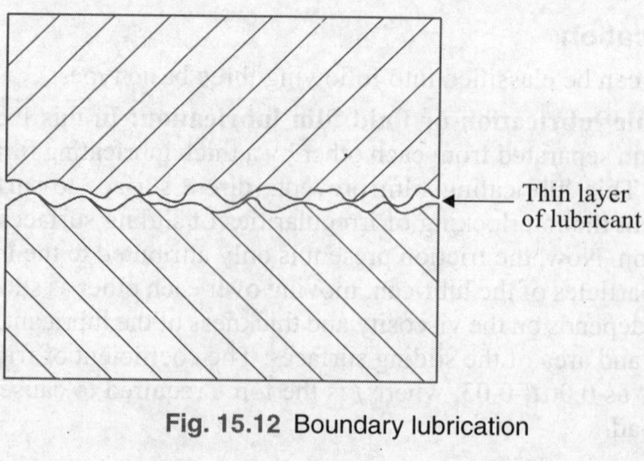

Fig. 15.12 Boundary lubrication

or chemical reaction of lubricant with metal. The thickness does not exceed one or two molecular layers. The load during motion is carried by the lubricant layers. The coefficient of friction in such cases usually remains in the range 0.05–0.15.

In boundary lubrication, the distance between the mating surfaces is quite less, sometimes of the order of height of the surface asperities (Fig. 15.12). Therefore, in case of squeezing out of lubricating film, the metal surfaces come in contact at the high spots of the journal and the bearing. This leads to generation of heat and the surfaces tend to become welded together, which prevents motion. This is known as *seizure*. If motion continues with the removal of some metal from one of the surfaces, the result is known as *scuffing*.

3. **Extreme pressure lubrication:** When moving surfaces remain under very high pressure, it leads to a rise in temperature where liquid lubricants may decompose or even vaporize. To meet these extreme conditions, blended mineral oils are used. The additives for blending are known as extreme pressure additives, e.g., chlorinated esters, sulfurized oils, and tricresyl phosphate. These additives present in lubricating oil react with metals at prevailing high temperature to form metallic chlorides, sulfides, or phosphides in the form of durable films, which are capable of withstanding very high loads and temperature. An advantage of high pressure lubrication is that the films with lower shear strength formed at the surface breaks down by the rubbing action of moving surfaces and immediately replenishes.

   Extreme pressure lubrication finds its application in for "hypoid" gears used in the rear axle drive of cars where both longitudinal sliding motion along with rolling motion occurs, in cutting fluids in machining of tough metals, in wire drawing through dies, etc.

Properties and Testing of Lubricating Oils

Properties & testing:

- Viscosity
- Flash/fire point
- Cloud/pour point
- Oiliness
- Carbon residue
- Volatility
- Neutralization number
- Saponification number
- Precipitation number
- Iodine value
- Aniline point
- Steam emulsion number

Viscosity

Viscosity is the property of the liquid by virtue of which it offers resistance to its own flow. A liquid having a steady flow on a surface may be assumed to be consisting of a series of parallel layers. The viscous drag between any two layers per unit area can be expressed as follows:

$$F = \eta \frac{v}{r}$$

where v is the relative velocity of the two layers, r is the distance between the two layers, and η is the coefficient of viscosity which is nothing but the force required per unit area to maintain an unit potential gradient between two parallel layers unit distance apart.

Unit: The unit of viscosity is poise.

Effect of temperature: In general, viscosity of lubricating oils decreases with increase in temperature. Therefore, a good lubricating oil is that whose viscosity does not change much with change in temperature. The rate at which the viscosity of a lubricating oil changes with increase in temperature is expressed in terms of an arbitrary scale known as viscosity index (VI).

Significance: For lubricating oil, viscosity determines its ability to lubricate. It is used in evaluating load-carrying capacity, effect of temperature changes, establishing the presence of contaminants in used oil during service.

Measurement: Viscosity of lubricating oil is measured by an instrument known as Redwood viscometer. It is of two types: Redwood viscometer 1, which is used for determining the viscosities of thin lubricating oils, whereas Redwood viscometer 2 is used for highly viscous oil. It consists of a cylindrical brass oil cup for holding the test sample of lubricating oil. The bottom of the cylinder is fitted with an agate discharge tube with an orifice of specified dimension. Valve rod is used to keep the orifice closed or opened. The oil cup is kept surrounded by water bath for adjusting the temperature. A calibrated flask (Kohlrausch flask) is provided for receiving the oil from the orifice. Thermometer and stirrer arrangement is made as shown in Fig. 15.13. The differences between the viscometers 1 and 2 are that the dimension of the orifice is much higher in viscometer 2 and also the receiving flask mouth is larger for viscometer 2.

Procedure: Oil is filled upto the mark in the cup and placed in the water bath. Water bath is slowly heated with constant stirring. When the oil reaches the required temperature, heating is stopped and the valve is lifted. The time taken for 50 ml of the sample to flow through the orifice is noted. Results are reported in seconds mentioning the test temperature and viscometer.

Viscosity index: The rate at which the viscosity of an oil changes with temperature is measured by an empirical number, known as the viscosity index (VI). A relatively small change in viscosity with temperature is indicated by high viscosity index, whereas relatively large change in viscosity is indicated by low viscosity index. "Pennsylvanian" oils consisting of mainly paraffins are assigned with a viscosity index of 100.,,On the other hand, oils of Gulf-Coast region consisting of mainly naphthenes are arbitrarily assigned with viscosity index of 0.

Determination of VI:

$$\text{VI} = \frac{L - U}{L - H} \times 100$$

where L is theviscosity at 100°F of the low viscosity standard oil, i.e., Gulf oil having a viscosity index 0 and also having the same viscosity at 210°F as the oil under test; U is the viscosity at 100°F of the oil under test; H is the viscosity at 100°F of the high viscosity standard oil,

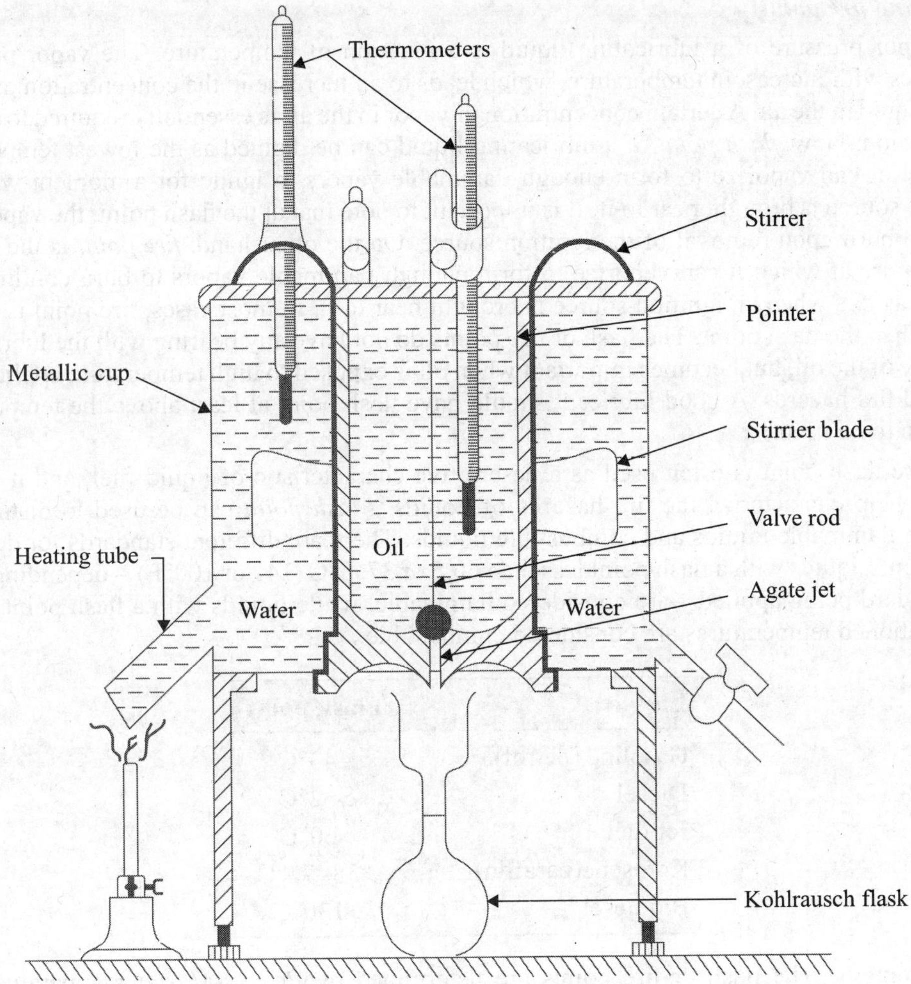

Fig. 15.13 Redwood viscometer

i.e., Pennsylvanianoil having a viscosity index 100 and also having the same viscosity at 210°F as the oil under test

Example 15.1

An oil sample has viscosity of 60 s at 210°F and 600 s at 100°F. The high viscosity index standard oil has viscosity of 60 s at 210°F and 500 s at 100°F, while the low viscosity index standard oil has viscosity of 60 s at 210°F and 800 s at 100°F. Calculate VI of unknown oil.

Solution

$$\text{VI} = \frac{L-U}{L-H} \times 100$$

$$= \frac{800-600}{800-500} \times 100$$

$$= 66.67$$

Flash and fire point

The vapor pressure of a lubricating liquid is a function of temperature. The vapor pressure increases with increasein temperature, which leads to an increase in the concentration of vapor of the liquid in the air. A certain concentration of vapor in the air is essentially required to sustain combustion. Now, *flash point* of a lubricating liquid can be defined as the lowest temperature at which it can vaporize to form enough flammable vapors to ignite for a moment when an ignition source is brought near to it. It is important to note that at the flash point, the vapor may cease to burn upon removal of the ignition source. On the other hand, *fire point* is the lowest temperature at which it can vaporize to form enough flammable vapors to burn continuously for at least 5 s when an ignition source is brought near to it. In most cases, fire point is ~10°C higher than the flash point. The flash or fire points do not have any bearing with the lubricating property of the oil, but becomes important when oil is exposed to high temperature applications to avoid fire hazards. A good lubricant should have flash point at least above the temperature at which to be used.

The flash point is often used as a descriptive characteristic of liquid fuel, and it is also used to help characterize the fire hazards of liquids. *Flash point* can be used to distinguish between flammable liquids and combustible liquids. There are different standards for defining each term. Liquids with a flash point less than 60.5 or 37. 8°C (141 or 100°F)—depending upon the standard being applied—are considered flammable, while liquids with a flash point above the mentioned temperatures are considered combustible.

Liquid	Flash point
Gasoline (petrol)	–43°C
Diesel	>62°C
Jet fuel	>60°C
Kerosene(paraffin)	>38–72°C
Biodiesel	>130°C

Measurement: The flash or fire points are determined by *Pensky-Marten's* apparatus. The apparatus consist of a brass cup with four openings. The openings are used for introducing stirrer, admission of air, thermometer, and to introduce test flame. At the top there is a shutter. When the shutter is turned, openings for the test flame and air are opened through which it is possible to insert the flame exposure device near to the surface of the oil. As the test flame is introduced in the opening, it gets extinguished, but as soon as it is brought to its original position, it is automatically lighted by the pilot burner. There is an indirect heating arrangement of the cup (Fig. 15.14).

Procedure: The oil sample is filled up to the mark in the cup which is then covered and properly placed in the stove. The sample is heated by heating the air bath by a burner at a rate of ~5°C/min with stirring. At every 1°C rise intemperature, the test film is introduced for a moment by working the shutter. The temperature at which a distinct flash appears inside the cup is recorded as the flash point. The heating is continued after that and the test flame is applied as before. The temperature is recorded at which the test flame burns for at least 5 s as the fire point.

Cloud and pour points

When lubricant oil is cooled slowly, the temperature at which it becomes cloudy in appearance is called its cloud temperature. The *pour point* of a lubricant liquid is the lowest temperature

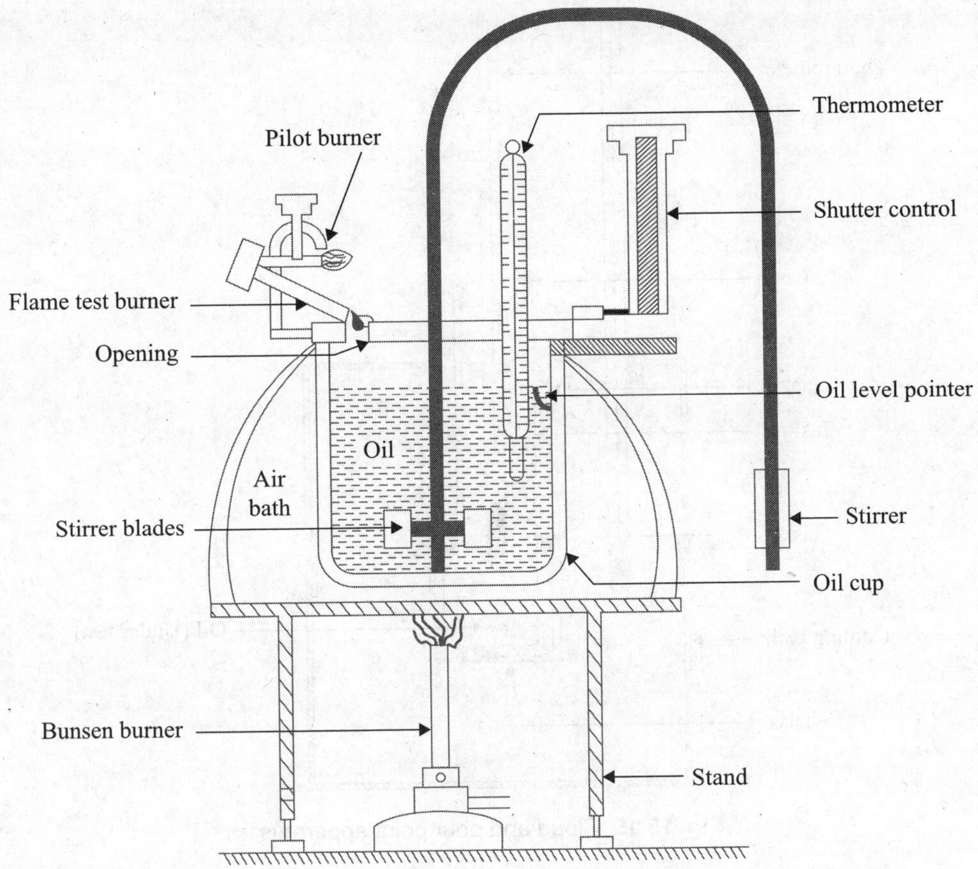

Fig. 15.14 Penskey–Marten's apparatus

at which it becomes semi-solid and loses its flow characteristics. These indicate the suitability of lubricants in cold conditions. Lubricants used at low temperatures should possess low pour point, otherwise solidification will result in jamming of machine.

Measurement: These are measured by an apparatus as shown in Fig. 15.15. The apparatus consists of a flat-bottomed tube enclosed in an air jacket. The air jacket is kept surrounded by freezing mixture, i.e., ice + NaCl contained in a jar.

Procedure: The tube is half filled with oil and a thermometer is introduced in it as shown. The temperature falls with progressive cooling. With every 1°C fall in temperature, the tube is withdrawn for a moment and examined. After this it is replaced immediately. The temperature at which distinct cloudiness is noticed at the bottom of the tube is recorded as the cloud point. The procedure is continued till a temperature at which the oil does not flow in the tube even when kept horizontal for 5 s. The corresponding temperature is recorded as the *pour point*.

Oiliness

Oiliness is an important property of lubricants used in high pressure lubrication. It is the capacity of a lubricant to stick on the surface of sliding machine parts under conditions of heavy load. Lubricants with poor oiliness usually squeeze out of the machine parts on application of load. Vegetable oils have good oiliness, whereas mineral oils have comparatively less oiliness.

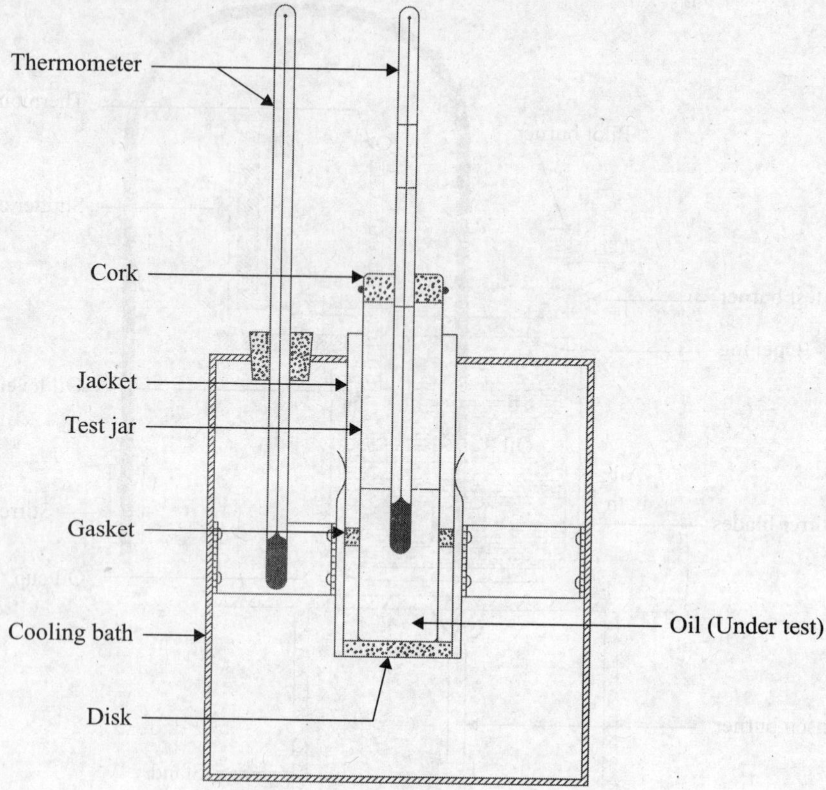

Fig. 15.15 Cloud and pour point apparatus

However, the oiliness of mineral oils can be improved by blending with vegetable oils and higher fatty acids such as oleic or stearic acids.

Carbon residue

Lubricating oils contain high percentage of carbon in combined form. When used at high temperatures, they decompose to deposit a certain amount of carbon. These carbon deposits create problems, particularly in internal combustion engines and air compressors. Excessive deposits of carbon in the combustion chamber results in a decreased volume of the charge at the end of the compression stroke, increasing the compression ratio which ultimately leads to detonation. A good lubricant is that which deposits the least amount of carbon during its use.

Volatility

Lubricating oils exposed to high temperature may volatilize off, leaving behind a residual oil which may exhibit different lubricating properties. Therefore, good lubricating oils should have low volatility.

Neutralization number

Neutralization number refers to the amount of acidic or basic constituents of oil. The presence of acidic constituents is more common and the amount of acidic constituents is known as "acid number." It is defined as the number of milligrams of KOH required to neutralize the free acids in 1g of the oil. The acid value of lubricating oil should be less than 0.1. Oil with acid value greater than 0.1 indicates that the oil has been oxidized, which may lead to corrosion besides gum and sludge formation. In a very similar manner, the "base number" may be defined as the number of milligrams of HCl required to neutralize the free bases in 1 g of the oil.

Saponification number

It is the number of milligrams of KOH required to saponify 1 g of oil. Unlike vegetable and animal oils, mineral oils do not saponify at all. Therefore, this test helps to distinguish between vegetable/animal oil, mineral oil, and blended oils having both of them.

Precipitation number

It refers to the percentage of asphalt present in oil. It is used to differentiate different classes of lubricants.

Iodine value

It is defined as the number of milligrams of iodine absorbed by one gram of the oil. It is the measure of degree of unsaturation and thereby the tendency of oil to absorb oxygen. Irrespective of composition, any oil exposed to air and heat eventually combines with oxygen in the air to form acids and gummy sludges unsuitable for use as lubricant. Oils with low iodine value, i.e., high resistance to oxidation is required for lubrication purpose, where it attains high temperatures and remains in use for an extended duration.

Aniline point

It is the minimum equilibrium solution temperature for equal volume of aniline and oil sample. It indicates the percentage of aromatic hydrocarbons present in lubricating oil. The more the percentage of aromatic hydrocarbon, the less is the aniline point. Thus, the less is the aniline point, the more is the possibility of deterioration an oil when it comes in contact with rubber sealings, packings, etc. A good lubricating oil has high aniline point.

Steam emulsion number

When water enters into oil, it forms emulsions. The emulsions so formed have poor lubricating properties, thereby causing abrasion and wearing out of the lubricated parts of the machines. Thus, the higher is the percentage of water, the worse is the lubricating properties. The tendency of lubricant oil–water emulsion to separate can be determined by bubbling steam at 100°C through 20 ml of oil taken in a test tube till temperature reaches 90°C and noting the time for separation of oil and water in to distinct layers as shown in Fig. 15.16. The time in seconds in which oil and water emulsion separate out in distinct layers is called steam emulsion number or SEN or demulsification number. Thus, a better lubricating oil is that having low SEN.

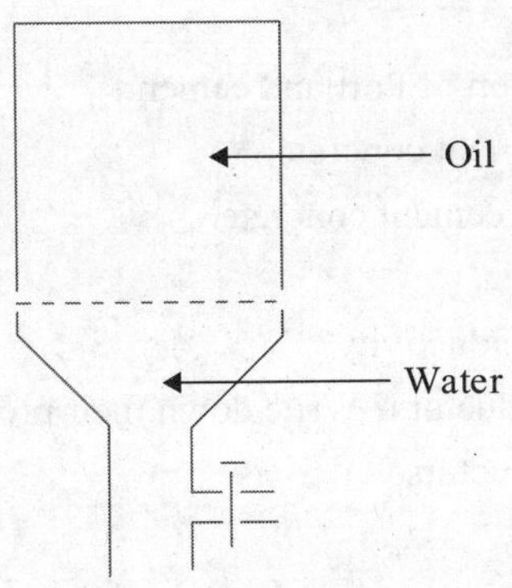

Fig. 15.16 Setup for testing demulsibility

QUESTIONS

1. What is an abrasive?
2. Give examples of two artificially prepared abrasives.
3. What are neutral refractories? Give example.
4. What are *Garnets*? Discuss their uses.
5. Discuss the properties and uses of carborundum.
6. What are refractories?
7. What is Mohs scale? Explain its use.
8. Discuss the classification of refractories.
9. How thermal conductivity of a refractory is related to porosity?
10. What do you mean by thermal spalling of refractories?
11. What do you mean by porosity of refractories?
12. Provide four essential properties of a good refractory material.
13. What are the requirements of a good refractory?
14. Explain "seger cone test" of refractory materials.
15. Discuss the basic steps involved in the manufacture of refractory materials.
16. Discuss preparation, properties, and uses of zirconia bricks.
17. What are acidic refractories? How do they differ from basic refractories?
18. What do you mean by neutral refractory? Explain with examples.
19. Discuss the manufacture and uses of fireclay refractories.
20. What is Portland cement?
21. What is the function of gypsum in cement?
22. Explain Puzzolana cement?
23. What are the raw materials required for manufacture of Portland cement?
24. Differentiate between dry and wet processes for the manufacture of Portland cement.
25. Draw a labeled diagram of rotary kiln used for the manufacture of Portland cement by wet process and explain.
26. Explain the mechanism of setting and hardening of cement.
27. What are the different temperature zones in rotary kiln. Explain the reactions that occur in these zones.
28. Discuss IS 269–1975 specification of Portland cement.
29. Explain the effect of CO_2 on cement concrete.
30. Explain the effect of sulfates on cement concrete.
31. What is superconductivity?
32. What is meant by T_c for superconductivity?
33. What do you mean by superconductors? Write down their properties and some applications.
34. Explain Type I and II superconductors.
35. What is a lubricant?

36. Which type of oils is suitable for thick film lubrication?
37. Why antioxidants are added to hydrocarbon oils?
38. What do you mean by oiliness of a lubricant?
39. What is the significance of steam emulsion number of lubricating oil?
40. Which type of lubricants is used in transformers?
41. What is the difference between flash point and fire point?
42. What is the significance of determining the pour point of a lubricant?
43. Explain solid lubricants with suitable examples.
44. Explain the mechanism of fluid lubrication.
45. What is grease? Name different types of greases with examples in each category.
46. Discuss the significance of viscosity for lubricating oil.
47. What is aniline point?
48. What is soda-based grease? Provide an example.
49. Explain boundary lubrication.
50. What is synthetic lubricant? Provide some examples.
51. What is the function of anti-foamant additive?
52. What is the function of a metal deactivator?
53. What is the function of depressant?
54. What are the different methods used for refining of petroleum oils?
55. Explain acid refining and solvent refining methods used during refining of petroleum oils.
56. Explain extreme pressure lubrication.
57. Give example of some extreme pressure lubricants.
58. What is the function of soap in grease?
59. Synthetic lubricants have added advantages over natural lubricants. Explain.
60. What is importance of saponification value of lubricating oil?
61. What is the importance of carbon residue of lubricating oil?
62. Discuss how to determine viscosity with the help of Redwood viscometer.
63. Describe determination of flash point by Penskey–Marten's apparatus.
64. Explain different types of additives used during preparation of lubricating oils along with their functions and examples.

CHAPTER

16 Composite Materials

Chapter Outline

- Constituents of composites
- Fiber-reinforced composites
- Micromechanics of fiber
- Particle-reinforced composites
- Layered composites
- Advantages of composites

Every individual conventional class of basic engineering materials such as metal, polymers, or ceramics has its own distinct characteristics as well as limitations. None of these materials can be used in situations that demand very specific requirements such as high strength and stiffness even at elevated temperatures, corrosion resistance and ability to withstand extreme temperature conditions. A new class of compounds has been developed in recent years called *composites* to meet these requirements. Composite may be defined as *multiphase materials consisting of two/more distinct phases with an interface separating them*. The properties of composites are different from those of the parent materials. Composite materials possess such combination of properties, which cannot be easily achieved. The important features which make these materials different from conventional materials are higher specific strength and stiffness, lower specific gravity, thermal expansion and electrical conductivity, low-cost easy fabrication, better corrosion resistance, toughness, impact and thermal shock resistance, better creep and fatigue strength, etc. These materials find their applications in automobile industries, turbine engines, valves, pump parts, spray nozzles, wire drawing dies, fabrication of roof and floors, furniture, sport goods, high-speed machinery, components of rockets, aircrafts, electronic circuit boards, etc. Wood is a composite of cellulose fibers and lignin cementing materials, bone is a composite of collagen (a soft but strong protein) with apatite (hard but brittle), packing paper impregnated with bitumen or wax, insulating tape, reinforced concrete, etc., are some of the common examples of composite materials.

Constituents of Composites

Composites in general consist of two phases: matrix and dispersed phase. The surface forming the common boundary between these two phases is known as interphase.

Matrix Phase

It is the continuous body constituent that encloses the composite and gives it its bulk form. Matrix phase may be metal, ceramic, or polymer. Composites using these matrixes are known as metal matrix composites (MMC), ceramic matrix composites (CMC), and polymer matrix composites (PMC), respectively. The essential requirements of a good matrix material are (i) it should be ductile, (ii) the bond strength between matrix and dispersed phase must be high for effective stress transmittance during application of load, and (iii) it should have resistance toward corrosion.

Functions of matrix phase

1. It binds the dispersed phase together through its cohesive and adhesive forces.
2. It acts as a medium for transmission and distribution of applied load to the dispersed phase.
3. It protects the dispersed phase from chemical action and keep in proper position and orientation so as to carry the intended load.
4. It prevents propagation of brittle cracks by virtue of its plasticity and softness.

Dispersed Phase

It is the structural constituent that determines the internal structure of a composite. The dispersed phases of composites may be fibers, particles, whiskers, or flakes. Let us discuss the important aspects of these structural constituents.

Fiber

It is a long and thin filament of any polymer, metal, or ceramic having high aspect ratio, i.e., the length-to-diameter rationears the crystal-sized diameter. They have high strength and stiffness. Effective transfer of load from one fiber to another requires the maintenance of characteristic aspect ratio. Orientation of fiber is very important as far as the properties of fibrous composites are concerned. If matrix is unidirectional, then the resulting composite is anisotropic. Some important fibers are glass fibers, carbon fibers, aramid fibers, boron fibers, etc.

1. ***Glass fibers*** are obtained by extruding glass melt through small orifices, rapid pulling, followed by cooling the emerging continuous filaments. Individual fiber is called monofilament which has a diameter of ~10 μ. Usually, a "sizing agent"in liquid form is applied to glass monofilaments so as to help in handling strands and protect them from abrasion. Sizing agent contains chemical coupling agent, a binder, and a lubricant. Glass fiber is very popular reinforcement material for several reasons such as (i) it is readily available in low cost, (ii) it is easy to draw from molten melt, (iii) it has high specific strength of 136 kNm and specific stiffness 2.9 kNm, (iv) it can be easily and economically used to prepare glass-reinforced polymer composites, (v) it can be coupled with polymer matrix to develop chemical inertness.
2. ***Carbon fibers*** are obtained by the pyrolys is of an organic carbon rich filamentary material such as cellulose and polyacrylonitrilein an inert atmosphere. The monofilaments have diameters of about 5–10 μ. They are used as reinforcing material with epoxy or polyester resins to form composites, which have higher specific strength, i.e., strength or weight ratio, than metals. These are high performancefibers. However, these fibers are quite costly. Carbon fibers as reinforcing material due to (i) high modulus, specific strength (123 kNm), and stiffness (14 kNm) even at elevated temperatures, (ii) resistant to moisture, acids, bases, and a number of solvents.
3. ***Aramid fibers*** are basically aromatic polyamides such as Kevlar and Nomex. It is prepared from a nematic liquid crystalline solution using a dry jet wet spinning technique or using H_2SO_4 as solvent and cold water as coagulant. These fibers are

weak in compression and susceptible to degradation by acids and strong bases. Aramid fiber is used as reinforcement material for several reasons due to (i) high modulus and tensile strength; (ii) stability at high temperatures and retention of mechanical properties in a wide range of temperature, i.e., –200°C to 200°C; (iii) resistant to creep and fatigue failure; (iv) excellent toughness and impact resistance.

Particulates

These are small pieces of hard solid metallic or non-metallic materials. The distribution of particles in a given matrix is mostlyrandom. Thus, the resulting composites are isotropic. Due to their inherent hardness, the particulates in composite cause constraints on the plastic deformation on the matrix phase. Addition of particulate fillers bring following changes in matrix:

1. Improvisation of performance at elevated temperatures.
2. Increase in surface hardness
3. Improvisation of wear and abrasion resistance
4. Changes in the thermal and electrical conductivities
5. Reduction in cost
6. Increase in strength

Note:

Particulate-matrix interaction that leads to strengthening may or may not occur at atomic or molecular level depending on the size of the particulates. Accordingly particulate fillers are classified as large particle and dispersion strengthening fillers.

Flakes

These are thin solids having a two-dimensional geometry, e.g., mica flakes. They impartequal strength in a plane compared to fibers, where reinforcement is unidirectional. Packing of flakes is more efficient than those of fibers and spherical particulates.

Whiskers

These are thin strong filaments or fibers made by growing a crystal with high aspect ratio, e.g., made of graphite, silicon carbide, sapphire, silicon nitride, and aluminum oxide. They possess high elastic modulus, highdegree of crystalline perfection, and exceptionally high strength. However, their use in composites is limited, which is attributed to their high cost and difficulty in incorporation in matrix.

Role of Interface

The transmission of stress from the matrix phase to reinforcement depends on the strength of interfacial bond. The stronger is the bond, the lesser is the possibility of failure. For composites with *good interfacial bond*, the fracture mode is, usually, a sharp and well-defined break. On the other hand, for composites with poor interfacial bond, the fracture is progressive one-bond failure, followed by matrix failure, and finally failure of fibers.

Classification of Composites

Composite can be broadly classified into different types on the basis of types of enforcement, matrix, and layers as shown in Fig. 16.1.

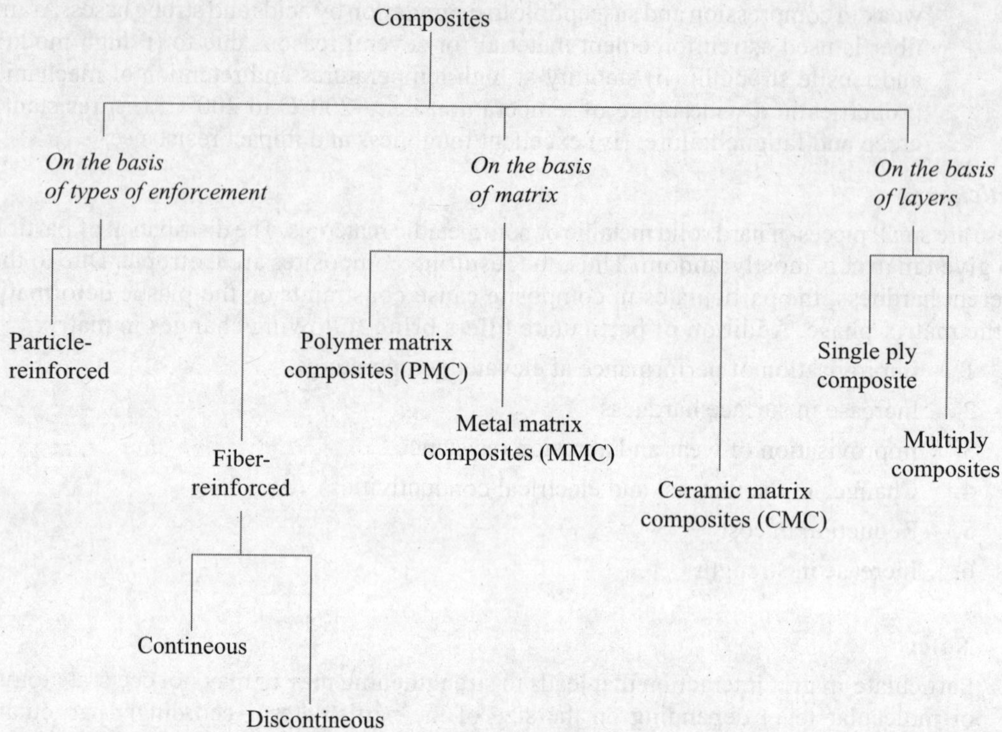

Fig. 16.1 Classification of composites

Let us discuss some important composites:

Fiber-reinforced Composites

Here fibers are used as dispersed phase for reinforcement of matrices. Such a composite involves three components, namely, filaments (i.e., fibers), a polymer matrix (i.e., encapsulating agent for the filaments), and a bonding agent, which ties fiber filaments to polymer. The fibers are used in the form of continuous lengths, staples, or whiskers. The reinforcement efficiency is maximum when continuous fibers are used. The characteristic of fiber-reinforced composites depends on the nature and properties of fibers as well as matrix phase and their relative volume fractions, orientation and distribution of fibers in the matrix phase, aspect ratio, i.e., length-to-diameter ratio of fibers, and the strength of the interfacial bond between the fiber phase and the matrix phase.

Characteristics

1. Such composites possess superior properties such as higher yield strength, fracture strength, and fatigue life. Fibers prevent slip and crack propagation in the complex and thereby increase mechanical properties. On application of load, there is a localized plastic flow in the matrix, which facilitates the transfer of load to fibers embedded in it. For maximum strength and modulus, there should be maximum number of fibers per unit volume, so that each fiber takes its full share of the load.
2. In general, the fiber-reinforced composites are anisotropic and the maximum strength is in the direction of alignment of fibers. For getting isotropic properties, fibers are oriented randomly within the matrix.

3. During preparation of fiber-reinforced composite, it is essential that the coefficient of expansion of the fiber should be same as that of the matrix, the fiber and the matrix should be chemically compatible with each other, the fiber should retain its strength in a wide range of temperature.

Some important types of fiber-reinforced composites

1. **Glass fiber-reinforced polymer composites:** In such composites, *glass fibers* are employed for improving the characteristics of polymeric matrices such as nylons and polyester. These composites possess less densities, high tensile strengths, and impact resistance, and exhibit excellent resistance to corrosion and chemicals. As majority of polymeric matrices start deteriorating or melting at high temperatures, these composites find application with limited temperature service conditions. Also due to lack of desired stiffness and rigidity, these composites cannot be employed as structural components.

   Applications

   Automobile parts, storage tanks, plasticpipes, and in transportation industries to reduce vehicle weight.

2. **Carbon fiber-reinforced polymer composites:** In such composites, high performance carbon fibers are used as reinforcement. These are also known as advance polymer matrix composites or high performance composites which are used in situations requiring excellent resistanceto corrosion, lighter density, and retention of required properties, at elevated temperatures.

   Applications

   The use of these composites is limited due to their high cost. However, they are used in structural components such as wing, body, stabilizer, etc., of aircrafts, helicopters, and sport materials.

3. **Aramid fiber-reinforced polymer composites:** These composites are of following two types:

   (i) ***Short fiber-reinforced composites:*** Short fibers of p-aramid have high aspect ratio and surface area which provides effective reinforcement. In addition, they have inherent toughness, strength, heat stability, and high wearresistance. These are widely used in automobile brakes and clutches.

Note:

The performance of these composites is better than those containing asbestos; therefore, these are better substitutes of asbestos in breaking applications. In addition, the use of asbestos in restricted nowadays as it poses serious health problems.

   (ii) ***Long (continuous) fiber-reinforced composites:*** These composites are metal-like in ductile energy absorption and respond non-catastrophically to compressive stresses as these fibers are capable of absorbing energy. The composites are excellent structural and advanced engineering materials and find wide applications in commercial aircrafts as structural materials, helicopter parts, protective apparel (thermal and ballistics), etc. Structural material of latest commercial aircrafts employ about 3–5% composites, containing fibers of p-aramid or hybrid of aramid and carbon.

Micromechanic of fiber and particle-reinforced composites

One can predict the properties of a composite from the relative proportions of the matrix and reinforcing material and their geometrical arrangement. Let us discuss some of the properties of fiber-reinforced composite.

1. **Density:** Let v_c, v_m, and v_f represent the *volume* of composite, matrix, and fiber, respectively. Then,

$$v_c = v_m + v_f \quad [16.1]$$

Now, volume fraction of the matrix, $V_m = \frac{v_m}{v_m + v_f} = \frac{v_m}{v_c}$ [16.2]

Volume fraction of fiber, $V_f = \frac{v_f}{v_c}$ [16.3]

Let w_c, w_m, and w_f be *weights* of the composite material, matrix, and fiber, respectively. Then,

$$w_c = w_m + w_f \quad [16.4]$$

Now,

Weight fraction of the matrix, $W_m = \frac{w_m}{w_m + w_f} = \frac{w_m}{w_c}$ [16.5]

Weight fraction of fiber, $W_f = \frac{w_f}{w_c}$ [16.6]

Weight fractions and volume fractions can be interconverted with the help of density of the composite material.

From relation [16.1], $v_c = v_m + v_f$

or $\frac{w_c}{\rho_c} = \frac{w_m}{\rho_m} + \frac{w_f}{\rho_f}$ [as, $\rho = \frac{w}{v}$]

or $\frac{1}{\rho_c} = \frac{w_m/w_c}{w_m} + \frac{w_f/w_c}{\rho_f}$ [Dividing w_c on both sides of equation]

$$= \frac{W_m}{\rho_m} + \frac{W_f}{\rho_f}$$

or $\rho_c = \frac{1}{W_m/\rho_m + W_f/\rho_f}$ [16.7]

From [4], $w_c = w_m + w_f$

or $\rho_c v_c = \rho_m v_m + \rho_f v_f$

or $\rho_c = \rho_m \frac{v_m}{v_c} + \rho_f \frac{v_f}{v_c}$ [Dividing v_c on both sides of equation]

$$= \rho_m V_m + \rho_f V_f \quad [16.8]$$

Note:

1. Relation between the volume and weight fractions

$$W_f = \frac{w_f}{w_c} = \frac{\rho_f v_f}{\rho_c v_c} = \frac{\rho_f}{\rho_c} V_f$$

or $V_f = \frac{\rho_c}{\rho_f} V_f$ [16.9]

Similarly, $V_m = \dfrac{\rho_c}{\rho_m} W_m$ [16.10]

2. Void content of the composite

If void remains present in the composite, theoretically calculated density using relation [16.7] does not match with experimentally determined density.

Volume fraction of voids is expressed as

$$V_f = \frac{\rho_{cT} - \rho_{cE}}{\rho_{cT}} \quad [16.11]$$

where ρ_{cT} is the theoretical density of composite, ρ_{cE} is the experimental density of composite, $(\rho_{cT} - \rho_{cE})$ is the void content.

2. **Longitudinal strength and stiffness:** Longitudinal strength and stiffness depend on the properties, relative proportions, extent of bonding of its constituents as well as the direction in which mechanical properties are measured. Longitudinal behavior can be predicted with the following assumptions:
   - (i) Composite is unidirectionalin which fibers are uniform in diameter and properties. They are continuous and parallel throughout the composite, i.e., $l_f = l_m = l$.
   - (ii) The stress is applied along the direction of alignment so that the deformation of matrix, fibers, and composites is same (iso-strain condition), i.e., $\in_f = \in_m = \in_c$.
   - (iii) A perfect bonding exists between the fibers and the matrix.

Under iso-strain conditions

Total load carried by the composite (P_c)

= Load carried by matrix + Load carried by fibers

$$= P_m + P_f \quad [16.12]$$

Let σ_c, σ_m and σ_f be the respective stresses on cross-sectional areas of composite (A_c), matrix (A_m), and fibers (A_f).

Now, Stress = Load/Area

$$\frac{P_c}{A_c} = \sigma_c; \quad \frac{P_m}{A_m} = \sigma_m \quad \text{and} \quad \frac{P_f}{A_f} = \sigma_f$$

or $P_c = \sigma_c A_c$, $P_m = \sigma_m A_m$, and $P_f = \sigma_f A_f$

From relation [16.12],

$$\sigma_c A_c = \sigma_m A_m + \sigma_f A_f$$

On dividing Eq. (16.7) by A_c throughout, we get

$$\sigma_c = \sigma_m \frac{A_m}{A_c} + \sigma_f \frac{A_f}{A_c}$$

$$= \sigma_m \frac{A_m \times l}{A_c \times l} + \sigma_f \frac{A_f \times l}{A_c \times l}$$

$$= \sigma_m \frac{v_m}{A_c} + \sigma_f \frac{v_f}{A_c}$$

$$= \sigma_m V_m + \sigma_f V_f \quad [16.13]$$

where V_m and V_f are volume fractions of matrix and fiber, respectively.

Dividing each term in relation [16.13] by its respective strain,

$$\frac{\sigma_c}{\epsilon_c} = \frac{\sigma_m}{\epsilon_m} V_m + \frac{\sigma_f}{\epsilon_f} V_f \qquad [16.14]$$

Modules of elasticity (E) = Stress (σ)/Strain ($\in$)

If the deformations of the composite, matrix, and fibers are all elastic, then

$$E_c = \frac{\sigma_c}{\epsilon_c}; \quad E_m = \frac{\sigma_m}{\epsilon_m}; \quad \text{and } E_f = \frac{\sigma_f}{\epsilon_f} \qquad [16.15]$$

From relations [16.14] and [16.15],

$$E_c\,(\text{Longitudinal}) = E_m V_m + E_f V_f \qquad [16.16]$$

Relations such as [16.13] and [16.16] are known as rule of mixtures, according to which the contributions of the matrix and the fibers to the average composite properties are proportional to their volume fractions. Relation [16.16] is applicable for composites in which both the constituents, i.e., fiber and matrix, deform elastically such as glass/ceramic fiber-reinforced composites.

Now, let us see how the load is shared between different constituents of the composite.

$$\frac{\sigma_f}{\sigma_m} = \frac{E_f \epsilon_f}{E_m \epsilon_m}$$

$$\text{or } \frac{\sigma_f}{\sigma_m} = \frac{E_f}{E_m} \; [\text{as } \epsilon_f = \epsilon_m = \epsilon_c] \qquad [16.17]$$

$$\text{Similarly, } \frac{\sigma_f}{\sigma_c} = \frac{E_f}{E_c} \qquad [16.18]$$

$$\text{Now, } \frac{P_f}{P_m} = \frac{\sigma_f A_f}{\sigma_m A_m} = \frac{\sigma_f V_f}{\sigma_m V_m} \; [\text{as } l_f = l_m = l] \qquad [16.19]$$

$$\text{From relation [16.17], } \frac{P_f}{P_m} = \frac{E_f V_f}{E_m V_m} \qquad [16.20]$$

$$\text{Similarly, } \frac{P_f}{P_c} = \frac{E_f / V_f}{E_m V_m + E_f V_f} \qquad [16.21]$$

$$\text{or } \frac{P_f}{P_c} = \frac{E_f / E_m}{V_m / V_f + E_f / E_m} \qquad [16.22]$$

3. **Transverse stiffness and strength:** Transverse loading is the stress applied perpendicular to the direction of alignment. Here again the loading is in iso-strain condition, i.e.,

   $\sigma_c = \sigma_w + \sigma_f = \sigma$

   Now the strain on the composite,

   $\in_c = \in_c V_m + \in_f V_f$

$$\text{or } \frac{\sigma_c}{E_c(t)} = \frac{\sigma_m V_m}{E_m} + \frac{\sigma_f V_f}{E_f} \qquad [16.23]$$

where $E_c(t)$ is the modulus of elasticity of transverse direction.

$$\frac{1}{E_c(f)} = \frac{V_m}{E_m} + \frac{V_f}{E_f} = \frac{V_m E_f + V_f E_m}{E_m E_f} \qquad [16.24]$$

$$\text{Hence, } E_c(t) = \frac{E_m E_f}{V_m E_f + V_f E_m} \qquad [16.25]$$

Relation [16.23] can be used to predict the *modulus of elasticity* of a matrix and fiber composite during transverse loading.

Example 16.1

Find the fraction of load carried by the fibers in two different epoxy matrix composites containing 25% and 65% glass fibers by volume. Given elastic moduli for the glass fibers and epoxy resins are 72 GN/m² and 3.5 GN/m², respectively.

Solution

For 25% fiber volume, $V_m/V_f = \dfrac{1-0.25}{0.25} = 3$

$$\frac{P_f}{P_c} = \frac{E_f/E_m}{V_m/V_f + E_f/E_m}$$

$$= \frac{72/3.5}{3+72/3.5} = \frac{20.57}{3+20.57}$$

$$= 0.87$$

For 65% fiber volume, $V_m/V_f = \dfrac{1-0.65}{0.65} = 0.54$

$$\frac{P_f}{P_c} = \frac{E_f/E_m}{V_m/V_f + E_f/E_m}$$

$$= \frac{72/3.5}{0.54+72/3.5} = \frac{20.57}{0.54+20.57}$$

$$= 0.97$$

Particulate-reinforced Composites

These are made by dispersion of particulates of different shape and size in a matrix of another material. In such composites, the matrix as well as particulates shares the load-bearing function. The behavior of these composites is governed by the nature of distribution of particles, i.e., uniform/non-uniform, relative volume fraction of constituents, strength of the force at the interface of particles and matrix. These composites are of two types, viz., large particle and dispersion strengthened composites.

1. **Large particle composites:** In such composites the interaction between particle and matrix phases is not on the atomic or molecular level. In these cases, elastic modulus fall between

$$E_c(u) = E_m(1 - V_P) + E_1 V_P$$

$$\text{and } E_c(l) = \frac{E_m E_P}{E_m(1-V_P) + E_m V_P}$$

where $E_c(u)$ and $E_c(l)$ represent upper and lower elastic modulus; E_m and E_P represent elastic modulus of matrix and particulate phases; V_P is the volume fraction of particulate phase, e.g., cements, i.e., ceramic–metal composites. To be specific, Al_2O_3 dispersed in Cr matrix, TiC or WC dispersed in Ni or Co matrix, etc.

2. **Dispersion strengthened composites:** In such a case, reinforcement is achieved by the uniform distribution of fine particles of very hard and inert material. Here interaction between particulate and matrix phases occurs at the atomic or molecular level. The composite formed is relatively more durable, e.g., thoria (ThO_2) dispersed in Ni matrix.

Layered Composites

These are broadly of two types, viz., laminar composites and sandwich panels.

1. Laminar composites: Laminar composites consist of a number of two-dimensional sheets that are stacked and cemented together so that the orientation of reinforcement varies with each successive layer. The properties of such composites depend upon the properties of the constituents and their geometrical design. Layered composites possess high strength in both directions of reinforcement, but their shear strength is comparatively low. For example, plywood (Fig. 16.2), which is a laminated composite of thin layers of wood with alternate layers cemented together so that the grain of each layer is at right angles of its neighbor.

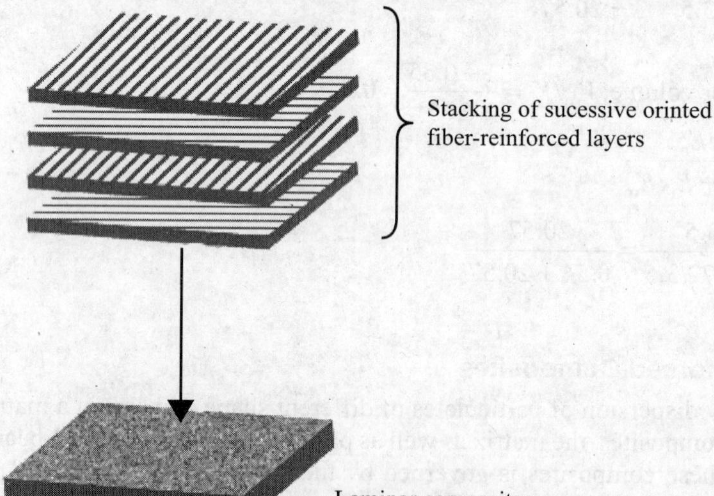

Fig. 16.2 Laminar composite

2. Sandwich panel: Another type of layered composite is sandwich panel which consists of two strong outer sheets known as faces and an intervening layer of comparatively less-dense core material. These three layers are joined by using adhesive. The function of core is to reduce the deformation perpendicular to the face plane by providing shear rigidity. The faces bear most of the in-plane loading as well as transverse bending stresses, if any. The stiffness of the sandwich panels increases

with thickness of the core. Honey combstructure (thin foils forming interlocked hexagonal cells with their axes oriented at right angles to the direction of face sheets) is one of the very popular types of core material (Fig. 16.3). Such sandwich panels find application in fabrication of wings of aircrafts boat hulls, snip structure parts, and building structures (roofs, floors, walls, etc.).

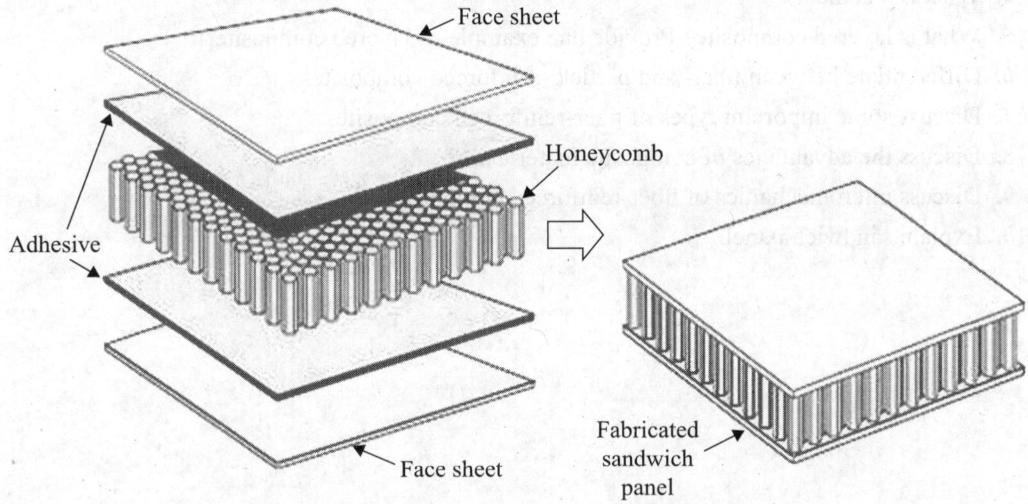

Fig. 16.3 Honeycomb core sandwich panel

Advantages of Composites

Composite materials have lots of advantage over conventional materials. Let us look into some important advantages.

1. These are cost-effective as compared to conventional metals and ceramics.
2. Weight of composite articles is less which can go upto 50% as compared to that of conventional metallic designs. Weight reduction using composites has created a huge market demand in automotive, industrial, aerospace, and other industries.
3. Composites show excellent mechanical properties such as high strength and stiffness, excellent impact and damage tolerance characteristics. Composites can be designed to be far stronger than aluminum or steel. Metals are equally strong in all directions. But composites can be engineered and designed to be strong in a specific direction.
4. These show excellent chemical properties. Composites resist damage from weather and from harsh chemicals that can destroy other materials. Therefore, these are good choices where chemicals are handled or stored. In outdoors, they stand up to severe weather and wide changes in temperature.
5. They provide improved insulation as compared to metallic materials.
6. Composites can be molded into complicated shapes more easily than most other materials, i.e., they have design flexibility. This gives designers the freedom to create almost any shape or form. The surface of composites can also be molded to mimic any surface finish or texture, from smooth to pebbly.

QUESTIONS

1. Explain fiber-reinforced composites with one suitable example.
2. What is a composite?
3. How carbon fibers are prepared?
4. What is a cement?
5. What is layered composite? Provide one example of layered composite.
6. Differentiate between fiber- and particle-reinforced composites.
7. Discuss some important types of fiber-reinforced composites.
8. Discuss the advantages of composite materials.
9. Discuss micromechanics of fiber-reinforced composites.
10. Explain sandwich panel.

CHAPTER

17 Nanomaterials

Chapter Outline

- Classification
- Self Assembly
- Preparation of Nanomaterials
- Carbon Nanomaterials
- Nano Scale Effect on Properties
- Applications of Nanomaterials

The word *nano* itself means dwarf in Greek. Nanometer (10^{-9} m) is a magical point on the dimensional scale as the bulk properties of material such as mechanical, electrical, optical, thermal, and catalytic change abruptly with the entry into this domain. Almost all micro-structured materials have similar properties to the corresponding bulk materials but properties of nanomaterials differ significantly from both those of atoms and bulk materials enabling their unique applications in modern era. To mention a few, an opaque substance such as copper becomes transparent, a stable material such as aluminium turns combustible, an insoluble material such as gold becomes soluble, and a chemically inert material such as gold serves as a potential catalyst at nanoscale. The reason behind the change in properties in moving from macro to nanoscale is mainly attributed to the significant hike in surface area to volume ratio and quantum effects.

The materials having structured components with at least one dimension less than 100 nm are known as *nanomaterials*. Materials with one dimension in nanoscale and are extended in other two dimensions are layers, such as thin films or surface coatings. Materials with two dimensions in nanoscale and extended in one dimension include nanowires and tubes. Materials that are in nanoscale in three dimensions are particles, e.g., precipitates, colloids, and quantum dots, i.e., tiny particles of semiconductor materials, and nanocrystalline materials. The study on fundamental relationships between properties and material dimensions in the nanometer scale is known as *nanoscience* while *nanotechnology* is the application of these nanostructures and principles behind them to make nanoscale devices and to produce new materials. In this chapter, emphasis has been given to have an idea on some very popular nanomaterials, an overview on their preparation, and their applications.

Classifying Nanostructured Materials

There are several ways of classification of nanomaterials. Let us look into the two extreme classifications. The first one focuses on the *macroscopic dimensions* of the material. On this basis, the definition of nanomaterials goes as materials containing structures having at least one dimension less than about 100 nm. As per this, a thin film with a thickness less than 100 nm is considered as a nanomaterial since one of the dimensions is nanometric. For nanofibers and nanowires, two dimensions are nanometric and for quantum dots all the three dimensions are nanometric. The *second one* deals with the *dimensionality* of the nanoscale component with which the material is made. A nanostructure is said to have one dimension, e.g., say length larger than 100 nm in one direction only. Asper this definition, a nanoparticle is considered to have zero dimension, i.e., it has no dimension with a length larger than 100 nm. A wire or a fiber is a 1-D object, and a thin film is a 2-D nanostructure. To summarize, 0-D nanomaterials contain spheres or clusters which are considered as point-like particles. 1-D nanomaterials contain nanofibers, wires, and rods. 2-D uses films, plates, multilayers, or networks. 3-D nanomaterials are nanophase materials consisting of equiaxed nanometer-sized grains (Fig. 17.1).

Fig. 17.1 (a) 0-D spheres and clusters; (b) 1-D nanofibers, wires, and rods; (c) 2-D films and networks; (d) 3-D nanomaterials

It is also possible to classify nanomaterials in families reflecting their composition, viz., carbon-based nanomaterials, metal-based nanomaterials, dendrimers, and composite nanomaterials. *Carbon-based nanomaterials* are composed mostly of carbon, taking the form of a hollow spheres, ellipsoids, or tubes. Spherical and ellipsoidal carbon nanomaterials are referred to as fullerenes, while cylindrical ones are called nanotubes. These particles have many potential applications, including improved films and coatings, stronger and lighter materials, and applications in electronics. *Metal-based nanomaterials* include quantum dots, nanogold, nanosilver, and metal oxides such as TiO_2. A quantum dot is a closely packed semiconductor crystal comprising hundreds or thousands of atoms, and whose size is on the order of a few nanometers to a few hundred nanometers. Changing the size of quantum dots changes their optical properties. Titanium dioxide (TiO_2) nanoparticles are extensively used in applications such as paint, sunscreen, and toothpaste. *Dendrimers* are nanosized polymers built from branched units. The surface of a dendrimer has numerous chain ends, which can be tailored or functionalized to perform specific chemical functions. This property could also be useful for catalysis. 3-D dendrimers contain interior cavities into which other molecules could be placed, which they used for drug delivery. *Composite nanomaterials* contain a mixture of simple nanoparticles or compounds such as nanosized clays within a bulk material. The nanoparticles give better physical, mechanical, and/or chemical properties to the initial bulk material.

Self-assembly

Molecular synthesis is a technology that chemists use to make molecules from atoms through the formation of covalent bonds. Molecular self-assembly is a process in which molecules spontaneously form ordered aggregates without human intervention. The interaction is usually the non-covalent forces, and the structures so generated through aggregation remain in equilibrium state. Although the focus on self-assemblyas astrategy for synthesis has been confined largely to molecules, with expanding contact of chemistry with biology and material science, the scope has broaden to include matter at all scales ranging from molecular, nanoscale (colloids, nanowires and nanospheres, and relatedstructures), and meso- to macroscopic (objects with dimensions from microns to centimeters). The rules for self-assembly in each of these ranges are similar but not identical. Because newtypes of aggregates, especially those with potential for application in microelectronics, photonics, and nanosciencehave become increasingly important technologically, interest in self-assembly as a route to aggregates of components larger than molecules has grown.

Now, self-assembly can be defined as a spontaneous reversible process in which pre-existing parts or disordered components of a pre-existing system unconstrained by scaleforms an organized structure or pattern as a result of non-covalent interactions among them without any external force or direction.

There are numerous examples of self-assembled systems found in nature. For example, protein molecules synthesized as linear chains spontaneously fold into functional three-dimensional structures, aggregates of proteins and nucleic acids which are used as catalyst and signal conduction in living tissues, nanomaterials, etc.

Principles of Molecular Self-assembly

The success of self-assembly in a molecular system is determined by five characteristics of the system.

Components: A self-assembling system consists of components at all scales ranging from molecules to macroscopic. Their interaction leads from some less-ordered state (a solution, disordered aggregate or random coil) to a final state (a crystal or folded macromolecule) that is more ordered.

Interactions: Self-assembly occurs when molecules interact with one another through a balance of attractive and repulsive forces. These forces are generally weak non-covalent forces (van der Waals, ionic, steric, entropic, magnetic, gravitational, electrostatic, and others) when using components larger than molecules, and often it is possible to adjust these interactions over wide ranges of strength, range, and selectivity.

Reversibility or adjustability: For self-assembly to generate ordered structures, the association either must be reversibleor must allow the components to adjust their positions within an aggregate once it has formed.

Environment: The self-assembly of molecules normally is carried out in solution or at an interface of its components. The interaction of the components with their environment can strongly influence the course of theprocess.

Mass transport and agitation: For self-assembly to occur, the components must be mobile. In solution, thermal motion provides the major part of the motion required to bring the molecules into contact. In nanoscale, mesoscopic, and macroscopic self-assembly systems, the components interact in ways that are analogous to those involving molecules. In designing such systems, the first challenge often is assuring the mobility of the components at a higher level of sizes than molecules as Brownian motion rapidly becomes irrelevant, and gravity and friction become important. The choice of interactions between the components (i.e., the choice of interactions allowing the system to approach equilibrium) is also important.

Self-assembled Monolayers

Self-assembled monolayers (SAM) are molecular assemblies that are formed spontaneously on surfaces. Sometimes, molecules that form the monolayer do not interact strongly with the substrate, e.g., porphyrins on highly oriented pyrolitic graphites. Other possibility is that the molecules possess a functional group that has a strong affinity to the substrate and anchors the molecule to it. A typical SAM consisting of a head group, tail, and functional end group is depicted in Fig. 17.2. Common head groups include thiols, silanes, phosphonates, etc.

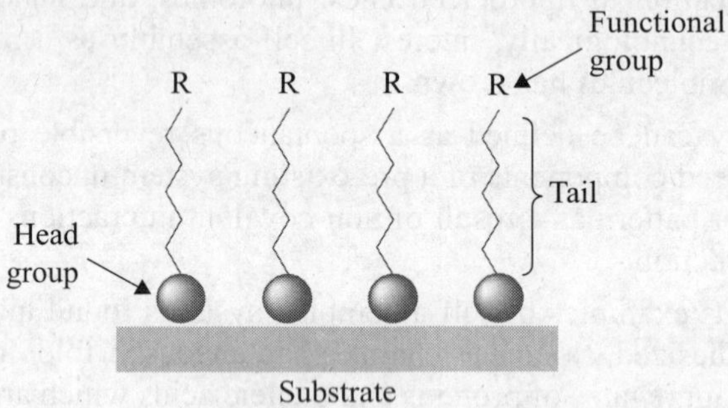

Fig. 17.2 Representation of a SAM structure

SAMs are created by the chemisorptions of "head groups" onto a substrate from either the vapor or liquid phase followed by a slow organization of "tail groups." Initially, at small molecular density on the surface, adsorbate molecules form either a disordered mass of molecules or form an ordered two-dimensional "lying down phase." However, at higher molecular density, over a period of time, adsorbate molecules begin to form three-dimensional crystalline or semi-crystalline structures on the substrate surface. The "head groups" assemble together on the substrate, while the tail groups assemble far from the substrate. Areas of close-packed molecules nucleate and grow until the surface of the substrate is covered in a single monolayer. Lowering of surface free energy is the driving force for the adsorption.

Note:

1. Types of SAM mostly depend on the head group. Selecting the type of head group in turn depends on the application of the SAM. Typically, head groups are connected to a molecular chain in which the terminal end can be functionalized by adding –OH, $-NH_2$, –COOH, or –SH groups to vary the wetting and interfacial properties.
2. An appropriate substrate is chosen to react with the head group. Substrates can be planar surfaces, such as silicon and metals, or curved surfaces, such as nanoparticles.
3. *Alkanethiols* are the most commonly used molecules for SAMs. Alkanethiols are molecules with an alkyl chain as the backbone, a tail group, and an S-H head group. They are used to form SAM on nobel metal substrates such as gold, as sulfur has a special affinity for them.
4. *Silanes* are used mostly on nonmetallic oxide substrates.
5. SAM is used as a tool for nano and micro-fabrication. Additional layers can be built on to the monolayers to make a self-assembling multilayer. It has a tremendous use in nanoelectromechanical systems (NEMS) and microelectromechanical systems (MEMS).

Mesoscale Self-assembly

Mesoscale self-assembly (MESA) refers to self-assembly of building units with size ranging from micrometers to millimeters. The components interact through a variety of forces such as magnetic, electrostatic, capillary interaction, fluidic shear, gravitational, etc. It offers a new strategy for fabrication of 3-D structures which are too large to be prepared by chemical synthesis, but too small to be assembled from individual components by manual or mechanical methods. For example, spontaneous folding resulting in self-assembly of elastomeric sheets patterned with magnetic dipole to 3-D spherical shell.

Nanocrystals

A *nanocrystal* is a material particle having at least one dimension less than 100 nm and made of atoms in either a single- or poly-crystalline arrangement. The size of nanocrystals makes them different from larger crystals. When embedded in solids nanocrystals may exhibit much more complex melting behavior than conventional solids and may form the basis of a special class of solids. They can behave as single-domain systems that can help to explain the behavior of macroscopic samples of a similar material. Semiconductor nanocrystals having dimensions smaller than 10 nm are also known as *quanum dots*. Nanocrystals made of metals, semiconductors, and oxides are of special interest. Copper nanocrystals are considered as super hard materials unlike bulk copper; zinc oxide nanocrystals have very effective UV blocking properties, and, therefore, are used in sunscreen lotions; clay nanocrystals upon incorporation into polymer matrix make a rise in glass transition temperature as well as other mechanical properties; semiconductor nanoparticles with typical size <10 nm, i.e., quantum dots, find a wide application in drug delivery; nanocrystalline silicon (nc-Si) is an allotropic form of silicon with paracrystalline structure which shows increased absorption in the red and IR wavelengths and thereby opted as an important material for use in a Si solar cell; and so on.

Supramolecular Systems

Molecular self-assembly is the key concept behind the supramolecular chemistry since assembly of the molecules is governed by non-covalent interactions such as hydrogen bonding and vander Walls forces. The supramolecular structures are formed by intermolecular self-assembly, e.g., micelles and vesicles.

A ***micelle*** is an aggregate of surfactant molecules dispersed in a liquid colloid. Individual surfactant molecules that are in the colloid but are not part of a micelle are called *monomers*. A typical micelle in aqueous solution forms an aggregate with the hydrophilic head regions in contact with surrounding solvent, sequestering the hydrophobic single-tail regions in the micelle center. Micelles are often roughly spherical in shape, but ellipsoids, cylinders, and bilayers are also possible. The shape and size of a micelle is a function of the molecular geometry of its surfactant molecules and solution conditions such as surfactant concentration, temperature, pH, and ionic strength. The process of forming micelles is known as micellization (refer to Chapter 8 for details).

A ***vesicle*** is a small organelle (i.e., a specialized subunit within a cell which has a specific function) within the cell consisting of fluid enclosed by a lipid bilayer membrane. Vesicles can form naturally as well as artificially. Artificially prepared vesicles are known as liposomes. Vesicles perform a variety of functions. These are a basic tool used by the cell for organizing cellular substances. Vesicles are involved in metabolism, transport, buoyancy control, and enzyme storage. They can also act as chemical reaction chambers.

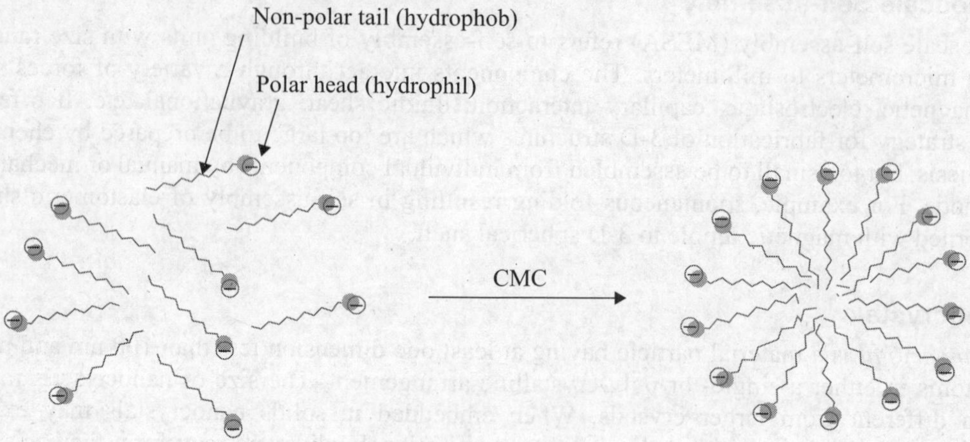

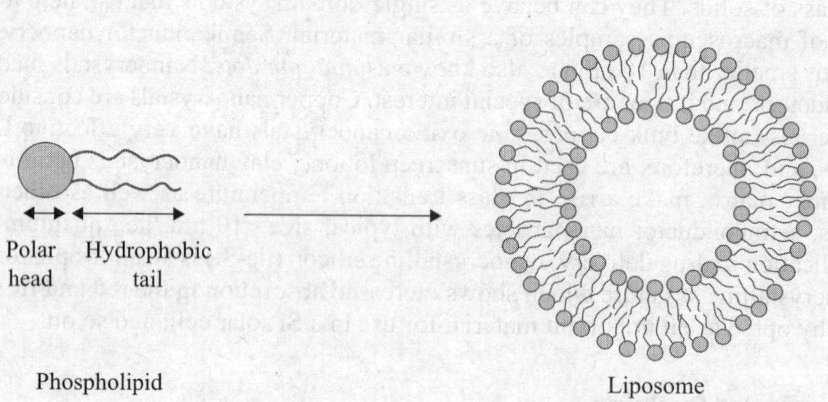

Preparation of Nanomaterials

There are two general approaches to the synthesis of nanomaterials and the fabrication of nanostructures (Fig. 17.3):

1. **Top-down approach:** These approaches use large (macroscopic) initial structures, which can be externally controlled in the processing of nanostructures. Typical examples are etching through the mask, ball milling, and application of severe plastic deformation. This method, by nature, is not cheap and quick to manufacture. Rather this method is slow and not suitable for a large scale production.
2. **Bottom-up approach:** These approaches include the miniaturization of materials components (up to atomic level) with further self-assembly process leading to the formation of nanostructures. During self-assembly, the physical forces operating at nanoscale are used to combine basic units into larger stable structures. By this method, fabrication is much less expensive. Typical examples are quantum dot formation during epitaxial growth and formation of nanoparticles from colloidal dispersion. The methods in this approach are of four types: gas-phase method, liquid-phase method, solid-phase methods, and biological method.

Let us discuss some basic and widely used methods to prepare nanomaterials.

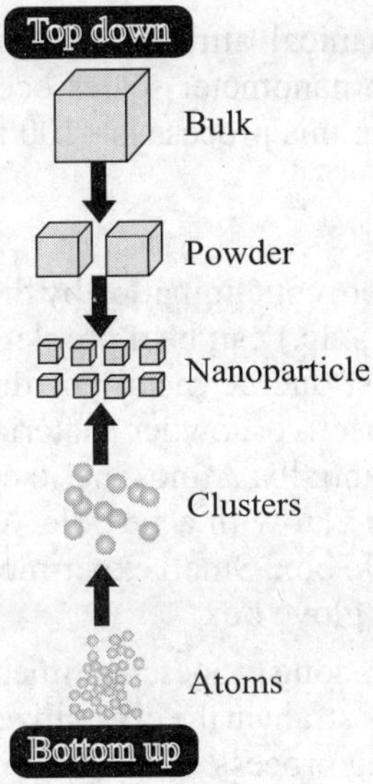

Fig. 17.3 Schematic presentation reflecting the principles used during preparation of nanomaterials

High-energy Ball Milling

The primary objectives of the milling are to reduce particle size, solid-state alloying, mixing or blending, and particle shape changes. This process was developed by Benjamin and his coworkers at the International Nickel Company in the late of 1960. A variety of ball mills have been developed for different purposes including tumbler mills, attrition mills, shaker mills, vibratory mills, and planetary mills. The basic process of mechanical attrition is illustrated in Fig. 17.4. Powders with typical particle diameters of about 50 μm are placed together with a number of hardened steel or tungsten carbide (WC) coated balls in a sealed container preferably in an inert atmosphere which is shaken or violently agitated. Since the kinetic energy of the balls is a function of their mass and velocity, dense materials (steel or tungsten carbide) are preferable to ceramic balls. By using high frequencies and small amplitudes of vibration, it is possible to generate high-energy milling forces. During the continuous severe plastic

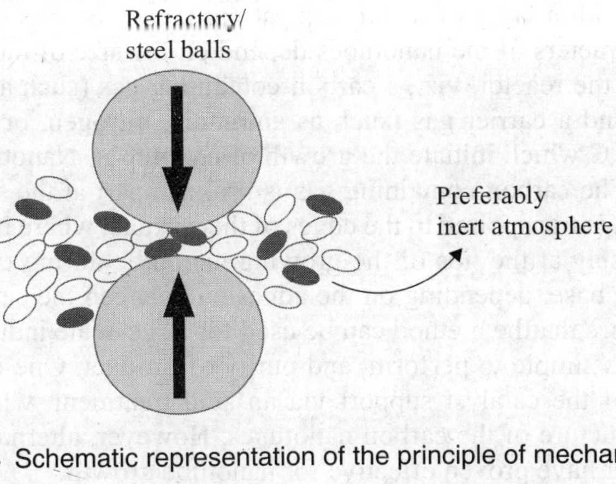

Fig. 17.4 Schematic representation of the principle of mechanical milling

deformation associated with mechanical attrition, a continuous refinement of the internal structure of the powder particles to nanometer scales occurs during high energy mechanical attrition. The temperature rise during this process is ~100 to 200°C.

Note:

1. During mechanical attrition, contamination by the milling tools (Fe) and atmosphere (trace elements of O_2, N_2, etc.) can be a problem. By minimizing the milling time and using the purest, most ductile metal powders available, a thin coating of the milling tools by the respective powder material can be obtained which reduces iron contamination substantially. Atmospheric contamination can be minimized or eliminated by sealing the vial with a flexible "O" ring after the powder has been loaded in an inert gas glove box. Small experimental ball mills can also be enclosed completely inan inert gas glove box.
2. Besides the contamination, long processing time, no control on particle morphology, agglomerates, and residual strain in the crystallized phase are the other disadvantages of high-energy ball milling process.

Chemical Vapor Deposition

Chemical vapor deposition (CVD) is a technique used to produce high purity solid materials, typically thin films. In a CVD process, substrates are exposed to one or more precursor materials in the gaseous state. The precursors react or decompose on the substrate surface to yield a coating of the required material. Frequently, volatile byproducts are also produced, which are removed by gas flow through the reaction chamber. The primary step is activating the reaction between the substrate surface and the precursor. The activation is achieved either by thermal means (thermal CVD) or by using plasma (plasma-assisted CVD). Both these techniques are schematically shown in Fig. 17.5. CVD schemes are employed widely for various processes throughout the semiconductor industry. CVD is widely employed in micro-fabrication processes to deposit materials in various forms, including monocrystalline, polycrystalline, amorphous, and epitaxial. The materials include silicon, carbon nanofibers, carbon nanotubes, silicon carbide, and various high κ-dielectrics. The term "high κ-dielectric" refers to a material with a high dielectric constant κ, as compared to silicon dioxide.

CVD method for preparation of carbon nanotubes

Substrate is prepared with a layer of metal catalyst particles (commonly nickel, cobalt, iron, or a combination). Diameters of the nanotubes depend on the size of the metal particles. Two gases are blended into the reactor, viz., a carbon-containing gas (such as acetylene, ethylene, ethanol, or methane) and a carrier gas (such as ammonia, nitrogen, or hydrogen). Substrate is now heated to ~700°C which initiate the growth of nanotubes. Nanotubes grow at the sites of the metal catalyst. The carbon-containing gas is broken apart at the surface of the catalyst particle, and the carbon is transported to the edges of the particle, where it forms the nanotubes. Catalyst particles can stay at the tips of the growing nanotube during the growth process, or remain at the nanotube base, depending on the adhesion between the catalyst particle and the substrate. Advantages are thatthe method can be used for large-scale industrial production, has large length of tubes, is simple to perform, and purity of product. One issue in this synthesis route is the removal of the catalyst support via an acid treatment, which sometimes could destroy the original structure of the carbon nanotubes. However, alternative catalyst supports that are soluble in water have proven effective for nanotube growth.

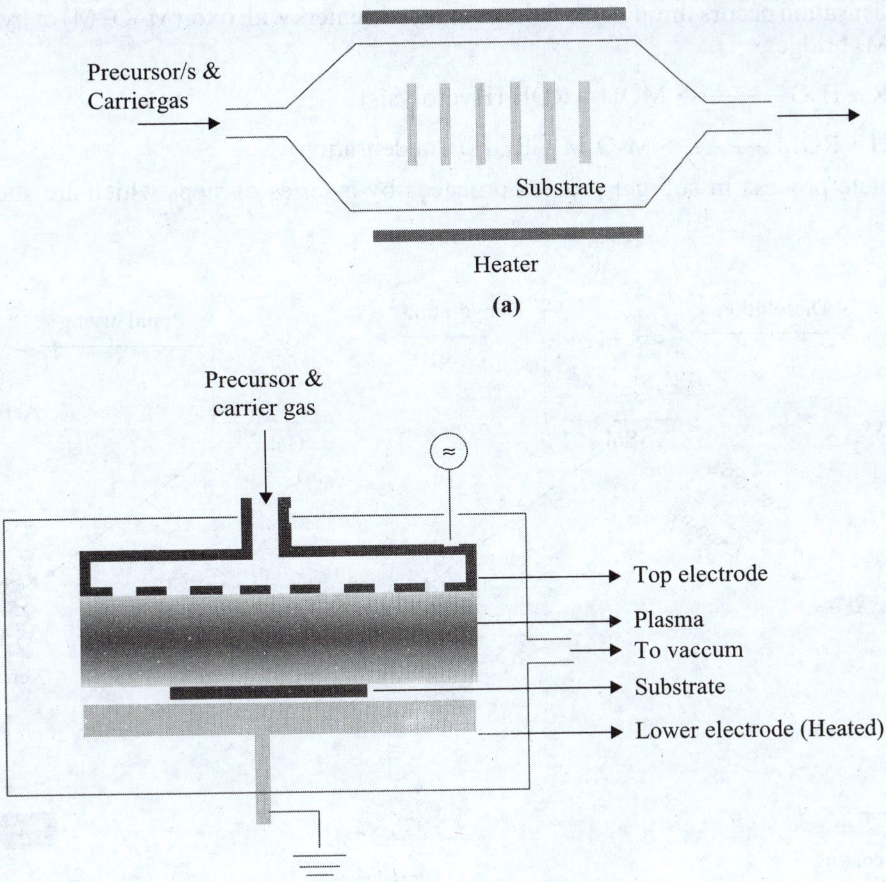

Fig. 17.5 A typical setup for (a) thermal CVD and (b) plasma-assisted CVD

Wet Chemical Synthesis

In principle, wet chemical synthesis of nanomaterials can be classified into two broad groups: *top-down method,* where single crystals are etched in an aqueous solution for producing nanomaterials, e.g., the synthesis of porous silicon by electrochemical etching; *bottom up method*, which consists of sol–gel method, precipitation, etc., where materials containing the desired precursors are mixed in a controlled fashion to form a colloidal solution. Let us discuss the sol–gel process in details.

Sol–gel method of synthesizing nanomaterials is widely employed to prepare oxide materials. The sol–gel process involves the fabrication of inorganic networks, mostly metal oxides, through the formation of a colloidal suspension, i.e., *sol* and its subsequent gelation to form a network in a continuous liquid phase, i.e., *gel*. Typical precursors for synthesizing such colloids are metal alkoxides such as $Si(OEt)_4$ (tetraethyl orthosilicate or TEOS). The precursor is processed to form a dispersible oxide, i.e., sol in contact with water or dilute acid. Removal of the liquid from the sol yields the gel, and the sol–gel transition controls the particle size and shape. Calcination of the gel produces the oxide. The reactions involved in the sol–gel chemistry based on the hydrolysis and condensation of metal alkoxides $M(OR)_n$ is described here. Condensation occurs through the linkage of metal centers with oxo-(M–O–M) or hydroxo-(M–OH–M) bridges.

$$MOR + H_2O \longrightarrow MOH + ROH \text{ (Hydrolysis)}$$

$$MOH + ROM \longrightarrow M\text{-}O\text{-}M + ROH \text{ (Condensation)}$$

The complete process in sol–gel process proceeds by a series of steps which are shown in Fig. 17.6.

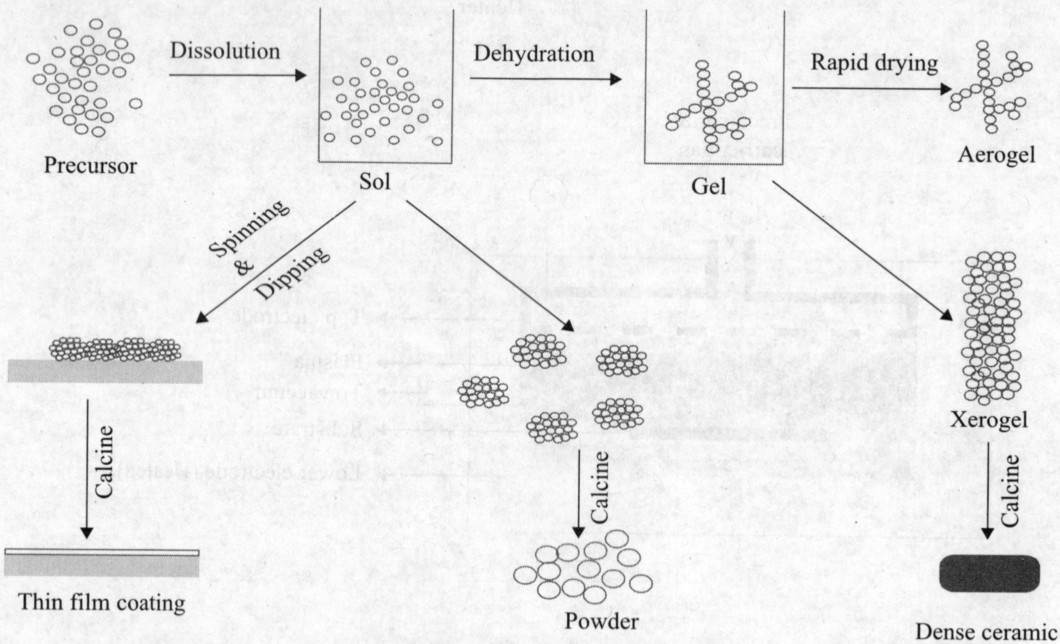

Fig. 17.6 Schematic representation of sol–gel process of synthesis of nanomaterials

1. *Step 1* involves formation of different stable solutions of the alkoxide or solvated metal precursor, i.e., the sol.
2. In *Step 2* gelation due to the formation of an oxo- or hydroxo-bridged network by a poly-condensation or poly-esterification reaction occurs which dramatically increases the viscosity of the solution.
3. *Step 3* involves syneresis, i.e., aging of the gel, during which the poly-condensation reactions continue so as to transform the gel into a solid mass, accompanied by contraction of the gel network and expulsion of solvent from gel pores. Syneresis also accompanies Ostwald ripening or coarsening, which is the phenomenon by which smaller particles are consumed by larger particles during the growth process and sometimes during phase transformations. The aging process of gels is critical for the prevention of cracks in gels casting.
4. *Step 4* involves drying of the gel, when water and other volatile liquids are removed from the gel network. This process is a complicated one due to fundamental changes in the structure of the gel. If isolation of solvent is achieved by thermal evaporation, the resulting monolith is termed a *xerogel*. However, if the solvent is extracted under supercritical or near supercritical conditions, the product is an *aerogel*.

5. *Step 5* involves calcination of the monolith at temperatures up to 800°C, during which surface-bound M–OH groups are removed, making the gel stabilized against rehydration.
6. *Step 6* which is the last stepis the densification and decomposition of the gels at high temperatures, i.e., at a temperature >800°C. In the process, pores of the gel network are collapsed, and remaining organic species are volatilized.

Advantages

1. The main advantage is that one can get monosized nanoparticles by any bottom-up approach.
2. It is a cheap and low-temperature technique.
3. This is widely used for synthesizing nonmetallic inorganic materials such as glasses, glass ceramics, or ceramic materials at very low temperatures as compared to the traditional high temperature processesthat require melting glass or firing ceramics.

Limitations

1. Difficulties in controlling the growth of the particles and stopping the newly formed particles from agglomeration.
2. Difficulty in ensuring the completion of reactions so thatno unwanted reactant is left on the product.
3. Production rates of nano powders are very low in this process.

Gas Condensation Processing (GPC)

The set up for gas condensation processing (GPC) consists of a vacuum chamber with evaporation arrangement and particle collection equipment. In the process, the metallic or inorganic material is vaporized using thermal evaporation sources such as Joule-heated refractory crucibles, electron beam evaporation devices, or sputtering sources in an inert atmosphere. Inert gas is continuously allowed to enter into the chamber and removed by pumps so that a dynamic vacuum is generated. The gas cools the vapor and nanoparticles form in the vicinity of the source by homogenous nucleation in the gas phase and grow by coalescence and incorporation of atoms from the gas phase. The particle size depends critically on the residence time of the particles in the growth regime and can be influenced by the gas pressure, kind of inert gas used, i.e., He, Ar, or Kr, and on the evaporation rate, i.e., vapor pressure of the evaporating material. The average particle size can be made to increase by increasing gas pressure, vapor pressure, and mass of the inert gas. A rotating cylindrical device cooled with liquid nitrogen (cold finger) is employed for the particle collection. The nanoparticles are extracted from the gas flow by thermophoretic forces and get deposited loosely on the surface of the collection device as a powder. Finally, the nanoparticles are removed from the surface of the cylinder by means of a scraper. The schematic presentation for GPC is shown in Fig. 17.7.

Note:

1. The method is extremely slow and therefore limited to a laboratory scale.
2. Control of the composition of the particles has been difficult and reproducibility is poor.

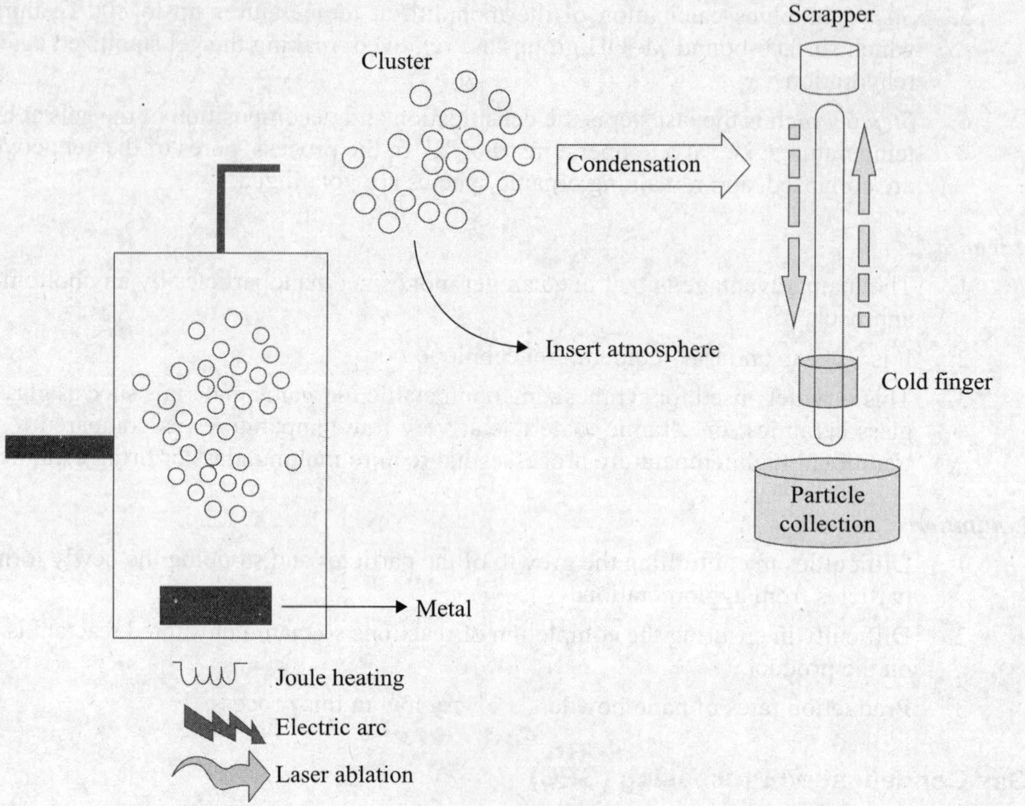

Fig. 17.7 Schematic representation of typical setup for GPC

3. Evaporation is usually achieved from refractory metal crucibles such as W, Ta, or Mo. However, for metals with high melting points and those that react with the crucibles, sputtering or laser or electron beam evaporation is used.
4. Sputtering is a non-thermal process in which surface atoms are physically ejected from the surface by momentum transfer from an energetic bombarding species of atomic or molecular size.
5. Synthesis of alloys or inter-metallic compounds by thermal evaporation can only be done in exceptional cases where the vapor pressures of the constituent elements are similar. As an alternative, sputtering from an alloy or mixed target can be employed.
6. Composite materials such as Cu/Bi or W/Ga can be synthesized by simultaneous evaporation from two separate crucibles onto a rotating collection device.

Chemical Vapor Condensation (CVC)

Chemical vapor condensation (CVC) was developed in Germany in 1994. The process involves pyrolysis of vapors of metal organic precursors in a reduced pressure atmosphere. Particles of ZrO_2 and Y_2O_3 have been prepared by CVC method. As shown schematically in Fig. 17.8, the evaporation source used in GPC is replaced by is a hot wall reactor. Originally, the process was intended to adjust the parameter field during the synthesis in order to suppress film formation and enhance homogeneous nucleation of particles in the gas flow. It is a matter of common observation that film or particle formation is controlled by the residence time of the precursor in the reactor. Adjustment of the residence time of the precursor molecules by changing the gas flow rate, the pressure difference between the precursor delivery system and the main chamber, and the temperature of the hot wall reactor leads to the significant production of nanosized particles of metals and ceramics instead of thin films as in CVD process.

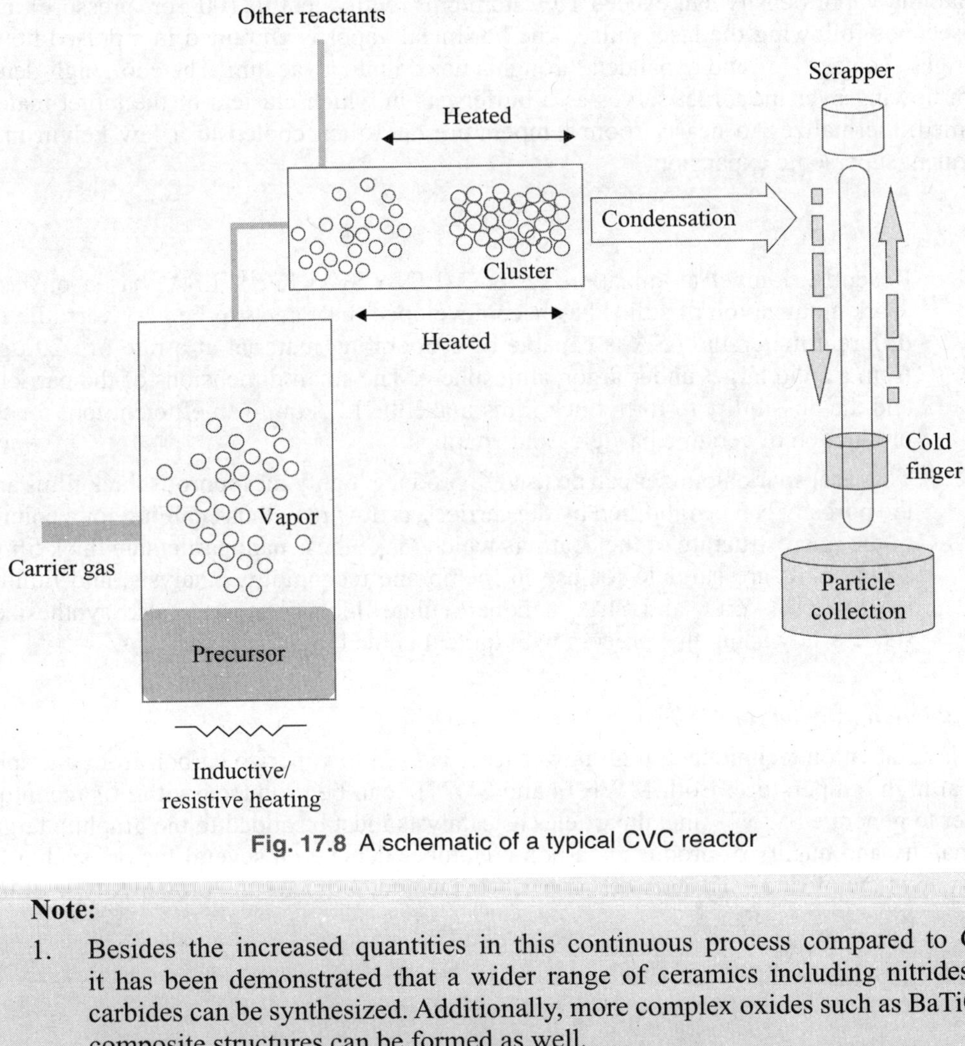

Fig. 17.8 A schematic of a typical CVC reactor

Note:

1. Besides the increased quantities in this continuous process compared to GPC, it has been demonstrated that a wider range of ceramics including nitrides and carbides can be synthesized. Additionally, more complex oxides such as $BaTiO_3$ or composite structures can be formed as well.
2. In addition to the formation of single-phase nanoparticles by CVC of a single precursor, the reactor allows the synthesis of mixtures of nanoparticles of two phases or doped nanoparticles by supplying two precursors at the front end of the reactor, and coated nanoparticles, i.e., n-ZrO_2 coated with n-Al_2O_3 or vice versa, by supplying a second precursor at the second stage of the reactor. In this case, nanoparticles which have been formed by homogeneous nucleation are coated by heterogeneous nucleation in the second stage of the reactor.

Laser Ablation

Laser ablation has been extensively used for the preparation of nanoparticles and particulate films. In this method, a high energy pulsed laser with an intensity flux exceeding 10^7 W/cm^3 is focused on a target containing the material to be made into clusters. These pulsed lasers can easily generate temperatures of $>10^4$K at the target material. This high temperature vaporizes all known substances so quickly that the rest of the source can operate at room temperature. Typical yields are 10^{14}–10^{15} atoms from a surface area of 0. 01 cm^2 in a 10^{-8} s pulse. The local atomic vapor density can exceed 10^{18} atom/cm^3 (equivalent to 100 Torr pressure) in the microseconds following the laser pulse. The hot metal vapor is entrained in a pulsed flow of carrier gas such as "He" and expanded through a nozzle into a vacuum. The cool, high-density helium flowing over the target serves as a buffer gas in which clusters of the target material is formed, thermalizes to nearly room temperature, and then cooled to a few kelvin in the subsequent supersonic expansion.

Note:

1. Recently a novel atomization system, (LINA-SPARK™), LSA, based on laser spark atomization of solids has been developed that seems to be very versatile for different materials. LSA is capable of evaporating material at a rate of ~20 μg/s from a solid target under argon atmosphere. The small dimensions of the particles and the possibility to form thick films make the LSA quite an efficient tool for the production of ceramic particles and coatings.
2. The laser spark atomizer can be used to produce highly mesoporous thick films and the porosity can be modified by the carrier gas flow rate, thus enabling for a control of the microstructure of the coatings which make these nanoparticulate thick films. These films are suitable for use in membrane technology, catalysis, and lithium ion batteries. ZrO_2 and SnO_2 nanoparticulate thick films were also synthesized successfully using this process with quite identical microstructure.

Laser ablation method for CNT preparation

In the laser ablation technique, a high power laser is used to vaporize carbon from a graphite target at high temperature. Both MWNTs and SWNTs can be produced with this technique. In order to generate SWNTs, metal particles as catalysts must be added to the graphite targets. The quantity and quality of produced carbon nanotubes depend on several factors such as the amount and type of catalysts, laser power and wavelength, temperature, pressure, type of inert

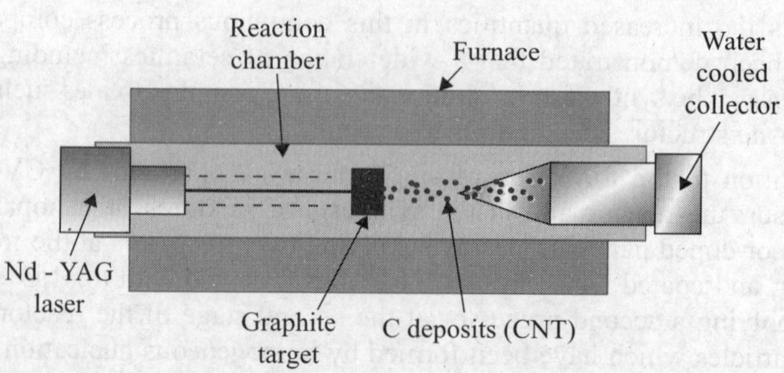

Fig. 17.9 Setup for preparation of CNT by laser ablation

gas, and the fluid dynamics near the carbon target. Schematic diagram of the laser ablation apparatus is shown in Fig. 17.9. In a typical method, the laser is focused onto a carbon targets containing ~1% cobalt/nickel with ~99% of graphite composite that is placed in a 1200°C quartz tube furnace under the argon atmosphere. In the process, argon gas carries the vapors from the high temperature chamber into a cooled collector positioned downstream. The nanotubes will self-assemble from carbon vapors and condense on the walls of the flow tube. The diameter distribution of SWNTs from this method varies about 1. 0–1.6 nm with a purity of about 90%.

Carbon Nanomaterials

In this chapter, emphasis is given on carbon nanomaterials. Typical examples of carbon nanomaterials are fullerenes and cylindrical nanotubes. The other shapes such as nanowires and nanocones are also found. Graphene is the mother of all carbon nanomaterials. It is nothing but a flat monolayer of carbon atoms tightly packed into a two-dimensional honeycomb lattice. These two-dimensional (2-D) graphene sheet can be wrapped up into zero-dimensional (0-D) fullerenes, rolled into one-dimensional (1-D) nanotubes or stacked into 3-D graphite and other structures (Fig. 17.10). Thus, carbon nanostructures are accordingly classified as zero-dimensional, one-dimensional, two-dimensional, and three-dimensional nanostructures.

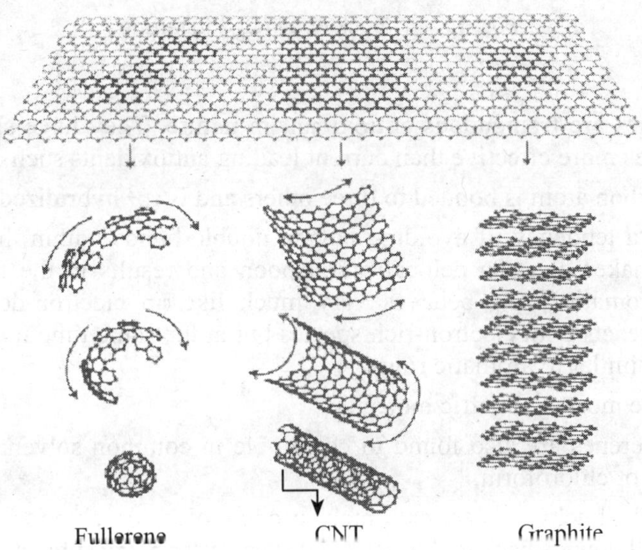

Fig. 17.10 Graphene and other types of carbon nanostructures (from **Geim AK, Novoselov KS. Nature Materials 6(3): 183–191, 2007)**

Fullerenes

In 1985, a new carbon material was discovered by H. Kroto and R. Smalley called carbon-60 (C_{60}). They named that as "buckminsterfullerene," after the name of an architect Buckminster Fuller, who was well known for building geodesic domes. The suffix "ene" represents the fact that each "C" is covalently bonded with other three carbon atoms ultimately indicating the presence of double bonds. C_{60} is a spherical molecule about 1 nm in diameter, comprising 60 carbon atoms arranged as 20 hexagons and 12 pentagons as the basis of icosahedral symmetry closed-cage structure. Fullerene is defined as a molecule composed entirely of carbon, in the form of hollow spheres. These spherical fullerenes are also called *buckyballs*, and they resemble more or less of a football-like architecture. Since that time the family of fullerene has increased and now it consists of numerous compounds such as C_{70}, C_{76}, C_{84}, C_{240}, and C_{540}. Fullerenes are a class of closed-cage carbon molecule, C_n, characteristically containing 12 pentagons and a variable number of hexagons:

$$\text{Number of hexagons} = \frac{(\text{Carbon atoms, } n) - 20}{2}$$

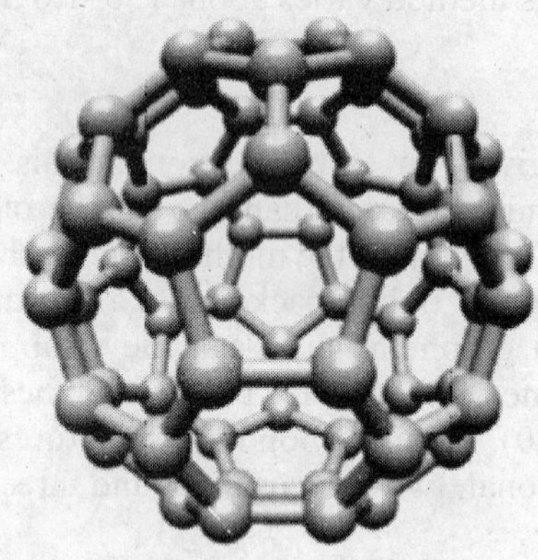

Fig. 17. 11 Bucky-ball (C_{60}) fullerene

Characteristics

1. Fullerenes are tremendous antioxidant in nature. They have shown performance 100 times more effective than current leading antioxidants such as vitamin E.
2. Each carbon atom is bonded to three others and is sp^2 hybridized.
3. C_{60} has a tendency of avoiding having double bonds within the pentagonal rings which makes electron delocalization poor, and results in the fact that C_{60} is not "superaromatic." C_{60} behaves very much like an electron-deficient alkene and readily reacts with electron-rich species but at the same time it can also sometimes behave similar to aromatic rings.
4. C_{60} is the most symmetric molecule.
5. The fullerenes are also found to be soluble in common solvents such as benzene, toluene, or chloroform.
6. Physically, buckyballs are extremely strong molecules, able to resist great pressure. They will bounce back to their original shape after being subjected to over 3000 atm.
7. Chemically, fullerenes are stable, but not totally unreactive. Breaking the balls requires temperatures of over 1000°C and the exact value depends on type of fullerene.

Applications

1. Several applications are envisaged for fullerenes, such as miniature "ball bearings" to lubricate surfaces, drug delivery vehicles, and electronic circuits.
2. Used as MRI agents in medical world.
3. Fullerenes can be added to polymer structures to create new copolymers with specific physical and mechanical properties.
4. Fullerenes have potential ability to transfer hydrogen. Therefore, they are used as catalysts for hydrogenation.
5. Fullerenes are used as proton exchange membranes for fuel cells.

6. Being strong anti-oxidant in nature, major pharmaceutical companies are exploring the use of fullerenes in controlling the neurological damage of such diseases as Alzheimer's disease and Lou Gehrig's disease (ALS), which are a result of radical damage.

Carbon nanotubes

In 1991, SumioIijima, a Japanese researcher observed carbon nanotubes (CNTs) which are hollow fibers. CNTs are extended tubes of rolled graphene sheets (a planner network of inter connected planner hexagonal rings of carbon atoms) which are typically closed at their ends by semi-fullerene-like structures. Defects in the structures result in bends and transitions overall. The diameter of a carbon nanotube remains in the order of one nanometer but can go up to several microns to centimeters long. There are two forms of CNTs namely:

1. **Single-walled carbon nanotubes (SWCNT):** These are of different types depending on the manner in which the graphene sheets are rolled. The basic varities being zigzag, armchair, and chiral. Identification of a particular variety can be made by following the pattern across the diameter of the tube and analyzing their cross-sectional structure.
2. **Multi-walled carbon nanotubes (MWCNT):** It consists of several concentric SWCNT with different diameters. The forms are more complex here as each SWCNT can have different structures resulting in a variety of sequential arrangements.

   The simplest form being the one in which the concentric layers are identical but of different diameter. In other varieties, two or more types of concentric SWCNTs remain arranged in different orders. These can have either regular layering or random layering.

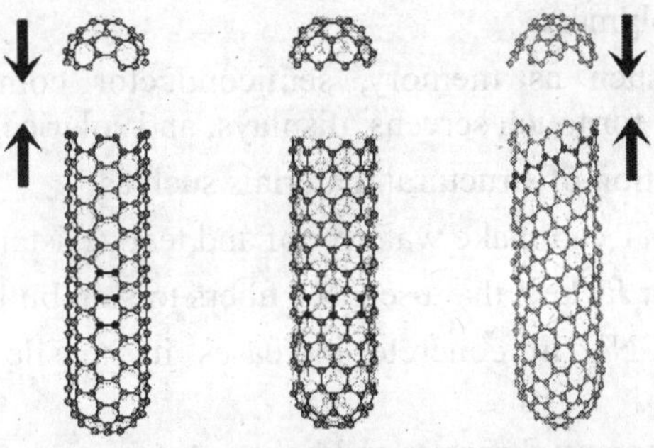

Fig. 17.12 Different types of SWCNT

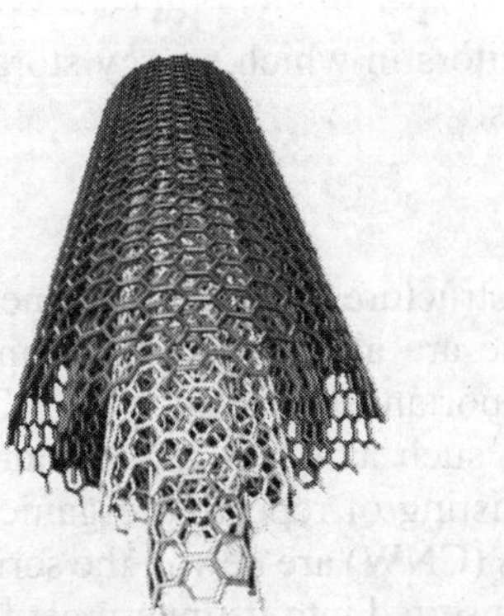

Fig. 17.13 MWCNT made of concentric SWCNTs

Note:
Another form with tubular structure is carbon nanofibers (CNF) which are not hollow fibers.

Characteristics

1. These materials have high thermal and electrical conductivity. Here, motion of electrons fall under the regime of ballistic transport. It is the transport of electrons in a medium with negligible electrical resistivity due to scattering. Ballistic transport is observed when the mean free path of the electron (the average length that the electron can travel freely, i.e., before hitting against something and deviating from its original path) is much bigger than the width of the wire through which the electron travels such that the electron alters its motion only by hitting against the walls.
2. Their mechanical strength is very high with more than one terapascal (TPa) making them as stiff as diamond. In case of multi-walled nanotubes, Young's modulus goes upto 1.8 TPa which is 100 times more than steel.
3. Aspect ratio (length to width ratio) is >1000.
4. Stable at high temperature.
5. Stable against strong acids and other regular chemicals including atmospheric components.

Applications

1. In conducting polymers.
2. In electronics such as memory, semiconductor components, and transparent conducting films for touch screens, displays, and solar cells.
3. Used for preparation of structural materials such as
   (a) Textiles: CNT can make waterproof and tear-resistant fabrics.
   (b) Body armor: Jackets that use CNT fibers to stop bullets.
   (c) Concrete: CNT in concrete increases its tensile strength and halt crack propagation.
   (d) Sports equipment: Stronger and lighter tennis rackets, bicycle parts, etc.
   (e) High-tensile strength fibers
   (f) Bridges: CNT may be able to replace steel in suspension and other bridges.
4. To build ultra-capacitors in which energy storage capacity is much higher than the traditional capacitors.

Nanowires

Nanowires can be defined as structures that have diameter of the order of a nanometer and an unconstrained length. These are also known as quantum wires as at this scale quantum mechanical effects become important. Different types of nanowires exist, viz., metallic such as Pt and Au, semiconducting such as C, Si, Ga, N, and insulating such as SiO_2 and TiO_2 and molecular nanowires consisting of repeating organic or inorganic molecular units DNA, Li2Mo6Se6. Carbon nanowires (CNW) are new in the series which consists of an MWNT with a long 1D linear carbon chain inserted into its innermost tube.

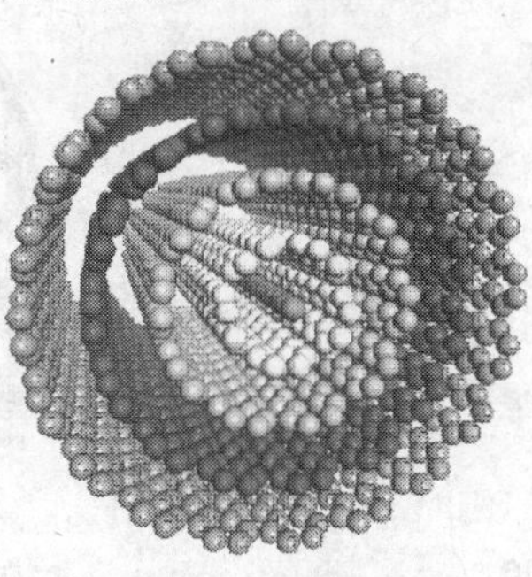

Fig. 17.14 Carbon nanowire inside an MWCNT

Characteristics

1. Often referred to as one-dimensional materials.
2. Aspect ratio (length to width ratio) is >1000.
3. Electrons in nanowires are quantum confined laterally and therefore occupy energy levels which are different from the quasi-continuous energy levels or bands found in bulk materials.
4. The conductivity of a nanowire is much less than that of the corresponding bulk material. This is due to the fact that the width of nanowire is much less than nanotubes which shorten the mean free path of electron of the bulk material to wire width. Again, conductivity is also reduced by edge effects which come from atoms that lay at the surface of nanowire and are not fully bonded to neighboring atoms.

Applications

1. Because of their high Young's modulus, they are used for enhancing mechanical properties of composites.
2. As nanowires appear in bundles, they may be used as tribological additives to improve friction characteristics and reliability of electronic transducers (electric or electronic devices that transform energy from one manifestation into another) and actuators (devices, such as valves and switches, that perform actions such as turning things on or off or making adjustments in an operational system).
3. Can be used to prepare active electronic components such as *p–n* junction and logic gates.
4. Semiconductor nanowire crossings are expected to play a very important role in future of digital computing.
5. Nanowires have potential applications in high-density data storage, either as magnetic read heads or as patterned storage media.

Nanocones

Carbon nanocones are conical structures discovered in 1994. Nanocones have height and base diameter of the same order of magnitude. These are made of graphene sheets which are composed solely of carbon hexagons with some pentagonal defects to be specific from one to five so as to form a curved cone tip. The opening angle, i.e., apex of the cones is not arbitrary, but has preferred values of approximately 20°, 40°, and 60°. There is one more kind of nanocones known as nono horns which look like animal horns with exact five defects on the tip.

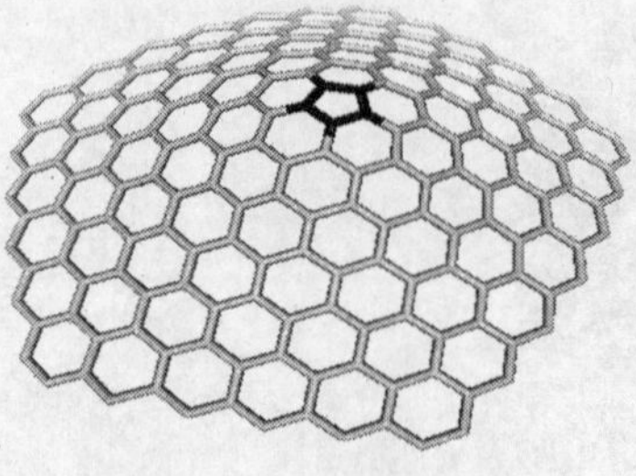

Fig. 17.15 **Nanocone**

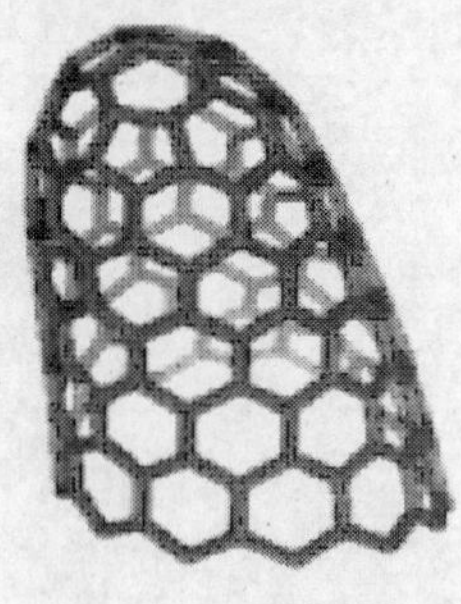

Fig. 17.16 **Nanohorn**

Characteristics

1. The spacing between each nanocone can be controlled or precisely regulated, instead of randomly arranged.
2. The reactive group and whatever molecule that is connected to it are projected away from the surface to minimize interferences between molecules and to expedite interactions between a probe and target molecules.
3. The number of molecules bound to the "tip" is minimized, down to a single molecule, allowing more precise molecule–molecule interaction.

Applications

1. Nanocone can be used as base polymer or in diluted form both in the catalyst and in the cross linker component.
2. Nanocone surface can be widely used in other fields such as ELISA, bio/chemical sensor, bead-based assays, affinity-based separation, and SPR spectroscopy.

Graphite

Nanographites are molecular systems, where graphene sheets of dimensions of the order of nanometres are stacked. They are also known as exfoliated graphite nanoplatelets (xGnP). xGnP consists of several graphene sheets stacked together to a total thickness between 1 and 15 nm (average 5 nm), whereas the platelet diameter ranges from sub-micron to over 100 microns. Exfoliated graphite nanoplatelets (xGnP) were typically produced by acid intercalation into multilayered graphite structure followed by thermal exfoliation and a controlled size reduction. Since graphite is the stiffest material found in nature (Young's Modulus = 1060 MPa), having a modulus several times that of clay, accompanied with excellent electrical and thermal conductivity, the xGnP should have similar properties to carbon-based nanomaterials, including carbon nanotubes, nanofibers, and fullerenes, yet the estimated cost is substantially low as compared to other carbon nanomaterials.

Characteristics

1. Because of the platelet shape, xGnP significantly improves the impermeability of composites when used at densities of ~3 wt% or greater.
2. Since xGnP is composed of the same material as carbon nanotubes, it shares many of their electrochemical characteristics, although not their tensile strength.
3. xGnP particles can be aligned using electric field.
4. Graphene is an extremely electrically conductive material.

5. Highly hydrophobic.
6. It can have surface area as high as 1500 m^2/g.
7. Evaluation of the properties of the resulting composites compared to other carbon-based nano reinforcements show that the xGnP improves the modulus of better than other commercially available reinforcements at equivalent volume fractions.
8. The thickness of the xGnP can be controlled in a range from 1 to 25 nm. The diameter of the platelet can be controlled from the sub-micron level to ten's of microns. Consequently, the surface area of xGnP can range from ~25 to over several hundred square meters per gram.

Applications

1. Composite materials made with polymers, such as plastics, nylon, or rubber, can be made electrically or thermally conductive with the addition of small amounts of xGnP.
2. These nanoparticles can change the fundamental properties of plastics, enabling them to perform more like metals with metallic properties.

Nano Scale Effect on Properties

Properties	Examples
Catalytic	Improved catalytic efficiency through the increase of surface-to-volume ratio.
Electrical	Enhanced electrical conductivity in ceramic and magnetic nanocomposites while increased electrical resistance in metals.
Mechanical	Improved hardness and toughness of metals and alloys, ductility, and superplasticity of ceramics.
Magnetic	Increased magnetic coercivity up to a critical grain size, super magnetic behavior. Coercivity, also called the coercive field or coercive force, is a measure of a ferromagnetic to withstand an external magnetic field.
Optical	Spectral shift of optical absorption, and fluorescence properties, increased quantum efficiency of semiconductor crystals.
Sterical	Increased selectivity, hollow spheres for specific drug transportation, and controlled release.
Biological	Increased permeability through biological barriers such as membranes, increased biocompatibility.

General Applications of Nanomaterials (Nanotechnology)

Nanotechnology is the cutting age technology to inspire in entering into new frontiers of research interests. It has already proved its tremendous potentiality to cater the necessity of modern society with user friendly as well as eco-friendly approach. A few specimen examples are discussed below.

In medicine

Nanotechnology has been used in the medical field in delivering drugs to specific cells using nanoparticles. The overall drug consumption and side-effects can be lowered significantly by depositing the active agent in the required region only and that to in no higher dose than needed.

This highly selective approach reduces costs and human suffering. Use of dendrimers and nanoparticles in targeted and controlled drug delivery, is an emerging field of research called Nano-biopharmacuetics. The basic steps in drug delivery are Step I-Efficient encapsulation of the drugs, Step II-Successful delivery of said drugs to the targeted region of the body, and Step III-successful release of the drug there. The carrier in nanodrug delivery may be coated solid particles, Vesicles, Liposomes, Micelles, Polymers or Solid lipid nanoparticles.

In catalysis

Nanocatalysts are basically heterogeneous catalysts defined as nanoscale materials which have at least one nanoscale dimension, or have been subjected to nanoscale structural modification. They could be classified into four distinct types, viz., nanoparticulate, nanoporous, nanocrystalline, and supramolecular catalysts. However, most catalysts consist of particles with size in nanoscale dispersed on a high-surface-area support. For example, rhodium nanocatalysts for hydrogenations, PdO nanoparticle supported on carbon nanotubes, graphene oxide useful for reduction of nitrophenols, hydrogen generation promoted by a $CuO/ZnO–ZrO_2$ nanocatalyst, and Pd-nanoparticlesmediated C-C bond forming reactions.

Advantages of nanocatalysts

1. Nanocatalyst can fit where many of the traditional catalyst will not.
2. By nanocatalyst being very small in size creates a very high surface to volume ratio. These increases the performances of the catalyst as now relatively more surface becomes available for reactants.
3. Some nanocatalysts can develop partials and net charges that help in the process of making and breaking bonds at a more efficient scale.
4. Nanocatalysts have already proven themselves as an important member of green chemistry zone.

In environment technology

1. **In household cleaning:** The most prominent application of nanotechnology in the household is self-cleaning or "easy-to-clean" surfaces on ceramics or glasses. Nanoceramic particles have improved the smoothness and heat resistance of common household equipment such as the flat iron. The use of engineered nanofibers already makes clothes water- and stain-repellent or wrinkle-free. Textiles with a nanotechnological "finish" can be washed less frequently and at lower temperatures. Nanotechnology has been used to integrate tiny carbon particles membrane and guarantee full-surface protection from electrostatic charges for the wearer.
2. **Fuel cells:** The effectiveness of potential capability of carbon nanotubes in storing hydrogen has inspired the scientists to start research work on carbon nanotube based fuel cells. This type of fuel cells has the potential to power cars, amongst other things, with water as the only emission, although this concept is yet to be commercialized.
3. **Photovoltaics:** Conventional solar cells are called photovoltaic cells. These cells are very costly due to use of silicon. Moreover, they can only achieve efficiencies around 10% which is not at all energy economy. Such costly solar cells can be substituted successfully with very cheap plastic solar cells made of tiny nanorods dispersed within in a polymer. The nanorods behave as wires because when they absorb light of a specific wavelength they generate electrons. These electrons flow through the

nanorods until they reach the aluminum electrode where they are combined to form a current and are used as electricity. Use of such nanophotovoltaic cells will definitely reduce the dependence of human society on traditional fossil fuels for making power generation in future.

In biomimicry

It is one of the favorite topics in nanotechnology, as scientists take clues from nature to inspire new creation. Biomimicry is becoming increasingly important due to the following reasons: (a) nature does not produce waste in a stable ecosystem, (b) biomimicry beautifully operates hierarchically which goes as follows: molecular → nano → cellular → organism → ecosystem; and (c) evolutionary pressure typically forces natural systems to become highly optimized and efficient. A few examples of biomimicry are as follows:

1. **Anti-reflection coatings**: Nano-engineered anti-reflective coating on an untreated silicon solar cell increases the sunlight absorption up to 97%.
2. **Adhesives**: Animals that adhere to walls and walk on ceilings owe their ability to micro- and nanoscale attachment elements. Similar to this observation it has been also understood that aligned CNTs spiking out of substrate surfaces showed strong nanometer-scale adhesion forces. Vertically aligned multiwalled carbon nanotubes have just recently been used to mimic the gecko feet as dry adhesives.
3. **High strength nanocomposites**: This class of nanocomposites is best fit for automotive, aerospace, and defence structures.
4. **Anti-corrosion coatings**: Chromium (VI) has remained an essential ingredient in the metal finishing industry for corrosion control. But chromium (VI) shows adverse effects on health and environment. The nanometer-thick polyelectrolyte/ inhibitor coating, on the other hand, is environment friendly. They simultaneously provide three mechanisms of corrosion protection: (a) passivation of the metal degradation by controlled release of inhibitor; (b) buffering of pH changes at the corrosive area by polyelectrolyte layers; and (c) self-curing of the film defects owing to the mobility of the polyelectrolyte constituents in the layer-by-layer assembly.

QUESTIONS

1. What are nanomaterials?
2. What do you mean by material self-assembly?
3. What is SAM? Explain with a suitable example.
4. Discuss the applications of SAM.
5. What do you mean by MESA?
6. What do you mean liposome?
7. How molecular self-assembly works in supramolecular system? Explain with a suitable example.
8. What is a micelle? Which factors control the size and shape of a micelle?
9. What is a vesicle?
10. What are nanocrystals?

11. What is graphene sheet?
12. What are fullerenes? Provide their uses.
13. Out of carbon nanotube and nanowire, which one is a better conductor and why?
14. What is biomimicry?
15. Explain nanocatalyst with suitable examples. Also suggest its advantages over traditional catalysts.
16. Provide the uses of nanowires.
17. Discuss the characteristics of nanowires.
18. What are different types of single-layer carbonnano tubes?
19. How nanotechnology is useful in medicine?
20. Discuss CVD technique for preparation of carbon nanotubes.
21. What are the limitations of ball milling method for preparation of nanoparticles?
22. Discuss laser ablation for preparation of CNTs.
23. What is the difference between CVD and CVC techniques used for preparation of nanomaterials?
24. Discuss sol–gel process for manufacture of nanomaterials.
25. What are the advantages and limitations of sol–gel process?
26. Discuss gas condensation processing (GPC) in detail.
27. What are the differences between top-down and bottom-up approaches in synthesis of nanomaterials?
28. What do you mean by nanomaterials? Explain different categories of nanomaterials with suitable examples.
29. What are carbon nanomaterials? Explain different types of carbon nanomaterials with suitable examples.
30. Discuss the uses of nanotechnology in the modern age.
31. What are carbon nanotubes and nanowires? Explain their characteristics and applications.
32. What are fullerenes and nanocones? Explain their characteristics and applications.
33. Discuss the effect of nanoscale on different properties of materials.
34. Discuss the applications of nanotechnology.

CHAPTER

18 Polymers

Chapter Outline

- Glass Transition Temperature
- Melting Point
- Molecular Weight of Polymers
- Classification of Polymers
- Polymerization
- Polymerization Techniques
- Plastics
- Polyesters
- Phenolic Resins
- Amino Resins
- Molding of Plastics
- Elastomers
- Conducting Polymers
- Biopolymers

Polymer is derived from a Greek word, which means many parts (*poly* meaning many and *meros* meaning parts). It is a class of materials consisting of many small molecules called monomers which are linked together to form long chains. A typical polymer may include few thousands of monomers. Because of their large sizes polymers are also known as macromolecules. People have taken advantage of the versatility of polymers for centuries in the form of oils, tars, resins, and gums. However, the modern polymer industry began to develop in the late 1830s with the success of Charles Goodyear in producing a useful form of natural rubber through a process known as *vulcanization*. The first ever semi-synthetic polymer *cellulose nitrate* came into the market in 1860. The progress in polymer science was slow until 1930s when materials such as vinyl polymers, neoprene, polystyrene, and nylon were developed. The introduction of these revolutionary materials began a real explosion in polymer research.

Today, polymer has become an integral part of human life. Due to its diverse structures and properties it has entered into almost all area of requirements, such as construction, transport, agriculture, education, and information technology. One should not forget that the very existence of living organism depends on the biopolymers, such as nucleic acids, proteins, and carbohydrates.

Terminologies

Functionality

It refers to the number of bonding sites present in a monomer molecule, for example, the double bond of ethylene can be considered as a site for two free valecies because with its breakage it makes available two single bonds for combination. Polymers can be classified on the basis of functionality into the following two types:

Bifunctional polymers

In bifunctional polymers, the functionality of monomer is two. Here linear and straight chain polymers are formed. For example, all vinyl polymers, adipic acid, and amino acid.

Trifunctional monomers

In trifunctional monomers, functionality of monomer is three. Here three-dimensional network polymers are formed. For example, phenol and melamine.

Degree of Polymerization

It is defined as the number of repeating units present in a polymer molecule. Therefore, in the following example the degree of polymerization (DP) is "*n*." The value of *n* is much large which may go up to few thousand units.

$$\underset{\text{Ethylene}}{nCH_2{=}CH_2} \xrightarrow{\text{Polymerization}} \underset{\text{Polyethylene}}{\left[CH_2{-}CH_2\right]_n}$$

Example 18.1

A 28 g of ethylene was polymerized and the average degree of polymerization of polyethylene was found to be 400. Calculate the number of polyethylene molecules in the sample.

Solution

$$DP = \frac{\text{Total number of ethylene molecules}}{\text{Number of polyethylene molecules}}$$

$$\text{or} \quad \text{Number of polyethylen molecules} = \frac{\text{Total number of ethylene molecules}}{\text{DP}}$$

$$= \frac{6.023 \times 10^{3}}{400} = 1.5 \times 10^{21} \text{ molecules}$$

Glass Transition Temperature

Glass transition temperature (T_g) is the temperature at which amorphous polymers undergo a transition from a rubbery, viscous amorphous liquid to a brittle, glassy amorphous solid. Below this temperature the amorphous polymer is brittle, hard, and glassy, and above this it becomes flexible, soft, and rubbery (Fig. 18.1). A polymer does not have a unique value of T_g because the glass phase is not at equilibrium. The measured value of T_r will depend on the molecular weight of the polymer, its thermal history and age, on the measurement method, and on the rate of heating or cooling. Therefore, the expressed value of T_g is an approximate one. Illustrative plot of heat supplied as a function of temperature is given as follows. When an amorphous polymer is heated, temperature increases. The rate of increase is determined by the heat capacity of the polymer. Only something peculiar happens at T_g that the temperature

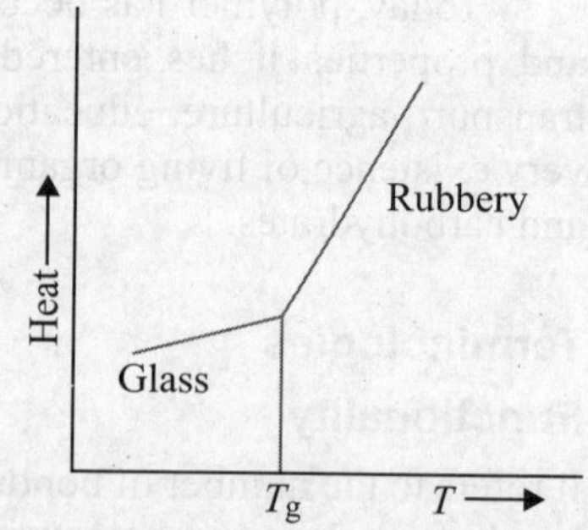

Fig. 18.1 Amorphous polymer

does not stop rising. There is no latent heat of glass transition. However, the temperature does not rise at the same rate above T_g, which is attributed to an increase in the heat capacity when it goes through the glass transition. Because the glass transition involves change in heat capacity, but does not involve a latent heat, this transition is called a *second-order transition*.

Glass transition temperature depends on

1. **Degree of branching:** T_g can be altered by changing the degree of branching or cross linking in the polymer. Branching hinders free rotation and thereby increases T_g.
2. **Additives:** Addition of plasticizer (additives that increase the plasticity or fluidity of the material to which they are added) reduces T_g.
3. **Molecular mass:** In general, T_g increases with increase in molecular mass upto a certain limit beyond which it remains unaltered.
4. **Stereo regularatiy:** Stereo regularity of polymers increases T_g. Therefore, T_g of different polymers remains in the order isotactic > syndiotactic > atactic.

Melting Point

The glass transition is a transition which happens to *amorphous* polymers. On the other hand, melting is a transition which occurs in *crystalline* polymers (Fig. 18.2). It happens at a temperature when the polymer chains fall out of their crystal structures and become a disordered liquid. However, even crystalline polymers carry some amorphous portion which may go up to 40–70% of the polymer sample. This is why the same sample of a polymer can have both a glass transition temperature (T_g) and a melting temperature (T_m). The point to be highlighted is that the amorphous portion undergoes the glass transition only and the crystalline portion undergoes melting only. When a crystalline polymer is heated at a constant rate, temperature continue to increase until the polymer reaches its melting point. The temperature holds steady for a while till the polymer has completely melted. Then the temperature of the polymer begins to increase once again, but with a slower rate. The molten polymer has a higher heat capacity than the solid crystalline polymer, so it can absorb more heat with a smaller increase in temperature. Any change brought about by heat, which has a change in heat capacity, and a latent heat is involved, is called a *first-order transition*.

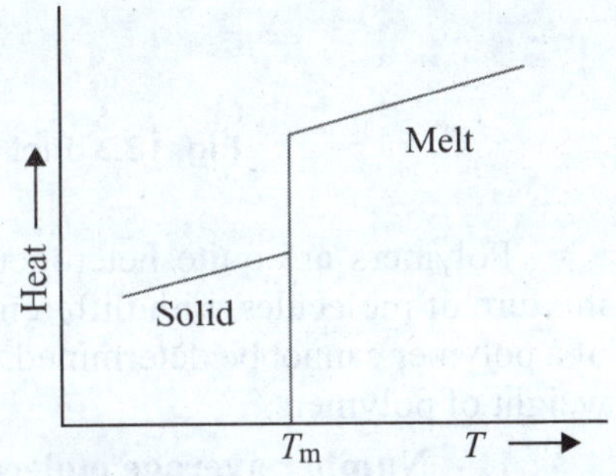

Fig. 18.2 Crystalline polymer

A comparison of glass temperature and melting points are summarized in the table below:

Glass transition	Melting point
1. Property of the amorphous region	1. Property of the crystalline region
2. Below T_g: disordered amorphous solid with immobile molecules	2. Below T_m: ordered crystalline solid
3. Above T_g: disordered amorphous solid in which portions of molecules can wiggle around	3. Above T_m: disordered melt
4. A second-order transition.	4. A first-order transition

Molecular Weight of Polymers

Molecular weight (MW) is important as it determines many physical properties such as temperature for transitions from liquids to waxes to rubbers to solids; mechanical properties such as stiffness, viscosity, and strength. The properties become more pronounced with increase in molecular weights. This can be revealed from the plot in Fig. 18.3. The curve shows that the goal of polymer synthesis is *not* to make the largest possible molecules, but to make molecules large enough to get onto the plateau region. Increasing the MW beyond this does not improve the physical properties much, but makes processing more difficult.

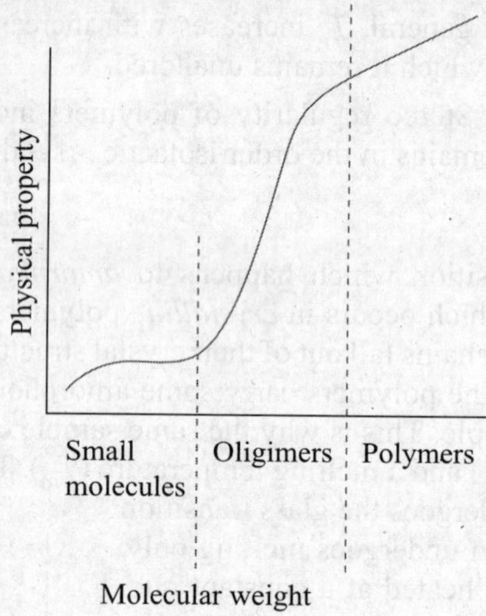

Fig. 18.3 Plot of molecular weight vs physical property

Polymers are quite heterogeneous in distribution of molecular weights, i.e., these are mixture of molecules with different molecular weights. Therefore, absolute molecular weight of a polymer cannot be determined. There are three different ways to find the average molecular weight of polymers.

1. **Number average molecular weight:** Here a polymer property that is not influenced by the size of any particle in the mixture is considered for the determination of molecular weight. Examples of such property (also known as colligative properties) are elevation in boiling point, depression in freezing point, and osmotic pressure. For these properties, the average molecular weight is the total weight of polymer sample divided by the number of molecules present. In polymer science, this weight is known as the number average molecular weight (M_n). This can be expressed as

$$\overline{M_n} = \frac{\text{Total weight}}{\text{Total number}}$$

$$= \frac{\Sigma N_i M_i}{\Sigma N_i} \quad [18.1]$$

$$= \Sigma x_i M_i \quad [18.2]$$

where N_i is the number of molecules with weight M_i.

The term $N_i/\Sigma N_i$ is physically the number fraction of polymers with molecular weight M_i. Therefore, it is also known as mole fraction and the relation [18.1] can also be expressed as relation [18.2].

2. **Weight average molecular weight**: Here a polymer property is considered which not only depends on the number of polymer molecules but also depends on the size or weight of each polymer molecule. An example of such a property is light scattering. Weight average molecular weight can be calculated by the following formula:

$$\overline{M_w} = \frac{\Sigma N_i M_i^2}{\Sigma N_i M_i} \qquad [18.3]$$

$$= \Sigma w_i M_i \qquad [18.4]$$

Here, $N_i M_i/\Sigma N_i M_i$ is the weight fraction of polymer with molecular weight w_i.

Note:

1. The weight average molecular weight is always greater than the number average molecular weight. However, in case of monodisperse system in which all molecules have same molecular weight, $\overline{M_w} = \overline{M_n}$.
2. The ratio of $\overline{M_w} / \overline{M_n}$ is often used as a measure of molecular mass distribution or *index of polydispersity.*

3. **Viscosity average molecular weight**: It is obtained from the viscosity measurement and can be expressed as

$$\overline{M_v} = \frac{\Sigma w_i M_i^a}{\Sigma w_i}$$

$$= \left[\frac{\Sigma w_i M_i^{a+1}}{\Sigma N_i M_i}\right]^{1/a} \qquad [18.5]$$

where a is a constant (and a = 1). Weight average molecular weight and viscosity average molecular weight are same. However, in practice a remains in the range 0.5 to 0.9; therefore, $\overline{M_v}$ is almost always less than $\overline{M_w}$.

Example 18.2

Calculate the number average and weight average molecular weights of polypropylene having following composition:

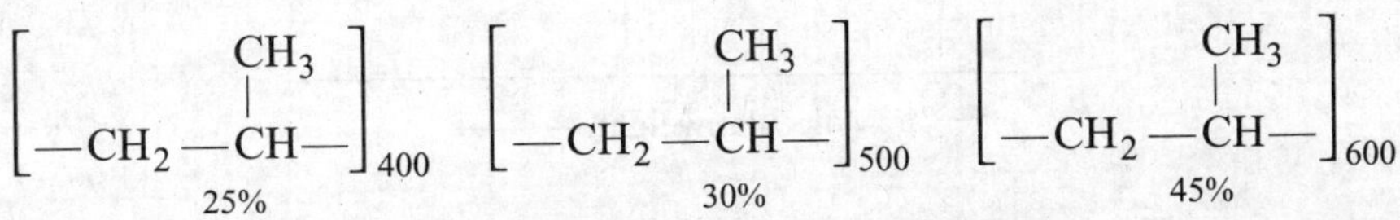

25% 30% 45%

Solution

Molecular mass of the repeating unit is 42.

$$\overline{M_n} = \frac{\Sigma N_i M_i}{\Sigma N_i}$$

$$= \frac{25 \times 16800 + 30 \times 21000 + 45 \times 25200}{100}$$

$$= 21840$$

$$\overline{M_w} = \frac{\Sigma N_i M_i^2}{\Sigma N_i M_i}$$

$$= \frac{25 \times (16800)^2 + 30 \times (21000)^2 + 45 \times (25200)^2}{25 \times 16800 + 30 \times 21000 + 45 \times 25200}$$

$$= 22373$$

Note:

The ratio of $\overline{M}_w/\overline{M}_n$ is often used as a measure of molecular mass distribution or index of polydispersity (PDI).

$$\text{PDI} = \frac{\overline{M}_w}{\overline{M}_n}$$

In case of monodisperse system, i.e., in which all molecules have identical molecular mass, PDI = 1, since $\overline{M}_n = \overline{M}_w$. In most of the cases, PDI $\geq$ 1. It should be noted that high-molecular-weight fractions have a greater influence on $\overline{M}_w$, while low-molecular-weight fractions have greater influence on $\overline{M}_n$. The following graph (Fig. 18.4) demonstrates the distribution of different molecular weights in a typical heterogeneous polymer sample.

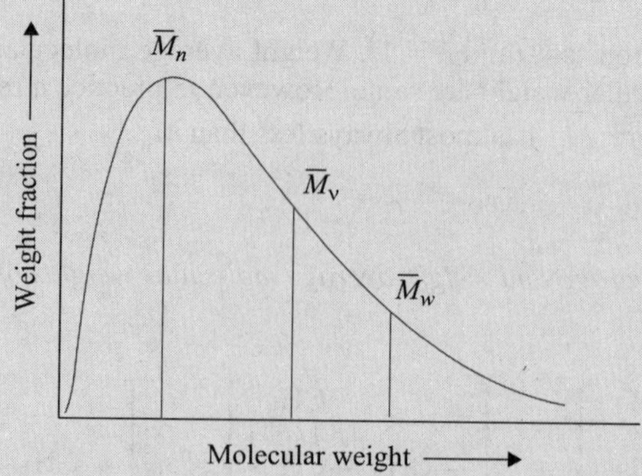

Fig. 18.4 Distribution of different molecular weights

Example 18.3

In a polymer, there are 150 molecules of molecular weight 100, 200 molecules of molecular weight 1000, and 300 molecules of molecular weight 10000. Find the number and weight average molecular mass of the polymer and PDI.

Solution

$$\overline{M_n} = \frac{\Sigma N_i M_i}{\Sigma N_i}$$

$$= \frac{150 \times 100 + 200 \times 1000 + 300 \times 10000}{650}$$

$$= 4.946 \times 10^3$$

$$\overline{M_w} = \frac{\Sigma N_i M_i^2}{\Sigma N_i M_i}$$

$$= \frac{150 \times (100)^2 + 200 \times (1000)^2 + 300 \times (10000)^2}{150 \times 100 + 200 \times 1000 + 300 \times 10000}$$

$$= 9.95 \times 10^2$$

$$\text{PDI} = \frac{\overline{M_w}}{\overline{M_n}} = 4.98$$

Classification of Polymers

Classification

- Origin/source
  - **Natural**: found in nature e.g., starch, cellulose, protein, nucleic acids, natural rubber, etc.
  - **Synthetic**: man made polymers e.g., polyethylene, polystyrene, nylon, bakelite, etc.
- Composition
  - **Homopolymer**: made of identical monomer units, e.g., polyethylene, polyvinyl chloride, etc.
  - **Copolymer**: made of two or more different type of monomers, e.g., nylon-6,6, bakelite, Buna-S, etc.
- Mechanism of polymerisation
  - **Addition polymers**: polyethylene, polystyrene, PVC, etc.
  - **Condensation polymers**: nylon 6,6, bakelite, etc.
- Heat treatment
  - **Thermoplastic**: soften on heating and stiffen on cooling, e.g., PE, PVC, PMMA, etc.
  - **Thermosetting**: these can be moulded once and don't soften on heating e.g., bakelite, urea-fomaldehyde resin, etc.
- Structure
  - **Linear**: e.g., HDPE
  - **Branched**: e.g., LDPE
  - Cross linked-vulcanized rubbers, bakelite, etc.
- Tacticity
  - **Isotactic**: the side groups are all on the same side of the main chain.
  - **Syndiotactic**: the side groups are arranged in alternatinf fashion.
  - **Atactic**: the side groups arranged in a random fashion around the main chain.
- Type of atom present
  - Organic polymers
  - Inorganic polymers like silicones

Polymerization

It is the process by virtue of which monomer molecules join together to form polymer. The polymerization reactions can be broadly classified into two types: addition and condensation polymerizations.

1. **Addition or chain growth polymerization:** Such a process proceeds without elimination of any small molecule. The molecular mass of the polymer is a whole number multiple of the monomer. The reaction can be initiated by the application of heat, light, pressure, or a catalyst. For example,

$$n\text{CH}_2{=}\underset{\displaystyle \text{G}}{\underset{|}{\text{CH}}} \xrightarrow{\text{Polymerization}} \left[\text{CH}_2{-}\underset{\displaystyle \text{G}}{\underset{|}{\text{CH}}}\right]_n$$

2. **Condensation or step growth polymerization:** It proceeds by condensation of two different bi- or poly-functional monomers having functional groups with affinity for each other. The reaction always accompanies with the elimination of small molecules such as H_2O and HCl. For example,

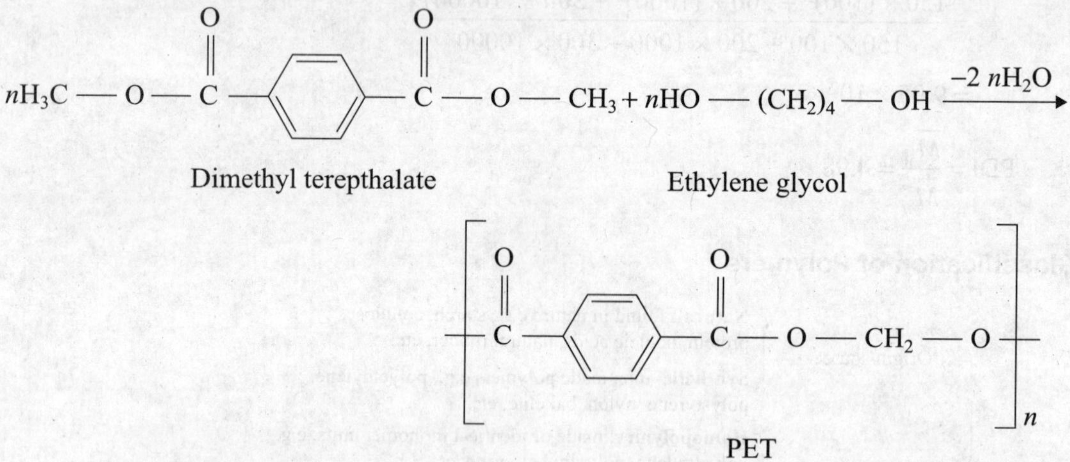

3. **Co-polymerization:** It involves the joint polymerization of two or more monomer species, e.g., styrene and butadiene polymerize together to form GR-S rubber.

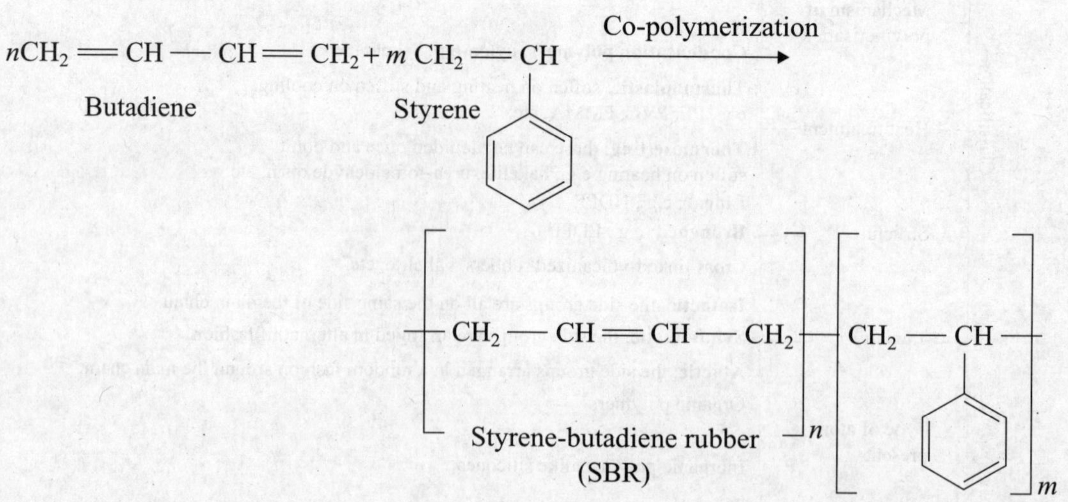

Mechanism of Addition Polymerization

Addition or chain growth polymerization takes place in compounds having multiple bonds such as vinyl monomers. The general mechanism can be represented as follows:

1. **Initiation:** In this step, the initiator interacts with a monomer molecule to form a chain initiating species.

   $M + In \longrightarrow M^*$

2. **Propagation:** It consists of a series of consecutive reactions to carry the chain growth process by the interaction of M^* with other monomer molecules as per the following equations:

$$\left\{\begin{array}{l} M^* + M \longrightarrow M_1^* \\ M_1^* + M \longrightarrow M_2^* \\ M_2^* + M \longrightarrow M_3^* \\ \cdot \\ \cdot \\ \cdot \\ \cdot \\ M_{n-1}^* + M \longrightarrow M_n^* \end{array}\right.$$

3. **Termination**: The chain growth finally terminates as per the following equation: $M_n^* \longrightarrow M_n$

Types of Addition Polymerization

Addition polymerization can be broadly divided into three types: free radical, ionic, and coordination polymerizations.

1. **Free-radical polymerization:** In this polymerization, monomer is transferred into radical by the action of light (photochemical initiation), heat (thermal initiation), or by adding chemicals, known as initiators (chemical initiation). Some common initiators are benzoyl peroxide and azobisisobutyronitrile (AIBN), which generate radicals as per the following equations:

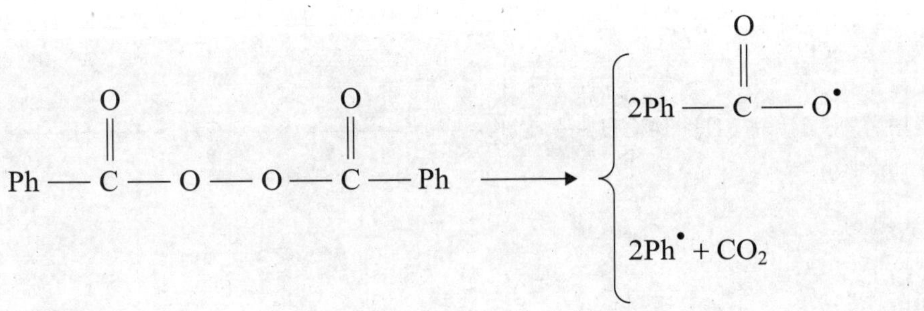

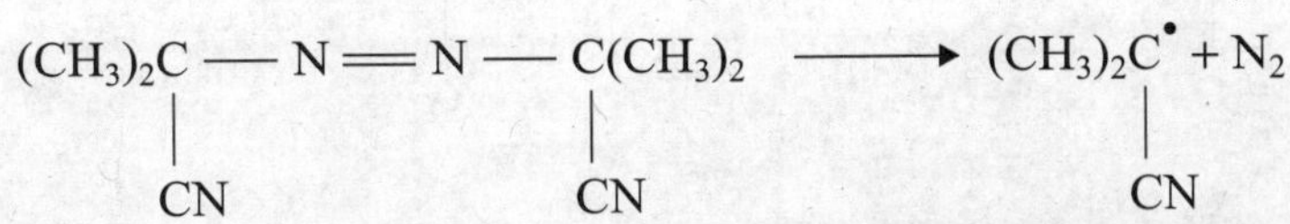

Let us discuss the mechanism by taking example of a vinyl polymer. Here "G" stands for substituted group which may be $-Cl$, $-CH_3$, $-CN$, $-Ph$, etc.

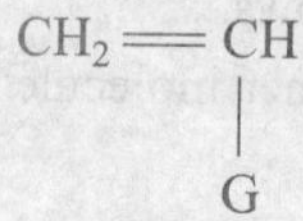

Initiation

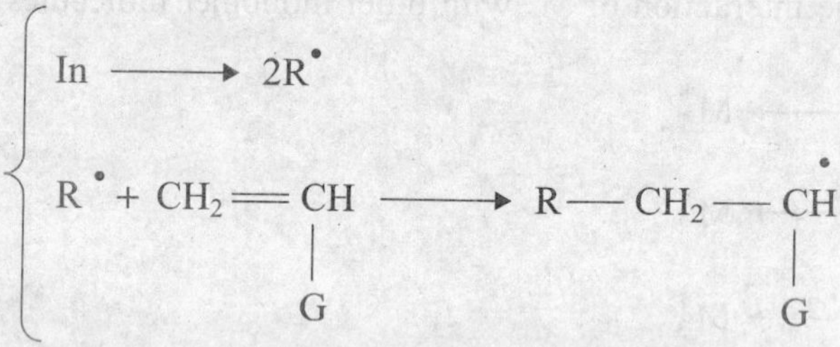

Propagation: The active radical so formed add to monomer molecules forming the macroradical. This step decides the rate of polymerization, the molecular weight of polymer, the structure of polymer, i.e., the degree of branching, and the mode of monomer addition. The important feature in mode of addition is that head-to-tail addition is both steric and resonance favored.

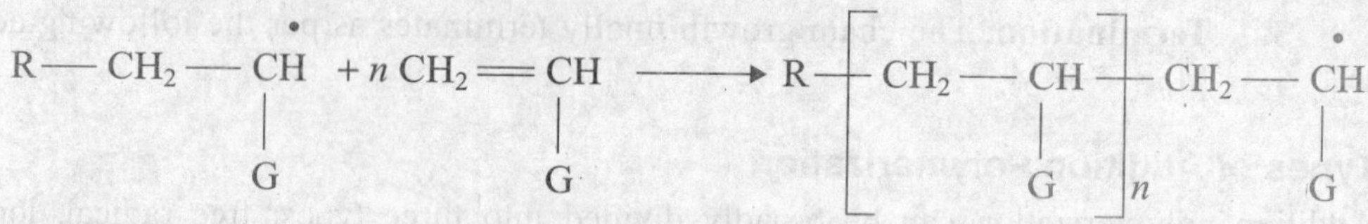

Termination: It happens by either combination of free radicals or by disproportionation. The latter one involves the transfer a hydrogen atom from one radical to another which results in the formation of two molecules, one saturated and one unsaturated. Termination can also be achieved by adding inhibitors such as hydroquinone and trinitrobenzene. Both these processes of coupling and disproportionation are shown here.

Coupling

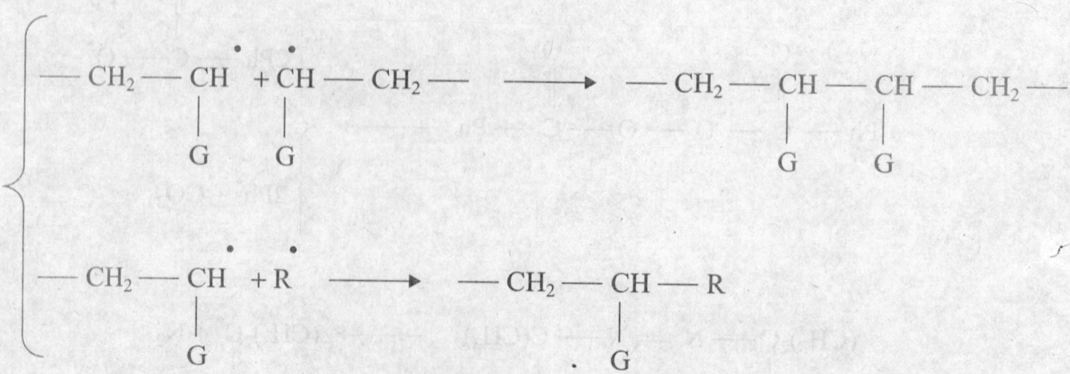

Disproportionation

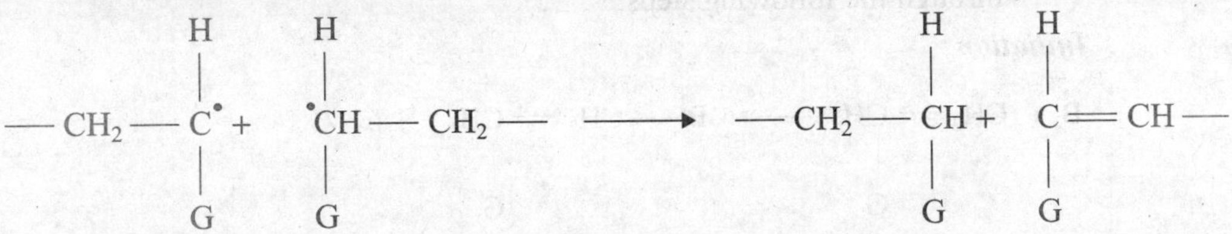

2. **Ionic polymerization:** This process depends on the formation and propagation of ionic species. It can be further discussed under cationic and anionic polymerization.

   (i) ***Cationic polymerization***: Monomers with electron-releasing substituents (such as –R, –OR, and –Ph) normally polymerize through cationic mechanism in the presence of Lewis acid catalysts such as $AlCl_3$, BF_3, and $SnCl_4$. The reaction proceeds through the following steps:

Initiation

$$FeCl_3 + H_2O \longrightarrow [FeCl_3.OH]^- + H^+$$

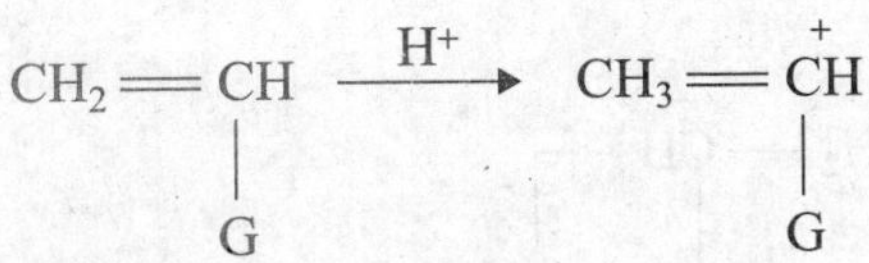

Propagation

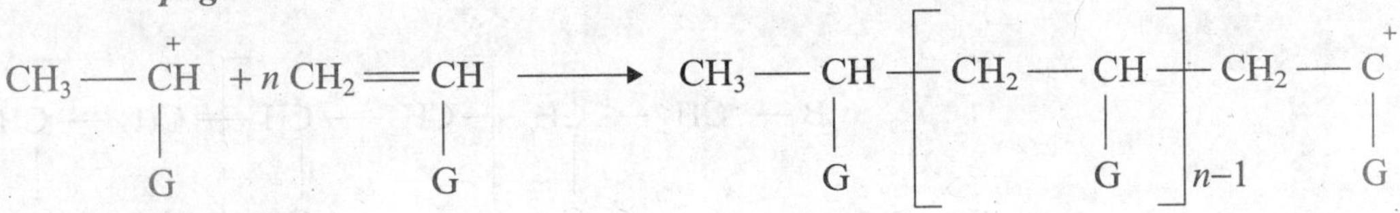

Termination

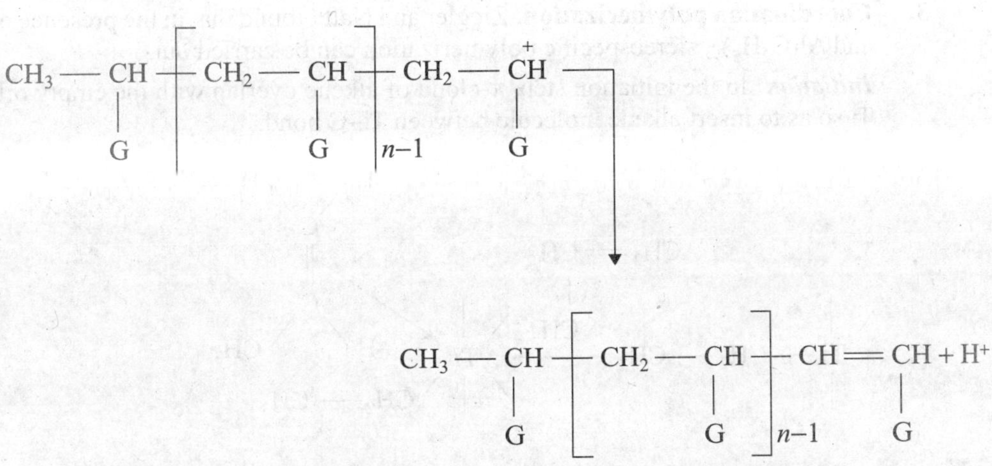

   (ii) ***Anionic polymerization***: Monomers with electron-withdrawing substituents (such as –CN, –COOR, and –Ph), normally polymerize through anionic mechanism in the presence of strong bases as catalysts such as sodium or potassium amide, alkali metal, and Grignard reagent. The reaction proceeds through the following steps:

Initiation

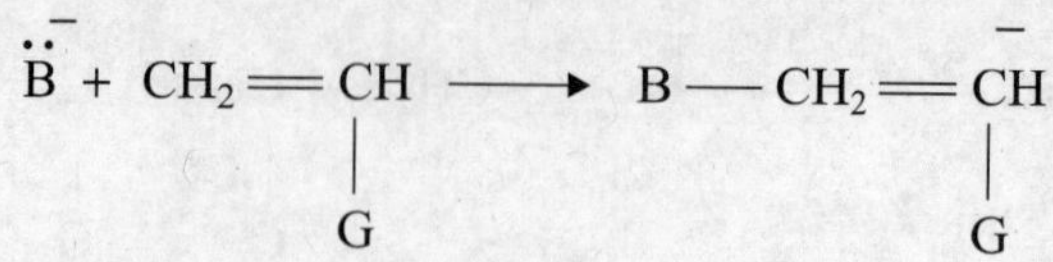

Propagation

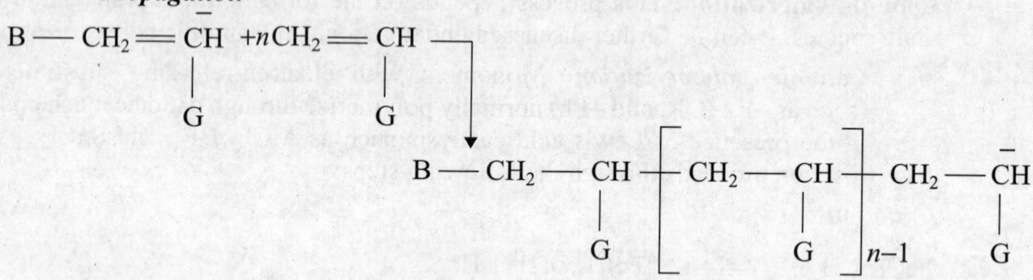

Termination

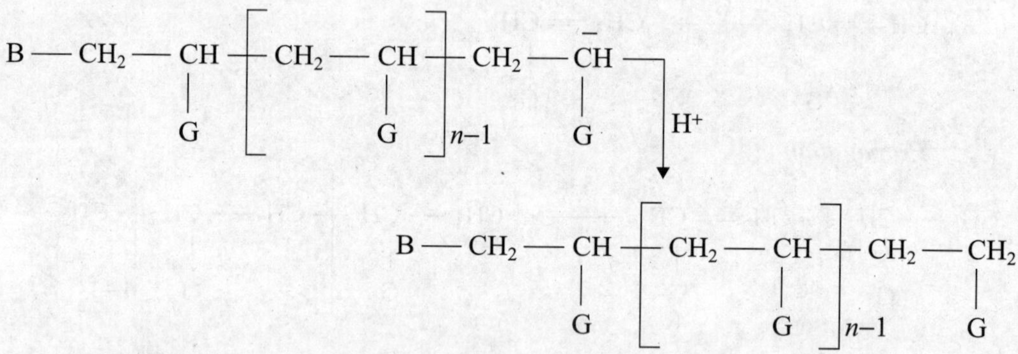

3. **Coordination polymerization:** Ziegler and Natta found that in the presence of $TiCl_3$ and $Al(C_2H_5)_3$, stereospecific polymerization can be carried out.

Initiation: In the initiation step, π-cloud of alkene overlap with the empty orbital of Ti so as to insert alkene molecule between Ti–C bond.

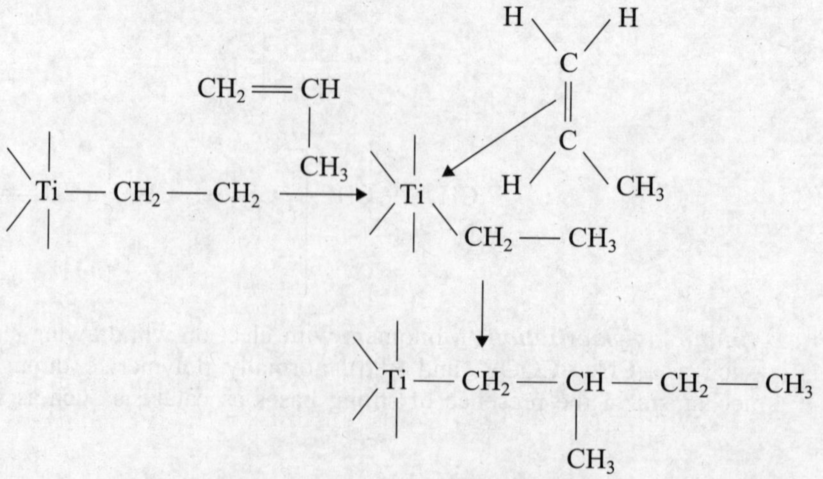

Propagation: Intermolecular rearrangement again generates a vacant site on Ti, each time facilitating the addition of one more molecule of alkene in a similar fashion.

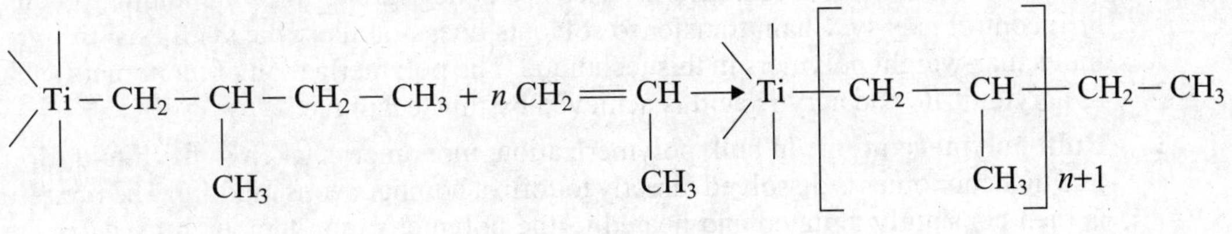

Termination: It is done by addition of molecules containing active hydrogen, such as HX.

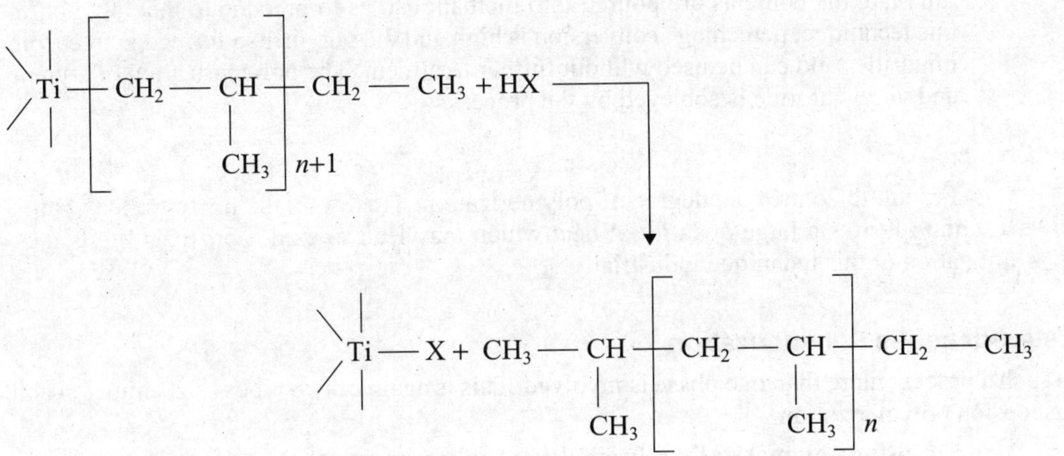

Polymerization Techniques

The main polymerization techniques are as follows:

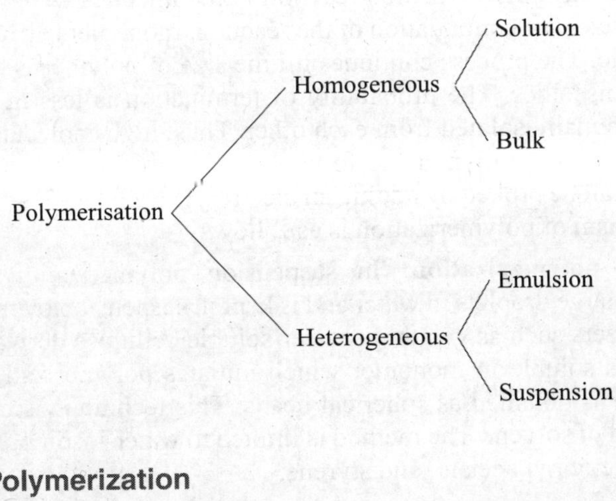

Homogeneous Polymerization

In this technique, polymerization takes place in one phase. This is possible either in solvent or in a reaction vessel containing only monomer, and hence the names are solution polymerization and bulk polymerization, respectively.

1. **Solution polymerization:** In this case, the monomer is allowed to dissolve in a suitable solvent followed by the addition of an initiator to initiate the polymerization

process. The mixture is kept at polymerization temperature with constant agitation. At the end of the reaction, the polymer is obtained as a precipitate which is filtered off, washed, and dried. Increase in viscosity is negligible, for which agitation and heat control is easy. Chain transfer to solvents does not allow the synthesis of high-molecular-weight polymers in this technique. The polymerization of monomers such as acrylonitrile and acrylic acid is achieved by this technique.

2. **Bulk polymerization:** In bulk polymerization, monomer is taken in the liquid form in which monomer is dissolved directly to form a homogeneous mixture. The mixture is then constantly agitated and heated to the polymerization temperature. After the starting of reaction, there is no need of heating since the reaction is exothermic and by controlling the conditions temperature can be maintained steadily. After a specific time lap, the contents are poured into methanol so as to precipitate the polymer. In this technique, percentage conversion is high and the polymer so formed is free from impurities and can be used without further treatment. The polymerization of styrene and vinyl chloride is achieved by the process.

Note:

It is difficult to control the degree of polymerization. Therefore, the uncontrolled chain reaction releases a huge quantity of heat which may lead to explosion. This limits the utilization of this technique industrially.

Heterogeneous Polymerization

In such a process more than one phase is involved. This is again of two types: viz. emulsion and suspension polymerization.

1. **Emulsion polymerization:** In emulsion polymerization, the monomer is dispersed in aqueous phase as fine droplets which is stabilized by adding surfactant or protective colloids. The surfactants lead to the formation of micelles when their concentration exceeds critical micelle concentration. Addition of water-soluble initiator at this stage initiates the polymerization reaction in the micelles which ultimately increase the micelle size. For continuation of the reaction, monomers diffuse from its droplets to the micelle. The process continues till the size of polymer is big enough to come out of the miscellies. The probability of termination is less in this process as the active sites remain isolated from each other. Thus, high-molecular-weight polymers can be formed. The polymers so formed can be used in the emulsion itself or the suspension can be broken by adding an electrolyte such as 3% solution of $Al_2(SO_4)_3$. The mechanism of polymerization is as follows:
2. **Suspension polymerization:** In suspension polymerization, the monomer is dispersed as large droplets in water and is kept in suspension by mechanical agitation using stabilizers such as gelatin or water-soluble cellulose derivatives. The initiator used remains soluble in monomer which initiates polymerization in each droplet. The polymer is obtained as spherical beads. This technique is cheap as it involves water instead of solvent. The method is limited to water-insoluble monomers such as vinyl chloride, vinyl acetate, and styrene.

Plastics

In general, usefulness of pure polymers is very limited as they cannot be processed into articles having required properties. Therefore, in practice, polymers blended with additives are used

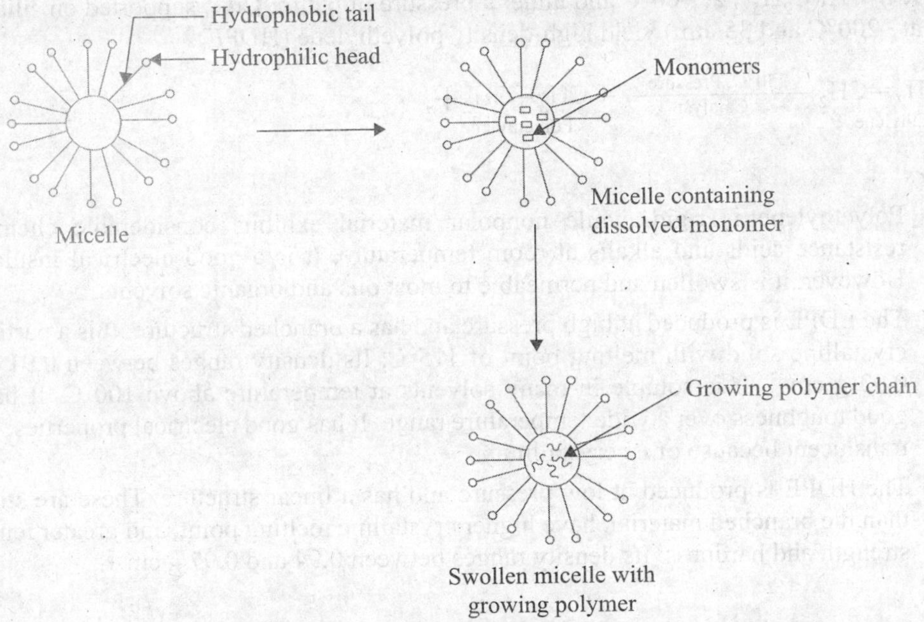

Fig. 18.5 Emulsion polymerization

which are referred to as plastics. In general, plastic may be defined as high-molecular-weight organic materials which can be molded into any desired form on application of heat and pressure in the presence of a catalyst. Broadly speaking plastics are classified into two types: thermoplastic and thermosetting. The basic difference among them is highlighted in the following table.

Thermoplastic	Thermosetting
1. Soften on heating and stiffen on cooling	1. Do not soften on heating
2. Can be remolded	2. Cannot be remolded
3. Can be obtained through addition/ condensation polymerization	3. Can be obtained through addition/ condensation polymerization
4. Linear or branched structure.	4. Three-dimensional cross-linked structure
5. Adjacent chains are held by weak molecular forces	5. Adjacent chains are held by strong covalent bonds
6. Tough	6. Brittle
7. Often soluble in suitable solvents	7. Insoluble in all solvents.
8. Examples: PE, PVC, PMMA, nylons, polyester, etc.	8. Example: Bakelite, urea–formaldehyde, resin, epoxy resin, etc.

Let us discuss some important thermoplastic and thermosetting polymers.

Polyethylene

It is prepared by addition polymerization of ethylene at high pressure (~1500 atm) and ~250°C in the presence of traces of oxygen which is a radical initiator. It is to be noted that free radical initiators yield low-density polyethylene (LDPE) while ionic catalysts (Zeiglar–Natta catalyst, that is, $TiCl_4 + Al(C_2H_5)_3$ at ~60°C and under a pressure of 6 atm; CrO_3 supported on silica or alumina at ~200°C and 35 atm) yield high-density polyethylene (HDPE).

$$\underset{\text{Ethylene}}{n\mathrm{CH_2{=}CH_2}} \xrightarrow[\text{Catalyst}]{250^\circ\text{C, Pressure}} \underset{\text{Polyethylene}}{\mathrm{+CH_2{-}CH_2+}_n}$$

Properties

1. Polyethylene is rigid, while nonpolar material exhibits considerable chemical resistance acids and alkalis at room temperature. It is a good electrical insulator. However, it is swollen and permeable to most oils and organic solvents.
2. The LDPE is produced at high pressure and has a branched structure. It is a partially crystalline solid with melting point of 115°C. Its density ranges between 0.91 and 0.93 g cm^{-3}. It is soluble in many solvents at temperature above 100°C. It has a good toughness over a wide temperature range. It has good electrical properties. It is translucent because of its crystallinity.
3. The HDPE is produced at low pressure and has a linear structure. These are stiffer than the branched material, have higher crystalline melting point, and greater tensile strength and hardness. Its density ranges between 0.94 and 0.97 g cm^{-3}.

Uses

1. LDPE is extensively used in electrical insulation industry.
2. It is used for making films and sheets.
3. It is used as packaging material because of its transparency, high tear strength and good chemical and moisture resistance properties.
4. It is used as storing bottles and containers for the kitchen and laboratory. It is used for making household utensils and toys.
5. The LDPE is used for blow moulding, injection molding; manufacture of film, sheet, and wire, and cable insulation; extrusion coating and pipe.

A comparative account of both LDPE and HDPE are shown as follows:

LDPE	HDPE
1. Molecular weight ranges from 5000 to 40000.	1. Molecular weight ranges from 15000 to 2×10^5.
2. The density is low	2. The density of HDPE is high
3. Softening temperature is 115°C	3. Softening temperature is 135°C
4. Tough and flexible	4. Stiff and hard
5. Refractive index of LDPE is 1.51.	5. Refractive index of HDPE is 1.54.
6. The tensile strength is low	6. The tensile strength is high.
7. The elongation of LDPE is 90–800%.	7. The elongation of HDPE is 50–1000 %.
8. Branched	8. Linear

Polystyrene

Polystyrene can be prepared by polymerization of styrene in the presence of benzoyl peroxide as catalyst. The process involved is free radical addition polymerization.

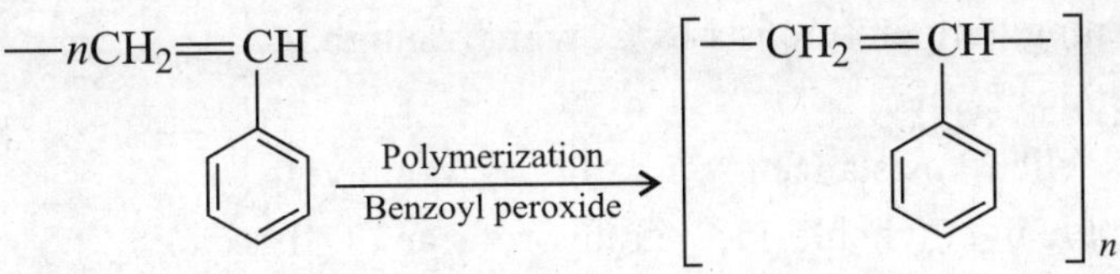

Properties

1. Commercially available polystyrene is mostly of the atactic variety. Due to the presence of bulky phenyl groups, packing of chains is not effective. Therefore, it is amorphous in nature and very light with a low specific gravity of ~1.05 g cm^{-3}.
2. It is transparent with a high refractive index of 1.59.
3. Polystyrene is chemically inert, that is, acids, alkalis, oxidizing, or reducing agents have little effect on it.
4. Due to chain stiffening effect of benzene ring, it is hard but brittle.
5. Being nonpolar amorphous polymer, its softening temperature is low and remains in the range 90–100°C. At about 100°C, it forms water-soluble emulsions.
6. It is excellent moisture resistant due to its nonpolar nature.

Uses

1. Polystyrene is very widely used in the manufacture of articles such as molded containers, lids, jars, bottles, radio and television cabinets, toys, foamed plastics, battery cases, indoor lighting panels, and many other household items.
2. Copolymers of styrene with acrylonitrile, vinyl carbazole, or diphenyl acrylamide are a few important ones. Introduction of the comonomer enhances the heat and impact resistance of the polymer without sacrificing the useful properties of the styrene homopolymer. For example, styrene–acrylonitrile (SAN) copolymer is a transparent plastic with a very good impact strength and is used for molding crockery items and machine components. Acrylonitrile–butadiene–styrene (ABS) terpolymer is another commercially important plastic which possesses good strength and toughness. It is most suitable for injection-molded articles of household items and packing containers.

Polyvinyl Chloride (PVC)

Polyvinyl chloride can be prepared by heating a water emulsion of vinyl chloride in the presence of benzoyl peroxide or hydrogen peroxide as catalyst under pressure.

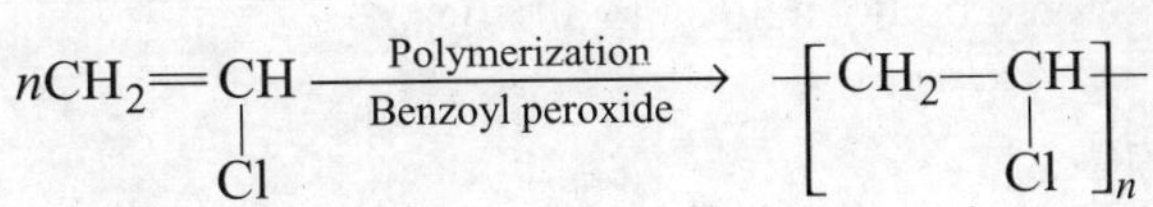

Properties

1. It is a colorless, odorless, noninflammable polymer with specific gravity of ~1.33 g cm^{-3}.
2. The presence of chlorine atoms at the alternate carbons creates polarity and hence the interchain attraction. The result being there is an increase in hardness and stiffness as compared to polyethylene. However, it remains brittle.

3. Its softening temperature is 148°C, which is high.
4. It is chemically inert.
5. It has excellent resistance toward oil and weathering.
6. It is soluble in ethyl chloride, tetrahydrofuran (THF), etc.

Uses

1. It is used in acid recovery plants and for handling hydrocarbons.
2. It is used for making tank-lining, safety helmets, refrigerator components, tyres, bottles for consumable liquids such as edible oil, vinegar, fruit juice, etc.
3. It has potential use in making water carrying pipes, pipes for drainage, as a wood substitute in making frames for doors and windows.
4. Plasticized PVC, which can be prepared by adding plasticizers such as dibutyl phthalate, dioctyl phthalate, etc. to rigid PVC, is a very good insulator for current and has completely replaced rubber insulation of wires. It is also used for making leathers which are used in bathroom curtains, handbags, car upholstery, rain wears, shoes, etc. These leathers are more abrasion resistance, flex resistance, washable, and in addition have low cost as compared to natural leather.

Polymethyl Methacrylate (PMMA)

PMMA can be prepared by polymerization of methyl acrylate in the presence of acetyl peroxide or hydrogen peroxide as catalyst. It is also known as *plexiglass* or Lucite.

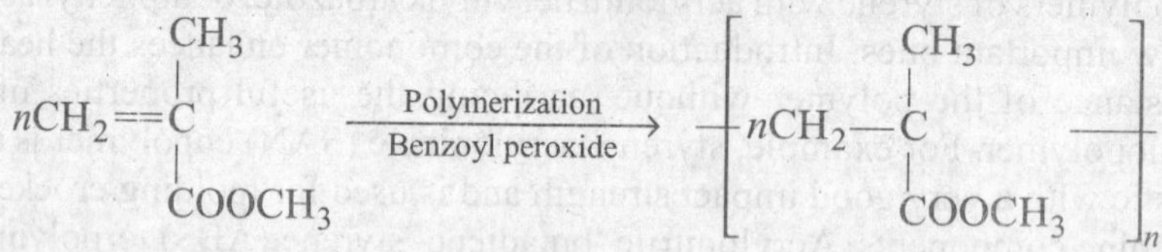

Properties

1. It is an amorphous, colorless, transparent thermoplastic with high optical transparency.
2. The bulky groups restrict chain flexibility for which it is hard and has a remarkable high T_g above 65°C.
3. It has high softening point in the range 130–140°C. This is due to the inter-molecular dipole–dipole forces.
4. It is easily affected by hot acids and alkalies.

Uses

For making lenses, artificial eyes, automotive appliances, optical fibres, aircraft light fixtures, emulsions, paints, adhesives, etc. Optical clarity is the main feature of this plastic. In many applications, it is an excellent substitute for glass, it has poor scratch resistance.

Polyacrylonitrile (PAN)

Polyacrylonitrile (PAN) is a synthetic, semicrystalline polymer prepared by free radical polymerization of acrylonitrile in the presence of peroxide initiator. The trade name is *Orlon*.

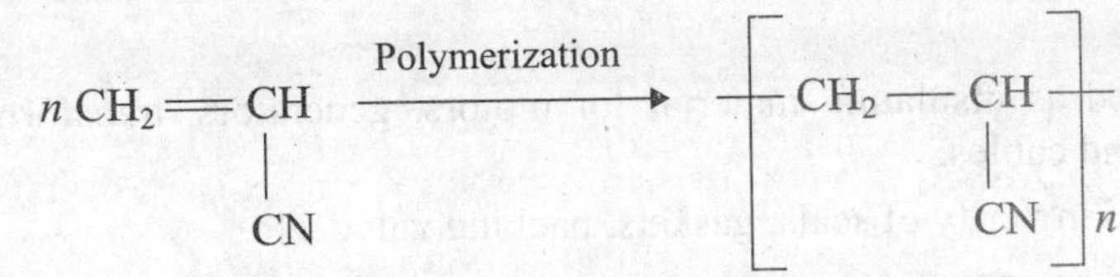

Properties

1. Although it is thermoplastic, it does not melt under normal conditions. It melts above 300°C.
2. PAN has low density, thermal stability, high strength, and modulus of elasticity. These unique properties have made PAN an essential polymer in high tech.
3. Depending on the application, a small amount (1–10%) of other vinyl co-monomers can be used along with acrylonitrile.
4. The orlon fibers are more resistant to the attack of acids and gases as compared to nylon fibers.

Uses

1. It is a versatile polymer used to produce variety of products such as ultrafiltration membranes, hollow fibers for reverse osmosis, fibers for textiles, etc.
2. PAN fibers are the chemical precursor of high-quality carbon fibers.
3. It is a repeat unit in several important copolymers such as styrene acrylonitrile (SAN) and acrylonitrile butadiene styrene (ABS) plastic.
4. It is used for making warm clothes, carpets, blankets, etc.

Polytetrafluoroethylene (Teflon)

Teflon is obtained by radical polymerization of tetrafluoroethylene in the presence of benzoyl peroxide as catalyst.

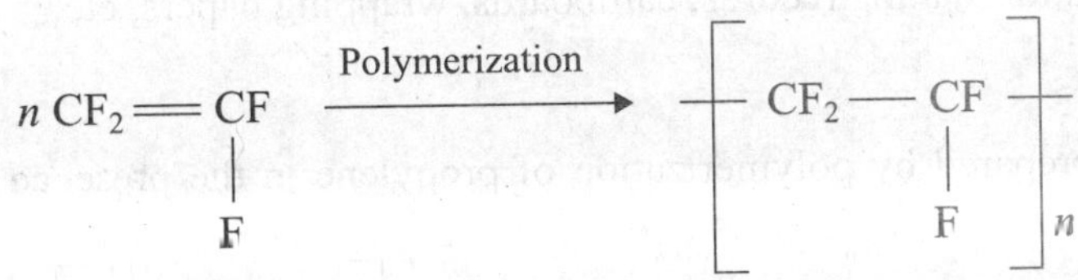

Properties

1. Due to the presence of highly electronegative fluorine atoms, there exist very strong attractive forces between different chains. These strong attractive forces are responsible for extreme strength, toughness, high softening temperature (327°C), and high density (2.3 g/cm^3).
2. It has excellent chemical resistance except toward alkali and hot fluorine.
3. It has very low coefficient of friction.
4. It exhibits exceptionally high electrical insulation properties.
5. It can be easily machined, punched, and drilled.

Uses

1. It is used as insulating material for motors, generators, transformers, capacitors, wires, and cables.
2. It is used in verity of seals, gaskets, packing valve, etc.
3. It is used as non-stick coating of frying pans, as it is not wetted by oil and water.
4. It is used in non-lubricating bearings.

Polyvinyl acetate (PVA)

Polyvinyl acetate (PVA) is prepared by emulsion polymerization of vinyl acetate in the presence of benzoyl peroxide as catalyst.

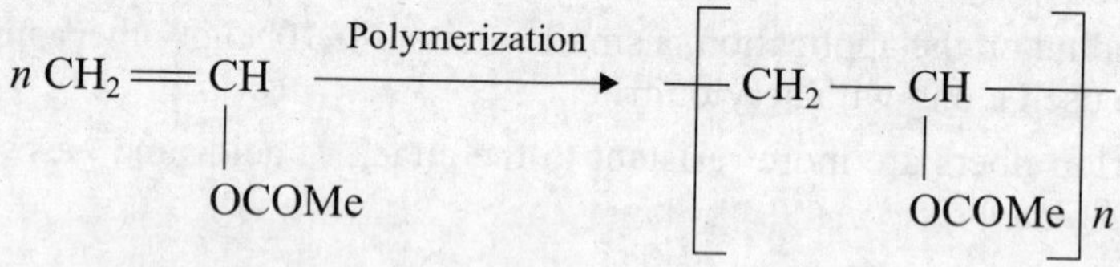

Properties

1. It is a colorless and transparent material.
2. It is an amorphous polymer with low T_g, i.e., 28°C. Thus, the materials made of PVA can be easily distorted even at room temperature.
3. It is fairly soluble in organic solvents.
4. It is harmless when taken orally.

Uses

1. It is used for preparation of water-based emulsion paints.
2. It is used in finishing textiles and other fabrics.
3. It is used for making chewing gums.
4. It is used for making records, cardboards, wrapping papers, etc.

Polypropylene

Polypropylene is prepared by polymerization of propylene in the presence of Ziegler–Natta catalyst.

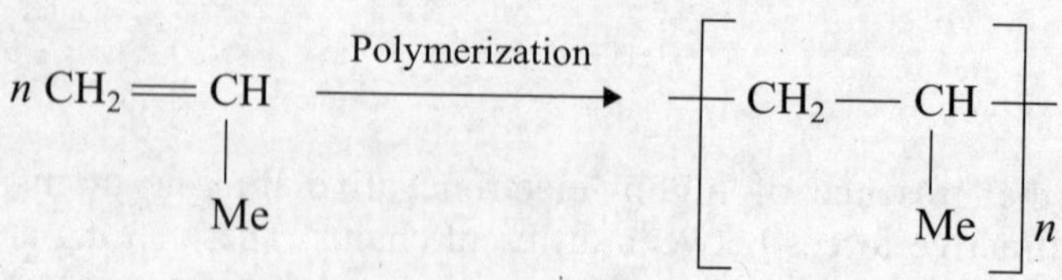

Properties

1. It is stereo-regular, isotatic, and highly crystalline polymer.
2. The presence of methyl group attached to alternate carbon on the parent chain interferes with molecular symmetry, which lowers the density (0.9 g/cm^3).
3. It is prone toward oxidation due to the presence of tertiary carbon.
4. It has good impact strength.

Uses

1. Thin sections have excellent resistant to flexing for which it is used for making boxes, cases, automobile accelerator paddles, etc.
2. Used for wrapping food materials such as biscuits and potato chips.
3. PP elastomers blend is used for making car bumpers, protective strips, radiator grill, etc.

Polycarbonates

Polycarbonates (PC), known by the trademarked names Laxen, Makrolon, Makroclear and others, are a particular group of thermoplastic polymers. These are prepared by copolymerization of diphenyl carbonate and bisphenol-A [2,2-bis(4-hydroxyphenyl)propane] as follows:

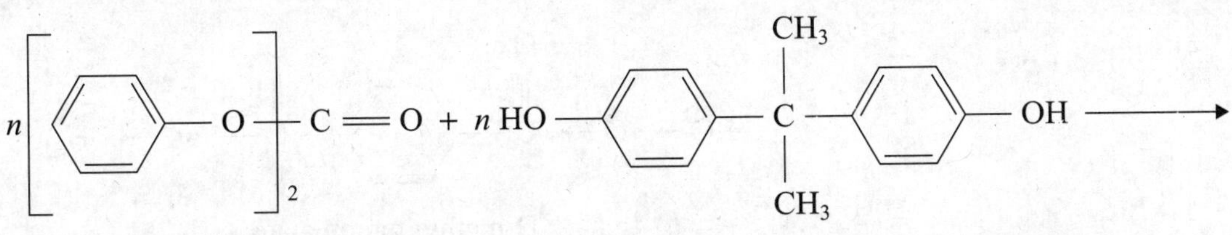

Diphenyl carbonate Bisphenol-A

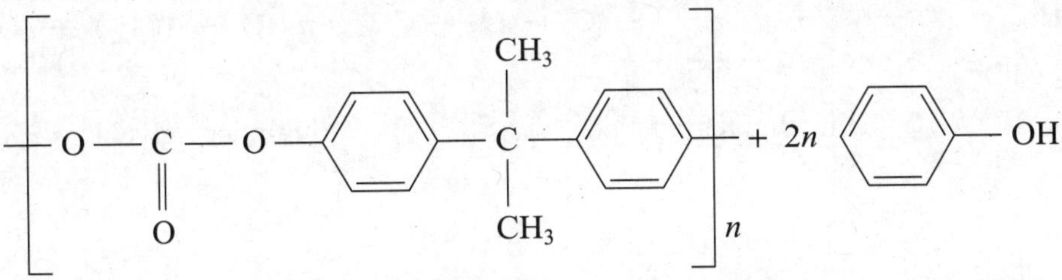

Polycarbonate

Properties

1. They have high impact and tensile strength over a wide range of temperature.
2. They are soluble in organic solvents and alkalis.
3. They are easily worked, molded, and thermoformed.
4. Polycarbonates are strong, lightweight, and heat-resistant.

Uses

1. These are used for preparing molded domestic ware.
2. These are used for insulation in electrical and electronics industries.
3. These are used to make lightweight alternatives to glass such as bicycle helmets, microwave cookware, and bulletproof windows.

Polyesters

Polyethylene Terephthalate (PET)

Polyethylene terephthalate (PET) is the most important polyester. It can be manufactured by condensing dimethyl terephthalate with ethylene glycol. It is also commercially known as terylene or decron. In the first step of its preparation, terephthalic acid is converted into its dimethyl ester by treatment with ethyl alcohol. In the subsequent step, dimethyl terephthalate is allowed to react with ethylene glycol in basic medium to yield PET.

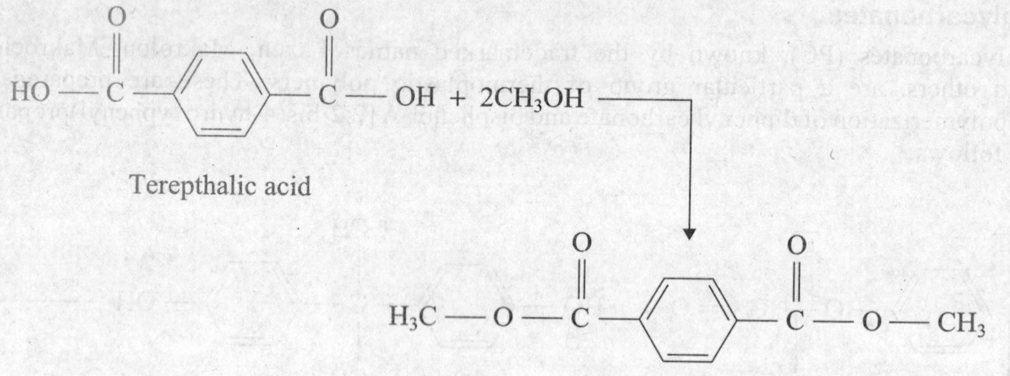

Terepthalic acid

Dimethyl terepthalate

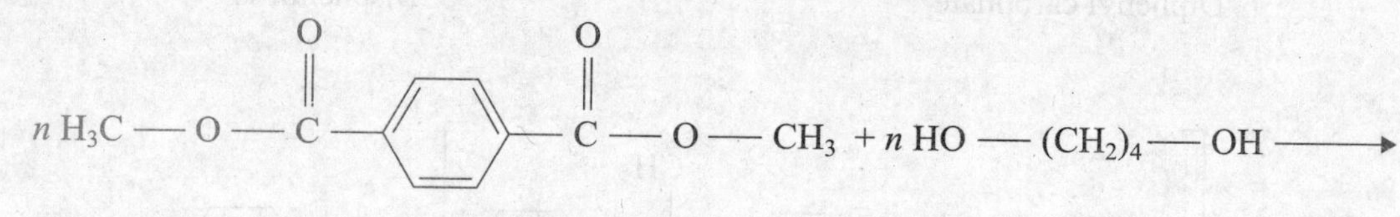

Dimethyl terepthalate

Ethylene glycol

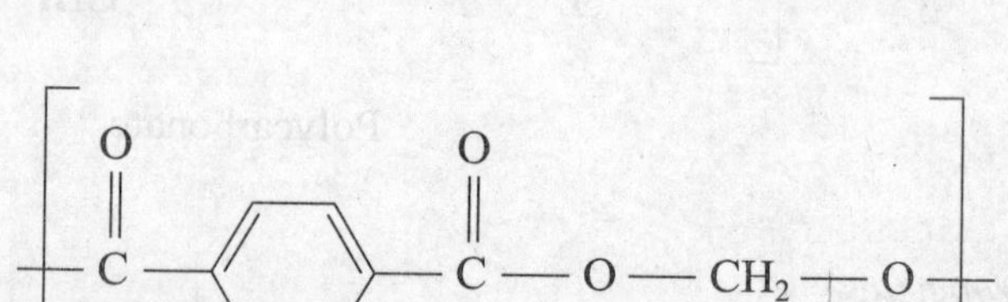

PET

Properties

1. PET readily crystallizes because of the symmetrical structure and numerous polar groups.
2. Its T_g and melting point are 80°C and 245°C, respectively.
3. It is effectively resistant to moisture, dilute mineral acids, and hydrocarbon solvents. However, it is readily affected by conc. HNO_3 and H_2SO_4. The polymer is also degraded by NaOH.
4. Due to stiffness in the polymer chain and strong dipole–dipole forces, it has high tensile strength and high impact strength which are also retained up to a temperature of 175°C.

5. It is a good durable fiber-forming materials which are proved to be outstanding crease resistance.
6. It is soluble in chloro- and fluoroacetic acids, phenols, and anhydrous hydrofluoric acid.
7. Glass-filled PET moldings have superior mechanical properties and high temperature resistance.

Uses

1. PET films are used as transparency in overhead projectors, containers for juice concentrates, cola drinks, beers, spirits, etc.
2. It is used in preparation of magnetic recording tapes.
3. Fiber applications are wearing apparel, curtain, thread, tyre cord, etc.
4. Another application of polyethylene terephthalate film is for manufacturing electrical insulation materials.

Alkyd Resin (Glyptal Resin)

Alkyd resin can be prepared by condensing polybasic acids or anhydrides with polyhydric alcohol such as glycerol in the presence of heat and catalyst. To be specific, the resin obtained from phthalic anhydride and glycerol is also known as glyptal resin.

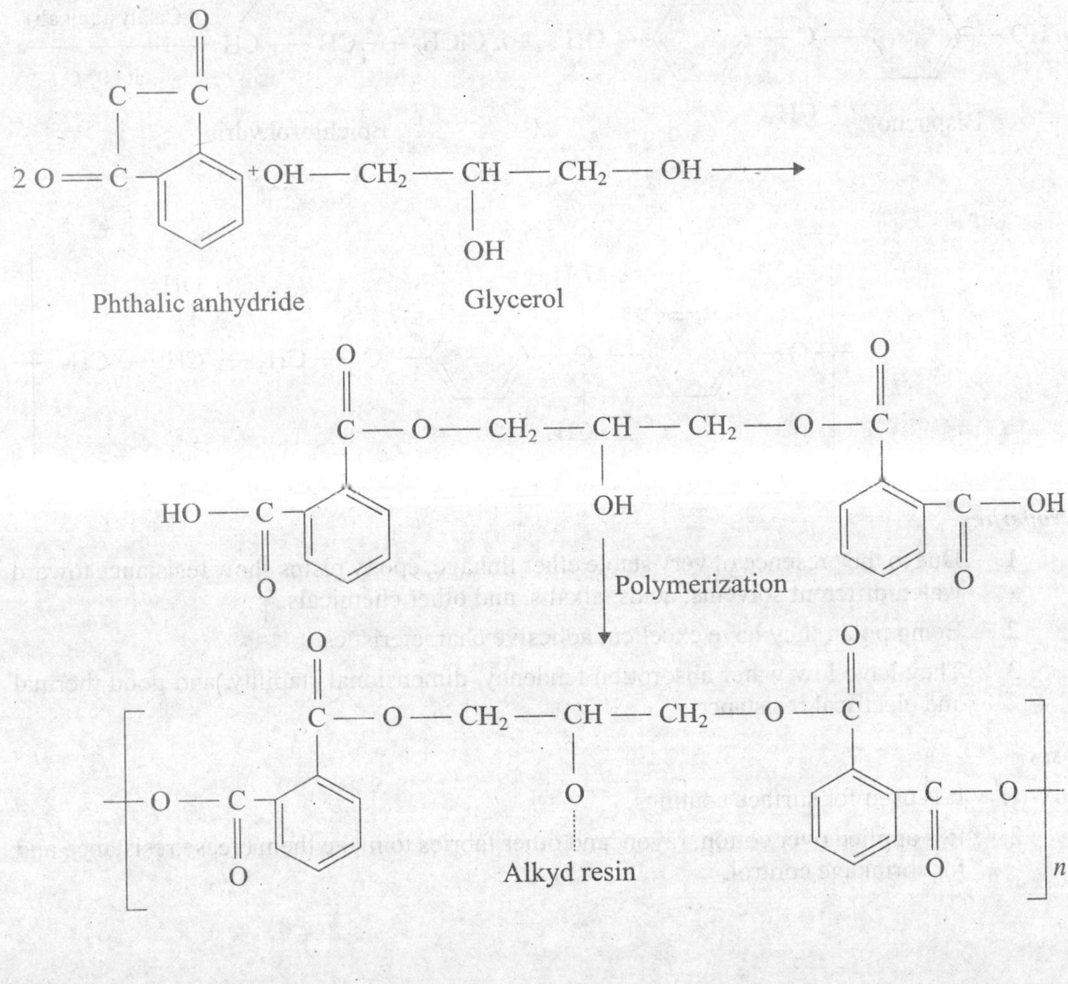

Properties

1. It is very hard.
2. It is infusible and insoluble.
3. It is resistant to chemicals and corrosion.
4. It is dimensionally stable.

Uses

1. It is used for making paints, enamels, and varnishes.
2. It is used as a binder in cement, asbestos, etc.
3. It is used for making switches, circuit breaker insulation, etc.

Epoxy Resins (Araldite)

Epoxy resins are prepared by the combination of bisphenol and epichlorohydrin in the presence of an alkali as catalyst at ~60°C. The active hydroxyl groups results in a 3-D cross-linked structure. The molecular weight varies from 350 which is for a flowing liquid to 8000 for a solid.

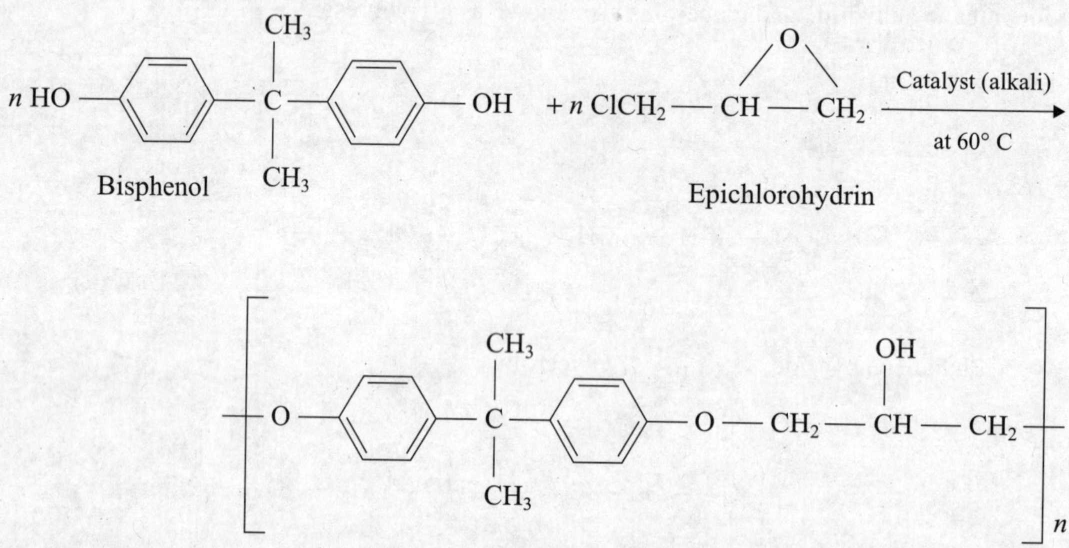

Properties

1. Due to the presence of very stable ether linkage, epoxy resins show resistance toward water, different solvents, acids, alkalis, and other chemicals.
2. Being polar, they have excellent adhesive characteristics.
3. They have low water absorption tendency, dimensional stability, and good thermal and electrical resistance.

Uses

1. It is used for surface coatings.
2. It is applied over cotton, rayon, and other fabrics to make them crease resistance and for shrinkage control.

3. Alkyds are used in paints and in molds for casting.
4. It is used as adhesives for glass, metals, etc., under the name araldite.

Phenolic Resin

Phenolic resins or phenoplasts are condensation polymers of phenolic derivatives such as phenol, resorcinol, etc., with aldehydes such as formaldehyde, furfural, etc. Most important member of this class is Bakelite or phenol–formaldehyde resin. It is prepared by the condensation of a phenol or a mixture of phenol with formaldehyde. The reaction between phenol and formaldehyde is catalyzed by acids or alkalies. The nature of the product depends on the type of catalyst and the molar ratio of the reactants. The reaction between phenol and formaldehyde in the acidic condition is given below.

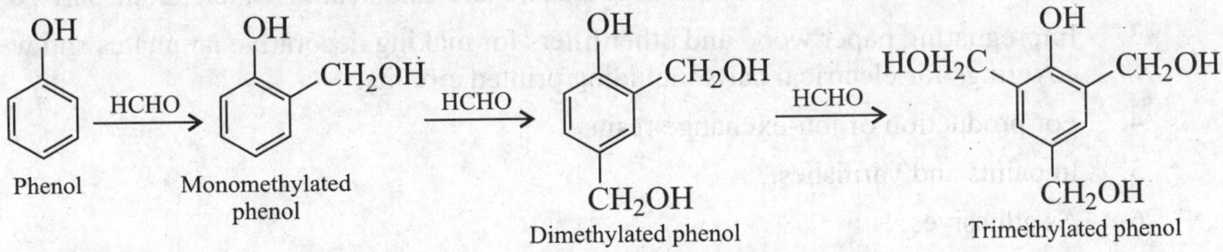

The monomethylated phenols condense with phenols to form low-molecular-weight linear polymers known as *novolacs*. These are fusible and soluble. Further heating of novolacs in the presence of curing agents such as hexamethylene tetramine (produces formaldehyde) yields three-dimensional cross-linked polymers known as *Bakelites*. These are hard, rigid, and infusible solid.

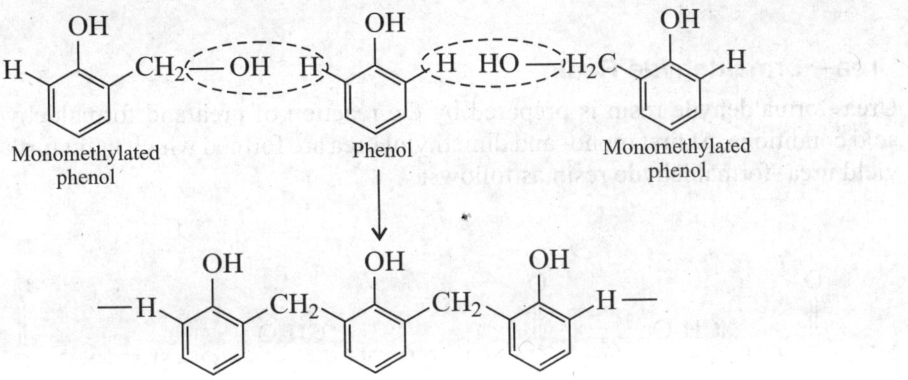

Novolac

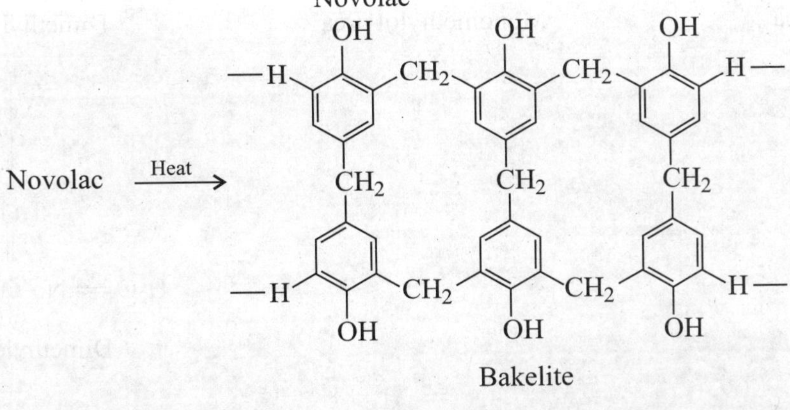

Bakelite

Properties

1. Bakelites are very hard and rigid materials.
2. These are scratch and water resistant infusible and insoluble solids.
3. These are resistant to nonoxidizing acids, salts, and many organic solvents but are easily attacked by alkalies due to the presence of free hydroxyl groups.
4. These are good electrical insulators.

Uses

1. For making electrical insulator parts such as switches, plugs, heater handles, etc.
2. In making molded articles such as radio and television cabinets, telephone parts, etc.
3. Impregnating paper wood and other fillers for making decorative laminates and wall coverings for electrical parts including printed circuits.
4. For production of ion-exchange resins.
5. In paints and varnishes.
6. As adhesives.

Amino Resins

These are prepared by the reaction of formaldehyde with urea or melamine to form urea–formaldehyde and melamine–formaldehyde resins, respectively.

Urea–Formaldehyde Resin

Urea–formaldehyde resin is prepared by the reaction of urea and formaldehyde in neutral or acid conditions. At first mono- and dimethylol urea are formed which upon further condensation yield urea–formaldehyde resin as follows:

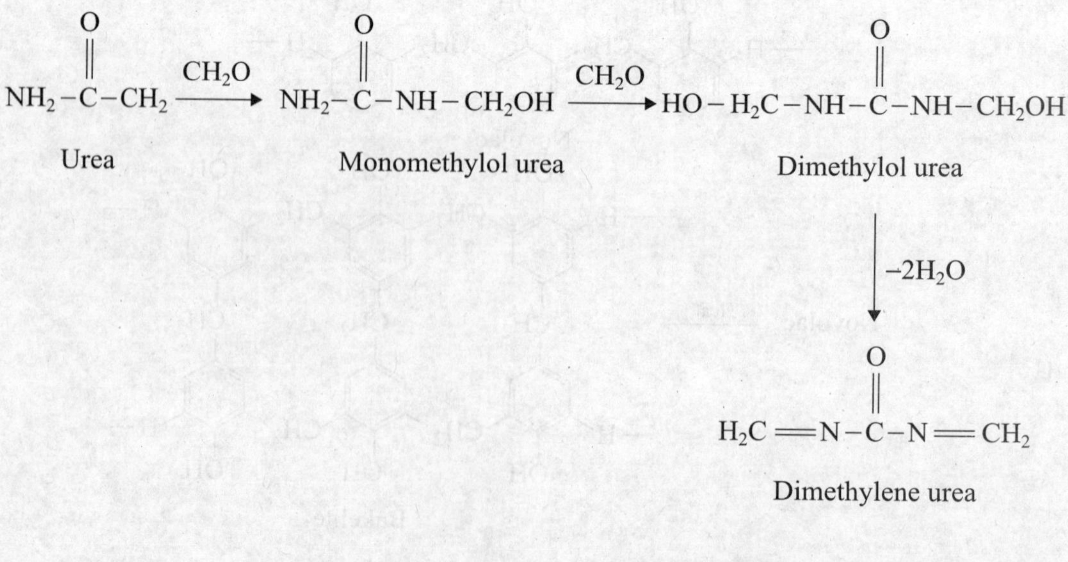

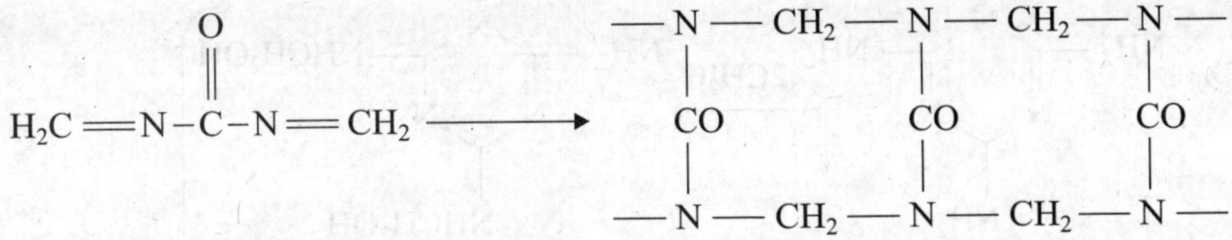

Urea–formaldehyde resin
(A cross linked polymer)

Properties

1. These are clear and colorless.
2. These are resistant toward solvents, chemicals, grease, and moisture.
3. These exhibit excellent abrasion resistance.
4. These are good electrical insulators.
5. These exhibits good tensile strength.

Uses

1. These are used as adhesive for plywood.
2. These are used for finishing cotton textiles. They impart crease resistance and also helpful for shrinkage control.
3. These are used for bonding grinding wheels.
4. These are used in utensils such as plates and glasses.

Melamine–Formaldehyde Resin

Melamine–formaldehyde resins are prepared by the reaction of melamine with formaldehyde under neutral or alkaline conditions. The reaction yields di- and tri-methylol melamine in the beginning. Subsequently with excess of formaldehyde, a cross-linked melamine–formaldehyde resin is formed.

Properties

1. MF resins have better hardness and tensile strength than PF resins.
2. These resins have better heat and moisture resistance than UF resins.
3. These have good adhesive characteristics.

Uses

1. These are used in plywood as boil-resistant adhesive.
2. These are used as textile finishing agent.
3. These are used for production of high-quality dinner wares.
4. These are used for preparation of decorative laminates.

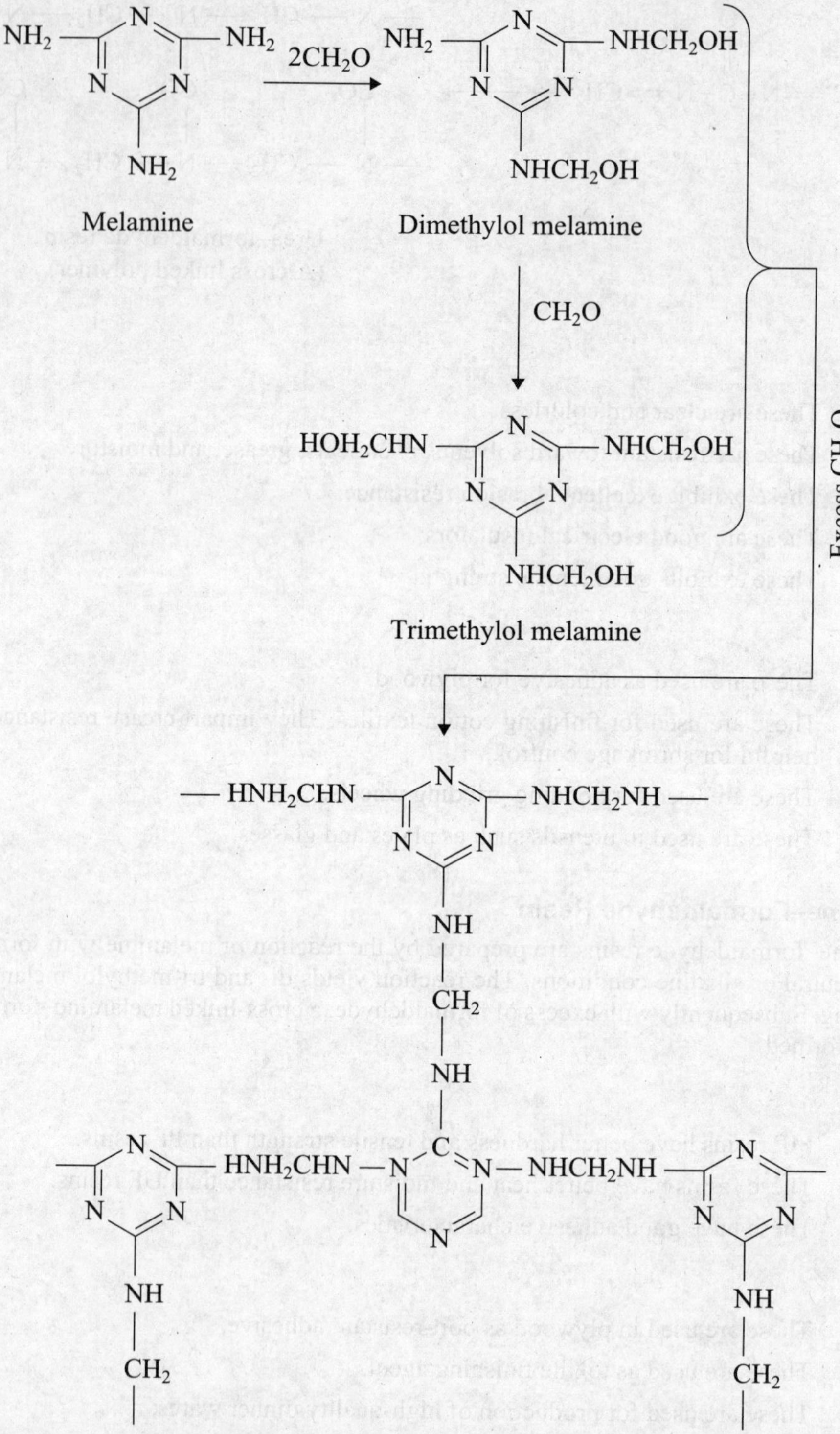

Cross–linked melamine–formaldehyde resin

Molding of Plastics

For fabrication of plastics into desired shapes, different techniques are employed, viz., compression molding, injection molding, and extrusion molding.

Compression Molding

It is the oldest mass production process for polymer products and is mostly used for shaping thermosets. In the process, the mold is held between the heated platens of a hydraulic press. Now, a required quantity of plastic ingredients in proper proportion is filled between the two half pieces of the mold. The two halves are then closed slowly so that the material flows to shape. Finally, curing is done by heating for thermosets. After curing, the molded article is taken out. The steps involved in the complete process are shown in Fig. 18.6.

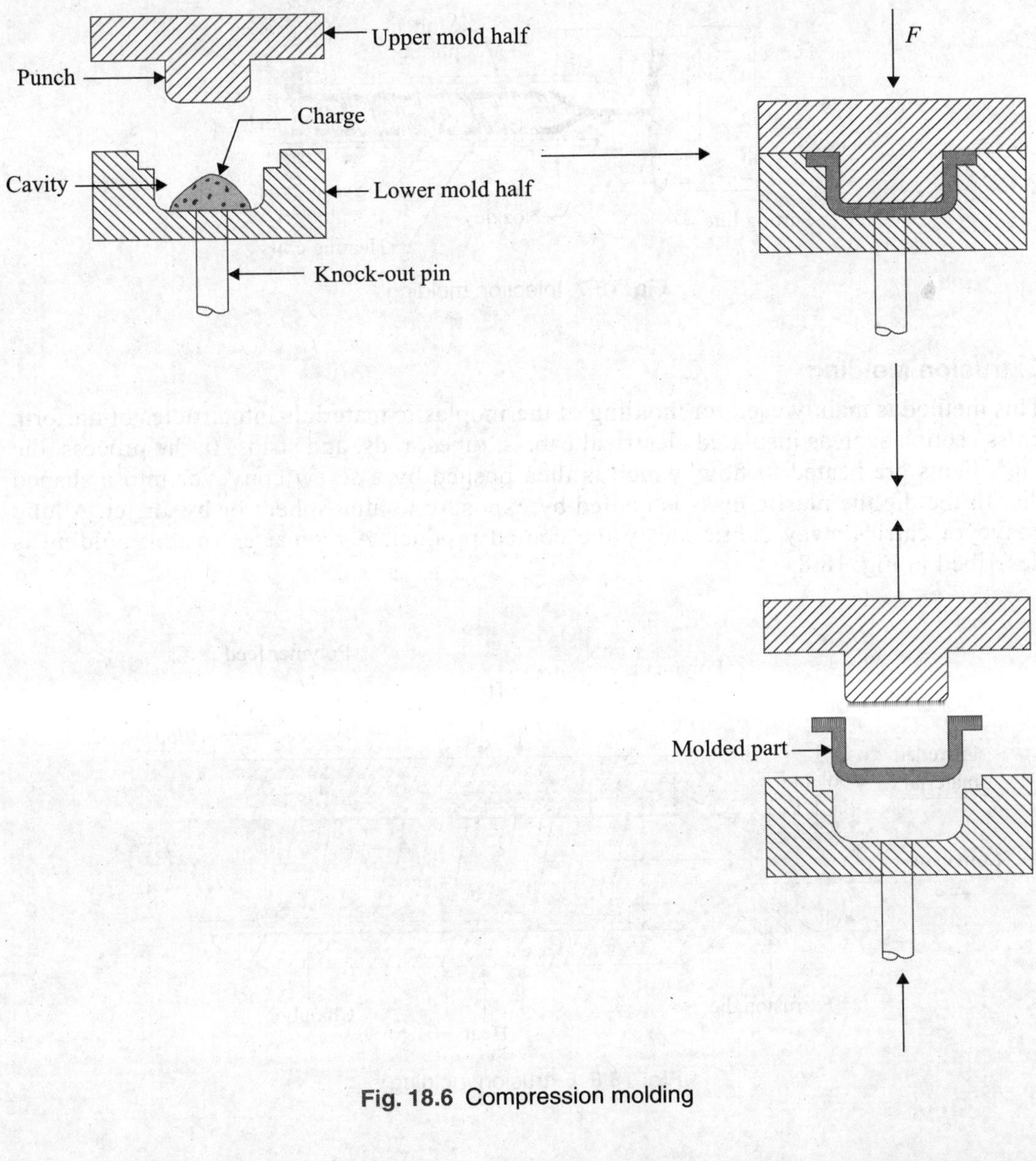

Fig. 18.6 Compression molding

Injection Molding

It is mostly used for shaping thermoplastics. The plastic ingredient is fed into a heated cylinder, which is injected at a controlled rate into the tightly locked cold mold by using a screw arrangement or by using piston plunger as shown in Fig. 18.7. As the plastic enters into the mold, it is cured and become rigid. After curing the article is removed from the mold. The major advantages of injection molding are its ability to make complex shapes in a single operation, its ability to make articles repeatedly with consistent reproducibility, and low loss of material, in addition to low finishing cost.

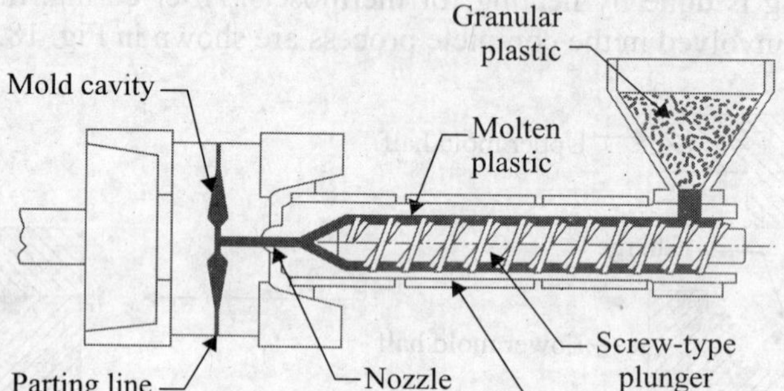

Fig. 18.7 Injection molding

Extrusion Molding

This method is mainly used for molding of thermoplastic materials into articles of uniform cross section such as insulated electrical cables, tubes, rods, and strips. In the process, the ingredients are heated to flow, which is then pushed by a screw conveyor into a shaped die. In the die the plastic mass is cooled by exposure to atmosphere or by air jet. A long conveyor carries away continuously the cooled product. A typical extrusion molding is described in Fig. 18.8.

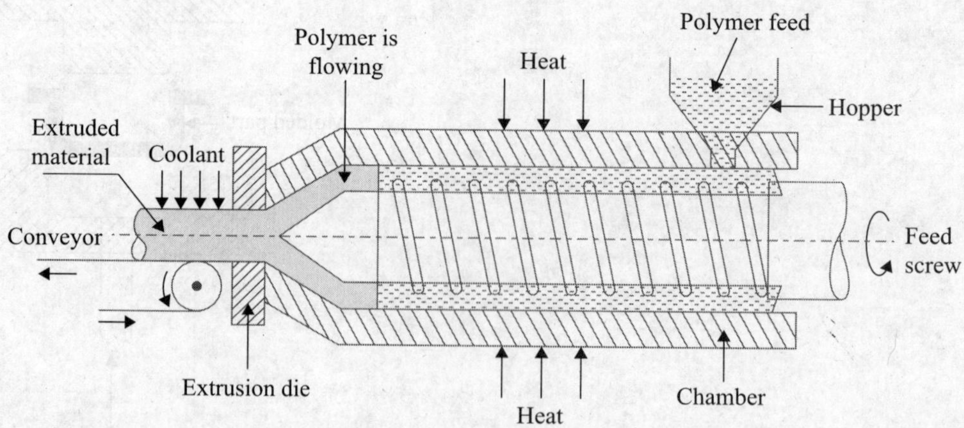

Fig. 18.8 Extrusion molding

Elastomers

Synthetic Rubber

Polyurethanes

These are prepared by rearrangement polymerization of di-/poly-isocynates with di-/poly-hydric alcohol. All these polymers carry characteristic urethane linkage. For example, the reaction of butane-1,4-diol with hexane-1,6-diisocyanate forms a crystalline polyurethane known as Perlon-U.

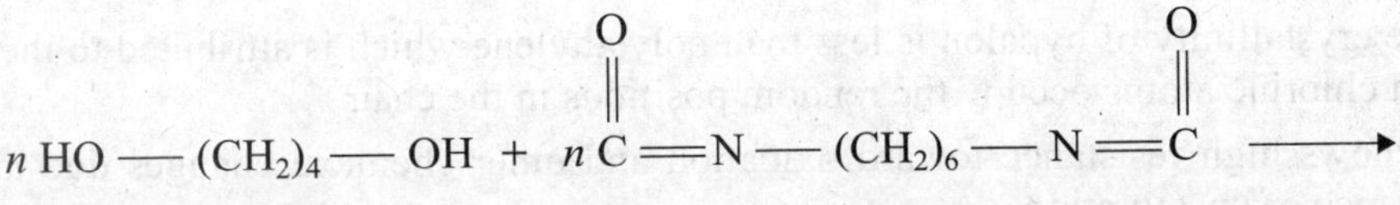

Butane-1,4-diol Hexane-1,6-diisocyanate

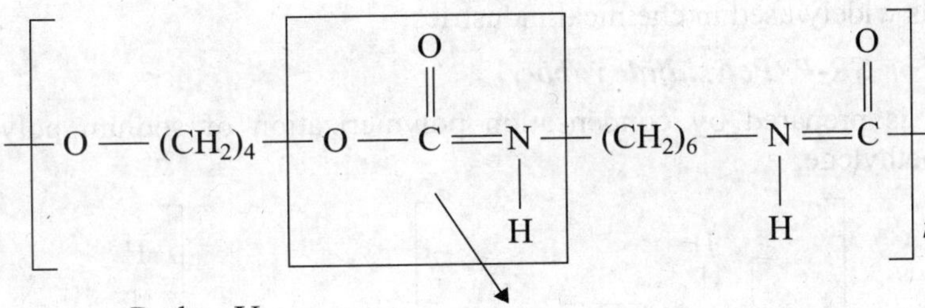

Perlon-U Urathane linkage

Properties

1. These are highly resistant to oxidation due to saturated character.
2. These are resistant to organic solvents and at the same time easily attacked by concentrated and hot acids and alkalis.
3. Appropriate choice of diol and diisocyanate results in the formation of urethanes which can be used as coatings, elastomers, fibers, and foams.

Uses

1. These are used as surface coatings.
2. Resilient PU fibers are used for making swimsuits and foundation garments.
3. Elastomeric PUs are used for enhancing the life of tyre treads.
4. Foamed PUs are used in making furniture cushions, pillows, mattresses, etc. These are also used as lather substitute.

Hypalon (chlorosulfonated polyethylene rubber)

These are prepared by the treatment of polyethylene with chlorine and sulfur dioxide. In the process, chlorine and chlorosulfonyl groups are introduced into the polyethylene chains.

$$(CH_2 - CH_2)_{x+y+z} + Cl_2 + SO_2 \longrightarrow$$

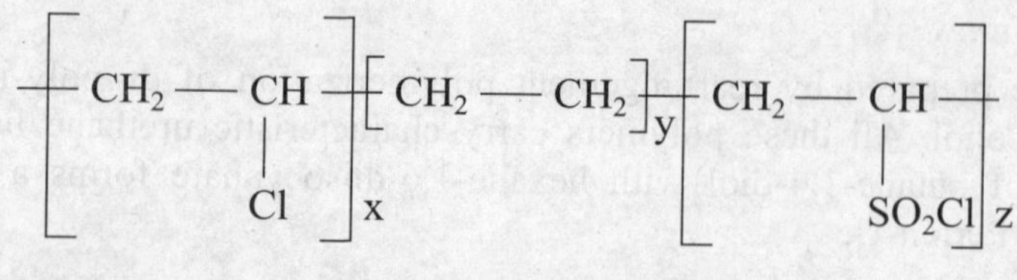

Properties

1. The crystallinity of hypalon is less than polyethylene which is attributed to the fact that chlorine atoms occupy the random positions in the chain.
2. It shows high resistance toward oxidation and other chemical changes due to the absence of unsaturation.
3. It can be easily vulcanized by using ZnO, MgO, and other bases due to the presence of chemically active sulfuryl groups.

Uses

It is widely used in chemical industries.

Thiokol or GR-P (Polysulfide rubber)

Thiokol is prepared by condensation polymerization of sodium polysulfide (Na_2S_x) and dichloroethylene.

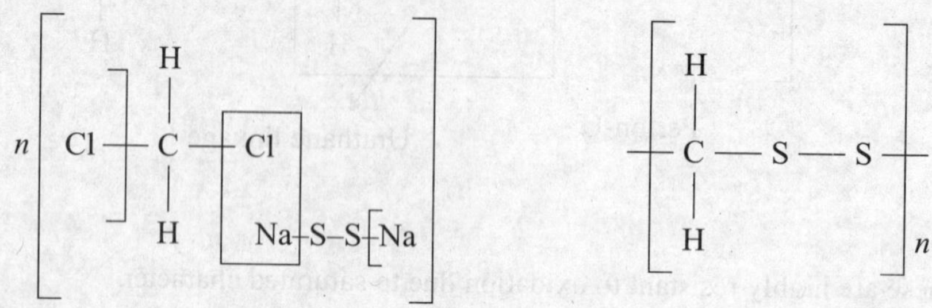

Properties

1. It has offensive mercaptan-like odor.
2. It has outstanding resistance to oxygen, ozone, and sunlight.
3. It has excellent resistance to swelling and disintegration by organic solvents and gasoline, kerosene and lubricating oils.
4. It has lower tensile strength and modulus than natural rubber.

Uses

1. It is used as diaphragms and seals in contact with solvents.
2. It is used as for chemically resistant tubing for conveying gasoline and oil.
3. It is used as printing rolls.
4. It is used in manufacture of oil hoses engine gaskets, etc.

Silicone Rubbers

Silicones are a group of organosilicon polymers. These are prepared by the treatment of silicon halide with Grignard reagent followed by controlled hydrolysis. In the beginning a mixture of organosilicon halides are formed, which are separated by fractional distillation before hydrolysis. Dialkyl silicon halides yield long-chain polymers while monoalkyl halides yield highly cross-linked polymers.

$$SiCl_4 + RMgCl \longrightarrow \begin{cases} R_2SiCl_2 \\ RSiCl_3 \end{cases}$$

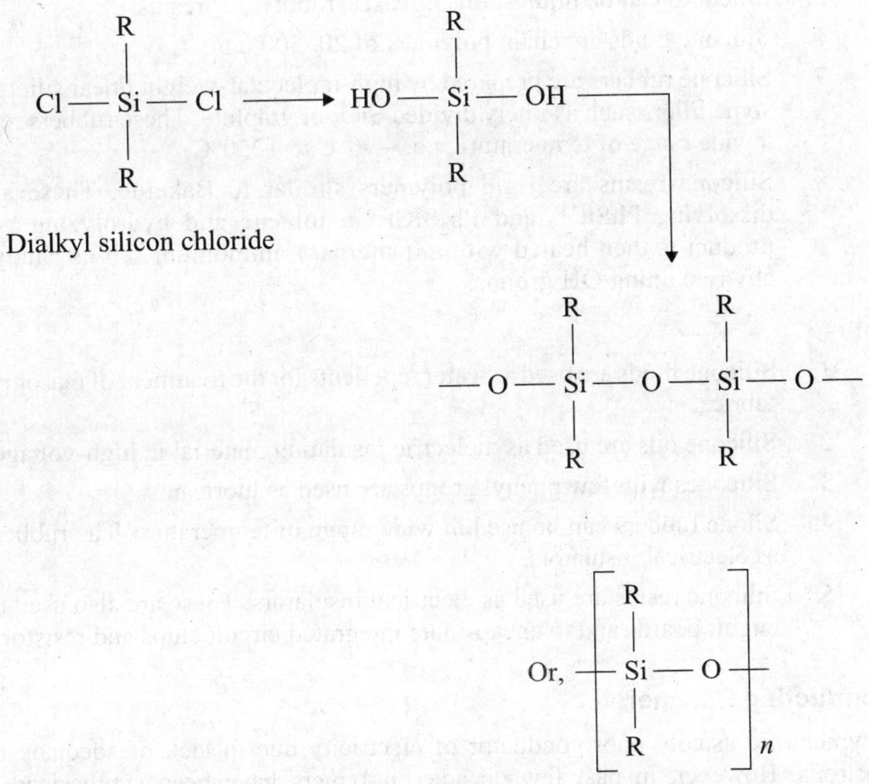

Dialkyl silicon chloride

Silicones

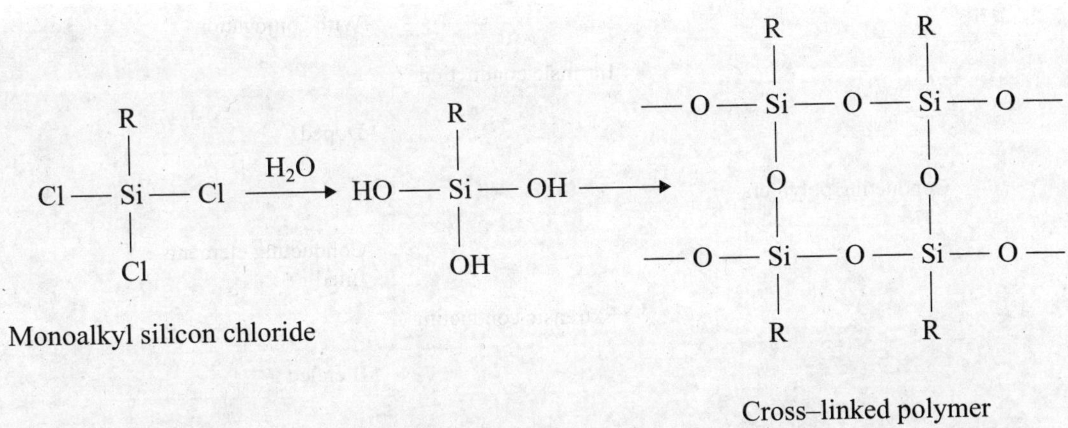

Monoalkyl silicon chloride

Cross–linked polymer

Properties

1. These are resistant to heat, oxidation, and most of the chemicals due to very stable Si–O and Si–C bonds.
2. These are strongly water repellent due to the presence of alkyl groups surrounding the silicone chain.
3. These are good electrical insulators.
4. These have non-stick and anti-foaming properties.
5. Silicones can be liquids, oils, greases, rubbers, or resins.
6. Silicone fluids are chain polymers of 20–500 units.
7. Silicone rubbers are prepared by high-molecular-weight linear silicon polymers with some fillers such as finely divided SiO_2 or graphite. These rubbers retain elasticity in a wide range of temperature, i.e., –90°C to +250°C.
8. Silicone resins are rigid polymers similar to Bakelite. These are prepared by dissolving $PhSiCl_3$ and Ph_2SiCl_2 in toluene and hydrolyzing with water. The product is then heated with a quaternary ammonium salt as catalyst to condense any remaining OH groups.

Uses

1. Silicone fluids are used as water repellents for the treatment of masonry and buildings, fabrics, etc.
2. Silicone oils are used as dielectric insulating material in high-voltage transformers.
3. Silicones with few phenyl groups are used as lubricants.
4. Silone rubbers can be used in wide range of temperature. The rubbers are also used as electrical insulators.
5. Silicone resins are used as electrical insulators. These are also used to make printed circuit boards and to encapsulate integrated circuit chips and resistors.

Conducting Polymers

Polymers are usually poor conductor of electricity due to lack of adequate number of free electrons. However, in past few decades, polymers have been synthesized which possess electrical conductivity at par with metals. Such polymers are called conducting polymers. The basic classification of conducting polymers is shown as follows:

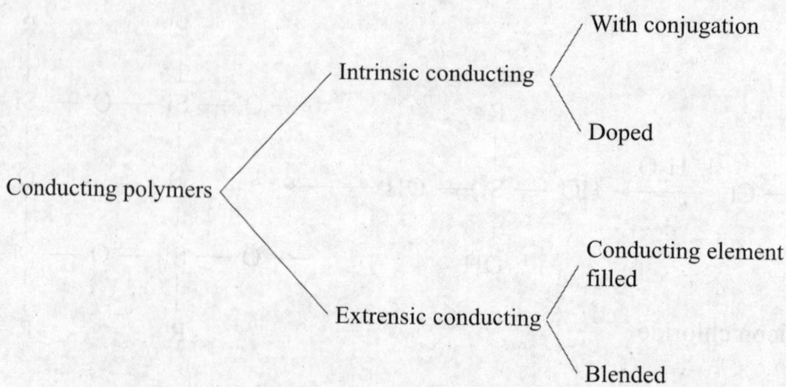

Intrinsic Conducting Polymers

Intrinsic conducting polymers (ICPs) polymers have extensive conjugation in the backbone which is responsible for conduction. These are further divided into two types: with conjugation and doped conducting polymers.

1. **With conjugated π-electrons in the backbone:** In such a case, overlapping of orbitals having conjugated π-electrons over the entire backbone forms the valency bands as well as conduction bands which remain extended over the entire polymer molecule. The band gap is significant for which conduction can occur only after thermal or photolytic activation of electrons. Examples of polymers in this category are polyacetylene polymers, polyaniline, polypyrrole, and polybutadienylene. Conductivity of such polymers is of the order of 10^{-10} S cm^{-1}.

$$n\,\mathrm{CH{\equiv}CH} \longrightarrow \mathrm{-\!\!\left(CH{=}CH\right)\!\!-}_n$$

Acetylene Polyacetylene

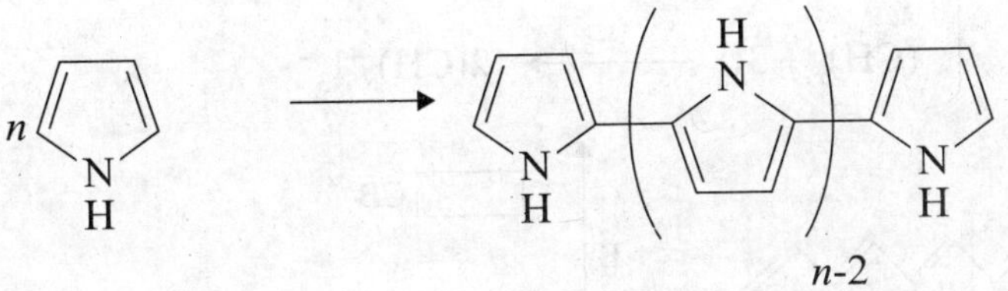

Pyrrole Polypyrrole

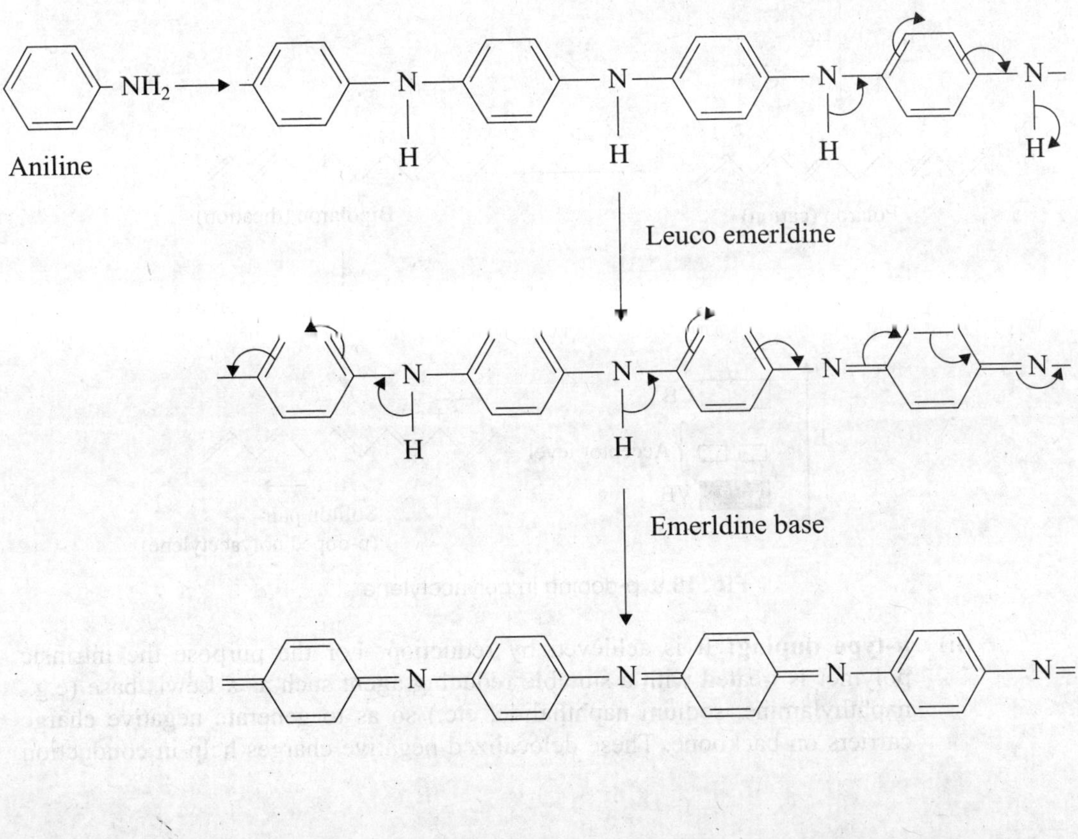

2. **Doped conducting polymers:** Intrinsic conducting polymers can be easily oxidized or reduced on account of their low ionization energy and high electron affinities. The conductivity of such polymers can be increased by creating either positive or negative charges on the polymer backbone by oxidation or reduction. By analogy with semiconductor technology, it is referred to as *doping*, which is of the following two types, viz., *p*- and *n*-type.

   (i) ***p*-type doping:** It is achieved by oxidation. For the purpose the intrinsic polymer is treated with a suitable oxidizing agent such as a Lewis acid or with I_2 vapor or iodine in CCl_4 so as to generate positive charge carriers on backbone. These delocalized positive charges help in conduction by forming an acceptor band between valence and conduction bands; hence, the name *p*-type semiconduction.

$$\underset{\text{Polyacetylene}}{(CH)_x} + \underset{\text{L. Acid}}{A} \longrightarrow \underset{\text{p-doped polyacetylene}}{(CH)_x^{+}A^{-}}$$

$$(CH)_x + 2FeCl_3 \longrightarrow (CH)_x^{+}FeCl_4^{-} + FeCl_2$$

$$(CH)_x + 3I_2 \longrightarrow 2(CH)_x^{+}I_3^{-}$$

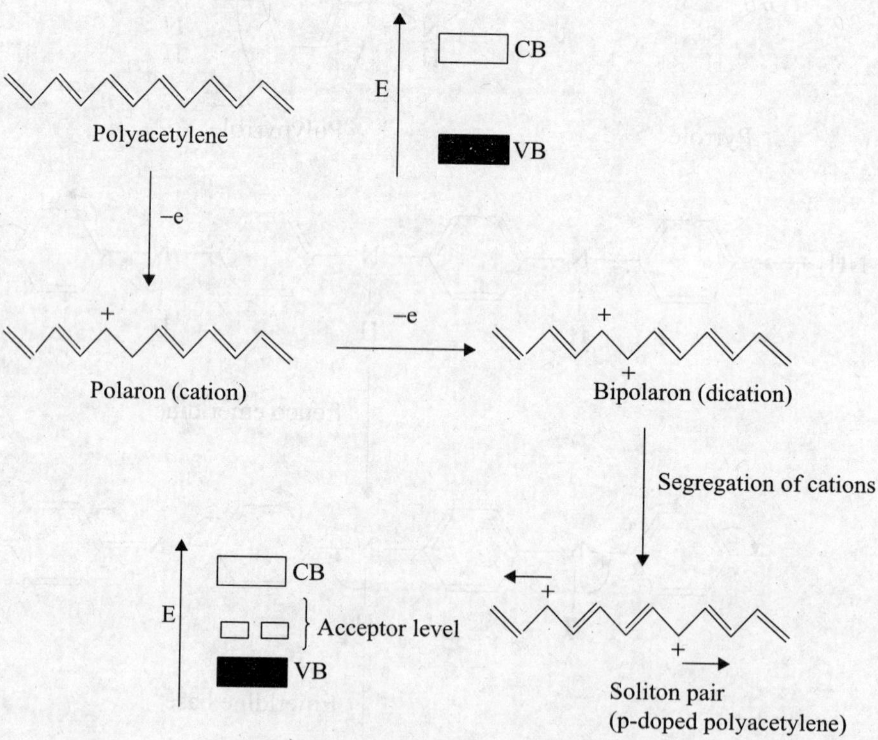

Fig. 18.9 p-doping in polyacetylene

   (ii) ***n*-type doping:** It is achieved by reduction. For the purpose the intrinsic polymer is treated with a suitable reducing agent such as a Lewis base (e.g., naphthylamine, sodium naphthalide, etc.) so as to generate negative charge carriers on backbone. These delocalized negative charges help in conduction by forming a donor band between the valence and conduction bands; hence, the name *n*-type semiconduction.

$$\left\{\begin{array}{l} \underset{\text{Polyacetylene}}{(CH)_x} + \underset{\text{L. Base}}{B} \longrightarrow \underset{\text{n-doped polyacetylene}}{(CH)_x^- B^+} \\ (CH)_x + Na^+(C_{10}H_8)^- \longrightarrow Na^+((CH)_x^- + C_{10}H_8 \end{array}\right.$$

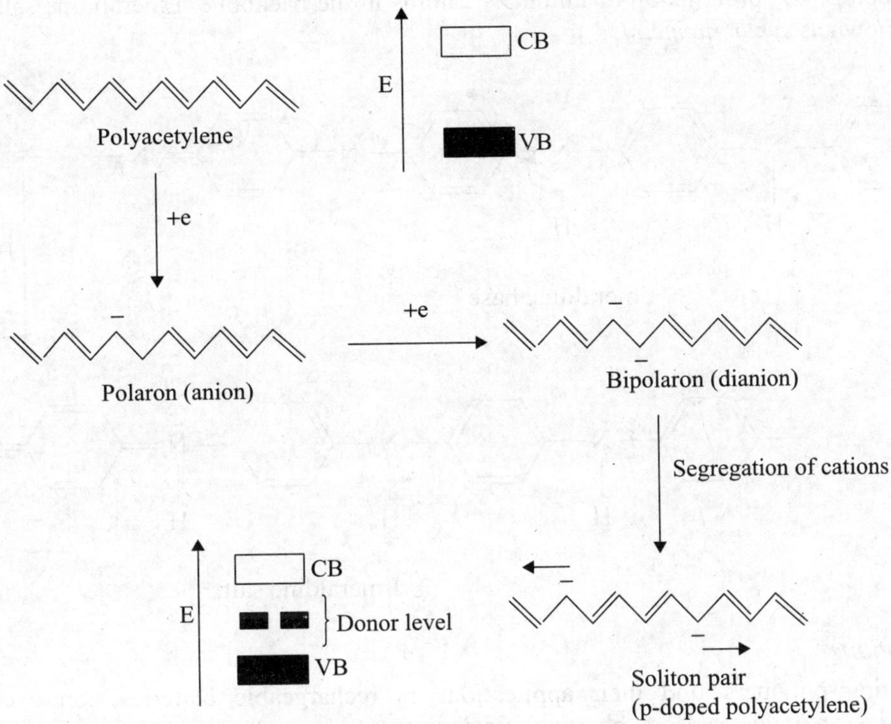

Extrinsic Conducting Polymers

The polymers in which conductivity is attributed to the presence of externally added ingredient to them are known as extrinsic conducting polymers. These are further of two types, viz., conductive element filled and blended polymers.

(i) **Conductive element filled polymers:** In such a case, polymer acts as a binder to hold the conducting elements such as carbon black, metallic fibers, and metallic oxides together in the solid matrix. The minimum concentration of conducting filler which should be added to the polymer so that it starts conducting is known as *percolation threshold*. At this concentration of filler, a conducting path is generated in the polymer matrix. These polymers possess quite good bulk conductivity, light in weight, mechanically durable; can be easily molded and are of low cost.

> **Note:**
> It is important to note that adding even 10% of carbon black to polymer substantially reduces the tensile strength, impact strength, and elongation at break.

(ii) **Blended conducting polymer:** These are obtained by blending a conventional polymer with a conducting polymer. Such polymers possess better physical, chemical, electrical, and mechanical properties.

Note:

In general doping brings a significant rise in surface conductivity of polymers. For example, emeralidine salt has a conductivity of ~10^3 S cm^{-1} as compared to emeralidine base whose conductivity is ~10^{-10} S cm^{-1}. Emeralidine salt is prepared by protonic doping, i.e., protonation of imine "N" atoms in the backbone. Emeralidine salt is also known as *synthetic metal*.

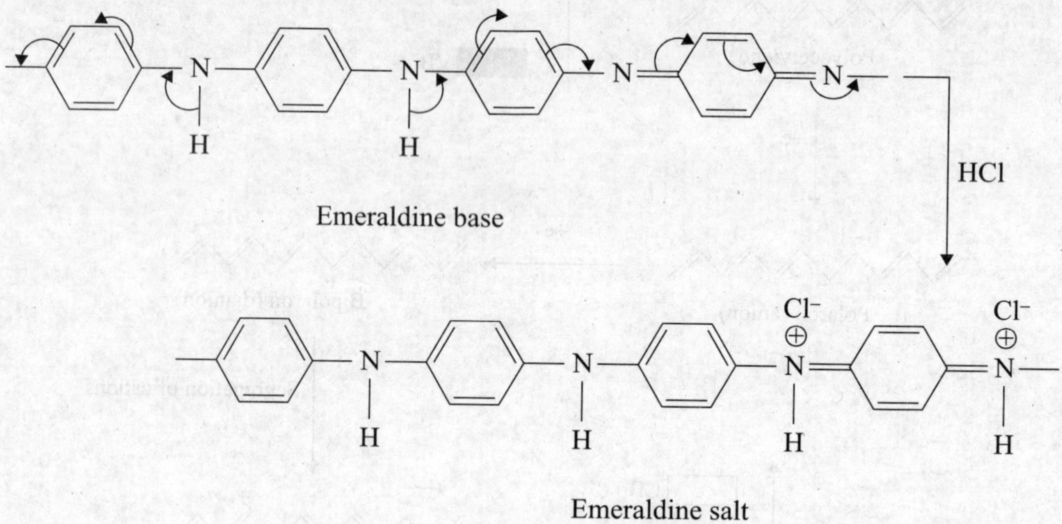

Applications

Conducting polymers find their applications in rechargeable batteries, ion exchangers, electronics, analytical sensors, photovoltaic devices, etc.

Biopolymers

The polymers present in animals or plants are known as biopolymers. Biopolymers can be broadly classified into four basic types: carbohydrates, protein, nucleic acids, and natural rubber.

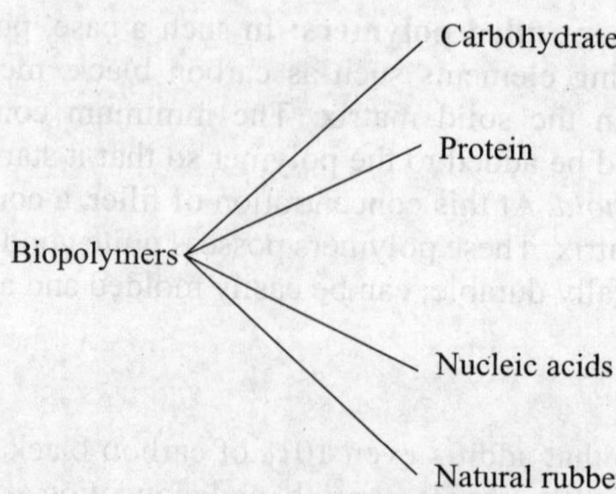

Carbohydrate (Polysaccharides)

Carbohydrates are polyhydroxy aldehydes or ketones. These compounds can be further subdivided into mono-, oligo-, and polysaccharides. Monosaccharides are the simplest carbohydrate (having 3–7 C atoms), which cannot be further hydrolyzed into smaller molecules, e.g., ribose ($C_5H_{10}O_5$), glucose ($C_6H_{12}O_6$), fructose ($C_6H_{12}O_6$), etc. Oligosaccharides yield 2–9 monosaccharides upon hydrolysis, e.g., maltose ($C_{12}H_{22}O_{11}$) and sucrose ($C_{12}H_{22}O_{11}$). Polysaccharides are biopolymers of monosaccharides having general formula $(C_5H_{10}O_5)_n$, where n have values of 1000–3000.

Starch

Starch is the polymer of monosaccharide (glucose). It is a mixture of two different polysaccharides, viz., amylose and amylopectin. Amylose is the liner macromolecule with α (1 $\rightarrow$ 4) glycosidic linkages and making up to 20–30% of the structure. It is insoluble in water. On the other hand, amylopectin is the branched one and insoluble. Glucose units are linked in a linear way with α (1 $\rightarrow$ 4) glycosidic bond. Branching takes place with α (1 $\rightarrow$ 6) bonds occurring every 24–30 glucose units, resulting in a soluble molecule that can be quickly degraded as it has many end points for enzymes to attach onto. It makes up 70–80% of the cellulose structure. Starch is used as a foodstuff (wheat, corn, rice, potato, etc.), for synthesis of alcohol, in sizing paper and textiles, etc.

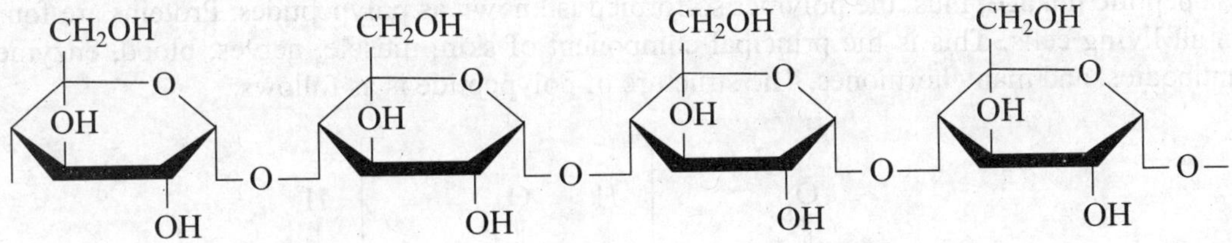

Amylose

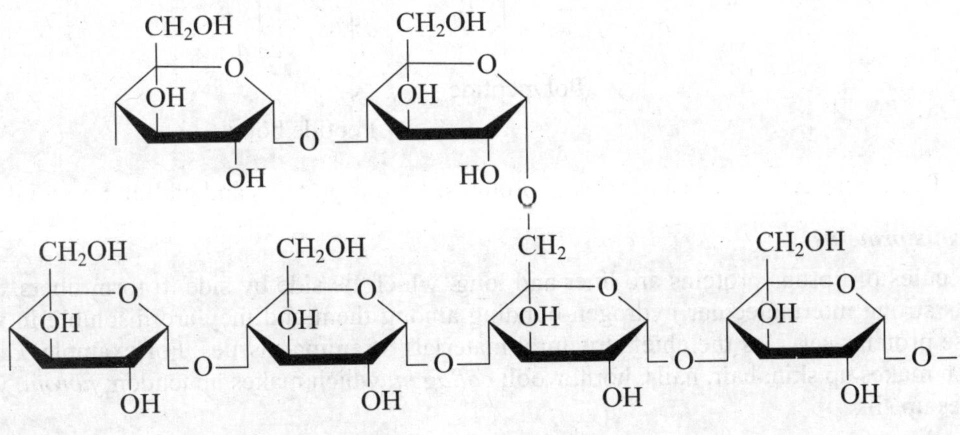

Amylopectin

Cellulose

Cellulose is the most abundant organic polymer on the Earth. Cellulose is a polysaccharides with formula $(C_5H_{10}O_5)_n$, consisting of a linear chain of several hundred to over ten thousand β (1 → 4) linked D-glucose units. Cellulose is an important structural component of the cell wall of green plants. The cellulose content of cotton fiber is 90% and that of wood is 40–50%. Cellulose contains several hydroxyl groups but still it is insoluble in water as the cellulose chains are held by hydrogen bonding between two –OH groups on adjacent chains. It is widely used in textile industry as thread, used in manufacture of paper, used for preparation of celluloid (a hard plastic) and cellophane (a film), etc.

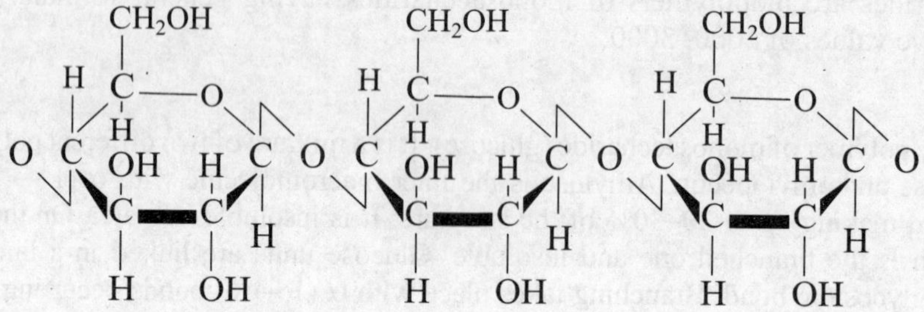

Protein (Polyamides)

Proteins are polyamides derived from α-amino carboxylic acids. The amino acids remain linked via peptide linkage; thus, the polymer so formed is known as polypeptides. Proteins are found in all living cells. This is the principal component of skin, muscle, nerves, blood, enzymes, antibodies, and many hormones. The structure of polypeptide is as follows:

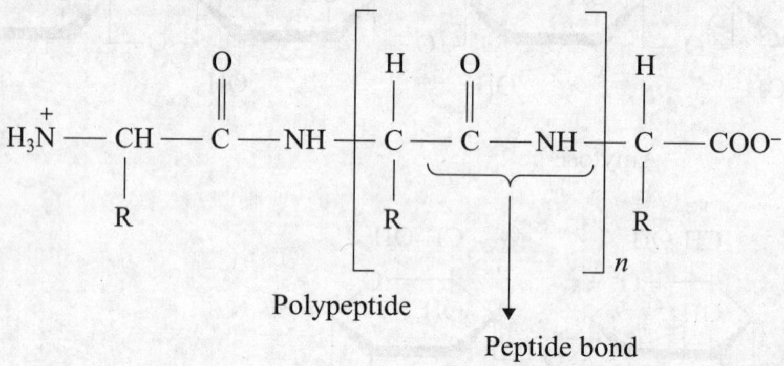

Polypeptide

There exist two broad categories of proteins: fibrous proteins and globular proteins.

Fibrous proteins

Molecules of fibrous proteins are liner and long, which lie side by side to form fibers. There exists strong intermolecular hydrogen bonding among them and they are insoluble in water. These proteins serve as the chief structural materials of animal tissues. For example, *keratin*, which makes up skin, hair, nails, horn, wool; *collagen*, which makes up tendon; *fibroin,* which makes up silk.

Globular proteins

In this case, the molecules are folded into spheroidal shapes in such a way that lipophilic parts are turned inward toward each other away from water while hydrophobic parts are turned outward. They have mainly intramolecular hydrogen bonding. The intermolecular forces are weak which make them soluble in water as well as in aqueous solutions of acids or bases or salts. These are essential for the maintenance and regulation of life process. These proteins make up *hemoglobin*, which is required for oxygen transport from lungs to tissues; *enzymes*, which catalyzes the biochemical reactions; *antibodies*, which provide defense against foreign organisms; *fibrinogen*, which helps in blood clotting.

Nucleic Acids

Nucleic acids are polymeric macromolecules essential for all known forms of life. Polynucleotide chains, which are the polymer of nucleotide, form the backbone of nucleic acids. Each nucleotide has three components, viz., a five carbon sugar, a phosphate group, and a nitrogenous base. On the basis of the sugar residue, there are two types of nucleic acids, viz., DNA and RNA. If the sugar is deoxyribose, then the polymer is DNA. On the other hand, if the sugar is ribose, the polymer is RNA. Nucleic acids control heredity in the molecular level and also play vital role in biosynthesis of proteins.

DNA

In DNA, the sugar is deoxyribose and the bases are adenine, guanine, cytosine, and thymine. The structure for the monomer nucleotide, the bases, and the generation of polynucleotide chain and finally the formation of double helix structure of DNA is shown in Fig. 18.10. The phosphate groups and sugar play the structural role, while the bases carry genetic information.

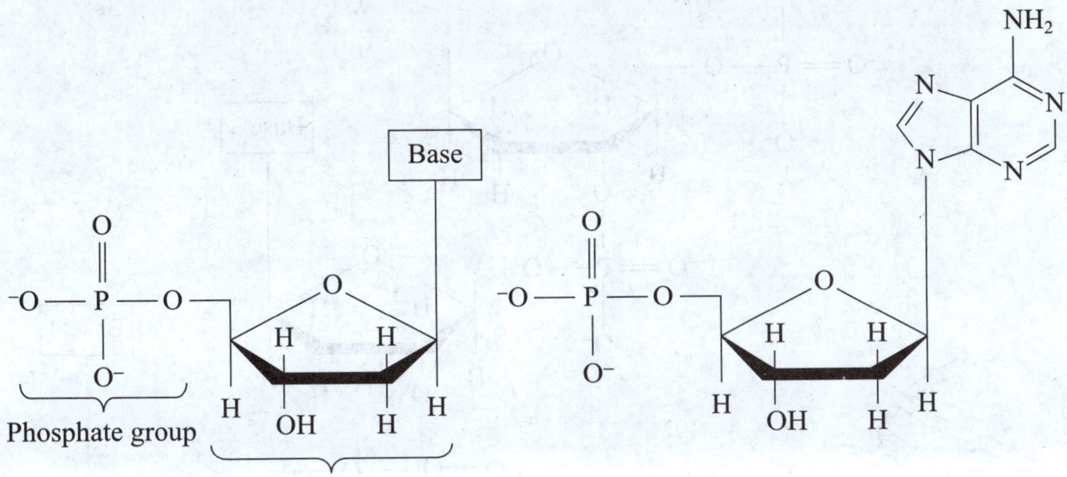

Sugar base (Deoxyribose) Nucleotide with a base (Adenine)

Nucleotide for DNA

Base

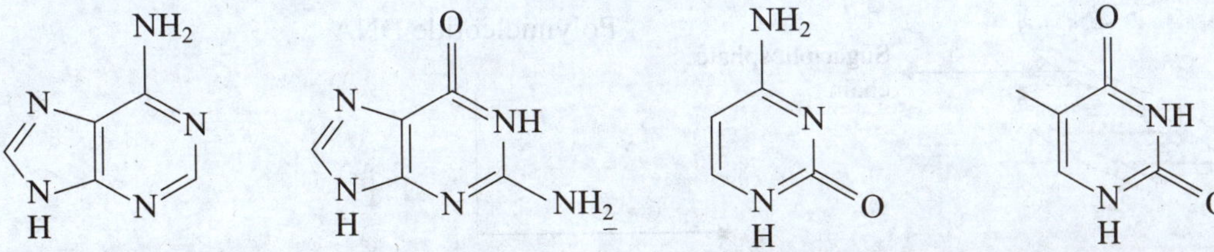

Adenine Guanine Cytosine Thymine

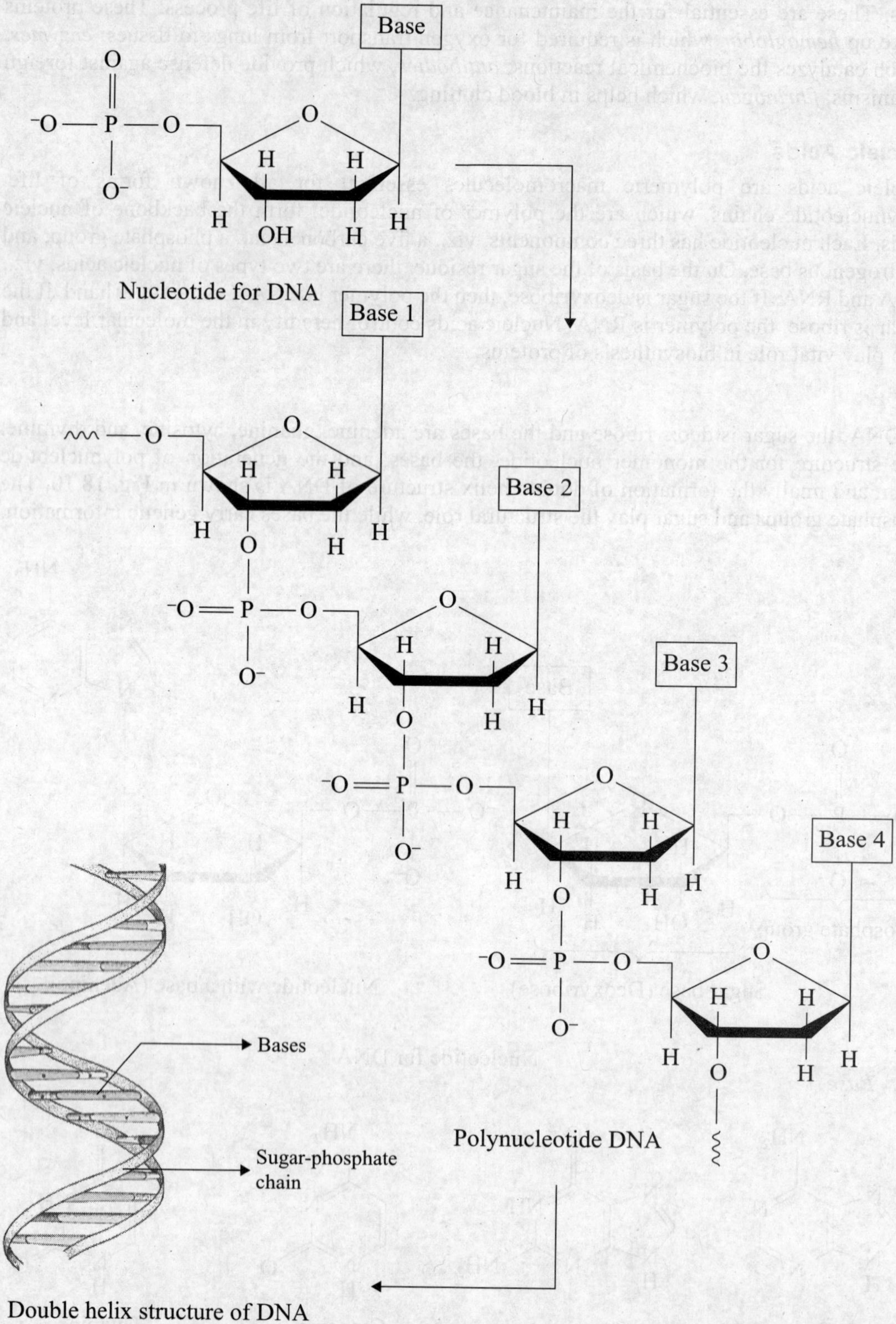

Fig. 18.10 Polynucleotide chain and double helix structure of DNA

RNA

In RNA, the sugar is ribose and the bases are adenine, guanine, cytosine, and uracil. The structure of the monomer nucleotide and the base is shown in Fig. 18.11. The polynuclotide chains are formed in a very similar manner to that of DNA. RNA exists as single helix. It is found in the cytoplasm of the cell and its main function is biosynthesis of protein.

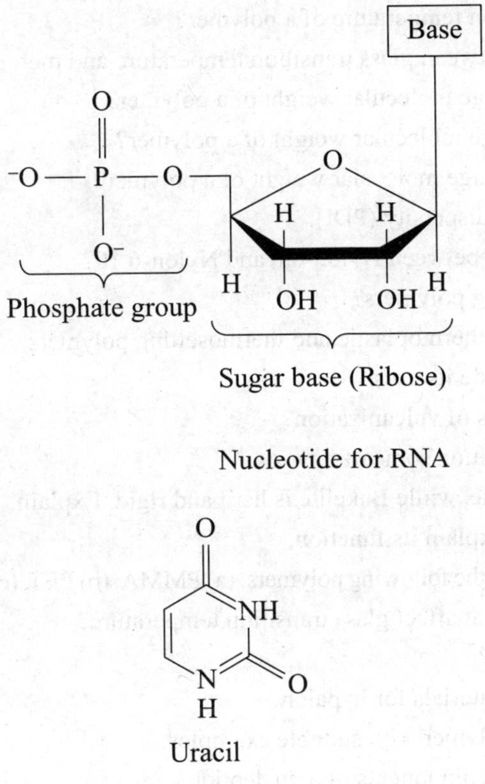

Fig. 18.11 Structure of the monomer nucleotide and the base

The comparative account of both nucleic acids is summarized here.

DNA	RNA
1. The sugar in DNA is 2-deoxyribose	The sugar in RNA is ribose
2. The bases are A, T, G, and C	The bases are A, G, C, and U
3. DNA structure is made of two right-handed helical polynucleotide chains that forms double helix around the one principal axis	RNA exists as single helix
4. Found in the nucleus of the cell	Found in cytoplasm of the cell
5. Prime function is to control heredity in molecular level	Function is synthesis of proteins

Natural Rubbers

This has been discussed separately under elastomers in this chapter.

QUESTIONS

1. What is degree of polymerization of a polymer?
2. What is copolymerization?
3. What is functionality of a monomer? Explain with suitable examples.
4. What is glass transition temperature of a polymer?
5. Give a comparison between glass transition temperature and melting point of a polymer.
6. What is number average molecular weight of a polymer?
7. What is weight average molecular weight of a polymer?
8. What is viscosity average molecular weight of a polymer?
9. Explain index of polydispersity (PDI).
10. What is the difference between Nylon-6,6 and Nylon-6,10?
11. What are thermosetting polymers?
12. Differentiate between thermoplastic and thermosetting polymers.
13. What is Kevlar? Provide its uses.
14. Provide the advantages of vulcanization?
15. What is Bakelite? Mention some of its uses.
16. PVC is soft and flexible, while Bakelite is hard and rigid. Explain.
17. What is plasticizer? Explain its function.
18. Name the monomers in the following polymers: (a) PMMA, (b) PET, (c) Nylon, (d) Natural rubber.
19. What are the factors that affect glass transition temperature?
20. What are biopolymers?
21. Provide the starting materials for hypalon.
22. Explain conducting polymer with suitable examples.
23. What are the different components of a nucleotide?
24. Why Kevlar is much less flexible than nylons?
25. What is copolymerization?
26. What is emulsion polymerization?
27. What is the structure of the recurring unit of natural rubber?
28. What are the applications of polyurethane foams?
29. What do you mean by compound of rubber?
30. What is the difference between compounding and vulcanization of rubber?
31. What are polycarbonates?
32. What are silicones?
33. What do you mean by Ziegler–Natta polymerization?
34. What are polyurethanes? What is the principal linkage in polyurethanes?
35. Name the monomer of Bakelite.
36. What are the monomers for the preparation of polyurethanes? Provide some of their examples.
37. What are silicones?
38. How silicone resins are prepared?

39. Provide some uses of silicones.
40. What is urea–fomaldehyde resin?
41. What is melamine–formaldehyde resin?
42. Distinguish between thermoplastic and thermosetting polymers. Explain both categories with at least one example from each.
43. What is an elastomer? Provide the limitations of raw rubber and suggest a remedial method.
44. What is synthetic rubber? Is vulcanization essential for all synthetic rubbers?
45. Provide the preparation properties and uses of Nylon-6, Nylon-6,6, and Nylon 6, 10.
46. Discuss preparation, properties, and uses of PET.
47. What is Gyptal resin? Give its uses.
48. Explain emulsion polymerization.
49. Explain suspension polymerization.
50. What do you mean by molding of plastics?
51. Explain different types of molding techniques.
52. What is extrusion molding? What for it is used?
53. Describe the process of compression molding. Also compare it with injection molding.
54. What are conducting polymers? Discuss possible categories of conducting polymers with suitable examples.
55. Explain different types of doped conducting polymers.
56. Explain extrinsic conducting polymers with suitable examples.
57. What do you mean by conductive element filled polymers?
58. Explain intrinsic conducting polymers with suitable examples.
59. What do you mean by blended conducting polymer?
60. Explain biopolymers with suitable examples.
61. What is nucleic acid?
62. What are the different components of a nucleotide?
63. What is DNA?
64. What are the bases in DNA and RNA?
65. Differentiate between DNA and RNA.
66. Explain structure of DNA.
67. What is protein?
68. Explain different categories of proteins.
69. What is a peptide linkage?
70. What is cellulose?
71. Explain the structure of starch.
72. Explain compounding of rubber.
73. Discuss different types of polymerization techniques.
74. Explain the conduction mechanism in p-type extrinsic semiconductors.
75. Discuss preparation and properties of urea–formaldehyde and melamine–formaldehyde resins.

CHAPTER

19

Corrosion

Chapter Outline

- Dry Corrosion
- Wet Corrosion
- Factors Affecting Rate of Corrosion
- Remedial Measures to Reduce Corrosion

Corrosion be defined as an unwanted destruction of a metallic substance due to chemical or electrochemical attack of environment on it. Metals are usually available in the form of compounds in the earth crust. During metallurgy a lot of energy is spent which gets stored in the metal as potential energy. Therefore when a metal is allowed to remain as such in the elemental form it always tends to interact with the atmospheric components and goes back to the compound form which is relatively more stable. Therefore corrosion may also be defined as the reverse process of metal extraction.

Dry Corrosion

This happens due to the direct interaction of atmospheric components such as O_2, X_2, SO_x, NO_x, H_2S, etc. with the metallic materials in the absence of moisture. This can be discussed under three basic categories.

Corrosion due to oxygen

Alkali and alkaline earth metals react with oxygen at room temperature. Other metals except Ag, Au and Pt, react with oxygen at elevated temperatures. Corrosion starts at the surface of metal, i.e., at the interface of the metal and atmosphere with the formation of a thin oxide film (the mechanism is given below). Further interaction depends on the nature of the oxide film formed.

$$\begin{aligned} 2M &\longrightarrow 2M^{n+} + 2ne \\ (n/2)O_2 + 2ne &\longrightarrow nO^{2-} \\ \hline 2M + (n/2)O_2 &\longrightarrow \underbrace{2M^{n+} + nO^{2-}}_{\text{Corrosion product at the metal surface (oxide film)}} \end{aligned}$$

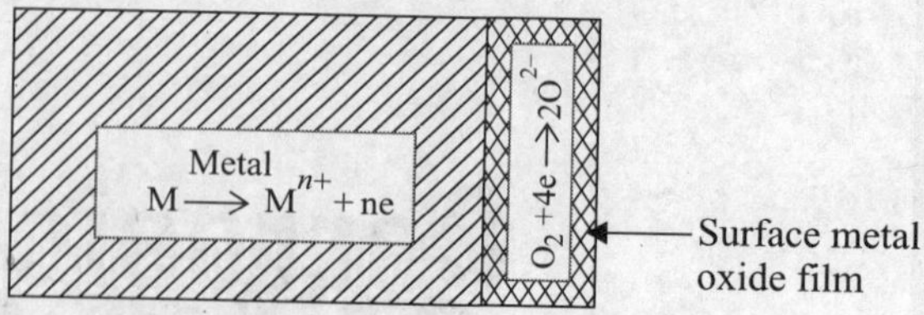

Fig. 19.1 Formation of surface oxide film

Stable film

If the oxide film is stable, it remains adhered to the surface strongly and there by acts as a physical barrier between metal and the atmosphere. This prevents further penetration of oxygen to the base metal. As a result, corrosion is restricted to the surface, e.g., in case of oxides of Al, Pb, Cu, etc.

Unstable film

If the oxide formed is unstable, it dissociates back to metal and oxygen. Therefore corrosion does not take place, e.g., oxides of Ag, Au and Pt.

Volatile

If the oxide film is volatile, it gets volatilized to expose new surface to interact with oxygen. Here corrosion continues to eat the whole metallic structure. Therefore corrosion is rapid and continuous, e.g., oxide of molybdenum.

Porous

Here the oxide film has pores or channels through which oxygen slowly diffuses to interact with the base metal. Therefore in this case corrosion is slow but continuous, e.g., oxide of iron.

Note:

1. **Pilling-Bedworth rule:** As per the rule, the lesser is the specific volume ratio, i.e., ratio between volume of metal oxide and volume of metal, the greater is the oxidation corrosion. For example, the specific volume ratio of W and Cr are 3.6 and 2.0, which indicates toward the fact that the corrosion rate of W is less as compared to Cr even at higher temperature.
2. The metal oxide formed is mostly non-stoichiometric. Such an oxide is either deficit or excess of metal ions which give rise to two types of semiconducting oxides, viz., *p*-type oxides such as NiO and FeO, which are deficient in metal ions, and *n*-type oxides such as ZnO and CdO, which are having excess of metal ions.
3. Alloying influence the rate of oxidation of host metal. This is governed by *Hauffe's valency rules*. The rules are summarized as follows:

Nature of oxide film	Valency of alloying metal in relation to host metal	Effect on rate of oxidation
p-type	Lower	Decreases
(NiO, FeO, Cu_2O)	Higher	Increases
n-type	Lower	Decreases
(ZnO, CdO, TiO_2, Fe_2O_3)	Higher	Increases

Example: Let us consider alloying of Ni with Li. In this case, some Li^+ ions occupy the vacant cationic sites in the non-stoichiometric NiO. For each doped Li^+ ion, a positive hole is created to maintain electrical neutrality. As the number of vacant sites decreases, the migration of Ni^{2+} via vacant sites in the lattice is hindered. The result is that the rate of corrosion is reduced. On the other hand, alloying of Ni with Cr increases the rate of corrosion. This is because Cr^{3+} decreases positive holes and increases the cationic vacancies.

Corrosion due to other corrosive gases

The extent of corrosion depends on the chemical affinity between the base metal and the atmospheric components. Again corrosion starts at the surface with the formation of surface film. The further course of reaction depends on the nature of the surface film formed, e.g., Fe forms a sulphide film at its surface upon reaction with hydrogen sulphide at elevated temperature which is a porous one and therefore corrosion is continuous but slow. On the other hand, Ag forms a chloride film upon reaction with atmospheric chlorine. The AgCl film so formed is very stable and sticks firmly to the surface preventing further corrosion.

$$Fe + H_2S \longrightarrow \underset{\text{Porous}}{FeS + H_2}$$

$$2Ag + Cl_2 \longrightarrow \underset{\text{Stable}}{2AgCl}$$

Liquid metal corrosion

This type of corrosion occurs when a molten liquid is passed continuously on a solid metal/alloy surface. The corrosion is attributed to either dissolution of the molten liquid or penetration of the molten liquid into the solid metal phase.

Wet Corrosion

This type of corrosion occurs due to the setup of an electrochemical cell, i.e., due to the development of separate anodic and cathodic areas between which current flows through the conducting liquid. Here anode is always destroyed or corroded while cathode is protected. The basic mechanism is that the metal is oxidized at anode releasing the metal ions and electrons. The electrons migrate to cathode where the dissolved constituents accept the electron to form oxide, hydroxide ions, etc. Now the metal ions formed at anode and non-metallic ions formed at cathode diffuse towards each other through the conducting medium to form corrosion product

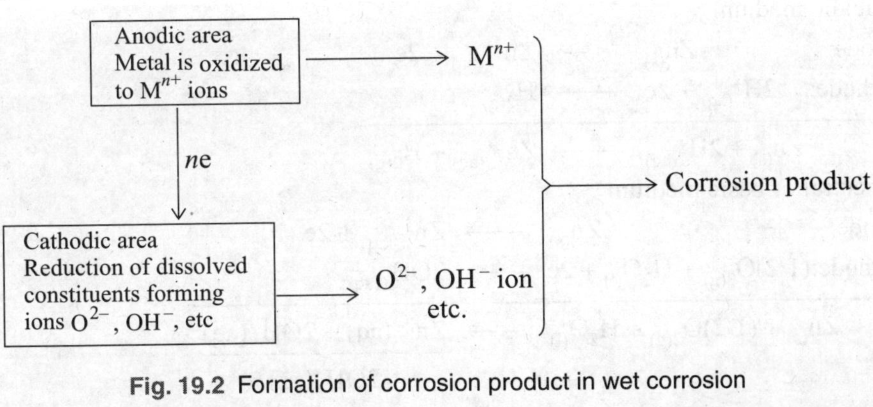

Fig. 19.2 Formation of corrosion product in wet corrosion

somewhere in between cathode and anode depending on the mobility of the ions. The corrosion product may dissolve into the medium or may get deposited on the surface.

Note:

1. During corrosion, the electrons released at anode migrate to the cathode through the conducting medium. The different possible cathodic reactions are as follows:
   (i) **Through evolution of hydrogen**
   $$\begin{cases} \text{Acidic medium:} & 2H^+ + 2e \longrightarrow H_2 \\ \text{Neutral/alkaline medium:} & 2H_2O + 2e \longrightarrow H_2 + 2OH^- \end{cases}$$
   (ii) **Through absorption of oxygen**
   $$\begin{cases} \text{Acidic medium:} & 4H^+ + O_2 + 4e \longrightarrow 2H_2O \\ \text{Neutral/alkaline medium:} & 2H_2O + O_2 + 4e \longrightarrow 4OH^- \end{cases}$$
2. A comparative account of dry and wet corrosion

Dry corrosion	Wet corrosion
Occurs in the absence of electrolyte or moisture	Occurs in the presence of electrolyte or moisture
It involves direct chemical attack of corrosive component of atmosphere on base metal	It occurs through the development of electrochemical cells
It is uniform	It is non-uniform
Rate is slow	Rate is relatively fast
Corrosion product accumulates at the site of corrosion	Accumulates somewhere in between anode and cathode

Types of Wet Corrosion

Wet or non-uniform corrosion is of different kinds. Some of them are as follows:

Galvanic cell corrosion

When two dissimilar metals remain in contact in the presence of a conducing liquid then the more electropositive metal acts as anode and gets corroded. Such corrosion is known as Galvanic corrosion, e.g., in Zn–Cu couple Zn being more electropositive acts as anode and gets corroded in preference. The possible mechanism in both acidic and neutral medium is given as follows:

In acidic medium

Anode: $Zn_{(s)} \longrightarrow Zn^{2+}_{(aq)} + 2e$

Cathode: $2H^+_{(aq)} + 2e \longrightarrow H_{2(g)}$

$$Zn_{(s)} + 2H^+_{(aq)} \longrightarrow Zn^{2+}_{(aq)} + H_{2(g)}$$

In neutral or basic medium

Anode: $Zn_{(s)} \longrightarrow Zn^{2+}_{(aq)} + 2e$

Cathode: $(1/2)O_{2(g)} + H_2O_{(l)} + 2e \longrightarrow 2OH^-_{(aq)}$

$$Zn_{(s)} + (1/2)O_{2(g)} + H_2O_{(l)} \longrightarrow \underbrace{Zn^{2+}(aq) + 2OH^-(aq)}_{2OH^-(aq)}$$

Concentration cell corrosion

Such corrosion occurs when a metal surface is exposed to a conducting liquid of varying concentration. The portion of the metal that remains in contact with lower concentration of metal ions acts as anode and gets corroded. This is known as metal ion concentration cell corrosion.

Another important type in this category is oxygen concentration cell corrosion or differential aeration corrosion. If two portions of a metal have different access to oxygen then the portion which has limited access to oxygen behaves anodic with respect to the portion which has more access to oxygen. This can be included in concentration cell corrosion. For example, a Zn rod kept partially immersed in water. Here the portion of the rod that is inside the water has lesser access to oxygen and behaves anodic with respect to the portion that remains outside. The reactions will be similar to those discussed in Galvanic corrosion.

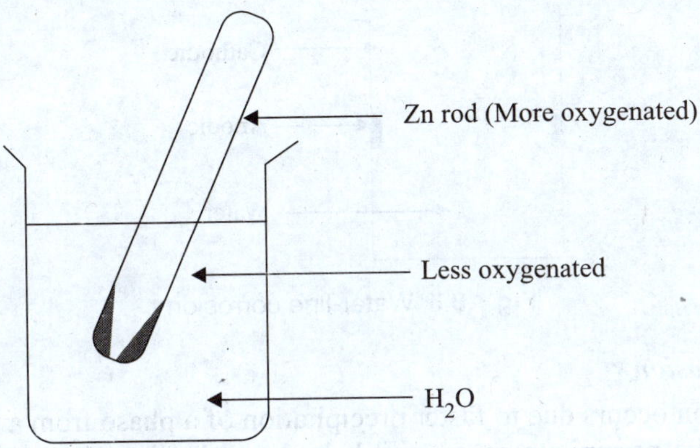

Fig. 19.3 Differential aeration corrosion

Pitting corrosion

The metal surface having pits or cavities undergo corrosion due to development of separate anodic and cathodic areas. Pitting is usually a result of breakdown or cracking of the protective film on a metal at specific points. Here pits/cavities act as anode with respect to the normal portion. A typical pitting corrosion cell in iron surface is illustrated below. Here corrosion is due to the development of an oxygen concentration cell (Fig. 19.4).

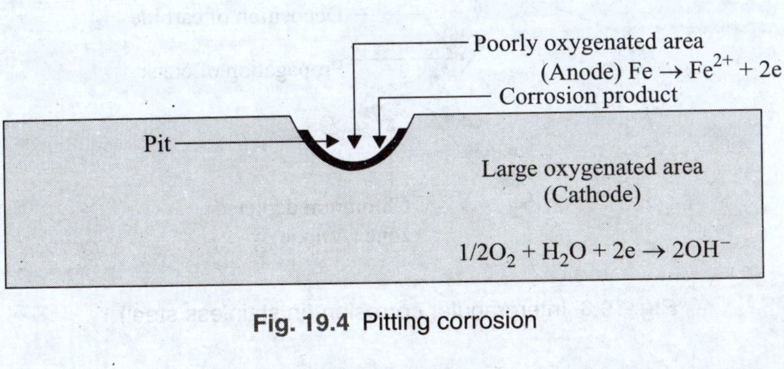

Fig. 19.4 Pitting corrosion

Water-line corrosion

This is an example of differential aeration corrosion. When water is stored in a steel tank, corrosion takes place along a line just beneath the level of water meniscus. In this case, the area above the water line having more access to oxygen acts as cathode, whereas the area below the water line having relatively less access to oxygen acts as anode. If the water relatively free from acidity, this corrosion is not significant. The reactions involved are as follows:

$$\begin{cases} \text{Anode} & Fe \longrightarrow Fe^{2+} + 2e \\ \text{Cathode} & 4H^{+} + O_2 + 4e \longrightarrow 2H_2O \longrightarrow 2H^{+} + 2OH^{-} \end{cases}$$

$$\text{Oveall reaction} \quad Fe^{2+} + 2OH^{-} \longrightarrow Fe(OH)_2 \xrightarrow{\text{Oxidation}} Fe(OH)_3$$

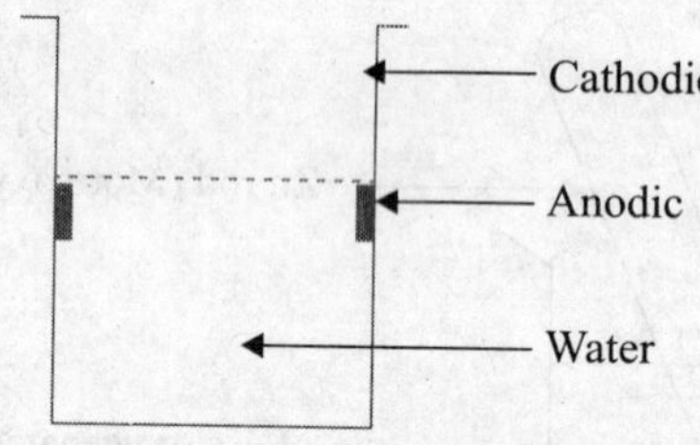

Fig. 19.5 Water-line corrosion

Inter-granular corrosion

This type of corrosion occurs due to faster precipitation of a phase from a solid solution at the grain boundaries. The precipitate compound behaves cathodic, whereas the grain boundary behaves anodic. Such corrosion is very popular in alloys. For example, stainless steel, an alloy of iron, carbon, and chromium. During welding of steel, chromium carbide ($M_{23}C_6$) precipitates at the grain boundaries. Thus, the concentration of Cr is relatively less in the region adjacent to grain boundaries as compared to grain center and the precipitate. The result is that the region adjacent to grain boundaries becomes anodic and susceptible to corrosion. Such corrosion occurs in microscopic level, follows a path along the grain boundaries until the grain is completely dislodged.

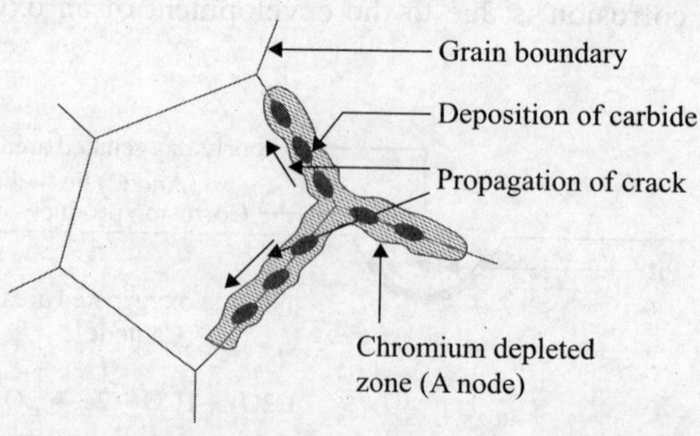

Fig. 19.6 Intergranular corrosion (in stainless steel)

Note:

1. Such a corrosion lead to sudden failure of structure without external indication of attack.
2. This corrosion can be minimized by preventing heterogeneous precipitation which mostly occurs due to slow cooling of alloy. Therefore, during alloying, proper heat treatment flowed by rapid quenching is required.

Microbial corrosion

Biological processes mediated by microorganisms can produce corrosion which is known as microbial/bio-corrosion/microbially influenced corrosion (MIC). Four distinct processes have been identified. The first one is microbial deposits. These deposits are bio-films which are used by bacteria to adhere to the surface of substrate. These deposits lead to the development of a differential aeration cell. The area of the metal directly under the bio-film has a less access to oxygen and behaves anodic, while the surface just outside the contact area having more access to oxygen behaves cathodic. Metal dissolution will occur under the microbial deposits forming pits, but the density of local dissolution areas depend on the density of the colony. The second one is that the microbial deposits may produce inorganic and organic acids which change the local environment and thereby induce corrosion at the colony to metal interface. The production of inorganic acids will also lead to hydrogen ion production which may contribute to hydrogen embrittlement of the colonized metal. Aerobic sulfur oxidizing bacteria of the type *thiobacillus sp.* can create an environment of up to 10% sulfuric acid, thereby encouraging rapid corrosion. Third possibility is that in anaerobic conditions, some bacteria such as *Desulfuromonas sp.* and *Desulfobacter sp.* reduce the sulfate ions to produce oxygen and the sulfide ion. The sulfide ion then combines with iron or other metal ions to form corresponding sulfides, the corrosion product. The fourth possibility is that some bacteria such as *Shewanella sp.* are there which can directly transfer electrons to metal surface for reduction. The reductive processes used for respiration do not cause the physical corrosion that is observed on metal surfaces, but breaks down the metals, allowing oxidation and visible corrosion. A typical case of microbial corrosion is shown in Fig. 19.7.

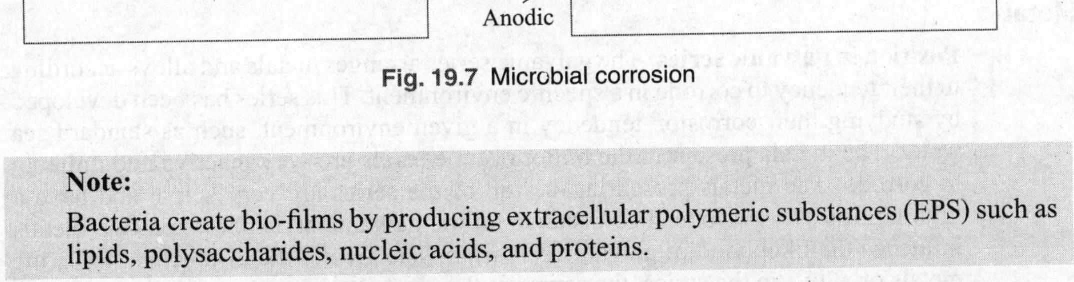

Fig. 19.7 Microbial corrosion

Note:

Bacteria create bio-films by producing extracellular polymeric substances (EPS) such as lipids, polysaccharides, nucleic acids, and proteins.

Soil or underground corrosion

Metals or alloys that remain in contact with soil often suffer corrosion which is known as soil or underground corrosion. Underground storage tanks, cables, transmission and distribution pipes, etc., are the primary facilities to be affected by this corrosion. The presence of moisture, electrolytes, microorganisms, soil acidity, etc., are responsible for underground corrosion which is further promoted by differential aeration. The type of corrosion depends on the particular metal and the nature of the soil environment.

Stress corrosion

Metallic materials remain under strain due to mechanical operations like welding, bending, pressing, hammering, etc. During corrosion the stressed portion acts as anode with respect to the normal portion leading to highly localised corrosion.

For example, *caustic embrittlement,* which occurs in mild steel exposed to alkaline solution at stressed areas such as crevices or rivets, joints and bent portions at high temperature. It is often found in steam boilers and heat transfer equipments in which water with alkalinity corrode the mild steel plates particularly at the crevices. Boiler water contains sodium carbonate that has been added as water softening agent and breaks down to give sodium hydroxide making the water alkaline. This alkaline water flows into the hair line cracks and crevices by capillary action where the water evaporates building up the caustic soda. It is this concentrated alkali which dissolves iron as sodium ferroate (Na_2FeO_2) in crevices and cracks where the metal is under stress. Sodium ferroate then decomposes to magnetite regenerating caustic soda. The caustic soda generated further enhances corrosion. The reactions involved are given as follows.

$$Na_2CO_3 + H_2O \longrightarrow 2NaOH + CO_2$$

$$Fe + NaOH \longrightarrow \underset{\text{Sodium ferroate}}{Na_2FeO_2}$$

$$3Na_2FeO_2 + 4H_2O \longrightarrow 6NaOH + \underset{\text{Magnetite}}{Fe_3O_4} + H_2$$

Season cracking

It is an example of stress corrosion of brass, which occurs in an atmosphere of NH_3 or RNH_2. Both the component metals Cu and Zn form complex ions such as $[Cu(NH_3)_4]^{2+}$ and $[Zn(NH_3)_4]^{2+}$ in ammonia solutions. This leads to dissolution of brass leading to cracks under stress.

Factors Affecting Corrosion

Basically the analysis is made with respect to the nature of metal and environment.

Metal

1. **Position in galvanic series:** The galvanic series arranges metals and alloys according to their tendency to corrode in a specific environment. This series has been developed by studying their corrosion tendency in a given environment, such as standard sea water. The metals present at the bottom of the series are very inactive and unlikely to corrode. The metals present at the top of the series are very active and have a high tendency to corrode. The distance on the galvanic series between two metals influence the likelihood of galvanic corrosion. The greater the distance between the metals or alloys in the series, the severe is the corrosion.

Anodic

Mg
Mg alloys
Zn
Al
Cd
Al alloys
Mild steel
Cast iron
Pb-Sn solder
Pb
Sn
Brass
Silver solder
Cu
Ni
Chromium stainless steel
18-8 Stainless steel
Ag
Ti
Au
Pt

Cathodic

Note:

Surface coating of some metals makes them passive, increasing their effective electrode potential and thereby making them cathodic. This is something opposite to that predicted by the electrochemical series. Thus, the electrochemical series does not provide the real corrosion tendency of metals and alloys in actual environment. Therefore, a more practical series known as Galvanic series has been developed. This series is not exactly similar to electrochemical series, rather this includes metals and alloys and predicts relative corrosion tendency of metals or alloys. In addition, another feature to be marked is that the position of a given metal or alloy may change in a galvanic series.

2. **Relative anodic and cathodic area:** Anode always has to fulfil the electron requirement of cathode and in the process gets corroded. Corrosion is severe and highly localized if the anodic area is small as compared to the cathodic area. This is because the current density is more and the demand of electrons by the larger cathodic area can be met by relatively smaller anodic area by undergoing rapid corrosion.
3. **Passivity:** There are some metals such as Al, Ti, Cr, Ni, etc., which form highly stable thin oxide films at their surface. As a result, the metals become passive to the environmental attack and show more corrosion-resistance behavior than expected with respect to their positions in the Galvanic series. An important example is stainless steel. The corrosion resistance in this case is attributed the passive character of chromium.

4. **Purity:** Impurities present in the metal result in heterogeneity and thereby help in the development of separate anodic and cathodic areas. The rate and severity of corrosion increase with increase in impurities.
5. **Nature of corrosion product formed:** Nature of surface thin film decides the extent and rate of corrosion. Particularly the *specific volume ratio*, i.e., the ratio of volumes of the metal compound and metal, plays an important role. The greater the specific volume ratio, the lesser is the corrosion rate.

Environment

1. **Temperature:** In general, elevated temperature enhances the rate of corrosion. This is because at elevated temperature the rate of reaction is enhanced.
2. **Humidity/moisture content:** Moisture or humidity present in the atmosphere helps in the setup of an electrochemical cell and facilitates corrosion. However, there is always a critical humidity depending on the nature of the metal and that of the corrosion product above which the rate of atmospheric corrosion increases rapidly.
3. **pH:** In general, acidic medium, i.e., $pH < 7$, is more corrosive than basic or neutral medium. However, amphoteric metals such as Zn, Al, and Pb form soluble complexes in basic medium, i.e., $pH > 7$, and get corroded.
4. **Conductance of the medium:** The greater the conductance of the medium, the easier is the current flow and severe is the corrosion, e.g., a metal piece buried in clayey soil is more intensely corroded than a piece buried in sand. This is because clay is enriched with charge carriers and is a better conductor.

Remedial Measures to Reduce Corrosion

Let us discuss the measures that can be taken to restrict corrosion separately with respect to metal and environment.

Metal

1. **Proper designing:** Care must be taken during the design of a metal structure so that corrosion will not occur, and if at all it occurs, it should not be intense and localized, rather it should be uniform. Some important design principles are as follows:

   (i) Avoid L, T, and U shaped profiles in constructions as far as possible. This is because, the more is the number of angles, corners, and edges in any design, the difficult is the surface treatment. Let us look into one example of efficient design (see Fig. 19.8).

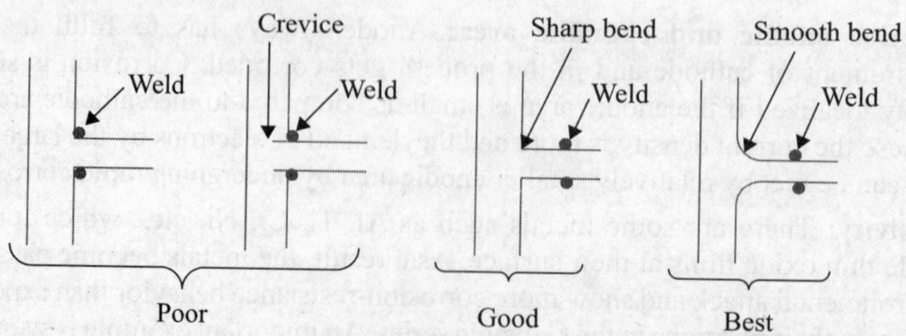

Fig. 19.8 Some improper and proper designs

(ii) Avoid contact of two dissimilar metals.

(iii) If at all two dissimilar metals are to be kept in contact, then they should be as close as possible in Galvanic series and if possible some insulating fitting may be used in between.

(iv) Design should be such that the anodic area should be larger than the cathodic area.

(v) Prevent the occurrence of any type of in-homogeneity in both metals and environment in immediate proximity.

(vi) The design should be such that it allows adequate cleaning and flushing of critical parts.

(vii) Design should avoid stressed portions in the structure.

2. **Cathodic protection:** The principle being the metal to be protected is made cathode so as to avoid corrosion. This can be achieved in two ways, viz., sacrificial anodic protection and impressed current cathodic protection.

***Sacrificial anodic protection**:* In the first method, the metal to be protected is allowed to be connected to a more electropositive metal so that the latter operate as anode. In the process of corrosion, the cathode is protected at the cost of anode which is sacrificed in the process, e.g., underground cables and pipes can be protected from corrosion by coupling them with more active metals such as Mg and Zn (see Fig. 19.9). Protection hulls of ships and boat from marine corrosion can be achieved by hanging sheets of Mg or Zn around the hull which behave anodic to iron. The sheets are replaced by fresh ones when they are completely consumed.

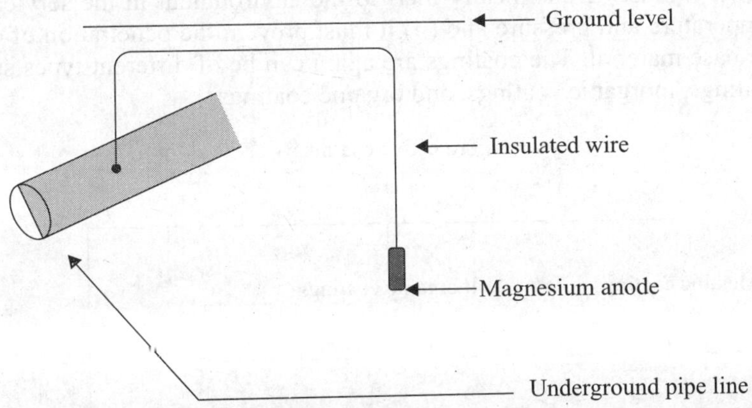

Fig. 19.9 Sacrificial anodic protection

Impressed current cathodic protection: In this method, an impressed current is allowed to pass through the circuit from an external DC source in the opposite direction to nullify the corrosion current. The result is that the anode is converted into cathode and protected from corrosion. Here the anode may be either an inert material or one which deteriorates and have to be replaced periodically, e.g., graphite, platinum, stainless steel, high silica iron, and scrap iron. The anode is buried in a back fill of gypsum to have better contact between itself and the surrounding soil as shown in Fig. 19.10.

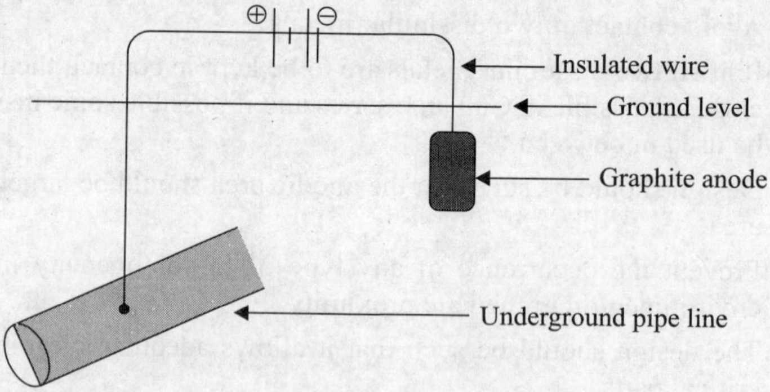

Fig. 19.10 Impressed current cathodic protection

Note:

This method is suitable for large structures and long term applications such as buried pipelines, tanks, and transmission line towers.

3. **By using protective coatings:** The metal can be protected from corrosion by applying protective coatings on the surface which acts as a barrier between the metal and the environment. Besides corrosion protection, protective coatings sometimes impart surface specific mechanical and physical properties such as wear resistance, hardness, electrical properties, and thermal insulating properties. The only limitation of the protective coating is its service behavior. However, the two basic requirements are (i) it must be chemically inert to the environment in the service conditions of temperature and pressure and (ii) it must prevent the penetration of environment to the base material. The coatings are again can be of different types such as metallic coatings, inorganic coatings, and organic coatings.

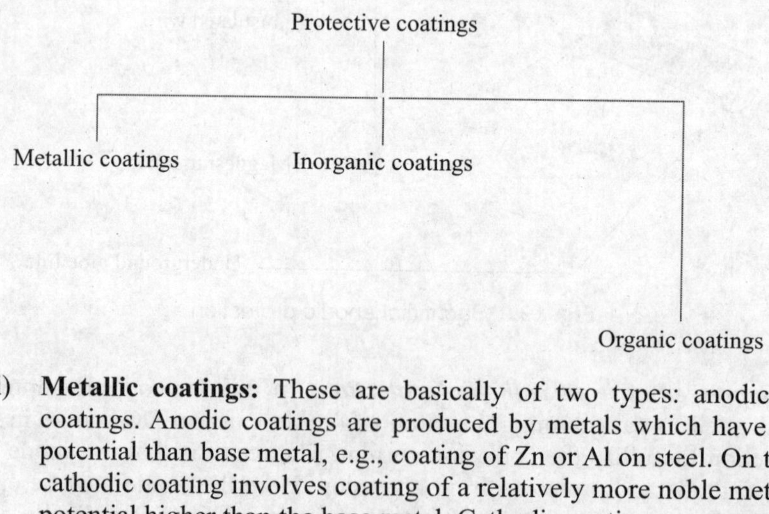

(i) **Metallic coatings:** These are basically of two types: anodic and cathodic coatings. Anodic coatings are produced by metals which have less electrode potential than base metal, e.g., coating of Zn or Al on steel. On the other hand, cathodic coating involves coating of a relatively more noble metal, i.e., having potential higher than the base metal. Cathodic coatings are more effective than anodic coatings only when they are continuous and free from pores and breaks. Evan a very small pit leads to intense localized corrosion. Coating of tin on iron is an example of cathodic coating. Metallic coating is applied by hot dipping. Let us discuss two widely used hot dipping methods.

(a) ***Galvanising:*** It is a process in which a thin coat of zinc is applied on an article of iron or steel. In the process, articles such as pipe and wire are first cleaned by dipping in dilute sulphuric acid solution at ~90°C for 15–20 min. The article is then washed, dried, and dipped in a bath of molten zinc maintained at ~430°C. The surface of the bath is kept covered with a flux of ammonium chloride to prevent formation of oxide. The article is then allowed to pass through a pair of hot rollers to remove any excess zinc and produce a thin film of uniform thickness. Finally, the article is subjected to annealing at ~650°C and then cooling slowly. The setup for the complete process is shown in Fig. 19.11.

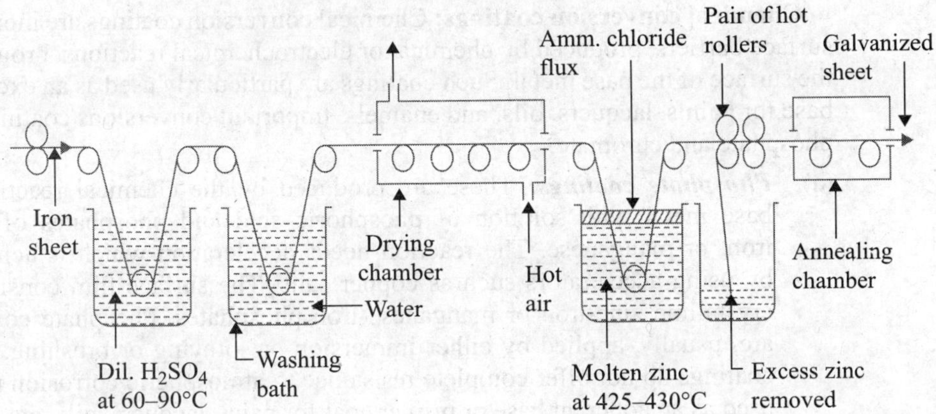

Fig. 19.11 Galvanizing

(b) ***Tinning:*** It is a process of coating tin on article of iron, steel, copper, or brass. The first step is same as that of galvanizing. The cleaned article is allowed to pass through a bath of zinc chloride flux followed by a bath of molten tin. Here flux helps in the adhering of molten tin on the article. The coated article is then passed through palm oil bath to prevent oxidation. The article is then allowed to pass through a pair of hot rollers to remove any excess tin and produce a thin film of uniform thickness. The setup for the complete process is shown in Fig. 19.12.

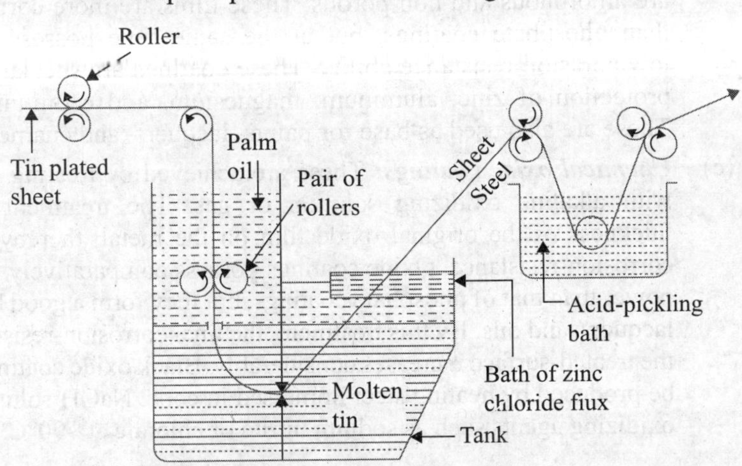

Fig. 19.12 Types of wet corrosion

Note:

Galvanized articles cannot be utilized for preparation and storing of foodstuffs, particularly acidic ones as zinc dissolves in acidic medium to form toxic compounds. In contrast, tin is non-toxic and therefore tinned copper sheets are used to make cooking utensils, manufacturing containers for storing and packing of foodstuffs.

(ii) **Inorganic coatings:** These are non-metallic protective coatings which include chemical conversion coatings, anodized oxide coatings, and vitreous enamel coatings. Let us discuss them in details.

Chemical conversion coatings: Chemical conversion coatings are inorganic surface barriers, produced by chemical or electrochemical reactions, brought at the surface of the base metal. Such coatings are particularly used as an excellent base for paints, lacquers, oils, and enamels. Important conversions coatings are phosphate and chromate.

(a) ***Phosphate coatings:*** These are produced by the chemical reaction of base metal with solution of phosphoric acid and phosphates of zinc, iron, or manganese. The reaction needs acceleration which is achieved by using accelerators such as copper salts. The surface film consists of crystalline zinc-iron or manganese-iron phosphates. Phosphate coatings are, usually, applied by either immersion or spraying or brushing. Such coatings do not offer complete resistance to atmospheric corrosion rather used as an adherent base or primer coat for paint, lacquers, oils, etc. Such coatings are applied frequently to iron, steel, and zinc, and sometimes to aluminum, cadmium, and tin. Phosphate coatings are, usually, grey in color. It is possible to turn them black by using a dye (bonderizing), if it is not intended to paint the phosphate-coated parts afterward. Such dyeing of the phosphate film is, usually, followed by oiling (packerizing).

(b) ***Chromate coatings:*** These are produced by immersion of the metal in a bath of acidified (dil. H_2SO_4) potassium dichromate. At some critical pH, basic chromium chromate ($Cr_2O_3 \cdot CrO_3 \cdot x\,H_2O$), a mixture of trivalent and hexavalent chromium, gets coated on the metal surface. Chromate films are amorphous and non-porous. These films are more corrosion resistant than phosphate coatings, but at the same time possess comparatively low abrasion-resistance ability. These coatings are specially used for the protection of zinc, aluminum, magnesium, and cadmium-plated parts. These are also used as base for paints, lacquers, and enamels.

(c) ***Chemical oxide coatings:*** These are achieved by treating the base metal with alkaline oxidizing solution or gas. The treatment increases the thickness of the original oxide film on the metal, thereby increasing its corrosion-resistance. Oxide coatings possess comparatively less absorptive power than that of phosphate coatings, but they form a good base for paints, lacquers, and oils. By this treatment, the final corrosion-resistance ability of the treated-surface increases considerably. Black oxide coatings on steel can be produced by heating steel immersed in conc. NaOH solution containing oxidizing agents such as sodium nitrite or chlorate at ~90°C.

Anodized oxide coatings: These are generally produced on non-ferrous metals such as Al, Zn, Mg and their alloys by anodic oxidation process in which the base metal is made anode. It is carried out by passing a direct electric current through a bath in which the metal or alloy is suspended from anode. Anodized oxide coatings are somewhat thicker than the natural oxide films and thereby possess improved resistance to corrosion as well as mechanical injury. For example, anodizing on aluminum is achieved by electrolysis in a suitable acid electrolyte such as sulfuric, chromic, oxalic, or phosphoric acid) at ~35 to 40°C and moderate current densities. Aluminum is made anode, while a plate of lead or stainless steel is made cathode. During electrolysis, oxygen liberated at anode combines with the metal forming the oxide film, thus thickening the natural oxide film. The outer part of the oxide film formed is very porous and considerably softer than the layer that remains adhered to the surface of metal. The sealing of pores can be done by exposing film to boiling water. This treatment changes porous aluminum oxide at the surface of coating into its monohydrate ($Al_2O_3 \cdot H_2O$), which occupies more volume, thereby the pores are sealed. Alternatively, sealing can be done by immersion of the film in boiling dilute sodium dichromate solution.

These coatings can be colored with organic dyes and inorganic pigments to provide aesthetic appeal. For the purpose, anodizing is done at higher temperature and in higher acid concentrations so as to provide a porous coating. Subsequently, the article is immersed in a dye solution or precipitating an inorganic pigment in the film before the sealing operation.

Vitreous or porcelain enamel coating: These coatings are generally applied on ferrous materials such as cast iron and steel. The vitreous material known as "frit" is prepared by fusing together refractory acidic substances such as quartz and feldspar with basic fluxes such as borax, fluorspar, soda ash, cryolite, and litharge in proper proportions. Application on metal can be done either by dry or wet processes.

In the wet process, the frit in smelted in a furnace at ~1400°C. The homogeneous melt so obtained is then quenched in cold water to friable pieces of frit. The frit is then ground with water and other additives such as coloring agents, opacifiers, and floating agents to get the slip. The cleaned metal is then dipped into the suspension of slip followed by air drying. However, in the dry process, the material is fired in a muffle furnace at ~500–650°C and the dry frit and additives are dusted on the red hot object. The material is then reheated in order to fuse the glass constituents.

These coatings can withstand high temperatures up to 1000°C and are resistant to acids, alkalies, and other corrosive agents with exception of hydrofluoric acid and conc. alkalies.

(iii) **Organic coatings:** Organic coatings are inert organic barriers which include paints, varnishes, lacquers, and enamels. These are used on metals or alloys for protection of corrosion and decoration. The protective value of such a coating depends on its chemical inertness to the corrosive environmental components, impermeability to water, salts, and gases, its surface adhesion property, as well as on its proper application method.

Paints

Paint is a mechanical dispersion of one or more pigments in a vehicle which is a liquid, consisting of non-volatile, film-forming material known as drying oil and a highly volatile solvent known as thinner. Upon application of paint on a metal or alloy surface, the thinner evaporates, while the drying oil slowly oxidizes forming a dry pigmented film. A good paint possesses the following characteristics:

1. It should spread easily over the protected surface and possess high covering power.
2. It should form a quite tough, uniform, adherent, and impervious film.
3. The film should not get cracked on drying.
4. It should protect the painted surface from corrosion effects of environment.
5. Its film should be glossy (i.e., having shine or luster).
6. It should have the required consistency so that it can be easily applied with brush or spraying device to yield a smooth and uniform surface.
7. It should possess high adhesion capacity to the material over which it is intended to be used.

Constituents of Paints

The important constituents of paints are pigment, vehicle or medium, thinner, driers, fillers, plasticizers, and sometimes anti-skinning agents. Let us discuss them individually.

1. **Pigment**: It is an essential constituent of paint. Its functions are of several fold, viz., to provide strength, capacity, and desired color to paint, to give aesthetic appeal, to give protection to the paint film by reflecting UV light, to provide resistance to paint film against abrasion or wear, and to increase weather-resistance of the film. A good pigment should be opaque, chemically inert, non-toxic, and freely miscible with film-forming constituent. The pigments can be white or colored. White lead, zinc oxide, lithophone (~71% $BaSO_4$ + 28% ZnS + <1% ZnO), etc., are white pigments, whereas Prussian blue, ultramarine blue, red lead, ferric oxide, basic lead chromate, chromium oxide, litharge, etc., are colored pigments. The pigments used in paints can be grouped into the following categories:

   (i) **Natural/mineral pigment**: Examples: clay, mica, talc, chalk, barites, iron ores, etc.

   (ii) **Synthetic pigments:** Examples: white lead, zinc oxide, lithophone, TiO_2, $BaSO_4$, and several other inorganic and organic coloring substances.

Note:

Color	Example of pigment
Blue	Prussian blue, ultramarine blue
Red	Red lead, ferric oxide, basic lead chromate
Black	Graphite, carbon black, lamp black
Green	Chromium oxide
Brown	Burnt sienna, burnt umber
Yellow	Chrome yellow, litharage

2. **Vehicle or drying oil:** It is the film-forming constituent of the paint. It is usually a drying oil or a mixture of drying and semi-drying oils. These are nothing but glyceryl esters of high-molecular-weight fatty acids such as oleic acid ($C_{17}H_{33}COOH$), linoleic acid ($C_{17}H_{31}COOH$), linolenic acid ($C_{17}H_{29}COOH$), eleostearic acid ($C_{17}H_{29}COOH$), etc. The primary functions of the drying oil are to provide the medium, toughness, adhesion, elasticity, and hydrophobic characteristics. Upon application of the paint, fatty acid component of vehicle absorb oxygen from air to undergo a series of reactions of oxidation and polymerization to form the highly cross-linked structured macromolecular film.

Note:

1. **Drying oils**: These are oils containing high percentage of conjugated fatty acid esters of glycerol. Such oils quickly dry up to form the film, e.g., linseed oil, perilla oil, dehydrated castor oil, etc.
2. **Semi-drying oils**: These are oils containing low percentage of conjugated fatty acid esters of glycerol. They dry very slowly in air and therefore cannot be used directly in paints as such. However, they are used as blending agent with other drying oils, to get desired film upon drying, e.g., soyabean oil, safflower oil, rosin oil, fish oil, etc.

3. **Thinner:** It is used to reduce the viscosity of the paint to suitable consistency, so that it can be easily applied. It is a volatile substance which evaporates easily after application of the paint. Common thinners used are turpentine, petroleum spirits, benzene, naphtha, toluol, xylol, kerosene, methylated naphthalene, etc. The primary functions are to dissolve film-forming material and other desirable additives in the vehicle, increase the penetration power of the vehicle, increase the elasticity of the paint film, and to help in the drying of the paint film.
4. **Drier**: It is an oxygen-carrier catalyst which accelerates the drying of the oil film through oxidation, polymerization, and condensation. The most effective driers are resinates, borates, linoleates, tungstates, and naphthenates of heavy metals such as Co, Mn, Pb, and Zn. The fact to be noted is that too much of a drier tends to produce hard and brittle films.
5. **Extender or filler:** It is an inert material of low refractive index. Important extenders used are barytes, talc, asbestos, ground silica, gypsum, ground mica, slate powder, china clay, $CaCO_3$, magnesium silicate, diatomite clay, calcium sulphate, etc. The main functions are to reduce the cost, increase durability of the paint, help in reducing the cracking of paint film, help in filling voids in film, increase random arrangement of pigment particles, and to act as carriers for the pigment color.
6. **Plasticizers:** Plasticizer is used in the paint to provide elasticity to the film so as to minimize its cracking. Some commonly used plasticizers are tricresyl phosphate, triphenyl phosphate, tributyl phthalate, diamyl phthalate, dibutyl tartarate, etc.
7. **Anti-skinning agent:** It is added to some paints with the objective of preventing gelling and skinning of the paint film, e.g., polyhydroxy phenols.

Formulation of Paints

Manufacture of paints depends upon proper composition of paint to meet the specific requirements which are met by proper choice of pigments, vehicles, and extenders by the paint formulator. The most important concept for a modern paint formulator is pigment volume concentration (PVC), which is the concentration by volume of the pigments expressed as a percentage of the total volume of non-volatile constituents of the paint. As non-volatile volume in paint is the sum of the volumes of pigment and non-volatile vehicle, PVC can be expressed as

$$\text{PVC} = \frac{\text{Volume of pigment in paint}}{\text{Total volume of non-volatile constituents of the paint}}$$

$$= \frac{\text{Volume of pigment in paint}}{\text{Volume of [pigment + non-volatile constituents of the paint]}}$$

Importance of PVC

PVC largely controls factors such as gloss, washability, durability, adhesion, consistency, etc.

1. With the decrease in PVC, gloss tends to increase until the paint becomes flat.
2. With the increase in PVC, the relative quantity of binder decreases; therefore, the resulting film loses cohesion and, hence, durability. Thus, with the increase in PVC, the adhesion and durability of paint-film decreases.
3. Increase in PVC, decreases the washability of paint-film.
4. Extenders, when added to paint, amounts to increase in PVC, and thus, decrease the gloss, washability, durability, and adhesion. So, in case the pigment is costly and its covering power is high, a portion of the pigment may economically be replaced by extenders, without sacrificing the covering power of pigment.
5. Opacity of white paint is created by the difference in the refractive indices of the pigment and vehicle. It is also influenced by the size of the dispersed pigment particles and PVC.

Varnishes

Varnish is a homogeneous dispersion of natural or synthetic resin in oil or spirit. It is used as a protective coating on suitable surfaces. It dries by evaporation, oxidation, and polymerization of its constituents, leaving behind a hard, transparent, glossy, lustrous, and durable film. There are two main types of varnishes:

1. **Oil varnish/oleo-resinous varnish:** It is a homogeneous solution of one or more natural or synthetic resins in a drying oil and a volatile solvent. Oil reduces the natural tendency of brittleness of the pure resin film. Such a varnish dries up by the evaporation of the volatile solvent, followed by oxidation and polymerization of the drying oil. Thus, it takes relatively longer period (~24 h) for drying, but the film produced is hard, quite lustrous, and durable. For example, copal varnish (prepared by dissolving copal in linseed oil and mixing a quantity of turpentine).
2. **Spirit varnish:** It consists of a resin dissolved in a completely volatile solvent. Such a varnish dries rapidly by the evaporation of the solvent. Spirit varnish dries quite rapidly and leaves behind a brittle film, which has a tendency to crack or peel off. Such varnishes are used, usually, for polishing wooden furniture. For example, shellac is a spirit varnish (a solution of shellac in alcohol).

Constituents of a Varnish

The important constituents of a varnish are resin, drying oil, thinner, driers, and anti-skinning agents.

1. **Resin**: It provides elasticity, good adhesion, color, and glossiness to the varnish film. It also provides resistance to weathering, durability, resistance to chemical action, and water-proofness. Both natural resins such as shellac, kauri, rosin, copal, etc., and synthetic resins such as phenol-formaldehyde, urea-formaldehyde, etc., are commonly used.
2. **Drying oils**: These are film-forming materials which dry by oxidation and polymerization. Principal oils used are linseed oil, tung oil, dehydrated castor oil, soyabean oil, perilla oil, fish oil, etc.
3. **Thinners**: Thinners are used to reduce viscosity of varnish in addition to helping in the drying process. The commonly used thinners are turpentine, petroleum spirits, kerosene, xylol, tolyl, butyl and ethyl alcohols, amyl acetate, acetone, etc.
4. **Driers**: These are added to enhance the drying rate of oil constituents. The commonly used driers are linoleates, napthenates, resonates of Pb, Co, and Mn.
5. **Anti-skinning agent**: These are used to prevent the peeling off of the varnish film, e.g., tert-amyl phenol.

Note:

Characteristics of a good varnish: A good varnish should possess the following characteristics:

1. It should produce glossy and shining film on drying.
2. It should be soft so that can adapt itself to the contraction and expansion of coated-material such as wood due to temperature variations
3. It should dry quickly to yield elastic film so that it does not crack or peel off on drying.
4. It should produce a hard, tough, durable, and resistant to wear and tear protective film.
5. It should yield aesthetical appealing film which does not change color on exposure to atmospheric weather.

Uses of Varnish

1. It is used as a brightening coat to painted surface. Thus, a surface is first coated with paint and over it is then applied a coat of varnish, which eliminates the effect of atmospheric oxygen, thereby preventing corrosion.
2. For improving the appearance of wooden furniture by intensifying the ornamental grains of wood surfaces.

Lacquers

A lacquer is a colloidal dispersion of solution of a cellulose derivative, resin, and plasticizer in solvent and diluents. Lacquer dries in air principally by evaporation of solvents yielding a transparent, hard, and water-proof film.

Constituents of Lacquers

1. **Cellulose derivatives**: These provide hardness, water proofness, and durability to the film, e.g., cellulose nitrate, cellulose acetate, cellulose acetobutyrate, etc.

2. **Resins**: These are used to enhance the thickness of the film with retention of original gloss. Resins also enhance the adhesion and water resistance, e.g., phenol-formaldehyde, alkyd, copal, etc.
3. **Plasticizers**: The function is to generate a smooth and flexible film with improved adherence, e.g., tricresyl phosphate, dibutyl phthalate, etc.
4. **Solvents**: These are used to dissolve the film-forming constituents such as cellulose derivatives and resins, e.g., ethyl acetate, butyl acetate, ethyl lactate, methyl ethyl ketone, etc.
5. **Diluents**: The function of diluents is to decrease viscosity or consistency of the medium. Diluents also reduce the cost, e.g., toluol, benzol, solvent naphtha, petroleum spirit, etc.

Uses of Lacquers

1. For paintings of wood work and furniture.
2. For giving a finishing coat to automobile bodies, due to their resistance to abrasion, cracking, chalking, etc.
3. In coating cotton fabrics used in preparing artificial leathers, etc.

Enamels

Enamel is a pigmented-varnish, i.e., an intimate dispersion of pigments in a varnish. Upon drying, enamels give lustrous, hard, and glossy finish. The properties of enamel vary widely, depending on the nature of the vehicle and resin. The drying of enamel may occur at room temperature by oxidation and/or polymerization or may be brought about at elevated temperatures either in the presence or absence of oxygen. The constituents of enamels are pigments, vehicle, driers, and thinner. The functions as well as examples of individual components are already discussed above.

Environment

Environment can be modified either by the removal of the corrosive components or by addition of some foreign reagents known as inhibitors to neutralize the effect of the corrosive components.

1. **Removal of corrosive components:** Let us look into some common methods of removal of corrosive components from environment. Oxygen and other dissolved corrosive gases can be removed from water by agitation with adjustment of temperature. The process is known as de-aeration. Moisture can be removed from atmosphere by using dehydrating agents such as alumina and silica gel. Acids present can be neutralized with lime. Salts can be removed by the use of ion-exchange resin.
2. **Addition of inhibitor:** Inhibitor is a substance which when added to the corrosive environment reduces the rate of corrosion. These are of three types, viz., anodic, cathodic, and vapor-phase inhibitors.
   (i) ***Anodic inhibitors*:** Chromates and phosphates can be added to form stable compounds with the metal ions formed at anode. The stable salts so formed stick to the anode surface making it passive. Such inhibitors are known as anodic inhibitor.

Note

There exist critical concentrations above which anodic inhibitors inhibit corrosion. If insufficient concentration is used, then all the anodic areas may not be covered and this leads to localized and intense corrosion.

(ii) ***Cathodic inhibitors***: The metals which form amphoteric oxides can be added at cathode to form stable hydroxides which precipitate out. Such inhibitors are known as cathodic inhibitor.

(iii) ***Vapor-phase inhibitors***: These are organic compounds which readily sublime and form a protective layer on the surface of metal, e.g., dicyclohexylammonium nitrite. These are used for protection of metallic parts in small and closed containers such as compressors and condensers.

QUESTIONS

1. What is dry corrosion?
2. Describe caustic embrittlement.
3. What is differential aeration corrosion?
4. Which gases in the atmosphere accelerate the rusting of iron?
5. Can Mg be used as a sacrificial anode?
6. What is microbial corrosion?
7. Discuss the mechanism of microbial corrosion.
8. What do you mean by passivity?
9. Iron corrodes faster than aluminum even though iron is placed below aluminum in the electrochemical series. Explain.
10. Describe stress corrosion with an example.
11. Explain water-line corrosion.
12. Explain how cathodic protection of iron is different from its galvanization.
13. Why galvanized utensils are not used in storing foodstuffs?
14. What are enamels? Explain with examples.
15. What is vehicle or drying oil? Explain with examples.
16. What is Galvanic series? In which way is it different from electrochemical series?
17. What is impressed current cathodic protection?
18. What do you mean by sacrificial anodic protection? Explain with a suitable example.
19. Explain cathodic and anodic inhibitors with suitable examples.
20. What is meant by wet corrosion?
21. Why coating of zinc on iron is called sacrificial anode?
22. Why anodic inhibitors are always not suitable?
23. What are the constituents of lacquers?
24. What are the characteristic of good varnishes?

25. Explain the mechanism of pitting corrosion with a suitable illustration.
26. What is the function of pigments in paints?
27. What is the function of thinner in paints?
28. What is chemical conversion coating? Explain phosphate coating in details.
29. Explain anodized oxide coatings.
30. What is varnish? Explain different types of varnishes with suitable examples.

CHAPTER

20 Catalysis

Chapter Outline

- Catalyst
- Terminologies
- Catalysis
- Theories of Catalysis
- Enzyme Catalysis

In 1836, Berzelius realized that there are substances which can increase the rate of a reaction without being consumed in the process. According to him, this was due to loosening of bonds which holds the atoms together. He coined the term catalyst for those substances and called this phenomenon as catalysis (Greek "Kata"—wholly, "lyein"—to loosen).

Catalyst

Catalyst refers to a substance that is capable of altering the rate of a reaction and is recovered unchanged with respect to composition and amount at the end of the reaction.

Characteristics

1. A catalyst remains unchanged with respect to composition and amount (mass) at the end of the reaction. However, there might be a change in physical state. For example, the granular MnO_2 which is used as a catalyst during the decomposition of $KClO_3$ is recovered as powdered MnO_2 at the end of the reaction.
2. A catalyst is very selective in its action.
3. A small amount of catalyst is enough to catalyze almost an unlimited reaction.
4. A catalyst does not initiate a reaction rather it only alters the rate of a feasible reaction.
5. Every catalyst has its own optimum temperature at which it shows maximum efficiency.
6. A catalyst does not change the position of equilibrium in a reversible reaction as it increases the rate of both forward and reverse reactions in the same proportion. Thus, the approach of equilibrium is quickened.
7. The activity of a catalyst can be changed by using small amount of foreign substance, i.e., promoter or poison in addition.

Terminologies

Promoter

A promoter is an additional substance used along with the catalyst to increase the efficiency and life span of a catalyst. It cannot catalyze a process by itself. For example,

1. Mo, in Haber's process for manufacture of ammonia is an example of promoter.

   $$N_2 + 3H_2 \xrightarrow{Fe\text{–}Mo} 2NH_3$$

2. Cr_2O_3 in the manufacture of CH_3OH

   $$CO + 2H_2O \xrightarrow{Zn\text{–}Cr_2O_3} CH_3OH$$

Poison

A poison is an additional substance used along with the catalyst that decreases its efficiency. For example,

1. Bromine vapor poisons Ni catalyst during hydrogenation of oil.
2. Lead acetate poisons Pd catalyst during preparation of alkene from alkyne.
3. As_2O_3 poisons Pt catalyst in contact during the process for manufacture of sulfuric acid.

   $$2SO_2 + O_2 \xrightarrow{Pt\text{–}As_2O_3} 2SO_3$$

4. Iron catalyst in Haber's process of manufacture of ammonia can be poisoned by hydrogen sulphide.

   $$N_2 + 3H_2 \xrightarrow{Fe\text{–}H_2S} 2NH_3$$

Negative Catalyst or Retarder

The catalyst that retards the rate of a reaction is referred to as negative catalyst. For examlple,

1. Glycerol can be used to control the rate of decomposition of H_2O_2,

   $$H_2O_2 \xrightarrow{Glycerol} H_2O + ½\, O_2$$

2. Ethyl alcohol can be used to control the rate of decomposition of $CHCl_3$,

   $$CHCl_3 \xrightarrow{2\%\ alcohol,\ air} COCl_2 + Cl_2$$

Self-Catalyst

Sometimes one of the reactants or products formed catalyzes the processes and such a process is known as self-catalysis. The corresponding substance is known as self-catalyst. For example,

1. During acid hydrolysis of ester, the acid formed in the processes operates as self-catalyst.

   $$CH_3COOC_2H_5 + H_2O \xrightarrow{H_2SO_4} CH_3COOH + C_2H_5OH$$

   (CH_3COOH →) Catalyst

   "As" acts as a self-catalyst during decomposition of arsine.

   $$2AsH_3 \longrightarrow 2As + 3H_2$$

   ($2As$ →) Catalyst

2. Mn^{2+} ions catalyze the reaction between $KMnO_4$ and oxalic acid.

$$2MnO_4^- + 5C_2O_4^{2-} + 16H^+ \longrightarrow \underbrace{2\,Mn^{2+}}_{\text{Catalyst}} + 10\,CO_2 + 8\,H_2O$$

Catalysis

Catalysis is the phenomenon by virtue of which a catalyst is able to alter the rate of a reaction.

Types of Catalysis

Homogeneous catalysis

Here, a catalyst remains in the same phase as that of the reactants and is uniformly distributed throughout. For example,

$$2SO_{2(g)} + O_{2(g)} \xrightarrow{NO_{(g)}} 2SO_{3(g)}$$

$$CH_3CHO_{(g)} \xrightarrow{I_{2(g)}} CH_{4(g)} + CO_{(g)}$$

$$C_{12}H_{22}O_{11(Solution)} + H_2O_{(l)} \xrightarrow{H_2SO_{4(l)}} C_6H_{12}O_{6\,(Solution)} + C_6H_{12}O_{6\,(Solution)}$$

Heterogeneous catalysis

Here, a catalyst remains in different phase than that of the reactants. It is also known as contact catalysis as the reaction occurs by contact of reactants with the catalyst surface. For example,

$$2SO_{2(g)} + O_{2(g)} \xrightarrow{Pt} 2SO_{3(g)}$$

$$N_{2(g)} + 3H_{2(g)} \xrightarrow{Fe} 2NH_{3\,(g)}$$

$$2\,H_2O_{2(l)} \xrightarrow{Fe} 2H_2O_{(l)} + O_{2(g)}$$

$$2KClO_{3(s)} \xrightarrow{MnO_{2(s)}} 2KCl_{(s)} + 3O_{2(g)}$$

Theories of Catalysis

This is the mechanism by virtue of which a catalyst operates. In general, a catalyst provides an alternate path with much less activation energy (Fig. 20.1). This path modulation in the presence of a catalyst can be discussed with respect to two theories.

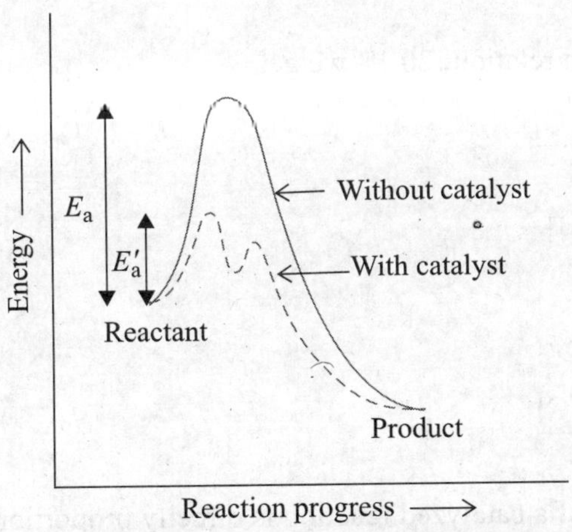

Fig. 20.1 Lowering of activation energy in the presence of a catalyst

Intermediate Compound Formation Theory

This theory is successful in explaining homogeneous catalysis. According to this theory, the complete process occurs via the following steps:

Step I: The catalyst reacts with the prime reactant to form an intermediate compound.

Step II: The intermediate compound subsequently reacts with the other reactant to yield the products. This step is the slowest one and regarded as the rate determining step.

Step III: The catalyst released in step II participates further in the reaction as per steps I and II.

Mathematical treatment

Let us consider a hypothetical process, $A + B \xrightarrow{\text{Catalyst (C)}} AB$

With respect to the theory, the different steps are

$$A + C \underset{k_2}{\overset{k_1}{\rightleftharpoons}} AC$$

Intermediate compound

$$AC + B \xrightarrow{k_3} AB + C \text{ (slow)}$$

Released

$$\text{Rate} = k_3 [AC] [B] \qquad ...[20.1]$$

At steady state, $\dfrac{d[AC]}{dt} = 0$

or $k_1 [A] [C] - k_2 [AC] - k_3 [AC] [B] = 0$

or $[AC] \{k_2 + k_3 [B]\} = k_1 [A] [C]$

or $$[AC] = \frac{k_1[A][C]}{k_1 + k_3[B]} \qquad ...[20.2]$$

Substituting [AC] in relation [20.1], we get

$$\text{Rate} = \frac{k_3\, k_1[A][B][C]}{k_2 + k_3[B]} \qquad ...[20.3]$$

Case I: If $k_2 \ll k_3$ [B],

$$\text{Rate} = k_1 [A] [C] \qquad ...[20.4]$$

Case II: If k_3 [B] $\ll k_2$,

$$\text{Rate} = \frac{k_3\, k_1[A][B][C]}{k_2} \qquad ...[20.5]$$

Therefore, the rate of a catalyzed reaction is directly proportional to the concentration of a catalyst, though it is neither produced nor consumed in the process.

Illustration

Let us illustrate this theory with a specific example of oxidation of sulfur dioxide.

$$2SO_2 + O_2 \longrightarrow 2SO_3$$

Steps

$$NO + O_2 \rightleftharpoons NO_2 \text{ (Intermediate compound)}$$

$$SO_2 + NO_2 \longrightarrow SO_3 + NO$$

Limitations

The limitations of the theory are as follows:

1. It cannot be applied in heterogeneous catalysis.
2. It fails to explain the increase or the decrease of efficiency of a catalyst in the presence of a foreign substance.
3. It fails to account for the negative catalysis.

Adsorption Theory

This theory is successful in explaining heterogeneous catalysis. The process takes place in the following steps:

Step I: As the reacting molecules are allowed to react in the presence of a catalyst, they get diffused on the surface of the catalyst.

Step II: The reactant molecules get adsorbed on the surface of a catalyst. This is through the development of van der Waals forces with the active centers or free valencies present on the surface of a catalyst.

Step III: The adsorbed reactant molecules then get transferred into an energy-rich activated complex.

Step IV: The activated complex decomposes to yield the product which diffuses away from the catalyst.

The complete process is explained schematically in Fig. 20.2.

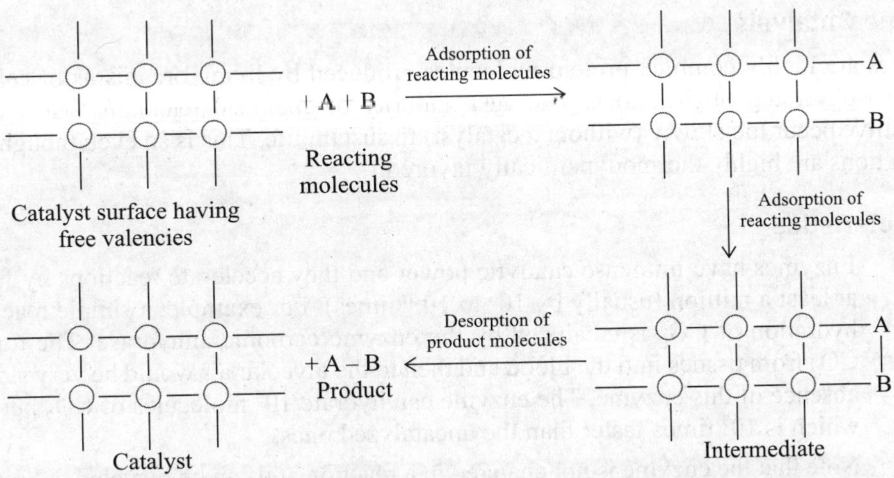

Fig. 20.2 Schematic presentation of different steps in adsorption theory

Mathematical treatment

$$\text{Rate} = \frac{dx}{dt} \propto \text{fraction of the surface of catalyst which is occupied } (\Theta)$$

or $$\frac{dx}{dt} = Z\Theta$$

or $$\frac{dx}{dt} = Z \times \frac{k_1 P}{1 + k_1 P}$$

where k_1 is the coefficient of adsorption; $\Theta = k_1P/(1 + k_1P)$ is the result of Langmuir adsorption isotherm (for details refer to Chapter 8); and P is the pressure due to reactant molecules.

Where $$k_1 = \frac{k_a}{k_d}$$

Advantages

It successfully explains

1. **Efficiency of finely divided catalysts:** Smaller is the particle size more is the surface area which ultimately makes available relatively larger number of free valencies (active sites). Therefore, finely divided catalysts are more effective than lumps.
2. **Catalyst remains unchanged during a reaction and is effective in small quantities:** Adsorption and desorption at the surface of a catalyst take place alternately making the site utilized in one step to become free in the next step. Therefore, the catalyst remains unchanged and only a small amount is sufficient to catalyze the whole reaction.
3. **Catalytic poisoning:** Poison gets adsorbed on the catalytic surface in preference to the reactants and renders the surface, i.e., the free valencies unavailable for further adsorption of reactants.
4. **Promoter action:** Promoter occupies the interstitial positions increasing the lattice spacing. This results in cracks and peaks on catalytic surface which leads to an increase in free valencies. Thus, an enhancement can be seen in the catalytic action.

Enzyme Catalysis

Enzymes are highly complex protein molecules produced by living organisms or cells which catalyzes physiological reactions. The vast majority of chemical reactions that keep living things alive occur too slowly (without a catalyst) to sustain life. This is so even though some of the reactions are highly thermodynamically favored.

Characteristics

1. Enzymes have immense catalytic power and they accelerate reactions by factors of at least a million (usually by 10^6 to 10^{20} times). For example, a simple reaction-like hydration of CO_2 is catalyzed by the enzyme carbonic anhydrase. The transfer of CO_2 from tissues into the blood and then to the alveolar air would be very slow in the absence of this enzyme. The enzyme can hydrate 10^5 molecules of CO_2 per second, which is 10^7 times faster than the uncatalyzed ones.
2. Note that the enzyme is not changed in a reaction and can be recycled to break down additional substrate molecules.

3. Each enzyme is specific for a particular reaction because its amino acid sequence is unique and causes it to have a unique three-dimensional structure.
4. The active site is the portion of the enzyme that interacts with the substrate, so that any substance that blocks or changes the shape of the active site affects the activity of the enzyme.

Examples of Common Enzymes

Amylase: degrades starches and sugars present in potatoes, fruits, vegetables; *lactase*: degrades lactose present in milk sugars; *diastase*: acts on vegetable starch; *sucrose*: breaks down sugars such as sucrose; *maltase*: breaks down disaccharides to monosaccharides; *protease*: cleaves proteins to peptides; *trypsin*: produced in pancreas and helps in protein degradation; *lipase*: degrades fats in dairy products, nuts, oils, and meat.

Classification of Enzymes

Enzymes can be grouped into different categories on the basis of their action.

1. **Oxidoreductases:** Catalyze oxidation and reduction of substrate, i.e., helps in transfer of hydrogen, oxygen or electron from one substrate to another.
2. **Transferases:** Involve catalytic transfer of functional group from one substrate to another.
3. **Hydrolases:** Involve hydrolysis of chemical bond with hydrolysis of water.
4. **Lyases:** Involve breakdown of chemical bond without hydrolysis of water.
5. **Isomerases:** Involve interchange of substrates based on isomerism.
6. **Ligases:** Help in sealing gaps in nucleotides.

Factors Affecting Enzyme Action

1. **Salt concentration:** If the salt concentration is very low, the charged amino acid side chains of the enzyme molecules attract each other which results in denaturation of enzyme and form an inactive precipitate. On the other hand, if the salt concentration is very high, normal interaction of charged groups will be blocked, new interactions will occur, and again the enzyme will precipitate. An intermediate salt concentration such as that of human blood (0.9%) or cytoplasm is the optimum for many enzymes.
2. **pH:** Amino acid side chains contain groups such as –COOR and $–NH_2$ that readily gain or lose H^+ ions. As the pH is lowered an enzyme will tend to gain H^+ ions, and eventually enough side chains will be affected so that the enzyme's shape is disrupted. Similarly, as the pH is raised, the enzyme will lose H^+ ions and eventually lose its active shape. Many enzymes perform up to their optimum in the neutral pH range and are denatured at either an extremely high or low pH with a few exceptions such as pepsin, which acts in the human stomach where the pH is very low to have optimum performance.
3. **Temperature:** Generally, enzyme reactions tend to go faster with increasing temperature. However, if the temperature of an enzyme-catalyzed reaction is raised still further, an optimum temperature is reached above which kinetic energy of the enzyme and water molecules are so great that the conformation of the enzyme molecules is disrupted. The positive effect of speeding up the reaction is now more than offset by the negative effect of changing the conformation of more and more enzyme molecules. Many proteins are denatured at temperatures around 40–50°C, while some are still active at 70–80°C, and a few even withstand boiling.

4. **Activators and inhibitors:** Many molecules other than the substrate may interact with an enzyme to increase the rate of the reaction (an activator) or to decrease the rate of the reaction (an inhibitor). These molecules can regulate the enzyme action. Any substance that tends to unfold the enzyme, such as an organic solvent or detergent, will act as an inhibitor. Some inhibitors act by reducing the —S—S— bridges that stabilize the enzyme's structure. Many inhibitors act by reacting with side chains in or near the active site to change its shape or block it. Many well-known poisons such as potassium cyanide and curare are enzyme inhibitors that interfere with the active site of critical enzymes.

Enzyme Action

1. Enzymes are very specific in their action, and it was suggested by the organic chemist Emil Fisher in 1894 that this was because both the enzyme and the substrate possess specific complementary geometric shapes that fit exactly into one another. This is often referred to as "*the lock and key*" model. However, while this model explains enzyme specificity, it fails to explain the stabilization of the transition state that enzymes achieve.
2. In 1958, Daniel Koshland suggested a modification to the lock and key model. Since enzymes are rather flexible structures, the active site is continually reshaped by interactions with the substrate as the substrate interacts with the enzyme. As a result, the substrate does not simply bind to a rigid active site in addition to the amino acid chains which make up the active site are molded into the precise positions that enable the enzyme to perform its catalytic function. In some cases, the substrate molecule also changes shape slightly as it enters the active site. The active site continues to change until the substrate is completely bound, at which point the final shape and charge is determined. This model is known as "*induced fit model*", which opposes the former Lock and Key model, that explained the formation of the E–S complex as a result of the binding of complementary geometrical rigid structures, as a lock and a key (see Fig. 20.3).

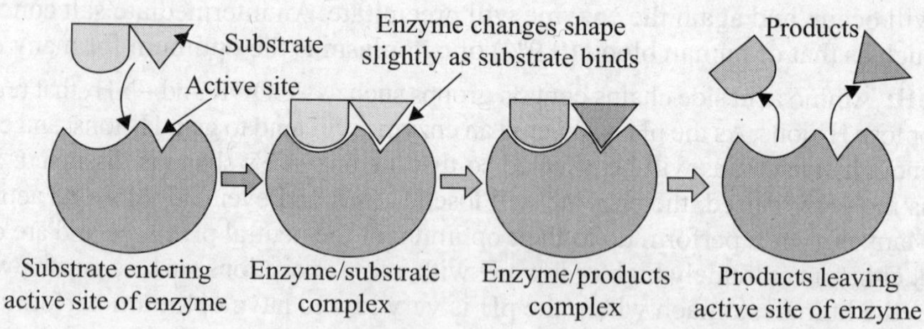

Fig. 20.3 Induced fit model of enzyme action

Kinetics of Enzyme Action (Michaelis and Menten Mechanism)

The Michaelis–Menten mechanism for the catalysis of biological chemical reactions is one of the most important chemical reaction mechanisms in biochemistry. On he basis of this mechanism, an enzyme-catalyzed reaction can be assumed to proceed through the following steps:

$$E + S \underset{k_{-1}}{\overset{k_1}{\rightleftharpoons}} ES$$

$$ES \xrightarrow{k_2} \text{Product (rate controlling factor)}$$

Applying steady-state approximation,

$$\frac{d[ES]}{dt} = 0$$

or $$k_1 [E] [S] - k_{-1} [ES] - k_2[ES] = 0$$

or $$[ES] (k_{-1} + k_2) = k_1 [E] [S]$$

or $$[ES] = \frac{k_1[E][S]}{k_{-1} + k_2}$$

or $$[ES] = \frac{[E][S]}{\dfrac{k_{-1} + k_2}{k_1}}$$

or $$[ES] = \frac{[E][S]}{K_M} \qquad ...[20.6]$$

where K_M is known as Michaelis constant.

Again,

$$[E] = [E_0] - [ES]$$

or $$[ES] = [E_0] - [E] \qquad ...[20.7]$$

where [E] is the concentration of free enzyme and $[E_0]$ is the total enzyme concentration.

Substituting [ES] in relation [20.6], we get

$$[E_0] - [E] = \frac{[E][S]}{K_M}$$

or $$[E_0] = [E]\left[1 + \frac{[S]}{K_M}\right]$$

or $$[E] = \frac{K_M[E_0]}{K_M + [S]} \qquad ...[20.8]$$

As the second step is the controlling step, the rate of the reaction

$$r = k_2 [ES]$$

$$= \frac{k_2}{K_M} [E] [S]$$

$$= \frac{k_2}{K_M} \times \frac{K_M[E_0][S]}{K_M + [S]}$$

$$= \frac{k_2[E_0][S]}{K_M + [S]} \qquad ...[20.9]$$

Under extreme conditions, the order with respect to substrate can be evaluated.

Case I: If $K_M \ll [S]$, then $K_M + [S] \cong [S]$

$$\text{Rate} = k_2\,[E_0] \qquad ...[20.10]$$

Thus, the order is zero with respect to the substrate.

Case II: If the substrate concentration $[S] \ll K_M$, then

$$\text{Rate} = \frac{k_2}{K_M}\,[E_0]\,[S]$$

Thus, the order is one with respect to the substrate.

Evaluation of Michaelis Constant

Let $[E_0] = [ES]$, then

$$\text{Rate} = r_{max} = k_2\,[ES]$$
$$= k_2\,[E_0]$$

Substituting [ES] in relation [20.7], we get

$$r = \frac{r_{max}[S]}{K_M + [S]}$$

or $$\frac{1}{r} = \frac{K_M + [S]}{r_{max}[S]}$$

or $$\frac{1}{r} = \frac{K_M}{r_{max}[S]} + \frac{1}{r_{max}} \qquad ...[20.11]$$

Now, K_M can be evaluated from the slope of the graph that has been plotted by taking $1/r$ as a function of $1/[S]$ (see Fig. 20.4).

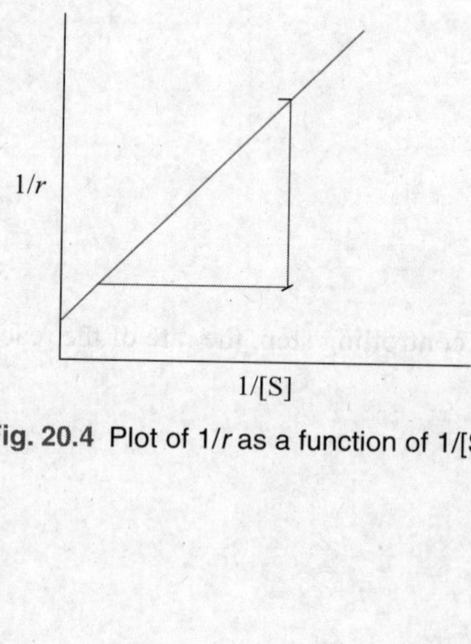

Fig. 20.4 Plot of $1/r$ as a function of $1/[S]$

$$\text{Slope} = \frac{K_M}{r_{max}}$$

$$\text{Intercept} = \frac{1}{r_{max}}$$

$$\text{Therefore, } K_M = \frac{\text{Slope}}{\text{Intercepet}}$$

Note:

Catalytic efficiency of enzymes

The catalytic efficiency, ε (epsilon), of an enzyme can be expressed as

$$\varepsilon = \frac{K_{cat}}{K_M} \qquad ...[20.12]$$

where K_{cat} is the catalytic constant or the turnover number is the number of catalytic cycles performed by the active site in a given interval divided by the duration of the interval. In terms of Michaelis–Menten mechanism, it is numerically equivalent to k_2, the rate constant of the reaction that forms product from enzyme–substrate complex. Now, substituting K_{cat} and K_M in relation,

$$\varepsilon = \frac{k_2}{\frac{k_{-1}+k_2}{k_1}}$$

$$= \frac{k_2 k_1}{k_{-1}+k_2} \qquad ...[20.13]$$

where $k_2 = \frac{r_{max}}{[E_0]}$ (from the relation).

QUESTIONS

1. What role does As_2O_3 play in the synthesis of H_2SO_4 by contact processes?
2. What do you mean by autocatalyst? Give an example of autocatalytic reaction.
3. What do you mean by homogeneous and heterogeneous catalysis? Explain with one example in each category.
4. What are the characteristics of a good catalyst?
5. Explain (i) active center and (ii) catalytic poison with respect to heterogeneous catalysis.
6. Explain with example the function of catalytic promoter.
7. Differentiate between catalytic poisoning and negative catalyst with example.
8. What is a promoter? Give an example.
9. Define autocatalyzed reaction with examples. Explain contact catalysis and active centers present in the catalytic surface.
10. What is the effect of temperature on enzyme action?
11. What is the effect of pH on enzyme action?
12. What is an enzyme? Provide examples of two enzymes along with their functions.
13. Why CO must be removed completely in Haber's process for manufacture of NH_3?
14. Why is it essential to remove arsenic in contact process for manufacture of H_2SO_4?
15. What are enzymes? The mechanism of an enzyme-catalyzed reaction is given as

$$E + S \underset{k_{-1}}{\overset{k_1}{\rightleftharpoons}} [ES] \xrightarrow{k_1} E + P$$

By applying steady-state approximation, prove that the rate of reaction will be equal to $\frac{k_2[E][S]}{K_M}$, where S is the substrate; E is the enzyme; ES is the enzyme–substrate complex; P is the product; and K_M is the Michaelis constant.

16. Give the kinetics of an enzyme-catalyzed reaction and explain the effect of pH on the reaction rate.
17. Explain intermediate compound formation theory.
18. Explain catalytic efficiency of enzymes.
19. Explain adsorption theory of catalytic action. How does this theory help in overcoming the limitations of intermediate compound formation theory?
20. Describe the factors which affect the enzyme action.
21. In which way is the induced fit model different from the lock and key model?
22. Show that the enzyme-catalyzed reaction follows zero-order kinetics with respect to substrate when $K_M \ll [S]$. Also discuss the graphical evaluation of Michaelis constant.

CHAPTER 21 Battery Technology

Chapter Outline

- Classifications
- Primary Cells
- Secondary Cells
- Fuel Cells
- Modern Batteries

A cell has two electrodes, and the emf generated depends on the magnitude of the electrode potentials of both the electrodes. With respect to the demand for a specific purpose, higher voltage output can be obtained by coupling a number of cells in series. Such an arrangement of two or more cells in series is known as battery. Commercial batteries are an assembly of electrochemical cells which satisfy some important requisites mentioned here.

(i) It should be compact and lightweight.

(ii) It should be easily portable.

(iii) It should be tolerant to different service conditions such as variation of temperature, vibration, shock, etc.

(iv) It should have long life of operation without much variation in output voltage.

(v) It should have high energy efficiency.

(vi) It should be rechargeable so that it can be used again and again. In addition, it should also have high cycle life.

(vii) It should be cost-effective.

Classification

The commercial cells or batteries can be discussed under three categories: primary cell, secondary cell, and fuel cell.

Primary Cell

Here the cell reaction cannot be made to proceed in the reverse direction. These are use and throw type, i.e., can be used once only. Examples are Weston cadmium cell, Leclanche dry cell, alkaline cell, etc.

Leclanche dry cell

It consists of a cylindrical zinc container filled with a paste of MnO_2, NH_4Cl, and carbon. There is a graphite rod placed at the center but not touching the base. The graphite rod is fitted with a metal cap and the container is sealed with a pitch at the top (Fig. 21.1). The Zn container acts as the anode, while the graphite rod acts as the cathode. There is an insulating cover protecting the container from the atmosphere. The schematic representation of inner core of a typical dry cell is as follows:

$$\overset{\ominus}{Zn} / MnO_2 + ZnCl_2 + C + Starch / \overset{\oplus}{Graphite}$$

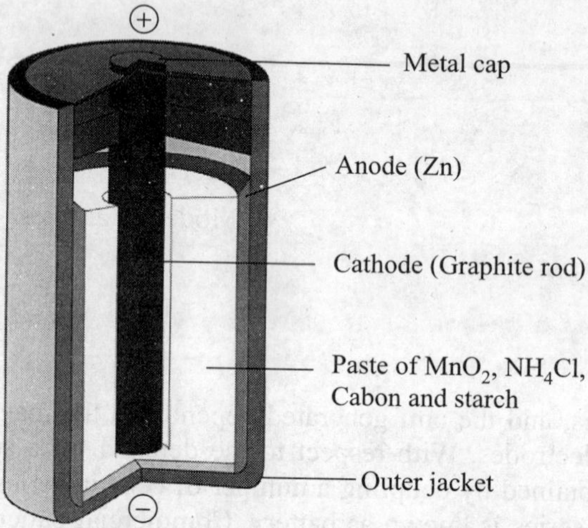

Fig. 21.1 Cross-sectional view of dry cell

The reactions that occur at the electrodes are summarized here. The important aspect of the reactions is the ammonia produced at the cathode, which reacts with zinc ions produced at the anode to form diamminezinc (II) complex. The voltage output of such a cell is in the range 1.25–1.50 V.

Anode:

$$Zn_{(s)} \longrightarrow Zn^{2+}_{(aq)} + 2e$$

Cathode:

$$2MnO_{2(s)} + H_2O_{(l)} + 2e \longrightarrow Mn_2O_{3(s)} + 2OH^-_{(aq)}$$

$$[NH_4{}^+_{(aq)} + OH^-_{(aq)} \longrightarrow NH_{3(g)} + H_2O_{(l)}] \times 2$$

$$Zn^{2+}_{(aq)} + 2NH_{3(g)} \longrightarrow [Zn(NH_3)_2]^{2+}_{(aq)}$$

$$2MnO_{2(s)} + Zn^{2+}_{(aq)} + 2NH_4{}^+_{(g)} + 2e \longrightarrow Mn_2O_{3(s)} + H_2O_{(l)} + [Zn(NH_3)_2]^{2+}_{(aq)}$$

Cell:

$$Zn_{(s)} + 2MnO_{2(s)} + 2NH_4{}^+_{(aq)} \longrightarrow Mn_2O_{3(s)} + [Zn(NH_3)_2]^{2+}_{(aq)}$$

Note:

Due to acidic nature of NH_4Cl, upon hydrolysis the zinc container is corroded even if the cell is not in use. Therefore, cell does not work for a longer period of time.

Alkaline cell

It is an improved form of Leclanche dry cell in which NH_4Cl is replaced by KOH as the electrolyte. The cell representation and reactions are summarized as follows:

$$\overset{\ominus}{Zn} / MnO_2 + KOH + C + Starch / \overset{\oplus}{Graphite}$$

Anode:

$$Zn_{(s)} + 2OH^-_{(aq)} \rightarrow Zn(OH)_{2(s)} + 2e$$

Cathode:

$$2MnO_{2(s)} + H_2O_{(1)} + 2e \rightarrow Mn_2O_{3(s)} + 2\,OH^-_{(aq)}$$

Cell:

$$Zn_{(s)} + 2MnO_{2(s)} + H_2O_{(1)} \rightarrow Zn(OH)_{2(s)} + Mn_2O_{3(s)}$$

The advantages of this alkaline cell over dry cell is that

1. Zn does not dissolve readily in alkaline medium. Thus, Zn container is not corroded, which ultimately increases the durability of the cell.
2. The cell has less internal resistance with high utilization coefficient.
3. It provides a constant voltage output of 1.5 V.

Mercury cell

It is a *modern dry cell* which finds its application in mini electronic appliances such as hearing aids, heart pacemakers, and digital watches. It is encased in a stainless steel case. In this cell, zinc amalgam is used as the anode, while a strong alkaline paste consisting of KOH and HgO acts as the cathode. A lining of porous paper keeps the electrodes apart (Fig. 21.2). As there is no change in the electrolyte composition during the cell operation, it provides a constant output voltage of 1.34 V for most of its life period and is widely used in watches and other electronic gadgets. The cell representation and reactions are summarized as follows:

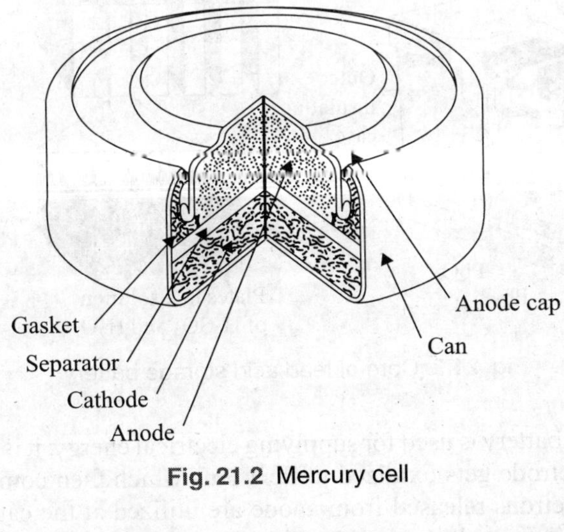

Fig. 21.2 Mercury cell

$$\overset{\ominus}{Zn\text{–}Hg} / Paper / KOH + \overset{\oplus}{HgO}$$

Anode:

$$Zn\text{–}Hg_{(s)} + 2OH^-_{(aq)} \rightarrow ZnO_{(s)} + H_2O_{(l)} + 2e$$

Cathode:

$$HgO_{(s)} + H_2O_{(l)} + 2e \rightarrow Hg_{(l)} + 2OH^-_{(aq)}$$

Cell:

$$Zn_{(s)} + HgO_{(s)} \rightarrow ZnO_{(s)} + Hg_{(l)}$$

Secondary Cell

In such a cell, the cell reaction can be made to proceed in the reverse direction by passing direct current through it from an external emf source. Therefore, it can operate in both ways, i.e., to receive electrical energy and also to supply it. When it supplies electrical energy, it operates like an *electrochemical cell* and eventually becomes run down. The cell then needs to be recharged. During recharging, it operates like *electrolytic cell*, e.g., lead storage battery, nickel-cadmium storage cell, etc.

Lead acid storage battery

The most common example of this type of cell is *lead acid storage cell.* It consists of usually six 2-V cells connected in a series. Each cell consists of several positive and negative electrodes made of spongy lead and lead (IV) oxide operating as the anode and the cathode, respectively (Fig. 21.3). The electrodes are connected in parallel and are kept immersed in 28% sulfuric acid with specific gravity 1.3 g/cm solution.

$$\underset{\ominus}{Pb / PbSO_4} / 38\%\ H_2SO_4 / \underset{\oplus}{PbO_2 / PbSO_4}$$

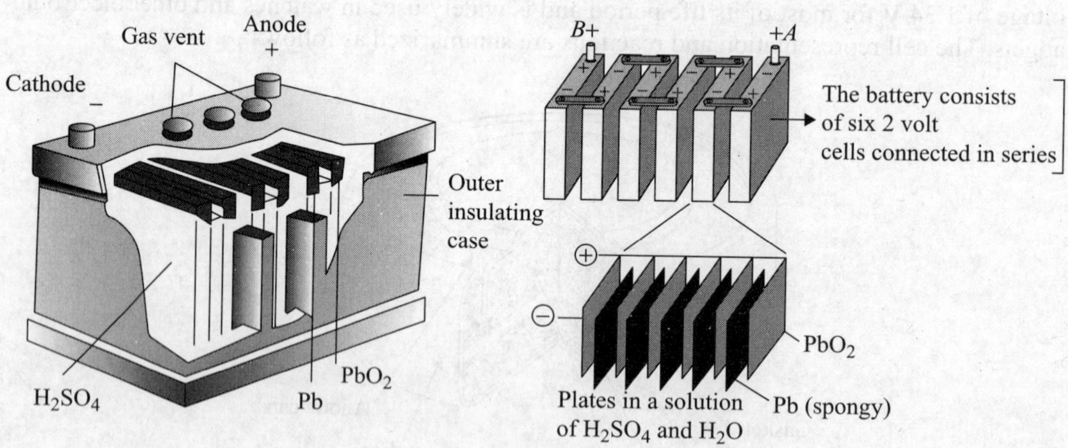

Fig. 21.3 Core of lead acid storage battery

Discharging: When the battery is used for supplying electrical energy, it is said to be discharged. In the process, lead electrode gets oxidized to Pb^{2+} ions which then combine with SO_4^{2-} ions to form $PbSO_4$. The electrons released from anode are utilized at the cathode to reduce PbO_2 to Pb^{2+} ions. These Pb^{2+} ions also combine with SO_4^{2-} ions to form $PbSO_4$. The reactions occurring at the electrodes and cell are as follows:

Anode:

$$Pb_{(s)} \longrightarrow Pb^{2+}_{(aq)} + 2e$$
$$Pb^{2+}_{(aq)} + SO_4^{2-}{}_{(aq)} \longrightarrow PbSO_{4(s)}$$
$$Pb_{(s)} + SO_4^{2-}{}_{(aq)} \quad PbSO_{4(s)} + 2e$$

Cathode:

$$PbO_{2(s)} + 4H^+_{(aq)} + 2e \longrightarrow Pb^{2+}_{(aq)} + 2H_2O$$
$$Pb^{2+}_{(aq)} + SO_4^{2-}{}_{(aq)} \longrightarrow PbSO_{4(s)}$$
$$PbO_{2(s)} + SO_4^{2-}{}_{(aq)} + 4H^+_{(aq)} + 2e \longrightarrow PbSO_{4(s)} + 2H_2O_{(l)}$$

Cell:

$$Pb_{(s)} + PbO_{2(s)} + 2SO_4^{2-}{}_{(aq)} + 4H^+_{(aq)} \longrightarrow 2PbSO_{4(s)} + 2H_2O_{(l)}$$

Charging: During use, $PbSO_4$ is precipitated at both the electrodes. When $PbSO_4$ covers completely both the electrodes, the cell stops working. For further use it needs to be recharged. The cell can be recharged by connecting it to an external direct current source so as to reverse the cell reaction. This is possible as $PbSO_4$ formed stick to the electrodes and is positioned to gain or lose electrons.

Cathode: $$PbSO_{4(s)} + 2e \longrightarrow Pb_{(s)} + SO_4^{2-}{}_{(aq)}$$
Anode: $$PbSO_{4(s)} + 2H_2O_{(l)} \longrightarrow PbO_{2(s)} + SO_4^{2-}{}_{(aq)} + 4H^+_{(aq)} + 2e$$
Cell: $$2PbSO_{4(s)} + 2H_2O_{(l)} \longrightarrow Pb_{(s)} + PbO_{2(s)} + 2SO_4^{2-}{}_{(aq)} + 4H^+_{(aq)}$$

Note:

1. Overcharging release hydrogen and oxygen gases due to electrolysis of water. This reduces the acid level, damaging the exposed electrodes. In addition the gases released sometimes lead to high pressure built up which may lead to explosion. Therefore, such batteries are not completely sealed and have vents to release the excesses gases. Nowadays Ca–Pb alloy electrodes are used to prevent the electrolysis of water. Such batteries with alloy electrodes can be sealed.
2. The large overvoltage for the oxidation of water allows lead storage batteries to be recharged. If it were not for this large overvoltage, the charging current would oxidize water to oxygen gas instead of $PbSO_4$ to PbO_2.
3. As concentration of H_2SO_4 decreases during discharging, the extent to which the battery has discharged can be checked by measuring the density of H_2SO_4 in the cell.
4. An interesting property of lead storage battery is its ability to deliver large amounts of current for a short period of time, making them ideal for powering the ignition system like in a car engine.
5. The battery can function for several years under extremes temperature from −30°F to 100°F.
6. In this cell, the oxidizing agent (PbO_2), reducing agent (Pb) as well as their oxidation and reduction product ($PbSO_4$) are solids. Thus, migration of oxidizing agent and/or reducing agent from one electrode to another is not possible and the salt does not require any salt bridge or porous partition.

Alkaline storage cell

In alkaline storage cell, electrolyte is an alkali. Unlike acid storage cell, concentration of electrolyte in alkaline storage cell does not undergo any net change during the cell operation. A popular example in this category is nickel-cadmium alkaline cell (*NiCad*). It consists of Cd-electrode as the anode and a metal grid containing nickel(IV) oxide as the cathode (Fig. 21.4). The electrodes are kept separated by an absorbent material soaked with 6M KOH as electrolyte. The reactions are as follows:

Anode:

$$Cd_{(s)} \longrightarrow Cd^{2+}_{(aq)} + 2e$$

$$Cd^{2+}_{(aq)} + 2OH^-_{(aq)} \longrightarrow Cd(OH)_{2(s)}$$

$$Cd_{(s)} + 2OH^-_{(aq)} \longrightarrow Cd(OH)_{2(s)} + 2e$$

Cathode:

$$NiO_{2(s)} + 2H_2O_{(l)} + 2e \longrightarrow Ni(OH)_{2(s)} + 2OH^-_{(aq)}$$

Cell

$$Cd_{(s)} + NiO_{2(s)} + 2H_2O_{(l)} + 2e \longrightarrow Cd(OH)_{2(s)} + Ni(OH)_{2(s)}$$

The reaction products adhere to the electrodes and therefore the reaction can be reversed by passing current from a direct current source. The voltage output of the cell is 1.4 V. Such a battery can be operated at high discharge rates and in a wide range of temperature. In addition, retention properties are excellent and therefore can be stored for a long time without deterioration independent of conditions. It is widely used in photography, computers, transmitters, hearing aids, etc.

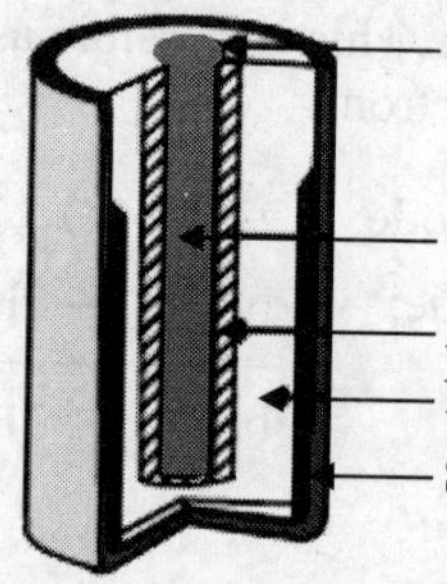

Fig. 21.4 NiCad cell

Fuel Cell

A *fuel cell* is an electrochemical device that converts the chemical energy of fuels such as hydrogen, methane, butane, and gasoline directly into electrical energy. It offers the opportunity to obtain the benefits of clean electric power without pollution-producing engines, heavy batteries, and even thermal power plants.

Construction: Every fuel cell is constructed with two porous electrodes impregnated with a catalyst which sandwich an electrolyte. The common electrolytes are alkali, molten carbonate, phosphoric acid, proton exchange membrane (PEM), and solid oxide. The first three are liquid electrolytes, while the last two are solids. The arrangements are made so as to pass fuel and oxidizer, i.e., oxygen from separate containers present outside the main body of the cell. The purpose of electrolyte is to carry charged particles from one electrode to the other, whereas the purpose of catalyst is to speed up the reactions at the electrodes. The specifications for electrodes, electrolyte, and catalyst decide the type of cell, e.g., hydrogen–oxygen fuel cell and propane–oxygen fuel cell. The general representation is as follows:

Fuel/Electrode/Electrolyte/Electrode/Oxidant

Types of fuel cell

Fuel cells are usually classified into different types on the basis of the electrolyte used. The basic categories are as follows.

Fuel cell

- *Alkaline fuel cell* (AFC)- aqueous solution of KOH soaked in a matrix is used as an electrolyte.
- *Polymer electrolyte membrane fuel cell (PEM)*: Nafion membrane is used which is a per-fluorinated cation exchange polymer membrane.
- *Solid oxide fuel cell (SOFC)*: Yettria stabilized zirconia is used as an electrolyte.
- *Phosphoric acid fuel cell (PAFC)*: Phosphoric acid soaked in a matrix in used as an electrolyte.
- *Molten carbonate fuel cell (MCFC)*: A solution of lithium, sodium, and potassium carbonates soaked in a matrix is used as an electrolyte.

1. **Alkaline fuel cells:** In alkaline fuel cells (AFCs), NaOH or KOH solution soaked in a matrix is used as electrolyte. Let us discuss the construction and working of a typical alkaline fuel cell which is hydrogen–oxygen alkaline fuel cell (Bacon cell). In this cell, electrodes are porous graphite electrodes impregnated with finely divided Pt or a 75 : 25 alloy of Pd with Ag and electrolyte is 25% KOH.

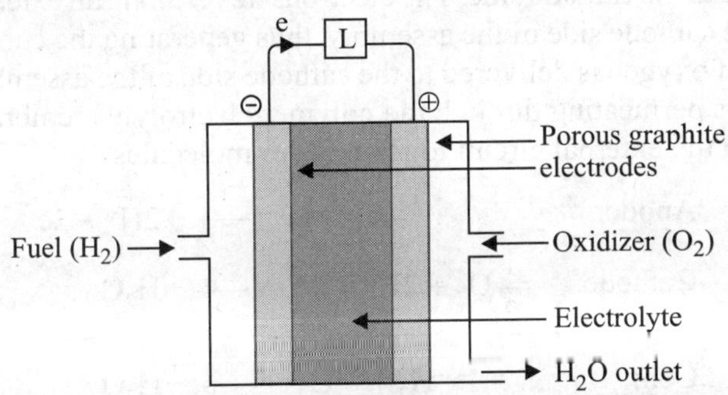

Fig. 21.5 H_2–O_2 fuel cell

Working: The hydrogen is oxidized and the electrons lost in the process migrate to cathode through the external metallic wire. Oxygen diffuses into the fuel cell at the cathode which receives the electrons and gets reduced to free OH^- ions. In the overall reaction, hydrogen and oxygen combine together to form water (shown below), which drains from the cell. As long as a fuel and oxidizer are supplied, the cell will generate electricity. The electrolyte plays a key role. It must permit only the appropriate ions to pass between the anode and cathode. If free electrons or other substances could travel through the electrolyte, they would disrupt the chemical reaction. The current generating is a DC current. The output voltage remains in the range 0.8–1.0 V.

$$\begin{array}{lll}
\text{Anode:} & 2H_{2(g)} + 4OH^-_{(aq)} \longrightarrow & 4H_2O_{(l)} + 4e \\
\text{Cathode:} & O_{2(g)} + 2H_2O_{(l)} + 4e \longrightarrow & 4OH^-_{(aq)} \\
\hline
\text{Cell:} & 2H_{2(g)} + O_{2(g)} \longrightarrow & 2H_2O_{(l)}
\end{array}$$

Note:

Other fuels such as hydrocarbons and alcohols can also be used as fuel in place of hydrogen. A popular example is methyl alcohol–oxygen fuel cell. The reactions occurring at the electrodes along with the complete cell reaction is as follows:

$$\begin{array}{lll}
\text{Anode:} & CH_3OH + H_2O \longrightarrow & 6H^+ + CO_2 + 6e^- \\
\text{Cathode:} & \frac{3}{2}O_2 + 6H^+ + 6e^- \longrightarrow & 3H_2O \\
\hline
\text{Cell Reaction:} & CH_3OH + \frac{3}{2}O_2 \longrightarrow & 2H_2O + CO_2
\end{array}$$

2. **Polymer electrolyte membrane fuel cells (PEMFCs):** These cells are also known as *proton exchange membrane* fuel cells. In these cells, the electrolyte consists of a layer of solid polymer which allows the transmission of proton from one electrode to another. Use of *nafion* membrane which is a perfluorinated cation exchange polymer membrane as electrolyte is very popular in this category. Such cells require H_2 and O_2 as their input. A stream of hydrogen is allowed to enter to the anode side of the membrane electrode assembly. At the anode side, it is catalytically split into protons and electrons. The newly formed protons permeate through the polymer electrolyte membrane to the cathode side. The electrons travel along an external circuit having the load to the cathode side of the assembly, thus generating the current. Simultaneously, a stream of oxygen is delivered to the cathode side of the assembly which reacts with the protons permeating through the polymer electrolyte membrane and the electrons arriving in the external circuit to form water molecules.

$$\begin{array}{lll}
\text{Anode:} & H_2 \longrightarrow & 2H^+ + 2e \\
\text{Cathode:} & \frac{1}{2}O_2 + 2H^+ + 2e \longrightarrow & H_2O \\
\hline
\text{Cell:} & H_2 + \frac{1}{2}O_2 \longrightarrow & H_2O
\end{array}$$

Note:

1. Platinum is by far the most effective element used as catalyst for PEMFCs, and nearly all current PEM fuel cells use platinum particles on porous carbon support. However, due to their high cost, Pt/C catalysts are not feasible for commercialization. The performance of platinum catalysts can be further increased by using the high-index facets of platinum nanoparticles, i.e., Miller indexes with large integers such as Pt (730). Platinum alloy, e.g., Pt_3Ni (111) is another alternative for the purpose.
2. The water management is a crucial aspect as far as performance is concerned. Too much water will flood the membrane, too little will dry it and in both cases,

power output will drop. A wide variety of solutions for managing the water exists including integration of electroosmotic (EO) pumps.

3. The platinum catalyst on the membrane gets easily poisoned by CO (acceptable range is ≤1 ppm). The membrane is also sensitive to metallic components in the fuel cell system or from contaminants in the fuel/oxidant.
4. The most commonly used membrane is Nafion. It is not feasible to use Nafion at temperatures above 80–90°C as the membrane would dry. Another more recent membrane is based on polybenzimidazole (PBI) which can reach up to 220°C without using any water management.

3. **Solid oxide fuel cells (SOFCs):** Such a cell uses all solid state materials. The electrolyte is a solid material, most commonly yttria stabilized zirconia (YSZ) which is a ceramic material is used. Such cells require high operating temperature of ~1000°C and can run on a variety of fuels. SOFCs are unique in that negatively charged oxygen ions travel from the cathode to the anode instead of positively charged hydrogen ions traveling from the anode to the cathode, as is the case in all other types of fuel cells. Oxygen gas is fed through cathode, where it reacts with electrons and transferred into oxide ions. The oxide ions then travel through the electrolyte to react with hydrogen gas at the anode. The reaction at the anode produces electricity and water as by-products. Carbon dioxide may also be a by-product depending on the fuel. However, the carbon emission from an SOFC system is less than that from a thermal power plant which is based on fossil fuel combustion. The chemical reactions for the SOFC system can be expressed as follows:

$$\begin{array}{lrcl} \text{Anode:} & 2H_2 + 2O^{2-} & \longrightarrow & 2H_2O + 4e^- \\ \text{Cathode:} & O_2 + 4e^- & \longrightarrow & 2O^{2-} \\ \hline \text{Cell reaction:} & 2H_2 + O_2 & \longrightarrow & 2H_2O \end{array}$$

(i) SOFCs can run on fuels other than pure hydrogen gas but the fuel must contain hydrogen atoms. SOFCs are capable of reforming internally light hydrocarbons such as methane (natural gas), propane, and butane to hydrogen. However, for heavier hydrocarbons including gasoline, diesel fuel, jet fuel, and biofuels, external reformer is required.

(ii) These are prone to "carbon coking," which refers to carbon build-up on the anode that result in reduced performance by slowing down the internal fuel reforming process.

(iii) Another disadvantage of SOFC systems is slow start-up time due to high operating temperature, which makes SOFCs less useful for mobile applications.

(iv) A high operating temperature provides an advantage by removing the need for a precious metal catalyst such as platinum and thereby reducing cost. In addition, waste heat from SOFC systems may be captured and reused, increasing the theoretical overall efficiency to as high as 80–85%.

(v) Lowering of temperature decreases the ionic conductivity of YSZ electrolyte and therefore to obtain optimum performance, a high operating temperature is maintained. Recently it has been reported that the operating temperature of

SOFC system can be reduced to 500–600°C with replacement of the YSZ electrolyte with a CGO (cerium gadolinium oxide) electrolyte. The lower operating temperature allows the use of stainless steel instead of ceramic as the cell substrate, which reduces cost as well as start-up time of the system.

4. **Phosphoric acid fuel cells (PAFCs)**: These fuel cells use liquid phosphoric acid as an electrolyte. These cells are very similar to alkaline fuel cells. Electrolyte is highly concentrated or pure liquid H_3PO_4 is saturated in a silicon carbide matrix (SiC). The electrodes are made of carbon paper coated with a finely dispersed platinum catalyst. Operating range is about 150–210°C. Reaction is similar to that described above in case of PEMFCs.

Note:

1. The expelled water can be converted into steam for air and water heating which potentially allows efficiency to increase up to 70%.
2. At lower temperatures, H_3PO_4 is a poor ionic conductor, and CO poisoning of the platinum electrocatalyst in the anode becomes severe. However, they are much less sensitive to CO than PEFCs and AFCs.
3. Disadvantages include rather low power density and aggressive electrolyte.

5. **Molten carbonate fuel cells (MCFCs):** These require a high operating temperature ~650°C, similar to solid oxide fuel cells. MCFCs use lithium potassium carbonate salt as an electrolyte, which melts into molten state that allows the movement of negative carbonate ions within the cell. Such cells are capable of converting fuel into a hydrogen-rich gas in the anode, eliminating the need of an external reformer. This reforming process is called internal reforming. The compatible fuels include natural gas, biogas, and gases produced from coal. The hydrogen in the gas reacts with carbonate ions from the electrolyte at the anode to produce water, carbon dioxide, and electrons. The electrons travel through the external circuit causing the flow of current. At cathode, oxygen from the air and carbon dioxide recycled from the anode react with the electrons to form carbonate ions that replenish the electrolyte, completing the circuit. The chemical reactions for an MCFC system can be expressed as follows:

Anode: $$CO_3^{2-} + H_2 \longrightarrow H_2O + CO_2 + 2e^-$$

Cathode: $$CO_2 + \frac{1}{2}O_2 + 2e^- \longrightarrow CO_3^{2-}$$

Cell reaction: $$H_2 + \frac{1}{2}O_2 \longrightarrow H_2O$$

Following are disadvantages of MCFCs:

1. Slow start-up times because of their high operating temperature. This makes MCFC systems not suitable for mobile applications.
2. The main challenge of MCFCs is their short life span. The high temperature and carbonate electrolyte lead to corrosion of the electrodes and thereby decrease the durability and cell life.

Advantages of MCFCs over other fuel cell technologies are as follows:

1. They are not prone to "carbon coking," which refers to carbon build-up on the anode resulting in performance reduction by slowing down the internal fuel reforming

process. This makes carbon-rich fuels, such as gases made from coal, compatible with the system.

2. MCFCs also have relatively high fuel-to-electricity efficiencies which may reach 50%, considerably higher than the 37–42% efficiency of a phosphoric acid fuel cell. Efficiencies can be as high as 65% when the fuel cell is paired with a turbine and 85% if heat is captured and used in a combined heat and power (CHP) system.

Note:

1. Since fuel cells create electricity chemically, rather than by combustion, they are not subject to the thermodynamic laws that limit a conventional power plant. Therefore, fuel cells are more efficient in extracting energy from a fuel.
2. Fuel cells have a lot of advantages such as (i) fuel efficiency is very high (75–80%) as compared to traditional thermal power plants where the maximum efficiency goes up to 40%; (ii) recharging is not required and it can operate as long as the fuel and oxidizer are supplied from outside; (iii) no thermal and noise pollution; (iv) environmental friendly by-product.
3. It also suffers from a lot of limitation which discourages their use in regular practice such as (i) not portable, as fuel and oxidizer cylinders need to be carried along with the cell; (ii) high cost of catalyst; (iii) a lot of energy is spent in keeping the fuel in liquid form; (iv) fuel free from impurities is also costly.

Modern Batteries

Zinc–Air Batteries

Zinc–air batteries are powered by the oxidation of Zn with oxygen from the air. In this battery, a mass of loose granulated zinc particles mixed with an electrolyte such as KOH forms a porous anode (Fig. 21.6). Oxygen from the air at the cathode forms hydroxyl ions which migrate into

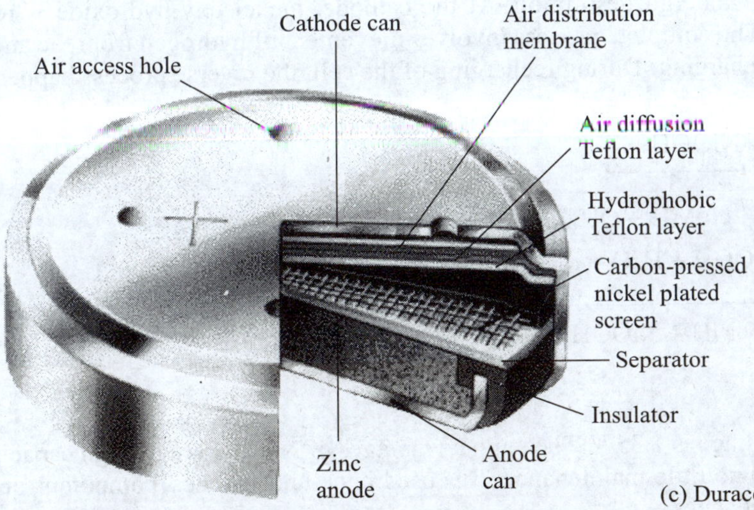

Fig. 21.6 Zinc–air batteries

the zinc paste and form zincate, i.e., $[Zn(OH)_4]^{2-}$, releasing electrons to travel to the cathode. The zincate decays into zinc oxide and water. The water and hydroxyls from the electrodes are recycled so the water is not consumed. The reactions produce a theoretical 1.65 V, but this is reduced to 1.35–1.4 V in available cells. The reaction rate can be controlled by varying the air flow, and oxidized zinc/electrolyte paste can be replaced with fresh paste.

$$\underbrace{\overset{\ominus}{\text{Grnulated Zn}}} \ / \ 6\text{M KOH} \ / \ \underbrace{\overset{\oplus}{\text{Air / C}}}$$

$$\begin{array}{llll}
\text{Anode:} & Zn + 4OH^- & \longrightarrow & [Zn\,(OH)_4]^{2-} + 2e^- \ (E_0 = -1.25\text{ V}) \\
\text{Fluid:} & [Zn\,(OH)_4]^{2-} & \longrightarrow & ZnO + H_2O + 2OH^- \\
\text{Cathode:} & \frac{1}{2}O_2 + H_2O + 2e^- & \longrightarrow & 2OH^- \ (E_0 = 0.34\text{ V; pH} = 11) \\
\hline
\text{Overall:} & 2Zn + O_2 & \longrightarrow & 2ZnO \ (E_0 = 1.59\text{ V})
\end{array}$$

Note:

These batteries have high energy densities and are relatively inexpensive to produce. Such a battery has long shelf life. It is available in different sizes. The sizes vary from very small button cells for hearing aids, larger batteries used in cameras, to very large batteries used in electric vehicles.

Nickel–Metal Hydride (Ni–MH) Batteries

Nickel metal hydride battery is a rechargeable *modern battery*. Ni–MH use nickel oxy-hydroxide (NiOOH) as the cathode and a hydrogen-absorbing alloy (the most common is AB_5, where A is a mixture of rare earths such as lanthanum, cerium, neodymium, and praseodymium and B is nickel, cobalt, manganese, and/or aluminum) as the anode (Fig. 21.7). Electrolyte is usually KOH. A hydrophilic polyolefin nonwoven material keeps the two electrodes separate, and serves as a medium for absorbing the electrolyte. During discharge of the battery, the hydrogen stored in the alloy undergo desorption. At the cathode, nickel oxy-hydroxide is reduced to nickel hydroxide. The complete process involves movement of hydrogen from the anode to the cathode during discharging. During recharging of the cell, the reverse process happens.

$$\underbrace{\overset{\ominus}{AB_5}} \ / \ KOH \ / \ \underbrace{\overset{\oplus}{\text{NiOOH/Ni}}}$$

$$\begin{array}{llll}
\text{Anode} & MH + OH^- & \rightleftharpoons & M + H_2O + e \\
\text{Cathode} & NiOOH + H_2O + e & \rightleftharpoons & Ni(OH)_2 + OH^- \\
\hline
\text{Cell} & MH + NiOOH & \rightleftharpoons & M + Ni(OH)_2
\end{array}$$

Note:

The output voltage is 1.35 V. The main advantages of Ni–MH are its high capacity, long cycle life, and no/little maintenance. It is used in cellular phones, computers, and other electronic appliances.

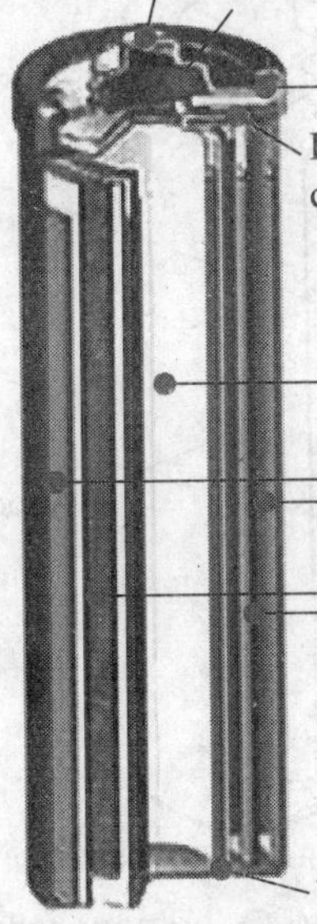

Fig. 21.7 Ni–MH battery

Lithium Batteries

Lithium batteries are primary batteries that use lithium metal or lithium compounds as the anode. They stand apart from other batteries in their high charge density (long life) and high cost per unit. Depending on the design and chemical compounds used, lithium cells can produce voltages from 1.5 to 3.7 V. In contrast *lithium-ion* batteries are rechargeable batteries in which lithium ions move between the anode and the cathode, using an intercalated lithium compound as the electrode material instead of the metallic lithium used in lithium batteries. Lithium batteries are widely used in products such as portable consumer electronic devices. Let us look into the details of both primary and secondary lithium cells.

Primary lithium battery

Primary lithium batteries are further classified on the basis of the type of electrolyte or solvent and material of cathode. The basic types are *soluble cathode, solid cathode,* and *solid electrolyte* cells. Let us discuss one example in the category of primary lithium battery.

Li-MnO_2 battery: It belongs to *solid cathode* lithium battery. In this battery, lithium is used as the anode, while a specially prepared heat-treated MnO_2 is used as the cathode (Fig. 21.8). Electrolyte is lithium salts (lithium perchlorate) in a mixed organic solvent propylene carbonate and dimethoxy ethane. The cell representation is as follows:

$$\underset{\ominus}{Li}/LiClO_4 \text{ in Propylene carbonate + Dimethoxy ethane}/\underset{\oplus}{MnO_2}$$

Reaction

During the reaction, Mn^{4+} is reduced to Mn^{3+} by the interstitially occupied lithium ions in the MnO_2 intercalation compound. $LiMnO_2$ indicates that Li^+ ions remain present in the host MnO_2 lattice. The cell reaction is as follows:

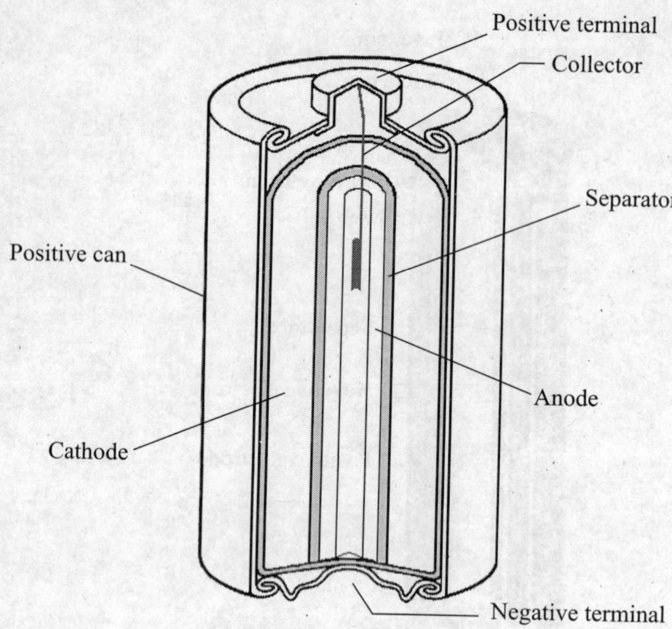

Fig. 21.8 Cylindrical Li–MnO_2 primary cell

Anode	xLi	$\longrightarrow$	x LI^+ + xe
Cathode	MnO_2 + xLi^+ + xe	$\longrightarrow$	$LiMn_{1-x}Mn_xO_2$
Cell	xLi + MnO_2	$\longrightarrow$	$LiMn_{1-x}Mn_xO_2$

Note:

The output voltage is 3.5 V. Operating temperature is –20 to 50°C. Such cells have wide applications such as in long-term memory back-up device, security devices, camera, and many other electronic devices.

Secondary lithium battery

Depending on the active cathodic material and electrolyte used, secondary lithium batteries or rechargeable lithium batteries are further classified into five basic categories: *liquid organic electrolyte cells*, *polymer electrolyte cells*, *inorganic electrolyte cells*, *lithium ion cells*, and *lithium alloy cells*. Here discussion is restricted only to lithium ion battery.

Lithium–ion battery: In Li–ion battery, lithium-doped graphite intercalation compound (Li–GIC) electrode is used as the cathode (Fig. 21.9), while the anode is an intercalated lithium compound such as a layered oxide such as lithium cobalt(III) oxide ($LiCoO_2$), a polyanion such as lithium iron phosphate ($LiFePO_4$) or a spinel-like lithium manganese oxide ($LiMn_2O_4$). The liquid electrolyte consists of a complex lithium compound such as lithium hexafluorophosphate ($LiPF_6$), lithium hexafluoroarsenate monohydrate ($LiAsF_6 \cdot H_2O$), lithium perchlorate ($LiClO_4$), lithium tetrafluoroborate ($LiBF_4$) or lithium triflate ($LiCF_3SO_3$) dissolved in an organic solvent such as dimethyl carbobnate and diethyl carbonate. The representation of a typical lithium ion cell is as follows:

$\ominus$ $\oplus$

$\underbrace{Li_nC}/LiFePO_4 + OC(OCH_3)_2/\underbrace{LiCoO_2}$

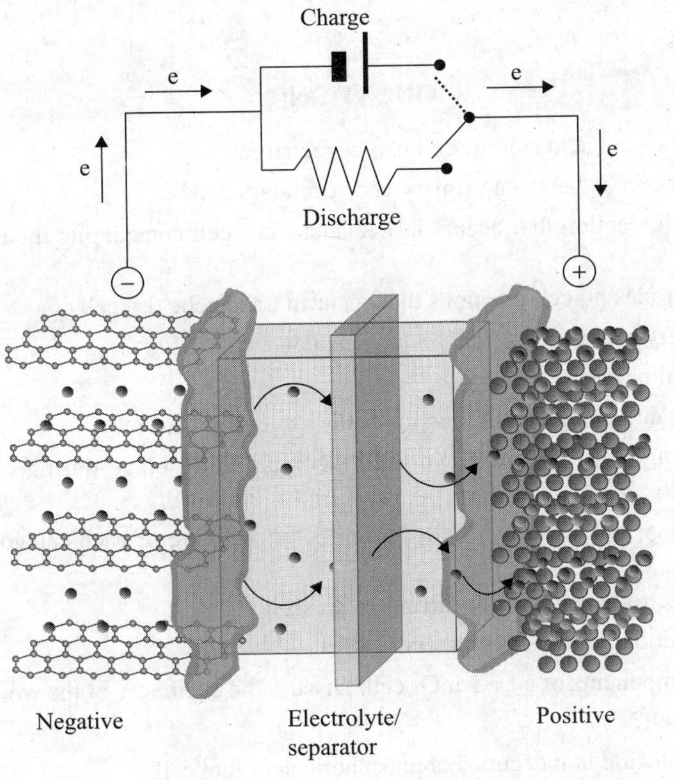

Fig. 21.9 Li–ion battery

Reaction

Both electrodes allow lithium ions to migrate toward and away from them. When a lithium-ion cell discharges, the positive ion is extracted from the negative electrode, i.e., graphite, and inserted into the positive electrode, i.e., intercalated lithium compound. During charging, the reverse occurs.

$$\text{Anode} \qquad Li_nC \rightleftharpoons nLi^+ + ne + C$$

$$\text{Cathode} \qquad Li_{1-n}CoO_2 + nLi^+ + ne \rightleftharpoons LiCoO_2$$

$$Li_nC + Li_{1-n}CoO_2 \rightleftharpoons C + LiCoO_2$$

Note:

1. As Li^+ ions migrate from anode to cathode and back from cathode to anode during discharging and charging, respectively, the lithium ion batteries are called "Swing" cells.

2. A typical Li-ion battery can store 150 watt-hours of electricity in 1 kg of battery as compared to lead acid batteries, which can store only 25 watt-hours of electricity in 1 kg.

QUESTIONS

1. Explain why the lead acid storage cell can be recharged.
2. What is the difference between primary and secondary cell?
3. Provide the cell reaction that occurs in Leclanche dry cell considering the reaction at anode and cathode.
4. Write the electrode and cell reactions that occur in Laclanche dry cell.
5. Lead acid battery is not completely sealed. Explain.
6. What is an alkaline cell?
7. What are the main advantages of alkaline battery over dry battery?
8. What is a storage cell? Write down the reactions taking place during charging of lead storage cell.
9. What are primary and secondary cells? Discuss the working of each category with suitable examples.
10. Mention the electrode reactions occurring in Zn/air cell.
11. Describe the working of Ni–MH battery.
12. Mention the components of a Li–MnO_2 cell. Discuss the chemistry of the working of the cell.
13. What is a fuel cell?
14. Write the cell reaction that occurs in a phosphoric acid fuel cell.
15. What is MCFC? Why it is preferred over AFC?
16. Write the cell reaction that occurs in a molten carbonate fuel cell.
17. Describe the working of CH_3OH–O_2 fuel cell.
18. Describe the construction and working of solid oxide fuel cell (SOFC).
19. What happens upon excess recharging of lead acid storage battery?
20. What is carbon coking?
21. What step should be taken to increase the efficiency of Pt catalyst in PEMFC?
22. Describe the construction and working of a lithium ion battery.
23. Why non-aqueous solvent is used in Li-ion battery?
24. What is the anode material in a Li-ion battery?
25. What is the difference between a lithium battery and lithium-ion battery?

CHAPTER

22 Green Chemistry

Chapter Outline

- Principles
- Examples of Green Chemistry in Industry
- Matrices to Express Greenness
- Green Chemistry and Catalysis
- Extra Element Detection in Organic Compounds (Safer Technique)
- R_4M_4 Principle
- Life Cycle Analysis

The term "Green Chemistry" was first coined by P. T. Anastas in 1991 during a special program launched by the United States Environmental Protection Agency (USEPA). As per him: *It's more effective, it's more efficient, it's more elegant, it's simply better chemistry.* Green chemistry incorporates a new approach to the synthesis, processing, and application of chemical substances in a manner so as to reduce threats to human health and the environment. It has changed the traditional concepts of efficiency of process that focus primarily on product yield in a process to the one that assigns economic value for eliminating waste at source and avoiding the use of toxic and/or hazardous substances. In other words, *green chemistry* is a proactive approach to pollution prevention. It targets pollution at the design stage, before it even begins.

Green chemistry may be defined as: *The design of chemical products and processes that are more environmentally benign and reduce negative impacts to human health and the environment.*

Principles

Green chemistry aims to protect the environment not by cleaning up, but by inventing new chemical processes that do not pollute. It is a rapidly developing and is an important area in the chemical sciences. Green chemistry must accomplish three things: (i) be more environmentally benign than the alternatives, (ii) be more economically viable than the alternatives, and (iii) functionally outperform the alternatives.

To provide a roadmap for chemists trying to implement green chemistry, the following 12 principles were implemented by Paul Anastas and John Warner:

1. **Prevention:** It is better to prevent waste than to treat or clean up waste after it has been created.
2. **Atom economy**: Synthetic methods should be designed to maximize the incorporation of all materials used in the process into the final product (discussed separately).
3. **Less hazardous chemical synthesis:** Wherever practicable, synthetic methods should be designed to use and generate substances that possess little or no toxicity to human health and the environment. This principle can be explained by the following examples:

   (i) Polycarbonate is a class of polymers which find wide applications in cases where high optical properties combined with strength are needed. The most

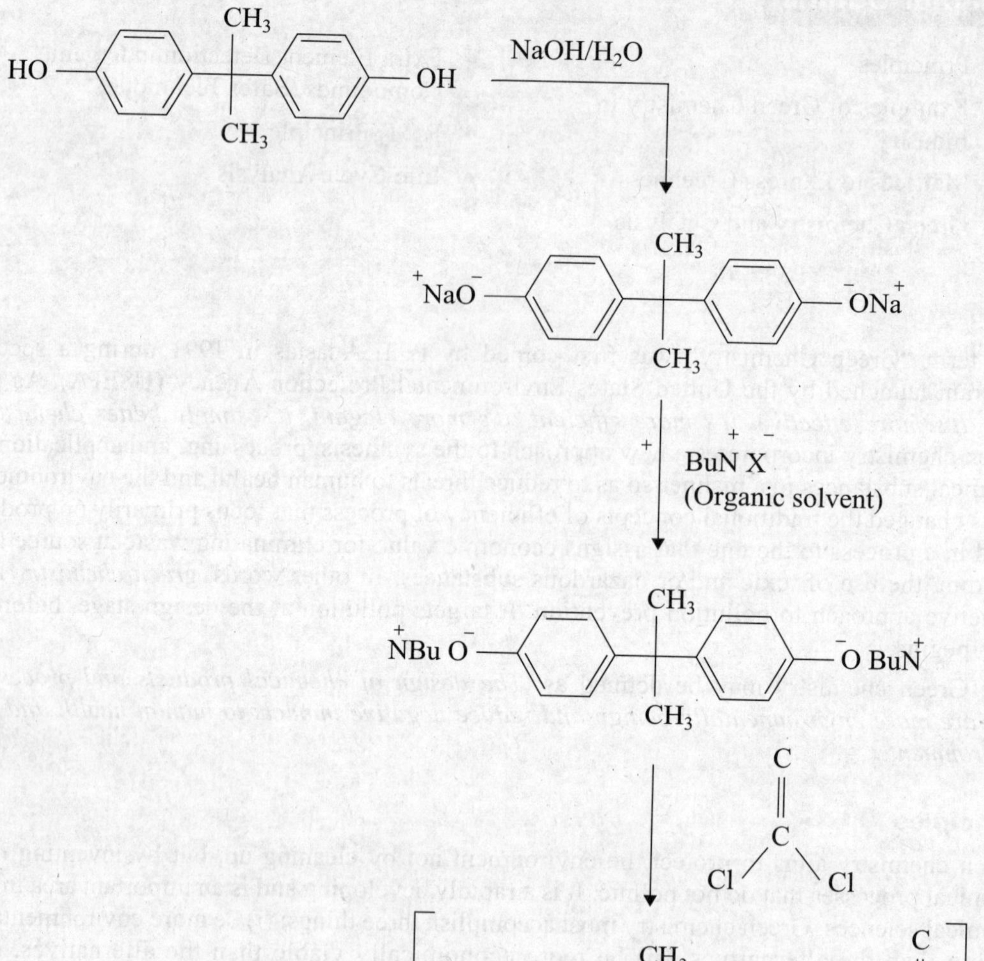

Polycarbonate (Lexan)

common one is manufactured from bisphenol A by condensation reaction with carbonyl chloride (phosgene). The reaction is a two-phase reaction (i.e., water + immiscible organic solvent). The Bu_4N^+ is a *phase transfer catalyst*, which improves the solubility of the phenolate in the organic phase and greatly speeds reaction. This is an example of an *interfacial polymerization.* Carbonyl chloride is a very poisonous gas, manufactured from other hazardous gases such as carbon monoxide and chlorine.

Greener method

Polycarbonates can also be made by ester exchange using dimethyl carbonate or diphenyl carbonate. The process for the production of polycarbonate that uses dimethyl/diphenyl carbonate is less hazardous than the process of using phosgene or carbonyl chloride. Dimethyl carbonate is readily manufactured from methanol, carbon monoxide, and oxygen in the liquid phase, in the presence of copper (II) chloride, $CuCl_2$. Diphenyl carbonate is produced from dimethyl carbonate by heating with phenol in the liquid phase.

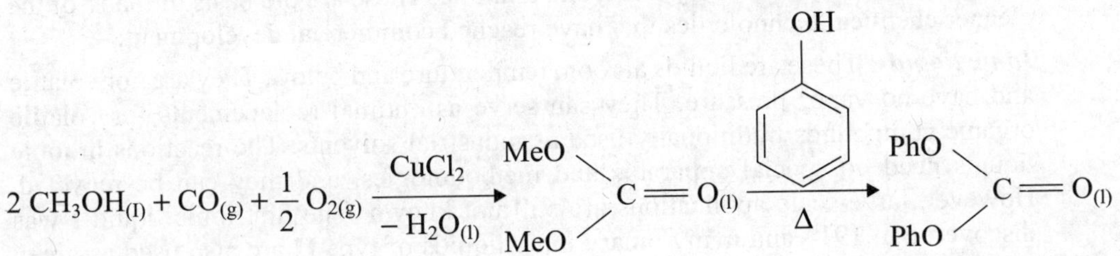

Dimethyl carbonate Diphenyl carbonate

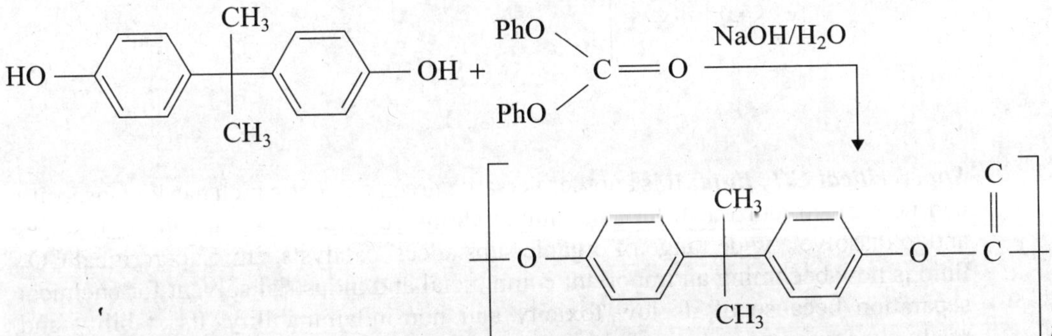

Polycarbonate (lexan)

(ii) In the manufacture of polystyrene foam sheet packing material, chlorofluorocarbons which contribute to O_3 depletion, global warming, and ground level smog have now been replaced by CO_2 as the blooming agent.

4. **Design of relatively safe chemicals**: Chemical products should be designed to cause their desired function keeping their toxicity at a minimum level. For example, racemic thalidomide (thalidomide marketed under the brand names Inmunoprin/

Talidex/Talizer/Thalomid is an immunomodulatory drug) when administered during pregnancy leads to horrible birth defects in many new born. Evidence indicates that only one of the enantiomers has the curing effect, while the other isomer is the cause of severe defects. This is why it is vital to produce the enantiomeric forms separately so that associated hazard can be reduced by maintaining their performance. Catalysts that can catalyze important reactions that produces only one of the two mirror image forms have been developed.

5. **Safer solvents and auxiliaries:** The use of auxiliary substances such as solvents and separating agents should be made unnecessary wherever possible and innocuous when used. Solvents such as alcohol, benzene (carcinogenic), CCl_4, $CHCl_3$, perchloroethylene, and CH_2Cl_2 are extensively used in most of the syntheses and most of them are toxic and volatile. Purification steps also utilize and generate large amounts of solvent and other wastes (e.g., chromatography supports). These have now been replaced by safer *green solvents* such as ionic liquids, supercritical CO_2 fluid, water or supercritical water, and also solvent-free systems that utilize the surfaces or interiors of clays, zeolites, silica, and alumina. These are the basis of many of the cleaner chemical technologies that have reached commercial development.

   Ionic liquids: These are liquids at room temperature and below. They are nonvolatile and have no vapor pressure. They can serve as optimal replacements for volatile organic compounds traditionally used as industrial solvents. The reactions in ionic liquids need no special apparatus and methodologies, and they can be recycled. However, large-scale applications are still not known. The first ionic liquid **I** was discovered in 1914 and many binary ionic liquids of type **II** are also used as green solvents.

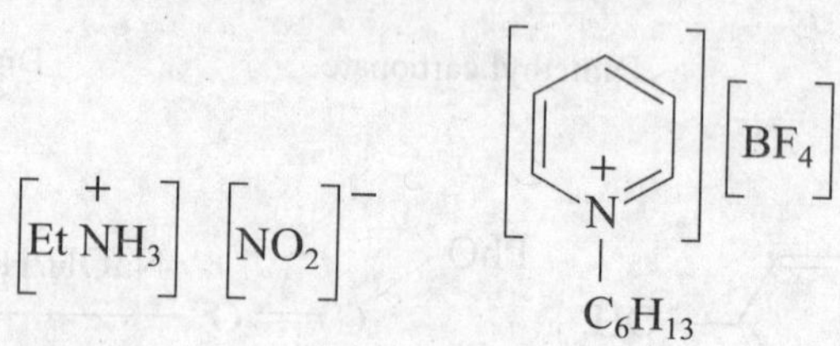

I **II**

   Supercritical CO_2 fluid: It is another versatile green solvent which has low viscosity and no surface tension. It has the unique ability to diffuse like gas through solids and to dissolve a wide range of organic substances, catalysts, etc. Supercritical CO_2 fluid is now becoming an important commercial and industrial solvent for chemical separation because of its low toxicity and non-inflammability. Its stability and relatively low temperature of the process allow most compounds to be extracted with little damage and denaturation (e.g., fragrance compounds used in perfumery). Because CO_2 is obtained as a byproduct of other industrial processes, it is inexpensive, and being a gas it is easily evaporated leaving no residue.

   Supercritical water: Organic substances are insoluble in water. Many compounds are soluble in water when it becomes supercritical at 374°C and 218 atm. Hence, this clean and cheap solvent is used as a green solvent for many synthetic reactions.

   Reactions in aqueous phase: The use of ordinary water for organic reactions was unknown till the middle of the 20th century. However, replacement of organic solvents with eco-friendly water has found success with many reactions, some of which may occur at higher rates because of its high polarity. Reactions carried out in aqueous medium include oxidations, reductions, epoxidations, polymerizations (with or without catalysts), and many name reactions. Li and Chan reported some case studies showing the innovative use of water as a reaction medium. For example, water with alcohol as co-solvent is used in Diels–Alder reactions. One example is shown here.

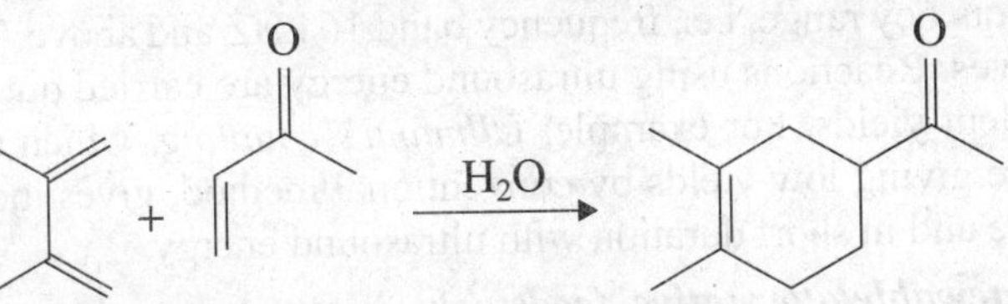

Reactions in solid phase: Large numbers of reactions occur in solid state without the solvent. These reactions are simple to operate and economical, and solvent–related pollution is avoided.

Immobilized Solvent material: Here the hazardous material is made immobilized so that its chance of release to environment can be minimized. For example, Hurter and Hatton developed a novel concept in which the hazardous substance under consideration such as THF is attached to a polymeric backbone using chlorinated styrene derivative. As THF remains attached to polymeric backbone is less likely to volatilize, it can be recovered easily by ultrafiltration.

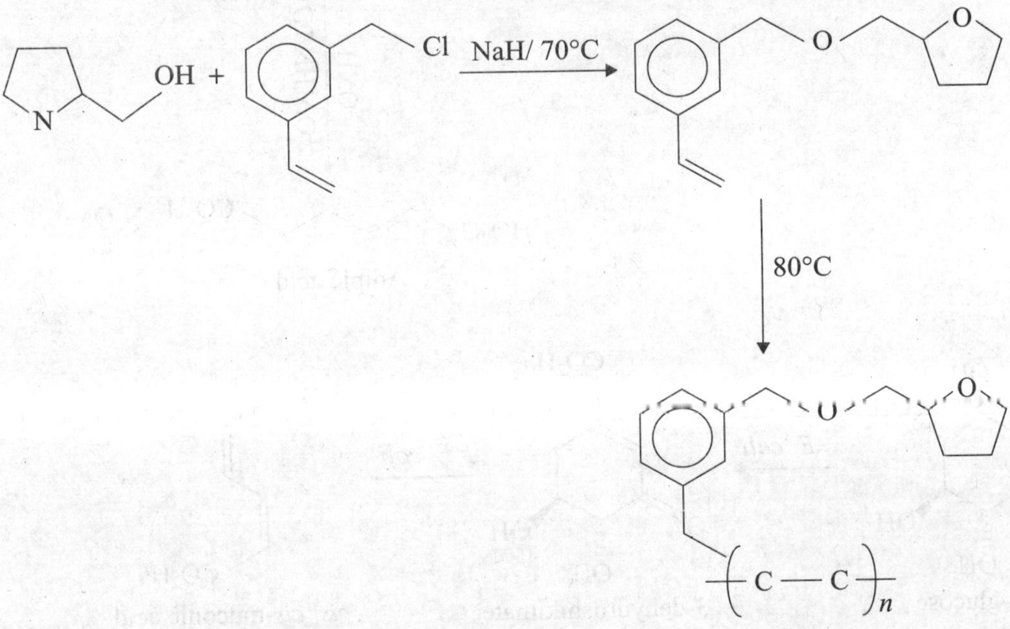

THF attached with polymer backbone

6. **Design for energy efficiency:** Energy requirements of chemical processes should be recognized for their environmental and economic impacts and should be minimized. If possible, synthetic methods should be carried out at ambient temperature and pressure.

Microwave irradiation: Reactions with microwave sources have been carried out in a solid support such as clay and silica gel, eliminating the use of solvents or with minimum amount of solvents. The reactions take place at a faster rate than thermal heating. For example, *Beckmann rearrangement* of oximes in the solid state with microwave irradiation gave quantitative yields of the products without the use of acid catalysts.

Sono-chemistry (ultrasound energy): Ultrasound is a mechanical wave beyond the audible frequency range, i.e., frequency band 16 kHZ and above. These waves are high energy waves. Reactions using ultrasound energy are carried out at room temperature with excellent yields. For example, *Ullmann's coupling,* which takes place at higher temperature giving low yields by conventional method, gives increased yields at low temperature and in short duration with ultrasound energy.

7. ***Use of renewable/alternative feedstock***: A raw material or feedstock should be renewable rather than depleting whenever technically and economically practicable. For green synthesis, the feedstock should replace the traditional petroleum sources, e.g., benzene used in the commercial synthesis of adipic acid, which is required in the manufacture of nylon, plasticizers, and lubricants, has been replaced to some extent by the renewable and nontoxic glucose and the reaction is carried out in water.

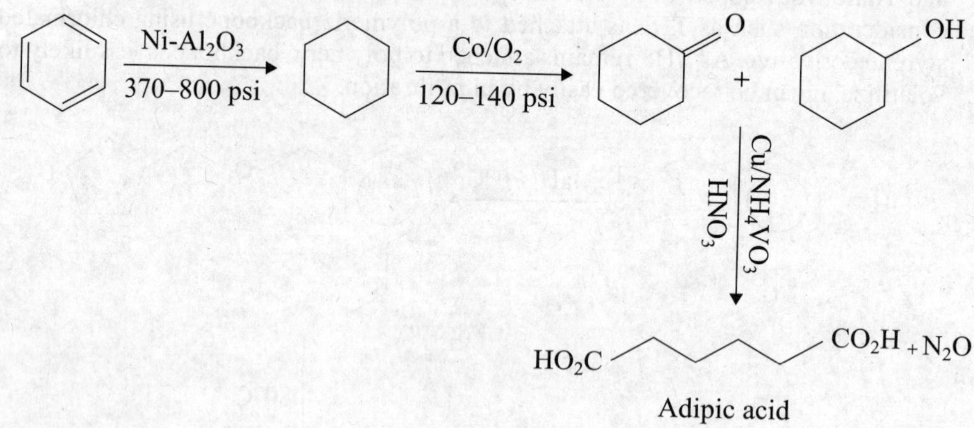

Greener

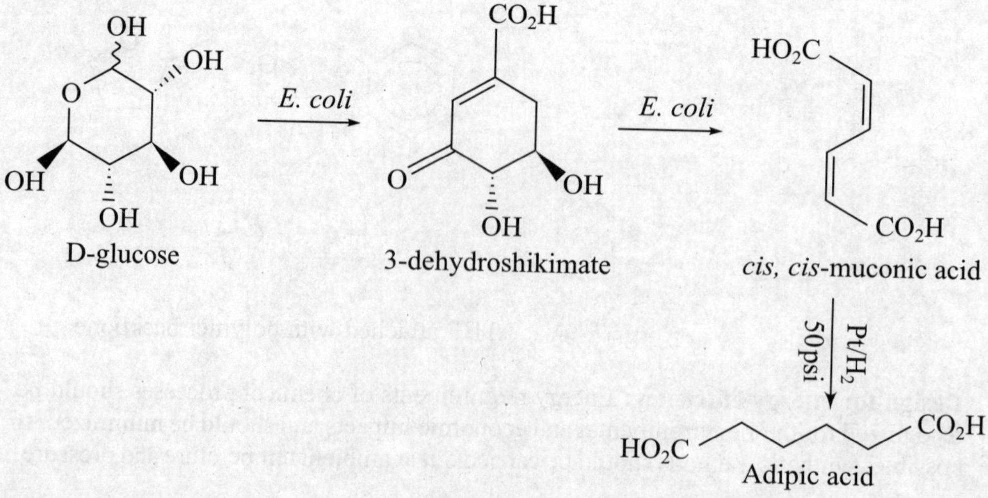

Indigo is a widely used dye. This is prepared by taking aniline as the starting material, which is highly toxic. In addition, the conventional process also generates considerable amount of waste salts. In the greener method, it is made by removal of side chain of tryptophan to give indole which is then hydroxylated and then oxidized to yield indigo.

Conventional route

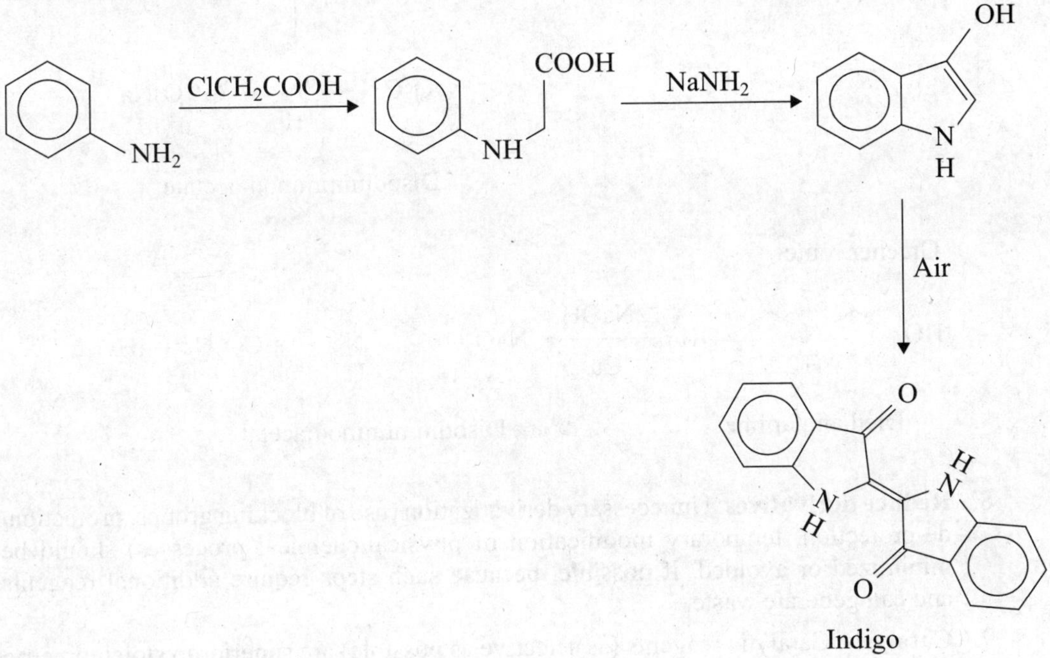

Greener route

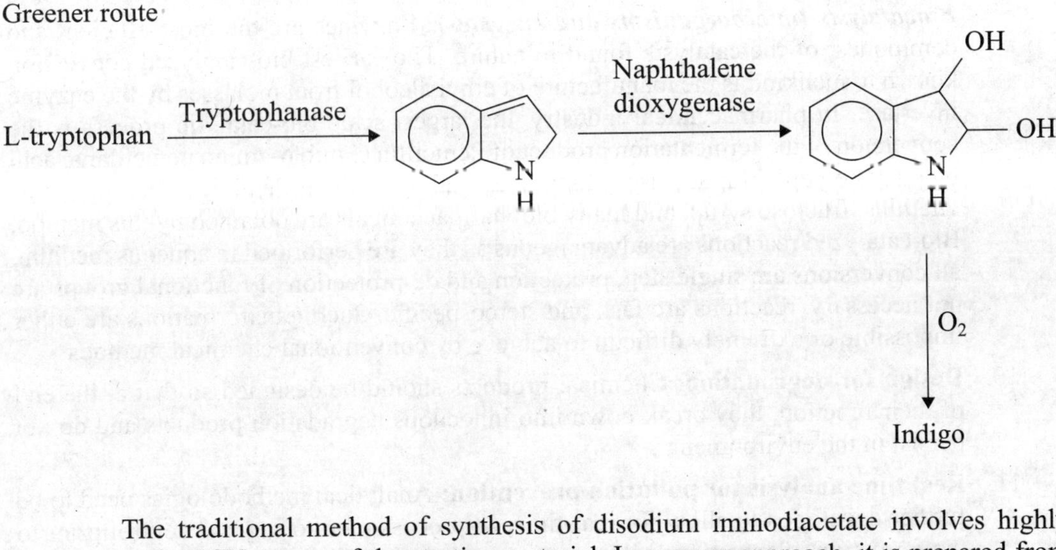

The traditional method of synthesis of disodium iminodiacetate involves highly toxic KCN as one of the starting material. In greener approach, it is prepared from diethanolamine as the starting material.

Conventional route

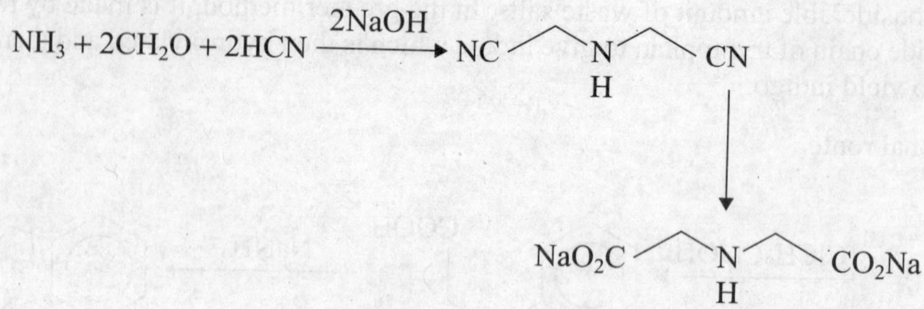

Disodiumiminodiacetate

Greener route

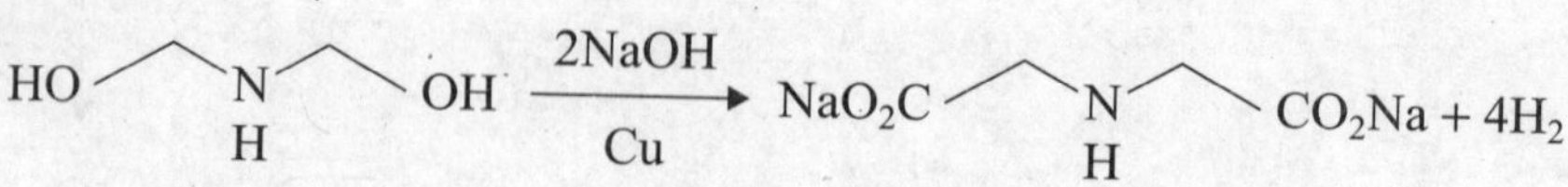

Diethanolamine Disodiumiminodiacetate

8. **Reduce derivatives**: Unnecessary derivatization (use of blocking groups, protection/de-protection, temporary modification of physical/chemical processes) should be minimized or avoided, if possible, because such steps require additional reagents and can generate waste.
9. **Catalysis**: Catalytic reagents (as selective as possible) are superior to stoichiometric reagents. Apart from heavy metal catalysts, *softer catalysts* such as zeolites and phase transfer catalysts, e.g., crown ethers, are finding increasing industrial applications.

   Biocatalysts (microorganisms and enzymes): Enzymes are the most efficient and commonest of the catalysts found in nature. The earliest bio-catalyzed conversion known to mankind is the manufacture of ethyl alcohol from molasses by the enzyme invertase. In pharmaceutical industry, the largest scale bio-catalytic process is the conversion of the fermentation product of Penicillin G into 6-amino penicillanic acid by enzyme penicillin acylase. Many chemically modified Penicillins, amino acids, vitamins, fructose syrup, and many biopharmaceuticals are obtained by this method. Bio-catalyzed reactions are advantageous as they are performed in aqueous medium, all conversions are single step, protection and de-protection of functional groups are not necessary, reactions are fast, and stereospecific. Such transformations are either impossible or extremely difficult to achieve by conventional chemical methods.
10. **Design for degradation**: Chemical products should be designed so that at the end of their function, they break down into innocuous degradation products and do not persist in the environment.
11. **Real time analysis for pollution prevention:** Analytical methodologies need to be further developed to allow for real-time, in-process monitoring and control prior to the formation of hazardous substances.
12. **Inherently safer chemistry for accident prevention**: Substances and the form of a substance used in a chemical process should be chosen to minimize the potential

for chemical accidents, including releases, explosions, and fires. Manufacture of gold atom nanoparticles used diborane (highly toxic and bursts into flame near room temperature) and cancer-causing benzene. Now, diborane has been replaced by environmentally benign sodium borohydride ($NaBH_4$), which also eliminates the use of benzene. Nanoscience and nanotechnology are another important contribution to green chemistry. Nanotechnology provides huge savings in materials by development of microscopic and submicroscopic electronic and mechanical devices.

Examples of Green Chemistry in Industry

Let us look into some common examples of Green chemistry in industries:

1. The most polluting reaction in industry is oxidation. Implementation of green chemistry has led to the use of alternative less polluting reagents, viz., metal ion contamination is minimized by using molecular O_2 as the primary oxidant and use of extremely high oxidation state transition metal complexes.
2. Diels–Alder reaction is 100% atom economy reaction as all the atoms of the reactants are incorporated in the cyclo-adduct. Other examples of reactions often exploited in industry are isomerization reaction, metathesis, and addition reactions, which are quite atom economical processes.
3. Conventional methylation reactions employing toxic alkyl halides or methylsulfate, leading to environmental hazard are replaced by dimethyl carbonate with no deposit of inorganic salts. For example, methylation of aryl acetonitrile in the presence of K_2CO_3 to 2-arylpropionitriles (>99%).
4. The use of phosgene and methylene chloride in the synthesis of polycarbonates has been replaced by diphenyl carbonate.
5. Use of CO_2 as a reaction medium for asymmetric catalytic reductions, particularly hydrogenation and H_2 transfer reactions.
6. A convenient green synthesis of acetaldehyde is by *Wackerchemie's oxidation* of ethylene with O_2 in the presence of a catalyst, in place of its synthesis by oxidation of ethanol or hydration of acelylene with H_2SO_4.

Matrices to Express Greenness

E-Factor

The greenness of a chemical process can be expressed by a term called E-Factor (environmental factor) which was introduced by Roger Sheldon. It is defined as the mass ratio of waste to desired product.

$$\text{E-Factor} = \frac{\text{Total mass of waste}}{\text{Product mass}} \tag{22.1}$$

Although the ideal E-factor of 0 is almost achieved in petroleum refining, the production of bulk and fine chemicals gives E-factors of between 1 and 50. Typical E-factors for the production of pharmaceuticals lie between 25 and 100. Note that water is not considered in this calculation, because this would lead to very high E-factors. However, inorganic and organic wastes that are diluted in the aqueous stream must be included. Sometimes it is easier to calculate the E-factor from a different viewpoint, since accounting for the losses and exact waste streams is difficult:

$$\text{E-Factor} = \frac{\text{Weight of raw materials} - \text{Weight of product}}{\text{Weight of product}} \quad [22.2]$$

A higher E-factor means more waste, which leads to a greater negative environmental impact. Note that water is not considered in this calculation, because this would lead to very high E-factor value. However, inorganic and organic wastes that are diluted in the aqueous stream must be included.

Atom Economy

The concept of atom economy or atom efficiency was first introduced by Barry Trost. This is an extremely useful tool for the evaluation of the amounts of waste that will be generated by different processes. It is the ratio of the molecular mass of the product and the total molecular mass of all substances formed as represented in the stoichiometric equation for the reaction. In contrast to the E-factor, it is a theoretical number based on stoichiometric amounts and disregards those substances which do not appear in the stoichiometric equation. For example, the atom efficiencies in oxidation of a secondary alcohol to the corresponding ketone are compared. In the first scheme, stoichiometric CrO_3 is used, whereas the second is carried out in the presence of a catalyst.

Scheme 1

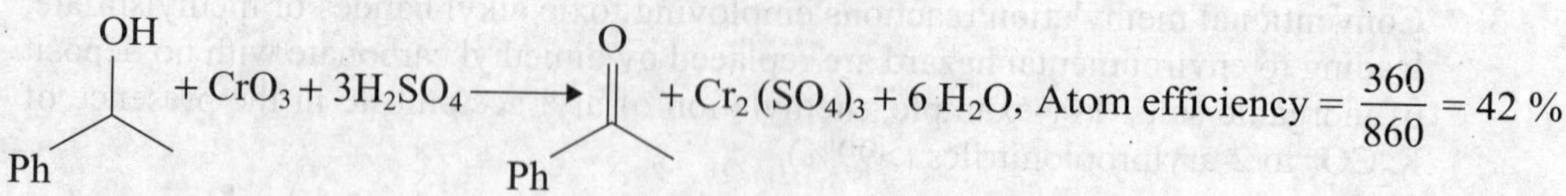

Scheme 2

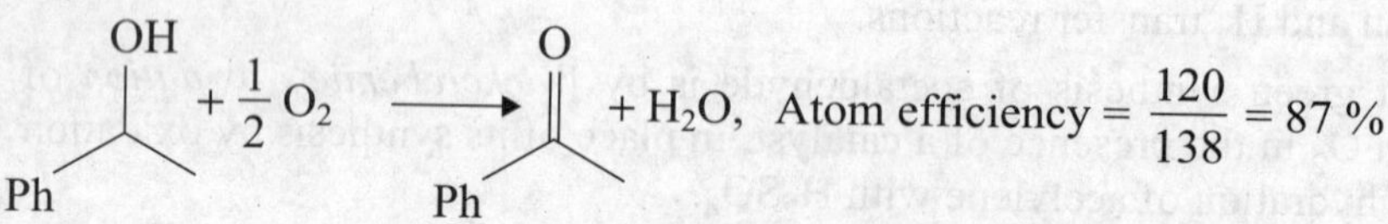

Environmental Quotient

The E-factor and atom economy can be used for comparing reaction alternatives, but we should remember that there are different types of wastes. The reaction described above has two by-products, i.e., chromium sulfate and water. Obviously, water is a good waste, while chromium sulfate is a bad waste. Therefore, evaluating synthetic processes on the basis of only the amount of waste produced is insufficient. To solve this problem, Sheldon put forward the concept of the environmental quotient (EQ). It is obtained by multiplying the E-factor by Q, an arbitrarily assigned hazard quotient. This measure takes into account both the amount and the nature of the waste. Assigning absolute Q-values to waste streams is difficult, because cases differ according to location and type of waste. Nevertheless, the EQ gives a better measure of the environmental impact of a process than the E-factor or the atom economy alone.

Green Chemistry and Catalysis

In the light of Green chemistry principles, a good catalyst possess the following qualities:

1. It plays a vital role in the environmentally benign synthesis of new and existing chemicals.
2. It is environmentally safe.
3. It produces fewer by-products, co-products, and other waste products and hence addresses the benefits of atom economy.
4. It reduces more number of steps into less number of steps.
5. It reduces the overall E-factor for a synthesis.
6. It minimizes the hazard.

Let us try to illustrate the above points through some specimen examples:

1. Conventional synthesis of methyl isocyanate (MIC) produces HCl as byproduct and uses phosgene. HCl is corrosive and hazardous, while phosgene is highly toxic. New catalytic synthesis of the same eliminates the hazardous use of toxic chemical phosgene.

   Conventional method

$$CH_3NH_2 + COCl_2 \longrightarrow \underset{\text{(MIC)}}{CH_3NCO} + HCl$$

   Catalytic method

$$CH_3NH_2 + CO \xrightarrow{\text{Catalyst}} \underset{\text{(MIC)}}{CH_3NHCHO}$$

$$CH_3NHCHO \xrightarrow[\text{Catalyst}]{O_2} CH_3NCO$$

2. Conventional synthesis of acryl amide utilizes corrosive acid and ammonia. Moreover, a huge amount of ammonium sulfate is generated as by-product. New enzymatic synthesis of acryl amide is a clean synthesis with high atom economy and low E factor.

   Conventional method

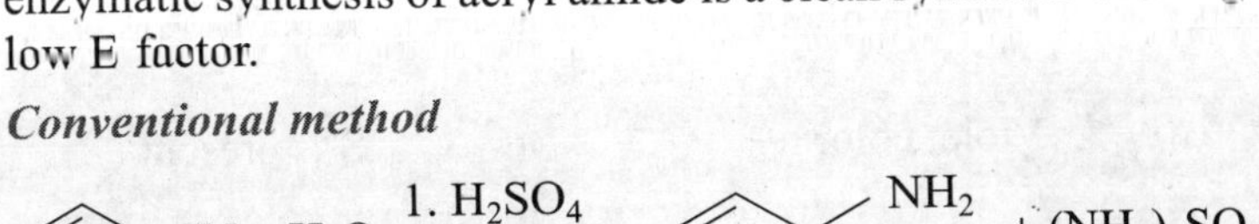

   Catalytic method

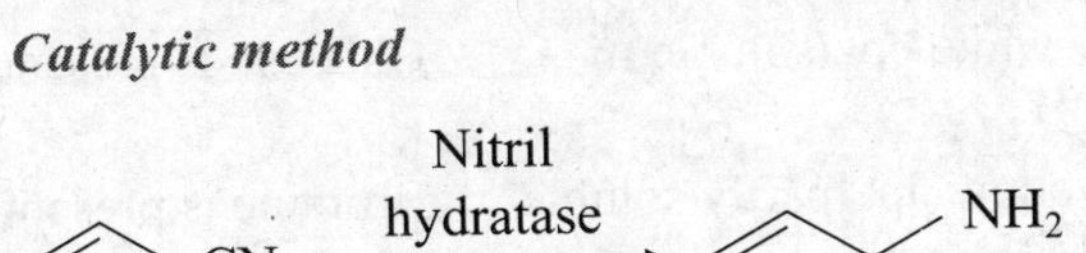

3. Conventionally, carboxylic acid cannot be directly converted into amide derivative. Preparation of the intermediate acid chloride demands the use of thionyl chloride or phosphorous pentachloride. Both these reagents are hazardous in nature. It also produces a lot of HCl as by-product, which is corrosive in nature. On the other hand, boric acid is non-toxic, safe, and inexpensive. So boric acid is a green catalyst. Moreover, the E-factor of this catalyzed reaction is much lower compared to the un-catalyzed version.

$$\textit{Conventional: } RCO_2H \xrightarrow[PCl_5]{SOCl_2 \textit{ or}} RCOCl \xrightarrow{R'NH_2} RCONHR'$$

$$\textit{Catalytic: } RCO_2H + R'NH_2 \xrightarrow[\text{toluene reflux}]{B(OH)_3} RCONHR' + H_2O$$

4. Conventionally, adipic acid is synthesized by oxidation of cyclohexanone/cyclohexanol under drastic reaction conditions of using HNO_3 acid. On the other hand, the same product may be obtained from D-glucose through the enzymatic oxidation and degradation process under mild reaction conditions (both the reactions are discussed above under renewable feedstock).

Extra Element Detection in Organic Compounds (Safer Technique)

In conventional practice (Lassaigen's test) for organic qualitative analysis, the organic compound is fused with metallic sodium so as to convert the water-insoluble organically bound elements to water-soluble sodium salts which can be easily detected. Here there is always a possibility of explosion and fire hazard. In *green approach,* the organic compound is fused with an intimate mixture of Zn dust and Na_2CO_3 in 2:3 weight ratios in a fusion tube. The fused mass is then extracted with distilled water and the filtrate is used to test sulfur, nitrogen, and halogens in a very similar manner as that used in Lassaigen's test (described below in a comprehensive manner). There is a possibility of explosion and fire hazard in this approach. In addition, the Zn–alkali fusion mixture can be prepared and stored in a bottle for months together.

Test	Observation	Inference
Filtrate + $FeSO_4$ crystals Heat + dil. H_2SO_4	Prussian blue color	N is present
Filtrate + Sodium nitroprusside $Na_2[Fe(CN)_5NO]$	Violet color	S is present
Filtrate + dil. CH_3COOH + $Pb(CH_3COO)_2$	Black ppt.	S is present
Filtrate + Conc. HNO_3 boil then cool + $AgNO_3$	Curdy white ppt. soluble in NH_4OH	Chlorine is present
	Pale yellow ppt. partly soluble in NH_4OH	Bromine is present
	Yellow ppt. insoluble in NH_4OH	Iodine is present

Precautions

1. During fusion, the fusion tube must be heated very slowly and uniformly keeping in red hot condition for at least 2 min for proper fusion.
2. The amount of distilled water used for extraction must be limited to ~5 ml.
3. During N test, $FeSO_4$ crystals must be added instead of solution to avoid excess dilution. In addition, H_2SO_4, instead of HCl, is used for acidification.

R_4M_4 Principles or Models

R_4 stands for reduce, reuse, recycle, redesign, whereas M_4 stands for multidimensional, multitasking, multitracking, and multifaceted. Here two instruments based on this model have been discussed.

Econoburette

Econoburette is developed for semimicro volumetric titration. These are used for risk-free titration where pipette is replaced by an inbuilt pipette and conical flask by an inbuilt bulb. Pipetting of stock solution by mouth is not required, which prevent exposure of user's body to chemicals. This allows titration of volatile and toxic solutions with full-proof safety. Econoburette minimizes the use of materials and time by 90% and prevent discharge of polluting effluent to the environment. A typical econoburette designed by Man Singh is shown in Fig. 22.1. The econoburette consists of three graduated tubes (graduated in 0.05 ml) which open in a common glass bulb attached below. The set up for acid–base titration in econoburette is shown in the figure. As shown, one limb is used for taking acid, another for base, and the third one is used for the indicator. During titration, the chemical—acid, base, and the indicator—can be released by the stopcock attached to each of the tubes. After finishing each titration, the mixture was removed from flask via valve below. The reaction mixture is stirred with glass stirrer. The process is repeated for 3 concordant readings.

Survismeter

There are numerous uses of viscosity, surface tension, and interfacial tension (IFT) measurements in industrial cleaning, wettabilities, surface designing, etc. Different individual instruments such as viscometer and stalgmoeter are used which requires separate infrastructure, time, resources, and laboratory occupation. However, with the emergence of Green chemistry, there has been much concern for clean and green environment where discharge of volatile organic liquids such as dioxin and benzene which are carcinogenic is not safe. Survismeter is a significant device that provides quick multitasking economic facility to users. This instrument is based on R_4M_4 principles for measurement of surface tension, interfacial tension, wetting coefficient, frictiohesity, and viscosity with the use of minimum quantity of resources and minimum discharge of effluents to environment after use. Poisonous and most volatile liquids or mixtures can also be studied without their escape to environment. It is excellent in study of liquid–liquid interface (LLI) of two immiscible solvents. A typical survismeter as designed by Man Singh is shown in Fig. 22.2.

The important parts of the survismeter being: (i) sample reservoir or master bulb-sample loading, (ii) control pressure unit (CPU)—carbureting and bypassing, (iii) uniform functional capillaries—fluid dynamics and monitoring, (iv) functional bulbs—for measurements and regulatory, (v) buffer bulbs—equilibrium and operational time, (vi) lock and key junctions—monitor sequential operations, (vii) connectors—integrated unit, (viii) liquid lifting device—pressure gradient pump, (ix) interfacial tension capillary—for IFT, (x) electronic timer—for viscous flow times, (xi) pendant drop counter—for drop counts, (xii) leveler—for vertical positions at 90° angle, (xiii) reflector—for column rise in IFT capillary.

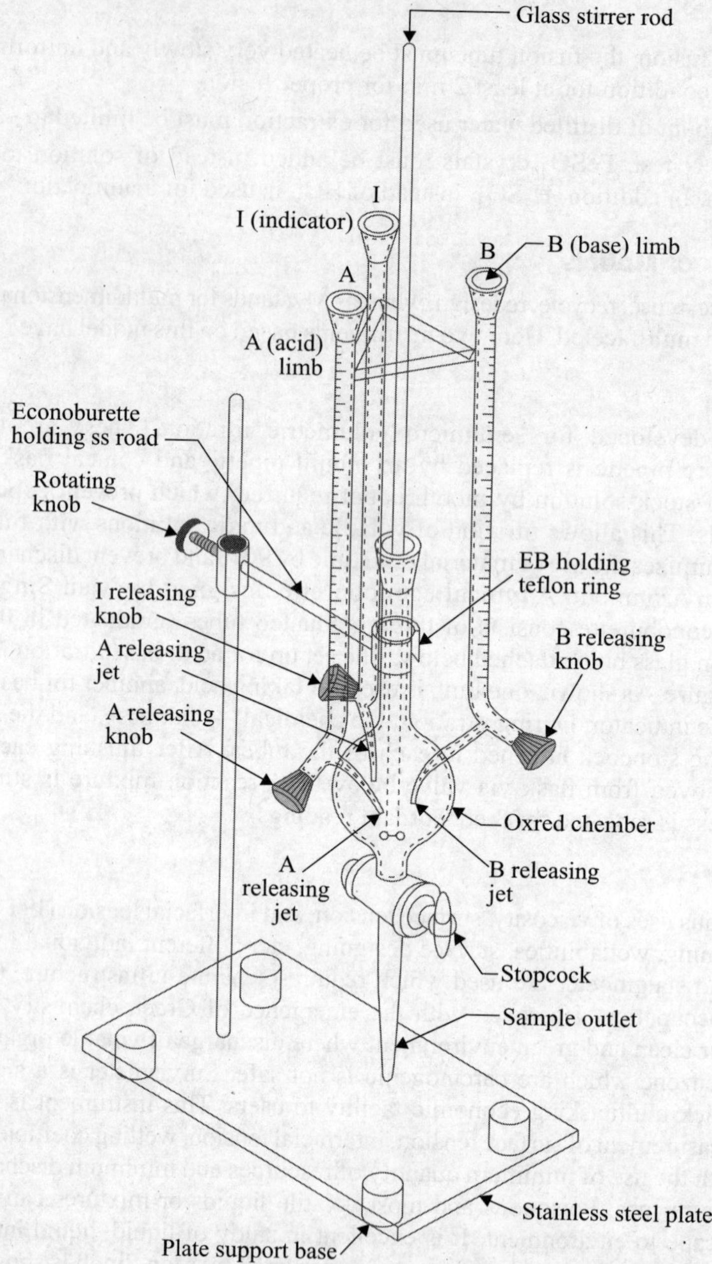

Fig. 22.1 Econoburette

Life Cycle Analysis

Society has now become seriously concerned about the issues of natural resource depletion and environmental degradation. Lot of focus has now been diverted toward developing *greener* products and using *greener* processes. Thus, companies are trying to explore pollution prevention strategies and environmental management systems to improve the environmental performance of their products and practiced processes. One such tool is life cycle analysis (LCA) which is a novel approach that provides a standard algorithm for assessment of the environment impact of a production operation. It was developed in the 1980s. The approach encompasses all stages

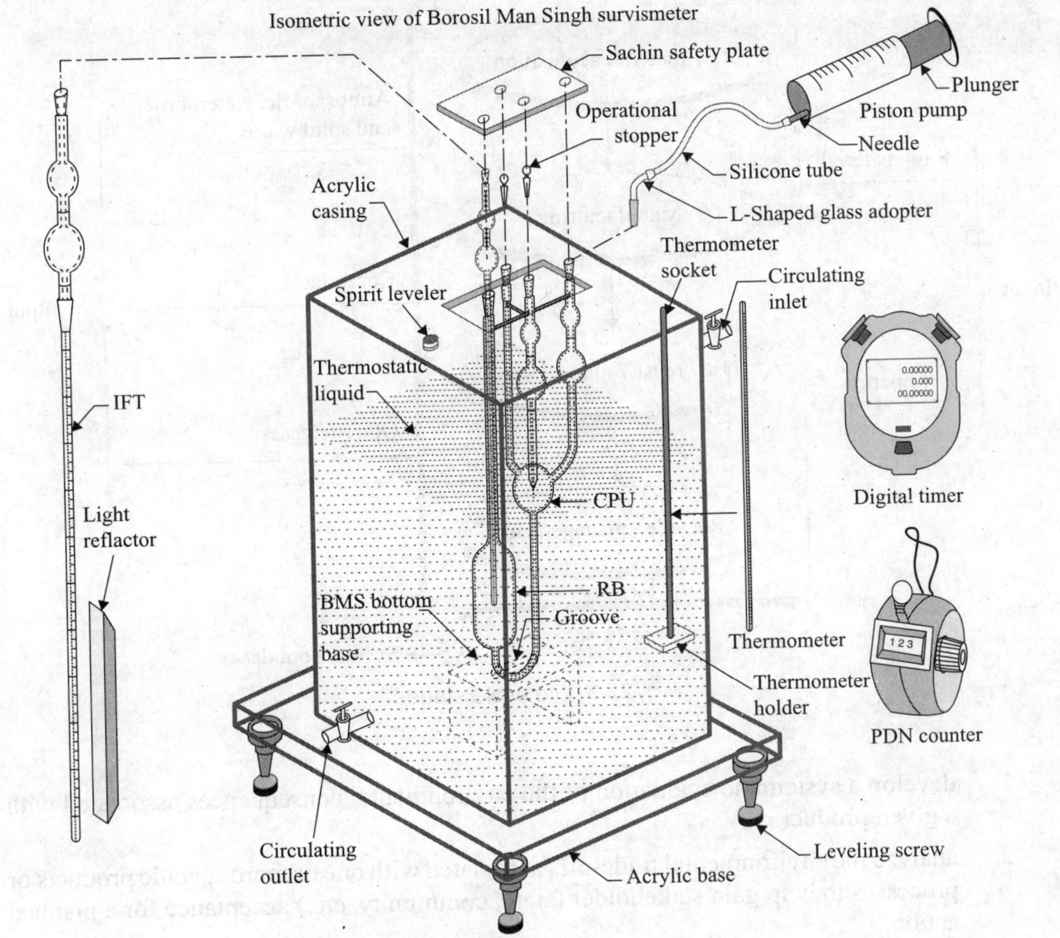

Fig. 22.2 Man Singh survismeter

Source: Survismeter, 3-in-1 Instrument for Simultaneous Measurements of Surface Tension, Inter Facial Tension (IFT) and Viscosity, Man Singh, *Pak. J. Anal. Environ. Chem.*, 8(1&2), 2007, 82–85.

of a product's life from raw material gathering through production and consumption, to waste, i.e., from *cradle to grave*. LCA enables scientists to estimate the cumulative environmental impacts resulting from all stages in the product's life cycle, often including impacts those are not considered in traditional analyses such as raw material extraction, material transportation, and ultimate product disposal. Figure 22.3 illustrates the possible life cycle stages that can be considered in an LCA and the typical inputs and outputs measured.

Benefits of Conducting LCA

An LCA can help decision makers to select the product or process that puts in the least impact to the environment. For selecting a product or process, LCA information can be coupled with other information such as cost and performance data. LCA data identify the transfer of environmental impacts from one media to another (e.g., eliminating air emissions by creating a wastewater effluent instead) and/or from one life cycle stage to another (e.g., from use and reuse of the product to the raw material acquisition phase). By performing an LCA, analysts[1] can

[1]*Life Cycle Assessment: Principles and Practice*, U.S. Environmental Protection Agency, EPA/600/R-06/060, May 2006.

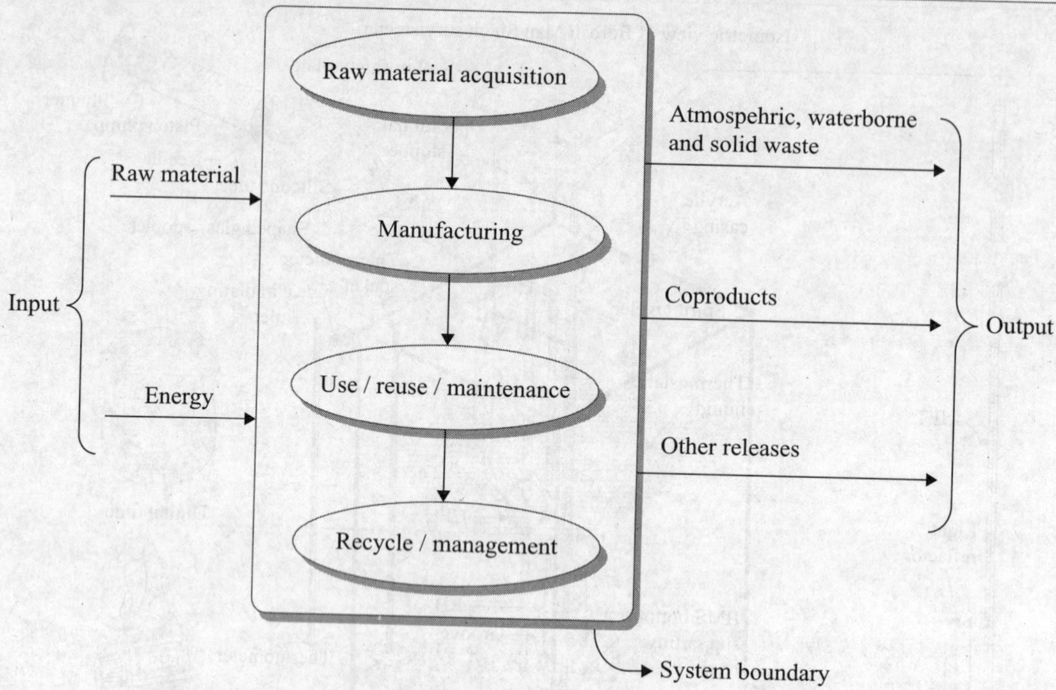

Fig. 22.3 Life cycle stages

1. develop a systematic evaluation of the environmental consequences associated with a given product.
2. analyze the environmental trade-offs associated with one or more specific products or processes to help gain stakeholder (state, community, etc.) acceptance for a planned action.
3. quantify environmental releases to air, water, and land in relation to each life cycle stage and/or major contributing process.
4. assist in identifying significant shifts in environmental impacts between life cycle stages and environmental media.
5. assess the human and ecological effects of material consumption and environmental releases to the local community, region, and world.
6. compare the health and ecological impacts between two or more rival products or processes or identify the impacts of a specific product or process.
7. identify impacts to one or more specific environmental areas of concern.

Limitation of Conducting LCA

The limitations of LCA are as follows:

1. LCA cannot determine which product or process is the most cost-effective or works the best. The information of an LCA study can only be used as one component of a more comprehensive decision-making process assessing the trade-offs with cost and performance, e.g., life cycle management (LCM). LCM is an integrated framework

of concepts and techniques to address environmental, economic, technological, and social aspects of products, services, and organizations.

2. A single model for LCA may not fit everywhere due to the complexity of environmental systems.
3. LCA helps to identify potential environmental trade-offs. However, converting the impact results into a single score requires the use of value judgments, which is made by the commissioner of the study or the modeler.

QUESTIONS

1. What do you mean by Green chemistry?
2. What are the principles of Green chemistry?
3. Explain green solvents with suitable examples.
4. What are the goals of Green chemistry perspective?
5. What are different matrices to express greenness?
6. Explain importance of "atom economy" with a suitable example.
7. Explain less hazardous chemical synthesis with suitable example.
8. Explain ionic liquids with suitable examples.
9. What do you mean by "Cradle to Grave" approach in Green chemistry?
10. What is LCA? Provide possible life cycle stages that can be considered in an LCA.
11. What are the advantages and disadvantages of LCA?
12. What do you mean by R_4M_4 approach?
13. What is survismeter? Why it is named so?
14. What is econoburette?
15. What are the advantages of an econoburette over the traditional one?
16. Discuss the safer and greener technique for detection of extra elements in organic compounds.
17. In which way Zn-alkali fusion is greener over traditional metallic sodium fusion?
18. Explain *E-factor* and *Environmental Quotient* (EQ).
19. Name two green solvents.
20. What is supercritical CO_2?
21. Explain catalytic reagents are superior to stoichiometric reagents.
22. What do you mean by "using alternate feedstock"? Explain with a suitable example.
23. Suggest how to minimize the energy requirements of chemical processes.
24. Explain dry media/solid phase reaction with a suitable example.

CHAPTER

23 Periodic Classification

Chapter Outline

- Periodic Table
- Block Classification Based on Electronic Configuration
- Shielding/Screening Effect
- Periodic Properties

Every matter in the Universe is made of elements. Till date 118 elements have been discovered. Among these, there are many elements which are plenty available in the earth crust while some of them are rarely available and termed as rare earths. There are some elements which are only prepared in the lab by nuclear transmutation process and are short lived, particularly elements after ^{92}U which are known as transuranic elements. All these elements are having versatile characteristics. It is difficult to study the properties of all these elements individually. Therefore, there is an urgent need of classifying elements into different groups so that similar elements can be placed together and can be kept separated from dissimilar elements to facilitate their property study. The tabular array so obtained is known as Periodic Table. As per Glenn T. Seaborg, Nobel Prize winner in Chemistry (1951), Periodic Table is a remarkable demonstration of the fact that the chemical elements are not a random cluster of entities but instead display trends and lie together in families. An awareness of the Periodic Table is essential to anyone who wishes to disentangle the world and see how it is built up from the fundamental building blocks of the chemistry, the chemical elements.

Periodic Table

The periodic table is a tabular array of the elements organized with respect to some characteristic aspect so that similar elements can be placed together and can be kept separated from dissimilar elements. Different workers such as Dobereiner, John Alexander Newlands, Dmitri Mendeleev, and many others have put their effort to develop the periodic table. However, the most successful effort was by Russian Chemist Mendeleev. He proposed that '*the properties of elements are a periodic function of their atomic weights*', which is also known as the Mendeleev's periodic law. Mendeleev arranged the elements according to his law in the increasing order of their atomic weights. The periodic table so developed suffers from several limitations viz. ambiguity with respect to the position of hydrogen, certain places of the periodic table are there where similar elements are placed at different places while dissimilar elements are placed together, no place is demarcated for putting isotopes, there are four anomalous pairs of elements where the rule of increasing atomic weight has been ignored and no separate position has been fixed for lanthanides and actinides. This is all about the history of the development of periodic table in brief.

The latest form periodic table which is in use now-a-days is the ***extended or long form of periodic table*** recommended by IUPAC which is based on the modern periodic law by Moseley (1911) i.e., '*the properties of elements are a periodic function of their atomic number*'. This periodic table has 18 vertical columns or groups and these group numbers arranged from Group-1, i.e., alkali metals through Group-18, i.e., noble gas elements. There are altogether seven horizontal rows or periods in this form of periodic table. The period number corresponds to the highest principal quantum number (n) of the elements in the period. The first period contains 2 elements. The subsequent periods consist of 8, 8, 18, 18, 32, and 32 elements, respectively. In this form of the Periodic Table, 14 elements each of the sixth and seventh periods (lanthanides and actinides, respectively) are placed separately below the main platform.

Block Classification Based on Electronic Configuration

The block classification of elements is based on the fact the last electron enters to which subshell of the principal shell.

***s-block*:** In the elements of s-block, the last electron enters to s-subshell of ultimate, or outermost shell i.e., ns-subshell. Here ns-subshell is progressively filled. As s-subshell can accommodate two electrons, this block consists of two groups viz. group 1 and 2 and is present at extreme left of the periodic table. The general electronic configuration is $ns^{1,\,2}$. The group 1 elements are known as alkali metals with valence shell configuration, ns^1, while group 2 are known as alkaline earth metals with valence shell configuration, ns^2. All elements belonging to this block, except hydrogen, are metals.

IUPAC Periodic Table of the Elements

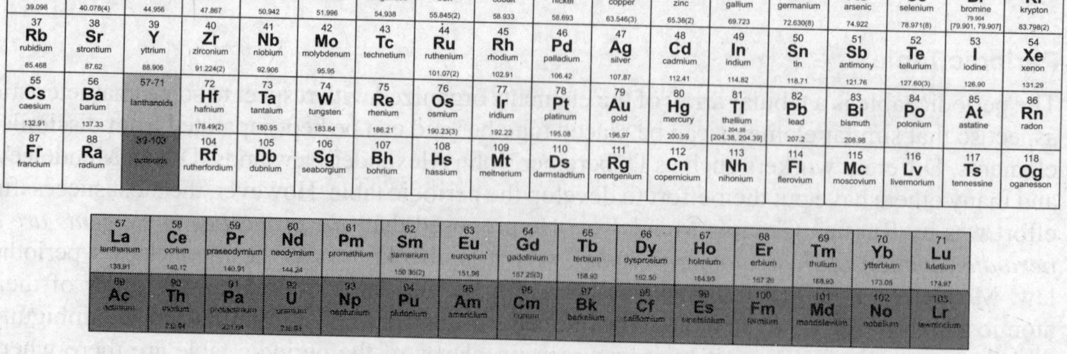

Fig. 23.1 Long form periodic table

***p-block*:** The last electron enters to p-subshell of the ultimate or outermost shell. In these elements np-subshell is progressively filled. As p-subshell can accommodate six electrons, this block consists of six groups viz. group 13 to 18 and is present at the extreme right of the periodic table. The general electronic configuration is ns^2, np^{1-6} (ns^2, np^1 for group 13 to ns^2, np^6 for group 18. s- and p-block elements together are known as normal or representative elements as in these elements, the ultimate shell is incomplete and progressively filled. This block consists of different types of elements such as some metals, all non-metals, all metalloids, and noble gases.

***d-block*:** In the elements of this block, either in their atomic state or in any of their common oxidation states, the last electron enters to d-subshell of the penultimate or inner to the outermost shell. In the elements belonging to this block *(n – 1)* d-subshell is progressively filled. As d-subshell can accommodate 10 electrons, this block consists of ten groups viz. group 3 to 12 and present at the middle of the periodic table in between s- and p-blocks. The general electronic configuration is: $(n-1)\ d^{1-10},\ ns^{0-2}$. The elements of d-block are also called *transition elements* as their properties are intermediate between those of s- and p-block elements. All these elements are metals and exhibit variable oxidation states. These elements exhibit all three different types of close packing viz. face cantered cubic (fcc), hexagonal close packing (hcp) and body cantered cubic (bcc) structures. These elements are again classified into four series corresponding to the filling of the *(n – 1)* d subshell.

- 3d-series (1st transition series): These elements are present in the 4th period and have general electronic configuration of $3d^{1-10}$, $4s^{1,2}$. There are 10 elements, ^{21}Sc ($3d^1$, $4s^2$) to ^{30}Zn ($3d^{10}$, $4s^2$) in this series.
- 4d-series (2nd transition series): This series is having configuration of $4d^{1-10}$, $4s^{0-2}$ and consists of 10 elements, ^{39}Y ($4d^1$, $5s^2$) to ^{48}Cd ($4d^{10}$, $5s^2$) which are present in the 5th period.
- 5d-series (3rd transition series): This series consists of 10 elements, ^{57}La ($4f^0$, $5d^1$, $6s^2$) and ^{72}Hf ($4f^{14}$, $5d^2$,$6s^2$) to ^{80}Hg ($4f^{14}$, $5d^{10}$,$6s^2$). The elements of this series lie in the 6th period. The 14 elements from ^{58}Ce to ^{71}Lu are placed outside the main body of the periodic table in a separate block.
- 6d-series (4th transition series): This series consists again of 10 elements, ^{89}Ac ($5f^0$, $6d^1$, $7s^2$) and ^{104}Rf ($5f^{14}$, $6d^2$,$7s^2$) to ^{118}Og ($5f^{14}$, $6d^{10}$,$7s^2$). The elements of this series lie in the 6th period. The 14 elements from ^{90}Th to ^{103}Lr are placed outside the main body of the periodic table in a separate f-block.

***f-block*:** In these elements, either in their atomic state or in any of the common oxidation states, the last electron enters to f-subshell of the antepenultimate or inner to the penultimate shell. The general configuration is: $(n-2)\ f^{2-7,\,9-14},\ (n-1)\ d^{0,1},\ ns^2$. This group is placed separately below the main frame of the periodic table. The location is in the group 3 of the main body. This block consists of two sets of 14 elements. The 1st one is the 4f-series which is from ^{58}Ce to ^{72}Lu along with the parent group-3 element ^{57}La. As per the name of the parent element, this group of 15 elements is known as lanthanides. This is also sometimes known as rare earths due their very low abundancy in earth crust. The general configuration being, $4f^{2-7,\,9-14}$, $5d^{0,1}$, $6s^2$. The 2nd one is the 5f-series which is from ^{90}Th to ^{103}Lr along with the parent group 3 element ^{89}Ac. As per the name of the parent element, this group of 15 elements is known as actinides. The general configuration being, $5f^{2-7,\,9-14}$, $6d^{0,1}$, $7s^2$. Actinides are radioactive elements. Many of the actinide elements have been made only in nanogram quantities or even less by nuclear reactions and their chemistry is not fully explored. The elements in this series after uranium are called *Trans-uranium Elements*.

Note:

- In 6th period, after s-block element 'Ba', in ^{57}La, the last electron goes to penultimate 5d subshell and the configuration being, *[Xe] $6s^2$, $4f^0$, $5d^1$*. This is something not exactly as per (n+l) rule. As per the rule, electron should go to 4f- before 5d-subshell. This abnormality can be explained by the fact that Z_{eff} (effective nuclear charge, discussed separately in this chapter) is not enough to contract 4f and 5d is a better choice. But afterwards, the Z_{eff} is enough to contract 4f and the energy of 4f- is much less than 5d. Therefore, from ^{58}Ce, the electron gets filled up in 4f orbital. As d-block has already started with ^{57}La and then electrons start entering f-subshell, f-block elements don't fit into the main body of periodic table and rather are placed separately below.
- In some other lanthanides like Gd and Lu, the last electron goes to 5d instead of 4f. The reason can be (i) the half and fully filled configurations are exceptionally stable, (ii) as Z_{eff} is capable of contracting f-orbitals more effectively, the inter electronic repulsions is more in f-orbital than d-orbitals.

Shielding/Screening Effect

In a multielectron element, the valence electrons experience less nuclear charge due to enter electronic repulsion among the inner shell electrons (Fig. 23.2). This effect is known as shielding/screening effect. The effective nuclear charge experienced by valence electron can be expressed as,

$$Z_{eff} = Z - \sigma \quad [1]$$

Where,

Z: Nuclear charge,

Z_{eff}: Effective nuclear charge

σ: Magnitude of screening effect and can be computed by using Slater's rules as described below

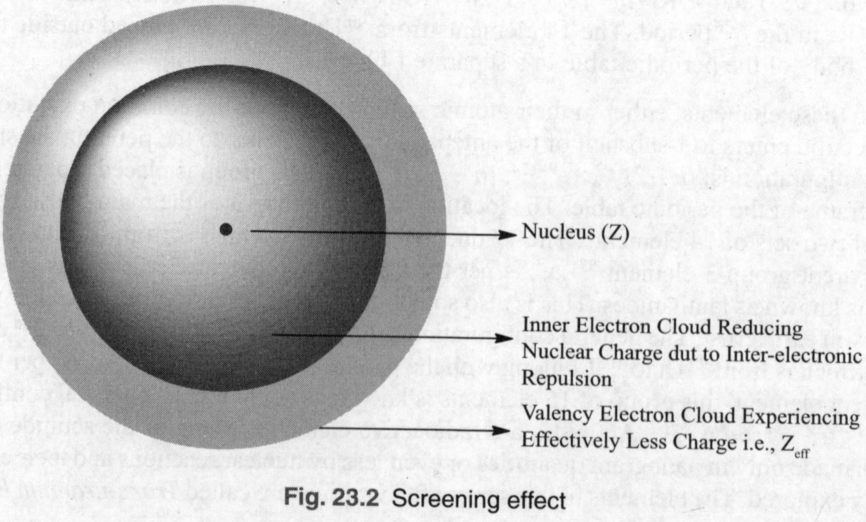

Fig. 23.2 Screening effect

Slater rules

Slater has utilised certain basic values to theoretically calculate the screening constant. The values so obtained is found to be close with the experimental findings. To apply the rules following steps are used.

Step 1: Write the electron configuration of the atom in the following form: (1s) (2s, 2p) (3s, 3p) (3d) (4s, 4p) (4d) (4f) (5s, 5p) . . .

Step 2: Identify the electron for which 'σ' is to be calculated and ignore all electrons present in higher group of orbitals as they don't shield the electrons in lower groups.

Step 3: The value of 'σ' can be computed by using some numerical values suggested by Slater which is summarized as follows.

(a) *For shielding experienced by s- and p-electrons*: The other electrons in the (ns, np) group contribute 0.35 each to 'σ' except for 1s for which the value is 0.30. All electrons in the (n – 1)th shell contribute 0.85 each to the 'σ' while the electrons in the (n – 2)th shell and so on contribute 1.0 each to the screening constant.

(b) *For shielding experienced by d- and f-electrons*: The other electrons in the (nd) or (nf) group contribute 0.35 each to 'σ'. All electrons in the (ns, np) along with (n –1), (n – 2)th shell and so on contribute 1.0 each to the screening constant.

Group	Contribution to 'σ'			
	Other electrons in the same group	**Electrons in group(s) with n, but l < 1**	**Electrons in group(s) with (n – 1)**	**Electrons in all group(s) with ≤ (n – 2)**
[1s]	0.30	–	–	–
[*ns*, *np*]	0.35	–	0.85	1
[*nd*] or [*nf*]	0.35	1	1	1

Illustration

Let's calculate the screening constant for different electrons of ^{24}Cr. The electronic configuration being, ($1s^2$), ($2s^2$, $2p^6$), ($3s^2$, $3p^6$), ($4s^1$), ($3d^5$)

For 3d electron, 4s-electron doesn't contribute to screening constant. Here, the nth shell is the 3rd shell where, the rest 12 electrons contribute 0.35 each to 'σ'. The 10 electrons in 2nd and 1st shell contribute 1.0 each to 'σ'. $\sigma = 4 \times 0.35 + 18 \times 1.00 = 19.5$

For 4s-electron, there is no further electron in 4s. The 13 electrons in 3rd shell contribute 0.85 each. The 8 electrons in 2nd shell contribute 0.85 while 2 electrons in 1st shell contribute 1.0 each to 'σ'. $\sigma = 13 \times 0.85 + 10 \times 1.00 = 21.05$

For 3s and 3p electron, 4s-electron doesn't contribute to screening constant. The 12 rest electrons in 3rd shell contribute 0.35. The 8 electrons in 2nd shell contribute 0.85 while 2 electrons in 1st shell contribute 1.0 each to 'σ'. $\sigma = 7 \times 0.35 + 8 \times 0.85 + 2 \times 1.00 = 11.25$

For 2s and 2p electron, the electrons in 3rd and 4th shell don't contribute to screening constant. The 7 rest electrons in nth shell i.e., 2nd shell contribute 0.35. The 8 electrons in 2nd shell contribute 0.85 while 2 electrons in 1st shell contribute 1.0 each to 'σ'. $\sigma = 7 \times 0.35 + 2 \times 0.85 = 4.15$

For 1s- electron, $\sigma = 1 \times 0.30 = 0.30$

Variation of 'σ' along a period and group

Along a period from left to right additional electrons progressively enter the same subshell. Therefore, variation of 'σ' is not much appreciable. However, as nuclear charge increases from left to right along a period, a steady increase is observed with respect to effective nuclear charge (Z_{eff}) values. Let's calculate the screening constant values for the valence electron of 2nd period elements. One can clearly see the trend.

Table 23.1 Screening constant 'σ' an Z_{eff} for 2nd period elements

Element/ Configuration	Screening constant (σ)	Z_{eff}
Li / $1s^2, 2s^1$	$\sigma = 2 \times 0.85 = 1.70$	$3 - 1.70 = 1.30$
Be / $1s^2, 2s^2$	$\sigma = 1 \times 0.35 + 2 \times 0.85 = 2.05$	$4 - 2.05 = 2.08$
B / $1s^2, 2s^2, 2p^1$	$\sigma = 2 \times 0.35 + 2 \times 0.85 = 2.40$	$5 - 2.40 = 2.76$
C / $1s^2, 2s^2, 2p^2$	$\sigma = 3 \times 0.35 + 2 \times 0.85 = 2.75$	$6 - 2.75 = 3.25$
N / $1s^2, 2s^2, 2p^3$	$\sigma = 4 \times 0.35 + 2 \times 0.85 = 3.10$	$7 - 3.10 = 3.90$
O / $1s^2, 2s^2, 2p^4$	$\sigma = 5 \times 0.35 + 2 \times 0.85 = 3.45$	$8 - 3.45 = 4.55$
F / $1s^2, 2s^2, 2p^5$	$\sigma = 6 \times 0.35 + 2 \times 0.85 = 3.80$	$9 - 3.80 = 5.20$
Ne / $1s^2, 2s^2, 2p^6$	$\sigma = 7 \times 0.35 + 2 \times 0.85 = 4.15$	$10 - 4.15 = 5.85$

Now, let's see the values in a group from top to bottom. Here, the value of 'σ' changes significantly from one element to another due to progressive addition of new inner shells. A clear observation is that though 'σ' vary significantly along a group, Z_{eff} remains the same (except the 1st element) in moving down along a group.

Table 23.2 Screening constant 'σ' an Z_{eff} for 1st group elements

Element/Configuration	Screening constant (σ)	Z_{eff}
Li / $1s^2, 2s^1$	$\sigma = 2 \times 0.85 = 1.70$	$3 - 1.70 = 1.30$
Na / $1s^2, 2s^2, 2p^6, 3s^1$	$\sigma = 8 \times 0.85 + 2 \times 1.00 = 8.80$	$11 - 8.80 = 2.20$
K / $1s^2, 2s^2, 2p^6, 3s^2 3p^6, 4s^1$	$\sigma = 8 \times 0.85 + 10 \times 1.00 = 16.80$	$19 - 16.80 = 2.20$
Rb / $1s^2, 2s^2 2p^6, 3s^2, 3p^6 3d^{10}, 4s^2 4p^6, 5s^1$	$\sigma = 8 \times 0.85 + 28 \times 1.00 = 34.80$	$37 - 34.80 = 2.20$
Cs / $1s^2, 2s^2 2p^6, 3s^2 3p^6 3d^{10}, 4s^2 4p^6 4d^{10}, 5s^2 5p^6, 6s^1$	$\sigma = 8 \times 0.85 + 46 \times 1.00 = 52.80$	$55 - 52.80 = 2.20$

Periodic Properties

In the periodic table, the elements with similar properties get repeated after certain regular interval of atomic number (Z), i.e., 2, 8, 8, 18, 18 and 32 which are also known as magic numbers. This periodic recurrence of elements having similar properties after regular intervals is called periodicity. The properties of an element depend upon the distribution of electrons in the various shells of an atom and in particular the valence shells. In a particular group of periodic table, all elements show a similar electronic distribution in the valence shell and hence they show similar with a varying, i.e., gradual increase or decrease in magnitude, e.g., one can see the elements present in group 1 of periodic table. All the elements have ns1 configuration in the valency shell.

Table 23.3 Electronic configuration of Gr-1 elements

Element (Gr-1)	Electronic Configuration
H	$1s^1$
Li	$1s^2, 2s^1$
Na	$1s^2, 2s^2, 2p^6, 3s^1$
K	$1s^2, 2s^2, 2p^6, 3s^2 3p^6, 4s^1$
Rb	$1s^2, 2s^2\, 2p^6, 3s^2, 3p^6\, 3d^{10}, 4s^2\, 4p^6, 5s^1$
Cs	$1s^2, 2s^2\, 2p^6, 3s^2 3p^6\, 3d^{10}, 4s^2\, 4p^6\, 4d^{10}, 5s^2\, 5p^6, 6s^1$

Properties such as atomic and ionic radii, ionization energy, electron affinity, and electronegativities, etc. are the properties of individual atoms. These properties directly dependent on their electronic configuration. Properties such as melting point, boiling point, the heat of fusion, heat of vaporization, density, atomic volume, etc., are collective properties of a group of atoms. These properties usually indirectly dependent on their electronic configuration. All such properties which directly or indirectly dependent on the electronic configuration of the elements are called atomic properties. Let's discuss some of these properties.

(a) Atomic Size

It is generally the distance between the centre of the nucleus and the outermost shell of electrons. Finding the size of an atom is a lot more complicated aspect and the precise value can't be measured. The reason is basically of two-fold. Firstly, it is impossible to isolate an individual atom because of its very small size. Secondly, the electron cloud surrounding the atom does not have a sharp boundary. Therefore, a more practical approach being developed where, the size is estimated in the environment itself. Accordingly, the size may be expressed as covalent radius (for non-metallic elements), metallic radius (for metals), and Vanderwall's radius (in a weak molecular force environment).

Covalent radius

A covalent radius may be defined as half of the distance between the nuclei of two identical atoms bonded together by a covalent bond. This radius is essentially single bond covalent radius. The most common methods of measuring covalent radius are x-ray diffraction and rotational spectroscopy. This is the most widely used value as far as atomic size is concerned. Let's consider a homonuclear diatomic molecule, A_2 where the atoms are held by a single covalent bond. Then by definition, covalent radius is the half of the distance between the nuclei of both the bonded atoms (Fig. 23.3).

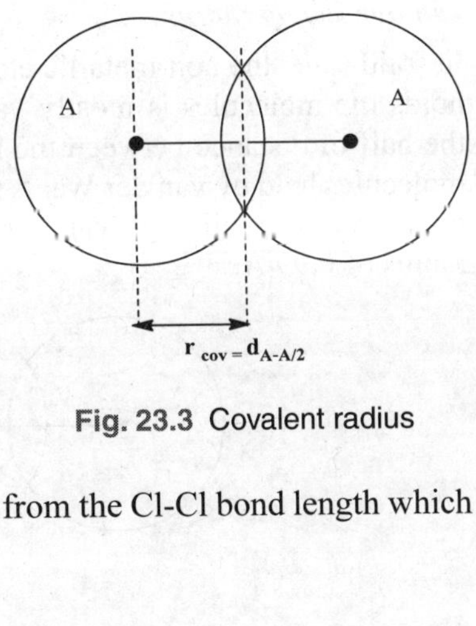

Fig. 23.3 Covalent radius

e.g., covalent radius of 'Cl' can be calculated from the Cl-Cl bond length which is 1.98 Å (from experiment).

$$r_{cov} = \frac{d_{Cl-Cl}}{2}$$

$$= \frac{1.98}{2} = 0.99\text{Å}$$

Note:

Covalent radii can be single-bond, double-bond and triple-bond covalent radii which involve single, double, and triple bond, respectively. Let's us look into single, double, and triple covalent radii in (Å) of some elements: B (0.82, 0.76, and 0.68), C (0.77, 0.67, and 0.60), N (0.75, 0.60, and 0.55) and so on.

Metallic radius

This is used for expressing size for the elements which are metals. In metals, the atoms are assumed to be spheres which are closely packed forming the lattice. In a close packed arrangement, the atoms are assumed to touch each other. Therefore, the metallic radius is defined as the half of distance between the nuclei of two adjacent metal atoms in the metal lattice. The value further depends on the nature of packing i.e., cubic close packing (ccp), hexagonal close packing (hcp) or body cantered close packing (bcc) which decides the proximity of atoms in the lattice. Metallic radii are 10 to 15% higher than the single bond covalent radii.

Table 23.4 Comparison of covalent and metallic radius of Gr-1 elements

Element (Gr 1)	r_{cov} (Å)	$r_{metallic}$ (Å)
Li	1.23	1.55
Na	1.54	1.90
K	2.03	2.35
Rb	2.16	2.48
Cs	2.35	2.67

van der Waals radius

In solid state, the non-metallic elements usually exist as aggregate of molecules. The force that holds the molecules is mostly van der Waals forces. The van der Waals radius is defined as the half of distance between the nuclei of two neighbouring atoms belonging to two adjacent molecules held by van der Waals forces (Fig. 23.4). van der Waals radii are substantially higher than covalent radii, e.g., van der Walls radius of chlorine is 1.80 Å as compared to covalent radius of 0.99 Å.

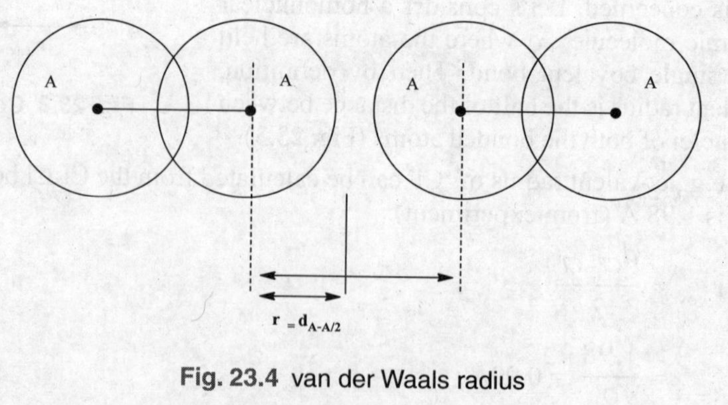

Fig. 23.4 van der Waals radius

Ionic radius

The removal of an electron from an atom result in the formation of a cation, whereas gain of an electron leads to an anion. The ionic radii can be estimated by measuring the distances between cations and anions in ionic crystals. In general, the ionic radii of elements exhibit the same trend as the atomic radii. A cation is smaller than its parent atom because it has fewer electrons while its nuclear charge remains the same which ultimately increases Z_{eff}. The size of an anion is larger than that of the parent atom because the addition of one or more electrons results in the increased repulsion among the electrons and a decrease in Z_{eff}. For example, the ionic radius of fluoride ion (F^-) is 1.36 Å whereas the atomic radius of fluorine is only 0.64 Å. On the other hand, the atomic radius of sodium is 1.86 Å compared to the ionic radius of 0.95 Å for Na^+.

> **Note:**
>
> *Size of isoelectronic species*: Isoelectronic species are the atoms and ions which contain the same number of electrons. For example, O^{2-}, F^-, Na^+, and Mg^{2+} have the same number of electrons, i.e., 10 electrons. Their radii are different because of their different effective nuclear charges. More is effective nuclear charge, smaller is the size. Therefore, Mg^{2+}, having the highest value of effective nuclear charge is the smallest one while O^{2-}, with lowest value of the Z_{eff} is the largest one. The size order is $O^{2-} > F^- > Na^+ > Mg^{2+}$.

Variation of atomic/ionic size along a period and group

For representative elements, the atomic/ionic size decreases steadily from left to right along a period. In a period, the additional electrons progressively enter the same shell for which the screening factor is not very significant rather Z_{eff} controls the size. As Z_{eff} increase from left to right, the size decreases along a period from left to right. Therefore, in a period, alkali metals have the largest size while halogens have the smallest size, e.g., let's look into the size (covalent radii) of 2nd period elements.

Table 23.5 Size variation of 2nd period elements

Element (2nd Period)	Li	Be	B	C	N	O	F
Size (Å)	1.23	0.90	0.82	0.77	0.75	0.73	0.72

Along a group, there is increase in Z, but Z_{eff} is almost the same (refer to screening effect). In a group, while moving down there is a progressive addition of new shells which control the size and regular increase is observed down the group.

Table 23.6 Size variation of Gr 2 elements

Element (Gr 2)	Be	Mg	Ca	Sr	Ba
Size (Å)	0.90	1.36	1.74	1.91	1.98

Note:

For transition elements, the variation is controlled by the competition between. Z_{eff} and the inter-electronic repulsion among d-electrons with progressive addition of electrons in d-subshell. Up to half filled Z_{eff} dominates the variation while after half filled the inter electronic repulsion plays the regulating role. Therefore, in the 1st half up to half filled the size decreases due to increase in Z_{eff} while after half filled the size again starts increasing due to dominance of inter electronic repulsion factor. In the mid-way as these two factors balance each other the variation is not much, e.g., let's look into the size variation of 3d-transition series.

Table 23.7 Size variation of 3d-transition series elements

Element (2nd Period)	Sc	Ti	V	Cr	Mn	Fe	Co	Ni	Cu	Zn
Size (Å)	1.44	1.32	1.22	1.18	1.17	1.17	1.16	1.15	1.17	1.25

(b) Ionisation Potential/Energy

Ionisation Energy is a quantitative measure of the tendency of an element to lose electron. It is the amount of energy required to remove the most loosely bound electron from an isolated neutral gaseous atom in its ground state. It is always positive.

$$A_{(g)} + IE \longrightarrow A_{(g)}^{+} + e$$

Note:

The ionisation energy defined above is also known as 1st ionisation energy (IE_1). The energy required to remove an electron from the univalent cation formed after the removal of the most loosely bound electron is known as 2nd ionisation energy (IE_2). Relatively more energy is required for the purpose as the effective nuclear charge per electron, is more in the cation than the neutral atom. Thus, the 2nd ionisation energy is always more than the 1st ionisation energy. In the same trend, 3rd ionisation energy is more than 2nd one and so on, i.e., $IE_1 < IE_2 < IE_3$.....

$$A_{(g)} + IE_1 \longrightarrow A_{(g)}^{+} + e$$
$$A_{(g)}^{+} + IE_2 \longrightarrow A_{(g)}^{2+} + e$$
$$A_{(g)}^{2+} + IE_3 \longrightarrow A_{(g)}^{3+} + e$$

Table 23.8 Successive Ionisation Energies of 2nd period elements (eV)

Element	Ionisation energy (eV)						
	IE_1	IE_2	IE_3	IE_4	IE_5	IE_6	IE_7
Li	5.4	75.6	122.4				
Be	9.3	18.2	153.9	217.7			
B	8.3	25.1	37.9	259.3	340.1		
C	11.3	24.4	47.9	64.5	39.2	489.8	

Element	Ionisation energy (eV)						
	IE_1	IE_2	IE_3	IE_4	IE_5	IE_6	IE_7
N	14.5	29.6	47.4	77.5	97.9	551.9	666.8
O	13.6	35.1	54.9	77.4	113.9	138.1	739.1
F	17.4	35.0	62.6	87.2	114.2	157.1	185.1
Ne	21.6	41.1	64.0	97.2	126.4	157.9	–

Factors affecting

(a) Size – Larger is the size less is ionisation energy. This factor is quite helpful in explaining the overall variation along a group or period. In general IE decrease down the group while the same increases along the period from left to right.

(b) Effective Nuclear Charge (Z_{eff}) – The greater is the Z_{eff}, the more difficult it would be to remove the electron from the atom and higher is the value of ionisation energy. Therefore, the value of ionisation energy mostly increases from left to right in moving along a period.

(c) Extent of orbital penetration – For a given value of principal quantum number (n), the magnitude of penetration of different orbitals follows the order s> p> d >f. Therefore, other factors being same, an s-electron will be tougher to remove than p-electron, p-electron will be tougher than d-electron and so on.

Let's look into the example of Be ($1s^2$, $2s^2$) and B ($1s^2$, $2s^2$, $2p^1$). The IE of B (8.3 eV) is less than Be (9.3 eV), since for B, electron has to remove from p-orbital while that for Be, it is to be removed from s-orbital.

(d) Electronic configuration – Half-filled and fully filled configurations are exceptionally stable due to maximum exchange energy and uniform/spherical distribution of charge. Therefore, ionisation energy of an elements with such a configuration is relatively higher than expected from its position in the periodic table.

Let's look into the ionisation of Be and N in the 2nd period. This can be explained based on extra stability associated with filled 2s-orbital in Be ($1s^2$, $2s^2$) and half-filled 2p-orbital in N ($1s^2$, $2s^2$, $2p^3$).

(e) The shielding or screening action of electrons in the inner shell – Ionisation energy decreases with the increase of screening effect. This is helpful in explaining the variation of IE along a group. In a group as one move down, screening effect increases substantially due addition of inner shells which lowers the Z_{eff} and in turn lowers the ionisation energy.

Variation of IE along a period and group

Along a period, effective nuclear charge mostly controls the variation of ionisation energy. Therefore, for representative elements, IE increases as one move from left to right in a period. However, some exceptions are there as several other factors also influence the IE. Let's look into the variation of IE for 2nd period elements (Fig. 23.5). The IE of B (8.3 eV) is less than Be (9.3 eV), since for B, electron has to remove from p-orbital while that for Be, it is to be removed from s-orbital. In addition, Be has fully filled s-orbital and has extra stability associated with it. Another exception is IE of O is less than N. This can be explained based on extra stability associated with half-filled 2p-orbital in N ($1s^2$, $2s^2$, $2p^3$).

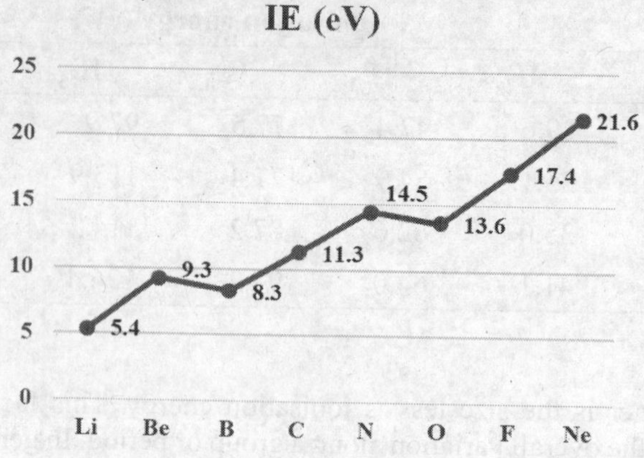

Fig. 23.5 Variation of IE of 2nd period elements

Along a group, atomic size plays a very significant role and controls the variation. From top to bottom in a group, size increases due to addition of new shells. Therefore, IE decreases from top to bottom in a group.

Note:

- An exception in the vertical trend of ionisation energy is observed for the elements with atomic number (Z) > 72. The IE of ^{73}Ta to ^{82}Pb are greater than those of the elements of the same group above them (Table 23.9, all values are in eV). The reason for this abnormal behaviour is attributed to the *lanthanide contraction*. As a result of lanthanide contraction, there occurs an increase in nuclear charge without a corresponding increase in size through the lanthanides. In fact, size decreases in this region.

Table 23.9 IE of 5th and 6th period elements in eV

Group/Period	5	6	7	8	9	10	11	12	13	14
5	^{41}Nb	Mo	Tc	Ru	Rh	Pd	Ag	^{48}Cd	In	^{50}Sn
	6.8	7.1	7.2	7.3	7.4	8.3	7.5	8.9	5.7	7.3
6	^{73}Ta	W	Re	Os	Ir	Pt	Au	^{80}Hg	Tl	^{82}Pb
	7.7	7.8	7.8	8.7	9.2	9.0	9.2	10.4	6.1	7.4

- After ^{57}La, the electrons enter in the f-subshell for ^{58}Ce to ^{71}Lu, i.e, lanthanides. As penetration of f-orbital towards nucleus is the least among the orbitals, the electrons present in them do not offer significant shielding. This is due to this imperfect shielding of f-electrons, a contraction of size is observed along lanthanides which is known as lanthanide contraction.

(c) Electron Affinity

The amount of energy released upon addition of an electron to the valency shell of an isolated neutral gaseous atom in its ground state is known as electron affinity. This is always negative as energy is released.

$$A_{(g)} + e \longrightarrow \overset{-}{A}_{(g)} + EA$$

> **Note:**
> The electron affinity defined above is also known as *1st electron affinity* (EA_1). In the process of adding an electron to the anion so formed against the electrostatic repulsive forces between the electron to be added and the negative charge on anion, extra energy needs to be supplied to the anion to form a divalent anion. The energy supplied to convert $A_{(g)}^-$ to $A_{(g)}^{2-}$ is known as *second electron affinity* (EA_2) which is negative. e.g., the 1st electron affinity of oxygen is –1.48 eV, while the 2nd electron affinity is +7.3 eV.

Factors affecting

Like ionisation energy, it is also influenced by size, effective nuclear charge, electronic configuration, and screening effect.

(a) Size – Larger is the size less is the ability of nucleus to attract the additional electron towards it and less amount of energy will be released upon addition of extra electron. Thus, EA decreases with increase of size. This factor is quite helpful in explaining the overall variation along a group or period. In general EA decrease down the group while the same increases along the period from left to right.

(b) Effective Nuclear Charge (Z_{eff}) – The greater is the Z_{eff}, the more is the tendency of an atom to attract the additional electron, and higher amount of energy will be released upon addition of extra electron. This leads to increase in with the increase of effective nuclear charge. Therefore, the value of ionisation energy mostly increases from left to right in moving along a period.

(c) Electronic configuration – Half-filled and fully filled configurations are exceptionally stable due to maximum exchange energy and uniform/spherical distribution of charge. Therefore, EA of an element with completely filled configuration is practically zero while the for an element having half-filled configuration is relatively lower than expected as per its position in periodic table.

Let's look into the of Be and N in the 2nd period. The EA of Be is zero due to extra stability associated with filled 2s-orbital in Be ($1s^2$, $2s^2$). The EA of N is relatively low (–1.2 eV). The reason is attributed to the half-filled 2p-orbital in N ($1s^2$, $2s^2$, $2p^3$).

Variation of EA along a period and group

Along a period for representative elements, from left to right, electron affinity values generally increase with a few exceptions. Let's look into the variation of electron affinities of 2nd period elements. Be has electron affinity equal to zero due to its completely filled s-orbital. N- has exceptionally low EA due to extra stability associated with the half-filled p-orbital. For noble gas Ne, the electron affinity is again equal to zero as the valence shell is completely filled.

In moving down a group, as size plays a dominating role, EA values generally decrease. However, some exceptions to this observation are noticed for 2nd and 3rd period elements. Although the elements of 2nd period are relatively smaller in size than those of the 3rd period elements, yet the EA values of 2nd period elements are smaller than those of 3rd period elements. This is because of the much smaller size of 2nd period elements leading to high charge densities for the respective ions. This high charge density opposes the addition of electron to some extent. The trend can be noticed in reference to the EA values of Group 17 elements. This follows the order, F (–3.6 eV) < Cl (–3.8 eV) > Br (–3.5 eV) > I (–3.2 eV).

Note:

Higher EA value refers to higher tendency to accept electron. Therefore, halogens with high EA values are observed to be very good oxidizing agents. Now as Cl has the highest EA is expected to be the best oxidizing agent. However, the oxidising ability among halogens follows the order, F > Cl > Br > I. In fact, oxidation potential does not include only EA, rather it also includes the hydration energy. Due to smaller size, fluoride is extensively hydrated and the process releases substantially high amount of hydration energy. In addition, dissociation energy of F_2 (1.64 eV/mol) molecule is also than that of Cl_2 (2.48 eV/mol). The low value of bond dissociation energy is attributed to the repulsion operating between the non-bonding 2p-electrons on the F-atoms while the higher values of bond dissociation energy in other halogens are attributed to possibility of bonding.

Applications of IE and EA

Metallic and non-metallic characteristics: Metals have high tendency to lose electron, i.e., they are highly electropositive. Again, it is a well-known fact that, lower is the value of IE of an element greater is the tendency to lose electron. Therefore, metallic character increases from top to bottom along a group with the decrease of IE. With the same argument, it can be easily explained that the metallic character decreases along a period from left to right with the increase of IE. On the other hand, non-metals are characterised by their higher affinity to accept electrons i.e., they are highly electronegative. Again, electron affinity is a measure of the tendency of an element to accept electron. Therefore, non-metallic character increases from left to right in a period with the increase in EA. Similarly. As the EA decreases along a group from top to bottom, non-metallic character of the elements also decreases in the same directions.

The elements present in the lower left-hand side of the periodic table exhibit maximum electropositive character and hence are metals while the elements lying at the upper right-hand side show minimum electropositive character and hence are non-metals. The elements lying between metals and non-metals show characteristics of both metals and non-metals and hence are called metalloids (Fig. 23.6).

Non-metals →

	13	14	15	16	17
2	B Boron	C Carbon	N Nitrogen	O Oxygen	F Fluorine
3	Al Aluminium	Si Silicon	P Phosphorus	S Sulfur	Cl Chlorine
4	Ga Gallium	Ge Germanium	As Arsenic	Se Selenium	Br Bromine
5	In Indium	Sn Tin	Sb Antimony	Te Tellurium	I Iodine
6	Tl Thallium	Pb Lead	Bi Bismuth	Po Polonium	At Astatine

← Metals

Metalloids

Fig. 23.6 Division of elements into metals, non-metals, and metalloids

Relative stability and reactivity: The IE is a quantitative measure of the stability of elements. More is IE, more is the difficulty in removing electron from an atom and more is the stability. Therefore, in a period, for metals (electropositive elements), stability increases with the increase of IE from left to right. e.g., in 3rd period the reactivity follows the order, Na > Mg > Al

On the other hand, in a group reactivity increases from top to bottom with the decrease in IE. E.g., for Gr-1, the relative reactivity follows the order Na < K < Rb < Cs

Note:

For electronegative elements, the trend is reversed. The elements with higher electron affinity are more reactive and vice versa.

Oxidising/ Reducing power of an element: An oxidising agent is that which helps in oxidation and itself get reduced in the process. Therefore, an element with higher electron affinity, i.e., higher potential to accept electron is a better oxidising agent. It is quite evident that, along a period from left to right the reducing power decreases with the increase of EA while along a group from top to bottom reducing power increases with decrease of EA, e.g., halogens with maximum value of electron affinity in the periodic table are the most powerful oxidising agents.

On the other hand, reducing agent is that which helps in reduction and itself get oxidised in the process. Therefore, an element with lower IE, i.e., higher potential to lose electron is a better reducing agent. In a period from left to right with the increase of IE, the reducing power decreases while along a group the same increases with decrease of IE, e.g., alkali metals with lowest values of IE are the most powerful reducing agents.

(d) Electronegativity

It is the measure of the relative ability of an atom in a bond to attract the shared pair of electrons towards itself. Unlike ionization enthalpy and electron gain enthalpy, it is not a measurable quantity. However, a few numerical scales of electronegativity of elements viz., Pauling scale, Mulliken-Jaffe scale, Allred-Rochow scale have been developed to measure electronegativity from various types of experimental data.

Pauling Scale

The most widely used is the Pauling scale. Linus Pauling, an American scientist, in 1922 assigned arbitrarily a value of 4.0 for electronegativity of fluorine, which is the highest one for any element and calculated the same for other elements by using the following formula.

$$\chi_A - \chi_B = 0.208\sqrt{\Delta} \quad [2]$$

Where, $\Delta = E_{A-B} - \sqrt{E_{A-A} \times E_{B-B}}$ and,

Δ, is the resonance energy,

E_{A-B}, E_{A-A} and E_{B-B} are the bond energies of AB, A_2 and B_2 molecules, respectively. Remember all these values are in electron-volts

Mulliken Scale

Robert S. Mulliken proposed electronegativity of an element as the arithmetic mean of the ionisation energy and electron affinity.

$$\chi = \frac{IE + EA}{2} \quad [3]$$

As this definition is not dependent on an arbitrary relative scale, it has also been termed as **absolute electronegativity**, having the units eV. However, it is more usual to use a linear transformation to transform these absolute values into values that resemble the more familiar Pauling scale values.

$$\chi = \frac{IE + EA}{2 \times 2.8} \quad [4]$$

Example: Find the electronegativity of 'Cl'. Given, the IE and EA are 13.0 and –3.8 eV/ atom, respectively.

Solution

$$\chi = \frac{IE + EA}{5.6} = \frac{13.0 + 3.8}{5.6} = 3.0$$

Allred-Rochow electronegativity

As per A. Louis Allred and Eugene G. Rochow, the electronegativity should be related to the charge experienced by an electron on the surface of an atom: The higher the charge per unit area of atomic surface the greater the tendency of that atom to attract electrons. The Z_{eff}, experienced by valence electrons can be estimated using Slater's rule while the surface area of an atom in a molecule can be taken to be proportional to the square of the covalent radius, r_{cov}. When, r_{cov} is expressed in Å,

$$\chi = 0.359 \frac{Z_{eff}}{r_{cov}^2} + 0.744 \quad [5]$$

Example

Find electronegativity of 82Pb. Given the covalent radius is 1.47 Å.

Solution

Electronic configuration of ^{82}Pb is *[^{54}Xe] $4f^{14}$, $5d^{10}$, $6s^2$, $6p^2$*. The screening constant for the incoming shared pair of electrons can be calculated by using Slater's rules.

$$\sigma = 4 \times 0.35 + 18 \times 0.85 + 60 \times 1.0 = 76.70$$

We know, $\chi = 0.359 \frac{Z_{eff}}{r_{cov}^2} + 0.744$

$$= 0.359 \frac{82 - 76.70}{(1.47)^2} + 0.744 = 1.62$$

Factors affecting

Electronegativity values depend on the size, Z_{eff}, screening magnitude, ionisation energy, electron affinity, and types of hybridisations.

(a) Size – Larger is the size less is electronegativity. This factor is quite helpful in explaining the overall variation along a group or period. In general electronegativity decrease down the group while the same increases along the period from left to right.

(b) Effective Nuclear Charge (Z_{eff}) – The greater is the Z_{eff}, the more is the ability to attract the shared pair, and more is electronegativity. Therefore, the value of 'χ' mostly increases from left to right in moving along a period.

(c) Ionisation energy and electron affinity – More is the numerical values of IE and EA, higher is the electronegativity.

(d) Type of hybridization –The magnitude of electronegativity of an atom also depends on the type of hybridisation which the atom adopts during formation of different bonds. The magnitude of electronegativity increases with the increase of s-character in hybrid orbitals.

Let's look into the example of carbon. Carbon adopts different hybridisation in saturated and unsaturated compounds. Electronegativity of 'C' is highest in acetylene as in that case it is sp-hybridised with highest s-character, i.e., 50%. Due to this fact acetylenic hydrogen is acidic and acetylene readily reacts with metals and other bases to form salts, i.e., acetylides.

Table 23.10 Variation of electronegativity with % of s- character

Hydrocarbon	**Methane**	**Ethane**	**Acetylene**
Type of hybridisation	sp^3	sp^2	sp
% of s-character	25%	33.3%	50%
Electronegative order	Lowest	Higher	Highest

Variation of Electronegativity along a period and group

Along a period from left to right, the electronegativity increases with the decrease of size and increase of Z_{eff}. Highest electronegativity for any specific period is associated with the halogens in group 17. Along a group, again the size is the dominating parameter and the result being in moving down, the electronegativity decreases in a regular fashion.

The above variation leads to the fact that Gr-17 elements, i.e., halogens are the most electronegative elements which lie on the extreme right of the periodic table while alkali metals, i.e., Gr-1 elements which lie on the extreme left are the least electronegative or most electropositive elements. Fluorine is the most electronegative element while cesium is the most electropositive one.

Applications

- ***Nature of a bond:*** The concept of electronegativity is quite useful in predicting the nature of the bond formed between two atoms (Fig. 23.7). If a covalent bond is formed between two atoms belonging to the same element, then there exists zero electronegativity difference and the bond is known as non-polar covalent bond. If the bond is formed between two atoms belonging to two different elements, then there exists some electronegativity difference and the bond is known as polar covalent bond. Such bonds possess some % of ionic character. When electronegativity difference between the bonded atoms is too high that % of ionic character is more than 50% then the bond is said to be ionic bond.

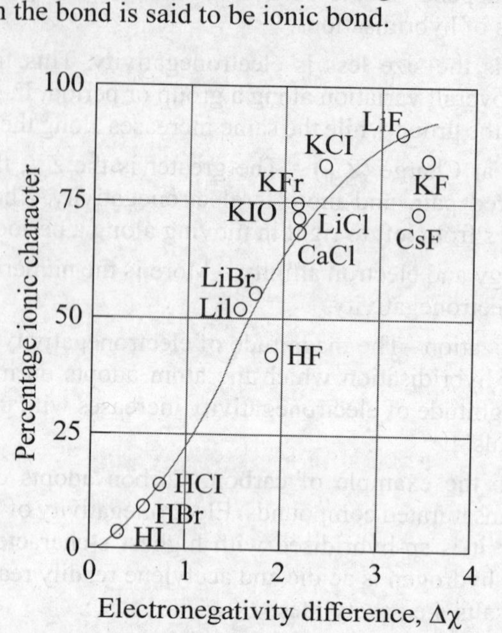

Fig. 23.7 % of ionic character as a function of Δχ

Pauling has developed an equation for calculating the % of ionic character in a covalent bond from electronegativity difference. It has been observed and established by Pauling that 'A – B' bond has 50% ionic character when the electronegativity difference between A and B is 1.7. An electronegativity difference of more than 1.7 refers to an ionic bond while less than 1.7 refers to a covalent bond. However, Pauling formula fails to explain the ionic character of bonds where the electronegativity difference is too high. One can look into the example of H – F bond where the $\Delta\chi$ value is 1.9 pointing towards more than 50% ionic character, i.e., the bond is expected to be ionic. However, in actual practice H – F bond is covalent which is also quite observable from the above graph. The modification to the above formula is done by Hanny and Smith which fits more effectively into the above graph. As per the modified formula, $\Delta\chi = 2.1$ refers to 50% ionic character. Thus, the bonds with $\Delta\chi > 2.1$ are essentially ionic and those with less than 2.1 are covalent. Both the formulae are cited below.

Pauling formula, % of ionic character $= [1 - e^{1-\frac{1}{4}(\chi_A \sim \chi_B)^2}] \times 100$ [5]

Hanny and Smith modified formula,

% of ionic character $= [\,0.16\,(\chi_A \sim \chi_B) + 0.035\,(\chi_A \sim \chi_B)^2\,] \times 100$ [6]

- ***Acid-base character of the normal oxides long a period:*** In moving from left to right along a period acidic character of the normal oxides increases. This is attributed to the fact that, with the progressive increase of the electronegativity values, the difference of electronegativities between the element of interest and oxygen decreases. This ultimately reduces polarity of 'X – O' (X- is the element of interest) bond and makes the ionisation of the same relatively difficult in aqueous solution.

Oxides	Na_2O	MgO	Al_2O_3	SiO_2	P_4O_{10}	SO_3	Cl_2O_7
χ_E	1.0	1.2	1.4	1.7	2.0	2.4	2.8
$\chi_E \sim \chi_O$ $[\chi_O = 3.5]$	2.5	2.3	2.1	1.8	1.5	1.1	0.7
Nature of oxide	*Strongly basic*	*Basic*	*Amphoteric*	*Weakly acidic*	*Acidic*	*Strongly acidic*	*Very strongly acidic*

- ***Metallic and non-metallic character of the elements:*** The elements with higher values of electronegativity are essentially non-metals while those with lower values of electronegativities are metals. This is quite observable in the periodic table. In a period from left to right metallic character decreases and their oxides become less and less basic. On the other hand, along a group from top to bottom metallic character decreases with decrease in electronegativity. The oxides become progressively basic. This situation is quite pronounced in Gr-14 and 15 elements. These groups start with non-metals like C and N but ends with metals like Pb and Bi, respectively.

Note:

Let's put the variation trend of different atomic properties along a period from left to right and along a group from top to bottom in one go in the following figure.

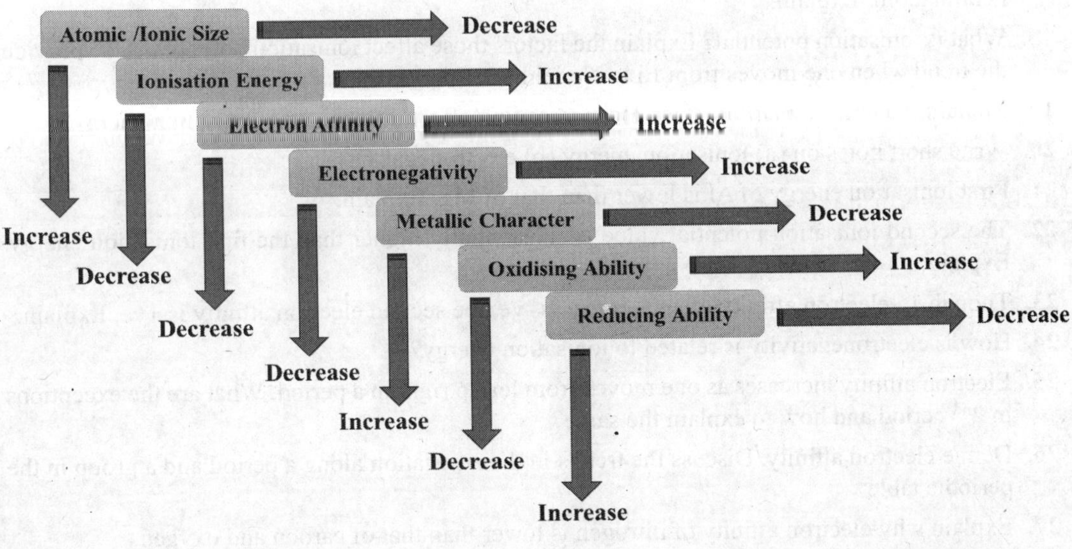

QUESTIONS

1. Discuss the block classification of elements based on electronic configuration.
2. What are the limitations of Mendeleev's periodic table? Also provide modern periodic law proposed by Moseley.
3. Discuss the merits of long form of periodic table over Mendeleev's periodic table.
4. Half-filled and completely-filled orbitals are relatively more stable. Explain with suitable examples.
5. What are s-block elements? How do they differ from p-block elements?
6. Discuss the characteristics of representative elements.
7. Discuss characteristics of d-block i.e., transition elements. Transition elements exhibit variable oxidation states. Explain.
8. What are s-, p-, d- and f- block elements. Discuss their main characteristics.
9. Why do lanthanides not find their place in the main body of the periodic table?
10. Explain lanthanide contraction and its consequences.
11. Explain different scales of electronegativity. What is the relation between Mulliken and Pauling approach?
12. Explain why absolute value of atomic size can't be measured.
13. Distinguish between covalent radius and van der wall's radius. Which one is relatively higher and why?
14. Discuss Hanny and Smith modification over Pauling's approach in prediction of nature of a covalent bond.
15. Discuss variation of atomic size in a period and along a group in the periodic table. Provide suitable reason for the same.
16. Arrange the following species in increasing order of their size. (a) Fe^{2+}, Fe, Fe^{3+} (b) O, O^{2-}, O^{-}, O^{2+} (c) Cl^{-}, Ca^{2+}, S^{2-}, Ar
17. Cationic size is always less than the neutral atom while anionic size is always more than the neutral atom. Explain.
18. What is ionisation potential? Explain the factors those affect ionisation potential. Also provide the trend when one moves from Li to Ne in the 2nd period.
19. Explain the term *screening effect.* How screening effect influence the ionisation energy?
20. Write short notes on (a) ionisation energy (b) electronegativity.
21. First ionisation energy of Al is lower than that of Mg. Explain.
22. The second ionisation potential value is substantially higher than the first ionisation energy. Explain.
23. Though 1st electron affinity of an element is -ve, the second electron affinity is +ve. Explain.
24. How is electronegativity is related to ionisation energy?
25. Electron affinity increases as one moves from left to right in a period. What are the exceptions in 2nd period and how to explain the same?
26. Define electron affinity. Discuss the trends in their variation along a period and a group in the periodic table.
27. Explain why electron affinity of nitrogen is lower than that of carbon and oxygen.

28. Discuss Slater's rules for calculation of screening constant and Z_{eff}.
29. Explain the trend in screening effect along a period and along a group.
30. Show that through the screening constant changes significantly along a group from top to bottom, Z_{eff} remain the same except for the ist element in the group.
31. Find screening constant of different electrons in iron atom. Also find the Z_{eff} for each one.
32. Explain how electronegativity is useful in estimation of % of ionic character in a covalent bond.
33. Calculate the % of ionic character in K-Cl bond and predict the nature of the molecule. The electronegativity values of K and Cl are 0.8 and 3.0 respectively.
34. Explain why metallic character increases as one moves down in a group.
35. Electron affinities of Be, Mg, and noble gases are zero while those for N and P are very low.
36. What is periodicity? Explain the underlaying reason for the same.
37. How is electronegativity related to the polarity of a covalent bond? As per Pauling what should be the difference of electronegativities of bonded atoms for the bond to be ionic.
38. Distinguish between electron affinity and electronegativity. Fluorine is more electronegative than chlorine, although its electron affinity is less than that of chlorine.
39. Chlorine has higher electron affinity than fluorine still fluorine is better oxidising agent than chlorine.
40. Find electronegativity of ^{83}Bi. Given the covalent radius of fluorine is 1.46 Å.